THE ART OF 64-BIT ASSEMBLY, VOLUME 1

T0073517

THE ART OF 64-BIT ASSEMBLY

Volume 1

x86-64 Machine Organization and Programming

Randall Hyde

no starch press

San Francisco

THE ART OF 64-BIT ASSEMBLY, VOLUME 1. Copyright © 2022 by Randall Hyde.

All rights reserved. No part of this work may be reproduced or transmitted in any form or by any means, electronic or mechanical, including photocopying, recording, or by any information storage or retrieval system, without the prior written permission of the copyright owner and the publisher.

Printed in the United States of America

First printing

25 24 23 22 21   1 2 3 4 5 6 7 8 9

ISBN-13: 978-1-7185-0108-9 (print)
ISBN-13: 978-1-7185-0109-6 (ebook)

Publisher: William Pollock
Production Manager: Rachel Monaghan
Production Editors: Katrina Taylor and Miles Bond
Developmental Editors: Athabasca Witschi and Nathan Heidelberger
Cover Design: Gina Redman
Interior Design: Octopod Studios
Technical Reviewer: Anthony Tribelli
Copyeditor: Sharon Wilkey
Compositor: Jeff Lytle, Happenstance Type-O-Rama
Proofreader: Sadie Barry

For information on book distributors or translations, please contact No Starch Press, Inc. directly:
No Starch Press, Inc.
245 8th Street, San Francisco, CA 94103
phone: 1-415-863-9900; info@nostarch.com
www.nostarch.com

Library of Congress Cataloging-in-Publication Data

```
Names: Hyde, Randall, author.
Title: The art of 64-bit assembly. Volume 1, x86-64 machine organization
  and programming / Randall Hyde.
Description: San Francisco : No Starch Press Inc, 2022. | Includes
   bibliographical references and index. |
Identifiers: LCCN 2021020214 (print) | LCCN 2021020215 (ebook) | ISBN
  9781718501089 (print) | ISBN 9781718501096 (ebook)
Subjects: LCSH: Assembly languages (Electronic computers)
Classification: LCC QA76.73.A8 H969 2022  (print) | LCC QA76.73.A8  (ebook)
  | DDC 005.13/6--dc23
LC record available at https://lccn.loc.gov/2021020214
LC ebook record available at https://lccn.loc.gov/2021020215
```

No Starch Press and the No Starch Press logo are registered trademarks of No Starch Press, Inc. Other product and company names mentioned herein may be the trademarks of their respective owners. Rather than use a trademark symbol with every occurrence of a trademarked name, we are using the names only in an editorial fashion and to the benefit of the trademark owner, with no intention of infringement of the trademark.

The information in this book is distributed on an "As Is" basis, without warranty. While every precaution has been taken in the preparation of this work, neither the author nor No Starch Press, Inc. shall have any liability to any person or entity with respect to any loss or damage caused or alleged to be caused directly or indirectly by the information contained in it.

To my wife, Mandy. In the second
edition of *The Art of Assembly Language,*
I mentioned that it had been a great 30 years
and I was looking forward to another 30.
Now it's been 40, so I get to look forward
to at least another 20!

About the Author

Randall Hyde is the author of *The Art of Assembly Language* and *Write Great Code,* Volumes 1, 2, and 3 (all from No Starch Press), as well as *Using 6502 Assembly Language and P-Source* (Datamost). He is also the coauthor of *Microsoft Macro Assembler 6.0 Bible* (The Waite Group). Over the past 40 years, Hyde has worked as an embedded software/hardware engineer developing instrumentation for nuclear reactors, traffic control systems, and other consumer electronics devices. He has also taught computer science at California State Polytechnic University, Pomona, and at the University of California, Riverside. His website is *http://www.randallhyde.com/.*

About the Tech Reviewer

Tony Tribelli has more than 35 years of experience in software development. This experience ranges, among other things, from embedded device kernels to molecular modeling and visualization to video games. The latter includes ten years at Blizzard Entertainment. He is currently a software development consultant and privately develops applications utilizing computer vision.

BRIEF CONTENTS

Foreword xxiii

Acknowledgments xxv

Introduction xxvii

PART I: MACHINE ORGANIZATION 1

Chapter 1: Hello, World of Assembly Language 3

Chapter 2: Computer Data Representation and Operations 43

Chapter 3: Memory Access and Organization 105

Chapter 4: Constants, Variables, and Data Types 147

PART II: ASSEMBLY LANGUAGE PROGRAMMING 213

Chapter 5: Procedures 215

Chapter 6: Arithmetic 287

Chapter 7: Low-Level Control Structures 377

Chapter 8: Advanced Arithmetic 453

Chapter 9: Numeric Conversion 491

Chapter 10: Table Lookups 583

Chapter 11: SIMD Instructions 595

Chapter 12: Bit Manipulation 707

Chapter 13: Macros and the MASM Compile-Time Language 747

Chapter 14: The String Instructions 825

Chapter 15: Managing Complex Projects 847

Chapter 16: Stand-Alone Assembly Language Programs 873

PART III: REFERENCE MATERIAL **899**

A: ASCII Character Set 901

B: Glossary 905

C: Installing and Using Visual Studio 919

D: The Windows Command Line Interpreter 925

E: Answers to Questions 935

Index 967

CONTENTS IN DETAIL

FOREWORD   xxiii

ACKNOWLEDGMENTS   xxv

INTRODUCTION   xxvii

PART I: MACHINE ORGANIZATION   1

1
HELLO, WORLD OF ASSEMBLY LANGUAGE   3

1.1 What You'll Need 4
1.2 Setting Up MASM on Your Machine 4
1.3 Setting Up a Text Editor on Your Machine 5
1.4 The Anatomy of a MASM Program 5
1.5 Running Your First MASM Program 6
1.6 Running Your First MASM/C++ Hybrid Program 7
1.7 An Introduction to the Intel x86-64 CPU Family 9
1.8 The Memory Subsystem 13
1.9 Declaring Memory Variables in MASM 14
     1.9.1 Associating Memory Addresses with Variables 16
     1.9.2 Associating Data Types with Variables 17
1.10 Declaring (Named) Constants in MASM. 18
1.11 Some Basic Machine Instructions 18
     1.11.1 The mov Instruction 18
     1.11.2 Type Checking on Instruction Operands 20
     1.11.3 The add and sub Instructions 21
     1.11.4 The lea Instruction 22
     1.11.5 The call and ret Instructions and MASM Procedures 22
1.12 Calling C/C++ Procedures. 24
1.13 Hello, World! 25
1.14 Returning Function Results in Assembly Language 27
1.15 Automating the Build Process 33
1.16 Microsoft ABI Notes. 35
     1.16.1 Variable Size 35
     1.16.2 Register Usage 38
     1.16.3 Stack Alignment 39
1.17 For More Information. 39
1.18 Test Yourself 40

2
COMPUTER DATA REPRESENTATION AND OPERATIONS   43

2.1 Numbering Systems. 44
    2.1.1 A Review of the Decimal System 44
    2.1.2 The Binary Numbering System 44
    2.1.3 Binary Conventions 45
2.2 The Hexadecimal Numbering System. 46
2.3 A Note About Numbers vs. Representation 48
2.4 Data Organization 50
    2.4.1 Bits 51
    2.4.2 Nibbles 51
    2.4.3 Bytes 52
    2.4.4 Words 53
    2.4.5 Double Words. 54
    2.4.6 Quad Words and Octal Words. 55
2.5 Logical Operations on Bits 55
    2.5.1 The AND Operation 55
    2.5.2 The OR Operation. 56
    2.5.3 The XOR Operation 57
    2.5.4 The NOT Operation 57
2.6 Logical Operations on Binary Numbers and Bit Strings 57
2.7 Signed and Unsigned Numbers. 62
2.8 Sign Extension and Zero Extension 67
2.9 Sign Contraction and Saturation 68
2.10 Brief Detour: An Introduction to Control Transfer Instructions 69
    2.10.1 The jmp Instruction. 69
    2.10.2 The Conditional Jump Instructions 70
    2.10.3 The cmp Instruction and Corresponding Conditional Jumps. 72
    2.10.4 Conditional Jump Synonyms 73
2.11 Shifts and Rotates 74
2.12 Bit Fields and Packed Data. 79
2.13 IEEE Floating-Point Formats 86
    2.13.1 Single-Precision Format 87
    2.13.2 Double-Precision Format. 88
    2.13.3 Extended-Precision Format 89
    2.13.4 Normalized Floating-Point Values 89
    2.13.5 Non-Numeric Values 90
    2.13.6 MASM Support for Floating-Point Values. 90
2.14 Binary-Coded Decimal Representation 91
2.15 Characters 92
    2.15.1 The ASCII Character Encoding 93
    2.15.2 MASM Support for ASCII Characters. 95
2.16 The Unicode Character Set. 96
    2.16.1 Unicode Code Points. 96
    2.16.2 Unicode Code Planes. 97
    2.16.3 Unicode Encodings 97
2.17 MASM Support for Unicode 98
2.18 For More Information. 99
2.19 Test Yourself 99

3
MEMORY ACCESS AND ORGANIZATION   **105**

3.1 Runtime Memory Organization 106
    3.1.1 The .code Section 108
    3.1.2 The .data Section 108
    3.1.3 The .const Section 109
    3.1.4 The .data? Section 110
    3.1.5 Organization of Declaration Sections Within Your Programs 110
    3.1.6 Memory Access and 4K Memory Management Unit Pages 111
3.2 How MASM Allocates Memory for Variables 113
3.3 The Label Declaration 114
3.4 Little-Endian and Big-Endian Data Organization 114
3.5 Memory Access 116
3.6 MASM Support for Data Alignment 119
3.7 The x86-64 Addressing Modes 122
    3.7.1 x86-64 Register Addressing Modes 122
    3.7.2 x86-64 64-Bit Memory Addressing Modes 123
    3.7.3 Large Address Unaware Applications 127
3.8 Address Expressions 130
3.9 The Stack Segment and the push and pop Instructions 134
    3.9.1 The Basic push Instruction 134
    3.9.2 The Basic pop Instruction 135
    3.9.3 Preserving Registers with the push and pop Instructions 137
3.10 The Stack Is a LIFO Data Structure 137
3.11 Other push and pop Instructions 140
3.12 Removing Data from the Stack Without Popping It 140
3.13 Accessing Data You've Pushed onto the Stack Without Popping It 142
3.14 Microsoft ABI Notes 144
3.15 For More Information 144
3.16 Test Yourself 145

4
CONSTANTS, VARIABLES, AND DATA TYPES   **147**

4.1 The imul Instruction 148
4.2 The inc and dec Instructions 149
4.3 MASM Constant Declarations 149
    4.3.1 Constant Expressions 152
    4.3.2 this and $ Operators 154
    4.3.3 Constant Expression Evaluation 156
4.4 The MASM typedef Statement 156
4.5 Type Coercion 157
4.6 Pointer Data Types 161
    4.6.1 Using Pointers in Assembly Language 162
    4.6.2 Declaring Pointers in MASM 163
    4.6.3 Pointer Constants and Pointer Constant Expressions 164
    4.6.4 Pointer Variables and Dynamic Memory Allocation 166
    4.6.5 Common Pointer Problems 167
4.7 Composite Data Types 174
4.8 Character Strings 174
    4.8.1 Zero-Terminated Strings 174
    4.8.2 Length-Prefixed Strings 175

     4.8.3 String Descriptors 176
     4.8.4 Pointers to Strings 177
     4.8.5 String Functions 177
4.9 Arrays 181
     4.9.1 Declaring Arrays in Your MASM Programs 182
     4.9.2 Accessing Elements of a Single-Dimensional Array 183
     4.9.3 Sorting an Array of Values 185
4.10 Multidimensional Arrays 189
     4.10.1 Row-Major Ordering 190
     4.10.2 Column-Major Ordering 193
     4.10.3 Allocating Storage for Multidimensional Arrays 194
     4.10.4 Accessing Multidimensional Array Elements in Assembly Language . 196
4.11 Records/Structs 197
     4.11.1 MASM Struct Declarations 198
     4.11.2 Accessing Record/Struct Fields 199
     4.11.3 Nesting MASM Structs 200
     4.11.4 Initializing Struct Fields 200
     4.11.5 Arrays of Structs 203
     4.11.6 Aligning Fields Within a Record 204
4.12 Unions 206
     4.12.1 Anonymous Unions 208
     4.12.2 Variant Types 209
4.13 Microsoft ABI Notes 210
4.14 For More Information 210
4.15 Test Yourself 210

PART II: ASSEMBLY LANGUAGE PROGRAMMING   213

5
PROCEDURES   215

5.1 Implementing Procedures 216
     5.1.1 The call and ret Instructions 218
     5.1.2 Labels in a Procedure 219
5.2 Saving the State of the Machine 220
5.3 Procedures and the Stack 224
     5.3.1 Activation Records 228
     5.3.2 The Assembly Language Standard Entry Sequence 231
     5.3.3 The Assembly Language Standard Exit Sequence 233
5.4 Local (Automatic) Variables 234
     5.4.1 Low-Level Implementation of Automatic (Local) Variables 235
     5.4.2 The MASM Local Directive 237
     5.4.3 Automatic Allocation 240
5.5 Parameters 240
     5.5.1 Pass by Value 241
     5.5.2 Pass by Reference 241
     5.5.3 Low-Level Parameter Implementation 243
     5.5.4 Declaring Parameters with the proc Directive 255
     5.5.5 Accessing Reference Parameters on the Stack 256

5.6 Calling Conventions and the Microsoft ABI 261
5.7 The Microsoft ABI and Microsoft Calling Convention 263
    5.7.1 Data Types and the Microsoft ABI 263
    5.7.2 Parameter Locations 264
    5.7.3 Volatile and Nonvolatile Registers 265
    5.7.4 Stack Alignment 267
    5.7.5 Parameter Setup and Cleanup (or "What's with
          These Magic Instructions?") 268
5.8 Functions and Function Results 270
5.9 Recursion 271
5.10 Procedure Pointers 278
5.11 Procedural Parameters 280
5.12 Saving the State of the Machine, Part II 280
5.13 Microsoft ABI Notes 283
5.14 For More Information 284
5.15 Test Yourself 284

6
ARITHMETIC 287

6.1 x86-64 Integer Arithmetic Instructions 287
    6.1.1 Sign- and Zero-Extension Instructions 288
    6.1.2 The mul and imul Instructions 289
    6.1.3 The div and idiv Instructions 291
    6.1.4 The cmp Instruction, Revisited 293
    6.1.5 The setcc Instructions 295
    6.1.6 The test Instruction 297
6.2 Arithmetic Expressions 299
    6.2.1 Simple Assignments 299
    6.2.2 Simple Expressions 300
    6.2.3 Complex Expressions 302
    6.2.4 Commutative Operators 307
6.3 Logical (Boolean) Expressions 308
6.4 Machine and Arithmetic Idioms 310
    6.4.1 Multiplying Without mul or imul 310
    6.4.2 Dividing Without div or idiv 312
    6.4.3 Implementing Modulo-N Counters with AND 312
6.5 Floating-Point Arithmetic 313
    6.5.1 Floating-Point on the x86-64 317
    6.5.2 FPU Registers 317
    6.5.3 FPU Data Types 324
    6.5.4 The FPU Instruction Set 325
    6.5.5 FPU Data Movement Instructions 326
    6.5.6 Conversions 328
    6.5.7 Arithmetic Instructions 330
    6.5.8 Comparison Instructions 350
    6.5.9 Constant Instructions 360
    6.5.10 Transcendental Instructions 361
    6.5.11 Miscellaneous Instructions 363
6.6 Converting Floating-Point Expressions to Assembly Language 364
    6.6.1 Converting Arithmetic Expressions to Postfix Notation 366
    6.6.2 Converting Postfix Notation to Assembly Language 367

6.7 SSE Floating-Point Arithmetic. 369
    6.7.1 SSE MXCSR Register 369
    6.7.2 SSE Floating-Point Move Instructions. 370
    6.7.3 SSE Floating-Point Arithmetic Instructions 371
    6.7.4 SSE Floating-Point Comparisons 372
    6.7.5 SSE Floating-Point Conversions 373
6.8 For More Information 374
6.9 Test Yourself 375

7
LOW-LEVEL CONTROL STRUCTURES   **377**

7.1 Statement Labels 378
    7.1.1 Using Local Symbols in Procedures 378
    7.1.2 Initializing Arrays with Label Addresses 381
7.2 Unconditional Transfer of Control (jmp) 382
    7.2.1 Register-Indirect Jumps 383
    7.2.2 Memory-Indirect Jumps. 389
7.3 Conditional Jump Instructions 390
7.4 Trampolines 393
7.5 Conditional Move Instructions 394
7.6 Implementing Common Control Structures in Assembly Language 396
    7.6.1 Decisions 396
    7.6.2 if/then/else Sequences 397
    7.6.3 Complex if Statements Using Complete Boolean Evaluation 400
    7.6.4 Short-Circuit Boolean Evaluation 401
    7.6.5 Short-Circuit vs. Complete Boolean Evaluation. 403
    7.6.6 Efficient Implementation of if Statements in Assembly Language. 405
    7.6.7 switch/case Statements 410
7.7 State Machines and Indirect Jumps 424
7.8 Loops. 433
    7.8.1 while Loops 433
    7.8.2 repeat/until Loops. 434
    7.8.3 forever/endfor Loops 436
    7.8.4 for Loops 437
    7.8.5 The break and continue Statements 438
    7.8.6 Register Usage and Loops 442
7.9 Loop Performance Improvements 443
    7.9.1 Moving the Termination Condition to the End of a Loop 443
    7.9.2 Executing the Loop Backward 445
    7.9.3 Using Loop-Invariant Computations 446
    7.9.4 Unraveling Loops. 447
    7.9.5 Using Induction Variables 448
7.10 For More Information 450
7.11 Test Yourself 450

8
ADVANCED ARITHMETIC   **453**

8.1 Extended-Precision Operations 454
    8.1.1 Extended-Precision Addition 454
    8.1.2 Extended-Precision Subtraction 457
    8.1.3 Extended-Precision Comparisons 458

      8.1.4 Extended-Precision Multiplication 461
      8.1.5 Extended-Precision Division. 466
      8.1.6 Extended-Precision Negation Operations 477
      8.1.7 Extended-Precision AND Operations 479
      8.1.8 Extended-Precision OR Operations 479
      8.1.9 Extended-Precision XOR Operations. 480
      8.1.10 Extended-Precision NOT Operations 480
      8.1.11 Extended-Precision Shift Operations. 480
      8.1.12 Extended-Precision Rotate Operations 484
  8.2 Operating on Different-Size Operands. 485
  8.3 Decimal Arithmetic 486
      8.3.1 Literal BCD Constants. 487
      8.3.2 Packed Decimal Arithmetic Using the FPU. 488
  8.4 For More Information. 489
  8.5 Test Yourself 489

9
NUMERIC CONVERSION   **491**
  9.1 Converting Numeric Values to Strings 491
      9.1.1 Converting Numeric Values to Hexadecimal Strings. 492
      9.1.2 Converting Extended-Precision Hexadecimal Values to Strings. 499
      9.1.3 Converting Unsigned Decimal Values to Strings. 500
      9.1.4 Converting Signed Integer Values to Strings 507
      9.1.5 Converting Extended-Precision Unsigned Integers to Strings 508
      9.1.6 Converting Extended-Precision Signed Decimal Values to Strings. . . . 513
      9.1.7 Formatting Conversions 514
      9.1.8 Converting Floating-Point Values to Strings 519
  9.2 String-to-Numeric Conversion Routines 546
      9.2.1 Converting Decimal Strings to Integers 546
      9.2.2 Converting Hexadecimal Strings to Numeric Form. 556
      9.2.3 Converting Unsigned Decimal Strings to Integers. 563
      9.2.4 Converting of Extended-Precision String to Unsigned Integer 566
      9.2.5 Converting of Extended-Precision Signed Decimal String to Integer . . . 569
      9.2.6 Converting of Real String to Floating-Point 570
  9.3 For More Information. 581
  9.4 Test Yourself 581

10
TABLE LOOKUPS   **583**
  10.1 Tables 583
      10.1.1 Function Computation via Table Lookup 584
      10.1.2 Generating Tables 590
      10.1.3 Table-Lookup Performance 593
  10.2 For More Information. 593
  10.3 Test Yourself 593

11
SIMD INSTRUCTIONS   **595**
  11.1 The SSE/AVX Architectures. 596
  11.2 Streaming Data Types 596

11.3 Using cpuid to Differentiate Instruction Sets. 599
11.4 Full-Segment Syntax and Segment Alignment 604
11.5 SSE, AVX, and AVX2 Memory Operand Alignment 606
11.6 SIMD Data Movement Instructions. 609
    11.6.1 The (v)movd and (v)movq Instructions. 609
    11.6.2 The (v)movaps, (v)movapd, and (v)movdqa Instructions 610
    11.6.3 The (v)movups, (v)movupd, and (v)movdqu Instructions. 612
    11.6.4 Performance of Aligned and Unaligned Moves 612
    11.6.5 The (v)movlps and (v)movlpd Instructions 615
    11.6.6 The movhps and movhpd Instructions. 617
    11.6.7 The vmovhps and vmovhpd Instructions 618
    11.6.8 The movlhps and vmovlhps Instructions. 619
    11.6.9 The movhlps and vmovhlps Instructions. 619
    11.6.10 The (v)movshdup and (v)movsldup Instructions. 620
    11.6.11 The (v)movddup Instruction 621
    11.6.12 The (v)lddqu Instruction. 622
    11.6.13 Performance Issues and the SIMD Move Instructions. 622
    11.6.14 Some Final Comments on the SIMD Move Instructions 624
11.7 The Shuffle and Unpack Instructions. 625
    11.7.1 The (v)pshufb Instructions 625
    11.7.2 The (v)pshufd Instructions 626
    11.7.3 The (v)pshuflw and (v)pshufhw Instructions 628
    11.7.4 The shufps and shufpd Instructions. 630
    11.7.5 The vshufps and vshufpd Instructions 632
    11.7.6 The (v)unpcklps, (v)unpckhps, (v)unpcklpd, and
        (v)unpckhpd Instructions 633
    11.7.7 The Integer Unpack Instructions 637
    11.7.8 The (v)pextrb, (v)pextrw, (v)pextrd, and (v)pextrq Instructions. 641
    11.7.9 The (v)pinsrb, (v)pinsrw, (v)pinsrd, and (v)pinsrq Instructions 642
    11.7.10 The (v)extractps and (v)insertps Instructions 643
11.8 SIMD Arithmetic and Logical Operations 644
11.9 The SIMD Logical (Bitwise) Instructions 645
    11.9.1 The (v)ptest Instructions. 646
    11.9.2 The Byte Shift Instructions 646
    11.9.3 The Bit Shift Instructions 647
11.10 The SIMD Integer Arithmetic Instructions 648
    11.10.1 SIMD Integer Addition 648
    11.10.2 Horizontal Additions 650
    11.10.3 Double-Word–Sized Horizontal Additions. 652
    11.10.4 SIMD Integer Subtraction 653
    11.10.5 SIMD Integer Multiplication. 654
    11.10.6 SIMD Integer Averages 657
    11.10.7 SIMD Integer Minimum and Maximum 657
    11.10.8 SIMD Integer Absolute Value. 659
    11.10.9 SIMD Integer Sign Adjustment Instructions. 659
    11.10.10 SIMD Integer Comparison Instructions 660
    11.10.11 Integer Conversions. 664
11.11 SIMD Floating-Point Arithmetic Operations 668
11.12 SIMD Floating-Point Comparison Instructions. 671
    11.12.1 SSE and AVX Comparisons. 671
    11.12.2 Unordered vs. Ordered Comparisons. 673
    11.12.3 Signaling and Quiet Comparisons. 673

11.12.4 Instruction Synonyms 673
11.12.5 AVX Extended Comparisons 674
11.12.6 Using SIMD Comparison Instructions 676
11.12.7 The (v)movmskps, (v)movmskpd Instructions. 676
11.13 Floating-Point Conversion Instructions 679
11.14 Aligning SIMD Memory Accesses 681
11.15 Aligning Word, Dword, and Qword Object Addresses 683
11.16 Filling an XMM Register with Several Copies of the Same Value 684
11.17 Loading Some Common Constants Into XMM and YMM Registers 685
11.18 Setting, Clearing, Inverting, and Testing a Single Bit in an SSE Register 687
11.19 Processing Two Vectors by Using a Single Incremented Index 688
11.20 Aligning Two Addresses to a Boundary 690
11.21 Working with Blocks of Data Whose Length Is Not
a Multiple of the SSE/AVX Register Size. 691
11.22 Dynamically Testing for a CPU Feature 692
11.23 The MASM Include Directive. 702
11.24 And a Whole Lot More 703
11.25 For More Information. 703
11.26 Test Yourself 705

**12
BIT MANIPULATION   707**

12.1 What Is Bit Data, Anyway?. 707
12.2 Instructions That Manipulate Bits 708
12.2.1 The and Instruction. 709
12.2.2 The or Instruction. 710
12.2.3 The xor Instruction 712
12.2.4 Flag Modification by Logical Instructions 712
12.2.5 The Bit Test Instructions 715
12.2.6 Manipulating Bits with Shift and Rotate Instructions 716
12.3 The Carry Flag as a Bit Accumulator 716
12.4 Packing and Unpacking Bit Strings 717
12.5 BMI1 Instructions to Extract Bits and Create Bit Masks 723
12.6 Coalescing Bit Sets and Distributing Bit Strings 728
12.7 Coalescing and Distributing Bit Strings Using BMI2 Instructions. 731
12.8 Packed Arrays of Bit Strings 733
12.9 Searching for a Bit. 736
12.10 Counting Bits 739
12.11 Reversing a Bit String 739
12.12 Merging Bit Strings 741
12.13 Extracting Bit Strings 742
12.14 Searching for a Bit Pattern 743
12.15 For More Information. 744
12.16 Test Yourself 744

**13
MACROS AND THE MASM COMPILE-TIME LANGUAGE   747**

13.1 Introduction to the Compile-Time Language. 748
13.2 The echo and .err Directives 748
13.3 Compile-Time Constants and Variables. 750
13.4 Compile-Time Expressions and Operators. 750

      13.4.1 The MASM Escape (!) Operator 750
      13.4.2 The MASM Evaluation (%) Operator 750
      13.4.3 The catstr Directive 751
      13.4.4 The instr Directive 751
      13.4.5 The sizestr Directive 752
      13.4.6 The substr Directive 752
13.5 Conditional Assembly (Compile-Time Decisions) 752
13.6 Repetitive Assembly (Compile-Time Loops) 756
13.7 Macros (Compile-Time Procedures) 760
13.8 Standard Macros 760
13.9 Macro Parameters 762
      13.9.1 Standard Macro Parameter Expansion 762
      13.9.2 Optional and Required Macro Parameters 766
      13.9.3 Default Macro Parameter Values 768
      13.9.4 Macros with a Variable Number of Parameters 769
      13.9.5 The Macro Expansion (&) Operator 770
13.10 Local Symbols in a Macro 770
13.11 The exitm Directive 772
13.12 MASM Macro Function Syntax 773
13.13 Macros as Compile-Time Procedures and Functions 775
13.14 Writing Compile-Time "Programs" 776
      13.14.1 Constructing Data Tables at Compile Time . . . . : . . . 776
      13.14.2 Unrolling Loops 779
13.15 Simulating HLL Procedure Calls 781
      13.15.1 HLL-Like Calls with No Parameters 781
      13.15.2 HLL-Like Calls with One Parameter 782
      13.15.3 Using opattr to Determine Argument Types 784
      13.15.4 HLL-Like Calls with a Fixed Number of Parameters 786
      13.15.5 HLL-Like Calls with a Varying Parameter List 791
13.16 The invoke Macro 794
13.17 Advanced Macro Parameter Parsing 795
      13.17.1 Checking for String Literal Constants 797
      13.17.2 Checking for Real Constants 798
      13.17.3 Checking for Registers 808
      13.17.4 Compile-Time Arrays 813
13.18 Using Macros to Write Macros 818
13.19 Compile-Time Program Performance 822
13.20 For More Information 822
13.21 Test Yourself 823

14
THE STRING INSTRUCTIONS   825

14.1 The x86-64 String Instructions 826
      14.1.1 The rep, repe, repz, and the repnz and repne Prefixes 826
      14.1.2 The Direction Flag 827
      14.1.3 The movs Instruction 827
      14.1.4 The cmps Instruction 832
      14.1.5 The scas Instruction 835
      14.1.6 The stos Instruction 835
      14.1.7 The lods Instruction 836
      14.1.8 Building Complex String Functions from lods and stos 837
14.2 Performance of the x86-64 String Instructions 837

14.3 SIMD String Instructions 838
    14.3.1 Packed Compare Operand Sizes 839
    14.3.2 Type of Comparison. 839
    14.3.3 Result Polarity 840
    14.3.4 Output Processing 841
    14.3.5 Packed String Compare Lengths 841
    14.3.6 Packed String Comparison Results 843
14.4 Alignment and Memory Management Unit Pages 844
14.5 For More Information 845
14.6 Test Yourself 845

15
MANAGING COMPLEX PROJECTS   **847**

15.1 The include Directive 848
15.2 Ignoring Duplicate Include Operations 849
15.3 Assembly Units and External Directives 849
15.4 Header Files in MASM 852
15.5 The externdef Directive 852
15.6 Separate Compilation 854
15.7 An Introduction to Makefiles 862
    15.7.1 Basic Makefile Syntax 863
    15.7.2 Make Dependencies 864
    15.7.3 Make Clean and Touch 867
15.8 The Microsoft Linker and Library Code 869
15.9 Object File and Library Impact on Program Size 870
15.10 For More Information 871
15.11 Test Yourself 871

16
STAND-ALONE ASSEMBLY LANGUAGE PROGRAMS   **873**

16.1 Hello World, by Itself 874
16.2 Header Files and the Windows Interface 876
16.3 The Win32 API and the Windows ABI 878
16.4 Building a Stand-Alone Console Application 878
16.5 Building a Stand-Alone GUI Application 879
16.6 A Brief Look at the MessageBox Windows API Function 880
16.7 Windows File I/O 881
16.8 Windows Applications 897
16.9 For More Information 897
16.10 Test Yourself 898

PART III: REFERENCE MATERIAL   **899**

A
ASCII CHARACTER SET   **901**

B
GLOSSARY   **905**

C

INSTALLING AND USING VISUAL STUDIO   919

C.1 Installing Visual Studio Community. 919
C.2 Creating a Command Line Prompt for MASM 920
C.3 Editing, Assembling, and Running a MASM Source File .922

D

THE WINDOWS COMMAND LINE INTERPRETER   925

D.1 Command Line Syntax 925
D.2 Directory Names and Drive Letters. 928
D.3 Some Useful Built-in Commands. 930
    D.3.1 The cd and chdir Commands 930
    D.3.2 The cls Command 931
    D.3.3 The copy Command 931
    D.3.4 The date Command. 931
    D.3.5 The del (erase) Command 932
    D.3.6 The dir Command 932
    D.3.7 The more Command 932
    D.3.8 The move Command 933
    D.3.9 The ren and rename Commands 933
    D.3.10 The rd and rmdir Commands 933
    D.3.11 The time Command 933
D.4 For More Information 934

E

ANSWERS TO QUESTIONS   935

INDEX   967

FOREWORD

Assembly language programmers often hear the question, "Why would you bother when there are so many other languages that are much easier to write and to understand?" There has always been one answer: you write assembly language because you can.

Free of any other assumptions, free of artificial structuring, and free of the restrictions that so many other languages impose on you, you can create anything that is within the capacity of the operating system and the processor hardware. The full capacity of the x86 and later x64 hardware is available to the programmer. Within the boundaries of the operating system, any structure that is imposed, is imposed by the programmer in the code design and layout that they choose to use.

There have been many good assemblers over time, but the use of the Microsoft assembler, commonly known as MASM, has one great advantage: it has been around since the early 1980s, and while others come and go, MASM is updated on an as-needed basis for technology and operating system changes by the operating system vendor Microsoft.

From its origins as a real-mode 16-bit assembler, over time and technology changes it has been updated to a 32-bit version. With the introduction of 64-bit Windows, there is a 64-bit version of MASM as well that produces 64-bit object modules. The 32- and 64-bit versions are components in the Visual Studio suite of tools and can be used by both C and C++ as well as pure assembler executable files and dynamic link libraries.

Randall Hyde's original *The Art of Assembly Language* has been a reference work for nearly 20 years, and with the author's long and extensive understanding of x86 hardware and assembly programming, a 64-bit version of the book is a welcome addition to the total knowledge base for future high-performance x64 programming.

—Steve Hutchesson
https://www.masm32.com/

ACKNOWLEDGMENTS

Several individuals at No Starch Press have contributed to the quality of this book and deserve appropriate kudos for all their effort:

Bill Pollock, president
Barbara Yien, executive editor
Katrina Taylor, production editor
Miles Bond, assistant production editor
Athabasca Witschi, developmental editor
Nathan Heidelberger, developmental editor
Natalie Gleason, marketing manager
Morgan Vega Gomez, marketing coordinator
Sharon Wilkey, copyeditor
Sadie Barry, proofreader
Jeff Lytle, compositor

—Randall Hyde

INTRODUCTION

This book is the culmination of 30 years' work. The very earliest versions of this book were notes I copied for my students at Cal Poly Pomona and UC Riverside under the title "How to Program the IBM PC Using 8088 Assembly Language." I had lots of input from students and a good friend of mine, Mary Philips, that softened the edges a bit. Bill Pollock rescued that early version from obscurity on the internet, and with the help of Karol Jurado, the first edition of *The Art of Assembly Language* became a reality in 2003.

Thousands of readers (and suggestions) later, along with input from Bill Pollock, Alison Peterson, Ansel Staton, Riley Hoffman, Megan Dunchak,

Linda Recktenwald, Susan Glinert Stevens, and Nancy Bell at No Starch Press (and a technical review by Nathan Baker), the second edition of this book arrived in 2010.

Ten years later, *The Art of Assembly Language* (or *AoA* as I refer to it) was losing popularity because it was tied to the 35-year-old 32-bit design of the Intel x86. Today, someone who was going to learn 80x86 assembly language would want to learn 64-bit assembly on the newer x86-64 CPUs. So in early 2020, I began the process of translating the old 32-bit *AoA* (based on the use of the High-Level Assembler, or HLA) to 64 bits by using the Microsoft Macro Assembler (MASM).

When I first started the project, I thought I'd translate a few HLA programs to MASM, tweak a little text, and wind up with *The Art of 64-Bit Assembly* with minimal effort. I was wrong. Between the folks at No Starch Press wanting to push the envelope on readability and understanding, and the incredible job Tony Tribelli has done in his technical review of every line of text and code in this book, this project turned out to be as much work as writing a new book from scratch. That's okay; I think you'll really appreciate the work that has gone into this book.

A Note About the Source Code in This Book

A considerable amount of x86-64 assembly language (and C/C++) source code is presented throughout this book. Typically, source code comes in three flavors: code snippets, single assembly language procedures or functions, and full-blown programs.

Code snippets are fragments of a program; they are not stand-alone, and you cannot compile (assemble) them using MASM (or a C++ compiler in the case of C/C++ source code). Code snippets exist to make a point or provide a small example of a programming technique. Here is a typical example of a code snippet you will find in this book:

```
someConst = 5
    .
    .
    .
mov eax, someConst
```

The vertical ellipsis (. . .) denotes arbitrary code that could appear in its place (not all snippets use the ellipsis, but it's worthwhile to point this out).

Assembly language procedures are also not stand-alone code. While you can assemble many assembly language procedures appearing in this book (by simply copying the code straight out of the book into an editor and then running MASM on the resulting text file), they will not execute on their own. Code snippets and assembly language procedures differ in one major way: procedures appear as part of the downloadable source files for this book (at *https://artofasm.randallhyde.com/*).

Full-blown programs, which you can compile and execute, are labeled as *listings* in this book. They have a listing number/identifier of the form

"Listing *C-N*," where *C* is the chapter number and *N* is a sequentially increasing listing number, starting at 1 for each chapter. Here is an example of a program listing that appears in this book:

```
; Listing 1-3

; A simple MASM module that contains
; an empty function to be called by
; the C++ code in Listing 1-2.

        .CODE

; The "option casemap:none" statement
; tells MASM to make all identifiers
; case-sensitive (rather than mapping
; them to uppercase). This is necessary
; because C++ identifiers are case-
; sensitive.

        option  casemap:none

; Here is the "asmFunc" function.

        public  asmFunc
asmFunc PROC

; Empty function just returns to C++ code.

        ret     ; Returns to caller

asmFunc ENDP
        END
```

Listing 1: A MASM program that the C++ program in Listing 1-2 calls

Like procedures, all listings are available in electronic form at my website: *https://artofasm.randallhyde.com/*. This link will take you to the page containing all the source files and other support information for this book (such as errata, electronic chapters, and other useful information). A few chapters attach listing numbers to procedures and macros, which are not full programs, for legibility purposes. A couple of listings demonstrate MASM syntax errors or are otherwise unrunnable. The source code still appears in the electronic distribution under that listing name.

Typically, this book follows executable listings with a build command and sample output. Here is a typical example (user input is given in a bold-face font):

```
C:\>build listing4-7

C:\>echo off
 Assembling: listing4-7.asm
c.cpp
```

```
C:\>listing4-7
Calling Listing 4-7:
aString: maxLen:20, len:20, string data:'Initial String Data'
Listing 4-7 terminated
```

Most of the programs in this text run from a Windows *command line* (that is, inside the *cmd.exe* application). By default, this book assumes you're running the programs from the root directory on the C: drive. Therefore, every build command and sample output typically has the text prefix `C:\>` before any command you would type from the keyboard on the command line. However, you can run the programs from any drive or directory.

If you are completely unfamiliar with the Windows command line, please take a little time to learn about the Windows command line interpreter (CLI). You can start the CLI by executing the *cmd.exe* program from the Windows run command. As you're going to be running the CLI frequently while reading this book, I recommend creating a shortcut to *cmd.exe* on your desktop. In Appendix C, I describe how to create this shortcut to automatically set up the environment variables you will need to easily run MASM (and the Microsoft Visual C++ compiler). Appendix D provides a quick introduction to the Windows CLI for those who are unfamiliar with it.

PART I

MACHINE ORGANIZATION

1

HELLO, WORLD OF ASSEMBLY LANGUAGE

 This chapter is a "quick-start" chapter that lets you begin writing basic assembly language programs as rapidly as possible. By the conclusion of this chapter, you should understand the basic syntax of a Microsoft Macro Assembler (MASM) program and the prerequisites for learning new assembly language features in the chapters that follow.

NOTE   *This book uses the MASM running under Windows because that is, by far, the most commonly used assembler for writing x86-64 assembly language programs. Furthermore, the Intel documentation typically uses assembly language examples that are syntax-compatible with MASM. If you encounter x86 source code in the real world, it will likely be written using MASM. That being said, many other popular x86-64 assemblers are out there, including the GNU Assembler (gas), Netwide Assembler (NASM), Flat Assembler (FASM), and others. These assemblers employ a different syntax from MASM (gas being the one most radically different). At some point, if you work in assembly language much, you'll probably encounter source code written with one of these other assemblers. Don't fret; learning the syntactical differences isn't that hard once you've mastered x86-64 assembly language using MASM.*

This chapter covers the following:

- Basic syntax of a MASM program
- The Intel central processing unit (CPU) architecture
- Setting aside memory for variables
- Using machine instructions to control the CPU
- Linking a MASM program with C/C++ code so you can call routines in the C Standard Library
- Writing some simple assembly language programs

1.1 What You'll Need

You'll need a few prerequisites to learn assembly language programming with MASM: a 64-bit version of MASM, plus a text editor (for creating and modifying MASM source files), a linker, various library files, and a C++ compiler.

Today's software engineers drop down into assembly language only when their C++, C#, Java, Swift, or Python code is running too slow and they need to improve the performance of certain modules (or functions) in their code. Because you'll typically be interfacing assembly language with C++, or other high-level language (HLL) code, when using assembly in the real world, we'll do so in this book as well.

Another reason to use C++ is for the C Standard Library. While different individuals have created several useful libraries for MASM (see *http:// www.masm32.com/* for a good example), there is no universally accepted standard set of libraries. To make the C Standard Library immediately accessible to MASM programs, this book presents examples with a short C/C++ main function that calls a single external function written in assembly language using MASM. Compiling the C++ main program along with the MASM source file will produce a single executable file that you can run and test.

Do you need to know C++ to learn assembly language? Not really. This book will spoon-feed you the C++ you'll need to run the example programs. Nevertheless, assembly language isn't the best choice for your first language, so this book assumes that you have some experience in a language such as C/C++, Pascal (or Delphi), Java, Swift, Rust, BASIC, Python, or any other imperative or object-oriented programming language.

1.2 Setting Up MASM on Your Machine

MASM is a Microsoft product that is part of the Visual Studio suite of developer tools. Because it's Microsoft's tool set, you need to be running some variant of Windows (as I write this, Windows 10 is the latest version; however, any later version of Windows will likely work as well). Appendix C provides a complete description of how to install Visual Studio Community (the "no-cost" version, which includes MASM and the Visual C++ compiler, plus other tools you will need). Please refer to that appendix for more details.

1.3 Setting Up a Text Editor on Your Machine

Visual Studio includes a text editor that you can use to create and edit MASM and C++ programs. Because you have to install the Visual Studio package to obtain MASM, you automatically get a production-quality programmer's text editor you can use for your assembly language source files.

However, you can use any editor that works with straight ASCII files (UTF-8 is also fine) to create MASM and C++ source files, such as Notepad++ or the text editor available from *https://www.masm32.com/*. Word processing programs, such as Microsoft Word, are not appropriate for editing program source files.

1.4 The Anatomy of a MASM Program

A typical (stand-alone) MASM program looks like Listing 1-1.

```
; Comments consist of all text from a semicolon character
; to the end of the line.

; The ".code" directive tells MASM that the statements following
; this directive go in the section of memory reserved for machine
; instructions (code).

        .code

; Here is the "main" function. (This example assumes that the
; assembly language program is a stand-alone program with its
; own main function.)

main    PROC

Machine instructions go here

        ret     ; Returns to caller

main    ENDP

; The END directive marks the end of the source file.

        END
```

Listing 1-1: Trivial shell program

A typical MASM program contains one or more *sections* representing the type of data appearing in memory. These sections begin with a MASM statement such as .code or .data. Variables and other memory values appear in a *data* section. Machine instructions appear in procedures that appear within a *code* section. And so on. The individual sections appearing in an assembly language source file are optional, so not every type of section will appear in a particular source file. For example, Listing 1-1 contains only a single code section.

The .code statement is an example of an assembler *directive*—a statement that tells MASM something about the program but is not an actual x86-64 machine instruction. In particular, the .code directive tells MASM to group the statements following it into a special section of memory reserved for machine instructions.

1.5   Running Your First MASM Program

A traditional first program people write, popularized by Brian Kernighan and Dennis Ritchie's *The C Programming Language* (Prentice Hall, 1978) is the "Hello, world!" program. The whole purpose of this program is to provide a simple example that someone learning a new programming language can use to figure out how to use the tools needed to compile and run programs in that language.

Unfortunately, writing something as simple as a "Hello, world!" program is a major production in assembly language. You have to learn several machine instruction and assembler directives, not to mention Windows system calls, to print the string "Hello, world!" At this point in the game, that's too much to ask from a beginning assembly language programmer (for those who want to blast on ahead, take a look at the sample program in Appendix C).

However, the program shell in Listing 1-1 is actually a complete assembly language program. You can compile (*assemble*) and run it. It doesn't produce any output. It simply returns back to Windows immediately after you start it. However, it does run, and it will serve as the mechanism for showing you how to assemble, link, and run an assembly language source file.

MASM is a traditional *command line assembler*, which means you need to run it from a Windows *command line prompt* (available by running the *cmd.exe* program). To do so, enter something like the following into the command line prompt or shell window:

```
C:\>ml64 programShell.asm /link /subsystem:console /entry:main
```

This command tells MASM to assemble the *programShell.asm* program (where I've saved Listing 1-1) to an executable file, link the result to produce a console application (one that you can run from the command line), and begin execution at the label main in the assembly language source file. Assuming that no errors occur, you can run the resulting program by typing the following command into your command prompt window:

```
C:\>programShell
```

Windows should immediately respond with a new command line prompt (as the programShell application simply returns control back to Windows after it starts running).

1.6 Running Your First MASM/C++ Hybrid Program

This book commonly combines an assembly language module (containing one or more functions written in assembly language) with a C/C++ main program that calls those functions. Because the compilation and execution process is slightly different from a stand-alone MASM program, this section demonstrates how to create, compile, and run a hybrid assembly/C++ program. Listing 1-2 provides the main C++ program that calls the assembly language module.

```
// Listing 1-2

// A simple C++ program that calls an assembly language function.
// Need to include stdio.h so this program can call "printf()".

#include <stdio.h>

// extern "C" namespace prevents "name mangling" by the C++
// compiler.

extern "C"
{
    // Here's the external function, written in assembly
    // language, that this program will call:

    void asmFunc(void);
};

int main(void)
{
    printf("Calling asmMain:\n");
    asmFunc();
    printf("Returned from asmMain\n");
}
```

Listing 1-2: A sample C/C++ program, listing1-2.cpp, that calls an assembly language function

Listing 1-3 is a slight modification of the stand-alone MASM program that contains the asmFunc() function that the C++ program calls.

```
; Listing 1-3

; A simple MASM module that contains an empty function to be
; called by the C++ code in Listing 1-2.

        .CODE

; (See text concerning option directive.)

        option  casemap:none

; Here is the "asmFunc" function.

        public  asmFunc
asmFunc PROC
```

```
; Empty function just returns to C++ code.

        ret     ; Returns to caller

asmFunc ENDP
        END
```

Listing 1-3: A MASM program, listing1-3.asm, *that the C++ program in Listing 1-2 calls*

Listing 1-3 has three changes from the original *programShell.asm* source file. First, there are two new statements: the option statement and the public statement.

The option statement tells MASM to make all symbols case-sensitive. This is necessary because MASM, by default, is case-insensitive and maps all identifiers to uppercase (so asmFunc() would become ASMFUNC()). C++ is a case-sensitive language and treats asmFunc() and ASMFUNC() as two different identifiers. Therefore, it's important to tell MASM to respect the case of the identifiers so as not to confuse the C++ program.

NOTE *MASM identifiers may begin with a dollar sign ($), underscore (_), or an alphabetic character and may be followed by zero or more alphanumeric, dollar sign, or underscore characters. An identifier may not consist of a $ character by itself (this has a special meaning to MASM).*

The public statement declares that the asmFunc() identifier will be visible outside the MASM source/object file. Without this statement, asmFunc() would be accessible only within the MASM module, and the C++ compilation would complain that asmFunc() is an undefined identifier.

The third difference between Listing 1-3 and Listing 1-1 is that the function's name was changed from main() to asmFunc(). The C++ compiler and linker would get confused if the assembly code used the name main(), as that's also the name of the C++ main() function.

To compile and run these source files, you use the following commands:

```
C:\>ml64 /c listing1-3.asm
Microsoft (R) Macro Assembler (x64) Version 14.15.26730.0
Copyright (C) Microsoft Corporation.  All rights reserved.

 Assembling: listing1-3.asm

C:\>cl listing1-2.cpp listing1-3.obj
Microsoft (R) C/C++ Optimizing Compiler Version 19.15.26730 for x64
Copyright (C) Microsoft Corporation.  All rights reserved.

listing1-2.cpp
Microsoft (R) Incremental Linker Version 14.15.26730.0
Copyright (C) Microsoft Corporation.  All rights reserved.

/out:listing1-2.exe
listing1-2.obj
listing1-3.obj
```

```
C:\>listing1-2
Calling asmFunc:
Returned from asmFunc
```

The ml64 command uses the /c option, which stands for *compile-only*, and does not attempt to run the linker (which would fail because *listing1-3.asm* is not a stand-alone program). The output from MASM is an object code file (*listing1-3.obj*), which serves as input to the Microsoft Visual C++ (MSVC) compiler in the next command.

The cl command runs the MSVC compiler on the *listing1-2.cpp* file and links in the assembled code (*listing1-3.obj*). The output from the MSVC compiler is the *listing1-2.exe* executable file. Executing that program from the command line produces the output we expect.

1.7   An Introduction to the Intel x86-64 CPU Family

Thus far, you've seen a single MASM program that will actually compile and run. However, the program does nothing more than return control to Windows. Before you can progress any further and learn some real assembly language, a detour is necessary: unless you understand the basic structure of the Intel x86-64 CPU family, the machine instructions will make little sense.

The Intel CPU family is generally classified as a *von Neumann architecture machine*. Von Neumann computer systems contain three main building blocks: the *central processing unit (CPU)*, *memory*, and *input/output (I/O) devices*. These three components are interconnected via the *system bus* (consisting of the address, data, and control buses). The block diagram in Figure 1-1 shows these relationships.

The CPU communicates with memory and I/O devices by placing a numeric value on the address bus to select one of the memory locations or I/O device port locations, each of which has a unique numeric *address*. Then the CPU, memory, and I/O devices pass data among themselves by placing the data on the data bus. The control bus contains signals that determine the direction of the data transfer (to/from memory and to/from an I/O device).

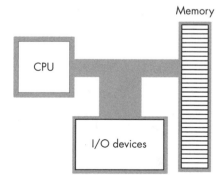

Figure 1-1: Von Neumann computer system block diagram

Within the CPU, special locations known as *registers* are used to manipulate data. The x86-64 CPU registers can be broken into four categories: general-purpose registers, special-purpose application-accessible registers, segment registers, and special-purpose kernel-mode registers. Because the segment registers aren't used much in modern 64-bit operating systems (such as Windows), there is little need to discuss them in this book. The special-purpose kernel-mode registers are intended for writing operating systems, debuggers, and other system-level tools. Such software construction is well beyond the scope of this text.

The x86-64 (Intel family) CPUs provide several *general-purpose registers* for application use. These include the following:

- Sixteen 64-bit registers that have the following names: RAX, RBX, RCX, RDX, RSI, RDI, RBP, RSP, R8, R9, R10, R11, R12, R13, R14, and R15
- Sixteen 32-bit registers: EAX, EBX, ECX, EDX, ESI, EDI, EBP, ESP, R8D, R9D, R10D, R11D, R12D, R13D, R14D, and R15D
- Sixteen 16-bit registers: AX, BX, CX, DX, SI, DI, BP, SP, R8W, R9W, R10W, R11W, R12W, R13W, R14W, and R15W
- Twenty 8-bit registers: AL, AH, BL, BH, CL, CH, DL, DH, DIL, SIL, BPL, SPL, R8B, R9B, R10B, R11B, R12B, R13B, R14B, and R15B

Unfortunately, these are not 68 independent registers; instead, the x86-64 overlays the 64-bit registers over the 32-bit registers, the 32-bit registers over the 16-bit registers, and the 16-bit registers over the 8-bit registers. Table 1-1 shows these relationships.

Because the general-purpose registers are not independent, modifying one register may modify as many as three other registers. For example, modifying the EAX register may very well modify the AL, AH, AX, and RAX registers. This fact cannot be overemphasized. A common mistake in programs written by beginning assembly language programmers is register value corruption due to the programmer not completely understanding the ramifications of the relationships shown in Table 1-1.

Table 1-1: General-Purpose Registers on the x86-64

Bits 0–63	Bits 0–31	Bits 0–15	Bits 8–15	Bits 0–7
RAX	EAX	AX	AH	AL
RBX	EBX	BX	BH	BL
RCX	ECX	CX	CH	CL
RDX	EDX	DX	DH	DL
RSI	ESI	SI		SIL
RDI	EDI	DI		DIL
RBP	FBP	BP		BPL
RSP	ESP	SP		SPL
R8	R8D	R8W		R8B

Bits 0–63	Bits 0–31	Bits 0–15	Bits 8–15	Bits 0–7
R9	R9D	R9W		R9B
R10	R10D	R10W		R10B
R11	R11D	R11W		R11B
R12	R12D	R12W		R12B
R13	R13D	R13W		R13B
R14	R14D	R14W		R14B
R15	R15D	R15W		R15B

In addition to the general-purpose registers, the x86-64 provides special-purpose registers, including eight *floating-point registers* implemented in the x87 *floating-point unit (FPU)*. Intel named these registers ST(0) to ST(7). Unlike with the general-purpose registers, an application program cannot directly access these. Instead, a program treats the floating-point register file as an eight-entry-deep stack and accesses only the top one or two entries (see "Floating-Point Arithmetic" in Chapter 6 for more details).

Each floating-point register is 80 bits wide, holding an extended-precision real value (hereafter just *extended precision*). Although Intel added other floating-point registers to the x86-64 CPUs over the years, the FPU registers still find common use in code because they support this 80-bit floating-point format.

In the 1990s, Intel introduced the MMX register set and instructions to support *single instruction, multiple data (SIMD)* operations. The *MMX register set* is a group of eight 64-bit registers that overlay the ST(0) to ST(7) registers on the FPU. Intel chose to overlay the FPU registers because this made the MMX registers immediately compatible with multitasking operating systems (such as Windows) without any code changes to those OSs. Unfortunately, this choice meant that an application could not simultaneously use the FPU and MMX instructions.

Intel corrected this issue in later revisions of the x86-64 by adding the *XMM register set*. For that reason, you rarely see modern applications using the MMX registers and instruction set. They are available if you really want to use them, but it is almost always better to use the XMM registers (and instruction set) and leave the registers in FPU mode.

To overcome the limitations of the MMX/FPU register conflicts, AMD/Intel added sixteen 128-bit XMM registers (XMM0 to XMM15) and the SSE/SSE2 instruction set. Each register can be configured as four 32-bit floating-point registers; two 64-bit double-precision floating-point registers; or sixteen 8-bit, eight 16-bit, four 32-bit, two 64-bit, or one 128-bit integer registers. In later variants of the x86-64 CPU family, AMD/Intel doubled the size of the registers to 256 bits each (renaming them YMM0 to YMM15) to support eight 32-bit floating-point values or four 64-bit double-precision floating-point values (integer operations were still limited to 128 bits).

The *RFLAGS* (or just *FLAGS*) register is a 64-bit register that encapsulates several single-bit Boolean (true/false) values.[1] Most of the bits in the RFLAGS register are either reserved for kernel mode (operating system) functions or are of little interest to the application programmer. Eight of these bits (or *flags*) are of interest to application programmers writing assembly language programs: the overflow, direction, interrupt disable,[2] sign, zero, auxiliary carry, parity, and carry flags. Figure 1-2 shows the layout of the flags within the lower 16 bits of the RFLAGS register.

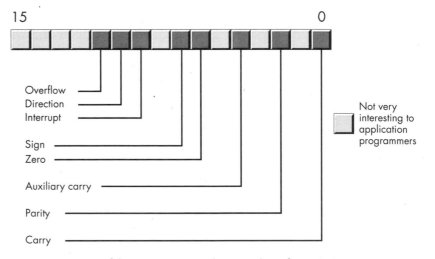

Figure 1-2: Layout of the FLAGS register (lower 16 bits of RFLAGS)

Four flags in particular are extremely valuable: the overflow, carry, sign, and zero flags, collectively called the *condition codes*.[3] The state of these flags lets you test the result of previous computations. For example, after comparing two values, the condition code flags will tell you whether one value is less than, equal to, or greater than a second value.

One important fact that comes as a surprise to those just learning assembly language is that almost all calculations on the x86-64 CPU involve a register. For example, to add two variables together and store the sum into a third variable, you must load one of the variables into a register, add the second operand to the value in the register, and then store the register away in the destination variable. Registers are a middleman in nearly every calculation.

You should also be aware that, although the registers are called *general-purpose*, you cannot use any register for any purpose. All the x86-64 registers have their own special purposes that limit their use in certain contexts. The RSP register, for example, has a very special purpose that effectively prevents

---

1. Technically, the I/O privilege level (IOPL) is 2 bits, but these bits are not accessible from user-mode programs, so this book ignores this field.

2. Application programs cannot modify the interrupt flag, but we'll look at this flag in Chapter 2; hence the discussion of this flag here.

3. Technically, the parity flag is also a condition code, but we will not use that flag in this text.

you from using it for anything else (it's the *stack pointer*). Likewise, the RBP register has a special purpose that limits its usefulness as a general-purpose register. For the time being, avoid the use of the RSP and RBP registers for generic calculations; also, keep in mind that the remaining registers are not completely interchangeable in your programs.

1.8   The Memory Subsystem

The *memory subsystem* holds data such as program variables, constants, machine instructions, and other information. Memory is organized into cells, each of which holds a small piece of information. The system can combine the information from these small cells (or *memory locations*) to form larger pieces of information.

The x86-64 supports *byte-addressable memory*, which means the basic memory unit is a byte, sufficient to hold a single character or a (very) small integer value (we'll talk more about that in Chapter 2).

Think of memory as a linear array of bytes. The address of the first byte is 0, and the address of the last byte is $2^{32} - 1$. For an x86 processor with 4GB memory installed,[4] the following pseudo-Pascal array declaration is a good approximation of memory:

```
Memory: array [0..4294967295] of byte;
```

C/C++ and Java users might prefer the following syntax:

```
byte Memory[4294967296];
```

For example, to execute the equivalent of the Pascal statement `Memory [125] := 0;`, the CPU places the value 0 on the data bus, places the address 125 on the address bus, and asserts the write line (this generally involves setting that line to 0), as shown in Figure 1-3.

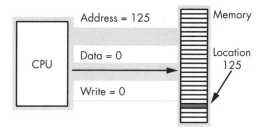

Figure 1-3: Memory write operation

To execute the equivalent of `CPU := Memory [125];`, the CPU places the address 125 on the address bus, asserts the read line (because the CPU is reading data from memory), and then reads the resulting data from the data bus (see Figure 1-4).

---

4. The following discussion will use the 4GB address space of the older 32-bit x86-64 processors. A typical x86-64 processor running a modern 64-bit OS can access a maximum of 2^{48} memory locations, or just over 256TB.

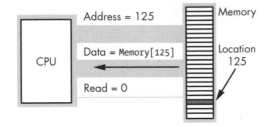

Figure 1-4: Memory read operation

To store larger values, the x86 uses a sequence of consecutive memory locations. Figure 1-5 shows how the x86 stores bytes, *words* (2 bytes), and *double words* (4 bytes) in memory. The memory address of each object is the address of the first byte of each object (that is, the lowest address).

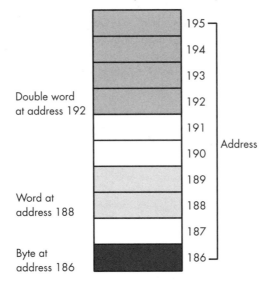

Figure 1-5: Byte, word, and double-word storage in memory

1.9 Declaring Memory Variables in MASM

Although it is possible to reference memory by using numeric addresses in assembly language, doing so is painful and error-prone. Rather than having your program state, "Give me the 32-bit value held in memory location 192 and the 16-bit value held in memory location 188," it's much nicer to state, "Give me the contents of elementCount and portNumber." Using variable names, rather than memory addresses, makes your program much easier to write, read, and maintain.

To create (writable) data variables, you have to put them in a data section of the MASM source file, defined using the .data directive. This directive tells MASM that all following statements (up to the next .code or other section-defining directive) will define data declarations to be grouped into a read/ write section of memory.

Within a .data section, MASM allows you to declare variable objects by using a set of data declaration directives. The basic form of a data declaration directive is

```
label   directive ?
```

where *label* is a legal MASM identifier and *directive* is one of the directives appearing in Table 1-2.

Table 1-2: MASM Data Declaration Directives

Directive	Meaning
byte (or db)	Byte (unsigned 8-bit) value
sbyte	Signed 8-bit integer value
word (or dw)	Unsigned 16-bit (word) value
sword	Signed 16-bit integer value
dword (or dd)	Unsigned 32-bit (double-word) value
sdword	Signed 32-bit integer value
qword (or dq)	Unsigned 64-bit (quad-word) value
sqword	Signed 64-bit integer value
tbyte (or dt)	Unsigned 80-bit (10-byte) value
oword	128-bit (octal-word) value
real4	Single-precision (32-bit) floating-point value
real8	Double-precision (64-bit) floating-point value
real10	Extended-precision (80-bit) floating-point value

The question mark (?) operand tells MASM that the object will not have an explicit value when the program loads into memory (the default initialization is zero). If you would like to initialize the variable with an explicit value, replace the ? with the initial value; for example:

```
hasInitialValue  sdword   -1
```

Some of the data declaration directives in Table 1-2 have a signed version (the directives with the s prefix). For the most part, MASM ignores this prefix. It is the machine instructions you write that differentiate between signed and unsigned operations; MASM itself usually doesn't care whether a variable holds a signed or an unsigned value. Indeed, MASM allows both of the following:

```
     .data
u8   byte    -1    ; Negative initializer is okay
i8   sbyte   250   ; even though +128 is maximum signed byte
```

All MASM cares about is whether the initial value will fit into a byte. The -1, even though it is not an unsigned value, will fit into a byte in memory. Even though 250 is too large to fit into a signed 8-bit integer (see

"Signed and Unsigned Numbers" in Chapter 2), MASM will happily accept this because 250 will fit into a byte variable (as an unsigned number).

It is possible to reserve storage for multiple data values in a single data declaration directive. The string multi-valued data type is critical to this chapter (later chapters discuss other types, such as arrays in Chapter 4). You can create a null-terminated string of characters in memory by using the byte directive as follows:

```
; Zero-terminated C/C++ string.
strVarName  byte 'String of characters', 0
```

Notice the , 0 that appears after the string of characters. In any data declaration (not just byte declarations), you can place multiple data values in the operand field, separated by commas, and MASM will emit an object of the specified size and value for each operand. For string values (surrounded by apostrophes in this example), MASM emits a byte for each character in the string (plus a zero byte for the , 0 operand at the end of the string). MASM allows you to define strings by using either apostrophes or quotes; you must terminate the string of characters with the same delimiter that begins the string (quote or apostrophe).

1.9.1   *Associating Memory Addresses with Variables*

One of the nice things about using an assembler/compiler like MASM is that you don't have to worry about numeric memory addresses. All you need to do is declare a variable in MASM, and MASM associates that variable with a unique set of memory addresses. For example, say you have the following declaration section:

```
      .data
i8    sbyte   ?
i16   sword   ?
i32   sdword  ?
i64   sqword  ?
```

MASM will find an unused 8-bit byte in memory and associate it with the i8 variable; it will find a pair of consecutive unused bytes and associate them with i16; it will find four consecutive locations and associate them with i32; finally, MASM will find 8 consecutive unused bytes and associate them with i64. You'll always refer to these variables by their name. You generally don't have to concern yourself with their numeric address. Still, you should be aware that MASM is doing this for you.

When MASM is processing declarations in a .data section, it assigns consecutive memory locations to each variable.[5] Assuming i8 (in the previous declarations) as a memory address of 101, MASM will assign the addresses appearing in Table 1-3 to i8, i16, i32, and i64.

_____

5. Technically, MASM assigns offsets into the .data section to variables. Windows converts these offsets to physical memory addresses when it loads the program into memory at runtime.

Table 1-3: Variable Address Assignment

Variable	Memory address
i8	101
i16	102 (address of i8 plus 1)
i32	104 (address of i16 plus 2)
i64	108 (address of i32 plus 4)

Whenever you have multiple operands in a data declaration statement, MASM will emit the values to sequential memory locations in the order they appear in the operand field. The label associated with the data declaration (if one is present) is associated with the address of the first (leftmost) operand's value. See Chapter 4 for more details.

1.9.2 Associating Data Types with Variables

During assembly, MASM associates a data type with every label you define, including variables. This is rather advanced for an assembly language (most assemblers simply associate a value or an address with an identifier).

For the most part, MASM uses the variable's size (in bytes) as its type (see Table 1-4).

Table 1-4: MASM Data Types

Type	Size	Description
byte (db)	1	1-byte memory operand, unsigned (generic integer)
sbyte	1	1-byte memory operand, signed integer
word (dw)	2	2-byte memory operand, unsigned (generic integer)
sword	2	2-byte memory operand, signed integer
dword (dd)	4	4-byte memory operand, unsigned (generic integer)
sdword	4	4-byte memory operand, signed integer
qword (dq)	8	8-byte memory operand, unsigned (generic integer)
sqword	8	8-byte memory operand, signed integer
tbyte (dt)	10	10-byte memory operand, unsigned (generic integer or BCD)
oword	16	16-byte memory operand, unsigned (generic integer)
real4	4	4-byte single-precision floating-point memory operand
real8	8	8-byte double-precision floating-point memory operand
real10	10	10-byte extended-precision floating-point memory operand
proc	N/A	Procedure label (associated with PROC directive)
label:	N/A	Statement label (any identifier immediately followed by a :)
constant	Varies	Constant declaration (equate) using = or EQU directive
text	N/A	Textual substitution using macro or TEXTEQU directive

Later sections and chapters fully describe the proc, label, constant, and text types.

1.10 Declaring (Named) Constants in MASM

MASM allows you to declare manifest constants by using the = directive. A *manifest constant* is a symbolic name (identifier) that MASM associates with a value. Everywhere the symbol appears in the program, MASM will directly substitute the value of that symbol for the symbol.

A manifest constant declaration takes the following form:

```
label = expression
```

Here, *label* is a legal MASM identifier, and *expression* is a constant arithmetic expression (typically, a single literal constant value). The following example defines the symbol dataSize to be equal to 256:

```
dataSize = 256
```

Most of the time, MASM's equ directive is a synonym for the = directive. For the purposes of this chapter, the following statement is largely equivalent to the previous declaration:

```
dataSize equ 256
```

Constant declarations (*equates* in MASM terminology) may appear anywhere in your MASM source file, prior to their first use. They may appear in a .data section, a .code section, or even outside any sections.

1.11 Some Basic Machine Instructions

The x86-64 CPU family provides from just over a couple hundred to many thousands of machine instructions, depending on how you define a machine instruction. But most assembly language programs use around 30 to 50 machine instructions,[6] and you can write several meaningful programs with only a few. This section provides a small handful of machine instructions so you can start writing simple MASM assembly language programs right away.

1.11.1 The mov Instruction

Without question, the mov instruction is the most oft-used assembly language statement. In a typical program, anywhere from 25 percent to 40 percent of the instructions are mov instructions. As its name suggests, this instruction moves data from one location to another.[7] Here's the generic MASM syntax for this instruction:

```
mov    destination_operand, source_operand
```

---

6. Different programs may use a different set of 30 to 50 instructions, but few programs use more than 50 distinct instructions.

7. Technically, mov copies data from one location to another. It does not destroy the original data in the source operand. Perhaps a better name for this instruction would have been copy. Alas, it's too late to change it now.

The *source_operand* may be a (general-purpose) register, a memory variable, or a constant. The *destination_operand* may be a register or a memory variable. The x86-64 instruction set does not allow both operands to be memory variables. In a high-level language like Pascal or C/C++, the mov instruction is roughly equivalent to the following assignment statement:

```
destination_operand = source_operand ;
```

The mov instruction's operands must both be the same size. That is, you can move data between a pair of byte (8-bit) objects, word (16-bit) objects, double-word (32-bit), or quad-word (64-bit) objects; you may not, however, mix the sizes of the operands. Table 1-5 lists all the legal combinations for the mov instruction.

You should study this table carefully because most of the general-purpose x86-64 instructions use this syntax.

Table 1-5: Legal x86-64 mov Instruction Operands

Source*	Destination
reg_8	reg_8
reg_8	mem_8
mem_8	reg_8
constant**	reg_8
constant	mem_8
reg_{16}	reg_{16}
reg_{16}	mem_{16}
mem_{16}	reg_{16}
constant	reg_{16}
constant	mem_{16}
reg_{32}	reg_{32}
reg_{32}	mem_{32}
mem_{32}	reg_{32}
constant	reg_{32}
constant	mem_{32}
reg_{64}	reg_{64}
reg_{64}	mem_{64}
mem_{64}	reg_{64}
constant	reg_{64}
$constant_{32}$	mem_{64}

* reg_n means an *n*-bit register, and mem_n means an *n*-bit memory location.
** The constant must be small enough to fit in the specified destination operand.

This table includes one important thing to note: the x86-64 allows you to move only a 32-bit constant value into a 64-bit memory location (it will sign-extend this value to 64 bits; see "Sign Extension and Zero Extension" in Chapter 2 for more information about sign extension). Moving a 64-bit constant into a 64-bit register is the only x86-64 instruction that allows a 64-bit constant operand. This inconsistency in the x86-64 instruction set is annoying. Welcome to the x86-64.

1.11.2 Type Checking on Instruction Operands

MASM enforces some type checking on instruction operands. In particular, the size of an instruction's operands must agree. For example, MASM will generate an error for the following:

```
i8 byte ?
    .
    .
    .
mov ax, i8
```

The problem is that you are attempting to load an 8-bit variable (i8) into a 16-bit register (AX). As their sizes are not compatible, MASM assumes that this is a logic error in the program and reports an error.[8]

For the most part, MASM ignores the difference between signed and unsigned variables. MASM is perfectly happy with both of these mov instructions:

```
i8 sbyte ?
u8 byte  ?
    .
    .
    .
mov al, i8
mov bl, u8
```

All MASM cares about is that you're moving a byte variable into a byte-sized register. Differentiating signed and unsigned values in those registers is up to the application program. MASM even allows something like this:

```
r4v real4 ?
r8v real8 ?
    .
    .
    .
mov eax, r4v
mov rbx, r8v
```

---

8. It is possible that you might actually want to do this, with the mov instruction loading AL with the byte at location i8 and AH with the byte immediately following i8 in memory. If you really want to do this (admittedly crazy) operation, see "Type Coercion" in Chapter 4.

Again, all MASM really cares about is the size of the memory operands, not that you wouldn't normally load a floating-point variable into a general-purpose register (which typically holds integer values).

In Table 1-4, you'll notice that there are proc, *label*, and *constant* types. MASM will report an error if you attempt to use a proc or *label* reserved word in a mov instruction. The procedure and label types are associated with addresses of machine instructions, not variables, and it doesn't make sense to "load a procedure" into a register.

However, you may specify a *constant* symbol as a source operand to an instruction; for example:

```
someConst = 5
    .
    .
    .
mov eax, someConst
```

As there is no size associated with constants, the only type checking MASM will do on a constant operand is to verify that the constant will fit in the destination operand. For example, MASM will reject the following:

```
wordConst = 1000
    .
    .
    .
mov al, wordConst
```

1.11.3 The add and sub Instructions

The x86-64 add and sub instructions add or subtract two operands, respectively. Their syntax is nearly identical to the mov instruction:

```
add destination_operand, source_operand
sub destination_operand, source_operand
```

However, constant operands are limited to a maximum of 32 bits. If your destination operand is 64 bits, the CPU allows only a 32-bit immediate source operand (it will sign-extend that operand to 64 bits; see "Sign Extension and Zero Extension" in Chapter 2 for more details on sign extension).

The add instruction does the following:

```
destination_operand = destination_operand + source_operand
```

The sub instruction does the calculation:

```
destination_operand = destination_operand - source_operand
```

With these three instructions, plus some MASM control structures, you can actually write sophisticated programs.

1.11.4 The lea Instruction

Sometimes you need to load the address of a variable into a register rather than the value of that variable. You can use the lea (*load effective address*) instruction for this purpose. The lea instruction takes the following form:

```
lea    reg64, memory_var
```

Here, *reg64* is any general-purpose 64-bit register, and *memory_var* is a variable name. Note that *memory_var*'s type is irrelevant; it doesn't have to be a qword variable (as is the case with mov, add, and sub instructions). Every variable has a memory address associated with it, and that address is always 64 bits. The following example loads the RCX register with the address of the first character in the strVar string:

```
strVar  byte "Some String", 0
        .
        .
        .
        lea rcx, strVar
```

The lea instruction is roughly equivalent to the C/C++ unary & (*address-of*) operator. The preceding assembly example is conceptually equivalent to the following C/C++ code:

```
char strVar[] = "Some String";
char *RCX;
        .
        .
        .
        RCX = &strVar[0];
```

1.11.5 The call and ret Instructions and MASM Procedures

To make function calls (as well as write your own simple functions), you need the call and ret instructions.

The ret instruction serves the same purpose in an assembly language program as the return statement in C/C++: it returns control from an assembly language procedure (assembly language functions are called *procedures*). For the time being, this book will use the variant of the ret instruction that does not have an operand:

```
ret
```

(The ret instruction does allow a single operand, but unlike in C/C++, the operand does not specify a function return value. You'll see the purpose of the ret instruction operand in Chapter 5.)

As you might guess, you call a MASM procedure by using the call instruction. This instruction can take a couple of forms. The most common is

```
call proc_name
```

where *proc_name* is the name of the procedure you want to call.

As you've seen in a couple code examples already, a MASM procedure consists of the line

```
proc_name proc
```

followed by the body of the procedure (typically ending with a ret instruction). At the end of the procedure (typically immediately after the ret instruction), you end the procedure with the following statement:

```
proc_name endp
```

The label on the endp directive must be identical to the one you supply for the proc statement.

In the stand-alone assembly language program in Listing 1-4, the main program calls myProc, which will immediately return to the main program, which then immediately returns to Windows.

```
; Listing 1-4

; A simple demonstration of a user-defined procedure.

        .code

; A sample user-defined procedure that this program can call.

myProc  proc
        ret     ; Immediately return to the caller
myProc  endp

; Here is the "main" procedure.

main    PROC

; Call the user-defined procedure.

        call  myProc

        ret     ; Returns to caller
main    endp
        end
```

Listing 1-4: A sample user-defined procedure in an assembly language program

You can compile this program and try running it by using the following commands:

```
C:\>ml64 listing1-4.asm /link /subsystem:console /entry:main
Microsoft (R) Macro Assembler (x64) Version 14.15.26730.0
Copyright (C) Microsoft Corporation.  All rights reserved.

 Assembling: listing1-4.asm
Microsoft (R) Incremental Linker Version 14.15.26730.0
Copyright (C) Microsoft Corporation.  All rights reserved.
```

```
/OUT:listing1-4.exe
listing1-4.obj
/subsystem:console
/entry:main

C:\>listing1-4
```

1.12 Calling C/C++ Procedures

While writing your own procedures and calling them are quite useful, the reason for introducing procedures at this point is not to allow you to write your own procedures, but rather to give you the ability to call procedures (functions) written in C/C++. Writing your own procedures to convert and output data to the console is a rather complex task (probably well beyond your capabilities at this point). Instead, you can call the C/C++ `printf()` function to produce program output and verify that your programs are actually doing something when you run them.

Unfortunately, if you call `printf()` in your assembly language code without providing a `printf()` procedure, MASM will complain that you've used an undefined symbol. To call a procedure outside your source file, you need to use the MASM `externdef` directive.[9] This directive has the following syntax:

```
externdef  symbol:type
```

Here, *symbol* is the external symbol you want to define, and *type* is the type of that symbol (which will be `proc` for external procedure definitions). To define the `printf()` symbol in your assembly language file, use this statement:

```
externdef  printf:proc
```

When defining external procedure symbols, you should put the `externdef` directive in your `.code` section.

The `externdef` directive doesn't let you specify parameters to pass to the `printf()` procedure, nor does the `call` instruction provide a mechanism for specifying parameters. Instead, you can pass up to four parameters to the `printf()` function in the x86-64 registers RCX, RDX, R8, and R9. The `printf()` function requires that the first parameter be the address of a format string. Therefore, you should load RCX with the address of a zero-terminated string prior to calling `printf()`. If the format string contains any format specifiers (for example, %d), you must pass appropriate parameter values in RDX, R8, and R9. Chapter 5 goes into great detail concerning procedure parameters, including how to pass floating-point values and more than four parameters.

---

9. MASM has two other directives, extrn and extern, that could also be used. This book uses the externdef directive because it is the most general directive.

1.13   Hello, World!

At this point (many pages into this chapter), you finally have enough information to write this chapter's namesake application: the "Hello, world!" program, shown in Listing 1-5.

```
; Listing 1-5

; A "Hello, world!" program using the C/C++ printf() function to
; provide the output.

        option  casemap:none
        .data

; Note: "10" value is a line feed character, also known as the
; "C" newline character.

fmtStr byte    'Hello, world!', 10, 0

        .code

; External declaration so MASM knows about the C/C++ printf()
; function.

        externdef  printf:proc

; Here is the "asmFunc" function.

        public  asmFunc
asmFunc proc

; "Magic" instruction offered without explanation at this point:

        sub     rsp, 56

; Here's where we'll call the C printf() function to print
; "Hello, world!" Pass the address of the format string
; to printf() in the RCX register. Use the LEA instruction
; to get the address of fmtStr.

        lea     rcx, fmtStr
        call    printf

; Another "magic" instruction that undoes the effect of the
; previous one before this procedure returns to its caller.

        add     rsp, 56

        ret     ; Returns to caller

asmFunc endp
        end
```

Listing 1-5: Assembly language code for the "Hello, world!" program

The assembly language code contains two "magic" statements that this chapter includes without further explanation. Just accept the fact that subtracting from the RSP register at the beginning of the function and then adding this value back to RSP at the end of the function are needed to make the calls to C/C++ functions work properly. Chapter 5 more fully explains the purpose of these statements.

The C++ function in Listing 1-6 calls the assembly code and makes the printf() function available for use.

```
// Listing 1-6

// C++ driver program to demonstrate calling printf() from assembly
// language.

// Need to include stdio.h so this program can call "printf()".

#include <stdio.h>

// extern "C" namespace prevents "name mangling" by the C++
// compiler.

extern "C"
{
    // Here's the external function, written in assembly
    // language, that this program will call:

    void asmFunc(void);
};

int main(void)
{
    // Need at least one call to printf() in the C program to allow
    // calling it from assembly.

    printf("Calling asmFunc:\n");
    asmFunc();
    printf("Returned from asmFunc\n");
}
```

Listing 1-6: C++ code for the "Hello, world!" program

Here's the sequence of steps needed to compile and run this code on my machine:

```
C:\>ml64 /c listing1-5.asm
Microsoft (R) Macro Assembler (x64) Version 14.15.26730.0
Copyright (C) Microsoft Corporation.  All rights reserved.

 Assembling: listing1-5.asm

C:\>cl listing1-6.cpp listing1-5.obj
Microsoft (R) C/C++ Optimizing Compiler Version 19.15.26730 for x64
```

```
Copyright (C) Microsoft Corporation.  All rights reserved.

listing1-6.cpp
Microsoft (R) Incremental Linker Version 14.15.26730.0
Copyright (C) Microsoft Corporation.  All rights reserved.

/out:listing1-6.exe
listing1-6.obj
listing1-5.obj

C:\>listing1-6
Calling asmFunc:
Hello, World!
Returned from asmFunc
```

You can finally print "Hello, world!" on the console!

1.14 Returning Function Results in Assembly Language

In a previous section, you saw how to pass up to four parameters to a procedure written in assembly language. This section describes the opposite process: returning a value to code that has called one of your procedures.

In pure assembly language (where one assembly language procedure calls another), passing parameters and returning function results are
strictly a convention that the caller and callee procedures share with one
another. Either the callee (the procedure being called) or the caller (the
procedure doing the calling) may choose where function results appear.

From the callee viewpoint, the procedure returning the value determines
where the caller can find the function result, and whoever calls that function must respect that choice. If a procedure returns a function result in the
XMM0 register (a common place to return floating-point results), whoever
calls that procedure must expect to find the result in XMM0. A different procedure could return its function result in the RBX register.

From the caller's viewpoint, the choice is reversed. Existing code expects
a function to return its result in a particular location, and the function being
called must respect that wish.

Unfortunately, without appropriate coordination, one section of code
might demand that functions it calls return their function results in one
location, while a set of existing library functions might insist on returning
their function results in another location. Clearly, such functions would not
be compatible with the calling code. While there are ways to handle this
situation (typically by writing facade code that sits between the caller and
callee and moves the return results around), the best solution is to ensure
that everybody agrees on things like where function return results will be
found prior to writing any code.

This agreement is known as an *application binary interface (ABI)*. An ABI
is a contract, of sorts, between different sections of code that describe *calling
conventions* (where things are passed, where they are returned, and so on),

data types, memory usage and alignment, and other attributes. CPU manufacturers, compiler writers, and operating system vendors all provide their own ABIs. For obvious reasons, this book uses the Microsoft Windows ABI.

Once again, it's important to understand that when you're writing your own assembly language code, the way you pass data between your procedures is totally up to you. One of the benefits of using assembly language is that you can decide the interface on a procedure-by-procedure basis. The only time you have to worry about adhering to an ABI is when you call code that is outside your control (or if that external code makes calls to your code). This book covers writing assembly language under Microsoft Windows (specifically, assembly code that interfaces with MSVC); therefore, when dealing with external code (Windows and C++ code), you have to use the Windows/MSVC ABI. The Microsoft ABI specifies that the first four parameters to printf() (or any C++ function, for that matter) must be passed in RCX, RDX, R8, and R9.

The Windows ABI also states that functions (procedures) return integer and pointer values (that fit into 64 bits) in the RAX register. So if some C++ code expects your assembly procedure to return an integer result, you would load the integer result into RAX immediately before returning from your procedure.

To demonstrate returning a function result, we'll use the C++ program in Listing 1-7 (*c.cpp*, a generic C++ program that this book uses for most of the C++/assembly examples hereafter). This C++ program includes two extra function declarations: getTitle() (supplied by the assembly language code), which returns a pointer to a string containing the title of the program (the C++ code prints this title), and readLine() (supplied by the C++ program), which the assembly language code can call to read a line of text from the user (and put into a string buffer in the assembly language code).

```
// Listing 1-7

// c.cpp

// Generic C++ driver program to demonstrate returning function
// results from assembly language to C++. Also includes a
// "readLine" function that reads a string from the user and
// passes it on to the assembly language code.

// Need to include stdio.h so this program can call "printf()"
// and string.h so this program can call strlen.

#include <errno.h>
#include <stdio.h>
#include <stdlib.h>
#include <string.h>

// extern "C" namespace prevents "name mangling" by the C++
// compiler.
```

```cpp
extern "C"
{
    // asmMain is the assembly language code's "main program":

    void asmMain(void);

    // getTitle returns a pointer to a string of characters
    // from the assembly code that specifies the title of that
    // program (that makes this program generic and usable
    // with a large number of sample programs in "The Art of
    // 64-Bit Assembly").

    char *getTitle(void);

    // C++ function that the assembly
    // language program can call:

    int readLine(char *dest, int maxLen);

};

// readLine reads a line of text from the user (from the
// console device) and stores that string into the destination
// buffer the first argument specifies. Strings are limited in
// length to the value specified by the second argument
// (minus 1).

// This function returns the number of characters actually
// read, or -1 if there was an error.

// Note that if the user enters too many characters (maxlen or
// more), then this function returns only the first maxlen-1
// characters. This is not considered an error.

int readLine(char *dest, int maxLen)
{
    // Note: fgets returns NULL if there was an error, else
    // it returns a pointer to the string data read (which
    // will be the value of the dest pointer).

    char *result = fgets(dest, maxLen, stdin);
    if(result != NULL)
    {
        // Wipe out the newline character at the
        // end of the string:

        int len = strlen(result);
        if(len > 0)
        {
            dest[len - 1] = 0;
        }
        return len;
    }
```

```
        return -1; // If there was an error
}

int main(void)
{
    // Get the assembly language program's title:

    try
    {
        char *title = getTitle();

        printf("Calling %s:\n", title);
        asmMain();
        printf("%s terminated\n", title);
    }
    catch(...)
    {
        printf
        (
            "Exception occurred during program execution\n"
            "Abnormal program termination.\n"
        );
    }
}
```

Listing 1-7: Generic C++ code for calling assembly language programs

The try..catch block catches any exceptions the assembly code generates, so you get some sort of indication if the program aborts abnormally.

Listing 1-8 provides assembly code that demonstrates several new concepts, foremost returning a function result (to the C++ program). The assembly language function getTitle() returns a pointer to a string that the calling C++ code will print as the title of the program. In the .data section, you'll see a string variable titleStr that is initialized with the name of this assembly code (Listing 1-8). The getTitle() function loads the address of that string into RAX and returns this string pointer to the C++ code (Listing 1-7) that prints the title before and after running the assembly code.

This program also demonstrates reading a line of text from the user. The assembly code calls the readLine() function appearing in the C++ code. The readLine() function expects two parameters: the address of a character buffer (C string) and a maximum buffer length. The code in Listing 1-8 passes the address of the character buffer to the readLine() function in RCX and the maximum buffer size in RDX. The maximum buffer length must include room for two extra characters: a newline character (line feed) and a zero-terminating byte.

Finally, Listing 1-8 demonstrates declaring a character buffer (that is, an array of characters). In the .data section, you will find the following declaration:

```
input byte maxLen dup (?)
```

The maxLen dup (?) operand tells MASM to duplicate the (?) (that is, an uninitialized byte) maxLen times. maxLen is a constant set to 256 by an equate directive (=) at the beginning of the source file. (For more details, see "Declaring Arrays in Your MASM Programs" in Chapter 4.)

```
; Listing 1-8

; An assembly language program that demonstrates returning
; a function result to a C++ program.

        option  casemap:none

nl      =       10  ; ASCII code for newline
maxLen  =       256 ; Maximum string size + 1

        .data
titleStr byte    'Listing 1-8', 0
prompt  byte     'Enter a string: ', 0
fmtStr  byte     "User entered: '%s'", nl, 0

; "input" is a buffer having "maxLen" bytes. This program
; will read a user string into this buffer.

; The "maxLen dup (?)" operand tells MASM to make "maxLen"
; duplicate copies of a byte, each of which is uninitialized.

input   byte    maxLen dup (?)

        .code

        externdef    printf:proc
        externdef    readLine:proc

; The C++ function calling this assembly language module
; expects a function named "getTitle" that returns a pointer
; to a string as the function result. This is that function:

        public getTitle
getTitle proc

; Load address of "titleStr" into the RAX register (RAX holds
; the function return result) and return back to the caller:

        lea rax, titleStr
        ret
getTitle endp

; Here is the "asmMain" function.

        public  asmMain
asmMain proc
        sub     rsp, 56
```

```
; Call the readLine function (written in C++) to read a line
; of text from the console.

; int readLine(char *dest, int maxLen)

; Pass a pointer to the destination buffer in the RCX register.
; Pass the maximum buffer size (max chars + 1) in EDX.
; This function ignores the readLine return result.
; Prompt the user to enter a string:

        lea     rcx, prompt
        call    printf

; Ensure the input string is zero-terminated (in the event
; there is an error):

        mov     input, 0

; Read a line of text from the user:

        lea     rcx, input
        mov     rdx, maxLen
        call    readLine

; Print the string input by the user by calling printf():

        lea     rcx, fmtStr
        lea     rdx, input
        call    printf

        add     rsp, 56
        ret     ; Returns to caller

asmMain endp
        end
```

Listing 1-8: Assembly language program that returns a function result

To compile and run the programs in Listings 1-7 and 1-8, use statements such as the following:

```
C:\>ml64 /c listing1-8.asm
Microsoft (R) Macro Assembler (x64) Version 14.15.26730.0
Copyright (C) Microsoft Corporation.  All rights reserved.

 Assembling: listing1-8.asm

C:\>cl /EHa /Felisting1-8.exe c.cpp listing1-8.obj
Microsoft (R) C/C++ Optimizing Compiler Version 19.15.26730 for x64
Copyright (C) Microsoft Corporation.  All rights reserved.

c.cpp
Microsoft (R) Incremental Linker Version 14.15.26730.0
```

Copyright (C) Microsoft Corporation. All rights reserved.

```
/out:listing1-8.exe
c.obj
listing1-8.obj
```

```
C:\> listing1-8
Calling Listing 1-8:
Enter a string: This is a test
User entered: 'This is a test'
Listing 1-8 terminated
```

The /Felisting1-8.exe command line option tells MSVC to name the executable file *listing1-8.exe*. Without the /Fe option, MSVC would name the resulting executable file *c.exe* (after *c.cpp*, the generic example C++ file from Listing 1-7).

1.15 Automating the Build Process

At this point, you're probably thinking it's a bit tiresome to type all these (long) command lines every time you want to compile and run your programs. This is especially true if you start adding more command line options to the ml64 and cl commands. Consider the following two commands:

```
ml64 /nologo /c /Zi /Cp listing1-8.asm
cl /nologo /O2 /Zi /utf-8 /EHa /Felisting1-8.exe c.cpp listing1-8.obj
listing1-8
```

The /Zi option tells MASM and MSVC to compile extra debug information into the code. The /nologo option tells MASM and MSVC to skip printing copyright and version information during compilation. The MASM /Cp option tells MASM to make compilations case-insensitive (so you don't need the options casemap:none directive in your assembly source file). The /O2 option tells MSVC to optimize the machine code the compiler produces. The /utf-8 option tells MSVC to use UTF-8 Unicode encoding (which is ASCII-compatible) rather than UTF-16 encoding (or other character encoding). The /EHa option tells MSVC to handle processor-generated exceptions (such as memory access faults—a common exception in assembly language programs). As noted earlier, the /Fe option specifies the executable output filename. Typing all these command line options every time you want to build a sample program is going to be a lot of work.

The easy solution is to create a batch file that automates this process. You could, for example, type the three previous command lines into a text file, name it *l8.bat*, and then simply type l8 at the command line to automatically execute those three commands. That saves a lot of typing and is much quicker (and less error-prone) than typing these three commands every time you want to compile and run the program.

The only drawback to putting those three commands into a batch file is that the batch file is specific to the *listing1-8.asm* source file, and you would have to create a new batch file to compile other programs. Fortunately, it is easy to create a batch file that will work with any single assembly source file that compiles and links with the generic *c.cpp* program. Consider the following *build.bat* batch file:

```
echo off
ml64 /nologo /c /Zi /Cp %1.asm
cl /nologo /O2 /Zi /utf-8 /EHa /Fe%1.exe c.cpp %1.obj
```

The %1 item in these commands tells the Windows command line processor to substitute a command line parameter (specifically, command line parameter number 1) in place of the %1. If you type the following from the command line

```
build listing1-8
```

then Windows executes the following three commands:

```
echo off
ml64 /nologo /c /Zi /Cp listing1-8.asm
cl /nologo /O2 /Zi /utf-8 /EHa /Felisting1-8.exe c.cpp listing1-8.obj
```

With this *build.bat* file, you can compile several projects simply by specifying the assembly language source file name (without the *.asm* suffix) on the build command line.

The *build.bat* file does not run the program after compiling and linking it. You could add this capability to the batch file by appending a single line containing %1 to the end of the file. However, that would always attempt to run the program, even if the compilation failed because of errors in the C++ or assembly language source files. For that reason, it's probably better to run the program manually after building it with the batch file, as follows:

```
C:\>build listing1-8
C:\>listing1-8
```

A little extra typing, to be sure, but safer in the long run.

Microsoft provides another useful tool for controlling compilations from the command line: *makefiles*. They are a better solution than batch files because makefiles allow you to conditionally control steps in the process (such as running the executable) based on the success of earlier steps. However, using Microsoft's make program (*nmake.exe*) is beyond the scope of this chapter. It's a good tool to learn (and Chapter 15 will teach you the basics). However, batch files are sufficient for the simple projects appearing throughout most of this book and require little extra knowledge or training to use. If you are interested in learning more about makefiles, see Chapter 15 or "For More Information" on page 39.

1.16　Microsoft ABI Notes

As noted earlier (see "Returning Function Results in Assembly Language" on page 27), the Microsoft ABI is a contract between modules in a program to ensure compatibility (between modules, especially modules written in different programming languages).[10] In this book, the C++ programs will be calling assembly language code, and the assembly modules will be calling C++ code, so it's important that the assembly language code adhere to the Microsoft ABI.

Even if you were to write stand-alone assembly language code, it would still be calling C++ code, as it would (undoubtedly) need to make Windows *application programming interface (API)* calls. The Windows API functions are all written in C++, so calls to Windows must respect the Windows ABI.

Because following the Microsoft ABI is so important, each chapter in this book (if appropriate) includes a section at the end discussing those components of the Microsoft ABI that the chapter introduces or heavily uses. This section covers several concepts from the Microsoft ABI: variable size, register usage, and stack alignment.

1.16.1　Variable Size

Although dealing with different data types in assembly language is completely up to the assembly language programmer (and the choice of machine instructions to use on that data), it's crucial to maintain the size of the data (in bytes) between the C++ and assembly language programs. Table 1-6 lists several common C++ data types and the corresponding assembly language types (that maintain the size information).

Table 1-6: C++ and Assembly Language Types

C++ type	Size (in bytes)	Assembly language type
char	1	sbyte
signed char	1	sbyte
unsigned char	1	byte
short int	2	sword
short unsigned	2	word
int	4	sdword
unsigned (unsigned int)	4	dword
long	4	sdword
long int	4	sdword
long unsigned	4	dword
long int	8	sqword
long unsigned	8	qword

(continued)

---

10. Microsoft also refers to the ABI as the *X64 Calling Conventions* in its documentation.

Table 1-6: C++ and Assembly Language Types *(continued)*

C++ type	Size (in bytes)	Assembly language type
__int64	8	sqword
unsigned __int64	8	qword
Float	4	real4
double	8	real8
pointer (for example, void *)	8	qword

Although MASM provides signed type declarations (sbyte, sword, sdword, and sqword), assembly language instructions do not differentiate between the unsigned and signed variants. You could process a signed integer (sdword) by using unsigned instruction sequences, and you could process an unsigned integer (dword) by using signed instruction sequences. In an assembly language source file, these different directives mainly serve as a documentation aid to help describe the programmer's intentions.[11]

Listing 1-9 is a simple program that verifies the sizes of each of these C++ data types.

NOTE *The %2zd format string displays size_t type values (the sizeof operator returns a value of type size_t). This quiets down the MSVC compiler (which generates warnings if you use only %2d). Most compilers are happy with %2d.*

```
// Listing 1-9

// A simple C++ program that demonstrates Microsoft C++ data
// type sizes:

#include <stdio.h>

int main(void)
{
        char            v1;
        unsigned char   v2;
        short           v3;
        short int       v4;
        short unsigned  v5;
        int             v6;
        unsigned        v7;
        long            v8;
        long int        v9;
        long unsigned   v10;
```

---

11. Earlier 32-bit versions of MASM included some high-level language control statements (for example, .if, .else, .endif) that made use of the signed versus unsigned declarations. However, Microsoft no longer supports these high-level statements. As a result, MASM no longer differentiates signed versus unsigned declarations.

```
        long long int      v11;
        long long unsigned v12;
        __int64            v13;
        unsigned __int64   v14;
        float              v15;
        double             v16;
        void *             v17;

    printf
    (
        "Size of char:             %2zd\n"
        "Size of unsigned char:    %2zd\n"
        "Size of short:            %2zd\n"
        "Size of short int:        %2zd\n"
        "Size of short unsigned:   %2zd\n"
        "Size of int:              %2zd\n"
        "Size of unsigned:         %2zd\n"
        "Size of long:             %2zd\n"
        "Size of long int:         %2zd\n"
        "Size of long unsigned:    %2zd\n"
        "Size of long long int:    %2zd\n"
        "Size of long long unsigned: %2zd\n"
        "Size of __int64:          %2zd\n"
        "Size of unsigned __int64: %2zd\n"
        "Size of float:            %2zd\n"
        "Size of double:           %2zd\n"
        "Size of pointer:          %2zd\n",
        sizeof v1,
        sizeof v2,
        sizeof v3,
        sizeof v4,
        sizeof v5,
        sizeof v6,
        sizeof v7,
        sizeof v8,
        sizeof v9,
        sizeof v10,
        sizeof v11,
        sizeof v12,
        sizeof v13,
        sizeof v14,
        sizeof v15,
        sizeof v16,
        sizeof v17
    );
}
```

Listing 1-9: Output sizes of common C++ data types

Here's the build command and output from Listing 1-9:

```
C:\>cl listing1-9.cpp
Microsoft (R) C/C++ Optimizing Compiler Version 19.15.26730 for x64
Copyright (C) Microsoft Corporation.  All rights reserved.
```

```
listing1-9.cpp
Microsoft (R) Incremental Linker Version 14.15.26730.0
Copyright (C) Microsoft Corporation.  All rights reserved.

/out:listing1-9.exe
listing1-9.obj

C:\>listing1-9
Size of char:               1
Size of unsigned char:      1
Size of short:              2
Size of short int:          2
Size of short unsigned:     2
Size of int:                4
Size of unsigned:           4
Size of long:               4
Size of long int:           4
Size of long unsigned:      4
Size of long long int:      8
Size of long long unsigned: 8
Size of __int64:            8
Size of unsigned __int64:   8
Size of float:              4
Size of double:             8
Size of pointer:            8
```

1.16.2 Register Usage

Register usage in an assembly language procedure (including the main assembly language function) is also subject to certain Microsoft ABI rules. Within a procedure, the Microsoft ABI has this to say about register usage):[12]

- Code that calls a function can pass the first four (integer) arguments to the function (procedure) in the RCX, RDX, R8, and R9 registers, respectively. Programs pass the first four floating-point arguments in XMM0, XMM1, XMM2, and XMM3.

- Registers RAX, RCX, RDX, R8, R9, R10, and R11 are *volatile*, which means that the function/procedure does not need to save the registers' values across a function/procedure call.

- XMM0/YMM0 through XMM5/YMM5 are also volatile. The function/procedure does not need to preserve these registers across a call.

- RBX, RBP, RDI, RSI, RSP, R12, R13, R14, and R15 are nonvolatile registers. A procedure/function must preserve these registers' values across a call. If a procedure modifies one of these registers, it must save the register's value before the first such modification and restore the register's value from the saved location prior to returning from the function/procedure.

---

12. For more details, see the Microsoft documentation at *https://docs.microsoft.com/en-us/cpp/build/x64-calling-convention?view=msvc-160/*.

- XMM6 through XMM15 are nonvolatile. A function must preserve these registers across a function/procedure call (that is, when a procedure returns, these registers must contain the same values they had upon entry to that procedure).

- Programs that use the x86-64's floating-point coprocessor instructions must preserve the value of the floating-point control word across procedure calls. Such procedures should also leave the floating-point stack cleared.

- Any procedure/function that uses the x86-64's direction flag must leave that flag cleared upon return from the procedure/function.

Microsoft C++ expects function return values to appear in one of two places. Integer (and other non-scalar) results come back in the RAX register (up to 64 bits). If the return type is smaller than 64 bits, the upper bits of the RAX register are undefined—for example, if a function returns a short int (16-bit) result, bits 16 to 63 in RAX may contain garbage. Microsoft's ABI specifies that floating-point (and vector) function return results shall come back in the XMM0 register.

1.16.3 Stack Alignment

Some "magic" instructions appear in various source listings throughout this chapter (they basically add or subtract values from the RSP register). These instructions have to do with stack alignment (as required by the Microsoft ABI). This chapter (and several that follow) supply these instructions in the code without further explanation. For more details on the purpose of these instructions, see Chapter 5.

1.17 For More Information

This chapter has covered a lot of ground! While you still have a lot to learn about assembly language programming, this chapter, combined with your knowledge of HLLs (especially C/C++), provides just enough information to let you start writing real assembly language programs.

Although this chapter covered many topics, the three primary ones of interest are the x86-64 CPU architecture, the syntax for simple MASM programs, and interfacing with the C Standard Library.

The following resources provide more information about makefiles:

- Wikipedia: *https://en.wikipedia.org/wiki/Make_(software)*
- *Managing Projects with GNU Make* by Robert Mecklenburg (O'Reilly Media, 2004)
- *The GNU Make Book,* First Edition, by John Graham-Cumming (No Starch Press, 2015)
- *Managing Projects with make,* by Andrew Oram and Steve Talbott (O'Reilly & Associates, 1993)

For more information about MVSC:

- Microsoft Visual Studio websites: *https://visualstudio.microsoft.com/* and *https://visualstudio.microsoft.com/vs/*
- Microsoft free developer offers: *https://visualstudio.microsoft.com/free-developer-offers/*

For more information about MASM:

- Microsoft, C++, C, and Assembler documentation: *https://docs.microsoft.com/en-us/cpp/assembler/masm/masm-for-x64-ml64-exe?view=msvc-160/*
- Waite Group MASM Bible (covers MASM 6, which is 32-bit only, but still contains lots of useful information about MASM): *https://www.amazon.com/Waite-Groups-Microsoft-Macro-Assembler/dp/0672301555/*

For more information about the ABI:

- The best documentation comes from Agner Fog's website: *https://www.agner.org/optimize/*.
- Microsoft's website also has information on Microsoft ABI calling conventions (see *https://docs.microsoft.com/en-us/cpp/build/x64-calling-convention?view=msvc-160* or search for *Microsoft calling conventions*).

1.18 Test Yourself

1. What is the name of the Windows command line interpreter program?
2. What is the name of the MASM executable program file?
3. What are the names of the three main system buses?
4. Which register(s) overlap the RAX register?
5. Which register(s) overlap the RBX register?
6. Which register(s) overlap the RSI register?
7. Which register(s) overlap the R8 register?
8. Which register holds the condition code bits?
9. How many bytes are consumed by the following data types?

    a. word

    b. dword

    c. oword

    d. qword with a 4 dup (?) operand

    e. real8

10. If an 8-bit (byte) memory variable is the destination operand of a mov instruction, what source operands are legal?
11. If a mov instruction's destination operand is the EAX register, what is the largest constant (in bits) you can load into that register?

12. For the add instruction, fill in the largest constant size (in bits) for all the destination operands specified in the following table:

Destination	Constant size
RAX	
EAX	
AX	
AL	
AH	
mem_{32}	
mem_{64}	

13. What is the destination (register) operand size for the lea instruction?

14. What is the source (memory) operand size of the lea instruction?

15. What is the name of the assembly language instruction you use to call a procedure or function?

16. What is the name of the assembly language instruction you use to return from a procedure or function?

17. What does *ABI* stand for?

18. In the Windows ABI, where do you return the following function return results?

    a. 8-bit byte values

    b. 16-bit word values

    c. 32-bit integer values

    d. 64-bit integer values

    e. Floating-point values

    f. 64-bit pointer values

19. Where do you pass the first parameter to a Microsoft ABI–compatible function?

20. Where do you pass the second parameter to a Microsoft ABI–compatible function?

21. Where do you pass the third parameter to a Microsoft ABI–compatible function?

22. Where do you pass the fourth parameter to a Microsoft ABI–compatible function?

23. What assembly language data type corresponds to a C/C++ long int?

24. What assembly language data type corresponds to a C/C++ long long unsigned?

COMPUTER DATA REPRESENTATION AND OPERATIONS

A major stumbling block many beginners encounter when attempting to learn assembly language is the common use of the binary and hexadecimal numbering systems. Although hexadecimal numbers are a little strange, their advantages outweigh their disadvantages by a large margin. Understanding the binary and hexadecimal numbering systems is important because their use simplifies the discussion of other topics, including bit operations, signed numeric representation, character codes, and packed data.

This chapter discusses several important concepts, including the following:

- The binary and hexadecimal numbering systems
- Binary data organization (bits, nibbles, bytes, words, and double words)
- Signed and unsigned numbering systems
- Arithmetic, logical, shift, and rotate operations on binary values

- Bit fields and packed data
- Floating-point and binary-code decimal formats
- Character data

This is basic material, and the remainder of this text depends on your understanding of these concepts. If you are already familiar with these terms from other courses or study, you should at least skim this material before proceeding to the next chapter. If you are unfamiliar with this material, or only vaguely familiar with it, you should study it carefully before proceeding. *All of the material in this chapter is important!* Do not skip over any material.

2.1 Numbering Systems

Most modern computer systems do not represent numeric values using the decimal (base-10) system. Instead, they typically use a binary, or two's complement, numbering system.

2.1.1 A Review of the Decimal System

You've been using the decimal numbering system for so long that you probably take it for granted. When you see a number like 123, you don't think about the value 123; rather, you generate a mental image of how many items this value represents. In reality, however, the number 123 represents the following:

$$(1 \times 10^2) + (2 \times 10^1) + (3 \times 10^0)$$

or

$$100 + 20 + 3$$

In a decimal *positional numbering system*, each digit appearing to the left of the decimal point represents a value between 0 and 9 times an increasing power of 10. Digits appearing to the right of the decimal point represent a value between 0 and 9 times an increasing negative power of 10. For example, the value 123.456 means this:

$$(1 \times 10^2) + (2 \times 10^1) + (3 \times 10^0) + (4 \times 10^{-1}) + (5 \times 10^{-2}) + (6 \times 10^{-3})$$

or

$$100 + 20 + 3 + 0.4 + 0.05 + 0.006$$

2.1.2 The Binary Numbering System

Most modern computer systems operate using *binary* logic. The computer represents values using two voltage levels (usually 0 V and +2.4 to 5 V). These two levels can represent exactly two unique values. These could be any two different values, but they typically represent the values 0 and 1, the two digits in the binary numbering system.

The binary numbering system works just like the decimal numbering system, except binary allows only the digits 0 and 1 (rather than 0 to 9) and uses powers of 2 rather than powers of 10. Therefore, converting a binary number to decimal is easy. For each 1 in a binary string, add 2^n, where n is the zero-based position of the binary digit. For example, the binary value 11001010_2 represents the following:

$$(1 \times 2^7) + (1 \times 2^6) + (0 \times 2^5) + (0 \times 2^4) + (1 \times 2^3) + (0 \times 2^2) + (1 \times 2^1) + (0 \times 2^0)$$

$$=$$

$$128_{10} + 64_{10} + 8_{10} + 2_{10}$$

$$=$$

$$202_{10}$$

Converting decimal to binary is slightly more difficult. You must find those powers of 2 that, when added together, produce the decimal result.

A simple way to convert decimal to binary is the *even/odd—divide-by-two* algorithm. This algorithm uses the following steps:

1. If the number is even, emit a 0. If the number is odd, emit a 1.
2. Divide the number by 2 and throw away any fractional component or remainder.
3. If the quotient is 0, the algorithm is complete.
4. If the quotient is not 0 and is odd, insert a 1 before the current string; if the number is even, prefix your binary string with 0.
5. Go back to step 2 and repeat.

Binary numbers, although they have little importance in high-level languages, appear everywhere in assembly language programs. So you should be comfortable with them.

2.1.3   Binary Conventions

In the purest sense, every binary number contains an infinite number of digits (or *bits*, which is short for *binary digits*). For example, we can represent the number 5 by any of the following:

101   00000101   0000000000101   . . . 000000000000101

Any number of leading-zero digits may precede the binary number without changing its value. Because the x86-64 typically works with groups of 8 bits, we'll zero-extend all binary numbers to a multiple of 4 or 8 bits. Following this convention, we'd represent the number 5 as 0101_2 or 00000101_2.

To make larger numbers easier to read, we will separate each group of 4 binary bits with an underscore. For example, we will write the binary value 1010111110110010 as 1010_1111_1011_0010.

NOTE   *MASM does not allow you to insert underscores into the middle of a binary number. This is a convention adopted in this book for readability purposes.*

We'll number each bit as follows:

1. The rightmost bit in a binary number is bit position 0.
2. Each bit to the left is given the next successive bit number.

An 8-bit binary value uses bits 0 to 7:

$$X_7 \; X_6 \; X_5 \; X_4 \; X_3 \; X_2 \; X_1 \; X_0$$

A 16-bit binary value uses bit positions 0 to 15:

$$X_{15} \; X_{14} \; X_{13} \; X_{12} \; X_{11} \; X_{10} \; X_9 \; X_8 \; X_7 \; X_6 \; X_5 \; X_4 \; X_3 \; X_2 \; X_1 \; X_0$$

A 32-bit binary value uses bit positions 0 to 31, and so on.

Bit 0 is the *low-order (LO)* bit; some refer to this as the *least significant bit*. The leftmost bit is called the *high-order (HO)* bit, or the *most significant bit*. We'll refer to the intermediate bits by their respective bit numbers.

In MASM, you can specify binary values as a string of 0 or 1 digits ending with the character b. Remember, MASM doesn't allow underscores in binary numbers.

2.2   The Hexadecimal Numbering System

Unfortunately, binary numbers are verbose. To represent the value 202_{10} requires eight binary digits, but only three decimal digits. When dealing with large values, binary numbers quickly become unwieldy. Unfortunately, the computer "thinks" in binary, so most of the time using the binary numbering system is convenient. Although we can convert between decimal and binary, the conversion is not a trivial task.

The hexadecimal (base-16) numbering system solves many of the problems inherent in the binary system: hexadecimal numbers are compact, and it's simple to convert them to binary, and vice versa. For this reason, most engineers use the hexadecimal numbering system.

Because the *radix* (base) of a hexadecimal number is 16, each hexadecimal digit to the left of the hexadecimal point represents a certain value multiplied by a successive power of 16. For example, the number 1234_{16} is equal to this:

$$(1 \times 16^3) + (2 \times 16^2) + (3 \times 16^1) + (4 \times 16^0)$$

or

$$4096 + 512 + 48 + 4 = 4660_{10}$$

Each hexadecimal digit can represent one of 16 values between 0 and 15_{10}. Because there are only 10 decimal digits, we need 6 additional digits to represent the values in the range 10_{10} to 15_{10}. Rather than create new symbols for these digits, we use the letters A to F. The following are all examples of valid hexadecimal numbers:

$$1234_{16} \quad DEAD_{16} \quad BEEF_{16} \quad 0AFB_{16} \quad F001_{16} \quad D8B4_{16}$$

Because we'll often need to enter hexadecimal numbers into the computer system, and on most computer systems you cannot enter a subscript to denote the radix of the associated value, we need a different mechanism for representing hexadecimal numbers. We'll adopt the following MASM conventions:

1. All hexadecimal values begin with a numeric character and have an *h* suffix; for example, 123A4h and 0DEADh.
2. All binary values end with a *b* character; for example, 10010b.
3. Decimal numbers do not have a suffix character.
4. If the radix is clear from the context, this book may drop the trailing *h* or *b* character.

Here are some examples of valid hexadecimal numbers using MASM notation:

1234h 0DEADh 0BEEFh 0AFBh 0F001h 0D8B4h

As you can see, hexadecimal numbers are compact and easy to read. In addition, you can easily convert between hexadecimal and binary. Table 2-1 provides all the information you'll ever need to convert any hexadecimal number into a binary number, or vice versa.

Table 2-1: Binary/Hexadecimal Conversion

Binary	Hexadecimal
0000	0
0001	1
0010	2
0011	3
0100	4
0101	5
0110	6
0111	7
1000	8
1001	9
1010	A
1011	B
1100	C
1101	D
1110	E
1111	F

To convert a hexadecimal number into a binary number, substitute the corresponding 4 bits for each hexadecimal digit in the number. For example, to convert 0ABCDh into a binary value, convert each hexadecimal digit according to Table 2-1, as shown here:

A	B	C	D	Hexadecimal
1010	1011	1100	1101	Binary

To convert a binary number into hexadecimal format is almost as easy:

1. Pad the binary number with 0s to make sure that the number contains a multiple of 4 bits. For example, given the binary number 1011001010, add 2 bits to the left of the number so that it contains 12 bits: 001011001010.

2. Separate the binary value into groups of 4 bits; for example, 0010_1100_1010.

3. Look up these binary values in Table 2-1 and substitute the appropriate hexadecimal digits: 2CAh.

Contrast this with the difficulty of conversion between decimal and binary, or decimal and hexadecimal!

Because converting between hexadecimal and binary is an operation you will need to perform over and over again, you should take a few minutes to memorize the conversion table. Even if you have a calculator that will do the conversion for you, you'll find manual conversion to be a lot faster and more convenient.

2.3   A Note About Numbers vs. Representation

Many people confuse numbers and their representation. A common question beginning assembly language students ask is, "I have a binary number in the EAX register. How do I convert that to a hexadecimal number in the EAX register?" The answer is, "You don't."

Although a strong argument could be made that numbers in memory or in registers are represented in binary, it is best to view values in memory or in a register as *abstract numeric quantities*. Strings of symbols like 128, 80h, or 10000000b are not different numbers; they are simply different representations for the same abstract quantity that we refer to as *one hundred twenty-eight*. Inside the computer, a number is a number regardless of representation; the only time representation matters is when you input or output the value in a human-readable form.

Human-readable forms of numeric quantities are always strings of characters. To print the value 128 in human-readable form, you must convert the numeric value 128 to the three-character sequence 1 followed by 2 followed by 8. This would provide the decimal representation of the numeric quantity. If you prefer, you could convert the numeric value 128 to the three-character sequence 80h. It's the same number, but we've converted it to a different sequence of characters because (presumably) we wanted to view the number using hexadecimal representation rather than decimal. Likewise, if we want to see the number in binary, we must convert this numeric value to a string containing a 1 followed by seven 0 characters.

Pure assembly language has no generic print or write functions you can call to display numeric quantities as strings on your console. You could write your own procedures to handle this process (and this book considers some of those procedures later). For the time being, the MASM code in this book relies on the C Standard Library printf() function to display numeric values. Consider the program in Listing 2-1, which converts various values to their hexadecimal equivalents.

```
; Listing 2-1

; Displays some numeric values on the console.

        option  casemap:none

nl      =       10  ; ASCII code for newline

        .data
i       qword   1
j       qword   123
k       qword   456789

titleStr byte   'Listing 2-1', 0

fmtStrI byte    "i=%d, converted to hex=%x", nl, 0
fmtStrJ byte    "j=%d, converted to hex=%x", nl, 0
fmtStrK byte    "k=%d, converted to hex=%x", nl, 0

        .code
        externdef   printf:proc

; Return program title to C++ program:

        public getTitle
getTitle proc

; Load address of "titleStr" into the RAX register (RAX holds
; the function return result) and return back to the caller:

        lea rax, titleStr
        ret
getTitle endp

; Here is the "asmMain" function.

        public  asmMain
asmMain proc

; "Magic" instruction offered without explanation at this point:

        sub     rsp, 56

; Call printf three times to print the three values i, j, and k:

; printf("i=%d, converted to hex=%x\n", i, i);
```

```
        lea     rcx, fmtStrI
        mov     rdx, i
        mov     r8, rdx
        call    printf

; printf("j=%d, converted to hex=%x\n", j, j);

        lea     rcx, fmtStrJ
        mov     rdx, j
        mov     r8, rdx
        call    printf

; printf("k=%d, converted to hex=%x\n", k, k);

        lea     rcx, fmtStrK
        mov     rdx, k
        mov     r8, rdx
        call    printf

; Another "magic" instruction that undoes the effect of the previous
; one before this procedure returns to its caller.

        add     rsp, 56

        ret     ; Returns to caller

asmMain endp
        end
```

Listing 2-1: Decimal-to-hexadecimal conversion program

Listing 2-1 uses the generic *c.cpp* program from Chapter 1 (and the generic *build.bat* batch file as well). You can compile and run this program by using the following commands at the command line:

```
C:\>build  listing2-1

C:\>echo off
 Assembling: listing2-1.asm
c.cpp

C:\> listing2-1
Calling Listing 2-1:
i=1, converted to hex=1
j=123, converted to hex=7b
k=456789, converted to hex=6f855
Listing 2-1 terminated
```

2.4 Data Organization

In pure mathematics, a value's representation may require an arbitrary number of bits. Computers, on the other hand, generally work with a specific number of bits. Common collections are single bits, groups of 4 bits (called *nibbles*), 8 bits (*bytes*), 16 bits (*words*), 32 bits (*double words*, or *dwords*), 64 bits (*quad words,* or *qwords*), 128 bits (*octal words,* or *owords*), and more.

2.4.1 Bits

The smallest unit of data on a binary computer is a single *bit*. With a single bit, you can represent any two distinct items. Examples include 0 or 1, true or false, and right or wrong. However, you are *not* limited to representing binary data types; you could use a single bit to represent the numbers 723 and 1245 or, perhaps, the colors red and blue, or even the color red and the number 3256. You can represent *any two* different values with a single bit, but *only two* values with a single bit.

Different bits can represent different things. For example, you could use 1 bit to represent the values 0 and 1, while a different bit could represent the values true and false. How can you tell by looking at the bits? The answer is that you can't. This illustrates the whole idea behind computer data structures: *data is what you define it to be*. If you use a bit to represent a Boolean (true/false) value, then that bit (by your definition) represents true or false. However, you must be consistent. If you're using a bit to represent true or false at one point in your program, you shouldn't use that value to represent red or blue later.

2.4.2 Nibbles

A nibble is a collection of 4 bits. With a nibble, we can represent up to 16 distinct values because a string of 4 bits has 16 unique combinations:

```
0000
0001
0010
0011
0100
0101
0110
0111
1000
1001
1010
1011
1100
1101
1110
1111
```

Nibbles are an interesting data structure because it takes 4 bits to represent a single digit in *binary-coded decimal (BCD)* numbers[1] and hexadecimal numbers. In the case of hexadecimal numbers, the values 0, 1, 2, 3, 4, 5, 6, 7,

---

1. *Binary-coded decimal* is a numeric scheme used to represent decimal numbers, using 4 bits for each decimal digit.

8, 9, A, B, C, D, E, and F are represented with 4 bits. BCD uses 10 different digits (0, 1, 2, 3, 4, 5, 6, 7, 8 and 9) and also requires 4 bits (because we can represent only eight different values with 3 bits, and the additional six values we can represent with 4 bits are never used in BCD representation). In fact, any 16 distinct values can be represented with a nibble, though hexadecimal and BCD digits are the primary items we can represent with a single nibble.

2.4.3 Bytes

Without question, the most important data structure used by the x86-64 microprocessor is the byte, which consists of 8 bits. Main memory and I/O addresses on the x86-64 are all byte addresses. This means that the smallest item that can be individually accessed by an x86-64 program is an 8-bit value. To access anything smaller requires that we read the byte containing the data and eliminate the unwanted bits. The bits in a byte are normally numbered from 0 to 7, as shown in Figure 2-1.

Figure 2-1: Bit numbering

Bit 0 is the LO bit, or least significant bit, and bit 7 is the HO bit, or most significant bit of the byte. We'll refer to all other bits by their number.

A byte contains exactly two nibbles (see Figure 2-2).

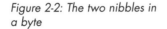

HO Nibble   LO Nibble

Figure 2-2: The two nibbles in a byte

Bits 0 to 3 compose the *low-order nibble*, and bits 4 to 7 form the *high-order nibble*. Because a byte contains exactly two nibbles, byte values require two hexadecimal digits.

Because a byte contains 8 bits, it can represent 2^8 (256) different values. Generally, we'll use a byte to represent numeric values in the range 0 through 255, signed numbers in the range –128 through +127 (see "Signed and Unsigned Numbers" on page 62), ASCII IBM character codes, and other special data types requiring no more than 256 different values. Many data types have fewer than 256 items, so 8 bits are usually sufficient.

Because the x86-64 is a byte-addressable machine, it's more efficient to manipulate a whole byte than an individual bit or nibble. So it's more efficient to use a whole byte to represent data types that require no more than 256 items, even if fewer than 8 bits would suffice.

Probably the most important use for a byte is holding a character value. Characters typed at the keyboard, displayed on the screen, and printed on the printer all have numeric values. To communicate with the rest of the world, PCs typically use a variant of the *ASCII character set* or the *Unicode character set*. The ASCII character set has 128 defined codes.

Bytes are also the smallest variable you can create in a MASM program. To create an arbitrary byte variable, you should use the byte data type, as follows:

```
        .data
byteVar  byte ?
```

The byte data type is a partially untyped data type. The only type information associated with a byte object is its size (1 byte).[2] You may store any 8-bit value (small signed integers, small unsigned integers, characters, and the like) into a byte variable. It is up to you to keep track of the type of object you've put into a byte variable.

2.4.4 Words

A word is a group of 16 bits. We'll number the bits in a word from 0 to 15, as Figure 2-3 shows. Like the byte, bit 0 is the low-order bit. For words, bit 15 is the high-order bit. When referencing the other bits in a word, we'll use their bit position number.

15 14 13 12 11 10 9 8 7 6 5 4 3 2 1 0

Figure 2-3: Bit numbers in a word

A word contains exactly 2 bytes (and, therefore, four nibbles). Bits 0 to 7 form the low-order byte, and bits 8 to 15 form the high-order byte (see Figures 2-4 and 2-5).

15 14 13 12 11 10 9 8 7 6 5 4 3 2 1 0

HO Byte   LO Byte

Figure 2-4: The 2 bytes in a word

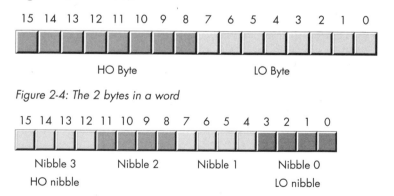

15 14 13 12 11 10 9 8 7 6 5 4 3 2 1 0

Nibble 3   Nibble 2   Nibble 1   Nibble 0
HO nibble   LO nibble

Figure 2-5: Nibbles in a word

---

2. For MASM's HLL statements, the byte directive also notes that the value is an unsigned, rather than signed, value. However, for most normal machine instructions, MASM ignores this extra type information.

With 16 bits, you can represent 2^{16} (65,536) values. These could be the values in the range 0 to 65,535 or, as is usually the case, the signed values –32,768 to +32,767, or any other data type with no more than 65,536 values.

The three major uses for words are short signed integer values, short unsigned integer values, and Unicode characters. Unsigned numeric values are represented by the binary value corresponding to the bits in the word. Signed numeric values use the two's complement form for numeric values (see "Sign Extension and Zero Extension" on page 67). As Unicode characters, words can represent up to 65,536 characters, allowing the use of non-Roman character sets in a computer program. Unicode is an international standard, like ASCII, that allows computers to process non-Roman characters such as Kanji, Greek, and Russian characters.

As with bytes, you can also create word variables in a MASM program. To create an arbitrary word variable, use the word data type as follows:

```
        .data
w       word   ?
```

2.4.5 Double Words

A double word is exactly what its name indicates: a pair of words. Therefore, a double-word quantity is 32 bits long, as shown in Figure 2-6.

Figure 2-6: Bit numbers in a double word

Naturally, this double word can be divided into a high-order word and a low-order word, 4 bytes, or eight different nibbles (see Figure 2-7).

Double words (dwords) can represent all kinds of things. A common item you will represent with a double word is a 32-bit integer value (which allows unsigned numbers in the range 0 to 4,294,967,295 or signed numbers in the range –2,147,483,648 to 2,147,483,647). 32-bit floating-point values also fit into a double word.

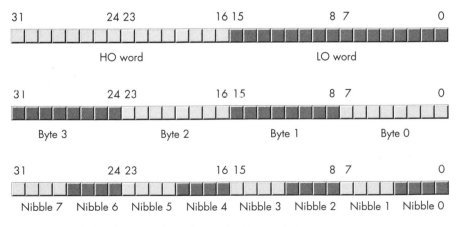

Figure 2-7: Nibbles, bytes, and words in a double word

You can create an arbitrary double-word variable by using the `dword` data type, as the following example demonstrates:

```
        .data
d       dword   ?
```

2.4.6   Quad Words and Octal Words

Quad-word (64-bit) values are also important because 64-bit integers, pointers, and certain floating-point data types require 64 bits. Likewise, the SSE/MMX instruction set of modern x86-64 processors can manipulate 64-bit values. In a similar vein, octal-word (128-bit) values are important because the AVX/SSE instruction set can manipulate 128-bit values. MASM allows the declaration of 64- and 128-bit values by using the `qword` and `oword` types, as follows:

```
        .data
o       oword ?
q       qword ?
```

You may not directly manipulate 128-bit integer objects using standard instructions like `mov`, `add`, and `sub` because the standard x86-64 integer registers process only 64 bits at a time. In Chapter 8, you will see how to manipulate these extended-precision values; Chapter 11 describes how to directly manipulate `oword` values by using SIMD instructions.

2.5   Logical Operations on Bits

We'll do four primary logical operations (Boolean functions) with hexadecimal and binary numbers: AND, OR, XOR (exclusive-or), and NOT.

2.5.1   The AND Operation

The *logical AND operation* is a *dyadic* operation (meaning it accepts exactly two operands).[3] These operands are individual binary bits. The AND operation is shown here:

```
0 and 0 = 0
0 and 1 = 0
1 and 0 = 0
1 and 1 = 1
```

A compact way to represent the logical AND operation is with a truth table. A *truth table* takes the form shown in Table 2-2.

Table 2-2: AND Truth Table

AND	0	1
0	0	0
1	0	1

---

3. Many texts call this a *binary operation*. The term *dyadic* means the same thing and avoids the confusion with the binary numbering system.

This is just like the multiplication tables you've encountered in school. The values in the left column correspond to the left operand of the AND operation. The values in the top row correspond to the right operand of the AND operation. The value located at the intersection of the row and column (for a particular pair of input values) is the result of logically ANDing those two values together.

In English, the logical AND operation is, "If the first operand is 1 and the second operand is 1, the result is 1; otherwise, the result is 0." We could also state this as, "If either or both operands are 0, the result is 0."

You can use the logical AND operation to force a 0 result: if one of the operands is 0, the result is always 0 regardless of the other operand. In Table 2-2, for example, the row labeled with a 0 input contains only 0s, and the column labeled with a 0 contains only 0s. Conversely, if one operand contains a 1, the result is exactly the value of the second operand. These results of the AND operation are important, particularly when we want to force bits to 0. We will investigate these uses of the logical AND operation in the next section.

2.5.2 The OR Operation

The *logical OR operation* is also a dyadic operation. Its definition is as follows:

```
0 or 0 = 0
0 or 1 = 1
1 or 0 = 1
1 or 1 = 1
```

Table 2-3 shows the truth table for the OR operation.

Table 2-3: OR Truth Table

OR	0	1
0	0	1
1	1	1

Colloquially, the logical OR operation is, "If the first operand or the second operand (or both) is 1, the result is 1; otherwise, the result is 0." This is also known as the *inclusive-or* operation.

If one of the operands to the logical OR operation is a 1, the result is always 1 regardless of the second operand's value. If one operand is 0, the result is always the value of the second operand. Like the logical AND operation, this is an important side effect of the logical OR operation that will prove quite useful.

Note that there is a difference between this form of the inclusive logical OR operation and the standard English meaning. Consider the sentence "I am going to the store *or* I am going to the park." Such a statement implies that the speaker is going to the store or to the park, but not to both places. Therefore, the English version of logical OR is slightly different from the inclusive-or operation; indeed, this is the definition of the *exclusive-or* operation.

2.5.3 The XOR Operation

The *logical XOR (exclusive-or) operation* is also a dyadic operation. Its definition follows:

```
0 xor 0 = 0
0 xor 1 = 1
1 xor 0 = 1
1 xor 1 = 0
```

Table 2-4 shows the truth table for the XOR operation.

Table 2-4: XOR Truth Table

XOR	0	1
0	0	1
1	1	0

In English, the logical XOR operation is, "If the first operand or the second operand, but not both, is 1, the result is 1; otherwise, the result is 0." The exclusive-or operation is closer to the English meaning of the word *or* than is the logical OR operation.

If one of the operands to the logical exclusive-or operation is a 1, the result is always the *inverse* of the other operand; that is, if one operand is 1, the result is 0 if the other operand is 1, and the result is 1 if the other operand is 0. If the first operand contains a 0, the result is exactly the value of the second operand. This feature lets you selectively invert bits in a bit string.

2.5.4 The NOT Operation

The logical NOT operation is a *monadic operation* (meaning it accepts only one operand):

```
not 0 = 1
not 1 = 0
```

The truth table for the NOT operation appears in Table 2-5.

Table 2-5: NOT Truth Table

NOT	0	1
	1	0

2.6 Logical Operations on Binary Numbers and Bit Strings

The previous section defines the logical functions for single-bit operands. Because the x86-64 uses groups of 8, 16, 32, 64, or more bits,[4] we need to extend the definition of these functions to deal with more than 2 bits.

---

4. The XMM and YMM registers process up to 128 or 256 bits, respectively. If you have a CPU that supports ZMM registers, it can process 512 bits at a time.

Logical functions on the x86-64 operate on a *bit-by-bit* (or *bitwise*) basis. Given two values, these functions operate on bit 0 of each value, producing bit 0 of the result; then they operate on bit 1 of the input values, producing bit 1 of the result, and so on. For example, if you want to compute the logical AND of the following two 8-bit numbers, you would perform the logical AND operation on each column independently of the others:

```
1011_0101b
1110_1110b
----------
1010_0100b
```

You may apply this bit-by-bit calculation to the other logical functions as well.

To perform a logical operation on two hexadecimal numbers, you should convert them to binary first.

The ability to force bits to 0 or 1 by using the logical AND/OR operations and the ability to invert bits using the logical XOR operation are very important when working with strings of bits (for example, binary numbers). These operations let you selectively manipulate certain bits within a bit string while leaving other bits unaffected.

For example, if you have an 8-bit binary value X and you want to guarantee that bits 4 to 7 contain 0s, you could logically AND the value X with the binary value 0000_1111b. This bitwise logical AND operation would force the HO 4 bits to 0 and pass the LO 4 bits of X unchanged. Likewise, you could force the LO bit of X to 1 and invert bit 2 of X by logically ORing X with 0000_0001b and logically XORing X with 0000_0100b, respectively.

Using the logical AND, OR, and XOR operations to manipulate bit strings in this fashion is known as *masking* bit strings. We use the term *masking* because we can use certain values (1 for AND, 0 for OR/XOR) to mask out or mask in certain bits from the operation when forcing bits to 0, 1, or their inverse.

The x86-64 CPUs support four instructions that apply these bitwise logical operations to their operands. The instructions are and, or, xor, and not. The and, or, and xor instructions use the same syntax as the add and sub instructions:

```
and   dest, source
or    dest, source
xor   dest, source
```

These operands have the same limitations as the add operands. Specifically, the *source* operand has to be a constant, memory, or register operand, and the *dest* operand must be a memory or register operand. Also, the operands must be the same size and cannot both be memory operands. If the destination operand is 64 bits and the source operand is a constant, that constant is limited to 32 bits (or fewer), and the CPU will sign-extend the value to 64 bits (see "Sign Extension and Zero Extension" on page 67).

These instructions compute the obvious bitwise logical operation via the following equation:

dest = *dest operator source*

The x86-64 logical not instruction, because it has only a single operand, uses a slightly different syntax. This instruction takes the following form:

not   *dest*

This instruction computes the following result:

dest = not(*dest*)

The *dest* operand must be a register or memory operand. This instruction inverts all the bits in the specified destination operand.

The program in Listing 2-2 inputs two hexadecimal values from the user and calculates their logical and, or, xor, and not.

```
; Listing 2-2

; Demonstrate AND, OR, XOR, and NOT logical instructions.

          option  casemap:none

nl        =       10  ; ASCII code for newline

          .data
leftOp    dword   0f0f0f0fh
rightOp1  dword   0f0f0f0f0h
rightOp2  dword   12345678h

titleStr  byte    'Listing 2-2', 0

fmtStr1   byte    "%lx AND %lx = %lx", nl, 0
fmtStr2   byte    "%lx OR  %lx = %lx", nl, 0
fmtStr3   byte    "%lx XOR %lx = %lx", nl, 0
fmtStr4   byte    "NOT %lx = %lx", nl, 0

          .code
          externdef    printf:proc

; Return program title to C++ program:

          public getTitle
getTitle  proc

;  Load address of "titleStr" into the RAX register (RAX holds the
;  function return result) and return back to the caller:

          lea rax, titleStr
          ret
getTitle  endp
```

```
; Here is the "asmMain" function.

            public  asmMain
asmMain     proc

; "Magic" instruction offered without explanation at this point:

            sub     rsp, 56

; Demonstrate the AND instruction:

            lea     rcx, fmtStr1
            mov     edx, leftOp
            mov     r8d, rightOp1
            mov     r9d, edx  ; Compute leftOp
            and     r9d, r8d  ; AND rightOp1
            call    printf

            lea     rcx, fmtStr1
            mov     edx, leftOp
            mov     r8d, rightOp2
            mov     r9d, r8d
            and     r9d, edx
            call    printf

; Demonstrate the OR instruction:

            lea     rcx, fmtStr2
            mov     edx, leftOp
            mov     r8d, rightOp1
            mov     r9d, edx  ; Compute leftOp
            or      r9d, r8d  ; OR rightOp1
            call    printf

            lea     rcx, fmtStr2
            mov     edx, leftOp
            mov     r8d, rightOp2
            mov     r9d, r8d
            or      r9d, edx
            call    printf

; Demonstrate the XOR instruction:

            lea     rcx, fmtStr3
            mov     edx, leftOp
            mov     r8d, rightOp1
            mov     r9d, edx  ; Compute leftOp
            xor     r9d, r8d  ; XOR rightOp1
            call    printf

            lea     rcx, fmtStr3
            mov     edx, leftOp
            mov     r8d, rightOp2
            mov     r9d, r8d
```

```
        xor     r9d, edx
        call    printf

; Demonstrate the NOT instruction:

        lea     rcx, fmtStr4
        mov     edx, leftOp
        mov     r8d, edx  ; Compute not leftOp
        not     r8d
        call    printf

        lea     rcx, fmtStr4
        mov     edx, rightOp1
        mov     r8d, edx  ; Compute not rightOp1
        not     r8d
        call    printf

        lea     rcx, fmtStr4
        mov     edx, rightOp2
        mov     r8d, edx  ; Compute not rightOp2
        not     r8d
        call    printf

; Another "magic" instruction that undoes the effect of the previous
; one before this procedure returns to its caller.

        add     rsp, 56

        ret     ; Returns to caller

asmMain endp
        end
```

Listing 2-2: and, or, xor, and not example

Here's the result of building and running this code:

```
C:\MASM64>build  listing2-2

C:\MASM64>ml64 /nologo /c /Zi /Cp  listing2-2.asm
 Assembling: listing2-2.asm

C:\MASM64>cl /nologo /O2 /Zi /utf-8 /Fe listing2-2.exe c.cpp  listing2-2.obj
c.cpp

C:\MASM64> listing2-2
Calling Listing 2-2:
f0f0f0f AND f0f0f0f0 = 0
f0f0f0f AND 12345678 = 2040608
f0f0f0f OR  f0f0f0f0 = ffffffff
f0f0f0f OR  12345678 = 1f3f5f7f
f0f0f0f XOR f0f0f0f0 = ffffffff
f0f0f0f XOR 12345678 = 1d3b5977
NOT f0f0f0f = f0f0f0f0
NOT f0f0f0f0 = f0f0f0f
```

```
NOT 12345678 = edcba987
Listing 2-2 terminated
```

By the way, you will often see the following "magic" instruction:

```
xor reg, reg
```

XORing a register with itself sets that register to 0. Except for 8-bit registers, the xor instruction is usually more efficient than moving the immediate constant into the register. Consider the following:

```
xor eax, eax  ; Just 2 bytes long in machine code
mov eax, 0    ; Depending on register, often 6 bytes long
```

The savings are even greater when dealing with 64-bit registers (as the immediate constant 0 is 8 bytes long by itself).

2.7 Signed and Unsigned Numbers

Thus far, we've treated binary numbers as unsigned values. The binary number . . . 00000 represents 0, . . . 00001 represents 1, . . . 00010 represents 2, and so on toward infinity. With n bits, we can represent 2^n unsigned numbers. What about negative numbers? If we assign half of the possible combinations to the negative values, and half to the positive values and 0, with n bits we can represent the signed values in the range -2^{n-1} to $+2^{n-1} -1$. So we can represent the negative values –128 to –1 and the non-negative values 0 to 127 with a single 8-bit byte. With a 16-bit word, we can represent values in the range –32,768 to +32,767. With a 32-bit double word, we can represent values in the range –2,147,483,648 to +2,147,483,647.

In mathematics (and computer science), the *complement method* encodes negative and non-negative (positive plus zero) numbers into two equal sets in such a way that they can use the same algorithm (or hardware) to perform addition and produce the correct result regardless of the sign.

The x86-64 microprocessor uses the *two's complement* notation to represent signed numbers. In this system, the HO bit of a number is a *sign bit* (dividing the integers into two equal sets). If the sign bit is 0, the number is positive (or zero); if the sign bit is 1, the number is negative (taking a complement form, which I'll describe in a moment). Following are some examples.

For 16-bit numbers:

- 8000h is negative because the HO bit is 1.
- 100h is positive because the HO bit is 0.
- 7FFFh is positive.
- 0FFFFh is negative.
- 0FFFh is positive.

If the HO bit is 0, the number is positive (or 0) and uses the standard binary format. If the HO bit is 1, the number is negative and uses the two's complement form (which is the magic form that supports addition of negative and non-negative numbers with no special hardware).

To convert a positive number to its negative, two's complement form, you use the following algorithm:

1. Invert all the bits in the number; that is, apply the logical NOT function.
2. Add 1 to the inverted result and ignore any carry out of the HO bit.

This produces a bit pattern that satisfies the mathematical definition of the complement form. In particular, adding negative and non-negative numbers using this form produces the expected result.

For example, to compute the 8-bit equivalent of –5:

- 0000_0101b   5 (in binary).
- 1111_1010b   Invert all the bits.
- 1111_1011b   Add 1 to obtain result.

If we take –5 and perform the two's complement operation on it, we get our original value, 0000_0101b, back again:

- 1111_1011b   Two's complement for –5.
- 0000_0100b   Invert all the bits.
- 0000_0101b   Add 1 to obtain result (+5).

Note that if we add +5 and –5 together (ignoring any carry out of the HO bit), we get the expected result of 0:

```
    1111_1011b      Two's complement for -5
  + 0000_0101b      Invert all the bits and add 1
    ----------
(1) 0000_0000b      Sum is zero, if we ignore carry
```

The following examples provide some positive and negative 16-bit signed values:

- 7FFFh: +32767, the largest 16-bit positive number
- 8000h: –32768, the smallest 16-bit negative number
- 4000h: +16384

To convert the preceding numbers to their negative counterpart (that is, to negate them), do the following:

```
7FFFh:    0111_1111_1111_1111b    +32,767
          1000_0000_0000_0000b    Invert all the bits (8000h)
          1000_0000_0000_0001b    Add 1 (8001h or -32,767)

4000h:    0100_0000_0000_0000b    16,384
          1011_1111_1111_1111b    Invert all the bits (0BFFFh)
          1100_0000_0000_0000b    Add 1 (0C000h or -16,384)
```

8000h:	1000_0000_0000_0000b	-32,768
	0111_1111_1111_1111b	Invert all the bits (7FFFh)
	1000_0000_0000_0000b	Add one (8000h or -32,768)

8000h inverted becomes 7FFFh. After adding 1, we obtain 8000h! Wait, what's going on here? – (–32,768) is –32,768? Of course not. But the value +32,768 cannot be represented with a 16-bit signed number, so we cannot negate the smallest negative value.

Usually, you will not need to perform the two's complement operation by hand. The x86-64 microprocessor provides an instruction, neg (*negate*), that performs this operation for you:

```
neg dest
```

This instruction computes *dest* = -*dest*; and the operand must be a memory location or a register. neg operates on byte-, word-, dword-, and qword-sized objects. Because this is a signed integer operation, it only makes sense to operate on signed integer values. The program in Listing 2-3 demonstrates the two's complement operation and the neg instruction on signed 8-bit integer values.

```
; Listing 2-3

; Demonstrate two's complement operation and input of numeric values.

        option  casemap:none

nl      =       10  ; ASCII code for newline
maxLen  =       256

        .data
titleStr byte   'Listing 2-3', 0

prompt1  byte   "Enter an integer between 0 and 127:", 0
fmtStr1  byte   "Value in hexadecimal: %x", nl, 0
fmtStr2  byte   "Invert all the bits (hexadecimal): %x", nl, 0
fmtStr3  byte   "Add 1 (hexadecimal): %x", nl, 0
fmtStr4  byte   "Output as signed integer: %d", nl, 0
fmtStr5  byte   "Using neg instruction: %d", nl, 0

intValue sqword ?
input    byte   maxLen dup (?)

        .code
        externdef printf:proc
        externdef atoi:proc
        externdef readLine:proc

; Return program title to C++ program:

        public getTitle
getTitle proc
        lea rax, titleStr
```

```
              ret
getTitle      endp

; Here is the "asmMain" function.

              public  asmMain
asmMain       proc

; "Magic" instruction offered without explanation at this point:

              sub     rsp, 56

; Read an unsigned integer from the user: This code will blindly
; assume that the user's input was correct. The atoi function returns
; zero if there was some sort of error on the user input. Later
; chapters in Ao64A will describe how to check for errors from the
; user.

              lea     rcx, prompt1
              call    printf

              lea     rcx, input
              mov     rdx, maxLen
              call    readLine

; Call C stdlib atoi function.

; i = atoi(str)

              lea     rcx, input
              call    atoi
              and     rax, 0ffh        ; Only keep LO 8 bits
              mov     intValue, rax

; Print the input value (in decimal) as a hexadecimal number:

              lea     rcx, fmtStr1
              mov     rdx, rax
              call    printf

; Perform the two's complement operation on the input number.
; Begin by inverting all the bits (just work with a byte here).

              mov     rdx, intValue
              not     dl               ; Only work with 8-bit values!
              lea     rcx, fmtStr2
              call    printf

; Invert all the bits and add 1 (still working with just a byte).

              mov     rdx, intValue
              not     rdx
              add     rdx, 1
              and     rdx, 0ffh        ; Only keep LO eight bits
```

```
            lea     rcx, fmtStr3
            call    printf

; Negate the value and print as a signed integer (work with a full
; integer here, because C++ %d format specifier expects a 32-bit
; integer). HO 32 bits of RDX get ignored by C++.

            mov     rdx, intValue
            not     rdx
            add     rdx, 1
            lea     rcx, fmtStr4
            call    printf

; Negate the value using the neg instruction.

            mov     rdx, intValue
            neg     rdx
            lea     rcx, fmtStr5
            call    printf

; Another "magic" instruction that undoes the effect of the previous
; one before this procedure returns to its caller.

            add     rsp, 56
            ret             ; Returns to caller
asmMain     endp
            end
```

Listing 2-3: Two's complement example

The following commands build and run the program in Listing 2-3:

```
C:\>build  listing2-3

C:\>echo off
 Assembling: listing2-3.asm
c.cpp

C:\> listing2-3
Calling Listing 2-3:
Enter an integer between 0 and 127:123
Value in hexadecimal: 7b
Invert all the bits (hexadecimal): 84
Add 1 (hexadecimal): 85
Output as signed integer: -123
Using neg instruction: -123
Listing 2-3 terminated
```

Beyond the two's complement operation (both by inversion/add 1 and using the neg instruction), this program demonstrates one new feature: user numeric input. *Numeric input* is accomplished by reading an input string from the user (using the readLine() function that is part of the *c.cpp* source file) and then calling the C Standard Library atoi() function. This function requires a single parameter (passed in RCX) that points to a string containing an integer value. It translates that string to the corresponding integer and returns the integer value in RAX.[5]

2.8 Sign Extension and Zero Extension

Converting an 8-bit two's complement value to 16 bits, and conversely converting a 16-bit value to 8 bits, can be accomplished via *sign extension* and *contraction* operations.

To extend a signed value from a certain number of bits to a greater number of bits, copy the sign bit into all the additional bits in the new format. For example, to sign-extend an 8-bit number to a 16-bit number, copy bit 7 of the 8-bit number into bits 8 to 15 of the 16-bit number. To sign-extend a 16-bit number to a double word, copy bit 15 into bits 16 to 31 of the double word.

You must use sign extension when manipulating signed values of varying lengths. For example, to add a byte quantity to a word quantity, you must sign-extend the byte quantity to a word before adding the two values. Other operations (multiplication and division, in particular) may require a sign extension to 32 bits; see Table 2-6.

Table 2-6: Sign Extension

8 Bits	16 Bits	32 Bits
80h	0FF80h	0FFFFFF80h
28h	0028h	00000028h
9Ah	0FF9Ah	0FFFFFF9Ah
7Fh	007Fh	0000007Fh
	1020h	00001020h
	8086h	0FFFF8086h

To extend an unsigned value to a larger one, you must zero-extend the value, as shown in Table 2-7. *Zero extension* is easy—just store a 0 into the HO byte(s) of the larger operand. For example, to zero-extend the 8-bit value 82h to 16 bits, you prepend a 0 to the HO byte, yielding 0082h.

Table 2-7: Zero Extension

8 Bits	16 Bits	32 Bits
80h	0080h	00000080h
28h	0028h	00000028h

(continued)

---

5. Technically, atoi() returns a 32-bit integer in EAX. This code goes ahead and uses 64-bit values; the C Standard Library code ignores the HO 32 bits in RAX.

Table 2-7: Zero Extension *(continued)*

8 Bits	16 Bits	32 Bits
9Ah	009Ah	0000009Ah
7Fh	007Fh	0000007Fh
	1020h	00001020h
	8086h	00008086h

2.9 Sign Contraction and Saturation

Sign contraction, converting a value with a certain number of bits to the identical value with a fewer number of bits, is a little more troublesome. Given an *n*-bit number, you cannot always convert it to an *m*-bit number if $m < n$. For example, consider the value −448. As a 16-bit signed number, its hexadecimal representation is 0FE40h. The magnitude of this number is too large for an 8-bit value, so you cannot sign-contract it to 8 bits (doing so would create an overflow condition).

To properly sign-contract a value, the HO bytes to discard must all contain either 0 or 0FFh, and the HO bit of your resulting value must match *every* bit you've removed from the number. Here are some examples (16 bits to 8 bits):

- 0FF80h can be sign-contracted to 80h.
- 0040h can be sign-contracted to 40h.
- 0FE40h cannot be sign-contracted to 8 bits.
- 0100h cannot be sign-contracted to 8 bits.

If you must convert a larger object to a smaller object, and you're willing to live with loss of precision, you can use *saturation*. To convert a value via saturation, you copy the larger value to the smaller value if it is not outside the range of the smaller object. If the larger value is outside the range of the smaller value, you *clip* the value by setting it to the largest (or smallest) value within the range of the smaller object.

For example, when converting a 16-bit signed integer to an 8-bit signed integer, if the 16-bit value is in the range −128 to +127, you copy the LO byte of the 16-bit object to the 8-bit object. If the 16-bit signed value is greater than +127, then you clip the value to +127 and store +127 into the 8-bit object. Likewise, if the value is less than −128, you clip the final 8-bit object to −128.

Although clipping the value to the limits of the smaller object results in loss of precision, sometimes this is acceptable because the alternative is to raise an exception or otherwise reject the calculation. For many applications, such as audio or video processing, the clipped result is still recognizable, so this is a reasonable conversion.

2.10 Brief Detour: An Introduction to Control Transfer Instructions

The assembly language examples thus far have limped along without making use of *conditional execution* (that is, the ability to make decisions while executing code). Indeed, except for the call and ret instructions, you haven't seen any way to affect the straight-line execution of assembly code.

However, this book is rapidly approaching the point where meaningful examples require the ability to conditionally execute different sections of code. This section provides a brief introduction to the subject of conditional execution and transferring control to other sections of your program.

2.10.1 The jmp Instruction

Perhaps the best place to start is with a discussion of the x86-64 unconditional transfer-of-control instruction—the jmp instruction. The jmp instruction takes several forms, but the most common form is

```
jmp statement_label
```

where *statement_label* is an identifier attached to a machine instruction in your .code section. The jmp instruction immediately transfers control to the statement prefaced by the label. This is semantically equivalent to a goto statement in an HLL.

Here is an example of a statement label in front of a mov instruction:

```
stmtLbl: mov eax, 55
```

Like all MASM symbols, statement labels have two major attributes associated with them: an address (which is the memory address of the machine instruction following the label) and a type. The type is label, which is the same type as a proc directive's identifier.

Statement labels don't have to be on the same physical source line as a machine instruction. Consider the following example:

```
anotherLabel:
   mov eax, 55
```

This example is semantically equivalent to the previous one. The value (address) bound to anotherLabel is the address of the machine instruction following the label. In this case, it's still the mov instruction even though that mov instruction appears on the next line (it still follows the label without any other MASM statements that would generate code occurring between the label and the mov statement).

Technically, you could also jump to a proc label instead of a statement label. However, the jmp instruction does not set up a return address, so if the procedure executes a ret instruction, the return location may be undefined. (Chapter 5 explores return addresses in greater detail.)

2.10.2 The Conditional Jump Instructions

Although the common form of the jmp instruction is indispensable in assembly language programs, it doesn't provide any ability to conditionally execute different sections of code—hence the name *unconditional jump*.[6] Fortunately, the x86-64 CPUs provide a wide array of *conditional jump instructions* that, as their name suggests, allow conditional execution of code.

These instructions test the condition code bits (see "An Introduction to the Intel x86-64 CPU Family" in Chapter 1) in the FLAGS register to determine whether a branch should be taken. There are four condition code bits in the FLAGs register that these conditional jump instructions test: the carry, sign, overflow, and zero flags.[7]

The x86-64 CPUs provide eight instructions that test each of these four flags (see Table 2-8). The basic operation of the conditional jump instructions is that they test a flag to see if it is set (1) or clear (0) and branch to a target label if the test succeeds. If the test fails, the program continues execution with the next instruction following the conditional jump instruction.

Table 2-8: Conditional Jump Instructions That Test the Condition Code Flags

Instruction	Explanation
jc *label*	Jump if carry set. Jump to label if the carry flag is set (1); fall through if carry is clear (0).
jnc *label*	Jump if no carry. Jump to label if the carry flag is clear (0); fall through if carry is set (1).
jo *label*	Jump if overflow. Jump to label if the overflow flag is set (1); fall through if overflow is clear (0).
jno *label*	Jump if no overflow. Jump to label if the overflow flag is clear (0); fall through if overflow is set (1).
js *label*	Jump if sign (negative). Jump to label if the sign flag is set (1); fall through if sign is clear (0).
jns *label*	Jump if not sign. Jump to label if the sign flag is clear (0); fall through if sign is set (1).
jz *label*	Jump if zero. Jump to label if the zero flag is set (1); fall through if zero is clear (0).
jnz *label*	Jump if not zero. Jump to label if the zero flag is clear (0); fall through if zero is set (1).

To use a conditional jump instruction, you must first execute an instruction that affects one (or more) of the condition code flags. For example, an unsigned arithmetic overflow will set the carry flag (and

---

6. Note that variants of the jmp instruction, known as *indirect jumps*, can provide conditional execution capabilities. For more information, see Chapter 7.

7. Technically, you can test a fifth condition code flag: the parity flag. This book does not cover its use. See the Intel documentation for more details about the parity flag.

likewise, if overflow does not occur, the carry flag will be clear). Therefore, you could use the jc and jnc instructions after an add instruction to see if an (unsigned) overflow occurred during the calculation. For example:

```
    mov eax, int32Var
    add eax, anotherVar
    jc  overflowOccurred

; Continue down here if the addition did not
; produce an overflow.

        .
        .
        .


overflowOccurred:

; Execute this code if the sum of int32Var and anotherVar
; does not fit into 32 bits.
```

Not all instructions affect the flags. Of all the instructions we've looked at thus far (mov, add, sub, and, or, not, xor, and lea), only the add, sub, and, or, xor, and not instructions affect the flags. The add and sub instructions affect the flags as shown in Table 2-9.

Table 2-9: Flag Settings After Executing add or sub

Flag	Explanation
Carry	Set if an unsigned overflow occurs (for example, adding the byte values 0FFh and 01h). Clear if no overflow occurs. Note that subtracting 1 from 0 will also clear the carry flag (that is, 0 – 1 is equivalent to 0 + (–1), and –1 is 0FFh in two's complement form).
Overflow	Set if a signed overflow occurs (for example, adding the byte values 07Fh and 01h). Signed overflow occurs when the next-to-HO-bit overflows into the HO bit (for example, 7Fh becomes 80h, or 0FFh becomes 0, when dealing with byte-sized calculations).
Sign	The sign flag is set if the HO bit of the result is set. The sign flag is clear otherwise (that is, the sign flag reflects the state of the HO bit of the result).
Zero	The zero flag is set if the result of a computation produces 0; it is clear otherwise.

The logical instructions (and, or, xor, and not) always clear the carry and overflow flags. They copy the HO bit of their result into the sign flag and set/clear the zero flag if they produce a zero/nonzero result.

In addition to the conditional jump instructions, the x86-64 CPUs also provide a set of conditional move instructions. Chapter 7 covers those instructions.

2.10.3 The cmp Instruction and Corresponding Conditional Jumps

The cmp (*compare*) instruction is probably the most useful instruction to execute prior to a conditional jump. The compare instruction has the same syntax as the sub instruction and, in fact, it also subtracts the second operand from the first operand and sets the condition code flags based on the result of the subtraction.[8] But the cmp instruction doesn't store the difference back into the first (destination) operand. The whole purpose of the cmp instruction is to set the condition code flags based on the result of the subtraction.

Though you could use the jc/jnc, jo/jno, js/jns, and jz/jnz instructions immediately after a cmp instruction (to test how cmp has set the individual flags), the flag names don't really mean much in the context of the cmp instruction. Logically, when you see the following instruction (note that the cmp instruction's operand syntax is identical to the add, sub, and mov instructions),

```
cmp left_operand, right_operand
```

you read this instruction as "compare the *left_operand* to the *right_operand*." Questions you would normally ask after such a comparison are as follows:

- Is the *left_operand* equal to the *right_operand*?
- Is the *left_operand* not equal to the *right_operand*?
- Is the *left_operand* less than the *right_operand*?
- Is the *left_operand* less than or equal to the *right_operand*?
- Is the *left_operand* greater than the *right_operand*?
- Is the *left_operand* greater than or equal to the *right_operand*?

The conditional jump instructions presented thus far don't (intuitively) answer any of these questions.

The x86-64 CPUs provide an additional set of conditional jump instructions, shown in Table 2-10, that allow you to test for comparison conditions.

Table 2-10: Conditional Jump Instructions for Use After a cmp Instruction

Instruction	Flags tested	Explanation
je *label*	ZF == 1	Jump if equal. Transfers control to target label if the *left_operand* is equal to the *right_operand*. This is a synonym for jz, as the zero flag will be set if the two operands are equal (their subtraction produces a 0 result in that case).
jne *label*	ZF == 0	Jump if not equal. Transfers control to target label if the *left_operand* is not equal to the *right_operand*. This is a synonym for jnz, as the zero flag will be clear if the two operands are not equal (their subtraction produces a non-zero result in that case).

---

8. Immediate operands for 64-bit instructions are also limited to 32 bits, which the CPU sign extends to 64 bits.

Instruction	Flags tested	Explanation
ja *label*	CF == 0 and ZF == 0	Jump if above. Transfers control to target label if the *unsigned left_operand* is greater than the *unsigned right_operand*.
jae *label*	CF == 0	Jump if above or equal. Transfers control to target label if the *unsigned left_operand* is greater than or equal to the *unsigned right_operand*. This is a synonym for jnc, as it turns out that an unsigned overflow (well, underflow, actually) will not occur if the *left_operand* is greater than or equal to the *right_operand*.
jb *label*	CF == 1	Jump if below. Transfers control to target label if the *unsigned left_operand* is less than the *unsigned right_operand*. This is a synonym for jc, as it turns out that an unsigned overflow (well, underflow, actually) occurs if the *left_operand* is less than the *right_operand*.
jbe *label*	CF == 1 or ZF == 1	Jump if below or equal. Transfers control to target label if the *unsigned left_operand* is less than or equal to the *unsigned right_operand*.
jg *label*	SF == OF and ZF == 0	Jump if greater. Transfers control to target label if the *signed left_operand* is greater than the *signed right_operand*.
jge *label*	SF == OF	Jump if greater or equal. Transfers control to target label if the *signed left_operand* is greater than or equal to the *signed right_operand*.
jl *label*	SF ≠ OF	Jump if less. Transfers control to target label if the *signed left_operand* is less than the *signed right_operand*.
jle *label*	ZF == 1 or SF ≠ OF	Jump if less or equal. Transfers control to target label if the *signed left_operand* is less than or equal to the *signed right_operand*.

Perhaps the most important thing to note in Table 2-10 is that separate conditional jump instructions test for signed and unsigned comparisons. Consider the two byte values 0FFh and 01h. From an unsigned perspective, 0FFh is greater than 01h. However, when we treat these as signed numbers (using the two's complement numbering system), 0FFh is actually –1, which is clearly less than 1. They have the same bit representations but two completely different comparison results when treating these values as signed or unsigned numbers.

2.10.4 Conditional Jump Synonyms

Some of the instructions are synonyms for other instructions. For example, jb and jc are the same instruction (that is, they have the same numeric *machine code* encoding). This is done for convenience and readability's sake. After a cmp instruction, jb is much more meaningful than jc, for example. MASM defines several synonyms for various conditional branch instructions that make coding a little easier. Table 2-11 lists many of these synonyms.

Table 2-11: Conditional Jump Synonyms

Instruction	Equivalents	Description
ja	jnbe	Jump if above, jump if not below or equal.
jae	jnb, jnc	Jump if above or equal, jump if not below, jump if no carry.
jb	jc, jnae	Jump if below, jump if carry, jump if not above or equal.
jbe	jna	Jump if below or equal, jump if not above.
jc	jb, jnae	Jump if carry, jump if below, jump if not above or equal.
je	jz	Jump if equal, jump if zero.
jg	jnle	Jump if greater, jump if not less or equal.
jge	jnl	Jump if greater or equal, jump if not less.
jl	jnge	Jump if less, jump if not greater or equal.
jle	jng	Jump if less or equal, jump if not greater.
jna	jbe	Jump if not above, jump if below or equal.
jnae	jb, jc	Jump if not above or equal, jump if below, jump if carry.
jnb	jae, jnc	Jump if not below, jump if above or equal, jump if no carry.
jnbe	ja	Jump if not below or equal, jump if above.
jnc	jnb, jae	Jump if no carry, jump if no below, jump if above or equal.
jne	jnz	Jump if not equal, jump if not zero.
jng	jle	Jump if not greater, jump if less or equal.
jnge	jl	Jump if not greater or equal, jump if less.
jnl	jge	Jump if not less, jump if greater or equal.
jnle	jg	Jump if not less or equal, jump if greater.
jnz	jne	Jump if not zero, jump if not equal.
jz	je	Jump if zero, jump if equal.

There is a very important thing to note about the cmp instruction: it sets the flags only for integer comparisons (which will also cover characters and other types you can encode with an integer number). Specifically, it does not compare floating-point values and set the flags as appropriate for a floating-point comparison. To learn more about floating-point arithmetic (and comparisons), see "Floating-Point Arithmetic" in Chapter 6.

2.11 Shifts and Rotates

Another set of logical operations that apply to bit strings is the *shift* and *rotate* operations. These two categories can be further broken down into left shifts, left rotates, right shifts, and right rotates.

The *shift-left operation* moves each bit in a bit string one position to the left, as shown in Figure 2-8.

Figure 2-8: Shift-left operation

Bit 0 moves into bit position 1, the previous value in bit position 1 moves into bit position 2, and so on. We'll shift a 0 into bit 0, and the previous value of the high-order bit will become the *carry* out of this operation.

The x86-64 provides a shift-left instruction, shl, that performs this useful operation. The syntax for the shl instruction is shown here:

```
shl dest, count
```

The *count* operand is either the CL register or a constant in the range 0 to n, where n is one less than the number of bits in the destination operand (for example, $n = 7$ for 8-bit operands, $n = 15$ for 16-bit operands, $n = 31$ for 32-bit operands, and $n = 63$ for 64-bit operands). The *dest* operand is a typical destination operand. It can be either a memory location or a register.

When the *count* operand is the constant 1, the shl instruction does the operation shown in Figure 2-9.

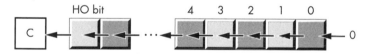

Figure 2-9: shl by 1 operation

In Figure 2-9, the *C* represents the carry flag—that is, the HO bit shifted out of the operand moves into the carry flag. Therefore, you can test for overflow after a shl *dest,* 1 instruction by testing the carry flag immediately after executing the instruction (for example, by using jc and jnc).

The shl instruction sets the zero flag based on the result (z=1 if the result is zero, z=0 otherwise). The shl instruction sets the sign flag if the HO bit of the result is 1. If the shift count is 1, then shl sets the overflow flag if the HO bit changes (that is, you shift a 0 into the HO bit when it was previously 1, or shift a 1 in when it was previously 0); the overflow flag is undefined for all other shift counts.

Shifting a value to the left one digit is the same thing as multiplying it by its radix (base). For example, shifting a decimal number one position to the left (adding a 0 to the right of the number) effectively multiplies it by 10 (the radix):

```
1234 shl 1 = 12340
```

(shl 1 means shift one digit position to the left.)

Because the radix of a binary number is 2, shifting it left multiplies it by 2. If you shift a value to the left n times, you multiply that value by 2^n.

A *shift-right* operation works the same way, except we're moving the data in the opposite direction. For a byte value, bit 7 moves into bit 6, bit 6 moves into bit 5, bit 5 moves into bit 4, and so on. During a right shift, we'll move a 0 into bit 7, and bit 0 will be the carry out of the operation (see Figure 2-10).

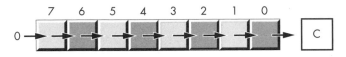

Figure 2-10: Shift-right operation

As you would probably expect, the x86-64 provides a shr instruction that will shift the bits to the right in a destination operand. The syntax is similar to that of the shl instruction:

shr *dest, count*

This instruction shifts a 0 into the HO bit of the destination operand; it shifts the other bits one place to the right (from a higher bit number to a lower bit number). Finally, bit 0 is shifted into the carry flag. If you specify a count of 1, the shr instruction does the operation shown in Figure 2-11.

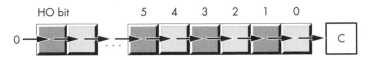

Figure 2-11: shr by 1 operation

The shr instruction sets the zero flag based on the result (ZF=1 if the result is zero, ZF=0 otherwise). The shr instruction clears the sign flag (because the HO bit of the result is always 0). If the shift count is 1, shl sets the overflow flag if the HO bit changes (that is, you shift a 0 into the HO bit when it was previously 1, or shift a 1 in when it was previously 0); the overflow flag is undefined for all other shift counts.

Because a left shift is equivalent to a multiplication by 2, it should come as no surprise that a right shift is roughly comparable to a division by 2 (or, in general, a division by the radix of the number). If you perform n right shifts, you will divide that number by 2^n.

However, a shift right is equivalent to only an *unsigned* division by 2. For example, if you shift the unsigned representation of 254 (0FEh) one place to the right, you get 127 (7Fh), exactly what you would expect. However, if you shift the two's complement representation of –2 (0FEh) to the right one position, you get 127 (7Fh), which is *not* correct. This problem occurs because we're shifting a 0 into bit 7. If bit 7 previously contained a 1, we're changing it from a negative to a positive number. Not a good thing to do when dividing by 2.

To use the shift right as a division operator, we must define a third shift operation: *arithmetic shift right*.[9] This works just like the normal shift-right operation (a logical shift right) except, instead of shifting a 0 into the high-order bit, an arithmetic shift-right operation copies the HO bit back into itself; that is, during the shift operation, it does not modify the HO bit, as Figure 2-12 shows.

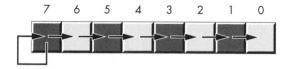

Figure 2-12: Arithmetic shift-right operation

An arithmetic shift right generally produces the result you expect. For example, if you perform the arithmetic shift-right operation on −2 (0FEh), you get −1 (0FFh). However, this operation always rounds the numbers to the closest integer that is *less than or equal to the actual result*. For example, if you apply the arithmetic shift-right operation on −1 (0FFh), the result is −1, not 0. Because −1 is less than 0, the arithmetic shift-right operation rounds toward −1. This is not a bug in the arithmetic shift-right operation; it just uses a different (though valid) definition of integer division.

The x86-64 provides an arithmetic shift-right instruction, sar (*shift arithmetic right*). This instruction's syntax is nearly identical to that of shl and shr:

---

sar *dest, count*

The usual limitations on the count and destination operands apply. This instruction operates as shown in Figure 2-13 if the count is 1.

Figure 2-13: sar dest, 1 operation

The sar instruction sets the zero flag based on the result (z=1 if the result is zero, and z=0 otherwise). The sar instruction sets the sign flag to the HO bit of the result. The overflow flag should always be clear after a sar instruction, as signed overflow is impossible with this operation.

The *rotate-left* and *rotate-right* operations behave like the shift-left and shift-right operations, except the bit shifted out from one end is shifted back in at the other end. Figure 2-14 diagrams these operations.

---

9. There is no need for an arithmetic shift left. The standard shift-left operation works for both signed and unsigned numbers, assuming no overflow occurs.

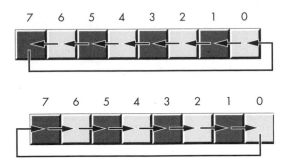

Figure 2-14: Rotate-left and rotate-right operations

The x86-64 provides rol (rotate left) and ror (rotate right) instructions that do these basic operations on their operands. The syntax for these two instructions is similar to the shift instructions:

```
rol dest, count
ror dest, count
```

If the shift count is 1, these two instructions copy the bit shifted out of the destination operand into the carry flag, as Figures 2-15 and 2-16 show.

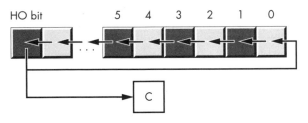

Figure 2-15: rol dest, 1 operation

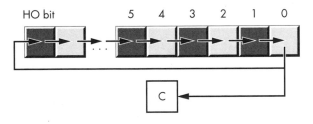

Figure 2-16: ror dest, 1 operation

Unlike the shift instructions, the rotate instructions do not affect the settings of the sign or zero flags. The OF flag is defined only for the 1-bit rotates; it is undefined in all other cases (except RCL and RCR instructions only: a zero-bit rotate does nothing—that is, it affects no flags). For left rotates, the OF flag is set to the exclusive-or of the original HO 2 bits. For right rotates, the OF flag is set to the exclusive-or of the HO 2 bits after the rotate.

It is often more convenient for the rotate operation to shift the output bit through the carry and to shift the previous carry value back into the input bit of the shift operation. The x86-64 rcl (*rotate through carry left*) and rcr (*rotate through carry right*) instructions achieve this for you. These instructions use the following syntax:

```
rcl dest, count
rcr dest, count
```

The *count* operand is either a constant or the CL register, and the *dest* operand is a memory location or register. The *count* operand must be a value that is less than the number of bits in the *dest* operand. For a count value of 1, these two instructions do the rotation shown in Figure 2-17.

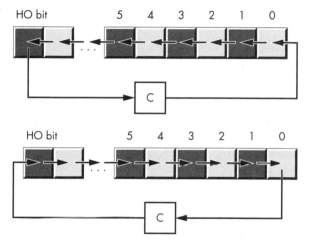

Figure 2-17: rcl dest, 1 and rcr dest, 1 operations

Unlike the shift instructions, the rotate-through-carry instructions do not affect the settings of the sign or zero flags. The OF flag is defined only for the 1-bit rotates. For left rotates, the OF flag is set if the original HO 2 bits change. For right rotates, the OF flag is set to the exclusive OR of the resultant HO 2 bits.

2.12　Bit Fields and Packed Data

Although the x86-64 operates most efficiently on byte, word, dword, and qword data types, occasionally you'll need to work with a data type that uses a number of bits other than 8, 16, 32, or 64. You can also zero-extend a non-standard data size to the next larger power of 2 (such as extending a 22-bit value to a 32-bit value). This turns out to be fast, but if you have a large array of such values, slightly more than 31 percent of the memory is going to waste (10 bits in every 32-bit value). However, suppose you were to repurpose those 10 bits for something else? By *packing* the separate 22-bit and 10-bit values into a single 32-bit value, you don't waste any space.

For example, consider a date of the form 04/02/01. Representing this date requires three numeric values: month, day, and year values. Months, of course, take on the values 1 to 12. At least 4 bits (a maximum of 16 different values) are needed to represent the month. Days range from 1 to 31. So it will take 5 bits (a maximum of 32 different values) to represent the day entry. The year value, assuming that we're working with values in the range

0 to 99, requires 7 bits (which can be used to represent up to 128 different values). So, $4 + 5 + 7 = 16$ bits, or 2 bytes.

In other words, we can pack our date data into 2 bytes rather than the 3 that would be required if we used a separate byte for each of the month, day, and year values. This saves 1 byte of memory for each date stored, which could be a substantial savings if you need to store many dates. The bits could be arranged as shown in Figure 2-18.

15 14 13 12 11 10 9   8   7   6   5   4   3   2   1   0

| M | M | M | M | D | D | D | D | D | Y | Y | Y | Y | Y | Y | Y |

Figure 2-18: Short packed date format (2 bytes)

MMMM represents the 4 bits making up the month value, *DDDDD* represents the 5 bits making up the day, and *YYYYYYY* is the 7 bits composing the year. Each collection of bits representing a data item is a *bit field*. For example, April 2, 2001, would be represented as 4101h:

0100	00010	0000001	= 0100_0001_0000_0001b or 4101h
4	2	01	

Although packed values are *space-efficient* (that is, they make efficient use of memory), they are computationally *inefficient* (slow!). The reason? It takes extra instructions to unpack the data packed into the various bit fields. These extra instructions take additional time to execute (and additional bytes to hold the instructions); hence, you must carefully consider whether packed data fields will save you anything. The sample program in Listing 2-4 demonstrates the effort that must go into packing and unpacking this 16-bit date format.

```
; Listing 2-4

; Demonstrate packed data types.

        option  casemap:none

NULL    =       0
nl      =       10  ; ASCII code for newline
maxLen  =       256

; New data declaration section.
; .const holds data values for read-only constants.

            .const
ttlStr      byte    'Listing 2-4', 0
moPrompt    byte    'Enter current month: ', 0
dayPrompt   byte    'Enter current day: ', 0
yearPrompt  byte    'Enter current year '
            byte    '(last 2 digits only): ', 0

packed      byte    'Packed date is %04x', nl, 0
```

```
theDate     byte    'The date is %02d/%02d/%02d'
            byte    nl, 0

badDayStr   byte    'Bad day value was entered '
            byte    '(expected 1-31)', nl, 0

badMonthStr byte    'Bad month value was entered '
            byte    '(expected 1-12)', nl, 0
badYearStr  byte    'Bad year value was entered '
            byte    '(expected 00-99)', nl, 0


            .data
month       byte    ?
day         byte    ?
year        byte    ?
date        word    ?

input       byte    maxLen dup (?)

            .code
            externdef printf:proc
            externdef readLine:proc
            externdef atoi:proc

; Return program title to C++ program:

            public getTitle
getTitle    proc
            lea rax, ttlStr
            ret
getTitle    endp

; Here's a user-written function that reads a numeric value from the
; user:

; int readNum(char *prompt);

; A pointer to a string containing a prompt message is passed in the
; RCX register.

; This procedure prints the prompt, reads an input string from the
; user, then converts the input string to an integer and returns the
; integer value in RAX.

readNum     proc

; Must set up stack properly (using this "magic" instruction) before
; we can call any C/C++ functions:

            sub     rsp, 56

; Print the prompt message. Note that the prompt message was passed to
; this procedure in RCX, we're just passing it on to printf:

            call    printf
```

```
        ; Set up arguments for readLine and read a line of text from the user.
        ; Note that readLine returns NULL (0) in RAX if there was an error.

                    lea     rcx, input
                    mov     rdx, maxLen
                    call    readLine

        ; Test for a bad input string:

                    cmp     rax, NULL
                    je      badInput

        ; Okay, good input at this point, try converting the string to an
        ; integer by calling atoi. The atoi function returns zero if there was
        ; an error, but zero is a perfectly fine return result, so we ignore
        ; errors.

                    lea     rcx, input      ; Ptr to string
                    call    atoi            ; Convert to integer

badInput:
                    add     rsp, 56         ; Undo stack setup
                    ret
readNum     endp

        ; Here is the "asmMain" function.

                    public  asmMain
asmMain     proc
                    sub     rsp, 56

        ; Read the date from the user. Begin by reading the month:

                    lea     rcx, moPrompt
                    call    readNum

        ; Verify the month is in the range 1..12:

                    cmp     rax, 1
                    jl      badMonth
                    cmp     rax, 12
                    jg      badMonth

        ; Good month, save it for now:

                    mov     month, al       ; 1..12 fits in a byte

        ; Read the day:

                    lea     rcx, dayPrompt
                    call    readNum
```

```
; We'll be lazy here and verify only that the day is in the range
; 1..31.

                cmp     rax, 1
                jl      badDay
                cmp     rax, 31
                jg      badDay

; Good day, save it for now:

                mov     day, al         ; 1..31 fits in a byte

; Read the year:

                lea     rcx, yearPrompt
                call    readNum

; Verify that the year is in the range 0..99.

                cmp     rax, 0
                jl      badYear
                cmp     rax, 99
                jg      badYear

; Good year, save it for now:

                mov     year, al        ; 0..99 fits in a byte

; Pack the data into the following bits:

;   15 14 13 12 11 10  9  8  7  6  5  4  3  2  1  0
;    m  m  m  m  d  d  d  d  d  y  y  y  y  y  y  y

                movzx   ax, month
                shl     ax, 5
                or      al, day
                shl     ax, 7
                or      al, year
                mov     date, ax

; Print the packed date:

                lea     rcx, packed
                movzx   rdx, date
                call    printf

; Unpack the date and print it:

                movzx   rdx, date
                mov     r9, rdx
                and     r9, 7fh         ; Keep LO 7 bits (year)
                shr     rdx, 7          ; Get day in position
                mov     r8, rdx
```

```
            and     r8, 1fh         ; Keep LO 5 bits
            shr     rdx, 5          ; Get month in position
            lea     rcx, theDate
            call    printf

            jmp     allDone

; Come down here if a bad day was entered:

badDay:
            lea     rcx, badDayStr
            call    printf
            jmp     allDone

; Come down here if a bad month was entered:

badMonth:
            lea     rcx, badMonthStr
            call    printf
            jmp     allDone

; Come down here if a bad year was entered:

badYear:
            lea     rcx, badYearStr
            call    printf

allDone:
            add     rsp, 56
            ret             ; Returns to caller
asmMain     endp
            end
```

Listing 2-4: Packing and unpacking date data

Here's the result of building and running this program:

```
C:\>build  listing2-4

C:\>echo off
 Assembling: listing2-4.asm
c.cpp

C:\> listing2-4
Calling Listing 2-4:
Enter current month: 2
Enter current day: 4
Enter current year (last 2 digits only): 68
Packed date is 2244
The date is 02/04/68
Listing 2-4 terminated
```

Of course, having gone through the problems with Y2K (Year 2000),[10] you know that using a date format that limits you to 100 years (or even 127 years) would be quite foolish. To future-proof the packed date format, we can extend it to 4 bytes packed into a double-word variable, as shown in Figure 2-19. (As you will see in Chapter 4, you should always try to create data objects whose length is an even power of 2—1 byte, 2 bytes, 4 bytes, 8 bytes, and so on—or you will pay a performance penalty.)

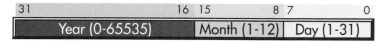

Figure 2-19: Long packed date format (4 bytes)

The Month and Day fields now consist of 8 bits each, so they can be extracted as a byte object from the double word. This leaves 16 bits for the year, with a range of 65,536 years. By rearranging the bits so the Year field is in the HO bit positions, the Month field is in the middle bit positions, and the Day field is in the LO bit positions, the long date format allows you to easily compare two dates to see if one date is less than, equal to, or greater than another date. Consider the following code:

```
mov eax, Date1  ; Assume Date1 and Date2 are dword variables
cmp eax, Date2  ; using the Long Packed Date format
jna d1LEd2

    Do something if Date1 > Date2

d1LEd2:
```

Had you kept the different date fields in separate variables, or organized the fields differently, you would not have been able to compare Date1 and Date2 as easily as for the short packed data format. Therefore, this example demonstrates another reason for packing data even if you don't realize any space savings—it can make certain computations more convenient or even more efficient (contrary to what normally happens when you pack data).

Examples of practical packed data types abound. You could pack eight Boolean values into a single byte, you could pack two BCD digits into a byte, and so on.

A classic example of packed data is the RFLAGS register. This register packs nine important Boolean objects (along with seven important system flags) into a single 16-bit register. You will commonly need to access many of these flags. You can test many of the condition code flags by using the conditional jump instructions and manipulate the individual bits in the FLAGS register with the instructions in Table 2-12 that directly affect certain flags.

---

10. If you're too young to remember this fiasco, programmers in the middle to late 1900s used to encode only the last two digits of the year in their dates. When the year 2000 rolled around, the programs were incapable of distinguishing dates like 2019 and 1919.

Table 2-12: Instructions That Affect Certain Flags

Instruction	Explanation
cld	Clears (sets to 0) the direction flag.
std	Sets (to 1) the direction flag.
cli	Clears the interrupt disable flag.
sti	Sets the interrupt disable flag.
clc	Clears the carry flag.
stc	Sets the carry flag.
cmc	Complements (inverts) the carry flag.
sahf	Stores the AH register into the LO 8 bits of the FLAGS register. (Warning: certain early x86-64 CPUs do not support this instruction.)
lahf	Loads AH from the LO 8 bits of the FLAGS register. (Warning: certain early x86-64 CPUs do not support this instruction.)

The lahf and sahf instructions provide a convenient way to access the LO 8 bits of the FLAGS register as an 8-bit byte (rather than as eight separate 1-bit values). See Figure 2-20 for a layout of the FLAGS register.

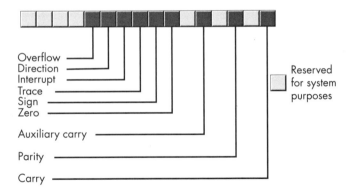

Figure 2-20: FLAGS register as packed Boolean data

The lahf (*load AH with the LO eight bits of the FLAGS register*) and the sahf (*store AH into the LO byte of the RFLAGS register*) use the following syntax:

```
lahf
sahf
```

2.13 IEEE Floating-Point Formats

When Intel planned to introduce a floating-point unit (the 8087 FPU) for its new 8086 microprocessor, it hired the best numerical analyst it could find to design a floating-point format. That person then hired two other experts in the field, and the three of them (William Kahan, Jerome Coonen, and Harold Stone) designed Intel's floating-point format. They did such a good job designing the KCS Floating-Point Standard that the Institute of Electrical and Electronics Engineers (IEEE) adopted this format for its floating-point format.[11]

To handle a wide range of performance and accuracy requirements, Intel actually introduced *three* floating-point formats: single-precision, double-precision, and extended-precision. The single- and double-precision formats corresponded to C's float and double types or FORTRAN's real and double-precision types. The extended-precision format contains 16 extra bits that long chains of computations could use as guard bits before rounding down to a double-precision value when storing the result.

2.13.1 Single-Precision Format

The *single-precision format* uses a one's complement 24-bit mantissa, an 8-bit excess-127 exponent, and a single sign bit. The *mantissa* usually represents a value from 1.0 to just under 2.0. The HO bit of the mantissa is always assumed to be 1 and represents a value just to the left of the *binary point*.[12] The remaining 23 mantissa bits appear to the right of the binary point. Therefore, the mantissa represents the value:

`1.mmmmmmmm mmmmmmmm`

The mmmm characters represent the 23 bits of the mantissa. Note that because the HO bit of the mantissa is always 1, the single-precision format doesn't actually store this bit within the 32 bits of the floating-point number. This is known as an *implied bit*.

Because we are working with binary numbers, each position to the right of the binary point represents a value (0 or 1) times a successive negative power of 2. The implied 1 bit is always multiplied by 2^0, which is 1. This is why the mantissa is always greater than or equal to 1. Even if the other mantissa bits are all 0, the implied 1 bit always gives us the value 1.[13] Of course, even if we had an almost infinite number of 1 bits after the binary point, they still would not add up to 2. This is why the mantissa can represent values in the range 1 to just under 2.

Although there is an infinite number of values between 1 and 2, we can represent only 8 million of them because we use a 23-bit mantissa (with the implied 24th bit always 1). This is the reason for inaccuracy in floating-point arithmetic—we are limited to a fixed number of bits in computations involving single-precision floating-point values.

The mantissa uses a *one's complement* format rather than two's complement to represent signed values. The 24-bit value of the mantissa is simply

---

11. Minor changes were made to the way certain degenerate operations were handled, but the bit representation remained essentially unchanged.

12. The *binary point* is the same thing as the *decimal point* except it appears in binary numbers rather than decimal numbers.

13. This isn't necessarily true. The IEEE floating-point format supports *denormalized* values where the HO bit is not 0. However, we will ignore denormalized values in our discussion.

an unsigned binary number, and the sign bit determines whether that value is positive or negative. One's complement numbers have the unusual property that there are two representations for 0 (with the sign bit set or clear). Generally, this is important only to the person designing the floating-point software or hardware system. We will assume that the value 0 always has the sign bit clear.

To represent values outside the range 1.0 to just under 2.0, the exponent portion of the floating-point format comes into play. The floating-point format raises 2 to the power specified by the exponent and then multiplies the mantissa by this value. The exponent is 8 bits and is stored in an *excess-127* format. In excess-127 format, the exponent 0 is represented by the value 127 (7Fh), negative exponents are values in the range 0 to 126, and positive exponents are values in the range 128 to 255. To convert an exponent to excess-127 format, add 127 to the exponent value. The use of excess-127 format makes it easier to compare floating-point values. The single-precision floating-point format takes the form shown in Figure 2-21.

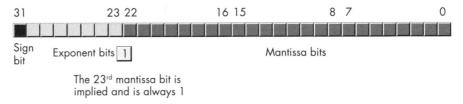

Figure 2-21: Single-precision (32-bit) floating-point format

With a 24-bit mantissa, you will get approximately six and a half (decimal) digits of precision (half a digit of precision means that the first six digits can all be in the range 0 to 9, but the seventh digit can be only in the range 0 to x, where $x < 9$ and is generally close to 5). With an 8-bit excess-127 exponent, the dynamic range[14] of single-precision floating-point numbers is approximately $2^{\pm 127}$, or about $10^{\pm 38}$.

Although single-precision floating-point numbers are perfectly suitable for many applications, the precision and dynamic range are somewhat limited and unsuitable for many financial, scientific, and other applications. Furthermore, during long chains of computations, the limited accuracy of the single-precision format may introduce serious error.

2.13.2 Double-Precision Format

The *double-precision format* helps overcome the problems of single-precision floating-point. Using twice the space, the double-precision format has an 11-bit excess-1023 exponent and a 53-bit mantissa (with an implied HO bit of 1) plus a sign bit. This provides a dynamic range of about $10^{\pm 308}$ and 14.5 digits of precision, sufficient for most applications. Double-precision floating-point values take the form shown in Figure 2-22.

14. The *dynamic range* is the difference in size between the smallest and largest positive values.

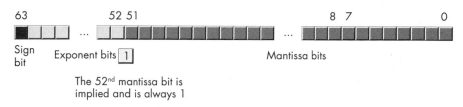

Figure 2-22: 64-bit double-precision floating-point format

2.13.3 Extended-Precision Format

To ensure accuracy during long chains of computations involving double-precision floating-point numbers, Intel designed the *extended-precision format*. It uses 80 bits. Twelve of the additional 16 bits are appended to the mantissa, and 4 of the additional bits are appended to the end of the exponent. Unlike the single- and double-precision values, the extended-precision format's mantissa does not have an implied HO bit. Therefore, the extended-precision format provides a 64-bit mantissa, a 15-bit excess-16383 exponent, and a 1-bit sign. Figure 2-23 shows the format for the extended-precision floating-point value.

Figure 2-23: 80-bit extended-precision floating-point format

On the x86-64 FPU, all computations are done using the extended-precision format. Whenever you load a single- or double-precision value, the FPU automatically converts it to an extended-precision value. Likewise, when you store a single- or double-precision value to memory, the FPU automatically rounds the value down to the appropriate size before storing it. By always working with the extended-precision format, Intel guarantees that a large number of guard bits are present to ensure the accuracy of your computations.

2.13.4 Normalized Floating-Point Values

To maintain maximum precision during computation, most computations use normalized values. A *normalized floating-point value* is one whose HO mantissa bit contains 1. Almost any non-normalized value can be normalized: shift the mantissa bits to the left and decrement the exponent until a 1 appears in the HO bit of the mantissa.

Remember, the exponent is a binary exponent. Each time you increment the exponent, you multiply the floating-point value by 2. Likewise, whenever you decrement the exponent, you divide the floating-point value by 2. By the same token, shifting the mantissa to the left one bit position multiplies the floating-point value by 2; likewise, shifting the mantissa to the right divides the floating-point value by 2. Therefore, shifting the mantissa to the left one position *and* decrementing the exponent does not change the value of the floating-point number at all.

Keeping floating-point numbers normalized is beneficial because it maintains the maximum number of bits of precision for a computation. If the HO *n* bits of the mantissa are all 0, the mantissa has that many fewer bits of precision available for computation. Therefore, a floating-point computation will be more accurate if it involves only normalized values.

In two important cases, a floating-point number cannot be normalized. Zero is one of these special cases. Obviously, it cannot be normalized because the floating-point representation for 0 has no 1 bits in the mantissa. This, however, is not a problem because we can exactly represent the value 0 with only a single bit.

In the second case, we have some HO bits in the mantissa that are 0, but the biased exponent is also 0 (and we cannot decrement it to normalize the mantissa). Rather than disallow certain small values, whose HO mantissa bits and biased exponent are 0 (the most negative exponent possible), the IEEE standard allows special *denormalized* values to represent these smaller values.[15] Although the use of denormalized values allows IEEE floating-point computations to produce better results than if underflow occurred, keep in mind that denormalized values offer fewer bits of precision.

2.13.5 Non-Numeric Values

The IEEE floating-point standard recognizes three special non-numeric values: –infinity, +infinity, and a special not-a-number (NaN). For each of these special numbers, the exponent field is filled with all 1 bits.

If the exponent is all 1 bits and the mantissa is all 0 bits, then the value is infinity. The sign bit will be 0 for +infinity, and 1 for –infinity.

If the exponent is all 1 bits and the mantissa is not all 0 bits, then the value is an invalid number (known as a *not-a-number* in IEEE 754 terminology). NaNs represent illegal operations, such as trying to take the square root of a negative number.

Unordered comparisons occur whenever either operand (or both) is a NaN. As NaNs have an indeterminate value, they cannot be compared (that is, they are incomparable). Any attempt to perform an unordered comparison typically results in an exception or some sort of error. Ordered comparisons, on the other hand, involve two operands, neither of which are NaNs.

2.13.6 MASM Support for Floating-Point Values

MASM provides several data types to support the use of floating-point data in your assembly language programs. MASM floating-point constants allow the following syntax:

- An optional + or - symbol, denoting the sign of the mantissa (if this is not present, MASM assumes that the mantissa is positive)
- Followed by one or more decimal digits

---

15. The alternative would be to underflow the values to 0.

- Followed by a decimal point and zero or more decimal digits
- Optionally followed by an e or E, optionally followed by a sign (+ or -) and one or more decimal digits

The decimal point or the e/E must be present in order to differentiate this value from an integer or unsigned literal constant. Here are some examples of legal literal floating-point constants:

```
1.234  3.75e2  -1.0  1.1e-1  1.e+4  0.1  -123.456e+789  +25.0e0  1.e3
```

A floating-point literal constant must begin with a decimal digit, so you must use, for example, 0.1 to represent .1 in your programs.

To declare a floating-point variable, you use the real4, real8, or real10 data types. The number at the end of these data type declarations specifies the number of bytes used for each type's binary representation. Therefore, you use real4 to declare single-precision real values, real8 to declare double-precision floating-point values, and real10 to declare extended-precision floating-point values. Aside from using these types to declare floating-point variables rather than integers, their use is nearly identical to that of byte, word, dword, and so on. The following examples demonstrate these declarations and their syntax:

```
          .data

fltVar1   real4   ?
fltVar1a  real4   2.7
pi        real4   3.14159
DblVar    real8   ?
DblVar2   real8   1.23456789e+10
XPVar     real10  ?
XPVar2    real10  -1.0e-104
```

As usual, this book uses the C/C++ printf() function to print floating-point values to the console output. Certainly, an assembly language routine could be written to do this same thing, but the C Standard Library provides a convenient way to avoid writing that (complex) code, at least for the time being.

NOTE *Floating-point arithmetic is different from integer arithmetic; you cannot use the x86-64 add and sub instructions to operate on floating-point values. Floating-point arithmetic is covered in Chapter 6.*

2.14   Binary-Coded Decimal Representation

Although the integer and floating-point formats cover most of the numeric needs of an average program, in some special cases other numeric representations are convenient. In this section, we'll discuss the *binary-coded decimal (BCD)* format because the x86-64 CPU provides a small amount of hardware support for this data representation.

BCD values are a sequence of nibbles, with each nibble representing a value in the range 0 to 9. With a single byte, we can represent values containing two decimal digits, or values in the range 0 to 99 (see Figure 2-24).

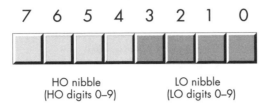

Figure 2-24: BCD data representation in memory

As you can see, BCD storage isn't particularly memory efficient. For example, an 8-bit BCD variable can represent values in the range 0 to 99, while that same 8 bits, when holding a binary value, can represent values in the range 0 to 255. Likewise, a 16-bit binary value can represent values in the range 0 to 65,535, while a 16-bit BCD value can represent only about one-sixth of those values (0 to 9999).

However, it's easy to convert BCD values between the internal numeric representation and their string representation, and to encode multi-digit decimal values in hardware (for example, using a thumb wheel or dial) using BCD. For these two reasons, you're likely to see people using BCD in embedded systems (such as toaster ovens, alarm clocks, and nuclear reactors) but rarely in general-purpose computer software.

The Intel x86-64 floating-point unit supports a pair of instructions for loading and storing BCD values. Internally, however, the FPU converts these BCD values to binary and performs all calculations in binary. It uses BCD only as an external data format (external to the FPU, that is). This generally produces more-accurate results and requires far less silicon than having a separate coprocessor that supports decimal arithmetic.

2.15   Characters

Perhaps the most important data type on a personal computer is the character data type. The term *character* refers to a human or machine-readable symbol that is typically a non-numeric entity, specifically any symbol that you can normally type on a keyboard (including some symbols that may require multiple keypresses to produce) or display on a video display. Letters (*alphabetic characters*), punctuation symbols, numeric digits, spaces, tabs, carriage returns (ENTER), other control characters, and other special symbols are all characters.

NOTE   *Numeric characters are distinct from numbers: the character "1" is different from the value 1. The computer (generally) uses two different internal representations for numeric characters ("0", "1", . . . , "9") versus the numeric values 0 to 9.*

Most computer systems use a 1- or 2-byte sequence to encode the various characters in binary form. Windows, macOS, FreeBSD, and Linux use either the ASCII or Unicode encodings for characters. This section discusses the ASCII and Unicode character sets and the character declaration facilities that MASM provides.

2.15.1 The ASCII Character Encoding

The *American Standard Code for Information Interchange (ASCII) character set* maps 128 textual characters to the unsigned integer values 0 to 127 (0 to 7Fh). Although the exact mapping of characters to numeric values is arbitrary and unimportant, using a standardized code for this mapping is important because when you communicate with other programs and peripheral devices, you all need to speak the same "language." ASCII is a standardized code that nearly everyone has agreed on: if you use the ASCII code 65 to represent the character A, then you know that a peripheral device (such as a printer) will correctly interpret this value as the character A whenever you transmit data to that device.

Despite some major shortcomings, ASCII data has become the standard for data interchange across computer systems and programs.[16] Most programs can accept ASCII data; likewise, most programs can produce ASCII data. Because you will be dealing with ASCII characters in assembly language, it would be wise to study the layout of the character set and memorize a few key ASCII codes (for example, for 0, A, a, and so on). See Appendix A for a list of all the ASCII character codes.

The ASCII character set is divided into four groups of 32 characters. The first 32 characters, ASCII codes 0 to 1Fh (31), form a special set of non-printing characters, the *control characters*. We call them control characters because they perform various printer/display control operations rather than display symbols. Examples include *carriage return*, which positions the cursor to the left side of the current line of characters;[17] line feed, which moves the cursor down one line on the output device; and backspace, which moves the cursor back one position to the left.

Unfortunately, different control characters perform different operations on different output devices. Little standardization exists among output devices. To find out exactly how a control character affects a particular device, you will need to consult its manual.

The second group of 32 ASCII character codes contains various punctuation symbols, special characters, and the numeric digits. The most notable characters in this group include the space character (ASCII code 20h) and the numeric digits (ASCII codes 30h to 39h).

---

16. Today, Unicode (especially the UTF-8 encoding) is rapidly replacing ASCII because the ASCII character set is insufficient for handling international alphabets and other special characters.

17. Historically, carriage return refers to the paper carriage used on typewriters: physically moving the carriage all the way to the right enabled the next character typed to appear at the left side of the paper.

The third group of 32 ASCII characters contains the uppercase alphabetic characters. The ASCII codes for the characters A to Z lie in the range 41h to 5Ah (65 to 90). Because there are only 26 alphabetic characters, the remaining 6 codes hold various special symbols.

The fourth, and final, group of 32 ASCII character codes represents the lowercase alphabetic symbols, 5 additional special symbols, and another control character (delete). The lowercase character symbols use the ASCII codes 61h to 7Ah. If you convert the codes for the upper- and lowercase characters to binary, you will notice that the uppercase symbols differ from their lowercase equivalents in exactly one bit position. For example, consider the character codes for E and e appearing in Figure 2-25.

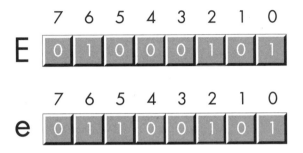

Figure 2-25: ASCII codes for E and e

The only place these two codes differ is in bit 5. Uppercase characters always contain a 0 in bit 5; lowercase alphabetic characters always contain a 1 in bit 5. You can use this fact to quickly convert between upper- and lowercase. If you have an uppercase character, you can force it to lowercase by setting bit 5 to 1. If you have a lowercase character, you can force it to uppercase by setting bit 5 to 0. You can toggle an alphabetic character between upper- and lowercase by simply inverting bit 5.

Indeed, bits 5 and 6 determine which of the four groups in the ASCII character set you're in, as Table 2-13 shows.

Table 2-13: ASCII Groups

Bit 6	Bit 5	Group
0	0	Control characters
0	1	Digits and punctuation
1	0	Uppercase and special
1	1	Lowercase and special

So you could, for instance, convert any upper- or lowercase (or corresponding special) character to its equivalent control character by setting bits 5 and 6 to 0.

Consider, for a moment, the ASCII codes of the numeric digit characters appearing in Table 2-14.

Table 2-14: ASCII Codes for Numeric Digits

Character	Decimal	Hexadecimal
0	48	30h
1	49	31h
2	50	32h
3	51	33h
4	52	34h
5	53	35h
6	54	36h
7	55	37h
8	56	38h
9	57	39h

The LO nibble of the ASCII code is the binary equivalent of the represented number. By stripping away (that is, setting to 0) the HO nibble of a numeric character, you can convert that character code to the corresponding binary representation. Conversely, you can convert a binary value in the range 0 to 9 to its ASCII character representation by simply setting the HO nibble to 3. You can use the logical AND operation to force the HO bits to 0; likewise, you can use the logical OR operation to force the HO bits to 0011b (3).

Unfortunately, you *cannot* convert a string of numeric characters to their equivalent binary representation by simply stripping the HO nibble from each digit in the string. Converting 123 (31h 32h 33h) in this fashion yields 3 bytes, 010203h, but the correct value for 123 is 7Bh. The conversion described in the preceding paragraph works only for single digits.

2.15.2 MASM Support for ASCII Characters

MASM provides support for character variables and literals in your assembly language programs. Character literal constants in MASM take one of two forms: a single character surrounded by apostrophes or a single character surrounded by quotes, as follows:

```
'A'  "A"
```

Both forms represent the same character (A).

If you wish to represent an apostrophe or a quote within a string, use the other character as the string delimiter. For example:

```
'A "quotation" appears within this string'
"Can't have quotes in this string"
```

Unlike the C/C++ language, MASM doesn't use different delimiters for single-character objects versus string objects, or differentiate between a character constant and a string constant with a single character. A character literal constant has a single character between the quotes (or apostrophes); a string literal has multiple characters between the delimiters.

To declare a character variable in a MASM program, you use the byte data type. For example, the following declaration demonstrates how to declare a variable named UserInput:

```
            .data
UserInput   byte ?
```

This declaration reserves 1 byte of storage that you could use to store any character value (including 8-bit extended ASCII/ANSI characters). You can also initialize character variables as follows:

```
              .data
TheCharA      byte 'A'
ExtendedChar  byte 128 ; Character code greater than 7Fh
```

Because character variables are 8-bit objects, you can manipulate them using 8-bit registers. You can move character variables into 8-bit registers, and you can store the value of an 8-bit register into a character variable.

2.16 The Unicode Character Set

The problem with ASCII is that it supports only 128 character codes. Even if you extend the definition to 8 bits (as IBM did on the original PC), you're limited to 256 characters. This is way too small for modern multinational/multilingual applications. Back in the 1990s, several companies developed an extension to ASCII, known as *Unicode*, using a 2-byte character size. Therefore, (the original) Unicode supported up to 65,536 character codes.

Alas, as well-thought-out as the original Unicode standard could be, systems engineers discovered that even 65,536 symbols were insufficient. Today, Unicode defines 1,112,064 possible characters, encoded using a variable-length character format.

2.16.1 Unicode Code Points

A Unicode *code point* is an integer value that Unicode associates with a particular character symbol. The convention for Unicode code points is to specify the value in hexadecimal with a preceding U+ prefix; for example, U+0041 is the Unicode code point for the A character (41h is also the ASCII code for A; Unicode code points in the range U+0000 to U+007F correspond to the ASCII character set).

2.16.2 Unicode Code Planes

The Unicode standard defines code points in the range U+000000 to U+10FFFF (10FFFFh is 1,114,111, which is where most of the 1,112,064 characters in the Unicode character set come from; the remaining 2047 code points are reserved for use as *surrogates*, which are Unicode extensions).[18] The Unicode standard breaks this range up into 17 *multilingual planes,* each supporting up to 65,536 code points. The HO two hexadecimal digits of the six-digit code point value specify the multilingual plane, and the remaining four digits specify the character within the plane.

The first multilingual plane, U+000000 to U+00FFFF, roughly corresponds to the original 16-bit Unicode definition; the Unicode standard calls this the *Basic Multilingual Plane (BMP).* Planes 1 (U+010000 to U+01FFFF), 2 (U+020000 to U+02FFFF), and 14 (U+0E0000 to U+0EFFFF) are supplementary (extension) planes. Unicode reserves planes 3 to 13 for future expansion, and planes 15 and 16 for user-defined character sets.

Obviously, representing Unicode code points outside the BMP requires more than 2 bytes. To reduce memory usage, Unicode (specifically the UTF-16 encoding; see the next section) uses 2 bytes for the Unicode code points in the BMP, and uses 4 bytes to represent code points outside the BMP. Within the BMP, Unicode reserves the surrogate code points (U+D800–U+DFFF) to specify the 16 planes after the BMP. Figure 2-26 shows the encoding.

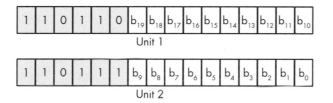

Unit 1

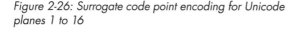

Unit 2

Figure 2-26: Surrogate code point encoding for Unicode planes 1 to 16

Note that the two words (unit 1 and unit 2) always appear together. The unit 1 value (with HO bits 110110b) specifies the upper 10 bits (b_{10} to b_{19}) of the Unicode scalar, and the unit 2 value (with HO bits 110111b) specifies the lower 10 bits (b_0 to b_9) of the Unicode scalar. Therefore, bits b_{16} to b_{19} (plus one) specify Unicode plane 1 to 16. Bits b_0 to b_{15} specify the Unicode scalar value within the plane.

2.16.3 Unicode Encodings

As of Unicode v2.0, the standard supports a 21-bit character space capable of handling over a million characters (though most of the code points remain reserved for future use). Rather than use a 3-byte (or worse, 4-byte) encoding to allow the larger character set, Unicode, Inc., allowed different encodings, each with its own advantages and disadvantages.

---

18. *Unicode scalars* is another term you might hear. A Unicode scalar is a value from the set of all Unicode code points *except* the 2047 surrogate code points.

UTF-32 uses 32-bit integers to hold Unicode scalars.[19] The advantage to this scheme is that a 32-bit integer can represent every Unicode scalar value (which requires only 21 bits). Programs that require random access to characters in strings (without having to search for surrogate pairs) and other constant-time operations are (mostly) possible when using UTF-32. The obvious drawback to UTF-32 is that each Unicode scalar value requires 4 bytes of storage (twice that of the original Unicode definition and four times that of ASCII characters).

The second encoding format the Unicode supports is *UTF-16*. As the name suggests, UTF-16 uses 16-bit (unsigned) integers to represent Unicode values. To handle scalar values greater than 0FFFFh, UTF-16 uses the surrogate pair scheme to represent values in the range 010000h to 10FFFFh (see the discussion of code planes and surrogate code points in the previous section). Because the vast majority of useful characters fit into 16 bits, most UTF-16 characters require only 2 bytes. For those rare cases where surrogates are necessary, UTF-16 requires two words (32 bits) to represent the character.

The last encoding, and unquestionably the most popular, is *UTF-8*. The UTF-8 encoding is upward compatible from the ASCII character set. In particular, all ASCII characters have a single-byte representation (their original ASCII code, where the HO bit of the byte containing the character contains a 0 bit). If the UTF-8 HO bit is 1, UTF-8 requires additional bytes (1 to 3 additional bytes) to represent the Unicode code point. Table 2-15 provides the UTF-8 encoding schema.

Table 2-15: UTF-8 Encoding

Bytes	Bits for code point	First code point	Last code point	Byte 1	Byte 2	Byte 3	Byte 4
1	7	U+00	U+7F	0xxxxxxx			
2	11	U+80	U+7FF	110xxxxx	10xxxxxx		
3	16	U+800	U+FFFF	1110xxxx	10xxxxxx	10xxxxxx	
4	21	U+10000	U+10FFFF	11110xxx	10xxxxxx	10xxxxxx	10xxxxxx

The *xxx...* bits are the Unicode code point bits. For multi-byte sequences, byte 1 contains the HO bits, byte 2 contains the next HO bits, and so on. For example, the 2-byte sequence 11011111b, 10000001b corresponds to the Unicode scalar 0000_0111_1100_0001b (U+07C1).

2.17 MASM Support for Unicode

Unfortunately, MASM provides almost zero support for Unicode text in a source file. Fortunately, MASM's macro facilities provide a way for you to create your own Unicode support for strings in MASM. See Chapter 13 for more details on MASM macros. I will also return to this subject in *The Art of*

---

19. *UTF* stands for *Universal Transformation Format*, if you were wondering.

64-Bit Assembly, Volume 2, where I will spend considerable time describing how to force MASM to accept and process Unicode strings in source and resource files.

2.18 For More Information

For general information about data representation and Boolean functions, consider reading my book *Write Great Code*, Volume 1, Second Edition (No Starch Press, 2020), or a textbook on data structures and algorithms (available at any bookstore).

ASCII, EBCDIC, and Unicode are all international standards. You can find out more about the Extended Binary Coded Decimal Interchange Code (EBCDIC) character set families on IBM's website (*http://www.ibm.com/*). ASCII and Unicode are both International Organization for Standardization (ISO) standards, and ISO provides reports for both character sets. Generally, those reports cost money, but you can also find out lots of information about the ASCII and Unicode character sets by searching for them by name on the internet. You can also read about Unicode at *http://www.unicode.org/*. *Write Great Code* also contains additional information on the history, use, and encoding of the Unicode character set.

2.19 Test Yourself

1. What does the decimal value 9384.576 represent (in terms of powers of 10)?

2. Convert the following binary values to decimal:

   a. 1010
   b. 1100
   c. 0111
   d. 1001
   e. 0011
   f. 1111

3. Convert the following binary values to hexadecimal:

   a. 1010
   b. 1110
   c. 1011
   d. 1101
   e. 0010
   f. 1100
   g. 1100_1111
   h. 1001_1000_1101_0001

4. Convert the following hexadecimal values to binary:

   a. 12AF

   b. 9BE7

   c. 4A

   d. 137F

   e. F00D

   f. BEAD

   g. 4938

5. Convert the following hexadecimal values to decimal:

   a. A

   b. B

   c. F

   d. D

   e. E

   f. C

6. How many bits are there in a

   a. Word

   b. Qword

   c. Oword

   d. Dword

   e. BCD digit

   f. Byte

   g. Nibble

7. How many bytes are there in a

   a. Word

   b. Dword

   c. Qword

   d. Oword

8. How different values can you represent with a

   a. Nibble

   b. Byte

   c. Word

   d. Bit

9. How many bits does it take to represent a hexadecimal digit?

10. How are the bits in a byte numbered?

11. Which bit number is the LO bit of a word?

12. Which bit number is the HO bit of a dword?

13. Compute the logical AND of the following binary values:

    a. 0 and 0

    b. 0 and 1

    c. 1 and 0

    d. 1 and 1

14. Compute the logical OR of the following binary values:

    a. 0 and 0

    b. 0 and 1

    c. 1 and 0

    d. 1 and 1

15. Compute the logical XOR of the following binary values:

    a. 0 and 0

    b. 0 and 1

    c. 1 and 0

    d. 1 and 1

16. The logical NOT operation is the same as XORing with what value?

17. Which logical operation would you use to force bits to 0 in a bit string?

18. Which logical operation would you use to force bits to 1 in a bit string?

19. Which logical operation would you use to invert all the bits in a bit string?

20. Which logical operation would you use to invert selected bits in a bit string?

21. Which machine instruction will invert all the bits in a register?

22. What is the two's complement of the 8-bit value 5 (00000101b)?

23. What is the two's complement of the signed 8-bit value –2 (11111110)?

24. Which of the following signed 8-bit values are negative?

    a. 1111_1111b

    b. 0111_0001b

    c. 1000_0000b

    d. 0000_0000b

    e. 1000_0001b

    f. 0000_0001b

25. Which machine instruction takes the two's complement of a value in a register or memory location?

26. Which of the following 16-bit values can be correctly sign-contracted to 8 bits?
   a. 1111_1111_1111_1111
   b. 1000_0000_0000_0000
   c. 000_0000_0000_0001
   d. 1111_1111_1111_0000
   e. 1111_1111_0000_0000
   f. 0000_1111_0000_1111
   g. 0000_0000_1111_1111
   h. 0000_0001_0000_0000

27. What machine instruction provides the equivalent of an HLL goto statement?

28. What is the syntax for a MASM statement label?

29. What flags are the condition codes?

30. *JE* is a synonym for what instruction that tests a condition code?

31. *JB* is a synonym for what instruction that tests a condition code?

32. Which conditional jump instructions transfer control based on an unsigned comparison?

33. Which conditional jump instructions transfer control based on a signed comparison?

34. How does the SHL instruction affect the zero flag?

35. How does the SHL instruction affect the carry flag?

36. How does the SHL instruction affect the overflow flag?

37. How does the SHL instruction affect the sign flag?

38. How does the SHR instruction affect the zero flag?

39. How does the SHR instruction affect the carry flag?

40. How does the SHR instruction affect the overflow flag?

41. How does the SHR instruction affect the sign flag?

42. How does the SAR instruction affect the zero flag?

43. How does the SAR instruction affect the carry flag?

44. How does the SAR instruction affect the overflow flag?

45. How does the SAR instruction affect the sign flag?

46. How does the RCL instruction affect the carry flag?

47. How does the RCL instruction affect the zero flag?

48. How does the RCR instruction affect the carry flag?

49. How does the RCR instruction affect the sign flag?

50. A shift left is equivalent to what arithmetic operation?

51. A shift right is equivalent to what arithmetic operation?

52. When performing a chain of floating-point addition, subtraction, multiplication, and division operations, which operations should you try to do first?

53. How should you compare floating-point values for equality?

54. What is a normalized floating-point value?

55. How many bits does a (standard) ASCII character require?

56. What is the hexadecimal representation of the ASCII characters 0 through 9?

57. What delimiter character(s) does MASM use to define character constants?

58. What are the three common encodings for Unicode characters?

59. What is a Unicode code point?

60. What is a Unicode code plane?

3

MEMORY ACCESS AND ORGANIZATION

Chapters 1 and 2 showcd you how to declare and access simple variables in an assembly language program. This chapter fully explains x86-64 memory access. In this chapter, you will learn how to efficiently organize your variable declarations to speed up access to their data. You'll also learn about the x86-64 stack and how to manipulate data on it.

This chapter discusses several important concepts, including the following:

- Memory organization
- Memory allocation by program
- x86-64 memory addressing modes

- Indirect and scaled-indexed addressing modes
- Data type coercion
- The x86-64 stack

This chapter will teach to you make efficient use of your computer's memory resources.

3.1 Runtime Memory Organization

A running program uses memory in many ways, depending on the data's type. Here are some common data classifications you'll find in an assembly language program:

Code

Memory values that encode machine instructions.

Uninitialized static data

An area in memory that the program sets aside for uninitialized variables that exist the whole time the program runs; Windows will initialize this storage area to 0s when it loads the program into memory.

Initialized static data

A section of memory that also exists the whole time the program runs. However, Windows loads values for all the variables appearing in this section from the program's executable file so they have an initial value when the program first begins execution.

Read-only data

Similar to initialized static data insofar as Windows loads initial data for this section of memory from the executable file. However, this section of memory is marked *read-only* to prevent inadvertent modification of the data. Programs typically store constants and other unchanging data in this section of memory (by the way, note that the code section is also marked read-only by the operating system).

Heap

This special section of memory is designated to hold dynamically allocated storage. Functions such as C's malloc() and free() are responsible for allocating and deallocating storage in the heap area. "Pointer Variables and Dynamic Memory Allocation" in Chapter 4 discusses dynamic storage allocation in greater detail.

Stack

In this special section in memory, the program maintains local variables for procedures and functions, program state information, and other transient data. See "The Stack Segment and the push and pop Instructions" on page 134 for more information about the stack section.

These are the typical sections you will find in common programs (assembly language or otherwise). Smaller programs won't use all of these sections (code, stack, and data sections are a good minimum number). Complex programs may create additional sections in memory for their own purposes. Some programs may combine several of these sections together. For example, many programs will combine the code and read-only sections into the same section in memory (as the data in both sections gets marked as read-only). Some programs combine the uninitialized and initialized data sections together (*initializing* the uninitialized variables to 0). Combining sections is generally handled by the linker program. See the Microsoft linker documentation for more details on combining sections.[1]

Windows tends to put different types of data into different sections (or *segments*) of memory. Although it is possible to reconfigure memory as you choose by running the linker and specifying various parameters, by default Windows loads a MASM program into memory by using an organization similar to that in Figure 3-1.[2]

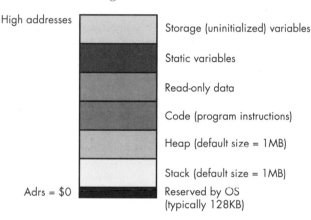

High addresses

Storage (uninitialized) variables

Static variables

Read-only data

Code (program instructions)

Heap (default size = 1MB)

Stack (default size = 1MB)

Adrs = $0

Reserved by OS
(typically 128KB)

Figure 3-1: MASM typical runtime memory organization

Windows reserves the lowest memory addresses. Generally, your application cannot access data (or execute instructions) at these low addresses. One reason the operating system reserves this space is to help trap NULL pointer references: if you attempt to access memory location 0 (NULL), the operating system will generate a *general protection fault* (also known as a *segmentation fault*), meaning you've accessed a memory location that doesn't contain valid data.

The remaining six areas in the memory map hold different types of data associated with your program. These sections of memory include the stack section, the heap section, the `.code` section, the `.data` (static) section,

---

1. The Microsoft linker documentation can be accessed at *https://docs.microsoft.com/en-us/cpp/build/reference/linking?view=msvc-160/*.

2. This is, of course, subject to change over time at the whims of Microsoft.

the .const section, and the .data? (storage) section. Each corresponds to a type of data you can create in your MASM programs. The .code, .data, .const, and .data? sections are described next in detail.[3]

3.1.1   The .code Section

The .code section contains the machine instructions that appear in a MASM program. MASM translates each machine instruction you write into a sequence of one or more byte values. The CPU interprets these byte values as machine instructions during program execution.

By default, when MASM links your program, it tells the system that your program can execute instructions and read data from the code segment but cannot write data to the code segment. The operating system will generate a general protection fault if you attempt to store any data into the code segment.

3.1.2   The .data Section

The .data section is where you will typically put your variables. In addition to declaring static variables, you can also embed lists of data into the .data declaration section. You use the same technique to embed data into your .data section that you use to embed data into the .code section: you use the byte, word, dword, qword, and so on, directives. Consider the following example:

```
     .data
b    byte   0
     byte   1,2,3

u    dword  1
     dword  5,2,10;

c    byte   ?
     byte   'a', 'b', 'c', 'd', 'e', 'f';

bn   byte   ?
     byte   true  ; Assumes true is defined as "1"
```

Values that MASM places in the .data memory segment by using these directives are written to the segment after the preceding variables. For example, the byte values 1, 2, and 3 are emitted to the .data section after b's 0 byte. Because there aren't any labels associated with these values, you do not have direct access to them in your program. You can use the indexed addressing modes to access these extra values.

In the preceding examples, note that the c and bn variables do not have an (explicit) initial value. However, if you don't provide an initial

---

3. The OS provides the stack and heap sections; you don't normally declare these two in an assembly language program. Therefore, there isn't anything more to discuss about them here.

value, MASM will initialize the variables in the .data section to 0, so MASM assigns the NULL character (ASCII code 0) to c as its initial value. Likewise, MASM assigns false as the initial value for bn (assuming false is defined as 0). Variable declarations in the .data section always consume memory, even if you haven't assigned them an initial value.

3.1.3   The .const Section

The .const data section holds constants, tables, and other data that your program cannot change during execution. You create read-only objects by declaring them in the .const declaration section. The .const section is similar to the .data section, with three differences:

- The .const section begins with the reserved word .const rather than .data.
- All declarations in the .const section have an initializer.
- The system does not allow you to write data to variables in a .const object while the program is running.

Here's an example:

```
        .const
pi      real4    3.14159
e       real4    2.71
MaxU16  word     65535
MaxI16  sword    32767
```

All .const object declarations must have an initializer because you cannot initialize the value under program control. For many purposes, you can treat .const objects as literal constants. However, because they are actually memory objects, they behave like (read-only) .data objects. You cannot use a .const object anywhere a literal constant is allowed; for example, you cannot use them as displacements in addressing modes (see "The x86-64 Addressing Modes" on page 122), and you cannot use them in constant expressions. In practice, you can use them anywhere that reading a .data variable is legal.

As with the .data section, you may embed data values in the .const section by using the byte, word, dword, and so on, data declarations, though all declarations must be initialized. For example:

```
          .const
roArray byte    0
        byte    1, 2, 3, 4, 5
qwVal   qword   1
        qword   0
```

Note that you can also declare constant values in the .code section. Data values you declare in this section are also read-only objects, as Windows write-protects the .code section. If you do place constant declarations in the .code section, you should take care to place them in a location that the program will not attempt to execute as code (such as after a jmp or ret instruction). Unless you're manually encoding x86 machine instructions using data declarations (which would be rare, and done only by expert programmers), you don't want your program to attempt to execute data as machine instructions; the result is usually undefined.[4]

3.1.4   The .data? Section

The .const section requires that you initialize all objects you declare. The .data section lets you optionally initialize objects (or leave them uninitialized, in which case they have the default initial value of 0). The .data? section lets you declare variables that are always uninitialized when the program begins running. The .data? section begins with the .data? reserved word and contains variable declarations without initializers. Here is an example:

```
            .data?
UninitUns32 dword   ?
i           sdword  ?
character   byte    ?
b           byte    ?
```

Windows will initialize all .data? objects to 0 when it loads your program into memory. However, it's probably not a good idea to depend on this implicit initialization. If you need an object initialized with 0, declare it in a .data section and explicitly set it to 0.

Variables you declare in the .data? section may consume less disk space in the executable file for the program. This is because MASM writes out initial values for .const and .data objects to the executable file, but it may use a compact representation for uninitialized variables you declare in the .data? section; note, however, that this behavior is dependent on the OS version and object-module format.

3.1.5   Organization of Declaration Sections Within Your Programs

The .data, .const, .data?, and .code sections may appear zero or more times in your program. The declaration sections may appear in any order, as the following example demonstrates:

```
            .data
i_static    sdword    0

            .data?
i_uninit    sdword    ?

            .const
i_readonly  dword     5
```

---

4. Technically, it is well defined: the machine will decode whatever bit pattern you place in memory as a machine instruction. However, few people will be able to look at a piece of data and interpret its meaning as a machine instruction.

```
           .data
j          dword     ?

           .const
i2         dword     9

           .data?
c          byte      ?

           .data?
d          dword     ?

           .code

    Code goes here

           end
```

The sections may appear in an arbitrary order, and a given declaration section may appear more than once in your program. As noted previously, when multiple declaration sections of the same type (for example, the three .data? sections in the preceding example) appear in a declaration section of your program, MASM combines them into a single group (in any order it pleases).

3.1.6 *Memory Access and 4K Memory Management Unit Pages*

The x86-64's *memory management unit (MMU)* divides memory into blocks known as *pages.*[5] The operating system is responsible for managing pages in memory, so application programs don't typically worry about page organization. However, you should be aware of a couple of issues when working with pages in memory: specifically, whether the CPU even allows access to a given memory location and whether it is read/write or read-only (write-protected).

Each program section appears in memory in contiguous MMU pages. That is, the .const section begins at offset 0 in an MMU page and sequentially consumes pages in memory for all the data appearing in that section. The next section in memory (perhaps .data) begins at offset 0 in the next MMU page following the last page of the previous section. If that previous section (for example, .const) did not consume an integral multiple of 4096 bytes, padding space will be present between the end of that section's data to the end of its last page (to guarantee that the next section begins on an MMU page boundary).

Each new section starts in its own MMU page because the MMU controls access to memory by using page *granularity*. For example, the MMU controls whether a page in memory is readable/writable or read-only. For

---

5. Unfortunately, early Intel documentation called 256-byte blocks *pages*, and some early MMUs used 512-byte pages, so this term elicits a lot of confusion. In memory, however, pages are always 4096-byte blocks on the x86-64.

.const sections, you want the memory to be read-only. For the .data section, you want to allow reads and writes. Because the MMU can enforce these attributes only on a page-by-page basis, you cannot have .data section information in the same MMU page as a .const section.

Normally, all of this is completely transparent to your code. Data you declare in a .data (or .data?) section is readable and writable, and data in a .const section (and .code section) is read-only (.code sections are also *executable*). Beyond placing data in a particular section, you don't have to worry too much about the page attributes.

You do have to worry about MMU page organization in memory in one situation. Sometimes it is convenient to access (read) data beyond the end of a data structure in memory (for legitimate reasons—see Chapter 11 on SIMD instructions and Chapter 14 on string instructions). However, if that data structure is aligned with the end of an MMU page, accessing the next page in memory could be problematic. Some pages in memory are *inaccessible*; the MMU does not allow reading, writing, or execution to occur on that page.

Attempting to do so will generate an x86-64 *general protection (segmentation) fault* and abort the normal execution of your program.[6] If you have a data access that crosses a page boundary, and the next page in memory is inaccessible, this will crash your program. For example, consider a word access to a byte object at the very end of an MMU page, as shown in Figure 3-2.

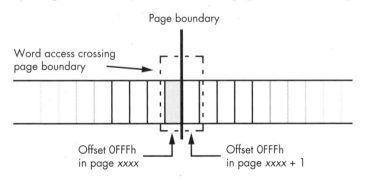

Figure 3-2: Word access at the end of an MMU page

As a general rule, you should never read data beyond the end of a data structure.[7] If for some reason you need to do so, you should ensure that it is legal to access the next page in memory (alas, there is no instruction on modern x86-64 CPUs to allow this; the only way to be sure that access is legal is to make sure there is valid data after the data structure you are accessing).

---

6. This will typically crash your program unless you have an exception handler in place to handle general protection faults.

7. It goes without saying that you should never write data beyond the end of a given data structure; this is always incorrect and can create far more problems than just crashing your program (including severe security issues).

3.2 How MASM Allocates Memory for Variables

MASM associates a current *location counter* with each of the four declaration sections (.code, .data, .const, and .data?). These location counters initially contain 0, and whenever you declare a variable in one of these sections (or write code in a code section), MASM associates the current value of that section's location counter with the variable; MASM also bumps up the value of that location counter by the size of the object you're declaring. As an example, assume that the following is the only .data declaration section in a program:

```
        .data
b       byte    ?       ; Location counter = 0,  size = 1
w       word    ?       ; Location counter = 1,  size = 2
d       dword   ?       ; Location counter = 3,  size = 4
q       qword   ?       ; Location counter = 7,  size = 8
o       oword   ?       ; Location counter = 15, size = 16
                        ; Location counter is now 31
```

As you can see, the variable declarations appearing in a (single) .data section have contiguous offsets (location counter values) into the .data section. Given the preceding declaration, w will immediately follow b in memory, d will immediately follow w in memory, q will immediately follow d, and so on. These offsets aren't the actual runtime address of the variables. At runtime, the system loads each section to a (base) address in memory. The linker and Windows add the base address of the memory section to each of these location counter values (which we call *displacements*, or *offsets*) to produce the actual memory address of the variables.

Keep in mind that you may link other modules with your program (for example, from the C Standard Library) or even additional .data sections in the same source file, and the linker has to merge the .data sections together. Each section has its own location counter that also starts from zero when allocating storage for the variables in the section. Hence, the offset of an individual variable may have little bearing on its final memory address.

Remember that MASM allocates memory objects you declare in .const, .data, and .data? sections in completely different regions of memory. Therefore, you cannot assume that the following three memory objects appear in adjacent memory locations (indeed, they probably will not):

```
        .data
b       byte    ?

        .const
w       word    1234h

        .data?
d       dword   ?
```

In fact, MASM will not even guarantee that variables you declare in separate .data (or whatever) sections are adjacent in memory, even if there is nothing between the declarations in your code. For example, you cannot assume that b, w, and d are in adjacent memory locations in the following declarations, nor can you assume that they *won't* be adjacent in memory:

```
        .data
b    byte    ?

        .data
w    word    1234h

        .data
d    dword   ?
```

If your code requires these variables to consume adjacent memory locations, you must declare them in the same .data section.

3.3 The Label Declaration

The label declaration lets you declare variables in a section (.code, .data, .const, and .data?) without allocating memory for the variable. The label directive tells MASM to assign the current address in a declaration section to a variable but not to allocate any storage for the object. That variable shares the same memory address as the next object appearing in the variable declaration section. Here is the syntax for the label declaration:

```
variable_name label type
```

The following code sequence provides an example of using the label declaration in the .const section:

```
        .const
abcd    label   dword
        byte 'a', 'b', 'c', 'd'
```

In this example, abcd is a double word whose LO byte contains 97 (the ASCII code for a), byte 1 contains 98 (b), byte 2 contains 99 (c), and the HO byte contains 100 (d). MASM does not reserve storage for the abcd variable, so MASM associates the following 4 bytes in memory (allocated by the byte directive) with abcd.

3.4 Little-Endian and Big-Endian Data Organization

Back in "The Memory Subsystem" in Chapter 1, this book pointed out that the x86-64 stores multi-byte data types in memory with the LO byte at the lowest address in memory and the HO byte at the highest address in memory (see Figure 1-5 in Chapter 1). This type of data organization in memory is known as *little endian*. Little-endian data organization (in which the LO byte comes first and the HO byte comes last) is a common memory organization shared by many modern CPUs. It is not, however, the only possible data organization.

The *big-endian* data organization reverses the order of the bytes in memory. The HO byte of the data structure appears first (in the lowest memory address), and the LO byte appears in the highest memory address. Tables 3-1, 3-2, and 3-3 describe the memory organization for words, double words, and quad words, respectively.

Table 3-1: Word Object Little- and Big-Endian Data Organizations

Data byte	Memory organization for little endian	Memory organization for big endian
0 (LO byte)	base + 0	base + 1
1 (HO byte)	base + 1	base + 0

Table 3-2: Double-Word Object Little- and Big-Endian Data Organizations

Data byte	Memory organization for little endian	Memory organization for big endian
0 (LO byte)	base + 0	base + 3
1	base + 1	base + 2
2	base + 2	base + 1
3 (HO byte)	base + 3	base + 0

Table 3-3: Quad-Word Object Little- and Big-Endian Data Organizations

Data byte	Memory organization for little endian	Memory organization for big endian
0 (LO byte)	base + 0	base + 7
1	base + 1	base + 6
2	base + 2	base + 5
3	base + 3	base + 4
4	base + 4	base + 3
5	base + 5	base + 2
6	base + 6	base + 1
7 (HO byte)	base + 7	base + 0

Normally, you wouldn't be too concerned with big-endian memory organization on an x86-64 CPU. However, on occasion you may need to deal with data produced by a different CPU (or by a protocol, such as TCP/IP, that uses big-endian organization as its canonical integer format). If you were to load a big-endian value in memory into a CPU register, your calculations would be incorrect.

If you have a 16-bit big-endian value in memory and you load it into a 16-bit register, it will have its bytes swapped. For 16-bit values, you can correct this issue by using the xchg instruction. It has the syntax

```
xchg reg, reg
xchg reg, mem
```

where *reg* is any 8-, 16-, 32-, or 64-bit general-purpose register, and *mem* is any appropriate memory location. The *reg* operands in the first instruction, or the *reg* and *mem* operands in the second instruction, must both be the same size.

Though you can use the xchg instruction to exchange the values between any two arbitrary (like-sized) registers, or a register and a memory location, it is also useful for converting between (16-bit) little- and big-endian formats. For example, if AX contains a big-endian value that you would like to convert to little-endian form prior to some calculations, you can use the following instruction to swap the bytes in the AX register to convert the value to little-endian form:

```
xchg al, ah
```

You can use the xchg instruction to convert between little- and big-endian form for any of the 16-bit registers AX, BX, CX, and DX by using the low/high register designations (AL/AH, BL/BH, CL/CH, and DL/DH).

Unfortunately, the xchg trick doesn't work for registers other than AX, BX, CX, and DX. To handle larger values, Intel introduced the bswap (*byte swap*) instruction. As its name suggests, this instruction swaps the bytes in a 32- or 64-bit register. It swaps the HO and LO bytes, and the (HO − 1) and (LO + 1) bytes (plus all the other bytes, in opposing pairs, for 64-bit registers). The bswap instruction works for all general-purpose 32-bit and 64-bit registers.

3.5 Memory Access

As you saw in "The Memory Subsystem" in Chapter 1, the x86-64 CPU fetches data from memory on the data bus. In an idealized CPU, the data bus is the size of the standard integer registers on the CPU; therefore, you would expect the x86-64 CPUs to have a 64-bit data bus. In practice, modern CPUs often make the physical data bus connection to main memory much larger in order to improve system performance. The bus brings in large chunks of data from memory in a single operation and places that data in the CPU's *cache*, which acts as a buffer between the CPU and physical memory.

From the CPU's point of view, the cache *is* memory. Therefore, when the remainder of this section discusses memory, it's generally talking about data sitting in the cache. As the system transparently maps memory accesses into the cache, we can discuss memory as though the cache were not present and discuss the advantages of the cache as necessary.

On early x86 processors, memory was arranged as an array of bytes (8-bit machines such as the 8088), words (16-bit machines such as the 8086 and 80286), or double words (on 32-bit machines such as the 80386). On a 16-bit machine, the LO bit of the address did not physically appear on the address bus. So the addresses 126 and 127 put the same bit pattern on the address bus (126, with an implicit 0 in bit position 0), as shown in Figure 3-3.[8]

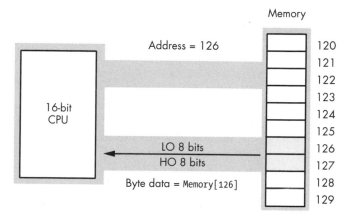

Figure 3-3: Address and data bus for 16-bit processors

When reading a byte, the CPU uses the LO bit of the address to select the LO byte or HO byte on the data bus. Figure 3-4 shows the process when accessing a byte at an even address (126 in this figure). Figure 3-5 shows the same operation when reading a byte from an odd address (127 in this figure). Note that in both Figures 3-4 and 3-5, the address appearing on the address bus is 126.

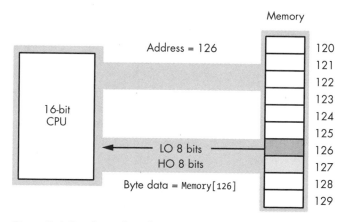

Figure 3-4: Reading a byte from an even address on a 16-bit CPU

8. 32-bit processors did not put the LO 2 bits onto the address bus, so addresses 124, 125, 126, and 127 would all have the value 124 on the address bus.

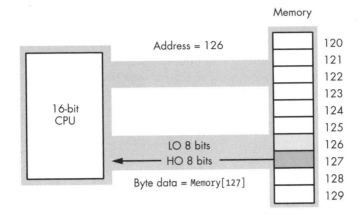

Figure 3-5: Reading a byte from an odd address on a 16-bit CPU

So, what happens when this 16-bit CPU wants to access 16 bits of data at an odd address? For example, suppose in these figures the CPU reads the word at address 125. When the CPU puts address 125 on the address bus, the LO bit doesn't physically appear. Therefore, the actual address on the bus is 124. If the CPU were to read the LO 8 bits off the data bus at this point, it would get the data at address 124, not address 125.

Fortunately, the CPU is smart enough to figure out what is going on here, and extracts the data from the HO 8 bits on the address bus and uses this as the LO 8 bits of the data operand. However, the HO 8 bits that the CPU needs are not found on the data bus. The CPU has to initiate a second read operation, placing address 126 on the address bus, to get the HO 8 bits (which will be sitting in the LO 8 bits of the data bus, but the CPU can figure that out). The bottom line is that it takes two memory cycles for this read operation to complete. Therefore, the instruction reading the data from memory will take longer to execute than had the data been read from an address that was an integral multiple of two.

The same problem exists on 32-bit processors, except the 32-bit data bus allows the CPU to read 4 bytes at a time. Reading a 32-bit value at an address that is not an integral multiple of four incurs the same performance penalty. Note, however, that accessing a 16-bit operand at an odd address doesn't always guarantee an extra memory cycle—only addresses whose remainder when divided by four is 3 incur the penalty. In particular, if you access a 16-bit value (on a 32-bit bus) at an address where the LO 2 bits contain 01b, the CPU can read the word in a single memory cycle, as shown in Figure 3-6.

Modern x86-64 CPUs, with cache systems, have largely eliminated this problem. As long as the data (1, 2, 4, 8, or 10 bytes in size) is fully within a cache line, there is no memory cycle penalty for an unaligned access. If the access does cross a cache line boundary, the CPU will run a bit slower while it executes two memory operations to get (or store) the data.

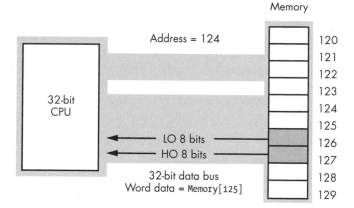

Figure 3-6: Accessing a word on a 32-bit data bus

3.6 MASM Support for Data Alignment

To write fast programs, you need to ensure that you properly align data objects in memory. Proper *alignment* means that the starting address for an object is a multiple of a certain size, usually the size of an object if the object's size is a power of 2 for values up to 32 bytes in length. For objects greater than 32 bytes, aligning the object on an 8-, 16-, or 32-byte address boundary is probably sufficient. For objects fewer than 16 bytes, aligning the object at an address that is the next power of 2 greater than the object's size is usually fine. Accessing data that is not aligned at an appropriate address may require extra time (as noted in the previous section); so, if you want to ensure that your program runs as rapidly as possible, you should try to align data objects according to their size.

Data becomes misaligned whenever you allocate storage for different-sized objects in adjacent memory locations. For example, if you declare a byte variable, it will consume 1 byte of storage, and the next variable you declare in that declaration section will have the address of that byte object plus 1. If the byte variable's address happens to be an even address, the variable following that byte will start at an odd address. If that following variable is a word or double-word object, its starting address will not be optimal. In this section, we'll explore ways to ensure that a variable is aligned at an appropriate starting address based on that object's size.

Consider the following MASM variable declarations:

```
    .data
dw  dword  ?
b   byte   ?
w   word   ?
dw2 dword  ?
w2  word   ?
b2  byte   ?
dw3 dword  ?
```

The first `.data` declaration in a program (running under Windows) places its variables at an address that is an even multiple of 4096 bytes. Whatever variable first appears in that `.data` declaration is guaranteed to be aligned on a reasonable address. Each successive variable is allocated at an address that is the sum of the sizes of all the preceding variables plus the starting address of that `.data` section. Therefore, assuming MASM allocates the variables in the previous example at a starting address of 4096, MASM will allocate them at the following addresses:

			; Start Adrs	Length
dw	dword	?	; 4096	4
b	byte	?	; 4100	1
w	word	?	; 4101	2
dw2	dword	?	; 4103	4
w2	word	?	; 4107	2
b2	byte	?	; 4109	1
dw3	dword	?	; 4110	4

With the exception of the first variable (which is aligned on a 4KB boundary) and the byte variables (whose alignment doesn't matter), all of these variables are misaligned. The `w`, `w2`, and `dw2` variables start at odd addresses, and the `dw3` variable is aligned on an even address that is not a multiple of four.

An easy way to guarantee that your variables are aligned properly is to put all the double-word variables first, the word variables second, and the byte variables last in the declaration, as shown here:

```
        .data
dw      dword   ?
dw2     dword   ?
dw3     dword   ?
w       word    ?
w2      word    ?
b       byte    ?
b2      byte    ?
```

This organization produces the following addresses in memory:

			; Start Adrs	Length
dw	dword	?	; 4096	4
dw2	dword	?	; 4100	4
dw3	dword	?	; 4104	4
w	word	?	; 4108	2
w2	word	?	; 4110	2
b	byte	?	; 4112	1
b2	byte	?	; 4113	1

As you can see, these variables are all aligned at reasonable addresses. Unfortunately, it is rarely possible for you to arrange your variables in this manner. While many technical reasons make this alignment impossible, a good practical reason for not doing this is that it doesn't let you organize your variable declarations by logical function (that is, you probably want to keep related variables next to one another regardless of their size).

To resolve this problem, MASM provides the align directive, which uses the following syntax:

```
align integer_constant
```

The integer constant must be one of the following small unsigned integer values: 1, 2, 4, 8, or 16. If MASM encounters the align directive in a .data section, it will align the very next variable on an address that is an even multiple of the specified alignment constant. The previous example could be rewritten, using the align directive, as follows:

```
        .data
        align   4
dw      dword   ?
b       byte    ?
        align   2
w       word    ?
        align   4
dw2     dword   ?
w2      word    ?
b2      byte    ?
        align   4
dw3     dword   ?
```

If MASM determines that the current address (location counter value) of an align directive is not an integral multiple of the specified value, MASM will quietly emit extra bytes of padding after the previous variable declaration until the current address in the .data section is a multiple of the specified value. This makes your program slightly larger (by a few bytes) in exchange for faster access to your data. Given that your program will grow by only a few bytes when you use this feature, this is probably a good trade-off.

As a general rule, if you want the fastest possible access, you should choose an alignment value that is equal to the size of the object you want to align. That is, you should align words to even boundaries by using an align 2 statement, double words to 4-byte boundaries by using align 4, quad words to 8-byte boundaries by using align 8, and so on. If the object's size is not a power of 2, align it to the next higher power of 2 (up to a maximum of 16 bytes). Note, however, that you need only align real80 (and tbyte) objects on an 8-byte boundary.

Note that data alignment isn't always necessary. The cache architecture of modern x86-64 CPUs actually handles most misaligned data. Therefore, you should use the alignment directives only with variables for which speedy access is absolutely critical. This is a reasonable space/speed trade-off.

3.7 The x86-64 Addressing Modes

Until now, you've seen only a single way to access a variable: the *PC-relative* addressing mode. In this section, you'll see additional ways your programs can access memory by using x86-64 memory addressing modes. An *addressing mode* is a mechanism the CPU uses to determine the address of a memory location an instruction will access.

The x86-64 memory addressing modes provide flexible access to memory, allowing you to easily access variables, arrays, records, pointers, and other complex data types. Mastery of the x86-64 addressing modes is the first step toward mastering x86-64 assembly language.

The x86-64 provides several addressing modes:

- Register addressing modes
- PC-relative memory addressing modes
- Register-indirect addressing modes: $[reg_{64}]$
- Indirect-plus-offset addressing modes: $[reg_{64} + expression]$
- Scaled-indexed addressing modes: $[reg_{64} + reg_{64} * scale]$ and $[reg_{64} + expression + reg_{64} * scale]$

The following sections describe each of these modes.

3.7.1 x86-64 Register Addressing Modes

The *register addressing modes* provide access to the x86-64's general-purpose register set. By specifying the name of the register as an operand to the instruction, you can access the contents of that register. This section uses the x86-64 mov (*move*) instruction to demonstrate the register addressing mode. The generic syntax for the mov instruction is shown here:

```
mov destination, source
```

The mov instruction copies the data from the *source* operand to the *destination* operand. The 8-, 16-, 32-, and 64-bit registers are all valid operands for this instruction. The only restriction is that both operands must be the same size. The following mov instructions demonstrate the use of various registers:

```
mov ax, bx      ; Copies the value from BX into AX
mov dl, al      ; Copies the value from AL into DL
mov esi, edx    ; Copies the value from EDX into ESI
mov rsp, rbp    ; Copies the value from RBP into RSP
mov ch, cl      ; Copies the value from CL into DH
mov ax, ax      ; Yes, this is legal! (Though not very useful)
```

The registers are the best place to keep variables. Instructions using the registers are shorter and faster than those that access memory. Because most computations require at least one register operand, the register addressing mode is popular in x86-64 assembly code.

3.7.2 x86-64 64-Bit Memory Addressing Modes

The addressing modes provided by the x86-64 family include PC-relative, register-indirect, indirect-plus-offset, and scaled-indexed. Variations on these four forms provide all the addressing modes on the x86-64.

3.7.2.1 The PC-Relative Addressing Mode

The most common addressing mode, and the one that's easiest to understand, is the *PC-relative* (or *RIP-relative*) addressing mode. This mode consists of a 32-bit constant that the CPU adds with the current value of the RIP (instruction pointer) register to specify the address of the target location.

The syntax for the PC-relative addressing mode is to use the name of a symbol you declare in one of the many MASM sections (.data, .data?, .const, .code, etc.), as this book has been doing all along:

```
mov al, symbol  ; PC-relative addressing mode automatically provides [RIP]
```

Assuming that variable j is an int8 variable appearing at offset 8088h from RIP, the instruction mov al, j loads the AL register with a copy of the byte at memory location RIP + 8088h. Likewise, if int8 variable K is at address RIP + 1234h in memory, then the instruction mov K, dl stores the value in the DL register to memory location RIP + 1234h (see Figure 3-7).

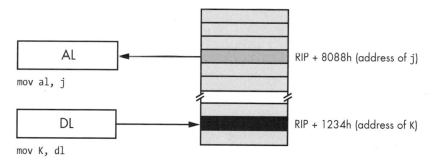

Figure 3-7: PC-relative addressing mode

MASM does not directly encode the address of j or K into the instruction's *operation code* (or *opcode*, the numeric machine encoding of the instruction). Instead, it encodes a signed displacement from the end of the current instruction's address to the variable's address in memory. For example, if the next instruction's opcode is sitting in memory at location 8000h (the end of the current instruction), then MASM will encode the value 88h as a 32-bit signed constant for j in the instruction opcode.

You can also access words and double words on the x86-64 processors by specifying the address of their first byte (see Figure 3-8).

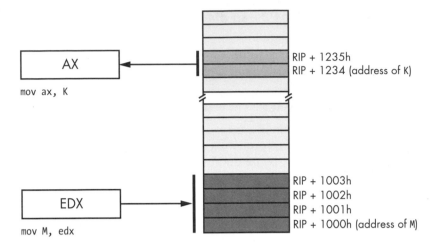

mov ax, K

mov M, edx

Figure 3-8: Accessing a word or dword by using the PC-relative addressing mode

3.7.2.2 The Register-Indirect Addressing Modes

The x86-64 CPUs let you access memory indirectly through a register by using the *register-indirect* addressing modes. The term *indirect* means that the operand is not the actual address, but the operand's value specifies the memory address to use. In the case of the register-indirect addressing modes, the value held in the register is the address of the memory location to access. For example, the instruction mov [rbx], eax tells the CPU to store EAX's value at the location whose address is currently in RBX (the square brackets around RBX tell MASM to use the register-indirect addressing mode).

The x86-64 has 16 forms of this addressing mode. The following instructions provide examples of these 16 forms:

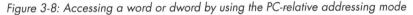

```
mov [reg64], al
```

where reg_{64} is one of the 64-bit general-purpose registers: RAX, RBX, RCX, RDX, RSI, RDI, RBP, RSP, R8, R9, R10, R11, R12, R13, R14, or R15. This addressing mode references the memory location at the offset found in the register enclosed by brackets.

The register-indirect addressing modes require a 64-bit register. You cannot specify a 32-, 16-, or 8-bit register in the square brackets when using an indirect addressing mode. Technically, you could load a 64-bit register with an arbitrary numeric value and access that location indirectly using the register-indirect addressing mode:

```
mov rbx, 12345678
mov [rbx], al   ; Attempts to access location 12345678
```

Unfortunately (or fortunately, depending on how you look at it), this will probably cause the operating system to generate a protection fault because it's not always legal to access arbitrary memory locations. As it turns out, there are better ways to load the address of an object into a register, and you'll see those shortly.

You can use the register-indirect addressing modes to access data referenced by a pointer, you can use them to step through array data, and, in general, you can use them whenever you need to modify the address of a variable while your program is running.

The register-indirect addressing mode provides an example of an *anonymous* variable; when using a register-indirect addressing mode, you refer to the value of a variable by its numeric memory address (the value you load into a register) rather than by the name of the variable.

MASM provides a simple instruction that you can use to take the address of a variable and put it into a 64-bit register, the lea (*load effective address*) instruction:

```
lea rbx, j
```

After executing this lea instruction, you can use the [rbx] register-indirect addressing mode to indirectly access the value of j.

3.7.2.3 Indirect-Plus-Offset Addressing Mode

The indirect-plus-offset addressing modes compute an *effective address* by adding a 32-bit signed constant to the value of a 64-bit register.[9] The instruction then uses the data at this effective address in memory.

The indirect-plus-offset addressing modes use the following syntax:

```
mov [reg₆₄ + constant], source
mov [reg₆₄ - constant], source
```

where reg_{64} is a 64-bit general-purpose register, *constant* is a 4-byte constant (±2 billion), and *source* is a register or constant value.

If *constant* is 1100h and RBX contains 12345678h, then

```
mov [rbx + 1100h], al
```

stores AL into the byte at address 12346778h in memory (see Figure 3-9).

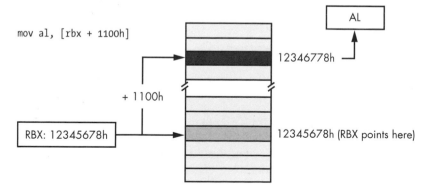

Figure 3-9: Indirect-plus-offset addressing mode

---

9. The *effective address* is the ultimate address in memory that an instruction will access, once all the address calculations are complete.

The indirect-plus-offset addressing modes are really handy for accessing fields of classes and records/structures. You will see how to use these addressing modes for that purpose in Chapter 4.

3.7.2.4 Scaled-Indexed Addressing Modes

The *scaled-indexed addressing modes* are similar to the indexed addressing modes, except the scaled-indexed addressing modes allow you to combine two registers plus a displacement, and multiply the index register by a (scaling) factor of 1, 2, 4, or 8 to compute the effective address by adding in the value of the second register multiplied by the scaling factor. (Figure 3-10 shows an example involving RBX as the base register and RSI as the index register.)

The syntax for the scaled-indexed addressing modes is shown here:

```
[base_reg₆₄ + index_reg₆₄*scale]
[base_reg₆₄ + index_reg₆₄*scale + displacement]
[base_reg₆₄ + index_reg₆₄*scale - displacement]
```

$base\_reg_{64}$ represents any general-purpose 64-bit register, $index\_reg_{64}$ represents any general-purpose 64-bit register except RSP, and *scale* must be one of the constants 1, 2, 4, or 8.

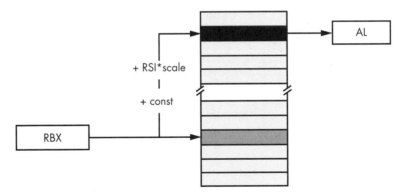

```
mov al, [rbx + rsi*scale + const]
```

Figure 3-10: Scaled-indexed addressing mode

In Figure 3-10, suppose that RBX contains 1000FF00h, RSI contains 20h, and *const* is 2000h; then the instruction

```
mov al, [rbx + rsi*4 + 2000h]
```

will move the byte at address 10011F80h—1000FF00h + (20h × 4) + 2000—into the AL register.

The scaled-indexed addressing modes are useful for accessing array elements that are 2, 4, or 8 bytes each. These addressing modes are also useful for accessing elements of an array when you have a pointer to the beginning of the array.

3.7.3 Large Address Unaware Applications

One advantage of 64-bit addresses is that they can access a frightfully large amount of memory (something like 8TB under Windows). By default, the Microsoft linker (when it links together the C++ and assembly language code) sets a flag named LARGEADDRESSAWARE to true (yes). This makes it possible for your programs to access a huge amount of memory. However, there is a price to be paid for operating in LARGEADDRESSAWARE mode: the *const* component of the $[reg_{64} + const]$ addressing mode is limited to 32 bits and cannot span the entire address space.

Because of instruction-encoding limitations, the *const* value is limited to a signed value in the range ±2GB. This is probably far more than enough when the register contains a 64-bit base address and you want to access a memory location at a fixed offset (less than ±2GB) around that base address. A typical way you would use this addressing mode is as follows:

```
lea rcx, someStructure
mov al, [rcx+fieldOffset]
```

Prior to the introduction of 64-bit addresses, the *const* offset appearing in the (32-bit) indirect-plus-offset addressing mode could span the entire (32-bit) address space. So if you had an array declaration such as

```
    .data
buf byte    256 dup (?)
```

you could access elements of this array by using the following addressing mode form:

```
mov al, buf[ebx]   ; EBX was used on 32-bit processors
```

If you were to attempt to assemble the instruction mov al, buf[rbx] in a 64-bit program (or any other addressing mode involving buf other than PC-relative), MASM would assemble the code properly, but the linker would report an error:

```
error LNK2017: 'ADDR32' relocation to 'buf' invalid without /LARGEADDRESSAWARE:NO
```

The linker is complaining that in an address space exceeding 32 bits, it is impossible to encode the offset to the buf buffer because the machine instruction opcodes provide only a 32-bit offset to hold the address of buf.

However, if we were to artificially limit the amount of memory that our application uses to 2GB, then MASM can encode the 32-bit offset to buf into the machine instruction. As long as we kept our promise and never used any more memory than 2GB, several new variations on the indirect-plus-offset and scaled-indexed addressing modes become possible.

To turn off the large address–aware flag, you need to add an extra command line option to the ml64 command. This is easily done in the *build.bat* file; let's create a new *build.bat* file and call it *sbuild.bat*. This file will have the following lines:

```
echo off
ml64 /nologo /c /Zi /Cp %1.asm
cl /nologo /O2 /Zi /utf-8 /EHa /Fe%1.exe c.cpp %1.obj /link /largeaddressaware:no
```

This set of commands (*sbuild.bat* for *small build*) tells MASM to pass a command to the linker that turns off the large address–aware file. MASM, MSVC, and the Microsoft linker will construct an executable file that requires only 32-bit addresses (ignoring the 32 HO bits in the 64-bit registers appearing in addressing modes).

Once you've disabled LARGEADDRESSAWARE, several new variants of the indirect-plus-offset and scaled-indexed addressing modes become available to your programs:

```
variable[reg₆₄]
variable[reg₆₄ + const]
variable[reg₆₄ - const]
variable[reg₆₄ * scale]
variable[reg₆₄ * scale + const]
variable[reg₆₄ * scale - const]
variable[reg₆₄ + reg_not_RSP₆₄ * scale]
variable[reg₆₄ + reg_not_RSP₆₄ * scale + const]
variable[reg₆₄ + reg_not_RSP₆₄ * scale - const]
```

where *variable* is the name of an object you've declared in your source file by using directives like byte, word, dword, and so on; *const* is a (maximum 32-bit) constant expression; and *scale* is 1, 2, 4, or 8. These addressing mode forms use the address of *variable* as the base address and add in the current value of the 64-bit registers (see Figures 3-11 through 3-16 for examples).

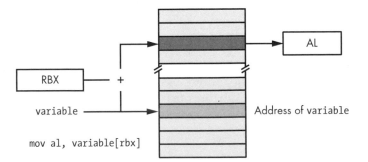

Figure 3-11: Base address form of indirect-plus-offset addressing mode

Although the small address forms (LARGEADDRESSAWARE:NO) are convenient and efficient, they can fail spectacularly if your program ever uses more than 2GB of memory. Should your programs ever grow beyond that point, you will have to completely rewrite every instruction that uses one of these addresses (that uses a global data object as the base address rather than loading the base address into a register). This can be very painful and error prone. Think twice before ever using the LARGEADDRESSAWARE:NO option.

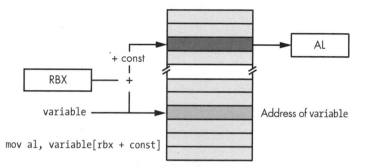

mov al, variable[rbx + const]

Figure 3-12: Small address plus constant form of indirect-plus-offset addressing mode

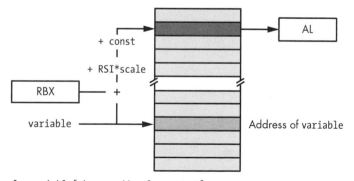

mov al, variable[rbx + rsi*scale]

Figure 3-13: Small address form of base-plus-scaled-indexed addressing mode

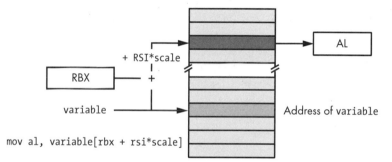

mov al, variable[rbx + rsi*scale + const]

Figure 3-14: Small address form of base-plus-scaled-indexed-plus-constant addressing mode

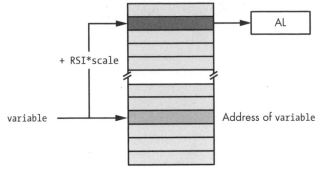

mov al, variable[rsi*scale]

Figure 3-15: Small address form of scaled-indexed addressing mode

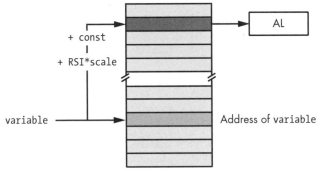

mov al, variable[rsi*scale + const]

Figure 3-16: Small address form of scaled-indexed-plus-constant addressing mode

3.8 Address Expressions

Often, when accessing variables and other objects in memory, we need to access memory locations immediately before or after a variable rather than the memory at the address specified by the variable. For example, when accessing an element of an array or a field of a structure/record, the exact element or field is probably not at the address of the variable itself. Address expressions provide a mechanism to attach an arithmetic expression to an address to access memory around a variable's address.

This book considers an *address expression* to be any legal x86-64 addressing mode that includes a displacement (that is, variable name) or an offset. For example, the following are legal address expressions:

$[reg_{64} + offset]$
$[reg_{64} + reg\_not\_RSP_{64} * scale + offset]$

Consider the following legal MASM syntax for a memory address, which isn't actually a new addressing mode but simply an extension of the PC-relative addressing mode:

---

variable_name[offset]

This extended form computes its effective address by adding the constant offset within the brackets to the variable's address. For example, the instruction mov al, Address[3] loads the AL register with the byte in memory that is 3 bytes beyond the Address object (see Figure 3-17).

The *offset* value in these examples must be a constant. If *index* is an int32 variable, then *variable*[*index*] is not a legal address expression. If you wish to specify an index that varies at runtime, you must use one of the indirect or scaled-indexed addressing modes.

Another important thing to remember is that the offset in *Address*[*offset*] is a byte address. Although this syntax is reminiscent of array indexing in a high-level language like C/C++ or Java, this does not properly index into an array of objects unless *Address* is an array of bytes.

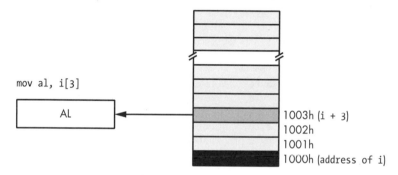

mov al, i[3]

Figure 3-17: Using an address expression to access data beyond a variable

Until this point, the offset in all the addressing mode examples has always been a single numeric constant. However, MASM also allows a *constant expression* anywhere an offset is legal. A constant expression consists of one or more constant terms manipulated by operators such as addition, subtraction, multiplication, division, modulo, and a wide variety of others. Most address expressions, however, will involve only addition, subtraction, multiplication, and sometimes division. Consider the following example:

---

mov al, X[2*4 + 1]

This instruction will move the byte at address X + 9 into the AL register.

The value of an address expression is always computed at compile time, never while the program is running. When MASM encounters the preceding instruction, it calculates $2 \times 4 + 1$ on the spot and adds this result to the base address of X in memory. MASM encodes this single sum (base address of X plus 9) as part of the instruction; MASM does not emit extra instructions to compute this sum for you at runtime (which is good, because doing so would be less efficient). Because MASM computes the value of address expressions at compile time, all components of the expression must be constants because MASM cannot know the runtime value of a variable while it is compiling the program.

Address expressions are useful for accessing the data in memory beyond a variable, particularly when you've used the byte, word, dword, and so on, statements in a .data or .const section to tack on additional bytes after a data declaration. For example, consider the program in Listing 3-1 that uses address expressions to access the four consecutive bytes associated with variable i.

```
; Listing 3-1

; Demonstrate address expressions.

        option  casemap:none

nl      =       10  ; ASCII code for newline

                .const
ttlStr          byte    'Listing 3-1', 0
fmtStr1         byte    'i[0]=%d ', 0
fmtStr2         byte    'i[1]=%d ', 0
fmtStr3         byte    'i[2]=%d ', 0
fmtStr4         byte    'i[3]=%d',nl, 0

        .data
i       byte    0, 1, 2, 3

        .code
        externdef printf:proc

; Return program title to C++ program:

        public getTitle
getTitle proc
        lea rax, ttlStr
        ret
getTitle endp

; Here is the "asmMain" function.

        public  asmMain
asmMain proc
        push    rbx
```

```
; "Magic" instruction offered without
; explanation at this point:

        sub     rsp, 48

        lea     rcx, fmtStr1
        movzx   rdx, i[0]
        call    printf

        lea     rcx, fmtStr2
        movzx   rdx, i[1]
        call    printf

        lea     rcx, fmtStr3
        movzx   rdx, i[2]
        call    printf

        lea     rcx, fmtStr4
        movzx   rdx, i[3]
        call    printf

        add     rsp, 48
        pop     rbx
        ret             ; Returns to caller
asmMain endp
        end
```

Listing 3-1: Demonstration of address expressions

Here's the output from the program:

```
C:\>build listing3-1

C:\>echo off
 Assembling: listing3-1.asm
c.cpp

C:\>listing3-1
Calling Listing 3-1:
i[0]=0 i[1]=1 i[2]=2 i[3]=3
Listing 3-1 terminated
```

The program in Listing 3-1 displays the four values 0, 1, 2, and 3 as though they were array elements. This is because the value at the address of i is 0. The address expression i[1] tells MASM to fetch the byte appearing at i's address plus 1. This is the value 1, because the byte statement in this program emits the value 1 to the .data segment immediately after the value 0. Likewise for i[2] and i[3], this program displays the values 2 and 3.

Note that MASM also provides a special operator, this, that returns the current location counter (current position) within a section. You can use the this operator to represent the address of the current instruction in an address expression. See "Constant Expressions" in Chapter 4 for more details.

3.9 The Stack Segment and the push and pop Instructions

The x86-64 maintains the stack in the stack segment of memory. The *stack* is a dynamic data structure that grows and shrinks according to certain needs of the program. The stack also stores important information about the program, including local variables, subroutine information, and temporary data.

The x86-64 controls its stack via the RSP (stack pointer) register. When your program begins execution, the operating system initializes RSP with the address of the last memory location in the stack memory segment. Data is written to the stack segment by "pushing" data onto the stack and "popping" data off the stack.

3.9.1 The Basic push Instruction

Here's the syntax for the x86-64 push instruction:

```
push   reg₁₆
push   reg₆₄
push   memory₁₆
push   memory₆₄
pushw  constant₁₆
push   constant₃₂   ; Sign extends constant₃₂ to 64 bits
```

These six forms allow you to push 16-bit or 64-bit registers, 16-bit or 64-bit memory locations, and 16-bit or 64-bit constants, but not 32-bit registers, memory locations, or constants.

The push instruction does the following:

```
RSP    := RSP - size_of_register_or_memory_operand (2 or 8)
[RSP] := operand's_value
```

For example, assuming that RSP contains 00FF_FFFCh, the instruction push rax will set RSP to 00FF_FFE4h and store the current value of RAX into memory location 00FF_FFE04, as Figures 3-18 and 3-19 show.

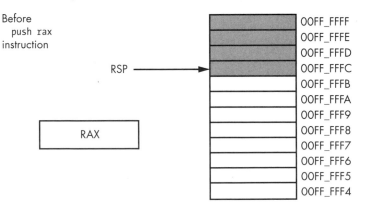

Figure 3-18: Stack segment before the push rax operation

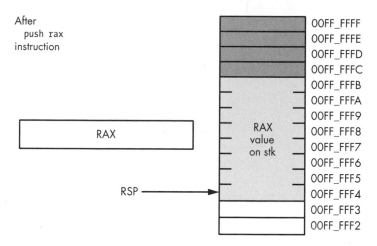

After
push rax
instruction

RAX

RSP

	00FF_FFFF
	00FF_FFFE
	00FF_FFFD
	00FF_FFFC
	00FF_FFFB
	00FF_FFFA
	00FF_FFF9
RAX value on stk	00FF_FFF8
	00FF_FFF7
	00FF_FFF6
	00FF_FFF5
	00FF_FFF4
	00FF_FFF3
	00FF_FFF2

Figure 3-19: Stack segment after the push rax operation

Although the x86-64 supports 16-bit push operations, their primary use is in 16-bit environments such as Microsoft Disk Operating System (MS-DOS). For maximum performance, the stack pointer's value should always be a multiple of eight; indeed, your program may malfunction under a 64-bit OS if RSP contains a value that is not a multiple of eight. The only practical reason for pushing fewer than 8 bytes at a time on the stack is to build up a quad word via four successive word pushes.

3.9.2 The Basic pop Instruction

To retrieve data you've pushed onto the stack, you use the pop instruction. The basic pop instruction allows the following forms:

```
pop reg16
pop reg64
pop memory16
pop memory64
```

Like the push instruction, the pop instruction supports only 16-bit and 64-bit operands; you cannot pop an 8-bit or 32-bit value from the stack. As with the push instruction, you should avoid popping 16-bit values (unless you do four 16-bit pops in a row) because 16-bit pops may leave the RSP register containing a value that is not a multiple of eight. One major difference between push and pop is that you cannot pop a constant value (which makes sense, because the operand for push is a source operand, while the operand for pop is a destination operand).

Formally, here's what the pop instruction does:

```
operand := [RSP]
RSP     := RSP + size_of_operand (2 or 8)
```

As you can see, the pop operation is the converse of the push operation. Note that the pop instruction copies the data from memory location [RSP] before adjusting the value in RSP. See Figures 3-20 and 3-21 for details on this operation.

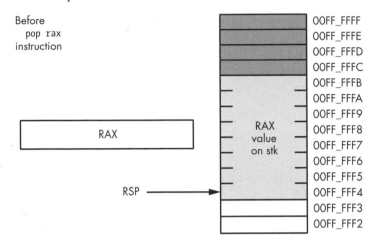

Figure 3-20: Memory before a pop rax operation

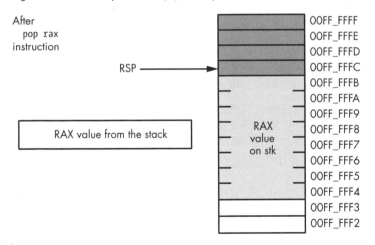

Figure 3-21: Memory after the pop rax operation

The value popped from the stack is still present in memory. Popping a value does not erase the value in memory; it just adjusts the stack pointer so that it points at the next value above the popped value. However, you should never attempt to access a value you've popped off the stack. The next time something is pushed onto the stack, the popped value will be obliterated. Because your code isn't the only thing that uses the stack (for example, the operating system uses the stack, as do subroutines), you cannot rely on data remaining in stack memory once you've popped it off the stack.

3.9.3   Preserving Registers with the push and pop Instructions

Perhaps the most common use of the push and pop instructions is to save register values during intermediate calculations. Because registers are the best place to hold temporary values, and registers are also needed for the various addressing modes, it is easy to run out of registers when writing code that performs complex calculations. The push and pop instructions can come to your rescue when this happens.

Consider the following program outline:

Some instructions that use the RAX register

Some instructions that need to use RAX, for a
different purpose than the above instructions

Some instructions that need the original value in RAX

The push and pop instructions are perfect for this situation. By inserting a push instruction before the middle sequence and a pop instruction after the middle sequence, you can preserve the value in RAX across those calculations:

Some instructions that use the RAX register

    push rax

Some instructions that need to use RAX, for a
different purpose than the above instructions

    pop rax

Some instructions that need the original value in RAX

This push instruction copies the data computed in the first sequence of instructions onto the stack. Now the middle sequence of instructions can use RAX for any purpose it chooses. After the middle sequence of instructions finishes, the pop instruction restores the value in RAX so the last sequence of instructions can use the original value in RAX.

3.10   The Stack Is a LIFO Data Structure

You can push more than one value onto the stack without first popping previous values off the stack. However, the stack is a *last-in, first-out (LIFO)* data structure, so you must be careful how you push and pop multiple values. For example, suppose you want to preserve RAX and RBX across a block of instructions; the following code demonstrates the obvious way to handle this:

```
push rax
push rbx
  Code that uses RAX and RBX goes here
pop rax
pop rbx
```

Unfortunately, this code will not work properly! Figures 3-22 through 3-25 show the problem. Because this code pushes RAX first and RBX second, the stack pointer is left pointing at RBX's value on the stack. When the pop rax instruction comes along, it removes the value that was originally in RBX from the stack and places it in RAX! Likewise, the pop rbx instruction pops the value that was originally in RAX into the RBX register. The result is that this code manages to swap the values in the registers by popping them in the same order that it pushes them.

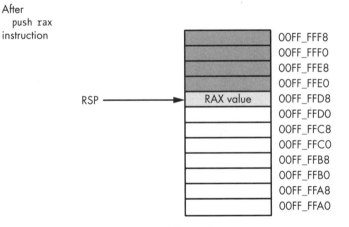

Figure 3-22: Stack after pushing RAX

To rectify this problem, you must note that the stack is a LIFO data structure, so the first thing you must pop is the last thing you push onto the stack. Therefore, you must always observe the following maxim: *always pop values in the reverse order that you push them.*

The correction to the previous code is shown here:

```
push rax
push rbx
  Code that uses RAX and RBX goes here
pop rbx
pop rax
```

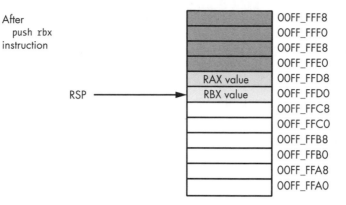

After
  push rbx
instruction

RSP

	00FF_FFF8
	00FF_FFF0
	00FF_FFE8
	00FF_FFE0
RAX value	00FF_FFD8
RBX value	00FF_FFD0
	00FF_FFC8
	00FF_FFC0
	00FF_FFB8
	00FF_FFB0
	00FF_FFA8
	00FF_FFA0

Each box in this diagram represents 8 bytes
on the stack (note the addresses).

Figure 3-23: Stack after pushing RBX

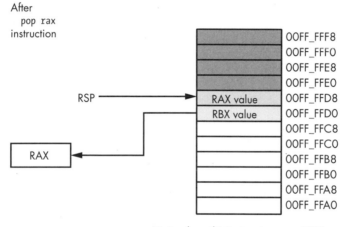

After
  pop rax
instruction

RSP

RAX

Notice how this instruction pops RBX's saved
value into the RAX register.

Figure 3-24: Stack after popping RAX

Another important maxim to remember is this: *always pop exactly the same number of bytes that you push.* This generally means that the number of pushes and pops must exactly agree. If you have too few pops, you will leave data on the stack, which may confuse the running program. If you have too many pops, you will accidentally remove previously pushed data, often with disastrous results.

A corollary to the preceding maxim is *be careful when pushing and popping data within a loop.* Often it is quite easy to put the pushes in a loop and leave the pops outside the loop (or vice versa), creating an inconsistent stack. Remember, it is the execution of the push and pop instructions that matters, not the number of push and pop instructions that appear in your program. At runtime, the number (and order) of the push instructions the program executes must match the number (and reverse order) of the pop instructions.

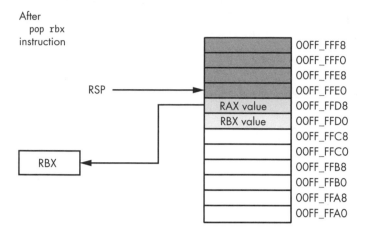

After
pop rbx
instruction

RSP

	OOFF_FFF8
	OOFF_FFF0
	OOFF_FFE8
	OOFF_FFE0
RAX value	OOFF_FFD8
RBX value	OOFF_FFD0
	OOFF_FFC8
	OOFF_FFC0
	OOFF_FFB8
	OOFF_FFB0
	OOFF_FFA8
	OOFF_FFA0

RBX

Notice how this instruction pops RAX's saved
value into the RBX register.

Figure 3-25: Stack after popping RBX

One final thing to note: *the Microsoft ABI requires the stack to be aligned on a 16-byte boundary.* If you push and pop items on the stack, make sure that the stack is aligned on a 16-byte boundary before calling any functions or procedures that adhere to the Microsoft ABI (and require the stack to be aligned on a 16-byte boundary).

3.11   Other push and pop Instructions

The x86-64 provides four additional push and pop instructions in addition to the basic ones:

```
pushf      popf
pushfq     popfq
```

The pushf, pushfq, popf, and popfq instructions push and pop the RFLAGS register. These instructions allow you to preserve condition code and other flag settings across the execution of a sequence of instructions. Unfortunately, unless you go to a lot of trouble, it is difficult to preserve individual flags. When using the pushf(q) and popf(q) instructions, it's an all-or-nothing proposition: you preserve all the flags when you push them; you restore all the flags when you pop them.

You should really use the pushfq and popfq instructions to push the full 64-bit version of the RFLAGS register (rather than pushing only the 16-bit FLAGs portion). Although the extra 48 bits you push and pop are essentially ignored when writing applications, you still want to keep the stack aligned by pushing and popping only quad words.

3.12   Removing Data from the Stack Without Popping It

Quite often you may discover that you've pushed data onto the stack that you no longer need. Although you could pop the data into an unused register or memory location, there is an easier way to remove unwanted data from the stack—simply adjust the value in the RSP register to skip over the unwanted data on the stack.

Consider the following dilemma (in pseudocode, not actual assembly language):

```
push rax
push rbx

  Some code that winds up computing some values we want to keep
  in RAX and RBX

if(Calculation_was_performed) then

    ; Whoops, we don't want to pop RAX and RBX!
    ; What to do here?

else

    ; No calculation, so restore RAX, RBX.

    pop rbx
    pop rax

endif;
```

Within the then section of the if statement, this code wants to remove the old values of RAX and RBX without otherwise affecting any registers or memory locations. How can we do this?

Because the RSP register contains the memory address of the item on the top of the stack, we can remove the item from the top of the stack by adding the size of that item to the RSP register. In the preceding example, we wanted to remove two quad-word items from the top of the stack. We can easily accomplish this by adding 16 to the stack pointer (see Figures 3-26 and 3-27 for the details):

```
push rax
push rbx

  Some code that winds up computing some values we want to keep
  in RAX and RBX

if(Calculation_was_performed) then

    ; Remove unneeded RAX/RBX values
    ; from the stack.

    add rsp, 16

else
```

```
; No calculation, so restore RAX, RBX.

pop rbx
pop rax
```

endif;

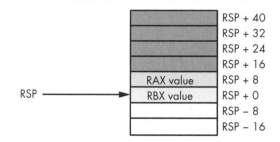

Figure 3-26: Removing data from the stack, before
add rsp, 16

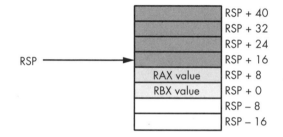

Figure 3-27: Removing data from the stack, after
add rsp, 16

Effectively, this code pops the data off the stack without moving it any-where. Also note that this code is faster than two dummy pop instructions because it can remove any number of bytes from the stack with a single add instruction.

NOTE *Remember to keep the stack aligned on a quad-word boundary. Therefore, you should always add a constant that is a multiple of eight to RSP when removing data from the stack.*

3.13 Accessing Data You've Pushed onto the Stack Without Popping It

Once in a while, you will push data onto the stack and will want to get a copy of that data's value, or perhaps you will want to change that data's value without actually popping the data off the stack (that is, you wish to pop the data off the stack at a later time). The x86-64 [reg_{64} ± $offset$] addressing mode provides the mechanism for this.

Consider the stack after the execution of the following two instructions (see Figure 3-28):

```
push rax
push rbx
```

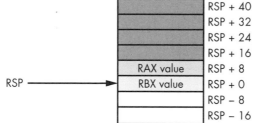

RSP ──────────────▶

	RSP + 40
	RSP + 32
	RSP + 24
	RSP + 16
RAX value	RSP + 8
RBX value	RSP + 0
	RSP – 8
	RSP – 16

Figure 3-28: Stack after pushing RAX and RBX

If you wanted to access the original RBX value without removing it from the stack, you could cheat and pop the value and then immediately push it again. Suppose, however, that you wish to access RAX's old value or another value even further up the stack. Popping all the intermediate values and then pushing them back onto the stack is problematic at best, impossible at worst. However, as you will notice from Figure 3-28, each value pushed on the stack is at a certain offset from the RSP register in memory. Therefore, we can use the [rsp ± *offset*] addressing mode to gain direct access to the value we are interested in. In the preceding example, you can reload RAX with its original value by using this single instruction:

```
mov rax, [rsp + 8]
```

This code copies the 8 bytes starting at memory address rsp + 8 into the RAX register. This value just happens to be the previous value of RAX that was pushed onto the stack. You can use this same technique to access other data values you've pushed onto the stack.

NOTE   *Don't forget that the offsets of values from RSP into the stack change every time you push or pop data. Abusing this feature can create code that is hard to modify; if you use this feature throughout your code, it will make it difficult to push and pop other data items between the point where you first push data onto the stack and the point where you decide to access that data again using the [rsp + offset] memory addressing mode.*

The previous section pointed out how to remove data from the stack by adding a constant to the RSP register. That pseudocode example could probably be written more safely as this:

```
push rax
push rbx
```

```
      Some code that winds up computing some values we want to keep
      in RAX and RBX

if(Calculation_was_performed) then

      Overwrite saved values on stack with
      new RAX/RBX values (so the pops that
      follow won't change the values in RAX/RBX)

         mov [rsp + 8], rax
         mov [rsp], rbx

endif
pop rbx
pop rax
```

In this code sequence, the calculated result was stored over the top of the values saved on the stack. Later, when the program pops the values, it loads these calculated values into RAX and RBX.

3.14 Microsoft ABI Notes

About the only feature this chapter introduces that affects the Microsoft ABI is data alignment. As a general rule, the Microsoft ABI requires all data to be aligned on a natural boundary for that data object. A *natural boundary* is an address that is a multiple of the object's size (up to 16 bytes). Therefore, if you intend to pass a word/sword, dword/sdword, or qword/sqword value to a C++ procedure, you should attempt to align that object on a 2-, 4-, or 8-byte boundary, respectively.

When calling code written in a Microsoft ABI–aware language, you must ensure that the stack is aligned on a 16-byte boundary before issuing a call instruction. This can severely limit the usefulness of the push and pop instructions. If you use the push instructions to save a register's value prior to a call, you must make sure you push two (64-bit) values, or otherwise make sure the RSP address is a multiple of 16 bytes, prior to making the call. Chapter 5 explores this issue in greater detail.

3.15 For More Information

An older, 16-bit version of my book *The Art of Assembly Language Programming* can be found at *https://artofasm.randallhyde.com/*. In that text, you will find information about the 8086 16-bit addressing modes and segmentation. The published edition of that book (No Starch Press, 2010) covers the 32-bit addressing modes. Of course, the Intel x86 documentation (found at *http://www.intel .com/*) provides complete information on x86-64 address modes and machine instruction encoding.

3.16 Test Yourself

1. The PC-relative addressing mode indexes off which 64-bit register?
2. What does *opcode* stand for?
3. What type of data is the PC-relative addressing mode typically used for?
4. What is the address range of the PC-relative addressing mode?
5. In a register-indirect addressing mode, what does the register contain?
6. Which of the following registers is valid for use with the register-indirect addressing mode?
   a. AL
   b. AX
   c. EAX
   d. RAX

7. What instruction would you normally use to load the address of a memory object into a register?
8. What is an effective address?
9. What scaling values are legal with the scaled-indexed addressing mode?
10. What is the memory limitation on a LARGEADDRESSAWARE:NO application?
11. What is the advantage of using the LARGEADDRESSAWARE:NO option when compiling a program?
12. What is the difference between the .data section and the .data? section?
13. Which (standard MASM) memory sections are read-only?
14. Which (standard MASM) memory sections are readable and writable?
15. What is the location counter?
16. Explain how to use the label directive to coerce data to a different type.
17. Explain what happens if two (or more) .data sections appear in a MASM source file.
18. How would you align a variable in the .data section to an 8-byte boundary?
19. What does *MMU* stand for?
20. If b is a byte variable in read/write memory, explain how a mov ax, b instruction could cause a general protection fault.
21. What is an address expression?
22. What is the purpose of the MASM PTR operator?
23. What is the difference between a big-endian value and a little-endian value?
24. If AX contains a big-endian value, what instruction could you use to convert it to a little-endian value?

25. If EAX contains a little-endian value, what instruction could you use to convert it to a big-endian value?

26. If RAX contains a big-endian value, what instruction could you use to convert it to a little-endian value?

27. Explain, step by step, what the push rax instruction does.

28. Explain, step by step, what the pop rax instruction does.

29. When using the push and pop instructions to preserve registers, you must always pop the registers in the _____ order that you pushed them.

30. What does *LIFO* stand for?

31. How do you access data on the stack without using the push and pop instructions?

32. How can pushing RAX onto the stack before calling a Windows ABI–compatible function create problems?

4

CONSTANTS, VARIABLES, AND DATA TYPES

Chapter 2 discussed the basic format for data in memory. Chapter 3 covered how a computer system physically organizes that data in memory. This chapter finishes the discussion by connecting the concept of *data representation* to its actual physical representation. As the title indicates, this chapter concerns itself with three main topics: constants, variables, and data structures. I do not assume that you've had a formal course in data structures, though such experience would be useful.

This chapter discusses how to declare and use constants, scalar variables, integers, data types, pointers, arrays, records/structures, and unions. You must master these subjects before going on to the next chapter. Declaring and accessing arrays, in particular, seem to present a multitude of problems to beginning assembly language programmers. However, the rest of this text depends on your understanding of these data structures and their memory representation. Do not try to skim over this material with the expectation that you will pick it up as you need it later. You will need it right away, and trying to learn this material along with later material will only confuse you more.

4.1 The imul Instruction

This chapter introduces arrays and other concepts that will require the expansion of your x86-64 instruction set knowledge. In particular, you will need to learn how to multiply two values; hence, this section looks at the imul (*integer multiply*) instruction.

The imul instruction has several forms. This section doesn't cover all of them, just the ones that are useful for array calculations (for the remaining imul instructions, see "Arithmetic Expressions" in Chapter 6). The imul variants of interest right now are as follows:

```
; The following computes destreg = destreg * constant:

imul destreg₁₆, constant
imul destreg₃₂, constant
imul destreg₆₄, constant₃₂

; The following computes dest = src * constant:

imul destreg₁₆, srcreg₁₆, constant
imul destreg₁₆, srcmem₁₆, constant

imul destreg₃₂, srcreg₃₂, constant
imul destreg₃₂, srcmem₃₂, constant

imul destreg₆₄, srcreg₆₄, constant₃₂
imul destreg₆₄, srcmem₆₄, constant₃₂

; The following computes dest = destreg * src:

imul destreg₁₆, srcreg₁₆
imul destreg₁₆, srcmem₁₆
imul destreg₃₂, srcreg₃₂
imul destreg₃₂, srcmem₃₂
imul destreg₆₄, srcreg₆₄
imul destreg₆₄, srcmem₆₄
```

Note that the syntax of the imul instruction is different from that of the add and sub instructions. In particular, the destination operand must be a register (add and sub both allow a memory operand as a destination). Also note that imul allows three operands when the last operand is a constant. Another important difference is that the imul instruction allows only 16-, 32-, and 64-bit operands; it does not multiply 8-bit operands. Finally, as is true for most instructions that support the immediate addressing mode, the CPU limits constant sizes to 32 bits. For 64-bit operands, the x86-64 will sign-extend the 32-bit immediate constant to 64 bits.

imul computes the product of its specified operands and stores the result into the destination register. If an overflow occurs (which is always a signed overflow, because imul multiplies only signed integer values), then this instruction sets both the carry and overflow flags. imul leaves the other condition code flags undefined (so, for example, you cannot meaningfully check the sign flag or the zero flag after executing imul).

4.2 The inc and dec Instructions

As several examples up to this point have indicated, adding or subtracting 1 from a register or memory location is a very common operation. In fact, these operations are so common that Intel's engineers included a pair of instructions to perform these specific operations: inc (*increment*) and dec (*decrement*).

The inc and dec instructions use the following syntax:

```
inc mem/reg
dec mem/reg
```

The single operand can be any legal 8-, 16-, 32-, or 64-bit register or memory operand. The inc instruction will add 1 to the specified operand, and the dec instruction will subtract 1 from the specified operand.

These two instructions are slightly shorter than the corresponding add or sub instructions (their encoding uses fewer bytes). There is also one slight difference between these two instructions and the corresponding add or sub instructions: they do not affect the carry flag.

4.3 MASM Constant Declarations

MASM provides three directives that let you define constants in your assembly language programs.[1] Collectively, these three directives are known as *equates*. You've already seen the most common form:

```
symbol = constant_expression
```

For example:

```
MaxIndex = 15
```

Once you declare a symbolic constant in this manner, you may use the symbolic identifier anywhere the corresponding literal constant is legal. These constants are known as *manifest constants*—symbolic representations that allow you to substitute the literal value for the symbol anywhere in the program.

Contrast this with .const variables; a .const variable is certainly a constant value because you cannot change its value at runtime. However, a memory

---

1. Technically, you could also use macro functions to define constants in MASM. See Chapter 13 for more details.

location is associated with a .const variable; the operating system, not the MASM compiler, enforces the read-only attribute. Although it will certainly crash your program when it runs, it is perfectly legal to write an instruction like mov ReadOnlyVar, eax. On the other hand, it is no more legal to write mov MaxIndex, eax (using the preceding declaration) than it is to write mov 15, eax. In fact, both statements are equivalent because the compiler substitutes 15 for MaxIndex whenever it encounters this manifest constant.

Constant declarations are great for defining "magic" numbers that might possibly change during program modification. Most of the listings throughout this book have used manifest constants like nl (*newline*), maxLen, and NULL.

In addition to the = directive, MASM provides the equ directive:

---

symbol equ *constant_expression*

With a couple exceptions, these two equate directives do the same thing: they define a manifest constant, and MASM will substitute the *constant_expression* value wherever the symbol appears in the source file.

The first difference between the two is that MASM allows you to redefine symbols that use the = directive. Consider the following code snippet:

```
maxSize  = 100

Code that uses maxSize, expecting it to be 100

maxSize  = 256

Code that uses maxSize, expecting it to be 256
```

You might question the term *constant* when it's pretty clear in this example that maxSize's value changes at various points in the source file. However, note that while maxSize's value does change during assembly, at runtime the particular literal constant (100 or 256 in this example) can never change.

You cannot redefine the value of a constant you declare with an equ directive (at runtime or assembly time). Any attempt to redefine an equ symbol results in a symbol redefinition error from MASM. So if you want to prevent the accidental redefinition of a constant symbol in your source file, you should use the equ directive rather than the = directive.

Another difference between the = and equ directives is that constants you define with = must be representable as a 64-bit (or smaller) integer. Short character strings are legal as = operands, but only if they have eight or fewer characters (which would fit into a 64-bit value). Equates using equ have no such limitation.

Ultimately, the difference between = and equ is that the = directive computes the value of a numeric expression and saves that value to substitute wherever that symbol appears in the program. The equ directive, if its operand can be reduced to a numeric value, will work the same way. However, if the equ operand cannot be converted to a numeric value, then the equ directive will save its operand as textual data and substitute that textual data in place of the symbol.

Because of the numeric/text processing, equ can get confused on occasion by its operand. Consider the following example:

```
SomeStr  equ   "abcdefgh"
         .
         .
         .
memStr   byte  SomeStr
```

MASM will report an error (initializer magnitude too large for specified size or something similar) because a 64-bit value (obtained by creating an integer value from the eight characters abcdefgh) will not fit into a byte variable. However, if we add one more character to the string, MASM will gladly accept this:

```
SomeStr  equ   "abcdefghi"
         .
         .
         .
memStr   byte  SomeStr
```

The difference between these two examples is that in the first case, MASM decides that it can represent the string as a 64-bit integer, so the constant is a quad-word constant rather than a string of characters. In the second example, MASM cannot represent the string of characters as an integer, so it treats the operand as a text operand rather than a numeric operand. When MASM does a textual substitution of the string abcdefghi for memStr in the second example, MASM assembles the code properly because strings are perfectly legitimate operands for the byte directive.

Assuming you really want MASM to treat a string of eight characters or fewer as a string rather than as an integer value, there are two solutions. The first is to surround the operand with *text delimiters*. MASM uses the symbols < and > as text delimiters in an equ operand field. So, you could use the following code to solve this problem:

```
SomeStr  equ   <"abcdefgh">
         .
         .
         .
memStr   byte  SomeStr
```

Because the equ directive's operand can be somewhat ambiguous at times, Microsoft introduced a third equate directive, textequ, to use when you want to create a text equate. Here's the current example using a text equate:

```
SomeStr  textequ   <"abcdefgh">
         .
         .
         .
memStr   byte      SomeStr
```

Note that `textequ` operands must always use the text delimiters (< and >) in the operand field.

Whenever MASM encounters a symbol defined with the text directive in a source file, it will immediately substitute the text associated with that directive for the identifier. This is somewhat similar to the C/C++ #define macro (except you don't get to specify any parameters). Consider the following example:

```
maxCnt  =        10
max     textequ <maxCnt>
max     =        max+1
```

MASM substitutes `maxCnt` for `max` throughout the program (after the `textequ` declaring `max`). In the third line of this example, this substitution yields the statement:

```
maxCnt  =        maxCnt+1
```

Thereafter in the program, MASM will substitute the value 11 everywhere it sees the symbol `maxCnt`. Whenever MASM sees `max` after that point, it will substitute `maxCnt`, and then it will substitute 11 for `maxCnt`.

You could even use MASM text equates to do something like the following:

```
mv      textequ  <mov>
        .
        .
        .
        mv       rax,0
```

MASM will substitute `mov` for `mv` and compile the last statement in this sequence into a `mov` instruction. Most people would consider this a huge violation of assembly language programming style, but it's perfectly legal.

4.3.1   Constant Expressions

Thus far, this chapter has given the impression that a symbolic constant definition consists of an identifier, an optional type, and a literal constant. Actually, MASM constant declarations can be a lot more sophisticated than this because MASM allows the assignment of a constant expression, not just a literal constant, to a symbolic constant. The generic constant declaration takes one of the following two forms:

```
identifier =   constant_expression
identifier equ constant_expression
```

Constant (integer) expressions take the familiar form you're used to in high-level languages like C/C++ and Python. They may contain literal constant values, previously declared symbolic constants, and various arithmetic operators.

The constant expression operators follow standard precedence rules (similar to those in C/C++); you may use the parentheses to override the precedence if necessary. In general, if the precedence isn't obvious, use parentheses to exactly state the order of evaluation. Table 4-1 lists the arithmetic operators MASM allows in constant (and address) expressions.

Table 4-1: Operations Allowed in Constant Expressions

Arithmetic operators	
- (unary negation)	Negates the expression immediately following -.
*	Multiplies the integer or real values around the asterisk.
/	Divides the left integer operand by the right integer operand, producing an integer (truncated) result.
mod	Divides the left integer operand by the right integer operand, producing an integer remainder.
/	Divides the left numeric operand by the second numeric operand, producing a floating-point result.
+	Adds the left and right numeric operands.
-	Subtracts the right numeric operand from the left numeric operand.
[]	$expr_1[expr_2]$ computes the sum of $expr_1 + expr_2$.
Comparison operators	
EQ	Compares left operand with right operand. Returns true if equal.[*]
NE	Compares left operand with right operand. Returns true if not equal.
LT	Returns true if left operand is less than right operand.
LE	Returns true if left operand is ≤ right operand.
GT	Returns true if left operand is greater than right operand.
GE	Returns true if left operand is ≥ right operand.
Logical operators**	
AND	For Boolean operands, returns the logical AND of the two operands.
OR	For Boolean operands, returns the logical OR of the two operands.
NOT	For Boolean operands, returns the logical negation (inverse).
Unary operators	
HIGH	Returns the HO byte of the LO 16 bits of the following expression.
HIGHWORD	Returns the HO word of the LO 32 bits of the following expression.
HIGH32	Returns the HO 32 bits of the 64-bit expression following the operator.
LENGTHOF	Returns the number of data elements of the variable name following the operator.
LOW	Returns the LO byte of the expression following the operator.
LOWWORD	Returns the LO word of the expression following the operator.

(continued)

Table 4-1: Operations Allowed in Constant Expressions *(continued)*

Unary operators	
LOW32	Returns the LO dword of the expression following the operator.
OFFSET	Returns the offset into its respective section for the symbol following the operator.
OPATTR	Returns the attributes of the expression following the operator. The attributes are returned as a bit map with the following meanings: bit 0: There is a code label in the expression. bit 1: The expression is relocatable. bit 2: The expression is a constant expression. bit 3: The expression uses direct addressing. bit 4: The expression is a register. bit 5: The expression contains no undefined symbols. bit 6: The expression is a stack-segment memory expression. bit 7: The expression references an external label. bits 8–11: Language type (probably 0 for 64-bit code).
SIZE	Returns the size, in bytes, of the first initializer in a symbol's declaration.
SIZEOF	Returns the size, in bytes, allocated for a given symbol.
THIS	Returns an address expression equal to the value of the current program counter within a section. Must include type after this; for example, this byte.
$	Synonym for this.

* MASM represents "true" by using all 1 bits (–1 or 0FFFFFF...FFh).
** Note to C/C++ and Java users: MASM's constant expressions use complete Boolean evaluation rather than short-circuit Boolean evaluation. Hence, MASM constant expressions do not behave identically to C/C++ and Java expressions.

4.3.2   *this* and *$* Operators

The last two operators in Table 4-1 deserve special mention. The this and $ operands (they are roughly synonyms for one another) return the current offset into the section containing them. The current offset into the section is known as the *location counter* (see "How MASM Allocates Memory for Variables" in Chapter 3). Consider the following:

```
someLabel equ $
```

This sets the label's offset to the current location in the program. The type of the symbol will be *statement label* (for example, proc). Typically, people use the $ operator for branch labels (and advanced features). For example, the following creates an infinite loop (effectively locking up the CPU):

```
jmp $     ; "$" is equivalent to the address of the jmp instr
```

You can also use instructions like this to skip a fixed number of bytes ahead (or behind) in the source file:

```
jmp $+5   ; Skip to a position 5 bytes beyond the jmp
```

For the most part, creating operands like this is crazy because it depends on knowing the number of bytes of machine code each machine instruction compiles into. Obviously, this is an advanced operation and not recommended for beginning assembly language programmers (it's even hard to recommend for most advanced assembly language programmers).

One practical use of the $ operator (and probably its most common use) is to compute the size of a block of data declarations in the source file:

```
someData      byte 1, 2, 3, 4, 5
sizeSomeData =     $-someData
```

The address expression $-someData computes the current offset minus the offset of someData in the current section. In this case, this produces 5, the number of bytes in the someData operand field. In this simple example, you're probably better off using the sizeof someData expression. This also returns the number of bytes required for the someData declaration. However, consider the following statements:

```
someData      byte 1, 2, 3, 4, 5
              byte 6, 7, 8, 9, 0
sizeSomeData =     $-someData
```

In this case, sizeof someData still returns 5 (because it returns only the length of the operands attached to someData), whereas sizeSomeData is set to 10.

If an identifier appears in a constant expression, that identifier must be a constant identifier that you have previously defined in your program in the equate directive. You may not use variable identifiers in a constant expression; their values are not defined at assembly time when MASM evaluates the constant expression. Also, don't confuse compile-time and runtime operations:

```
; Constant expression, computed while MASM
; is assembling your program:

x     = 5
y     = 6
Sum   = x + y

; Runtime calculation, computed while your program
; is running, long after MASM has assembled it:

    mov al, x
    add al, y
```

The this operator differs from the $ operator in one important way: the $ has a default type of statement label. The this operator, on the other hand, allows you to specify a type. The syntax for the this operator is the following:

```
this type
```

where *type* is one of the usual data types (byte, sbyte, word, sword, and so forth). Therefore, this proc is what is directly equivalent to $. Note that the following two MASM statements are equivalent:

```
someLabel label byte
someLabel equ   this byte
```

4.3.3 Constant Expression Evaluation

MASM immediately interprets the value of a constant expression during assembly. It does not emit any machine instructions to compute x + y in the constant expression of the example in the previous section. Instead, it directly computes the sum of these two constant values. From that point forward in the program, MASM associates the value 11 with the constant Sum just as if the program had contained the statement Sum = 11 rather than Sum = x + y. On the other hand, MASM does not precompute the value 11 in AL for the mov and add instructions in the previous section; it faithfully emits the object code for these two instructions, and the x86-64 computes their sum when the program is run (sometime after the assembly is complete).

In general, constant expressions don't get very sophisticated in assembly language programs. Usually, you're adding, subtracting, or multiplying two integer values. For example, the following set of equates defines a set of constants that have consecutive values:

```
TapeDAT         = 0
Tape8mm         = TapeDAT + 1
TapeQIC80       = Tape8mm + 1
TapeTravan      = TapeQIC80 + 1
TapeDLT         = TapeTravan + 1
```

These constants have the following values: TapeDAT = 0, Tape8mm = 1, TapeQIC80 = 2, TapeTravan = 3, and TapeDLT = 4. This example, by the way, demonstrates how you would create a list of enumerated data constants in MASM.

4.4 The MASM typedef Statement

Let's say that you do not like the names that MASM uses for declaring byte, word, dword, real4, and other variables. Let's say that you prefer Pascal's naming convention or perhaps C's naming convention. You want to use terms like *integer, float, double*, or whatever. If MASM were Pascal, you could redefine the names in the type section of the program. With C, you could use a typedef statement to accomplish the task. Well, MASM, like C/C++, has its own type statement that also lets you create aliases of these names. The MASM typedef statement takes the following form:

```
new_type_name  typedef  existing_type_name
```

The following example demonstrates how to set up some names in your MASM programs that are compatible with C/C++ or Pascal:

```
integer   typedef  sdword
float     typedef  real4
double    typedef  real8
colors    typedef  byte
```

Now you can declare your variables with more meaningful statements like these:

```
          .data
i         integer  ?
x         float    1.0
HouseColor colors  ?
```

If you program in Ada, C/C++, or FORTRAN (or any other language, for that matter), you can pick type names you're more comfortable with. Of course, this doesn't change how the x86-64 or MASM reacts to these variables one iota, but it does let you create programs that are easier to read and understand because the type names are more indicative of the actual underlying types. One warning for C/C++ programmers: don't get too excited and go off and define an int data type. Unfortunately, int is an x86-64 machine instruction (*interrupt*), and therefore this is a reserved word in MASM.

4.5 Type Coercion

Although MASM is fairly loose when it comes to type checking, MASM does ensure that you specify appropriate operand sizes to an instruction. For example, consider the following (incorrect) program in Listing 4-1.

```
; Listing 4-1

; Type checking errors.

        option  casemap:none

nl      =       10  ; ASCII code for newline

        .data
i8      sbyte   ?
i16     sword   ?
i32     sdword  ?
i64     sqword  ?

        .code

; Here is the "asmMain" function.

        public  asmMain
asmMain proc
```

```
            mov     eax, i8
            mov     al, i16
            mov     rax, i32
            mov     ax, i64

            ret     ; Returns to caller
asmMain endp
            end
```

Listing 4-1: MASM type checking

MASM will generate errors for these four mov instructions because the operand sizes are incompatible. The mov instruction requires both operands to be the same size. The first instruction attempts to move a byte into EAX, the second instruction attempts to move a word into AL, and the third instruction attempts to move a double word into RAX. The fourth instruction attempts to move a qword into AX. Here's the output from the compiler when you attempt to assemble this file:

```
C:\>ml64 /c listing4-1.asm
Microsoft (R) Macro Assembler (x64) Version 14.15.26730.0
Copyright (C) Microsoft Corporation.  All rights reserved.

 Assembling: listing4-1.asm
listing4-1.asm(24) : error A2022:instruction operands must be the same size
listing4-1.asm(25) : error A2022:instruction operands must be the same size
listing4-1.asm(26) : error A2022:instruction operands must be the same size
listing4-1.asm(27) : error A2022:instruction operands must be the same size
```

While this is a good feature in MASM,[2] sometimes it gets in the way. Consider the following code fragments:

```
            .data
byte_values label byte
            byte  0, 1

              .
              .
              .

            mov ax, byte_values
```

In this example, let's assume that the programmer really wants to load the word starting at the address of byte_values into the AX register because they want to load AL with 0, and AH with 1, by using a single instruction (0 is held in the LO memory byte, and 1 is held in the HO memory byte). MASM will refuse, claiming a type mismatch error (because byte_values is a byte object and AX is a word object).

---

2. After all, if the two operand sizes are different, this usually indicates an error in the program.

The programmer could break this into two instructions, one to load AL with the byte at address byte_values and the other to load AH with the byte at address byte_values[1]. Unfortunately, this decomposition makes the program slightly less efficient (which was probably the reason for using the single mov instruction in the first place). To tell MASM that we know what we're doing and we want to treat the byte_values variable as a word object, we can use type coercion.

Type coercion is the process of telling MASM that you want to treat an object as an explicit type, regardless of its actual type.[3] To coerce the type of a variable, you use the following syntax:

```
new_type_name ptr address_expression
```

The *new_type_name* item is the new type you wish to associate with the memory location specified by *address_expression*. You may use this coercion operator anywhere a memory address is legal. To correct the previous example, so MASM doesn't complain about type mismatches, you would use the following statement:

```
mov ax, word ptr byte_values
```

This instruction tells MASM to load the AX register with the word starting at address byte_values in memory. Assuming byte_values still contains its initial value, this instruction will load 0 into AL and 1 into AH.

Table 4-2 lists all the MASM type-coercion operators.

Table 4-2: MASM Type-Coercion Operators

Directive	Meaning
byte ptr	Byte (unsigned 8-bit) value
sbyte ptr	Signed 8-bit integer value
word ptr	Unsigned 16-bit (word) value
sword ptr	Signed 16-bit integer value
dword ptr	Unsigned 32-bit (double-word) value
sdword ptr	Signed 32-bit integer value
qword ptr	Unsigned 64-bit (quad-word) value
sqword ptr	Signed 64-bit integer value
tbyte ptr	Unsigned 80-bit (10-byte) value
oword ptr	128-bit (octal-word) value
xmmword ptr	128-bit (octal-word) value—same as oword ptr
ymmword ptr	256-bit value (for use with AVX YMM registers)
zmmword ptr	512-bit value (for use with AVX-512 ZMM registers)

(continued)

---

3. Type coercion is also called *type casting* in some languages.

Table 4-2: MASM Type-Coercion Operator *(continued)*

Directive	Meaning
real4 ptr	Single-precision (32-bit) floating-point value
real8 ptr	Double-precision (64-bit) floating-point value
real10 ptr	Extended-precision (80-bit) floating-point value

Type coercion is necessary when you specify an anonymous variable as the operand to an instruction that directly modifies memory (for example, neg, shl, not, and so on). Consider the following statement:

```
not [rbx]
```

MASM will generate an error on this instruction because it cannot determine the size of the memory operand. The instruction does not supply sufficient information to determine whether the program should invert the bits in the byte pointed at by RBX, the word pointed at by RBX, the double word pointed at by RBX, or the quad word pointed at by RBX. You must use type coercion to explicitly specify the size of anonymous references with these types of instructions:

```
not byte ptr [rbx]
not dword ptr [rbx]
```

WARNING   *Do not use the type-coercion operator unless you know exactly what you are doing and fully understand the effect it has on your program. Beginning assembly language programmers often use type coercion as a tool to quiet the assembler when it complains about type mismatches, without solving the underlying problem.*

Consider the following statement (where byteVar is an 8-bit variable):

```
mov dword ptr byteVar, eax
```

Without the type-coercion operator, MASM complains about this instruction because it attempts to store a 32-bit register in an 8-bit memory location. Beginning programmers, wanting their programs to assemble, may take a shortcut and use the type-coercion operator, as shown in this instruction; this certainly quiets the assembler—it will no longer complain about a type mismatch—so the beginning programmers are happy.

However, the program is still incorrect; the only difference is that MASM no longer warns you about your error. The type-coercion operator does not fix the problem of attempting to store a 32-bit value into an 8-bit memory location—it simply allows the instruction to store a 32-bit value *starting at the address specified by the 8-bit variable*. The program still stores 4 bytes, overwriting the 3 bytes following byteVar in memory.

This often produces unexpected results, including the phantom modification of variables in your program.[4] Another, rarer possibility is for the

---

4. If you have a variable immediately following byteVar in this example, the mov instruction will surely overwrite the value of that variable, whether or not you intend for this to happen.

program to abort with a general protection fault, if the 3 bytes following byteVar are not allocated in real memory or if those bytes just happen to fall in a read-only section of memory. The important thing to remember about the type-coercion operator is this: if you cannot exactly state the effect this operator has, don't use it.

Also keep in mind that the type-coercion operator does not perform any translation of the data in memory. It simply tells the assembler to treat the bits in memory as a different type. It will not automatically extend an 8-bit value to 32 bits, nor will it convert an integer to a floating-point value. It simply tells the compiler to treat the bit pattern of the memory operand as a different type.

4.6 Pointer Data Types

You've probably experienced pointers firsthand in the Pascal, C, or Ada programming languages, and you're probably getting worried right now. Almost everyone has a bad experience when they first encounter pointers in a high-level language. Well, fear not! Pointers are actually easier to deal with in assembly language than in high-level languages.

Besides, most of the problems you had with pointers probably had nothing to do with pointers but rather with the linked list and tree data structures you were trying to implement with them. Pointers, on the other hand, have many uses in assembly language that have nothing to do with linked lists, trees, and other scary data structures. Indeed, simple data structures like arrays and records often involve the use of pointers. So, if you have some deep-rooted fear about pointers, forget everything you know about them. You're going to learn how great pointers really are.

Probably the best place to start is with the definition of a pointer. A *pointer* is a memory location whose value is the address of another memory location. Unfortunately, high-level languages like C/C++ tend to hide the simplicity of pointers behind a wall of abstraction. This added complexity (which exists for good reason, by the way) tends to frighten programmers because *they don't understand what's going on.*

To illuminate what's really happening, consider the following array declaration in Pascal:

```
M: array [0..1023] of integer;
```

Even if you don't know Pascal, the concept here is pretty easy to understand. M is an array with 1024 integers in it, indexed from M[0] to M[1023]. Each one of these array elements can hold an integer value that is independent of all the others. In other words, this array gives you 1024 different integer variables, each of which you refer to by number (the array index) rather than by name.

If you encounter a program that has the statement M[0] := 100;, you probably won't have to think at all about what is happening with this statement. It is storing the value 100 into the first element of the array M. Now consider the following two statements:

```
i := 0;       (Assume "i" is an integer variable)
M [i] := 100;
```

You should agree, without too much hesitation, that these two statements perform the same operation as M[0] := 100;. Indeed, you're probably willing to agree that you can use any integer expression in the range 0 to 1023 as an index into this array. The following statements still perform the same operation as our single assignment to index 0:

```
i := 5;       (Assume all variables are integers)
j := 10;
k := 50;
m [i*j-k] := 100;
```

"Okay, so what's the point?" you're probably thinking. "Anything that produces an integer in the range 0 to 1023 is legal. So what?" Okay, how about the following:

```
M [1] := 0;
M [M [1]] := 100;
```

Whoa! Now that takes a few moments to digest. However, if you take it slowly, it makes sense, and you'll discover that these two instructions perform the same operation you've been doing all along. The first statement stores 0 into array element M[1]. The second statement fetches the value of M[1], which is an integer so you can use it as an array index into M, and uses that value (0) to control where it stores the value 100.

If you're willing to accept this as reasonable—perhaps bizarre, but usable nonetheless—then you'll have no problems with pointers. Because M[1] is a pointer! Well, not really, but if you were to change M to *memory* and treat this array as all of memory, this is the exact definition of a pointer: a memory location whose value is the address (or index, if you prefer) of another memory location. Pointers are easy to declare and use in an assembly language program. You don't even have to worry about array indices or anything like that.

4.6.1   Using Pointers in Assembly Language

A MASM pointer is a 64-bit value that may contain the address of another variable. If you have a dword variable p that contains 1000_0000h, then p "points" at memory location 1000_0000h. To access the dword that p points at, you could use code like the following:

```
mov  rbx, p      ; Load RBX with the value of pointer p
mov  rax, [rbx]  ; Fetch the data that p points at
```

By loading the value of p into RBX, this code loads the value 1000_0000h into RBX (assuming p contains 1000_0000h). The second instruction loads the RAX register with the qword starting at the location whose offset appears in RBX. Because RBX now contains 1000_0000h, this will load RAX from locations 1000_0000h through 1000_0007h.

Why not just load RAX directly from location 1000_0000h by using an instruction like mov rax, mem (assuming mem is at address 1000_0000h)? Well, there are several reasons. But the primary reason is that this mov instruction always loads RAX from location mem. You cannot change the address from where it loads RAX. The former instructions, however, always load RAX from the location where p is pointing. This is easy to change under program control. In fact, the two instructions mov rax, offset mem2 and mov p, rax will cause those previous two instructions to load RAX from mem2 the next time they execute. Consider the following code fragment:

```
mov rax, offset i
mov p, rax

    .
    .
    .        ; Code that sets or clears the carry flag.

jc skipSetp

   mov rax, offset j
   mov p, rax

   .
   .
   .

skipSetp:
   mov rbx, p         ; Assume both code paths wind up
   mov rax, [rbx]     ; down here
```

This short example demonstrates two execution paths through the program. The first path loads the variable p with the address of the variable i. The second path through the code loads p with the address of the variable j. Both execution paths converge on the last two mov instructions that load RAX with i or j depending on which execution path was taken. In many respects, this is like a parameter to a procedure in a high-level language like Swift. Executing the same instructions accesses different variables depending on whose address (i or j) winds up in p.

4.6.2   Declaring Pointers in MASM

Because pointers are 64 bits long, you could use the qword type to allocate storage for your pointers. However, rather than use qword declarations, an arguably better approach is to use typedef to create a pointer type:

```
        .data
pointer typedef qword
```

```
b          byte    ?
d          dword   ?
pByteVar   pointer b
pDWordVar  pointer d
```

This example demonstrates that it is possible to initialize as well as declare pointer variables in MASM. Note that you may specify addresses of static variables (.data, .const, and .data? objects) in the operand field of a qword/pointer directive, so you can initialize only pointer variables with the addresses of static objects.

4.6.3   Pointer Constants and Pointer Constant Expressions

MASM allows very simple constant expressions wherever a pointer constant is legal. Pointer constant expressions take one of the three following forms:[5]

```
offset StaticVarName [PureConstantExpression]
offset StaticVarName + PureConstantExpression
offset StaticVarName - PureConstantExpression
```

The PureConstantExpression term is a numeric constant expression that does not involve any pointer constants. This type of expression produces a memory address that is the specified number of bytes before or after (- or +, respectively) the StaticVarName variable in memory. Note that the first two forms shown here are semantically equivalent; both return a pointer constant whose address is the sum of the static variable and the constant expression.

Because you can create pointer constant expressions, it should come as no surprise to discover that MASM lets you define manifest pointer constants by using equates. The program in Listing 4-2 demonstrates how you can do this.

```
; Listing 4-2

; Pointer constant demonstration.

        option  casemap:none

nl      =       10

        .const
ttlStr  byte    "Listing 4-2", 0
fmtStr  byte    "pb's value is %ph", nl
        byte    "*pb's value is %d", nl, 0

        .data
b       byte    0
        byte    1, 2, 3, 4, 5, 6, 7
```

---

5. In MASM syntax, the form x[y] is equivalent to x + y. Likewise, [x][y] is also equivalent to x + y.

```
pb        textequ <offset b[2]>

          .code
          externdef printf:proc

; Return program title to C++ program:

          public getTitle
getTitle proc
          lea rax, ttlStr
          ret
getTitle endp

; Here is the "asmMain" function.

          public  asmMain
asmMain proc

; "Magic" instruction offered without
; explanation at this point:

          sub       rsp, 48

          lea       rcx, fmtStr
          mov       rdx, pb
          movzx     r8, byte ptr [rdx]
          call      printf

          add       rsp, 48
          ret       ; Returns to caller

asmMain endp
          end
```

Listing 4-2: Pointer constant expressions in a MASM program

Here's the assembly and execution of this code:

```
C:\>build listing4-2

C:\>echo off
 Assembling: listing4-2.asm
c.cpp

C:\>listing4-2
Calling Listing 4-2:
pb's value is 00007FF6AC381002h
*pb's value is 2
Listing 4-2 terminated
```

Note that the address printed may vary on different machines and different versions of Windows.

4.6.4 Pointer Variables and Dynamic Memory Allocation

Pointer variables are the perfect place to store the return result from the C Standard Library malloc() function. This function returns the address of the storage it allocates in the RAX register; therefore, you can store the address directly into a pointer variable with a single mov instruction immediately after a call to malloc(). Listing 4-3 demonstrates calls to the C Standard Library malloc() and free() functions.

```
; Listing 4-3

; Demonstration of calls
; to C standard library malloc
; and free functions.

        option  casemap:none

nl      =       10

        .const
ttlStr  byte    "Listing 4-3", 0
fmtStr  byte    "Addresses returned by malloc: %ph, %ph", nl, 0

        .data
ptrVar  qword   ?
ptrVar2 qword   ?

        .code
        externdef printf:proc
        externdef malloc:proc
        externdef free:proc

; Return program title to C++ program:

        public getTitle
getTitle proc
        lea rax, ttlStr
        ret
getTitle endp

; Here is the "asmMain" function.

        public  asmMain
asmMain proc

; "Magic" instruction offered without
; explanation at this point:

        sub     rsp, 48

; C standard library malloc function.

; ptr = malloc(byteCnt);
```

```
        mov     rcx, 256        ; Allocate 256 bytes
        call    malloc
        mov     ptrVar, rax     ; Save pointer to buffer

        mov     rcx, 1024       ; Allocate 1024 bytes
        call    malloc
        mov     ptrVar2, rax    ; Save pointer to buffer

        lea     rcx, fmtStr
        mov     rdx, ptrVar
        mov     r8, rax         ; Print addresses
        call    printf

; Free the storage by calling
; C standard library free function.

; free(ptrToFree);

        mov     rcx, ptrVar
        call    free

        mov     rcx, ptrVar2
        call    free

        add     rsp, 48
        ret     ; Returns to caller

asmMain endp
        end
```

Listing 4-3: Demonstration of `malloc()` *and* `free()` *calls*

Here's the output I obtained when building and running this program. Note that the addresses that malloc() returns may vary by system, by operating system version, and for other reasons. Therefore, you will likely get different numbers than I obtained on my system.

```
C:\>build listing4-3

C:\>echo off
 Assembling: listing4-3.asm
c.cpp

C:\>listing4-3
Calling Listing 4-3:
Addresses returned by malloc: 0000013B2BC43AD0h, 0000013B2BC43BE0h
Listing 4-3 terminated
```

4.6.5 Common Pointer Problems

Programmers encounter five common problems when using pointers. Some of these errors will cause your programs to immediately stop with a diagnostic message; other problems are subtler, yielding incorrect results without otherwise reporting an error or simply affecting the performance of your program without displaying an error. These five problems are as follows:

1. Using an uninitialized pointer
2. Using a pointer that contains an illegal value (for example, NULL)
3. Continuing to use malloc()'d storage after that storage has been freed
4. Failing to free() storage once the program is finished using it
5. Accessing indirect data by using the wrong data type

The first problem is using a pointer variable before you have assigned a valid memory address to the pointer. Beginning programmers often don't realize that declaring a pointer variable reserves storage only for the pointer itself; it does not reserve storage for the data that the pointer references. The short program in Listing 4-4 demonstrates this problem (don't try to compile and run this program; it will crash).

```
; Listing 4-4

; Uninitialized pointer demonstration.
; Note that this program will not
; run properly.

        option  casemap:none

nl      =       10

        .const
ttlStr  byte    "Listing 4-4", 0
fmtStr  byte    "Pointer value= %p", nl, 0

        .data
ptrVar  qword   ?

        .code
        externdef printf:proc

; Return program title to C++ program:

        public getTitle
getTitle proc
        lea rax, ttlStr
        ret
getTitle endp

; Here is the "asmMain" function.

        public  asmMain
asmMain proc

; "Magic" instruction offered without
; explanation at this point:

        sub     rsp, 48
```

```
        lea     rcx, fmtStr
        mov     rdx, ptrVar
        mov     rdx, [rdx]      ; Will crash system
        call    printf

        add     rsp, 48
        ret     ; Returns to caller

asmMain endp
        end
```

Listing 4-4: Uninitialized pointer demonstration

Although variables you declare in the .data section are, technically, initialized, static initialization still doesn't initialize the pointer in this program with a valid address (it initializes the pointer with 0, which is NULL).

Of course, there is no such thing as a truly uninitialized variable on the x86-64. What you really have are variables that you've explicitly given an initial value to and variables that just happen to inherit whatever bit pattern was in memory when storage for the variable was allocated. Much of the time, these garbage bit patterns lying around in memory don't correspond to a valid memory address. Attempting to *dereference* such a pointer (that is, access the data in memory at which it points) typically raises a *memory access violation* exception.

Sometimes, however, those random bits in memory just happen to correspond to a valid memory location you can access. In this situation, the CPU will access the specified memory location without aborting the program. Although to a naive programmer this situation may seem preferable to stopping the program, in reality this is far worse because your defective program continues to run without alerting you to the problem. If you store data through an uninitialized pointer, you may very well overwrite the values of other important variables in memory. This defect can produce some very difficult-to-locate problems in your program.

The second problem programmers have with pointers is storing invalid address values into a pointer. The first problem is actually a special case of this second problem (with garbage bits in memory supplying the invalid address rather than you producing it via a miscalculation). The effects are the same; if you attempt to dereference a pointer containing an invalid address, you either will get a memory access violation exception or will access an unexpected memory location.

The third problem listed is also known as the *dangling pointer problem*. To understand this problem, consider the following code fragment:

```
mov  rcx, 256
call malloc        ; Allocate some storage
mov  ptrVar, rax   ; Save address away in ptrVar
    .
    .              ; Code that uses the pointer variable ptrVar.
    .
```

```
mov    rcx, ptrVar
call   free          ; Free storage associated with ptrVar
    .
    .             ; Code that does not change the value in ptrVar.
    .
mov rbx, ptrVar
mov [rbx], al
```

In this example, the program allocates 256 bytes of storage and saves the address of that storage in the ptrVar variable. Then the code uses this block of 256 bytes for a while and frees the storage, returning it to the system for other uses. Note that calling free() does not change the value of ptrVar in any way; ptrVar still points at the block of memory allocated by malloc() earlier. Indeed, free() does not change any data in this block, so upon return from free(), ptrVar still points at the data stored into the block by this code.

However, note that the call to free() tells the system that the program no longer needs this 256-byte block of memory and the system can use this region of memory for other purposes. The free() function cannot enforce the fact that you will never access this data again; you are simply promising that you won't. Of course, the preceding code fragment breaks this promise; as you can see in the last two instructions, the program fetches the value in ptrVar and accesses the data it points at in memory.

The biggest problem with dangling pointers is that you can get away with using them a good part of the time. As long as the system doesn't reuse the storage you've freed, using a dangling pointer produces no ill effects in your program. However, with each new call to malloc(), the system may decide to reuse the memory released by that previous call to free(). When this happens, any attempt to dereference the dangling pointer may produce unintended consequences. The problems range from reading data that has been overwritten (by the new, legal use of the data storage), to overwriting the new data, to (the worst case) overwriting system heap management pointers (doing so will probably cause your program to crash). The solution is clear: *never use a pointer value once you free the storage associated with that pointer.*

Of all the problems, the fourth (failing to free allocated storage) will probably have the least impact on the proper operation of your program. The following code fragment demonstrates this problem:

```
mov   rcx, 256
call malloc
mov   ptrVar, rax
    .                 ; Code that uses ptrVar.
    .                 ; This code does not free up the storage
    .                 ; associated with ptrVar.
mov   rcx, 512
call malloc
mov   ptrVar, rax

; At this point, there is no way to reference the original
; block of 256 bytes pointed at by ptrVar.
```

In this example, the program allocates 256 bytes of storage and references this storage by using the ptrVar variable. At some later time, the program allocates another block of bytes and overwrites the value in ptrVar with the address of this new block. Note that the former value in ptrVar is lost. Because the program no longer has this address value, there is no way to call free() to return the storage for later use.

As a result, this memory is no longer available to your program. While making 256 bytes of memory inaccessible to your program may not seem like a big deal, imagine that this code is in a loop that repeats over and over again. With each execution of the loop, the program loses another 256 bytes of memory. After a sufficient number of loop iterations, the program will exhaust the memory available on the heap. This problem is often called a *memory leak* because the effect is the same as though the memory bits were leaking out of your computer (yielding less and less available storage) during program execution.

Memory leaks are far less damaging than dangling pointers. Indeed, memory leaks create only two problems: the danger of running out of heap space (which, ultimately, may cause the program to abort, though this is rare) and performance problems due to virtual memory page swapping. Nevertheless, you should get in the habit of always freeing all storage once you have finished using it. When your program quits, the operating system reclaims all storage, including the data lost via memory leaks. Therefore, memory lost via a leak is lost only to your program, not the whole system.

The last problem with pointers is the lack of type-safe access. This can occur because MASM cannot and does not enforce pointer type checking. For example, consider the program in Listing 4-5.

```
; Listing 4-5

; Demonstration of lack of type
; checking in assembly language
; pointer access.

        option  casemap:none

nl        =      10
maxLen    =      256


        .const
ttlStr   byte    "Listing 4-5", 0
prompt   byte    "Input a string: ", 0
fmtStr   byte    "%d: Hex value of char read: %x", nl, 0


        .data
bufPtr   qword   ?
bytesRead qword  ?

        .code
        externdef readLine:proc
        externdef printf:proc
```

```
        externdef malloc:proc
        externdef free:proc

; Return program title to C++ program:

        public getTitle
getTitle proc
        lea  rax, ttlStr
        ret
getTitle endp

; Here is the "asmMain" function.

        public  asmMain
asmMain proc
        push  rbx              ; Preserve RBX

; "Magic" instruction offered without
; explanation at this point:

        sub   rsp, 40

; C standard library malloc function.
; Allocate sufficient characters
; to hold a line of text input
; by the user:

        mov   rcx, maxLen      ; Allocate 256 bytes
        call  malloc
        mov   bufPtr, rax      ; Save pointer to buffer

; Read a line of text from the user and place in
; the newly allocated buffer:

        lea   rcx, prompt      ; Prompt user to input
        call  printf           ; a line of text

        mov   rcx, bufPtr      ; Pointer to input buffer
        mov   rdx, maxLen      ; Maximum input buffer length
        call  readLine         ; Read text from user
        cmp   rax, -1          ; Skip output if error
        je    allDone
        mov   bytesRead, rax   ; Save number of chars read

; Display the data input by the user:

        xor   rbx, rbx         ; Set index to zero
displp: mov   r9, bufPtr       ; Pointer to buffer
        mov   rdx, rbx         ; Display index into buffer
        mov   r8d, [r9+rbx*1]  ; Read dword rather than byte!
        lea   rcx, fmtStr
        call  printf
```

```
        inc     rbx                ; Repeat for each char in buffer
        cmp     rbx, bytesRead
        jb      dispLp

; Free the storage by calling
; C standard library free function.

; free(bufPtr);

allDone:
        mov     rcx, bufPtr
        call    free

        add     rsp, 40
        pop     rbx     ; Restore RBX
        ret             ; Returns to caller
asmMain endp
        end
```

Listing 4-5: Type-unsafe pointer access example

Here are the commands to build and run this sample program:

```
C:\>build listing4-5

C:\>echo off
 Assembling: listing4-5.asm
c.cpp

C:\>listing4-5
Calling Listing 4-5:
Input a string: Hello, World!
0: Hex value of char read: 6c6c6548
1: Hex value of char read: 6f6c6c65
2: Hex value of char read: 2c6f6c6c
3: Hex value of char read: 202c6f6c
4: Hex value of char read: 57202c6f
5: Hex value of char read: 6f57202c
6: Hex value of char read: 726f5720
7: Hex value of char read: 6c726f57
8: Hex value of char read: 646c726f
9: Hex value of char read: 21646c72
10: Hex value of char read: 21646c
11: Hex value of char read: 2164
12: Hex value of char read: 21
13: Hex value of char read: 5c000000
Listing 4-5 terminated
```

The program in Listing 4-5 reads data from the user as character values and then displays the data as double-word hexadecimal values. While a powerful feature of assembly language is that it lets you ignore data types at will and automatically coerce the data without any effort, this power is a two-edged sword. If you make a mistake and access indirect data by using the wrong data type, MASM and the x86-64 may not catch the mistake, and your program may produce inaccurate results. Therefore, when using pointers and indirection in your programs, you need to take care that you use the data consistently with respect to data type.

This demonstration program has one fundamental flaw that could create a problem for you: when reading the last two characters of the input buffer, the program accesses data beyond the characters input by the user. If the user inputs 255 characters (plus the zero-terminating byte that readLine() appends), this program will access data beyond the end of the buffer allocated by malloc(). In theory, this could cause the program to crash. This is yet another problem that can occur when accessing data by using the wrong type via pointers.

4.7 Composite Data Types

Composite data types, also known as *aggregate data types*, are those that are built up from other (generally scalar) data types. The next sections cover several of the more important composite data types—character strings, arrays, multi-dimensional arrays, records/structs, and unions. A string is a good example of a composite data type; it is a data structure built up from a sequence of individual characters and other data.

4.8 Character Strings

After integer values, *character strings* are probably the most common data type that modern programs use. The x86-64 does support a handful of string instructions, but these instructions are really intended for block memory operations, not a specific implementation of a character string. Therefore, this section will provide a couple of definitions of character strings and discuss how to process them.

In general, a character string is a sequence of ASCII characters that possesses two main attributes: a *length* and *character data*. Different languages use different data structures to represent strings. Assembly language (at least, sans any library routines) doesn't really care how you implement strings. All you need to do is create a sequence of machine instructions to process the string data in whatever format the strings take.

4.8.1 Zero-Terminated Strings

Without question, *zero-terminated strings* are the most common string representation in use today because this is the native string format for C, C++, and other languages. A zero-terminated string consists of a sequence of zero or more ASCII characters ending with a 0 byte. For example, in C/C++, the string "abc" requires 4 bytes: the three characters a, b, and c followed by a 0. As you'll soon see, MASM character strings are upward compatible with zero-terminated strings, but in the meantime, you should note that creating zero-terminated strings in MASM is easy. The easiest place to do this is in the .data section by using code like the following:

```
        .data
zeroString byte    "This is the zero-terminated string", 0
```

Whenever a character string appears in the byte directive as it does here, MASM emits each character in the string to successive memory locations. The zero value at the end of the string terminates this string.

Zero-terminated strings have two principal attributes: they are simple to implement, and the strings can be any length. On the other hand, zero-terminated strings have a few drawbacks. First, though not usually important, zero-terminated strings cannot contain the NUL character (whose ASCII code is 0). Generally, this isn't a problem, but it does create havoc once in a while. The second problem with zero-terminated strings is that many operations on them are somewhat inefficient. For example, to compute the length of a zero-terminated string, you must scan the entire string looking for that 0 byte (counting characters up to the 0). The following program fragment demonstrates how to compute the length of the preceding string:

```
        lea rbx, zeroString
        xor rax, rax     ; Set RAX to zero
whileLp: cmp byte ptr [rbx+rax*1], 0
        je  endwhile

        inc rax
        jmp whileLp

endwhile:

; String length is now in RAX.
```

As you can see from this code, the time it takes to compute the length of the string is proportional to the length of the string; as the string gets longer, it takes longer to compute its length.

4.8.2 Length-Prefixed Strings

The *length-prefixed string* format overcomes some of the problems with zero-terminated strings. Length-prefixed strings are common in languages like Pascal; they generally consist of a length byte followed by zero or more character values. The first byte specifies the string length, and the following bytes (up to the specified length) are the character data. In a length-prefixed scheme, the string "abc" would consist of the 4 bytes: 03 (the string length) followed by a, b, and c. You can create length-prefixed strings in MASM by using code like the following:

```
        .data
lengthPrefixedString label byte;
        byte 3, "abc"
```

Counting the characters ahead of time and inserting them into the byte statement, as was done here, may seem like a major pain. Fortunately, there are ways to have MASM automatically compute the string length for you.

Length-prefixed strings solve the two major problems associated with zero-terminated strings. It is possible to include the NUL character in length-prefixed strings, and those operations on zero-terminated strings that are relatively inefficient (for example, string length) are more efficient when using length-prefixed strings. However, length-prefixed strings have their own drawbacks. The principal drawback is that they are limited to a maximum of 255 characters in length (assuming a 1-byte length prefix).

Of course, if you have a problem with a string length limitation of 255 characters, it's perfectly possible to create a length-prefixed string by using any number of bytes for the length as needed. For example, the *High-Level Assembler (HLA)* uses a 4-byte length variant of length-prefixed strings, allowing strings up to 4GB long.[6] The point is that in assembly language, you can define string formats however you like.

If you want to create length-prefixed strings in your assembly language programs, you don't want to have to manually count the characters in the string and emit that length in your code. It's far better to have the assembler do this kind of grunge work for you. This is easily accomplished using the location counter operator ($) as follows:

```
      .data
lengthPrefixedString label byte;
      byte lpsLen, "abc"
lpsLen = $-lengthPrefixedString-1
```

The `lpsLen` operand subtracts 1 in the address expression because `$-lengthPrefixedString` also includes the length prefix byte, which isn't considered part of the string length.

4.8.3   String Descriptors

Another common string format is a *string descriptor*. A string descriptor is typically a small data structure (record or structure, see "Records/Structs" on page 197) that contains several pieces of data describing a string. At a bare minimum, a string descriptor will probably have a pointer to the actual string data and a field specifying the number of characters in the string (that is, the string length). Other possible fields might include the number of bytes currently occupied by the string,[7] the maximum number of bytes the string could occupy, the string encoding (for example, ASCII, Latin-1, UTF-8, or UTF-16), and any other information the string data structure's designer could dream up.

---

6. Visit *https://artofasm.randallhyde.com/* for more details on the High-Level Assembler.

7. The number of bytes could be different from the number of characters in the string if the string encoding includes multi-byte character sequences, such as what you would find in UTF-8 or UTF-16 encodings.

By far, the most common descriptor format incorporates a pointer to the string's data and a size field specifying the number of bytes currently occupied by that string data. Note that this particular string descriptor is not the same thing as a length-prefixed string. In a length-prefixed string, the length immediately precedes the character data itself. In a descriptor, the length and a pointer are kept together, and this pair is (usually) separate from the character data itself.

4.8.4 Pointers to Strings

Most of the time, an assembly language program won't directly work with strings appearing in the .data (or .const or .data?) section. Instead, the program will work with pointers to strings (including strings whose storage the program has dynamically allocated with a call to a function like malloc()). Listing 4-5 provided a simple (if not broken) example. In such applications, your assembly code will typically load a pointer to a string into a base register and then use a second (index) register to access individual characters in the string.

4.8.5 String Functions

Unfortunately, very few assemblers provide a set of string functions you can call from your assembly language programs.[8] As an assembly language programmer, you're expected to write these functions on your own. Fortunately, a couple of solutions are available if you don't quite feel up to the task.

The first set of string functions you can call (without having to write them yourself) is the C Standard Library string functions (from the *string.h* header file in C). Of course, you'll have to use C strings (zero-terminated strings) in your code when calling C Standard Library functions, but this generally isn't a big problem. Listing 4-6 provides examples of calls to various C string functions.

```
; Listing 4-6

; Calling C Standard Library string functions.

        option  casemap:none

nl      =       10
maxLen  =       256

        .const
ttlStr  byte    "Listing 4-6", 0
prompt  byte    "Input a string: ", 0
fmtStr1 byte    "After strncpy, resultStr='%s'", nl, 0
```

---

8. The High-Level Assembler (HLA) is a notable exception. The HLA Standard Library includes a wide set of string functions written in HLA. Were it not for the HLA Standard Library being all 32-bit code, you would have been able to call those functions from your MASM code. That being said, it isn't that difficult to rewrite the HLA library functions in MASM. You can obtain the HLA Standard Library source code from *https://artofasm .randallhyde.com/* if you care to try this.

```
fmtStr2     byte    "After strncat, resultStr='%s'", nl, 0
fmtStr3     byte    "After strcmp (3), eax=%d", nl, 0
fmtStr4     byte    "After strcmp (4), eax=%d", nl, 0
fmtStr5     byte    "After strcmp (5), eax=%d", nl, 0
fmtStr6     byte    "After strchr, rax='%s'", nl, 0
fmtStr7     byte    "After strstr, rax='%s'", nl, 0
fmtStr8     byte    "resultStr length is %d", nl, 0

str1        byte    "Hello, ", 0
str2        byte    "World!", 0
str3        byte    "Hello, World!", 0
str4        byte    "hello, world!", 0
str5        byte    "HELLO, WORLD!", 0

            .data
strLength dword ?
resultStr byte  maxLen dup (?)

            .code
            externdef readLine:proc
            externdef printf:proc
            externdef malloc:proc
            externdef free:proc

; Some C standard library string functions:

; size_t strlen(char *str)

            externdef strlen:proc

; char *strncat(char *dest, const char *src, size_t n)

            externdef strncat:proc

; char *strchr(const char *str, int c)

            externdef strchr:proc

; int strcmp(const char *str1, const char *str2)

            externdef strcmp:proc

; char *strncpy(char *dest, const char *src, size_t n)

            externdef strncpy:proc

; char *strstr(const char *inStr, const char *search4)

            externdef strstr:proc

; Return program title to C++ program:

            public getTitle
getTitle proc
            lea rax, ttlStr
```

```
        ret
getTitle endp

; Here is the "asmMain" function.

        public  asmMain
asmMain proc

; "Magic" instruction offered without
; explanation at this point:

        sub     rsp, 48

; Demonstrate the strncpy function to copy a
; string from one location to another:

        lea     rcx, resultStr  ; Destination string
        lea     rdx, str1       ; Source string
        mov     r8, maxLen      ; Max number of chars to copy
        call    strncpy

        lea     rcx, fmtStr1
        lea     rdx, resultStr
        call    printf

; Demonstrate the strncat function to concatenate str2 to
; the end of resultStr:

        lea     rcx, resultStr
        lea     rdx, str2
        mov     r8, maxLen
        call    strncat

        lea     rcx, fmtStr2
        lea     rdx, resultStr
        call    printf

; Demonstrate the strcmp function to compare resultStr
; with str3, str4, and str5:

        lea     rcx, resultStr
        lea     rdx, str3
        call    strcmp

        lea     rcx, fmtStr3
        mov     rdx, rax
        call    printf

        lea     rcx, resultStr
        lea     rdx, str4
        call    strcmp

        lea     rcx, fmtStr4
        mov     rdx, rax
        call    printf
```

```
        lea     rcx, resultStr
        lea     rdx, str5
        call    strcmp

        lea     rcx, fmtStr5
        mov     rdx, rax
        call    printf

; Demonstrate the strchr function to search for
; "," in resultStr:

        lea     rcx, resultStr
        mov     rdx, ','
        call    strchr

        lea     rcx, fmtStr6
        mov     rdx, rax
        call    printf

; Demonstrate the strstr function to search for
; str2 in resultStr:

        lea     rcx, resultStr
        lea     rdx, str2
        call    strstr

        lea     rcx, fmtStr7
        mov     rdx, rax
        call    printf

; Demonstrate a call to the strlen function:

        lea     rcx, resultStr
        call    strlen

        lea     rcx, fmtStr8
        mov     rdx, rax
        call    printf

        add     rsp, 48
        ret             ; Returns to caller
asmMain endp
        end
```

Listing 4-6: Calling C Standard Library string function from MASM source code

Here are the commands to build and run Listing 4-6:

```
C:\>build listing4-6

C:\>echo off
 Assembling: listing4-6.asm
c.cpp
```

```
C:\>listing4-6
Calling Listing 4-6:
After strncpy, resultStr='Hello, '
After strncat, resultStr='Hello, World!'
After strcmp (3), eax=0
After strcmp (4), eax=-1
After strcmp (5), eax=1
After strchr, rax=', World!'
After strstr, rax='World!'
resultStr length is 13
Listing 4-6 terminated
```

Of course, you could make a good argument that if all your assembly code does is call a bunch of C Standard Library functions, you should have written your application in C in the first place. Most of the benefits of writing code in assembly language happen only when you "think" in assembly language, not C. In particular, you can dramatically improve the performance of your string function calls if you stop using zero-terminated strings and switch to another string format (such as length-prefixed or descriptor-based strings that include a length component).

In addition to the C Standard Library, you can find lots of x86-64 string functions written in assembly language out on the internet. A good place to start is the MASM Forum at *https://masm32.com/board/* (despite the name, this message forum supports 64-bit as well as 32-bit MASM programming). Chapter 14 discusses string functions written in assembly language in greater detail.

4.9 Arrays

Along with strings, arrays are probably the most commonly used composite data. Yet most beginning programmers don't understand how arrays operate internally and their associated efficiency trade-offs. It's surprising how many novice (and even advanced!) programmers view arrays from a completely different perspective once they learn how to deal with arrays at the machine level.

Abstractly, an *array* is an aggregate data type whose members (elements) are all the same type. Selection of a member from the array is by an integer index.[9] Different indices select unique elements of the array. This book assumes that the integer indices are contiguous (though this is by no means required). That is, if the number x is a valid index into the array and y is also a valid index, with $x < y$, then all i such that $x < i < y$ are valid indices.

Whenever you apply the indexing operator to an array, the result is the specific array element chosen by that index. For example, A[i] chooses the *i*th element from array A. There is no formal requirement that element i be anywhere near element i+1 in memory. As long as A[i] always refers to the

---

9. Or it could be a value whose underlying representation is integer, such as character, enumerated, and Boolean types.

same memory location and A[i+1] always refers to its corresponding location (and the two are different), the definition of an array is satisfied.

In this book, we assume that array elements occupy contiguous locations in memory. An array with five elements will appear in memory as Figure 4-1 shows.

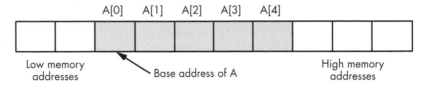

Figure 4-1: Array layout in memory

The *base address* of an array is the address of the first element in the array and always appears in the lowest memory location. The second array element directly follows the first in memory, the third element follows the second, and so on. Indices are not required to start at zero. They may start with any number as long as they are contiguous. However, for the purposes of discussion, this book will start all indexes at zero.

To access an element of an array, you need a function that translates an array index to the address of the indexed element. For a single-dimensional array, this function is very simple:

element_address = base_address + ((index - initial_index) * element_size)

where *initial_index* is the value of the first index in the array (which you can ignore if it's zero), and the value *element_size* is the size, in bytes, of an individual array element.

4.9.1 Declaring Arrays in Your MASM Programs

Before you can access elements of an array, you need to set aside storage for that array. Fortunately, array declarations build on the declarations you've already seen. To allocate *n* elements in an array, you would use a declaration like the following in one of the variable declaration sections:

array_name *base_type* n dup (?)

array_name is the name of the array variable, and *base_type* is the type of an element of that array. This declaration sets aside storage for the array. To obtain the base address of the array, just use *array_name*.

The n dup (?) operand tells MASM to duplicate the object n times. Now let's look at some specific examples:

```
        .data

; Character array with elements 0 to 127.

CharArray  byte 128 dup (?)
```

```
; Array of bytes with elements 0 to 9.

ByteArray  byte  10 dup (?)

; Array of double words with elements 0 to 3.

DWArray    dword  4 dup (?)
```

These examples all allocate storage for uninitialized arrays. You may also specify that the elements of the arrays be initialized using declarations like the following in the .data and .const sections:

```
RealArray   real4  1.0, 1.0, 1.0, 1.0, 1.0, 1.0, 1.0, 1.0
IntegerAry  sdword 1, 1, 1, 1, 1, 1, 1, 1
```

Both definitions create arrays with eight elements. The first definition initializes each 4-byte real value to 1.0, and the second declaration initializes each 32-bit integer (sdword) element to 1.

If all the array elements have the same initial value, you can save a little work by using the following declarations:

```
RealArray   real4  8 dup (1.0)
IntegerAry  sdword 8 dup (1)
```

These operand fields tell MASM to make eight copies of the value inside the parentheses. In past examples, this has always been ? (an uninitialized value). However, you can put an initial value inside the parentheses, and MASM will duplicate that value. In fact, you can put a comma-separated list of values, and MASM will duplicate everything inside the parentheses:

```
RealArray   real4  4 dup (1.0, 2.0)
IntegerAry  sdword 4 dup (1, 2)
```

These two examples also create eight-element arrays. Their initial values will be 1.0, 2.0, 1.0, 2.0, 1.0, 2.0, 1.0, 2.0, and 1, 2, 1, 2, 1, 2, 1, 2, respectively.

4.9.2 Accessing Elements of a Single-Dimensional Array

To access an element of a zero-based array, you can use this formula:

```
element_address = base_address + index * element_size
```

If you are operating in LARGEADDRESSAWARE:NO mode, for the *base_address* entry you can use the name of the array (because MASM associates the address of the first element of an array with the name of that array). If you are operating in a large address mode, you'll need to load the base address of the array into a 64-bit (base) register; for example:

```
lea rbx, base_address
```

The *element_size* entry is the number of bytes for each array element. If the object is an array of bytes, the *element_size* field is 1 (resulting in a very simple computation). If each element of the array is a word (or other 2-byte type), then *element_size* is 2, and so on. To access an element of the IntegerAry array in the previous section, you'd use the following formula (the size is 4 because each element is an sdword object):

```
element_address = IntegerAry + (index * 4)
```

Assuming LARGEADDRESSAWARE:NO, the x86-64 code equivalent to the statement eax = IntegerAry[index] is as follows:

```
mov rbx, index
mov eax, IntegerAry[rbx*4]
```

In large address mode (LARGEADDRESSAWARE:YES), you'd have to load the address of the array into a base register; for example:

```
lea rdx, IntegerAry
mov rbx, index
mov eax, [rdx + rbx*4]
```

These two instructions don't explicitly multiply the index register (RBX) by 4 (the size of a 32-bit integer element in IntegerAry). Instead, they use the scaled-indexed address mode to perform the multiplication.

Another thing to note about this instruction sequence is that it does not explicitly compute the sum of the base address plus the index times 4. Instead, it relies on the scaled-indexed addressing mode to implicitly compute this sum. The instruction mov eax, IntegerAry[rbx*4] loads EAX from location IntegerAry + rbx*4, which is the base address plus index*4 (because RBX contains index*4). Similarly, mov eax, [rdx+rbx*4] computes this same sum as part of the addressing mode. Sure, you could have used

```
lea rax, IntegerAry
mov rbx, index
shl rbx, 2      ; Sneaky way to compute 4 * RBX
add rbx, rax    ; Compute base address plus index * 4
mov eax, [rbx]
```

in place of the previous sequence, but why use five instructions when two or three will do the same job? This is a good example of why you should know your addressing modes inside and out. Choosing the proper addressing mode can reduce the size of your program, thereby speeding it up.

However, if you need to multiply by a constant other than 1, 2, 4, or 8, then you cannot use the scaled-indexed addressing modes. Similarly, if you need to multiply by an element size that is not a power of 2, you will not be able to use the shl instruction to multiply the index by the element size; instead, you will have to use imul or another instruction sequence to do the multiplication.

The indexed addressing mode on the x86-64 is a natural for accessing elements of a single-dimensional array. Indeed, its syntax even suggests an array access. The important thing to keep in mind is that you must remember to multiply the index by the size of an element. Failure to do so will produce incorrect results.

The examples appearing in this section assume that the index variable is a 64-bit value. In reality, integer indexes into arrays are generally 32-bit integers or 32-bit unsigned integers. Therefore, you'd typically use the following instruction to load the index value into RBX:

```
mov ebx, index  ; Zero-extends into RBX
```

Because loading a 32-bit value into a general-purpose register automatically zero-extends that register to 64 bits, the former instruction sequences (which expect a 64-bit index value) will still work properly when you're using 32-bit integers as indexes into an array.

4.9.3 Sorting an Array of Values

Almost every textbook on this planet gives an example of a sort when introducing arrays. Because you've probably seen how to do a sort in high-level languages already, it's instructive to take a quick look at a sort in MASM. Listing 4-7 uses a variant of the bubble sort, which is great for short lists of data and lists that are nearly sorted, but horrible for just about everything else.[10]

```
; Listing 4-7

; A simple bubble sort example.

; Note: This example must be assembled
; and linked with LARGEADDRESSAWARE:NO.

        option  casemap:none

nl      =       10
maxLen  =       256
true    =       1
false   =       0

bool    typedef ptr byte

        .const
ttlStr  byte    "Listing 4-7", 0
fmtStr  byte    "Sortme[%d] = %d", nl, 0

        .data
```

---

10. Fear not, you'll see some better sorting algorithms in Chapter 5.

```
        ; sortMe - A 16-element array to sort:

sortMe  label   dword
        dword   1, 2, 16, 14
        dword   3, 9, 4,  10
        dword   5, 7, 15, 12  ·
        dword   8, 6, 11, 13
sortSize = ($ - sortMe) / sizeof dword     ; Number of elements

        ; didSwap - A Boolean value that indicates
        ;           whether a swap occurred on the
        ;           last loop iteration.

didSwap bool    ?

        .code
        externdef printf:proc

; Return program title to C++ program:

        public getTitle
getTitle proc
        lea     rax, ttlStr
        ret
getTitle endp

; Here's the bubblesort function.

;       sort(dword *array, qword count);

; Note: this is not an external (C)
; function, nor does it call any
; external functions. So it will
; dispense with some of the Windows
; calling sequence stuff.

; array - Address passed in RCX.
; count - Element count passed in RDX.

sort    proc
        push    rax             ; In pure assembly language
        push    rbx             ; it's always a good idea
        push    rcx             ; to preserve all registers
        push    rdx             ; you modify
        push    r8

        dec     rdx             ; numElements - 1

; Outer loop:

outer:  mov     didSwap, false

        xor     rbx, rbx        ; RBX = 0
inner:  cmp     rbx, rdx        ; while RBX < count - 1
        jnb     xInner
```

```
        mov     eax, [rcx + rbx*4]      ; EAX = sortMe[RBX]
        cmp     eax, [rcx + rbx*4 + 4]  ; If EAX > sortMe[RBX + 1]
        jna     dontSwap                ; then swap

        ; sortMe[RBX] > sortMe[RBX + 1], so swap elements:

        mov     r8d, [rcx + rbx*4 + 4]
        mov     [rcx + rbx*4 + 4], eax
        mov     [rcx + rbx*4], r8d
        mov     didSwap, true

dontSwap:
        inc     rbx                     ; Next loop iteration
        jmp     inner

; Exited from inner loop, test for repeat
; of outer loop:

xInner: cmp     didSwap, true
        je      outer

        pop     r8
        pop     rdx
        pop     rcx
        pop     rbx
        pop     rax
        ret
sort    endp

; Here is the "asmMain" function.

        public  asmMain
asmMain proc
        push    rbx

; "Magic" instruction offered without
; explanation at this point:

        sub     rsp, 40

; Sort the "sortMe" array:

        lea     rcx, sortMe
        mov     rdx, sortSize           ; 16 elements in array
        call    sort

; Display the sorted array:

        xor     rbx, rbx
displp: mov     r8d, sortMe[rbx*4]
        mov     rdx, rbx
        lea     rcx, fmtStr
        call    printf
```

```
          inc     rbx
          cmp     rbx, sortSize
          jb      displp

          add     rsp, 40
          pop     rbx
          ret     ; Returns to caller
asmMain endp
          end
```

Listing 4-7: A simple bubble sort example

Here are the commands to assemble and run this sample code:

```
C:\>sbuild listing4-7

C:\>echo off
 Assembling: listing4-7.asm
c.cpp

C:\>listing4-7
Calling Listing 4-7:
Sortme[0] = 1
Sortme[1] = 2
Sortme[2] = 3
Sortme[3] = 4
Sortme[4] = 5
Sortme[5] = 6
Sortme[6] = 7
Sortme[7] = 8
Sortme[8] = 9
Sortme[9] = 10
Sortme[10] = 11
Sortme[11] = 12
Sortme[12] = 13
Sortme[13] = 14
Sortme[14] = 15
Sortme[15] = 16
Listing 4-7 terminated
```

The bubble sort works by comparing adjacent elements in an array. The cmp instruction (before ; if EAX > sortMe[RBX + 1]) compares EAX (which contains sortMe[rbx*4]) against sortMe[rbx*4 + 4]. Because each element of this array is 4 bytes (dword), the index [rbx*4 + 4] references the next element beyond [rbx*4].

As is typical for a bubble sort, this algorithm terminates if the innermost loop completes without swapping any data. If the data is already presorted, the bubble sort is very efficient, making only one pass over the data. Unfortunately, if the data is not sorted (worst case, if the data is sorted in reverse order), then this algorithm is extremely inefficient. However, the bubble sort is easy to implement and understand (which is why introductory texts continue to use it in examples).

4.10 Multidimensional Arrays

The x86-64 hardware can easily handle single-dimensional arrays. Unfortunately, there is no magic addressing mode that lets you easily access elements of multidimensional arrays. That's going to take some work and several instructions.

Before discussing how to declare or access multidimensional arrays, it would be a good idea to figure out how to implement them in memory. The first problem is to figure out how to store a multidimensional object into a one-dimensional memory space.

Consider for a moment a Pascal array of the form A:array[0..3,0..3] of char;. This array contains 16 bytes organized as four rows of four characters. Somehow, you've got to draw a correspondence with each of the 16 bytes in this array and 16 contiguous bytes in main memory. Figure 4-2 shows one way to do this.

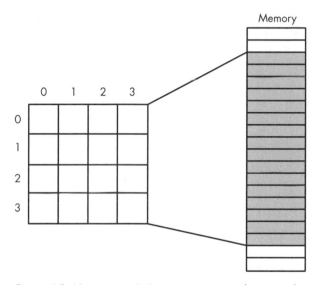

Figure 4-2: Mapping a 4×4 array to sequential memory locations

The actual mapping is not important as long as two things occur: (1) each element maps to a unique memory location (that is, no two entries in the array occupy the same memory locations) and (2) the mapping is consistent (that is, a given element in the array always maps to the same memory location). So, what you really need is a function with two input parameters (row and column) that produces an offset into a linear array of 16 memory locations.

Now any function that satisfies these constraints will work fine. Indeed, you could randomly choose a mapping as long as it was consistent. However, what you really want is a mapping that is efficient to compute at runtime and works for any size array (not just 4×4 or even limited to two dimensions). While a large number of possible functions fit this bill, two functions in particular are used by most programmers and high-level languages: row-major ordering and column-major ordering.

4.10.1 Row-Major Ordering

Row-major ordering assigns successive elements, moving across the rows and then down the columns, to successive memory locations. This mapping is demonstrated in Figure 4-3.

Memory

A:array[0..3, 0..3] of char;

	0	1	2	3
0	0	1	2	3
1	4	5	6	7
2	8	9	10	11
3	12	13	14	15

15 A[3,3]
14 A[3,2]
13 A[3,1]
12 A[3,0]
11 A[2,3]
10 A[2,2]
9 A[2,1]
8 A[2,0]
7 A[1,3]
6 A[1,2]
5 A[1,1]
4 A[1,0]
3 A[0,3]
2 A[0,2]
1 A[0,1]
0 A[0,0]

Figure 4-3: Row-major array element ordering

Row-major ordering is the method most high-level programming languages employ. It is easy to implement and use in machine language. You start with the first row (row 0) and then concatenate the second row to its end. You then concatenate the third row to the end of the list, then the fourth row, and so on (see Figure 4-4).

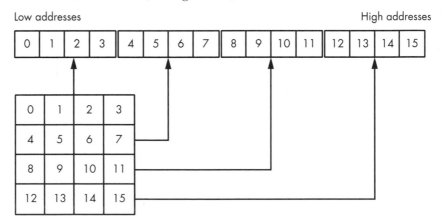

Figure 4-4: Another view of row-major ordering for a 4×4 array

The actual function that converts a list of index values into an offset is a slight modification of the formula for computing the address of an element of a single-dimensional array. The formula to compute the offset for a two-dimensional row-major ordered array is as follows:

```
element_address =
    base_address + (col_index * row_size + row_index) * element_size
```

As usual, *base_address* is the address of the first element of the array (A[0][0] in this case), and *element_size* is the size of an individual element of the array, in bytes. *col_index* is the leftmost index, and *row_index* is the rightmost index into the array. *row_size* is the number of elements in one row of the array (4, in this case, because each row has four elements). Assuming *element_size* is 1, this formula computes the following offsets from the base address:

Column Index	Row Index	Offset into Array
0	0	0
0	1	1
0	2	2
0	3	3
1	0	4
1	1	5
1	2	6
1	3	7
2	0	8
2	1	9
2	2	10
2	3	11
3	0	12
3	1	13
3	2	14
3	3	15

For a three-dimensional array, the formula to compute the offset into memory is the following:

```
Address = Base +
    ((depth_index * col_size + col_index) * row_size + row_index) * element_size
```

The *col_size* is the number of items in a column, and *row_size* is the number of items in a row. In C/C++, if you've declared the array as *type* A[i][j][k];, then *row_size* is equal to k and *col_size* is equal to j.

For a four-dimensional array, declared in C/C++ as *type* A[i][j][k][m];, the formula for computing the address of an array element is shown here:

```
Address = Base +
    (((left_index * depth_size + depth_index) * col_size + col_index) *
    row_size + row_index) * element_size
```

The *depth_size* is equal to j, *col_size* is equal to k, and *row_size* is equal to m. *left_index* represents the value of the leftmost index.

By now you're probably beginning to see a pattern. There is a generic formula that will compute the offset into memory for an array with *any* number of dimensions; however, you'll rarely use more than four.

Another convenient way to think of row-major arrays is as arrays of arrays. Consider the following single-dimensional Pascal array definition:

```
A: array [0..3] of sometype;
```

where sometype is the type sometype = array [0..3] of char;.

A is a single-dimensional array. Its individual elements happen to be arrays, but you can safely ignore that for the time being. The formula to compute the address of an element of a single-dimensional array is as follows:

```
element_address = Base + index * element_size
```

In this case, *element_size* happens to be 4 because each element of A is an array of four characters. So, this formula computes the base address of each row in this 4×4 array of characters (see Figure 4-5).

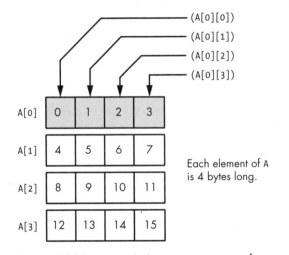

Figure 4-5: Viewing a 4×4 array as an array of arrays

Of course, once you compute the base address of a row, you can reapply the single-dimensional formula to get the address of a particular element. While this doesn't affect the computation, it's probably a little easier to deal with several single-dimensional computations rather than a complex multi-dimensional array computation.

Consider a Pascal array defined as A:array [0..3, 0..3, 0..3, 0..3, 0..3] of char;. You can view this five-dimensional array as a single-dimensional array of arrays. The following Pascal code provides such a definition:

```
type
  OneD   = array[0..3] of char;
  TwoD   = array[0..3] of OneD;
  ThreeD = array[0..3] of TwoD;
  FourD  = array[0..3] of ThreeD;
var
  A: array[0..3] of FourD;
```

The size of OneD is 4 bytes. Because TwoD contains four OneD arrays, its size is 16 bytes. Likewise, ThreeD is four TwoDs, so it is 64 bytes long. Finally, FourD is four ThreeDs, so it is 256 bytes long. To compute the address of A [b, c, d, e, f], you could use the following steps:

1. Compute the address of A[b] as *Base* + b * *size*. Here *size* is 256 bytes. Use this result as the new base address in the next computation.

2. Compute the address of A[b, c] by the formula *Base* + c * *size*, where *Base* is the value obtained in the previous step and *size* is 64. Use the result as the new base in the next computation.

3. Compute the base address of A [b, c, d] by *Base* + d * *size*, where *Base* comes from the previous computation, and *size* is 16. Use the result as the new base in the next computation.

4. Compute the address of A[b, c, d, e] with the formula *Base* + e * *size*, where *Base* comes from the previous computation, and *size* is 4. Use this value as the base for the next computation.

5. Finally, compute the address of A[b, c, d, e, f] by using the formula *Base* + f * *size*, where *Base* comes from the previous computation and *size* is 1 (obviously, you can ignore this final multiplication). The result you obtain at this point is the address of the desired element.

One of the main reasons you won't find higher-dimensional arrays in assembly language is that assembly language emphasizes the inefficiencies associated with such access. It's easy to enter something like A[b, c, d, e, f] into a Pascal program, not realizing what the compiler is doing with the code. Assembly language programmers are not so cavalier—they see the mess you wind up with when you use higher-dimensional arrays. Indeed, good assembly language programmers try to avoid two-dimensional arrays and often resort to tricks in order to access data in such an array when its use becomes absolutely mandatory.

4.10.2 Column-Major Ordering

Column-major ordering is the other function high-level languages frequently use to compute the address of an array element. FORTRAN and various dialects of BASIC (for example, older versions of Microsoft BASIC) use this method.

In row-major ordering, the rightmost index increases the fastest as you move through consecutive memory locations. In column-major ordering, the leftmost index increases the fastest. Pictorially, a column-major ordered array is organized as shown in Figure 4-6.

The formula for computing the address of an array element when using column-major ordering is similar to that for row-major ordering. You reverse the indexes and sizes in the computation.

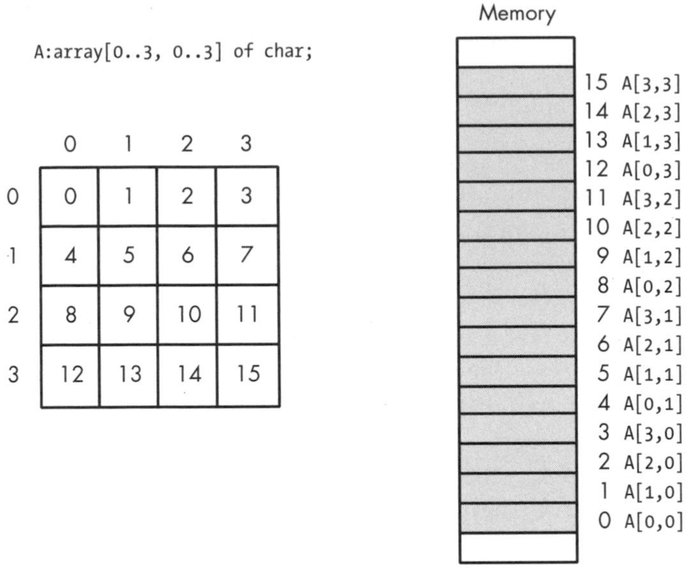

```
A:array[0..3, 0..3] of char;
```

Memory

	0	1	2	3
0	0	1	2	3
1	4	5	6	7
2	8	9	10	11
3	12	13	14	15

```
15 A[3,3]
14 A[2,3]
13 A[1,3]
12 A[0,3]
11 A[3,2]
10 A[2,2]
 9 A[1,2]
 8 A[0,2]
 7 A[3,1]
 6 A[2,1]
 5 A[1,1]
 4 A[0,1]
 3 A[3,0]
 2 A[2,0]
 1 A[1,0]
 0 A[0,0]
```

Figure 4-6: Column-major array element ordering

For a two-dimension column-major array:

```
element_address = base_address + (row_index * col_size + col_index) *
    element_size
```

For a three-dimension column-major array:

```
Address = Base +
    ((row_index * col_size + col_index) *
    depth_size + depth_index) * element_size
```

For a four-dimension column-major array:

```
Address =
    Base + (((row_index * col_size + col_index) * depth_size + depth_index)
    left_size + left_index) * element_size
```

4.10.3 Allocating Storage for Multidimensional Arrays

If you have an $m \times n$ array, it will have $m \times n$ elements and require $m \times n \times$ element_size bytes of storage. To allocate storage for an array, you must reserve this memory. As usual, there are several ways of accomplishing this task. To declare a multidimensional array in MASM, you could use a declaration like the following:

```
array_name element_type size₁*size₂*size₃*...*sizeₙ dup (?)
```

where $size_1$ to $size_n$ are the sizes of each of the dimensions of the array.

For example, here is a declaration for a 4×4 array of characters:

```
GameGrid byte 4*4 dup (?)
```

Here is another example that shows how to declare a three-dimensional array of strings (assuming the array holds 64-bit pointers to the strings):

```
NameItems qword 2 * 3 * 3 dup (?)
```

As was the case with single-dimensional arrays, you may initialize every element of the array to a specific value by following the declaration with the values of the array constant. Array constants ignore dimension information; all that matters is that the number of elements in the array constant corresponds to the number of elements in the actual array. The following example shows the GameGrid declaration with an initializer:

```
GameGrid byte 'a', 'b', 'c', 'd'
         byte 'e', 'f', 'g', 'h'
         byte 'i', 'j', 'k', 'l'
         byte 'm', 'n', 'o', 'p'
```

This example was laid out to enhance readability (which is always a good idea). MASM does not interpret the four separate lines as representing rows of data in the array. Humans do, which is why it's good to write the data in this manner. All that matters is that there are 16 (4 × 4) characters in the array constant. You'll probably agree that this is much easier to read than

```
GameGrid byte  'a', 'b', 'c', 'd', 'e', 'f', 'g', 'h', 'i', 'j',
'k', 'l', 'm', 'n', 'o', 'p'
```

Of course, if you have a large array, an array with really large rows, or an array with many dimensions, there is little hope for winding up with something readable. That's when comments that carefully explain everything come in handy.

As for single-dimensional arrays, you can use the dup operator to initialize each element of a large array with the same value. The following example initializes a 256×64 array of bytes so that each byte contains the value 0FFh:

```
StateValue byte 256*64 dup (0FFh)
```

The use of a constant expression to compute the number of array elements rather than simply using the constant 16,384 (256 × 64) more clearly suggests that this code is initializing each element of a 256×64 element array than does the simple literal constant 16,384.

Another MASM trick you can use to improve the readability of your programs is to use *nested dup declarations*. The following is an example of a MASM nested dup declaration:

```
StateValue byte 256 dup (64 dup (0FFh))
```

MASM replicates anything inside the parentheses the number of times specified by the constant preceding the dup operator; this includes nested dup declarations. This example says, "Duplicate the stuff inside the parentheses 256 times." Inside the parentheses, there is a dup operator that says, "Duplicate 0FFh 64 times," so the outside dup operator duplicates the duplication of 64 0FFh values 256 times.

It is probably a good programming convention to declare multidimensional arrays by using the "dup of dup (. . . of dup)" syntax. This can make it clearer that you're creating a multidimensional array rather than a single-dimensional array with a large number of elements.

4.10.4 *Accessing Multidimensional Array Elements in Assembly Language*

Well, you've seen the formulas for computing the address of a multidimensional array element. Now it's time to see how to access elements of those arrays by using assembly language.

The mov, shl, and imul instructions make short work of the various equations that compute offsets into multidimensional arrays. Let's consider a two-dimensional array first:

```
        .data
i       sdword  ?
j       sdword  ?
TwoD    sdword  4 dup (8 dup (?))



            .
            .
            .


; To perform the operation TwoD[i,j] := 5;
; you'd use code like the following.
; Note that the array index computation is (i*8 + j)*4.

        mov ebx, i   ; Remember, zero-extends into RBX
        shl rbx, 3   ; Multiply by 8
        add ebx, j   ; Also zero-extends result into RBX[11]
        mov TwoD[rbx*4], 5
```

Note that this code does *not* require the use of a two-register addressing mode on the x86-64 (at least, not when using the LARGEADDRESSAWARE:NO option). Although an addressing mode like TwoD[rbx][rsi] looks like it should be a natural for accessing two-dimensional arrays, that isn't the purpose of this addressing mode.

Now consider a second example that uses a three-dimensional array (again, assuming LARGEADDRESSAWARE:NO):

```
        .data
i       dword   ?
```

---

11. The add instruction zero-extends into RBX, assuming the HO 32 bits of RBX were zero after the shl operation. This is generally a safe assumption, but something to keep in mind if i's value is large.

```
j        dword   ?
k        dword   ?
ThreeD   sdword  3 dup (4 dup (5 dup (?)))
                 .
                 .
                 .

; To perform the operation ThreeD[i,j,k] := ESI;
; you'd use the following code that computes
; ((i*4 + j)*5 + k)*4 as the address of ThreeD[i,j,k].

         mov  ebx, i    ; Zero-extends into RBX
         shl  ebx, 2    ; Four elements per column
         add  ebx, j
         imul ebx, 5    ; Five elements per row
         add  ebx, k
         mov  ThreeD[rbx*4], esi
```

This code uses the imul instruction to multiply the value in RBX by 5, because the shl instruction can multiply a register by only a power of 2. While there are ways to multiply the value in a register by a constant other than a power of 2, the imul instruction is more convenient.[12] Also remember that operations on the 32-bit general-purpose registers automatically zero-extend their result into the 64-bit register.

4.11 Records/Structs

Another major composite data structure is the Pascal *record* or C/C++/C# *structure*.[13] The Pascal terminology is probably better, because it tends to avoid confusion with the more general term *data structure*. However, MASM uses the term *struct*, so this book favors that term.

Whereas an array is homogeneous, with elements that are all the same type, the elements in a struct can have different types. Arrays let you select a particular element via an integer index. With structs, you must select an element (known as a *field*) by name.

The whole purpose of a structure is to let you encapsulate different, though logically related, data into a single package. The Pascal record declaration for a student is a typical example:

```
student =
    record
        Name:     string[64];
        Major:    integer;
        SSN:      string[11];
        Midterm1: integer;
```

---

12. A full discussion of multiplication by constants other than a power of 2 appears in Chapter 6.

13. Records and structures also go by other names in other languages, but most people recognize at least one of these names.

```
        Midterm2: integer;
        Final:    integer;
        Homework: integer;
        Projects: integer;
end;
```

Most Pascal compilers allocate each field in a record to contiguous memory locations. This means that Pascal will reserve the first 65 bytes for the name,[14] the next 2 bytes hold the major code (assuming a 16-bit integer), the next 12 bytes hold the Social Security number, and so on.

4.11.1 MASM Struct Declarations

In MASM, you can create record types by using the struct/ends declaration. You would encode the preceding record in MASM as follows:

```
student   struct
sName     byte    65 dup (?)  ; "Name" is a MASM reserved word
Major     word    ?
SSN       byte    12 dup (?)
Midterm1  word    ?
Midterm2  word    ?
Final     word    ?
Homework  word    ?
Projects  word    ?
student   ends
```

As you can see, the MASM declaration is similar to the Pascal declaration. To be true to the Pascal declaration, this example uses character arrays rather than strings for the sName and SSN (US Social Security number) fields. Also, the MASM declaration assumes that integers are unsigned 16-bit values (which is probably appropriate for this type of data structure).

The field names within the struct must be unique; the same name may not appear two or more times in the same record. However, all field names are local to that record. Therefore, you may reuse those field names elsewhere in the program or in different records.

The struct/ends declaration may appear anywhere in the source file as long as you define it before you use it. A struct declaration does not actually allocate any storage for a student variable. Instead, you have to explicitly declare a variable of type student. The following example demonstrates how to do this:

```
        .data
John    student  {}
```

The funny operand ({}) is a MASM-ism, just something you'll have to remember.

---

14. Strings require an extra byte, in addition to all the characters in the string, to encode the length.

The John variable declaration allocates 89 bytes of storage laid out in memory, as shown in Figure 4-7.

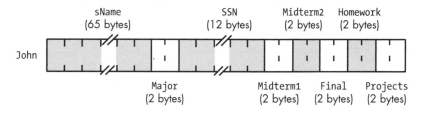

Figure 4-7: Student data structure storage in memory

If the label John corresponds to the base address of this record, the sName field is at offset John + 0, the Major field is at offset John + 65, the SSN field is at offset John + 67, and so on.

4.11.2 Accessing Record/Struct Fields

To access an element of a structure, you need to know the offset from the beginning of the structure to the desired field. For example, the Major field in the variable John is at offset 65 from the base address of John. Therefore, you could store the value in AX into this field by using this instruction:

```
mov word ptr John[65], ax
```

Unfortunately, memorizing all the offsets to fields in a struct defeats the whole purpose of using them in the first place. After all, if you have to deal with these numeric offsets, why not just use an array of bytes instead of a struct?

Fortunately, MASM lets you refer to field names in a record by using the same mechanism most HLLs use: the dot operator. To store AX into the Major field, you could use mov John.Major, ax instead of the previous instruction. This is much more readable and certainly easier to use.

The use of the dot operator does not introduce a new addressing mode. The instruction mov John.Major, ax still uses the PC-relative addressing mode. MASM simply adds the base address of John with the offset to the Major field (65) to get the actual displacement to encode into the instruction.

The dot operator works quite well when dealing with struct variables you declare in one of the static sections (.data, .const, or .data?) and access via the PC-relative addressing mode. However, what happens when you have a pointer to a record object? Consider the following code fragment:

```
mov  rcx, sizeof student  ; Size of student struct
call malloc               ; Returns pointer in RAX
mov [rax].Final, 100
```

Unfortunately, the Final field name is local to the student structure. As a result, MASM will complain that the name Final is undefined in this code sequence. To get around this problem, you add the structure name to the dotted name list when using pointer references. Here's the correct form of the preceding code:

```
mov  rcx, sizeof student  ; Size of student struct
call malloc
mov [rax].student.Final, 100
```

4.11.3 Nesting MASM Structs

MASM allows you to define fields of a structure that are themselves structure types. Consider the following two struct declarations:

```
grades    struct
Midterm1  word  ?
Midterm2  word  ?
Final     word  ?
Homework  word  ?
Projects  word  ?
grades    ends

student   struct
sName     byte  65 dup (?)  ; "Name" is a MASM reserved word
Major     word  ?
SSN       byte  12 dup (?)
sGrades   grades {}
student   ends
```

The sGrades field now holds all the individual grade fields that were formerly individual fields in the grades structure. Note that this particular example has the same memory layout as the previous examples (see Figure 4-7). The grades structure itself doesn't add any new data; it simply organizes the grade fields under its own substructure.

To access the subfields, you use the same syntax you'd use with C/C++ (and most other HLLs supporting records/structures). If the John variable declaration appearing in previous sections was of this new struct type, you'd access the Homework field by using a statement such as the following:

```
mov ax, John.sGrades.Homework
```

4.11.4 Initializing Struct Fields

A typical structure declaration such as the following

```
          .data
structVar  structType  {}
```

leaves all fields in structType uninitialized (similar to having the ? operand in other variable declarations). MASM will allow you to provide initial values for all the fields of a structure by supplying a list of comma-separated items between the braces in the operand field of a structure variable declaration, as shown in Listing 4-8.

```
; Listing 4-8

; Sample struct initialization example.

        option  casemap:none

nl      =       10

        .const
ttlStr  byte    "Listing 4-8", 0
fmtStr  byte    "aString: maxLen:%d, len:%d, string data:'%s'"
        byte    nl, 0

; Define a struct for a string descriptor:

strDesc struct
maxLen  dword   ?
len     dword   ?
strPtr  qword   ?
strDesc ends

        .data

; Here's the string data we will initialize the
; string descriptor with:

charData byte   "Initial String Data", 0
len     =       lengthof charData ; Includes zero byte

; Create a string descriptor initialized with
; the charData string value:

aString strDesc {len, len, offset charData}

        .code
        externdef printf:proc

; Return program title to C++ program:

        public getTitle
getTitle proc
        lea rax, ttlStr
        ret
getTitle endp

; Here is the "asmMain" function.

        public  asmMain
asmMain proc
```

```
; "Magic" instruction offered without
; explanation at this point:

        sub     rsp, 48

; Display the fields of the string descriptor.

        lea     rcx, fmtStr
        mov     edx, aString.maxLen ; Zero-extends!
        mov     r8d, aString.len    ; Zero-extends!
        mov     r9, aString.strPtr
        call    printf

        add     rsp, 48 ; Restore RSP
        ret             ; Returns to caller
asmMain endp
        end
```

Listing 4-8: Initializing the fields of a structure

Here are the build commands and output for Listing 4-8:

```
C:\>build listing4-8

C:\>echo off
 Assembling: listing4-8.asm
c.cpp

C:\>listing4-8
Calling Listing 4-8:
aString: maxLen:20, len:20, string data:'Initial String Data'
Listing 4-8 terminated
```

If a structure field is an array object, you'll need special syntax to initialize that array data. Consider the following structure definition:

```
aryStruct struct
aryField1 byte    8 dup (?)
aryField2 word    4 dup (?)
aryStruct ends
```

The initialization operands must either be a string or a single item. Therefore, the following is not legal:

```
a aryStruct {1,2,3,4,5,6,7,8,  1,2,3,4}
```

This (presumably) is an attempt to initialize aryField1 with {1,2,3,4,5,6,7,8} and aryField2 with {1,2,3,4}. MASM, however, won't accept this. MASM wants only two values in the operand field (one for aryField1 and one for aryField2). The solution is to place the array constants for the two arrays in their own set of braces:

```
a aryStruct {{1,2,3,4,5,6,7,8}, {1,2,3,4}}
```

If you supply too many initializers for a given array element, MASM will report an error. If you supply too few initializers, MASM will quietly fill in the remaining array entries with 0 values:

```
a aryStruct {{1,2,3,4}, {1,2,3,4}}
```

This example initializes a.aryField1 with {1,2,3,4,0,0,0,0} and initializes a.aryField2 with {1,2,3,4}.

If the field is an array of bytes, you can substitute a character string (with no more characters than the array size) for the list of byte values:

```
b aryStruct {"abcdefgh", {1,2,3,4}}
```

If you supply too few characters, MASM will fill out the rest of the byte array with 0 bytes; too many characters produce an error.

4.11.5 Arrays of Structs

It is a perfectly reasonable operation to create an array of structures. To do so, you create a struct type and then use the standard array declaration syntax. The following example demonstrates how you could do this:

```
recElement struct
    Fields for this record
recElement ends
            .
            .
            .
        .data
recArray    recElement 4 dup ({})
```

To access an element of this array, you use the standard array-indexing techniques. Because recArray is a single-dimensional array, you'd compute the address of an element of this array by using the formula *base_address* + *index* * lengthof(recElement). For example, to access an element of recArray, you'd use code like the following:

```
; Access element i of recArray:
; RBX := i*lengthof(recElement)

 imul ebx, i, sizeOf recElement    ; Zero-extends EBX to RBX!
 mov  eax, recArray.someField[rbx] ; LARGEADDRESSAWARE:NO!
```

The index specification follows the entire variable name; remember, this is assembly, not a high-level language (in a high-level language, you'd probably use recArray[i].someField).

Naturally, you can create multidimensional arrays of records as well. You would use the row-major or column-major order functions to compute the address of an element within such records. The only thing that really changes (from the discussion of arrays) is that the size of each element is the size of the record object:

```
        .data
rec2D   recElement 4 dup (6 dup ({}))

         .
         .
         .

; Access element [i,j] of rec2D and load someField into EAX:

    imul ebx, i, 6
    add  ebx, j
    imul ebx, sizeof recElement
    lea  rcx, rec2D  ; To avoid requiring LARGEADDRESS...
    mov  eax, [rcx].recElement.someField[rbx*1]
```

4.11.6 Aligning Fields Within a Record

To achieve maximum performance in your programs, or to ensure that MASM's structures properly map to records or structures in a high-level language, you will often need to be able to control the alignment of fields within a record. For example, you might want to ensure that a double-word field's offset is a multiple of four. You can use the align directive to do this. The following creates a structure with unaligned fields:

```
Padded  struct
b       byte    ?
d       dword   ?
b2      byte    ?
b3      byte    ?
w       word    ?
Padded  ends
```

Here's how MASM organizes this structure's fields in memory:[15]

Name	Size Offset	Type
Padded	00000009	
b	00000000	byte
d	00000001	dword
b2	00000005	byte
b3	00000006	byte
w	00000007	word

As you can see from this example, the d and w fields are both aligned on odd offsets, which may result in slower performance. Ideally, you would like d to be aligned on a double-word offset (multiple of four) and w aligned on an even offset.

---

15. By the way, if you would like MASM to provide you with this information, supply a /Fl command line option to *ml64.exe*. This tells MASM to produce a listing file, which contains this information.

You can fix this problem by adding `align` directives to the structure, as follows:

```
Padded  struct
b       byte    ?
        align   4
d       dword   ?
b2      byte    ?
b3      byte    ?
        align   2
w       word    ?
Padded  ends
```

Now, MASM uses the following offsets for each of these fields:

Padded	0000000C	
b	00000000	byte
d	00000004	dword
b2	00000008	byte
b3	00000009	byte
w	0000000A	word

As you can see, d is now aligned on a 4-byte offset, and w is aligned at an even offset.

MASM provides one additional option that lets you automatically align objects in a struct declaration. If you supply a value (which must be 1, 2, 4, 8, or 16) as the operand to the struct statement, MASM will automatically align all fields in the structure to an offset that is a multiple of that field's size or to the value you specify as the operand, *whichever is smaller.* Consider the following example:

```
Padded  struct  4
b       byte    ?
d       dword   ?
b2      byte    ?
b3      byte    ?
w       word    ?
Padded  ends
```

Here's the alignment MASM produces for this structure:

Padded	0000000C	
b	00000000	byte
d	00000004	dword
b2	00000008	byte
b3	00000009	byte
w	0000000A	word

Note that MASM properly aligns d on a dword boundary and w on a word boundary (within the structure). Also note that w is not aligned on a dword boundary (even though the struct operand was 4). This is because MASM uses the smaller of the operand or the field's size as the alignment value (and w's size is 2).

4.12 Unions

A record/struct definition assigns different offsets to each field in the record according to the size of those fields. This behavior is quite similar to the allocation of memory offsets in a .data?, .data, or .const section. MASM provides a second type of structure declaration, the union, that does not assign different addresses to each object; instead, each field in a union declaration has the same offset: zero. The following example demonstrates the syntax for a union declaration:

```
unionType union
 Fields (syntactically identical to struct declarations)
unionType ends
```

Yes, it seems rather weird that MASM still uses ends for the end of the union (rather than endu). If this really bothers you, just create a textequ for endu as follows:

```
endu   textequ <ends>
```

Now, you can use endu to your heart's content to mark the end of a union.

You access the fields of a union exactly the same way you access the fields of a struct: using dot notation and field names. The following is a concrete example of a union type declaration and a variable of the union type:

```
numeric  union
i        sdword  ?
u        dword   ?
q        qword   ?
numeric  ends
         .
         .
         .
         .data
number   numeric  {}
         .
         .
         .
     mov number.u, 55
         .
         .
         .
     mov number.i, -62
         .
         .
         .
     mov rbx, number.q
```

The important thing to note about union objects is that all the fields of a union have the same offset in the structure. In the preceding example, the number.u, number.i, and number.q fields all have the same offset: zero. Therefore, the fields of a union overlap in memory; this is similar to the way the x86-64 8-, 16-, 32-, and 64-bit general-purpose registers overlap one another. Usually, you may access only one field of a union at a time; you do not manipulate separate fields of a particular union variable concurrently because writing to one field overwrites the other fields. In the preceding example, any modification of number.u would also change number.i and number.q.

Programmers typically use unions for two reasons: to conserve memory or to create aliases. Memory conservation is the intended use of this data structure facility. To see how this works, let's compare the numeric union in the preceding example with a corresponding structure type:

```
numericRec   struct
i            sdword  ?
u            dword   ?
q            qword   ?
numericRec   ends
```

If you declare a variable, say n, of type numericRec, you access the fields as n.i, n.u, and n.q exactly as though you had declared the variable to be type numeric. The difference between the two is that numericRec variables allocate separate storage for each field of the structure, whereas numeric (union) objects allocate the same storage for all fields. Therefore, sizeof numericRec is 16 because the record contains two double-word fields and a quad-word (real64) field. The sizeof numeric, however, is 8. This is because all the fields of a union occupy the same memory locations, and the size of a union object is the size of the largest field of that object (see Figure 4-8).

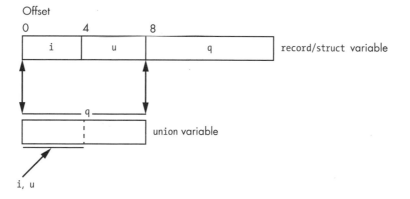

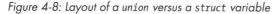

Figure 4-8: Layout of a union versus a struct variable

In addition to conserving memory, programmers often use unions to create aliases in their code. As you may recall, an *alias* is a different name for the same memory object. Aliases are often a source of confusion in a program, so you should use them sparingly; sometimes, however, using an alias can be quite convenient. For example, in one section of your program, you might need to constantly use type coercion to refer to an object using a different type. Although you can use a MASM textequ to simplify this process, another way to do this is to use a union variable with the fields representing the different types you want to use for the object. As an example, consider the following code:

```
CharOrUns union
chr       byte      ?
u         dword     ?
CharOrUns ends

          .data
v         CharOrUns {}
```

With a declaration like this, you can manipulate an uns32 object by accessing v.u. If, at some point, you need to treat the LO byte of this dword variable as a character, you can do so by accessing the v.chr variable; for example:

```
mov v.u, eax
mov ch, v.chr
```

You can use unions exactly the same way you use structures in a MASM program. In particular, union declarations may appear as fields in structures, struct declarations may appear as fields in unions, array declarations may appear within unions, you can create arrays of unions, and so on.

4.12.1 Anonymous Unions

Within a struct declaration, you can place a union declaration without specifying a field name for the union object. The following example demonstrates the syntax:

```
HasAnonUnion struct
r            real8     ?

             union
u            dword     ?
i            sdword    ?
             ends

s            qword     ?
HasAnonUnion ends

             .data
v            HasAnonUnion {}
```

Whenever an anonymous union appears within a record, you can access the fields of the union as though they were unenclosed fields of the record. In the preceding example, for instance, you would access v's u and i fields by using the syntax v.u and v.i, respectively. The u and i fields have the same offset in the record (8, because they follow a real8 object). The fields of v have the following offsets from v's base address:

v.r	0
v.u	8
v.i	8
v.s	12

sizeof(v) is 20 because the u and i fields consume only 4 bytes.

MASM also allows anonymous structures within unions. Please see the MASM documentation for more details, though the syntax and usage are identical to anonymous unions within structures.

4.12.2 Variant Types

One big use of unions in programs is to create *variant* types. A variant variable can change its type dynamically while the program is running. A variant object can be an integer at one point in the program, switch to a string at a different part of the program, and then change to a real value at a later time. Many very high-level language (VHLL) systems use a dynamic type system (that is, variant objects) to reduce the overall complexity of the program; indeed, proponents of many VHLLs insist that the use of a dynamic typing system is one of the reasons you can write complex programs with so few lines of code using those languages.

Of course, if you can create variant objects in a VHLL, you can certainly do it in assembly language. In this section, we'll look at how we can use the union structure to create variant types.

At any one given instant during program execution, a variant object has a specific type, but under program control, the variable can switch to a different type. Therefore, when the program processes a variant object, it must use an if statement or switch statement (or something similar) to execute different instructions based on the object's current type. VHLLs do this transparently.

In assembly language, you have to provide the code to test the type yourself. To achieve this, the variant type needs additional information beyond the object's value. Specifically, the variant object needs a field that specifies the current type of the object. This field (often known as the *tag* field) is an enumerated type or integer that specifies the object's type at any given instant. The following code demonstrates how to create a variant type:

```
VariantType struct
tag         dword    ?  ; 0-uns32, 1-int32, 2-real64

            union
u           dword    ?
i           sdword   ?
r           real8    ?
```

```
            ends
VariantType ends

            .data
v           VariantType {}
```

The program would test the v.tag field to determine the current type of the v object. Based on this test, the program would manipulate the v.i, v.u, or v.r field.

Of course, when operating on variant objects, the program's code must constantly be testing the tag field and executing a separate sequence of instructions for dword, sdword, or real8 values. If you use the variant fields often, it makes a lot of sense to write procedures to handle these operations for you (for example, vadd, vsub, vmul, and vdiv).

4.13 Microsoft ABI Notes

The Microsoft ABI expects fields of an array to be aligned on their *natural* size: the offset from the beginning of the structure to a given field must be a multiple of the field's size. On top of this, the whole structure must be aligned at a memory address that is a multiple of the size of the largest object in the structure (up to 16 bytes). Finally, the entire structure's size must be a multiple of the largest element in the structure (you must add padding bytes to the end of the structure to appropriately fill out the structure's size).

The Microsoft ABI expects arrays to begin at an address in memory that is a multiple of the element size. For example, if you have an array of 32-bit objects, the array must begin on a 4-byte boundary.

Of course, if you're not passing an array or structure data to another language (you're only processing the struct or array in your assembly code), you can align (or misalign) the data however you want.

4.14 For More Information

For additional information about data structure representation in memory, consider reading my book *Write Great Code*, Volume 1 (No Starch Press, 2004). For an in-depth discussion of data types, consult a textbook on data structures and algorithms. Of course, the MASM online documentation (at *https://www.microsoft.com/*) is a good source of information.

4.15 Test Yourself

1. What is the two-operand form of the imul instruction that multiplies a register by a constant?

2. What is the three-operand form of the imul instruction that multiplies a register by a constant and leaves the result in a destination register?

3. What is the syntax for the imul instruction that multiplies one register by another?

4. What is a manifest constant?

5. Which directive(s) would you use to create a manifest constant?

6. What is the difference between a text equate and a numeric equate?

7. Explain how you would use an equate to define literal strings whose length is greater than eight characters.

8. What is a constant expression?

9. What operator would you use to determine the number of data elements in the operand field of a byte directive?

10. What is the location counter?

11. What operator(s) return(s) the current location counter?

12. How would you compute the number of bytes between two declarations in the .data section?

13. How would you create a set of enumerated data constants using MASM?

14. How do you define your own data types using MASM?

15. What is a pointer (how is it implemented)?

16. How do you dereference a pointer in assembly language?

17. How do you declare pointer variables in assembly language?

18. What operator would you use to obtain the address of a static data object (for example, in the .data section)?

19. What are the five common problems encountered when using pointers in a program?

20. What is a dangling pointer?

21. What is a memory leak?

22. What is a composite data type?

23. What is a zero-terminated string?

24. What is a length-prefixed string?

25. What is a descriptor-based string?

26. What is an array?

27. What is the base address of an array?

28. Provide an example of an array declaration using the dup operator.

29. Describe how to create an array whose elements you initialize at assembly time.

30. What is the formula for accessing elements of a

    a. Single-dimension array dword A[10]?

    b. Two-dimensional array word W[4, 8]?

    c. Three-dimensional array real8 R[2, 4, 6]?

31. What is row-major order?

32. What is column-major order?

33. Provide an example of a two-dimensional array declaration (word array W[4, 8]) using nested dup operators.

34. What is a record/struct?

35. What MASM directives do you use to declare a record data structure?

36. What operator do you use to access fields of a record/struct?

37. What is a union?

38. What directives do you use to declare unions in MASM?

39. What is the difference between the memory organization of fields in a union versus those in a record/struct?

40. What is an anonymous union in a struct?

PART II

ASSEMBLY LANGUAGE PROGRAMMING

5

PROCEDURES

In a procedural programming language, the basic unit of code is the procedure. A *procedure* is a set of instructions that compute a value or take an action (such as printing or reading a character value). This chapter discusses how MASM implements procedures, parameters, and local variables. By the end of this chapter, you should be well versed in writing your own procedures and functions, and fully understand parameter passing and the Microsoft ABI calling convention.

5.1 Implementing Procedures

Most procedural programming languages implement procedures by using the call/return mechanism. The code calls a procedure, the procedure does its thing, and then the procedure returns to the caller. The call and return instructions provide the x86-64's *procedure invocation mechanism*. The calling code calls a procedure with the call instruction, and the procedure returns to the caller with the ret instruction. For example, the following x86-64 instruction calls the C Standard Library printf() function:

```
call printf
```

Alas, the C Standard Library does not supply all the routines you will ever need. Most of the time you'll have to write your own procedures. To do this, you will use MASM's procedure-declaration facilities. A basic MASM procedure declaration takes the following form:

```
proc_name proc options
          Procedure statements
proc_name endp
```

Procedure declarations appear in the .code section of your program. In the preceding syntax example, *proc_name* represents the name of the procedure you wish to define. This can be any valid (and unique) MASM identifier.

Here is a concrete example of a MASM procedure declaration. This procedure stores 0s into the 256 double words that RCX points at upon entry into the procedure:

```
zeroBytes proc
          mov eax, 0
          mov edx, 256
repeatlp: mov [rcx+rdx*4-4], eax
          dec rdx
          jnz repeatlp
          ret
zeroBytes endp
```

As you've probably noticed, this simple procedure doesn't bother with the "magic" instructions that add and subtract a value to and from the RSP register. Those instructions are a requirement of the Microsoft ABI when the procedure will be calling other C/C++ code (or other code written in a Microsoft ABI–compliant language). Because this little function doesn't call any other procedures, it doesn't bother executing such code. Also note that this code uses the loop index to count down from 256 to 0, filling in the 256 dword array backward (from end to beginning) rather than filling it in from beginning to end. This is a common technique in assembly language.

You can use the x86-64 call instruction to call this procedure. When, during program execution, the code falls into the ret instruction, the procedure returns to whoever called it and begins executing the first instruction beyond the call instruction. The program in Listing 5-1 provides an example of a call to the zeroBytes routine.

```
; Listing 5-1

; Simple procedure call example.

        option  casemap:none

nl      =       10

        .const
ttlStr  byte    "Listing 5-1", 0

        .data
dwArray dword   256 dup (1)

        .code

; Return program title to C++ program:

        public getTitle
getTitle proc
        lea rax, ttlStr
        ret
getTitle endp

; Here is the user-written procedure
; that zeroes out a buffer.

zeroBytes proc
        mov eax, 0
        mov edx, 256
repeatlp: mov [rcx+rdx*4-4], eax
        dec rdx
        jnz repeatlp
        ret
zeroBytes endp

; Here is the "asmMain" function.

        public  asmMain
asmMain proc

; "Magic" instruction offered without
; explanation at this point:

        sub     rsp, 48
```

```
        lea     rcx, dwArray
        call    zeroBytes

        add     rsp, 48     ; Restore RSP
        ret                 ; Returns to caller
asmMain endp
        end
```

Listing 5-1: Example of a simple procedure

5.1.1 The call and ret Instructions

The x86-64 call instruction does two things. First, it pushes the (64-bit) address of the instruction immediately following the call onto the stack; then it transfers control to the address of the specified procedure. The value that call pushes onto the stack is known as the *return address.*

When the procedure wants to return to the caller and continue execution with the first statement following the call instruction, most procedures return to their caller by executing a ret (*return*) instruction. The ret instruction pops a (64-bit) return address off the stack and transfers control indirectly to that address.

The following is an example of the minimal procedure:

```
minimal proc
        ret
minimal endp
```

If you call this procedure with the call instruction, minimal will simply pop the return address off the stack and return to the caller. If you fail to put the ret instruction in the procedure, the program will not return to the caller upon encountering the endp statement. Instead, the program will fall through to whatever code happens to follow the procedure in memory.

The example program in Listing 5-2 demonstrates this problem. The main program calls noRet, which falls straight through to followingProc (printing the message followingProc was called).

```
; Listing 5-2

; A procedure without a ret instruction.

        option  casemap:none

nl              =       10

        .const
ttlStr          byte    "Listing 5-2", 0
fpMsg           byte    "followingProc was called", nl, 0

        .code
        externdef printf:proc
```

```
; Return program title to C++ program:

            public getTitle
getTitle    proc
            lea rax, ttlStr
            ret
getTitle    endp

; noRet - Demonstrates what happens when a procedure
;         does not have a return instruction.

noRet       proc
noRet       endp

followingProc proc
            sub   rsp, 28h
            lea   rcx, fpMsg
            call printf
            add   rsp, 28h
            ret
followingProc endp

; Here is the "asmMain" function.

            public  asmMain
asmMain     proc
            push    rbx

            sub     rsp, 40   ; "Magic" instruction

            call    noRct

            add     rsp, 40   ; "Magic" instruction
            pop     rbx
            ret               ; Returns to caller
asmMain     endp
            end
```

Listing 5-2: Effect of a missing ret instruction in a procedure

Although this behavior might be desirable in certain rare circumstances, it usually represents a defect in most programs. Therefore, always remember to explicitly return from the procedure by using the ret instruction.

5.1.2 Labels in a Procedure

Procedures may contain statement labels, just like the main procedure in your assembly language program (after all, the main procedure, asmMain in most of the examples in this book, is just another procedure declaration as far as MASM is concerned). Note, however, that statement labels defined within a procedure are *local* to that procedure; such symbols are not *visible* outside the procedure.

In most situations, having *scoped symbols* in a procedure is nice (see "Local (Automatic) Variables" on page 234 for a discussion of scope). You don't have to worry about *namespace pollution* (conflicting symbol names) among the different procedures in your source file. Sometimes, however, MASM's name scoping can create problems. You might actually want to refer to a statement label outside a procedure.

One way to do this on a label-by-label basis is to use a global statement label declaration. *Global statement labels* are similar to normal statement labels in a procedure except you follow the symbol with two colons instead of a single colon, like so:

```
globalSymbol:: mov eax, 0
```

Global statement labels are visible outside the procedure. You can use an unconditional or conditional jump instruction to transfer control to a global symbol from outside the procedure; you can even use a `call` instruction to call that global symbol (in which case, it becomes a second entry point to the procedure). Generally, having multiple entry points to a procedure is considered bad programming style, and the use of multiple entry points often leads to programming errors. As such, you should rarely use global symbols in assembly language procedures.

If, for some reason, you don't want MASM to treat all the statement labels in a procedure as local to that procedure, you can turn scoping on and off with the following statements:

```
option scoped
option noscoped
```

The `option noscoped` directive disables scoping in procedures (for all procedures following the directive). The `option scoped` directive turns scoping back on. Therefore, you can turn scoping off for a single procedure (or set of procedures) and turn it back on immediately afterward.

5.2   Saving the State of the Machine

Take a look at Listing 5-3. This program attempts to print 20 lines of 40 spaces and an asterisk. Unfortunately, a subtle bug creates an infinite loop. The main program uses the `jnz printLp` instruction to create a loop that calls `PrintSpaces` 20 times. This function uses EBX to count off the 40 spaces it prints, and then returns with ECX containing 0. The main program then prints an asterisk and a newline, decrements ECX, and then repeats because ECX isn't 0 (it will always contain 0FFFF_FFFFh at this point).

The problem here is that the `print40Spaces` subroutine doesn't preserve the EBX register. *Preserving a register* means you save it upon entry into the subroutine and restore it before leaving. Had the `print40Spaces` subroutine preserved the contents of the EBX register, Listing 5-3 would have functioned properly.

```
; Listing 5-3

; Preserving registers (failure) example.

                option  casemap:none

nl              =       10

                .const
ttlStr          byte    "Listing 5-3", 0
space           byte    " ", 0
asterisk        byte    '*, %d', nl, 0

                .code
                externdef printf:proc

; Return program title to C++ program:

                public getTitle
getTitle        proc
                lea rax, ttlStr
                ret
getTitle        endp

; print40Spaces - Prints out a sequence of 40 spaces
;                 to the console display.

print40Spaces proc
                sub  rsp, 48    ; "Magic" instruction
                mov  ebx, 40
printLoop:      lea  rcx, space
                call printf
                dec  ebx
                jnz  printLoop ; Until EBX == 0
                add  rsp, 48    ; "Magic" instruction
                ret
print40Spaces endp

; Here is the "asmMain" function.

                public  asmMain
asmMain         proc
                push    rbx

; "Magic" instruction offered without
; explanation at this point:

                sub     rsp, 40   ; "Magic" instruction

                mov     rbx, 20
astLp:          call    print40Spaces
                lea     rcx, asterisk
                mov     rdx, rbx
                call    printf
```

```
              dec    rbx
              jnz    astLp

              add    rsp, 40   ; "Magic" instruction
              pop    rbx
              ret              ; Returns to caller
asmMain       endp
              end
```

Listing 5-3: Program with an unintended infinite loop

You can use the x86-64's push and pop instructions to preserve register values while you need to use them for something else. Consider the following code for PrintSpaces:

```
print40Spaces proc
              push rbx
              sub  rsp, 40    ; "Magic" instruction
              mov  ebx, 40
printLoop:    lea  rcx, space
              call printf
              dec  ebx
              jnz  printLoop ; Until EBX == 0
              add  rsp, 40    ; "Magic" instruction
              pop  rbx
              ret
print40Spaces endp
```

print40Spaces saves and restores RBX by using push and pop instructions. Either the caller (the code containing the call instruction) or the callee (the subroutine) can take responsibility for preserving the registers. In the preceding example, the callee preserves the registers.

Listing 5-4 shows what this code might look like if the caller preserves the registers (for reasons that will become clear in "Saving the State of the Machine, Part II" on page 280, the main program saves the value of RBX in a static memory location rather than using the stack).

```
; Listing 5-4

; Preserving registers (caller) example.

              option  casemap:none

nl            =       10

              .const
ttlStr        byte    "Listing 5-4", 0
space         byte    " ", 0
asterisk      byte    '*, %d', nl, 0

              .data
saveRBX       qword   ?
```

```
                .code
                externdef printf:proc

; Return program title to C++ program:

                public getTitle
getTitle        proc
                lea rax, ttlStr
                ret
getTitle        endp

; print40Spaces - Prints out a sequence of 40 spaces
;                 to the console display.

print40Spaces proc
                sub  rsp, 48   ; "Magic" instruction
                mov  ebx, 40
printLoop:      lea  rcx, space
                call printf
                dec  ebx
                jnz  printLoop ; Until EBX == 0
                add  rsp, 48   ; "Magic" instruction
                ret
print40Spaces endp

; Here is the "asmMain" function.

                public  asmMain
asmMain         proc
                push    rbx

; "Magic" instruction offered without
; explanation at this point:

                sub     rsp, 40

                mov     rbx, 20
astLp:          mov     saveRBX, rbx
                call    print40Spaces
                lea     rcx, asterisk
                mov     rdx, saveRBX
                call    printf
                mov     rbx, saveRBX
                dec     rbx
                jnz     astLp

                add     rsp, 40
                pop     rbx
                ret          ; Returns to caller
asmMain         endp
                end
```

Listing 5-4: Demonstration of caller register preservation

Callee preservation has two advantages: space and maintainability. If the callee (the procedure) preserves all affected registers, only one copy of the push and pop instructions exists—those the procedure contains. If the caller saves the values in the registers, the program needs a set of preservation instructions around every call. This makes your programs not only longer but also harder to maintain. Remembering which registers to save and restore on each procedure call is not easily done.

On the other hand, a subroutine may unnecessarily preserve some registers if it preserves all the registers it modifies. In the preceding examples, the print40Spaces procedure didn't save RBX. Although print40Spaces changes RBX, this won't affect the program's operation. If the caller is preserving the registers, it doesn't have to save registers it doesn't care about.

One big problem with having the caller preserve registers is that your program may change over time. You may modify the calling code or the procedure to use additional registers. Such changes, of course, may change the set of registers that you must preserve. Worse still, if the modification is in the subroutine itself, you will need to locate *every* call to the routine and verify that the subroutine does not change any registers the calling code uses.

Assembly language programmers use a common convention with respect to register preservation: unless there is a good reason (performance) for doing otherwise, most programmers will preserve all registers that a procedure modifies (and that doesn't explicitly return a value in a modified register). This reduces the likelihood of defects occurring in a program because a procedure modifies a register the caller expects to be preserved. Of course, you could follow the rules concerning the Microsoft ABI with respect to volatile and nonvolatile registers; however, such calling conventions impose their own inefficiencies on programmers (and other programs).

Preserving registers isn't all there is to preserving the environment. You can also push and pop variables and other values that a subroutine might change. Because the x86-64 allows you to push and pop memory locations, you can easily preserve these values as well.

5.3 Procedures and the Stack

Because procedures use the stack to hold the return address, you must exercise caution when pushing and popping data within a procedure. Consider the following simple (and defective) procedure:

```
MessedUp    proc

            push rax
            ret

MessedUp    endp
```

At the point the program encounters the ret instruction, the x86-64 stack takes the form shown in Figure 5-1.

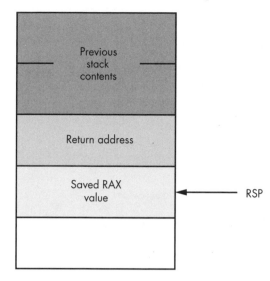

Figure 5-1: Stack contents before ret in the MessedUp procedure

The ret instruction isn't aware that the value on the top of the stack is not a valid address. It simply pops whatever value is on top and jumps to that location. In this example, the top of the stack contains the saved RAX value. Because it is very unlikely that RAX's value pushed on the stack was the proper return address, this program will probably crash or exhibit another undefined behavior. Therefore, when pushing data onto the stack within a procedure, you must take care to properly pop that data prior to returning from the procedure.

Popping extra data off the stack prior to executing the ret statement can also create havoc in your programs. Consider the following defective procedure:

```
MessedUp2  proc

           pop rax
           ret

MessedUp2  endp
```

Upon reaching the ret instruction in this procedure, the x86-64 stack looks something like Figure 5-2.

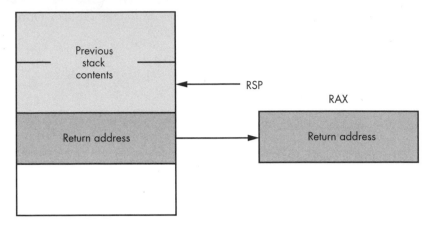

Figure 5-2: Stack contents before ret in MessedUp2

Once again, the ret instruction blindly pops whatever data happens to be on the top of the stack and attempts to return to that address. Unlike the previous example, in which the top of the stack was unlikely to contain a valid return address (because it contained the value in RAX), there is a small possibility that the top of the stack in this example *does* contain a return address. However, this will not be the proper return address for the messedUp2 procedure; instead, it will be the return address for the procedure that called messedUp2. To understand the effect of this code, consider the program in Listing 5-5.

```
; Listing 5-5

; Popping a return address by mistake.

            option  casemap:none

nl          =       10

            .const
ttlStr      byte    "Listing 5-5", 0
calling     byte    "Calling proc2", nl, 0
call1       byte    "Called proc1", nl, 0
rtn1        byte    "Returned from proc 1", nl, 0
rtn2        byte    "Returned from proc 2", nl, 0

            .code
            externdef printf:proc

; Return program title to C++ program:

            public getTitle
getTitle    proc
            lea rax, ttlStr
            ret
getTitle    endp
```

```
; proc1 - Gets called by proc2, but returns
;          back to the main program.

proc1          proc
               pop    rcx      ; Pops return address off stack
               ret
proc1          endp

proc2          proc
               call   proc1    ; Will never return

; This code never executes because the call to proc1
; pops the return address off the stack and returns
; directly to asmMain.

               sub    rsp, 40
               lea    rcx, rtn1
               call   printf
               add    rsp, 40
               ret
proc2          endp

; Here is the "asmMain" function.

               public asmMain
asmMain        proc

               sub    rsp, 40

               lea    rcx, calling
               call   printf

               call   proc2
               lea    rcx, rtn2
               call   printf

               add    rsp, 40
               ret              ; Returns to caller
asmMain        endp
               end
```

Listing 5-5: Effect of popping too much data off the stack

Because a valid return address is sitting on the top of the stack when proc1 is entered, you might think that this program will actually work (properly). However, when returning from the proc1 procedure, this code returns directly to the asmMain program rather than to the proper return address in the proc2 procedure. Therefore, all code in the proc2 procedure that follows the call to proc1 does not execute.

When reading the source code, you may find it very difficult to figure out why those statements are not executing, because they immediately follow the call to the proc1 procedure. It isn't clear, unless you look very closely, that the program is popping an extra return address off the stack and therefore doesn't return to proc2 but rather returns directly to whoever calls proc2.

Therefore, you should always be careful about pushing and popping data in a procedure, and verify that a one-to-one relationship exists between the pushes in your procedures and the corresponding pops.[1]

5.3.1 Activation Records

Whenever you call a procedure, the program associates certain information with that procedure call, including the return address, parameters, and automatic local variables, using a data structure called an *activation record*.[2] The program creates an activation record when calling (activating) a procedure, and the data in the structure is organized in a manner identical to records.

NOTE   *This section begins by discussing traditional activation records created by a hypothetical compiler, ignoring the parameter-passing conventions of the Microsoft ABI. Once this initial discussion is complete, this chapter will incorporate the Microsoft ABI conventions.*

Construction of an activation record begins in the code that calls a procedure. The caller makes room for the parameter data (if any) on the stack and copies the data onto the stack. Then the call instruction pushes the return address onto the stack. At this point, construction of the activation record continues within the procedure itself. The procedure pushes registers and other important state information and then makes room in the activation record for local variables. The procedure might also update the RBP register so that it points at the base address of the activation record.

To see what a traditional activation record looks like, consider the following C++ procedure declaration:

```
void ARDemo(unsigned i, int j, unsigned k)
{
    int a;
    float r;
    char c;
    bool b;
    short w
    .
    .
    .
}
```

Whenever a program calls this ARDemo procedure, it begins by pushing the data for the parameters onto the stack. In the original C/C++ calling convention (ignoring the Microsoft ABI), the calling code pushes the parameters onto the stack in the opposite order that they appear in the parameter list,

---

1. One possible recommendation is to always push registers in the same order: RAX, RBX, RCX, RDX, RSI, RDI, R8, . . . , R15 (leaving out the registers you don't push). This makes visual inspections of the code easier.

2. *Stack frame* is another term used to describe the activation record.

from right to left. Therefore, the calling code first pushes the value for the k parameter, then it pushes the value for the j parameter, and it finally pushes the data for the i parameter. After pushing the parameters, the program calls the ARDemo procedure. Immediately upon entry into the ARDemo procedure, the stack contains these four items arranged as shown in Figure 5-3. By pushing the parameters in the reverse order, they appear on the stack in the correct order (with the first parameter at the lowest address in memory).

NOTE *The x86-64 push instruction is capable of pushing 16-bit or 64-bit objects onto the stack. For performance reasons, you always want to keep RSP aligned on an 8-byte boundary (which largely eliminates using 16-bit pushes). For this and other reasons, modern programs always reserve at least 8 bytes for each parameter, regardless of the actual parameter size.*

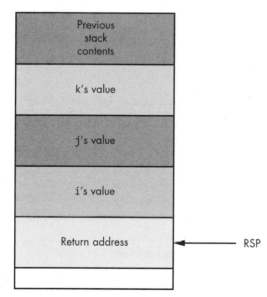

Figure 5-3: Stack organization immediately upon entry into ARDemo

NOTE *The Microsoft ABI requires the stack to be aligned on a 16-byte boundary when making system calls. Assembly programs don't require this, but it's often convenient to keep the stack aligned this way for those times when you need to make a system call (OS or C Standard Library call).*

The first few instructions in ARDemo will push the current value of RBP onto the stack and then copy the value of RSP into RBP.[3] Next, the code drops the stack pointer down in memory to make room for the local variables. This produces the stack organization shown in Figure 5-4.

---

3. Technically speaking, few actual optimizing C/C++ compilers will do this unless you have certain options turned on. However, this chapter ignores such optimizations in favor of an easier-to-understand example.

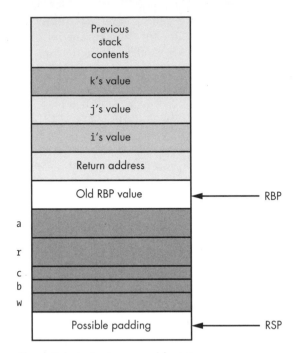

Figure 5-4: Activation record for ARDemo

NOTE *Unlike parameters, local variables do not have to be a multiple of 8 bytes in the activation record. However, the entire block of local variables must be a multiple of 16 bytes in size so that RSP remains aligned on a 16-byte boundary as required by the Microsoft ABI. Hence the presence of* possible padding *in Figure 5-4.*

5.3.1.1 Accessing Objects in the Activation Record

To access objects in the activation record, you must use offsets from the RBP register to the desired object. The two items of immediate interest to you are the parameters and the local variables. You can access the parameters at positive offsets from the RBP register; you can access the local variables at negative offsets from the RBP register, as Figure 5-5 shows.

Intel specifically reserves the RBP (Base Pointer) register for use as a pointer to the base of the activation record. This is why you should avoid using the RBP register for general calculations. If you arbitrarily change the value in the RBP register, you could lose access to the current procedure's parameters and local variables.

The local variables are aligned on offsets that are equal to their native size (chars are aligned on 1-byte addresses, shorts/words are aligned on 2-byte addresses, longs/ints/unsigneds/dwords are aligned on 4-byte addresses, and so forth). In the ARDemo example, all of the locals just happen to be allocated on appropriate addresses (assuming a compiler allocates storage in the order of declaration).

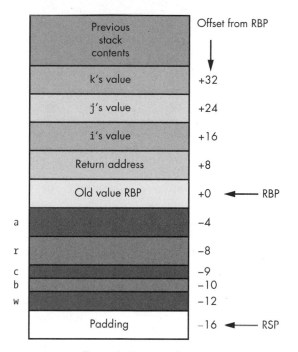

	Offset from RBP
Previous stack contents	↓
k's value	+32
j's value	+24
i's value	+16
Return address	+8
Old value RBP	+0 ◄—— RBP
a	−4
r	−8
c	−9
b	−10
w	−12
Padding	−16 ◄—— RSP

Figure 5-5: Offsets of objects in the ARDemo activation record

5.3.1.2 Using Microsoft ABI Parameter Conventions

The Microsoft ABI makes several modifications to the activation record model, in particular:

- The caller passes the first four parameters in registers rather than on the stack (though it must still reserve storage on the stack for those parameters).

- Parameters are always 8-byte values.

- The caller must reserve (at least) 32 bytes of parameter data on the stack, even if there are fewer than five parameters (plus 8 bytes for each additional parameter if there are five or more parameters).

- RSP must be 16-byte-aligned immediately before the call instruction pushes the return address onto the stack.

For more information, see "Microsoft ABI Notes" in Chapter 1. You must follow these conventions only when calling Windows or other Microsoft ABI–compliant code. For assembly language procedures that you write and call, you can use any convention you like.

5.3.2 The Assembly Language Standard Entry Sequence

The caller of a procedure is responsible for allocating storage for parameters on the stack and moving the parameter data to its appropriate location. In the simplest case, this just involves pushing the data onto the stack by using

64-bit push instructions. The call instruction pushes the return address onto the stack. It is the procedure's responsibility to construct the rest of the activation record. You can accomplish this by using the following assembly language *standard entry sequence* code:

```
push rbp           ; Save a copy of the old RBP value
mov rbp, rsp       ; Get ptr to activation record into RBP
sub rsp, num_vars  ; Allocate local variable storage plus padding
```

If the procedure doesn't have any local variables, the third instruction shown here, sub rsp, *num_vars*, isn't necessary.

num_vars represents the number of *bytes* of local variables needed by the procedure, a constant that should be a multiple of 16 (so the RSP register remains aligned on a 16-byte boundary).[4] If the number of bytes of local variables in the procedure is not a multiple of 16, you should round up the value to the next higher multiple of 16 before subtracting this constant from RSP. Doing so will slightly increase the amount of storage the procedure uses for local variables but will not otherwise affect the operation of the procedure.

If a Microsoft ABI–compliant program calls your procedure, the stack will be aligned on a 16-byte boundary immediately prior to the execution of the call instruction. As the return address adds 8 bytes to the stack, immediately upon entry into your procedure, the stack will be aligned on an (*RSP mod 16*) == *8* address (aligned on an 8-byte address but not on a 16-byte address). Pushing RBP onto the stack (to save the old value before copying RSP into RBP) adds another 8 bytes to the stack so that RSP is now 16-byte-aligned. Therefore, assuming the stack was 16-byte-aligned prior to the call, and the number you subtract from RSP is a multiple of 16, the stack will be 16-byte-aligned after allocating storage for local variables.

If you cannot ensure that RSP is 16-byte-aligned (*RSP mod 16 == 8*) upon entry into your procedure, you can always force 16-byte alignment by using the following sequence at the beginning of your procedure:

```
push rbp
mov rbp, rsp
sub rsp, num_vars  ; Make room for local variables
and rsp, -16       ; Force qword stack alignment
```

The –16 is equivalent to 0FFFF_FFFF_FFFF_FFF0h. The and instruction sequence forces the stack to be aligned on a 16-byte boundary (it reduces the value in the stack pointer so that it is a multiple of 16).

The ARDemo activation record has only 12 bytes of local storage. Therefore, subtracting 12 from RSP for the local variables will not leave the stack 16-byte-aligned. The and instruction in the preceding sequence, however, guarantees that RSP is 16-byte-aligned regardless of RSP's value upon entry

---

4. Alignment of the stack on a 16-byte boundary is a Microsoft ABI requirement, not a hardware requirement. The hardware is happy with an 8-byte address alignment. However, if you make any calls to Microsoft ABI–compliant code, you will need to keep the stack aligned on a 16-byte boundary.

into the procedure (this adds in the padding bytes shown in Figure 5-5). The few bytes and CPU cycles needed to execute this instruction would pay off handsomely if RSP was not oword aligned. Of course, if you know that the stack was properly aligned before the call, you could dispense with the extra and instruction and simply subtract 16 from RSP rather than 12 (in other words, reserving 4 more bytes than the ARDemo procedure needs, to keep the stack aligned).

5.3.3   The Assembly Language Standard Exit Sequence

Before a procedure returns to its caller, it needs to clean up the activation record. Standard MASM procedures and procedure calls, therefore, assume that it is the procedure's responsibility to clean up the activation record, although it is possible to share the cleanup duties between the procedure and the procedure's caller.

If a procedure does not have any parameters, the exit sequence is simple. It requires only three instructions:

```
mov rsp, rbp    ; Deallocate locals and clean up stack
pop rbp         ; Restore pointer to caller's activation record
ret             ; Return to the caller
```

In the Microsoft ABI (as opposed to pure assembly procedures), it is the caller's responsibility to clean up any parameters pushed on the stack. Therefore, if you are writing a function to be called from C/C++ (or other Microsoft ABI–compliant code), your procedure doesn't have to do anything at all about the parameters on the stack.

If you are writing procedures that will be called only from your assembly language programs, it is possible to have the callee (the procedure) rather than the caller clean up the parameters on the stack upon returning to the caller, using the following standard exit sequence:

```
mov rsp, rbp      ; Deallocate locals and clean up stack
pop rbp           ; Restore pointer to caller's activation record
ret parm_bytes    ; Return to the caller and pop the parameters
```

The *parm_bytes* operand of the ret instruction is a constant that specifies the number of bytes of parameter data to remove from the stack after the return instruction pops the return address. For example, the ARDemo example code in the previous sections has three quad words reserved for the parameters (because we want to keep the stack qword aligned). Therefore, the standard exit sequence would take the following form:

```
mov rsp, rbp
pop rbp
ret 24
```

If you do not specify a 16-bit constant operand to the ret instruction, the x86-64 will not pop the parameters off the stack upon return. Those parameters will still be sitting on the stack when you execute the first instruction following the call to the procedure. Similarly, if you specify a value that is too small, some of the parameters will be left on the stack upon return from the procedure. If the ret operand you specify is too large, the ret instruction will actually pop some of the caller's data off the stack, usually with disastrous consequences.

By the way, Intel has added a special instruction to the instruction set to shorten the standard exit sequence: leave. This instruction copies RBP into RSP and then pops RBP. The following is equivalent to the standard exit sequence presented thus far:

```
leave
ret optional_const
```

The choice is up to you. Most compilers generate the leave instruction (because it's shorter), so using it is the standard choice.

5.4   Local (Automatic) Variables

Procedures and functions in most high-level languages let you declare *local variables*. These are generally accessible only within the procedure; they are not accessible by the code that calls the procedure.

Local variables possess two special attributes in HLLs: scope and lifetime. The *scope* of an identifier determines where that identifier is visible (accessible) in the source file during compilation. In most HLLs, the scope of a procedure's local variable is the body of that procedure; the identifier is inaccessible outside that procedure.

Whereas scope is a compile-time attribute of a symbol, *lifetime* is a runtime attribute. The lifetime of a variable is from that point when storage is first bound to the variable until the point where the storage is no longer available for that variable. Static objects (those you declare in the .data, .const, .data?, and .code sections) have a lifetime equivalent to the total runtime of the application. The program allocates storage for such variables when the program first loads into memory, and those variables maintain that storage until the program terminates.

Local variables (or, more properly, *automatic variables*) have their storage allocated upon entry into a procedure, and that storage is returned for other use when the procedure returns to its caller. The name *automatic* refers to the program automatically allocating and deallocating storage for the variable on procedure invocation and return.

A procedure can access any global .data, .data?, or .const object the same way the main program accesses such variables—by referencing the name (using the PC-relative addressing mode). Accessing global objects is convenient and easy. Of course, accessing global objects makes your programs harder to read, understand, and maintain, so you should avoid using global variables within procedures. Although accessing global variables within a procedure may sometimes be the best solution to a given problem, you likely won't be writing such code at this point, so you should carefully consider your options before doing so.[5]

5.4.1   Low-Level Implementation of Automatic (Local) Variables

Your program accesses local variables in a procedure by using negative offsets from the activation record base address (RBP). Consider the following MASM procedure in Listing 5-6 (which admittedly doesn't do much, other than demonstrate the use of local variables).

```
; Listing 5-6

; Accessing local variables.

            option  casemap:none
            .code

; sdword a is at offset -4 from RBP.
; sdword b is at offset -8 from RBP.

; On entry, ECX and EDX contain values to store
; into the local variables a and b (respectively):

localVars   proc
            push rbp
            mov  rbp, rsp
            sub  rsp, 16        ; Make room for a and b

            mov  [rbp-4], ecx  ; a = ECX
            mov  [rbp-8], edx  ; b = EDX

    ; Additional code here that uses a and b:

            mov  rsp, rbp
            pop  rbp
            ret
localVars   endp
```

Listing 5-6: Sample procedure that accesses local variables

The standard entry sequence allocates 16 bytes of storage even though locals a and b require only 8. This keeps the stack 16-byte-aligned. If this isn't necessary for a particular procedure, subtracting 8 would work just as well.

The activation record for localVars appears in Figure 5-6.

Of course, having to refer to the local variables by the offset from the RBP register is truly horrible. This code is not only difficult to read (is [RBP-4] the a or the b variable?) but also hard to maintain. For example, if you decide you no longer need the a variable, you'd have to go find every occurrence of [RBP-8] (accessing the b variable) and change it to [RBP-4].

---

5. This argument against accessing global variables does not apply to other global symbols. It is perfectly reasonable to access global constants, types, procedures, and other objects in your programs.

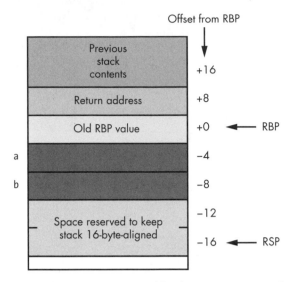

Figure 5-6: Activation record for the LocalVars *procedure*

A slightly better solution is to create equates for your local variable names. Consider the modification to Listing 5-6 shown here in Listing 5-7.

```
; Listing 5-7

; Accessing local variables #2.

            option  casemap:none
            .code

; localVars - Demonstrates local variable access.

; sdword a is at offset -4 from RBP.
; sdword b is at offset -8 from RBP.

; On entry, ECX and EDX contain values to store
; into the local variables a and b (respectively):

a           equ     <[rbp-4]>
b           equ     <[rbp-8]>
localVars   proc
            push    rbp
            mov     rbp, rsp
            sub     rsp, 16  ; Make room for a and b

            mov     a, ecx
            mov     b, edx

    ; Additional code here that uses a and b:

            mov     rsp, rbp
            pop     rbp
```

```
          ret
localVars  endp
```

Listing 5-7: Local variables using equates

This is considerably easier to read and maintain than the former program in Listing 5-6. It's possible to improve on this equate system. For example, the following four equates are perfectly legitimate:

```
a   equ <[rbp-4]>
b   equ a-4
d   equ b-4
e   equ d-4
```

MASM will associate [RBP-4] with a, [RBP-8] with b, [RBP-12] with d, and [RBP-16] with e. However, getting too crazy with fancy equates doesn't pay; MASM provides a high-level-like declaration for local variables (and parameters) you can use if you really want your declarations to be as maintainable as possible.

5.4.2 The MASM Local Directive

Creating equates for local variables is a lot of work and error prone. It's easy to specify the wrong offset when defining equates, and adding and removing local variables from a procedure is a headache. Fortunately, MASM provides a directive that lets you specify local variables, and MASM automatically fills in the offsets for the locals. That directive, local, uses the following syntax:

```
local  list_of_declarations
```

The *list_of_declarations* is a list of local variable declarations, separated by commas. A local variable declaration has two main forms:

```
identifier:type
identifier [elements]:type
```

Here, *type* is one of the usual MASM data types (byte, word, dword, and so forth), and *identifier* is the name of the local variable you are declaring. The second form declares local arrays, where *elements* is the number of array elements. *elements* must be a constant expression that MASM can resolve at assembly time.

local directives, if they appear in a procedure, must be the first statement(s) after a procedure declaration (the proc directive). A procedure may have more than one local statement; if there is more than one local directive, all must appear together after the proc declaration. Here's a code snippet with examples of local variable declarations:

```
procWithLocals proc
          local  var1:byte, local2:word, dVar:dword
          local  qArray[4]:qword, rlocal:real4
```

```
        local   ptrVar:qword
        local   userTypeVar:userType
        .
    .       ; Other statements in the procedure.
        .
procWithLocals endp
```

MASM automatically associates appropriate offsets with each variable you declare via the local directive. MASM assigns offsets to the variables by subtracting the variable's size from the current offset (starting at zero) and then rounding down to an offset that is a multiple of the object's size. For example, if userType is typedef'd to real8, MASM assigns offsets to the local variables in procWithLocals as shown in the following MASM listing output:

```
var1 . . . . . . . . . . . . . .    byte    rbp - 00000001
local2 . . . . . . . . . . . .      word    rbp - 00000004
dVar . . . . . . . . . . . . .      dword   rbp - 00000008
qArray . . . . . . . . . . . .      qword   rbp - 00000028
rlocal . . . . . . . . . . . .      dword   rbp - 0000002C
ptrVar . . . . . . . . . . . .      qword   rbp - 00000034
userTypeVar . . . . . . . . .       qword   rbp - 0000003C
```

In addition to assigning an offset to each local variable, MASM associates the [RBP-constant] addressing mode with each of these symbols. Therefore, if you use a statement like mov ax, local2 in the procedure, MASM will substitute [RBP-4] for the symbol local2.

Of course, upon entry into the procedure, you must still allocate storage for the local variables on the stack; that is, you must still provide the code for the standard entry (and standard exit) sequence. This means you must add up all the storage needed for the local variables so you can subtract this value from RSP after moving RSP's value into RBP. Once again, this is grunt work that could turn out to be a source of defects in the procedure (if you miscount the number of bytes of local variable storage), so you must take care when manually computing the storage requirements.

MASM does provide a solution (of sorts) for this problem: the option directive. You've seen the option casemap:none, option noscoped, and option scoped directives already; the option directive actually supports a wide array of arguments that control MASM's behavior. Two option operands control procedure code generation when using the local directive: prologue and epilogue. These operands typically take the following two forms:

```
option prologue:PrologueDef
option prologue:none
option epilogue:EpilogueDef
option epilogue:none
```

By default, MASM assumes prologue:none and epilogue:none. When you specify none as the prologue and epilogue values, MASM will not generate any extra code to support local variable storage allocation and deallocation in a procedure; you will be responsible for supplying the standard entry and exit sequences for the procedure.

If you insert the `option prologue:PrologueDef` (default prologue generation) and `option epilogue:EpilogueDef` (default epilogue generation) into your source file, all following procedures will automatically generate the appropriate standard entry and exit sequences for you (assuming local directives are in the procedure). MASM will quietly generate the standard entry sequence (the *prologue*) immediately after the last local directive (and before the first machine instruction) in a procedure, consisting of the usual standard entry sequence instructions

```
push  rbp
mov   rbp, rsp
sub   rsp, local_size
```

where *local_size* is a constant specifying the number of local variables plus a (possible) additional amount to leave the stack aligned on a 16-byte boundary. (MASM usually assumes the stack was aligned on a *mod 16 == 8* boundary prior to the `push rbp` instruction.)

For MASM's automatically generated prologue code to work, the procedure must have exactly one entry point. If you define a global statement label as a second entry point, MASM won't know that it is supposed to generate the prologue code at that point. Entering the procedure at that second entry point will create problems unless you explicitly include the standard entry sequence yourself. Moral of the story: procedures should have exactly one entry point.

Generating the standard exit sequence for the epilogue is a bit more problematic. Although it is rare for an assembly language procedure to have more than a single *entry* point, it's common to have multiple *exit* points. After all, the exit point is controlled by the programmer's placement of a ret instruction, not by a directive (like `endp`). MASM deals with the issue of multiple exit points by automatically translating any ret instruction it finds into the standard exit sequence:

```
leave
ret
```

Assuming, of course, that `option epilogue:EpilogueDef` is active.

You can control whether MASM generates prologues (standard entry sequences) and epilogues (standard exit sequences) independently of one another. So if you would prefer to write the leave instruction yourself (while having MASM generate the standard entry sequence), you can.

One final note about the `prologue:` and `epilogue:` options. In addition to specifying `prologue:PrologueDef` and `epilogue:EpilogueDef`, you can also supply a *macro identifier* after the `prologue:` or `epilogue:` options. If you supply a macro identifier, MASM will expand that macro for the standard entry or exit sequence. For more information on macros, see "Macros and the MASM Compile-Time Language" in Chapter 13.

Most of the example programs throughout the remainder of this book continue to use texequ declarations for local variables rather than the local directive to make the use of the [RBP-constant] addressing mode and local variable offsets more explicit.

5.4.3   Automatic Allocation

One big advantage to automatic storage allocation is that it efficiently shares a fixed pool of memory among several procedures. For example, say you call three procedures in a row, like so:

```
call ProcA
call ProcB
call ProcC
```

The first procedure (ProcA in this code) allocates its local variables on the stack. Upon return, ProcA deallocates that stack storage. Upon entry into ProcB, the program allocates storage for ProcB's local variables by *using the same memory locations just freed by ProcA*. Likewise, when ProcB returns and the program calls ProcC, ProcC uses the same stack space for its local variables that ProcB recently freed up. This memory reuse makes efficient use of the system resources and is probably the greatest advantage to using automatic variables.

Now that you've seen how assembly language allocates and deallocates storage for local variables, it's easy to understand why automatic variables do not maintain their values between two calls to the same procedure. Once the procedure returns to its caller, the storage for the automatic variable is lost, and, therefore, the value is lost as well. Thus, *you must always assume that a local var object is uninitialized upon entry into a procedure.* If you need to maintain the value of a variable between calls to a procedure, you should use one of the static variable declaration types.

5.5   Parameters

Although many procedures are totally self-contained, most require input data and return data to the caller. *Parameters* are values that you pass to and from a procedure. In straight assembly language, passing parameters can be a real chore.

The first thing to consider when discussing parameters is how we pass them to a procedure. If you are familiar with Pascal or C/C++, you've probably seen two ways to pass parameters: *pass by value* and *pass by reference.* Anything that can be done in an HLL can be done in assembly language (obviously, as HLL code compiles into machine code), but you have to provide the instruction sequence to access those parameters in an appropriate fashion.

Another concern you will face when dealing with parameters is *where* you pass them. There are many places to pass parameters: in registers, on the stack, in the code stream, in global variables, or in a combination of these. This chapter covers several of the possibilities.

5.5.1 Pass by Value

A parameter passed by value is just that—the caller passes a value to the procedure. Pass-by-value parameters are input-only parameters. You can pass them to a procedure, but the procedure cannot return values through them. Consider this C/C++ function call:

```
CallProc(I);
```

If you pass I by value, CallProc() does not change the value of I, regardless of what happens to the parameter inside CallProc().

Because you must pass a copy of the data to the procedure, you should use this method only for passing small objects like bytes, words, double words, and quad words. Passing large arrays and records by value is inefficient (because you must create and pass a copy of the object to the procedure).[6]

5.5.2 Pass by Reference

To pass a parameter by reference, you must pass the address of a variable rather than its value. In other words, you must pass a pointer to the data. The procedure must dereference this pointer to access the data. Passing parameters by reference is useful when you must modify the actual parameter or when you pass large data structures between procedures. Because pointers on the x86-64 are 64 bits wide, a parameter that you pass by reference will consist of a quad-word value.

You can compute the address of an object in memory in two common ways: the offset operator or the lea instruction. You can use the offset operator to take the address of any static variable you've declared in your .data, .data?, .const, or .code sections. Listing 5-8 demonstrates how to obtain the address of a static variable (staticVar) and pass that address to a procedure (someFunc) in the RCX register.

```
; Listing 5-8

; Demonstrate obtaining the address
; of a static variable using offset
; operator.

            option  casemap:none

            .data
staticVar   dword   ?

            .code
            externdef someFunc:proc

getAddress  proc
```

---

6. The Microsoft ABI doesn't allow passing objects larger than 64 bits by value. If you're writing Microsoft ABI–compliant code, the inefficiency of passing large objects is irrelevant.

```
            mov     rcx, offset staticVar
            call    someFunc

            ret
getAddress  endp

            end
```

Listing 5-8: Using the `offset` operator to obtain the address of a static variable

Using the `offset` operator raises a couple of issues. First of all, it can compute the address of only a static variable; you cannot obtain the address of an automatic (local) variable or parameter, nor can you compute the address of a memory reference involving a complex memory addressing mode (for example, `[RBX+RDX*1-5]`). Another problem is that an instruction like `mov rcx, offset staticVar` assembles into a large number of bytes (because the `offset` operator returns a 64-bit constant). If you look at the assembly listing MASM produces (with the `/Fl` command line option), you can see how big this instruction is:

```
00000000  48/ B9              mov     rcx, offset staticVar
          0000000000000000 R
0000000A  E8 00000000 E       call    someFunc
```

As you can see here, the `mov` instruction is 10 (0Ah) bytes long.

You've seen numerous examples of the second way to obtain the address of a variable: the `lea` instruction (for example, when loading the address of a format string into RCX prior to calling `printf()`). Listing 5-9 shows the example in Listing 5-8 recoded to use the `lea` instruction.

```
; Listing 5-9

; Demonstrate obtaining the address
; of a variable using the lea instruction.

            option  casemap:none

            .data
staticVar   dword   ?

            .code
            externdef someFunc:proc

getAddress  proc

            lea     rcx, staticVar
            call    someFunc

            ret
getAddress  endp
            end
```

Listing 5-9: Obtaining the address of a variable using the `lea` instruction

Looking at the listing MASM produces for this code, we find that the lea instruction is only 7 bytes long:

```
00000000  48/ 8D 0D      lea    rcx, staticVar
          00000000 R
00000007  E8 00000000 E  call   someFunc
```

So, if nothing else, your programs will be shorter if you use the lea instruction rather than the offset operator.

Another advantage to using lea is that it will accept any memory addressing mode, not just the name of a static variable. For example, if staticVar were an array of 32-bit integers, you could load the current element address, indexed by the RDX register, in RCX by using an instruction such as this:

```
lea rcx, staticVar[rdx*4]  ; Assumes LARGEADDRESSAWARE:NO
```

Pass by reference is usually less efficient than pass by value. You must dereference all pass-by-reference parameters on each access; this is slower than simply using a value because it typically requires at least two instructions. However, when passing a large data structure, pass by reference is faster because you do not have to copy the large data structure before calling the procedure. Of course, you'd probably need to access elements of that large data structure (for example, an array) by using a pointer, so little efficiency is lost when you pass large arrays by reference.

5.5.3   Low-Level Parameter Implementation

A parameter-passing mechanism is a contract between the caller and the callee (the procedure). Both parties have to agree on where the parameter data will appear and what form it will take (for example, value or address). If your assembly language procedures are being called only by other assembly language code that you've written, you control both sides of the contract negotiation and get to decide where and how you're going to pass parameters.

However, if external code is calling your procedure, or your procedure is calling external code, your procedure will have to adhere to whatever *calling convention* that external code uses. On 64-bit Windows systems, that calling convention will, undoubtedly, be the Windows ABI.

Before discussing the Windows calling conventions, we'll consider the situation of calling code that you've written (and, therefore, have complete control over the calling conventions). The following sections provide insight into the various ways you can pass parameters in pure assembly language code (without the overhead associated with the Microsoft ABI).

5.5.3.1   Passing Parameters in Registers

Having touched on *how* to pass parameters to a procedure, the next thing to discuss is *where* to pass parameters. This depends on the size and number of those parameters. If you are passing a small number of parameters to a procedure, the registers are an excellent place to pass them. If you are passing a single parameter to a procedure, you should use the registers listed in Table 5-1 for the accompanying data types.

Table 5-1: Parameter Location by Size

Data size	Pass in this register
Byte	CL
Word	CX
Double word	ECX
Quad word	RCX

This is not a hard-and-fast rule. However, these registers are convenient because they mesh with the first parameter register in the Microsoft ABI (which is where most people will pass a single parameter).

If you are passing several parameters to a procedure in the x86-64's registers, you should probably use up the registers in the following order:

```
First                                                    Last
RCX, RDX, R8, R9, R10, R11, RAX, XMM0/YMM0-XMM5/YMM5
```

In general, you should pass integer and other non-floating-point values in the general-purpose registers, and floating-point values in the XMMx/YMMx registers. This is not a hard requirement, but Microsoft reserves these registers for passing parameters and for local variables (*volatile*), so using these registers to pass parameters won't mess with Microsoft ABI nonvolatile registers. Of course, if you intend to have Microsoft ABI–compliant code call your procedure, you must exactly observe the Microsoft calling conventions (see "Calling Conventions and the Microsoft ABI" on page 261).

NOTE *You can use the* movsd *instruction to load a double-precision value into one of the XMM registers.[7] This instruction has the following syntax:*

```
movsd   XMMn, mem64
```

Of course, if you're writing pure assembly language code (no calls to or from any code you didn't write), you can use most of the general-purpose registers as you see fit (RSP is an exception, and you should avoid RBP, but the others are fair game). Ditto for the XMM/YMM registers.

As an example, consider the strfill(s,c) procedure that copies the character c (passed by value in AL) to each character position in s (passed by reference in RDI) up to a zero-terminating byte (Listing 5-10).

---

7. Intel has overloaded the meaning of the *movsd* mnemonic. When it has two operands (the first being an XMM register and the second being a 64-bit memory location), *movsd* stands for *move scalar double-precision*. When it has no operands, *movsd* is a string instruction and stands for *move string double*.

```
; Listing 5-10

; Demonstrate passing parameters in registers.

            option  casemap:none

            .data
staticVar   dword   ?

            .code
            externdef someFunc:proc

; strfill - Overwrites the data in a string with a character.

;      RDI -  Pointer to zero-terminated string
;             (for example, a C/C++ string).
;       AL -  Character to store into the string.

strfill     proc
            push    rdi     ; Preserve RDI because it changes

; While we haven't reached the end of the string:

whlNot0:    cmp     byte ptr [rdi], 0
            je      endOfStr

; Overwrite character in string with the character
; passed to this procedure in AL:

            mov     [rdi], al

; Move on to the next character in the string and
; repeat this process:

            inc     rdi
            jmp     whlNot0

endOfStr:   pop     rdi
            ret
strfill     endp
            end
```

Listing 5-10: Passing parameters in registers to the strfill procedure

To call the strfill procedure, you would load the address of the string data into RDI and the character value into AL prior to the call. The following code fragment demonstrates a typical call to strfill:

```
lea  rdi, stringData ; Load address of string into RDI
mov  al, ' '         ; Fill string with spaces
call strfill
```

This code passes the string by reference and the character data by value.

5.5.3.2 Passing Parameters in the Code Stream

Another place where you can pass parameters is in the code stream immediately after the call instruction. Consider the following print routine that prints a literal string constant to the standard output device:

```
call print
byte "This parameter is in the code stream.",0
```

Normally, a subroutine returns control to the first instruction immediately following the call instruction. Were that to happen here, the x86-64 would attempt to interpret the ASCII codes for "This..." as an instruction. This would produce undesirable results. Fortunately, you can skip over this string before returning from the subroutine.

So how do you gain access to these parameters? Easy. The return address on the stack points at them. Consider the implementation of print appearing in Listing 5-11.

```
; Listing 5-11

; Demonstration passing parameters in the code stream.

        option  casemap:none

nl          =       10
stdout      =       -11

            .const
ttlStr      byte    "Listing 5-11", 0

            .data
soHandle    qword   ?
bWritten    dword   ?

            .code

            ; Magic equates for Windows API calls:

            extrn __imp_GetStdHandle:qword
            extrn __imp_WriteFile:qword

; Return program title to C++ program:

            public  getTitle
getTitle    proc
            lea     rax, ttlStr
            ret
getTitle    endp

; Here's the print procedure.
; It expects a zero-terminated string
; to follow the call to print.
```

```
print       proc
            push    rbp
            mov     rbp, rsp
            and     rsp, -16        ; Ensure stack is 16-byte-aligned
            sub     rsp, 48         ; Set up stack for MS ABI

; Get the pointer to the string immediately following the
; call instruction and scan for the zero-terminating byte.

            mov     rdx, [rbp+8]    ; Return address is here
            lea     r8, [rdx-1]     ; R8 = return address - 1
search4_0:  inc     r8              ; Move on to next char
            cmp     byte ptr [R8], 0 ; At end of string?
            jne     search4_0

; Fix return address and compute length of string:

            inc     r8              ; Point at new return address
            mov     [rbp+8], r8     ; Save return address
            sub     r8, rdx         ; Compute string length
            dec     r8              ; Don't include 0 byte

; Call WriteFile to print the string to the console:

; WriteFile(fd, bufAdrs, len, &bytesWritten);

; Note: pointer to the buffer (string) is already
; in RDX. The len is already in R8. Just need to
; load the file descriptor (handle) into RCX:

            mov     rcx, soHandle   ; Zero-extends!
            lea     r9, bWritten    ; Address of "bWritten" in R9
            call    __imp_WriteFile

            leave
            ret
print       endp

; Here is the "asmMain" function.

            public  asmMain
asmMain     proc
            push    rbp
            mov     rbp, rsp
            sub     rsp, 40

; Call getStdHandle with "stdout" parameter
; in order to get the standard output handle
; we can use to call write. Must set up
; soHandle before first call to print procedure.

            mov     ecx, stdout     ; Zero-extends!
            call    __imp_GetStdHandle
            mov     soHandle, rax   ; Save handle
```

```
; Demonstrate passing parameters in code stream
; by calling the print procedure:

            call    print
            byte    "Hello, world!", nl, 0

; Clean up, as per Microsoft ABI:

            leave
            ret     ; Returns to caller

asmMain     endp
            end
```

Listing 5-11: Print procedure implementation (using code stream parameters)

One quick note about a machine idiom in Listing 5-11. The instruction

```
lea  r8, [rdx-1]
```

isn't actually loading an address into R8, per se. This is really an arithmetic instruction that is computing R8 = RDX − 1 (with a single instruction rather than two as would normally be required). This is a common usage of the lea instruction in assembly language programs. Therefore, it's a little programming trick that you should become comfortable with.

Besides showing how to pass parameters in the code stream, the print routine also exhibits another concept: *variable-length parameters*. The string following the call can be any practical length. The zero-terminating byte marks the end of the parameter list.

We have two easy ways to handle variable-length parameters: either use a special terminating value (like 0) or pass a special length value that tells the subroutine the number of parameters you are passing. Both methods have their advantages and disadvantages.

Using a special value to terminate a parameter list requires that you choose a value that never appears in the list. For example, print uses 0 as the terminating value, so it cannot print the NUL character (whose ASCII code is 0). Sometimes this isn't a limitation. Specifying a length parameter is another mechanism you can use to pass a variable-length parameter list. While this doesn't require any special codes, or limit the range of possible values that can be passed to a subroutine, setting up the length parameter and maintaining the resulting code can be a real nightmare.[8]

Despite the convenience afforded by passing parameters in the code stream, passing parameters there has disadvantages. First, if you fail to provide the exact number of parameters the procedure requires, the subroutine will get confused. Consider the print example. It prints a string of characters up to a zero-terminating byte and then returns control to the first instruction following that byte. If you leave off the zero-terminating

---

8. This is especially true if the parameter list changes frequently.

byte, the print routine happily prints the following opcode bytes as ASCII characters until it finds a zero byte. Because zero bytes often appear in the middle of an instruction, the print routine might return control into the middle of another instruction, which will probably crash the machine.

Inserting an extra 0, which occurs more often than you might think, is another problem programmers have with the print routine. In such a case, the print routine would return upon encountering the first zero byte and attempt to execute the following ASCII characters as machine code. Problems notwithstanding, however, the code stream is an efficient place to pass parameters whose values do not change.

5.5.3.3   Passing Parameters on the Stack

Most high-level languages use the stack to pass a large number of parameters because this method is fairly efficient. Although passing parameters on the stack is slightly less efficient than passing parameters in registers, the register set is limited (especially if you're limiting yourself to the four registers the Microsoft ABI sets aside for this purpose), and you can pass only a few value or reference parameters through registers. The stack, on the other hand, allows you to pass a large amount of parameter data without difficulty. This is the reason that most programs pass their parameters on the stack (at least, when passing more than about three to six parameters).

To manually pass parameters on the stack, push them immediately before calling the subroutine. The subroutine then reads this data from the stack memory and operates on it appropriately. Consider the following high-level language function call:

```
CallProc(i,j,k);
```

Back in the days of 32-bit assembly language, you could have passed these parameters to CallProc by using an instruction sequence such as the following:

```
push  k  ; Assumes i, j, and k are all 32-bit
push  j  ; variables
push  i
call  CallProc
```

Unfortunately, with the advent of the x86-64 64-bit CPU, the 32-bit push instruction was removed from the instruction set (the 64-bit push instruction replaced it). If you want to pass parameters to a procedure by using the push instruction, they must be 64-bit operands.[9]

Because keeping RSP aligned on an appropriate boundary (8 or 16 bytes) is crucial, the Microsoft ABI simply requires that every parameter

---

9. Actually, the x86-64 allows you to push 16-bit operands onto the stack. However, keeping RSP properly aligned on an 8- or 16-byte boundary when using 16-bit push instructions will be a big source of bugs in your program. Furthermore, it winds up taking two instructions to push a 32-bit value with 16-bit push instructions, so it is hardly cost-effective to use those instructions.

consume 8 bytes on the stack, and thus doesn't allow larger arguments on the stack. If you're controlling both sides of the parameter contract (caller and callee), you can pass larger arguments to your procedures. However, it is a good idea to ensure that all parameter sizes are a multiple of 8 bytes.

One simple solution is to make all your variables qword objects. Then you can directly push them onto the stack by using the push instruction prior to calling a procedure. However, not all objects fit nicely into 64 bits (characters, for example). Even those objects that could be 64 bits (for example, integers) often don't require the use of so much storage.

One sneaky way to use the push instruction on smaller objects is to use type coercion. Consider the following calling sequence for CallProc:

```
push   qword ptr k
push   qword ptr j
push   qword ptr i
call   CallProc
```

This sequence pushes the 64-bit values starting at the addresses associated with variables i, j, and k, regardless of the size of these variables. If the i, j, and k variables are smaller objects (perhaps 32-bit integers), these push instructions will push their values onto the stack along with additional data beyond these variables. As long as CallProc treats these parameter values as their actual size (say, 32 bits) and ignores the HO bits pushed for each argument onto the stack, this will usually work out properly.

Pushing extra data beyond the bounds of the variable onto the stack creates one possible problem. If the variable is at the very end of a page in memory and the following page is not readable, then pushing data beyond the variable may attempt to push data from that next memory page, resulting in a memory access violation (which will crash your program). Therefore, if you use this technique, you must ensure that such variables do not appear at the very end of a memory page (with the possibility that the next page in memory is inaccessible). The easiest way to do this is to make sure the variables you push on the stack in this fashion are never the last variables you declare in your data sections; for example:

```
i     dword ?
j     dword ?
k     dword ?
pad   qword ?   ; Ensures that there are at least 64 bits
                ; beyond the k variable
```

While pushing extra data beyond a variable will work, it's still a questionable programming practice. A better technique is to abandon the push instructions altogether and use a different technique to move the parameter data onto the stack.

Another way to "push" data onto the stack is to drop the RSP register down an appropriate amount in memory and then simply move data onto the stack by using a mov (or similar) instruction. Consider the following calling sequence for CallProc:

```
sub  rsp, 12
mov  eax, k
mov  [rsp+8], eax
mov  eax, j
mov  [rsp+4], eax
mov  eax, i
mov  [rsp], eax
call CallProc
```

Although this takes twice as many instructions as the previous examples (eight versus four), this sequence is safe (no possibility of accessing inaccessible memory pages). Furthermore, it pushes exactly the amount of data needed for the parameters onto the stack (32 bits for each object, for a total of 12 bytes).

The major problem with this approach is that it is a really bad idea to have an address in the RSP register that is not aligned on an 8-byte boundary. In the worst case, having a nonaligned (to 8 bytes) stack will crash your program; in the very best case, it will affect the performance of your program. So even if you want to pass the parameters as 32-bit integers, you should always allocate a multiple of 8 bytes for parameters on the stack prior to a call. The previous example would be encoded as follows:

```
sub  rsp, 16   ; Allocate a multiple of 8 bytes
mov  eax, k
mov  [rsp+8], eax
mov  eax, j
mov  [rsp+4], eax
mov  eax, i
mov  [rsp], eax
call CallProc
```

Note that CallProc will simply ignore the extra 4 bytes allocated on the stack in this fashion (don't forget to remove this extra storage from the stack on return).

To satisfy the requirement of the Microsoft ABI (and, in fact, of most application binary interfaces for the x86-64 CPUs) that each parameter consume exactly 8 bytes (even if their native data size is smaller), you can use the following code (same number of instructions, just uses a little more stack space):

```
sub  rsp, 24   ; Allocate a multiple of 8 bytes
mov  eax, k
mov  [rsp+16], eax
mov  eax, j
mov  [rsp+8], eax
mov  eax, i
mov  [rsp], eax
call CallProc
```

The mov instructions spread out the data on 8-byte boundaries. The HO dword of each 64-bit entry on the stack will contain garbage (whatever data was in stack memory prior to this sequence). That's okay; the CallProc procedure (presumably) will ignore that extra data and operate only on the LO 32 bits of each parameter value.

Upon entry into CallProc, using this sequence, the x86-64's stack looks like Figure 5-7.

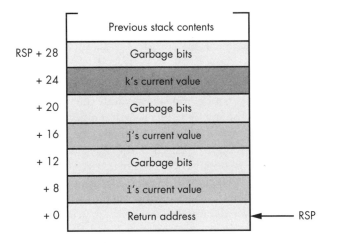

Figure 5-7: Stack layout upon entry into CallProc

If your procedure includes the standard entry and exit sequences, you may directly access the parameter values in the activation record by indexing off the RBP register. Consider the layout of the activation record for CallProc that uses the following declaration:

```
CallProc proc
         push   rbp      ; This is the standard entry sequence
         mov    rbp, rsp ; Get base address of activation record into RBP
         .
         .
         .
         leave
         ret    24
```

Assuming you've pushed three quad-word parameters onto the stack, it should look something like Figure 5-8 immediately after the execution of mov rbp, rsp in CallProc.

Now you can access the parameters by indexing off the RBP register:

```
mov eax, [rbp+32]    ; Accesses the k parameter
mov ebx, [rbp+24]    ; Accesses the j parameter
mov ecx, [rbp+16]    ; Accesses the i parameter
```

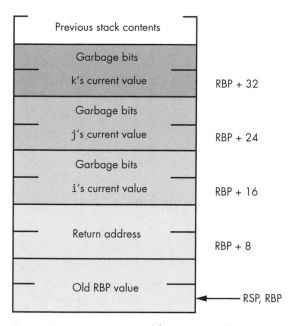

Figure 5-8: Activation record for CallProc *after standard entry sequence execution*

5.5.3.4 Accessing Value Parameters on the Stack

Accessing parameters passed by value is no different from accessing a local variable object. One way to accomplish this is by using equates, as was demonstrated for local variables earlier. Listing 5-12 provides an example program whose procedure accesses a parameter that the main program passes to it by value.

```
; Listing 5-12

; Accessing a parameter on the stack.

        option  casemap:none

nl          =       10
stdout      =       -11

            .const
ttlStr      byte    "Listing 5-12", 0
fmtStr1     byte    "Value of parameter: %d", nl, 0

            .data
value1      dword   20
value2      dword   30

            .code
            externdef printf:proc
```

```
; Return program title to C++ program:

            public  getTitle
getTitle    proc
            lea     rax, ttlStr
            ret
getTitle    endp

theParm     equ     <[rbp+16]>
ValueParm   proc
            push    rbp
            mov     rbp, rsp

            sub     rsp, 32         ; "Magic" instruction

            lea     rcx, fmtStr1
            mov     edx, theParm
            call    printf

            leave
            ret
ValueParm   endp

; Here is the "asmMain" function.

            public  asmMain
asmMain     proc
            push    rbp
            mov     rbp, rsp
            sub     rsp, 40

            mov     eax, value1
            mov     [rsp], eax      ; Store parameter on stack
            call    ValueParm

            mov     eax, value2
            mov     [rsp], eax
            call    ValueParm

; Clean up, as per Microsoft ABI:

            leave
            ret                     ; Returns to caller

asmMain     endp
            end
```

Listing 5-12: Demonstration of value parameters

Although you could access the value of theParm by using the anonymous
address [RBP+16] within your code, using the equate in this fashion makes
your code more readable and maintainable.

5.5.4 Declaring Parameters with the proc Directive

MASM provides another solution for declaring parameters for procedures using the proc directive. You can supply a list of parameters as operands to the proc directive, as follows:

```
proc_name  proc  parameter_list
```

where *parameter_list* is a list of one or more parameter declarations separated by commas. Each parameter declaration takes the form

```
parm_name:type
```

where *parm_name* is a valid MASM identifier, and *type* is one of the usual MASM types (proc, byte, word, dword, and so forth). With one exception, the parameter list declarations are identical to the local directive's operands: the exception is that MASM doesn't allow arrays as parameters. (MASM parameters assume that the Microsoft ABI is being used, and the Microsoft ABI allows only 64-bit parameters.)

The parameter declarations appearing as proc operands assume that a standard entry sequence is executed and that the program will access parameters off the RBP register, with the saved RBP and return address values at offsets 0 and 8 from the RBP register (so the first parameter will start at offset 16). MASM assigns offsets for each parameter that are 8 bytes apart (per the Microsoft ABI). As an example, consider the following parameter declaration:

```
procWithParms proc  k:byte, j:word, i:dword
              .
              .
              .
procWithParms endp
```

k will have the offset [RBP+16], j will have the offset [RBP+24], and i will have the offset [RBP+32]. Again, the offsets are always 8 bytes, regardless of the parameter data type.

As per the Microsoft ABI, MASM will allocate storage on the stack for the first four parameters, even though you would normally pass these parameters in RCX, RDX, R8, and R9. These 32 bytes of storage (starting at RBP+16) are called *shadow storage* in Microsoft ABI nomenclature. Upon entry into the procedure, the parameter values do not appear in this shadow storage (instead, the values are in the registers). The procedure can save the register values in this preallocated storage, or it can use the shadow storage for any purpose it desires (such as for additional local variable storage). However, if the procedure refers to the parameter names declared in the proc operand field, expecting to access the parameter data, the procedure should store the values from these registers into that shadow storage (assuming the parameters were passed in the RCX, RDX, R8, and R9 registers). Of course, if you push these arguments on the stack prior to the call (in assembly language, ignoring the Microsoft ABI calling convention), then the data is already in place, and you don't have to worry about shadow storage issues.

When calling a procedure whose parameters you declare in the operand field of a proc directive, don't forget that MASM assumes you push the parameters onto the stack in the reverse order they appear in the parameter list, to ensure that the first parameter in the list is at the lowest memory address on the stack. For example, if you call the procWithParms procedure from the previous code snippet, you'd typically use code like the following to push the parameters:

```
mov    eax, dwordValue
push   rax              ; Parms are always 64 bits
mov    ax, wordValue
push   rax
mov    al, byteValue
push   rax
call   procWithParms
```

Another possible solution (a few bytes longer, but often faster) is to use the following code:

```
sub    rsp, 24          ; Reserve storage for parameters
mov    eax, dwordValue ; i
mov    [rsp+16], eax
mov    ax, wordValue
mov    [rsp+8], ax      ; j
mov    al, byteValue
mov    [rsp], al        ; k
call   procWithParms
```

Don't forget that if it is the callee's responsibility to clean up the stack, you'd probably use an add rsp, 24 instruction after the preceding two sequences to remove the parameters from the stack. Of course, you can also have the procedure itself clean up the stack by specifying the number to add to RSP as a ret instruction operand, as explained earlier in this chapter.

5.5.5 Accessing Reference Parameters on the Stack

Because you pass the addresses of objects as reference parameters, accessing the reference parameters within a procedure is slightly more difficult than accessing value parameters because you have to dereference the pointers to the reference parameters.

In Listing 5-13, the RefParm procedure has a single pass-by-reference parameter. A pass-by-reference parameter is always a (64-bit) pointer to an object. To access the value associated with the parameter, this code has to load that quad-word address into a 64-bit register and access the data indirectly. The mov rax, theParm instruction in Listing 5-13 fetches this pointer into the RAX register, and then the procedure RefParm uses the [RAX] addressing mode to access the actual value of theParm.

```
; Listing 5-13

; Accessing a reference parameter on the stack.

        option  casemap:none

nl          =       10

            .const
ttlStr      byte    "Listing 5-13", 0
fmtStr1     byte    "Value of parameter: %d", nl, 0

            .data
value1      dword   20
value2      dword   30

            .code
            externdef printf:proc

; Return program title to C++ program:

            public  getTitle
getTitle    proc
            lea     rax, ttlStr
            ret
getTitle    endp

theParm     equ     <[rbp+16]>
RefParm     proc
            push    rbp
            mov     rbp, rsp

            sub     rsp, 32         ; "Magic" instruction

            lea     rcx, fmtStr1
            mov     rax, theParm    ; Dereference parameter
            mov     edx, [rax]
            call    printf

            leave
            ret
RefParm     endp

; Here is the "asmMain" function.

            public  asmMain
asmMain     proc
            push    rbp
            mov     rbp, rsp
            sub     rsp, 40

            lea     rax, value1
            mov     [rsp], rax      ; Store address on stack
            call    RefParm
```

```
            lea     rax, value2
            mov     [rsp], rax
            call    RefParm

; Clean up, as per Microsoft ABI:

            leave
            ret     ; Returns to caller

asmMain     endp
            end
```

Listing 5-13: Accessing a reference parameter

Here are the build commands and program output for Listing 5-13:

```
C:\>build listing5-13

C:\>echo off
 Assembling: listing5-13.asm
c.cpp

C:\>listing5-13
Calling Listing 5-13:
Value of parameter: 20
Value of parameter: 30
Listing 5-13 terminated
```

As you can see, accessing (small) pass-by-reference parameters is a little less efficient than accessing value parameters because you need an extra instruction to load the address into a 64-bit pointer register (not to mention you have to reserve a 64-bit register for this purpose). If you access reference parameters frequently, these extra instructions can really begin to add up, reducing the efficiency of your program. Furthermore, it's easy to forget to dereference a reference parameter and use the address of the value in your calculations. Therefore, unless you really need to affect the value of the actual parameter, you should use pass by value to pass small objects to a procedure.

Passing large objects, like arrays and records, is where using reference parameters becomes efficient. When passing these objects by value, the calling code has to make a copy of the actual parameter; if it is a large object, the copy process can be inefficient. Because computing the address of a large object is just as efficient as computing the address of a small scalar object, no efficiency is lost when passing large objects by reference. Within the procedure, you must still dereference the pointer to access the object, but the efficiency loss due to indirection is minimal when you contrast this with the cost of copying that large object. The program in Listing 5-14 demonstrates how to use pass by reference to initialize an array of records.

```
; Listing 5-14

; Passing a large object by reference.
```

```
        option  casemap:none

nl          =       10
NumElements =       24

Pt          struct
x           byte    ?
y           byte    ?
Pt          ends

            .const
ttlStr      byte    "Listing 5-14", 0
fmtStr1     byte    "RefArrayParm[%d].x=%d ", 0
fmtStr2     byte    "RefArrayParm[%d].y=%d", nl, 0

            .data
index       dword   ?
Pts         Pt      NumElements dup ({})

            .code
            externdef printf:proc

; Return program title to C++ program:

            public  getTitle
getTitle    proc
            lea     rax, ttlStr
            ret
getTitle    endp

ptArray     equ     <[rbp+16]>
RefAryParm  proc
            push    rbp
            mov     rbp, rsp

            mov     rdx, ptArray
            xor     rcx, rcx        ; RCX = 0

; While ECX < NumElements, initialize each
; array element. x = ECX/8, y = ECX % 8.

ForEachEl:  cmp     ecx, NumElements
            jnl     LoopDone

            mov     al, cl
            shr     al, 3           ; AL = ECX / 8
            mov     [rdx][rcx*2].Pt.x, al

            mov     al, cl
            and     al, 111b        ; AL = ECX % 8
            mov     [rdx][rcx*2].Pt.y, al
            inc     ecx
            jmp     ForEachEl

LoopDone:   leave
```

```
            ret
RefAryParm  endp

; Here is the "asmMain" function.

            public  asmMain
asmMain     proc
            push    rbp
            mov     rbp, rsp
            sub     rsp, 40

; Initialize the array of points:

            lea     rax, Pts
            mov     [rsp], rax      ; Store address on stack
            call    RefAryParm

; Display the array:

            mov     index, 0
displLp:    cmp     index, NumElements
            jnl     dispDone

            lea     rcx, fmtStr1
            mov     edx, index              ; Zero-extends!
            lea     r8, Pts                 ; Get array base
            movzx   r8, [r8][rdx*2].Pt.x    ; Get x field
            call    printf

            lea     rcx, fmtStr2
            mov     edx, index              ; Zero-extends!
            lea     r8, Pts                 ; Get array base
            movzx   r8, [r8][rdx*2].Pt.y    ; Get y field
            call    printf

            inc     index
            jmp     displLp

; Clean up, as per Microsoft ABI:

dispDone:
            leave
            ret     ; Returns to caller

asmMain     endp
            end
```

Listing 5-14: Passing an array of records by referencing

Here are the build commands and output for Listing 5-14:

```
C:\>build listing5-14

C:\>echo off
```

```
Assembling: listing5-14.asm
c.cpp

C:\>listing5-14
Calling Listing 5-14:
RefArrayParm[0].x=0 RefArrayParm[0].y=0
RefArrayParm[1].x=0 RefArrayParm[1].y=1
RefArrayParm[2].x=0 RefArrayParm[2].y=2
RefArrayParm[3].x=0 RefArrayParm[3].y=3
RefArrayParm[4].x=0 RefArrayParm[4].y=4
RefArrayParm[5].x=0 RefArrayParm[5].y=5
RefArrayParm[6].x=0 RefArrayParm[6].y=6
RefArrayParm[7].x=0 RefArrayParm[7].y=7
RefArrayParm[8].x=1 RefArrayParm[8].y=0
RefArrayParm[9].x=1 RefArrayParm[9].y=1
RefArrayParm[10].x=1 RefArrayParm[10].y=2
RefArrayParm[11].x=1 RefArrayParm[11].y=3
RefArrayParm[12].x=1 RefArrayParm[12].y=4
RefArrayParm[13].x=1 RefArrayParm[13].y=5
RefArrayParm[14].x=1 RefArrayParm[14].y=6
RefArrayParm[15].x=1 RefArrayParm[15].y=7
RefArrayParm[16].x=2 RefArrayParm[16].y=0
RefArrayParm[17].x=2 RefArrayParm[17].y=1
RefArrayParm[18].x=2 RefArrayParm[18].y=2
RefArrayParm[19].x=2 RefArrayParm[19].y=3
RefArrayParm[20].x=2 RefArrayParm[20].y=4
RefArrayParm[21].x=2 RefArrayParm[21].y=5
RefArrayParm[22].x=2 RefArrayParm[22].y=6
RefArrayParm[23].x=2 RefArrayParm[23].y=7
Listing 5-14 terminated
```

As you can see from this example, passing large objects by reference is very efficient.

5.6   Calling Conventions and the Microsoft ABI

Back in the days of 32-bit programs, different compilers and languages typically used completely different parameter-passing conventions. As a result, a program written in Pascal could not call a C/C++ function (at least, using the native Pascal parameter-passing conventions). Similarly, C/C++ programs couldn't call FORTRAN, or BASIC, or functions written in other languages, without special help from the programmer. It was literally a Tower of Babel situation, as the languages were incompatible with one another.[10]

To resolve these problems, CPU manufacturers, such as Intel, devised a set of protocols known as the *application binary interface (ABI)* to provide conformity to procedure calls. Languages that conformed to the CPU

10. In the Tower of Babel story, from Genesis in the Bible, God changed the spoken languages of the people constructing the tower so they couldn't communicate with one another.

manufacturer's ABI were able to call functions and procedures written in other languages that also conformed to the same ABI. This brought a modicum of sanity to the world of programming language interoperability.

For programs running under Windows, Microsoft took a subset of the Intel ABI and created the Microsoft calling convention (which most people call the *Microsoft ABI*). The next section covers the Microsoft calling conventions in detail. However, first it's worthwhile to discuss many of the other calling conventions that existed prior to the Microsoft ABI.[11]

One of the older *formal* calling conventions is the *Pascal calling convention.* In this convention, a caller pushes parameters on the stack in the order that they appear in the actual parameter list (from left to right). On the 80x86/x86-64 CPUs, where the stack grows down in memory, the first parameter winds up at the highest address on the stack, and the last parameter winds up at the lowest address on the stack.

While it might look like the parameters appear backward on the stack, the computer doesn't really care. After all, the procedure will access the parameters by using a numeric offset, and it doesn't care about the offset's value.[12] On the other hand, for simple compilers, it's much easier to generate code that pushes the parameters in the order they appear in the source file, so the Pascal calling convention makes life a little easier for compiler writers (though optimizing compilers often rearrange the code anyway).

Another feature of the Pascal calling convention is that the callee (the procedure itself) is responsible for removing parameter data from the stack upon subroutine return. This localizes the cleanup code to the procedure so that parameter cleanup isn't duplicated across every call to the procedure.

The big drawback to the Pascal calling sequence is that handling variable parameter lists is difficult. If one call to a procedure has three parameters, and a second call has four parameters, the offset to the first parameter will vary depending on the actual number of parameters. Furthermore, it's more difficult (though certainly not impossible) for a procedure to clean up the stack after itself if the number of parameters varies. This is not an issue for Pascal programs, as standard Pascal does not allow user-written procedures and functions to have varying parameter lists. For languages like C/C++, however, this is an issue.

Because C (and other C-based programming languages) supports varying parameter lists (for example, the printf() function), C adopted a different calling convention: the *C calling convention*, also known as the *cdecl calling convention*. In C, the caller pushes parameters on the stack in the reverse order that they appear in the actual parameter list. So, it pushes the last parameter first and pushes the first parameter last.

---

11. It's important to note here that Intel's ABI and Microsoft's ABI are not exactly the same. A compiler that adheres to the Intel ABI is not necessarily compatible with Microsoft languages (and other languages that adhere to the Microsoft ABI).

12. Strictly speaking, this is not true. Offsets in the range ±127 require only a 1-byte encoding, so smaller offsets are preferable to larger offsets. However, having more than 128 bytes of parameters is rare, so this isn't a big issue for most programs.

Because the stack is a LIFO data structure, the first parameter winds up at the lowest address on the stack (and at a fixed offset from the return address, typically right above it in memory; this is true regardless of how many actual parameters appear on the stack). Also, because C supports varying parameter lists, it is up to the caller to clean up the parameters on the stack after the return from the function.

The third common calling convention in use on 32-bit Intel machines, *STDCALL*, is basically a combination of the Pascal and C/C++ calling conventions. Parameters are passed right to left (as in C/C++). However, the callee is responsible for cleaning up the parameters on the stack before returning.

One problem with these three calling conventions is that they all use only memory to pass their parameters to a procedure. Of course, the most efficient place to pass parameters is in machine registers. This led to a fourth common calling convention known as the *FASTCALL calling convention*. In this convention, the calling program passes parameters in registers to a procedure. However, as registers are a limited resource on most CPUs, the FASTCALL calling convention typically passes only the first three to six parameters in registers. If more parameters are needed, the FASTCALL passes the remaining parameters on the stack (typically in reverse order, like the C/C++ and STDCALL calling conventions).

5.7   The Microsoft ABI and Microsoft Calling Convention

This chapter has repeatedly referred to the Microsoft ABI. Now it's time to formally describe the Microsoft calling convention.

NOTE   *Remember that adhering to the Microsoft ABI is necessary only if you need to call another function that uses it, or if outside code is calling your function and expects the function to use the Microsoft ABI. If this is not the case, you can use any calling conventions that are convenient for your code.*

5.7.1   Data Types and the Microsoft ABI

As noted in "Microsoft ABI Notes" in Chapters 1, 3, and 4, the native data type sizes are 1, 2, 4, and 8 bytes (see Table 1-6 in Chapter 1). All such variables should be aligned in memory on their native size.

For parameters, all procedure/function parameters must consume exactly 64 bits. If a data object is smaller than 64 bits, the HO bits of the parameter value (the bits beyond the actual parameter's native size) are undefined (and not guaranteed to be zero). Procedures should access only the actual data bits for the parameter's native type and ignore the HO bits.

If a parameter's native type is larger than 64 bits, the Microsoft ABI requires the caller to pass the parameter by reference rather than by value (that is, the caller must pass the address of the data).

5.7.2 Parameter Locations

The Microsoft ABI uses a variant of the FASTCALL calling convention that requires the caller to pass the first four parameters in registers. Table 5-2 lists the register locations for these parameters.

Table 5-2: FASTCALL Parameter Locations

Parameter	If scalar/reference	If floating point
1	RCX	XMM0
2	RDX	XMM1
3	R8	XMM2
4	R9	XMM3
5 to n	On stack, right to left	On stack, right to left

If the procedure has floating-point parameters, the calling convention skips the use of the general-purpose register for that same parameter location. Say you have the following C/C++ function:

```
void someFunc(int a, double b, char *c, double d)
```

Then the Microsoft calling convention would expect the caller to pass a in (the LO 32 bits of) RCX, b in XMM1, a pointer to c in R8, and d in XMM3, skipping RDX, R9, XMM0, and XMM2. This rule has an exception: for vararg (variable number of parameters) or unprototyped functions, floating-point values must be duplicated in the corresponding general-purpose register (see *https://docs.microsoft.com/en-us/cpp/build/x64-calling-convention?view=msvc-160#parameter-passing/*).

Although the Microsoft calling convention passes the first four parameters in registers, it still requires the caller to allocate storage on the stack for these parameters (*shadow storage*).[13] In fact, the Microsoft calling convention requires the caller to allocate storage for four parameters on the stack even if the procedure doesn't have four parameters (or any parameters at all). The caller doesn't need to copy the parameter data into this stack storage area—leaving the parameter data only in the registers is sufficient. However, that stack space must be present. Microsoft compilers assume the stack space is there and will use that stack space to save the register values (for example, if the procedure calls another procedure and needs to preserve the registers across that other call). Sometimes Microsoft's compilers use this shadow storage as local variables.

If you're calling an external function (such as a C/C++ library function) that adheres to the Microsoft calling convention and you do not allocate the shadow storage, the application will almost certainly crash.

---

13. Also called *shadow store* in various documents.

5.7.3 Volatile and Nonvolatile Registers

As noted way back in Chapter 1, the Microsoft ABI declares certain registers to be volatile and others to be nonvolatile. *Volatile* means that a procedure can modify the contents of the register without preserving its value. *Nonvolatile* means that a procedure must preserve a register's value if it modifies that value. Table 5-3 lists the registers and their volatility.

Table 5-3: Register Volatility

Register	Volatile/nonvolatile
RAX	Volatile
RBX	Nonvolatile
RCX	Volatile
RDX	Volatile
RDI	Nonvolatile
RSI	Nonvolatile
RBP	Nonvolatile
RSP	Nonvolatile
R8	Volatile
R9	Volatile
R10	Volatile
R11	Volatile
R12	Nonvolatile
R13	Nonvolatile
R14	Nonvolatile
R15	Nonvolatile
XMM0/YMM0	Volatile
XMM1/YMM1	Volatile
XMM2/YMM2	Volatile
XMM3/YMM3	Volatile
XMM4/YMM4	Volatile
XMM5/YMM5	Volatile
XMM6/YMM6	XMM6 Nonvolatile, upper half of YMM6 volatile
XMM7/YMM7	XMM7 Nonvolatile, upper half of YMM7 volatile
XMM8/YMM8	XMM8 Nonvolatile, upper half of YMM8 volatile
XMM9/YMM9	XMM9 Nonvolatile, upper half of YMM9 volatile
XMM10/YMM10	XMM10 Nonvolatile, upper half of YMM10 volatile
XMM11/YMM11	XMM11 Nonvolatile, upper half of YMM11 volatile

(continued)

Table 5-3: Register Volatility *(continued)*

Register	Volatile/nonvolatile
XMM12/YMM12	XMM12 Nonvolatile, upper half of YMM12 volatile
XMM13/YMM13	XMM13 Nonvolatile, upper half of YMM13 volatile
XMM14/YMM14	XMM14 Nonvolatile, upper half of YMM14 volatile
XMM15/YMM15	XMM15 Nonvolatile, upper half of YMM15 volatile
FPU	Volatile, but FPU stack must be empty upon return
Direction flag	Must be cleared upon return

It is perfectly reasonable to use nonvolatile registers within a procedure. However, you must preserve those register values so that they are unchanged upon return from a function. If you're not using the shadow storage for anything else, this is a good place to save and restore nonvolatile register values during a procedure call; for example:

```
someProc  proc
          push  rbp
          mov   rbp, rsp
          mov   [rbp+16], rbx    ; Save RBX in parm 1's shadow
            .
            .  ; Procedure's code
            .
          mov   rbx, [rbp+16]    ; Restore RBX from shadow
          leave
          ret
someProc  endp
```

Of course, if you're using the shadow storage for another purpose, you can always save nonvolatile register values in local variables or can even push and pop the register values:

```
someProc  proc           ; Save RBX via push
          push  rbx  ; Note that this affects parm offsets
          push  rbp
          mov   rbp, rsp
            .
            .  ; Procedure's code
            .
          leave
          pop   rbx  ; Restore RBX from stack
          ret
someProc  endp

someProc2 proc           ; Save RBX in a local
          push  rbp
          mov   rbp, rsp
          sub   rsp, 16        ; Keep stack aligned
          mov   [rbp-8], rbx  ; Save RBX
            .
            .  ; Procedure's code
            .
```

```
        mov    rbx, [rbp-8]   ; Restore RBX
        leave
        ret
someProc2 endp
```

5.7.4 Stack Alignment

As I've mentioned many times now, the Microsoft ABI requires the stack to
be aligned on a 16-byte boundary whenever you make a call to a procedure.
When Windows transfers control to your assembly code (or when another
Windows ABI–compliant code calls your assembly code), you're guaranteed that the stack will be aligned on an 8-byte boundary that is not also a
16-byte boundary (because the return address consumed 8 bytes after the
stack was 16-byte-aligned). If, within your assembly code, you don't care
about 16-byte alignment, you can do anything you like with the stack (however, you should keep it aligned on at least an 8-byte boundary).

On the other hand, if you ever plan on calling code that uses the
Microsoft calling conventions, you need to be able to ensure that the stack
is properly aligned before the call. There are two ways to do this: carefully
manage any modifications to the RSP register after entry into your code (so
you know the stack is 16-byte-aligned whenever you make a call), or force
the stack to an appropriate alignment prior to making a call. Forcing alignment to 16 bytes is easily achieved using this instruction:

```
and rsp, -16
```

However, you must execute this instruction *before* setting up parameters
for a call. If you execute this instruction immediately before a call instruction (but after placing all the parameters on the stack), this could shift RSP
down in memory, and then the parameters will not be at the expected offset upon entry into the procedure.

Suppose you don't know the state of RSP and need to make a call to a
procedure that expects five parameters (40 bytes, which is not a multiple of
16 bytes). Here's a typical calling sequence you would use:

```
sub rsp, 40  ; Make room for 4 shadow parms plus a 5th parm
and rsp, -16 ; Guarantee RSP is now 16-byte-aligned

; Code to move four parameters into registers and the
; 5th parameter to location [RSP+32]:

mov rcx, parm1
mov rdx, parm2
mov r8,  parm3
mov r9,  parm4
mov rax, parm5
mov [rsp+32], rax
call procWith5Parms
```

The only problem with this code is that it is hard to clean up the stack
upon return (because you don't know exactly how many bytes you reserved

on the stack as a result of the and instruction). However, as you'll see in the next section, you'll rarely clean up the stack after an individual procedure call, so you don't have to worry about the stack cleanup here.

5.7.5   Parameter Setup and Cleanup (or "What's with These Magic Instructions?")

The Microsoft ABI requires the caller to set up the parameters and then clean them up (remove them from the stack) upon return from the function. In theory, this means that a call to a Microsoft ABI–compliant function is going to look something like the following:

```
; Make room for parameters. parm_size is a constant
; with the number of bytes of parameters required
; (including 32 bytes for the shadow parameters).

    sub rsp, parm_size

    Code that copies parameters to the stack

    call procedure

; Clean up the stack after the call:

    add rsp, parm_size
```

This allocation and cleanup sequence has two problems. First, you have to repeat the sequence (sub rsp, *parm_size* and add rsp, *parm_size*) for every call in your program (which can be rather inefficient). Second, as you saw in the preceding section, sometimes aligning the stack to a 16-byte boundary forces you to adjust the stack downward by an unknown amount, so you don't know how many bytes to add to RSP in order to clean up the stack.

If you have several calls sprinkled through a given procedure, you can optimize the process of allocating and deallocating parameters on the stack by doing this operation just once. To understand how this works, consider the following code sequence:

```
; 1st procedure call:

    sub rsp, parm_size    ; Allocate storage for proc1 parms
    Code that copies parameters to the registers and stack
    call proc1
    add  rsp, parm_size   ; Clean up the stack

; 2nd procedure call:

    sub rsp, parm_size2   ; Allocate storage for proc2 parms
    Code that copies parameters to the registers and stack
    call proc2
    add rsp, parm_size2   ; Clean up the stack
```

If you study this code, you should be able to convince yourself that the first add and second sub are somewhat redundant. If you were to modify the first sub instruction to reduce the stack size by the greater of *parm_size* and *parm_size2*, and replace the final add instruction with this same value, you could eliminate the add and sub instructions appearing between the two calls:

```
; 1st procedure call:

    sub rsp, max_parm_size    ; Allocate storage for all parms
    Code that copies parameters to the registers and stack for proc1
    call proc1

    Code that copies parameters to the registers and stack for proc2
    call proc2
    add rsp, max_parm_size     ; Clean up the stack
```

If you determine the maximum number of bytes of parameters needed by all calls within your procedure, you can eliminate all the individual stack allocations and cleanups throughout the procedure (don't forget, the minimum parameter size is 32 bytes, even if the procedure has no parameters at all, because of the shadow storage requirements).

It gets even better, though. If your procedure has local variables, you can combine the sub instruction that allocates local variables with the one that allocates storage for your parameters. Similarly, if you're using the standard entry/exit sequence, the leave instruction at the end of your procedure will automatically deallocate all the parameters (as well as the local variables) when you exit your procedure.

Throughout this book, you've seen lots of "magic" add and subtract instructions that have been offered without much in the way of explanation. Now you know what those instructions have been doing: they've been allocating storage for local variables and all the parameter space for the procedures being called as well as keeping the stack 16-byte-aligned.

Here's one last example of a procedure that uses the standard entry/exit procedure to set up locals and parameter space:

```
rbxSave   equ   [rbp-8]
someProc  proc
          push  rbp
          mov   rbp, rsp
          sub   rsp, 48        ; Also leave stack 16-byte-aligned
          mov   rbxSave, rbx   ; Preserve RBX
            .
            .
            .
          lea   rcx, fmtStr
          mov   rdx, rbx       ; Print value in RBX (presumably)
          call  printf
            .
            .
            .
          mov   rbx, rbxSave   ; Restore RBX
          leave                ; Clean up stack
          ret
someProc  endp
```

However, if you use this trick to allocate storage for your procedures' parameters, you will not be able to use the push instructions to move the data onto the stack. The storage has already been allocated on the stack for the parameters; you must use mov instructions to copy the data onto the stack (using the [RSP+constant] addressing mode) when copying the fifth and greater parameters.

5.8   Functions and Function Results

Functions are procedures that return a result to the caller. In assembly language, few syntactical differences exist between a procedure and a function, which is why MASM doesn't provide a specific declaration for a function. Nevertheless, there are some semantic differences; although you can declare them the same way in MASM, you use them differently.

Procedures are a sequence of machine instructions that fulfill a task. The result of the execution of a procedure is the accomplishment of that activity. Functions, on the other hand, execute a sequence of machine instructions specifically to compute a value to return to the caller. Of course, a function can perform an activity as well, and procedures can undoubtedly compute values, but the main difference is that the purpose of a function is to return a computed result; procedures don't have this requirement.

In assembly language, you don't specifically define a function by using special syntax. To MASM, everything is a proc. A section of code becomes a function by virtue of the fact that the programmer explicitly decides to return a function result somewhere (typically in a register) via the procedure's execution.

The x86-64's registers are the most common place to return function results. The strlen() routine in the C Standard Library is a good example of a function that returns a value in one of the CPU's registers. It returns the length of the string (whose address you pass as a parameter) in the RAX register.

By convention, programmers try to return 8-, 16-, 32-, and 64-bit (non-real) results in the AL, AX, EAX, and RAX registers, respectively. This is where most high-level languages return these types of results, and it's where the Microsoft ABI states that you should return function results. The exception is floating-point values. The Microsoft ABI states that you should return floating-point values in the XMM0 register.

Of course, there is nothing particularly sacred about the AL, AX, EAX, and RAX registers. You could return function results in any register if it is more convenient to do so. Of course, if you're calling a Microsoft ABI–compliant function (such as strlen()), you have no choice but to expect the function's return result in the RAX register (strlen() returns a 64-bit integer in RAX, for example).

If you need to return a function result that is larger than 64 bits, you obviously must return it somewhere other than in RAX (which can hold only 64-bit values). For values slightly larger than 64 bits (for example, 128 bits or maybe even as many as 256 bits), you can split the result into pieces and return those parts in two or more registers. It is common to see functions returning 128-bit values in the RDX:RAX register pair. Of course, the XMM/YMM registers are another good place to return large values. Just remember that these schemes are not Microsoft ABI–compliant, so they're practical only when calling code you've written.

If you need to return a large object as a function result (say, an array of 1000 elements), you obviously are not going to be able to return the function result in the registers. You can deal with large function return results in two common ways: either pass the return value as a reference parameter or allocate storage on the heap (for example, using the C Standard Library malloc() function) for the object and return a pointer to it in a 64-bit register. Of course, if you return a pointer to storage you've allocated on the heap, the calling program must free this storage when it has finished with it.

5.9   Recursion

Recursion occurs when a procedure calls itself. The following, for example, is a recursive procedure:

```
Recursive proc

        call Recursive
        ret

Recursive endp
```

Of course, the CPU will never return from this procedure. Upon entry into Recursive, this procedure will immediately call itself again, and control will never pass to the end of the procedure. In this particular case, runaway recursion results in an infinite loop.[14]

Like a looping structure, recursion requires a termination condition in order to stop infinite recursion. Recursive could be rewritten with a termination condition as follows:

```
Recursive proc

        dec  eax
        jz   allDone
        call Recursive
allDone:
        ret

Recursive endp
```

This modification to the routine causes Recursive to call itself the number of times appearing in the EAX register. On each call, Recursive decrements the EAX register by 1 and then calls itself again. Eventually, Recursive decrements EAX to 0 and returns from each call until it returns to the original caller.

---

14. Well, not really infinite. The stack will overflow, and Windows will raise an exception at that point.

So far, however, there hasn't been a real need for recursion. After all, you could efficiently code this procedure as follows:

```
Recursive proc
iterLp:
        dec   eax
        jnz   iterLp
        ret
Recursive endp
```

Both examples would repeat the body of the procedure the number of times passed in the EAX register.[15] As it turns out, there are only a few recursive algorithms that you cannot implement in an iterative fashion. However, many recursively implemented algorithms are more efficient than their iterative counterparts, and most of the time the recursive form of the algorithm is much easier to understand.

The *quicksort algorithm* is probably the most famous algorithm that usually appears in recursive form. A MASM implementation of this algorithm appears in Listing 5-15.

```
; Listing 5-15

; Recursive quicksort.

        option  casemap:none

nl          =       10
numElements =       10

            .const
ttlStr      byte    "Listing 5-15", 0
fmtStr1     byte    "Data before sorting: ", nl, 0
fmtStr2     byte    "%d "    ; Use nl and 0 from fmtStr3
fmtStr3     byte    nl, 0
fmtStr4     byte    "Data after sorting: ", nl, 0

            .data
theArray    dword   1,10,2,9,3,8,4,7,5,6

            .code
            externdef printf:proc

; Return program title to C++ program:

            public  getTitle
getTitle    proc
            lea     rax, ttlStr
            ret
getTitle    endp
```

---

15. The latter version will do it considerably faster because it doesn't have the overhead of the call/ret instructions.

```
; quicksort - Sorts an array using the
;               quicksort algorithm.

; Here's the algorithm in C, so you can follow along:

    void quicksort(int a[], int low, int high)
    {
        int i,j,Middle;
        if(low < high)
        {
            Middle = a[(low+high)/2];
            i = low;
            j = high;
            do
            {
                while(a[i] <= Middle) i++;
                while(a[j] > Middle) j--;
                if(i <= j)
                {
                    swap(a[i],a[j]);
                    i++;
                    j--;
                }
            } while(i <= j);

            // Recursively sort the two subarrays.

            if(low < j) quicksort(a,low,j-1);
            if(i < high) quicksort(a,j+1,high);
        }
    }

; Args:
    ; RCX (_a):       Pointer to array to sort
    ; RDX (_lowBnd): Index to low bound of array to sort
    ; R8 (_highBnd): Index to high bound of array to sort

_a          equ     [rbp+16]        ; Ptr to array
_lowBnd     equ     [rbp+24]        ; Low bounds of array
_highBnd    equ     [rbp+32]        ; High bounds of array

; Local variables (register save area):

saveR9      equ     [rbp+40]        ; Shadow storage for R9
saveRDI     equ     [rbp-8]
saveRSI     equ     [rbp-16]
saveRBX     equ     [rbp-24]
saveRAX     equ     [rbp-32]

; Within the procedure body, these registers
; have the following meaning:

; RCX: Pointer to base address of array to sort.
; EDX: Lower bound of array (32-bit index).
; R8D: Higher bound of array (32-bit index).
```

```
; EDI: index (i) into array.
; ESI: index (j) into array.
; R9D: Middle element to compare against.

quicksort   proc
            push    rbp
            mov     rbp, rsp
            sub     rsp, 32
```

; This code doesn't mess with RCX. No
; need to save it. When it does mess
; with RDX and R8, it saves those registers
; at that point.

; Preserve other registers we use:

```
            mov     saveRAX, rax
            mov     saveRBX, rbx
            mov     saveRSI, rsi
            mov     saveRDI, rdi
            mov     saveR9, r9

            mov     edi, edx        ; i = low
            mov     esi, r8d        ; j = high
```

; Compute a pivotal element by selecting the
; physical middle element of the array.

```
            lea     rax, [rsi+rdi*1]  ; RAX = i+j
            shr     rax, 1            ; (i + j)/2
            mov     r9d, [rcx][rax*4] ; Middle = ary[(i + j)/2]
```

; Repeat until the EDI and ESI indexes cross one
; another (EDI works from the start toward the end
; of the array, ESI works from the end toward the
; start of the array).

rptUntil:

; Scan from the start of the array forward
; looking for the first element greater or equal
; to the middle element):

```
            dec     edi     ; To counteract inc, below
while1:     inc     edi     ; i = i + 1
            cmp     r9d, [rcx][rdi*4] ; While Middle > ary[i]
            jg      while1
```

; Scan from the end of the array backward, looking
; for the first element that is less than or equal
; to the middle element.

```
            inc     esi     ; To counteract dec, below
while2:     dec     esi     ; j = j - 1
```

```
                cmp     r9d, [rcx][rsi*4] ; While Middle < ary[j]
                jl      while2
```

; If we've stopped before the two pointers have
; passed over one another, then we've got two
; elements that are out of order with respect
; to the middle element, so swap these two elements.

```
                cmp     edi, esi  ; If i <= j
                jnle    endif1

                mov     eax, [rcx][rdi*4] ; Swap ary[i] and ary[j]
                mov     r9d, [rcx][rsi*4]
                mov     [rcx][rsi*4], eax
                mov     [rcx][rdi*4], r9d

                inc     edi       ; i = i + 1
                dec     esi       ; j = j - 1

endif1:         cmp     edi, esi  ; Until i > j
                jng     rptUntil
```

; We have just placed all elements in the array in
; their correct positions with respect to the middle
; element of the array. So all elements at indexes
; greater than the middle element are also numerically
; greater than this element. Likewise, elements at
; indexes less than the middle (pivotal) element are
; now less than that element. Unfortunately, the
; two halves of the array on either side of the pivotal
; element are not yet sorted. Call quicksort recursively
; to sort these two halves if they have more than one
; element in them (if they have zero or one elements, then
; they are already sorted).

```
                cmp     edx, esi  ; If lowBnd < j
                jnl     endif2
```

                ; Note: a is still in RCX,
                ; low is still in RDX.
                ; Need to preserve R8 (high).
                ; Note: quicksort doesn't require stack alignment.

```
                push    r8
                mov     r8d, esi
                call    quicksort ; (a, low, j)
                pop     r8

endif2:         cmp     edi, r8d  ; If i < high
                jnl     endif3
```

                ; Note: a is still in RCX,
                ; High is still in R8D.
                ; Need to preserve RDX (low).
                ; Note: quicksort doesn't require stack alignment.

```
                push    rdx
                mov     edx, edi
                call    quicksort ; (a, i, high)
                pop     rdx

; Restore registers and leave:

endif3:
                mov     rax, saveRAX
                mov     rbx, saveRBX
                mov     rsi, saveRSI
                mov     rdi, saveRDI
                mov     r9, saveR9
                leave
                ret
quicksort       endp

; Little utility to print the array elements:

printArray  proc
                push    r15
                push    rbp
                mov     rbp, rsp
                sub     rsp, 40    ; Shadow parameters

                lea     r9, theArray
                mov     r15d, 0
whileLT10:  cmp     r15d, numElements
                jnl     endwhile1

                lea     rcx, fmtStr2
                lea     r9, theArray
                mov     edx, [r9][r15*4]
                call    printf

                inc     r15d
                jmp     whileLT10

endwhile1:  lea     rcx, fmtStr3
                call    printf
                leave
                pop     r15
                ret
printArray  endp

; Here is the "asmMain" function.

                public  asmMain
asmMain     proc
                push    rbp
                mov     rbp, rsp
                sub     rsp, 32    ; Shadow storage
```

```
; Display unsorted array:

        lea     rcx, fmtStr1
        call    printf
        call    printArray

; Sort the array:

        lea     rcx, theArray
        xor     rdx, rdx            ; low = 0
        mov     r8d, numElements-1  ; high = 9
        call    quicksort           ; (theArray, 0, 9)

; Display sorted results:

        lea     rcx, fmtStr4
        call    printf
        call    printArray

        leave
        ret     ; Returns to caller

asmMain endp
        end
```

Listing 5-15: Recursive quicksort program

Here is the build command and sample output for the quicksort program:

```
C:\>build listing5-15

C:\>echo off
 Assembling: listing5-15.asm
c.cpp

C:\>listing5-15
Calling Listing 5-15:
Data before sorting:
1
10
2
9
3
8
4
7
5
6

Data after sorting:
1
2
3
```

```
4
5
6
7
8
9
10
```

Listing 5-15 terminated

Note that this quicksort procedure uses registers for all local variables. The quicksort function is a *leaf function*; it doesn't call any other functions. Therefore, it doesn't need to align the stack on a 16-byte boundary. Also, as is a good idea for any pure-assembly procedure (that will be called only by other assembly language procedures), this quicksort procedure preserves all the registers whose values it modifies (even the volatile registers). That's just good programming practice even if it is a little less efficient.

5.10 Procedure Pointers

The x86-64 call instruction allows three basic forms: PC-relative calls (via a procedure name), indirect calls through a 64-bit general-purpose register, and indirect calls through a quad-word pointer variable. The call instruction supports the following (low-level) syntax:

```
call proc_name   ; Direct call to procedure proc_name
call reg64       ; Indirect call to procedure whose address
                 ; appears in the reg₆₄
call qwordVar    ; Indirect call to the procedure whose address
                 ; appears in the qwordVar quad-word variable
```

We've been using the first form throughout this book, so there is little need to discuss it here. The second form, the register indirect call, calls the procedure whose address is held in the specified 64-bit register. The address of a procedure is the byte address of the first instruction to execute within that procedure. On a von Neumann architecture machine (like the x86-64), the system stores machine instructions in memory along with other data. The CPU fetches the instruction opcode values from memory prior to executing them. When you execute the register indirect call instruction, the x86-64 first pushes the return address onto the stack and then begins fetching the next opcode byte (instruction) from the address specified by the register's value.

The third form of the preceding call instruction fetches the address of a procedure's first instruction from a quad-word variable in memory. Although this instruction suggests that the call uses the direct addressing of the procedure, you should realize that any legal memory addressing mode is also legal here. For example, call procPtrTable[rbx*8] is perfectly legitimate; this statement fetches the quad word from the array of quad words (procPtrTable) and calls the procedure whose address is the value contained within that quad word.

MASM treats procedure names like static objects. Therefore, you can compute the address of a procedure by using the offset operator along with the procedure's name or by using the lea instruction. For example, offset *proc_name* is the address of the very first instruction of the *proc_name* procedure. So, all three of the following code sequences wind up calling the *proc_name* procedure:

```
call proc_name
  .
  .
  .
mov  rax, offset proc_name
call rax
  .
  .
  .
lea  rax, proc_name
call rax
```

Because the address of a procedure fits in a 64-bit object, you can store such an address into a quad-word variable; in fact, you can initialize a quad-word variable with the address of a procedure by using code like the following:

```
p       proc
          .
          .
          .
p       endp
          .
          .
          .
        .data
ptrToP qword    offset p
          .
          .
          .
        call ptrToP ; Calls p if ptrToP has not changed
```

As with all pointer objects, you should not attempt to indirectly call a procedure through a pointer variable unless you've initialized that variable with an appropriate address. You can initialize a procedure pointer variable in two ways: .data and .const objects allow an initializer, or you can compute the address of a routine (as a 64-bit value) and store that 64-bit address directly into the procedure pointer at runtime. The following code fragment demonstrates both ways to initialize a procedure pointer:

```
        .data
ProcPointer qword  offset p   ; Initialize ProcPointer with
                              ; the address of p
          .
          .
          .
        call ProcPointer  ; First invocation calls p
```

```
; Reload ProcPointer with the address of q.

            lea   rax, q
            mov   ProcPointer, rax
            .
            .
            .
            call  ProcPointer ; This invocation calls q
```

Although all the examples in this section use static variable declarations (.data, .const, .data?), don't think you can declare simple procedure pointers only in the static variable declaration sections. You can also declare procedure pointers (which are just qword variables) as local variables, pass them as parameters, or declare them as fields of a record or a union.

5.11 Procedural Parameters

One place where procedure pointers are quite invaluable is in parameter lists. Selecting one of several procedures to call by passing the address of a procedure is a common operation. Of course, a *procedural parameter* is just a quad-word parameter containing the address of a procedure, so this is really no different from using a local variable to hold a procedure pointer (except, of course, that the caller initializes the parameter with the address of the procedure to call indirectly).

When using parameter lists with the MASM proc directive, you can specify a procedure pointer type by using the proc type specifier; for example:

```
procWithProcParm proc  parm1:word, procParm:proc
```

You can call the procedure pointed at by this parameter by using the following call instruction:

```
call procParm
```

5.12 Saving the State of the Machine, Part II

"Saving the State of the Machine" on page 220 described the use of the push and pop instructions to save the state of the registers across a procedure call (callee register preservation). While this is certainly one way to preserve registers across a procedure call, it certainly isn't the only way, nor is it always (or even usually) the best way to save and restore registers.

The push and pop instructions have a couple of major benefits: they are short (pushing or popping a 64-bit register uses a 1-byte instruction opcode), and they work with constant and memory operands. These instructions do have drawbacks, however: they modify the stack pointer, they work with only 2- or 8-byte registers, they work only with the general-purpose integer registers (and the FLAGS register), and they might be slower than an equivalent instruction that moves the register data onto the stack. Often, a better solution is to reserve storage in the local variable space and simply move the registers to/from those local variables on the stack.

Consider the following procedure declaration that preserves registers by using push and pop instructions:

```
preserveRegs proc
             push    rax
             push    rbx
             push    rcx
               .
               .
               .
             pop     rcx
             pop     rbx
             pop     rax
             ret
preserveRegs endp
```

You can achieve the same thing with the following code:

```
preserveRegs proc
saveRAX        textequ <[rsp+16]>
saveRBX        textequ <[rsp+8]>
saveRCX        textequ <[rsp]>

             sub     rsp, 24      ; Make room for locals
             mov     saveRAX, rax
             mov     saveRBX, rbx
             mov     saveRCX, rcx
               .
               .
               .
             mov     rcx, saveRCX
             mov     rbx, saveRBX
             mov     rax, saveRAX
             add     rsp, 24      ; Deallocate locals
             ret
preserveRegs endp
```

The disadvantage to this code is that two extra instructions are needed to allocate (and deallocate) storage on the stack for the local variables that hold the register values. The push and pop instructions automatically allocate this storage, sparing you from having to supply these extra instructions. For a simple situation such as this, the push and pop instructions probably are the better solution.

For more complex procedures, especially those that expect parameters on the stack or have local variables, the procedure is already setting up the activation record, and subtracting a larger number from RSP doesn't require any additional instructions:

```
             option  prologue:PrologueDef
             option  epilogue:EpilogueDef
preserveRegs proc    parm1:byte, parm2:dword
```

```
                    local   localVar1:dword, localVar2:qword
                    local   saveRAX:qword, saveRBX:qword
                    local   saveRCX:qword

                    mov     saveRAX, rax
                    mov     saveRBX, rbx
                    mov     saveRCX, rcx
                      .
                      .
                      .
                    mov     rcx, saveRCX
                    mov     rbx, saveRBX
                    mov     rax, saveRAX
                    ret
preserveRegs endp
```

MASM automatically generates the code to allocate the storage for saveRAX, saveRBX, and saveRCX (along with all the other local variables) on the stack, as well as clean up the local storage on return.

When allocating local variables on the stack along with storage for any parameters a procedure might pass to functions it calls, pushing and popping registers to preserve them becomes problematic. For example, consider the following procedure:

```
callsFuncs   proc
saveRAX      textequ <[rbp-8]>
saveRBX      textequ <[rbp-16]>
saveRCX      textequ <[rbp-24]>
             push    rbp
             mov     rbp, rsp
             sub     rsp, 48       ; Make room for locals and parms
             mov     saveRAX, rax  ; Preserve registers in
             mov     saveRBX, rbx  ; local variables
             mov     saveRCX, rcx

               .
               .
               .
             mov     [rsp], rax    ; Store parm1
             mov     [rsp+8], rbx  ; Store parm2
             mov     [rsp+16], rcx ; Store parm3
             call    theFunction
               .
               .
               .
             mov     rcx, saveRCX  ; Restore registers
             mov     rbx, saveRBX
             mov     rax, saveRAX
             leave                 ; Deallocate locals
             ret
callsFuncs   endp
```

Had this function pushed RAX, RBX, and RCX on the stack after subtracting 48 from RSP, those save registers would have wound up on the stack where the function passes parm1, parm2, and parm3 to theFunction. That's why the push and pop instructions don't work well when working with functions that build an activation record containing local storage.

5.13 Microsoft ABI Notes

This chapter has all but completed the discussion of the Microsoft calling conventions. Specifically, a Microsoft ABI–compliant function must follow these rules:

- (Scalar) parameters must be passed in RCX, RDX, R8, and R9, then pushed on the stack. Floating-point parameters substitute XMM0, XMM1, XMM2, and XMM3 for RCX, RDX, R8, and R9, respectively.

- Varargs functions (functions with a variable number of parameters, such as printf()) and unprototyped functions must pass floating-point values in both the general-purpose (integer) registers and in the XMM registers. (For what it's worth, printf() seems to be happy with just passing the floating-point values in the integer registers, though that might be a happy accident with the version of MSVC used in the preparation of this book.)

- All parameters must be less than or equal to 64 bits in size; larger parameters must be passed by reference.

- On the stack, parameters always consume 64 bits (8 bytes) regardless of their actual size; the HO bits of smaller objects are undefined.

- Immediately before a call instruction, the stack must be aligned on a 16-byte boundary.

- Registers RAX, RCX, RDX, R8, R9, R10, R11, and XMM0/YMM0 to XMM5/YMM5 are volatile. The caller must preserve the registers across a call if it needs their values to be saved across the call. Also note that the HO 128 bits of YMM0 to YMM15 are volatile, and the caller must preserve these registers if it needs these bits to be preserved across a call.

- Registers RBX, RSI, RDI, RBP, RSP, R12 to R15, and XMM6 to XMM15 are nonvolatile. The callee must preserve these registers if it changes their values. As noted earlier, while YMM0L to YMM15L (the LO 128 bits) are nonvolatile, the upper 128 bits of these registers can be considered volatile. However, if a procedure is saving the LO 128 bits of YMM0 to YMM15, it may as well preserve all the bits (this inconsistency in the Microsoft ABI is to support legacy code running on CPUs that don't support the YMM registers).

- Scalar function returns (64 bits or fewer) come back in the RAX register. If the data type is smaller than 64 bits, the HO bits of RAX are undefined.

- Functions that return values larger than 64 bits must allocate storage for the return value and pass the address of that storage in the first parameter (RCX) to the function. On return, the function must return this pointer in the RAX register.

- Functions return floating-point results (double or single) in the XMM0 register.

5.14 For More Information

The electronic edition of the 32-bit edition this book (found at *https://artofasm .randallhyde.com/*) contains a whole "volume" on advanced and intermediate procedures. Though that book covers 32-bit assembly language programming, the concepts apply directly to 64-bit assembly by simply using 64-bit addresses rather than 32-bit addresses.

While the information appearing in this chapter covers 99 percent of the material that assembly programmers typically use, there is additional information on procedures and parameters that you may find interesting. In particular, the electronic edition covers additional parameter-passing mechanisms (pass by value/result, pass by result, pass by name, and pass by lazy evaluation) and goes into greater detail about the places you can pass parameters. The electronic version also covers iterators, thunks, and other advanced procedure types. Finally, a good compiler construction textbook will cover additional details about runtime support for procedures.

For more information on the Microsoft ABI, search for *Microsoft calling conventions* on the Microsoft website (or on the internet).

5.15 Test Yourself

1. Explain, step by step, how the call instruction works.
2. Explain, step by step, how the ret instruction works.
3. What does the ret instruction, with a numeric constant operand, do?
4. What value is pushed on the stack for a return address?
5. What is namespace pollution?
6. How do you define a single global symbol in a procedure?
7. How would you make all symbols in a procedure non-scoped (that is, all the symbols in a procedure would be global)?
8. Explain how to use the push and pop instructions to preserve registers in a function.
9. What is the main disadvantage of caller preservation?
10. What is the main problem with callee preservation?
11. What happens if you fail to pop a value in a function that you pushed on the stack at the beginning of the function?

12. What happens if you pop extra data off the stack in a function (data that you did not push on the stack in the function)?

13. What is an activation record?

14. What register usually points at an activation record, providing access to the data in that record?

15. How many bytes are reserved for a typical parameter on the stack when using the Microsoft ABI?

16. What is the standard entry sequence for a procedure (the instructions)?

17. What is the standard exit sequence for a procedure (the instructions)?

18. What instruction can you use to force 16-byte alignment of the stack pointer if the current value in RSP is unknown?

19. What is the scope of a variable?

20. What is the lifetime of a variable?

21. What is an automatic variable?

22. When does the system allocate storage for an automatic variable?

23. Explain two ways to declare local/automatic variables in a procedure.

24. Given the following procedure source code snippet, provide the offsets for each of the local variables:

```
procWithLocals proc
            local   var1:word, local2:dword, dVar:byte
            local   qArray[2]:qword, rlocal[2]:real4
            local   ptrVar:qword
            .
            .       ; Other statements in the procedure.
            .
        procWithLocals endp
```

25. What statement(s) would you insert in the source file to tell MASM to automatically generate the standard entry and standard exit sequences for a procedure?

26. When MASM automatically generates a standard entry sequence for a procedure, how does it determine where to put the code sequence?

27. When MASM automatically generates a standard exit sequence for a procedure, how does it determine where to put the code sequence?

28. What value does a pass-by-value parameter pass to a function?

29. What value does a pass-by-reference parameter pass to a function?

30. When passing four integer parameters to a function, where does the Windows ABI state those parameters are to be passed?

31. When passing a floating-point value as one of the first four parameters, where does the Windows ABI insist the values will be passed?

32. When passing more than four parameters to a function, where does the Windows ABI state the parameters will be passed?

33. What is the difference between a volatile and nonvolatile register in the Windows ABI?

34. Which registers are volatile in the Windows ABI?

35. Which registers are nonvolatile in the Windows ABI?

36. When passing parameters in the code stream, how does a function access the parameter data?

37. What is a shadow parameter?

38. How many bytes of shadow storage will a function require if it has a single 32-bit integer parameter?

39. How many bytes of shadow storage will a function require if it has two 64-bit integer parameters?

40. How many bytes of shadow storage will a function require if it has six 64-bit integer parameters?

41. What offsets will MASM associate with each of the parameters in the following proc declaration?

```
procWithParms proc   parm1:byte, parm2:word, parm3:dword, parm4:qword
```

42. Suppose that parm4 in the preceding question is a pass-by-reference character parameter. How would you load that character into the AL register (provide a code sequence)?

43. What offsets will MASM associate with each of the local variables in the following proc snippet?

```
procWithLocals proc
            local lclVar1:byte, lclVar2:word, lclVar3:dword,
lclVar4:qword
```

44. What is the best way to pass a large array to a procedure?

45. What does *ABI* stand for?

46. Where is the most common place to return a function result?

47. What is a procedural parameter?

48. How would you call a procedure passed as a parameter to a function/procedure?

49. If a procedure has local variables, what is the best way to preserve registers within that procedure?

6

ARITHMETIC

This chapter discusses arithmetic computation in assembly language. By the end of this chapter, you should be able to translate arithmetic expressions and assignment statements from high-level languages like Pascal and C/C++ into x86-64 assembly language.

6.1 x86-64 Integer Arithmetic Instructions

Before you learn how to encode arithmetic expressions in assembly language, it would be a good idea to first discuss the remaining arithmetic instructions in the x86-64 instruction set. Previous chapters have covered most of the arithmetic and logical instructions, so this section covers the few remaining instructions you'll need.

6.1.1 Sign- and Zero-Extension Instructions

Several arithmetic operations require sign- or zero-extended values before the operation. So let's first consider the sign- and zero-extension instructions. The x86-64 provides several instructions to sign- or zero-extend a smaller number to a larger number. Table 6-1 lists instructions that will sign-extend the AL, AX, EAX, and RAX registers.

Table 6-1: Instructions for Extending AL, AX, EAX, and RAX

Instruction	Explanation
cbw	Converts the byte in AL to a word in AX via sign extension
cwd	Converts the word in AX to a double word in DX:AX via sign extension
cdq	Converts the double word in EAX to a quad word in EDX:EAX via sign extension
cqo	Converts the quad word in RAX to an octal word in RDX:RAX via sign extension
cwde	Converts the word in AX to a double word in EAX via sign extension
cdqe	Converts the double word in EAX to a quad word in RAX via sign extension

Note that the cwd (*convert word to double word*) instruction does not sign-extend the word in AX to a double word in EAX. Instead, it stores the HO word of the sign extension into the DX register (the notation DX:AX indicates that you have a double-word value, with DX containing the upper 16 bits and AX containing the lower 16 bits of the value). If you want the sign extension of AX to go into EAX, you should use the cwde (*convert word to double word, extended*) instruction. In a similar fashion, the cdq instruction sign-extends EAX into EDX:EAX. Use the cdqe instruction if you want to sign-extend EAX into RAX.

For general sign-extension operations, the x86-64 provides an extension of the mov instruction, movsx (*move with sign extension*), that copies data and sign-extends the data while copying it. The movsx instruction's syntax is similar to that of mov:

```
movsxd dest, source ; If dest is 64 bits and source is 32 bits
movsx  dest, source ; For all other operand combinations
```

The big difference in syntax between these instructions and the mov instruction is that the destination operand must usually be larger than the source operand.[1] For example, if the source operand is a byte, then the destination operand must be a word, dword, or qword. The destination operand must also be a register; the source operand, however, can be a memory location.[2] The movsx instruction does not allow constant operands.

---

1. In two special cases, the operands are the same size. Those two instructions, however, aren't especially useful.

2. This doesn't turn out to be much of a limitation because sign extension almost always precedes an arithmetic operation that must take place in a register.

For whatever reason, MASM requires a different instruction mnemonic (instruction name) when sign-extending a 32-bit operand into a 64-bit register (movsxd rather than movsx).

To zero-extend a value, you can use the movzx instruction. It does not have the restrictions of movsx; as long as the destination operand is larger than the source operand, the instruction works fine. It allows 8 to 16, 32, or 64 bits, and 16 to 32 or 64 bits. There is no 32- to 64-bit version (it turns out this is unnecessary).

The x86-64 CPUs, for historical reasons, will always zero-extend a register from 32 bits to 64 bits when performing 32-bit operations. Therefore, to zero-extend a 32-bit register into a 64-bit register, you need only move the (32-bit) register into itself; for example:

```
mov eax, eax  ; Zero-extends EAX into RAX
```

Zero-extending certain 8-bit registers (AL, BL, CL, and DL) into their corresponding 16-bit registers is easily accomplished without using movzx by loading the complementary HO register (AH, BH, CH, or DH) with 0. To zero-extend AX into DX:AX or EAX into EDX:EAX, all you need to do is load DX or EDX with 0.[3]

Because of instruction-encoding limitations, the x86-64 does not allow you to zero- or sign-extend the AH, BH, CH, or DH registers into any of the 64-bit registers.

6.1.2 The mul and imul Instructions

You've already seen a subset of the imul instructions available in the x86-64 instruction set (see "The imul Instruction" in Chapter 4). This section presents the extended-precision version of imul along with the unsigned mul instruction.

The multiplication instructions provide you with another taste of irregularity in the x86-64's instruction set. Instructions like add, sub, and many others in the x86-64 instruction set support two operands, just like the mov instruction. Unfortunately, there weren't enough bits in the original 8086 opcode byte to support all instructions, so the x86-64 treats the mul (*unsigned multiply*) and imul (*signed integer multiply*) instructions as single-operand instructions, just like the inc, dec, and neg instructions. Of course, multiplication *is* a two-operand function. To work around this fact, the x86-64 always assumes the accumulator (AL, AX, EAX, or RAX) is the destination operand.

Another problem with the mul and imul instructions is that you cannot use them to multiply the accumulator by a constant. Intel quickly discovered the need to support multiplication by a constant and added the more general versions of the imul instruction to overcome this problem. Nevertheless, you must be aware that the basic mul and imul instructions do not support the full range of operands as the imul appearing in Chapter 4 does.

---

3. Zero-extending into DX:AX or EDX:EAX is just as necessary as the cwd and cdq instructions, as you will eventually see.

The multiply instruction has two forms: unsigned multiplication (mul) and signed multiplication (imul). Unlike addition and subtraction, you need separate instructions for signed and unsigned operations.

The single-operand multiply instructions take the following forms: Unsigned multiplication:

```
mul reg8    ; Returns AX
mul reg16   ; Returns DX:AX
mul reg32   ; Returns EDX:EAX
mul reg64   ; Returns RDX:RAX

mul mem8    ; Returns AX
mul mem16   ; Returns DX:AX
mul mem32   ; Returns EDX:EAX
mul mem64   ; Returns RDX:RAX
```

Signed (integer) multiplication:

```
imul reg8  ; Returns AX
imul reg16 ; Returns DX:AX
imul reg32 ; Returns EDX:EAX
imul reg64 ; Returns RDX:RAX

imul mem8  ; Returns AX
imul mem16 ; Returns DX:AX
imul mem32 ; Returns EDX:EAX
imul mem64 ; Returns RDX:RAX
```

The result of multiplying two n-bit values may require as many as $2 \times n$ bits. Therefore, if the operand is an 8-bit quantity, the result could require 16 bits. Likewise, a 16-bit operand produces a 32-bit result, a 32-bit operand produces 64 bits, and a 64-bit operand requires as many as 128 bits to hold the result. Table 6-2 lists the various computations.

Table 6-2: mul and imul Operations

Instruction	Computes
mul $operand_8$	AX = AL × $operand_8$ (unsigned)
imul $operand_8$	AX = AL × $operand_8$ (signed)
mul $operand_{16}$	DX:AX = AX × $operand_{16}$ (unsigned)
imul $operand_{16}$	DX:AX = AX × $operand_{16}$ (signed)
mul $operand_{32}$	EDX:EAX = EAX × $operand_{32}$ (unsigned)
imul $operand_{32}$	EDX:EAX = EAX × $operand_{32}$ (signed)
mul $operand_{64}$	RDX:RAX = RAX × $operand_{64}$ (unsigned)
imul $operand_{64}$	RDX:RAX = RAX × $operand_{64}$ (signed)

If an 8×8-, 16×16-, 32×32-, or 64×64-bit product requires more than 8, 16, 32, or 64 bits (respectively), the mul and imul instructions set the carry and overflow flags. mul and imul scramble the sign and zero flags.

NOTE *The sign and zero flags do not contain meaningful values after the execution of these two instructions.*

You'll use the single-operand `mul` and `imul` instructions quite a lot when you learn about extended-precision arithmetic in Chapter 8. Unless you're doing multiprecision work, however, you'll probably want to use the more generic multi-operand version of the `imul` instruction in place of the extended-precision `mul` or `imul`. However, the generic `imul` (see Chapter 4) is not a complete replacement for these two instructions; in addition to the number of operands, several differences exist. The following rules apply specifically to the generic (multi-operand) `imul` instruction:

- There isn't an 8×8-bit multi-operand `imul` instruction available.
- The generic `imul` instruction does not produce a 2×n-bit result, but truncates the result to n bits. That is, a 16×16-bit multiplication produces a 16-bit result. Likewise, a 32×32-bit multiplication produces a 32-bit result. These instructions set the carry and overflow flags if the result does not fit into the destination register.

6.1.3   The div and idiv Instructions

The x86-64 divide instructions perform a 128/64-bit division, a 64/32-bit division, a 32/16-bit division, or a 16/8-bit division. These instructions take the following forms:

```
div reg₈
div reg₁₆
div reg₃₂
div reg₆₄

div mem₈
div mem₁₆
div mem₃₂
div mem₆₄

idiv reg₈
idiv reg₁₆
idiv reg₃₂
idiv reg₆₄

idiv mem₈
idiv mem₁₆
idiv mem₃₂
idiv mem₆₄
```

The `div` instruction is an unsigned division operation. If the operand is an 8-bit operand, `div` divides the AX register by the operand, leaving the quotient in AL and the remainder (modulo) in AH. If the operand is a 16-bit quantity, the `div` instruction divides the 32-bit quantity in DX:AX by the operand, leaving the quotient in AX and the remainder in DX. With

32-bit operands, div divides the 64-bit value in EDX:EAX by the operand, leaving the quotient in EAX and the remainder in EDX. Finally, with 64-bit operands, div divides the 128-bit value in RDX:RAX by the operand, leaving the quotient in RAX and the remainder in RDX.

There is no variant of the div or idiv instructions that allows you to divide a value by a constant. If you want to divide a value by a constant, you need to create a memory object (preferably in the .const section) that is initialized with the constant, and then use that memory value as the div/idiv operand. For example:

```
        .const
ten     dword   10
          .
          .
          .
        div     ten ; Divides EDX:EAX by 10
```

The idiv instruction computes a signed quotient and remainder. The syntax for the idiv instruction is identical to div (except for the use of the idiv mnemonic), though creating signed operands for idiv may require a different sequence of instructions prior to executing idiv than for div.

You cannot, on the x86-64, simply divide one unsigned 8-bit value by another. If the denominator is an 8-bit value, the numerator must be a 16-bit value. If you need to divide one unsigned 8-bit value by another, you must zero-extend the numerator to 16 bits by loading the numerator into the AL register and then moving 0 into the AH register. *Failing to zero-extend AL before executing div may cause the x86-64 to produce incorrect results!* When you need to divide two 16-bit unsigned values, you must zero-extend the AX register (which contains the numerator) into the DX register. To do this, just load 0 into the DX register. If you need to divide one 32-bit value by another, you must zero-extend the EAX register into EDX (by loading a 0 into EDX) before the division. Finally, to divide one 64-bit number by another, you must zero-extend RAX into RDX (for example, using an xor rdx, rdx instruction) prior to the division.

When dealing with signed integer values, you will need to sign-extend AL into AX, AX into DX, EAX into EDX, or RAX into RDX before executing idiv. To do so, use the cbw, cwd, cdq, or cqo instructions.[4] Failure to do so may produce incorrect results.

The x86-64's divide instructions have one other issue: you can get a fatal error when using this instruction. First, of course, you can attempt to divide a value by 0. Another problem is that the quotient may be too large to fit into the RAX, EAX, AX, or AL register. For example, the 16/8-bit division 8000h/2 produces the quotient 4000h with a remainder of 0. 4000h will not fit into 8 bits. If this happens, or you attempt to divide by 0, the x86-64 will generate a division exception or integer overflow exception. This usually means your program will crash. If this happens to you, chances are you

---

4. You could also use movsx to sign-extend AL into AX.

didn't sign- or zero-extend your numerator before executing the division operation. Because this error may cause your program to crash, you should be very careful about the values you select when using division.

The x86-64 leaves the carry, overflow, sign, and zero flags undefined after a division operation. Therefore, you cannot test for problems after a division operation by checking the flag bits.

6.1.4   The cmp Instruction, Revisited

As noted in "The cmp Instruction and Corresponding Conditional Jumps" in Chapter 2, the cmp instruction updates the x86-64's flags according to the result of the subtraction operation (*leftOperand* - *rightOperand*). The x86-64 sets the flags in an appropriate fashion so that we can read this instruction as "compare *leftOperand* to *rightOperand*." You can test the result of the comparison by using the conditional set instructions to check the appropriate flags in the FLAGS register (see "The setcc Instructions" on page 295) or the conditional jump instructions (Chapter 2 or Chapter 7).

Probably the first place to start when exploring the cmp instruction is to look at exactly how it affects the flags. Consider the following cmp instruction:

```
cmp ax, bx
```

This instruction performs the computation AX – BX and sets the flags depending on the result of the computation. The flags are set as follows (also see Table 6-3):

ZF

The zero flag is set if and only if AX = BX. This is the only time AX – BX produces a 0 result. Hence, you can use the zero flag to test for equality or inequality.

SF

The sign flag is set to 1 if the result is negative. At first glance, you might think that this flag would be set if AX is less than BX, but this isn't always the case. If AX = 7FFFh and BX = –1 (0FFFFh), then subtracting AX from BX produces 8000h, which is negative (and so the sign flag will be set). So, for signed comparisons anyway, the sign flag doesn't contain the proper status. For unsigned operands, consider AX = 0FFFFh and BX = 1. Here, AX is greater than BX, but their difference is 0FFFEh, which is still negative. As it turns out, the sign flag and the overflow flag, taken together, can be used for comparing two signed values.

OF

The overflow flag is set after a cmp operation if the difference of AX and BX produced an overflow or underflow. As mentioned previously, the sign and overflow flags are both used when performing signed comparisons.

CF

The carry flag is set after a cmp operation if subtracting BX from AX requires a borrow. This occurs only when AX is less than BX, where AX and BX are both unsigned values.

Table 6-3: Condition Code Settings After cmp

Unsigned operands	Signed operands
ZF: Equality/inequality	ZF: Equality/inequality
CF: Left < Right (C = 1) Left ≥ Right (C = 0)	CF: No meaning
SF: No meaning	SF: See discussion in this section
OF: No meaning	OF: See discussion in this section

Given that the cmp instruction sets the flags in this fashion, you can test the comparison of the two operands with the following flags:

cmp *Left, Right*

For signed comparisons, the SF (sign) and OF (overflow) flags, taken together, have the following meanings:

- If [(SF = 0) and (OF = 1)] or [(SF = 1) and (OF = 0)], then *Left* < *Right* for a signed comparison.
- If [(SF = 0) and (OF = 0)] or [(SF = 1) and (OF = 1)], then *Left* ≥ *Right* for a signed comparison.

Note that (SF xor OF) is 1 if the left operand is less than the right operand. Conversely, (SF xor OF) is 0 if the left operand is greater than or equal to the right operand.

To understand why these flags are set in this manner, consider the examples in Table 6-4.

Table 6-4: Sign and Overflow Flag Settings After Subtraction

Left	Minus	Right	SF	OF
OFFFFh (−1)	−	OFFFEh (−2)	0	0
8000h (−32,768)	−	0001h	0	1
OFFFEh (−2)	−	OFFFFh (−1)	1	0
7FFFh (32767)	−	OFFFFh (−1)	1	1

Remember, the cmp operation is really a subtraction; therefore, the first example in Table 6-4 computes (−1) − (−2), which is (+1). The result is positive and an overflow did not occur, so both the S and O flags are 0. Because (SF xor OF) is 0, *Left* is greater than or equal to *Right*.

In the second example, the cmp instruction computes (−32,768) − (+1), which is (−32,769). Because a 16-bit signed integer cannot represent this value, the value wraps around to 7FFFh (+32,767) and sets the overflow flag. The result is positive (at least as a 16-bit value), so the CPU clears the sign flag. (SF xor OF) is 1 here, so *Left* is less than *Right*.

In the third example, cmp computes (−2) − (−1), which produces (−1). No overflow occurred, so the OF is 0, and the result is negative, so the SF is 1. Because (SF xor OF) is 1, *Left* is less than *Right*.

In the fourth (and final) example, cmp computes (+32,767) − (−1). This produces (+32,768), setting the overflow flag. Furthermore, the value wraps around to 8000h (−32,768), so the sign flag is set as well. Because (SF xor OF) is 0, *Left* is greater than or equal to *Right*.

6.1.5 *The setcc Instructions*

The setcc (*set on condition*) instructions set a single-byte operand (register or memory) to 0 or 1 depending on the values in the FLAGS register. The general formats for the setcc instructions are as follows:

```
setcc reg_8
setcc mem_8
```

The setcc represents a mnemonic appearing in Tables 6-5, 6-6, and 6-7. These instructions store a 0 in the corresponding operand if the condition is false, and they store a 1 in the 8-bit operand if the condition is true.

Table 6-5: setcc Instructions That Test Flags

Instruction	Description	Condition	Comments
setc	Set if carry	Carry = 1	Same as setb, setnae
setnc	Set if no carry	Carry = 0	Same as setnb, setae
setz	Set if zero	Zero = 1	Same as sete
setnz	Set if not zero	Zero = 0	Same as setne
sets	Set if sign	Sign = 1	
setns	Set if no sign	Sign = 0	
seto	Set if overflow	Overflow = 1	
setno	Set if no overflow	Overflow = 0	
setp	Set if parity	Parity = 1	Same as setpe
setpe	Set if parity even	Parity = 1	Same as setp
setnp	Set if no parity	Parity = 0	Same as setpo
setpo	Set if parity odd	Parity = 0	Same as setnp

The setcc instructions in Table 6-5 simply test the flags without any other meaning attached to the operation. You could, for example, use setc to check the carry flag after a shift, rotate, bit test, or arithmetic operation.

The setp/setpe and setnp/setpo instructions check the parity flag. These instructions appear here for completeness, but this book will not spend much time discussing the parity flag; in modern code, it's typically used only to check for an FPU not-a-number (NaN) condition.

The cmp instruction works synergistically with the setcc instructions. Immediately after a cmp operation, the processor flags provide information concerning the relative values of those operands. They allow you to see if one operand is less than, equal to, or greater than the other.

Two additional groups of setcc instructions are useful after a cmp operation. The first group deals with the result of an unsigned comparison (Table 6-6); the second group deals with the result of a signed comparison (Table 6-7).

Table 6-6: setcc Instructions for Unsigned Comparisons

Instruction	Description	Condition	Comments
seta	Set if above (>)	Carry = 0, Zero = 0	Same as setnbe
setnbe	Set if not below or equal (not ≤)	Carry = 0, Zero = 0	Same as seta
setae	Set if above or equal (≥)	Carry = 0	Same as setnc, setnb
setnb	Set if not below (not <)	Carry = 0	Same as setnc, setae
setb	Set if below (<)	Carry = 1	Same as setc, setnae
setnae	Set if not above or equal (not ≥)	Carry = 1	Same as setc, setb
setbe	Set if below or equal (≤)	Carry = 1 or Zero = 1	Same as setna
setna	Set if not above (not >)	Carry = 1 or Zero = 1	Same as setbe
sete	Set if equal (==)	Zero = 1	Same as setz
setne	Set if not equal (≠)	Zero = 0	Same as setnz

Table 6-7: setcc Instructions for Signed Comparisons

Instruction	Description	Condition	Comments
setg	Set if greater (>)	Sign == Overflow and Zero == 0	Same as setnle
setnle	Set if not less than or equal (not ≤)	Sign == Overflow or Zero == 0	Same as setg

Instruction	Description	Condition	Comments
setge	Set if greater than or equal (≥)	Sign == Overflow	Same as setnl
setnl	Set if not less than (not <)	Sign == Overflow	Same as setge
setl	Set if less than (<)	Sign ≠ Overflow	Same as setnge
setnge	Set if not greater or equal (not ≥)	Sign ≠ Overflow	Same as setl
setle	Set if less than or equal (≤)	Sign ≠ Overflow or Zero == 1	Same as setng
setng	Set if not greater than (not >)	Sign ≠ Overflow or Zero == 1	Same as setle
sete	Set if equal (=)	Zero == 1	Same as setz
setne	Set if not equal (≠)	Zero == 0	Same as setnz

The setcc instructions are particularly valuable because they can convert the result of a comparison to a Boolean value (false/true or 0/1). This is especially important when translating statements from a high-level language like Swift or C/C++ into assembly language. The following example shows how to use these instructions in this manner:

```
; bool = a <= b:

        mov eax, a
        cmp eax, b
        setle bool      ; bool is a byte variable
```

Because the setcc instructions always produce 0 or 1, you can use the results with the and and or instructions to compute complex Boolean values:

```
; bool = ((a <= b) && (d == e)):

        mov     eax, a
        cmp     eax, b
        setle bl
        mov     eax, d
        cmp     eax, e
        sete    bh
        and     bh, bl
        mov     bool, bh
```

6.1.6   The test Instruction

The x86-64 test instruction is to the and instruction what the cmp instruction is to sub. That is, the test instruction computes the logical AND of its two operands and sets the condition code flags based on the result; it does not, however, store the result of the logical AND back into the destination operand. The syntax for the test instruction is similar to and:

```
test operand1, operand2
```

The test instruction sets the zero flag if the result of the logical AND operation is 0. It sets the sign flag if the HO bit of the result contains a 1. The test instruction always clears the carry and overflow flags.

The primary use of the test instruction is to check whether an individual bit contains a 0 or a 1. Consider the instruction test al, 1. This instruction logically ANDs AL with the value 1; if bit 0 of AL contains 0, the result will be 0 (setting the zero flag) because all the other bits in the constant 1 are 0. Conversely, if bit 0 of AL contains 1, then the result is not 0, so test clears the zero flag. Therefore, you can test the zero flag after this test instruction to see if bit 0 contains a 0 or a 1 (for example, using setz or setnz instructions, or the jz/jnz instructions).

The test instruction can also check whether all the bits in a specified set of bits contain 0. The instruction test al, 0fh sets the zero flag if and only if the LO 4 bits of AL all contain 0.

One important use of the test instruction is to check whether a register contains 0. The instruction test reg, reg, where both operands are the same register, will logically AND that register with itself. If the register contains 0, the result is 0 and the CPU will set the zero flag. However, if the register contains a nonzero value, logically ANDing that value with itself produces that same nonzero value, so the CPU clears the zero flag. Therefore, you can check the zero flag immediately after the execution of this instruction (for example, using the setz or setnz instructions or the jz and jnz instructions) to see if the register contains 0. Here are some examples:

```
    test eax, eax
    setz bl          ; BL is set to 1 if EAX contains 0
         .
         .
         .
    test bl, bl
    jz   bxIs0

  Do something if BL != 0

bxIs0:
```

One major failing of the test instruction is that immediate (constant) operands can be no larger than 32 bits (as is the case with most instructions), which makes it difficult to use this instruction to test for set bits beyond bit position 31. For testing individual bits, you can use the bt (*bit test*) instruction (see "Instructions That Manipulate Bits" in Chapter 12). Otherwise, you'll have to move the 64-bit constant into a register (the mov instruction does support 64-bit immediate operands) and then test your target register against the 64-bit constant value in the newly loaded register.

6.2   Arithmetic Expressions

Probably the biggest shock to beginners facing assembly language for the first time is the lack of familiar arithmetic expressions. *Arithmetic expressions*, in most high-level languages, look similar to their algebraic equivalents. For example:

```
x = y * z;
```

In assembly language, you'll need several statements to accomplish this same task:

```
mov  eax, y
imul eax, z
mov  x, eax
```

Obviously, the HLL version is much easier to type, read, and understand. Although a lot of typing is involved, converting an arithmetic expression into assembly language isn't difficult at all. By attacking the problem in steps, the same way you would solve the problem by hand, you can easily break any arithmetic expression into an equivalent sequence of assembly language statements.

6.2.1   Simple Assignments

The easiest expressions to convert to assembly language are simple assignments. *Simple assignments* copy a single value into a variable and take one of two forms:

```
variable = constant
```

or

```
var1 = var2
```

Converting the first form to assembly language is simple—just use this assembly language statement:

```
mov variable, constant
```

This `mov` instruction copies the constant into the variable.

The second assignment is slightly more complicated because the x86-64 doesn't provide a memory-to-memory `mov` instruction. Therefore, to copy one memory variable into another, you must move the data through a register. By convention (and for slight efficiency reasons), most programmers tend to favor AL, AX, EAX, or RAX for this purpose. For example:

```
var1 = var2;
```

becomes

```
mov eax, var2
mov var1, eax
```

assuming that *var1* and *var2* are 32-bit variables. Use AL if they are 8-bit variables, use AX if they are 16-bit variables, or use RAX if they are 64-bit variables.

Of course, if you're already using AL, AX, EAX, or RAX for something else, one of the other registers will suffice. Regardless, you will generally use a register to transfer one memory location to another.

6.2.2 Simple Expressions

The next level of complexity is a simple expression. A *simple expression* takes the form

---

```
var1 = term1 op term2;
```

---

where *var1* is a variable, *term1* and *term2* are variables or constants, and *op* is an arithmetic operator (addition, subtraction, multiplication, and so on). Most expressions take this form. It should come as no surprise, then, that the x86-64 architecture was optimized for just this type of expression.

A typical conversion for this type of expression takes the form

---

```
mov eax, term1
op  eax, term2
mov var1, eax
```

---

where *op* is the mnemonic that corresponds to the specified operation (for example, + is add, – is sub, and so forth).

Note that the simple expression *var1* = *const1 op const2*; is easily handled with a compile-time expression and a single mov instruction. For example, to compute *var1* = 5 + 3;, use the single instruction mov *var1*, 5 + 3.

You need to be aware of a few inconsistencies. When dealing with the (*i*)mul and (*i*)div instructions on the x86-64, you must use the AL, AX, EAX, and RAX registers and the AH, DX, EDX, and RDX registers. You cannot use arbitrary registers as you can with other operations. Also, don't forget the sign-extension instructions if you're performing a division operation to divide one 16-, 32-, or 64-bit number by another. Finally, don't forget that some instructions may cause overflow. You may want to check for an overflow (or underflow) condition after an arithmetic operation.

Here are examples of common simple expressions:

```
; x = y + z:

        mov eax, y
        add eax, z
        mov x, eax

; x = y - z:

        mov eax, y
```

```
        sub eax, z
        mov x, eax

; x = y * z; (unsigned):

        mov eax, y
        mul z                ; Don't forget this wipes out EDX
        mov x, eax

; x = y * z; (signed):

        mov  eax, y
        imul eax, z          ; Does not affect EDX!
        mov x, eax

; x = y div z; (unsigned div):

        mov eax, y
        xor edx, edx         ; Zero-extend EAX into EDX
        div z
        mov x, eax

; x = y idiv z; (signed div):

        mov eax, y
        cdq                  ; Sign-extend EAX into EDX
        idiv z
        mov x, eax

; x = y % z; (unsigned remainder):

        mov  eax, y
        xor  edx, edx        ; Zero-extend EAX into EDX
        div  z
        mov  x, edx          ; Note that remainder is in EDX

; x = y % z; (signed remainder):

        mov  eax, y
        cdq                  ; Sign-extend EAX into EDX
        idiv z
        mov  x, edx          ; Remainder is in EDX
```

Certain unary operations also qualify as simple expressions, producing additional inconsistencies to the general rule. A good example of a unary operation is *negation*. In a high-level language, negation takes one of two possible forms:

var = -var

or

var1 = -var2

Note that *var* = *−constant* is really a simple assignment, not a simple expression. You can specify a negative constant as an operand to the mov instruction:

```
mov var, -14
```

To handle *var1* = *−var1*, use this single assembly language statement:

```
; var1 = -var1;

neg var1
```

If two different variables are involved, use the following:

```
; var1 = -var2;

mov eax, var2
neg eax
mov var1, eax
```

6.2.3   Complex Expressions

A *complex expression* is any arithmetic expression involving more than two terms and one operator. Such expressions are commonly found in programs written in a high-level language. Complex expressions may include parentheses to override operator precedence, function calls, array accesses, and so on. This section outlines the rules for converting such expressions.

A complex expression that is easy to convert to assembly language is one that involves three terms and two operators. For example:

```
w = w - y - z;
```

Clearly the straightforward assembly language conversion of this statement requires two sub instructions. However, even with an expression as simple as this, the conversion is not trivial. There are actually *two ways* to convert the preceding statement into assembly language:

```
mov eax, w
sub eax, y
sub eax, z
mov w, eax
```

and

```
mov eax, y
sub eax, z
sub w, eax
```

The second conversion, because it is shorter, looks better. However, it produces an incorrect result (assuming C-like semantics for the original statement). Associativity is the problem. The second sequence in the preceding example computes w = w − (y − z), which is not the same as w = (w − y) − z.

How we place the parentheses around the subexpressions can affect the result. Note that if you are interested in a shorter form, you can use the following sequence:

```
mov eax, y
add eax, z
sub w, eax
```

This computes w = w - (y + z), equivalent to w = (w - y) - z.
Precedence is another issue. Consider this expression:

```
x = w * y + z;
```

Once again, we can evaluate this expression in two ways:

```
x = (w * y) + z;
```

or

```
x = w * (y + z);
```

By now, you're probably thinking that this explanation is crazy. Everyone knows the correct way to evaluate these expressions is by the former form. However, you'd be wrong. The APL programming language, for example, evaluates expressions solely from right to left and does not give one operator precedence over another. Which way is "correct" depends entirely on how you define precedence in your arithmetic system.

Consider this expression:

```
x op1 y op2 z
```

If *op1* takes precedence over *op2*, then this evaluates to (x *op1* y) *op2* z. Otherwise, if *op2* takes precedence over *op1*, this evaluates to x *op1* (y *op2* z). Depending on the operators and operands involved, these two computations could produce different results.

Most high-level languages use a fixed set of precedence rules to describe the order of evaluation in an expression involving two or more different operators. Such programming languages usually compute multiplication and division before addition and subtraction. Those that support exponentiation (for example, FORTRAN and BASIC) usually compute that before multiplication and division. These rules are intuitive because almost everyone learns them before high school.

When converting expressions into assembly language, you must be sure to compute the subexpression with the highest precedence first. The following example demonstrates this technique:

```
; w = x + y * z:

        mov ebx, x
        mov eax, y     ; Must compute y * z first because "*"
        imul eax, z    ; has higher precedence than "+"
```

```
        add eax, ebx
        mov w, eax
```

If two operators appearing within an expression have the same precedence, you determine the order of evaluation by using associativity rules. Most operators are *left-associative*, meaning they evaluate from left to right. Addition, subtraction, multiplication, and division are all left-associative. A *right-associative* operator evaluates from right to left. The exponentiation operator in FORTRAN is a good example of a right-associative operator:

```
2**2**3
```

is equal to

```
2**(2**3)
```

not

```
(2**2)**3
```

The precedence and associativity rules determine the order of evaluation. Indirectly, these rules tell you where to place parentheses in an expression to determine the order of evaluation. Of course, you can always use parentheses to override the default precedence and associativity. However, the ultimate point is that your assembly code must complete certain operations before others to correctly compute the value of a given expression. The following examples demonstrate this principle:

```
; w = x - y - z:

        mov eax, x      ; All the same operator precedence,
        sub eax, y      ; so we need to evaluate from left
        sub eax, z      ; to right because they are left-
        mov w, eax      ; associative

; w = x + y * z:

        mov  eax, y     ; Must compute y * z first because
        imul eax, z     ; multiplication has a higher
        add eax, x      ; precedence than addition
        mov w, eax

; w = x / y - z:

        mov  eax, x     ; Here we need to compute division
        cdq             ; first because it has the highest
        idiv y          ; precedence
        sub eax, z
        mov w, eax
```

```
; w = x * y * z:

        mov  eax, y     ; Addition and multiplication are
        imul eax, z     ; commutative; therefore, the order
        imul eax, x     ; of evaluation does not matter
        mov  w, eax
```

The associativity rule has one exception: if an expression involves multiplication and division, it is generally better to perform the multiplication first. For example, given an expression of the form

```
w = x / y * z       ; Note: This is (x * z) / y, not x / (y * z)
```

it is usually better to compute x * z and then divide the result by y rather than divide x by y and multiply the quotient by z.

This approach is better for two reasons. First, remember that the imul instruction always produces a 64-bit result (assuming 32-bit operands). By doing the multiplication first, you automatically *sign-extend* the product into the EDX register so you do not have to sign-extend EAX prior to the division.

A second reason for doing the multiplication first is to increase the accuracy of the computation. Remember, (integer) division often produces an inexact result. For example, if you compute 5 / 2, you will get the value 2, not 2.5. Computing (5 / 2) × 3 produces 6. However, if you compute (5 × 3) / 2, you get the value 7, which is a little closer to the real quotient (7.5). Therefore, if you encounter an expression of the form

```
w = x / y * z;
```

you can usually convert it to the following assembly code:

```
mov  eax, x
imul z      ; Note the use of extended imul!
idiv y
mov  w, eax
```

If the algorithm you're encoding depends on the truncation effect of the division operation, you cannot use this trick to improve the algorithm. Moral of the story: always make sure you fully understand any expression you are converting to assembly language. If the semantics dictate that you must perform the division first, then do so.

Consider the following statement:

```
w = x - y * x;
```

Because subtraction is not commutative, you cannot compute y * x and then subtract x from this result. Rather than use a straightforward multiplication-and-addition sequence, you'll have to load x into a register, multiply y and x (leaving their product in a different register), and then subtract this product from x. For example:

```
mov  ecx, x
mov  eax, y
imul eax, x
sub  ecx, eax
mov  w, ecx
```

This trivial example demonstrates the need for *temporary variables* in an expression. The code uses the ECX register to temporarily hold a copy of x until it computes the product of y and x. As your expressions increase in complexity, the need for temporaries grows. Consider the following C statement:

```
w = (a + b) * (y + z);
```

Following the normal rules of algebraic evaluation, you compute the subexpressions inside the parentheses first (that is, the two subexpressions with the highest precedence) and set their values aside. When you've computed the values for both subexpressions, you can compute their product. One way to deal with a complex expression like this is to reduce it to a sequence of simple expressions whose results wind up in temporary variables. For example, you can convert the preceding single expression into the following sequence:

```
temp1 = a + b;
temp2 = y + z;
w = temp1 * temp2;
```

Because converting simple expressions to assembly language is quite easy, it's now a snap to compute the former complex expression in assembly. The code is shown here:

```
mov  eax, a
add  eax, b
mov  temp1, eax
mov  eax, y
add  eax, z
mov  temp2, eax
mov  eax, temp1
imul eax, temp2
mov  w, eax
```

This code is grossly inefficient and requires that you declare a couple of temporary variables in your data segment. However, it is easy to optimize this code by keeping temporary variables, as much as possible, in x86-64 registers. By using x86-64 registers to hold the temporary results, this code becomes the following:

```
mov  eax, a
add  eax, b
```

```
mov   ebx, y
add   ebx, z
imul  eax, ebx
mov   w, eax
```

Here's yet another example:

```
x = (y + z) * (a - b) / 10;
```

This can be converted to a set of four simple expressions:

```
temp1 = (y + z)
temp2 = (a - b)
temp1 = temp1 * temp2
x = temp1 / 10
```

You can convert these four simple expressions into the following assembly language statements:

```
      .const
ten   dword   10
        .
        .
        .
      mov   eax, y    ; Compute EAX = y + z
      add   eax, z
      mov   ebx, a    ; Compute EBX = a - b
      sub   ebx, b
      imul  ebx       ; This sign-extends EAX into EDX
      idiv  ten
      mov x, eax
```

The most important thing to keep in mind is that you should keep temporary values in registers for efficiency. Use memory locations to hold temporaries only if you've run out of registers.

Ultimately, converting a complex expression to assembly language is very similar to solving the expression by hand, except instead of actually computing the result at each stage of the computation, you simply write the assembly code that computes the result.

6.2.4   Commutative Operators

If *op* represents an operator, that operator is *commutative* if the following relationship is always true:

```
(A op B) = (B op A)
```

As you saw in the previous section, commutative operators are nice because the order of their operands is immaterial, and this lets you rearrange a computation, often making it easier or more efficient. Often, rearranging a computation allows you to use fewer temporary variables. Whenever you encounter a commutative operator in an expression, you should always check whether you can use a better sequence to improve the size or speed of your code.

Tables 6-8 and 6-9, respectively, list the commutative and noncommutative operators you typically find in high-level languages.

Table 6-8: Common Commutative Binary Operators

Pascal	C/C++	Description
+	+	Addition
*	*	Multiplication
and	&& or &	Logical or bitwise AND
or	|| or |	Logical or bitwise OR
xor	^	(Logical or) bitwise exclusive-OR
=	==	Equality
<>	!=	Inequality

Table 6-9: Common Noncommutative Binary Operators

Pascal	C/C++	Description
-	-	Subtraction
/ or div	/	Division
mod	%	Modulo or remainder
<	<	Less than
<=	<=	Less than or equal
>	>	Greater than
>=	>=	Greater than or equal

6.3 Logical (Boolean) Expressions

Consider the following expression from a C/C++ program:

```
b = ((x == y) && (a <= c)) || ((z - a) != 5);
```

Here, b is a Boolean variable, and the remaining variables are all integers.

Although it takes only a single bit to represent a Boolean value, most assembly language programmers allocate a whole byte or word to represent Boolean variables. Most programmers (and, indeed, some programming languages like C) choose 0 to represent false and anything else to represent true. Some people prefer to represent true and false with 1 and 0 (respectively) and not allow any other values. Others select all 1 bits (0FFFF_FFFF _FFFF_FFFFh, 0FFFF_FFFFh, 0FFFFh, or 0FFh) for true and 0 for false. You could also use a positive value for true and a negative value for false. All these mechanisms have their advantages and drawbacks.

Using only 0 and 1 to represent false and true offers two big advantages. First, the setcc instructions produce these results, so this scheme is compatible with those instructions. Second, the x86-64 logical instructions (and, or, xor, and, to a lesser extent, not) operate on these values exactly as you would expect. That is, if you have two Boolean variables a and b, then the following instructions perform the basic logical operations on these two variables:

```
; d = a AND b:

    mov al, a
    and al, b
    mov d, al

; d = a || b:

    mov al, a
    or al, b
    mov d, al

; d = a XOR b:

    mov al, a
    xor al, b
    mov d, al

; b = NOT a:

    mov al, a      ; Note that the NOT instruction does not
    not al         ; properly compute AL = NOT all by itself.
    and al, 1      ; That is, (NOT 0) does not equal 1. The AND
    mov b, al      ; instruction corrects this problem

    mov al, a      ; Another way to do b = NOT a;
    xor al, 1      ; Inverts bit 0
    mov b, al
```

As pointed out here, the not instruction will not properly compute logical negation. The bitwise not of 0 is 0FFh, and the bitwise not of 1 is 0FEh. Neither result is 0 or 1. However, by ANDing the result with 1, you get the proper result. Note that you can implement the not operation more efficiently by using the xor al, 1 instruction because it affects only the LO bit.

As it turns out, using 0 for false and anything else for true has a lot of subtle advantages. Specifically, the test for true or false is often implicit in the execution of any logical instruction. However, this mechanism suffers from a big disadvantage: you cannot use the x86-64 and, or, xor, and not instructions to implement the Boolean operations of the same name. Consider the two values 55h and 0AAh. They're both nonzero, so they both represent the value true. However, if you logically AND 55h and 0AAh together by using the x86-64 and instruction, the result is 0. True AND true should produce true, not false. Although you can account for situations like this, it usually requires a few extra instructions and is somewhat less efficient when computing Boolean operations.

A system that uses nonzero values to represent true and 0 to represent false is an *arithmetic logical system*. A system that uses two distinct values like 0 and 1 to represent false and true is called a *Boolean logical system*, or simply a Boolean system. You can use either system, as convenient. Consider again this Boolean expression:

```
b = ((x == y) and (a <= d)) || ((z - a) != 5);
```

The resulting simple expressions might be as follows:

```
mov    eax, x
cmp    eax, y
sete   al        ; AL = x == y;

mov    ebx, a
cmp    ebx, d
setle  bl        ; BL = a <= d;
and    bl, al    ; BL = (x = y) and (a <= d);

mov    eax, z
sub    eax, a
cmp    eax, 5
setne  al
or     al, bl    ; AL = ((x == y) && (a <= d)) ||
mov    b, al     ;      ((z - a) != 5);
```

When working with Boolean expressions, don't forget that you might be able to optimize your code by simplifying them with algebraic transformations. In Chapter 7, you'll also see how to use control flow to calculate a Boolean result, which is generally quite a bit more efficient than using *complete Boolean evaluation*, as the examples in this section teach.

6.4   Machine and Arithmetic Idioms

An *idiom* is an idiosyncrasy (a peculiarity). Several arithmetic operations and x86-64 instructions have idiosyncrasies that you can take advantage of when writing assembly language code. Some people refer to the use of machine and arithmetic idioms as *tricky programming* that you should always avoid in well-written programs. While it is wise to avoid tricks just for the sake of tricks, many machine and arithmetic idioms are well known and commonly found in assembly language programs. You will see some important idioms all the time, so it makes sense to discuss them.

6.4.1   *Multiplying Without mul or imul*

When multiplying by a constant, you can sometimes write faster code by using shifts, additions, and subtractions in place of multiplication instructions.

Remember, a `shl` instruction computes the same result as multiplying the specified operand by 2. Shifting to the left two bit positions multiplies the operand by 4. Shifting to the left three bit positions multiplies the operand by 8. In general, shifting an operand to the left n bits multiplies it by 2^n. You can multiply any value by a constant by using a series of shifts and additions or shifts and subtractions. For example, to multiply the AX register by 10, you need only multiply it by 8 and then add two times the original value. That is, $10 \times AX = 8 \times AX + 2 \times AX$. The code to accomplish this is as follows:

```
shl ax, 1        ; Multiply AX by 2
mov bx, ax       ; Save 2 * AX for later
shl ax, 2        ; Multiply AX by 8 (*4 really,
                 ; but AX contains *2)
add ax, bx       ; Add in AX * 2 to AX * 8 to get AX * 10
```

If you look at the instruction timings, the preceding shift-and-add example requires fewer clock cycles on some processors in the 80x86 family than the mul instruction. Of course, the code is somewhat larger (by a few bytes), but the performance improvement is usually worth it.

You can also use subtraction with shifts to perform a multiplication operation. Consider the following multiplication by 7:

```
mov ebx, eax     ; Save EAX * 1
shl eax, 3       ; EAX = EAX * 8
sub eax, ebx     ; EAX * 8 - EAX * 1 is EAX * 7
```

A common error that beginning assembly language programmers make is subtracting or adding 1 or 2 rather than EAX × 1 or EAX × 2. The following does not compute EAX × 7:

```
shl eax, 3
sub eax, 1
```

It computes $(8 \times EAX) - 1$, something entirely different (unless, of course, EAX = 1). Beware of this pitfall when using shifts, additions, and subtractions to perform multiplication operations.

You can also use the lea instruction to compute certain products. The trick is to use the scaled-index addressing modes. The following examples demonstrate some simple cases:

```
lea eax, [ecx][ecx]        ; EAX = ECX * 2
lea eax, [eax][eax * 2]    ; EAX = ECX * 3
lea eax, [eax * 4]         ; EAX = ECX * 4
lea eax, [ebx][ebx * 4]    ; EAX = EBX * 5
lea eax, [eax * 8]         ; EAX = EAX * 8
lea eax, [edx][edx * 8]    ; EAX = EDX * 9
```

As time has progressed, Intel (and AMD) has improved the performance of the imul instruction to the point that it rarely makes sense to try to improve performance by using *strength-reduction optimizations* such as substituting shifts and additions for a multiplication. You should consult the Intel and AMD documentation (particularly the section on instruction timing) to see if a multi-instruction sequence is faster. Generally, a single shift instruction (for multiplication by a power of 2) or lea is going to produce better results than imul; beyond that, it's best to measure and see.

6.4.2 Dividing Without div or idiv

Just as the shl instruction is useful for simulating a multiplication by a power of 2, the shr and sar instructions can simulate a division by a power of two. Unfortunately, you cannot easily use shifts, additions, and subtractions to perform division by an arbitrary constant. Therefore, this trick is useful only when dividing by powers of 2. Also, don't forget that the sar instruction rounds toward negative infinity, unlike the idiv instruction, which rounds toward 0.

You can also divide by a value by multiplying by its reciprocal. Because the mul instruction is faster than the div instruction, multiplying by a reciprocal is usually faster than division.

To multiply by a reciprocal when dealing with integers, we must cheat. If you want to multiply by 1/10, there is no way you can load the value 1/10 into an x86-64 integer register prior to performing the multiplication. However, we could multiply 1/10 by 10, perform the multiplication, and then divide the result by 10 to get the final result. Of course, this wouldn't buy you anything; in fact, it would make things worse because you're now doing a multiplication by 10 as well as a division by 10. However, suppose you multiply 1/10 by 65,536 (6554), perform the multiplication, and then divide by 65,536. This would still perform the correct operation, and, as it turns out, if you set up the problem correctly, you can get the division operation for free. Consider the following code that divides AX by 10:

```
mov dx, 6554        ; 6554 = round(65,536 / 10)
mul dx
```

This code leaves AX/10 in the DX register.

To understand how this works, consider what happens when you use the mul instruction to multiply AX by 65,536 (1_0000h). This moves AX into DX and sets AX to 0 (a multiplication by 1_0000h is equivalent to a shift left by 16 bits). Multiplying by 6554 (65,536 divided by 10) puts AX divided by 10 into the DX register. Because mul is faster than div, this technique runs a little faster than using division.

Multiplying by a reciprocal works well when you need to divide by a constant. You could even use this approach to divide by a variable, but the overhead to compute the reciprocal pays off only if you perform the division many, many times by the same value.

6.4.3 Implementing Modulo-N Counters with AND

If you want to implement a counter variable that counts up to $2^n - 1$ and then resets to 0, use the following code:

```
inc CounterVar
and CounterVar, n_bits
```

where *n_bits* is a binary value containing *n* bits of 1s right-justified in the number. For example, to create a counter that cycles between 0 and 15 ($2^4 - 1$), you could use the following:

```
inc CounterVar
and CounterVar, 00001111b
```

6.5 Floating-Point Arithmetic

Integer arithmetic does not let you represent fractional numeric values. Therefore, modern CPUs support an approximation of *real* arithmetic: *floating-point arithmetic*. To represent real numbers, most floating-point formats employ scientific notation and use a certain number of bits to represent a mantissa and a smaller number of bits to represent an exponent.

For example, in the number 3.456e+12, the mantissa consists of 3.456, and the exponent digits are 12. Because the number of bits is fixed in computer-based representations, computers can represent only a certain number of digits (known as *significant digits*) in the mantissa. For example, if a floating-point representation could handle only three significant digits, then the fourth digit in 3.456e+12 (the 6) could not be accurately represented with that format, as three significant digits can represent only 3.45e+12 correctly.

Because computer-based floating-point representations also use a finite number of bits to represent the exponent, it also has a limited range of values, ranging from $10^{\pm38}$ for the single-precision format to $10^{\pm308}$ for the double-precision format (and up to $10^{\pm4932}$ for the extended-precision format). This is known as the *dynamic range* of the value.

A big problem with floating-point arithmetic is that it does not follow the standard rules of algebra. Normal algebraic rules apply only to *infinite-precision* arithmetic.

Consider the simple statement $x = x + 1$, where *x* is an integer. On any modern computer, this statement follows the normal rules of algebra *as long as overflow does not occur.* That is, this statement is valid only for certain values of *x* (*minint* ≤ *x* < *maxint*). Most programmers do not have a problem with this because they are well aware that integers in a program do not follow the standard algebraic rules (for example, 5 / 2 does not equal 2.5).

Integers do not follow the standard rules of algebra because the computer represents them with a finite number of bits. You cannot represent any of the (integer) values above the maximum integer or below the minimum integer. Floating-point values suffer from this same problem, only worse. After all, integers are a subset of real numbers. Therefore, the floating-point values must represent the same infinite set of integers. However, an infinite number of real values exists between any two integer values. In addition to having to limit your values between a maximum and minimum range, you cannot represent all the values between any pair of integers, either.

To demonstrate the impact of limited-precision arithmetic, we will adopt a simplified decimal floating-point format for our examples. Our floating-point format will provide a mantissa with three significant digits and a decimal exponent with two digits. The mantissa and exponents are both signed values, as shown in Figure 6-1.

Figure 6-1: A floating-point format

When adding and subtracting two numbers in scientific notation, we must adjust the two values so that their exponents are the same. Multiplication and division don't require the exponents to be the same; instead, the exponent after a multiplication is the sum of the two operand exponents, and the exponent after a division is the difference of the dividend and divisor's exponents.

For example, when adding 1.2e1 and 4.5e0, we must adjust the values so they have the same exponent. One way to do this is to convert 4.5e0 to 0.45e1 and then add. This produces 1.65e1. Because the computation and result require only three significant digits, we can compute the correct result via the representation shown in Figure 6-1. However, suppose we want to add the two values 1.23e1 and 4.56e0. Although both values can be represented using the three-significant-digit format, the computation and result do not fit into three significant digits. That is, 1.23e1 + 0.456e1 requires four digits of precision in order to compute the correct result of 1.686, so we must either *round* or *truncate* the result to three significant digits. Rounding generally produces the most accurate result, so let's round the result to obtain 1.69e1.

In fact, the rounding does not occur after adding the two values together (that is, producing the sum 1.686e1 and then rounding this to 1.69e1). The rounding actually occurs when converting 4.56e0 to 0.456e1, because the value 0.456e1 requires four digits of precision to maintain. Therefore, during the conversion, we have to round it to 0.46e1 so that the result fits into three significant digits. Then, the sum of 1.23e1 and 0.46e1 produces the final (rounded) sum of 1.69e1.

As you can see, the lack of *precision* (the number of digits or bits we maintain in a computation) affects the *accuracy* (the correctness of the computation).

In the addition/subtraction example, we were able to round the result because we maintained *four* significant digits *during* the calculation (specifically, when converting 4.56e0 to 0.456e1). If our floating-point calculation had been limited to three significant digits during computation, we would have had to truncate the last digit of the smaller number, obtaining 0.45e1, resulting in a sum of 1.68e1, a value that is even less accurate.

To improve the accuracy of floating-point calculations, it is useful to maintain one or more extra digits for use during the calculation (such as the extra digit used to convert 4.56e0 to 0.456e1). Extra digits available during a computation are known as *guard digits* (or *guard bits* in the case of a binary format). They greatly enhance accuracy during a long chain of computations.

In a sequence of floating-point operations, the error can *accumulate* and greatly affect the computation itself. For example, suppose we were to add 1.23e3 to 1.00e0. Adjusting the numbers so their exponents are the same before the addition produces 1.23e3 + 0.001e3. The sum of these two values, even after rounding, is 1.23e3. This might seem perfectly reasonable to you; after all, we can maintain only three significant digits, so adding in a small value shouldn't affect the result at all. However, suppose we were to add 1.00e0 to 1.23e3 *10 times.*[5] The first time we add 1.00e0 to 1.23e3, we get 1.23e3. Likewise, we get this same result the second, third, fourth . . . and tenth times when we add 1.00e0 to 1.23e3. On the other hand, had we added 1.00e0 to itself 10 times, then added the result (1.00e1) to 1.23e3, we would have gotten a different result, 1.24e3. This is an important fact to know about limited-precision arithmetic:

> The order of evaluation can affect the accuracy of the result.

You will get more accurate results if the relative magnitudes (the exponents) are close to one another when adding and subtracting floating-point values. If you are performing a chain calculation involving addition and subtraction, you should attempt to group the values appropriately.

Another problem with addition and subtraction is that you can wind up with *false precision*. Consider the computation 1.23e0 – 1.22e0, which produces 0.01e0. Although the result is mathematically equivalent to 1.00e – 2, this latter form suggests that the last two digits are exactly 0. Unfortunately, we have only a single significant digit at this time (remember, the original result was 0.01e0, and those two leading 0s were significant digits). Indeed, some floating-point unit (FPU) or software packages might actually insert random digits (or bits) into the LO positions. This brings up a second important rule concerning limited-precision arithmetic:

> Subtracting two numbers with the same signs (or adding two numbers with different signs) can produce high-order significant digits (bits) that are 0. This reduces the number of significant digits (bits) by a like amount in the final result.

By themselves, multiplication and division do not produce particularly poor results. However, they tend to multiply any error that already exists in a value. For example, if you multiply 1.23e0 by 2, when you should be multiplying 1.24e0 by 2, the result is even less accurate. This brings up a third important rule when working with limited-precision arithmetic:

> When performing a chain of calculations involving addition, subtraction, multiplication, and division, try to perform the multiplication and division operations first.

Often, by applying normal algebraic transformations, you can arrange a calculation so the multiply and divide operations occur first. For example, suppose you want to compute x * (y + z). Normally, you would add y and

---

5. But not in the same calculation, where guard digits could maintain the fourth digit during the calculation.

z together and multiply their sum by x. However, you will get a little more accuracy if you transform x * (y + z) to get x * y + x * z and compute the result by performing the multiplications first.[6]

Multiplication and division are not without their own problems. When two very large or very small numbers are multiplied, it is quite possible for *overflow* or *underflow* to occur. The same situation occurs when dividing a small number by a large number, or dividing a large number by a small (fractional) number. This brings up a fourth rule you should attempt to follow when multiplying or dividing values:

> When multiplying and dividing sets of numbers, try to arrange the multiplications so that they multiply large and small numbers together; likewise, try to divide numbers that have the same relative magnitudes.

Given the inaccuracies present in any computation (including converting an input string to a floating-point value), you should *never* compare two floating-point values to see if they are equal. In a binary floating-point format, different computations that produce the same (mathematical) result may differ in their least significant bits. For example, 1.31e0 + 1.69e0 should produce 3.00e0. Likewise, 1.50e0 + 1.50e0 should produce 3.00e0. However, if you were to compare (1.31e0 + 1.69e0) against (1.50e0 + 1.50e0), you might find out that these sums are *not* equal to one another. The test for equality succeeds if and only if all bits (or digits) in the two operands are exactly the same. Because this is not necessarily true after two different floating-point computations that should produce the same result, a straight test for equality may not work. Instead, you should use the following test:

```
if Value1 >= (Value2 - error) and Value1 <= (Value2 + error) then ...
```

Another common way to handle this same comparison is to use a statement of this form:

```
if abs(Value1 - Value2) <= error then ...
```

error should be a value slightly greater than the largest amount of error that will creep into your computations. The exact value will depend on the particular floating-point format you use. Here is the final rule we will state in this section:

> When comparing two floating-point numbers, always compare one value to see if it is in the range given by the second value plus or minus a small error value.

Many other little problems can occur when using floating-point values. This book can point out only some of the major problems and make you aware that you cannot treat floating-point arithmetic like real arithmetic

---

6. Of course, the drawback is that you must now perform two multiplications rather than one, so the result may be slower.

because of the inaccuracies present in limited-precision arithmetic. A good text on numerical analysis or even scientific computing can help fill in the details. If you are going to be working with floating-point arithmetic *in any language,* you should take the time to study the effects of limited-precision arithmetic on your computations.

6.5.1 Floating-Point on the x86-64

When the 8086 CPU first appeared in the late 1970s, semiconductor technology was not to the point where Intel could put floating-point instructions directly on the 8086 CPU. Therefore, Intel devised a scheme to use a second chip to perform the floating-point calculations—the *8087 floating-point unit (or x87 FPU).*[7] By the release of the Intel Pentium chip, semiconductor technology had advanced to the point that the FPU was fully integrated onto the x86 CPU. Today, the x86-64 still contains the x87 FPU device, but it has also expanded the floating-point capabilities by using the SSE, SSE2, AVX, and AVX2 instruction sets.

This section describes the x86 FPU instruction set. Later sections (and chapters) discuss the more advanced floating-point capabilities of the SSE through AVX2 instruction sets.

6.5.2 FPU Registers

The x87 FPUs add 14 registers to the x86-64: eight floating-point data registers, a control register, a status register, a tag register, an instruction pointer, a data pointer, and an opcode register. The *data registers* are similar to the x86-64's general-purpose register set insofar as all floating-point calculations take place in these registers. The *control register* contains bits that let you decide how the FPU handles certain degenerate cases like rounding of inaccurate computations; it also contains bits that control precision and so on. The *status register* is similar to the x86-64's FLAGS register; it contains the condition code bits and several other floating-point flags that describe the state of the FPU. The *tag register* contains several groups of bits that determine the state of the value in each of the eight floating-point data registers. The *instruction, data pointer,* and *opcode* registers contain certain state information about the last floating-point instruction executed. We do not consider the last four registers here; see the Intel documentation for more details.

6.5.2.1 FPU Data Registers

The FPUs provide eight 80-bit data registers organized as a stack, a significant departure from the organization of the general-purpose registers on the x86-64 CPU. MASM refers to these registers as ST(0), ST(1), . . . ST(7).[8]

---

7. Intel has also referred to this device as the *Numeric Data Processor (NDP), Numeric Processor Extension (NPX),* and *math coprocessor.*

8. Often, programmers will create text equates for these register names to use the identifiers ST0 to ST7.

The biggest difference between the FPU register set and the x86-64 register set is the stack organization. On the x86-64 CPU, the AX register is always the AX register, no matter what happens. On the FPU, however, the register set is an eight-element stack of 80-bit floating-point values (Figure 6-2).

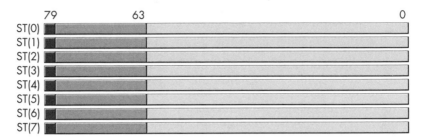

Figure 6-2: FPU floating-point register stack

ST(0) refers to the item on the top of stack, ST(1) refers to the next item on the stack, and so on. Many floating-point instructions push and pop items on the stack; therefore, ST(1) will refer to the previous contents of ST(0) after you push something onto the stack. Getting used to the register numbers changing will take some thought and practice, but this is an easy problem to overcome.

6.5.2.2 The FPU Control Register

When Intel designed the 8087 (and, essentially, the IEEE floating-point standard), there were no standards in floating-point hardware. Different (mainframe and mini) computer manufacturers all had different and incompatible floating-point formats. Unfortunately, several applications had been written taking into account the idiosyncrasies of these different floating-point formats.

Intel wanted to design an FPU that could work with the majority of the software out there (keep in mind that the IBM PC was three to four years away when Intel began designing the 8087, so Intel couldn't rely on that "mountain" of software available for the PC to make its chip popular). Unfortunately, many of the features found in these older floating-point formats were mutually incompatible. For example, in some floating-point systems, rounding would occur when there was insufficient precision; in others, truncation would occur. Some applications would work with one floating-point system but not with the other.

Intel wanted as many applications as possible to work with as few changes as possible on its 8087 FPUs, so it added a special register, the *FPU control register*, that lets the user choose one of several possible operating modes for the FPU. The 80x87 control register contains 16 bits organized as shown in Figure 6-3.

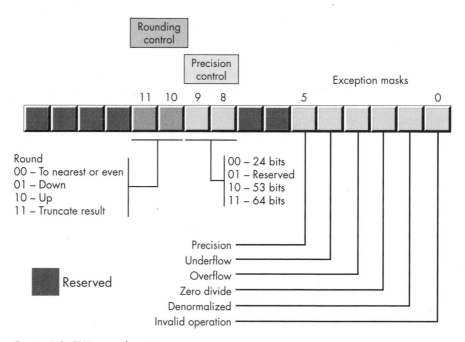

Figure 6-3: FPU control register

Bits 10 and 11 of the FPU control register provide rounding control according to the values in Table 6-10.

Table 6-10: Rounding Control

Bits 10 and 11	Function
00	To nearest or even
01	Round down
10	Round up
11	Truncate

The 00 setting is the default. The FPU rounds up values above one-half of the least significant bit. It rounds down values below one-half of the least significant bit. If the value below the least significant bit is exactly one-half of the least significant bit, the FPU rounds the value toward the value whose least significant bit is 0. For long strings of computations, this provides a reasonable, automatic way to maintain maximum precision.

The round-up and round-down options are present for those computations requiring accuracy. By setting the rounding control to round down and performing the operation, then repeating the operation with the rounding control set to round up, you can determine the minimum and maximum ranges between which the true result will fall.

The truncate option forces all computations to truncate any excess bits. You will rarely use this option if accuracy is important. However, you might use this option to help when porting older software to the FPU. This option is also extremely useful when converting a floating-point value to an integer. Because most software expects floating-point–to–integer conversions to truncate the result, you will need to use the truncation/rounding mode to achieve this.

Bits 8 and 9 of the control register specify the precision during computation. This capability is provided to allow compatibility with older software as required by the IEEE 754 standard. The precision-control bits use the values in Table 6-11.

Table 6-11: Mantissa Precision-Control Bits

Bits 8 and 9	Precision control
00	24 bits
01	Reserved
10	53 bits
11	64 bits

Some CPUs may operate faster with floating-point values whose precision is 53 bits (that is, 64-bit floating-point format) rather than 64 bits (that is, 80-bit floating-point format). See the documentation for your specific processor for details. Generally, the CPU defaults these bits to 11 to select the 64-bit mantissa precision.

Bits 0 to 5 are the *exception masks*. These are similar to the interrupt enable bit in the x86-64's FLAGS register. If these bits contain a 1, the corresponding condition is ignored by the FPU. However, if any bit contains 0s, and the corresponding condition occurs, then the FPU immediately generates an interrupt so the program can handle the degenerate condition.

Bit 0 corresponds to an invalid operation error, which generally occurs as the result of a programming error. Situations that raise the invalid operation exception include pushing more than eight items onto the stack or attempting to pop an item off an empty stack, taking the square root of a negative number, or loading a non-empty register.

Bit 1 masks the *denormalized* interrupt that occurs whenever you try to manipulate denormalized values. Denormalized exceptions occur when you load arbitrary extended-precision values into the FPU or work with very small numbers just beyond the range of the FPU's capabilities. Normally, you would probably *not* enable this exception. If you enable this exception and the FPU generates this interrupt, the Windows runtime system raises an exception.

Bit 2 masks the *zero-divide* exception. If this bit contains 0, the FPU will generate an interrupt if you attempt to divide a nonzero value by 0. If you do not enable the zero-divide exception, the FPU will produce NaN whenever you perform a zero division. It's probably a good idea to enable this exception by programming a 0 into this bit. Note that if your program generates this interrupt, the Windows runtime system will raise an exception.

Bit 3 masks the *overflow* exception. The FPU will raise the overflow exception if a calculation overflows or if you attempt to store a value that is too large to fit into the destination operand (for example, storing a large extended-precision value into a single-precision variable). If you enable this exception and the FPU generates this interrupt, the Windows runtime system raises an exception.

Bit 4, if set, masks the *underflow* exception. Underflow occurs when the result is too small to fit in the destination operand. Like overflow, this exception can occur whenever you store a small extended-precision value into a smaller variable (single or double precision) or when the result of a computation is too small for extended precision. If you enable this exception and the FPU generates this interrupt, the Windows runtime system raises an exception.

Bit 5 controls whether the *precision* exception can occur. A precision exception occurs whenever the FPU produces an imprecise result, generally the result of an internal rounding operation. Although many operations will produce an exact result, many more will not. For example, dividing 1 by 10 will produce an inexact result. Therefore, this bit is usually 1 because inexact results are common. If you enable this exception and the FPU generates this interrupt, the Windows runtime system raises an exception.

Bits 6 and 7, and 12 to 15, in the control register are currently undefined and reserved for future use (bits 7 and 12 were valid on older FPUs but are no longer used).

The FPU provides two instructions, `fldcw` (*load control word*) and `fstcw` (*store control word*), that let you load and store the contents of the control register, respectively. The single operand to these instructions must be a 16-bit memory location. The `fldcw` instruction loads the control register from the specified memory location. `fstcw` stores the control register into the specified memory location. The syntax for these instructions is shown here:

```
fldcw mem16
fstcw mem16
```

Here's some example code that sets the rounding control to *truncate result* and sets the rounding precision to 24 bits:

```
        .data
fcw16   word    ?
        .
        .
        .
        fstcw fcw16
        mov   ax, fcw16
        and   ax, 0f0ffh ; Clears bits 8-11
        or    ax, 0c00h  ; Rounding control = %11, Precision = %00
        mov   fcw16, ax
        fldcw fcw16
```

6.5.2.3 The FPU Status Register

The 16-bit FPU status register provides the status of the FPU at the instant you read it; its layout appears in Figure 6-4. The `fstsw` instruction stores the 16-bit floating-point status register into a word variable.

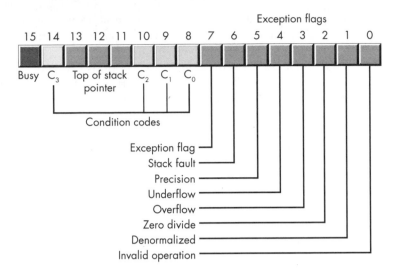

Figure 6-4: The FPU status register

Bits 0 through 5 are the exception flags. These bits appear in the same order as the exception masks in the control register. If the corresponding condition exists, the bit is set. These bits are independent of the exception masks in the control register. The FPU sets and clears these bits regardless of the corresponding mask setting.

Bit 6 indicates a *stack fault*. A stack fault occurs whenever a stack overflow or underflow occurs. When this bit is set, the C_1 condition code bit determines whether there was a stack overflow ($C_1 = 1$) or stack underflow ($C_1 = 0$) condition.

Bit 7 of the status register is set if *any* error condition bit is set. It is the logical or of bits 0 through 5. A program can test this bit to quickly determine if an error condition exists.

Bits 8, 9, 10, and 14 are the coprocessor condition code bits. Various instructions set the condition code bits, as shown in Tables 6-12 and 6-13, respectively.

Table 6-12: FPU Comparison Condition Code Bits (X = "Don't care")

Instruction	Condition code bits				Condition
	C_3	C_2	C_1	C_0	
fcom	0	0	X	0	ST > source
fcomp	0	0	X	1	ST < source
fcompp	1	0	X	0	ST = source
ficom	1	1	X	1	ST or source not comparable
ficomp					
ftst	0	0	X	0	ST is positive
	0	0	X	1	ST is negative
	1	0	X	0	ST is 0 (+ or −)
	1	1	X	1	ST is not comparable

Instruction	Condition code bits				Condition
	C_3	C_2	C_1	C_0	
fxam	0	0	0	0	Unsupported
	0	0	1	0	Unsupported
	0	1	0	0	+ Normalized
	0	1	1	0	− Normalized
	1	0	0	0	+ 0
	1	0	1	0	− 0
	1	1	0	0	+ Denormalized
	1	1	1	0	− Denormalized
	0	0	0	1	+ NaN
	0	0	1	1	− NaN
	0	1	0	1	+ Infinity
	0	1	1	1	− Infinity
	1	0	X	1	Empty register
fucom	0	0	X	0	ST > source
fucomp	0	0	X	1	ST < source
fucompp	1	0	X	0	ST = source
	1	1	X	1	Unordered/not comparable

Table 6-13: FPU Condition Code Bits (X = "Don't care")

Instruction	Condition code bits			
	C_3	C_2	C_1	C_0
fcom, fcomp, fcompp, ftst, fucom, fucomp, fucompp, ficom, ficomp	Result of comparison, see Table 6-12.	Operands are not comparable.	Set to 0.	Result of comparison, see Table 6-12.
fxam	See Table 6-12.	See Table 6-12.	Sign of result, or stack overflow/ underflow if stack exception bit is set.	See Table 6-12.
fprem, fprem1	Bit 0 of quotient	0—reduction done 1—reduction incomplete	Bit 0 of quotient, or stack overflow/ underflow if stack exception bit is set.	Bit 2 of quotient
fist, fbstp, frndint, fst, fstp, fadd, fmul, fdiv, fdivr, fsub, fsubr, fscale, fsqrt, fpatan, f2xm1, fyl2x, fyl2xp1	Undefined	Undefined	Rounding direction if exception; otherwise, set to 0.	Undefined
fptan, fsin, fcos, fsincos	Undefined	Set to 1 if within range; otherwise, 0.	Round-up occurred or stack overflow/ underflow if stack exception bit is set. Undefined if C_2 is set.	Undefined

(continued)

Table 6-13: FPU Condition Code Bits (X = "Don't care") *(continued)*

Instruction	Condition code bits			
	C_3	C_2	C_1	C_0
fchs, fabs, fxch, fincstp, fdecstp, const loads, fxtract, fld, fild, fbld, fstp (80 bit)	Undefined	Undefined	Set to 0 or stack overflow/underflow if stack exception bit is set.	Undefined
fldenv, frstor	Restored from memory operand	Restored from memory operand	Restored from memory operand	Restored from memory operand
fldcw, fstenv, fstcw, fstsw, fclex	Undefined	Undefined	Undefined	Undefined
finit, fsave	Cleared to 0	Cleared to 0	Cleared to 0	Cleared to 0

Bits 11 to 13 of the FPU status register provide the register number of the top of stack. During computations, the FPU adds (modulo 8) the logical register numbers supplied by the programmer to these 3 bits to determine the *physical* register number at runtime.

Bit 15 of the status register is the *busy bit*. It is set whenever the FPU is busy. This bit is a historical artifact from the days when the FPU was a separate chip; most programs will have little reason to access this bit.

6.5.3   FPU Data Types

The FPU supports seven data types: three integer types, a packed decimal type, and three floating-point types. The *integer type* supports 16-, 32-, and 64-bit integers, although it is often faster to do the integer arithmetic by using the integer unit of the CPU. The *packed decimal type* provides an 18-digit signed decimal (BCD) integer. The primary purpose of the BCD format is to convert between strings and floating-point values. The remaining three data types are the 32-, 64-, and 80-bit *floating-point data types*. The 80x87 data types appear in Figures 6-5, 6-6, and 6-7. Just note, for future reference, that the largest BCD value the x87 supports is an 18-digit BCD value (bits 72 to 78 are unused in this format).

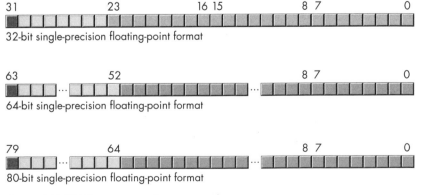

31   23   16 15   8 7   0

32-bit single-precision floating-point format

63   52   8 7   0

64-bit single-precision floating-point format

79   64   8 7   0

80-bit single-precision floating-point format

Figure 6-5: FPU floating-point formats

The FPU generally stores values in a *normalized* format. The HO bit of the mantissa is always 1 when a floating-point number is normalized. In the 32- and 64-bit floating-point formats, the FPU does not actually store this bit; the FPU always assumes that it is 1. Therefore, 32- and 64-bit floating-point numbers are always normalized. In the extended-precision 80-bit floating-point format, the FPU does *not* assume that the HO bit of the mantissa is 1; the HO bit of the mantissa appears as part of the string of bits.

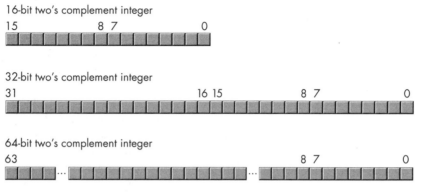

Figure 6-6: FPU integer formats

Normalized values provide the greatest precision for a given number of bits. However, many non-normalized values *cannot* be represented with the 80-bit format. These values are very close to 0 and represent the set of values whose mantissa HO bit is not 0. The FPUs support a special 80-bit form known as *denormalized* values. Denormalized values allow the FPU to encode very small values it cannot encode using normalized values, but denormalized values offer fewer bits of precision than normalized values. Therefore, using denormalized values in a computation may introduce slight inaccuracy. Of course, this is always better than underflowing the denormalized value to 0 (which could make the computation even less accurate), but you must keep in mind that if you work with very small values, you may lose some accuracy in your computations. The FPU status register contains a bit you can use to detect when the FPU uses a denormalized value in a computation.

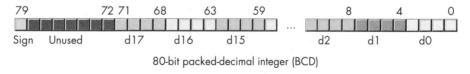

80-bit packed-decimal integer (BCD)

Figure 6-7: FPU packed decimal format

6.5.4 The FPU Instruction Set

The FPU adds many instructions to the x86-64 instruction set. We can classify these instructions as data movement instructions, conversions, arithmetic instructions, comparisons, constant instructions, transcendental instructions, and miscellaneous instructions. The following sections describe each of the instructions in these categories.

6.5.5 FPU Data Movement Instructions

The *data movement instructions* transfer data between the internal FPU registers and memory. The instructions in this category are fld, fst, fstp, and fxch. The fld instruction always pushes its operand onto the floating-point stack. The fstp instruction always pops the top of stack after storing it. The remaining instructions do not affect the number of items on the stack.

6.5.5.1 The fld Instruction

The fld instruction loads a 32-, 64-, or 80-bit floating-point value onto the stack. This instruction converts 32- and 64-bit operands to an 80-bit extended-precision value before pushing the value onto the floating-point stack.

The fld instruction first decrements the TOS pointer (bits 11 to 13 of the status register) and then stores the 80-bit value in the physical register specified by the new TOS pointer. If the source operand of the fld instruction is a floating-point data register, st(*i*), then the actual register that the FPU uses for the load operation is the register number *before* decrementing the TOS pointer. Therefore, fld st(0) duplicates the value on the top of stack.

The fld instruction sets the stack fault bit if stack overflow occurs. It sets the denormalized exception bit if you load an 80-bit denormalized value. It sets the invalid operation bit if you attempt to load an empty floating-point register onto the TOS (or perform another invalid operation).

Here are some examples:

```
fld st(1)
fld real4_variable
fld real8_variable
fld real10_variable
fld real8 ptr [rbx]
```

There is no way to directly load a 32-bit integer register onto the floating-point stack, even if that register contains a real4 value. To do so, you must first store the integer register into a memory location, and then push that memory location onto the FPU stack by using the fld instruction. For example:

```
mov tempReal4, eax  ; Save real4 value in EAX to memory
fld tempReal4       ; Push that value onto the FPU stack
```

6.5.5.2 The fst and fstp Instructions

The fst and fstp instructions copy the value on the top of the floating-point stack to another floating-point register or to a 32-, 64-, or (fstp only) 80-bit memory variable. When copying data to a 32- or 64-bit memory variable, the FPU rounds the 80-bit extended-precision value on the TOS to the smaller format as specified by the rounding control bits in the FPU control register.

By incrementing the TOS pointer in the status register after accessing the data in ST(0), the fstp instruction pops the value off the top of stack when moving it to the destination location. If the destination operand is a floating-point register, the FPU stores the value at the specified register number *before* popping the data off the top of stack.

Executing an `fstp st(0)` instruction effectively pops the data off the top of stack with no data transfer. Here are some examples:

```
fst real4_variable
fst real8_variable
fst realArray[rbx * 8]
fst st(2)
fstp st(1)
```

The last example effectively pops ST(1) while leaving ST(0) on the top of stack.

The `fst` and `fstp` instructions will set the stack exception bit if a stack underflow occurs (attempting to store a value from an empty register stack). They will set the precision bit if a loss of precision occurs during the store operation (for example, when storing an 80-bit extended-precision value into a 32- or 64-bit memory variable and some bits are lost during conversion). They will set the underflow exception bit when storing an 80-bit value into a 32- or 64-bit memory variable, but the value is too small to fit into the destination operand. Likewise, these instructions will set the overflow exception bit if the value on the top of stack is too big to fit into a 32- or 64-bit memory variable. They set the invalid operation flag if an invalid operation (such as storing into an empty register) occurs. Finally, these instructions set the C_1 condition bit if rounding occurs during the store operation (this occurs only when storing into a 32- or 64-bit memory variable and you have to round the mantissa to fit into the destination) or if a stack fault occurs.

NOTE *Because of an idiosyncrasy in the FPU instruction set related to the encoding of the instructions, you cannot use the `fst` instruction to store data into a `real10` memory variable. You may, however, store 80-bit data by using the `fstp` instruction.*

6.5.5.3 The fxch Instruction

The `fxch` instruction exchanges the value on the top of stack with one of the other FPU registers. This instruction takes two forms: one with a single FPU register as an operand and the second without any operands. The first form exchanges the top of stack with the specified register. The second form of `fxch` swaps the top of stack with ST(1).

Many FPU instructions (for example, `fsqrt`) operate only on the top of the register stack. If you want to perform such an operation on a value that is not on top, you can use the `fxch` instruction to swap that register with TOS, perform the desired operation, and then use `fxch` to swap the TOS with the original register. The following example takes the square root of ST(2):

```
fxch st(2)
fsqrt
fxch st(2)
```

The fxch instruction sets the stack exception bit if the stack is empty; it sets the invalid operation bit if you specify an empty register as the operand; and it always clears the C_1 condition code bit.

6.5.6 Conversions

The FPU performs all arithmetic operations on 80-bit real quantities. In a sense, the fld and fst/fstp instructions are conversion instructions because they automatically convert between the internal 80-bit real format and the 32- and 64-bit memory formats. Nonetheless, we'll classify them as data movement operations, rather than conversions, because they are moving real values to and from memory. The FPU provides six other instructions that convert to or from integer or BCD format when moving data. These instructions are fild, fist, fistp, fisttp, fbld, and fbstp.

6.5.6.1 The fild Instruction

The fild (*integer load*) instruction converts a 16-, 32-, or 64-bit two's complement integer to the 80-bit extended-precision format and pushes the result onto the stack. This instruction always expects a single operand: the address of a word, double-word, or quad-word integer variable. You cannot specify one of the x86-64's 16-, 32-, or 64-bit general-purpose registers. If you want to push the value of an x86-64 general-purpose register onto the FPU stack, you must first store it into a memory variable and then use fild to push that memory variable.

The fild instruction sets the stack exception bit and C_1 (accordingly) if stack overflow occurs while pushing the converted value. Look at these examples:

```
fild word_variable
fild dword_val[rcx * 4]
fild qword_variable
fild sqword ptr [rbx]
```

6.5.6.2 The fist, fistp, and fisttp Instructions

The fist, fistp, and fisttp instructions convert the 80-bit extended-precision variable on the top of stack to a 16-, 32-, or (fistp/fistpp only) 64-bit integer and store the result away into the memory variable specified by the single operand. The fist and fistp instructions convert the value on TOS to an integer according to the rounding setting in the FPU control register (bits 10 and 11). The fisttp instruction always does the conversion using the truncation mode. As with the fild instruction, the fist, fistp, and fisttp instructions will not let you specify one of the x86-64's general-purpose 16-, 32-, or 64-bit registers as the destination operand.

The fist instruction converts the value on the top of stack to an integer and then stores the result; it does not otherwise affect the floating-point register stack. The fistp and fisttp instructions pop the value off the floating-point register stack after storing the converted value.

These instructions set the stack exception bit if the floating-point register stack is empty (this will also clear C_1). They set the precision (imprecise operation) and C_1 bits if rounding occurs (that is, if the value in ST(0) has any fractional component). These instructions set the underflow exception bit if the result is too small (less than 1 but greater than 0, or less than 0 but greater than –1). Here are some examples:

```
fist   word_var[rbx * 2]
fist   dword_var
fisttp dword_var
fistp  qword_var
```

The fist and fistp instructions use the rounding control settings to determine how they will convert the floating-point data to an integer during the store operation. By default, the rounding control is usually set to round mode; yet, most programmers expect fist/fistp to truncate the decimal portion during conversion. If you want fist/fistp to truncate floating-point values when converting them to an integer, you will need to set the rounding control bits appropriately in the floating-point control register (or use the fisttp instruction to truncate the result regardless of the rounding control bits). Here's an example:

```
          .data
fcw16     word    ?
fcw16_2   word    ?
IntResult sdword  ?
             .
             .
             .
    fstcw fcw16
    mov   ax, fcw16
    or    ax, 0c00h      ; Rounding = %11 (truncate)
    mov   fcw16_2, ax    ; Store and reload the ctrl word
    fldcw fcw16_2

    fistp IntResult      ; Truncate ST(0) and store as int32

    fldcw fcw16          ; Restore original rounding control
```

6.5.6.3   The fbld and fbstp Instructions

The fbld and fbstp instructions load and store 80-bit BCD values. The fbld instruction converts a BCD value to its 80-bit extended-precision equivalent and pushes the result onto the stack. The fbstp instruction pops the extended-precision real value on TOS, converts it to an 80-bit BCD value (rounding according to the bits in the floating-point control register), and stores the converted result at the address specified by the destination memory operand. There is no fbst instruction.

The fbld instruction sets the stack exception bit and C_1 if stack overflow occurs. The results are undefined if you attempt to load an invalid BCD value. The `fbstp` instruction sets the stack exception bit and clears C_1 if stack underflow occurs (the stack is empty). It sets the underflow flag under the same conditions as `fist` and `fistp`. Look at these examples:

```
; Assuming fewer than eight items on the stack, the following
; code sequence is equivalent to an fbst instruction:

        fld   st(0)
        fbstp tbyte_var

; The following example easily converts an 80-bit BCD value to
; a 64-bit integer:

        fbld  tbyte_var
        fistp qword_var
```

These two instructions are especially useful for converting between string and floating-point formats. Along with the `fild` and `fist` instructions, you can use `fbld` and `fbstp` to convert between integer and string formats (see "Converting Unsigned Decimal Values to Strings" in Chapter 9).

6.5.7   Arithmetic Instructions

Arithmetic instructions make up a small but important subset of the FPU's instruction set. These instructions fall into two general categories: those that operate on real values and those that operate on a real and an integer value.

6.5.7.1   The fadd, faddp, and fiadd Instructions

The `fadd`, `faddp`, and `fiadd` instructions take the following forms:

```
fadd
faddp
fadd    st(i), st(0)
fadd    st(0), st(i)
faddp   st(i), st(0)
fadd    mem32
fadd    mem64
fiadd   mem16
fiadd   mem32
```

The `fadd` instruction, with no operands, is a synonym for `faddp`. The `faddp` instruction (also with no operands) pops the two values on the top of stack, adds them, and pushes their sum back onto the stack.

The next two forms of the `fadd` instruction, those with two FPU register operands, behave like the x86-64's `add` instruction. They add the value in the source register operand to the value in the destination register operand. One of the register operands must be ST(0).

The faddp instruction with two operands adds ST(0) (which must always be the source operand) to the destination operand and then pops ST(0). The destination operand must be one of the other FPU registers.

The last two forms, fadd with a memory operand, adds a 32- or 64-bit floating-point variable to the value in ST(0). This instruction will convert the 32- or 64-bit operands to an 80-bit extended-precision value before performing the addition. Note that this instruction does *not* allow an 80-bit memory operand. There are also instructions for adding 16- and 32-bit integers in memory to ST(0): fiadd mem_{16} and fiadd mem_{32}.

These instructions can raise the stack, precision, underflow, overflow, denormalized, and illegal operation exceptions, as appropriate. If a stack fault exception occurs, C_1 denotes stack overflow or underflow, or the rounding direction (see Table 6-13).

Listing 6-1 demonstrates the various forms of the fadd instruction.

```
; Listing 6-1

; Demonstration of various forms of fadd.

        option  casemap:none

nl          =       10

            .const
ttlStr      byte    "Listing 6-1", 0
fmtSt0St1   byte    "st(0):%f, st(1):%f", nl, 0
fmtAdd1     byte    "fadd: st0:%f", nl, 0
fmtAdd2     byte    "faddp: st0:%f", nl, 0
fmtAdd3     byte    "fadd st(1), st(0): st0:%f, st1:%f", nl, 0
fmtAdd4     byte    "fadd st(0), st(1): st0:%f, st1:%f", nl, 0
fmtAdd5     byte    "faddp st(1), st(0): st0:%f", nl, 0
fmtAdd6     byte    "fadd mem: st0:%f", nl, 0

zero        real8   0.0
one         real8   1.0
two         real8   2.0
minusTwo    real8   -2.0

            .data
st0         real8   0.0
st1         real8   0.0

            .code
            externdef printf:proc

; Return program title to C++ program:

            public  getTitle
getTitle    proc
            lea     rax, ttlStr
            ret
getTitle    endp
```

```
; printFP - Prints values of st0 and (possibly) st1.
;           Caller must pass in ptr to fmtStr in RCX.

printFP    proc
           sub    rsp, 40

; For varargs (for example, printf call), double
; values must appear in RDX and R8 rather
; than XMM1, XMM2.
; Note: if only one double arg in format
; string, printf call will ignore 2nd
; value in R8.

           mov    rdx, qword ptr st0
           mov    r8, qword ptr st1
           call   printf
           add    rsp, 40
           ret
printFP    endp

; Here is the "asmMain" function.

           public asmMain
asmMain    proc
           push   rbp
           mov    rbp, rsp
           sub    rsp, 48          ; Shadow storage

; Demonstrate various fadd instructions:

           mov    rax, qword ptr one
           mov    qword ptr st1, rax
           mov    rax, qword ptr minusTwo
           mov    qword ptr st0, rax
           lea    rcx, fmtSt0St1
           call   printFP

; fadd (same as faddp):

           fld    one
           fld    minusTwo
           fadd                    ; Pops st(0)!
           fstp   st0

           lea    rcx, fmtAdd1
           call   printFP

; faddp:

           fld    one
           fld    minusTwo
           faddp                   ; Pops st(0)!
           fstp   st0
```

```
                lea     rcx, fmtAdd2
                call    printFP

; fadd st(1), st(0):

                fld     one
                fld     minusTwo
                fadd    st(1), st(0)
                fstp    st0
                fstp    st1

                lea     rcx, fmtAdd3
                call    printFP

; fadd st(0), st(1):

                fld     one
                fld     minusTwo
                fadd    st(0), st(1)
                fstp    st0
                fstp    st1

                lea     rcx, fmtAdd4
                call    printFP

; faddp st(1), st(0):

                fld     one
                fld     minusTwo
                faddp   st(1), st(0)
                fstp    st0

                lea     rcx, fmtAdd5
                call    printFP

; faddp mem64:

                fld     one
                fadd    two
                fstp    st0

                lea     rcx, fmtAdd6
                call    printFP

                leave
                ret     ; Returns to caller

asmMain         endp
                end
```

Listing 6-1: Demonstration of fadd instructions

Here's the build command and output for the program in Listing 6-1:

```
C:\>build listing6-1

C:\>echo off
 Assembling: listing6-1.asm
c.cpp

C:\>listing6-1
Calling Listing 6-1:
st(0):-2.000000, st(1):1.000000
fadd: st0:-1.000000
faddp: st0:-1.000000
fadd st(1), st(0): st0:-2.000000, st1:-1.000000
fadd st(0), st(1): st0:-1.000000, st1:1.000000
faddp st(1), st(0): st0:-1.000000
fadd mem: st0:3.000000
Listing 6-1 terminated
```

6.5.7.2 The fsub, fsubp, fsubr, fsubrp, fisub, and fisubr Instructions

These six instructions take the following forms:

```
fsub
fsubp
fsubr
fsubrp

fsub    st(i), st(0)
fsub    st(0), st(i)
fsubp   st(i), st(0)
fsub    mem32
fsub    mem64

fsubr   st(i), st(0)
fsubr   st(0), st(i)
fsubrp  st(i), st(0)
fsubr   mem32
fsubr   mem64

fisub   mem16
fisub   mem32
fisubr  mem16
fisubr  mem32
```

With no operands, fsub is the same as fsubp (without operands). With no operands, the fsubp instruction pops ST(0) and ST(1) from the register stack, computes ST(1) − ST(0), and then pushes the difference back onto the stack. The fsubr and fsubrp instructions (*reverse subtraction*) operate in an identical fashion except they compute ST(0) − ST(1).

With two register operands (*destination, source*), the fsub instruction computes *destination = destination − source*. One of the two registers must be

ST(0). With two registers as operands, the fsubp also computes *destination = destination − source*, and then it pops ST(0) off the stack after computing the difference. For the fsubp instruction, the source operand must be ST(0).

With two register operands, the fsubr and fsubrp instructions work in a similar fashion to fsub and fsubp, except they compute *destination = source − destination*.

The fsub mem_{32}, fsub mem_{64}, fsubr mem_{32}, and fsubr mem_{64} instructions accept a 32- or 64-bit memory operand. They convert the memory operand to an 80-bit extended-precision value and subtract this from ST(0) (fsub) or subtract ST(0) from this value (fsubr) and store the result back into ST(0). There are also instructions for subtracting 16- and 32-bit integers in memory from ST(0): fisub mem_{16} and fisub mem_{32} (also fisubr mem_{16} and fisubr mem_{32}).

These instructions can raise the stack, precision, underflow, overflow, denormalized, and illegal operation exceptions, as appropriate. If a stack fault exception occurs, C_1 denotes stack overflow or underflow, or indicates the rounding direction (see Table 6-13).

Listing 6-2 demonstrates the fsub/fsubr instructions.

```
; Listing 6-2

; Demonstration of various forms of fsub/fsubrl.

        option  casemap:none

nl          =       10

            .const
ttlStr      byte    "Listing 6-2", 0
fmtStoSt1   byte    "st(0):%f, st(1):%f", nl, 0
fmtSub1     byte    "fsub: st0:%f", nl, 0
fmtSub2     byte    "fsubp: st0:%f", nl, 0
fmtSub3     byte    "fsub st(1), st(0): st0:%f, st1:%f", nl, 0
fmtSub4     byte    "fsub st(0), st(1): st0:%f, st1:%f", nl, 0
fmtSub5     byte    "fsubp st(1), st(0): st0:%f", nl, 0
fmtSub6     byte    "fsub mem: st0:%f", nl, 0
fmtSub7     byte    "fsubr st(1), st(0): st0:%f, st1:%f", nl, 0
fmtSub8     byte    "fsubr st(0), st(1): st0:%f, st1:%f", nl, 0
fmtSub9     byte    "fsubrp st(1), st(0): st0:%f", nl, 0
fmtSub10    byte    "fsubr mem: st0:%f", nl, 0

zero        real8   0.0
three       real8   3.0
minusTwo    real8   -2.0

            .data
st0         real8   0.0
st1         real8   0.0

            .code
            externdef printf:proc
```

```
            ; Return program title to C++ program:

                    public  getTitle
    getTitle        proc
                    lea     rax, ttlStr
                    ret
    getTitle        endp

            ; printFP - Prints values of st0 and (possibly) st1.
            ;           Caller must pass in ptr to fmtStr in RCX.

    printFP         proc
                    sub     rsp, 40

            ; For varargs (for example, printf call), double
            ; values must appear in RDX and R8 rather
            ; than XMM1, XMM2.
            ; Note: if only one double arg in format
            ; string, printf call will ignore 2nd
            ; value in R8.

                    mov     rdx, qword ptr st0
                    mov     r8, qword ptr st1
                    call    printf
                    add     rsp, 40
                    ret
    printFP         endp

            ; Here is the "asmMain" function.

                    public  asmMain
    asmMain         proc
                    push    rbp
                    mov     rbp, rsp
                    sub     rsp, 48    ; Shadow storage

            ; Demonstrate various fsub instructions:

                    mov     rax, qword ptr three
                    mov     qword ptr st1, rax
                    mov     rax, qword ptr minusTwo
                    mov     qword ptr st0, rax
                    lea     rcx, fmtSt0St1
                    call    printFP

            ; fsub (same as fsubp):

                    fld     three
                    fld     minusTwo
                    fsub                        ; Pops st(0)!
                    fstp    st0

                    lea     rcx, fmtSub1
                    call    printFP
```

```
; fsubp:

            fld     three
            fld     minusTwo
            fsubp                       ; Pops st(0)!
            fstp    st0

            lea     rcx, fmtSub2
            call    printFP

; fsub st(1), st(0):

            fld     three
            fld     minusTwo
            fsub    st(1), st(0)
            fstp    st0
            fstp    st1

            lea     rcx, fmtSub3
            call    printFP

; fsub st(0), st(1):

            fld     three
            fld     minusTwo
            fsub    st(0), st(1)
            fstp    st0
            fstp    st1

            lea     rcx, fmtSub4
            call    printFP

; fsubp st(1), st(0):

            fld     three
            fld     minusTwo
            fsubp   st(1), st(0)
            fstp    st0

            lea     rcx, fmtSub5
            call    printFP

; fsub mem64:

            fld     three
            fsub    minusTwo
            fstp    st0

            lea     rcx, fmtSub6
            call    printFP

; fsubr st(1), st(0):

            fld     three
            fld     minusTwo
```

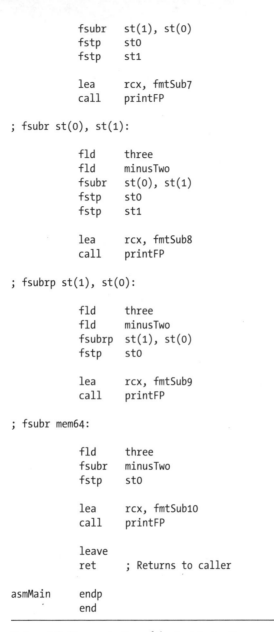

```
        fsubr    st(1), st(0)
        fstp     st0
        fstp     st1

        lea      rcx, fmtSub7
        call     printFP

; fsubr st(0), st(1):

        fld      three
        fld      minusTwo
        fsubr    st(0), st(1)
        fstp     st0
        fstp     st1

        lea      rcx, fmtSub8
        call     printFP

; fsubrp st(1), st(0):

        fld      three
        fld      minusTwo
        fsubrp   st(1), st(0)
        fstp     st0

        lea      rcx, fmtSub9
        call     printFP

; fsubr mem64:

        fld      three
        fsubr    minusTwo
        fstp     st0

        lea      rcx, fmtSub10
        call     printFP

        leave
        ret      ; Returns to caller

asmMain endp
        end
```

Listing 6-2: Demonstration of the fsub instructions

Here's the build command and output for Listing 6-2:

```
C:\>build listing6-2

C:\>echo off
 Assembling: listing6-2.asm
c.cpp
```

```
C:\>listing6-2
Calling Listing 6-2:
st(0):-2.000000, st(1):3.000000
fsub: st0:5.000000
fsubp: st0:5.000000
fsub st(1), st(0): st0:-2.000000, st1:5.000000
fsub st(0), st(1): st0:-5.000000, st1:3.000000
fsubp st(1), st(0): st0:5.000000
fsub mem: st0:5.000000
fsubr st(1), st(0): st0:-2.000000, st1:-5.000000
fsubr st(0), st(1): st0:5.000000, st1:3.000000
fsubrp st(1), st(0): st0:-5.000000
fsubr mem: st0:-5.000000
Listing 6-2 terminated
```

6.5.7.3 The fmul, fmulp, and fimul Instructions

The fmul and fmulp instructions multiply two floating-point values. The fimul instruction multiples an integer and a floating-point value. These instructions allow the following forms:

```
fmul
fmulp

fmul   st(0), st(i)
fmul   st(i), st(0)
fmul   mem_{32}
fmul   mem_{64}

fmulp st(i), st(0)

fimul mem_{16}
fimul mem_{32}
```

With no operands, fmul is a synonym for fmulp. The fmulp instruction, with no operands, will pop ST(0) and ST(1), multiply these values, and push their product back onto the stack. The fmul instructions with two register operands compute *destination = destination × source*. One of the registers (source or destination) must be ST(0).

The fmulp st(0), st(i) instruction computes $ST(i) = ST(i) \times ST(0)$ and then pops ST(0). This instruction uses the value for i before popping ST(0). The fmul mem_{32} and fmul mem_{64} instructions require a 32- or 64-bit memory operand, respectively. They convert the specified memory variable to an 80-bit extended-precision value and then multiply ST(0) by this value. There are also instructions for multiplying 16- and 32-bit integers in memory by ST(0): fimul mem_{16} and fimul mem_{32}.

These instructions can raise the stack, precision, underflow, overflow, denormalized, and illegal operation exceptions, as appropriate. If rounding occurs during the computation, these instructions set the C_1 condition code bit. If a stack fault exception occurs, C_1 denotes stack overflow or underflow.

Listing 6-3 demonstrates the various forms of the fmul instruction.

```
; Listing 6-3

; Demonstration of various forms of fmul.

        option  casemap:none

nl          =       10

            .const
ttlStr      byte    "Listing 6-3", 0
fmtStoSt1   byte    "st(0):%f, st(1):%f", nl, 0
fmtMul1     byte    "fmul: st0:%f", nl, 0
fmtMul2     byte    "fmulp: st0:%f", nl, 0
fmtMul3     byte    "fmul st(1), st(0): st0:%f, st1:%f", nl, 0
fmtMul4     byte    "fmul st(0), st(1): st0:%f, st1:%f", nl, 0
fmtMul5     byte    "fmulp st(1), st(0): st0:%f", nl, 0
fmtMul6     byte    "fmul mem: st0:%f", nl, 0

zero        real8   0.0
three       real8   3.0
minusTwo    real8   -2.0

            .data
st0         real8   0.0
st1         real8   0.0

            .code
            externdef printf:proc

; Return program title to C++ program:

            public  getTitle
getTitle    proc
            lea     rax, ttlStr
            ret
getTitle    endp

; printFP - Prints values of st0 and (possibly) st1.
;           Caller must pass in ptr to fmtStr in RCX.

printFP     proc
            sub     rsp, 40

; For varargs (for example, printf call), double
; values must appear in RDX and R8 rather
; than XMM1, XMM2.
; Note: if only one double arg in format
; string, printf call will ignore 2nd
; value in R8.

            mov     rdx, qword ptr st0
            mov     r8, qword ptr st1
            call    printf
```

```
            add     rsp, 40
            ret
printFP     endp

; Here is the "asmMain" function.

            public  asmMain
asmMain     proc
            push    rbp
            mov     rbp, rsp
            sub     rsp, 48         ; Shadow storage

; Demonstrate various fmul instructions:

            mov     rax, qword ptr three
            mov     qword ptr st1, rax
            mov     rax, qword ptr minusTwo
            mov     qword ptr st0, rax
            lea     rcx, fmtSt0St1
            call    printFP

; fmul (same as fmulp):

            fld     three
            fld     minusTwo
            fmul                    ; Pops st(0)!
            fstp    st0

            lea     rcx, fmtMul1
            call    printFP

; fmulp:

            fld     three
            fld     minusTwo
            fmulp                   ; Pops st(0)!
            fstp    st0

            lea     rcx, fmtMul2
            call    printFP

; fmul st(1), st(0):

            fld     three
            fld     minusTwo
            fmul    st(1), st(0)
            fstp    st0
            fstp    st1

            lea     rcx, fmtMul3
            call    printFP

; fmul st(0), st(1):

            fld     three
```

```
                fld     minusTwo
                fmul    st(0), st(1)
                fstp    st0
                fstp    st1

                lea     rcx, fmtMul4
                call    printFP

; fmulp st(1), st(0):

                fld     three
                fld     minusTwo
                fmulp   st(1), st(0)
                fstp    st0

                lea     rcx, fmtMul5
                call    printFP

; fmulp mem64:

                fld     three
                fmul    minusTwo
                fstp    st0

                lea     rcx, fmtMul6
                call    printFP

                leave
                ret     ; Returns to caller

asmMain         endp
                end
```

Listing 6-3: Demonstration of the fmul *instruction*

Here is the build command and output for Listing 6-3:

```
C:\>build listing6-3

C:\>echo off
 Assembling: listing6-3.asm
c.cpp

C:\>listing6-3
Calling Listing 6-3:
st(0):-2.000000, st(1):3.000000
fmul: st0:-6.000000
fmulp: st0:-6.000000
fmul st(1), st(0): st0:-2.000000, st1:-6.000000
fmul st(0), st(1): st0:-6.000000, st1:3.000000
fmulp st(1), st(0): st0:-6.000000
fmul mem: st0:-6.000000
Listing 6-3 terminated
```

6.5.7.4 The fdiv, fdivp, fdivr, fdivrp, fidiv, and fidivr Instructions

These six instructions allow the following forms:

```
fdiv
fdivp
fdivr
fdivrp

fdiv   st(0), st(i)
fdiv   st(i), st(0)
fdivp  st(i), st(0)

fdivr  st(0), st(i)
fdivr  st(i), st(0)
fdivrp st(i), st(0)

fdiv   mem₃₂
fdiv   mem₆₄
fdivr  mem₃₂
fdivr  mem₆₄

fidiv  mem₁₆
fidiv  mem₃₂
fidivr mem₁₆
fidivr mem₃₂
```

With no operands, the fdiv instruction is a synonym for fdivp. The fdivp instruction with no operands computes $ST(1) = ST(1) / ST(0)$. The fdivr and fdivrp instructions work in a similar fashion to fdiv and fdivp except that they compute $ST(0) / ST(1)$ rather than $ST(1) / ST(0)$.

With two register operands, these instructions compute the following quotients:

```
fdiv   st(0), st(i)    ; st(0) = st(0)/st(i)
fdiv   st(i), st(0)    ; st(i) = st(i)/st(0)
fdivp  st(i), st(0)    ; st(i) = st(i)/st(0) then pop st0
fdivr  st(0), st(i)    ; st(0) = st(i)/st(0)
fdivr  st(i), st(0)    ; st(i) = st(0)/st(i)
fdivrp st(i), st(0)    ; st(i) = st(0)/st(i) then pop st0
```

The fdivp and fdivrp instructions also pop $ST(0)$ after performing the division operation. The value for i in these two instructions is computed before popping $ST(0)$.

These instructions can raise the stack, precision, underflow, overflow, denormalized, zero divide, and illegal operation exceptions, as appropriate. If rounding occurs during the computation, these instructions set the C_1 condition code bit. If a stack fault exception occurs, C_1 denotes stack overflow or underflow.

Listing 6-4 provides a demonstration of the fdiv/fdivr instructions.

```
; Listing 6-4

; Demonstration of various forms of fsub/fsubrl.

        option  casemap:none

nl            =       10

              .const
ttlStr        byte    "Listing 6-4", 0
fmtSt0St1     byte    "st(0):%f, st(1):%f", nl, 0
fmtDiv1       byte    "fdiv: st0:%f", nl, 0
fmtDiv2       byte    "fdivp: st0:%f", nl, 0
fmtDiv3       byte    "fdiv st(1), st(0): st0:%f, st1:%f", nl, 0
fmtDiv4       byte    "fdiv st(0), st(1): st0:%f, st1:%f", nl, 0
fmtDiv5       byte    "fdivp st(1), st(0): st0:%f", nl, 0
fmtDiv6       byte    "fdiv mem: st0:%f", nl, 0
fmtDiv7       byte    "fdivr st(1), st(0): st0:%f, st1:%f", nl, 0
fmtDiv8       byte    "fdivr st(0), st(1): st0:%f, st1:%f", nl, 0
fmtDiv9       byte    "fdivrp st(1), st(0): st0:%f", nl, 0
fmtDiv10      byte    "fdivr mem: st0:%f", nl, 0

three         real8   3.0
minusTwo      real8   -2.0

              .data
st0           real8   0.0
st1           real8   0.0

              .code
              externdef printf:proc

; Return program title to C++ program:

              public  getTitle
getTitle      proc
              lea     rax, ttlStr
              ret
getTitle      endp

; printFP - Prints values of st0 and (possibly) st1.
;           Caller must pass in ptr to fmtStr in RCX.

printFP       proc
              sub     rsp, 40

; For varargs (for example, printf call), double
; values must appear in RDX and R8 rather
; than XMM1, XMM2.
; Note: if only one double arg in format
; string, printf call will ignore 2nd
; value in R8.
```

```
                mov     rdx, qword ptr st0
                mov     r8, qword ptr st1
                call    printf
                add     rsp, 40
                ret
printFP         endp

; Here is the "asmMain" function.

                public  asmMain
asmMain         proc
                push    rbp
                mov     rbp, rsp
                sub     rsp, 48         ; Shadow storage

; Demonstrate various fdiv instructions:

                mov     rax, qword ptr three
                mov     qword ptr st1, rax
                mov     rax, qword ptr minusTwo
                mov     qword ptr st0, rax
                lea     rcx, fmtSt0St1
                call    printFP

; fdiv (same as fdivp):

                fld     three
                fld     minusTwo
                fdiv                    ; Pops st(0)!
                fstp    st0

                lea     rcx, fmtDiv1
                call    printFP

; fdivp:

                fld     three
                fld     minusTwo
                fdivp                   ; Pops st(0)!
                fstp    st0

                lea     rcx, fmtDiv2
                call    printFP

; fdiv st(1), st(0):

                fld     three
                fld     minusTwo
                fdiv    st(1), st(0)
                fstp    st0
                fstp    st1

                lea     rcx, fmtDiv3
                call    printFP
```

```
; fdiv st(0), st(1):

                fld     three
                fld     minusTwo
                fdiv    st(0), st(1)
                fstp    st0
                fstp    st1

                lea     rcx, fmtDiv4
                call    printFP

; fdivp st(1), st(0):

                fld     three
                fld     minusTwo
                fdivp   st(1), st(0)
                fstp    st0

                lea     rcx, fmtDiv5
                call    printFP

; fdiv mem64:

                fld     three
                fdiv    minusTwo
                fstp    st0

                lea     rcx, fmtDiv6
                call    printFP

; fdivr st(1), st(0):

                fld     three
                fld     minusTwo
                fdivr   st(1), st(0)
                fstp    st0
                fstp    st1

                lea     rcx, fmtDiv7
                call    printFP

; fdivr st(0), st(1):

                fld     three
                fld     minusTwo
                fdivr   st(0), st(1)
                fstp    st0
                fstp    st1

                lea     rcx, fmtDiv8
                call    printFP

; fdivrp st(1), st(0):

                fld     three
```

```
            fld     minusTwo
            fdivrp  st(1), st(0)
            fstp    st0

            lea     rcx, fmtDiv9
            call    printFP

; fdivr mem64:

            fld     three
            fdivr   minusTwo
            fstp    st0

            lea     rcx, fmtDiv10
            call    printFP

            leave
            ret     ; Returns to caller

asmMain     endp
            end
```

Listing 6-4: Demonstration of the fdiv/fdivr instructions

Here's the build command and sample output for Listing 6-4:

```
C:\>build listing6-4

C:\>echo off
 Assembling: listing6-4.asm
c.cpp

C:\>listing6-4
Calling Listing 6-4:
st(0):-2.000000, st(1):3.000000
fdiv: st0:-1.500000
fdivp: st0:-1.500000
fdiv st(1), st(0): st0:-2.000000, st1:-1.500000
fdiv st(0), st(1): st0:-0.666667, st1:3.000000
fdivp st(1), st(0): st0:-1.500000
fdiv mem: st0:-1.500000
fdivr st(1), st(0): st0:-2.000000, st1:-0.666667
fdivr st(0), st(1): st0:-1.500000, st1:3.000000
fdivrp st(1), st(0): st0:-0.666667
fdivr mem: st0:-0.666667
Listing 6-4 terminated
```

6.5.7.5   The fsqrt Instruction

The fsqrt routine does not allow any operands. It computes the square root of the value on TOS and replaces ST(0) with this result. The value on TOS must be 0 or positive; otherwise, fsqrt will generate an invalid operation exception.

This instruction can raise the stack, precision, denormalized, and invalid operation exceptions, as appropriate. If rounding occurs during the computation, fsqrt sets the C_1 condition code bit. If a stack fault exception occurs, C_1 denotes stack overflow or underflow.

Here's an example:

```
; Compute z = sqrt(x**2 + y**2):

        fld x                ; Load x
        fld st(0)            ; Duplicate x on TOS
        fmulp                ; Compute x**2

        fld y                ; Load y
        fld st(0)            ; Duplicate y
        fmul                 ; Compute y**2

        faddp                ; Compute x**2 + y**2
        fsqrt                ; Compute sqrt(x**2 + y**2)
        fstp z               ; Store result away into z
```

6.5.7.6   The fprem and fprem1 Instructions

The fprem and fprem1 instructions compute a *partial remainder* (a value that may require additional computation to produce the actual remainder). Intel designed the fprem instruction before the IEEE finalized its floating-point standard. In the final draft of that standard, the definition of fprem was a little different from Intel's original design. To maintain compatibility with the existing software that used the fprem instruction, Intel designed a new version to handle the IEEE partial remainder operation, fprem1. You should always use fprem1 in new software; therefore, we will discuss only fprem1 here, although you use fprem in an identical fashion.

fprem1 computes the partial remainder of ST(0) / ST(1). If the difference between the exponents of ST(0) and ST(1) is less than 64, fprem1 can compute the exact remainder in one operation. Otherwise, you will have to execute fprem1 two or more times to get the correct remainder value. The C_2 condition code bit determines when the computation is complete. Note that fprem1 does *not* pop the two operands off the stack; it leaves the partial remainder in ST(0) and the original divisor in ST(1) in case you need to compute another partial product to complete the result.

The fprem1 instruction sets the stack exception flag if there aren't two values on the top of stack. It sets the underflow and denormal exception bits if the result is too small. It sets the invalid operation bit if the values on TOS are inappropriate for this operation. It sets the C_2 condition code bit if the partial remainder operation is not complete (or on stack underflow). Finally, it loads C_1, C_2, and C_0 with bits 0, 1, and 2 of the quotient, respectively.

An example follows:

```
; Compute z = x % y:

        fld y
        fld x
repeatLp:

        fprem1
        fstsw ax       ; Get condition code bits into AX
        and   ah, 1    ; See if C2 is set
        jnz   repeatLp ; Repeat until C2 is clear
        fstp z         ; Store away the remainder
        fstp st(0)     ; Pop old y value
```

6.5.7.7 The frndint Instruction

The frndint instruction rounds the value on TOS to the nearest integer by using the rounding algorithm specified in the control register.

This instruction sets the stack exception flag if there is no value on the TOS (it will also clear C_1 in this case). It sets the precision and denormal exception bits if a loss of precision occurred. It sets the invalid operation flag if the value on the TOS is not a valid number. Note that the result on the TOS is still a floating-point value; it simply does not have a fractional component.

6.5.7.8 The fabs Instruction

fabs computes the absolute value of ST(0) by clearing the mantissa sign bit of ST(0). It sets the stack exception bit and invalid operation bits if the stack is empty.

Here's an example:

```
; Compute x = sqrt(abs(x)):

        fld   x
        fabs
        fsqrt
        fstp  x
```

6.5.7.9 The fchs Instruction

fchs changes the sign of ST(0)'s value by inverting the mantissa sign bit (this is the floating-point negation instruction). It sets the stack exception bit and invalid operation bits if the stack is empty.

Look at this example:

```
; Compute x = -x if x is positive, x = x if x is negative.
; That is, force x to be a negative value.
```

```
fld   x
fabs
fchs
fstp x
```

6.5.8 Comparison Instructions

The FPU provides several instructions for comparing real values. The fcom, fcomp, and fcompp instructions compare the two values on the top of stack and set the condition codes appropriately. The ftst instruction compares the value on the top of stack with 0.

Generally, most programs test the condition code bits immediately after a comparison. Unfortunately, no instructions test the FPU condition codes. Instead, you use the fstsw instruction to copy the floating-point status register into the AX register, then the sahf instruction to copy the AH register into the x86-64's condition code bits. Then you can test the standard x86-64 flags to check for a condition. This technique copies C_0 into the carry flag, C_2 into the parity flag, and C_3 into the zero flag. The sahf instruction does not copy C_1 into any of the x86-64's flag bits.

Because sahf does not copy any FPU status bits into the sign or overflow flags, you cannot use signed comparison instructions. Instead, use unsigned operations (for example, seta, setb, ja, jb) when testing the results of a floating-point comparison. Yes, these instructions normally test unsigned values, and *floating-point numbers are signed values.* However, use the unsigned operations anyway; the fstsw and sahf instructions set the x86-64 FLAGS register as though you had compared unsigned values with the cmp instruction.

The x86-64 processors provide an extra set of floating-point comparison instructions that directly affect the x86-64 condition code flags. These instructions circumvent having to use fstsw and sahf to copy the FPU status into the x86-64 condition codes. These instructions include fcomi and fcomip. You use them just like the fcom and fcomp instructions, except, of course, you do not have to manually copy the status bits to the FLAGS register.

6.5.8.1 The fcom, fcomp, and fcompp Instructions

The fcom, fcomp, and fcompp instructions compare ST(0) to the specified operand and set the corresponding FPU condition code bits based on the result of the comparison. The legal forms for these instructions are as follows:

```
fcom
fcomp
fcompp

fcom  st(i)
fcomp st(i)

fcom   mem32
fcom   mem64
fcomp  mem32
fcomp  mem64
```

With no operands, fcom, fcomp, and fcompp compare ST(0) against ST(1) and set the FPU flags accordingly. In addition, fcomp pops ST(0) off the stack, and fcompp pops both ST(0) and ST(1) off the stack.

With a single-register operand, fcom and fcomp compare ST(0) against the specified register. fcomp also pops ST(0) after the comparison.

With a 32- or 64-bit memory operand, the fcom and fcomp instructions convert the memory variable to an 80-bit extended-precision value and then compare ST(0) against this value, setting the condition code bits accordingly. fcomp also pops ST(0) after the comparison.

These instructions set C_2 (which winds up in the parity flag when using sahf) if the two operands are not comparable (for example, NaN). If it is possible for an illegal floating-point value to wind up in a comparison, you should check the parity flag for an error before checking the desired condition (for example, with the setp/setnp or jp/jnp instructions).

These instructions set the stack fault bit if there aren't two items on the top of the register stack. They set the denormalized exception bit if either or both operands are denormalized. They set the invalid operation flag if either or both operands are NaNs. These instructions always clear the C_1 condition code.

Let's look at an example of a floating-point comparison:

```
        fcompp
        fstsw ax
        sahf
        setb al     ; AL = true if st(0) < st(1)
            .
            .
            .
        fcompp
        fstsw ax
        sahf
        jnb st1GEst0

    ; Code that executes if st(0) < st(1).

st1GEst0:
```

Because all x86-64 64-bit CPUs support the fcomi and fcomip instructions (described in the next section), you should consider using those instructions as they spare you from having to store the FPU status word into AX and then copy AH into the FLAGS register before testing the condition. On the other hand, fcomi and fcomip support only a limited number of operand forms (the fcom and fcomp instructions are more general).

Listing 6-5 is a sample program that demonstrates the use of the various fcom instructions.

```
; Listing 6-5

; Demonstration of fcom instructions.

        option   casemap:none
```

```
nl              =       10

                .const
ttlStr          byte    "Listing 6-5", 0
fcomFmt         byte    "fcom %f < %f is %d", nl, 0
fcomFmt2        byte    "fcom(2) %f < %f is %d", nl, 0
fcomFmt3        byte    "fcom st(1) %f < %f is %d", nl, 0
fcomFmt4        byte    "fcom st(1) (2) %f < %f is %d", nl, 0
fcomFmt5        byte    "fcom mem %f < %f is %d", nl, 0
fcomFmt6        byte    "fcom mem %f (2) < %f is %d", nl, 0
fcompFmt        byte    "fcomp %f < %f is %d", nl, 0
fcompFmt2       byte    "fcomp (2) %f < %f is %d", nl, 0
fcompFmt3       byte    "fcomp st(1) %f < %f is %d", nl, 0
fcompFmt4       byte    "fcomp st(1) (2) %f < %f is %d", nl, 0
fcompFmt5       byte    "fcomp mem %f < %f is %d", nl, 0
fcompFmt6       byte    "fcomp mem (2) %f < %f is %d", nl, 0
fcomppFmt       byte    "fcompp %f < %f is %d", nl, 0
fcomppFmt2      byte    "fcompp (2) %f < %f is %d", nl, 0


three           real8   3.0
zero            real8   0.0
minusTwo        real8   -2.0

                .data
st0             real8   ?
st1             real8   ?

                .code
                externdef printf:proc

; Return program title to C++ program:

                public  getTitle
getTitle        proc
                lea     rax, ttlStr
                ret
getTitle        endp

; printFP - Prints values of st0 and (possibly) st1.
;           Caller must pass in ptr to fmtStr in RCX.

printFP         proc
                sub     rsp, 40

; For varargs (for example, printf call), double
; values must appear in RDX and R8 rather
; than XMM1, XMM2.
; Note: if only one double arg in format
; string, printf call will ignore 2nd
; value in R8.

                mov     rdx, qword ptr st0
                mov     r8, qword ptr st1
                movzx   r9, al
```

```
            call    printf
            add     rsp, 40
            ret
printFP     endp

; Here is the "asmMain" function.

            public  asmMain
asmMain     proc
            push    rbp
            mov     rbp, rsp
            sub     rsp, 48    ; Shadow storage

; fcom demo:

            xor     eax, eax
            fld     three
            fld     zero
            fcom
            fstsw   ax
            sahf
            setb    al
            fstp    st0
            fstp    st1
            lea     rcx, fcomFmt
            call    printFP

; fcom demo 2:

            xor     eax, eax
            fld     zero
            fld     three
            fcom
            fstsw   ax
            sahf
            setb    al
            fstp    st0
            fstp    st1
            lea     rcx, fcomFmt2
            call    printFP

; fcom st(i) demo:

            xor     eax, eax
            fld     three
            fld     zero
            fcom    st(1)
            fstsw   ax
            sahf
            setb    al
            fstp    st0
            fstp    st1
            lea     rcx, fcomFmt3
            call    printFP
```

```
; fcom st(i) demo 2:

            xor     eax, eax
            fld     zero
            fld     three
            fcom    st(1)
            fstsw   ax
            sahf
            setb    al
            fstp    st0
            fstp    st1
            lea     rcx, fcomFmt4
            call    printFP

; fcom mem64 demo:

            xor     eax, eax
            fld     three           ; Never on stack so
            fstp    st1             ; copy for output
            fld     zero
            fcom    three
            fstsw   ax
            sahf
            setb    al
            fstp    st0
            lea     rcx, fcomFmt5
            call    printFP

; fcom mem64 demo 2:

            xor     eax, eax
            fld     zero            ; Never on stack so
            fstp    st1             ; copy for output
            fld     three
            fcom    zero
            fstsw   ax
            sahf
            setb    al
            fstp    st0
            lea     rcx, fcomFmt6
            call    printFP

; fcomp demo:

            xor     eax, eax
            fld     zero
            fld     three
            fst     st0             ; Because this gets popped
            fcomp
            fstsw   ax
            sahf
            setb    al
            fstp    st1
            lea     rcx, fcompFmt
            call    printFP
```

```
; fcomp demo 2:

                xor     eax, eax
                fld     three
                fld     zero
                fst     st0             ; Because this gets popped
                fcomp
                fstsw   ax
                sahf
                setb    al
                fstp    st1
                lea     rcx, fcompFmt2
                call    printFP

; fcomp demo 3:

                xor     eax, eax
                fld     zero
                fld     three
                fst     st0             ; Because this gets popped
                fcomp   st(1)
                fstsw   ax
                sahf
                setb    al
                fstp    st1
                lea     rcx, fcompFmt3
                call    printFP

; fcomp demo 4:

                xor     eax, eax
                fld     three
                fld     zero
                fst     st0             ; Because this gets popped
                fcomp   st(1)
                fstsw   ax
                sahf
                setb    al
                fstp    st1
                lea     rcx, fcompFmt4
                call    printFP

; fcomp demo 5:

                xor     eax, eax
                fld     three
                fstp    st1
                fld     zero
                fst     st0             ; Because this gets popped
                fcomp   three
                fstsw   ax
                sahf
                setb    al
                lea     rcx, fcompFmt5
                call    printFP
```

```
; fcomp demo 6:

            xor     eax, eax
            fld     zero
            fstp    st1
            fld     three
            fst     st0             ; Because this gets popped
            fcomp   zero
            fstsw   ax
            sahf
            setb    al
            lea     rcx, fcompFmt6
            call    printFP

; fcompp demo:

            xor     eax, eax
            fld     zero
            fst     st1             ; Because this gets popped
            fld     three
            fst     st0             ; Because this gets popped
            fcompp
            fstsw   ax
            sahf
            setb    al
            lea     rcx, fcomppFmt
            call    printFP

; fcompp demo 2:

            xor     eax, eax
            fld     three
            fst     st1             ; Because this gets popped
            fld     zero
            fst     st0             ; Because this gets popped
            fcompp
            fstsw   ax
            sahf
            setb    al
            lea     rcx, fcomppFmt2
            call    printFP

            leave
            ret     ; Returns to caller

asmMain     endp
            end
```

Listing 6-5: Program that demonstrates the fcom instructions

Here's the build command and output for the program in Listing 6-5:

```
C:\>build listing6-5

C:\>echo off
```

```
Assembling: listing6-5.asm
c.cpp
```

C:\>listing6-5
```
Calling Listing 6-5:
fcom 0.000000 < 3.000000 is 1
fcom(2) 3.000000 < 0.000000 is 0
fcom st(1) 0.000000 < 3.000000 is 1
fcom st(1) (2) 3.000000 < 0.000000 is 0
fcom mem 0.000000 < 3.000000 is 1
fcom mem 3.000000 (2) < 0.000000 is 0
fcomp 3.000000 < 0.000000 is 0
fcomp (2) 0.000000 < 3.000000 is 1
fcomp st(1) 3.000000 < 0.000000 is 0
fcomp st(1) (2) 0.000000 < 3.000000 is 1
fcomp mem 0.000000 < 3.000000 is 1
fcomp mem (2) 3.000000 < 0.000000 is 0
fcompp 3.000000 < 0.000000 is 0
fcompp (2) 0.000000 < 3.000000 is 1
Listing 6-5 terminated
```

NOTE *The x87 FPU also provides instructions that do* unordered comparisons*: fucom, fucomp, and fucompp. These are functionally equivalent to fcom, fcomp, and fcompp except they raise an exception under different conditions. See the Intel documentation for more details.*

6.5.8.2 The fcomi and fcomip Instructions

The fcomi and fcomip instructions compare ST(0) to the specified operand and set the corresponding FLAGS condition code bits based on the result of the comparison. You use these instructions in a similar manner to fcom and fcomp except you can test the CPU's flag bits directly after the execution of these instructions without first moving the FPU status bits into the FLAGS register. The legal forms for these instructions are as follows:

```
fcomi    st(0), st(i)
fcomip   st(0), st(i)
```

Note that a *pop-pop* version (fcomipp) does not exist. If all you want to do is compare the top two items on the FPU stack, you will have to explicitly pop that item yourself (for example, by using the fstp st(0) instruction).

Listing 6-6 is a sample program that demonstrates the operation of the fcomi and fcomip instructions.

```
; Listing 6-6

; Demonstration of fcomi and fcomip instructions.

        option  casemap:none

nl          =       10
```

```
                .const
ttlStr          byte        "Listing 6-6", 0
fcomiFmt        byte        "fcomi %f < %f is %d", nl, 0
fcomiFmt2       byte        "fcomi(2) %f < %f is %d", nl, 0
fcomipFmt       byte        "fcomip %f < %f is %d", nl, 0
fcomipFmt2      byte        "fcomip (2) %f < %f is %d", nl, 0

three           real8       3.0
zero            real8       0.0
minusTwo        real8       -2.0

                .data
st0             real8       ?
st1             real8       ?

                .code
                externdef printf:proc

; Return program title to C++ program:

                public  getTitle
getTitle        proc
                lea     rax, ttlStr
                ret
getTitle        endp

; printFP - Prints values of st0 and (possibly) st1.
;           Caller must pass in ptr to fmtStr in RCX.

printFP         proc
                sub     rsp, 40

; For varargs (for example, printf call), double
; values must appear in RDX and R8 rather
; than XMM1, XMM2.
; Note: if only one double arg in format
; string, printf call will ignore 2nd
; value in R8.

                mov     rdx, qword ptr st0
                mov     r8, qword ptr st1
                movzx   r9, al
                call    printf
                add     rsp, 40
                ret
printFP         endp

; Here is the "asmMain" function.

                public  asmMain
asmMain         proc
                push    rbp
                mov     rbp, rsp
                sub     rsp, 48     ; Shadow storage
```

```
; Test to see if 0 < 3.
; Note: ST(0) contains 0, ST(1) contains 3.

            xor     eax, eax
            fld     three
            fld     zero
            fcomi   st(0), st(1)
            setb    al
            fstp    st0
            fstp    st1
            lea     rcx, fcomiFmt
            call    printFP

; Test to see if 3 < 0.
; Note: ST(0) contains 0, ST(1) contains 3.

            xor     eax, eax
            fld     zero
            fld     three
            fcomi   st(0), st(1)
            setb    al
            fstp    st0
            fstp    st1
            lea     rcx, fcomiFmt2
            call    printFP

; Test to see if 3 < 0.
; Note: ST(0) contains 0, ST(1) contains 3.

            xor     eax, eax
            fld     zero
            fld     three
            fst     st0             ; Because this gets popped
            fcomip  st(0), st(1)
            setb    al
            fstp    st1
            lea     rcx, fcomipFmt
            call    printFP

; Test to see if 0 < 3.
; Note: ST(0) contains 0, ST(1) contains 3.

            xor     eax, eax
            fld     three
            fld     zero
            fst     st0             ; Because this gets popped
            fcomip  st(0), st(1)
            setb    al
            fstp    st1
            lea     rcx, fcomipFmt2
            call    printFP

            leave
            ret     ; Returns to caller
```

```
asmMain     endp
            end
```

Listing 6-6: Sample program demonstrating floating-point comparisons

Here's the build command and output for the program in Listing 6-6:

```
C:\>build listing6-6

C:\>echo off
 Assembling: listing6-6.asm
c.cpp

C:\>listing6-6
Calling Listing 6-6:
fcomi 0.000000 < 3.000000 is 1
fcomi(2) 3.000000 < 0.000000 is 0
fcomip 3.000000 < 0.000000 is 0
fcomip (2) 0.000000 < 3.000000 is 1
Listing 6-6 terminated
```

NOTE   *The x87 FPU also provides two instructions that do* unordered *comparisons:* fucomi *and* fucomip. *These are functionally equivalent to* fcomi *and* fcomip *except they raise an exception under different conditions. See the Intel documentation for more details.*

6.5.8.3 The ftst Instruction

The ftst instruction compares the value in ST(0) against 0.0. It behaves just like the fcom instruction would if ST(1) contained 0.0. This instruction does not differentiate −0.0 from +0.0. If the value in ST(0) is either of these values, ftst will set C_3 to denote equality (or unordered). This instruction does *not* pop ST(0) off the stack.

Here's an example:

```
ftst
fstsw ax
sahf
sete al       ; Set AL to 1 if TOS = 0.0
```

6.5.9 Constant Instructions

The FPU provides several instructions that let you load commonly used constants onto the FPU's register stack. These instructions set the stack fault, invalid operation, and C_1 flags if a stack overflow occurs; they do not otherwise affect the FPU flags. The specific instructions in this category include the following:

```
fldz            ; Pushes +0.0
fld1            ; Pushes +1.0
fldpi           ; Pushes pi (3.14159...)
fldl2t          ; Pushes log2(10)
```

```
fldl2e          ; Pushes log2(e)
fldlg2          ; Pushes log10(2)
fldln2          ; Pushes ln(2)
```

6.5.10 Transcendental Instructions

The FPU provides eight *transcendental* (logarithmic and trigonometric) instructions to compute sine, cosine, partial tangent, partial arctangent, $2^x - 1$, $y \times \log_2(x)$, and $y \times \log_2(x + 1)$. Using various algebraic identities, you can easily compute most of the other common transcendental functions by using these instructions.

6.5.10.1 The f2xm1 Instruction

f2xm1 computes $2^{ST(0)} - 1$. The value in ST(0) must be in the range −1.0 to +1.0. If ST(0) is out of range, f2xm1 generates an undefined result but raises no exceptions. The computed value replaces the value in ST(0).

Here's an example computing 10^i using the identity $10^i = 2^{i \times \log2(10)}$. This is useful for only a small range of i that doesn't put ST(0) outside the previously mentioned valid range:

```
fld i
fldl2t
fmul
f2xm1
fld1
fadd
```

Because f2xm1 computes $2^x - 1$, the preceding code adds 1.0 to the result at the end of the computation.

6.5.10.2 The fsin, fcos, and fsincos Instructions

These instructions pop the value off the top of the register stack and compute the sine, cosine, or both, and push the result(s) back onto the stack. The fsincos instruction pushes the sine followed by the cosine of the original operand; hence, it leaves cos(ST(0)) in ST(0) and sin(ST(0)) in ST(1).

These instructions assume ST(0) specifies an angle in radians, and this angle must be in the range $-2^{63} < ST(0) < +2^{63}$. If the original operand is out of range, these instructions set the C_2 flag and leave ST(0) unchanged. You can use the fprem1 instruction, with a divisor of 2π, to reduce the operand to a reasonable range.

These instructions set the stack fault (or rounding)/C_1, precision, underflow, denormalized, and invalid operation flags according to the result of the computation.

6.5.10.3 The fptan Instruction

fptan computes the tangent of ST(0), replaces ST(0) with this value, and then pushes 1.0 onto the stack. Like the fsin and fcos instructions, the value of ST(0) must be in radians and in the range $-2^{63} < ST(0) < +2^{63}$. If the value is outside this range, fptan sets C_2 to indicate that the conversion did not take place. As with the fsin, fcos, and fsincos instructions, you can use the fprem1 instruction to reduce this operand to a reasonable range by using a divisor of 2π.

If the argument is invalid (that is, 0 or π radians, which causes a division by 0), the result is undefined and this instruction raises no exceptions. fptan will set the stack fault/rounding, precision, underflow, denormal, invalid operation, C_2, and C_1 bits as required by the operation.

6.5.10.4 The fpatan Instruction

fpatan expects two values on the top of stack. It pops them and computes $ST(0) = \tan^{-1}(ST(1) / ST(0))$. The resulting value is the arctangent of the ratio on the stack expressed in radians. If you want to compute the arctangent of a particular value, use fld1 to create the appropriate ratio and then execute the fpatan instruction.

This instruction affects the stack fault/C_1, precision, underflow, denormal, and invalid operation bits if a problem occurs during the computation. It sets the C_1 condition code bit if it has to round the result.

6.5.10.5 The fyl2x Instruction

The fyl2x instruction computes $ST(0) = ST(1) \times \log_2(ST(0))$. The instruction itself has no operands, but expects two operands on the FPU stack in $ST(1)$ and $ST(0)$, thus using the following syntax:

```
fyl2x
```

To compute the log of any other base, you can use the arithmetic identity $\log_n(x) = \log_2(x) / \log_2(n)$. So if you first compute $\log_2(n)$ and put its reciprocal on the stack, then push x onto the stack and execute fyl2x, you wind up with $\log n(x)$.

The fyl2x instruction sets the C_1 condition code bit if it has to round up the value. It clears C_1 if no rounding occurs or if a stack overflow occurs. The remaining floating-point condition codes are undefined after the execution of this instruction. fyl2x can raise the following floating-point exceptions: invalid operation, denormal result, overflow, underflow, and inexact result. Note that the fldl2t and fldl2e instructions turn out to be quite handy when using the fyl2x instruction (for computing $\log_{10}$ and ln).

6.5.10.6 The fyl2xp1 Instruction

fyl2xp1 computes $ST(0) = ST(1) \times \log_2(ST(0) + 1.0)$ from two operands on the FPU stack. The syntax for this instruction is as follows:

```
fyl2xp1
```

Otherwise, the instruction is identical to fyl2x.

6.5.11 *Miscellaneous Instructions*

The FPU includes several additional instructions that control the FPU, synchronize operations, and let you test or set various status bits: finit/fninit, fldcw, fstcw, fclex/fnclex, and fstsw.

6.5.11.1 The finit and fninit Instructions

The finit and fninit instructions initialize the FPU for proper operation. Your code should execute one of these instructions before executing any other FPU instructions. They initialize the control register to 37Fh, the status register to 0, and the tag word to 0FFFFh. The other registers are unaffected.

Here are some examples:

```
finit
fninit
```

The difference between finit and fninit is that finit first checks for any pending floating-point exceptions before initializing the FPU; fninit does not.

6.5.11.2 The fldcw and fstcw Instructions

The fldcw and fstcw instructions require a single 16-bit memory operand:

```
fldcw mem₁₆
fstcw mem₁₆
```

These two instructions load the control word from a memory location (fldcw) or store the control word to a 16-bit memory location (fstcw).

When you use fldcw to turn on one of the exceptions, if the corresponding exception flag is set when you enable that exception, the FPU will generate an immediate interrupt before the CPU executes the next instruction. Therefore, you should use fclex to clear any pending interrupts before changing the FPU exception enable bits.

6.5.11.3 The fclex and fnclex Instructions

The fclex and fnclex instructions clear all exception bits, the stack fault bit, and the busy flag in the FPU status register.

Here are examples:

```
fclex
fnclex
```

The difference between these instructions is the same as that between finit and fninit: fclex first checks for pending floating-point exceptions.

6.5.11.4 The fstsw and fnstsw Instructions

These instructions store the FPU status word into a 16-bit memory location or the AX register:

```
fstsw   ax
fnstsw  ax
fstsw   mem₁₆
fnstsw  mem₁₆
```

These instructions are unusual in the sense that they can copy an FPU value into one of the x86-64 general-purpose registers (specifically, AX). The purpose is to allow the CPU to easily test the condition code register with the sahf instruction. The difference between fstsw and fnstsw is the same as that for fclex and fnclex.

6.6 Converting Floating-Point Expressions to Assembly Language

Because the FPU register organization is different from the x86-64 integer register set, translating arithmetic expressions involving floating-point operands is a little different from translating integer expressions. Therefore, it makes sense to spend some time discussing how to manually translate floating-point expressions into assembly language.

The FPU uses *postfix notation* (also called *reverse Polish notation*, or *RPN*) for arithmetic operations. Once you get used to using postfix notation, it's actually a bit more convenient for translating expressions because you don't have to worry about allocating temporary variables—they always wind up on the FPU stack. Postfix notation, as opposed to standard *infix notation*, places the operands before the operator. Table 6-14 provides simple examples of infix notation and the corresponding postfix notation.

Table 6-14: Infix-to-Postfix Translation

Infix notation	Postfix notation
5 + 6	5 6 +
7 − 2	7 2 −
y × z	y z ×
a / b	a b /

A postfix expression like 5 6 + says, "Push 5 onto the stack, push 6 onto the stack, and then pop the value off the top of stack (6) and add it to the new top of stack." Sound familiar? This is exactly what the fld and fadd instructions do. In fact, you can calculate the result by using the following code:

```
fld five   ; Declared somewhere as five real8 5.0 (or real4/real10)
fld six    ; Declared somewhere as six real8 6.0 (or real4/real10)
fadd       ; 11.0 is now on the top of the FPU stack
```

As you can see, postfix is a convenient notation because it's easy to translate this code into FPU instructions.

Another advantage to postfix notation is that it doesn't require any parentheses. The examples in Table 6-15 demonstrate some slightly more complex infix-to-postfix conversions.

Table 6-15: More-Complex Infix-to-Postfix Translations

Infix notation	Postfix notation
(y + z) * 2	y z + 2 *
y * 2 – (a + b)	y 2 * a b + –
(a + b) * (c + d)	a b + c d + *

The postfix expression y z + 2 * says, "Push *y*, then push *z*; next, add those values on the stack (producing y + z on the stack). Next, push 2 and then multiply the two values (2 and y + z) on the stack to produce two times the quantity y + z." Once again, we can translate these postfix expressions directly into assembly language. The following code demonstrates the conversion for each of the preceding expressions:

```
; y z + 2 *

        fld y
        fld z
        fadd
        fld const2   ; const2 real8 2.0 in .data section
        fmul

; y 2 * a b + -

        fld y
        fld const2   ; const2 real8 2.0 in .data section
        fmul
        fld a
        fld b
        fadd
        fsub

; a b + c d + *

        fld a
        fld b
        fadd
        fld c
        fld d
        fadd
        fmul
```

6.6.1 Converting Arithmetic Expressions to Postfix Notation

For simple expressions, those involving two operands and a single expression, the translation from infix to postfix notation is trivial: simply move the operator from the infix position to the postfix position (that is, move the operator from between the operands to after the second operand). For example 5 + 6 becomes 5 6 +. Other than separating your operands so you don't confuse them (that is, is it 5 and 6 or 56?), converting simple infix expressions into postfix notation is straightforward.

For complex expressions, the idea is to convert the simple subexpressions into postfix notation and then treat each converted subexpression as a single operand in the remaining expression. The following discussion surrounds completed conversions with square brackets so it is easy to see which text needs to be treated as a single operand in the conversion.

As for integer expression conversion, the best place to start is in the innermost parenthetical subexpression and then work your way outward, considering precedence, associativity, and other parenthetical subexpressions. As a concrete working example, consider the following expression:

```
x = ((y − z) * a) − (a + b * c) / 3.14159
```

A possible first translation is to convert the subexpression (y - z) into postfix notation:

```
x = ([y z -] * a) - (a + b * c) / 3.14159
```

Square brackets surround the converted postfix code just to separate it from the infix code, for readability. Remember, for the purposes of conversion, we will treat the text inside the square brackets as a single operand. Therefore, you would treat [y z -] as though it were a single variable name or constant.

The next step is to translate the subexpression ([y z -] * a) into postfix form. This yields the following:

```
x = [y z - a *] - (a + b * c) / 3.14159
```

Next, we work on the parenthetical expression (a + b * c). Because multiplication has higher precedence than addition, we convert b * c first:

```
x = [y z - a *] - (a + [b c *]) / 3.14159
```

After converting b * c, we finish the parenthetical expression:

```
x = [y z - a *] - [a b c * +] / 3.14159
```

This leaves only two infix operators: subtraction and division. Because division has the higher precedence, we'll convert that first:

```
x = [y z - a *] - [a b c * + 3.14159 /]
```

Finally, we convert the entire expression into postfix notation by dealing with the last infix operation, subtraction:

```
x = [y z - a *] [a b c * + 3.14159 /] -
```

Removing the square brackets yields the following postfix expression:

```
x = y z - a * a b c * + 3.14159 / -
```

The following steps demonstrate another infix-to-postfix conversion for this expression:

```
a = (x * y - z + t) / 2.0
```

1. Work inside the parentheses. Because multiplication has the highest precedence, convert that first:

   ```
   a = ([x y *] - z + t) / 2.0
   ```

2. Still working inside the parentheses, we note that addition and subtraction have the same precedence, so we rely on associativity to determine what to do next. These operators are left-associative, so we must translate the expressions from left to right. This means translate the subtraction operator first:

   ```
   a = ([x y * z -] + t) / 2.0
   ```

3. Now translate the addition operator inside the parentheses. Because this finishes the parenthetical operators, we can drop the parentheses:

   ```
   a = [x y * z - t +] / 2.0
   ```

4. Translate the final infix operator (division). This yields the following:

   ```
   a = [x y * z - t + 2.0 /]
   ```

5. Drop the square brackets, and we're done:

   ```
   a = x y * z - t + 2.0 /
   ```

6.6.2   Converting Postfix Notation to Assembly Language

Once you've translated an arithmetic expression into postfix notation, finishing the conversion to assembly language is easy. All you have to do is issue an fld instruction whenever you encounter an operand and issue an appropriate arithmetic instruction when you encounter an operator. This section uses the completed examples from the previous section to demonstrate how little there is to this process.

```
x = y z - a * a b c * + 3.14159 / -
```

1. Convert y to `fld y`.
2. Convert z to `fld z`.
3. Convert - to `fsub`.
4. Convert a to `fld a`.
5. Convert * to `fmul`.
6. Continuing in a left-to-right fashion, generate the following code for the expression:

```
fld    y
fld    z
fsub
fld    a
fmul
fld    a
fld    b
fld    c
fmul
fadd
fldpi          ; Loads pi (3.14159)
fdiv
fsub

fstp   x     ; Store result away into x
```

Here's the translation for the second example in the previous section:

```
a = x y * z - t + 2.0 /
        fld    x
        fld    y
        fmul
        fld    z
        fsub
        fld    t
        fadd
        fld    const2     ; const2 real8 2.0 in .data section
        fdiv

        fstp   a          ; Store result away into a
```

As you can see, the translation is fairly simple once you've converted the infix notation to postfix notation. Also note that, unlike integer expression conversion, you don't need any explicit temporaries. It turns out that the

FPU stack provides the temporaries for you.[9] For these reasons, converting floating-point expressions into assembly language is actually easier than converting integer expressions.

6.7 SSE Floating-Point Arithmetic

Although the x87 FPU is relatively easy to use, the stack-based design of the FPU created performance bottlenecks as CPUs became more powerful. After introducing the *Streaming SIMD Extensions (SSE)* in its Pentium III CPUs (way back in 1999), Intel decided to resolve the FPU performance bottleneck and added scalar (non-vector) floating-point instructions to the SSE instruction set that could use the XMM registers. Most modern programs favor the use of the SSE (and later) registers and instructions for floating-point operations over the x87 FPU, using only those x87 operations available exclusively on the x87.

The SSE instruction set supports two floating-point data types: 32-bit single-precision (Intel calls these *scalar single* operations) and 64-bit double-precision values (Intel calls these *scalar double* operations).[10] The SSE does not support the 80-bit extended-precision floating-point data types of the x87 FPU. If you need the extended-precision format, you'll have to use the x87 FPU.

6.7.1 SSE MXCSR Register

The SSE MXCSR register is a 32-bit status and control register that controls SSE floating-point operations. Bits 16 to 32 are reserved and currently have no meaning. Table 6-16 lists the functions of the LO 16 bits.

Table 6-16: SSE MXCSR Register

Bit	Name	Function
0	IE	Invalid operation exception flag. Set if an invalid operation was attempted.
1	DE	Denormal exception flag. Set if operations produced a denormalized value.
2	ZE	Zero exception flag. Set if an attempt to divide by 0 was made.
3	OE	Overflow exception flag. Set if there was an overflow.
4	UE	Underflow exception flag. Set if there was an underflow.
5	PE	Precision exception flag. Set if there was a precision exception.

(continued)

---

9. This assumes, of course, that your calculations aren't so complex that you exceed the eight-element limitation of the FPU stack.

10. This book has typically used *scalar* to denote atomic (noncomposite) data types that were not floating-point (chars, Booleans, integers, and so forth). In fact, floating-point values (that are not part of a larger composite data type) are also scalars. Intel uses *scalar* as opposed to *vector* (the SSE also supports vector operations).

Table 6-16: SSE MXCSR Register *(continued)*

Bit	Name	Function
6	DAZ	Denormals are 0. If set, treat denormalized values as 0.
7	IM	Invalid operation mask. If set, ignore invalid operation exceptions.
8	DM	Denormal mask. If set, ignore denormal exceptions.
9	ZM	Divide-by-zero mask. If set, ignore division-by-zero exceptions.
10	OM	Overflow mask. If set, ignore overflow exceptions.
11	UM	Underflow mask. If set, ignore underflow exceptions.
12	PM	Precision mask. If set, ignore precision exceptions.
13 14	Rounding Control	00: Round to nearest 01: Round toward −infinity 10: Round toward +infinity 11: Round toward 0 (truncate)
15	FTZ	Flush to zero. When set, all underflow conditions set the register to 0.

Access to the SSE MXCSR register is via the following two instructions:

```
ldmxcsr mem32
stmxcsr mem32
```

The `ldmxcsr` instruction loads the MXCSR register from the specified 32-bit memory location. The `stmxcsr` instruction stores the current contents of the MXCSR register to the specified memory location.

By far, the most common use of these two instructions is to set the rounding mode. In typical programs using the SSE floating-point instructions, it is common to switch between the round-to-nearest and round-to-zero (truncate) modes.

6.7.2   SSE Floating-Point Move Instructions

The SSE instruction set provides two instructions to move floating-point values between XMM registers and memory: `movss` (*move scalar single*) and `movsd` (*move scalar double*). Here is their syntax:

```
movss xmmn, mem32
movss mem32, xmmn
movsd xmmn, mem64
movsd mem64, xmmn
```

As for the standard general-purpose registers, the `movss` and `movsd` instructions move data between an appropriate memory location (containing a 32- or 64-bit floating-point value) and one of the 16 XMM registers (XMM0 to XMM15).

For maximum performance, `movss` memory operands should appear at a double-word-aligned memory address, and `movsd` memory operands should appear at a quad-word-aligned memory address. Though these instructions will function properly if the memory operands are not properly aligned in memory, there is a performance hit for misaligned accesses.

In addition to the `movss` and `movsd` instructions that move floating-point values between XMM registers or XMM registers and memory, you'll find a couple of other SSE move instructions useful that move data between XMM and general-purpose registers, `movd` and `movq`:

```
movd   reg_32,  xmm_n
movd   xmm_n,  reg_32
movq   reg_64,  xmm_n
movq   xmm_n,  reg_64
```

These instructions also have a form that allows a source memory operand. However, you should use `movss` and `movsd` to move floating-point variables into XMM registers.

The `movq` and `movd` instructions are especially useful for copying XMM registers into 64-bit general-purpose registers prior to a call to `printf()` (when printing floating-point values). As you'll see in a few sections, these instructions are also useful for floating-point comparisons on the SSE.

6.7.3   SSE Floating-Point Arithmetic Instructions

The Intel SSE instruction set adds the following floating-point arithmetic instructions:

```
addss  xmm_n,  xmm_n
addss  xmm_n,  mem_32
addsd  xmm_n,  xmm_n
addsd  xmm_n,  mem_64

subss  xmm_n,  xmm_n
subss  xmm_n,  mem_32
subsd  xmm_n,  xmm_n
subsd  xmm_n,  mem_64

mulss  xmm_n,  xmm_n
mulss  xmm_n,  mem_32
mulsd  xmm_n,  xmm_n
mulsd  xmm_n,  mem_64

divss  xmm_n,  xmm_n
divss  xmm_n,  mem_32
divsd  xmm_n,  xmm_n
divsd  xmm_n,  mem_64

minss  xmm_n,  xmm_n
minss  xmm_n,  mem_32
minsd  xmm_n,  xmm_n
minsd  xmm_n,  mem_64

maxss  xmm_n,  xmm_n
maxss  xmm_n,  mem_32
maxsd  xmm_n,  xmm_n
maxsd  xmm_n,  mem_64
```

```
sqrtss   xmm_n,  xmm_n
sqrtss   xmm_n,  mem_32
sqrtsd   xmm_n,  xmm_n
sqrtsd   xmm_n,  mem_64

rcpss    xmm_n,  xmm_n
rcpss    xmm_n,  mem_32

rsqrtss  xmm_n,  xmm_n
rsqrtss  xmm_n,  mem_32
```

The addsx, subsx, mulsx, and divsx instructions perform the expected floating-point arithmetic operations. The minsx instructions compute the minimum value of the two operands, storing the minimum value into the destination (first) operand. The maxsx instructions do the same thing, but compute the maximum of the two operands. The sqrtsx instructions compute the square root of the source (second) operand and store the result into the destination (first) operand. The rcpsx instructions compute the reciprocal of the source, storing the result into the destination.[11] The rsqrtsx instructions compute the reciprocal of the square root.[12]

The operand syntax is somewhat limited for the SSE instructions (compared with the generic integer instructions): the destination operand must always be an XMM register.

6.7.4 SSE Floating-Point Comparisons

The *SSE floating-point comparisons* work quite a bit differently from the integer and x87 FPU compare instructions. Rather than having a single generic instruction that sets flags (to be tested by setcc or jcc instructions), the SSE provides a set of condition-specific comparison instructions that store true (all 1 bits) or false (all 0 bits) into the destination operand. You can then test the result value for true or false. Here are the instructions:

```
cmpss xmm_n,  xmm_m/mem_32,  imm_8
cmpsd xmm_n,  xmm_m/mem_64,  imm_8

cmpeqss    xmm_n,  xmm_m/mem_32
cmpltss    xmm_n,  xmm_m/mem_32
cmpless    xmm_n,  xmm_m/mem_32
cmpunordss xmm_n,  xmm_m/mem_32
cmpne qss  xmm_n,  xmm_m/mem_32
cmpnltss   xmm_n,  xmm_m/mem_32
cmpnless   xmm_n,  xmm_m/mem_32
cmpordss   xmm_n,  xmm_m/mem_32
```

---

11. Intel's documentation claims that the reciprocal operation is just an approximation. Then again, by definition, the square root operation is also an approximation because it produces irrational results.

12. Also an approximation.

```
cmpeqsd    xmm_n,  xmm_m/mem_64
cmpltsd    xmm_n,  xmm_m/mem_64
cmplesd    xmm_n,  xmm_m/mem_64
cmpunordsd xmm_n,  xmm_m/mem_64
cmpneqsd   xmm_n,  xmm_m/mem_64
cmpnltsd   xmm_n,  xmm_m/mem_64
cmpnlesd   xmm_n,  xmm_m/mem_64
cmpordsd   xmm_n,  xmm_m/mem_64
```

The immediate constant is a value in the range 0 to 7 and represents one of the comparisons in Table 6-17.

Table 6-17: SSE Compare Immediate Operand

imm_8	Comparison
0	First operand == second operand
1	First operand < second operand
2	First operand <= second operand
3	First operand unordered second operand
4	First operand ≠ second operand
5	First operand not less than second operand (≥)
6	First operand not less than or equal to second operand (>)
7	First operand ordered second operand

The instructions without the third (immediate) operand are special *pseudo-ops* MASM provides that automatically supply the appropriate third operand. You can use the nlt form for ge and nle form for gt, assuming the operands are ordered.

The *unordered* comparison returns true if either (or both) operands are unordered (typically, NaN values). Likewise, the ordered comparison returns true if both operands are ordered.

As noted, these instructions leave 0 or all 1 bits in the destination register to represent false or true. If you want to branch based on these conditions, you should move the destination XMM register into a general-purpose register and test that register for zero/not zero. You can use the movq or movd instructions to accomplish this:

```
cmpeqsd xmm0, xmm1
movd    eax, xmm0      ; Move true/false to EAX
test    eax, eax       ; Test for true/false
jnz     xmm0EQxmm1     ; Branch if xmm0 == xmm1

; Code to execute if xmm0 != xmm1.
```

6.7.5 SSE Floating-Point Conversions

The x86-64 provides several floating-point conversion instructions that convert between floating-point and integer formats. Table 6-18 lists these instructions and their syntax.

Table 6-18: SSE Conversion Instructions

Instruction syntax	Description
cvtsd2si $reg_{32/64}$, xmm_n/mem_{64}	Converts scalar double-precision FP to 32- or 64-bit integer. Uses the current rounding mode in the MXCSR to determine how to deal with fractional components. Result is stored in a general-purpose 32- or 64-bit register.
cvtsd2ss xmm_n, xmm_n/mem_{64}	Converts scalar double-precision FP (in an XMM register or memory) to scalar single-precision FP and leaves the result in the destination XMM register. Uses the current rounding mode in the MXCSR to determine how to deal with inexact conversions.
cvtsi2sd xmm_n, $reg_{32/64}$/$mem_{32/64}$	Converts a 32- or 64-bit integer in an integer register or memory to a double-precision floating-point value, leaving the result in an XMM register.
cvtsi2ss xmm_n, $reg_{32/64}$/$mem_{32/64}$	Converts a 32- or 64-bit integer in an integer register or memory to a single-precision floating-point value, leaving the result in an XMM register.
cvtss2sd xmm_n, xmm_n/mem_{32}	Converts a single-precision floating-point value in an XMM register or memory to a double-precision value, leaving the result in the destination XMM register.
cvtss2si $reg_{32/64}$, xmm_n/mem_{32}	Converts a single-precision floating-point value in an XMM register or memory to an integer and leaves the result in a general-purpose 32- or 64-bit register. Uses the current rounding mode in the MXCSR to determine how to deal with inexact conversions.
cvttsd2si $reg_{32/64}$, xmm_n/mem_{64}	Converts scalar double-precision FP to a 32- or 64-bit integer. Conversion is done using truncation (does not use the rounding control setting in the MXCSR). Result is stored in a general-purpose 32- or 64-bit register.
cvttss2si $reg_{32/64}$, xmm_n/mem_{32}	Converts scalar single-precision FP to a 32- or 64-bit integer. Conversion is done using truncation (does not use the rounding control setting in the MXCSR). Result is stored in a general-purpose 32- or 64-bit register.

6.8   For More Information

The Intel and AMD processor manuals fully describe the operation of each of the integer and floating-point arithmetic instructions, including a detailed description of how these instructions affect the condition code bits and other flags in the FLAGS and FPU status registers. To write the best possible assembly language code, you need to be intimately familiar with how the arithmetic instructions affect the execution environment, so spending time with the Intel and AMD manuals is a good idea.

Chapter 8 discusses multiprecision integer arithmetic. See that chapter for details on handling integer operands that are greater than 64 bits in size.

The x86-64 SSE instruction set found on later iterations of the CPU provides support for floating-point arithmetic using the AVX register set. Consult the Intel and AMD documentation for details concerning the AVX floating-point instruction set.

6.9 Test Yourself

1. What are the implied operands for the single-operand imul and mul instructions?

2. What is the result size for an 8-bit mul operation? A 16-bit mul operation? A 32-bit mul operation? A 64-bit mul operation? Where does the CPU put the products?

3. What result(s) does an x86 div instruction produce?

4. When performing a signed 16×16–bit division using idiv, what must you do before executing the idiv instruction?

5. When performing an unsigned 32×32–bit division using div, what must you do before executing the div instruction?

6. What are the two conditions that will cause a div instruction to produce an exception?

7. How do the mul and imul instructions indicate overflow?

8. How do the mul and imul instructions affect the zero flag?

9. What is the difference between the extended-precision (single operand) imul instruction and the more generic (multi-operand) imul instruction?

10. What instructions would you normally use to sign-extend the accumulator prior to executing an idiv instruction?

11. How do the div and idiv instructions affect the carry, zero, overflow, and sign flags?

12. How does the cmp instruction affect the zero flag?

13. How does the cmp instruction affect the carry flag (with respect to an unsigned comparison)?

14. How does the cmp instruction affect the sign and overflow flags (with respect to a signed comparison)?

15. What operands do the setcc instructions take?

16. What do the setcc instructions do to their operand?

17. What is the difference between the test instruction and the and instruction?

18. What are the similarities between the test instruction and the and instruction?

19. Explain how you would use the test instruction to see if an individual bit is 1 or 0 in an operand.

20. Convert the following expressions to assembly language (assume all variables are signed 32-bit integers):

```
x = x + y
x = y - z
x = y * z
x = y + z * t
```

```
x = (y + z) * t
x = -((x * y) / z)
x = (y == z) && (t != 0)
```

21. Compute the following expressions without using an `imul` or `mul` instruction (assume all variables are signed 32-bit integers):

```
x = x * 2
x = y * 5
x = y * 8
```

22. Compute the following expressions without using a `div` or `idiv` instruction (assume all variables are unsigned 16-bit integers):

```
x = x / 2
x = y / 8
x = z / 10
```

23. Convert the following expressions to assembly language by using the FPU (assume all variables are real8 floating-point values):

```
x = x + y
x = y - z
x = y * z
x = y + z * t
x = (y + z) * t
x = -((x * y) / z)
```

24. Convert the following expressions to assembly language by using SSE instructions (assume all variables are real4 floating-point values):

```
x = x + y
x = y - z
x = y * z
x = y + z * t
```

25. Convert the following expressions to assembly language by using FPU instructions; assume b is a one-byte Boolean variable and x, y, and z are real8 floating-point variables:

```
b = x < y
b = x >= y && x < z
```

7

LOW-LEVEL CONTROL STRUCTURES

 This chapter discusses how to convert high-level–language control structures into assembly language control statements. The examples up to this point have created assembly control structures in an ad hoc manner. Now it's time to formalize how to control the operation of your assembly language programs. By the time you finish this chapter, you should be able to convert HLL control structures into assembly language.

Control structures in assembly language consist of conditional branches and indirect jumps. This chapter discusses those instructions and how to emulate HLL control structures (such as if/else, switch, and loop statements).

This chapter also discusses labels (the targets of conditional branches and jump statements) as well as the scope of labels in an assembly language source file.

7.1 Statement Labels

Before discussing jump instructions and how to emulate control structures using them, an in-depth discussion of assembly language statement labels is necessary. In an assembly language program, *labels* stand in as symbolic names for addresses. It is far more convenient to refer to a position in your code by using a name such as LoopEntry rather than a numeric address such as 0AF1C002345B7901Eh. For this reason, assembly language low-level control structures make extensive use of labels within source code (see "Brief Detour: An Introduction to Control Transfer Instructions" in Chapter 2).

You can do three things with (code) labels: transfer control to a label via a (conditional or unconditional) jump instruction, call a label via the call instruction, and take the address of a label. Taking the address of a label is useful when you want to indirectly transfer control to that address at a later point in your program.

The following code sequence demonstrates two ways to take the address of a label in your program (using the lea instruction and using the offset operator):

```
stmtLbl:
    .
    .
    .
  mov rcx, offset stmtLbl2
    .
    .
    .
  lea rax, stmtLbl
    .
    .
    .
stmtLbl2:
```

Because addresses are 64-bit quantities, you'll typically load an address into a 64-bit general-purpose register by using the lea instruction. Because that instruction uses a 32-bit relative displacement from the current instruction, the instruction encoding is significantly shorter than the mov instruction (which encodes a full 8-byte constant in addition to the opcode bytes).

7.1.1 Using Local Symbols in Procedures

Statement labels you define within a proc/endp procedure are *local* to that procedure, in the sense of *lexical scope*: the statement label is visible only within that procedure; you cannot refer to that statement label outside the procedure. Listing 7-1 demonstrates that you cannot refer to a symbol inside another procedure (note that this program will not assemble because of this error).

```
; Listing 7-1

; Demonstration of local symbols.
; Note that this program will not
; compile; it fails with an
; undefined symbol error.

        option  casemap:none

        .code

hasLocalLbl proc

localStmLbl:
        ret
hasLocalLbl endp

; Here is the "asmMain" function.

asmMain     proc

asmLocal:   jmp     asmLocal        ; This is okay
            jmp     localStmtLbl    ; Undefined in asmMain
asmMain     endp
            end
```

Listing 7-1: Demonstration of lexically scoped symbols

The command to assemble this file (and the corresponding diagnostic message) is as follows:

```
C:\>ml64 /c listing7-1.asm
Microsoft (R) Macro Assembler (x64) Version 14.15.26730.0
Copyright (C) Microsoft Corporation.  All rights reserved.

 Assembling: listing7-1.asm
listing7-1.asm(26) : error A2006:undefined symbol : localStmtLbl
```

If you really want to access a statement (or any other) label outside a procedure, you can use the option directive to turn off local scope within a section of your program, as noted in Chapter 5:

```
option noscoped
option scoped
```

The first form tells MASM to stop making symbols (inside proc/endp) local to the procedure containing them. The second form restores the lexical scoping of symbols in procedures. Therefore, using these two directives, you can turn scoping on or off for various sections of your source file (including as little as a single statement, if you like). Listing 7-2 demonstrates how to use the option directive to make a single symbol global outside the procedure containing it (note that this program still has compile errors).

```
; Listing 7-2

; Demonstration of local symbols #2.
; Note that this program will not
; compile; it fails with two
; undefined symbol errors.

            option  casemap:none

            .code

hasLocalLbl proc

localStmLbl:
            option noscoped
notLocal:
            option scoped
isLocal:
            ret
hasLocalLbl endp

; Here is the "asmMain" function.

asmMain     proc

            lea     rcx, localStmtLbl  ; Generates an error
            lea     rcx, notLocal      ; Assembles fine
            lea     rcx, isLocal       ; Generates an error
asmMain     endp
            end
```

Listing 7-2: The option scoped *and* option noscoped *directives*

Here's the build command (and diagnostic output) for Listing 7-2:

```
C:\>ml64 /c listing7-2.asm
Microsoft (R) Macro Assembler (x64) Version 14.15.26730.0
Copyright (C) Microsoft Corporation.  All rights reserved.

 Assembling: listing7-2.asm
listing7-2.asm(29) : error A2006:undefined symbol : localStmtLbl
listing7-2.asm(31) : error A2006:undefined symbol : isLocal
```

As you can see from MASM's output, the notLocal symbol (appearing after the option noscoped directive) did not generate an undefined symbol error. However, the localStmtLbl and isLocal symbols, which are local to hasLocalLbl, are undefined outside that procedure.

7.1.2 Initializing Arrays with Label Addresses

MASM also allows you to initialize quad-word variables with the addresses of statement labels. However, labels that appear in the initialization portions of variable declarations have some restrictions. The most important restriction is that the symbol must be in the same lexical scope as the data declaration attempting to use it. So, either the qword directive must appear inside the same procedure as the statement label, or you must use the option noscoped directive to make the symbol(s) global to the procedure. Listing 7-3 demonstrates these two ways to initialize a qword variable with statement label addresses.

```
; Listing 7-3

; Initializing qword values with the
; addresses of statement labels.

        option  casemap:none

            .data
lblsInProc  qword   globalLbl1, globalLbl2  ; From procWLabels

            .code

; procWLabels - Just a procedure containing private (lexically scoped)
;               and global symbols. This really isn't an executable
;               procedure.

procWLabels proc
privateLbl:
            nop     ; "No operation" just to consume space
            option  noscoped
globalLbl1: jmp     globalLbl2
globalLbl2: nop
            option  scoped
privateLbl2:
            ret
dataInCode  qword   privateLbl, globalLbl1
            qword   globalLbl2, privateLbl2
procWLabels endp

            end
```

Listing 7-3: Initializing qword variables with the address of statement labels

If you compile Listing 7-3 with the following command, you'll get no assembly errors:

```
ml64 /c /Fl listing7-3.asm
```

If you look at the *listing7-3.lst* output file that MASM produces, you can see that MASM properly initializes the qword declarations with the (section-relative/relocatable) offsets of the statement labels:

```
00000000                           .data
00000000          lblsInProc   qword   globalLbl1, globalLbl2
        0000000000000001 R
        0000000000000003 R
                 .
                 .
                 .
 00000005          dataInCode   qword   privateLbl, globalLbl1
        0000000000000000 R
        0000000000000001 R
 00000015  0000000000000003 R   qword   globalLbl2, privateLbl2
        0000000000000004 R
```

Transferring control to a statement label inside a procedure is generally considered bad programming practice. Unless you have a good reason to do so, you probably shouldn't.

As addresses on the x86-64 are 64-bit quantities, you will typically use the qword directive (as in the previous examples) to initialize a data object with the address of a statement label. However, if your program is (always going to be) smaller than 2GB, and you set the LARGEADDRESSAWARE:NO flag (using *sbuild.bat*), you can get away with using dword data declarations to hold the address of a label. Of course, as this book has pointed out many times, using 32-bit addresses in your 64-bit programs can lead to problems if you ever exceed 2GB of storage for your program.

7.2 Unconditional Transfer of Control (jmp)

The jmp (*jump*) instruction unconditionally transfers control to another point in the program. This instruction has three forms: a direct jump and two indirect jumps. These take the following forms:

```
jmp label
jmp reg₆₄
jmp mem₆₄
```

The first instruction is a *direct jump*, which you've seen in various sample programs up to this point. For direct jumps, you normally specify the target address by using a statement label. The label appears either on the same line as an executable machine instruction or by itself on a line preceding an executable machine instruction. The direct jump is completely equivalent to a goto statement in a high-level language.[1]

---

1. Unlike HLLs, for which your instructors usually forbid you to use goto statements, you will find that the use of the jmp instruction in assembly language is essential.

Here's an example:

```
        Statements
        jmp laterInPgm
                .
                .
                .

laterInPgm:
        Statements
```

7.2.1   Register-Indirect Jumps

The second form of the jmp instruction given earlier—jmp reg_{64}—is a *register-indirect jump* instruction that transfers control to the instruction whose address appears in the specified 64-bit general-purpose register. To use this form of the jmp instruction, you must load a 64-bit register with the address of a machine instruction prior to the execution of the jmp. When several paths, each loading the register with a different address, converge on the same jmp instruction, control transfers to an appropriate location determined by the path up to that point.

Listing 7-4 reads a string of characters from the user that contain an integer value. It uses the C Standard Library function strtol() to convert that string to a binary integer value. The strtol() function doesn't do the greatest job of reporting an error, so this program tests the return results to verify a correct input and uses register-indirect jumps to transfer control to different code paths based on the result.

The first part of Listing 7-4 contains constants, variables, external declarations, and the (usual) getTitle() function.

```
; Listing 7-4

; Demonstration of register-indirect jumps.

        option  casemap:none

nl          =       10
maxLen      =       256
EINVAL      =       22      ; "Magic" C stdlib constant, invalid argument
ERANGE      =       34      ; Value out of range

            .const
ttlStr      byte    "Listing 7-4", 0
fmtStr1     byte    "Enter an integer value between "
            byte    "1 and 10 (0 to quit): ", 0

badInpStr   byte    "There was an error in readLine "
            byte    "(ctrl-Z pressed?)", nl, 0

invalidStr  byte    "The input string was not a proper number"
            byte    nl, 0
```

```
rangeStr    byte    "The input value was outside the "
            byte    "range 1-10", nl, 0

unknownStr  byte    "There was a problem with strToInt "
            byte    "(unknown error)", nl, 0

goodStr     byte    "The input value was %d", nl, 0

fmtStr      byte    "result:%d, errno:%d", nl, 0

            .data
            externdef _errno:dword  ; Error return by C code
endStr      qword   ?
inputValue  dword   ?
buffer      byte    maxLen dup (?)

            .code
            externdef readLine:proc
            externdef strtol:proc
            externdef printf:proc

; Return program title to C++ program:

            public  getTitle
getTitle    proc
            lea     rax, ttlStr
            ret
getTitle    endp
```

The next section of Listing 7-4 is the strToInt() function, a wrapper around the C Standard Library strtol() function that does a more thorough job of handling erroneous inputs from the user. See the comments for the function's return values.

```
; strToInt - Converts a string to an integer, checking for errors.

; Argument:
;   RCX -   Pointer to string containing (only) decimal
;           digits to convert to an integer.

; Returns:
;   RAX -   Integer value if conversion was successful.
;   RCX -   Conversion state. One of the following:
;           0 - Conversion successful.
;           1 - Illegal characters at the beginning of the
;               string (or empty string).
;           2 - Illegal characters at the end of the string.
;           3 - Value too large for 32-bit signed integer.

strToInt    proc
strToConv   equ     [rbp+16]        ; Flush RCX here
endPtr      equ     [rbp-8]         ; Save ptr to end of str
            push    rbp
```

```
                mov     rbp, rsp
                sub     rsp, 32h        ; Shadow + 16-byte alignment

                mov     strToConv, rcx  ; Save, so we can test later

                ; RCX already contains string parameter for strtol:

                lea     rdx, endPtr     ; Ptr to end of string goes here
                mov     r8d, 10         ; Decimal conversion
                call    strtol

; On return:

;    RAX     - Contains converted value, if successful.
;    endPtr  - Pointer to 1 position beyond last char in string.

; If strtol returns with endPtr == strToConv, then there were no
; legal digits at the beginning of the string.

                mov     ecx, 1          ; Assume bad conversion
                mov     rdx, endPtr
                cmp     rdx, strToConv
                je      returnValue

; If endPtr is not pointing at a zero byte, then we've got
; junk at the end of the string.

                mov     ecx, 2          ; Assume junk at end
                mov     rdx, endPtr
                cmp     byte ptr [rdx], 0
                jne     returnValue

; If the return result is 7FFF_FFFFh or 8000_0000h (max long and
; min long, respectively), and the C global _errno variable
; contains ERANGE, then we've got a range error.

                mov     ecx, 0          ; Assume good input
                cmp     _errno, ERANGE
                jne     returnValue
                mov     ecx, 3          ; Assume out of range
                cmp     eax, 7fffffffh
                je      returnValue
                cmp     eax, 80000000h
                je      returnValue

; If we get to this point, it's a good number.

                mov     ecx, 0

returnValue:
                leave
                ret
strToInt    endp
```

The final section of Listing 7-4 is the main program. This is the part of code most interesting to us. It loads the RBX register with the address of code to execute based on the strToInt() return results. The strToInt() function returns one of the following states (see the comments in the previous code for an explanation):

- Valid input
- Illegal characters at the beginning of the string
- Illegal characters at the end of the string
- Range error

The program then transfers control to different sections of asmMain() based on the value held in RBX (which specifies the type of result strToInt() returns).

```
; Here is the "asmMain" function.

            public  asmMain
asmMain     proc
saveRBX     equ     qword ptr [rbp-8]     ; Must preserve RBX
            push    rbp
            mov     rbp, rsp
            sub     rsp, 48              ; Shadow storage

            mov     saveRBX, rbx         ; Must preserve RBX

            ; Prompt the user to enter a value
            ; between 1 and 10:

repeatPgm:  lea     rcx, fmtStr1
            call    printf

            ; Get user input:

            lea     rcx, buffer
            mov     edx, maxLen       ; Zero-extends!
            call    readLine
            lea     rbx, badInput     ; Initialize state machine
            test    rax, rax          ; RAX is -1 on bad input
            js      hadError          ; (only neg value readLine returns)

            ; Call strToInt to convert string to an integer and
            ; check for errors:

            lea     rcx, buffer       ; Ptr to string to convert
            call    strToInt
            lea     rbx, invalid
            cmp     ecx, 1
            je      hadError
            cmp     ecx, 2
            je      hadError
```

```
        lea     rbx, range
        cmp     ecx, 3
        je      hadError

        lea     rbx, unknown
        cmp     ecx, 0
        jne     hadError
```

; At this point, input is valid and is sitting in EAX.

; First, check to see if the user entered 0 (to quit
; the program).

```
        test    eax, eax        ; Test for zero
        je      allDone
```

; However, we need to verify that the number is in the
; range 1-10.

```
        lea     rbx, range
        cmp     eax, 1
        jl      hadError
        cmp     eax, 10
        jg      hadError
```

; Pretend a bunch of work happens here dealing with the
; input number.

```
        lea     rbx, goodInput
        mov     inputValue, eax
```

; The different code streams all merge together here to
; execute some common code (we'll pretend that happens;
; for brevity, no such code exists here).

hadError:

; At the end of the common code (which doesn't mess with
; RBX), separate into five different code streams based
; on the pointer value in RBX:

```
        jmp     rbx
```

; Transfer here if readLine returned an error:

```
badInput:   lea     rcx, badInpStr
            call    printf
            jmp     repeatPgm
```

; Transfer here if there was a non-digit character
; in the string:

```
invalid:    lea     rcx, invalidStr
```

```
                call    printf
                jmp     repeatPgm

; Transfer here if the input value was out of range:

range:          lea     rcx, rangeStr
                call    printf
                jmp     repeatPgm

; Shouldn't ever get here. Happens if strToInt returns
; a value outside the range 0-3.

unknown:        lea     rcx, unknownStr
                call    printf
                jmp     repeatPgm

; Transfer down here on a good user input.

goodInput:      lea     rcx, goodStr
                mov     edx, inputValue ; Zero-extends!
                call    printf
                jmp     repeatPgm

; Branch here when the user selects "quit program" by
; entering the value zero:

allDone:        mov     rbx, saveRBX    ; Must restore before returning
                leave
                ret                     ; Returns to caller

asmMain         endp
                end
```

Listing 7-4: Using register-indirect jmp instructions

Here's the build command and a sample run of the program in Listing 7-4:

```
C:\>build listing7-4

C:\>echo off
 Assembling: listing7-4.asm
c.cpp

C:\>listing7-4
Calling Listing 7-4:
Enter an integer value between 1 and 10 (0 to quit): ^Z
There was an error in readLine (ctrl-Z pressed?)
Enter an integer value between 1 and 10 (0 to quit): a123
The input string was not a proper number
```

```
Enter an integer value between 1 and 10 (0 to quit): 123a
The input string was not a proper number
Enter an integer value between 1 and 10 (0 to quit): 1234567890123
The input value was outside the range 1-10
Enter an integer value between 1 and 10 (0 to quit): -1
The input value was outside the range 1-10
Enter an integer value between 1 and 10 (0 to quit): 11
The input value was outside the range 1-10
Enter an integer value between 1 and 10 (0 to quit): 5
The input value was 5
Enter an integer value between 1 and 10 (0 to quit): 0
Listing 7-4 terminated
```

7.2.2 Memory-Indirect Jumps

The third form of the jmp instruction is a *memory-indirect jump*, which fetches the quad-word value from the memory location and jumps to that address. This is similar to the register-indirect jmp except the address appears in a memory location rather than in a register.

Listing 7-5 demonstrates a rather trivial use of this form of the jmp instruction.

```
; Listing 7-5

; Demonstration of memory-indirect jumps.

        option  casemap:none

nl          =       10

            .const
ttlStr      byte    "Listing 7-5", 0
fmtStr1     byte    "Before indirect jump", nl, 0
fmtStr2     byte    "After indirect jump", nl, 0

            .code
            externdef printf:proc

; Return program title to C++ program:

            public  getTitle
getTitle    proc
            lea     rax, ttlStr
            ret
getTitle    endp

; Here is the "asmMain" function.

            public  asmMain
asmMain     proc
            push    rbp
```

```
          mov     rbp, rsp
          sub     rsp, 48              ; Shadow storage

          lea     rcx, fmtStr1
          call    printf
          jmp     memPtr

memPtr    qword   ExitPoint

ExitPoint: lea    rcx, fmtStr2
          call    printf

          leave
          ret     ; Returns to caller

asmMain   endp
          end
```

Listing 7-5: Using memory-indirect jmp instructions

Here's the build command and output for Listing 7-5:

```
C:\>build listing7-5

C:\>echo off
 Assembling: listing7-5.asm
c.cpp

C:\>listing7-5
Calling Listing 7-5:
Before indirect jump
After indirect jump
Listing 7-5 terminated
```

Note that you can easily crash your system if you execute an indirect jump with an invalid pointer value.

7.3   Conditional Jump Instructions

Although Chapter 2 provided an overview of the conditional jump instructions, repeating that discussion and expanding upon it here is worthwhile as conditional jumps are the principal tool for creating control structures in assembly language.

Unlike the unconditional jmp instruction, the conditional jump instructions do not provide an indirect form. They only allow a branch to a statement label in your program.

Intel's documentation defines various synonyms or instruction aliases for many conditional jump instructions. Tables 7-1, 7-2, and 7-3 list all the aliases for a particular instruction, as well as the opposite branches. You'll soon see the purpose of the opposite branches.

Table 7-1: jcc Instructions That Test Flags

Instruction	Description	Condition	Aliases	Opposite
jc	Jump if carry	Carry = 1	jb, jnae	jnc
jnc	Jump if no carry	Carry = 0	jnb, jae	jc
jz	Jump if zero	Zero = 1	je	jnz
jnz	Jump if not zero	Zero = 0	jne	jz
js	Jump if sign	Sign = 1		jns
jns	Jump if no sign	Sign = 0		js
jo	Jump if overflow	Overflow = 1		jno
jno	Jump if no overflow	Overflow = 0		jo
jp	Jump if parity	Parity = 1	jpe	jnp
jpe	Jump if parity even	Parity = 1	jp	jpo
jnp	Jump if no parity	Parity = 0	jpo	jp
jpo	Jump if parity odd	Parity = 0	jnp	jpe

Table 7-2: jcc Instructions for Unsigned Comparisons

Instruction	Description	Condition	Aliases	Opposite
ja	Jump if above (>)	Carry = 0, Zero = 0	jnbe	jna
jnbe	Jump if not below or equal (not ≤)	Carry = 0, Zero = 0	ja	jbe
jae	Jump if above or equal (≥)	Carry = 0	jnc, jnb	jnae
jnb	Jump if not below (not <)	Carry = 0	jnc, jae	jb
jb	Jump if below (<)	Carry = 1	jc, jnae	jnb
jnae	Jump if not above or equal (not ≥)	Carry = 1	jc, jb	jae
jbe	Jump if below or equal (≤)	Carry = 1 or Zero = 1	jna	jnbe
jna	Jump if not above (not >)	Carry = 1 or Zero = 1	jbe	ja
je	Jump if equal (=)	Zero = 1	jz	jne
jne	Jump if not equal (≠)	Zero = 0	jnz	je

Table 7-3: jcc Instructions for Signed Comparisons

Instruction	Description	Condition	Aliases	Opposite
jg	Jump if greater (>)	Sign = Overflow or Zero = 0	jnle	jng
jnle	Jump if not less than or equal (not ≤)	Sign = Overflow or Zero = 0	jg	jle

(continued)

Table 7-3: jcc Instructions for Signed Comparisons *(continued)*

Instruction	Description	Condition	Aliases	Opposite
jge	Jump if greater than or equal (≥)	Sign = Overflow	jnl	jnge
jnl	Jump if not less than (not <)	Sign = Overflow	jge	jl
jl	Jump if less than (<)	Sign ≠ Overflow	jnge	jnl
jnge	Jump if not greater or equal (not ≥)	Sign ≠ Overflow	jl	jge
jle	Jump if less than or equal (≤)	Sign ≠ Oveflow or Zero = 1	jng	jnle
jng	Jump if not greater than (not >)	Sign ≠ Overflow or Zero = 1	jle	jg
je	Jump if equal (=)	Zero = 1	jz	jne
jne	Jump if not equal (≠)	Zero = 0	jnz	je

In many instances, you will need to generate the opposite of a specific branch instruction (examples appear later in this section). With only two exceptions, the *opposite branch (N/No N)* rule describes how to generate an opposite branch:

- If the second letter of the jcc instruction is not an n, insert an n after the j. For example, je becomes jne, and jl becomes jnl.

- If the second letter of the jcc instruction is an n, remove that n from the instruction. For example, jng becomes jg, and jne becomes je.

The two exceptions to this rule are jpe (*jump if parity is even*) and jpo (*jump if parity is odd*).[2] However, you can use the aliases jp and jnp as synonyms for jpe and jpo, and the N/No N rule applies to jp and jnp.

NOTE *Though you know that jge is the opposite of jl, get in the habit of using jnl rather than jge as the opposite jump instruction for jl. It's too easy in an important situation to start thinking, "Greater is the opposite of less," and substitute jg instead. You can avoid this confusion by always using the N/No N rule.*

The x86-64 conditional jump instructions give you the ability to split program flow into one of two paths depending on a certain condition. Suppose you want to increment the AX register if BX is equal to CX. You can accomplish this with the following code:

```
        cmp bx, cx
        jne SkipStmts;
        inc ax
SkipStmts:
```

2. Technically, this opposite branch rule doesn't apply to the jcxz, jecxz, and jrcxz instructions either, in addition to the jpe and jpo instructions. So, arguably, the rule has five exceptions. However, this section doesn't mention the jcxz, jecxz, and jrcxz instructions, so it mentions only the two exceptions.

Instead of checking for equality directly and branching to code to handle that condition, the common approach is to use the opposite branch to skip over the instructions you want to execute if the condition is true. That is, if BX is *not* equal to CX, jump over the increment instruction. Always use the opposite branch (N/No N) rule given earlier to select the opposite branch.

You can also use the conditional jump instructions to synthesize loops. For example, the following code sequence reads a sequence of characters from the user and stores each character in successive elements of an array until the user presses ENTER (newline):

```
        mov edi, 0
RdLnLoop:
        call getchar        ; Some function that reads a character
                            ; into the AL register
        mov Input[rdi], al  ; Store away the character
        inc rdi             ; Move on to the next character
        cmp al, nl          ; See if the user pressed ENTER
        jne RdLnLoop
```

The conditional jump instructions only test the x86-64 flags; they do not affect any of them.

From an efficiency point of view, it's important to note that each conditional jump has two machine code encodings: a 2-byte form and a 6-byte form.

The 2-byte form consists of the jcc opcode followed by a 1-byte PC-relative displacement. The 1-byte displacement allows the instruction to transfer control to a target instruction within about ±127 bytes around the current instruction. Given that the average x86-64 instruction is probably 4 to 5 bytes long, the 2-byte form of jcc is capable of branching to a target instruction within about 20 to 25 instructions.

Because a range of 20 to 25 instructions is insufficient for all conditional jumps, the x86-64 provides a second (6-byte) form with a 2-byte opcode and a 4-byte displacement. The 6-byte form gives you the ability to jump to an instruction within approximately ±2GB of the current instruction, which is probably sufficient for any reasonable program out there.

If you have the opportunity to branch to a nearby label rather than one that is far away (and still achieve the same result), branching to the nearby label will make your code shorter and possibly faster.

7.4 Trampolines

In the rare case you need to branch to a location beyond the range of the 6-byte jcc instructions, you can use an instruction sequence such as the following:

```
        jncc  skipJmp  ; Opposite jump of the one you want to use
        jmp   destPtr  ; JMP PC-relative is also limited to ±2GB
destPtr qword destLbl  ; so code must use indirect jump
skipJmp:
```

The opposite conditional branch transfers control to the normal *fall-though point* in the code (the code you'd normally fall through to if the condition is false). If the condition is true, control transfers to a memory-indirect jump that jumps to the original target location via a 64-bit pointer.

This sequence is known as a *trampoline*, because a program jumps to this point to jump even further in the program (much like how jumping on a trampoline lets you jump higher and higher). Trampolines are useful for call and unconditional jump instructions that use the PC-relative addressing mode (and, thus, are limited to a ±2GB range around the current instruction).

You'll rarely use trampolines to transfer to another location within your program. However, trampolines are useful when transferring control to a dynamically linked library or OS subroutine that could be far away in memory.

7.5   Conditional Move Instructions

Sometimes all you need to do after a comparison or other conditional test is to load a value into a register (and, conversely, not load that value if the test or comparison fails). Because branches can be somewhat expensive to execute, the x86-64 CPUs support a set of conditional move instructions, cmov*cc*. These instructions appear in Tables 7-4, 7-5, and 7-6; the generic syntax for these instructions is as follows:

```
cmovcc reg16, reg16
cmovcc reg16, mem16
cmovcc reg32, reg32
cmovcc reg32, mem32
cmovcc reg64, reg64
cmovcc reg64, mem64
```

The destination is always a general-purpose register (16, 32, or 64 bits). You can use these instructions only to load a register from memory or copy data from one register to another; you cannot use them to conditionally store data to memory.

Table 7-4: cmov*cc* Instructions That Test Flags

Instruction	Description	Condition	Aliases
cmovc	Move if carry	Carry = 1	cmovb, cmovnae
cmovnc	Move if no carry	Carry = 0	cmovnb, cmovae
cmovz	Move if zero	Zero = 1	cmove
cmovnz	Move if not zero	Zero = 0	cmovne
cmovs	Move if sign	Sign = 1	
cmovns	Move if no sign	Sign = 0	
cmovo	Move if overflow	Overflow = 1	

Instruction	Description	Condition	Aliases
cmovno	Move if no overflow	Overflow = 0	
cmovp	Move if parity	Parity = 1	cmovpe
cmovpe	Move if parity even	Parity = 1	cmovp
cmovnp	Move if no parity	Parity = 0	cmovpo
cmovpo	Move if parity odd	Parity = 0	cmovnp

Table 7-5: cmov*cc* Instructions for Unsigned Comparisons

Instruction	Description	Condition	Aliases
cmova	Move if above (>)	Carry = 0, Zero = 0	cmovnbe
cmovnbe	Move if not below or equal (not ≤)	Carry = 0, Zero = 0	cmova
cmovae	Move if above or equal (≥)	Carry = 0	cmovnc, cmovnb
cmovnb	Move if not below (not <)	Carry = 0	cmovnc, cmovae
cmovb	Move if below (<)	Carry = 1	cmovc, cmovnae
cmovnae	Move if not above or equal (not ≥)	Carry = 1	cmovc, cmovb
cmovbe	Move if below or equal (≤)	Carry = 1 or Zero = 1	cmovna
cmovna	Move if not above (not >)	Carry = 1 or Zero = 1	cmovbe
cmove	Move if equal (=)	Zero = 1	cmovz
cmovne	Move if not equal (≠)	Zero = 0	cmovnz

Table 7-6: cmov*cc* Instructions for Signed Comparisons

Instruction	Description	Condition	Aliases
cmovg	Move if greater (>)	Sign = Overflow or Zero = 0	cmovnle
cmovnle	Move if not less than or equal (not ≤)	Sign = Overflow or Zero = 0	cmovg
cmovge	Move if greater than or equal (≥)	Sign = Overflow	cmovnl
cmovnl	Move if not less than (not <)	Sign = Overflow	cmovge
cmovl	Move if less than (<)	Sign != Overflow	cmovnge
cmovnge	Move if not greater or equal (not ≥)	Sign != Overflow	cmovl
cmovle	Move if less than or equal (≤)	Sign != Overflow or Zero = 1	cmovng
cmovng	Move if not greater than (not >)	Sign != Overflow or Zero = 1	cmovle
cmove	Move if equal (=)	Zero = 1	cmovz
cmovne	Move if not equal (≠)	Zero = 0	cmovnz

In addition, a set of conditional floating-point move instructions (fcmovcc) will move data between ST0 and one of the other FPU registers on the FPU stack. Sadly, these instructions aren't all that useful in modern programs. See the Intel documentation for more details if you're interested in using them.

7.6 Implementing Common Control Structures in Assembly Language

This section shows you how to implement decisions, loops, and other control constructs using pure assembly language.

7.6.1 Decisions

In its most basic form, a *decision* is a branch within the code that switches between two possible execution paths based on a certain condition. Normally (though not always), conditional instruction sequences are implemented with the conditional jump instructions. Conditional instructions correspond to the if/then/endif statement in an HLL:

```
if(expression) then
    Statements
endif;
```

To convert this to assembly language, you must write statements that evaluate the *expression* and then branch around the *statements* if the result is false. For example, if you had the C statements

```
if(a == b)
{
    printf("a is equal to b \ n");
}
```

you could translate this to assembly as follows:

```
        mov  eax, a          ; Assume a and b are 32-bit integers
        cmp  eax, b
        jne  aNEb
        lea  rcx, aIsEqlBstr  ; "a is equal to b \ n"
        call printf
aNEb:
```

In general, conditional statements may be broken into three basic categories: if statements, switch/case statements, and indirect jumps. The following sections describe these program structures, how to use them, and how to write them in assembly language.

7.6.2 if/then/else Sequences

The most common conditional statements are the if/then/endif and if/then/else/endif statements. These two statements take the form shown in Figure 7-1.

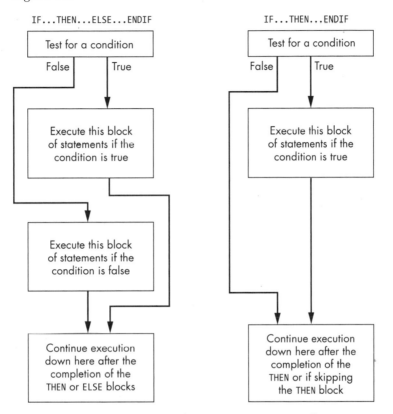

Figure 7-1: if/then/else/endif and if/then/endif statement flow

The if/then/endif statement is just a special case of the if/then/else/endif statement (with an empty else block). The basic implementation of an if/then/else/endif statement in x86-64 assembly language looks something like

```
Sequence of statements to test a condition
        jcc ElseCode;

Sequence of statements corresponding to the THEN block
        jmp EndOfIf

ElseCode:
Sequence of statements corresponding to the ELSE block

EndOfIf:
```

where jcc represents a conditional jump instruction.

For example, to convert the C/C++ statement

```
if(a == b)
    c = d;
else
    b = b + 1;
```

to assembly language, you could use the following x86-64 code:

```
        mov eax, a
        cmp eax, b
        jne ElseBlk
        mov eax, d
        mov c, eax
        jmp EndOfIf;

ElseBlk:
        inc b

EndOfIf:
```

For simple expressions like (a == b), generating the proper code for an if/then/else/endif statement is almost trivial. Should the expression become more complex, the code complexity increases as well. Consider the following C/C++ if statement presented earlier:

```
if(((x > y) && (z < t)) || (a != b))
    c = d;
```

To convert complex if statements such as this one, break it into a sequence of three if statements as follows:

```
if(a != b) c = d;
else if(x > y)
    if(z < t)
        c = d;
```

This conversion comes from the following C/C++ equivalences:

```
if(expr1 && expr2) Stmt;
```

is equivalent to

```
if(expr1) if(expr2) Stmt;
```

and

```
if(expr1 || expr2) Stmt;
```

is equivalent to

```
if(expr1) Stmt;
else if(expr2) Stmt;
```

In assembly language, the former if statement becomes

```
; if(((x > y) && (z < t)) || (a != b))c = d;

        mov eax, a
        cmp eax, b
        jne DoIf;
        mov eax, x
        cmp eax, y
        jng EndOfIf;
        mov eax, z
        cmp eax, t
        jnl EndOfIf;
DoIf:
        mov eax, d
        mov c, eax
EndOfIf:
```

Probably the biggest problem with complex conditional statements in assembly language is trying to figure out what you've done after you've written the code. High-level language expressions are much easier to read and comprehend. Well-written comments are essential for clear assembly language implementations of if/then/else/endif statements. An elegant implementation of the preceding example follows:

```
; if ((x > y) && (z < t)) or (a != b)  c = d;
; Implemented as:
; if (a != b) then goto DoIf:

        mov eax, a
        cmp eax, b
        jne DoIf

; if not (x > y) then goto EndOfIf:

        mov eax, x
        cmp eax, y
        jng EndOfIf

; if not (z < t) then goto EndOfIf:

        mov eax, z
        cmp eax, t
        jnl EndOfIf

; THEN block:

DoIf:
        mov eax, d
        mov c, eax

; End of IF statement.

EndOfIf:
```

Admittedly, this goes overboard for such a simple example. The following would probably suffice:

```
; if (((x > y) && (z < t)) || (a != b))  c = d;
; Test the Boolean expression:

        mov eax, a
        cmp eax, b
        jne DoIf
        mov eax, x
        cmp eax, y
        jng EndOfIf
        mov eax, z
        cmp eax, t
        jnl EndOfIf

; THEN block:

DoIf:
        mov eax, d
        mov c, eax

; End of IF statement.

EndOfIf:
```

However, as your if statements become complex, the density (and quality) of your comments becomes more and more important.

7.6.3   Complex if Statements Using Complete Boolean Evaluation

Many Boolean expressions involve conjunction (and) or disjunction (or) operations. This section describes how to convert such Boolean expressions into assembly language. We can do this in two ways: using *complete Boolean evaluation* or using *short-circuit Boolean evaluation*. This section discusses complete Boolean evaluation. The next section discusses short-circuit Boolean evaluation.

Conversion via complete Boolean evaluation is almost identical to converting arithmetic expressions into assembly language, as covered in Chapter 6. However, for Boolean evaluation, you do not need to store the result in a variable; once the evaluation of the expression is complete, you check whether you have a false (0) or true (1, or nonzero) result to take whatever action the Boolean expression dictates. Usually, the last logical instruction (and/or) sets the zero flag if the result is false and clears the zero flag if the result is true, so you don't have to explicitly test for the result. Consider the following if statement and its conversion to assembly language using complete Boolean evaluation:

```
;       if(((x < y) && (z > t)) || (a != b))
;           Stmt1

        mov  eax, x
```

```
        cmp    eax, y
        setl   bl        ; Store x < y in BL
        mov    eax, z
        cmp    eax, t
        setg   bh        ; Store z > t in BH
        and    bl, bh    ; Put (x < y) && (z > t) into BL
        mov    eax, a
        cmp    eax, b
        setne  bh        ; Store a != b into BH
        or     bl, bh    ; Put (x < y) && (z > t) || (a != b) into BL
        je     SkipStmt1 ; Branch if result is false

    Code for Stmt1 goes here

SkipStmt1:
```

This code computes a Boolean result in the BL register and then, at the end of the computation, tests this value to see whether it contains true or false. If the result is false, this sequence skips over the code associated with Stmt1. The important thing to note in this example is that the program will execute every instruction that computes this Boolean result (up to the je instruction).

7.6.4   Short-Circuit Boolean Evaluation

If you are willing to expend a little more effort, you can usually convert a Boolean expression to a much shorter and faster sequence of assembly language instructions by using *short-circuit Boolean evaluation*. This approach attempts to determine whether an expression is true or false by executing only some of the instructions that would compute the complete expression.

Consider the expression a && b. Once we determine that a is false, there is no need to evaluate b because there is no way the expression can be true. If b represents a complex subexpression rather than a single Boolean variable, it should be clear that evaluating only a is more efficient.

As a concrete example, consider the subexpression ((x < y) && (z > t)) from the previous section. Once you determine that x is not less than y, there is no need to check whether z is greater than t because the expression will be false regardless of z's and t's values. The following code fragment shows how you can implement short-circuit Boolean evaluation for this expression:

```
; if((x < y) && (z > t)) then ...

        mov eax, x
        cmp eax, y
        jnl TestFails
        mov eax, z
        cmp eax, t
        jng TestFails

    Code for THEN clause of IF statement

TestFails:
```

The code skips any further testing once it determines that x is not less than y. Of course, if x is less than y, the program has to test z to see if it is greater than t; if not, the program skips over the then clause. Only if the program satisfies both conditions does the code fall through to the then clause.

For the logical or operation, the technique is similar. If the first subexpression evaluates to true, there is no need to test the second operand. Whatever the second operand's value is at that point, the full expression still evaluates to true. The following example demonstrates the use of short-circuit evaluation with disjunction (or):

```
; if(ch < 'A' || ch > 'Z')
;     then printf("Not an uppercase char");
; endif;

        cmp ch, 'A'
        jb ItsNotUC
        cmp ch, 'Z'
        jna ItWasUC

ItsNotUC:
  Code to process ch if it's not an uppercase character

ItWasUC:
```

Because the conjunction and disjunction operators are commutative, you can evaluate the left or right operand first if it is more convenient to do so.[3] As one last example in this section, consider the full Boolean expression from the previous section:

```
; if(((x < y) && (z > t)) || (a != b))   Stmt1 ;

        mov eax, a
        cmp eax, b
        jne DoStmt1
        mov eax, x
        cmp eax, y
        jnl SkipStmt1
        mov eax, z
        cmp eax, t
        jng SkipStmt1

DoStmt1:
        Code for Stmt1 goes here

SkipStmt1:
```

3. However, be aware that some expressions depend on the leftmost subexpression evaluating one way in order for the rightmost subexpression to be valid; for example, a common test in C/C++ is if(x != NULL && x -> y) .... .

The code in this example evaluates a != b first, because it is shorter and faster,[4] and the remaining subexpression last. This is a common technique assembly language programmers use to write better code.[5]

7.6.5 Short-Circuit vs. Complete Boolean Evaluation

When using complete Boolean evaluation, every statement in the sequence for that expression will execute; short-circuit Boolean evaluation, on the other hand, may not require the execution of every statement associated with the Boolean expression. As you've seen in the previous two sections, code based on short-circuit evaluation is usually shorter and faster.

However, short-circuit Boolean evaluation may not produce the correct result in some cases. Given an expression with *side effects*, short-circuit Boolean evaluation will produce a different result than complete Boolean evaluation. Consider the following C/C++ example:

```
if((x == y) && (++z != 0))  Stmt ;
```

Using complete Boolean evaluation, you might generate the following code:

```
        mov    eax, x      ; See if x == y
        cmp    eax, y
        sete   bl
        inc    z           ; ++z
        cmp    z, 0        ; See if incremented z is 0
        setne  bh
        and    bl, bh      ; Test x == y && ++z != 0
        jz     SkipStmt

        Code for Stmt goes here

SkipStmt:
```

Using short-circuit Boolean evaluation, you might generate this:

```
        mov eax, x        ; See if x == y
        cmp eax, y
        jne SkipStmt
        inc z             ; ++z - sets ZF if z becomes zero
        je  SkipStmt      ; See if incremented z is 0

        Code for Stmt goes here

SkipStmt:
```

---

4. Of course, if you can predict that the subexpression a != b will be false the vast majority of the time, it would be best to test that condition last.

5. This assumes, of course, that all comparisons are equally likely to be true or false.

Notice a subtle but important difference between these two conversions: if x is equal to y, the first version still *increments z and compares it to 0* before it executes the code associated with Stmt; the short-circuit version, on the other hand, skips the code that increments z if it turns out that x is equal to y. Therefore, the behavior of these two code fragments is different if x is equal to y.

Neither implementation is particularly wrong; depending on the circumstances, you may or may not want the code to increment z if x is equal to y. However, it is important to realize that these two schemes produce different results, so you can choose an appropriate implementation if the effect of this code on z matters to your program.

Many programs take advantage of short-circuit Boolean evaluation and rely on the program not evaluating certain components of the expression. The following C/C++ code fragment demonstrates perhaps the most common example that requires short-circuit Boolean evaluation:

```
if(pntr != NULL && *pntr == 'a')  Stmt ;
```

If it turns out that pntr is NULL, the expression is false, and there is no need to evaluate the remainder of the expression. This statement relies on short-circuit Boolean evaluation for correct operation. Were C/C++ to use complete Boolean evaluation, the second half of the expression would attempt to dereference a NULL pointer, when pntr is NULL.

Consider the translation of this statement using complete Boolean evaluation:

```
; Complete Boolean evaluation:

        mov   rax, pntr
        test  rax, rax   ; Check to see if RAX is 0 (NULL is 0)
        setne bl
        mov   al, [rax]  ; Get *pntr into AL
        cmp   al, 'a'
        sete  bh
        and   bl, bh
        jz    SkipStmt

        Code for Stmt goes here

SkipStmt:
```

If pntr contains NULL (0), this program will attempt to access the data at location 0 in memory via the mov al, [rax] instruction. Under most operating systems, this will cause a memory access fault (general protection fault).

Now consider the short-circuit Boolean conversion:

```
; Short-circuit Boolean evaluation:

    mov  rax, pntr   ; See if pntr contains NULL (0) and
    test rax, rax    ; immediately skip past Stmt if this
    jz   SkipStmt    ; is the case
```

```
        mov  al, [rax]   ; If we get to this point, pntr contains
        cmp  al, 'a'     ; a non-NULL value, so see if it points
        jne  SkipStmt    ; at the character "a"

             Code for Stmt goes here

SkipStmt:
```

In this example, the problem with dereferencing the NULL pointer doesn't exist. If pntr contains NULL, this code skips over the statements that attempt to access the memory address pntr contains.

7.6.6 Efficient Implementation of if Statements in Assembly Language

Encoding if statements efficiently in assembly language takes a bit more thought than simply choosing short-circuit evaluation over complete Boolean evaluation. To write code that executes as quickly as possible in assembly language, you must carefully analyze the situation and generate the code appropriately. The following paragraphs provide suggestions you can apply to your programs to improve their performance.

7.6.6.1 Know Your Data!

Programmers often mistakenly assume that data is random. In reality, data is rarely random, and if you know the types of values that your program commonly uses, you can write better code. To see how, consider the following C/C++ statement:

```
if((a == b) && (c < d)) ++i;
```

Because C/C++ uses short-circuit evaluation, this code will test whether a is equal to b. If so, it will test whether c is less than d. If you expect a to be equal to b most of the time but don't expect c to be less than d most of the time, this statement will execute slower than it should. Consider the following MASM implementation of this code:

```
        mov eax, a
        cmp eax, b
        jne DontIncI

        mov eax, c
        cmp eax, d
        jnl DontIncI

        inc i

DontIncI:
```

As you can see, if a is equal to b most of the time and c is not less than d most of the time, you will have to execute all six instructions nearly every time in order to determine that the expression is false. Now consider the following implementation that takes advantage of this knowledge and the fact that the && operator is commutative:

```
        mov eax, c
        cmp eax, d
        jnl DontIncI

        mov eax, a
        cmp eax, b
        jne DontIncI

        inc i

DontIncI:
```

The code first checks whether c is less than d. If most of the time c is less than d, this code determines that it has to skip to the label DontIncI after executing only three instructions in the typical case (compared with six instructions in the previous example).

This fact is much more obvious in assembly language than in a high-level language, one of the main reasons assembly programs are often faster than their HLL counterparts: optimizations are more obvious in assembly language than in a high-level language. Of course, the key here is to understand the behavior of your data so you can make intelligent decisions such as the preceding one.

7.6.6.2 Rearranging Expressions

Even if your data is random (or you can't determine how the input values will affect your decisions), rearranging the terms in your expressions may still be beneficial. Some calculations take far longer to compute than others. For example, the div instruction is much slower than a simple cmp instruction. Therefore, if you have a statement like the following, you may want to rearrange the expression so that the cmp comes first:

```
if((x % 10 = 0) && (x != y) ++x;
```

Converted to assembly code, this if statement becomes the following:

```
        mov  eax, x        ; Compute X % 10
        cdq                ; Must sign-extend EAX -> EDX:EAX
        idiv ten           ; "ten dword 10" in .const section
        test edx, edx      ; Remainder is in EDX, test for 0
        jnz  SkipIf

        mov  eax, x
        cmp  eax, y
        je   SkipIf

        inc  x

SkipIf:
```

The `idiv` instruction is expensive (often 50 to 100 times slower than most of the other instructions in this example). Unless it is 50 to 100 times more likely that the remainder is 0 rather than x is equal to y, it would be better to do the comparison first and the remainder calculation afterward:

```
mov  eax, x
cmp  eax, y
je   SkipIf

mov  eax, x      ; Compute X % 10
cdq              ; Must sign-extend EAX -> EDX:EAX
idiv ten         ; "ten dword 10" in .const section
test edx, edx    ; See if remainder (EDX) is 0
jnz  SkipIf

inc  x

SkipIf:
```

Because the && and || operators are not commutative when short-circuit evaluation occurs, do consider such transformations carefully when making them. This example works fine because there are no side effects or possible exceptions being shielded by the reordered evaluation of the && operator.

7.6.6.3 Destructuring Your Code

Structured code is sometimes less efficient than unstructured code because it introduces code duplication or extra branches that might not be present in unstructured code.[6] Most of the time, this is tolerable because unstructured code is difficult to read and maintain; sacrificing some performance in exchange for maintainable code is often acceptable. In certain instances, however, you may need all the performance you can get and might choose to compromise the readability of your code.

Taking previously written structured code and rewriting it in an unstructured fashion to improve performance is known as *destructuring code*. The difference between unstructured code and destructured code is that unstructured code was written that way in the first place; destructured code started out as structured code and was purposefully written in an unstructured fashion to make it more efficient. Pure unstructured code is usually hard to read and maintain. Destructured code isn't quite as bad because you limit the damage (unstructuring the code) to only those sections where it is absolutely necessary.

One classic way to destructure code is to use *code movement* (physically moving sections of code elsewhere in the program) to move code that your program rarely uses out of the way of code that executes most of the time. Code movement can improve the efficiency of a program in two ways.

---

6. In IILLs, you can often get away with this because the compiler will optimize the code, producing unstructured machine code. Unfortunately, when writing in assembly language, you get machine code that is exactly equivalent to the assembly code you write.

First, a branch that is taken is more expensive (time-consuming) than a branch that is not taken.[7] If you move the rarely used code to another spot in the program and branch to it on the rare occasion the branch is taken, most of the time you will fall straight through to the code that executes most frequently.

Second, sequential machine instructions consume cache storage. If you move rarely executed statements out of the normal code stream to another section of the program (that is rarely loaded into cache), this will improve the cache performance of the system.

For example, consider the following pseudo C/C++ statement:

```
if(see_if_an_error_has_occurred)
{
    Statements to execute if no error
}
else
{
    Error-handling statements
}
```

In normal code, we don't expect errors to be frequent. Therefore, you would normally expect the then section of the preceding if to execute far more often than the else clause. The preceding code could translate into the following assembly code:

```
    cmp see_if_an_error_has_occurred, true
    je HandleTheError

        Statements to execute if no error

    jmp EndOfIf;

HandleTheError:
        Error-handling statements
EndOfIf:
```

If the expression is false, this code falls through to the normal statements and then jumps over the error-handling statements. Instructions that transfer control from one point in your program to another (for example, jmp instructions) tend to be slow. It is much faster to execute a sequential set of instructions rather than jump all over the place in your program. Unfortunately, the preceding code doesn't allow this.

One way to rectify this problem is to move the else clause of the code somewhere else in your program. You could rewrite the code as follows:

```
    cmp see_if_an_error_has_occurred, true
    je HandleTheError
```

7. Most of the time, this is true. On some architectures, special *branch-prediction hardware* reduces the cost of branches.

```
    Statements to execute if no error

EndOfIf:
```

At some other point in your program (typically after a jmp instruction), you would insert the following code:

```
HandleTheError:
  Error-handling statements
     jmp EndOfIf;
```

The program isn't any shorter. The jmp you removed from the original sequence winds up at the end of the else clause. However, because the else clause rarely executes, moving the jmp instruction from the then clause (which executes frequently) to the else clause is a big performance win because the then clause executes using only straight-line code. This technique is surprisingly effective in many time-critical code segments.

7.6.6.4 Calculation Rather Than Branching

On many processors in the x86-64 family, branches (jumps) are expensive compared to many other instructions. For this reason, it is sometimes better to execute more instructions in a sequence than fewer instructions that involve branching.

For example, consider the simple assignment eax = abs(eax). Unfortunately, no x86-64 instruction computes the absolute value of an integer. The obvious way to handle this is with an instruction sequence that uses a conditional jump to skip over the neg instruction (which creates a positive value in EAX if EAX was negative):

```
        test eax, eax
        jns ItsPositive;

        neg eax

ItsPositive:
```

Now consider the following sequence that will also do the job:

```
; Set EDX to 0FFFF_FFFFh if EAX is negative, 0000_0000 if EAX is
; 0 or positive:

        cdq

; If EAX was negative, the following code inverts all the bits in
; EAX; otherwise, it has no effect on EAX.

        xor eax, edx

; If EAX was negative, the following code adds 1 to EAX;
; otherwise, it doesn't modify EAX's value.
```

```
and edx, 1   ; EDX = 0 or 1 (1 if EAX was negative)
add eax, edx
```

This code will invert all the bits in EAX and then add 1 to EAX if EAX was negative prior to the sequence; that is, it negates the value in EAX. If EAX was zero or positive, this code does not change the value in EAX.

Though this sequence takes four instructions rather than the three that the previous example requires, there are no transfer-of-control instructions, so it may execute faster on many CPUs in the x86-64 family. Of course, if you use the cmovns instruction presented earlier, this can be done with the following three instructions (with no transfer of control):

```
mov     edx, eax
neg     edx
cmovns eax, edx
```

This demonstrates why it's good to know the instruction set!

7.6.7   switch/case Statements

The C/C++ switch statement takes the following form:

```
switch(expression)
{
    case const1:
      Stmts1: Code to execute if
              expression equals const1

    case const2:
      Stmts2: Code to execute if
              expression equals const2

      .
      .
      .
    case constn:
      Stmtsn: Code to execute if
              expression equals constn

    default:  ; Note that the default section is optional
      Stmts_default: Code to execute if expression
                     does not equal
                     any of the case values
}
```

When this statement executes, it checks the value of the *expression* against the constants *const1* to *constn*. If it finds a match, the corresponding statements execute.

C/C++ places a few restrictions on the switch statement. First, the switch statement allows only an integer expression (or something whose underlying type can be an integer). Second, all the constants in the case clauses must be unique. The reason for these restrictions will become clear in a moment.

7.6.7.1 switch Statement Semantics

Most introductory programming texts introduce the switch/case statement by explaining it as a sequence of if/then/elseif/else/endif statements. They might claim that the following two pieces of C/C++ code are equivalent:

```
switch(expression)
{
    case 0: printf("i=0"); break;
    case 1: printf("i=1"); break;
    case 2: printf("i=2"); break;
}

if(eax == 0)
    printf("i=0");
else if(eax == 1)
    printf("i=1");
else if(eax == 2)
    printf("i=2");
```

While semantically these two code segments may be the same, their implementation is usually different. Whereas the if/then/elseif/else/endif chain does a comparison for each conditional statement in the sequence, the switch statement normally uses an indirect jump to transfer control to any one of several statements with a single computation.

7.6.7.2 if/else Implementation of switch

The switch (and if/else/elseif) statements could be written in assembly language with the following code:

```
; if/then/else/endif form:

            mov eax, i
            test eax, eax    ; Check for 0
            jnz Not0

            Code to print "i = 0"
            jmp EndCase

Not0:
            cmp eax, 1
            jne Not1

            Code to print "i = 1"
            jmp EndCase

Not1:
            cmp eax, 2
            jne EndCase;

            Code to print "i = 2"
EndCase:
```

Probably the only thing worth noting about this code is that it takes longer to determine the last case than it does to determine whether the first case executes. This is because the if/else/elseif version implements a *linear search* through the case values, checking them one at a time from first to last until it finds a match.

7.6.7.3   Indirect Jump switch Implementation

A faster implementation of the switch statement is possible using an *indirect jump table*. This implementation uses the switch expression as an index into a table of addresses; each address points at the target case's code to execute. Consider the following example:

```
; Indirect Jump Version.


        mov eax, i
        lea rcx, JmpTbl
        jmp qword ptr [rcx][rax * 8]

JmpTbl  qword Stmt0, Stmt1, Stmt2

Stmt0:
        Code to print "i = 0"
        jmp EndCase;

Stmt1:
        Code to print "i = 1"
        jmp EndCase;

Stmt2:
        Code to print "i = 2"

EndCase:
```

To begin with, a switch statement requires that you create an array of pointers with each element containing the address of a statement label in your code (those labels must be attached to the sequence of instructions to execute for each case in the switch statement). In the preceding example, the JmpTbl array, initialized with the address of the statement labels Stmt0, Stmt1, and Stmt2, serves this purpose. I've placed this array in the procedure itself because the labels are local to the procedure. Note, however, that you must place the array in a location that will never be executed as code (such as immediately after a jmp instruction, as in this example).

The program loads the RAX register with i's value (assuming i is a 32-bit integer, the mov instruction zero-extends EAX into RAX), then uses this value as an index into the JmpTbl array (RCX holds the base address of the JmpTbl array) and transfers control to the 8-byte address found at the specified location. For example, if RAX contains 0, the jmp [rcx][rax * 8] instruction will fetch the quad word at address JmpTbl+0 (RAX × 8 = 0). Because the first quad word in the table contains the address of Stmt0, the jmp instruction transfers control to the first instruction following the Stmt0 label. Likewise, if i (and therefore, RAX) contains 1, then the indirect jmp instruction fetches the quad word at offset 8 from the table and transfers control to the first instruction following the Stmt1 label (because the address of Stmt1 appears at offset 8 in the table). Finally, if i / RAX contains 2, then this code fragment transfers control to the statements following the Stmt2 label because it appears at offset 16 in the JmpTbl table.

As you add more (consecutive) cases, the jump table implementation becomes more efficient (in terms of both space and speed) than the if/elseif form. Except for simple cases, the switch statement is almost always faster, and usually by a large margin. As long as the case values are consecutive, the switch statement version is usually smaller as well.

7.6.7.4   Noncontiguous Jump Table Entries and Range Limiting

What happens if you need to include nonconsecutive case labels or cannot be sure that the switch value doesn't go out of range? With the C/C++ switch statement, such an occurrence will transfer control to the first statement after the switch statement (or to a default case, if one is present in the switch).

However, this doesn't happen in the preceding example. If variable i does not contain 0, 1, or 2, executing the previous code produces undefined results. For example, if i contains 5 when you execute the code, the indirect jmp instruction will fetch the qword at offset 40 (5 × 8) in JmpTbl and transfer control to that address. Unfortunately, JmpTbl doesn't have six entries, so the program will fetch the value of the sixth quad word following JmpTbl and use that as the target address, which will often crash your program or transfer control to an unexpected location.

The solution is to place a few instructions before the indirect jmp to verify that the switch selection value is within a reasonable range. In the previous example, we'd probably want to verify that i's value is in the range 0 to 2 before executing the jmp instruction. If i's value is outside this range, the program should simply jump to the endcase label (this corresponds to dropping down to the first statement after the entire switch statement). The following code provides this modification:

```
        mov eax, i
        cmp eax, 2
        ja  EndCase
        lea rcx, JmpTbl
        jmp qword ptr [rcx][rax * 8]

JmpTbl  qword Stmt0, Stmt1, Stmt2

Stmt0:

        Code to print "i = 0"
        jmp EndCase;

Stmt1:

        Code to print "i = 1"
        jmp EndCase;
```

```
Stmt2:
        Code to print "i = 2"


EndCase:
```

Although the preceding example handles the problem of selection values being outside the range 0 to 2, it still suffers from a couple of severe restrictions:

- The cases must start with the value 0. That is, the minimum case constant has to be 0 in this example.
- The case values must be contiguous.

Solving the first problem is easy, and you deal with it in two steps. First, you compare the case selection value against a lower and upper bound before determining if the case value is legal. For example:

```
; SWITCH statement specifying cases 5, 6, and 7:
; WARNING: This code does *NOT* work.
; Keep reading to find out why.

        mov eax, i
        cmp eax, 5
        jb  EndCase
        cmp eax, 7              ; Verify that i is in the range
        ja  EndCase            ; 5 to 7 before the indirect jmp
        lea rcx, JmpTbl
        jmp qword ptr [rcx][rax * 8]

JmpTbl  qword Stmt5, Stmt6, Stmt7

Stmt5:
        Code to print "i = 5"
        jmp EndCase;

Stmt6:
        Code to print "i = 6"
        jmp EndCase;

Stmt7:
        Code to print "i = 7"

EndCase:
```

This code adds a pair of extra instructions, cmp and jb, to test the selection value to ensure it is in the range 5 to 7. If not, control drops down to the EndCase label; otherwise, control transfers via the indirect jmp instruction. Unfortunately, as the comments point out, this code is broken.

Consider what happens if variable i contains the value 5: the code will verify that 5 is in the range 5 to 7 and then will fetch the dword at offset 40 (5×8) and jump to that address. As before, however, this loads 8 bytes outside the bounds of the table and does not transfer control to a defined location.

One solution is to subtract the smallest case selection value from EAX before executing the jmp instruction, as shown in the following example:

```
; SWITCH statement specifying cases 5, 6, and 7.
; WARNING: There is a better way to do this; keep reading.

        mov eax, i
        cmp eax, 5
        jb  EndCase
        cmp eax, 7              ; Verify that i is in the range
        ja  EndCase             ; 5 to 7 before the indirect jmp
        sub eax, 5              ; 5 to 7 -> 0 to 2
        lea rcx, JmpTbl
        jmp qword ptr [rcx][rax * 8]

JmpTbl  qword Stmt5, Stmt6, Stmt7

Stmt5:

        Code to print "i = 5"
        jmp EndCase;

Stmt6:

        Code to print "i = 6"
        jmp EndCase;

Stmt7:

        Code to print "i = 7"

EndCase:
```

By subtracting 5 from the value in EAX, we force EAX to take on the value 0, 1, or 2 prior to the jmp instruction. Therefore, case-selection value 5 jumps to Stmt5, case-selection value 6 transfers control to Stmt6, and case-selection value 7 jumps to Stmt7.

To improve this code, you can eliminate the sub instruction by merging it into the jmp instruction's address expression. The following code does this:

```
; SWITCH statement specifying cases 5, 6, and 7:

        mov eax, i
        cmp eax, 5
        jb  EndCase
        cmp eax, 7                          ; Verify that i is in the range
        ja  EndCase                         ; 5 to 7 before the indirect jmp
        lea rcx, JmpTbl
        jmp qword ptr [rcx][rax * 8 - 5 * 8] ; 5 * 8 compensates for zero index

JmpTbl  qword Stmt5, Stmt6, Stmt7

Stmt5:

        Code to print "i = 5"
        jmp EndCase;

Stmt6:

        Code to print "i = 6"
```

```
        jmp EndCase;

Stmt7:

        Code to print "i = 7"


EndCase:
```

The C/C++ switch statement provides a default clause that executes if the case-selection value doesn't match any of the case values. For example:

```
switch(expression)
{

    case 5:  printf("ebx = 5"); break;
    case 6:  printf("ebx = 6"); break;
    case 7:  printf("ebx = 7"); break;
    default
        printf("ebx does not equal 5, 6, or 7");
}
```

Implementing the equivalent of the default clause in pure assembly language is easy. Just use a different target label in the jb and ja instructions at the beginning of the code. The following example implements a MASM switch statement similar to the preceding one:

```
; SWITCH statement specifying cases 5, 6, and 7
; with a DEFAULT clause:

    mov eax, i
    cmp eax, 5
    jb  DefaultCase
    cmp eax, 7                     ; Verify that i is in the range
    ja  DefaultCase                ; 5 to 7 before the indirect jmp
    lea rcx, JmpTbl
    jmp qword ptr [rcx][rax * 8 - 5 * 8] ; 5 * 8 compensates for zero index


JmpTbl  qword Stmt5, Stmt6, Stmt7

Stmt5:

        Code to print "i = 5"
        jmp EndCase


Stmt6:

        Code to print "i = 6"
        jmp EndCase


Stmt7:

        Code to print "i = 7"
        jmp EndCase


DefaultCase:
        Code to print "EBX does not equal 5, 6, or 7"


EndCase:
```

The second restriction noted earlier, (that is, the case values need to be contiguous) is easy to handle by inserting extra entries into the jump table. Consider the following C/C++ switch statement:

```
switch(i)
{
    case 1  printf("i = 1"); break;
    case 2  printf("i = 2"); break;
    case 4  printf("i = 4"); break;
    case 8  printf("i = 8"); break;
    default:
        printf("i is not 1, 2, 4, or 8");
}
```

The minimum switch value is 1, and the maximum value is 8. Therefore, the code before the indirect jmp instruction needs to compare the value in i against 1 and 8. If the value is between 1 and 8, it's still possible that i might not contain a legal case-selection value. However, because the jmp instruction indexes into a table of quad words using the case-selection table, the table must have eight quad-word entries.

To handle the values between 1 and 8 that are not case-selection values, simply put the statement label of the default clause (or the label specifying the first instruction after the endswitch if there is no default clause) in each of the jump table entries that don't have a corresponding case clause. The following code demonstrates this technique:

```
; SWITCH statement specifying cases 1, 2, 4, and 8
; with a DEFAULT clause:

        mov eax, i
        cmp eax, 1
        jb  DefaultCase
        cmp eax, 8                      ; Verify that i is in the range
        ja  DefaultCase                 ; 1 to 8 before the indirect jmp
        lea rcx, JmpTbl
        jmp qword ptr [rcx][rax * 8 - 1 * 8] ; 1 * 8 compensates for zero index

JmpTbl  qword Stmt1, Stmt2, DefaultCase, Stmt4
        qword DefaultCase, DefaultCase, DefaultCase, Stmt8

Stmt1:

        Code to print "i = 1"
        jmp EndCase

Stmt2:

        Code to print "i = 2"
        jmp EndCase

Stmt4:

        Code to print "i = 4"
        jmp EndCase
```

```
Stmt8:
        Code to print "i = 8"
        jmp EndCase

DefaultCase:
        Code to print "i does not equal 1, 2, 4, or 8"

EndCase:
```

7.6.7.5 Sparse Jump Tables

The current implementation of the switch statement has a problem. If the case values contain nonconsecutive entries that are widely spaced, the jump table could become exceedingly large. The following switch statement would generate an extremely large code file:

```
switch(i)
{
    case 1:        Stmt1 ;
    case 100:      Stmt2 ;
    case 1000:     Stmt3 ;
    case 10000:    Stmt4 ;
    default:       Stmt5 ;

}
```

In this situation, your program will be much smaller if you implement the switch statement with a sequence of if statements rather than using an indirect jump statement. However, keep one thing in mind: the size of the jump table does not normally affect the execution speed of the program. If the jump table contains two entries or two thousand, the switch statement will execute the multiway branch in a constant amount of time. The if statement implementation requires a linearly increasing amount of time for each case label appearing in the case statement.

Probably the biggest advantage to using assembly language over an HLL like Pascal or C/C++ is that you get to choose the actual implementation of statements like switch. In some instances, you can implement a switch statement as a sequence of if/then/elseif statements, or you can implement it as a jump table, or you can use a hybrid of the two:

```
switch(i)
{
    case 0:     Stmt0 ;
    case 1:     Stmt1 ;
    case 2:     Stmt2 ;
    case 100:   Stmt3 ;
    default:    Stmt4 ;

}
```

That could become the following:

```
mov eax, i
cmp eax, 100
je  DoStmt3;
cmp eax, 2
ja  TheDefaultCase
lea rcx, JmpTbl
jmp qword ptr [rcx][rax * 8]
   .
   .
   .
```

If you are willing to live with programs that cannot exceed 2GB in size (and use the LARGEADDRESSAWARE:NO command linc option), you can improve the implementation of the switch statement and save one instruction:

```
; SWITCH statement specifying cases 5, 6, and 7
; with a DEFAULT clause:

      mov eax, i
      cmp eax, 5
      jb  DefaultCase
      cmp eax, 7                  ; Verify that i is in the range
      ja  DefaultCase             ; 5 to 7 before the indirect jmp
      jmp JmpTbl[rax * 8 - 5 * 8] ; 5 * 8 compensates for zero index

JmpTbl  qword Stmt5, Stmt6, Stmt7

Stmt5:
      Code to print "i = 5"
      jmp EndCase

Stmt6:
      Code to print "i = 6"
      jmp EndCase

Stmt7:
      Code to print "i = 7"
      jmp EndCase

DefaultCase:
      Code to print "EBX does not equal 5, 6, or 7"

EndCase:
```

This code removed the lea rcx, JmpTbl instruction and replaced jmp [rcx][rax * 8 - 5 * 8] with jmp JmpTbl[rax * 8 - 5 * 8]. This is a small improvement, but an improvement nonetheless (this sequence not only is one instruction shorter but also uses one less register). Of course, constantly be aware of the danger of writing 64-bit programs that are not large-address aware.

Some switch statements have sparse cases but with groups of contiguous cases within the overall set of cases. Consider the following C/C++ switch statement:

```
switch(expression)
{
    case 0:
        Code for case 0
        break;

    case 1:
        Code for case 1
        break;

    case 2:
        Code for case 2
        break;

    case 10:
        Code for case 10
        break;

    case 11:
        Code for case 11
        break;

    case 100:
        Code for case 100
        break;

    case 101:
        Code for case 101
        break;

    case 103:
        Code for case 101
        break;

    case 1000:
        Code for case 1000
        break;

    case 1001:
        Code for case 1001
        break;

    case 1003:
        Code for case 1001
        break;

    default:
        Code for default case
        break;
} // end switch
```

You can convert a switch statement that consists of widely separated groups of (nearly) contiguous cases to assembly language code using one jump table implementation for each contiguous group, and you can then use compare instructions to determine which jump table instruction sequence to execute. Here's one possible implementation of the previous C/C++ code:

```
; Assume expression has been computed and is sitting in EAX/RAX
; at this point...

        cmp     eax, 100
        jb      try0_11
        cmp     eax, 103
        ja      try1000_1003
        cmp     eax, 100
        jb      default
        lea     rcx, jt100
        jmp     qword ptr [rcx][rax * 8 - 100 * 8]
jt100   qword   case100, case101, default, case103

try0_11: cmp    ecx, 11 ; Handle cases 0-11 here
        ja      defaultCase
        lea     rcx, jt0_11
        jmp     qword ptr [rcx][rax * 8]
jt0_11  qword   case0, case1, case2, defaultCase
        qword   defaultCase, defaultCase, defaultCase
        qword   defaultCase, defaultCase, defaultCase
        qword   case10, case11

try1000_1003:
        cmp     eax, 1000
        jb      defaultCase
        cmp     eax, 1003
        ja      defaultCase
        lea     rcx, jt1000
        jmp     qword ptr [rcx][rax * 8 - 1000 * 8]
jt1000  qword   case1000, case1001, defaultCase, case1003
          .
          .
          .
Code for the actual cases here
```

This code sequence combines groups 0 to 2 and 10 to 11 into a single group (requiring seven additional jump table entries) in order to save having to write an additional jump table sequence.

Of course, for a set of cases this simple, it's probably easier to just use compare-and-branch sequences. This example was simplified a bit just to make a point.

7.6.7.6   Other switch Statement Alternatives

What happens if the cases are too sparse to do anything but compare the expression's value case by case? Is the code doomed to being translated into the equivalent of an if/elseif/else/endif sequence? Not necessarily. However, before we consider other alternatives, it's important to mention that not all if/elseif/else/endif sequences are created equal. Look back at the previous example. A straightforward implementation might have been something like this:

```
if(unsignedExpression <= 11)
{
  Switch for 0 to 11
}
else if(unsignedExpression >= 100 && unsignedExpression <= 101)
{
  Switch for 100 to 101
}
else if(unsignedExpression >= 1000 && unsignedExpression <= 1001)
{
  Switch for 1000 to 1001
}
else
{
  Code for default case
}
```

Instead, the former implementation first tests against the value 100 and branches based on the comparison being less than (cases 0 to 11) or greater than (cases 1000 to 1001), effectively creating a small *binary search* that reduces the number of comparisons. It's hard to see the savings in the HLL code, but in assembly code you can count the number of instructions that would be executed in the best and worst cases and see an improvement over the standard linear search approach of simply comparing the values in the cases in the order they appear in the switch statement.[8]

If your cases are too sparse (no meaningful groups at all), such as the 1, 10, 100, 1000, 10,000 example given earlier in this chapter, you're not going to be able to (reasonably) implement the switch statement by using a jump table. Rather than devolving into a straight linear search (which can be slow), a better solution is to sort your cases and test them using a binary search.

With a binary search, you first compare the expression value against the middle case value. If it's less than the middle value, you repeat the search on the first half of the list of values; if it's greater than the middle value, you repeat the test on the second half of the values; if it's equal, obviously you drop into the code to handle that test. Here's the binary search version of the 1, 10, 100, . . . example:

```
; Assume expression has been calculated into EAX.

        cmp eax, 100
        jb  try1_10
```

---

8. Of course, if you have a large number of groups in a sparse switch statement, a binary search will be much faster, on average, than a linear search.

```
        ja   try1000_10000

    Code to handle case 100 goes here
        jmp AllDone

try1_10:
        cmp eax,1
        je  case1
        cmp eax, 10
        jne defaultCase

    Code to handle case 10 goes here
        jmp AllDone
case1:
    Code to handle case 1 goes here
        jmp AllDone

try1000_10000:
        cmp eax, 1000
        je  case1000
        cmp eax, 10000
        jne defaultCase

    Code to handle case 10000 goes here
        jmp AllDone

case1000:
    Code to handle case 1000 goes here
        jmp AllDone

defaultCase:
    Code to handle defaultCase goes here

AllDone:
```

The techniques presented in this section have many possible alternatives. For example, one common solution is to create a table containing a set of records (structures), with each record entry a two-tuple containing a case value and a jump address. Rather than having a long sequence of compare instructions, a short loop can sequence through all the table elements, searching for the case value and transferring control to the corresponding jump address if there is a match. This scheme is slower than the other techniques in this section but can be much shorter than the traditional if/elseif/else/endif implementation.[9]

Note, by the way, that the defaultCase label often appears in several jcc instructions in a (non-jump-table) switch implementation. Since the conditional jump instructions have two encodings, a 2-byte form and a 6-byte form, you should try to place the defaultCase near these conditional jumps so you can use the short form of the instruction as much as possible. Although the examples in this section have typically put the jump tables (which consume a

---

9. With a bit of effort, you could use a binary search if the table is sorted.

large number of bytes) immediately after their corresponding indirect jump, you could move these tables elsewhere in the procedure to help keep the conditional jump instructions short. Here's the earlier 1, 10, 100, . . . example coded with this in mind:

```
; Assume expression has been computed and is sitting in EAX/RAX
; at this point...

            cmp    eax, 100
            jb     try0_13
            cmp    eax, 103
            ja     try1000_1003
            lea    rcx, jt100
            jmp    qword ptr [rcx][rax * 8 - 100 * 8]

try0_13: cmp    ecx, 13     ; Handle cases 0 to 13 here
            ja     defaultCase
            lea    rcx, jt0_13
            jmp    qword ptr [rcx][rax * 8]

try1000_1003:
            cmp    eax, 1000    ; Handle cases 1000 to 1003 here
            jb     defaultCase
            cmp    eax, 1003
            ja     defaultCase
            lea    rcx, jt1000
            jmp    qword ptr [rcx][rax * 8 - 1000 * 8]

defaultCase:
    Put defaultCase here to keep it near all the
        conditional jumps to defaultCase

            jmp    AllDone

jt0_13   qword case0, case1, case2, case3
            qword defaultCase, defaultCase, defaultCase
            qword defaultCase, defaultCase, defaultCase
            qword case10, case11, case12, case13
jt100    qword case100, case101, case102, case103
jt1000   qword case1000, case1001, case1002, case1003
            .
            .
            .

Code for the actual cases here
```

7.7 State Machines and Indirect Jumps

Another control structure commonly found in assembly language programs is the *state machine*. A state machine uses a *state variable* to control program flow. The FORTRAN programming language provides this capability with the assigned goto statement. Certain variants of C (for example, GNU's GCC from the Free Software Foundation) provide similar features. In assembly language, the indirect jump can implement state machines.

So what is a state machine? In basic terms, it is a piece of code that keeps track of its execution history by entering and leaving certain *states*. For the purposes of this chapter, we'll just assume that a state machine is a piece of code that (somehow) remembers the history of its execution (its *state*) and executes sections of code based on that history.

In a real sense, all programs are state machines. The CPU registers and values in memory constitute the state of that machine. However, we'll use a much more constrained view. Indeed, for most purposes, only a single variable (or the value in the RIP register) will denote the current state.

Now let's consider a concrete example. Suppose you have a procedure and want to perform one operation the first time you call it, a different operation the second time you call it, yet something else the third time you call it, and then something new again on the fourth call. After the fourth call, it repeats these four operations in order.

For example, suppose you want the procedure to add EAX and EBX the first time, subtract them on the second call, multiply them on the third, and divide them on the fourth. You could implement this procedure as shown in Listing 7-6.

```
; Listing 7-6

; A simple state machine example.

        option  casemap:none

nl        =       10

          .const
ttlStr    byte    "Listing 7-6", 0
fmtStr0   byte    "Calling StateMachine, "
          byte    "state=%d, EAX=5, ECX=6", nl, 0

fmtStr0b  byte    "Calling StateMachine, "
          byte    "state=%d, EAX=1, ECX=2", nl, 0

fmtStrx   byte    "Back from StateMachine, "
          byte    "state=%d, EAX=%d", nl, 0

fmtStr1   byte    "Calling StateMachine, "
          byte    "state=%d, EAX=50, ECX=60", nl, 0

fmtStr2   byte    "Calling StateMachine, "
          byte    "state=%d, EAX=10, ECX=20", nl, 0

fmtStr3   byte    "Calling StateMachine, "
          byte    "state=%d, EAX=50, ECX=5", nl, 0

          .data
state     byte    0
```

```
                .code
                externdef printf:proc

; Return program title to C++ program:

                public  getTitle
getTitle        proc
                lea     rax, ttlStr
                ret
getTitle        endp

StateMachine proc
                cmp     state, 0
                jne     TryState1

; State 0: Add ECX to EAX and switch to state 1:

                add     eax, ecx
                inc     state           ; State 0 becomes state 1
                jmp     exit

TryState1:
                cmp     state, 1
                jne     TryState2

; State 1: Subtract ECX from EAX and switch to state 2:

                sub     eax, ecx
                inc     state           ; State 1 becomes state 2
                jmp     exit

TryState2:      cmp     state, 2
                jne     MustBeState3

; If this is state 2, multiply ECX by EAX and switch to state 3:

                imul    eax, ecx
                inc     state           ; State 2 becomes state 3
                jmp     exit

; If it isn't one of the preceding states, we must be in state 3,
; so divide EAX by ECX and switch back to state 0.

MustBeState3:
                push    rdx             ; Preserve this 'cause it
                                        ; gets whacked by div
                xor     edx, edx        ; Zero-extend EAX into EDX
                div     ecx
                pop     rdx             ; Restore EDX's value preserved above
                mov     state, 0        ; Reset the state back to 0

exit:           ret

StateMachine endp
```

```
; Here is the "asmMain" function.

            public  asmMain
asmMain     proc
            push    rbp
            mov     rbp, rsp
            sub     rsp, 48         ; Shadow storage

            mov     state, 0        ; Just to be safe

; Demonstrate state 0:

            lea     rcx, fmtStr0
            movzx   rdx, state
            call    printf

            mov     eax, 5
            mov     ecx, 6
            call    StateMachine

            lea     rcx, fmtStrx
            mov     r8, rax
            movzx   edx, state
            call    printf

; Demonstrate state 1:

            lea     rcx, fmtStr1
            movzx   rdx, state
            call    printf

            mov     eax, 50
            mov     ecx, 60
            call    StateMachine

            lea     rcx, fmtStrx
            mov     r8, rax
            movzx   edx, state
            call    printf

; Demonstrate state 2:

            lea     rcx, fmtStr2
            movzx   rdx, state
            call    printf

            mov     eax, 10
            mov     ecx, 20
            call    StateMachine

            lea     rcx, fmtStrx
            mov     r8, rax
            movzx   edx, state
            call    printf
```

```
; Demonstrate state 3:

        lea     rcx, fmtStr3
        movzx   rdx, state
        call    printf

        mov     eax, 50
        mov     ecx, 5
        call    StateMachine

        lea     rcx, fmtStrx
        mov     r8, rax
        movzx   edx, state
        call    printf

; Demonstrate back in state 0:

        lea     rcx, fmtStr0b
        movzx   rdx, state
        call    printf

        mov     eax, 1
        mov     ecx, 2
        call    StateMachine

        lea     rcx, fmtStrx
        mov     r8, rax
        movzx   edx, state
        call    printf

        leave
        ret     ; Returns to caller

asmMain endp
        end
```

Listing 7-6: A state machine example

Here's the build command and program output:

```
C:\>build listing7-6

C:\>echo off
 Assembling: listing7-6.asm
c.cpp

C:\>listing7-6
Calling Listing 7-6:
Calling StateMachine, state=0, EAX=5, ECX=6
Back from StateMachine, state=1, EAX=11
Calling StateMachine, state=1, EAX=50, ECX=60
Back from StateMachine, state=2, EAX=-10
Calling StateMachine, state=2, EAX=10, ECX=20
Back from StateMachine, state=3, EAX=200
Calling StateMachine, state=3, EAX=50, ECX=5
```

```
Back from StateMachine, state=0, EAX=10
Calling StateMachine, state=0, EAX=1, ECX=2
Back from StateMachine, state=1, EAX=3
Listing 7-6 terminated
```

Technically, this procedure is not the state machine. Instead, the variable state and the cmp/jne instructions constitute the state machine. The procedure is little more than a switch statement implemented via the if/then/elseif construct. The only unique thing is that it remembers how many times it has been called[10] and behaves differently depending upon the number of calls.

While this is a *correct* implementation of the desired state machine, it is not particularly efficient. The astute reader, of course, would recognize that this code could be made a little faster using an actual switch statement rather than the if/then/elseif/endif implementation. However, an even better solution exists.

It's common to use an indirect jump to implement a state machine in assembly language. Rather than having a state variable that contains a value like 0, 1, 2, or 3, we could load the state variable with the *address* of the code to execute upon entry into the procedure. By simply jumping to that address, the state machine could save the tests needed to select the proper code fragment. Consider the implementation in Listing 7-7 using the indirect jump.

```
; Listing 7-7

; An indirect jump state machine example.

        option  casemap:none

nl          =       10

            .const
ttlStr      byte    "Listing 7-7", 0
fmtStr0     byte    "Calling StateMachine, "
            byte    "state=0, EAX=5, ECX=6", nl, 0

fmtStr0b    byte    "Calling StateMachine, "
            byte    "state=0, EAX=1, ECX=2", nl, 0

fmtStrx     byte    "Back from StateMachine, "
            byte    "EAX=%d", nl, 0

fmtStr1     byte    "Calling StateMachine, "
            byte    "state=1, EAX=50, ECX=60", nl, 0

fmtStr2     byte    "Calling StateMachine, "
            byte    "state=2, EAX=10, ECX=20", nl, 0
```

---

10. Actually, it remembers how many times, modulo 4, that it has been called.

```
fmtStr3      byte    "Calling StateMachine, "
             byte    "state=3, EAX=50, ECX=5", nl, 0

             .data
state        qword   state0

             .code
             externdef printf:proc

; Return program title to C++ program:

             public  getTitle
getTitle     proc
             lea     rax, ttlStr
             ret
getTitle     endp

; StateMachine version 2.0 - using an indirect jump.

             option noscoped      ; statex labels must be global
StateMachine proc

             jmp     state

; State 0: Add ECX to EAX and switch to state 1:

state0:      add     eax, ecx
             lea     rcx, state1
             mov     state, rcx
             ret

; State 1: Subtract ECX from EAX and switch to state 2:

state1:      sub     eax, ecx
             lea     rcx, state2
             mov     state, rcx
             ret

; If this is state 2, multiply ECX by EAX and switch to state 3:

state2:      imul    eax, ecx
             lea     rcx, state3
             mov     state, rcx
             ret

state3:      push    rdx           ; Preserve this 'cause it
                                   ; gets whacked by div
             xor     edx, edx      ; Zero-extend EAX into EDX
             div     ecx
             pop     rdx           ; Restore EDX's value preserved above
             lea     rcx, state0
             mov     state, rcx
             ret
```

```
        StateMachine endp
                    option scoped

; Here is the "asmMain" function.

                public  asmMain
asmMain         proc
                push    rbp
                mov     rbp, rsp
                sub     rsp, 48         ; Shadow storage

                lea     rcx, state0
                mov     state, rcx      ; Just to be safe

; Demonstrate state 0:

                lea     rcx, fmtStr0
                call    printf

                mov     eax, 5
                mov     ecx, 6
                call    StateMachine

                lea     rcx, fmtStrx
                mov     rdx, rax
                call    printf

; Demonstrate state 1:

                lea     rcx, fmtStr1
                call    printf

                mov     eax, 50
                mov     ecx, 60
                call    StateMachine

                lea     rcx, fmtStrx
                mov     rdx, rax
                call    printf

; Demonstrate state 2:

                lea     rcx, fmtStr2
                call    printf

                mov     eax, 10
                mov     ecx, 20
                call    StateMachine

                lea     rcx, fmtStrx
                mov     rdx, rax
                call    printf
```

```
; Demonstrate state 3:

            lea     rcx, fmtStr3
            call    printf

            mov     eax, 50
            mov     ecx, 5
            call    StateMachine

            lea     rcx, fmtStrx
            mov     rdx, rax
            call    printf

; Demonstrate back in state 0:

            lea     rcx, fmtStr0b
            call    printf

            mov     eax, 1
            mov     ecx, 2
            call    StateMachine

            lea     rcx, fmtStrx
            mov     rdx, rax
            call    printf

            leave
            ret     ; Returns to caller

asmMain     endp
            end
```

Listing 7-7: A state machine using an indirect jump

Here's the build command and program output:

```
C:\>build listing7-7

C:\>echo off
 Assembling: listing7-7.asm
c.cpp

C:\>listing7-7
Calling Listing 7-7:
Calling StateMachine, state=0, EAX=5, ECX=6
Back from StateMachine, EAX=11
Calling StateMachine, state=1, EAX=50, ECX=60
Back from StateMachine, EAX=-10
Calling StateMachine, state=2, EAX=10, ECX=20
Back from StateMachine, EAX=200
Calling StateMachine, state=3, EAX=50, ECX=5
Back from StateMachine, EAX=10
Calling StateMachine, state=0, EAX=1, ECX=2
Back from StateMachine, EAX=3
Listing 7-7 terminated
```

The jmp instruction at the beginning of the StateMachine procedure transfers control to the location pointed at by the state variable. The first time you call StateMachine, it points at the State0 label. Thereafter, each subsection of code sets the state variable to point at the appropriate successor code.

7.8 Loops

Loops represent the final basic control structure (sequences, decisions, and loops) that make up a typical program. As with so many other structures in assembly language, you'll find yourself using loops in places you've never dreamed of using loops.

Most HLLs have implied loop structures hidden away. For example, consider the BASIC statement if A$ = B$ then 100. This if statement compares two strings and jumps to statement 100 if they are equal. In assembly language, you would need to write a loop to compare each character in A$ to the corresponding character in B$ and then jump to statement 100 if and only if all the characters matched.[11]

Program loops consist of three components: an optional *initialization component*, an optional *loop-termination test*, and the *body* of the loop. The order in which you assemble these components can dramatically affect the loop's operation. Three permutations of these components appear frequently in programs: while loops, repeat/until loops (do/while in C/C++), and infinite loops (for example, for(;;) in C/C++).

7.8.1 while Loops

The most general loop is the while loop. In C/C++, it takes the following form:

```
while(expression) statement(s);
```

In the while loop, the termination test appears at the beginning of the loop. As a direct consequence of the position of the termination test, the body of the loop may never execute if the Boolean expression is always false.

Consider the following C/C++ while loop:

```
i = 0;
while(i < 100)
{
    ++i;
}
```

The i = 0; statement is the initialization code for this loop. i is a loop-control variable, because it controls the execution of the body of the loop. i < 100 is the loop-termination condition: the loop will not terminate as long as i is less than 100. The single statement ++i; (*increment i*) is the loop body that executes on each loop iteration.

---

11. Of course, the C Standard Library provides the strcmp routine that compares the strings for you, effectively hiding the loop. However, if you were to write this function yourself, the looping nature of the operation would be obvious.

A C/C++ while loop can be easily synthesized using if and goto statements. For example, you may replace the previous C while loop with the following C code:

```
i = 0;
WhileLp:
if(i < 100)
{

    ++i;
      goto WhileLp;

}
```

More generally, you can construct any while loop as follows:

```
Optional initialization code

UniqueLabel:
if(not_termination_condition)
{
    Loop body
    goto UniqueLabel;

}
```

Therefore, you can use the techniques from earlier in this chapter to convert if statements to assembly language and add a single jmp instruction to produce a while loop. The example in this section translates to the following pure x86-64 assembly code:[12]

```
        mov i, 0
WhileLp:
        cmp i, 100
        jnl WhileDone
        inc i
        jmp WhileLp;

WhileDone:
```

7.8.2   repeat/until Loops

The repeat/until (do/while) loop tests for the termination condition at the end of the loop rather than at the beginning. In Pascal, the repeat/until loop takes the following form:

```
Optional initialization code
repeat
```

---

12. MASM will actually convert most while statements to different x86-64 code than this section presents. The reason for the difference appears in "Moving the Termination Condition to the End of a Loop" on page 443, when we explore how to write more efficient loop code.

```
    Loop body

until(termination_condition);
```

This is comparable to the following C/C++ do/while loop:

```
Optional initialization code
do
{
    Loop body

}while(not_termination_condition);
```

This sequence executes the initialization code, then executes the loop body, and finally tests a condition to see whether the loop should repeat. If the Boolean expression evaluates to false, the loop repeats; otherwise, the loop terminates. The two things you should note about the repeat/until loop are that the termination test appears at the end of the loop and, as a direct consequence, the loop body always executes at least once.

Like the while loop, the repeat/until loop can be synthesized with an if statement and a jmp. You could use the following:

```
Initialization code
SomeUniqueLabel:

    Loop body

if(not_termination_condition) goto SomeUniqueLabel;
```

Based on the material presented in the previous sections, you can easily synthesize repeat/until loops in assembly language. The following is a simple example:

```
    repeat (Pascal code)

        write('Enter a number greater than 100:');
        readln(i);

    until(i > 100);

// This translates to the following if/jmp code:

    RepeatLabel:

        write('Enter a number greater than 100:');
        readln(i);

    if(i <= 100) then goto RepeatLabel;

// It also translates into the following assembly code:

RepeatLabel:
```

```
        call print
        byte "Enter a number greater than 100: ", 0
        call readInt  ; Function to read integer from user

        cmp  eax, 100 ; Assume readInt returns integer in EAX
        jng  RepeatLabel
```

7.8.3   forever/endfor Loops

If while loops test for termination at the beginning of the loop and repeat/until/do/while loops check for termination at the end of the loop, the only place left to test for termination is in the middle of the loop. The C/C++ high-level for(;;) loop, combined with the break statement, provides this capability. The C/C++ infinite loop takes the following form:

```
for(;;)
{
    Loop body

}
```

There is no explicit termination condition. Unless otherwise provided, the for(;;) construct forms an infinite loop. A break statement usually handles loop termination. Consider the following C++ code that employs a for(;;) construct:

```
for(;;)
{
    cin >> character;
    if(character == '.') break;
    cout << character;

}
```

Converting a for(ever) loop to pure assembly language is easy. All you need is a label and a jmp instruction. The break statement in this example is also nothing more than a jmp instruction (or conditional jump). The pure assembly language version of the preceding code looks something like the following:

```
foreverLabel:

        call getchar    ; Assume it returns char in AL
        cmp  al, '.'
        je   ForIsDone

        mov  cl, al     ; Pass char read from getchar to putchar
        call putcchar   ; Assume this prints the char in CL
        jmp  foreverLabel

ForIsDone:
```

7.8.4 for Loops

The standard for loop is a special form of the while loop that repeats the loop body a specific number of times (this is known as a *definite* loop). In C/C++, the for loop takes the form

```
for(initialization_Stmt; termination_expression; inc_Stmt)
{
    Statements

}
```

which is equivalent to the following:

```
initialization_Stmt;
while(termination_expression)
{
    Statements

    inc_Stmt;

}
```

Traditionally, programs use the for loop to process arrays and other objects accessed in sequential order. We normally initialize a loop-control variable with the initialization statement and then use the loop-control variable as an index into the array (or other data type). For example:

```
for(i = 0; i < 7; ++i)
{
    printf("Array Element = %d \ n", SomeArray[i]);

}
```

To convert this to pure assembly language, begin by translating the for loop into an equivalent while loop:

```
i = 0;
while(i < 7)
{
    printf("Array Element = %d \ n", SomeArray[i]);
    ++i;
}
```

Now, using the techniques from "while Loops" on page 433, translate the code into pure assembly language:

```
        xor  rbx, rbx      ; Use RBX to hold loop index
WhileLp: cmp ebx, 7
        jnl  EndWhileLp

        lea  rcx, fmtStr   ; fmtStr = "Array Element = %d", nl, 0
        lea  rdx, SomeArray
```

```
        mov  rdx, [rdx][rbx * 4] ; Assume SomeArray is 4-byte ints
        call printf

        inc  rbx
        jmp  WhileLp;

EndWhileLp:
```

7.8.5   The break and continue Statements

The C/C++ break and continue statements both translate into a single jmp instruction. The break instruction exits the loop that immediately contains the break statement; the continue statement restarts the loop that contains the continue statement.

To convert a break statement to pure assembly language, just emit a goto/jmp instruction that transfers control to the first statement following the end of the loop to exit. You can do this by placing a label after the loop body and jumping to that label. The following code fragments demonstrate this technique for the various loops.

```
// Breaking out of a FOR(;;) loop:

for(;;)
{
     Stmts
        // break;
        goto BreakFromForever;
     Stmts
}
BreakFromForever:

// Breaking out of a FOR loop:

for(initStmt; expr; incStmt)
{
     Stmts
        // break;
        goto BrkFromFor;
     Stmts
}
BrkFromFor:

// Breaking out of a WHILE loop:

while(expr)
{
     Stmts
        // break;
        goto BrkFromWhile;
     Stmts
}
```

```
BrkFromWhile:

// Breaking out of a REPEAT/UNTIL loop (DO/WHILE is similar):

repeat
      Stmts
          // break;
          goto BrkFromRpt;
      Stmts
until(expr);
BrkFromRpt:
```

In pure assembly language, convert the appropriate control structures to assembly and replace the goto with a jmp instruction.

The continue statement is slightly more complex than the break statement. The implementation is still a single jmp instruction; however, the target label doesn't wind up going in the same spot for each of the different loops. Figures 7-2, 7-3, 7-4, and 7-5 show where the continue statement transfers control for each of the loops.

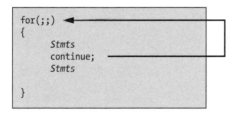

Figure 7-2: continue destination for the
for(;;) loop

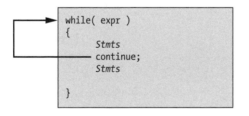

Figure 7-3: continue destination and the while loop

```
for( initStmt; expr; incStmt )
{
      Stmts
      continue;
      Stmts

}
```

Note: CONTINUE forces the execution of the
incStmt clause and then transfers control
to the test for loop termination.

Figure 7-4: continue destination and the for loop

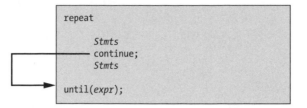

Figure 7-5: continue destination and the repeat/until *loop*

The following code fragments demonstrate how to convert the continue statement into an appropriate jmp instruction for each of these loop types:

for(;;)/continue/endfor

```
; Conversion of FOREVER loop with continue
; to pure assembly:
 for(;;)
 {
     Stmts
     continue;
     Stmts
 }

; Converted code:

foreverLbl:
     Stmts
         ; continue;
         jmp foreverLbl
     Stmts
     jmp foreverLbl
```

while/continue/endwhile

```
; Conversion of WHILE loop with continue
; into pure assembly:

 while(expr)
 {
     Stmts
     continue;
     Stmts
 }

; Converted code:

whlLabel:
 Code to evaluate expr
     jcc EndOfWhile    ; Skip loop on expr failure
       Stmts
         ; continue;
         jmp whlLabel ; Jump to start of loop on continue
```

```
        Stmts
    jmp whlLabel        ; Repeat the code
EndOfWhile:
```

for/continue/endfor

```
; Conversion for a FOR loop with continue
; into pure assembly:

 for(initStmt; expr; incStmt)
 {
     Stmts
    continue;
     Stmts
 }

; Converted code:

        initStmt
ForLpLbl:
    Code to evaluate expr
        jcc EndOfFor      ; Branch if expression fails
         Stmts

        ; continue;
        jmp ContFor       ; Branch to incStmt on continue

         Stmts

ContFor:
        incStmt
        jmp ForLpLbl

EndOfFor:
```

repeat/continue/until

```
 repeat
     Stmts
    continue;
     Stmts
 until(expr);

 do
 {
     Stmts
    continue;
     Stmts

 }while(!expr);

; Converted code:
```

```
RptLpLbl:
    Stmts
        ; continue;
        jmp ContRpt   ; Continue branches to termination test
            Stmts
ContRpt:
    Code to test expr
    jcc RptLpLbl        ; Jumps if expression evaluates false
```

7.8.6   Register Usage and Loops

Given that the x86-64 accesses registers more efficiently than memory locations, registers are the ideal spot to place loop-control variables (especially for small loops). However, registers are a limited resource; there are only 16 general-purpose registers (and some, such as RSP and RBP, are reserved for special purposes). Compared with memory, you cannot place much data in the registers, despite them being more efficient to use than memory.

Loops present a special challenge for registers. Registers are perfect for loop-control variables because they're efficient to manipulate and can serve as indexes into arrays and other data structures (a common use for loop-control variables). However, the limited availability of registers often creates problems when using registers in this fashion. Consider the following code that will not work properly because it attempts to reuse a register (CX) that is already in use (leading to the corruption of the outer loop's loop-control variable):

```
        mov cx, 8
loop1:
        mov cx, 4
loop2:
         Stmts
        dec cx
        jnz loop2

        dec cx
        jnz loop1
```

The intent here, of course, was to create a set of nested loops; that is, one loop inside another. The inner loop (loop2) should repeat four times for each of the eight executions of the outer loop (loop1). Unfortunately, both loops use the same register as a loop-control variable. Therefore, this will form an infinite loop. Because CX is always 0 upon encountering the second dec instruction, control will always transfer to the loop1 label (because decrementing 0 produces a nonzero result). The solution here is to save and restore the CX register or to use a different register in place of CX for the outer loop:

```
        mov cx, 8
loop1:
        push rcx
        mov  cx, 4
```

```
loop2:
            Stmts
            dec cx
            jnz loop2;

            pop rcx
            dec cx
            jnz loop1
or
            mov dx,8
loop1:
            mov cx, 4
loop2:
            Stmts
            dec cx
            jnz loop2

            dec dx
            jnz loop1
```

Register corruption is one of the primary sources of bugs in loops in assembly language programs, so always keep an eye out for this problem.

7.9   Loop Performance Improvements

Because loops are the primary source of performance problems within a program, they are the place to look when attempting to speed up your software. While a treatise on how to write efficient programs is beyond the scope of this chapter, you should be aware of the following concepts when designing loops in your programs. They're all aimed at removing unnecessary instructions from your loops in order to reduce the time it takes to execute a single iteration of the loop.

7.9.1   Moving the Termination Condition to the End of a Loop

Consider the following flow graphs for the three types of loops presented earlier:

```
REPEAT/UNTIL loop:
     Initialization code
          Loop body
     Test for termination
     Code following the loop

WHILE loop:
     Initialization code
     Loop-termination test
          Loop body
          Jump back to test
     Code following the loop
```

```
FOREVER/ENDFOR loop:
    Initialization code
            Loop body part one
            Loop-termination test
            Loop body part two
            Jump back to Loop body part one
    Code following the loop
```

As you can see, the repeat/until loop is the simplest of the bunch. This is reflected in the assembly language implementation of these loops. Consider the following repeat/until and while loops that are semantically identical:

```
; Example involving a WHILE loop:

        mov  esi, edi
        sub  esi, 20

; while(ESI <= EDI)

whileLp: cmp  esi, edi
        jnle endwhile

            Stmts

        inc  esi
        jmp  whileLp
endwhile:

; Example involving a REPEAT/UNTIL loop:

        mov esi, edi
        sub esi, 20
repeatLp:

            Stmts

        inc  esi
        cmp  esi, edi
        jng  repeatLp
```

Testing for the termination condition at the end of the loop allows us to remove a jmp instruction from the loop, which can be significant if the loop is nested inside other loops. Given the definition of the loop, you can easily see that the loop will execute exactly 20 times, which suggests that the conversion to a repeat/until loop is trivial and always possible.

Unfortunately, it's not always quite this easy. Consider the following C code:

```
while(esi <= edi)
{
    Stmts
    ++esi;
}
```

In this particular example, we haven't the slightest idea what ESI contains upon entry into the loop. Therefore, we cannot assume that the loop body will execute at least once. So, we must test for loop termination before executing the body of the loop. The test can be placed at the end of the loop with the inclusion of a single jmp instruction:

```
          jmp WhlTest
TopOfLoop:
          Stmts
          inc  esi
WhlTest:  cmp  esi, edi
          jle TopOfLoop
```

Although the code is as long as the original while loop, the jmp instruction executes only once rather than on each repetition of the loop. However, the slight gain in efficiency is obtained via a slight loss in readability (so be sure to comment it). The second code sequence is closer to spaghetti code than the original implementation. Such is often the price of a small performance gain. Therefore, you should carefully analyze your code to ensure that the performance boost is worth the loss of clarity.

7.9.2   Executing the Loop Backward

Because of the nature of the flags on the x86-64, loops that repeat from some number down to (or up to) 0 are more efficient than loops that execute from 0 to another value. Compare the following C/C++ for loop and the comparable assembly language code:

```
for(j = 1; j <= 8; ++j)
{
     Stmts
}

; Conversion to pure assembly (as well as using a
; REPEAT/UNTIL form):

mov j, 1
ForLp:
     Stmts
     inc j
     cmp j, 8
     jle ForLp
```

Now consider another loop that also has eight iterations but runs its loop-control variable from 8 down to 1 rather than 1 up to 8, thereby saving a comparison on each repetition of the loop:

```
    mov j, 8
LoopLbl:
    Stmts
    dec j
    jnz LoopLbl
```

Saving the execution time of the cmp instruction on each iteration of the loop may result in faster code. Unfortunately, you cannot force all loops to run backward. However, with a little effort and some coercion, you should be able to write many for loops so that they operate backward.

The preceding example worked out well because the loop ran from 8 down to 1. The loop terminated when the loop-control variable became 0. What happens if you need to execute the loop when the loop-control variable goes to 0? For example, suppose that the preceding loop needed to range from 7 down to 0. As long as the lower bound is non-negative, you can substitute the jns instruction in place of the jnz instruction in the earlier code:

```
    mov j, 7
LoopLbl:
    Stmts
    dec j
    jns LoopLbl
```

This loop will repeat eight times, with j taking on the values 7 to 0. When it decrements 0 to –1, it sets the sign flag and the loop terminates.

Keep in mind that some values may look positive but are actually negative. If the loop-control variable is a byte, values in the range 128 to 255 are negative in the two's complement system. Therefore, initializing the loop-control variable with any 8-bit value in the range 129 to 255 (or, of course, 0) terminates the loop after a single execution. This can get you into trouble if you're not careful.

7.9.3 Using Loop-Invariant Computations

A *loop-invariant computation* is a calculation that appears within a loop that always yields the same result. You needn't do such computations inside the loop. You can compute them outside the loop and reference the value of the computations inside the loop. The following C code demonstrates an invariant computation:

```
for(i = 0; i < n; ++i)
{
    k = (j - 2) + i
}
```

Because j never changes throughout the execution of this loop, the subexpression j - 2 can be computed outside the loop:

```
jm2 = j - 2;
for(i = 0; i < n; ++i)
{
    k = jm2 + i;
}
```

Although we've eliminated a single instruction by computing the sub-expression j - 2 outside the loop, there is still an invariant component to this calculation: adding j - 2 to i n times. Because this invariant component executes n times in the loop, we can translate the previous code to the following:

```
k = (j - 2) * n;
for(i = 0; i < n; ++i)
{
    k = k + i;
}
```

This translates to the following assembly code:

```
        mov  eax, j
        sub  eax, 2
        imul eax, n
        mov  ecx, 0
lp:     cmp  ecx, n
        jnl  loopDone
        add  eax, ecx   ; Single instruction implements loop body!
        inc  ecx
        jmp  lp
loopDone:
        mov  k, eax
```

For this particular loop, you can actually compute the result without using a loop at all (a formula corresponds to the preceding iterative calculation). Still, this simple example demonstrates how to eliminate loop-invariant calculations from a loop.

7.9.4 Unraveling Loops

For small loops—those whose body is only a few statements—the overhead required to process a loop may constitute a significant percentage of the total processing time. For example, look at the following Pascal code and its associated x86-64 assembly language code:

```
    for i := 3 downto 0 do A[i] := 0;

        mov i, 3
        lea rcx, A
LoopLbl:
        mov ebx, i
        mov [rcx][rbx * 4], 0
        dec i
        jns LoopLbl
```

Four instructions execute on each repetition of the loop. Only one instruction is doing the desired operation (moving a 0 into an element of

A). The remaining three instructions control the loop. Therefore, it takes 16 instructions to do the operation logically required by 4.

While we could make many improvements to this loop based on the information presented thus far, consider carefully exactly what this loop is doing—it's storing four 0s into A[0] through A[3]. A more efficient approach is to use four mov instructions to accomplish the same task. For example, if A is an array of double words, the following code initializes A much faster than the preceding code:

```
mov   A[0], 0
mov   A[4], 0
mov   A[8], 0
mov   A[12], 0
```

Although this is a simple example, it shows the benefit of *loop unraveling* (also known as *loop unrolling*). If this simple loop appeared buried inside a set of nested loops, the 4:1 instruction reduction could possibly double the performance of that section of your program.

Of course, you cannot unravel all loops. Loops that execute a variable number of times are difficult to unravel because there is rarely a way to determine at assembly time the number of loop iterations. Therefore, unraveling a loop is a process best applied to loops that execute a known number of times, with the number of times known at assembly time.

Even if you repeat a loop a fixed number of iterations, it may not be a good candidate for loop unraveling. Loop unraveling produces impressive performance improvements when the number of instructions controlling the loop (and handling other overhead operations) represents a significant percentage of the total number of instructions in the loop. Had the previous loop contained 36 instructions in the body (exclusive of the four overhead instructions), the performance improvement would be, at best, only 10 percent (compared with the 300 to 400 percent it now enjoys).

Therefore, the costs of unraveling a loop—all the extra code that must be inserted into your program—quickly reach a point of diminishing returns as the body of the loop grows larger or as the number of iterations increases. Furthermore, entering that code into your program can become quite a chore. Therefore, loop unraveling is a technique best applied to small loops.

Note that the superscalar 80x86 chips (Pentium and later) have *branch-prediction hardware* and use other techniques to improve performance. Loop unrolling on such systems may actually *slow* the code because these processors are optimized to execute short loops. Whenever applying "improvements" to speed up your code, you should always measure the performance before and after to ensure there was sufficient gain to justify the change.

7.9.5   Using Induction Variables

Consider the following Pascal loop:

```
for i := 0 to 255 do csetVar[i] := [];
```

Here the program is initializing each element of an array of character sets to the empty set. The straightforward code to achieve this is the following:

```
         mov  i, 0
         lea  rcx, csetVar
FLp:

         ; Compute the index into the array (assume that each
         ; element of a csetVar array contains 16 bytes).

         mov  ebx, i  ; Zero-extends into RBX!
         shl  ebx, 4

         ; Set this element to the empty set (all 0 bits).

         xor  rax, rax
         mov  qword ptr [rcx][rbx], rax
         mov  qword ptr [rcx][rbx + 8], rax

         inc  i
         cmp  i, 256
         jb   FLp;
```

Although unraveling this code will still improve performance, it will take 1024 instructions to accomplish this task, too many for all but the most time-critical applications. However, you can reduce the execution time of the body of the loop by using induction variables. An *induction variable* is one whose value depends entirely on the value of another variable.

In the preceding example, the index into the array csetVar tracks the loop-control variable (it's always equal to the value of the loop-control variable times 16). Because i doesn't appear anywhere else in the loop, there is no sense in performing the computations on i. Why not operate directly on the array index value? The following code demonstrates this technique:

```
         xor  rbx, rbx    ; i * 16 in RBX
         xor  rax, rax    ; Loop invariant
         lea  rcx, csetVar ; Base address of csetVar array
FLp:
         mov  qword ptr [rcx][rbx], rax
         mov  qword ptr [rcx][rbx + 8], rax

         add  ebx, 16
         cmp  ebx, 256 * 16
         jb   FLp
;        mov  ebx, 256    ; If you care to maintain same semantics as C code
```

The induction that takes place in this example occurs when the code increments the loop-control variable (moved into EBX for efficiency) by 16 on each iteration of the loop rather than by 1. Multiplying the loop-control variable by 16 (and the final loop-termination constant value) allows the code to eliminate multiplying the loop-control variable by 16 on each iteration of the loop (that is, this allows us to remove the shl instruction from the previous code). Further, because this code no longer refers to the original loop-control variable (i), the code can maintain the loop-control variable strictly in the EBX register.

7.10 For More Information

Write Great Code, Volume 2, by this author (Second Edition, No Starch Press, 2020) provides a good discussion of the implementation of various HLL control structures in low-level assembly language. It also discusses optimizations such as induction, unrolling, strength reduction, and so on, that apply to optimizing loops.

7.11 Test Yourself

1. What are the two typical mechanisms for obtaining the address of a label appearing in a program?
2. What statement can you use to make all symbols global that appear within a procedure?
3. What statement can you use to make all symbols local that appear within a procedure?
4. What are the two forms of the indirect jmp instruction?
5. What is a state machine?
6. What is the general rule for converting a branch to its opposite branch?
7. What are the two exceptions to the rule for converting a branch to its opposite branch?
8. What is a trampoline?
9. What is the general syntax of the conditional move instruction?
10. What is the advantage of a conditional move instruction over a conditional jump?
11. What are some disadvantages of conditional moves?
12. Explain the difference between short-circuit and complete Boolean evaluation.
13. Convert the following if statements to assembly language sequences by using complete Boolean evaluation (assume all variables are unsigned 32-bit integer values):

```
if(x == y || z > t)
{
    Do something
}
```

```
if(x != y && z < t)
{
    THEN statements
}
else
{
    ELSE statements
}
```

14. Convert the preceding statements to assembly language by using short-circuit Boolean evaluation (assume all variables are signed 16-bit integer values).

15. Convert the following switch statements to assembly language (assume all variables are unsigned 32-bit integers):

```
switch(s)
{
    case 0:    case 0 code   break;
    case 1:    case 1 code   break;
    case 2:    case 2 code   break;
    case 3:    case 3 code   break;
}

switch(t)
{
    case 2:    case 0 code   break;
    case 4:    case 4 code   break;
    case 5:    case 5 code   break;
    case 6:    case 6 code   break;
    default:   Default code
}

switch(u)
{
    case 10:   case 10 code   break;
    case 11:   case 11 code   break;
    case 12:   case 12 code   break;
    case 25:   case 25 code   break;
    case 26:   case 26 code   break;
    case 27:   case 27 code   break;
    default:   Default code
}
```

16. Convert the following while loops to assembly code (assume all variables are signed 32-bit integers):

```
while(i < j)
{
    Code for loop body
}
```

```
while(i < j && k != 0)
{
     Code for loop body, part a
   if(m == 5) continue;
     Code for loop body, part b
   if(n < 6) break;
     Code for loop body, part c
}

do
{
   Code for loop body
} while(i != j);

do
{
     Code for loop body, part a
   if(m != 5) continue;
     Code for loop body, part b
   if(n == 6) break;
     Code for loop body, part c
} while(i < j && k > j);

for(int i = 0; i < 10; ++i)
{
   Code for loop body
}
```

8

ADVANCED ARITHMETIC

This chapter covers extended-precision arithmetic, arithmetic on operands whose sizes are different, and decimal arithmetic. By the conclusion of this chapter, you will know how to apply arithmetic and logical operations to integer operands of any size, including those larger than 64 bits, and how to convert operands of different sizes into a compatible format. Finally, you'll learn to perform decimal arithmetic by using the x86-64 BCD instructions on the x87 FPU, which lets you use decimal arithmetic in those few applications that absolutely require base-10 operations.

8.1 Extended-Precision Operations

One big advantage of assembly language over high-level languages is that assembly language does not limit the size of integer operations. For example, the standard C programming language defines three integer sizes: short int, int, and long int.[1] On the PC, these are often 16- and 32-bit integers.

Although the x86-64 machine instructions limit you to processing 8-, 16-, 32-, or 64-bit integers with a single instruction, you can use multiple instructions to process integers of any size. If you want to add 256-bit integer values together, it's no problem. This section describes how to extend various arithmetic and logical operations from 16, 32, or 64 bits to as many bits as you please.

8.1.1 Extended-Precision Addition

The x86-64 add instruction adds two 8-, 16-, 32-, or 64-bit numbers. After the execution of add, the x86-64 carry flag is set if you have an overflow out of the HO bit of the sum. You can use this information to do extended-precision addition operations.[2] Consider the way you manually perform a multiple-digit addition operation (as shown in Figure 8-1).

Step 1: Add the least significant digits together

```
  289                      289
+ 456      produces      + 456
                           5 with carry 1
```

Step 2: Add the next significant digits plus carry

```
  1 (carry)                1 (carry)
  289                      289
+ 456      produces      + 456
    5                      45 with carry 1
```

Step 3: Add the most significant digits together

```
  1 (carry)                1 (carry)
  289                      289
+ 456      produces      + 456
   45                      745
```

Figure 8-1: Multi-digit addition

The x86-64 handles extended-precision arithmetic the same way, except instead of adding the numbers a digit at a time, it adds them together a byte, word, double word, or quad word at a time. Consider the three-quad-word (192-bit) addition operation in Figure 8-2.

---

1. Newer C standards also provide for a long long int, which is usually a 64-bit integer.

2. This book uses *multi-digit* and *multi-byte* as synonyms for *extended precision*.

Step 1: Add the least significant qwords together

Step 2: Add the middle qwords together

Step 3: Add the most significant qwords together

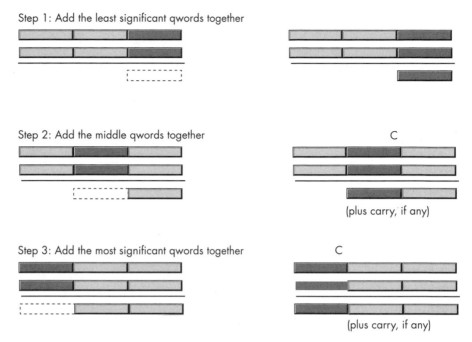

(plus carry, if any)

(plus carry, if any)

Figure 8-2: Adding two 192-bit objects together

As you can see, the idea is to break a larger operation into a sequence of smaller ones. Since the x86 processor family is capable of adding together at most 64 bits at a time (using general-purpose registers), the operation must proceed in blocks of 64 bits or fewer. Here are the steps:

1. Add the two LO quad words together just as you would add the two LO digits of a decimal number together in the manual algorithm, using the add instruction. If there is a carry out of the LO addition, add sets the carry flag to 1; otherwise, it clears the carry flag.

2. Add together the second pair of quad words in the two 192-bit values, plus the carry out of the previous addition (if any), using the adc (*add with carry*) instruction. The adc instruction uses the same syntax as add and performs almost the same operation:

```
adc dest, source ; dest := dest + source + C
```

The only difference is that adc adds in the value of the carry flag along with the source and destination operands. It sets the flags the same way add does (including setting the carry flag if there is an unsigned overflow). This is exactly what we need to add together the middle two double words of our 192-bit sum.

3. Add the HO double words of the 192-bit value with the carry out of the sum of the middle two quad words, once again using adc.

To summarize, the add instruction adds the LO quad words together, and adc adds all other quad word pairs together. At the end of the extended-precision addition sequence, the carry flag indicates unsigned overflow (if set), a set overflow flag indicates signed overflow, and the sign flag indicates the sign of the result. The zero flag doesn't have any real meaning at the end of the extended-precision addition (it simply means that the sum of the two HO quad words is 0 and does not indicate that the whole result is 0).

For example, suppose that you have two 128-bit values you wish to add together, defined as follows:

```
        .data
X       oword   ?
Y       oword   ?
```

Suppose also that you want to store the sum in a third variable, Z, which is also an oword. The following x86-64 code will accomplish this task:

```
mov rax, qword ptr X    ; Add together the LO 64 bits
add rax, qword ptr Y    ; of the numbers and store the
mov qword ptr Z, rax    ; result into the LO qword of Z

mov rax, qword ptr X[8] ; Add together (with carry) the
adc rax, qword ptr Y[8] ; HO 64 bits and store the result
mov qword ptr Z[8], rax ; into the HO qword of Z
```

The first three instructions add the LO quad words of X and Y together and store the result into the LO quad word of Z. The last three instructions add the HO quad words of X and Y together, along with the carry from the LO word, and store the result in the HO quad word of Z.

Remember, X, Y, and Z are oword objects (128 bits), and an instruction of the form mov rax, X would attempt to load a 128-bit value into a 64-bit register. To load a 64-bit value, specifically the LO 64 bits, the qword ptr operator coerces symbols X, Y, and Z to 64 bits. To load the HO qwords, you use address expressions of the form X[8], along with the qword ptr operator, because the x86 memory space addresses bytes, and it takes 8 consecutive bytes to form a quad word.

You can extend this algorithm to any number of bits by using adc to add in the higher-order values. For example, to add together two 256-bit values declared as arrays of four quad words, you could use code like the following:

```
        .data
BigVal1 qword  4 dup (?)
BigVal2 qword  4 dup (?)
BigVal3 qword  4 dup (?)    ; Holds the sum
     .
     .
     .
```

```
; Note that there is no need for "qword ptr"
; because the base type of BitValx is qword.

    mov rax, BigVal1[0]
    add rax, BigVal2[0]
    mov BigVal3[0], rax

    mov rax, BigVal1[8]
    adc rax, BigVal2[8]
    mov BigVal3[8], rax

    mov rax, BigVal1[16]
    adc rax, BigVal2[16]
    mov BigVal3[16], rax

    mov rax, BigVal1[24]
    adc rax, BigVal2[24]
    mov BigVal3[24], rax
```

8.1.2   Extended-Precision Subtraction

Just as it does addition, the x86-64 performs multi-byte subtraction the same way you would manually, except it subtracts whole bytes, words, double words, or quad words at a time rather than decimal digits. You use the sub instruction on the LO byte, word, double word, or quad word and the sbb (*subtract with borrow*) instruction on the high-order values.

The following example demonstrates a 128-bit subtraction using the 64-bit registers on the x86-64:

```
        .data
Left    oword   ?
Right   oword   ?
Diff    oword   ?
            .
            .
            .
    mov rax, qword ptr Left
    sub rax, qword ptr Right
    mov qword ptr Diff, rax

    mov rax, qword ptr Left[8]
    sbb rax, qword ptr Right[8]
    mov qword ptr Diff[8], rax
```

The following example demonstrates a 256-bit subtraction:

```
        .data
BigVal1 qword 4 dup (?)
BigVal2 qword 4 dup (?)
BigVal3 qword 4 dup (?)
```

.
.
.

```
; Compute BigVal3 := BigVal1 - BigVal2.

; Note: don't need to coerce types of
; BigVa1, BigVal2, or BigVal3 because
; their base types are already qword.

    mov rax, BigVal1[0]
    sub rax, BigVal2[0]
    mov BigVal3[0], rax

    mov rax, BigVal1[8]
    sbb rax, BigVal2[8]
    mov BigVal3[8], rax

    mov rax, BigVal1[16]
    sbb rax, BigVal2[16]
    mov BigVal3[16], rax

    mov rax, BigVal1[24]
    sbb rax, BigVal2[24]
    mov BigVal3[24], rax
```

8.1.3   Extended-Precision Comparisons

Unfortunately, there isn't a "compare with borrow" instruction that you can use to perform extended-precision comparisons. Fortunately, you can compare extended-precision values by using just a cmp instruction, as you'll soon see.

Consider the two unsigned values 2157h and 1293h. The LO bytes of these two values do not affect the outcome of the comparison. Simply comparing the HO bytes, 21h with 12h, tells us that the first value is greater than the second.

You need to look at both bytes of a pair of values only if the HO bytes are equal. In all other cases, comparing the HO bytes tells you everything you need to know about the values. This is true for any number of bytes, not just two. The following code compares two signed 128-bit integers by comparing their HO quad words first and comparing their LO quad words only if the HO quad words are equal:

```
; This sequence transfers control to location "IsGreater" if
; QwordValue > QwordValue2. It transfers control to "IsLess" if
; QwordValue < QwordValue2. It falls through to the instruction
; following this sequence if QwordValue = QwordValue2.
; To test for inequality, change the "IsGreater" and "IsLess"
; operands to "NotEqual" in this code.
```

```
        mov rax, qword ptr QWordValue[8]   ; Get HO qword
        cmp rax, qword ptr QWordValue2[8]
        jg  IsGreater
        jl  IsLess;

        mov rax, qword ptr QWordValue[0]   ; If HO qwords equal,
        cmp rax, qword ptr QWordValue2[0]  ; then we must compare
        jg  IsGreater;                     ; the LO dwords
        jl  IsLess;

; Fall through to this point if the two values were equal.
```

To compare unsigned values, use the ja and jb instructions in place of jg and jl.

You can synthesize any comparison from the preceding sequence, as shown in the following examples that demonstrate signed comparisons; just substitute ja, jae, jb, and jbe for jg, jge, jl, and jle (respectively) if you want unsigned comparisons. Each of the following examples assumes these declarations:

```
        .data
OW1     oword  ?
OW2     oword  ?

OW1q    textequ <qword ptr OW1>
OW2q    textequ <qword ptr OW2>
```

The following code implements a 128-bit test to see if OW1 < OW2 (signed). Control transfers to the IsLess label if OW1 < OW2. Control falls through to the next statement if this is not true:

```
        mov rax, OW1q[8]     ; Get HO dword
        cmp rax, OW2q[8]
        jg  NotLess
        jl  IsLess

        mov rax, OW1q[0]     ; Fall through to here if the HO
        cmp rax, OW2q[0]     ; qwords are equal
        jl  IsLess
NotLess:
```

Here is a 128-bit test to see if OW1 <= OW2 (signed). This code jumps to IsLessEq if the condition is true:

```
        mov rax, OW1q[8]     ; Get HO dword
        cmp rax, OW2q[8]
        jg  NotLessEQ
        jl  IsLessEQ
```

```
        mov rax, QW1q[0]    ; Fall through to here if the HO
        cmp rax, QW2q[0]    ; qwords are equal
        jle IsLessEQ
NotLessEQ:
```

This is a 128-bit test to see if OW1 > OW2 (signed). It jumps to IsGtr if this condition is true:

```
        mov rax, QW1q[8]    ; Get HO dword
        cmp rax, QW2q[8]
        jg  IsGtr
        jl  NotGtr

        mov rax, QW1q[0]    ; Fall through to here if the HO
        cmp rax, QW2q[0]    ; qwords are equal
        jg  IsGtr
NotGtr:
```

The following is a 128-bit test to see if OW1 >= OW2 (signed). This code jumps to label IsGtrEQ if this is the case:

```
        mov rax, QW1q[8]    ; Get HO dword
        cmp rax, QW2q[8]
        jg  IsGtrEQ
        jl  NotGtrEQ

        mov rax, QW1q[0]    ; Fall through to here if the HO
        cmp rax, QW2q[0]    ; qwords are equal
        jge IsGtrEQ
NotGtrEQ:
```

Here is a 128-bit test to see if OW1 == OW2 (signed or unsigned). This code branches to the label IsEqual if OW1 == OW2. It falls through to the next instruction if they are not equal:

```
        mov rax, QW1q[8]    ; Get HO dword
        cmp rax, QW2q[8]
        jne NotEqual

        mov rax, QW1q[0]    ; Fall through to here if the HO
        cmp rax, QW2q[0]    ; qwords are equal
        je  IsEqual
NotEqual:
```

The following is a 128-bit test to see if OW1 != OW2 (signed or unsigned). This code branches to the label IsNotEqual if OW1 != OW2. It falls through to the next instruction if they are equal:

```
        mov rax, QW1q[8]    ; Get HO dword
        cmp rax, QW2q[8]
        jne IsNotEqual
```

```
        mov rax, QW1q[0]     ; Fall through to here if the HO
        cmp rax, QW2q[0]     ; qwords are equal
        jne IsNotEqual

; Fall through to this point if they are equal.
```

To generalize the preceding code for objects larger than 128 bits, start the comparison with the objects' HO quad words and work your way down to their LO quad words, as long as the corresponding double words are equal. The following example compares two 256-bit values to see if the first is less than or equal (unsigned) to the second:

```
        .data
Big1    qword  4 dup (?)
Big2    qword  4 dup (?)
          .
          .
          .
        mov rax, Big1[24]
        cmp rax, Big2[24]
        jb  isLE
        ja  notLE

        mov rax, Big1[16]
        cmp rax, Big2[16]
        jb  isLE
        ja  notLE

        mov rax, Big1[8]
        cmp rax, Big2[8]
        jb  isLE
        ja  notLE

        mov  rax, Big1[0]
        cmp  rax, Big2[0]
        jnbe notLE
isLE:
        Code to execute if Big1 <= Big2
          .
          .
          .
notLE:
        Code to execute if Big1 > Big2
```

8.1.4   Extended-Precision Multiplication

Although an 8×8-, 16×16-, 32×32-, or 64×64-bit multiplication is usually sufficient, sometimes you may want to multiply larger values. You use the x86-64 single-operand mul and imul instructions for extended-precision multiplication operations, using the same techniques that you employ when manually multiplying two values. Consider the way you perform multi-digit multiplication by hand (Figure 8-3).

Step 1: Multiply 5×3

```
   123
 × 45
   15  (5×3)
```

Step 2: Multiply 5×2

```
   123
 × 45
   15
  100  (5×20)
```

Step 3: Multiply 5×1

```
   123
 × 45
   15
  100
  500  (5×100)
```

Step 4: Multiply 4×3

```
   123
 × 45
   15
  100
  500
  120  (40×3)
```

Step 5: Multiply 4×2

```
   123
 × 45
   15
  100
  500
  120
  800  (40×20)
```

Step 6: Multiply 4×1

```
   123
 × 45
   15
  100
  500
  120
  800
 4000  (40×100)
```

Step 7: Add partial products together

```
     123
   × 45
     15
    100
    500
    120
    800
 + 4000
   5535
```

Figure 8-3: Multi-digit multiplication

The x86-64 does extended-precision multiplication in the same manner except that it works with bytes, words, double words, and quad words rather than digits, as shown in Figure 8-4.

Probably the most important thing to remember when performing an extended-precision multiplication is that you must also perform an extended-precision addition at the same time. Adding up all the partial products requires several additions.

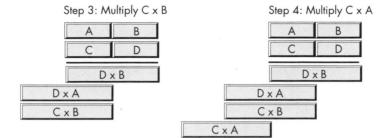

Step 1: Multiply the LO words

Step 2: Multiply D x A

Step 3: Multiply C x B

Step 4: Multiply C x A

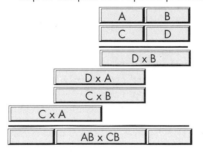

Step 5: Compute sum of partial products

Figure 8-4: Extended-precision multiplication

Listing 8-1 demonstrates how to multiply two 64-bit values (producing a 128-bit result) by using 32-bit instructions. Technically, you can do a 64-bit multiplication with a single instruction, but this example demonstrates a method you can easily extend to 128 bits by using the x86-64 64-bit registers rather than the 32-bit registers.

```
; Listing 8-1

; 128-bit multiplication.

        option  casemap:none

nl          =       10

            .const
ttlStr      byte    "Listing 8-1", 0
fmtStr1     byte    "%d * %d = %I64d (verify:%I64d)", nl, 0
```

```
                .data
op1             qword   123456789
op2             qword   234567890
product         oword   ?
product2        oword   ?

                .code
                externdef printf:proc

; Return program title to C++ program:

                public  getTitle
getTitle        proc
                lea     rax, ttlStr
                ret
getTitle        endp

; mul64 - Multiplies two 64-bit values passed in RDX and RAX by
;         doing a 64x64-bit multiplication, producing a 128-bit result.
;         Algorithm is easily extended to 128x128 bits by switching the
;         32-bit registers for 64-bit registers.

; Stores result to location pointed at by R8.

mul64           proc
mp              equ     <dword ptr [rbp - 8]>     ; Multiplier
mc              equ     <dword ptr [rbp - 16]>    ; Multiplicand
prd             equ     <dword ptr [r8]>          ; Result

                push    rbp
                mov     rbp, rsp
                sub     rsp, 24

                push    rbx     ; Preserve these register values
                push    rcx

; Save parameters passed in registers:

                mov     qword ptr mp, rax
                mov     qword ptr mc, rdx

; Multiply the LO dword of multiplier times multiplicand.

                mov eax, mp
                mul mc              ; Multiply LO dwords
                mov prd, eax        ; Save LO dword of product
                mov ecx, edx        ; Save HO dword of partial product result

                mov eax, mp
                mul mc[4]           ; Multiply mp(LO) * mc(HO)
                add eax, ecx        ; Add to the partial product
                adc edx, 0          ; Don't forget the carry!
```

```
                mov ebx, eax     ; Save partial product for now
                mov ecx, edx

; Multiply the HO word of multiplier with multiplicand.

                mov eax, mp[4]   ; Get HO dword of multiplier
                mul mc           ; Multiply by LO word of multiplicand
                add eax, ebx     ; Add to the partial product
                mov prd[4], eax  ; Save the partial product
                adc ecx, edx     ; Add in the carry!

                mov eax, mp[4]   ; Multiply the two HO dwords together
                mul mc[4]
                add eax, ecx     ; Add in partial product
                adc edx, 0       ; Don't forget the carry!

                mov prd[8], eax  ; Save HO qword of result
                mov prd[12], edx

; EDX:EAX contains 64-bit result at this point.

                pop     rcx      ; Restore these registers
                pop     rbx
                leave
                ret
mul64           endp

; Here is the "asmMain" function.

                public  asmMain
asmMain         proc
                push    rbp
                mov     rbp, rsp
                sub     rsp, 64          ; Shadow storage

; Test the mul64 function:

                mov     rax, op1
                mov     rdx, op2
                lea     r8, product
                call    mul64

; Use a 64-bit multiply to test the result:

                mov     rax, op1
                mov     rdx, op2
                imul    rax, rdx
                mov     qword ptr product2, rax

; Print the results:

                lea     rcx, fmtStr1
                mov     rdx, op1
```

```
        mov     r8,  op2
        mov     r9,  qword ptr product
        mov     rax, qword ptr product2
        mov     [rsp + 32], rax
        call    printf

        leave
        ret     ; Returns to caller

asmMain endp
        end
```

Listing 8-1: Extended-precision multiplication

The code works only for unsigned operands. To multiply two signed values, you must note the signs of the operands before the multiplication, take the absolute value of the two operands, do an unsigned multiplication, and then adjust the sign of the resulting product based on the signs of the original operands. Multiplication of signed operands is left as an exercise for you.

The example in Listing 8-1 was fairly straightforward because it was possible to keep the partial products in various registers. If you need to multiply larger values together, you will need to maintain the partial products in temporary (memory) variables. Other than that, the algorithm that Listing 8-1 uses generalizes to any number of double words.

8.1.5   Extended-Precision Division

You cannot synthesize a general n-bit / m-bit division operation by using the div and idiv instructions—though a less general operation, dividing an n-bit quantity by a 64-bit quantity can be done using the div instruction. A generic extended-precision division requires a sequence of shift and subtract instructions (which takes quite a few instructions and runs much slower). This section presents both methods (using div and shift and subtract) for extended-precision division.

8.1.5.1   Special Case Form Using div Instruction

Dividing a 128-bit quantity by a 64-bit quantity is handled directly by the div and idiv instructions, as long as the resulting quotient fits into 64 bits. However, if the quotient does not fit into 64 bits, then you have to perform extended-precision division.

For example, suppose you want to divide 0004_0000_0000_1234h by 2. The naive approach would look something like the following (assuming the value is held in a pair of qword variables named dividend, and divisor is a quad word containing 2):

```
; This code does *NOT* work!

mov rax, qword ptr dividend[0]    ; Get dividend into EDX:EAX
mov rdx, qword ptr dividend[8]
div divisor                       ; Divide RDX:RAX by divisor
```

Although this code is syntactically correct and will compile, it will raise a divide error exception when run. The quotient must fit into the RAX register when using div, and 2_0000_091Ah will not fit, being a 66-bit quantity (try dividing by 8 if you want to see it produce a result that will fit).

Instead, the trick is to divide the (zero- or sign-extended) HO double word of the dividend by the divisor and then repeat the process with the remainder and the LO dword of the dividend, as follows:

```
          .data
dividend  qword     1234h, 4
divisor   qword     2      ; dividend/divisor = 2_0000_091Ah
quotient  qword     2 dup (?)
remainder qword     ?
   .
   .
   .
mov rax, dividend[8]
xor edx, edx               ; Zero-extend for unsigned division
div divisor
mov quotient[8], rax       ; Save HO qword of the quotient
mov rax, dividend[0]       ; This code doesn't zero-extend
div divisor                ; RAX into RDX before div instr
mov quotient[0], rax       ; Save LO qword of the quotient (91Ah)
mov remainder, rdx         ; Save the remainder
```

The quotient variable is 128 bits because it's possible for the result to require as many bits as the dividend (for example, if you divide by 1). Regardless of the size of the dividend and divisor operands, the remainder is never larger than 64 bits (in this case). Hence, the remainder variable in this example is just a quad word.

To correctly compute the 128 / 64 quotient, begin by computing the 64 / 64 quotient of dividend[8] / divisor. The quotient from this first division becomes the HO double word of the final quotient. The remainder from this division becomes the extension in RDX for the second half of the division operation. The second half of the code divides rdx:dividend[0] by divisor to produce the LO quad word of the quotient and the remainder from the division. The code does not zero-extend RAX into RDX prior to the second div instruction, because RDX already contains valid bits that must not be disturbed.

The preceding 128 / 64 division operation is a special case of the general division algorithm to divide an arbitrary-size value by a 64-bit divisor. The general algorithm is as follows:

1. Move the HO quad word of the dividend into RAX and zero-extend it into RDX.

2. Divide by the divisor.

3. Store the value in RAX into the corresponding qword position of the quotient result variable (position of the dividend qword loaded into RAX prior to the division).

4. Load RAX with the next-lower quad word in the dividend, without modifying RDX.

5. Repeat steps 2 to 4 until you've processed all the quad words in the dividend.

At the end, the RDX register will contain the remainder, and the quotient will appear in the destination variable, where step 3 was storing the results. Listing 8-2 demonstrates how to divide a 256-bit quantity by a 64-bit divisor, producing a 256-bit quotient and a 64-bit remainder.

```
; Listing 8-2

; 256-bit by 64-bit division.

        option  casemap:none

nl          =       10

            .const
ttlStr      byte    "Listing 8-2", 0
fmtStr1     byte    "quotient  = "
            byte    "%08x_%08x_%08x_%08x_%08x_%08x_%08x_%08x"
            byte    nl, 0

fmtStr2     byte    "remainder = %I64x", nl, 0

            .data

; op1 is a 256-bit value. Initial values were chosen
; to make it easy to verify the result.

op1         oword   2222eeeeccccaaaa8888666644440000h
            oword   2222eeeeccccaaaa8888666644440000h

op2         qword   2
result      oword   2 dup (0) ; Also 256 bits
remain      qword   0

            .code
            externdef printf:proc

; Return program title to C++ program:

            public  getTitle
getTitle    proc
            lea     rax, ttlStr
            ret
getTitle    endp

; div256 - Divides a 256-bit number by a 64-bit number.
```

```
; Dividend  - passed by reference in RCX.
; Divisor   - passed in RDX.

; Quotient  - passed by reference in R8.
; Remainder - passed by reference in R9.

div256      proc
divisor     equ     <qword ptr [rbp - 8]>
dividend    equ     <qword ptr [rcx]>
quotient    equ     <qword ptr [r8]>
remainder   equ     <qword ptr [r9]>

            push    rbp
            mov     rbp, rsp
            sub     rsp, 8

            mov     divisor, rdx

            mov     rax, dividend[24]  ; Begin div with HO qword
            xor     rdx, rdx           ; Zero-extend into RDS
            div     divisor            ; Divide HO word
            mov     quotient[24], rax  ; Save HO result

            mov     rax, dividend[16]  ; Get dividend qword #2
            div     divisor            ; Continue with division
            mov     quotient[16], rax  ; Store away qword #2

            mov     rax, dividend[8]   ; Get dividend qword #1
            div     divisor            ; Continue with division
            mov     quotient[8], rax   ; Store away qword #1

            mov     rax, dividend[0]   ; Get LO dividend qword
            div     divisor            ; Continue with division
            mov     quotient[0], rax   ; Store away LO qword

            mov     remainder, rdx     ; Save remainder

            leave
            ret
div256      endp

; Here is the "asmMain" function.

            public  asmMain
asmMain     proc
            push    rbp
            mov     rbp, rsp
            sub     rsp, 80            ; Shadow storage

; Test the div256 function:

            lea     rcx, op1
            mov     rdx, op2
```

```
            lea     r8, result
            lea     r9, remain
            call    div256

; Print the results:

            lea     rcx, fmtStr1
            mov     edx, dword ptr result[28]
            mov     r8d, dword ptr result[24]
            mov     r9d, dword ptr result[20]
            mov     eax, dword ptr result[16]
            mov     [rsp + 32], rax
            mov     eax, dword ptr result[12]
            mov     [rsp + 40], rax
            mov     eax, dword ptr result[8]
            mov     [rsp + 48], rax
            mov     eax, dword ptr result[4]
            mov     [rsp + 56], rax
            mov     eax, dword ptr result[0]
            mov     [rsp + 64], rax
            call    printf

            lea     rcx, fmtStr2
            mov     rdx, remain
            call    printf

            leave
            ret     ; Returns to caller

asmMain     endp
            end
```

Listing 8-2: Unsigned 128 / 32-bit extended-precision division

Here's the build command and program output (note that you can verify that the division was correct by simply looking at the result, noting that each digit is one-half the original value):

```
C:\>build listing8-2

C:\>echo off
 Assembling: listing8-2.asm
c.cpp

C:\>listing8-2
Calling Listing 8-2:
quotient = 11117777_66665555_44443333_22220000_11117777_66665555_44443333_22
220000
remainder = 0
Listing 8-2 terminated
```

You can extend this code to any number of bits by adding additional mov-div-mov instructions to the sequence. Like the extended-precision multiplication in the previous section, this extended-precision division algorithm works only for unsigned operands. To divide two signed quantities, you must note their signs, take their absolute values, do the unsigned division, and then set the sign of the result based on the signs of the operands.

8.1.5.2 Generic N-bit by M-bit Division

To use a divisor larger than 64 bits, you have to implement the division by using a shift-and-subtract strategy, which works but is very slow. As with multiplication, the best way to understand how the computer performs division is to study how you were taught to do long division by hand. Consider the operation 3456 / 12 and the steps you would take to manually perform this operation, as shown in Figure 8-5.

```
      2                                        2
12 | 3456     Step 1: 12 goes into 34    12 | 3456    Step 2: Subtract 24 from 35
     24       two times                       24      to get 10 and drop down the 5
                                            -----
                                             105


     28                                       28
12 | 3456     Step 3: 12 goes into 105   12 | 3456    Step 4: Subtract 96 from 105
     24       eight times                     24      to get 9 and drop down the 6
    -----                                    -----
     105                                      105
      96                                        96
                                             -----
                                               96


     28                                      288
12 | 3456     Step 5: 12 goes into 96    12 | 3456    Step 6: Therefore, 12 goes
     24       exactly eight times             24      into 3456 exactly 288 times
    -----                                    -----
     105                                      105
      96                                        96
     -----                                    -----
        96                                       96
        96                                       96
                                                 ---
                                                  0
```

Figure 8-5: Manual digit-by-digit division operation

This algorithm is actually easier in binary because at each step you do not have to guess how many times 12 goes into the remainder, nor do you have to multiply 12 by your guess to obtain the amount to subtract. At each step in the binary algorithm, the divisor goes into the remainder exactly 0 or 1 time. As an example, consider the division of 27 (11011) by 3 (11) that is shown in Figure 8-6.

```
       1                                            1
    _____                                        _____
11 | 11011   Step 1: 11 goes into 11      11 | 11011   Step 2: Subtract the 11,
     11        one time                        11        producing 0, and bring
     ──                                         ──        down the 0
                                               00


      10                                          10
    _____                                      _____
11 | 11011   Step 3: 11 goes into 00      11 | 11011   Step 4: Subtract out the 0
     11        zero times                      11        and bring down the 1
     ──                                         ──
     00                                         00
     00                                         00
                                                ──
                                                 01


     100                                         100
    _____                                      _____
11 | 11011   Step 5: 11 goes into 01      11 | 11011   Step 6: Subtract out the zero
     11        zero times                      11        and bring down the 1
     ──                                         ──
     00                                         00
     00                                         00
     ──                                         ──
      01                                          01
      00                                          00
                                                  ──
                                                   11


    1001                                        1001
    _____                                      _____
11 | 11011   Step 7: 11 goes into 11      11 | 11011   Step 8: This produces the
     11        exactly one time                11        final result of 1001
     ──                                         ──
     00                                         00
     00                                         00
     ──                                         ──
      01                                          01
      00                                          00
      ──                                          ──
       11                                          11
                                                   11
                                                   ──
                                                   00
```

Figure 8-6: Longhand division in binary

The following algorithm implements this binary division operation in a way that computes the quotient and the remainder at the same time:

```
Quotient := Dividend;
Remainder := 0;
for i := 1 to NumberBits do

    Remainder:Quotient := Remainder:Quotient SHL 1;
    if Remainder >= Divisor then

        Remainder := Remainder - Divisor;
        Quotient := Quotient + 1;

    endif
endfor
```

NumberBits is the number of bits in the Remainder, Quotient, Divisor, and Dividend variables. SHL is the left-shift operator. The Quotient := Quotient + 1; statement sets the LO bit of Quotient to 1 because this algorithm previously shifts Quotient 1 bit to the left. Listing 8-3 implements this algorithm.

```
; Listing 8-3

; 128-bit by 128-bit division.

        option  casemap:none

nl          =       10

            .const
ttlStr      byte    "Listing 8-3", 0
fmtStr1     byte    "quotient  = "
            byte    "%08x_%08x_%08x_%08x"
            byte    nl, 0

fmtStr2     byte    "remainder = "
            byte    "%08x_%08x_%08x_%08x"
            byte    nl, 0

fmtStr3     byte    "quotient (2)  = "
            byte    "%08x_%08x_%08x_%08x"
            byte    nl, 0

            .data

; op1 is a 128-bit value. Initial values were chosen
; to make it easy to verify the result.

op1         oword   2222eeeeccccaaaa8888666644440000h
op2         oword   2
op3         oword   1111777766665555444433332222ode0000h
result      oword   ?
remain      oword   ?

            .code
            externdef printf:proc

; Return program title to C++ program:

            public  getTitle
getTitle    proc
            lea     rax, ttlStr
            ret
getTitle    endp

; div128 - This procedure does a general 128 / 128 division operation
;           using the following algorithm (all variables are assumed
;           to be 128-bit objects).
```

```
; Quotient := Dividend;
; Remainder := 0;
; for i := 1 to NumberBits do

;     Remainder:Quotient := Remainder:Quotient SHL 1;
;     if Remainder >= Divisor then

;         Remainder := Remainder - Divisor;
;         Quotient := Quotient + 1;

; endif
; endfor

; Data passed:

; 128-bit dividend, by reference in RCX.
; 128-bit divisor, by reference in RDX.

; Data returned:

; Pointer to 128-bit quotient in R8.
; Pointer to 128-bit remainder in R9.

div128      proc
remainder   equ      <[rbp - 16]>
dividend    equ      <[rbp - 32]>
quotient    equ      <[rbp - 32]>      ; Aliased to dividend
divisor     equ      <[rbp - 48]>

            push     rbp
            mov      rbp, rsp
            sub      rsp, 48

            push     rax
            push     rcx

            xor      rax, rax          ; Initialize remainder to 0
            mov      remainder, rax
            mov      remainder[8], rax

; Copy the dividend to local storage:

            mov      rax, [rcx]
            mov      dividend, rax
            mov      rax, [rcx+8]
            mov      dividend[8], rax

; Copy the divisor to local storage:

            mov      rax, [rdx]
            mov      divisor, rax
            mov      rax, [rdx + 8]
            mov      divisor[8], rax

            mov      cl, 128           ; Count off bits in CL
```

```
        ; Compute Remainder:Quotient := Remainder:Quotient SHL 1:

repeatLp:   shl     qword ptr dividend[0], 1  ; 256-bit extended-
            rcl     qword ptr dividend[8], 1  ; precision shift
            rcl     qword ptr remainder[0], 1 ; through remainder
            rcl     qword ptr remainder[8], 1

        ; Do a 128-bit comparison to see if the remainder
        ; is greater than or equal to the divisor.

            mov     rax, remainder[8]
            cmp     rax, divisor[8]
            ja      isGE
            jb      notGE

            mov     rax, remainder
            cmp     rax, divisor
            ja      isGE
            jb      notGE

        ; Remainder := Remainder - Divisor;

isGE:       mov     rax, divisor
            sub     remainder, rax
            mov     rax, divisor[8]
            sbb     remainder[8], rax

        ; Quotient := Quotient + 1;

            add     qword ptr quotient, 1
            adc     qword ptr quotient[8], 0

notGE:      dec     cl
            jnz     repeatLp

        ; Okay, copy the quotient (left in the dividend variable)
        ; and the remainder to their return locations.

            mov     rax, quotient[0]
            mov     [r8], rax
            mov     rax, quotient[8]
            mov     [r8][8], rax

            mov     rax, remainder[0]
            mov     [r9], rax
            mov     rax, remainder[8]
            mov     [r9][8], rax

            pop     rcx
            pop     rax
            leave
            ret

div128      endp
```

```
; Here is the "asmMain" function.

          public  asmMain
asmMain   proc
          push    rbp
          mov     rbp, rsp
          sub     rsp, 64        ; Shadow storage

; Test the div128 function:

          lea     rcx, op1
          lea     rdx, op2
          lea     r8, result
          lea     r9, remain
          call    div128

; Print the results:

          lea     rcx, fmtStr1
          mov     edx, dword ptr result[12]
          mov     r8d, dword ptr result[8]
          mov     r9d, dword ptr result[4]
          mov     eax, dword ptr result[0]
          mov     [rsp + 32], rax
          call    printf

          lea     rcx, fmtStr2
          mov     edx, dword ptr remain[12]
          mov     r8d, dword ptr remain[8]
          mov     r9d, dword ptr remain[4]
          mov     eax, dword ptr remain[0]
          mov     [rsp + 32], rax
          call    printf

; Test the div128 function:

          lea     rcx, op1
          lea     rdx, op3
          lea     r8, result
          lea     r9, remain
          call    div128

; Print the results:

          lea     rcx, fmtStr3
          mov     edx, dword ptr result[12]
          mov     r8d, dword ptr result[8]
          mov     r9d, dword ptr result[4]
          mov     eax, dword ptr result[0]
          mov     [rsp + 32], rax
          call    printf

          lea     rcx, fmtStr2
          mov     edx, dword ptr remain[12]
```

```
        mov     r8d, dword ptr remain[8]
        mov     r9d, dword ptr remain[4]
        mov     eax, dword ptr remain[0]
        mov     [rsp + 32], rax
        call    printf

        leave
        ret     ; Returns to caller

asmMain endp
        end
```

Listing 8-3: Extended-precision division

Here's the build command and program output:

```
C:\>build listing8-3

C:\>echo off
 Assembling: listing8-3.asm
c.cpp

C:\>listing8-3
Calling Listing 8-3:
quotient  = 11117777_66665555_44443333_22220000
remainder = 00000000_00000000_00000000_00000000
quotient (2)  = 00000000_00000000_00000000_00000002
remainder = 00000000_00000000_00000000_00000000
Listing 8-3 terminated
```

This code does not check for division by 0 (it will produce the value
0FFFF_FFFF_FFFF_FFFFh if you attempt to divide by 0); it handles only
unsigned values and is very slow (an order of magnitude or two worse than
the div and idiv instructions). To handle division by 0, check the divisor
against 0 prior to running this code and return an appropriate error code
if the divisor is 0. Dealing with signed values is the same as the earlier division algorithm: note the signs, take the operands' absolute values, do the
unsigned division, and then fix the sign afterward.

You can use the following technique to boost the performance of this
division by a fair amount. Check to see if the divisor variable uses only 32 bits.
Often, even though the divisor is a 128-bit variable, the value itself fits into
32 bits (that is, the HO double words of Divisor are 0) and you can use the
div instruction, which is much faster. The improved algorithm is a bit
more complex because you have to first compare the HO quad words for 0,
but on average, it runs much faster while remaining capable of dividing any
two pairs of values.

8.1.6   *Extended-Precision Negation Operations*

The neg instruction doesn't provide a generic extended-precision form.
However, a negation is equivalent to subtracting a value from 0, so we
can easily simulate an extended-precision negation by using the sub and sbb

instructions. The following code provides a simple way to negate a (320-bit) value by subtracting that value from 0, using an extended-precision subtraction:

```
      .data
Value  qword 5 dup (?) ; 320-bit value
        .
        .
        .
    xor rax, rax        ; RAX = 0
    sub rax, Value
    mov Value, rax

    mov eax, 0          ; Cannot use XOR here:
    sbb rax , Value[8]  ; must preserve carry!
    mov Value[8], rax

    mov eax, 0          ; Zero-extends!
    sbb rax, Value[16]
    mov Value[16], rax

    mov eax, 0
    sbb rax, Value[24]
    mov Value[24], rax

    mov rax, 0
    sbb rax, Value[32]
    mov Value[32], rax
```

A slightly more efficient way to negate smaller values (128 bits) uses a combination of neg and sbb instructions. This technique uses the fact that neg subtracts its operand from 0. In particular, it sets the flags the same way the sub instruction would if you subtracted the destination value from 0. This code takes the following form (assuming you want to negate the 128-bit value in RDX:RAX):

```
neg rdx
neg rax
sbb rdx, 0
```

The first two instructions negate the HO and LO qwords of the 128-bit result. However, if there is a borrow out of the LO negation (think of neg rax as subtracting 0 from RAX, possibly producing a carry/borrow), that borrow is not subtracted from the HO qword. The sbb instruction at the end of this sequence subtracts nothing from RDX if no borrow occurs when negating RAX; it subtracts 1 from RDX if a borrow was needed when subtracting 0 from RAX.

With a lot of work, it is possible to extend this scheme to more than 128 bits. However, around 256 bits (and certainly, once you get beyond 256 bits), it actually takes fewer instructions to use the general subtract-from-zero scheme.

8.1.7 Extended-Precision AND Operations

Performing an *n*-byte AND operation is easy: simply AND the corresponding bytes between the two operands, saving the result. For example, to perform the AND operation with all operands 128 bits long, you could use the following code:

```
mov rax,   qword ptr source1
and rax,   qword ptr source2
mov qword ptr dest, rax

mov rax,   qword ptr source1[8]
and rax,   qword ptr source2[8]
mov qword ptr dest[8], rax
```

To extend this technique to any number of qwords, logically AND the corresponding bytes, words, double words, or quad words together in the operands.

This sequence sets the flags according to the value of the last *and* operation. If you AND the HO quad words last, this sets all but the zero flag correctly. If you need to test the zero flag after this sequence, logically OR the two resulting double words together (or otherwise compare them both against 0).

NOTE   *You can also use the XMM and YMM registers to perform extended-precision logical operations (up to 256 bits at a time). See Chapter 11 for more details.*

8.1.8 Extended-Precision OR Operations

Multi-byte logical OR operations are performed in the same way as multi-byte AND operations. You OR the corresponding bytes in the two operands together. For example, to logically OR two 192-bit values, use the following code:

```
mov rax,   qword ptr source1
or  rax,   qword ptr source2
mov qword ptr dest, rax

mov rax,   qword ptr source1[8]
or  rax,   qword ptr source2[8]
mov qword ptr dest[8], rax

mov rax,   qword ptr source1[16]
or  rax,   qword ptr source2[16]
mov qword ptr dest[16], rax
```

As in the previous example, this does not set the zero flag properly for the entire operation. If you need to test the zero flag after an extended-precision OR, you must logically OR all the resulting double words together.

8.1.9 Extended-Precision XOR Operations

As with other logical operations, extended-precision XOR operations exclusive-ORs the corresponding bytes in the two operands to obtain the extended-precision result. The following code sequence operates on two 64-bit operands, computes their exclusive-or, and stores the result into a 64-bit variable:

```
mov rax,   qword ptr source1
xor rax,   qword ptr source2
mov qword ptr dest, rax

mov rax,   qword ptr source1[8]
xor rax,   qword ptr source2[8]
mov qword ptr dest[8], rax
```

The comment about the zero flag in the previous two sections, as well as the comment about the XMM and YMM registers, apply here.

8.1.10 Extended-Precision NOT Operations

The not instruction inverts all the bits in the specified operand. An extended-precision NOT is performed by executing the not instruction on all the affected operands. For example, to perform a 128-bit NOT operation on the value in RDX:RAX, execute the following instructions:

```
not rax
not rdx
```

Keep in mind that if you execute the NOT instruction twice, you wind up with the original value. Also, exclusive-ORing a value with all 1s (0FFh, 0FFFFh, 0FFFF_FFFFh, or 0FFFF_FFFF_FFFF_FFFFh) performs the same operation as the not instruction.

8.1.11 Extended-Precision Shift Operations

Extended-precision shift operations require a shift and a rotate instruction. This section describes how to construct these operations.

8.1.11.1 Extended-Precision Shift Left

A 128-bit shl (*shift left*) takes the form shown in Figure 8-7.

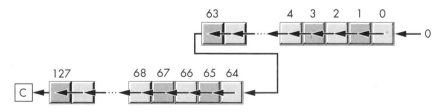

Figure 8-7: 128-bit shift-left operation

To accomplish this with machine instructions, we must first shift the LO qword to the left (for example, using the shl instruction) and capture the output from bit 63 (conveniently, the carry flag does this for us). We must then shift this bit into the LO bit of the HO qword while simultaneously shifting all the other bits to the left (and capturing the output by using the carry flag).

You can use the shl and rcl instructions to implement this 128-bit shift. For example, to shift the 128-bit quantity in RDX:RAX one position to the left, you'd use the following instructions:

```
shl rax, 1
rcl rdx, 1
```

The shl instruction shifts a 0 into bit 0 of the 128-bit operand and shifts bit 63 into the carry flag. The rcl instruction then shifts the carry flag into bit 64 and shifts bit 127 into the carry flag. The result is exactly what we want.

Using this technique, you can shift an extended-precision value only 1 bit at a time. You cannot shift an extended-precision operand several bits by using the CL register, nor can you specify a constant value greater than 1 when using this technique.

To perform a shift left on an operand larger than 128 bits, use additional rcl instructions. An extended-precision shift-left operation always starts with the least-significant quad word, and each succeeding rcl instruction operates on the next-most-significant double word. For example, to perform a 192-bit shift-left operation on a memory location, you could use the following instructions:

```
shl qword ptr Operand[0], 1
rcl qword ptr Operand[8], 1
rcl qword ptr Operand[16], 1
```

If you need to shift your data by 2 or more bits, you can either repeat the preceding sequence the desired number of times (for a constant number of shifts) or place the instructions in a loop to repeat them a certain number of times. For example, the following code shifts the 192-bit value Operand to the left by the number of bits specified in CL:

```
ShiftLoop:
    shl qword ptr Operand[0], 1
    rcl qword ptr Operand[8], 1
    rcl qword ptr Operand[16], 1
    dec cl
    jnz ShiftLoop
```

8.1.11.2 Extended-Precision Shift Right and Shift Arithmetic Right

You implement shr (*shift right*) and sar (*shift arithmetic right*) in a similar way, except you must start at the HO word of the operand and work your way down to the LO word:

```
; Extended-precision SAR:

    sar qword ptr Operand[16], 1
    rcr qword ptr Operand[8], 1
    rcr qword ptr Operand[0], 1

; Extended-precision SHR:

    shr qword ptr Operand[16], 1
    rcr qword ptr Operand[8], 1
    rcr qword ptr Operand[0], 1
```

The extended-precision shifts set the flags differently than their 8-, 16-, 32-, and 64-bit counterparts, because the rotate instructions affect the flags differently than the shift instructions. Fortunately, the carry flag is the one you'll test most often after a shift operation, and the extended-precision shift operations (that is, rotate instructions) properly set this flag.

8.1.11.3 Efficient Multi-bit Extended-Precision Shifts

The shld and shrd instructions let you efficiently implement extended-precision shifts of several bits. These instructions have the following syntax:

```
shld Operand₁, Operand₂, constant
shld Operand₁, Operand₂, cl
shrd Operand₁, Operand₂, constant
shrd Operand₁, Operand₂, cl
```

The shld instruction works as shown in Figure 8-8.

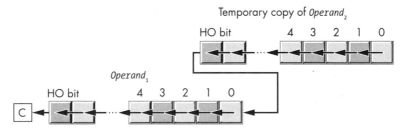

Figure 8-8: shld operation

$Operand_2$ must be a 16-, 32-, or 64-bit register. $Operand_1$ can be a register or a memory location. Both operands must be the same size. The third operand, *constant* or *cl*, specifies the number of bits to shift, and may be a value in the range 0 through $n - 1$, where n is the size of the first two operands.

The shld instruction shifts a copy of the bits in $Operand_2$ to the left by the number of bits specified by the third operand, storing the result into the location specified by the first operand. The HO bits shift into the carry flag, and the HO bits of *Operand₂* shift into the LO bits of *Operand₁*. The third operand specifies the number of bits to shift. If the count is n, then shld shifts bit $n-1$ into the carry flag (obviously, this instruction maintains only the last bit shifted into the carry). The shld instruction sets the flag bits as follows:

- If the shift count is 0, shld doesn't affect any flags.
- The carry flag contains the last bit shifted out of the HO bit of *Operand₁*.
- If the shift count is 1, the overflow flag will contain 1 if the sign bit of *Operand₁* changes during the shift. If the count is not 1, the overflow flag is undefined.
- The zero flag will be 1 if the shift produces a 0 result.
- The sign flag will contain the HO bit of the result.

The shrd instruction is similar to shld except, of course, it shifts its bits right rather than left. To get a clear picture of the shrd instruction, consider Figure 8-9.

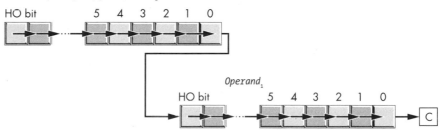

Figure 8-9: shrd operation

The shrd instruction sets the flag bits as follows:

- If the shift count is 0, shrd doesn't affect any flags.
- The carry flag contains the last bit shifted out of the LO bit of *Operand₁*.
- If the shift count is 1, the overflow flag will contain 1 if the HO bit of *Operand₁* changes. If the count is not 1, the overflow flag is undefined.
- The zero flag will be 1 if the shift produces a 0 result.
- The sign flag will contain the HO bit of the result.

Consider the following code sequence:

```
        .data
ShiftMe qword    012345678h, 90123456h, 78901234h
        .
        .
        .
    mov   rax, ShiftMe[8]
    shld  ShiftMe[16], rax, 6
```

```
mov   rax, ShiftMe[0]
shld ShiftMe[8], rax, 6
shl  ShiftMe[0], 6
```

The first shld instruction shifts the bits from ShiftMe[8] into ShiftMe[16] without affecting the value in ShiftMe[8]. The second shld instruction shifts the bits from ShiftMe into ShiftMe[8]. Finally, the shl instruction shifts the LO double word the appropriate amount.

There are two important things to note about this code. First, unlike the other extended-precision shift-left operations, this sequence works from the HO quad word down to the LO quad word. Second, the carry flag does not contain the carry from the HO shift operation. If you need to preserve the carry flag at that point, you will need to push the flags after the first shld instruction and pop the flags after the shl instruction.

You can do an extended-precision shift-right operation by using the shrd instruction. It works almost the same way as the preceding code sequence, except you work from the LO quad word to the HO quad word. The solution is left as an exercise for you.

8.1.12 Extended-Precision Rotate Operations

The rcl and rcr operations extend in a manner similar to shl and shr. For example, to perform 192-bit rcl and rcr operations, use the following instructions:

```
rcl qword ptr Operand[0], 1
rcl qword ptr Operand[8], 1
rcl qword ptr Operand[16], 1

rcr qword ptr Operand[16], 1
rcr qword ptr Operand[8], 1
rcr qword ptr Operand[0], 1
```

The only difference between this code and the code for the extended-precision shift operations is that the first instruction is a rcl or rcr rather than a shl or shr.

Performing an extended-precision rol or ror operation isn't quite as simple because of the way the incoming bit is processed. You can use the bt, shld, and shrd instructions to implement an extended-precision rol or ror instruction.[3] The following code shows how to use the shld and bt instructions to do a 128-bit extended-precision rol:

```
; Compute rol RDX:RAX, 4:

        mov   rbx, rdx
        shld rdx, rax, 4
        shld rax, rbx, 4
        bt    rbx, 28         ; Set carry flag, if desired
```

---

3. See Chapter 12 for a discussion of the bt (*bit test*) instruction.

An extended-precision ror instruction is similar; just keep in mind that you work on the LO end of the object first, and the HO end last.

8.2 Operating on Different-Size Operands

Occasionally, you may need to do a computation on a pair of operands that are not the same size. For example, you may need to add a word and a double word together or subtract a byte value from a word value. To do so, extend the smaller operand to the size of the larger operand and then operate on two same-size operands. For signed operands, you sign-extend the smaller operand to the same size as the larger operand; for unsigned values, you zero-extend the smaller operand. This works for any operation.

The following examples demonstrate adding a byte variable and a word variable:

```
        .data
var1    byte    ?
var2    word    ?
        .
        .
        .
; Unsigned addition:

        movzx   ax, var1
        add     ax, var2

; Signed addition:

        movsx   ax, var1
        add     ax, var2
```

In both cases, the byte variable was loaded into the AL register, extended to 16 bits, and then added to the word operand. This code works out really well if you can choose the order of the operations (for example, adding the 8-bit value to the 16-bit value).

Sometimes you cannot specify the order of the operations. Perhaps the 16-bit value is already in the AX register, and you want to add an 8-bit value to it. For unsigned addition, you could use the following code:

```
mov ax, var2     ; Load 16-bit value into AX
.                ; Do some other operations, leaving
.                ; a 16-bit quantity in AX
add al, var1     ; Add in the 8-bit value
adc ah, 0        ; Add carry into the HO word
```

The first add instruction adds the byte at var1 to the LO byte of the value in the accumulator. The adc instruction adds the carry from the addition of the LO bytes into the HO byte of the accumulator. If you leave out adc, you may not get the correct result.

Adding an 8-bit signed operand to a 16-bit signed value is a little more difficult. Unfortunately, you cannot add an immediate value (as in the preceding example) to the HO word of AX, because the HO extension byte can be either 0 or 0FFh. If a register is available, the best thing to do is the following:

```
mov   bx, ax      ; BX is the available register
movsx ax, var1
add   ax, bx
```

If an extra register is not available, you might try the following code:

```
push  ax          ; Save word value
movsx ax, var1    ; Sign-extend 8-bit operand to 16 bits
add   ax, [rsp]   ; Add in previous word value
add   rsp, 2      ; Pop junk from stack
```

This works because the x86-64 can push 16-bit registers. One word of advice: don't leave the RSP register misaligned (not on an 8-byte boundary) for very long. If you're working with 32- or 64-bit registers, you'll have to push the full 64-bit register and add 8 to RSP when you're done with the stack.

Another alternative is to store the 16-bit value in the accumulator into a memory location and then proceed as before:

```
mov   temp, ax
movsx ax, var1
add   ax, temp
```

All these examples add a byte value to a word value. By zero- or sign-extending the smaller operand to the size of the larger operand, you can easily add any two different-size variables together.

As a last example, consider adding an 8-bit signed value to an oword (128-bit) value:

```
      .data
OVal  qword    ?
BVal  byte     ?
      .
      .
      .
movsx rax, BVal
cqo
add   rax, qword ptr OVal
adc   rdx, qword ptr OVal[8]
```

8.3 Decimal Arithmetic

The x86-64 CPUs use the binary numbering system for their native internal representation. In the early days of computing, designers thought that decimal (base-10) arithmetic was more accurate for business calculations.

Mathematicians have shown that this is not the case; nevertheless, some algorithms depend on decimal calculations to produce correct results. Therefore, although decimal arithmetic is generally less efficient and less accurate than using binary arithmetic, the need for decimal arithmetic persists.

To represent decimal numbers in the native binary format, the most common technique is to use the *binary-coded decimal (BCD)* representation. This uses 4 bits to represent the 10 possible decimal digits (see Table 8-1). The binary value of those 4 bits is equal to the corresponding decimal value in the range 0 to 9. Of course, with 4 bits we can actually represent 16 different values; the BCD format ignores the remaining six bit combinations. Because each BCD digit requires 4 bits, we can represent a two-digit BCD value with a single byte. This means that we can represent the decimal values in the range 0 to 99 by using a single byte (as opposed to 0 to 255 with a byte in binary format).

Table 8-1: Binary-Coded Decimal Representation

BCD representation	Decimal equivalent
0000	0
0001	1
0010	2
0011	3
0100	4
0101	5
0110	6
0111	7
1000	8
1001	9
1010	Illegal
1011	Illegal
1100	Illegal
1101	Illegal
1110	Illegal
1111	Illegal

8.3.1 Literal BCD Constants

MASM does not provide, nor do you need, a literal BCD constant. Because BCD is just a form of hexadecimal notation that does not allow the values 0Ah to 0Fh, you can easily create BCD constants by using MASM's hexadecimal notation. For example, the following mov instruction copies the BCD value 99 into the AL register:

```
mov al, 99h
```

The important thing to keep in mind is that you must not use MASM literal decimal constants for BCD values. That is, mov al, 95 does not load the BCD representation for 95 into the AL register. Instead, it loads 5Fh into AL, and that's an illegal BCD value.

8.3.2 Packed Decimal Arithmetic Using the FPU

To improve the performance of applications that rely on decimal arithmetic, Intel incorporated support for decimal arithmetic directly into the FPU. The FPU supports values with up to 18 decimal digits of precision, with computations using all the arithmetic capabilities of the FPU, from addition to transcendental operations. Assuming you can live with only 18 digits of precision and a few other restrictions, decimal arithmetic on the FPU is the right way to go.

The FPU supports only one BCD data type: a 10-byte 18-digit packed decimal value. The packed decimal format uses the first 9 bytes to hold the BCD value in a standard packed decimal format. The first byte contains the two LO digits, and the ninth byte holds the two HO digits. The HO bit of the tenth byte holds the sign bit, and the FPU ignores the remaining bits in the tenth byte (as using those bits would create possible BCD values that the FPU could not exactly represent in the native floating-point format).

The FPU uses a one's complement notation for negative BCD values. The sign bit contains a 1 if the number is negative, and it contains a 0 if the number is positive. If the number is 0, the sign bit may be either 0 or 1, because, like the binary one's complement format, there are two distinct representations for 0.

MASM's tbyte type is the standard data type used to define packed BCD variables. The fbld and fbstp instructions require a tbyte operand (which you can initialize with a hexadecimal/BCD value).

Instead of fully supporting decimal arithmetic, the FPU provides two instructions, fbld and fbstp, that convert between packed decimal and binary floating-point formats when moving data to and from the FPU. The fbld (*float/BCD load*) instruction loads an 80-bit packed BCD value onto the top of the FPU stack after converting that BCD value to the binary floating-point format. Likewise, the fbstp (*float/BCD store and pop*) instruction pops the floating-point value off the top of stack, converts it to a packed BCD value, and stores the BCD value into the destination memory location. This means calculations are done using binary arithmetic. If you have an algorithm that absolutely, positively depends on the use of decimal arithmetic, it may fail if you use the FPU to implement it.[4]

The conversion between packed BCD and the floating-point format is not a cheap operation. The fbld and fbstp instructions can be quite slow

---

4. An example of such an algorithm might be a multiplication by 10 by shifting the number one digit to the left. However, such operations are not possible within the FPU itself, so algorithms that misbehave inside the FPU are rare.

(more than two orders of magnitude slower than `fld` and `fstp`, for example). Therefore, these instructions can be costly if you're doing simple additions or subtractions.

Because the FPU converts packed decimal values to the internal floating-point format, you can mix packed decimal, floating point, and (binary) integer formats in the same calculation. The following code fragment demonstrates how you might achieve this:

```
        .data
tb      tbyte    654321h
two     real8    2.0
one     dword    1

        fbld     tb
        fmul     two
        fiadd    one
        fbstp    tb

; TB now contains: 1308643h.
```

The FPU treats packed decimal values as integer values. Therefore, if your calculations produce fractional results, the `fbstp` instruction will round the result according to the current FPU rounding mode. If you need to work with fractional values, you need to stick with floating-point results.

8.4 For More Information

Donald Knuth's *The Art of Computer Programming*, Volume 2: *Seminumerical Algorithms* (Addison-Wesley Professional, 1997) contains a lot of useful information about decimal arithmetic and extended-precision arithmetic, though that text is generic and doesn't describe how to do this in x86-64 assembly language. Additional information on BCD arithmetic can also be found at the following websites:

- BCD Arithmetic, a Tutorial, *http://homepage.divms.uiowa.edu/~jones/bcd/bcd.html*
- General Decimal Arithmetic, *http://speleotrove.com/decimal/*
- Intel Decimal Floating-Point Math Library, *https://software.intel.com/en-us/articles/intel-decimal-floating-point-math-library/*

8.5 Test Yourself

1. Provide the code to compute $x = y + z$, assuming the following:

   a. x, y, and z are 128-bit integers

   b. x and y are 96-bit integers, and z is a 64-bit integer

   c. x, y, and z are 48-bit integers

2. Provide the code to compute $x = y - z$, assuming the following:
   a. x, y, and z are 192-bit integers
   b. x, y, and z are 96-bit integers

3. Provide the code to compute $x = y \times z$, assuming x, y, and z are 128-bit unsigned integers.

4. Provide the code to compute $x = y / z$, assuming x and y are 128-bit signed integers, and z is a 64-bit signed integer.

5. Assuming x and y are unsigned 128-bit integers, convert the following to assembly language:
   a. if($x == y$) *then code*
   b. if($x < y$) *then code*
   c. if($x > y$) *then code*
   d. if($x \neq y$) *then code*

6. Assuming x and y are signed 96-bit integers, convert the following to assembly language:
   a. if($x == y$) *then code*
   b. if($x < y$) *then code*
   c. if($x > y$) *then code*

7. Assuming x and y are signed 128-bit integers, provide two distinct ways to convert the following to assembly language:
   a. $x = -x$
   b. $x = -y$

8. Assuming x, y, and z are all 128-bit integer values, convert the following to assembly language:
   a. $x = y \& z$ (bitwise logical AND)
   b. $x = y \mid z$ (bitwise logical OR)
   c. $x = y \wedge z$ (bitwise logical XOR)
   d. $x = \sim y$ (bitwise logical NOT)
   e. $x = y \ll 1$ (bitwise shift left)
   f. $x = y \gg 1$ (bitwise shift right)

9. Assuming x and y are signed 128-bit values, convert $x = y \gg 1$ to assembly language (bitwise arithmetic shift right).

10. Provide the assembly code to rotate the 128-bit value in x through the carry flag (left by 1 bit).

11. Provide the assembly code to rotate the 128-bit value in x through the carry flag (right by 1 bit).

9

NUMERIC CONVERSION

 This chapter discusses the conversion between various numeric formats, including integer to decimal string, integer to hexadecimal string, floating-point to string, hexadecimal string to integer, decimal string to integer, and real string to floating-point. In addition to the basic conversions, this chapter discusses error handling (for string-to-numeric conversions) and performance enhancements. This chapter discusses standard-precision conversions (for 8-, 16-, 32-, and 64-bit integer formats) as well as extended-precision conversions (for example, 128-bit integer and string conversions).

9.1 Converting Numeric Values to Strings

Up to this point, this book has relied upon the C Standard Library to perform numeric I/O (writing numeric data to the display and reading numeric data from the user). However, the C Standard Library doesn't provide extended-precision numeric I/O facilities (and even 64-bit numeric I/O is questionable; this book has been using a Microsoft extension to printf() to do 64-bit numeric output). Therefore, it's time to break down and discuss how to do numeric I/O in assembly language—well, sort of. Because most operating systems support only character or string input and output, we aren't going to do actual numeric I/O. Instead, we're going write functions that convert between numeric values and strings, and then do string I/O.

The examples in this section work specifically with 64-bit (non-extended-precision) and 128-bit values, but the algorithms are general and extend to any number of bits.

9.1.1 Converting Numeric Values to Hexadecimal Strings

Converting a numeric value to a hexadecimal string is relatively straightforward. Just take each nibble (4 bits) in the binary representation and convert that to one of the 16 characters "0" through "9" or "A" through "F". Consider the btoh function in Listing 9-1 that takes a byte in the AL register and returns the two corresponding characters in AH (HO nibble) and AL (LO nibble).

NOTE   *For brevity, only the btoh function appears in Listing 9-1. The full Listing 9-1 is available online at* https://artofasm.randallhyde.com/.

```
; btoh - This procedure converts the binary value
;        in the AL register to two hexadecimal
;        characters and returns those characters
;        in the AH (HO nibble) and AL (LO nibble)
;        registers.

btoh        proc

            mov     ah, al      ; Do HO nibble first
            shr     ah, 4       ; Move HO nibble to LO
            or      ah, '0'     ; Convert to char
            cmp     ah, '9' + 1 ; Is it "A" through "F"?
            jb      AHisGood

; Convert 3Ah to 3Fh to "A" through "F":

            add     ah, 7

; Process the LO nibble here:

AHisGood:   and     al, 0Fh     ; Strip away HO nibble
            or      al, '0'     ; Convert to char
            cmp     al, '9' + 1 ; Is it "A" through "F"?
            jb      ALisGood

; Convert 3Ah to 3Fh to "A" through "F":

            add     al, 7
```

```
ALisGood:   ret
btoh        endp
```

Listing 9-1: A function that converts a byte to two hexadecimal characters

You can convert any numeric value in the range 0 to 9 to its corresponding ASCII character by ORing the numeric value with 0 (30h). Unfortunately,
this maps numeric values in the range 0Ah through 0Fh to 3Ah through 3Fh.
So, the code in Listing 9-1 checks to see if it produces a value greater than
3Ah and adds 7 to produce a final character code in the range 41h to 46h
("A" through "F").

Once we can convert a single byte to a pair of hexadecimal characters,
creating a string, output to the display is straightforward. We can call the
btoh (*byte to hex*) function for each byte in the number and store the corresponding characters away in a string. Listing 9-2 provides examples of btoStr
(*byte to string*), wtoStr (*word to string*), dtoStr (*double word to string*), and qtoStr
(*quad word to string*) functions.

```
; Listing 9-2

; Numeric-to-hex string functions.

        option  casemap:none

nl      =       10

        .const
ttlStr  byte    "Listing 9-2", 0
fmtStr1 byte    "btoStr: Value=%I64x, string=%s"
        byte    nl, 0

fmtStr2 byte    "wtoStr: Value=%I64x, string=%s"
        byte    nl, 0

fmtStr3 byte    "dtoStr: Value=%I64x, string=%s"
        byte    nl, 0

fmtStr4 byte    "qtoStr: Value=%I64x, string=%s"
        byte    nl, 0

        .data
buffer  byte    20 dup (?)

        .code
        externdef printf:proc

; Return program title to C++ program:

        public  getTitle
getTitle proc
        lea     rax, ttlStr
```

```
                    ret
getTitle        endp

; btoh - This procedure converts the binary value
;           in the AL register to two hexadecimal
;           characters and returns those characters
;           in the AH (HO nibble) and AL (LO nibble)
;           registers.

btoh            proc

                mov     ah, al      ; Do HO nibble first
                shr     ah, 4       ; Move HO nibble to LO
                or      ah, '0'     ; Convert to char
                cmp     ah, '9' + 1 ; Is it "A" to "F"?
                jb      AHisGood

; Convert 3Ah through 3Fh to "A" to "F":

                add     ah, 7

; Process the LO nibble here:

AHisGood:       and     al, 0Fh     ; Strip away HO nibble
                or      al, '0'     ; Convert to char
                cmp     al, '9' + 1 ; Is it "A" to "F"?
                jb      ALisGood

; Convert 3Ah through 3Fh to "A" to "F":

                add     al, 7
ALisGood:       ret

btoh            endp

; btoStr - Converts the byte in AL to a string of hexadecimal
;            characters and stores them at the buffer pointed at
;            by RDI. Buffer must have room for at least 3 bytes.
;            This function zero-terminates the string.

btoStr          proc
                push    rax
                call    btoh        ; Do conversion here

; Create a zero-terminated string at [RDI] from the
; two characters we converted to hex format:

                mov     [rdi], ah
                mov     [rdi + 1], al
                mov     byte ptr [rdi + 2], 0
                pop     rax
                ret
btoStr          endp
```

```
; wtoStr - Converts the word in AX to a string of hexadecimal
;          characters and stores them at the buffer pointed at
;          by RDI. Buffer must have room for at least 5 bytes.
;          This function zero-terminates the string.

wtoStr      proc
            push    rdi
            push    rax     ; Note: leaves LO byte at [RSP]

; Use btoStr to convert HO byte to a string:

            mov     al, ah
            call    btoStr

            mov     al, [rsp]       ; Get LO byte
            add     rdi, 2          ; Skip HO chars
            call    btoStr

            pop     rax
            pop     rdi
            ret
wtoStr      endp

; dtoStr - Converts the dword in EAX to a string of hexadecimal
;          characters and stores them at the buffer pointed at
;          by RDI. Buffer must have room for at least 9 bytes.
;          This function zero-terminates the string.

dtoStr      proc
            push    rdi
            push    rax     ; Note: leaves LO word at [RSP]

; Use wtoStr to convert HO word to a string:

            shr     eax, 16
            call    wtoStr

            mov     ax, [rsp]       ; Get LO word
            add     rdi, 4          ; Skip HO chars
            call    wtoStr

            pop     rax
            pop     rdi
            ret
dtoStr      endp

; qtoStr - Converts the qword in RAX to a string of hexadecimal
;          characters and stores them at the buffer pointed at
;          by RDI. Buffer must have room for at least 17 bytes.
;          This function zero-terminates the string.

qtoStr      proc
            push    rdi
            push    rax     ; Note: leaves LO dword at [RSP]
```

```
; Use dtoStr to convert HO dword to a string:

            shr     rax, 32
            call    dtoStr

            mov     eax, [rsp]      ; Get LO dword
            add     rdi, 8          ; Skip HO chars
            call    dtoStr

            pop     rax
            pop     rdi
            ret
qtoStr      endp

; Here is the "asmMain" function.

            public  asmMain
asmMain     proc
            push    rdi
            push    rbp
            mov     rbp, rsp
            sub     rsp, 64         ; Shadow storage

; Because all the (x)toStr functions preserve RDI,
; we need to do the following only once:

            lea     rdi, buffer

; Demonstrate call to btoStr:

            mov     al, 0aah
            call    btoStr

            lea     rcx, fmtStr1
            mov     edx, eax
            mov     r8, rdi
            call    printf

; Demonstrate call to wtoStr:

            mov     ax, 0a55ah
            call    wtoStr

            lea     rcx, fmtStr2
            mov     edx, eax
            mov     r8, rdi
            call    printf

; Demonstrate call to dtoStr:

            mov     eax, 0aa55FF00h
            call    dtoStr

            lea     rcx, fmtStr3
            mov     edx, eax
```

```
                mov     r8, rdi
                call    printf

; Demonstrate call to qtoStr:

                mov     rax, 1234567890abcdefh
                call    qtoStr

                lea     rcx, fmtStr4
                mov     rdx, rax
                mov     r8, rdi
                call    printf

                leave
                pop     rdi
                ret     ; Returns to caller

asmMain         endp
                end
```

Listing 9-2: btoStr, wtoStr, dtoStr, and qtoStr functions

Here's the build command and sample output:

```
C:\>build listing9-2

C:\>echo off
 Assembling: listing9-2.asm
c.cpp

C:\>listing9-2
Calling Listing 9-2:
btoStr: Value=aa, string=AA
wtoStr: Value=a55a, string=A55A
dtoStr: Value=aa55ff00, string=AA55FF00
qtoStr: Value=1234567890abcdef, string=1234567890ABCDEF
Listing 9-2 terminated
```

Each successive function in Listing 9-2 builds on the work done in the previous functions. For example, wtoStr calls btoStr twice to convert the 2 bytes in AX to a string of four hexadecimal characters. The code would be faster (but a lot larger) if you were to inline-expand each of these functions wherever the code calls them. If you needed only *one* of these functions, an inline expansion of any calls it makes would be worth the extra effort.

Here's a version of qtoStr with two improvements: inline expansion of the calls to dtoStr, wtoStr, and btoStr, plus the use of a simple table lookup (array access) to do the nibble-to-hex-character conversion (see Chapter 10 for more information on table lookups). The framework for this faster version of qtoStr appears in Listing 9-3.

NOTE *Because of the length and redundancy of Listing 9-3, a large part has been removed, but the missing code is obvious; the full Listing 9-3 is available online at* https://artofasm.randallhyde.com/.

```
; qtoStr - Converts the qword in RAX to a string of hexadecimal
;           characters and stores them at the buffer pointed at
;           by RDI. Buffer must have room for at least 17 bytes.
;           This function zero-terminates the string.

hexChar             byte    "0123456789ABCDEF"

qtoStr      proc
            push    rdi
            push    rcx
            push    rdx
            push    rax                 ; Leaves LO dword at [RSP]

            lea     rcx, hexChar

            xor     edx, edx            ; Zero-extends!
            shld    rdx, rax, 4
            shl     rax, 4
            mov     dl, [rcx][rdx * 1] ; Table lookup
            mov     [rdi], dl

; Emit bits 56-59:

            xor     edx, edx
            shld    rdx, rax, 4
            shl     rax, 4
            mov     dl, [rcx][rdx * 1]
            mov     [rdi + 1], dl

; Emit bits 52-55:

            xor     edx, edx
            shld    rdx, rax, 4
            shl     rax, 4
            mov     dl, [rcx][rdx * 1]
            mov     [rdi + 2], dl
                    .
                    .
                    .
```

Code to emit bits 8-51 was deleted for length reasons.
The code should be obvious if you look at the output
for the other nibbles appearing here.

```
                    .
                    .
                    .
; Emit bits 4-7:

            xor     edx, edx
            shld    rdx, rax, 4
            shl     rax, 4
            mov     dl, [rcx][rdx * 1]
            mov     [rdi + 14], dl
```

```
; Emit bits 0-3:

            xor     edx, edx
            shld    rdx, rax, 4
            shl     rax, 4
            mov     dl, [rcx][rdx * 1]
            mov     [rdi + 15], dl

; Zero-terminate string:

            mov     byte ptr [rdi + 16], 0

            pop     rax
            pop     rdx
            pop     rcx
            pop     rdi
            ret
qtoStr      endp
```

Listing 9-3: Faster implementation of qtoStr

Writing a short main program that contains the following loop

```
            lea     rdi, buffer
            mov     rax, 07fffffffh
loopit:     call    qtoStr
            dec     eax
            jnz     loopit
```

and then using a stopwatch on an old 2012-era 2.6 GHz Intel Core i7 processor, I got the approximate timings for the inline and original versions of qtoStr:

- Inline version: 19 seconds
- Original version: 85 seconds

As you can see, the inline version is significantly (four times) faster, but you probably won't convert 64-bit numbers to hexadecimal strings often enough to justify the kludgy code of the inline version.

For what it's worth, you could probably cut the time almost in half by using a much larger table (256 16-bit entries) for the hex characters and convert a whole byte at a time rather than a nibble. This would require half the instructions of the inline version (though the table would be 32 times bigger).

9.1.2 Converting Extended-Precision Hexadecimal Values to Strings

Extended-precision hexadecimal-to-string conversion is easy. It's simply an extension of the normal hexadecimal conversion routines from the previous section. For example, here's a 128-bit hexadecimal conversion function:

```
; otoStr - Converts the oword in RDX:RAX to a string of hexadecimal
;          characters and stores them at the buffer pointed at
;          by RDI. Buffer must have room for at least 33 bytes.
;          This function zero-terminates the string.
```

```
otoStr      proc
            push    rdi
            push    rax     ; Note: leaves LO dword at [RSP]

; Use qtoStr to convert each qword to a string:

            mov     rax, rdx
            call    qtoStr

            mov     rax, [rsp]      ; Get LO qword
            add     rdi, 16         ; Skip HO chars
            call    qtoStr

            pop     rax
            pop     rdi
            ret
otoStr      endp
```

9.1.3   Converting Unsigned Decimal Values to Strings

Decimal output is a little more complicated than hexadecimal output because the HO bits of a binary number affect the LO digits of the decimal representation (this was not true for hexadecimal values, which is why hexadecimal output is so easy). Therefore, we will have to create the decimal representation for a binary number by extracting one decimal digit at a time from the number.

The most common solution for unsigned decimal output is to successively divide the value by 10 until the result becomes 0. The remainder after the first division is a value in the range 0 to 9, and this value corresponds to the LO digit of the decimal number. Successive divisions by 10 (and their corresponding remainder) extract successive digits from the number.

Iterative solutions to this problem generally allocate storage for a string of characters large enough to hold the entire number. Then the code extracts the decimal digits in a loop and places them in the string one by one. At the end of the conversion process, the routine prints the characters in the string in reverse order (remember, the divide algorithm extracts the LO digits first and the HO digits last, the opposite of the way you need to print them).

This section employs a *recursive solution* because it is a little more elegant. This solution begins by dividing the value by 10 and saving the remainder in a local variable. If the quotient is not 0, the routine recursively calls itself to output any leading digits first. On return from the recursive call (which outputs all the leading digits), the recursive algorithm outputs the digit associated with the remainder to complete the operation. Here's how the operation works when printing the decimal value 789:

1. Divide 789 by 10. The quotient is 78, and the remainder is 9.
2. Save the remainder (9) in a local variable and recursively call the routine with the quotient.
3. *Recursive entry 1*: Divide 78 by 10. The quotient is 7, and the remainder is 8.

4. Save the remainder (8) in a local variable and recursively call the routine with the quotient.

5. *Recursive entry 2*: Divide 7 by 10. The quotient is 0, and the remainder is 7.

6. Save the remainder (7) in a local variable. Because the quotient is 0, don't call the routine recursively.

7. Output the remainder value saved in the local variable (7). Return to the caller (recursive entry 1).

8. *Return to recursive entry 1*: Output the remainder value saved in the local variable in recursive entry 1 (8). Return to the caller (original invocation of the procedure).

9. *Original invocation*: Output the remainder value saved in the local variable in the original call (9). Return to the original caller of the output routine.

Listing 9-4 implements the recursive algorithm.

```
; Listing 9-4

; Numeric unsigned integer-to-string function.

        option  casemap:none

nl              =       10

                .const
ttlStr          byte    "Listing 9-4", 0
fmtStr1         byte    "utoStr: Value=%I64u, string=%s"
                byte    nl, 0

                .data
buffer          byte    24 dup (?)

                .code
                externdef printf:proc

; Return program title to C++ program:

                public  getTitle
getTitle        proc
                lea     rax, ttlStr
                ret
getTitle        endp

; utoStr - Unsigned integer to string.

; Inputs:

;    RAX:   Unsigned integer to convert.
;    RDI:   Location to hold string.

; Note: for 64-bit integers, resulting
; string could be as long as 21 bytes
; (including the zero-terminating byte).
```

```
utoStr      proc
            push    rax
            push    rdx
            push    rdi

; Handle zero specially:

            test    rax, rax
            jnz     doConvert

            mov     byte ptr [rdi], '0'
            inc     rdi
            jmp     allDone

doConvert:  call    rcrsvUtoStr

; Zero-terminate the string and return:

allDone:    mov     byte ptr [rdi], 0
            pop     rdi
            pop     rdx
            pop     rax
            ret
utoStr      endp

ten         qword   10

; Here's the recursive code that does the
; actual conversion:

rcrsvUtoStr proc

            xor     rdx, rdx          ; Zero-extend RAX -> RDX
            div     ten
            push    rdx               ; Save output value
            test    eax, eax          ; Quit when RAX is 0
            jz      allDone

; Recursive call to handle value % 10:

            call    rcrsvUtoStr

allDone:    pop     rax               ; Retrieve char to print
            and     al, 0Fh           ; Convert to "0" to "9"
            or      al, '0'
            mov     byte ptr [rdi], al ; Save in buffer
            inc     rdi                ; Next char position
            ret
rcrsvUtoStr endp

; Here is the "asmMain" function.

            public  asmMain
asmMain     proc
            push    rdi
```

```
            push    rbp
            mov     rbp, rsp
            sub     rsp, 56         ; Shadow storage

; Because all the (x)toStr functions preserve RDI,
; we need to do the following only once:

            lea     rdi, buffer
            mov     rax, 1234567890
            call    utoStr

; Print the result:

            lea     rcx, fmtStr1
            mov     rdx, rax
            mov     r8, rdi
            call    printf

            leave
            pop     rdi
            ret             ; Returns to caller

asmMain     endp
            end
```

Listing 9-4: Unsigned integer-to-string function (recursive)

Here's the build command and program output:

```
C:\>build listing9-4

C:\>echo off
 Assembling: listing9-4.asm
c.cpp

C:\>listing9-4
Calling Listing 9-4:
utoStr: Value=1234567890, string=1234567890
Listing 9-4 terminated
```

Unlike hexadecimal output, there really is no need to provide a byte-size, word-size, or dword-size numeric-to-decimal-string conversion function. Simply zero-extending the smaller values to 64 bits is sufficient. Unlike the hexadecimal conversions, there are no leading zeros emitted by the qtoStr function, so the output is the same for all sizes of variables (64 bits and smaller).

Unlike the hexadecimal conversion (which is very fast to begin with, plus you don't really call it that often), you will frequently call the integer-to-string conversion function. Because it uses the div instruction, it can be fairly slow. Fortunately, we can speed it up by using the fist and fbstp instructions.

The fbstp instruction converts the 80-bit floating-point value currently sitting on the top of stack to an 18-digit packed BCD value (using the format appearing in Figure 6-7 in Chapter 6). The fist instruction allows you to load a 64-bit integer onto the FPU stack. So, by using these two instructions, you can (mostly) convert a 64-bit integer to a packed BCD value, which encodes a single decimal digit per 4 bits. Therefore, you can convert the packed BCD result that fbstp produces to a character string by using the same algorithm you use for converting hexadecimal numbers to a string.

There is only one catch with using fist and fbstp to convert an integer to a string: the Intel packed BCD format (see Figure 6-7 in Chapter 6) supports only 18 digits, whereas a 64-bit integer can have up to 19 digits. Therefore, any fbstp-based utoStr function will have to handle that 19th digit as a special case. With all this in mind, Listing 9-5 provides this new version of the utoStr function.

```
; Listing 9-5

; Fast unsigned integer-to-string function
; using fist and fbstp.

        option  casemap:none

nl              =       10

                .const
ttlStr          byte    "Listing 9-5", 0
fmtStr1         byte    "utoStr: Value=%I64u, string=%s"
                byte    nl, 0

                .data
buffer          byte    30 dup (?)

                .code
                externdef printf:proc

; Return program title to C++ program:

                public  getTitle
getTitle        proc
                lea     rax, ttlStr
                ret
getTitle        endp

; utoStr - Unsigned integer to string.

; Inputs:

;    RAX:   Unsigned integer to convert.
;    RDI:   Location to hold string.

; Note: for 64-bit integers, resulting
; string could be as long as 21 bytes
; (including the zero-terminating byte).
```

```
bigNum     qword   1000000000000000000
utoStr     proc
           push    rcx
           push    rdx
           push    rdi
           push    rax
           sub     rsp, 10
```

; Quick test for zero to handle that special case:

```
           test    rax, rax
           jnz     not0
           mov     byte ptr [rdi], '0'
           jmp     allDone
```

; The FBSTP instruction supports only 18 digits.
; 64-bit integers can have up to 19 digits.
; Handle that 19th possible digit here:

```
not0:      cmp     rax, bigNum
           jb      lt19Digits
```

; The number has 19 digits (which can be 0-9).
; Pull off the 19th digit:

```
           xor     edx, edx
           div     bigNum             ; 19th digit in AL
           mov     [rsp + 10], rdx    ; Remainder
           or      al, '0'
           mov     [rdi], al
           inc     rdi
```

; The number to convert is nonzero.
; Use BCD load and store to convert
; the integer to BCD:

```
lt19Digits: fild   qword ptr [rsp + 10]
           fbstp   tbyte ptr [rsp]
```

; Begin by skipping over leading zeros in
; the BCD value (max 19 digits, so the most
; significant digit will be in the LO nibble
; of DH).

```
           mov     dx, [rsp + 8]
           mov     rax, [rsp]
           mov     ecx, 20
           jmp     testFor0
```

```
SkipOs:    shld    rdx, rax, 4
           shl     rax, 4
testFor0:  dec     ecx               ; Count digits we've processed
           test    dh, 0fh           ; Because the number is not 0
           jz      SkipOs            ; this always terminates
```

```
; At this point the code has encountered
; the first nonzero digit. Convert the remaining
; digits to a string:

cnvrtStr:   and     dh, 0fh
            or      dh, '0'
            mov     [rdi], dh
            inc     rdi
            mov     dh, 0
            shld    rdx, rax, 4
            shl     rax, 4
            dec     ecx
            jnz     cnvrtStr

; Zero-terminate the string and return:

allDone:    mov     byte ptr [rdi], 0
            add     rsp, 10
            pop     rax
            pop     rdi
            pop     rdx
            pop     rcx
            ret
utoStr      endp

; Here is the "asmMain" function.

            public  asmMain
asmMain     proc
            push    rbp
            mov     rbp, rsp
            sub     rsp, 64         ; Shadow storage

; Because all the (x)toStr functions preserve RDI,
; we need to do the following only once:

            lea     rdi, buffer
            mov     rax, 9123456789012345678
            call    utoStr

            lea     rcx, fmtStr1
            mov     rdx, 9123456789012345678
            lea     r8, buffer
            call    printf

            leave
            ret             ; Returns to caller
asmMain     endp
            end
```

Listing 9-5: A *fist* and *fbstp*-based utoStr function

Here's the build command and sample output from this program:

```
C:\>build listing9-5

C:\>echo off
 Assembling: listing9-5.asm
c.cpp

C:\>listing9-5
Calling Listing 9-5:
utoStr: Value=9123456789012345678, string=9123456789012345678
Listing 9-5 terminated
```

The program in Listing 9-5 does use a div instruction, but it executes only once or twice, and only if there are 19 or 20 digits in the number. Therefore, the execution time of this div instruction will have little overall impact on the speed of the utoStr function (especially when you consider how often you actually print 19-digit numbers).

I got the following execution times on a 2.6 GHz circa-2012 Core i7 processor:

- Original utoStr: 108 seconds
- fist and fbstp implementation: 11 seconds

Clearly, the fist and fbstp implementation is the winner.

9.1.4   Converting Signed Integer Values to Strings

To convert a signed integer value to a string, you first check to see if the number is negative; if it is, you emit a hyphen (-) character and negate the value. Then you call the utoStr function to finish the job. Listing 9-6 shows the relevant code.

NOTE   *The full Listing 9-6 is available online at* https://artofasm.randallhyde.com/.

```
; itoStr - Signed integer-to-string conversion.

; Inputs:
;    RAX -   Signed integer to convert.
;    RDI -   Destination buffer address.

itoStr      proc
            push    rdi
            push    rax
            test    rax, rax
            jns     notNeg

; Number was negative, emit "-" and negate
; value.
```

```
            mov     byte ptr [rdi], '-'
            inc     rdi
            neg     rax

; Call utoStr to convert non-negative number:

notNeg:     call    utoStr
            pop     rax
            pop     rdi
            ret
itoStr      endp
```

Listing 9-6: Signed integer-to-string conversion

9.1.5   Converting Extended-Precision Unsigned Integers to Strings

For extended-precision output, the only operation through the entire
string-conversion algorithm that requires extended-precision arithmetic is
the divide-by-10 operation. Because we are dividing an extended-precision
value by a value that easily fits into a quad word, we can use the fast (and
easy) extended-precision division algorithm that uses the div instruction
(see "Special Case Form Using div Instruction" in "Extended-Precision
Division" in Chapter 8). Listing 9-7 implements a 128-bit decimal output
routine utilizing this technique.

```
; Listing 9-7

; Extended-precision numeric unsigned
; integer-to-string function.

        option  casemap:none

nl              =       10

                .const
ttlStr          byte    "Listing 9-7", 0
fmtStr1         byte    "otoStr(0): string=%s", nl, 0
fmtStr2         byte    "otoStr(1234567890): string=%s", nl, 0
fmtStr3         byte    "otoStr(2147483648): string=%s", nl, 0
fmtStr4         byte    "otoStr(4294967296): string=%s", nl, 0
fmtStr5         byte    "otoStr(FFF...FFFF): string=%s", nl, 0

                .data
buffer          byte    40 dup (?)

b0              oword   0
b1              oword   1234567890
b2              oword   2147483648
b3              oword   4294967296

; Largest oword value
; (decimal=340,282,366,920,938,463,463,374,607,431,768,211,455):

b4              oword   0FFFFFFFFFFFFFFFFFFFFFFFFFFFFFFFFh
```

```
            .code
            externdef printf:proc

; Return program title to C++ program:

            public  getTitle
getTitle    proc
            lea     rax, ttlStr
            ret
getTitle    endp

; DivideBy10 - Divides "divisor" by 10 using fast
;              extended-precision division algorithm
;              that employs the div instruction.

; Returns quotient in "quotient."
; Returns remainder in RAX.
; Trashes RDX.

; RCX - Points at oword dividend and location to
;       receive quotient.

ten         qword   10

DivideBy10  proc
parm        equ     <[rcx]>

            xor     edx, edx        ; Zero-extends!
            mov     rax, parm[8]
            div     ten
            mov     parm[8], rax

            mov     rax, parm
            div     ten
            mov     parm, rax
            mov     eax, edx        ; Remainder (always "0" to "9"!)
            ret
DivideBy10  endp

; Recursive version of otoStr.
; A separate "shell" procedure calls this so that
; this code does not have to preserve all the registers
; it uses (and DivideBy10 uses) on each recursive call.

; On entry:
;     Stack - Contains oword in/out parameter (dividend in/quotient out).
;     RDI   - Contains location to place output string.

; Note: this function must clean up stack (parameters)
;       on return.

rcrsvOtoStr proc
value       equ     <[rbp + 16]>
remainder   equ     <[rbp - 8]>
            push    rbp
```

```
                mov     rbp, rsp
                sub     rsp, 8
                lea     rcx, value
                call    DivideBy10
                mov     remainder, al

; If the quotient (left in value) is not 0, recursively
; call this routine to output the HO digits.

                mov     rax, value
                or      rax, value[8]
                jz      allDone

                mov     rax, value[8]
                push    rax
                mov     rax, value
                push    rax
                call    rcrsv0toStr

allDone:        mov     al, remainder
                or      al, '0'
                mov     [rdi], al
                inc     rdi
                leave
                ret     16        ; Remove parms from stack
rcrsv0toStr endp

; Nonrecursive shell to the above routine so we don't bother
; saving all the registers on each recursive call.

; On entry:

;    RDX:RAX - Contains oword to print.
;    RDI     - Buffer to hold string (at least 40 bytes).

otostr          proc

                push    rax
                push    rcx
                push    rdx
                push    rdi

; Special-case zero:

                test    rax, rax
                jnz     not0
                test    rdx, rdx
                jnz     not0
                mov     byte ptr [rdi], '0'
                inc     rdi
                jmp     allDone

not0:           push    rdx
```

```
            push    rax
            call    rcrsvOtoStr

; Zero-terminate string before leaving:

allDone:    mov     byte ptr [rdi], 0

            pop     rdi
            pop     rdx
            pop     rcx
            pop     rax
            ret

otostr      endp

; Here is the "asmMain" function.

            public  asmMain
asmMain     proc
            push    rdi
            push    rbp
            mov     rbp, rsp
            sub     rsp, 56         ; Shadow storage
```

; Because all the (*x*)toStr functions preserve RDI,
; we need to do the following only once:

```
            lea     rdi, buffer
```

; Convert b0 to a string and print the result:

```
            mov     rax, qword ptr b0
            mov     rdx, qword ptr b0[8]
            call    otostr

            lea     rcx, fmtStr1
            lea     rdx, buffer
            call    printf
```

; Convert b1 to a string and print the result:

```
            mov     rax, qword ptr b1
            mov     rdx, qword ptr b1[8]
            call    otostr

            lea     rcx, fmtStr2
            lea     rdx, buffer
            call    printf
```

; Convert b2 to a string and print the result:

```
            mov     rax, qword ptr b2
            mov     rdx, qword ptr b2[8]
```

```
                call    otostr

                lea     rcx, fmtStr3
                lea     rdx, buffer
                call    printf

; Convert b3 to a string and print the result:

                mov     rax, qword ptr b3
                mov     rdx, qword ptr b3[8]
                call    otostr

                lea     rcx, fmtStr4
                lea     rdx, buffer
                call    printf

; Convert b4 to a string and print the result:

                mov     rax, qword ptr b4
                mov     rdx, qword ptr b4[8]
                call    otostr

                lea     rcx, fmtStr5
                lea     rdx, buffer
                call    printf

                leave
                pop     rdi
                ret     ; Returns to caller

asmMain         endp
                end
```

Listing 9-7: 128-bit extended-precision decimal output routine

Here's the build command and program output:

```
C:\>build listing9-7

C:\>echo off
 Assembling: listing9-7.asm
c.cpp

C:\>listing9-7
Calling Listing 9-7:
otoStr(0): string=0
otoStr(1234567890): string=1234567890
otoStr(2147483648): string=2147483648
otoStr(4294967296): string=4294967296
otoStr(FFF...FFFF):
        string=340282366920938463463374607431768211455
Listing 9-7 terminated
```

Sadly, we cannot use the fbstp instruction to improve the performance of this algorithm as fbstp is limited to 80-bit BCD values.

9.1.6 Converting Extended-Precision Signed Decimal Values to Strings

Once you have an extended-precision unsigned decimal output routine, writing an extended-precision signed decimal output routine is easy. The basic algorithm is similar to that for 64-bit integers given earlier:

1. Check the sign of the number.
2. If it is positive, call the unsigned output routine to print it. If the number is negative, print a minus sign. Then negate the number and call the unsigned output routine to print it.

To check the sign of an extended-precision integer, test the HO bit of the number. To negate a large value, the best solution is probably to subtract that value from 0. Listing 9-8 is a quick version of i128toStr that uses the otoStr routine from the previous section.

NOTE   *The full Listing 9-8 is available online at* https://artofasm.randallhyde.com/.

```
; i128toStr - Converts a 128-bit signed integer to a string.

; Inputs:
;    RDX:RAX - Signed integer to convert.
;    RDI     - Pointer to buffer to receive string.

i128toStr   proc
            push    rax
            push    rdx
            push    rdi

            test    rdx, rdx  ; Is number negative?
            jns     notNeg

            mov     byte ptr [rdi], '-'
            inc     rdi
            neg     rdx          ; 128-bit negation
            neg     rax
            sbb     rdx, 0

notNeg:     call    otostr
            pop     rdi
            pop     rdx
            pop     rax
            ret
i128toStr   endp
```

Listing 9-8: 128-bit signed integer-to-string conversion

9.1.7 Formatted Conversions

The code in the previous sections converted signed and unsigned integers to strings by using the minimum number of necessary character positions. To create nicely formatted tables of values, you will need to write functions that provide appropriate padding in front of the string of digits before actually emitting the digits. Once you have the "unformatted" versions of these routines, implementing the formatted versions is easy.

The first step is to write iSize and uSize routines that compute the minimum number of character positions needed to display the value. One algorithm to accomplish this is similar to the numeric string conversion routines. In fact, the only difference is that you initialize a counter to 0 upon entry into the routine (for example, the nonrecursive shell routine), and you increment this counter rather than outputting a digit on each recursive call. (Don't forget to increment the counter inside iSize if the number is negative; you must allow for the output of the minus sign.) After the calculation is complete, these routines should return the size of the operand in the EAX register.

The only problem is that such a conversion scheme is slow (using recursion and div is not very fast). As it turns out, a brute-force version that simply compares the integer value against 1, 10, 100, 1000, and so on, works much faster. Here's the code that will do this:

```
; uSize - Determines how many character positions it will take
;         to hold a 64-bit numeric-to-string conversion.

; Input:
;   RAX -   Number to check.

; Returns:
;   RAX -   Number of character positions required.

dig2        qword   10
dig3        qword   100
dig4        qword   1000
dig5        qword   10000
dig6        qword   100000
dig7        qword   1000000
dig8        qword   10000000
dig9        qword   100000000
dig10       qword   1000000000
dig11       qword   10000000000
dig12       qword   100000000000
dig13       qword   1000000000000
dig14       qword   10000000000000
dig15       qword   100000000000000
dig16       qword   1000000000000000
dig17       qword   10000000000000000
dig18       qword   100000000000000000
dig19       qword   1000000000000000000
dig20       qword   10000000000000000000
```

```
uSize       proc
            push    rdx
            cmp     rax, dig10
            jae     ge10
            cmp     rax, dig5
            jae     ge5
            mov     edx, 4
            cmp     rax, dig4
            jae     allDone
            dec     edx
            cmp     rax, dig3
            jae     allDone
            dec     edx
            cmp     rax, dig2
            jae     allDone
            dec     edx
            jmp     allDone

ge5:        mov     edx, 9
            cmp     rax, dig9
            jae     allDone
            dec     edx
            cmp     rax, dig8
            jae     allDone
            dec     edx
            cmp     rax, dig7
            jae     allDone
            dec     edx
            cmp     rax, dig6
            jae     allDone
            dec     edx         ; Must be 5
            jmp     allDone

ge10:       cmp     rax, dig14
            jae     ge14
            mov     edx, 13
            cmp     rax, dig13
            jae     allDone
            dec     edx
            cmp     rax, dig12
            jae     allDone
            dec     edx
            cmp     rax, dig11
            jae     allDone
            dec     edx         ; Must be 10
            jmp     allDone

ge14:       mov     edx, 20
            cmp     rax, dig20
            jae     allDone
            dec     edx
            cmp     rax, dig19
            jae     allDone
            dec     edx
            cmp     rax, dig18
```

```
        jae     allDone
        dec     edx
        cmp     rax, dig17
        jae     allDone
        dec     edx
        cmp     rax, dig16
        jae     allDone
        dec     edx
        cmp     rax, dig15
        jae     allDone
        dec     edx         ; Must be 14

allDone:    mov     rax, rdx ; Return digit count
        pop     rdx
        ret
uSize   endp
```

For signed integers, you can use the following code:

```
; iSize - Determines the number of print positions required by
;         a 64-bit signed integer.

iSize       proc
        test    rax, rax
        js      isNeg

        jmp     uSize   ; Effectively a call and ret

; If the number is negative, negate it, call uSize,
; and then bump the size up by 1 (for the "-" character):

isNeg:      neg     rax
        call    uSize
        inc     rax
        ret
iSize   endp
```

For extended-precision size operations, the brute-force approach quickly becomes unwieldy (64 bits is bad enough). The best solution is to divide your extended-precision value by a power of 10 (say, 1e+18). This will reduce the size of the number by 18 digits. Repeat this process as long as the quotient is greater than 64 bits (keeping track of the number of times you've divided the number by 1e+18). When the quotient fits into 64 bits (19 or 20 digits), call the 64-bit uSize function and add in the number of digits you eliminated with the division operation (18 for each division by 1e+18). The implementation is left to you on this one . . .

Once you have the iSize and uSize routines, writing the formatted output routines, utoStrSize or itoStrSize, is easy. On initial entry, these routines call the corresponding iSize or uSize routine to determine the number of character positions for the number. If the value that the iSize or uSize routine returns is greater than the value of the minimum size parameter (passed into utoStrSize or itoStrSize), no other formatting is necessary. If the value of the parameter size is greater than the value iSize or uSize returns, the program must compute the difference between these two values and emit that many spaces (or other filler characters) to the output string before the numeric conversion. Listing 9-9 shows the utoStrSize and itoStrSize functions.

NOTE *The full Listing 9-9 is available online at* https://artofasm.randallhyde.com/. *The following listing omits everything except the actual utoStrSize and itoStrSize functions.*

```
; utoStrSize - Converts an unsigned integer to a formatted string
;               having at least "minDigits" character positions.
;               If the actual number of digits is smaller than
;               "minDigits" then this procedure inserts enough
;               "pad" characters to extend the size of the string.

; Inputs:
;     RAX -   Number to convert to string.
;     CL  -   minDigits (minimum print positions).
;     CH  -   Padding character.
;     RDI -   Buffer pointer for output string.

utoStrSize  proc
            push    rcx
            push    rdi
            push    rax

            call    uSize           ; Get actual number of digits
            sub     cl, al          ; >= the minimum size?
            jbe     justConvert

; If the minimum size is greater than the number of actual
; digits, we need to emit padding characters here.

; Note that this code used "sub" rather than "cmp" above.
; As a result, CL now contains the number of padding
; characters to emit to the string (CL is always positive
; at this point as negative and zero results would have
; branched to justConvert).

padLoop:    mov     [rdi], ch
            inc     rdi
            dec     cl
            jne     padLoop

; Okay, any necessary padding characters have already been
; added to the string. Call utoStr to convert the number
; to a string and append to the buffer:

justConvert:
            mov     rax, [rsp]      ; Retrieve original value
            call    utoStr

            pop     rax
            pop     rdi
```

```
                pop     rcx
                ret
utoStrSize  endp

; itoStrSize - Converts a signed integer to a formatted string
;               having at least "minDigits" character positions.
;               If the actual number of digits is smaller than
;               "minDigits" then this procedure inserts enough
;               "pad" characters to extend the size of the string.

; Inputs:
;   RAX -   Number to convert to string.
;   CL  -   minDigits (minimum print positions).
;   CH  -   Padding character.
;   RDI -   Buffer pointer for output string.

itoStrSize  proc
                push    rcx
                push    rdi
                push    rax

                call    iSize           ; Get actual number of digits
                sub     cl, al          ; >= the minimum size?
                jbe     justConvert

; If the minimum size is greater than the number of actual
; digits, we need to emit padding characters here.

; Note that this code used "sub" rather than "cmp" above.
; As a result, CL now contains the number of padding
; characters to emit to the string (CL is always positive
; at this point as negative and zero results would have
; branched to justConvert).

padLoop:        mov     [rdi], ch
                inc     rdi
                dec     cl
                jne     padLoop

; Okay, any necessary padding characters have already been
; added to the string. Call utoStr to convert the number
; to a string and append to the buffer:

justConvert:
                mov     rax, [rsp]      ; Retrieve original value
                call    itoStr

                pop     rax
                pop     rdi
                pop     rcx
                ret
itoStrSize  endp
```

Listing 9-9: Formatted integer-to-string conversion functions

9.1.8 Converting Floating-Point Values to Strings

The code appearing thus far in this chapter has dealt with converting integer numeric values to character strings (typically for output to the user). Converting floating-point values to a string is just as important. This section (and its subsections) covers that conversion.

Floating-point values can be converted to strings in one of two forms:

- Decimal notation conversion (for example, ± *xxx.yyy* format)
- Exponential (or scientific) notation conversion (for example, ± *x.yyyyye* ± *zz* format)

Regardless of the final output format, two distinct operations are needed to convert a value in floating-point form to a character string. First, you must convert the mantissa to an appropriate string of digits. Second, you must convert the exponent to a string of digits.

However, this isn't a simple case of converting two integer values to a decimal string and concatenating them (with an *e* between the mantissa and exponent). First of all, the mantissa is not an integer value: it is a fixed-point fractional binary value. Simply treating it as an *n*-bit binary value (where *n* is the number of mantissa bits) will almost always result in an incorrect conversion. Second, while the exponent is, more or less, an integer value,[1] it represents a power of 2, not a power of 10. Displaying that power of 2 as an integer value is not appropriate for decimal floating-point representation. Dealing with these two issues (fractional mantissa and binary exponent) is the major complication associated with converting a floating-point value to a string.

Though there are three floating-point formats on the x86-64— single-precision (32-bit real4), double-precision (64-bit real8), and extended-precision (80-bit real10)—the x87 FPU automatically converts the real4 and real8 formats to real10 upon loading the value into the FPU. Therefore, by using the x87 FPU for all floating-point arithmetic during the conversion, all we need to do is write code to convert real10 values into string form.

real10 floating-point values have a 64-bit mantissa. This is not a 64-bit integer. Instead, those 64 bits represent a value between 0 and slightly less than 2. (See "IEEE Floating-Point Formats" in Chapter 2 for more details on the IEEE 80-bit floating-point format.) Bit 63 is usually 1. If bit 63 is 0, the mantissa is denormalized, representing numbers between 0 and about 3.65×10^{-4951}.

To output the mantissa in decimal form with approximately 18 digits of precision, the trick is to successively multiply or divide the floating-point value by 10 until the number is between 1e+18 and just less than 1e+19 (that is, 9.9999 . . . e+18). Once the exponent is in the appropriate range, the mantissa bits form an 18-digit integer value (no fractional part), which can be converted to a decimal string to obtain the 18 digits that make up the mantissa value (using our friend, the fbstp instruction). In practice,

---

1. It's actually a biased-exponent value. However, that's easy to convert to a signed binary integer.

you would multiply or divide by large powers of 10 to get the value into the range 1e+18 to 1e+19. This is faster (fewer floating-point operations) and more accurate (also because of fewer floating-point operations).

NOTE *As discussed in "Converting Unsigned Decimal Values to Strings" on page 500, a 64-bit integer can produce slightly more than 18 significant digits (the maximum unsigned 64-bit value is 18,446,744,073,709,551,615, or 20 digits), but the fbstp instruction produces only an 18-digit result. Also, the sequence of floating-point operations that divide or multiply the value by 10 to get the number into the range 1e+18 to 1e+19 will introduce a small amount of error such that the LO digits produced by fbstp won't be completely accurate. Therefore, limiting the output to 18 significant digits is reasonable.[2]*

To convert the exponent to an appropriate decimal string, you need to track the number of multiplications or divisions by 10. For each division by 10, add 1 to the decimal exponent value; for each multiplication by 10, subtract 1 from the decimal exponent value. At the end of the process, subtract 18 from the decimal exponent value (as this process produces a value whose exponent is 18) and convert the decimal exponent value to a string.

9.1.8.1   Converting Floating-Point Exponents

To convert the exponent to a string of decimal digits, use the following algorithm:

1. If the number is 0.0, directly produce the mantissa output string of " 000000000000000000" (notice the space at the beginning of the string).
2. Initialize the decimal exponent to 0.
3. If the exponent is negative, emit a hyphen (-) character and negate the value; if it is positive, emit a space character.
4. If the value of the (possibly negated) exponent is less than 1.0, go to step 8.
5. *Positive exponents*: Compare the number against successively smaller powers of 10, starting with 10^{+4096}, then 10^{+2048}, then 10^{+1024}, then . . . , then 10^{0}. After each comparison, if the current value is greater than the power of 10, divide by that power of 10 and add the power of 10 exponent (4096, 2048, . . . , 0) to the decimal exponent value.
6. Repeat step 5 until the exponent is 0 (that is, the value is in the range $1.0 \le \text{value} < 10.0$).
7. Go to step 10.
8. *Negative exponents*: Compare the number against successful larger powers of 10 starting with 10^{-4096}, then 10^{-2048}, then 10^{-1024}, then . . . , then 10^{0}. After each comparison, if the current value is less than the power

---

2. Most programs deal with 64-bit double-precision floating-point values that have around 16 digits of precision, so the 18-digit limitation is more than sufficient when dealing with double-precision values.

of 10, divide by that power of 10 and subtract the power of 10 exponent (4096, 2048, . . . , 0) from the decimal exponent value.

9. Repeat step 8 until the exponent is 0 (that is, the value is in the range $1.0 \leq \text{value} < 10.0$).

10. Certain legitimate floating-point values are too large to represent with 18 digits (for example, 9,223,372,036,854,775,807 fits into 63 bits but requires more than 18 significant digits to represent). Specifically, values in the range 403A_DE0B_6B3A_763F_FF01h to 403A_DE0B_6B3A _763F_FFFFh are greater than 999,999,999,999,999,999 but still fit within a 64-bit mantissa. The fbstp instruction will not be able to convert these values to a packed BCD value.

    To resolve this issue, the code should explicitly test for values in this range and round them up to 1e+17 (and increment the decimal exponent value, should this happen). In some cases, values could be greater than 1e+19. In such instances, one last division by 10.0 will solve the problem.

11. At this point, the floating-point value is a reasonable number that the fbstp instruction can convert to a packed BCD value, so the conversion function uses fbstp to do this conversion.

12. Finally, convert the packed BCD value to a string of ASCII characters using an operation converting numeric values to hexadecimal (BCD) to strings (see "Converting Unsigned Decimal Values to Strings" on page 500 and Listing 9-5).

Listing 9-10 provides the (abbreviated) code and data to implement the mantissa-to-string conversion function, FPDigits. FPDigits converts the mantissa to a sequence of 18 digits and returns the decimal exponent value in the EAX register. It doesn't place a decimal point anywhere in the string, nor does it process the exponent at all.

NOTE   *The full Listing 9-10 is available online at* https://artofasm.randallhyde.com/.

```
            .data

            align   4

; TenTo17 - Holds the value 1.0e+17. Used to get a floating-
;           point number into the range x.xxxxxxxxxxxxe+17.

TenTo17     real10  1.0e+17

; PotTblN - Hold powers of 10 raised to negative powers of 2.

PotTblN     real10  1.0,
                    1.0e-1,
                    1.0e-2,
                    1.0e-4,
                    1.0e-8,
                    1.0e-16,
                    1.0e-32,
```

```
                        1.0e-64,
                        1.0e-128,
                        1.0e-256,
                        1.0e-512,
                        1.0e-1024,
                        1.0e-2048,
                        1.0e-4096


; PotTblP - Hold powers of 10 raised to positive powers of 2.

            align   4
PotTblP     real10  1.0,
                        1.0e+1,
                        1.0e+2,
                        1.0e+4,
                        1.0e+8,
                        1.0e+16,
                        1.0e+32,
                        1.0e+64,
                        1.0e+128,
                        1.0e+256,
                        1.0e+512,
                        1.0e+1024,
                        1.0e+2048,
                        1.0e+4096


; ExpTbl - Integer equivalents to the powers
;          in the tables above.

            align   4
ExpTab      dword   0,
                        1,
                        2,
                        4,
                        8,
                        16,
                        32,
                        64,
                        128,
                        256,
                        512,
                        1024,
                        2048,
                        4096

                        .
                        .
                        .


*************************************************************

; FPDigits - Used to convert a floating-point number on the FPU
;            stack (ST(0)) to a string of digits.
```

```
; Entry Conditions:

; ST(0) -    80-bit number to convert.
;            Note: code requires two free FPU stack elements.
; RDI  -     Points at array of at least 18 bytes where
;            FPDigits stores the output string.

; Exit Conditions:

; RDI  -     Converted digits are found here.
; RAX  -     Contains exponent of the number.
; CL   -     Contains the sign of the mantissa (" " or "-").
; ST(0) -    Popped from stack.


;*************************************************************

P10TblN     equ     <real10 ptr [r8]>
P10TblP     equ     <real10 ptr [r9]>
xTab        equ     <dword ptr [r10]>

FPDigits    proc
            push    rbx
            push    rdx
            push    rsi
            push    r8
            push    r9
            push    r10

; Special case if the number is zero.

            ftst
            fstsw   ax
            sahf
            jnz     fpdNotZero

; The number is zero, output it as a special case.

            fstp    tbyte ptr [rdi] ; Pop value off FPU stack
            mov     rax, "00000000"
            mov     [rdi], rax
            mov     [rdi + 8], rax
            mov     [rdi + 16], ax
            add     rdi, 18
            xor     edx, edx        ; Return an exponent of 0
            mov     bl, ' '         ; Sign is positive
            jmp     fpdDone

fpdNotZero:

; If the number is not zero, then fix the sign of the value.

            mov     bl, ' '         ; Assume it's positive
            jnc     WasPositive     ; Flags set from sahf above
```

```
                fabs                    ; Deal only with positive numbers
                mov     bl, '-'         ; Set the sign return result

WasPositive:

; Get the number between 1 and 10 so we can figure out
; what the exponent is.  Begin by checking to see if we have
; a positive or negative exponent.

                xor     edx, edx        ; Initialize exponent to 0
                fld1
                fcomip  st(0), st(1)
                jbe     PosExp

; We've got a value between zero and one, exclusive,
; at this point.  That means this number has a negative
; exponent.  Multiply the number by an appropriate power
; of 10 until we get it in the range 1 through 10.

                mov     esi, sizeof PotTblN  ; After last element
                mov     ecx, sizeof ExpTab   ; Ditto
                lea     r8, PotTblN
                lea     r9, PotTblP
                lea     r10, ExpTab

CmpNegExp:
                sub     esi, 10         ; Move to previous element
                sub     ecx, 4          ; Zeroes HO bytes
                jz      test1

                fld     P10TblN[rsi * 1] ; Get current power of 10
                fcomip  st(0), st(1)     ; Compare against NOS
                jbe     CmpNegExp        ; While Table >= value

                mov     eax, xTab[rcx * 1]
                test    eax, eax
                jz      didAllDigits

                sub     edx, eax
                fld     P10TblP[rsi * 1]
                fmulp
                jmp     CmpNegExp

; If the remainder is *exactly* 1.0, then we can branch
; on to InRange1_10; otherwise, we still have to multiply
; by 10.0 because we've overshot the mark a bit.

test1:
                fld1
                fcomip  st(0), st(1)
                je      InRange1_10

didAllDigits:
```

; If we get to this point, then we've indexed through
; all the elements in the PotTblN and it's time to stop.

```
                fld      P10TblP[10]   ; 10.0
                fmulp
                dec      edx
                jmp      InRange1_10
```

; At this point, we've got a number that is 1 or greater.
; Once again, our task is to get the value between 1 and 10.

PosExp:

```
                mov      esi, sizeof PotTblP ; After last element
                mov      ecx, sizeof ExpTab  ; Ditto
                lea      r9, PotTblP
                lea      r10, ExpTab
```

CmpPosExp:

```
                sub      esi, 10               ; Move back 1 element in
                sub      ecx, 4                ; PotTblP and ExpTbl
                fld      P10TblP[rsi * 1]
                fcomip   st(0), st(1)
                ja       CmpPosExp;
                mov      eax, xTab[rcx * 1]
                test     eax, eax
                jz       InRange1_10

                add      edx, eax
                fld      P10TblP[rsi * 1]
                fdivp
                jmp      CmpPosExp
```

InRange1_10:

; Okay, at this point the number is in the range 1 <= x < 10.
; Let's multiply it by 1e+18 to put the most significant digit
; into the 18th print position. Then convert the result to
; a BCD value and store away in memory.

```
                sub      rsp, 24       ; Make room for BCD result
                fld      TenTo17
                fmulp
```

; We need to check the floating-point result to make sure it
; is not outside the range we can legally convert to a BCD
; value.

; Illegal values will be in the range:

; >999,999,999,999,999,999 ... <1,000,000,000,000,000,000
; $403a_de0b_6b3a_763f_ff01 ... $403a_de0b_6b3a_763f_ffff

```
                    ; Should one of these values appear, round the result up to
                    ; $403a_de0b_6b3a_7640_0000:

                            fstp    real10 ptr [rsp]
                            cmp     word ptr [rsp + 8], 403ah
                            jne     noRounding

                            cmp     dword ptr [rsp + 4], 0de0b6b3ah
                            jne     noRounding

                            mov     eax, [rsp]
                            cmp     eax, 763fff01h
                            jb      noRounding;
                            cmp     eax, 76400000h
                            jae     TooBig

                            fld     TenTo17
                            inc     edx             ; Inc exp as this is really 10^18
                            jmp     didRound

                    ; If we get down here, there were problems getting the
                    ; value in the range 1 <= x <= 10 above and we've got a value
                    ; that is 10e+18 or slightly larger. We need to compensate for
                    ; that here.

            TooBig:
                            lea     r9, PotTblP
                            fld     real10 ptr [rsp]
                            fld     P10TblP[10]    ; /10
                            fdivp
                            inc     edx             ; Adjust exp due to fdiv
                            jmp     didRound

            noRounding:
                            fld     real10 ptr [rsp]
            didRound:
                            fbstp   tbyte ptr [rsp]

                    ; The data on the stack contains 18 BCD digits. Convert these
                    ; to ASCII characters and store them at the destination location
                    ; pointed at by EDI.

                            mov     ecx, 8
            repeatLp:
                            mov     al, byte ptr [rsp + rcx]
                            shr     al, 4           ; Always in the
                            or      al, '0'         ; range "0" to "9"
                            mov     [rdi], al
                            inc     rdi

                            mov     al, byte ptr [rsp + rcx]
                            and     al, 0fh
```

```
                or      al, '0'
                mov     [rdi], al
                inc     rdi

                dec     ecx
                jns     repeatLp

                add     rsp, 24         ; Remove BCD data from stack

fpdDone:

                mov     eax, edx        ; Return exponent in EAX
                mov     cl, bl          ; Return sign in CL
                pop     r10
                pop     r9
                pop     r8
                pop     rsi
                pop     rdx
                pop     rbx
                ret


FPDigits        endp
```

Listing 9-10: Floating-point mantissa-to-string conversion

9.1.8.2   Converting a Floating-Point Value to a Decimal String

The FPDigits function does most of the work needed to convert a floating-point value to a string in decimal notation: it converts the mantissa to a string of digits and provides the exponent in a decimal integer form. Although the decimal format does not explicitly display the exponent value, a procedure that converts the floating-point value to a decimal string will need the (decimal) exponent value to determine where to put the decimal point. Along with a few additional arguments that the caller supplies, it's relatively easy to take the output from FPDigits and convert it to an appropriately formatted decimal string of digits.

The final function to write is r10ToStr, the main function to call when converting a real10 value to a string. This is a formatted output function that translates the binary floating-point value by using standard formatting options to control the output width, the number of positions after the decimal point, and any fill characters to write where digits don't appear (usually, this is a space). The r10ToStr function call will need the following arguments:

r10

> The real10 value to convert to a string (if r10 is a real4 or real8 value, the FPU will automatically convert it to a real10 value when loading it into the FPU).

fWidth

The field width. This is the total number of character positions that the string will consume. This count includes room for a sign (which could be a space or a hyphen) but does not include space for a zero-terminating byte for the string. The field width must be greater than 0 and less than or equal to 1024.

decDigits

The number of digits to the right of the decimal point. This value must be at least 3 less than fWidth because there must be room for a sign character, at least one digit to the left of the decimal point, and the decimal point. If this value is 0, the conversion routine will not emit a decimal point to the string. This is an unsigned value; if the caller supplies a negative number here, the procedure will treat it as a very large positive value (and will return an error).

fill

The fill character. If the numeric string that r10ToStr produces uses fewer characters than fWidth, the procedure will right-justify the numeric value in the output string and fill the leftmost characters with this fill character (which is usually a space character).

buffer

A buffer to receive the numeric string.

maxLength

The size of the buffer (including the zero-terminating byte). If the conversion routine attempts to create a string larger than this value (meaning fWidth is greater than or equal to this value), then it returns an error.

The string output operation has only three real tasks: properly position the decimal point (if present), copy only those digits specified by the fWidth value, and round the truncated digits into the output digits.

The rounding operation is the most interesting part of the procedure. The r10ToStr function converts the real10 value to ASCII characters before rounding because it's easier to round the result after the conversion. So the rounding operation consists of adding 5 to the (ASCII) digit just beyond the least significant displayed digit. If this sum exceeds (the character) 9, the rounding algorithm has to add 1 to the least significant displayed digit. If that sum exceeds 9, the algorithm must subtract (the value) 10 from the character and add 1 to the next least significant digit. This process repeats until reaching the most significant digit or until there is no carry out of a given digit (that is, the sum does not exceed 9). In the (rare) case that rounding bubbles through all the digits (for example, the string is "999999 . . . 9"), then the rounding algorithm has to replace the string with "10000 . . . 0" and increment the decimal exponent by 1.

The algorithm for emitting the string differs for values with negative and non-negative exponents. Negative exponents are probably the easiest to process. Here's the algorithm for emitting values with a negative exponent:

1. The function begins by adding 3 to decDigits.

2. If decDigits is less than 4, the function sets it to 4 as a default value.[3]

3. If decDigits is greater than fWidth, the function emits fWidth "#" characters to the string and returns.

4. If decDigits is less than fWidth, then output (fWidth - decDigits) padding characters (fill) to the output string.

5. If r10 was negative, emit -0. to the string; otherwise, emit 0. to the string (with a leading space in front of the 0 if non-negative).

6. Next, output the digits from the converted number. If the field width is less than 21 (18 digits plus the 3 leading 0. or -0. characters), then the function outputs the specified (fWidth) characters from the converted digit string. If the width is greater than 21, the function emits all 18 digits from the converted digits and follows it by however many 0 characters are necessary to fill out the field width.

7. Finally, the function zero-terminates the string and returns.

If the exponent is positive or 0, the conversion is slightly more complicated. First, the code has to determine the number of character positions required by the result. This is computed as follows:

---

exponent + 2 + decDigits + (0 if decDigits is 0, 1 otherwise)

The *exponent* value is the number of digits to the left of the decimal point (minus 1). The 2 component is present because there is always a position for the sign character (space or hyphen) and there is always at least one digit to the left of the decimal point. The decDigits component adds in the number of digits to appear after the decimal point. Finally, this equation adds in 1 for the dot character if a decimal point is present (that is, if decDigits is greater than 0).

Once the required width is computed, the function compares this value against the fWidth value the caller supplies. If the computed value is greater than fWidth, the function emits fWidth "#" characters and returns. Otherwise, it can emit the digits to the output string.

As happens with negative exponents, the code begins by determining whether the number will consume all the character positions in the output string. If not, it computes the difference between fWidth and the actual number of characters and outputs the fill character to pad the numeric string. Next, it outputs a space or a hyphen character (depending on the sign of the original value). Then the function outputs the digits to the left of the decimal point (by counting down the exponent value). If the decDigits value is nonzero, the function emits the dot character and any digits remaining in the digit

---

3. This is because fractional values (those with negative exponents) always have a leading - or space character, a 0, a decimal point (.), and at least one digit, for a total of four digits.

string that FPDigits produced. If the function ever exceeds the 18 digits that FPDigits produces (either before or after the decimal point), then the function fills the remaining positions with the 0 character. Finally, the function emits the zero-terminating byte for the string and returns to the caller.

Listing 9-11 provides the source code for the r10ToStr function.

NOTE   *The full Listing 9-11 is available online at* https://artofasm.randallhyde.com/. *For brevity, the following listing only provides the actual r10ToStr function.*

```
*********************************************************

; r10ToStr - Converts a real10 floating-point number to the
;            corresponding string of digits.  Note that this
;            function always emits the string using decimal
;            notation.  For scientific notation, use the e10ToBuf
;            routine.

; On Entry:

;    r10        -    real10 value to convert.
;                    Passed in ST(0).

;    fWidth     -    Field width for the number (note that this
;                    is an *exact* field width, not a minimum
;                    field width).
;                    Passed in EAX (RAX).

;    decimalpts -    # of digits to display after the decimal pt.
;                    Passed in EDX (RDX).

;    fill       -    Padding character if the number is smaller
;                    than the specified field width.
;                    Passed in CL (RCX).

;    buffer     -    Stores the resulting characters in
;                    this string.
;                    Address passed in RDI.

;    maxLength  -    Maximum string length.
;                    Passed in R8d (R8).

; On Exit:

; Buffer contains the newly formatted string.  If the
; formatted value does not fit in the width specified,
; r10ToStr will store "#" characters into this string.

; Carry -    Clear if success; set if an exception occurs.
;            If width is larger than the maximum length of
;            the string specified by buffer, this routine
;            will return with the carry set and RAX = -1,
;            -2, or -3.

*********************************************************
```

```
r10ToStr    proc

; Local variables:

fWidth      equ     <dword ptr [rbp - 8]>      ; RAX: uns32
decDigits   equ     <dword ptr [rbp - 16]>     ; RDX: uns32
fill        equ     <[rbp - 24]>               ; CL: char
bufPtr      equ     <[rbp - 32]>               ; RDI: pointer
exponent    equ     <dword ptr [rbp - 40]>     ; uns32
sign        equ     <byte ptr [rbp - 48]>      ; char
digits      equ     <byte ptr [rbp - 128]>     ; char[80]
maxWidth    =       64                  ; Must be smaller than 80 - 2

            push    rdi
            push    rbx
            push    rcx
            push    rdx
            push    rsi
            push    rax
            push    rbp
            mov     rbp, rsp
            sub     rsp, 128            ; 128 bytes of local vars

; First, make sure the number will fit into the
; specified string.

            cmp     eax, r8d            ; R8d = max length
            jae     strOverflow

; If the width is zero, raise an exception:

            test    eax, eax
            jz      voor                ; Value out of range

            mov     bufPtr, rdi
            mov     qword ptr decDigits, rdx
            mov     fill, rcx
            mov     qword ptr fWidth, rax

; If the width is too big, raise an exception:

            cmp     eax, maxWidth
            ja      badWidth

; Okay, do the conversion.
; Begin by processing the mantissa digits:

            lea     rdi, digits         ; Store result here
            call    FPDigits            ; Convert r80 to string
            mov     exponent, eax       ; Save exp result
            mov     sign, cl            ; Save mantissa sign char
```

```
                ; Round the string of digits to the number of significant
                ; digits we want to display for this number:

                        cmp     eax, 17
                        jl      dontForceWidthZero

                        xor     rax, rax        ; If the exp is negative or
                                                ; too large, set width to 0
dontForceWidthZero:
                        mov     rbx, rax        ; Really just 8 bits
                        add     ebx, decDigits  ; Compute rounding position
                        cmp     ebx, 17
                        jge     dontRound       ; Don't bother if a big #

                ; To round the value to the number of significant digits,
                ; go to the digit just beyond the last one we are considering
                ; (EAX currently contains the number of decimal positions)
                ; and add 5 to that digit.  Propagate any overflow into the
                ; remaining digit positions.

                        inc     ebx                     ; Index + 1 of last sig digit
                        mov     al, digits[rbx * 1]     ; Get that digit
                        add     al, 5                   ; Round (for example, +0.5)
                        cmp     al, '9'
                        jbe     dontRound

                        mov     digits[rbx * 1], '0' + 10 ; Force to zero

whileDigitGT9:                                          ; (See sub 10 below)
                        sub     digits[rbx * 1], 10     ; Sub out overflow,
                        dec     ebx                     ; carry, into prev
                        js      hitFirstDigit;          ; digit (until 1st
                                                        ; digit in the #)
                        inc     digits[rbx * 1]
                        cmp     digits[rbx], '9'        ; Overflow if > "9"
                        ja      whileDigitGT9
                        jmp     dontRound

hitFirstDigit:

                ; If we get to this point, then we've hit the first
                ; digit in the number.  So we've got to shift all
                ; the characters down one position in the string of
                ; bytes and put a "1" in the first character position.

                        mov     ebx, 17

repeatUntilEBXeq0:

                        mov     al, digits[rbx * 1]
                        mov     digits[rbx * 1 + 1], al
                        dec     ebx
                        jnz     repeatUntilEBXeq0

                        mov     digits, '1'
```

```
                inc     exponent    ; Because we added a digit

dontRound:

; Handle positive and negative exponents separately.

                mov     rdi, bufPtr ; Store the output here
                cmp     exponent, 0
                jge     positiveExponent

; Negative exponents:
; Handle values between 0 and 1.0 here (negative exponents
; imply negative powers of 10).

; Compute the number's width.  Since this value is between
; 0 and 1, the width calculation is easy: it's just the
; number of decimal positions they've specified plus three
; (since we need to allow room for a leading "-0.").

                mov     ecx, decDigits
                add     ecx, 3
                cmp     ecx, 4
                jae     minimumWidthIs4

                mov     ecx, 4      ; Minimum possible width is four

minimumWidthIs4:
                cmp     ecx, fWidth
                ja      widthTooBig

; This number will fit in the specified field width,
; so output any necessary leading pad characters.

                mov     al, fill
                mov     edx, fWidth
                sub     edx, ecx
                jmp     testWhileECXltWidth

whileECXltWidth:
                mov     [rdi], al
                inc     rdi
                inc     ecx

testWhileECXltWidth:
                cmp     ecx, fWidth
                jb      whileECXltWidth

; Output " 0." or "-0.", depending on the sign of the number.

                mov     al, sign
                cmp     al, '-'
                je      isMinus

                mov     al, ' '
```

```
isMinus:    mov     [rdi], al
            inc     rdi
            inc     edx

            mov     word ptr [rdi], '.0'
            add     rdi, 2
            add     edx, 2

; Now output the digits after the decimal point:

            xor     ecx, ecx        ; Count the digits in ECX
            lea     rbx, digits     ; Pointer to data to output d

; If the exponent is currently negative, or if
; we've output more than 18 significant digits,
; just output a zero character.

repeatUntilEDXgeWidth:
            mov     al, '0'
            inc     exponent
            js      noMoreOutput

            cmp     ecx, 18
            jge     noMoreOutput

            mov     al, [rbx]
            inc     ebx

noMoreOutput:
            mov     [rdi], al
            inc     rdi
            inc     ecx
            inc     edx
            cmp     edx, fWidth
            jb      repeatUntilEDXgeWidth
            jmp     r10BufDone

; If the number's actual width was bigger than the width
; specified by the caller, emit a sequence of "#" characters
; to denote the error.

widthTooBig:

; The number won't fit in the specified field width,
; so fill the string with the "#" character to indicate
; an error.

            mov     ecx, fWidth
            mov     al, '#'
fillPound:  mov     [rdi], al
            inc     rdi
            dec     ecx
            jnz     fillPound
            jmp     r10BufDone
```

; Handle numbers with a positive exponent here.

positiveExponent:

; Compute # of digits to the left of the ".".
; This is given by:

```
;                       Exponent        ; # of digits to left of "."
;               +       2               ; Allow for sign and there
;                                       ; is always 1 digit left of "."
;               +       decimalpts      ; Add in digits right of "."
;               +       1               ; If there is a decimal point

                mov     edx, exponent   ; Digits to left of "."
                add     edx, 2          ; 1 digit + sign posn
                cmp     decDigits, 0
                je      decPtsIs0

                add     edx, decDigits  ; Digits to right of "."
                inc     edx             ; Make room for the "."

decPtsIs0:
```

; Make sure the result will fit in the
; specified field width.

```
                cmp     edx, fWidth
                ja      widthTooBig
```

; If the actual number of print positions
; is fewer than the specified field width,
; output leading pad characters here.

```
                cmp     edx, fWidth
                jae     noFillChars

                mov     ecx, fWidth
                sub     ecx, edx
                jz      noFillChars
                mov     al, fill
fillChars:      mov     [rdi], al
                inc     rdi
                dec     ecx
                jnz     fillChars

noFillChars:
```

; Output the sign character.

```
                mov     al, sign
                cmp     al, '-'
                je      outputMinus;

                mov     al, ' '
```

```
outputMinus:
            mov     [rdi], al
            inc     rdi

; Okay, output the digits for the number here.

            xor     ecx, ecx        ; Counts # of output chars
            lea     rbx, digits     ; Ptr to digits to output

; Calculate the number of digits to output
; before and after the decimal point.

            mov     edx, decDigits  ; Chars after "."
            add     edx, exponent   ; # chars before "."
            inc     edx             ; Always one digit before "."

; If we've output fewer than 18 digits, go ahead
; and output the next digit.  Beyond 18 digits,
; output zeros.

repeatUntilEDXeq0:
            mov     al, '0'
            cmp     ecx, 18
            jnb     putChar

            mov     al, [rbx]
            inc     rbx

putChar:    mov     [rdi], al
            inc     rdi

; If the exponent decrements to zero,
; then output a decimal point.

            cmp     exponent, 0
            jne     noDecimalPt
            cmp     decDigits, 0
            je      noDecimalPt

            mov     al, '.'
            mov     [rdi], al
            inc     rdi

noDecimalPt:
            dec     exponent        ; Count down to "." output
            inc     ecx             ; # of digits thus far
            dec     edx             ; Total # of digits to output
            jnz     repeatUntilEDXeq0

; Zero-terminate string and leave:

r10BufDone: mov     byte ptr [rdi], 0
            leave
            clc                     ; No error
            jmp     popRet
```

```
badWidth:    mov    rax, -2     ; Illegal width
             jmp    ErrorExit

strOverflow:
             mov    rax, -3     ; String overflow
             jmp    ErrorExit

voor:        or     rax, -1     ; Range error
ErrorExit:   leave
             stc    ; Error
             mov    [rsp], rax  ; Change RAX on return

popRet:      pop    rax
             pop    rsi
             pop    rdx
             pop    rcx
             pop    rbx
             pop    rdi
             ret

r10ToStr     endp
```

Listing 9-11: r10ToStr conversion function

9.1.8.3 Converting a Floating-Point Value to Exponential Form

Converting a floating-point value to exponential (scientific) form is a bit
easier than converting it to decimal form. The mantissa always takes the
form *sx.y* where *s* is a hyphen or a space, *x* is exactly one decimal digit, and
y is one or more decimal digits. The FPDigits function does almost all the
work to create this string. The exponential conversion function needs to
output the mantissa string with sign and decimal point characters and then
output the decimal exponent for the number. Converting the exponent
value (returned as a decimal integer in the EAX register by FPDigits) to a
string is just the numeric-to-decimal string conversion given earlier in this
chapter, using different output formatting.

The function this chapter presents allows you to specify the number of
digits for the exponent as 1, 2, 3, or 4. If the exponent requires more digits
than the caller specifies, the function returns a failure. If it requires fewer
digits than the caller specifies, the function pads the exponent with leading
0s. To emulate the typical floating-point conversion forms, specify an exponent size of 2 for single-precision values, 3 for double-precision values, and
4 for extended-precision values.

Listing 9-12 provides a quick-and-dirty function that converts the decimal
exponent value to the appropriate string form and emits those characters to
a buffer. This function leaves RDI pointing beyond the last exponent digit
and doesn't zero-terminate the string. It's really just a helper function to
output characters for the e10ToStr function that will appear in the next listing.

NOTE   *The full Listing 9-12 is available online at* https://artofasm.randallhyde.com/.
For brevity, the following listing only provides the actual expToBuf function.

```
*************************************************************

; expToBuf - Unsigned integer to buffer.
;            Used to output up to 4-digit exponents.

; Inputs:

;    EAX:    Unsigned integer to convert.
;    ECX:    Print width 1-4.
;    RDI:    Points at buffer.

;    FPU:    Uses FPU stack.

; Returns:

;    RDI:    Points at end of buffer.

expToBuf    proc

expWidth    equ     <[rbp + 16]>
exp         equ     <[rbp + 8]>
bcd         equ     <[rbp - 16]>

            push    rdx
            push    rcx             ; At [RBP + 16]
            push    rax             ; At [RBP + 8]
            push    rbp
            mov     rbp, rsp
            sub     rsp, 16

; Verify exponent digit count is in the range 1-4:

            cmp     rcx, 1
            jb      badExp
            cmp     rcx, 4
            ja      badExp
            mov     rdx, rcx

; Verify the actual exponent will fit in the number of digits:

            cmp     rcx, 2
            jb      oneDigit
            je      twoDigits
            cmp     rcx, 3
            ja      fillZeros       ; 4 digits, no error
            cmp     eax, 1000
            jae     badExp
            jmp     fillZeros

oneDigit:   cmp     eax, 10
            jae     badExp
            jmp     fillZeros
```

```
twoDigits:  cmp     eax, 100
            jae     badExp

; Fill in zeros for exponent:

fillZeros:  mov     byte ptr [rdi + rcx * 1 - 1], '0'
            dec     ecx
            jnz     fillZeros

; Point RDI at the end of the buffer:

            lea     rdi, [rdi + rdx * 1 - 1]
            mov     byte ptr [rdi + 1], 0
            push    rdi             ; Save pointer to end

; Quick test for zero to handle that special case:

            test    eax, eax
            jz      allDone

; The number to convert is nonzero.
; Use BCD load and store to convert
; the integer to BCD:

            fild    dword ptr exp   ; Get integer value
            fbstp   tbyte ptr bcd   ; Convert to BCD

; Begin by skipping over leading zeros in
; the BCD value (max 10 digits, so the most
; significant digit will be in the HO nibble
; of byte 4).

            mov     eax, bcd        ; Get exponent digits
            mov     ecx, expWidth   ; Number of total digits

OutputExp:  mov     dl, al
            and     dl, 0fh
            or      dl, '0'
            mov     [rdi], dl
            dec     rdi
            shr     ax, 4
            jnz     OutputExp

; Zero-terminate the string and return:

allDone:    pop     rdi
            leave
            pop     rax
            pop     rcx
            pop     rdx
            clc
            ret

badExp:     leave
            pop     rax
```

```
            pop     rcx
            pop     rdx
            stc
            ret

exptoBuf    endp
```

Listing 9-12: Exponent conversion function

The actual e10ToStr function in Listing 9-13 is similar to the r10ToStr function. The output of the mantissa is less complex because the form is fixed, but there is a little additional work at the end to output the exponent. Refer back to "Converting a Floating-Point Value to a Decimal String" on page 527 for details on the operation of this code.

NOTE *The full Listing 9-13 is available online at* https://artofasm.randallhyde.com/. *For brevity, the following listing only provides the actual e10ToStr function.*

```
;************************************************************

; e10ToStr - Converts a real10 floating-point number to the
;            corresponding string of digits.  Note that this
;            function always emits the string using scientific
;            notation; use the r10ToStr routine for decimal notation.

; On Entry:

;    e10         -  real10 value to convert.
;                   Passed in ST(0).

;    width       -  Field width for the number (note that this
;                   is an *exact* field width, not a minimum
;                   field width).
;                   Passed in RAX (LO 32 bits).

;    fill        -  Padding character if the number is smaller
;                   than the specified field width.
;                   Passed in RCX.

;    buffer      -  e10ToStr stores the resulting characters in
;                   this buffer (passed in RDI).

;    expDigs     -  Number of exponent digits (2 for real4,
;                   3 for real8, and 4 for real10).
;                   Passed in RDX (LO 8 bits).

;    maxLength   -  Maximum buffer size.
;                   Passed in R8.

; On Exit:

;    RDI         -  Points at end of converted string.
```

```
; Buffer contains the newly formatted string.  If the
; formatted value does not fit in the width specified,
; e10ToStr will store "#" characters into this string.

; If there was an error, EAX contains -1, -2, or -3
; denoting the error (value out of range, bad width,
; or string overflow, respectively).


;**********************************************************

; Unlike the integer-to-string conversions, this routine
; always right-justifies the number in the specified
; string.  Width must be a positive number; negative
; values are illegal (actually, they are treated as
; *really* big positive numbers that will always raise
; a string overflow exception).


;**********************************************************

e10ToStr        proc

fWidth          equ     <[rbp - 8]>         ; RAX
buffer          equ     <[rbp - 16]>        ; RDI
expDigs         equ     <[rbp - 24]>        ; RDX
rbxSave         equ     <[rbp - 32]>
rcxSave         equ     <[rbp - 40]>
rsiSave         equ     <[rbp - 48]>
Exponent        equ     <dword ptr [rbp - 52]>
MantSize        equ     <dword ptr [rbp - 56]>
Sign            equ     <byte ptr [rbp - 60]>
Digits          equ     <byte ptr [rbp - 128]>

                push    rbp
                mov     rbp, rsp
                sub     rsp, 128

                mov     buffer, rdi
                mov     rsiSave, rsi
                mov     rcxSave, rcx
                mov     rbxSave, rbx
                mov     fWidth, rax
                mov     expDigs, rdx

                cmp     eax, r8d
                jae     strOvfl
                mov     byte ptr [rdi + rax * 1], 0 ; Zero-terminate str

; First, make sure the width isn't zero.

                test    eax, eax
                jz      voor
```

```
                ; Just to be on the safe side, don't allow widths greater
                ; than 1024:

                        cmp     eax, 1024
                        ja      badWidth

        ; Okay, do the conversion.

                        lea     rdi, Digits     ; Store result string here
                        call    FPDigits        ; Convert e80 to digit str
                        mov     Exponent, eax   ; Save away exponent result
                        mov     Sign, cl        ; Save mantissa sign char

        ; Verify that there is sufficient room for the mantissa's sign,
        ; the decimal point, two mantissa digits, the "E", and the
        ; exponent's sign.  Also add in the number of digits required
        ; by the exponent (2 for real4, 3 for real8, 4 for real10).

        ; -1.2e+00     :real4
        ; -1.2e+000    :real8
        ; -1.2e+0000   :real10

                        mov     ecx, 6          ; Char posns for above chars
                        add     ecx, expDigs    ; # of digits for the exp
                        cmp     ecx, fWidth
                        jbe     goodWidth

        ; Output a sequence of "#...#" chars (to the specified width)
        ; if the width value is not large enough to hold the
        ; conversion:

                        mov     ecx, fWidth
                        mov     al, '#'
                        mov     rdi, buffer
        fillPound:      mov     [rdi], al
                        inc     rdi
                        dec     ecx
                        jnz     fillPound
                        jmp     exit_eToBuf

        ; Okay, the width is sufficient to hold the number; do the
        ; conversion and output the string here:

        goodWidth:

                        mov     ebx, fWidth     ; Compute the # of mantissa
                        sub     ebx, ecx        ; digits to display
                        add     ebx, 2          ; ECX allows for 2 mant digs
                        mov     MantSize,ebx

        ; Round the number to the specified number of print positions.
        ; (Note: since there are a maximum of 18 significant digits,
        ; don't bother with the rounding if the field width is greater
        ; than 18 digits.)
```

```
                cmp     ebx, 18
                jae     noNeedToRound

; To round the value to the number of significant digits,
; go to the digit just beyond the last one we are considering
; (EBX currently contains the number of decimal positions)
; and add 5 to that digit.  Propagate any overflow into the
; remaining digit positions.

                mov     al, Digits[rbx * 1] ; Get least sig digit + 1
                add     al, 5               ; Round (for example, +0.5)
                cmp     al, '9'
                jbe     noNeedToRound
                mov     Digits[rbx * 1], '9' + 1
                jmp     whileDigitGT9Test

whileDigitGT9:

; Subtract out overflow and add the carry into the previous
; digit (unless we hit the first digit in the number).

                sub     Digits[rbx * 1], 10
                dec     ebx
                cmp     ebx, 0
                jl      firstDigitInNumber

                inc     Digits[rbx * 1]
                jmp     whileDigitGT9Test

firstDigitInNumber:

; If we get to this point, then we've hit the first
; digit in the number.  So we've got to shift all
; the characters down one position in the string of
; bytes and put a "1" in the first character position.

                mov     ebx, 17
repeatUntilEBXeq0:

                mov     al, Digits[rbx * 1]
                mov     Digits[rbx * 1 + 1], al
                dec     ebx
                jnz     repeatUntilEBXeq0

                mov     Digits, '1'
                inc     Exponent        ; Because we added a digit
                jmp     noNeedToRound

whileDigitGT9Test:
                cmp     Digits[rbx], '9' ; Overflow if char > "9"
                ja      whileDigitGT9

noNeedToRound:
```

```
                ; Okay, emit the string at this point.  This is pretty easy
                ; since all we really need to do is copy data from the
                ; digits array and add an exponent (plus a few other simple chars).

                        xor     ecx, ecx    ; Count output mantissa digits
                        mov     rdi, buffer
                        xor     edx, edx    ; Count output chars
                        mov     al, Sign
                        cmp     al, '-'
                        je      noMinus

                        mov     al, ' '

noMinus:        mov     [rdi], al

                ; Output the first character and a following decimal point
                ; if there are more than two mantissa digits to output.

                        mov     al, Digits
                        mov     [rdi + 1], al
                        add     rdi, 2
                        add     edx, 2
                        inc     ecx
                        cmp     ecx, MantSize
                        je      noDecPt

                        mov     al, '.'
                        mov     [rdi], al
                        inc     rdi
                        inc     edx

noDecPt:

                ; Output any remaining mantissa digits here.
                ; Note that if the caller requests the output of
                ; more than 18 digits, this routine will output zeros
                ; for the additional digits.

                        jmp     whileECXltMantSizeTest

whileECXltMantSize:

                        mov     al, '0'
                        cmp     ecx, 18
                        jae     justPut0

                        mov     al, Digits[rcx * 1]

justPut0:
                        mov     [rdi], al
                        inc     rdi
                        inc     ecx
                        inc     edx
```

```
whileECXltMantSizeTest:
            cmp     ecx, MantSize
            jb      whileECXltMantSize

; Output the exponent:

            mov     byte ptr [rdi], 'e'
            inc     rdi
            inc     edx
            mov     al, '+'
            cmp     Exponent, 0
            jge     noNegExp

            mov     al, '-'
            neg     Exponent

noNegExp:
            mov     [rdi], al
            inc     rdi
            inc     edx

            mov     eax, Exponent
            mov     ecx, expDigs
            call    expToBuf
            jc      error

exit_eToBuf:
            mov     rsi, rsiSave
            mov     rcx, rcxSave
            mov     rbx, rbxSave
            mov     rax, fWidth
            mov     rdx, expDigs
            leave
            clc
            ret

strOvfl:    mov     rax, -3
            jmp     error

badWidth:   mov     rax, -2
            jmp     error

voor:       mov     rax, -1
error:      mov     rsi, rsiSave
            mov     rcx, rcxSave
            mov     rbx, rbxSave
            mov     rdx, expDigs
            leave
            stc
            ret

e10ToStr    endp
```

Listing 9-13: e10ToStr conversion function

9.2 String-to-Numeric Conversion Routines

The routines converting numeric values to strings, and strings to numeric values, have a couple of fundamental differences. First of all, numeric-to-string conversions generally occur without possibility of error;[4] string-to-numeric conversion, on the other hand, must handle the real possibility of errors such as illegal characters and numeric overflow.

A typical numeric input operation consists of reading a string of characters from the user and then translating this string of characters into an internal numeric representation. For example, in C++ a statement like `cin >> i32;` reads a line of text from the user and converts a sequence of digits appearing at the beginning of that line of text into a 32-bit signed integer (assuming `i32` is a 32-bit `int` object). The `cin >> i32;` statement skips over certain characters, like leading spaces, in the string that may appear before the actual numeric characters. The input string may also contain additional data beyond the end of the numeric input (for example, it is possible to read two integer values from the same input line), and therefore the input conversion routine must determine where the numeric data ends in the input stream.

Typically, C++ achieves this by looking for a character from a set of *delimiter* characters. The delimiter character set could be something as simple as "any character that is not a numeric digit" or the set of whitespace characters (space, tab, and so on), and perhaps few other characters such as a comma (,) or some other punctuation character. For the sake of example, the code in this section will assume that any leading spaces or tab characters (ASCII code 9) may precede any numeric digits, and the conversion stops on the first nondigit character it encounters. Possible error conditions are as follows:

- No numeric digits at all at the beginning of the string (following any spaces or tabs).
- The string of digits is a value that would be too large for the intended numeric size (for example, 64 bits).

It will be up to the caller to determine if the numeric string ends with an invalid character (upon return from the function call).

9.2.1 Converting Decimal Strings to Integers

The basic algorithm to convert a string containing decimal digits to a number is the following:

1. Initialize an accumulator variable to 0.
2. Skip any leading spaces or tabs in the string.
3. Fetch the first character after the spaces or tabs.

---

4. Well, assuming you have allocated a sufficiently large buffer so that the conversion routines don't write data beyond the end of the buffer.

4. If the character is not a numeric digit, return an error. If the character is a numeric digit, fall through to step 5.

5. Convert the numeric character to a numeric value (using AND 0Fh).

6. Set the accumulator = (accumulator × 10) + current numeric value.

7. If overflow occurs, return and report an error. If no overflow occurs, fall through to step 8.

8. Fetch the next character from the string.

9. If the character is a numeric digit, go back to step 5, else fall through to step 10.

10. Return success, with accumulator containing the converted value.

For signed integer input, you use this same algorithm with the following modifications:

- If the first non-space or tab character is a hyphen (-), set a flag denoting that the number is negative and skip the "-" character (if the first character is not -, then clear the flag).

- At the end of a successful conversion, if the flag is set, then negate the integer result before return (must check for overflow on the negate operation).

Listing 9-14 implements the conversion algorithm.

```
; Listing 9-14

; String-to-numeric conversion.

        option  casemap:none

false    =      0
true     =      1
tab      =      9
nl       =      10

         .const
ttlStr   byte   "Listing 9-14", 0
fmtStr1  byte   "strtou: String='%s'", nl
         byte   "    value=%I64u", nl, 0

fmtStr2  byte   "Overflow: String='%s'", nl
         byte   "    value=%I64x", nl, 0

fmtStr3  byte   "strtoi: String='%s'", nl
         byte   "    value=%I64i",nl, 0

unexError byte  "Unexpected error in program", nl, 0

value1   byte   "  1", 0
value2   byte   "12 ", 0
value3   byte   " 123 ", 0
value4   byte   "1234", 0
```

```
value5      byte    "1234567890123456789", 0
value6      byte    "18446744073709551615", 0
OFvalue     byte    "18446744073709551616", 0
OFvalue2    byte    "99999999999999999999", 0

ivalue1     byte    "  -1", 0
ivalue2     byte    "-12 ", 0
ivalue3     byte    " -123 ", 0
ivalue4     byte    "-1234", 0
ivalue5     byte    "-1234567890123456789", 0
ivalue6     byte    "-9223372036854775807", 0
OFivalue    byte    "-9223372036854775808", 0
OFivalue2   byte    "-99999999999999999999", 0

            .data
buffer      byte    30 dup (?)

            .code
            externdef printf:proc

; Return program title to C++ program:

            public  getTitle
getTitle    proc
            lea     rax, ttlStr
            ret
getTitle    endp

; strtou -  Converts string data to a 64-bit unsigned integer.

; Input:
;   RDI -   Pointer to buffer containing string to convert.

; Output:
;   RAX -   Contains converted string (if success), error code
;           if an error occurs.

;   RDI -   Points at first char beyond end of numeric string.
;           If error, RDI's value is restored to original value.
;           Caller can check character at [RDI] after a
;           successful result to see if the character following
;           the numeric digits is a legal numeric delimiter.

;   C   -   (carry flag) Set if error occurs, clear if
;           conversion was successful. On error, RAX will
;           contain 0 (illegal initial character) or
;           0FFFFFFFFFFFFFFFFh (overflow).

strtou      proc
            push    rdi     ; In case we have to restore RDI
            push    rdx     ; Munged by mul
            push    rcx     ; Holds input char
```

```
            xor     edx, edx ; Zero-extends!
            xor     eax, eax ; Zero-extends!
```

; The following loop skips over any whitespace (spaces and
; tabs) that appears at the beginning of the string.

```
            dec     rdi      ; Because of inc below
skipWS:     inc     rdi
            mov     cl, [rdi]
            cmp     cl, ' '
            je      skipWS
            cmp     al, tab
            je      skipWS
```

; If we don't have a numeric digit at this point,
; return an error.

```
            cmp     cl, '0'  ; Note: "0" < "1" < ... < "9"
            jb      badNumber
            cmp     cl, '9'
            ja      badNumber
```

; Okay, the first digit is good. Convert the string
; of digits to numeric form:

```
convert:    and     ecx, 0fh ; Convert to numeric in RCX
            mul     ten      ; Accumulator *= 10
            jc      overflow
            add     rax, rcx ; Accumulator += digit
            jc      overflow
            inc     rdi      ; Move on to next character
            mov     cl, [rdi]
            cmp     cl, '0'
            jb      endOfNum
            cmp     cl, '9'
            jbe     convert
```

; If we get to this point, we've successfully converted
; the string to numeric form:

```
endOfNum:   pop     rcx
            pop     rdx
```

; Because the conversion was successful, this procedure
; leaves RDI pointing at the first character beyond the
; converted digits. As such, we don't restore RDI from
; the stack. Just bump the stack pointer up by 8 bytes
; to throw away RDI's saved value.

```
            add     rsp, 8
            clc              ; Return success in carry flag
            ret
```

```
; badNumber - Drop down here if the first character in
;             the string was not a valid digit.

badNumber:  mov     rax, 0
            pop     rcx
            pop     rdx
            pop     rdi
            stc                 ; Return error in carry flag
            ret

overflow:   mov     rax, -1  ; 0FFFFFFFFFFFFFFFFh
            pop     rcx
            pop     rdx
            pop     rdi
            stc                 ; Return error in carry flag
            ret

ten         qword   10

strtou      endp

; strtoi - Converts string data to a 64-bit signed integer.

; Input:
;   RDI  -  Pointer to buffer containing string to convert.

; Output:
;   RAX  -  Contains converted string (if success), error code
;           if an error occurs.

;   RDI  -  Points at first char beyond end of numeric string.
;           If error, RDI's value is restored to original value.
;           Caller can check character at [RDI] after a
;           successful result to see if the character following
;           the numeric digits is a legal numeric delimiter.

;   C    -  (carry flag) Set if error occurs, clear if
;           conversion was successful. On error, RAX will
;           contain 0 (illegal initial character) or
;           0FFFFFFFFFFFFFFFFh (-1, indicating overflow).

strtoi      proc
negFlag     equ     <byte ptr [rsp]>

            push    rdi         ; In case we have to restore RDI
            sub     rsp, 8

; Assume we have a non-negative number.

            mov     negFlag, false

; The following loop skips over any whitespace (spaces and
; tabs) that appears at the beginning of the string.

            dec     rdi         ; Because of inc below
```

```
skipWS:     inc     rdi
            mov     al, [rdi]
            cmp     al, ' '
            je      skipWS
            cmp     al, tab
            je      skipWS

; If the first character we've encountered is "-",
; then skip it, but remember that this is a negative
; number.

            cmp     al, '-'
            jne     notNeg
            mov     negFlag, true
            inc     rdi             ; Skip "-"

notNeg:     call    strtou          ; Convert string to integer
            jc      hadError

; strtou returned success. Check the negative flag and
; negate the input if the flag contains true.

            cmp     negFlag, true
            jne     itsPosOr0

            cmp     rax, tooBig     ; Number is too big
            ja      overflow
            neg     rax
itsPosOr0:  add     rsp, 16         ; Success, so don't restore RDI
            clc                     ; Return success in carry flag
            ret

; If we have an error, we need to restore RDI from the stack:

overflow:   mov     rax, -1         ; Indicate overflow
hadError:   add     rsp, 8          ; Remove locals
            pop     rdi
            stc                     ; Return error in carry flag
            ret

tooBig      qword   7fffffffffffffffh
strtoi      endp

; Here is the "asmMain" function.

            public  asmMain
asmMain     proc
            push    rbp
            mov     rbp, rsp
            sub     rsp, 64         ; Shadow storage

; Test unsigned conversions:

            lea     rdi, value1
            call    strtou
```

```
        jc      UnexpectedError

                lea     rcx, fmtStr1
                lea     rdx, value1
                mov     r8, rax
                call    printf

                lea     rdi, value2
                call    strtou
                jc      UnexpectedError

                lea     rcx, fmtStr1
                lea     rdx, value2
                mov     r8, rax
                call    printf

                lea     rdi, value3
                call    strtou
                jc      UnexpectedError

                lea     rcx, fmtStr1
                lea     rdx, value3
                mov     r8, rax
                call    printf

                lea     rdi, value4
                call    strtou
                jc      UnexpectedError

                lea     rcx, fmtStr1
                lea     rdx, value4
                mov     r8, rax
                call    printf

                lea     rdi, value5
                call    strtou
                jc      UnexpectedError

                lea     rcx, fmtStr1
                lea     rdx, value5
                mov     r8, rax
                call    printf

                lea     rdi, value6
                call    strtou
                jc      UnexpectedError

                lea     rcx, fmtStr1
                lea     rdx, value6
                mov     r8, rax
                call    printf
```

```
        lea     rdi, OFvalue
        call    strtou
        jnc     UnexpectedError
        test    rax, rax        ; Nonzero for overflow
        jz      UnexpectedError

        lea     rcx, fmtStr2
        lea     rdx, OFvalue
        mov     r8, rax
        call    printf

        lea     rdi, OFvalue2
        call    strtou
        jnc     UnexpectedError
        test    rax, rax        ; Nonzero for overflow
        jz      UnexpectedError

        lea     rcx, fmtStr2
        lea     rdx, OFvalue2
        mov     r8, rax
        call    printf

; Test signed conversions:

        lea     rdi, ivalue1
        call    strtoi
        jc      UnexpectedError

        lea     rcx, fmtStr3
        lea     rdx, ivalue1
        mov     r8, rax
        call    printf

        lea     rdi, ivalue2
        call    strtoi
        jc      UnexpectedError

        lea     rcx, fmtStr3
        lea     rdx, ivalue2
        mov     r8, rax
        call    printf

        lea     rdi, ivalue3
        call    strtoi
        jc      UnexpectedError

        lea     rcx, fmtStr3
        lea     rdx, ivalue3
        mov     r8, rax
        call    printf
```

```
        lea     rdi, ivalue4
        call    strtoi
        jc      UnexpectedError

        lea     rcx, fmtStr3
        lea     rdx, ivalue4
        mov     r8, rax
        call    printf

        lea     rdi, ivalue5
        call    strtoi
        jc      UnexpectedError

        lea     rcx, fmtStr3
        lea     rdx, ivalue5
        mov     r8, rax
        call    printf

        lea     rdi, ivalue6
        call    strtoi
        jc      UnexpectedError

        lea     rcx, fmtStr3
        lea     rdx, ivalue6
        mov     r8, rax
        call    printf

        lea     rdi, OFivalue
        call    strtoi
        jnc     UnexpectedError
        test    rax, rax        ; Nonzero for overflow
        jz      UnexpectedError

        lea     rcx, fmtStr2
        lea     rdx, OFivalue
        mov     r8, rax
        call    printf

        lea     rdi, OFivalue2
        call    strtoi
        jnc     UnexpectedError
        test    rax, rax        ; Nonzero for overflow
        jz      UnexpectedError

        lea     rcx, fmtStr2
        lea     rdx, OFivalue2
        mov     r8, rax
        call    printf

        jmp     allDone

UnexpectedError:
        lea     rcx, unexError
        call    printf
```

```
allDone:    leave
            ret     ; Returns to caller
asmMain     endp
            end
```

Listing 9-14: Numeric-to-string conversions

Here's the build command and sample output for this program:

```
C:\>build listing9-14

C:\>echo off
 Assembling: listing9-14.asm
c.cpp

C:\>listing9-14
Calling Listing 9-14:
strtou: String='  1'
    value=1
strtou: String='12 '
    value=12
strtou: String=' 123 '
    value=123
strtou: String='1234'
    value=1234
strtou: String='1234567890123456789'
    value=1234567890123456789
strtou: String='18446744073709551615'
    value=18446744073709551615
Overflow: String='18446744073709551616'
    value=ffffffffffffffff
Overflow: String='999999999999999999999'
    value=ffffffffffffffff
strtoi: String='  -1'
    value=-1
strtoi: String='-12 '
    value=-12
strtoi: String=' -123 '
    value=-123
strtoi: String='-1234'
    value=-1234
strtoi: String='-1234567890123456789'
    value=-1234567890123456789
strtoi: String='-9223372036854775807'
    value=-9223372036854775807
Overflow: String='-9223372036854775808'
    value=ffffffffffffffff
Overflow: String='-999999999999999999999'
    value=ffffffffffffffff
Listing 9-14 terminated
```

For an extended-precision string-to-numeric conversion, you simply modify the strtou function to have an extend-precision accumulator and then do an extended-precision multiplication by 10 (rather than a standard multiplication).

9.2.2 Converting Hexadecimal Strings to Numeric Form

As was the case for numeric output, hexadecimal input is the easiest numeric input routine to write. The basic algorithm for hexadecimal-string-to-numeric conversion is the following:

1. Initialize an extended-precision accumulator value to 0.
2. For each input character that is a valid hexadecimal digit, repeat steps 3 through 6; drop down to step 7 when it is not a valid hexadecimal digit.
3. Convert the hexadecimal character to a value in the range 0 to 15 (0h to 0Fh).
4. If the HO 4 bits of the extended-precision accumulator value are non-zero, raise an exception.
5. Multiply the current extended-precision value by 16 (that is, shift left 4 bits).
6. Add the converted hexadecimal digit value to the accumulator.
7. Check the current input character to ensure it is a valid delimiter. Raise an exception if it is not.

Listing 9-15 implements this extended-precision hexadecimal input routine for 64-bit values.

```
; Listing 9-15

; Hexadecimal string-to-numeric conversion.

            option  casemap:none

false       =       0
true        =       1
tab         =       9
nl          =       10


            .const
ttlStr      byte    "Listing 9-15", 0
fmtStr1     byte    "strtoh: String='%s' "
            byte    "value=%I64x", nl, 0

fmtStr2     byte    "Error, RAX=%I64x, str='%s'", nl, 0
fmtStr3     byte    "Error, expected overflow: RAX=%I64x, "
            byte    "str='%s'", nl, 0

fmtStr4     byte    "Error, expected bad char: RAX=%I64x, "
            byte    "str='%s'", nl, 0

hexStr      byte    "1234567890abcdef", 0
hexStrOVFL  byte    "1234567890abcdef0", 0
hexStrBAD   byte    "x123", 0

            .code
            externdef printf:proc
```

```
              ; Return program title to C++ program:

                         public   getTitle
              getTitle   proc
                         lea      rax, ttlStr
                         ret
              getTitle   endp

              ; strtoh -   Converts string data to a 64-bit unsigned integer.

              ; Input:
              ;   RDI  -   Pointer to buffer containing string to convert.

              ; Output:
              ;   RAX  -   Contains converted string (if success), error code
              ;            if an error occurs.

              ;   RDI  -   Points at first char beyond end of hexadecimal string.
              ;            If error, RDI's value is restored to original value.
              ;            Caller can check character at [RDI] after a
              ;            successful result to see if the character following
              ;            the numeric digits is a legal numeric delimiter.

              ;   C    -   (carry flag) Set if error occurs, clear if
              ;            conversion was successful. On error, RAX will
              ;            contain 0 (illegal initial character) or
              ;            0FFFFFFFFFFFFFFFFh (overflow).

              strtoh     proc
                         push     rcx      ; Holds input char
                         push     rdx      ; Special mask value
                         push     rdi      ; In case we have to restore RDI

              ; This code will use the value in RDX to test and see if overflow
              ; will occur in RAX when shifting to the left 4 bits:

                         mov      rdx, 0F000000000000000h
                         xor      eax, eax ; Zero out accumulator

              ; The following loop skips over any whitespace (spaces and
              ; tabs) that appears at the beginning of the string.

                         dec      rdi      ; Because of inc below
              skipWS:    inc      rdi
                         mov      cl, [rdi]
                         cmp      cl, ' '
                         je       skipWS
                         cmp      al, tab
                         je       skipWS

              ; If we don't have a hexadecimal digit at this point,
              ; return an error.
```

```
                    cmp     cl, '0'   ; Note: "0" < "1" < ... < "9"
                    jb      badNumber
                    cmp     cl, '9'
                    jbe     convert
                    and     cl, 5fh   ; Cheesy LC -> UC conversion
                    cmp     cl, 'A'
                    jb      badNumber
                    cmp     cl, 'F'
                    ja      badNumber
                    sub     cl, 7     ; Maps 41h to 46h -> 3Ah to 3Fh

; Okay, the first digit is good. Convert the string
; of digits to numeric form:

convert:      test    rdx, rax  ; See if adding in the current
              jnz     overflow  ; digit will cause an overflow

              and     ecx, 0fh  ; Convert to numeric in RCX

; Multiply 64-bit accumulator by 16 and add in new digit:

                    shl     rax, 4
                    add     al, cl    ; Never overflows outside LO 4 bits

; Move on to next character:

                    inc     rdi
                    mov     cl, [rdi]
                    cmp     cl, '0'
                    jb      endOfNum
                    cmp     cl, '9'
                    jbe     convert

                    and     cl, 5fh   ; Cheesy LC -> UC conversion
                    cmp     cl, 'A'
                    jb      endOfNum
                    cmp     cl, 'F'
                    ja      endOfNum
                    sub     cl, 7     ; Maps 41h to 46h -> 3Ah to 3Fh
                    jmp     convert

; If we get to this point, we've successfully converted
; the string to numeric form:

endOfNum:

; Because the conversion was successful, this procedure
; leaves RDI pointing at the first character beyond the
; converted digits. As such, we don't restore RDI from
; the stack. Just bump the stack pointer up by 8 bytes
; to throw away RDI's saved value.
```

```
            add     rsp, 8    ; Remove original RDI value
            pop     rdx       ; Restore RDX
            pop     rcx       ; Restore RCX
            clc               ; Return success in carry flag
            ret

; badNumber- Drop down here if the first character in
;            the string was not a valid digit.

badNumber:  xor     rax, rax
            jmp     errorExit

overflow:   or      rax, -1   ; Return -1 as error on overflow
errorExit:  pop     rdi       ; Restore RDI if an error occurs
            pop     rdx
            pop     rcx
            stc               ; Return error in carry flag
            ret

strtoh      endp

; Here is the "asmMain" function.

            public  asmMain
asmMain     proc
            push    rbp
            mov     rbp, rsp
            sub     rsp, 64   ; Shadow storage

; Test hexadecimal conversion:

            lea     rdi, hexStr
            call    strtoh
            jc      error

            lea     rcx, fmtStr1
            mov     r8, rax
            lea     rdx, hexStr
            call    printf

; Test overflow conversion:

            lea     rdi, hexStrOVFL
            call    strtoh
            jnc     unexpected

            lea     rcx, fmtStr2
            mov     rdx, rax
            mov     r8, rdi
            call    printf
```

```
; Test bad character:

                lea     rdi, hexStrBAD
                call    strtoh
                jnc     unexp2

                lea     rcx, fmtStr2
                mov     rdx, rax
                mov     r8, rdi
                call    printf
                jmp     allDone

unexpected: lea     rcx, fmtStr3
                mov     rdx, rax
                mov     r8, rdi
                call    printf
                jmp     allDone

unexp2:         lea     rcx, fmtStr4
                mov     rdx, rax
                mov     r8, rdi
                call    printf
                jmp     allDone

error:          lea     rcx, fmtStr2
                mov     rdx, rax
                mov     r8, rdi
                call    printf

allDone:        leave
                ret     ; Returns to caller
asmMain         endp
                end
```

Listing 9-15: Hexadecimal string-to-numeric conversion

Here's the build command and program output:

```
C:\>build listing9-15

C:\>echo off
 Assembling: listing9-15.asm
c.cpp

C:\>listing9-15
Calling Listing 9-15:
strtoh: String='1234567890abcdef' value=1234567890abcdef
Error, RAX=ffffffffffffffff, str='1234567890abcdef0'
Error, RAX=0, str='x123'
Listing 9-15 terminated
```

For hexadecimal string conversions that handle numbers greater than 64 bits, you have to use an extended-precision shift left by 4 bits. Listing 9-16 demonstrates the necessary modifications to the strtoh function for a 128-bit conversion.

NOTE *Because of the length and redundancy of Listing 9-16, a large part of the uninteresting code has been removed. The full Listing 9-16 is available online at* https://artofasm.randallhyde.com/.

```
; strtoh128 - Converts string data to a 128-bit unsigned integer.

; Input:
;   RDI     - Pointer to buffer containing string to convert.

; Output:
;   RDX:RAX - Contains converted string (if success), error code
;               if an error occurs.

;   RDI     - Points at first char beyond end of hex string.
;               If error, RDI's value is restored to original value.
;               Caller can check character at [RDI] after a
;               successful result to see if the character following
;               the numeric digits is a legal numeric delimiter.

;   C       - (carry flag) Set if error occurs, clear if
;               conversion was successful. On error, RAX will
;               contain 0 (illegal initial character) or
;               0FFFFFFFFFFFFFFFFh (overflow).

strtoh128   proc
            push    rbx         ; Special mask value
            push    rcx         ; Input char to process
            push    rdi         ; In case we have to restore RDI

; This code will use the value in RDX to test and see if overflow
; will occur in RAX when shifting to the left 4 bits:

            mov     rbx, 0F000000000000000h
            xor     eax, eax    ; Zero out accumulator
            xor     edx, edx

; The following loop skips over any whitespace (spaces and
; tabs) that appears at the beginning of the string.

            dec     rdi         ; Because of inc below
skipWS:     inc     rdi
            mov     cl, [rdi]
            cmp     cl, ' '
            je      skipWS
            cmp     al, tab
            je      skipWS

; If we don't have a hexadecimal digit at this point,
; return an error.

            cmp     cl, '0'     ; Note: "0" < "1" < ... < "9"
            jb      badNumber
            cmp     cl, '9'
            jbe     convert
```

```
                and     cl, 5fh  ; Cheesy LC -> UC conversion
                cmp     cl, 'A'
                jb      badNumber
                cmp     cl, 'F'
                ja      badNumber
                sub     cl, 7    ; Maps 41h to 46h -> 3Ah to 3Fh

; Okay, the first digit is good. Convert the string
; of digits to numeric form:

convert:        test    rdx, rbx ; See if adding in the current
                jnz     overflow ; digit will cause an overflow

                and     ecx, 0fh ; Convert to numeric in RCX

; Multiply 64-bit accumulator by 16 and add in new digit:

                shld    rdx, rax, 4
                shl     rax, 4
                add     al, cl   ; Never overflows outside LO 4 bits

; Move on to next character:

                inc     rdi
                mov     cl, [rdi]
                cmp     cl, '0'
                jb      endOfNum
                cmp     cl, '9'
                jbe     convert

                and     cl, 5fh  ; Cheesy LC -> UC conversion
                cmp     cl, 'A'
                jb      endOfNum
                cmp     cl, 'F'
                ja      endOfNum
                sub     cl, 7    ; Maps 41h to 46h -> 3Ah to 3Fh
                jmp     convert

; If we get to this point, we've successfully converted
; the string to numeric form:

endOfNum:

; Because the conversion was successful, this procedure
; leaves RDI pointing at the first character beyond the
; converted digits. As such, we don't restore RDI from
; the stack. Just bump the stack pointer up by 8 bytes
; to throw away RDI's saved value.

                add     rsp, 8   ; Remove original RDI value
                pop     rcx      ; Restore RCX
                pop     rbx      ; Restore RBX
                clc              ; Return success in carry flag
                ret
```

```
; badNumber - Drop down here if the first character in
;              the string was not a valid digit.

badNumber:  xor     rax, rax
            jmp     errorExit

overflow:   or      rax, -1  ; Return -1 as error on overflow
errorExit:  pop     rdi      ; Restore RDI if an error occurs
            pop     rcx
            pop     rbx
            stc              ; Return error in carry flag
            ret

strtoh128   endp
```

Listing 9-16: 128-bit hexadecimal string-to-numeric conversion

9.2.3 Converting Unsigned Decimal Strings to Integers

The algorithm for unsigned decimal input is nearly identical to that for
hexadecimal input. In fact, the only difference (beyond accepting only decimal digits) is that you multiply the accumulating value by 10 rather than 16
for each input character (in general, the algorithm is the same for any base;
just multiply the accumulating value by the input base). Listing 9-17 demonstrates how to write a 64-bit unsigned decimal input routine.

```
; Listing 9-17

; 64-bit unsigned decimal string-to-numeric conversion.

        option  casemap:none

false    =       0
true     =       1
tab      =       9
nl       =       10

         .const
ttlStr   byte    "Listing 9-17", 0
fmtStr1  byte    "strtou: String='%s' value=%I64u", nl, 0
fmtStr2  byte    "strtou: error, rax=%d", nl, 0

qStr     byte    "12345678901234567", 0

         .code
         externdef printf:proc

; Return program title to C++ program:

         public  getTitle
getTitle proc
         lea     rax, ttlStr
```

```
                ret
getTitle    endp

; strtou -   Converts string data to a 64-bit unsigned integer.

; Input:
;   RDI  -   Pointer to buffer containing string to convert.

; Output:
;   RAX  -   Contains converted string (if success), error code
;            if an error occurs.

;   RDI  -   Points at first char beyond end of numeric string.
;            If error, RDI's value is restored to original value.
;            Caller can check character at [RDI] after a
;            successful result to see if the character following
;            the numeric digits is a legal numeric delimiter.

;   C    -   (carry flag) Set if error occurs, clear if
;            conversion was successful. On error, RAX will
;            contain 0 (illegal initial character) or
;            0FFFFFFFFFFFFFFFFh (overflow).

strtou      proc
            push    rcx         ; Holds input char
            push    rdx         ; Save, used for multiplication
            push    rdi         ; In case we have to restore RDI

            xor     rax, rax    ; Zero out accumulator

; The following loop skips over any whitespace (spaces and
; tabs) that appears at the beginning of the string.

            dec     rdi         ; Because of inc below
skipWS:     inc     rdi
            mov     cl, [rdi]
            cmp     cl, ' '
            je      skipWS
            cmp     al, tab
            je      skipWS

; If we don't have a numeric digit at this point,
; return an error.

            cmp     cl, '0'     ; Note: "0" < "1" < ... < "9"
            jb      badNumber
            cmp     cl, '9'
            ja      badNumber

; Okay, the first digit is good. Convert the string
; of digits to numeric form:

convert:    and     ecx, 0fh    ; Convert to numeric in RCX
```

; Multiple 64-bit accumulator by 10:

```
            mul     ten
            test    rdx, rdx ; Test for overflow
            jnz     overflow

            add     rax, rcx
            jc      overflow
```

; Move on to next character:

```
            inc     rdi
            mov     cl, [rdi]
            cmp     cl, '0'
            jb      endOfNum
            cmp     cl, '9'
            jbe     convert
```

; If we get to this point, we've successfully converted
; the string to numeric form:

endOfNum:

; Because the conversion was successful, this procedure
; leaves RDI pointing at the first character beyond the
; converted digits. As such, we don't restore RDI from
; the stack. Just bump the stack pointer up by 8 bytes
; to throw away RDI's saved value.

```
            add     rsp, 8   ; Remove original RDI value
            pop     rdx
            pop     rcx      ; Restore RCX
            clc              ; Return success in carry flag
            ret
```

; badNumber - Drop down here if the first character in
;   the string was not a valid digit.

```
badNumber:  xor     rax, rax
            jmp     errorExit

overflow:   mov     rax, -1  ; 0FFFFFFFFFFFFFFFFh
errorExit:  pop     rdi
            pop     rdx
            pop     rcx
            stc              ; Return error in carry flag
            ret

ten         qword   10

strtou      endp
```

; Here is the "asmMain" function.

```
                public  asmMain
asmMain         proc
                push    rbp
                mov     rbp, rsp
                sub     rsp, 64  ; Shadow storage

; Test hexadecimal conversion:

                lea     rdi, qStr
                call    strtou
                jc      error

                lea     rcx, fmtStr1
                mov     r8, rax
                lea     rdx, qStr
                call    printf
                jmp     allDone

error:          lea     rcx, fmtStr2
                mov     rdx, rax
                call    printf

allDone:        leave
                ret     ; Returns to caller
asmMain         endp
                end
```

Listing 9-17: Unsigned decimal string-to-numeric conversion

Here's the build command and sample output for the program in
Listing 9-17:

```
C:\>build listing9-17

C:\>echo off
 Assembling: listing9-17.asm
c.cpp

C:\>listing9-17
Calling Listing 9-17:
strtou: String='12345678901234567' value=12345678901234567
Listing 9-17 terminated
```

Is it possible to create a faster function that uses the fbld (x87 FPU BCD
store) instruction? Probably not. The fbstp instruction was much faster for
integer conversions because the standard algorithm used multiple executions of the (very slow) div instruction. Decimal-to-numeric conversion uses
the mul instruction, which is much faster than div. Though I haven't actually
tried it, I suspect using fbld won't produce faster running code.

9.2.4   Conversion of Extended-Precision String to Unsigned Integer

The algorithm for (decimal) string-to-numeric conversion is the same regardless of integer size. You read a decimal character, convert it to an integer,

multiply the accumulating result by 10, and add in the converted character. The only things that change for larger-than-64-bit values are the multiplication by 10 and addition operations. For example, to convert a string to a 128-bit integer, you would need to be able to multiply a 128-bit value by 10 and add an 8-bit value (zero-extended to 128 bits) to a 128-bit value.

Listing 9-18 demonstrates how to write a 128-bit unsigned decimal input routine. Other than the 128-bit multiplication by 10 and 128-bit addition operations, this code is functionally identical to the 64-bit string to integer conversion.

NOTE *Because of the length and redundancy of Listing 9-18, a large part has been removed; the full Listing 9-18 is available online at* https://artofasm.randallhyde.com/.

```
; strtou128 - Converts string data to a 128-bit unsigned integer.

; Input:
;   RDI      - Pointer to buffer containing string to convert.

; Output:
;   RDX:RAX - Contains converted string (if success), error code
;             if an error occurs.

;   RDI      - Points at first char beyond end of numeric string.
;             If error, RDI's value is restored to original value.
;             Caller can check character at [RDI] after a
;             successful result to see if the character following
;             the numeric digits is a legal numeric delimiter.

;   C        - (carry flag) Set if error occurs, clear if
;             conversion was successful. On error, RAX will
;             contain 0 (illegal initial character) or
;             0FFFFFFFFFFFFFFFFh (overflow).

strtou128   proc
accumulator equ     <[rbp - 16]>
partial     equ     <[rbp - 24]>
            push    rcx      ; Holds input char
            push    rdi      ; In case we have to restore RDI
            push    rbp
            mov     rbp, rsp
            sub     rsp, 24  ; Accumulate result here

            xor     edx, edx ; Zero-extends!
            mov     accumulator, rdx
            mov     accumulator[8], rdx

; The following loop skips over any whitespace (spaces and
; tabs) that appears at the beginning of the string.

            dec     rdi      ; Because of inc below
skipWS:     inc     rdi
            mov     cl, [rdi]
```

```
                cmp     cl, ' '
                je      skipWS
                cmp     al, tab
                je      skipWS

; If we don't have a numeric digit at this point,
; return an error.

                cmp     cl, '0'          ; Note: "0" < "1" < ... < "9"
                jb      badNumber
                cmp     cl, '9'
                ja      badNumber

; Okay, the first digit is good. Convert the string
; of digits to numeric form:

convert:        and     ecx, 0fh         ; Convert to numeric in RCX

; Multiply 128-bit accumulator by 10:

                mov     rax, accumulator
                mul     ten
                mov     accumulator, rax
                mov     partial, rdx     ; Save partial product
                mov     rax, accumulator[8]
                mul     ten
                jc      overflow1
                add     rax, partial
                mov     accumulator[8], rax
                jc      overflow1

; Add in the current character to the 128-bit accumulator:

                mov     rax, accumulator
                add     rax, rcx
                mov     accumulator, rax
                mov     rax, accumulator[8]
                adc     rax, 0
                mov     accumulator[8], rax
                jc      overflow2

; Move on to next character:

                inc     rdi
                mov     cl, [rdi]
                cmp     cl, '0'
                jb      endOfNum
                cmp     cl, '9'
                jbe     convert

; If we get to this point, we've successfully converted
; the string to numeric form:

endOfNum:
```

```
        ; Because the conversion was successful, this procedure
        ; leaves RDI pointing at the first character beyond the
        ; converted digits. As such, we don't restore RDI from
        ; the stack. Just bump the stack pointer up by 8 bytes
        ; to throw away RDI's saved value.

                mov     rax, accumulator
                mov     rdx, accumulator[8]
                leave
                add     rsp, 8   ; Remove original RDI value
                pop     rcx      ; Restore RCX
                clc              ; Return success in carry flag
                ret

; badNumber - Drop down here if the first character in
;             the string was not a valid digit.

badNumber:      xor     rax, rax
                xor     rdx, rdx
                jmp     errorExit

overflow1:      mov     rax, -1
                cqo              ; RDX = -1, too
                jmp     errorExit

overflow2:      mov     rax, -2  ; 0FFFFFFFFFFFFFFFEh
                cqo              ; Just to be consistent
errorExit:      leave            ; Remove accumulator from stack
                pop     rdi
                pop     rcx
                stc              ; Return error in carry flag
                ret

ten             qword   10

strtou128       endp
```

Listing 9-18: Extended-precision unsigned decimal input

9.2.5   Conversion of Extended-Precision Signed Decimal String to Integer

Once you have an unsigned decimal input routine, writing a signed decimal input routine is easy, as described by the following algorithm:

1. Consume any delimiter characters at the beginning of the input stream.

2. If the next input character is a minus sign, consume this character and set a flag noting that the number is negative; else just drop down to step 3.

3. Call the unsigned decimal input routine to convert the rest of the string to an integer.

4. Check the return result to make sure its HO bit is clear. Raise a value out of range exception if the HO bit of the result is set.

5. If the code encountered a minus sign in step 2, negate the result.

I'll leave the actual code implementation as a programming exercise for you.

9.2.6   *Conversion of Real String to Floating-Point*

Converting a string of characters representing a floating-point number to the 80-bit real10 format is slightly easier than the real10-to-string conversion appearing earlier in this chapter. Because decimal conversion (with no exponent) is a subset of the more general scientific notation conversion, if you can handle scientific notation, you get decimal conversion for free. Beyond that, the basic algorithm is to convert the mantissa characters to a packed BCD form (so the function can use the fbld instruction to do the string-to-numeric conversion) and then read the (optional) exponent and adjust the real10 exponent accordingly. The algorithm to do the conversion is the following:

1. Begin by stripping away any leading space or tab characters (and any other delimiters).

2. Check for a leading plus (+) or minus (-) sign character. Skip it if one is present. Set a sign flag to true if the number is negative (false if non-negative).

3. Initialize an exponent value to −18. The algorithm will create a left-justified packed BCD value from the mantissa digits in the string to provide to the fbld instruction, and left-justified packed BCD values are always greater than or equal to 10^{18}. Initializing the exponent to −18 accounts for this.

4. Initialize a significant-digit-counter variable that counts the number of significant digits processed thus far to 18.

5. If the number begins with any leading zeros, skip over them (do not change the exponent or significant digit counters for leading zeros to the left of the decimal point).

6. If the scan encounters a decimal point after processing any leading zeros, go to step 11; else fall through to step 7.

7. For each nonzero digit to the left of the decimal point, if the significant digit counter is not zero, insert the nonzero digit into a "digit string" array at the position specified by the significant digit counter (minus 1).[5] Note that this will insert the characters into the string in a reversed position.

---

5. If the significant digit counter is zero, the algorithm has already processed 18 significant digits and will ignore any additional digits as the real10 format cannot represent more than 18 significant digits.

8. For each digit to the left of the decimal point, increment the exponent value (originally initialized to −18) by 1.

9. If the significant digit counter is not zero, decrement the significant digit counter (this will also provide the index into the digit string array).

10. If the first nondigit encountered is not a decimal point, skip to step 14.

11. Skip over the decimal point character.

12. For each digit encountered to the right of the decimal point, continue adding the digits (in reverse order) to the digit string array as long as the significant digit counter is not zero. If the significant digit counter is greater than zero, decrement it. Also, decrement the exponent value.

13. *If the algorithm hasn't encountered at least one decimal digit by this point, report an illegal character exception and return.*

14. If the current character is not e or E, then go to step 20.[6] Otherwise, skip over the e or E character and continue with step 15.

15. If the next character is + or -, skip over it. Set a flag to true if the sign character is -, and set it to false otherwise (note that this exponent sign flag is different from the mantissa sign flag set earlier in this algorithm).

16. If the next character is not a decimal digit, report an error.

17. Convert the string of digits (starting with the current decimal digit character) to an integer.

18. Add the converted integer to the exponent value (which was initialized to −18 at the start of this algorithm).

19. If the exponent value is outside the range −4930 to +4930, report an out-of-range exception.

20. Convert the digit string array of characters to an 18-digit (9-byte) packed BCD value by stripping the HO 4 bits of each character, merging pairs of characters into a single byte (by shifting the odd-indexed byte to the left 4 bits and logically ORing with the even-indexed byte of each pair), and then setting the HO (10th) byte to 0.

21. Convert the packed BCD value to a real10 value (using the fbld instruction).

22. Take the absolute value of the exponent (though preserve the sign of the exponent). This value will be 13 bits or less (4096 has bit 12 set, so 4930 or less will have some combination of bits 0 to 13 set to 1, with all other bits 0).

23. If the exponent was positive, then for each set bit in the exponent, multiply the current real10 value by 10 raised to the power specified by that bit. For example, if bits 12, 10, and 1 are set, multiply the real10 value by 10^{4096}, 10^{1024}, and 10^2.

---

6. Some string formats also allow d or D to denote a double-precision value. The choice is up to you whether you wish to also allow this (and possibly check the range of the value if the algorithm encounters e or E versus d or D).

24. If the exponent was negative, then for each set bit in the exponent, divide the current real10 value by 10 raised to the power specified by that bit. For example, if bits 12, 10, and 1 are set, divide the real10 value by 10^{4096}, 10^{1024}, and 10^2.

25. If the mantissa is negative (the first sign flag set at the beginning of the algorithm), then negate the floating-point number.

Listing 9-19 provides an implementation of this algorithm.

```
; Listing 9-19

; Real string-to-floating-point conversion.

        option  casemap:none

false       =       0
true        =       1
tab         =       9
nl          =       10

            .const
ttlStr      byte    "Listing 9-19", 0
fmtStr1     byte    "strToR10: str='%s', value=%e", nl, 0

fStr1a      byte    "1.234e56",0
fStr1b      byte    "-1.234e56",0
fStr1c      byte    "1.234e-56",0
fStr1d      byte    "-1.234e-56",0
fStr2a      byte    "1.23",0
fStr2b      byte    "-1.23",0
fStr3a      byte    "1",0
fStr3b      byte    "-1",0
fStr4a      byte    "0.1",0
fStr4b      byte    "-0.1",0
fStr4c      byte    "0000000.1",0
fStr4d      byte    "-0000000.1",0
fStr4e      byte    "0.1000000",0
fStr4f      byte    "-0.1000000",0
fStr4g      byte    "0.0000001",0
fStr4h      byte    "-0.0000001",0
fStr4i      byte    ".1",0
fStr4j      byte    "-.1",0

values      qword   fStr1a, fStr1b, fStr1c, fStr1d,
                    fStr2a, fStr2b,
                    fStr3a, fStr3b,
                    fStr4a, fStr4b, fStr4c, fStr4d,
                    fStr4e, fStr4f, fStr4g, fStr4h,
                    fStr4i, fStr4j,
                    0

            align   4
PotTbl      real10  1.0e+4096,
                    1.0e+2048,
```

```
                    1.0e+1024,
                    1.0e+512,
                    1.0e+256,
                    1.0e+128,
                    1.0e+64,
                    1.0e+32,
                    1.0e+16,
                    1.0e+8,
                    1.0e+4,
                    1.0e+2,
                    1.0e+1,
                    1.0e+0

            .data
r8Val       real8   ?

            .code
            externdef printf:proc

; Return program title to C++ program:

            public  getTitle
getTitle    proc
            lea     rax, ttlStr
            ret
getTitle    endp


;*******************************************************

; strToR10 - RSI points at a string of characters that represent a
;            floating-point value. This routine converts that string
;            to the corresponding FP value and leaves the result on
;            the top of the FPU stack. On return, ESI points at the
;            first character this routine couldn't convert.

; Like the other ATOx routines, this routine raises an
; exception if there is a conversion error or if ESI
; contains NULL.

;*******************************************************

strToR10    proc

sign        equ     <cl>
expSign     equ     <ch>

DigitStr    equ     <[rbp - 20]>
BCDValue    equ     <[rbp - 30]>
rsiSave     equ     <[rbp - 40]>

            push    rbp
            mov     rbp, rsp
            sub     rsp, 40

            push    rbx
```

```
            push    rcx
            push    rdx
            push    r8
            push    rax

; Verify that RSI is not NULL.

            test    rsi, rsi
            jz      refNULL

; Zero out the DigitStr and BCDValue arrays.

            xor     rax, rax
            mov     qword ptr DigitStr, rax
            mov     qword ptr DigitStr[8], rax
            mov     dword ptr DigitStr[16], eax

            mov     qword ptr BCDValue, rax
            mov     word ptr BCDValue[8], ax

; Skip over any leading space or tab characters in the sequence.

            dec     rsi
whileDelimLoop:
            inc     rsi
            mov     al, [rsi]
            cmp     al, ' '
            je      whileDelimLoop
            cmp     al, tab
            je      whileDelimLoop

; Check for "+" or "-".

            cmp     al, '-'
            sete    sign
            je      doNextChar
            cmp     al, '+'
            jne     notPlus
doNextChar: inc     rsi             ; Skip the "+" or "-"
            mov     al, [rsi]

notPlus:

; Initialize EDX with -18 since we have to account
; for BCD conversion (which generates a number * 10^18 by
; default). EDX holds the value's decimal exponent.

            mov     rdx, -18

; Initialize EBX with 18, which is the number of significant
; digits left to process and it is also the index into the
; DigitStr array.
```

```
            mov     ebx, 18          ; Zero-extends!

; At this point, we're beyond any leading sign character.
; Therefore, the next character must be a decimal digit
; or a decimal point.

            mov     rsiSave, rsi     ; Save to look ahead 1 digit
            cmp     al, '.'
            jne     notPeriod

; If the first character is a decimal point, then the
; second character needs to be a decimal digit.

            inc     rsi
            mov     al, [rsi]

notPeriod:
            cmp     al, '0'
            jb      convError
            cmp     al, '9'
            ja      convError
            mov     rsi, rsiSave     ; Go back to orig char
            mov     al, [rsi]
            jmp     testWhlAL0

; Eliminate any leading zeros (they do not affect the value or
; the number of significant digits).

whileAL0:    inc     rsi
             mov     al, [rsi]
testWhlAL0:  cmp     al, '0'
             jc      whileAL0

; If we're looking at a decimal point, we need to get rid of the
; zeros immediately after the decimal point since they don't
; count as significant digits.  Unlike zeros before the decimal
; point, however, these zeros do affect the number's value as
; we must decrement the current exponent for each such zero.

            cmp     al, '.'
            jne     testDigit

            inc     edx              ; Counteract dec below
repeatUntilALnot0:
            dec     edx
            inc     rsi
            mov     al, [rsi]
            cmp     al, '0'
            je      repeatUntilALnot0
            jmp     testDigit2

; If we didn't encounter a decimal point after removing leading
; zeros, then we've got a sequence of digits before a decimal
; point.  Process those digits here.
```

```
        ; Each digit to the left of the decimal point increases
        ; the number by an additional power of 10.  Deal with
        ; that here.

whileADigit:
                inc     edx

; Save all the significant digits, but ignore any digits
; beyond the 18th digit.

                test    ebx, ebx
                jz      Beyond18

                mov     DigitStr[rbx * 1], al
                dec     ebx

Beyond18:       inc     rsi
                mov     al, [rsi]

testDigit:
                sub     al, '0'
                cmp     al, 10
                jb      whileADigit

                cmp     al, '.'-'0'
                jne     testDigit2

                inc     rsi             ; Skip over decimal point
                mov     al, [rsi]
                jmp     testDigit2

; Okay, process any digits to the right of the decimal point.

whileDigit2:
                test    ebx, ebx
                jz      Beyond18_2

                mov     DigitStr[rbx * 1], al
                dec     ebx

Beyond18_2:     inc     rsi
                mov     al, [rsi]

testDigit2:     sub     al, '0'
                cmp     al, 10
                jb      whileDigit2

; At this point, we've finished processing the mantissa.
; Now see if there is an exponent we need to deal with.

                mov     al, [rsi]
                cmp     al, 'E'
                je      hasExponent
                cmp     al, 'e'
                jne     noExponent
```

```
hasExponent:
            inc     rsi
            mov     al, [rsi]        ; Skip the "E".
            cmp     al, '-'
            sete    expSign
            je      doNextChar_2
            cmp     al, '+'
            jne     getExponent;

doNextChar_2:
            inc     rsi              ; Skip "+" or "-"
            mov     al, [rsi]

; Okay, we're past the "E" and the optional sign at this
; point.  We must have at least one decimal digit.

getExponent:
            sub     al, '0'
            cmp     al, 10
            jae     convError

            xor     ebx, ebx         ; Compute exponent value in EBX
ExpLoop:    movzx   eax, byte ptr [rsi] ; Zero-extends to RAX!
            sub     al, '0'
            cmp     al, 10
            jae     ExpDone

            imul    ebx, 10
            add     ebx, eax
            inc     rsi
            jmp     ExpLoop

; If the exponent was negative, negate our computed result.

ExpDone:
            cmp     expSign, false
            je      noNegExp

            neg     ebx

noNegExp:

; Add in the BCD adjustment (remember, values in DigitStr, when
; loaded into the FPU, are multiplied by 10^18 by default.
; The value in EDX adjusts for this).

            add     edx, ebx

noExponent:

; Verify that the exponent is between -4930 and +4930 (which
; is the maximum dynamic range for an 80-bit FP value).

            cmp     edx, 4930
            jg      voor             ; Value out of range
```

```
              cmp      edx, -4930
              jl       voor

; Now convert the DigitStr variable (unpacked BCD) to a packed
; BCD value.

              mov      r8, 8
for9:         mov      al, DigitStr[r8 * 2 + 2]
              shl      al, 4
              or       al, DigitStr[r8 * 2 + 1]
              mov      BCDValue[r8 * 1], al

              dec      r8
              jns      for9

              fbld     tbyte ptr BCDValue

; Okay, we've got the mantissa into the FPU.  Now multiply the
; mantissa by 10 raised to the value of the computed exponent
; (currently in EDX).

; This code uses power of 10 tables to help make the
; computation a little more accurate.

; We want to determine which power of 10 is just less than the
; value of our exponent.  The powers of 10 we are checking are
; 10**4096, 10**2048, 10**1024, 10**512, and so on. A slick way to
; do this check is by shifting the bits in the exponent
; to the left.  Bit #12 is the 4096 bit.  So if this bit is set,
; our exponent is >= 10**4096.  If not, check the next bit down
; to see if our exponent >= 10**2048, etc.

              mov      ebx, -10 ; Initial index into power of 10 table
              test     edx, edx
              jns      positiveExponent

; Handle negative exponents here.

              neg      edx
              shl      edx, 19 ; Bits 0 to 12 -> 19 to 31
              lea      r8, PotTbl

whileEDXne0:
              add      ebx, 10
              shl      edx, 1
              jnc      testEDX0

              fld      real10 ptr [r8][rbx * 1]
              fdivp

testEDX0:     test     edx, edx
              jnz      whileEDXne0
              jmp      doMantissaSign
```

```
; Handle positive exponents here.

positiveExponent:
            lea     r8, PotTbl
            shl     edx, 19 ; Bits 0 to 12 -> 19 to 31
            jmp     testEDX0_2

whileEDXne0_2:
            add     ebx, 10
            shl     edx, 1
            jnc     testEDX0_2

            fld     real10 ptr [r8][rbx * 1]
            fmulp

testEDX0_2: test    edx, edx
            jnz     whileEDXne0_2

; If the mantissa was negative, negate the result down here.

doMantissaSign:
            cmp     sign, false
            je      mantNotNegative

            fchs

mantNotNegative:
            clc                     ; Indicate success
            jmp     Exit

refNULL:    mov     rax, -3
            jmp     ErrorExit

convError:  mov     rax, -2
            jmp     ErrorExit

voor:       mov     rax, -1         ; Value out of range
            jmp     ErrorExit

illChar:    mov     rax, -4

ErrorExit:  stc                     ; Indicate failure
            mov     [rsp], rax      ; Save error code
Exit:       pop     rax
            pop     r8
            pop     rdx
            pop     rcx
            pop     rbx
            leave
            ret

strToR10    endp
```

```
; Here is the "asmMain" function.

            public  asmMain
asmMain     proc
            push    rbx
            push    rsi
            push    rbp
            mov     rbp, rsp
            sub     rsp, 64         ; Shadow storage

; Test floating-point conversion:

            lea     rbx, values
ValuesLp:   cmp     qword ptr [rbx], 0
            je      allDone

            mov     rsi, [rbx]
            call    strToR10
            fstp    r8Val

            lea     rcx, fmtStr1
            mov     rdx, [rbx]
            mov     r8, qword ptr r8Val
            call    printf
            add     rbx, 8
            jmp     ValuesLp

allDone:    leave
            pop     rsi
            pop     rbx
            ret     ; Returns to caller
asmMain     endp
            end
```

Listing 9-19: A strToR10 function

Here's the build command and sample output for Listing 9-19.

```
C:\>build listing9-19

C:\>echo off
 Assembling: listing9-19.asm
c.cpp

C:\>listing9-19
Calling Listing 9-19:
strToR10: str='1.234e56', value=1.234000e+56
strToR10: str='-1.234e56', value=-1.234000e+56
strToR10: str='1.234e-56', value=1.234000e-56
strToR10: str='-1.234e-56', value=-1.234000e-56
strToR10: str='1.23', value=1.230000e+00
strToR10: str='-1.23', value=-1.230000e+00
```

```
strToR10: str='1', value=1.000000e+00
strToR10: str='-1', value=-1.000000e+00
strToR10: str='0.1', value=1.000000e-01
strToR10: str='-0.1', value=-1.000000e-01
strToR10: str='0000000.1', value=1.000000e-01
strToR10: str='-0000000.1', value=-1.000000e-01
strToR10: str='0.1000000', value=1.000000e-01
strToR10: str='-0.1000000', value=-1.000000e-01
strToR10: str='0.0000001', value=1.000000e-07
strToR10: str='-0.0000001', value=-1.000000e-07
strToR10: str='.1', value=1.000000e-01
strToR10: str='-.1', value=-1.000000e-01
Listing 9-19 terminated
```

9.3   For More Information

Donald Knuth's *The Art of Computer Programming*, Volume 2: *Seminumerical Algorithms* (Addison-Wesley Professional, 1997) contains a lot of useful information about decimal arithmetic and extended-precision arithmetic, though that text is generic and doesn't describe how to do this in x86 assembly language.

9.4   Test Yourself

1. What is the code that will convert an 8-bit hexadecimal value in AL into two hexadecimal digits (in AH and AL)?

2. How many hexadecimal digits will dToStr produce?

3. Explain how to use qToStr to write a 128-bit hexadecimal output routine.

4. What instruction should you use to produce the fastest 64-bit decimal-to-string conversion function?

5. How do you write a signed decimal-to-string conversion if you're given a function that does an unsigned decimal-to-string conversion?

6. What are the parameters for the utoStrSize function?

7. What string will uSizeToStr produce if the number requires more print positions than specified by the minDigits parameter?

8. What are the parameters for the r10ToStr function?

9. What string will r10ToStr produce if the output won't fit in the string size specified by the fWidth argument?

10. What are the arguments to the e10ToStr function?

11. What is a delimiter character?

12. What are two possible errors that could occur during a string-to-numeric conversion?

10

TABLE LOOKUPS

This chapter discusses how to speed up or reduce the complexity of computations by using table lookups. Back in the early days of x86 programming, replacing expensive computations with table lookups was a common way to improve program performance. Today, memory speeds in modern systems limit performance gains that can be obtained by using table lookups. However, for complex calculations, this is still a viable technique for writing high-performance code. This chapter demonstrates the space/speed trade-offs when using table lookups.

10.1 Tables

To an assembly language programmer, a *table* is an array containing initialized values that do not change once created. In assembly language, you can use tables for a variety of purposes: computing functions, controlling program flow, or simply looking things up. In general, tables provide a fast mechanism for performing an operation at the expense of space in your program (the extra space holds the tabular data). In this section, we'll explore some of the many possible uses of tables in an assembly language program.

NOTE *Because tables typically contain initialized data that does not change during program execution, the* .const *section is a good place to put your table objects.*

10.1.1 Function Computation via Table Lookup

A simple-looking high-level-language arithmetic expression can be equivalent to a considerable amount of x86-64 assembly language code and, therefore, could be expensive to compute. Assembly language programmers often precompute many values and use a table lookup of those values to speed up their programs. This has the advantage of being easier, and it's often more efficient as well.

Consider the following Pascal statement:

```
if (character >= 'a') and (character <= 'z') then
    character := chr(ord(character) - 32);
```

This Pascal if statement converts the character variable's value from lowercase to uppercase if character is in the range a to z. The MASM code that does the same thing requires a total of seven machine instructions, as follows:

```
        mov al, character
        cmp al, 'a'
        jb  notLower
        cmp al, 'z'
        ja  notLower

        and al, 5fh  ; Same as sub(32, al) in this code
        mov character, al
notLower:
```

Using a table lookup, however, allows you to reduce this sequence to just four instructions:

```
mov    al, character
lea    rbx, CnvrtLower
xlat
mov    character, al
```

The xlat, or translate, instruction does the following:

```
mov al, [rbx + al * 1]
```

This instruction uses the current value of the AL register as an index into the array whose base address is found in RBX. It fetches the byte at that index in the array and copies that byte into the AL register. Intel calls this instruction *translate* because programmers typically use it to translate characters from one form to another by using a lookup table, exactly the way we are using it here.

In the previous example, CnvrtLower is a 256-byte table that contains the values 0 to 60h at indices 0 to 60h, 41h to 5Ah at indices 61h to 7Ah, and 7Bh to 0FFh at indices 7Bh to 0FFh. Therefore, if AL contains a value in the range 0 to 60h or 7Ah to 0FFh, the xlat instruction returns the same value, effectively leaving AL unchanged. However, if AL contains a value in the range 61h to 7Ah (the ASCII codes for a to z), then the xlat instruction replaces the value in AL with a value in the range 41h to 5Ah (the ASCII codes for A to Z), thereby converting lowercase to uppercase.

As the complexity of a function increases, the performance benefits of the table-lookup method increase dramatically. While you would almost never use a lookup table to convert lowercase to uppercase, consider what happens if you want to swap cases; for example, via computation:

```
        mov al, character
        cmp al, 'a'
        jb  notLower
        cmp al, 'z'
        ja  allDone

        and al, 5fh
        jmp allDone

notLower:
        cmp al, 'A'
        jb  allDone
        cmp al, 'Z'
        ja  allDone

        or  al, 20h
allDone:
        mov character, al
```

This code has 13 machine instructions.

The table-lookup code to compute this same function is as follows:

```
mov    al, character
lea    rbx, SwapUL
xlat
mov    character, al
```

As you can see, when using a table lookup to compute a function, only the table changes; the code remains the same.

10.1.1.1 Function Domains and Range

Functions computed via table lookup have a limited *domain* (the set of possible input values they accept), because each element in the domain of a function requires an entry in the lookup table. For example, our previous uppercase/lowercase conversion functions have the 256-character extended ASCII character set as their domain. A function such as sin or cos accepts the (infinite) set of real numbers as possible input values. You won't find it very practical to implement a function via table lookup whose domain is the set of real numbers, because you must limit the domain to a small set.

Most lookup tables are quite small, usually 10 to 256 entries. Rarely do lookup tables grow beyond 1000 entries. Most programmers don't have the patience to create (and verify the correctness) of a 1000-entry table (though see "Generating Tables" on page 590 for a discussion of generating tables programmatically).

Another limitation of functions based on lookup tables is that the elements in the domain must be fairly contiguous. Table lookups use the input value to a function as an index into the table, and return the value at that entry in the table. A function that accepts values 0, 100, 1000, and 10,000 would require 10,001 different elements in the lookup table because of the range of input values. Therefore, you cannot efficiently create such a function via a table lookup. Throughout this section on tables, we'll assume that the domain of the function is a fairly contiguous set of values.

The *range* of a function is the set of possible output values it produces. From the perspective of a table lookup, a function's range determines the size of each table entry. For example, if a function's range is the integer values 0 through 255, then each table entry requires a single byte; if the range is 0 through 65,535, each table entry requires 2 bytes, and so on.

The best functions you can implement via table lookups are those whose domain and range are always 0 to 255 (or a subset of this range). Any such function can be computed using the same two instructions: lea rbx, table and xlat. The only thing that ever changes is the lookup table. The uppercase/lowercase conversion routines presented earlier are good examples of such a function.

You cannot (conveniently) use the xlat instruction to compute a function value once the range or domain of the function takes on values outside 0 to 255. There are three situations to consider:

- The domain is outside 0 to 255, but the range is within 0 to 255.
- The domain is inside 0 to 255, but the range is outside 0 to 255.
- Both the domain and range of the function take on values outside 0 to 255.

We will consider these cases in the following sections.

10.1.1.2 Domain Outside 0 to 255, Range Within 0 to 255

If the domain of a function is outside 0 to 255, but the range of the function falls within this set of values, our lookup table will require more than 256 entries, but we can represent each entry with a single byte. Therefore, the lookup table can be an array of bytes. Other than those lookups that can use the xlat instruction, functions falling into this class are the most efficient. The following Pascal function invocation

```
B := Func(X);
```

where Func is

```
function Func(X:dword):byte;
```

is easily converted to the following MASM code:

```
mov edx, X      ; Zero-extends into RDX!
lea rbx, FuncTable
mov al, [rbx][rdx * 1]
mov B, al
```

This code loads the function parameter into RDX, uses this value (in the range 0 to ??) as an index into the FuncTable table, fetches the byte at that location, and stores the result into B. Obviously, the table must contain a valid entry for each possible value of X. For example, suppose you wanted to map a cursor position on an 80×25 text-based video display in the range 0 to 1999 (there are 2000 character positions on an 80×25 video display) to its X (0 to 79) or Y (0 to 24) coordinate on the screen. You could compute the X coordinate via the function

```
X = Posn % 80;
```

and the Y coordinate with the formula

```
Y = Posn / 80;
```

(where Posn is the cursor position on the screen). This can be computed using this x86-64 code:

```
mov ax, Posn
mov cl, 80
div cl

; X is now in AH, Y is now in AL.
```

However, the div instruction on the x86-64 is very slow. If you need to do this computation for every character you write to the screen, you will seriously degrade the speed of your video-display code. The following code, which realizes these two functions via table lookup, may improve the performance of your code considerably:

```
lea    rbx, yCoord
movzx ecx, Posn          ; Use a plain mov instr if Posn
mov    al, [rbx][rcx * 1] ; is uns32 rather than an
lea    rbx, xCoord        ; uns16 value
mov    ah, [rbx][rcx * 1]
```

Keep in mind that loading a value into ECX automatically zero-extends that value into RCX. Therefore, the movzx instruction in this code sequence actually zero-extends Posn into RCX, not just ECX.

If you're willing to live with the limitations of the LARGEADDRESSAWARE:NO linking option (see "Large Address Unaware Applications" in Chapter 3), you can simplify this code somewhat:

```
movzx ecx, Posn          ; Use a plain mov instr if Posn
mov   al, yCoord[rcx * 1] ; is uns32 rather than an
mov   ah, xCoord[rcx * 1] ; uns16 value
```

10.1.1.3 Domain in 0 to 255 and Range Outside 0 to 255, or Both Outside 0 to 255

If the domain of a function is within 0 to 255, but the range is outside this set, the lookup table will contain 256 or fewer entries, but each entry will require 2 or more bytes. If both the range and domains of the function are outside 0 to 255, each entry will require 2 or more bytes and the table will contain more than 256 entries.

Recall from Chapter 4 that the formula for indexing into a single-dimensional array (of which a table is a special case) is as follows:

```
element_address = Base + index * element_size
```

If elements in the range of the function require 2 bytes, you must multiply the index by 2 before indexing into the table. Likewise, if each entry requires 3, 4, or more bytes, the index must be multiplied by the size of each table entry before being used as an index into the table. For example, suppose you have a function, F(x), defined by the following (pseudo) Pascal declaration:

```
function F(x:dword):word;
```

You can create this function by using the following x86-64 code (and, of course, the appropriate table named F):

```
movzx ebx, x
lea   r8, F
mov   ax, [r8][rbx * 2]
```

If you can live with the limitations of LARGEADDRESSAWARE:NO, you can reduce this as follows:

```
movzx ebx, x
mov   ax, F[rbx * 2]
```

Any function whose domain is small and mostly contiguous is a good candidate for computation via table lookup. In some cases, noncontiguous domains are acceptable as well, as long as the domain can be coerced into an appropriate set of values (an example you've already seen is processing switch statement expressions). Such operations, called *conditioning*, are the subject of the next section.

10.1.1.4 Domain Conditioning

Domain conditioning is taking a set of values in the domain of a function and massaging them so that they are more acceptable as inputs to that function. Consider the following function:

sin x = sin x|(x∈[-2π,2π])

This says that the (computer) function sin(x) is equivalent to the (mathematical) function sin *x* where

−2π <= x <= 2π

As we know, sine is a circular function, which will accept any real-value input. The formula used to compute sine, however, accepts only a small set of these values.

This range limitation doesn't present any real problems; by simply computing sin(x mod (2 * pi)), we can compute the sine of any input value. Modifying an input value so that we can easily compute a function is called *conditioning the input*. In the preceding example, we computed *x* mod 2 * pi and used the result as the input to the sin function. This truncates *x* to the domain sin needs without affecting the result. We can apply input conditioning to table lookups as well. In fact, scaling the index to handle word entries is a form of input conditioning. Consider the following Pascal function:

```
function val(x:word):word; begin
    case x of
        0: val := 1;
        1: val := 1;
        2: val := 4;
        3: val := 27;
        4: val := 256;
        otherwise val := 0;
    end;
end;
```

This function computes a value for *x* in the range 0 to 4 and returns 0 if *x* is outside this range. Since *x* can take on 65,536 different values (being a 16-bit word), creating a table containing 65,536 words where only the first five entries are nonzero seems to be quite wasteful. However, we can still compute this function by using a table lookup if we use input conditioning. The following assembly language code presents this principle:

```
        mov    ax, 0       ; AX = 0, assume x > 4
        movzx  ebx, x      ; Note that HO bits of RBX must be 0!
        lea    r8, val
        cmp    bx, 4
        ja     defaultResult
```

```
        mov    ax, [r8][rbx * 2]

defaultResult:
```

This code checks to see if *x* is outside the range 0 to 4. If so, it manually sets AX to 0; otherwise, it looks up the function value through the val table. With input conditioning, you can implement several functions that would otherwise be impractical to do via table lookup.

10.1.2 *Generating Tables*

One big problem with using table lookups is creating the table in the first place. This is particularly true if the table has many entries. Figuring out the data to place in the table, then laboriously entering the data and, finally, checking that data to make sure it is valid, is very time-consuming and boring. For many tables, there is no way around this process. For other tables, there is a better way: using the computer to generate the table for you.

An example is probably the best way to describe this. Consider the following modification to the sine function:

$$\sin(x) \times r = \langle \; \frac{(r \times (1000 \times \sin x))}{1000} \; \Big| \; [\; x \in 0,359]\rangle$$

This states that *x* is an integer in the range 0 to 359 and *r* must be an integer. The computer can easily compute this with the following code:

```
Thousand dword 1000

    .
    .
    .

lea    r8, Sines
movzx  ebx, x
mov    eax, [r8][rbx * 2] ; Get sin(x) * 1000
imul   r                  ; Note that this extends EAX into EDX
idiv   Thousand           ; Compute (r *(sin(x) * 1000)) / 1000
```

(This provides the usual improvement if you can live with the limitations of LARGEADDRESSAWARE:NO.)

Note that integer multiplication and division are not associative. You cannot remove the multiplication by 1000 and the division by 1000 because they appear to cancel each other out. Furthermore, this code must compute this function in exactly this order.

All that we need to complete this function is Sines, a table containing 360 different values corresponding to the sine of the angle (in degrees) times 1000. The C/C++ program in Listing 10-1 generates this table for you.

```
// Listing 10-1: GenerateSines

// A C program that generates a table of sine values for
// an assembly language lookup table.
```

```c
#include <stdlib.h>
#include <stdio.h>
#include <math.h>

int main(int argc, char **argv)
{
    FILE *outFile;
    int angle;
    int r;

    // Open the file:

    outFile = fopen("sines.asm", "w");

    // Emit the initial part of the declaration to
    // the output file:

    fprintf
    (
        outFile,
        "Sines:"  // sin(0) = 0
    );

    // Emit the sines table:

    for(angle = 0; angle <= 359; ++angle)
    {
        // Convert angle in degrees to an angle in
        // radians using:

        // radians = angle * 2.0 * pi / 360.0;

        // Multiply by 1000 and store the rounded
        // result into the integer variable r.

        double theSine =
            sin
            (
                angle * 2.0 *
                3.14159265358979323846 /
                360.0
            );
        r = (int) (theSine * 1000.0);

        // Write out the integers eight per line to the
        // source file.
        // Note: If (angle AND %111) is 0, then angle
        // is divisible by 8 and we should output a
        // newline first.

        if((angle & 7) == 0)
        {
            fprintf(outFile, "\n\tword\t");
        }
        fprintf(outFile, "%5d", r);
```

```
        if ((angle & 7) != 7)
        {
            fprintf(outFile, ",");
        }

    } // endfor
    fprintf(outFile, "\n");

    fclose(outFile);
    return 0;

} // end main
```

Listing 10-1: A C program that generates a table of sines

This program produces the following output (truncated for brevity):

```
Sines:
    word      0,   17,   34,   52,   69,   87,  104,  121
    word    139,  156,  173,  190,  207,  224,  241,  258
    word    275,  292,  309,  325,  342,  358,  374,  390
    word    406,  422,  438,  453,  469,  484,  499,  515
    word    529,  544,  559,  573,  587,  601,  615,  629
    word    642,  656,  669,  681,  694,  707,  719,  731
    word    743,  754,  766,  777,  788,  798,  809,  819
    word    829,  838,  848,  857,  866,  874,  882,  891
    word    898,  906,  913,  920,  927,  933,  939,  945
    word    951,  956,  961,  965,  970,  974,  978,  981
    word    984,  987,  990,  992,  994,  996,  997,  998
    word    999,  999, 1000,  999,  999,  998,  997,  996
    word    994,  992,  990,  987,  984,  981,  978,  974
    word    970,  965,  961,  956,  951,  945,  939,  933
    word    927,  920,  913,  906,  898,  891,  882,  874
                               .
                               .
                               .
    word   -898, -891, -882, -874, -866, -857, -848, -838
    word   -829, -819, -809, -798, -788, -777, -766, -754
    word   -743, -731, -719, -707, -694, -681, -669, -656
    word   -642, -629, -615, -601, -587, -573, -559, -544
    word   -529, -515, -500, -484, -469, -453, -438, -422
    word   -406, -390, -374, -358, -342, -325, -309, -292
    word   -275, -258, -241, -224, -207, -190, -173, -156
    word   -139, -121, -104,  -87,  -69,  -52,  -34,  -17
```

Obviously, it's much easier to write the C program that generated this data than to enter (and verify) this data by hand. Of course, you don't even have to write the table-generation program in C (or Pascal/Delphi, Java, C#, Swift, or another high-level language). Because the program will execute only once, the performance of the table-generation program is not an issue.

Once you run your table-generation program, all that remains to be done is to cut and paste the table from the file (*sines.asm* in this example) into the program that will actually use the table.

10.1.3 Table-Lookup Performance

In the early days of PCs, table lookups were a preferred way to do high-performance computations. Today, it is not uncommon for a CPU to be 10 to 100 times faster than main memory. As a result, using a table lookup may not be faster than doing the same calculation with machine instructions. However, the on-chip CPU cache memory subsystems operate at near CPU speeds. Therefore, table lookups can be cost-effective if your table resides in cache memory on the CPU. This means that the way to get good performance using table lookups is to use small tables (because there's only so much room on the cache) and use tables whose entries you reference frequently (so the tables stay in the cache).

See *Write Great Code*, Volume 1 (No Starch Press, 2020) or the electronic version of *The Art of Assembly Language* at *https://www.randallhyde.com/* for details concerning the operation of cache memory and how you can optimize your use of cache memory.

10.2 For More Information

Donald Knuth's *The Art of Computer Programming*, Volume 3: *Searching and Sorting* (Addison-Wesley Professional, 1998) contains a lot of useful information about searching for data in tables. Searching for data is an alternative when a straight array access won't work in a given situation.

10.3 Test Yourself

1. What is the domain of a function?
2. What is the range of a function?
3. What does the xlat instruction do?
4. Which domain and range values allow you to use the xlat instruction?
5. Provide the code that implements the following functions (using pseudo-C prototypes and f as the table name):
   a. byte f(byte input)
   b. word f(byte input)
   c. byte f(word input)
   d. word f(word input)
6. What is domain conditioning?
7. Why might table lookups not be effective on modern processors?

11

SIMD INSTRUCTIONS

This chapter discusses the *vector instructions* on the x86-64. This special class of instructions provides parallel processing, traditionally known as *single-instruction, multiple-data (SIMD)* instructions because, quite literally, a single instruction operates on several pieces of data concurrently. As a result of this concurrency, SIMD instructions can often execute several times faster (in theory, as much as 32 to 64 times faster) than the comparable *single-instruction, single-data (SISD),* or *scalar,* instructions that compose the standard x86-64 instruction set.

The x86-64 actually provides three sets of vector instructions: the Multimedia Extensions (MMX) instruction set, the Streaming SIMD Extensions (SSE) instruction set, and the Advanced Vector Extensions (AVX) instruction set. This book does not consider the MMX instructions as they are obsolete (SSE equivalents exist for the MMX instructions).

The x86-64 vector instruction set (SSE/AVX) is almost as large as the scalar instruction set. A whole book could be written about SSE/AVX programming and algorithms. However, this is not that book; SIMD and parallel algorithms are an advanced subject beyond the scope of this book, so this chapter settles for introducing a fair number of SSE/AVX instructions and leaves it at that.

This chapter begins with some prerequisite information. First, it begins with a discussion of the x86-64 vector architecture and streaming data types. Then, it discusses how to detect the presence of various vector instructions (which are not present on all x86-64 CPUs) by using the cpuid instruction. Because most vector instructions require special memory alignment for data operands, this chapter also discusses MASM segments.

11.1 The SSE/AVX Architectures

Let's begin by taking a quick look at the SSE and AVX features in the x64-86 CPUs. The SSE and AVX instructions have several variants: the original SSE, plus SSE2, SSE3, SSE3, SSE4 (SSE4.1 and SSE4.2), AVX, AVX2 (AVX and AVX2 are sometimes called AVX-256), and AVX-512. SSE3 was introduced along with the Pentium 4F (Prescott) CPU, Intel's first 64-bit CPU. Therefore, you can assume that all Intel 64-bit CPUs support the SSE3 and earlier SIMD instructions.

The SSE/AVX architectures have three main generations:

- The SSE architecture, which (on 64-bit CPUs) provided sixteen 128-bit XMM registers supporting integer and floating-point data types
- The AVX/AVX2 architecture, which supported sixteen 256-bit YMM registers (also supporting integer and floating-point data types)
- The AVX-512 architecture, which supported up to thirty-two 512-bit ZMM registers

As a general rule, this chapter sticks to AVX2 and earlier instructions in its examples. Please see the Intel and AMD CPU manuals for a discussion of the additional instruction set extensions such as AVX-512. This chapter does not attempt to describe every SSE or AVX instruction. Most streaming instructions have very specialized purposes and aren't particularly useful in generic applications.

11.2 Streaming Data Types

The SSE and AVX programming models support two basic data types: scalars and vectors. *Scalars* hold one single- or double-precision floating-point value. *Vectors* hold multiple floating-point or integer values (between 2 and 32 values, depending on the scalar data type of byte, word, dword, qword, single precision, or double precision, and the register and memory size of 128 or 256 bits).

The XMM registers (XMM0 to XMM15) can hold a single 32-bit floating-point value (a scalar) or four single-precision floating-point values (a vector). The YMM registers (YMM0 to YMM15) can hold eight single-precision (32-bit) floating-point values (a vector); see Figure 11-1.

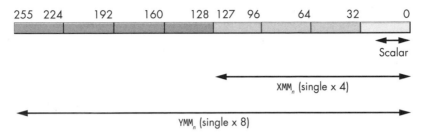

Figure 11-1: Packed and scalar single-precision floating-point data type

The XMM registers can hold a single double-precision scalar value or a vector containing a pair of double-precision values. The YMM registers can hold a vector containing four double-precision floating-point values, as shown in Figure 11-2.

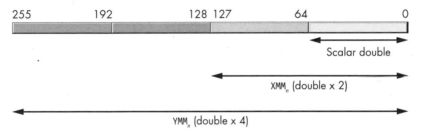

Figure 11-2: Packed and scalar double-precision floating-point type

The XMM registers can hold 16 byte values (YMM registers can hold 32 byte values), allowing the CPU to perform 16 (32) byte-sized computations with one instruction (Figure 11-3).

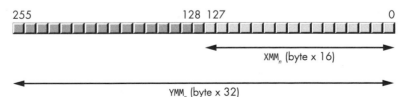

Figure 11-3: Packed byte data type

The XMM registers can hold eight word values (YMM registers can hold sixteen word values), allowing the CPU to perform eight (sixteen) 16-bit word-sized integer computations with one instruction (Figure 11-4).

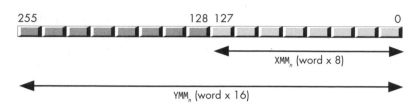

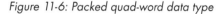

Figure 11-4: Packed word data type

The XMM registers can hold four dword values (YMM registers can hold eight dword values), allowing the CPU to perform four (eight) 32-bit dword-sized integer computations with one instruction (Figure 11-5).

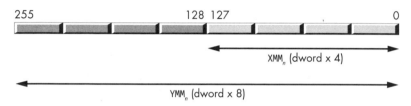

Figure 11-5: Packed double-word data type

The XMM registers can hold two qword values (YMM registers can hold four qword values), allowing the CPU to perform two (four) 64-bit qword computations with one instruction (Figure 11-6).

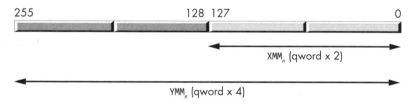

Figure 11-6: Packed quad-word data type

Intel's documentation calls the vector elements in an XMM and a YMM register *lanes*. For example, a 128-bit XMM register has 16 bytes. Bits 0 to 7 are lane 0, bits 8 to 15 are lane 1, bits 16 to 23 are lane 2, . . . , and bits 120 to 127 are lane 15. A 256-bit YMM register has 32 byte-sized lanes, and a 512-bit ZMM register has 64 byte-sized lanes.

Similarly, a 128-bit XMM register has eight word-sized lanes (lanes 0 to 7). A 256-bit YMM register has sixteen word-sized lanes (lanes 0 to 15). On AVX-512-capable CPUs, a ZMM register (512 bits) has thirty-two word-sized lanes, numbered 0 to 31.

An XMM register has four dword-sized lanes (lanes 0 to 3); it also has four single-precision (32-bit) floating-point lanes (also numbered 0 to 3). A YMM register has eight dword or single-precision lanes (lanes 0 to 7). An AVX2 ZMM register has sixteen dword or single-precision-sized lanes (numbers 0 to 15).

XMM registers support two qword-sized lanes (or two double-precision lanes), numbered 0 to 1. As expected, a YMM register has twice as many (four lanes, numbered 0 to 3), and an AVX2 ZMM register has four times as many lanes (0 to 7).

Several SSE/AVX instructions refer to various lanes within these registers. In particular, the shuffle and unpack instructions allow you to move data between lanes in SSE and AVX operands. See "The Shuffle and Unpack Instructions" on page 625 for examples of lane usage.

11.3   Using cpuid to Differentiate Instruction Sets

Intel introduced the 8086 (and shortly thereafter, the 8088) microprocessor in 1978. With almost every succeeding CPU generation, Intel added new instructions to the instruction set. Until this chapter, this book has used instructions that are generally available on all x86-64 CPUs (Intel and AMD). This chapter presents instructions that are available only on later-model x86-64 CPUs. To allow programmers to determine which CPU their applications were using so they could dynamically avoid using newer instructions on older processors, Intel introduced the cpuid instruction.

The cpuid instruction expects a single parameter (called a *leaf* function) passed in the EAX register. It returns various pieces of information about the CPU in different 32-bit registers based on the value passed in EAX. An application can test the return information to see if certain CPU features are available.

As Intel introduced new instructions, it changed the behavior of cpuid to reflect those changes. Specifically, Intel changed the range of values a program could legally pass in EAX to cpuid; this is known as the *highest function supported*. As a result, some 64-bit CPUs accept only values in the range 0h to 05h. The instructions this chapter discusses may require passing values in the range 0h to 07h. Therefore, the first thing you have to do when using cpuid is to verify that it accepts EAX = 07h as a valid parameter.

To determine the highest function supported, you load EAX with 0 or 8000_0000h and execute the cpuid instruction (all 64-bit CPUs support these two function values). The return value is the maximum you can pass to cpuid in EAX. The Intel and AMD documentation (also see *https://en.wikipedia.org/wiki/CPUID*) will list the values cpuid returns for various CPUs; for the purposes of this chapter, we need only verify that the highest function supported is 01h (which is true for all 64-bit CPUs) or 07h for certain instructions.

In addition to providing the highest function supported, the cpuid instruction with EAX = 0h (or 8000_0002h) also returns a 12-character vendor ID in the EBX, ECX, and EDX registers. For x86-64 chips, this will be either of the following:

- GenuineIntel (EBX is 756e_6547h, EDX is 4965_6e69h, and ECX is 6c65_746eh)
- AuthenticAMD (EBX is 6874_7541h, EDX is 6974_6E65h, and ECX is 444D_4163h)

To determine if the CPU can execute most SSE and AVX instructions, you must execute cpuid with EAX = 01h and test various bits placed in the ECX register. For a few of the more advanced features (advanced bit-manipulation functions and AVX2 instructions), you'll need to execute cpuid with EAX = 07h and check the results in the EBX register. The cpuid instruction (with EAX = 1) returns an interesting SSE/AVX feature flag in the following bits in ECX, as shown in Table 11-1; with EAX = 07h, it returns the bit manipulation or AVX2 flag in EBX, as shown in Table 11-2. If the bit is set, the CPU supports the specific instruction(s).

Table 11-1: Intel cpuid Feature Flags (EAX = 1)

Bit	ECX
0	SSE3 support
1	PCLMULQDQ support
9	SSSE3 support
19	CPU supports SSE4.1 instructions
20	CPU supports SSE4.2 instructions
28	Advanced Vector Extensions

Table 11-2: Intel cpuid Extended Feature Flags (EAX = 7, ECX = 0)

Bit	EBX
3	Bit Manipulation Instruction Set 1
5	Advanced Vector Extensions 2 (AVX2)
8	Bit Manipulation Instruction Set 2

Listing 11-1 queries the vendor ID and basic feature flags on a CPU.

```
; Listing 11-1

; CPUID Demonstration.

        option  casemap:none

nl          =       10

            .const
ttlStr      byte    "Listing 11-1", 0

            .data
maxFeature  dword   ?
VendorID    byte    14 dup (0)

            .code
            externdef printf:proc
```

```
        ; Return program title to C++ program:

                public  getTitle
getTitle        proc
                lea     rax, ttlStr
                ret
getTitle        endp

        ; Used for debugging:

print           proc
                push    rax
                push    rbx
                push    rcx
                push    rdx
                push    r8
                push    r9
                push    r10
                push    r11

                push    rbp
                mov     rbp, rsp
                sub     rsp, 40
                and     rsp, -16

                mov     rcx, [rbp + 72]   ; Return address
                call    printf

                mov     rcx, [rbp + 72]
                dec     rcx
skipToO:        inc     rcx
                cmp     byte ptr [rcx], 0
                jne     skipToO
                inc     rcx
                mov     [rbp + 72], rcx

                leave
                pop     r11
                pop     r10
                pop     r9
                pop     r8
                pop     rdx
                pop     rcx
                pop     rbx
                pop     rax
                ret
print           endp

        ; Here is the "asmMain" function.

                public  asmMain
asmMain         proc
                push    rbx
                push    rbp
                mov     rbp, rsp
```

```
            sub     rsp, 56             ; Shadow storage

            xor     eax, eax
            cpuid
            mov     maxFeature, eax
            mov     dword ptr VendorID, ebx
            mov     dword ptr VendorID[4], edx
            mov     dword ptr VendorID[8], ecx

            lea     rdx, VendorID
            mov     r8d, eax
            call    print
            byte    "CPUID(0): Vendor ID='%s',   "
            byte    "max feature=0%xh", nl, 0

; Leaf function 1 is available on all CPUs that support
; CPUID, no need to test for it.

            mov     eax, 1
            cpuid
            mov     r8d, edx
            mov     edx, ecx
            call    print
            byte    "cpuid(1), ECX=%08x, EDX=%08x", nl, 0

; Most likely, leaf function 7 is supported on all modern CPUs
; (for example, x86-64), but we'll test its availability nonetheless.

            cmp     maxFeature, 7
            jb      allDone

            mov     eax, 7
            xor     ecx, ecx
            cpuid
            mov     edx, ebx
            mov     r8d, ecx
            call    print
            byte    "cpuid(7), EBX=%08x, ECX=%08x", nl, 0

allDone:    leave
            pop     rbx
            ret             ; Returns to caller
asmMain     endp
            end
```

Listing 11-1: cpuid demonstration program

On an old MacBook Pro Retina with an Intel i7-3720QM CPU, running under Parallels, you get the following output:

```
C:\>build listing11-1

C:\>echo off
 Assembling: listing11-1.asm
c.cpp
```

```
C:\>listing11-1
Calling Listing 11-1:
CPUID(0): Vendor ID='GenuineIntel', max feature=0dh
cpuid(1), ECX=ffba2203, EDX=1f8bfbff
cpuid(7), EBX=00000281, ECX=00000000
Listing 11-1 terminated
```

This CPU supports SSE3 instructions (bit 0 of ECX is 1), SSE4.1 and SSE4.2 instructions (bits 19 and 20 of ECX are 1), and the AVX instructions (bit 28 is 1). Those, largely, are the instructions this chapter describes. Most modern CPUs will support these instructions (the i7-3720QM was released by Intel in 2012). The processor doesn't support some of the more interesting extended features on the Intel instruction set (the extended bit-manipulation instructions and the AVX2 instruction set). Programs using those instructions will not execute on this (ancient) MacBook Pro.

Running this on a more recent CPU (an iMac Pro 10-core Intel Xeon W-2150B) produces the following output:

```
C:\>listing11-1
Calling Listing 11-1:
CPUID(0): Vendor ID='GenuineIntel', max feature=016h
cpuid(1), ECX=fffa3203, EDX=1f8bfbff
cpuid(7), EBX=d09f47bb, ECX=00000000
Listing 11-1 terminated
```

As you can see, looking at the extended feature bits, the newer Xeon CPU does support these additional instructions. The code fragment in Listing 11-2 provides a quick modification to Listing 11-1 that tests for the availability of the BMI1 and BMI2 bit-manipulation instruction sets (insert the following code right before the allDone label in Listing 11-1).

```
; Test for extended bit manipulation instructions
; (BMI1 and BMI2):

            and     ebx, 108h       ; Test bits 3 and 8
            cmp     ebx, 108h       ; Both must be set
            jne     Unsupported
            call    print
            byte    "CPU supports BMI1 & BMI2", nl, 0
            jmp     allDone

Unsupported:
            call    print
            byte    "CPU does not support BMI1 & BMI2 "
            byte    "instructions", nl, 0

allDone:    leave
            pop     rbx
            ret             ; Returns to caller
asmMain     endp
```

Listing 11-2: Test for BMI1 and BMI2 instruction sets

Here's the build command and program output on the Intel
i7-3720QM CPU:

```
C:\>build listing11-2

C:\>echo off
 Assembling: listing11-2.asm
c.cpp

C:\>listing11-2
Calling Listing 11-2:
CPUID(0): Vendor ID='GenuineIntel', max feature=0dh
cpuid(1), ECX=ffba2203, EDX=1f8bfbff
cpuid(7), EBX=00000281, ECX=00000000
CPU does not support BMI1 & BMI2 instructions
Listing 11-2 terminated
```

Here's the same program running on the iMac Pro (Intel Xeon
W-2150B):

```
C:\>listing11-2
Calling Listing 11-2:
CPUID(0): Vendor ID='GenuineIntel', max feature=016h
cpuid(1), ECX=fffa3203, EDX=1f8bfbff
cpuid(7), EBX=d09f47bb, ECX=00000000
CPU supports BMI1 & BMI2
Listing 11-2 terminated
```

11.4 Full-Segment Syntax and Segment Alignment

As you will soon see, SSE and AVX memory data require alignment on 16-,
32-, and even 64-byte boundaries. Although you can use the align directive
to align data (see "MASM Support for Data Alignment" in Chapter 3), it
doesn't work beyond 16-byte alignment when using the simplified segment
directives presented thus far in this book. If you need alignment beyond
16 bytes, you have to use MASM full-segment declarations.

If you want to create a segment with complete control over segment
attributes, you need to use the segment and ends directives.[1] The generic syntax for a segment declaration is as follows:

```
segname  segment readonly alignment 'class'
         statements
segname  ends
```

segname is an identifier. This is the name of the segment (which must
also appear before the closing ends directive). It need not be unique; you can
have several segment declarations that share the same name. MASM will

---

1. Yes, MASM uses the same directive, ends, for ending both structures and segments.

combine segments with the same name when emitting code to the object file. Avoid the segment names _TEXT, _DATA, _BSS, and _CONST, as MASM uses these names for the .code, .data, .data?, and .const directives, respectively.

The *readonly* option is either blank or the MASM-reserved word readonly. This is a hint to MASM that the segment will contain read-only (constant) data. If you attempt to (directly) store a value into a variable that you declare in a read-only segment, MASM will complain that you cannot modify a read-only segment.

The *alignment* option is also optional and allows you to specify one of the following options:

- byte
- word
- dword
- para
- page
- align(*n*) (*n* is a constant that must be a power of 2)

The alignment options tell MASM that the first byte emitted for this particular segment must appear at an address that is a multiple of the alignment option. The byte, word, and dword reserved words specify 1-, 2-, or 4-byte alignments. The para alignment option specifies paragraph alignment (16 bytes). The page alignment option specifies an address alignment of 256 bytes. Finally, the align(*n*) alignment option lets you specify any address alignment that is a power of 2 (1, 2, 4, 8, 16, 32, and so on).

The default segment alignment, if you don't explicitly specify one, is paragraph alignment (16 bytes). This is also the default alignment for the simplified segment directives (.code, .data, .data?, and .const).

If you have some (SSE/AVX) data objects that must start at an address that is a multiple of 32 or 64 bytes, then creating a new data segment with 64-byte alignment is what you want. Here's an example of such a segment:

```
dseg64   segment align(64)
obj64    oword   0, 1, 2, 3    ; Starts on 64-byte boundary
b        byte    0             ; Messes with alignment
         align   32            ; Sets alignment to 32 bytes
obj32    oword   0, 1          ; Starts on 32-byte boundary
dseg64   ends
```

The optional *class* field is a string (delimited by apostrophes and single quotes) that is typically one of the following names: CODE, DATA, or CONST. Note that MASM and the Microsoft linker will combine segments that have the same class name even if their segment names are different.

This chapter presents examples of these segment declarations as they are needed.

11.5 SSE, AVX, and AVX2 Memory Operand Alignment

SSE and AVX instructions typically allow access to a variety of memory operand sizes. The so-called scalar instructions, which operate on single data elements, can access byte-, word-, dword-, and qword-sized memory operands. In many respects, these types of memory accesses are similar to memory accesses by the non-SIMD instructions. The SSE, AVX, and AVX2 instruction set extensions also access *packed* or *vector* operands in memory. Unlike with the scalar memory operands, stringent rules limit the access of packed memory operands. This section discusses those rules.

The SSE instructions can access up to 128 bits of memory (16 bytes) with a single instruction. Most multi-operand SSE instructions can specify an XMM register or a 128-bit memory operand as their source (second) operand. As a general rule, these memory operands must appear on a 16-byte-aligned address in memory (that is, the LO 4 bits of the memory address must contain 0s).

NOTE *Almost all SSE, AVX, and AVX2 instructions will generate a memory alignment fault if you attempt to access a 128-bit object at an address that is not 16-byte-aligned. Always ensure that your SSE packed operands are properly aligned.*

Because segments have a default alignment of para (16 bytes), you can easily ensure that any 16-byte packed data objects are 16-byte-aligned by using the align directive:

```
align 16
```

MASM will report an error if you attempt to use align 16 in a segment you've defined with the byte, word, or dword alignment type. It will work properly with para, page, or any align(*n*) option where *n* is greater than or equal to 16.

If you are using AVX instructions to access 256-bit (32-byte) memory operands, you must ensure that those memory operands begin on a 32-byte address boundary. Unfortunately, align 32 won't work, because the default segment alignment is para (16-byte) alignment, and the segment's alignment must be greater than or equal to the operand field of any align directives appearing within that segment. Therefore, to be able to define 256-bit variables usable by AVX instructions, you must explicitly define a (data) segment that is aligned on a (minimum) 32-byte boundary, such as the following:

```
avxData    segment  align(32)
           align    32    ; This is actually redundant here
someData   oword    0, 1  ; 256 bits of data
             .
             .
             .
avxData    ends
```

Though it's somewhat redundant to say this, it's so important it's worth repeating:

> Almost all AVX/AVX2 instructions will generate an alignment fault if you attempt to access a 256-bit object at an address that is not 32-byte-aligned. Always ensure that your AVX packed operands are properly aligned.

If you are using the AVX2 extended instructions with 512-bit memory operands, you must ensure that those operands appear on an address in memory that is a multiple of 64 bytes. As for AVX instructions, you will have to define a segment that has an alignment greater than or equal to 64 bytes, such as this:

```
avx2Data    segment  align(64)
someData    oword    0, 1, 2, 3  ; 512 bits of data
              .
              .
              .
avx2Data    ends
```

Forgive the redundancy, but it's important to remember:

> Almost all AVX-512 instructions will generate an alignment fault if you attempt to access a 512-bit object at an address that is not 64-byte-aligned. Always ensure that your AVX-512 packed operands are properly aligned.

If you're using SSE, AVX, and AVX2 data types in the same application, you can create a single data segment to hold all these data values by using a 64-byte alignment option for the single section, instead of a segment for each data type size. Remember, the segment's alignment has to be *greater than* or equal to the alignment required by the specific data type. Therefore, a 64-byte alignment will work fine for SSE and AVX/AVX2 variables, as well as AVX-512 variables:

```
SIMDData    segment  align(64)
sseData     oword    0   ; 64-byte-aligned is also 16-byte-aligned
            align    32  ; Alignment for AVX data
avxData     oword    0, 1 ; 32 bytes of data aligned on 32 bytes
            align    64
avx2Data    oword    0, 1, 2, 3  ; 64 bytes of data
              .
              .
              .
SIMDData    ends
```

If you specify an alignment option that is much larger than you need (such as 256-byte page alignment), you might unnecessarily waste memory.

The align directive works well when your SSE, AVX, and AVX2 data values are static or global variables. What happens when you want to create local variables on the stack or dynamic variables on the heap? Even if your program adheres to the Microsoft ABI, you're guaranteed only 16-byte alignment on the stack upon entry to your program (or to a procedure). Similarly, depending on your heap management functions, there is no guarantee that a `malloc` (or similar) function returns an address that is properly aligned for SSE, AVX, or AVX2 data objects.

Inside a procedure, you can allocate storage for a 16-, 32-, or 64-byte-aligned variable by over-allocating the storage, adding the size minus 1 of the object to the allocated address, and then using the `and` instruction to zero out LO bits of the address (4 bits for 16-byte-aligned objects, 5 bits for 32-byte-aligned objects, and 6 bits for 64-byte-aligned objects). Then you reference the object by using this pointer. The following sample code demonstrates how to do this:

```
sseproc    proc
sseptr     equ      <[rbp - 8]>
avxptr     equ      <[rbp - 16]>
avx2ptr    equ      <[rbp - 24]>
           push     rbp
           mov      rbp, rsp
           sub      rsp, 160

; Load RAX with an address 64 bytes
; above the current stack pointer. A
; 64-byte-aligned address will be somewhere
; between RSP and RSP + 63.

           lea      rax, [rsp + 63]

; Mask out the LO 6 bits of RAX. This
; generates an address in RAX that is
; aligned on a 64-byte boundary and is
; between RSP and RSP + 63:

           and      rax, -64 ; 0FFFF...FC0h

; Save this 64-byte-aligned address as
; the pointer to the AVX2 data:

           mov      avx2ptr, rax

; Add 64 to AVX2's address. This skips
; over AVX2's data. The address is also
; 64-byte-aligned (which means it is
; also 32-byte-aligned). Use this as
; the address of AVX's data:

           add      rax, 64
           mov      avxptr, rax

; Add 32 to AVX's address. This skips
; over AVX's data. The address is also
; 32-byte-aligned (which means it is
; also 16-byte-aligned). Use this as
```

```
; the address of SSE's data:

            add     rax, 32
            mov     sseptr, rax
            .
            . Code that accesses the
            . AVX2, AVX, and SSE data
            . areas using avx2ptr,
            . avxptr, and sseptr

            leave
            ret
sseproc     endp
```

For data you allocate on the heap, you do the same thing: allocate extra storage (up to twice as many bytes minus 1), add the size of the object minus 1 (15, 31, or 63) to the address, and then mask the newly formed address with −64, −32, or −16 to produce a 64-, 32-, or 16-byte-aligned object, respectively.

11.6   SIMD Data Movement Instructions

The x86-64 CPUs provide a variety of data move instructions that copy data between (SSE/AVX) registers, load registers from memory, and store register values to memory. The following subsections describe each of these instructions.

11.6.1   The (v)movd and (v)movq Instructions

For the SSE instruction set, the movd (*move dword*) and movq (*move qword*) instructions copy the value from a 32- or 64-bit general-purpose register or memory location into the LO dword or qword of an XMM register:[2]

```
movd xmm_n,  reg_32/mem_32
movq xmm_n,  reg_64/mem_64
```

These instructions zero-extend the value to remaining HO bits in the XMM register, as shown in Figures 11-7 and 11-8.

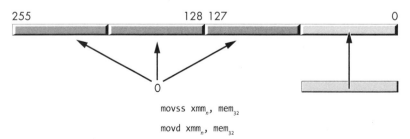

Figure 11-7: Moving a 32-bit value from memory to an XMM register (with zero extension)

---

2. xmm_n represents XMM0 through XMM15.

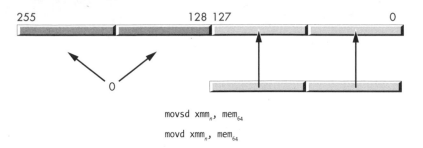

```
255              128 127                    0
```

movsd xmm$_n$, mem$_{64}$

movd xmm$_n$, mem$_{64}$

Figure 11-8: Moving a 64-bit value from memory to an XMM register (with zero extension)

The following instructions store the LO 32 or 64 bits of an XMM register into a dword or qword memory location or general-purpose register:

movd reg$_{32}$/mem$_{32}$, xmm$_n$
movq reg$_{64}$/mem$_{64}$, xmm$_n$

The movq instruction also allows you to copy data from the LO qword of one XMM register to another, but for whatever reason, the movd instruction does not allow two XMM register operands:

movq xmm$_n$, xmm$_n$

For the AVX instructions, you use the following instructions:[3]

vmovd xmm$_n$, reg$_{32}$/mem$_{32}$
vmovd reg$_{32}$/mem$_{32}$, xmm$_n$
vmovq xmm$_n$, reg$_{64}$/mem$_{64}$
vmovq reg$_{64}$/mem$_{64}$, xmm$_n$

The instructions with the XMM destination operands also zero-extend their values into the HO bits (up to bit 255, unlike the standard SSE instructions that do not modify the upper bits of the YMM registers).

Because the movd and movq instructions access 32- and 64-bit values in memory (rather than 128-, 256-, or 512-bit values), these instructions do not require their memory operands to be 16-, 32-, or 64-byte-aligned. Of course, the instructions may execute faster if their operands are dword (movd) or qword (movq) aligned in memory.

11.6.2 The (v)movaps, (v)movapd, and (v)movdqa Instructions

The movaps (*move aligned, packed single*), movapd (*move aligned, packed double*), and movdqa (*move double quad-word aligned*) instructions move 16 bytes of data between memory and an XMM register or between two XMM registers. The AVX versions (with the v prefix) move 16 or 32 bytes between memory and an XMM or a YMM register or between two XMM or YMM registers (moves involving XMM registers zero out the HO bits of the corresponding YMM

---

3. ymm$_n$ represents YMM0 through YMM15.

register). The memory locations must be aligned on a 16-byte or 32-byte boundary (respectively), or the CPU will generate an unaligned access fault.

All three mov* instructions load 16 bytes into an XMM register and are, in theory, interchangeable. In practice, Intel may optimize the operations for the type of data they move (single-precision floating-point values, double-precision floating-point values, or integer values), so it's always a good idea to choose the appropriate instruction for the data type you are using (see "Performance Issues and the SIMD Move Instructions" on page 622 for an explanation). Likewise, all three vmov* instructions load 16 or 32 bytes into an XMM or a YMM register and are interchangeable.

These instructions take the following forms:

movaps xmm_n, mem_{128}	vmovaps xmm_n, mem_{128}	vmovaps ymm_n, mem_{256}
movaps mem_{128}, xmm_n	vmovaps mem_{128}, xmm_n	vmovaps mem_{256}, ymm_n
movaps xmm_n, xmm_n	vmovaps xmm_n, xmm_n	vmovaps ymm_n, ymm_n
movapd xmm_n, mem_{128}	vmovapd xmm_n, mem_{128}	vmovapd ymm_n, mem_{256}
movapd mem_{128}, xmm_n	vmovapd mem_{128}, xmm_n	vmovapd mem_{256}, ymm_n
movapd xmm_n, xmm_n	vmovapd xmm_n, xmm_n	vmovapd ymm_n, ymm_n
movdqa xmm_n, mem_{128}	vmovdqa xmm_n, mem_{128}	vmovdqa ymm_n, mem_{256}
movdqa mem_{128}, xmm_n	vmovdqa mem_{128}, xmm_n	vmovdqa mem_{256}, ymm_n
movdqa xmm_n, xmm_n	vmovdqa xmm_n, xmm_n	vmovdqa ymm_n, ymm_n

The mem_{128} operand should be a vector (array) of four single-precision floating-point values for the (v)movaps instruction; it should be a vector of two double-precision floating-point values for the (v)movapd instruction; it should be a 16-byte value (16 bytes, 8 words, 4 dwords, or 2 qwords) when using the (v)movdqa instruction. If you cannot guarantee that the operands are aligned on a 16-byte boundary, use the movups, movupd, or movdqu instructions, instead (see the next section).

The mem_{256} operand should be a vector (array) of eight single-precision floating-point values for the vmovaps instruction; it should be a vector of four double-precision floating-point values for the vmovapd instruction; it should be a 32-byte value (32 bytes, 16 words, 8 dwords, or 4 qwords) when using the vmovdqa instruction. If you cannot guarantee that the operands are 32-byte-aligned, use the vmovups, vmovupd, or vmovdqu instructions instead.

Although the physical machine instructions themselves don't particularly care about the data type of the memory operands, MASM's assembly syntax certainly does care. You will need to use operand type coercion if the instruction doesn't match one of the following types:

- The movaps instruction allows real4, dword, and oword operands.
- The movapd instruction allows real8, qword, and oword operands.
- The movdqa instruction allows only oword operands.
- The vmovaps instruction allows real4, dword, and ymmword ptr operands (when using a YMM register).
- The vmovapd instruction allows real8, qword, and ymmword ptr operands (when using a YMM register).
- The vmovdqa instruction allows only ymmword ptr operands (when using a YMM register).

Often you will see memcpy (*memory copy*) functions use the (v)movapd instructions for very high-performance operations. See Agner Fog's website at *https://www.agner.org/optimize/* for more details.

11.6.3 The (v)movups, (v)movupd, and (v)movdqu Instructions

When you cannot guarantee that packed data memory operands lie on a 16- or 32-byte address boundary, you can use the (v)movups (*move unaligned packed single-precision*), (v)movupd (*move unaligned packed double-precision*), and (v)movdqu (*move double quad-word unaligned*) instructions to move data between XMM or YMM registers and memory.

NOTE *These instructions typically run slower than their aligned equivalents. Therefore, you should use the aligned instructions if you are moving data between XMM or YMM registers or know the memory operands lie on 16-byte-aligned or 32-byte-aligned addresses.*

As for the aligned moves, all the unaligned moves do the same thing: copying 16 (32) bytes of data to and from memory. The convention for the various data types is the same as it is for the aligned data movement instructions.

11.6.4 Performance of Aligned and Unaligned Moves

Listings 11-3 and 11-4 provide sample programs that demonstrate the performance of the mova* and movu* instructions using aligned and unaligned memory accesses.

```
; Listing 11-3

; Performance test for packed versus unpacked
; instructions. This program times aligned accesses.

        option  casemap:none

nl          =       10

            .const
ttlStr      byte    "Listing 11-3", 0

dseg        segment align(64) 'DATA'

; Aligned data types:

            align   64
alignedData byte    64 dup (0)
dseg        ends

            .code
            externdef printf:proc
```

```
            ; Return program title to C++ program:

                    public  getTitle
            getTitle  proc
                    lea     rax, ttlStr
                    ret
            getTitle  endp

            ; Used for debugging:

            print     proc

            ; Print code removed for brevity.
            ; See Listing 11-1 for actual code.

            print     endp

            ; Here is the "asmMain" function.

                    public  asmMain
            asmMain   proc
                    push    rbx
                    push    rbp
                    mov     rbp, rsp
                    sub     rsp, 56         ; Shadow storage

                    call    print
                    byte    "Starting", nl, 0

                    mov     rcx, 4000000000 ; 4,000,000,000
                    lea     rdx, alignedData
                    mov     rbx, 0
            rptLp:    mov     rax, 15
            rptLp2:   movaps  xmm0, xmmword ptr [rdx + rbx * 1]
                    movapd  xmm0, real8 ptr   [rdx + rbx * 1]
                    movdqa  xmm0, xmmword ptr [rdx + rbx * 1]
                    vmovaps ymm0, ymmword ptr [rdx + rbx * 1]
                    vmovapd ymm0, ymmword ptr [rdx + rbx * 1]
                    vmovdqa ymm0, ymmword ptr [rdx + rbx * 1]
                    vmovaps zmm0, zmmword ptr [rdx + rbx * 1]
                    vmovapd zmm0, zmmword ptr [rdx + rbx * 1]

                    dec     rax
                    jns     rptLp2

                    dec     rcx
                    jnz     rptLp

                    call    print
                    byte    "Done", nl, 0

            allDone:  leave
                    pop     rbx
```

```
                ret      ; Returns to caller
asmMain         endp
                end
```

Listing 11-3: Aligned memory-access timing code

```
; Listing 11-4

; Performance test for packed versus unpacked
; instructions. This program times unaligned accesses.

        option  casemap:none

nl              =        10

                .const
ttlStr          byte     "Listing 11-4", 0

dseg            segment align(64) 'DATA'

; Aligned data types:

                align    64
alignedData byte         64 dup (0)
dseg            ends

                .code
                externdef printf:proc

; Return program title to C++ program:

                public  getTitle
getTitle        proc
                lea      rax, ttlStr
                ret
getTitle        endp

; Used for debugging:

print           proc

; Print code removed for brevity.
; See Listing 11-1 for actual code.

print           endp

; Here is the "asmMain" function.

                public  asmMain
asmMain         proc
                push     rbx
                push     rbp
                mov      rbp, rsp
```

```
            sub     rsp, 56         ; Shadow storage

            call    print
            byte    "Starting", nl, 0

            mov     rcx, 4000000000 ; 4,000,000,000
            lea     rdx, alignedData
rptLp:      mov     rbx, 15
rptLp2:
            movups  xmm0, xmmword ptr [rdx + rbx * 1]
            movupd  xmm0, real8 ptr  [rdx + rbx * 1]
            movdqu  xmm0, xmmword ptr [rdx + rbx * 1]
            vmovups ymm0, ymmword ptr [rdx + rbx * 1]
            vmovupd ymm0, ymmword ptr [rdx + rbx * 1]
            vmovdqu ymm0, ymmword ptr [rdx + rbx * 1]
            vmovups zmm0, zmmword ptr [rdx + rbx * 1]
            vmovupd zmm0, zmmword ptr [rdx + rbx * 1]
            dec     rbx
            jns     rptLp2

            dec     rcx
            jnz     rptLp

            call    print
            byte    "Done", nl, 0

allDone:    leave
            pop     rbx
            ret     ; Returns to caller
asmMain     endp
            end
```

Listing 11-4: Unaligned memory-access timing code

The code in Listing 11-3 took about 1 minute and 7 seconds to execute on a 3GHz Xeon W CPU. The code in Listing 11-4 took 1 minute and 55 seconds to execute on the same processor. As you can see, there is sometimes an advantage to accessing SIMD data on an aligned address boundary.

11.6.5 The (v)movlps and (v)movlpd Instructions

The (v)movl* instructions and (v)movh* instructions (from the next section) might look like normal move instructions. Their behavior is similar to many other SSE/AVX move instructions. However, they were designed to support packing and unpacking floating-point vectors. Specifically, these instructions allow you to merge two pairs of single-precision or a pair of double-precision floating-point operands from two different sources into a single XMM register.

The (v)movlps instructions use the following syntax:

```
movlps   xmm_dest, mem_64
movlps   mem_64,   xmm_src
vmovlps  xmm_dest, xmm_src, mem_64
vmovlps  mem_64,   xmm_src
```

The movlps xmm_{dest}, mem_{64} form copies a pair of single-precision floating-point values into the two LO 32-bit lanes of a destination XMM register, as shown in Figure 11-9. This instruction leaves the HO 64 bits unchanged.

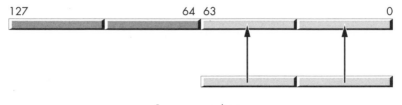

movlps xmm_n, xmm/mem_{64}

Figure 11-9: movlps instruction

The movlps mem_{64}, xmm_{src} form copies the LO 64 bits (the two LO single-precision lanes) from the XMM source register to the specified memory location. Functionally, this is equivalent to the movq or movsd instructions (as it copies 64 bits to memory), though this instruction might be slightly faster if the LO 64 bits of the XMM register actually contain two single-precision values (see "Performance Issues and the SIMD Move Instructions" on page 622 for an explanation).

The vmovlps instruction has three operands: a destination XMM register, a source XMM register, and a source (64-bit) memory location. This instruction copies the two single-precision values from the memory location into the LO 64 bits of the destination XMM register. It copies the HO 64 bits of the source register (which also hold two single-precision values) into the HO 64 bits of the destination register. Figure 11-10 shows the operation. Note that this instruction merges the pair of operands with a single instruction.

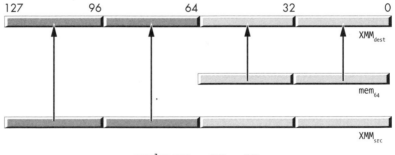

vmovlps xmm_{dest}, xmm_{src}, mem_{64}

Figure 11-10: vmovlps instruction

Like movsd, the movlpd (*move low packed double*) instruction copies the LO 64 bits (a double-precision floating-point value) of the source operand to the LO 64 bits of the destination operand. The difference is that the movlpd instruction doesn't zero-extend the value when moving data from memory into an XMM register, whereas the movsd instruction will zero-extend the value into the upper 64 bits of the destination XMM register. (Neither the movsd nor movlpd will zero-extend when copying data between XMM registers; of course, zero extension doesn't apply when storing data to memory.)[4]

11.6.6 The movhps and movhpd Instructions

The movhps and movhpd instructions move a 64-bit value (either two single-precision floats in the case of movhps, or a single double-precision value in the case of movhpd) into the HO quad word of a destination XMM register. Figure 11-11 shows the operation of the movhps instruction; Figure 11-12 shows the movhpd instruction.

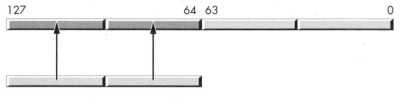

movhps xmm$_n$, mem$_{64}$

Figure 11-11: movhps instruction

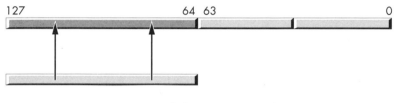

movhpd xmm$_n$, mem$_{64}$

Figure 11-12: movhpd instruction

The movhps and movhpd instructions can also store the HO quad word of an XMM register into memory. The allowable syntax is shown here:

```
movhps xmm_n, mem_64
movhps mem_64, xmm_n
movhpd xmm_n, mem_64
movhpd mem_64, xmm_n
```

These instructions do not affect bits 128 to 255 of the YMM registers (if present on the CPU).

You would normally use a movlps instruction followed by a movhps instruction to load four single-precision floating-point values into an XMM register, taking the floating-point values from two different data sources (similarly, you could use the movlpd and movhpd instructions to load a pair of double-precision values into a single XMM register from different sources).

---

4. The vmovlps and vmovlpd instructions will zero-extend to the HO bits of the corresponding YMM register, regardless of what happens in the XMM register.

Conversely, you could also use this instruction to split a vector result in half and store the two halves in different data streams. This is probably the intended purpose of this instruction. Of course, if you can use it for other purposes, have at it.

MASM (version 14.15.26730.0, at least) seems to require movhps operands to be a 64-bit data type and does not allow real4 operands.[5] Therefore, you may have to explicitly coerce an array of two real4 values with qword ptr when using this instruction:

```
r4m         real4   1.0, 2.0, 3.0, 4.0
r8m         real8   1.0, 2.0
             .
             .
             .
            movhps  xmm0, qword ptr r4m2
            movhpd  xmm0, r8m
```

11.6.7 The vmovhps and vmovhpd Instructions

Although the AVX instruction extensions provide vmovhps and vmovhpd instructions, they are not a simple extension of the SSE movhps and movhpd instructions. The syntax for these instructions is as follows:

```
vmovhps xmm_dest, xmm_src, mem_64
vmovhps mem_64, xmm_src
vmovhpd xmm_dest, xmm_src, mem_64
vmovhpd mem_64, xmm_src
```

The instructions that store data into a 64-bit memory location behave similarly to the movhps and movhpd instructions. The instructions that load data into an XMM register have two source operands. They load a full 128 bits (four single-precision values or two double-precision values) into the destination XMM register. The HO 64 bits come from the memory operand; the LO 64 bits come from the LO quad word of the source XMM register, as Figure 11-13 shows. These instructions also zero-extend the value into the upper 128 bits of the (overlaid) YMM register.

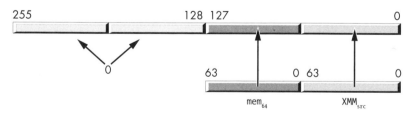

Figure 11-13: vmovhpd and vmovhps instructions

5. This is probably a bug. It may be corrected in later versions of MASM.

Unlike for the movhps instruction, MASM properly accepts real4 source operands for the vmovhps instruction:

```
r4m        real4   1.0, 2.0, 3.0, 4.0
r8m        real8   1.0, 2.0
            .
            .
            .
           vmovhps xmm0, xmm1, r4m
           vmovhpd xmm0, xmm1, r8m
```

11.6.8 The movlhps and vmovlhps Instructions

The movlhps instruction moves a pair of 32-bit single-precision floating-point values from the LO qword of the source XMM register into the HO 64 bits of a destination XMM register. It leaves the LO 64 bits of the destination register unchanged. If the destination register is on a CPU that supports 256-bit AVX registers, this instruction also leaves the HO 128 bits of the overlaid YMM register unchanged.

The syntax for these instructions is as follows:

```
movlhps   xmm_dest, xmm_src
vmovlhps  xmm_dest, xmm_src1, xmm_src2
```

You cannot use this instruction to move data between memory and an XMM register; it transfers data only between XMM registers. No double-precision version of this instruction exists.

The vmovlhps instruction is similar to movlhps, with the following differences:

- vmovlhps requires three operands: two source XMM registers and a destination XMM register.
- vmovlhps copies the LO quad word of the first source register into the LO quad word of the destination register.
- vmovlhps copies the LO quad word of the second source register into bits 64 to 127 of the destination register.
- vmovlhps zero-extends the result into the upper 128 bits of the overlaid YMM register.

There is no vmovlhpd instruction.

11.6.9 The movhlps and vmovhlps Instructions

The movhlps instruction has the following syntax:

```
movhlps xmm_dest, xmm_src
```

The `movhlps` instruction copies the pair of 32-bit single-precision floating-point values from the HO qword of the source operand to the LO qword of the destination register, leaving the HO 64 bits of the destination register unchanged (this is the converse of `movlhps`). This instruction copies data only between XMM registers; it does not allow a memory operand.

The `vmovhlps` instruction requires three XMM register operands; here is its syntax:

---

vmovhlps xmm_{dest}, xmm_{src1}, xmm_{src2}

This instruction copies the HO 64 bits of the first source register into the HO 64 bits of the destination register, copies the HO 64 bits of the second source register into bits 0 to 63 of the destination register, and finally, zero-extends the result into the upper bits of the overlaid YMM register.

There are no `movhlpd` or `vmovhlpd` instructions.

11.6.10   The (v)movshdup and (v)movsldup Instructions

The `movshdup` instruction moves the two odd-index single-precision floating-point values from the source operand (memory or XMM register) and duplicates each element into the destination XMM register, as shown in Figure 11-14.

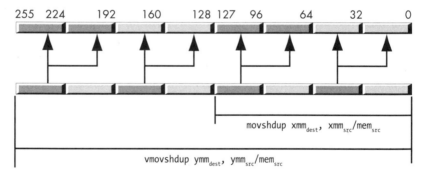

Figure 11-14: movshdup and vmovshdup instructions

This instruction ignores the single-precision floating-point values at even-lane indexes into the XMM register. The `vmovshdup` instruction works the same way but on YMM registers, copying four single-precision values rather than two (and, of course, zeroing the HO bits). The syntax for these instructions is shown here:

---

movshdup xmm_{dest}, mem_{128}/xmm_{src}
vmovshdup xmm_{dest}, mem_{128}/xmm_{src}
vmovshdup ymm_{dest}, mem_{256}/ymm_{src}

The `movsldup` instruction works just like the `movshdup` instruction, except it copies and duplicates the two single-precision values at even indexes in the source XMM register to the destination XMM register. Likewise, the vmovsldup instruction copies and duplicates the four double-precision values in the source YMM register at even indexes, as shown in Figure 11-15.

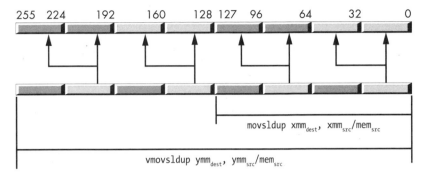

Figure 11-15: movsldup and vmovsldup instructions

The syntax is as follows:

```
movsldup   xmm_dest,  mem_128/xmm_src
vmovsldup  xmm_dest,  mem_128/xmm_src
vmovsldup  ymm_dest,  mem_256/ymm_src
```

11.6.11   The (v)movddup Instruction

The movddup instruction copies and duplicates a double-precision value from the LO 64 bits of an XMM register or a 64-bit memory location into the LO 64 bits of a destination XMM register; then it also duplicates this value into bits 64 to 127 of that same destination register, as shown in Figure 11-16.

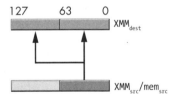

movddup xmm_dest, xmm_src/mem_src

Figure 11-16: movddup instruction behavior

This instruction does not disturb the HO 128 bits of a YMM register (if applicable). The syntax for this instruction is as follows:

```
movddup xmm_dest, mem_64/xmm_src
```

The vmovddup instruction operates on an XMM or a YMM destination register and an XMM or a YMM source register or 128- or 256-bit memory location. The 128-bit version works just like the movddup instruction except it zeroes the HO bits of the destination YMM register. The 256-bit version copies a pair of double-precision values at even indexes (0 and 2) in the source value to their corresponding indexes in the destination YMM register and duplicates those values at the odd indexes in the destination, as Figure 11-17 shows.

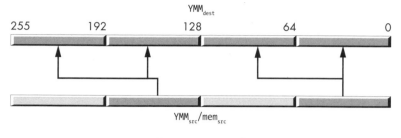

Figure 11-17: vmovddup instruction behavior

Here is the syntax for this instruction:

```
movddup   xmm_dest,  mem_64/xmm_src
vmovddup ymm_dest,  mem_256/ymm_src
```

11.6.12   The (v)lddqu Instruction

The (v)lddqu instruction is operationally identical to (v)movdqu. You can sometimes use this instruction to improve performance if the (memory) source operand is not aligned properly and crosses a cache line boundary in memory. For more details on this instruction and its performance limitations, refer to the Intel or AMD documentation (specifically, the optimization manuals).

These instructions always take the following form:

```
lddqu   xmm_dest,  mem_128
vlddqu  xmm_dest,  mem_128
vlddqu  ymm_dest,  mem_256
```

11.6.13   Performance Issues and the SIMD Move Instructions

When you look at the SSE/AVX instructions' semantics at the programming model level, you might question why certain instructions appear in the instruction set. For example, the movq, movsd, and movlps instructions can all load 64 bits from a memory location into the LO 64 bits of an XMM register. Why bother doing this? Why not have a single instruction that copies the 64 bits from a quad word in memory to the LO 64 bits of an XMM register (be it a 64-bit integer, a pair of 32-bit integers, a 64-bit double-precision floating-point value, or a pair of 32-bit single-precision floating-point values)? The answer lies in the term *microarchitecture.*

The x86-64 *macroarchitecture* is the programming model that a software engineer sees. In the macroarchitecture, an XMM register is a 128-bit resource that, at any given time, could hold a 128-bit array of bits (or an integer), a pair of 64-bit integer values, a pair of 64-bit double-precision floating-point values, a set of four single-precision floating-point values, a set of four double-word integers, eight words, or 16 bytes. All these data types overlay one another, just like the 8-, 16-, 32-, and 64-bit general-purpose registers overlay one another (this is known as *aliasing*). If you load two double-precision floating-point values into an XMM register and then modify the (integer) word at bit positions 0 to 15, you're also changing those same bits (0 to 15) in the double-precision value in the LO qword of the XMM register. The semantics of the x86-64 programming model require this.

At the microarchitectural level, however, there is no requirement that the CPU use the same physical bits in the CPU for integer, single-precision, and double-precision values (even when they are aliased to the same register). The microarchitecture could set aside a separate set of bits to hold integers, single-precision, and double-precision values for a single register. So, for example, when you use the movq instruction to load 64 bits into an XMM register, that instruction might actually copy the bits into the underlying integer register (without affecting the single-precision or double-precision subregisters). Likewise, movlps would copy a pair of single-precision values into the single-precision register, and movsd would copy a double-precision value into the double-precision register (Figure 11-18). These separate subregisters (integer, single-precision, and double-precision) could be connected directly to the arithmetic or logical unit that handles their specific data types, making arithmetic and logical operations on those subregisters more efficient. As long as the data is sitting in the appropriate subregister, everything works smoothly.

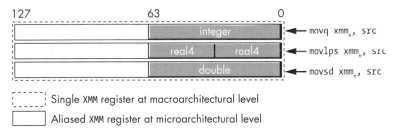

Figure 11-18: Register aliasing at the microarchitectural level

However, what happens if you use movq to load a pair of single-precision floating-point values into an XMM register and then try to perform a single-precision vector operation on those two values? At the macroarchitectural level, the two single-precision values are sitting in the appropriate bit positions of the XMM register, so this has to be a legal operation. At the microarchitectural level, however, those two single-precision floating-point values are sitting in the integer subregister, not the single-precision subregister. The underlying microarchitecture has to note that the values are in the wrong subregister and move them to the appropriate (single-precision) subregister before performing the single-precision arithmetic or logical operation. This may introduce a slight delay (while the microarchitecture moves the data around), which is why you should always pick the appropriate move instructions for your data types.

There is no guarantee that your programs will run faster by using the appropriate instructions for your data type, but at least they won't run slower.

11.6.14   Some Final Comments on the SIMD Move Instructions

The SIMD data movement instructions are a confusing bunch. Their syntax is inconsistent, many instructions duplicate the actions of other instructions, and they have some perplexing irregularity issues. Someone new to the x86-64 instruction set might ask, "Why was the instruction set designed this way?" Why, indeed?

The answer to that question is historical. The SIMD instructions did not exist on the earliest x86 CPUs. Intel added the MMX instruction set to the Pentium-series CPUs. At that time (the early 1990s), current technology allowed Intel to add only a few additional instructions, and the MMX registers were limited to 64 bits in size. Furthermore, software engineers and computer systems designers were only beginning to explore the multimedia capabilities of modern computers, so it wasn't entirely clear which instructions (and data types) were necessary to support the type of software we see several decades later. As a result, the earliest SIMD instructions and data types were limited in scope.

As time passed, CPUs gained additional silicon resources, and software/systems engineers discovered new uses for computers (and new algorithms to run on those computers), so Intel (and AMD) responded by adding new SIMD instructions to support these more modern multimedia applications. The original MMX instructions, for example, supported only integer data types, so Intel added floating-point support in the SSE instruction set, because multimedia applications needed real data types. Then Intel extended the integer types from 64 bits to 128, 256, and even 512 bits. With each extension, Intel (and AMD) had to retain the older instruction set extensions in order to allow preexisting software to run on the new CPUs.

As a result, the newer instruction sets kept piling on new instructions that did the same work as the older ones (with some additional capabilities). This is why instructions like movaps and vmovaps have considerable overlap in their functionality. If the CPU resources had been available earlier (for example, to put 256-bit YMM registers on the CPU), there would have been almost no need for the movaps instruction—the vmovaps could have done all the work.[6]

In theory, we could create an architecturally elegant variant of the x86-64 by starting over from scratch and designing a minimal instruction set that handles all the activities of the current x86-64 without all the kruft and kludges present in the existing instruction set. However, such a CPU would lose the primary advantage of the x86-64: the ability to run decades of software written for the Intel architecture. The cost of being able to run all this old software is that assembly language programmers (and compiler writers) have to deal with all these irregularities in the instruction set.

---

6. Other than, of course, the issue of zeroing and preserving the HO bits of YMM registers when operating on 128-bit data sets.

11.7 The Shuffle and Unpack Instructions

The SSE/AVX *shuffle and unpack instructions* are variants of the move instructions. In addition to moving data around, these instructions can also rearrange the data appearing in different lanes of the XMM and YMM registers.

11.7.1 The (v)pshufb Instructions

The `pshufb` instruction was the first packed byte shuffle SIMD instruction (it first appeared with the MMX instruction set). Because of its origin, its syntax and behavior are a bit different from the other shuffle instructions in the instruction set. The syntax is the following:

---

pshufb xmm_{dest}, xmm/mem₁₂₈

The first (destination) operand is an XMM register whose byte lanes `pshufb` will shuffle (rearrange). The second operand (either an XMM register or a 128-bit oword memory location) is an array of 16 byte values holding indexes that control the shuffle operation. If the second operand is a memory location, that oword value must be aligned on a 16-byte boundary.

Each byte (lane) in the second operand selects a value for the corresponding byte lane in the first operand, as shown in Figure 11-19.

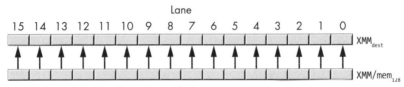

Figure 11-19: Lane index correspondence for pshufb instruction

The 16-byte indexes in the second operand each take the form shown in Figure 11-20.

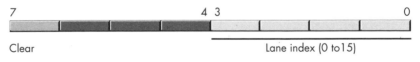

Figure 11-20: phsufb byte index

The `pshufb` instruction ignores bits 4 to 6 in an index byte. Bit 7 is the clear bit; if this bit contains a 1, the `pshufb` instruction ignores the lane index bits and stores a 0 into the corresponding byte in XMM$_{dest}$. If the clear bit contains a 0, the `pshufb` instruction does a shuffle operation.

The `pshufb` shuffle operation takes place on a lane-by-lane basis. The instruction first makes a temporary copy of XMM$_{dest}$. Then for each index byte (whose HO bit is 0), the `pshufb` copies the lane specified by the LO 4 bits of the index from the XMM$_{dest}$ lane that matches the index's lane, as shown in Figure 11-21. In this example, the index appearing in lane 6 contains the value 00000011b. This selects the value in lane 3 of the temporary (original XMM$_{dest}$) value and copies it to lane 6 of XMM$_{dest}$. The pshufb instruction repeats this operation for all 16 lanes.

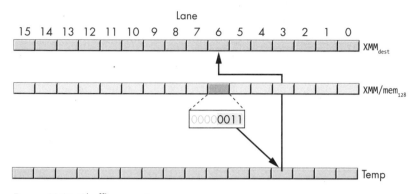

Figure 11-21: Shuffle operation

The AVX instruction set extensions introduced the vpshufb instruction. Its syntax is the following:

```
vpshufb xmm_dest, xmm_src, xmm_index/mem_128
vpshufb ymm_dest, ymm_src, ymm_index/mem_256
```

The AVX variant adds a source register (rather than using XMM$_{dest}$ as both the source and destination registers), and, rather than creating a temporary copy of XMM$_{dest}$ prior to the operation and picking the values from that copy, the vpshufb instructions select the source bytes from the XMM$_{src}$ register. Other than that, and the fact that these instructions zero the HO bits of YMM$_{dest}$, the 128-bit variant operates identically to the SSE pshufb instruction.

The AVX instruction allows you to specify 256-bit YMM registers in addition to 128-bit XMM registers.[7]

11.7.2 The (v)pshufd Instructions

The SSE extensions first introduced the pshufd instruction. The AVX extensions added the vpshufd instruction. These instructions shuffle dwords in XMM and YMM registers (*not* double-precision values) similarly to the (v)pshufb instructions. However, the shuffle index is specified differently from (v)pshufb. The syntax for the (v)pshufd instructions is as follows:

```
pshufd  xmm_dest, xmm_src/mem_128, imm_8
vpshufd xmm_dest, xmm_src/mem_128, imm_8
vpshufd ymm_dest, ymm_src/mem_256, imm_8
```

---

7. The AVX-512 extensions also allow the use of 512-bit ZMM registers for the vshufb instruction.

The first operand (XMM_{dest} or YMM_{dest}) is the destination operand where the shuffled values will be stored. The second operand is the source from which the instruction will select the double words to place in the destination register; as usual, if this is a memory operand, you must align it on the appropriate (16- or 32-byte) boundary. The third operand is an 8-bit immediate value that specifies the indexes for the double words to select from the source operand.

For the (v)pshufd instructions with an XMM_{dest} operand, the imm_8 operand has the encoding shown in Table 11-3. The value in bits 0 to 1 selects a particular dword from the source operand to place in dword 0 of the XMM_{dest} operand. The value in bits 2 to 3 selects a dword from the source operand to place in dword 1 of the XMM_{dest} operand. The value in bits 4 to 5 selects a dword from the source operand to place in dword 2 of the XMM_{dest} operand. Finally, the value in bits 6 to 7 selects a dword from the source operand to place in dword 3 of the XMM_{dest} operand.

Table 11-3: (v)pshufd imm_8 Operand Values

Bit positions	Destination lane
0 to 1	0
2 to 3	1
4 to 5	2
6 to 7	3

The difference between the 128-bit pshufd and vpshufd instructions is that pshufd leaves the HO 128 bits of the underlying YMM register unchanged and vpshufd zeroes the HO 128 bits of the underlying YMM register.

The 256-bit variant of vpshufd (when using YMM registers as the source and destination operands) still uses an 8-bit immediate operand as the index value. Each 2-bit index value manipulates two dword values in the YMM registers. Bits 0 to 1 control dwords 0 and 4, bits 2 to 3 control dwords 1 and 5, bits 4 to 5 control dwords 2 and 6, and bits 6 to 7 control dwords 3 and 7, as shown in Table 11-4.

Table 11-4: Double-Word Transfers for vpshufd YMM_{dest}, YMM_{src}/mem_{src}, imm_8

Index	YMM/mem_{src} [index] copied into	YMM/mem_{src} [index + 4] copied into
Bits 0 to 1 of imm_8	$YMM_{dest}[0]$	$YMM_{dest}[4]$
Bits 2 to 3 of imm_8	$YMM_{dest}[1]$	$YMM_{dest}[5]$
Bits 4 to 5 of imm_8	$YMM_{dest}[2]$	$YMM_{dest}[6]$
Bits 6 to 7 of imm_8	$YMM_{dest}[3]$	$YMM_{dest}[7]$

The 256-bit version is slightly less flexible as it copies two dwords at a time, rather than one. It processes the LO 128 bits exactly the same way as the 128-bit version of the instruction; it also copies the corresponding lanes in the upper 128 bits of the source to the YMM destination register by using the same shuffle pattern. Unfortunately, you can't independently control the HO and LO halves of the YMM register by using the vpshufd instruction. If you really need to shuffle dwords independently, you can use vshufb with appropriate indexes that copy 4 bytes (in place of a single dword).

11.7.3 The (v)pshuflw and (v)pshufhw Instructions

The pshuflw and vpshuflw and the pshufhw and vpshufhw instructions provide support for 16-bit word shuffles within an XMM or a YMM register. The syntax for these instructions is the following:

```
pshuflw   xmm_dest, xmm_src/mem_128, imm_8
pshufhw   xmm_dest, xmm_src/mem_128, imm_8

vpshuflw  xmm_dest, xmm_src/mem_128, imm_8
vpshufhw  xmm_dest, xmm_src/mem_128, imm_8

vpshuflw  ymm_dest, ymm_src/mem_256, imm_8
vpshufhw  ymm_dest, ymm_src/mem_256, imm_8
```

The 128-bit lw variants copy the HO 64 bits of the source operand to the same positions in the XMM_{dest} operand. Then they use the index (imm_8) operand to select word lanes 0 to 3 in the LO qword of the XMM_{src}/ mem_{128} operand to move to the LO 4 lanes of the destination operand. For example, if the LO 2 bits of imm_8 are 10b, then the pshuflw instruction copies lane 2 from the source into lane 0 of the destination operand (Figure 11-22). Note that pshuflw does not modify the HO 128 bits of the overlaid YMM register, whereas vpshuflw zeroes those HO bits.

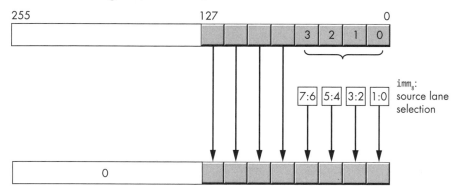

128-bit vpshuflw sets HO 128 bits to 0; pshuflw leaves HO 128 bits unmodified.

Figure 11-22: (v)pshuflw xmm, xmm/mem, imm_8 operation

The 256-bit vpshuflw instruction (with a YMM destination register) copies two pairs of words at a time—one pair in the HO 128 bits and one pair in the LO 128 bits of the YMM destination register and 256-bit source locations, as shown in Figure 11-23. The index (imm_8) selection is the same for the LO and HO 128 bits.

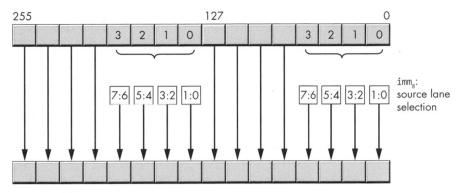

Figure 11-23: *vpshuflw ymm, ymm/mem, imm₈ operation*

The 128-bit hw variants copy the LO 64 bits of the source operand to the same positions in the destination operand. Then they use the index operand to select words 4 to 7 (indexed as 0 to 3) in the 128-bit source operand to move to the HO four word lanes of the destination operand (Figure 11-24).

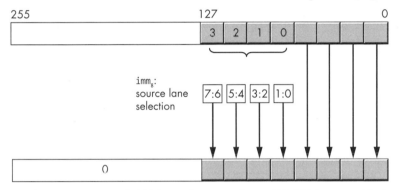

128-bit vpshufhw sets HO 128 bits to 0; pshufhw leaves HO 128 bits unmodified.

Figure 11-24: *(v)pshufhw operation*

The 256-bit vpshufhw instruction (with a YMM destination register) copies two pairs of words at a time—one in the HO 128 bits and one in the LO 128 bits of the YMM destination register and 256-bit source locations, as shown in Figure 11-25.

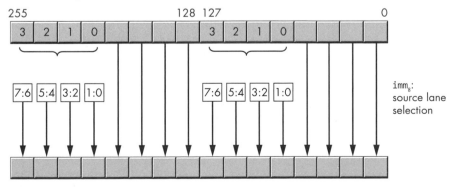

Figure 11-25: *vpshufhw operation*

11.7.4 The shufps and shufpd Instructions

The shuffle instructions (shufps and shufpd) extract single- or double-precision values from the source operands and place them in specified positions in the destination operand. The third operand, an 8-bit immediate value, selects which values to extract from the source to move into the destination register. The syntax for these two instructions is as follows:

shufps $xmm_{src1/dest}$, xmm_{src2}/mem_{128}, imm_8
shufpd $xmm_{src1/dest}$, xmm_{src2}/mem_{128}, imm_8

For the shufps instruction, the second source operand is an 8-bit immediate value that is actually a four-element array of 2-bit values.

imm_8 bits 0 and 1 select a single-precision value from one of the four lanes in the $XMM_{src1/dest}$ operand to store into lane 0 of the destination operation. Bits 2 and 3 select a single-precision value from one of the four lanes in the $XMM_{src1/dest}$ operand to store into lane 1 of the destination operation (the destination operand is also $XMM_{src1/dest}$).

imm_8 bits 4 and 5 select a single-precision value from one of the four lanes in the XMM_{src2}/mem_{src2} operand to store into lane 2 of the destination operation. Bits 6 and 7 select a single-precision value from one of the four lanes in the XMM_{src2}/mem_{src2} operand to store into lane 3 of the destination operation.

Figure 11-26 shows the operation of the shufps instruction.

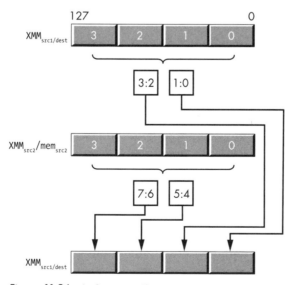

Figure 11-26: shufps operation

For example, the instruction

```
shufps xmm0, xmm1, 0E4h   ; 0E4h = 11 10 01 00
```

loads XMM0 with the following single-precision values:

- XMM0[0 to 31] from XMM0[0 to 32]
- XMM0[32 to 63] from XMM0[32 to 63]
- XMM0[64 to 95] from XMM1[63 to 95]
- XMM0[96 to 127] from XMM1[96 to 127]

If the second operand (XMM_{src2}/mem_{src2}) is the same as the first operand ($XMM_{src1/dest}$), it's possible to rearrange the four single-precision values in the XMM_{dest} register (which is probably the source of the instruction name *shuffle*).

The shufpd instruction works similarly, shuffling double-precision values. As there are only two double-precision values in an XMM register, it takes only a single bit to choose between the values. Likewise, as there are only two double-precision values in the destination register, the instruction requires only two (single-bit) array elements to choose the destination. As a result, the third operand, the imm_8 value, is actually just a 2-bit value; the instruction ignores bits 2 to 7 in the imm_8 operand. Bit 0 of the imm_8 operand selects either lane 0 and bits 0 to 63 (if it is 0) or lane 1 and bits 64 to 127 (if it is 1) from the $XMM_{src1/dest}$ operand to place into lane 0 and bits 0 to 63 of XMM_{dest}. Bit 1 of the imm_8 operand selects either lane 0 and bits 0 to 63 (if it is 0) or lane 1 and bits 64 to 127 (if it is 1) from the XMM_{src}/mem_{128} operand to place into lane 1 and bits 64 to 127 of XMM_{dest}. Figure 11-27 shows this operation.

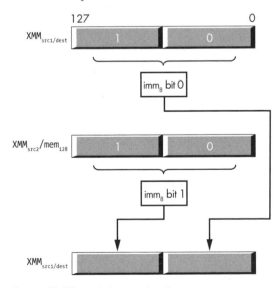

Figure 11-27: shufpd operation

NOTE *These instructions do not modify the upper 128 bits of any overlaid YMM register.*

11.7.5 The vshufps and vshufpd Instructions

The vshufps and vshufpd instructions are similar to shufps and shufpd. They allow you to shuffle the values in 128-bit XMM registers or 256-bit YMM registers.[8] The vshufps and vshufpd instructions have four operands: a destination XMM or YMM register, two source operands (src_1 must be an XMM or a YMM register, and src_2 can be an XMM or a YMM register or a 128- or 256-bit memory location), and an imm_8 operand. Their syntax is the following:

vshufps xmm_{dest}, xmm_{src1}, xmm_{src2}/mem_{128}, imm_8
vshufpd xmm_{dest}, xmm_{src1}, xmm_{src2}/mem_{128}, imm_8

vshufps ymm_{dest}, ymm_{src1}, ymm_{src2}/mem_{256}, imm_8
vshufpd ymm_{dest}, ymm_{src1}, ymm_{src2}/mem_{256}, imm_8

Whereas the SSE shuffle instructions use the destination register as an implicit source operand, the AVX shuffle instructions allow you to specify explicit destination and source operands (they can all be different, or all the same, or any combination thereof).

For the 256-bit vshufps instructions, the imm_8 operand is an array of four 2-bit values (bits 0:1, 2:3, 4:5, and 6:7). These 2-bit values select one of four single-precision values from the source locations, as described in Table 11-5.

Table 11-5: vshufps Destination Selection

	Destination	imm_8 value			
imm_8 bits		00	01	10	11
76 54 32 **10**	Dest[0 to 31]	Src_1[0 to 31]	Src_1[32 to 63]	Src_1[64 to 95]	Src_1[96 to 127]
	Dest[128 to 159]	Src_1[128 to 159]	Src_1[160 to 191]	Src_1[192 to 223]	Src_1[224 to 255]
76 54 **32** 10	Dest[32 to 63]	Src_1[0 to 31]	Src_1[32 to 63]	Src_1[64 to 95]	Src_1[96 to 127]
	Dest[160 to 191]	Src_1[128 to 159]	Src_1[160 to 191]	Src_1[192 to 223]	Src_1[224 to 255]
76 **54** 32 10	Dest[64 to 95]	Src_2[0 to 31]	Src_2[32 to 63]	Src_2[64 to 95]	Src_2[96 to 127]
	Dest[192 to 223]	Src_2[128 to 159]	Src_2[160 to 191]	Src_2[192 to 223]	Src_2[224 to 255]
76 54 32 10	Dest[96 to 127]	Src_2[0 to 31]	Src_2[32 to 63]	Src_2[64 to 95]	Src_2[96 to 127]
	Dest[224 to 255]	Src_2[128 to 159]	Src_2[160 to 191]	Src_2[192 to 223]	Src_2[224 to 255]

If both source operands are the same, you can shuffle around the single-precision values in any order you choose (and if the destination and both source operands are the same, you can arbitrarily shuffle the dwords within that register).

---

8. They also allow you to shuffle values in ZMM registers. However, this book is largely ignoring the AVX-512 instruction set extensions. See the Intel and AMD documentation if you are interested in using the 512-bit variants of these instructions.

The vshufps instruction also allows you to specify XMM and 128-bit memory operands. In this form, it behaves quite similarly to the shufps instruction except that you get to specify two different 128-bit source operands (rather than only one 128-bit source operand), and it zeroes the HO 128 bits of the corresponding YMM register. If the destination operand is different from the first source operand, this can be useful. If the vshufps's first source operand is the same XMM register as the destination operand, you should use the shufps instruction as its machine encoding is shorter.

The vshufpd instruction is an extension of shufpd to 256 bits (plus the addition of a second source operand). As there are four double-precision values present in a 256-bit YMM register, vshufpd needs 4 bits to select the source indexes (rather than the 2 bits that shufpd requires). Table 11-6 describes how vshufpd copies the data from the source operands to the destination operand.

Table 11-6: vshufpd Destination Selection

imm$_8$ bits	Destination	imm$_8$ value 0	imm$_8$ value 1
7654 3 2 1 **0**	Dest[0 to 63]	Src$_1$[0 to 63]	Src$_1$[64 to 127]
7654 3 2 1 0	Dest[64 to 127]	Src$_2$[0 to 63]	Src$_2$[64 to 127]
7654 3 **2** 1 0	Dest[128 to 191]	Src$_1$[128 to 191]	Src$_1$[192 to 255]
7654 **3** 2 1 0	Dest[192 to 255]	Src$_2$[128 to 191]	Src$_2$[192 to 255]

Like the vshufps instruction, vshufpd also allows you to specify XMM registers if you want a three-operand version of shufpd.

11.7.6 The (v)unpcklps, (v)unpckhps, (v)unpcklpd, and (v)unpckhpd Instructions

The unpack (and merge) instructions are a simplified variant of the shuffle instructions. These instructions copy single- and double-precision values from fixed locations in their source operands and insert those values into fixed locations in the destination operand. They are, essentially, shuffle instructions without the imm$_8$ operand and with fixed shuffle patterns.

The unpcklps and unpckhps instructions choose half their single-precision operands from one of two sources, merge these values (interleaving them), and then store the merged result into the destination operand (which is the same as the first source operand). The syntax for these two instructions is as follows:

```
unpcklps xmm_dest, xmm_src/mem_128
unpckhps xmm_dest, xmm_src/mem_128
```

The XMM$_{dest}$ operand serves as both the first source operand and the destination operand. The XMM$_{src}$/mem$_{128}$ operand is the second source operand.

The difference between the two is the way they select their source operands. The `unpcklps` instruction copies the two LO single-precision values from the source operand to bit positions 32 to 63 (dword 1) and 96 to 127 (dword 3). It leaves dword 0 in the destination operand alone and copies the value originally in dword 1 to dword 2 in the destination. Figure 11-28 diagrams this operation.

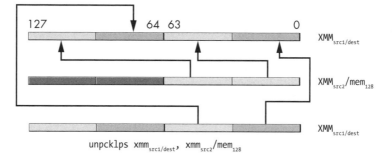

Figure 11-28: unpcklps instruction operation

The `unpckhps` instruction copies the two HO single-precision values from the two sources to the destination register, as shown in Figure 11-29.

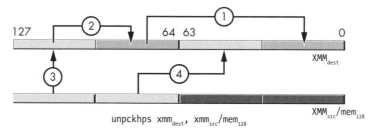

Bubbles denote logical order of operations

Figure 11-29: unpckhps instruction operation

The `unpcklpd` and `unpckhpd` instructions do the same thing as `unpcklps` and `unpckhps` except, of course, they operate on double-precision values rather than single-precision values. Figures 11-30 and 11-31 show the operation of these two instructions.

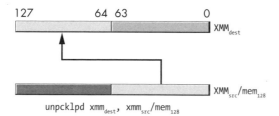

Figure 11-30: unpcklpd instruction operation

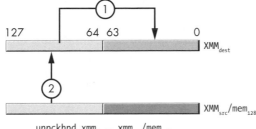

unpckhpd xmm$_{dest}$, xmm$_{src}$/mem$_{128}$

Figure 11-31: unpckhpd instruction operation

NOTE *These instructions do not modify the upper 128 bits of any overlaid YMM register.*

The vunpcklps, vunpckhps, vunpcklpd, and vunpckhpd instructions have the following syntax:

---

vunpcklps xmm$_{dest}$, xmm$_{src1}$, xmm$_{src2}$/mem$_{128}$
vunpckhps xmm$_{dest}$, xmm$_{src1}$, xmm$_{src2}$/mem$_{128}$

vunpcklps ymm$_{dest}$, ymm$_{src1}$, ymm$_{src2}$/mem$_{256}$
vunpckhps ymm$_{dest}$, ymm$_{src1}$, ymm$_{src2}$/mem$_{256}$

They work similarly to the non-v variants, with a couple of differences:

- The AVX variants support using the YMM registers as well as the XMM registers.

- The AVX variants require three operands. The first (destination) and second (source$_1$) operands must be XMM or YMM registers. The third (source$_2$) operand can be an XMM or a YMM register or a 128- or 256-bit memory location. The two-operand form is just a special case of the three-operand form, where the first and second operands specify the same register name.

- The 128-bit variants zero out the HO bits of the YMM register rather than leaving those bits unchanged.

Of course, the AVX instructions with the YMM registers interleave twice as many single- or double-precision values. The interleaving extension happens in the intuitive way, with vunpcklps (Figure 11-32):

- The single-precision values in source$_1$, bits 0 to 31, are first written to bits 0 to 31 of the destination.

- The single-precision values in source$_2$, bits 0 to 31, are written to bits 32 to 63 of the destination.

- The single-precision values in source$_1$, bits 32 to 63, are written to bits 64 to 95 of the destination.

- The single-precision values in source$_2$, bits 32 to 63, are written to bits 96 to 127 of the destination.

- The single-precision values in source$_1$, bits 128 to 159, are first written to bits 128 to 159 of the destination.
- The single-precision values in source$_2$, bits 128 to 159, are written to bits 160 to 191 of the destination.
- The single-precision values in source$_1$, bits 160 to 191, are written to bits 192 to 223 of the destination.
- The single-precision values in source$_2$, bits 160 to 191, are written to bits 224 to 256 of the destination.

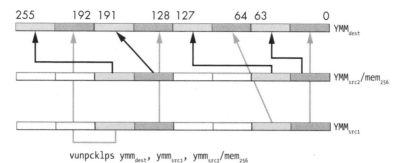

vunpcklps ymm$_{dest}$, ymm$_{src1}$, ymm$_{src2}$/mem$_{256}$

Figure 11-32: vunpcklps instruction operation

The vunpckhps instruction (Figure 11-33) does the following:

- The single-precision values in source$_1$, bits 64 to 95, are first written to bits 0 to 31 of the destination.
- The single-precision values in source$_2$, bits 64 to 95, are written to bits 32 to 63 of the destination.
- The single-precision values in source$_1$, bits 96 to 127, are written to bits 64 to 95 of the destination.
- The single-precision values in source$_2$, bits 96 to 127, are written to bits 96 to 127 of the destination.

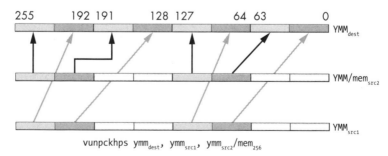

vunpckhps ymm$_{dest}$, ymm$_{src1}$, ymm$_{src2}$/mem$_{256}$

Figure 11-33: vunpckhps instruction operation

Likewise, vunpcklpd and vunpckhpd move double-precision values.

11.7.7 The Integer Unpack Instructions

The punpck* instructions provide a set of integer unpack instructions to complement the floating-point variants. These instructions appear in Table 11-7.

Table 11-7: Integer Unpack Instructions

Instruction	Description
punpcklbw	Unpacks low bytes to words
punpckhbw	Unpacks high bytes to words
punpcklwd	Unpacks low words to dwords
punpckhwd	Unpacks high words to dwords
punpckldq	Unpacks low dwords to qwords
punpckhdq	Unpacks high dwords to qwords
punpcklqdq	Unpacks low qwords to owords (double qwords)
punpckhqdq	Unpacks high qwords to owords (double qwords)

11.7.7.1 The punpck* Instructions

The punpck* instructions extract half the bytes, words, dwords, or qwords from two different sources and merge these values into a destination SSE register. The syntax for these instructions is shown here:

```
punpcklbw   xmm_dest, xmm_src
punpcklbw   xmm_dest, mem_src
punpckhbw   xmm_dest, xmm_src
punpckhbw   xmm_dest, mem_src
punpcklwd   xmm_dest, xmm_src
punpcklwd   xmm_dest, mem_src
punpckhwd   xmm_dest, xmm_src
punpckhwd   xmm_dest, mem_src
punpckldq   xmm_dest, xmm_src
punpckldq   xmm_dest, mem_src
punpckhdq   xmm_dest, xmm_src
punpckhdq   xmm_dest, mem_src
punpcklqdq  xmm_dest, xmm_src
punpcklqdq  xmm_dest, mem_src
punpckhqdq  xmm_dest, xmm_src
punpckhqdq  xmm_dest, mem_src
```

Figures 11- 34 through 11-41 show the data transfers for each of these instructions.

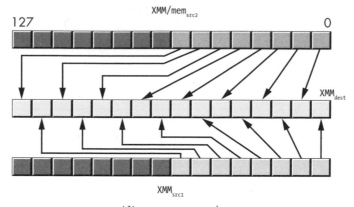

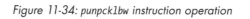

punpcklbw xmm$_{dest/src1}$, xmm/mem$_{src2}$

Figure 11-34: punpcklbw instruction operation

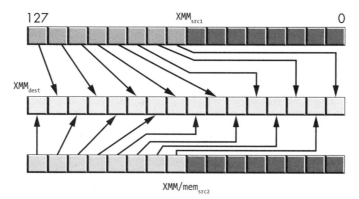

punpckhbw xmm$_{dest/src1}$, xmm/mem$_{src2}$

Figure 11-35: punpckhbw operation

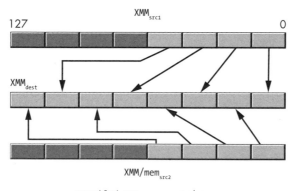

punpcklwd xmm$_{dest/src1}$, xmm/mem$_{src2}$

Figure 11-36: punpcklwd operation

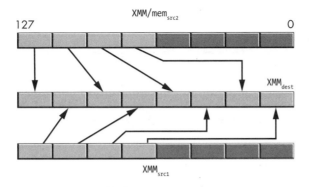

punpckhwd xmm$_{dest/src1}$, xmm/mem$_{src2}$

Figure 11-37: punpckhwd operation

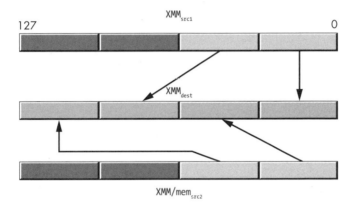

punpckldq xmm$_{dest/src1}$, xmm/mem$_{src2}$

Figure 11-38: punpckldq operation

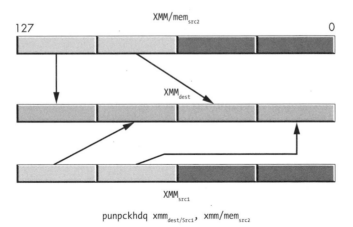

punpckhdq xmm$_{dest/Src1}$, xmm/mem$_{src2}$

Figure 11-39: punpckhdq operation

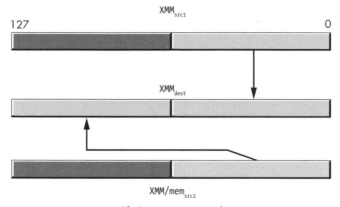

$$XMM_{src1}$$

punpcklqdq xmm$_{dest/src1}$, xmm/mem$_{src2}$

Figure 11-40: punpcklqdq operation

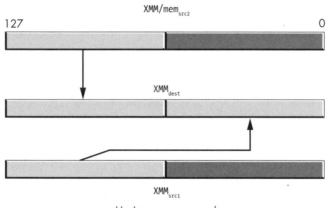

$$XMM/mem_{src2}$$

punpckhqdq xmm$_{dest/src1}$, xmm/mem$_{src2}$

Figure 11-41: punpckhqdq operation

> **NOTE** *These instructions do not modify the upper 128 bits of any overlaid YMM register.*

11.7.7.2 The vpunpck* SSE Instructions

The AVX vpunpck* instructions provide a set of AVX integer unpack instructions to complement the SSE variants. These instructions appear in Table 11-8.

Table 11-8: AVX Integer Unpack Instructions

Instruction	Description
vpunpcklbw	Unpacks low bytes to words
vpunpckhbw	Unpacks high bytes to words
vpunpcklwd	Unpacks low words to dwords
vpunpckhwd	Unpacks high words to dwords
vpunpckldq	Unpacks low dwords to qwords

Instruction	Description
vpunpckhdq	Unpacks high dwords to qwords
vpunpcklqdq	Unpacks low qwords to owords (double qwords)
vpunpckhqdq	Unpacks high qwords to owords (double qwords)

The `vpunpck*` instructions extract half the bytes, words, dwords, or qwords from two different sources and merge these values into a destination AVX or SSE register. Here is the syntax for the SSE forms of these instructions:

```
vpunpcklbw   xmm_dest, xmm_src1, xmm_src2/mem_128
vpunpckhbw   xmm_dest, xmm_src1, xmm_src2/mem_128
vpunpcklwd   xmm_dest, xmm_src1, xmm_src2/mem_128
vpunpckhwd   xmm_dest, xmm_src1, xmm_src2/mem_128
vpunpckldq   xmm_dest, xmm_src1, xmm_src2/mem_128
vpunpckhdq   xmm_dest, xmm_src1, xmm_src2/mem_128
vpunpcklqdq  xmm_dest, xmm_src1, xmm_src2/mem_128
vpunpckhqdq  xmm_dest, xmm_src1, xmm_src2/mem_128
```

Functionally, the only difference between these AVX instructions (`vunpck*`) and the SSE (`unpck*`) instructions is that the SSE variants leave the upper bits of the YMM AVX registers (bits 128 to 255) unchanged, whereas the AVX variants zero-extend the result to 256 bits. See Figures 11-34 through 11-41 for a description of the operation of these instructions.

11.7.7.3 The vpunpck* AVX Instructions

The AVX `vunpck*` instructions also support the use of the AVX YMM registers, in which case the unpack and merge operation extends from 128 bits to 256 bits. The syntax for these instructions is as follows:

```
vpunpcklbw   ymm_dest, ymm_src1, ymm_src2/mem_256
vpunpckhbw   ymm_dest, ymm_src1, ymm_src2/mem_256
vpunpcklwd   ymm_dest, ymm_src1, ymm_src2/mem_256
vpunpckhwd   ymm_dest, ymm_src1, ymm_src2/mem_256
vpunpckldq   ymm_dest, ymm_src1, ymm_src2/mem_256
vpunpckhdq   ymm_dest, ymm_src1, ymm_src2/mem_256
vpunpcklqdq  ymm_dest, ymm_src1, ymm_src2/mem_256
vpunpckhqdq  ymm_dest, ymm_src1, ymm_src2/mem_256
```

11.7.8   The (v)pextrb, (v)pextrw, (v)pextrd, and (v)pextrq Instructions

The (v)pextrb, (v)pextrw, (v)pextrd, and (v)pextrq instructions extract a byte, word, dword, or qword from a 128-bit XMM register and copy this data to a general-purpose register or memory location. The syntax for these instructions is the following:

```
pextrb reg_32, xmm_src, imm_8    ; imm_8 = 0 to 15
pextrb reg_64, xmm_src, imm_8    ; imm_8 = 0 to 15
pextrb mem_8,  xmm_src, imm_8    ; imm_8 = 0 to 15
```

```
vpextrb  reg₃₂, xmm_src, imm₈   ; imm₈ = 0 to 15
vpextrb  reg₆₄, xmm_src, imm₈   ; imm₈ = 0 to 15
vpextrb  mem₈,  xmm_src, imm₈   ; imm₈ = 0 to 15


pextrw   reg₃₂, xmm_src, imm₈   ; imm₈ = 0 to 7
pextrw   reg₆₄, xmm_src, imm₈   ; imm₈ = 0 to 7
pextrw   mem₁₆, xmm_src, imm₈   ; imm₈ = 0 to 7
vpextrw  reg₃₂, xmm_src, imm₈   ; imm₈ = 0 to 7
vpextrw  reg₆₄, xmm_src, imm₈   ; imm₈ = 0 to 7
vpextrw  mem₁₆, xmm_src, imm₈   ; imm₈ = 0 to 7


pextrd   reg₃₂, xmm_src, imm₈   ; imm₈ = 0 to 3
pextrd   mem₃₂, xmm_src, imm₈   ; imm₈ = 0 to 3
vpextrd  mem₆₄, xmm_src, imm₈   ; imm₈ = 0 to 3
vpextrd  reg₃₂, xmm_src, imm₈   ; imm₈ = 0 to 3
vpextrd  reg₆₄, xmm_src, imm₈   ; imm₈ = 0 to 3
vpextrd  mem₃₂, xmm_src, imm₈   ; imm₈ = 0 to 3


pextrq   reg₆₄, xmm_src, imm₈   ; imm₈ = 0 to 1
pextrq   mem₆₄, xmm_src, imm₈   ; imm₈ = 0 to 1
vpextrq  reg₆₄, xmm_src, imm₈   ; imm₈ = 0 to 1
vpextrq  mem₆₄, xmm_src, imm₈   ; imm₈ = 0 to 1
```

The byte and word instructions expect a 32- or 64-bit general-purpose register as their destination (first operand) or a memory location that is the same size as the instruction (that is, pextrb expects a byte-sized memory operand, pextrw expects a word-sized operand, and so on). The source (second) operand is a 128-bit XMM register. The index (third) operand is an 8-bit immediate value that specifies an index (lane number). These instructions fetch the byte, word, dword, or qword in the lane specified by the 8-bit immediate value and copy that value into the destination operand. The double-word and quad-word variants require a 32-bit or 64-bit general-purpose register, respectively. If the destination operand is a 32- or 64-bit general-purpose register, the instruction zero-extends the value to 32 or 64 bits, if necessary.

NOTE *These instructions do not support extracting data from the upper 128 bits of a YMM register.*

11.7.9 The (v)pinsrb, (v)pinsrw, (v)pinsrd, and (v)pinsrq Instructions

The (v)pinsr{b,w,d,q} instructions take a byte, word, dword, or qword from a general-purpose register or memory location and store that data to a lane of an XMM register. The syntax for these instructions is the following:[9]

```
pinsrb   xmm_dest, reg₃₂, imm₈            ; imm₈ = 0 to 15
pinsrb   xmm_dest, mem₈, imm₈             ; imm₈ = 0 to 15
vpinsrb  xmm_dest, xmm_src2, reg₃₂, imm₈  ; imm₈ = 0 to 15
vpinsrb  xmm_dest, xmm_src2, mem₈, imm₈   ; imm₈ = 0 to 15
```

---

9. Intel and AMD's documentation swap the second and third operands. This book uses the Intel syntax.

```
pinsrw  xmm_dest, reg_32, imm_8              ; imm_8 = 0 to 7
pinsrw  xmm_dest, mem_16, imm_8              ; imm_8 = 0 to 7
vpinsrw xmm_dest, xmm_src2, reg_32, imm_8    ; imm_8 = 0 to 7
vpinsrw xmm_dest, xmm_src2, mem_16, imm_8    ; imm_8 = 0 to 7


pinsrd  xmm_dest, reg_32, imm_8              ; imm_8 = 0 to 3
pinsrd  xmm_dest, mem_32, imm_8              ; imm_8 = 0 to 3
vpinsrd xmm_dest, xmm_src2, reg_32, imm_8    ; imm_8 = 0 to 3
vpinsrd xmm_dest, xmm_src2, mem_32, imm_8    ; imm_8 = 0 to 3


pinsrq  xmm_dest, reg_64, imm_8              ; imm_8 = 0 to 1
pinsrq  xmm_dest, xmm_src2, mem_64, imm_8    ; imm_8 = 0 to 1
vpinsrq xmm_dest, xmm_src2, reg_64, imm_8    ; imm_8 = 0 to 1
vpinsrq xmm_dest, xmm_src2, mem_64, imm_8    ; imm_8 = 0 to 1
```

The destination (first) operand is a 128-bit XMM register. The `pinsr*` instructions expect a memory location or a 32-bit general-purpose register as their source (second) operand (except the `pinsrq` instructions, which require a 64-bit register). The index (third) operand is an 8-bit immediate value that specifies an index (lane number).

These instructions fetch a byte, word, dword, or qword from the general-purpose register or memory location and copy that to the lane in the XMM register specified by the 8-bit immediate value. The `pinsr{b,w,d,q}` instructions leave any HO bits in the underlying YMM register unchanged (if applicable).

The `vpinsr{b,w,d,q}` instructions copy the data from the XMM source register into the destination register and then copy the byte, word, dword, or quad word to the specified location in the destination register. These instructions zero-extend the value throughout the HO bits of the underlying YMM register.

11.7.10 The (v)extractps and (v)insertps Instructions

The `extractps` and `vextractps` instructions are functionally equivalent to `pextrd` and `vpextrd`. They extract a 32-bit (single-precision floating-point) value from an XMM register and move it into a 32-bit general-purpose register or a 32-bit memory location. The syntax for the (v)extractps instructions is shown here:

```
extractps  reg_32, xmm_src, imm_8
extractps  mem_32, xmm_src, imm_8
vextractps reg_32, xmm_src, imm_8
vextractps mem_32, xmm_src, imm_8
```

The `insertps` and `vinsertps` instructions insert a 32-bit floating-point value into an XMM register and, optionally, zero out other lanes in the XMM register. The syntax for these instructions is as follows:

```
insertps  xmm_dest, xmm_src, imm_8
insertps  xmm_dest, mem_32, imm_8
vinsertps xmm_dest, xmm_src1, xmm_src2, imm_8
vinsertps xmm_dest, xmm_src1, mem_32, imm_8
```

For the `insertps` and `vinsertps` instructions, the imm$_8$ operand has the fields listed in Table 11-9.

Table 11-9: imm$_8$ Bit Fields for `insertps` and `vinsertps` Instructions

Bit(s)	Meaning
6 to 7	(Only if the source operand is an XMM register): Selects the 32-bit lane from the source XMM register (0, 1, 2, or 3). If the source operand is a 32-bit memory location, the instruction ignores this field and uses the full 32 bits from memory.
4 to 5	Specifies the lane in the destination XMM register in which to store the single-precision value.
3	If set, zeroes lane 3 of XMM$_{dest}$.
2	If set, zeroes lane 2 of XMM$_{dest}$.
1	If set, zeroes lane 1 of XMM$_{dest}$.
0	If set, zeroes lane 0 of XMM$_{dest}$.

On CPUs with the AVX extensions, `insertps` does not modify the upper bits of the YMM registers; `vinsertps` zeroes the upper bits.

The `vinsertps` instruction first copies the XMM$_{src1}$ register to XMM$_{dest}$ before performing the insertion operation. The HO bits of the corresponding YMM register are set to 0.

The x86-64 does not provide `(v)extractpd` or `(v)insertpd` instructions.

11.8 SIMD Arithmetic and Logical Operations

The SSE and AVX instruction set extensions provide a variety of scalar and vector arithmetic and logical operations.

"SSE Floating-Point Arithmetic" in Chapter 6 has already covered floating-point arithmetic using the scalar SSE instruction set, so this section does not repeat that discussion. Instead, this section covers the *vector* (or *packed*) arithmetic and logical instructions.

The vector instructions perform multiple operations in parallel on the different data lanes in an SSE or AVX register. Given two source operands, a typical SSE instruction will calculate two double-precision floating-point results, two quad-word integer calculations, four single-precision floating-point operations, four double-word integer calculations, eight word integer calculations, or sixteen byte calculations, simultaneously. The AVX registers (YMM) double the number of lanes and therefore double the number of concurrent calculations.

Figure 11-42 shows how the SSE and AVX instructions perform concurrent calculations; a value is taken from the same lane in two source locations, the calculation is performed, and the instruction stores the result to the same lane in the destination location. This process happens simultaneously for each lane in the source and destination operands. For example, if a pair of

XMM registers contains four single-precision floating-point values, a SIMD packed floating-point addition instruction would add the single-precision values in the corresponding lanes of the source operands and store the single-precision sums into the corresponding lanes of the destination XMM register.

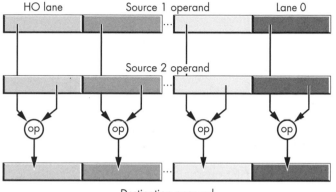

Figure 11-42: SIMD concurrent arithmetic and logical operations

Certain operations—for example, logical AND, ANDN (*and not*), OR, and XOR—don't have to be broken into lanes, because those operations perform the same result regardless of the instruction size. The lane size is a single bit. Therefore, the corresponding SSE/AVX instructions operate on their entire operands without regard for a lane size.

11.9   The SIMD Logical (Bitwise) Instructions

The SSE and AVX instruction set extensions provide the logical operations shown in Table 11-10 (using C/C++ bitwise operator syntax).

Table 11-10: SSE/AVX Logical Instructions

Operation	Description
andpd	dest = dest and source (128-bit operands)
vandpd	dest = source1 and source2 (128-bit or 256-bit operands)
andnpd	dest = dest and ~source (128-bit operands)
vandnpd	dest = source1 and ~source2 (128-bit or 256-bit operands)
orpd	dest = dest | source (128-bit operands)
vorpd	dest = source1 | source2 (128-bit or 256-bit operands)
xorpd	dest = dest ^ source (128-bit operands)
vxorpd	dest = source1 ^ source2 (128-bit or 256-bit operands)

The syntax for these instructions is the following:

```
andpd    xmm_dest, xmm_src/mem_128
vandpd   xmm_dest, xmm_src1, xmm_src2/mem_128
vandpd   ymm_dest, ymm_src1, ymm_src2/mem_256

andnpd   xmm_dest, xmm_src/mem_128
vandnpd  xmm_dest, xmm_src1, xmm_src2/mem_128
vandnpd  ymm_dest, ymm_src1, ymm_src2/mem_256

orpd     xmm_dest, xmm_src/mem_128
vorpd    xmm_dest, xmm_src1, xmm_src2/mem_128
vorpd    ymm_dest, ymm_src1, ymm_src2/mem_256

xorpd    xmm_dest, xmm_src/mem_128
vxorpd   xmm_dest, xmm_src1, xmm_src2/mem_128
vxorpd   ymm_dest, ymm_src1, ymm_src2/mem_256
```

The SSE instructions (without the v prefix) leave the HO bits of the underlying YMM register unchanged (if applicable). The AVX instructions (with the v prefix) that have 128-bit operands will zero-extend their result into the HO bits of the YMM register.

If the (second) source operand is a memory location, it must be aligned on an appropriate boundary (for example, 16 bytes for mem_{128} values and 32 bytes for mem_{256} values). Failure to do so will result in a runtime memory alignment fault.

11.9.1 The (v)ptest Instructions

The ptest instruction (*packed test*) is similar to the standard integer test instruction. The ptest instruction performs a logical AND between the two operands and sets the zero flag if the result is 0. The ptest instruction sets the carry flag if the logical AND of the second operand with the inverted bits of the first operand produces 0. The ptest instruction supports the following syntax:

```
ptest   xmm_src1, xmm_src2/mem_128
vptest  xmm_src1, xmm_src2/mem_128
vptest  ymm_src1, ymm_src2/mem_256
```

NOTE   *The ptest instruction is available only on CPUs that support the SSE4.1 instruction set (and later) extensions; vptest requires AVX support. The 128-bit SSE (ptest) and AVX (vptest) instructions do exactly the same thing, but the SSE encoding is more efficient.*

11.9.2 The Byte Shift Instructions

The SSE and AVX instruction set extensions also support a set of logical and arithmetic shift instructions. The first two to consider are pslldq and psrldq. Although they begin with a p, suggesting they are packed (vector) instructions, these instructions really are just 128-bit logical shift-left and shift-right instructions. Their syntax is as follows:

```
pslldq  xmm_dest, imm_8
vpslldq xmm_dest, xmm_src, imm_8
vpslldq ymm_dest, ymm_src, imm_8
psrldq  xmm_dest, imm_8
vpsrldq xmm_dest, xmm_src, imm_8
vpsrldq ymm_dest, ymm_src, imm_8
```

The `pslldq` instruction shifts its destination XMM register to the left by the number of *bytes* specified by the imm_8 operand. This instruction shifts 0s into the vacated LO bytes.

The `vpslldq` instruction takes the value in the source register (XMM or YMM), shifts that value to the left by imm_8 bytes, and then stores the result into the destination register. For the 128-bit variant, this instruction zero-extends the result into bits 128 to 255 of the underlying YMM register (on AVX-capable CPUs).

The `psrldq` and `vpsrldq` instructions operate similarly to `(v)pslldq` except, of course, they shift their operands to the right rather than to the left. These are logical shift-right operations, so they shift 0s into the HO bytes of their operand, and bits shifted out of bit 0 are lost.

The `pslldq` and `psrldq` instructions shift *bytes* rather than bits. For example, many SSE instructions produce byte masks 0 or 0FFh, representing Boolean results. These instructions shift the equivalent of a bit in one of these byte masks by shifting whole bytes at a time.

11.9.3 The Bit Shift Instructions

The SSE/AVX instruction set extensions also provide vector bit shift operations that work on two or more integer lanes, concurrently. These instructions provide word, dword, and qword variants of the logical shift-left, logical shift-right, and arithmetic shift-right operations, using the syntax

```
shift   xmm_dest, imm_8
shift   xmm_dest, xmm_src/mem_128
vshift  xmm_dest, xmm_src, imm_8
vshift  xmm_dest, xmm_src, mem_128
vshift  ymm_dest, ymm_src, imm_8
vshift  ymm_dest, ymm_src, xmm/mem_128
```

where *shift* = psllw, pslld, psllq, psrlw, psrld, psrlq, psraw, or psrad, and *vshift* = vpsllw, vpslld, vpsllq, vpsrlw, vpsrld, vpsrlq, vpsraw, or vpsraq.

The `(v)psl*` instructions shift their operands to the left; the `(v)psr*` instructions shift their operands to the right. The `(v)psll*` and `(v)psrl*` instructions are logical shift instructions and shift 0s into the bits vacated by the shift. Any bits shifted out of the operand are lost. The `(v)psra*` instructions are arithmetic shift-right instructions. They replicate the HO bit in each lane when shifting that lane's bits to the right; all bits shifted out of the LO bit are lost.

The SSE two-operand instructions treat their first operand as both the source and destination operand. The second operand specifies the number of bits to shift (which is either an 8-bit immediate constant or a value held in an XMM register or a 128-bit memory location). Regardless of the shift count's size, only the LO 4, 5, or 6 bits of the count are meaningful (depending on the lane size).

The AVX three-operand instructions specify a separate source and destination register for the shift operation. These instructions take the value from the source register, shift it the specified number of bits, and store the shifted result into the destination register. The source register remains unmodified (unless, of course, the instruction specifies the same register for the source and destination operands). For the AVX instructions, the source and destination registers can be XMM (128-bit) or YMM (256-bit) registers. The third operand is either an 8-bit immediate constant, an XMM register, or a 128-bit memory location. The third operand specifies the bit shift count (the same as the SSE instructions). You specify an XMM register for the count even when the source and destination registers are 256-bit YMM registers.

The w suffix instructions shift 16-bit operands (eight lanes for 128-bit destination operands, sixteen lanes for 256-bit destinations). The d suffix instructions shift 32-bit dword operands (four lanes for 128-bit destination operands, eight lanes for 256-bit destination operands). The q suffix instructions shift 64-bit operands (two lanes for 128-bit operands, four lanes for 256-bit operands).

11.10　The SIMD Integer Arithmetic Instructions

The SSE and AVX instruction set extensions deal mainly with floating-point calculations. They do, however, include a set of signed and unsigned integer arithmetic operations. This section describes the SSE/AVX integer arithmetic instructions.

11.10.1　SIMD Integer Addition

The SIMD integer addition instructions appear in Table 11-11. These instructions do not affect any flags and thus do not indicate when an overflow (signed or unsigned) occurs during the execution of these instructions. The program itself must ensure that the source operands are all within the appropriate range before performing an addition. If carry occurs during an addition, the carry is lost.

Table 11-11: SIMD Integer Addition Instructions

Instruction	Operands	Description
paddb	xmm_{dest}, xmm/mem_{128}	16-lane byte addition
vpaddb	xmm_{dest}, xmm_{src1}, xmm_{src2}/mem_{128}	16-lane byte addition
vpaddb	ymm_{dest}, ymm_{src1}, ymm_{src2}/mem_{256}	32-lane byte addition
paddw	xmm_{dest}, xmm/mem_{128}	8-lane word addition
vpaddw	xmm_{dest}, xmm_{src1}, xmm_{src2}/mem_{128}	8-lane word addition

Instruction	Operands	Description
vpaddw	ymm_{dest}, ymm_{src1}, ymm_{src2}/mem_{256}	16-lane word addition
paddd	xmm_{dest}, xmm/mem_{128}	4-lane dword addition
vpaddd	xmm_{dest}, xmm_{src1}, xmm_{src2}/mem_{128}	4-lane dword addition
vpaddd	ymm_{dest}, ymm_{src1}, ymm_{src2}/mem_{256}	8-lane dword addition
paddq	xmm_{dest}, xmm/mem_{128}	2-lane qword addition
vpaddq	xmm_{dest}, xmm_{src1}, xmm_{src2}/mem_{128}	2-lane qword addition
vpaddq	ymm_{dest}, ymm_{src1}, ymm_{src2}/mem_{256}	4-lane qword addition

These addition instructions are known as *vertical additions* because if we stack the two source operands on top of each other (on a printed page), the lane additions occur vertically (one source lane is directly above the second source lane for the corresponding addition operation).

The packed additions ignore any overflow from the addition operation, keeping only the LO byte, word, dword, or qword of each addition. As long as overflow is never possible, this is not an issue. However, for certain algorithms (especially audio and video, which commonly use packed addition), truncating away the overflow can produce bizarre results.

A cleaner solution is to use *saturation arithmetic*. For unsigned addition, saturation arithmetic *clips* (or *saturates*) an overflow to the largest possible value that the instruction's size can handle. For example, if the addition of two byte values exceeds 0FFh, saturation arithmetic produces 0FFh—the largest possible unsigned 8-bit value (likewise, saturation subtraction would produce 0 if underflow occurs). For signed saturation arithmetic, clipping occurs at the largest positive and smallest negative values (for example, 7Fh/+127 for positive values and 80h/−128 for negative values).

The x86 SIMD instructions provide both signed and unsigned saturation arithmetic, though the operations are limited to 8- and 16-bit quantities.[10] The instructions appear in Table 11-12.

Table 11-12: SIMD Integer Saturation Addition Instructions

Instruction	Operands	Description
paddsb	xmm_{dest}, xmm/mem_{128}	16-lane byte signed saturation addition
vpaddsb	xmm_{dest}, xmm_{src1}, xmm_{src2}/mem_{128}	16-lane byte signed saturation addition
vpaddsb	ymm_{dest}, ymm_{src1}, ymm_{src2}/mem_{256}	32-lane byte signed saturation addition
paddsw	xmm_{dest}, xmm/mem_{128}	8-lane word signed saturation addition
vpaddsw	xmm_{dest}, xmm_{src1}, xmm_{src2}/mem_{128}	8-lane word signed saturation addition
vpaddsw	ymm_{dest}, ymm_{src1}, ymm_{src2}/mem_{256}	16-lane word signed saturation addition
paddusb	xmm_{dest}, xmm/mem_{128}	16-lane byte unsigned saturation addition

(continued)

---

10. 8-bit addition is generally sufficient for video, with 16-bit addition certainly sufficient for high-end video encoding. 16-bit saturation is suitable for normal audio, though high-end audio requires 24-bit arithmetic.

Table 11-12: SIMD Integer Saturation Addition Instructions *(continued)*

Instruction	Operands	Description
vpaddusb	xmm_{dest}, xmm_{src1}, xmm_{src2}/mem_{128}	16-lane byte unsigned saturation addition
vpaddusb	ymm_{dest}, ymm_{src1}, ymm_{src2}/mem_{256}	32-lane byte unsigned saturation addition
paddusw	xmm_{dest}, xmm/mem_{128}	8-lane word unsigned saturation addition
vpaddusw	xmm_{dest}, xmm_{src1}, xmm_{src2}/mem_{128}	8-lane word unsigned saturation addition
vpaddusw	ymm_{dest}, ymm_{src1}, ymm_{src2}/mem_{256}	16-lane word unsigned saturation addition

As usual, both padd* and vpadd* instructions accept 128-bit XMM registers (sixteen 8-bit additions or eight 16-bit additions). The padd* instructions leave the HO bits of any corresponding YMM destination undisturbed; the vpadd* variants clear the HO bits. Also note that the padd* instructions have only two operands (the destination register is also a source), whereas the vpadd* instructions have two source operands and a single destination operand. The vpadd* instructions with the YMM register provide double the number of parallel additions.

11.10.2   Horizontal Additions

The SSE/AVX instruction sets also support three *horizontal addition* instructions, listed in Table 11-13.

Table 11-13: Horizontal Addition Instructions

Instruction	Description
(v)phaddw	16-bit (word) horizontal add
(v)phaddd	32-bit (dword) horizontal add
(v)phaddsw	16-bit (word) horizontal add and saturate

The horizontal addition instructions add adjacent words or dwords in their two source operands and store the sum of the result into a destination lane, as shown in Figure 11-43.

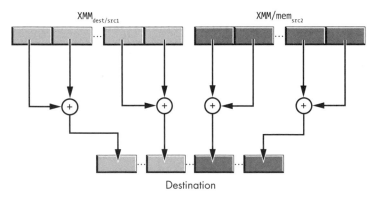

Figure 11-43: Horizontal addition operation

The `phaddw` instruction has the following syntax:

phaddw xmm$_{dest}$, xmm$_{src}$/mem$_{128}$

It computes the following:

```
temp[0 to 15]     = xmm_dest[0 to 15]          + xmm_dest[16 to 31]
temp[16 to 31]    = xmm_dest[32 to 47]         + xmm_dest[48 to 63]
temp[32 to 47]    = xmm_dest[64 to 79]         + xmm_dest[80 to 95]
temp[48 to 63]    = xmm_dest[96 to 111]        + xmm_dest[112 to 127]
temp[64 to 79]    = xmm_src/mem_128[0 to 15]   + xmm_src/mem_128[16 to 31]
temp[80 to 95]    = xmm_src/mem_128[32 to 47]  + xmm_src/mem_128[48 to 63]
temp[96 to 111]   = xmm_src/mem_128[64 to 79]  + xmm_src/mem_128[80 to 95]
temp[112 to 127]  = xmm_src/mem_128[96 to 111] + xmm_src/mem_128[112 to 127]
xmm_dest = temp
```

As is the case with most SSE instructions, `phaddw` does not affect the HO bits of the corresponding YMM destination register, only the LO 128 bits.

The 128-bit `vphaddw` instruction has the following syntax:

vphaddw xmm$_{dest}$, xmm$_{src1}$, xmm$_{src2}$/mem$_{128}$

It computes the following:

```
xmm_dest[0 to 15]     = xmm_src1[0 to 15]          + xmm_src1[16 to 31]
xmm_dest[16 to 31]    = xmm_src1[32 to 47]         + xmm_src1[48 to 63]
xmm_dest[32 to 47]    = xmm_src1[64 to 79]         + xmm_src1[80 to 95]
xmm_dest[48 to 63]    = xmm_src1[96 to 111]        + xmm_src1[112 to 127]
xmm_dest[64 to 79]    = xmm_src2/mem_128[0 to 15]  + xmm_src2/mem_128[16 to 31]
xmm_dest[80 to 95]    = xmm_src2/mem_128[32 to 47] + xmm_src2/mem_128[48 to 63]
xmm_dest[96 to 111]   = xmm_src2/mem_128[64 to 79] + xmm_src2/mem_128[80 to 95]
xmm_dest[111 to 127]  = xmm_src2/mem_128[96 to 111]+ xmm_src2/mem_128[112 to 127]
```

The `vphaddw` instruction zeroes out the HO 128 bits of the corresponding YMM destination register.

The 256-bit `vphaddw` instruction has the following syntax:

vphaddw ymm$_{dest}$, ymm$_{src1}$, ymm$_{src2}$/mem$_{256}$

`vphaddw` does not simply extend the 128-bit version in the intuitive way. Instead, it mixes up computations as follows (where SRC1 is YMM$_{src1}$ and SRC2 is YMM$_{src2}$/mem$_{256}$):

```
ymm_dest[0 to 15]     = SRC1[16 to 31]    + SRC1[0 to 15]
ymm_dest[16 to 31]    = SRC1[48 to 63]    + SRC1[32 to 47]
ymm_dest[32 to 47]    = SRC1[80 to 95]    + SRC1[64 to 79]
ymm_dest[48 to 63]    = SRC1[112 to 127]  + SRC1[96 to 111]
ymm_dest[64 to 79]    = SRC2[16 to 31]    + SRC2[0 to 15]
ymm_dest[80 to 95]    = SRC2[48 to 63]    + SRC2[32 to 47]
ymm_dest[96 to 111]   = SRC2[80 to 95]    + SRC2[64 to 79]
ymm_dest[112 to 127]  = SRC2[112 to 127]  + SRC2[96 to 111]
ymm_dest[128 to 143]  = SRC1[144 to 159]  + SRC1[128 to 143]
ymm_dest[144 to 159]  = SRC1[176 to 191]  + SRC1[160 to 175]
```

$$ymm_{dest}[160 \text{ to } 175] = SRC1[208 \text{ to } 223] + SRC1[192 \text{ to } 207]$$
$$ymm_{dest}[176 \text{ to } 191] = SRC1[240 \text{ to } 255] + SRC1[224 \text{ to } 239]$$
$$ymm_{dest}[192 \text{ to } 207] = SRC2[144 \text{ to } 159] + SRC2[128 \text{ to } 143]$$
$$ymm_{dest}[208 \text{ to } 223] = SRC2[176 \text{ to } 191] + SRC2[160 \text{ to } 175]$$
$$ymm_{dest}[224 \text{ to } 239] = SRC2[208 \text{ to } 223] + SRC2[192 \text{ to } 207]$$
$$ymm_{dest}[240 \text{ to } 255] = SRC2[240 \text{ to } 255] + SRC2[224 \text{ to } 239]$$

11.10.3   Double-Word–Sized Horizontal Additions

The phaddd instruction has the following syntax:

phaddd xmm_{dest}, xmm_{src}/mem_{128}

It computes the following:

$$temp[0 \text{ to } 31] \quad= xmm_{dest}[0 \text{ to } 31] \quad\quad + xmm_{dest}[32 \text{ to } 63]$$
$$temp[32 \text{ to } 63] \quad= xmm_{dest}[64 \text{ to } 95] \quad\quad + xmm_{dest}[96 \text{ to } 127]$$
$$temp[64 \text{ to } 95] \quad= xmm_{src}/mem_{128}[0 \text{ to } 31] \quad + xmm_{src}/mem_{128}[32 \text{ to } 63]$$
$$temp[96 \text{ to } 127] = xmm_{src}/mem_{128}[64 \text{ to } 95] + xmm_{src}/mem_{128}[96 \text{ to } 127]$$
$$xmm_{dest} = temp$$

The 128-bit vphaddd instruction has this syntax:

vphaddd xmm_{dest}, xmm_{src1}, xmm_{src2}/mem_{128}

It computes the following:

$$xmm_{dest}[0 \text{ to } 31] \quad\quad= xmm_{src1}[0 \text{ to } 31] \quad\quad + xmm_{src1}[32 \text{ to } 63]$$
$$xmm_{dest}[32 \text{ to } 63] \quad\quad= xmm_{src1}[64 \text{ to } 95] \quad\quad + xmm_{src1}[96 \text{ to } 127]$$
$$xmm_{dest}[64 \text{ to } 95] \quad\quad= xmm_{src2}/mem_{128}[0 \text{ to } 31] \quad + xmm_{src2}/mem_{128}[32 \text{ to } 63]$$
$$xmm_{dest}[96 \text{ to } 127] \quad= xmm_{src2}/mem_{128}[64 \text{ to } 95] + xmm_{src2}/mem_{128}[96 \text{ to } 127]$$
$$(ymm_{dest}[128 \text{ to } 255] = 0)$$

Like vphaddw, the 256-bit vphaddd instruction has the following syntax:

vphaddd ymm_{dest}, ymm_{src1}, ymm_{src2}/mem_{256}

It calculates the following:

$$ymm_{dest}[0 \text{ to } 31] \quad\quad= ymm_{src1}[32 \text{ to } 63] \quad\quad\quad + ymm_{src1}[0 \text{ to } 31]$$
$$ymm_{dest}[32 \text{ to } 63] \quad\quad= ymm_{src1}[96 \text{ to } 127] \quad\quad\quad + ymm_{src1}[64 \text{ to } 95]$$
$$ymm_{dest}[64 \text{ to } 95] \quad\quad= ymm_{src2}/mem_{128}[32 \text{ to } 63] \quad + ymm_{src2}/mem_{128}[0 \text{ to } 31]$$
$$ymm_{dest}[96 \text{ to } 127] \quad= ymm_{src2}/mem_{128}[96 \text{ to } 127] + ymm_{src2}/mem_{128}[64 \text{ to } 95]$$
$$ymm_{dest}[128 \text{ to } 159] = ymm_{src1}[160 \text{ to } 191] \quad\quad + ymm_{src1}[128 \text{ to } 159]$$
$$ymm_{dest}[160 \text{ to } 191] = ymm_{src1}[224 \text{ to } 255] \quad\quad + ymm_{src1}[192 \text{ to } 223]$$
$$ymm_{dest}[192 \text{ to } 223] = ymm_{src2}/mem_{128}[160 \text{ to } 191] + ymm_{src2}/mem_{128}[128 \text{ to } 159]$$
$$ymm_{dest}[224 \text{ to } 255] = ymm_{src2}/mem_{128}[224 \text{ to } 255] + ymm_{src2}/mem_{128}[192 \text{ to } 223]$$

If an overflow occurs during the horizontal addition, (v)phaddw and (v)phaddd simply ignore the overflow and store the LO 16 or 32 bits of the result into the destination location.

The (v)phaddsw instructions take the following forms:

```
phaddsw   xmm_dest, xmm_src/mem_128
vphaddsw  xmm_dest, xmm_src1, xmm_src2/mem_128
vphaddsw  ymm_dest, ymm_src1, ymm_src2/mem_256
```

The (v)phaddsw instruction (*horizontal signed integer add with saturate, word*) is a slightly different form of (v)phaddw: rather than storing only the LO bits into the result in the destination lane, this instruction saturates the result. *Saturation* means that any (positive) overflow results in the value 7FFFh, regardless of the actual result. Likewise, any negative underflow results in the value 8000h.

Saturation arithmetic works well for audio and video processing. If you were using standard (wraparound/modulo) addition when adding two sound samples together, the result would be horrible clicking sounds. Saturation, on the other hand, simply produces a clipped audio signal. While this is not ideal, it sounds considerably better than the results from modulo arithmetic. Similarly, for video processing, saturation produces a washed-out (white) color versus the bizarre colors that result from modulo arithmetic.

Sadly, there is no horizontal add with saturation for double-word operands (for example, to handle 24-bit audio).

11.10.4   SIMD Integer Subtraction

The SIMD integer subtraction instructions appear in Table 11-14. As for the SIMD addition instructions, they do not affect any flags; any carry, borrow, overflow, or underflow information is lost. These instructions subtract the second source operand from the first source operand (which is also the destination operand for the SSE-only instructions) and store the result into the destination operand.

Table 11-14: SIMD Integer Subtraction Instructions

Instruction	Operands	Description
psubb	xmm_dest, xmm/mem_128	16-lane byte subtraction
vpsubb	xmm_dest, xmm_src, xmm/mem_128	16-lane byte subtraction
vpsubb	ymm_dest, ymm_src, ymm/mem_256	32-lane byte subtraction
psubw	xmm_dest, xmm/mem_128	8-lane word subtraction
vpsubw	xmm_dest, xmm_src, xmm/mem_128	8-lane word subtraction
vpsubw	ymm_dest, ymm_src, ymm/mem_256	16-lane word subtraction
psubd	xmm_dest, xmm/mem_128	4-lane dword subtraction
vpsubd	xmm_dest, xmm_src, xmm/mem_128	4-lane dword subtraction
vpsubd	ymm_dest, ymm_src, ymm/mem_256	8-lane dword subtraction
psubq	xmm_dest, xmm/mem_128	2-lane qword subtraction
vpsubq	xmm_dest, xmm_src, xmm/mem_128	2-lane qword subtraction
vpsubq	ymm_dest, ymm_src, ymm/mem_256	4-lane qword subtraction

The (v)phsubw, (v)phsubd, and (v)phsubsw horizontal subtraction instructions work just like the horizontal addition instructions, except (of course) they compute the difference of the two source operands rather than the sum. See the previous sections for details on the horizontal addition instructions.

Likewise, there is a set of signed and unsigned byte and word saturating subtraction instructions (see Table 11-15). For the signed instructions, the byte-sized instructions saturate positive overflow to 7Fh (+127) and negative underflow to 80h (−128). The word-sized instructions saturate to 7FFFh (+32,767) and 8000h (−32,768). The unsigned saturation instructions saturate to 0FFFFh (+65,535) and 0.

Table 11-15: SIMD Integer Saturating Subtraction Instructions

Instruction	Operands	Description
psubsb	xmm_{dest}, xmm/mem_{128}	16-lane byte signed saturation subtraction
vpsubsb	xmm_{dest}, xmm_{src}, xmm/mem_{128}	16-lane byte signed saturation subtraction
vpsubsb	ymm_{dest}, ymm_{src}, ymm/mem_{256}	32-lane byte signed saturation subtraction
psubsw	xmm_{dest}, xmm/mem_{128}	8-lane word signed saturation subtraction
vpsubsw	xmm_{dest}, xmm_{src}, xmm/mem_{128}	8-lane word signed saturation subtraction
vpsubsw	ymm_{dest}, ymm_{src}, ymm/mem_{256}	16-lane word signed saturation subtraction
psubusb	xmm_{dest}, xmm/mem_{128}	16-lane byte unsigned saturation subtraction
vpsubusb	xmm_{dest}, xmm_{src}, xmm/mem_{128}	16-lane byte unsigned saturation subtraction
vpsubusb	ymm_{dest}, ymm_{src}, ymm/mem_{256}	32-lane byte unsigned saturation subtraction
psubusw	xmm_{dest}, xmm/mem_{128}	8-lane word unsigned saturation subtraction
vpsubusw	xmm_{dest}, xmm_{src}, xmm/mem_{128}	8-lane word unsigned saturation subtraction
vpsubusw	ymm_{dest}, ymm_{src}, ymm/mem_{256}	16-lane word unsigned saturation subtraction

11.10.5 SIMD Integer Multiplication

The SSE/AVX instruction set extensions *somewhat* support multiplication. Lane-by-lane multiplication requires that the result of an operation on two n-bit values fits in n bits, but $n \times n$ multiplication can produce a $2 \times n$-bit result. So a lane-by-lane multiplication operation creates problems as overflow is lost. The basic packed integer multiplication multiplies a pair of lanes and stores the LO bits of the result in the destination lane. For extended arithmetic, packed integer multiplication instructions produce the HO bits of the result.

The instructions in Table 11-16 handle 16-bit multiplication operations. The (v)pmullw instruction multiplies the 16-bit values appearing in the lanes of the source operand and stores the LO word of the result into the corresponding destination lane. This instruction is applicable to both signed and unsigned values. The (v)pmulhw instruction computes the product of two signed word values and stores the *HO word* of the result into the destination lanes. For unsigned operands, (v)pmulhuw performs the same task. By executing both (v)pmullw and (v)pmulh(u)w with the same operands, you can compute the full 32-bit result of a 16×16-bit multiplication. (You can use the punpck* instructions to merge the results into 32-bit integers.)

Table 11-16: SIMD 16-Bit Packed Integer Multiplication Instructions

Instruction	Operands	Description
pmullw	xmm_{dest}, xmm/mem_{128}	8-lane word multiplication, producing the LO word of the product
vpmullw	xmm_{dest}, xmm_{src}, xmm/mem_{128}	8-lane word multiplication, producing the LO word of the product
vpmullw	ymm_{dest}, ymm_{src}, ymm/mem_{256}	16-lane word multiplication, producing the LO word of the product
pmulhuw	xmm_{dest}, xmm/mem_{128}	8-lane word unsigned multiplication, producing the HO word of the product
vpmulhuw	xmm_{dest}, xmm_{src}, xmm/mem_{128}	8-lane word unsigned multiplication, producing the HO word of the product
vpmulhuw	ymm_{dest}, ymm_{src}, ymm/mem_{256}	16-lane word unsigned multiplication, producing the HO word of the product
pmulhw	xmm_{dest}, xmm/mem_{128}	8-lane word signed multiplication, producing the HO word of the product
vpmulhw	xmm_{dest}, xmm_{src}, xmm/mem_{128}	8-lane word signed multiplication, producing the HO word of the product
vpmulhw	ymm_{dest}, ymm_{src}, ymm/mem_{256}	16-lane word signed multiplication, producing the HO word of the product

Table 11-17 lists the 32- and 64-bit versions of the packed multiplication instructions. There are no (v)pmulhd or (v)pmulhq instructions; see (v)pmuludq and (v)pmuldq to handle 32- and 64-bit packed multiplication.

Table 11-17: SIMD 32- and 64-Bit Packed Integer Multiplication Instructions

Instruction	Operands	Description
pmulld	xmm_{dest}, xmm/mem_{128}	4-lane dword multiplication, producing the LO dword of the product
vpmulld	xmm_{dest}, xmm_{src}, xmm/mem_{128}	4-lane dword multiplication, producing the LO dword of the product
vpmulld	ymm_{dest}, ymm_{src}, ymm/mem_{256}	8-lane dword multiplication, producing the LO dword of the product
vpmullq	xmm_{dest}, xmm_{src}, xmm/mem_{128}	2-lane qword multiplication, producing the LO qword of the product
vpmullq	ymm_{dest}, ymm_{src}, ymm/mem_{256}	4-lane qword multiplication, producing the LO qword of the product (available on only AVX-512 CPUs)

At some point along the way, Intel introduced (v)pmuldq and (v)pmuludq to perform signed and unsigned 32×32-bit multiplications, producing a 64-bit result. The syntax for these instructions is as follows:

```
pmuldq    xmm_dest, xmm/mem_128
vpmuldq   xmm_dest, xmm_src1, xmm/mem_128
vpmuldq   ymm_dest, ymm_src1, ymm/mem_256

pmuludq   xmm_dest, xmm/mem_128
vpmuludq  xmm_dest, xmm_src1, xmm/mem_128
vpmuludq  ymm_dest, ymm_src1, ymm/mem_256
```

The 128-bit variants multiply the double words appearing in lanes 0 and 2 and store the 64-bit results into qword lanes 0 and 1 (dword lanes 0 and 1 and 2 and 3). On CPUs with AVX registers,[11] pmuldq and pmuludq do not affect the HO 128 bits of the YMM register. The vpmuldq and vpmuludq instructions zero-extend the result to 256 bits. The 256-bit variants multiply the double words appearing in lanes 0, 2, 4, and 6, producing 64-bit results that they store in qword lanes 0, 1, 2, and 3 (dword lanes 0 and 1, 2 and 3, 4 and 5, and 6 and 7).

The pclmulqdq instruction provides the ability to multiply two qword values, producing a 128-bit result. Here is the syntax for this instruction:

```
pclmulqdq   xmm_dest, xmm/mem_128, imm_8
vpclmulqdq  xmm_dest, xmm_src1, xmm_src2/mem_128, imm_8
```

These instructions multiply a pair of qword values found in XMM_{dest} and XMM_{src} and leave the 128-bit result in XMM_{dest}. The imm_8 operand specifies which qwords to use as the source operands. Table 11-18 lists the possible combinations for pclmulqdq. Table 11-19 lists the combinations for vpclmulqdq.

Table 11-18: imm_8 Operand Values for pclmulqdq Instruction

imm_8	Result
00h	$XMM_{dest} = XMM_{dest}[0 \text{ to } 63]$ * $XMM/mem_{128}[0 \text{ to } 63]$
01h	$XMM_{dest} = XMM_{dest}[64 \text{ to } 127]$ * $XMM/mem_{128}[0 \text{ to } 63]$
10h	$XMM_{dest} = XMM_{dest}[0 \text{ to } 63]$ * $XMM/mem_{128}[64 \text{ to } 127]$
11h	$XMM_{dest} = XMM_{dest}[64 \text{ to } 127]$ * $XMM/mem_{128}[64 \text{ to } 127]$

Table 11-19: imm_8 Operand Values for vpclmulqdq Instruction

imm_8	Result
00h	$XMM_{dest} = XMM_{src1}[0 \text{ to } 63]$ * $XMM_{src2}/mem_{128}[0 \text{ to } 63]$
01h	$XMM_{dest} = XMM_{src1}[64 \text{ to } 127]$ * $XMM_{src2}/mem_{128}[0 \text{ to } 63]$
10h	$XMM_{dest} = XMM_{src1}[0 \text{ to } 63]$ * $XMM_{src2}/mem_{128}[64 \text{ to } 127]$
11h	$XMM_{dest} = XMM_{src1}[64 \text{ to } 127]$ * $XMM_{src2}/mem_{128}[64 \text{ to } 127]$

---

11. Where the SSE4_1 feature flag for the legacy 128-bit version is set. See the Intel documentation for full details.

As usual, `pclmulqdq` leaves the HO 128 bits of the corresponding YMM destination register unchanged, while `vpcmulqdq` zeroes those bits.

11.10.6 SIMD Integer Averages

The (v)pavgb and (v)pavgw instructions compute the average of two sets of bytes or words. These instructions sum the value in the byte or word lanes of their source and destination operands, divide the result by 2, round the results, and leave the averaged results sitting in the destination operand lanes. The syntax for these instructions is shown here:

```
pavgb    xmm_dest, xmm/mem_128
vpavgb   xmm_dest, xmm_src1, xmm_src2/mem_128
vpavgb   ymm_dest, ymm_src1, ymm_src2/mem_256
pavgw    xmm_dest, xmm/mem_128
vpavgw   xmm_dest, xmm_src1, xmm_src2/mem_128
vpavgw   ymm_dest, ymm_src1, ymm_src2/mem_256
```

The 128-bit pavgb and vpavgb instructions compute 16 byte-sized averages (for the 16 lanes in the source and destination operands). The 256-bit variant of the vpavgb instruction computes 32 byte-sized averages.

The 128-bit pavgw and vpavgw instructions compute eight word-sized averages (for the eight lanes in the source and destination operands). The 256-bit variant of the vpavgw instruction computes 16 byte-sized averages.

The vpavgb and vpavgw instructions compute the average of the first XMM or YMM source operand and the second XMM, YMM, or mem source operand, storing the average in the destination XMM or YMM register.

Unfortunately, there are no (v)pavgd or (v)pavgq instructions. No doubt, these instructions were originally intended for mixing 8- and 16-bit audio or video streams (or photo manipulation), and the x86-64 CPU designers never felt the need to extend this beyond 16 bits (even though 24-bit audio is common among professional audio engineers).

11.10.7 SIMD Integer Minimum and Maximum

The SSE4.1 instruction set extensions added eight packed integer *minimum* and *maximum* instructions, as shown in Table 11-20. These instructions scan the lanes of a pair of 128- or 256-bit operands and copy the maximum or minimum value from that lane to the same lane in the destination operand.

Table 11-20: SIMD Minimum and Maximum Instructions

Instruction	Description
(v)pmaxsb	Destination byte lanes set to the maximum value of the two signed byte values found in the corresponding source lanes.
(v)pmaxsw	Destination word lanes set to the maximum value of the two signed word values found in the corresponding source lanes.

(continued)

Table 11-20: SIMD Minimum and Maximum Instructions *(continued)*

Instruction	Description
(v)pmaxsd	Destination dword lanes set to the maximum value of the two signed dword values found in the corresponding source lanes.
vpmaxsq	Destination qword lanes set to the maximum value of the two signed qword values found in the corresponding source lanes. (AVX-512 required for this instruction.)
(v)pmaxub	Destination byte lanes set to the maximum value of the two unsigned byte values found in the corresponding source lanes.
(v)pmaxuw	Destination word lanes set to the maximum value of the two unsigned word values found in the corresponding source lanes.
(v)pmaxud	Destination dword lanes set to the maximum value of the two unsigned dword values found in the corresponding source lanes.
vpmaxuq	Destination qword lanes set to the maximum value of the two unsigned qword values found in the corresponding source lanes. (AVX-512 required for this instruction.)
(v)pminsb	Destination byte lanes set to the minimum value of the two signed byte values found in the corresponding source lanes.
(v)pminsw	Destination word lanes set to the minimum value of the two signed word values found in the corresponding source lanes.
(v)pminsd	Destination dword lanes set to the minimum value of the two signed dword values found in the corresponding source lanes.
vpminsq	Destination qword lanes set to the minimum value of the two signed qword values found in the corresponding source lanes. (AVX-512- required for this instruction.)
(v)pminub	Destination byte lanes set to the minimum value of the two unsigned byte values found in the corresponding source lanes.
(v)pminuw	Destination word lanes set to the minimum value of the two unsigned word values found in the corresponding source lanes.
(v)pminud	Destination dword lanes set to the minimum value of the two unsigned dword values found in the corresponding source lanes.
vpminuq	Destination qword lanes set to the minimum value of the two unsigned qword values found in the corresponding source lanes. (AVX-512 required for this instruction.)

The generic syntax for these instructions is as follows:[12]

```
pmxxyz   xmm_dest, xmm_src/mem_128
vpmxxyz  xmm_dest, xmm_src1, xmm_src2/mem_128
vpmxxyz  ymm_dest, ymm_src1, ymm_src2/mem_256
```

The SSE instructions compute the minimum or maximum of the corresponding lanes in the source and destination operands and store the minimum or maximum result into the corresponding lanes in the destination register. The AVX instructions compute the minimum or maximum of the

---

12. *xx* = ax or in, *y* = s or u, and *z* = b, w, d, or q.

values in the same lanes of the two source operands and store the minimum or maximum result into the corresponding lanes of the destination register.

11.10.8   SIMD Integer Absolute Value

The SSE/AVX instruction set extensions provide three sets of instructions for computing the absolute values of signed byte, word, and double-word integers: (v)pabsb, (v)pabsw, and (v)pabsd.[13] The syntax for these instructions is the following:

```
pabsb   xmm_dest, xmm_src/mem_128
vpabsb  xmm_dest, xmm_src/mem_128
vpabsb  ymm_dest, ymm_src/mem_256

pabsw   xmm_dest, xmm_src/mem_128
vpabsw  xmm_dest, xmm_src/mem_128
vpabsw  ymm_dest, ymm_src/mem_256

pabsd   xmm_dest, xmm_src/mem_128
vpabsd  xmm_dest, xmm_src/mem_128
vpabsd  ymm_dest, ymm_src/mem_256
```

When operating on a system that supports AVX registers, the SSE pabsb, pabsw, and pabsd instructions leave the upper bits of the YMM registers unmodified. The 128-bit versions of the AVX instructions (vpabsb, vpabsw, and vpabsd) zero-extend the result through the upper bits.

11.10.9   SIMD Integer Sign Adjustment Instructions

The (v)psignb, (v)psignw, and (v)psignd instructions apply the sign found in a source lane to the corresponding destination lane. The algorithm works as follows:

```
if source lane value is less than zero then
    negate the corresponding destination lane
else if source lane value is equal to zero then
    set the corresponding destination lane to zero
else
    leave the corresponding destination lane unchanged
```

The syntax for these instructions is the following:

```
psignb   xmm_dest, xmm_src/mem_128
vpsignb  xmm_dest, xmm_src1, xmm_src2/mem_128
vpsignb  ymm_dest, ymm_src1, ymm_src2/mem_256

psignw   xmm_dest, xmm_src/mem_128
vpsignw  xmm_dest, xmm_src1, xmm_src2/mem_128
vpsignw  ymm_dest, ymm_src1, ymm_src2/mem_256
```

---

13. The AVX-512 instruction set actually includes a fourth set of absolute value instructions (vpvasq); see the Intel documentation for more details.

```
psignd   xmm_dest, xmm_src/mem_128
vpsignd  xmm_dest, xmm_src1, xmm_src2/mem_128
vpsignd  ymm_dest, ymm_src1, ymm_src2/mem_256
```

As usual, the 128-bit SSE instructions leave the upper bits of the YMM register unchanged (if applicable), and the 128-bit AVX instructions zero-extend the result into the upper bits of the YMM register.

11.10.10 SIMD Integer Comparison Instructions

The (v)pcmpeqb, (v)pcmpeqw, (v)pcmpeqd, (v)pcmpeqq, (v)pcmpgtb, (v)pcmpgtw, (v)pcmpgtd, and (v)pcmpgtq instructions provide packed signed integer comparisons. These instructions compare corresponding bytes, word, dwords, or qwords (depending on the instruction suffix) in the various lanes of their operands.[14] They store the result of the comparison instruction in the corresponding destination lanes.

11.10.10.1 SSE Compare-for-Equality Instructions

The syntax for the SSE *compare-for-equality* instructions (pcmpeq*) is shown here:

```
pcmpeqb xmm_dest, xmm_src/mem_128   ; Compares 16 bytes
pcmpeqw xmm_dest, xmm_src/mem_128   ; Compares 8 words
pcmpeqd xmm_dest, xmm_src/mem_128   ; Compares 4 dwords
pcmpeqq xmm_dest, xmm_src/mem_128   ; Compares 2 qwords
```

These instructions compute

$$xmm_{dest}[lane] = xmm_{dest}[lane] == xmm_{src}/mem_{128}[lane]$$

where *lane* varies from 0 to 15 for pcmpeqb, 0 to 7 for pcmpeqw, 0 to 3 for pcmpeqd, and 0 to 1 for pcmpeqq. The == operator produces a value of all 1 bits if the two values in the same lane are equal; it produces all 0 bits if the values are not equal.

11.10.10.2 SSE Compare-for-Greater-Than Instructions

The following is the syntax for the SSE *compare-for-greater-than* instructions (pcmpgt*):

```
pcmpgtb xmm_dest, xmm_src/mem_128   ; Compares 16 bytes
pcmpgtw xmm_dest, xmm_src/mem_128   ; Compares 8 words
pcmpgtd xmm_dest, xmm_src/mem_128   ; Compares 4 dwords
pcmpgtq xmm_dest, xmm_src/mem_128   ; Compares 2 qwords
```

These instructions compute

$$xmm_{dest}[lane] = xmm_{dest}[lane] > xmm_{src}/mem_{128}[lane]$$

---

14. Qword comparisons are available only on CPUs that support the SSE4.1 instruction set extensions.

where *lane* is the same as for the compare-for-equality instructions, and the > operator produces a value of all 1 bits if the signed integer in the XMM_{dest} lane is greater than the signed value in the corresponding XMM_{src}/MEM_{128} lane.

On AVX-capable CPUs, the SSE packed integer comparisons preserve the value in the upper bits of the underlying YMM register.

11.10.10.3   AVX Comparison Instructions

The 128-bit variants of these instructions have the following syntax:

```
vpcmpeqb xmm_dest, xmm_src1, xmm_src2/mem_128   ; Compares 16 bytes
vpcmpeqw xmm_dest, xmm_src1, xmm_src2/mem_128   ; Compares 8 words
vpcmpeqd xmm_dest, xmm_src1, xmm_src2/mem_128   ; Compares 4 dwords
vpcmpeqq xmm_dest, xmm_src1, xmm_src2/mem_128   ; Compares 2 qwords

vpcmpgtb xmm_dest, xmm_src1, xmm_src2/mem_128   ; Compares 16 bytes
vpcmpgtw xmm_dest, xmm_src1, xmm_src2/mem_128   ; Compares 8 words
vpcmpgtd xmm_dest, xmm_src1, xmm_src2/mem_128   ; Compares 4 dwords
vpcmpgtq xmm_dest, xmm_src1, xmm_src2/mem_128   ; Compares 2 qwords
```

These instructions compute as follows:

```
xmm_dest[lane] = xmm_src1[lane] == xmm_src2/mem_128[lane]
xmm_dest[lane] = xmm_src1[lane] >  xmm_src2/mem_128[lane]
```

These AVX instructions write 0s to the upper bits of the underlying YMM register.

The 256-bit variants of these instructions have the following syntax:

```
vpcmpeqb ymm_dest, ymm_src1, ymm_src2/mem_256   ; Compares 32 bytes
vpcmpeqw ymm_dest, ymm_src1, ymm_src2/mem_256   ; Compares 16 words
vpcmpeqd ymm_dest, ymm_src1, ymm_src2/mem_256   ; Compares 8 dwords
vpcmpeqq ymm_dest, ymm_src1, ymm_src2/mem_256   ; Compares 4 qwords

vpcmpgtb ymm_dest, ymm_src1, ymm_src2/mem_256   ; Compares 32 bytes
vpcmpgtw ymm_dest, ymm_src1, ymm_src2/mem_256   ; Compares 16 words
vpcmpgtd ymm_dest, ymm_src1, ymm_src2/mem_256   ; Compares 8 dwords
vpcmpgtq ymm_dest, ymm_src1, ymm_src2/mem_256   ; Compares 4 qwords
```

These instructions compute as follows:

```
ymm_dest[lane] = ymm_src1[lane] == ymm_src2/mem_256[lane]
ymm_dest[lane] = ymm_src1[lane] >  ymm_src2/mem_256[lane]
```

Of course, the principal difference between the 256- and the 128-bit instructions is that the 256-bit variants support twice as many byte (32), word (16), dword (8), and qword (4) signed-integer lanes.

11.10.10.4   Compare-for-Less-Than Instructions

There are no packed *compare-for-less-than* instructions. You can synthesize a less-than comparison by reversing the operands and using a greater-than comparison. That is, if $x < y$, then it is also true that $y > x$. If both packed operands are sitting in XMM or YMM registers, swapping the registers is relatively easy (especially when using the three-operand AVX instructions). If the second operand is a memory operand, you must first load that operand into a register so you can reverse the operands (a memory operand must always be the second operand).

11.10.10.5   Using Packed Comparison Results

The question remains of what to do with the result you obtain from a packed comparison. SSE/AVX packed signed integer comparisons do not affect condition code flags (because they compare multiple values and only one of those comparisons could be moved into the flags). Instead, the packed comparisons simply produce Boolean results. You can use these results with the packed AND instructions (pand, vpand, pandn, and vpandn), the packed OR instructions (por and vpor), or the packed XOR instructions (pxor and vpxor) to mask or otherwise modify other packed data values. Of course, you could also extract the individual lane values and test them (via a conditional jump). The following section describes a straightforward way to achieve this.

11.10.10.6   The (v)pmovmskb Instructions

The (v)pmovmskb instruction extracts the HO bit from all the bytes in an XMM or YMM register and stores the 16 or 32 bits (respectively) into a general-purpose register. These instructions set all HO bits of the general-purpose register to 0 (beyond those needed to hold the mask bits). The syntax is

```
pmovmskb    reg, xmm_src
vpmovmskb   reg, xmm_src
vpmovmskb   reg, ymm_src
```

where reg is any 32-bit or 64-bit general-purpose integer register. The semantics for the pmovmskb and vpmovmskb instructions with an XMM source register are the same, but the encoding of pmovmskb is more efficient.

The (v)pmovmskb instruction copies the sign bits from each of the byte lanes into the corresponding bit position of the general-purpose register. It copies bit 7 from the XMM register (the sign bit for lane 0) into bit 0 of the destination register; it copies bit 15 from the XMM register (the sign bit for lane 1) into bit 1 of the destination register; it copies bit 23 from the XMM register (the sign bit for lane 2) into bit 2 of the destination register; and so on.

The 128-bit instructions fill only bits 0 through 15 of the destination register (zeroing out all other bits). The 256-bit form of the vpmovmskb instruction fills bits 0 through 31 of the destination register (zeroing out HO bits if you specify a 64-bit register).

You can use the pmovmskb instruction to extract a single bit from each byte lane in an XMM or a YMM register after a (v)pcmpeqb or (v)pcmpgtb instruction. Consider the following code sequence:

```
pcmpeqb  xmm0, xmm1
pmovmskb eax,  xmm0
```

After the execution of these two instructions, EAX bit 0 will be 1 or 0 if byte 0 of XMM0 was equal, or not equal, to byte 0 of XMM1, respectively. Likewise, EAX bit 1 will contain the result of comparing byte 1 of XMM0 to XMM1, and so on for each of the following bytes (up to bit 15, which compares 16-byte values in XMM0 and XMM1).

Unfortunately, there are no pmovmskw, pmovmskd, and pmovmsq instructions. You can achieve the same result as pmovmskw by using the following code sequence:

```
pcmpeqw  xmm0, xmm1
pmovmskb eax, xmm0
mov      cl, 0     ; Put result here
shr      ax, 1     ; Shift out lane 7 result
rcl      cl, 1     ; Shift bit into CL
shr      ax, 1     ; Ignore this bit
shr      ax, 1     ; Shift out lane 6 result
rcl      cl, 1     ; Shift lane 6 result into CL
shr      ax, 1     ; Ignore this bit
shr      ax, 1     ; Shift out lane 5 result
rcl      cl, 1     ; Shift lane 5 result into CL
shr      ax, 1     ; Ignore this bit
shr      ax, 1     ; Shift out lane 4 result
rcl      cl, 1     ; Shift lane 4 result into CL
shr      ax, 1     ; Ignore this bit
shr      ax, 1     ; Shift out lane 3 result
rcl      cl, 1     ; Shift lane 3 result into CL
shr      ax, 1     ; Ignore this bit
shr      ax, 1     ; Shift out lane 2 result
rcl      cl, 1     ; Shift lane 2 result into CL
shr      ax, 1     ; Ignore this bit
shr      ax, 1     ; Shift out lane 1 result
rcl      cl, 1     ; Shift lane 1 result into CL
shr      ax, 1     ; Ignore this bit
shr      ax, 1     ; Shift out lane 0 result
rcl      cl, 1     ; Shift lane 0 result into CL
```

Because pcmpeqw produces a sequence of words (which contain either 0000h or 0FFFFh) and pmovmskb expects byte values, pmovmskb produces twice as many results as we expect, and every odd-numbered bit that pmovmskb produces is a duplicate of the preceding even-numbered bit (because the inputs are either 0000h or 0FFFFh). This code grabs every odd-numbered bit (starting with bit 15 and working down) and skips over the even-numbered bits. While this code is easy enough to follow, it is rather long and slow. If you're willing to live with an 8-bit result for which the lane numbers don't match the bit numbers, you can use more efficient code:

```
pcmpeqw   xmm0, xmm1
pmovmskb  eax, xmm0
shr       al, 1     ; Move odd bits to even positions
and       al, 55h   ; Zero out the odd bits, keep even bits
and       ah, 0aah  ; Zero out the even bits, keep odd bits
or        al, ah    ; Merge the two sets of bits
```

This interleaves the lanes in the bit positions as shown in Figure 11-44. Usually, it's easy enough to work around this rearrangement in the software. Of course, you can also use a 256-entry lookup table (see Chapter 10) to rearrange the bits however you desire. Of course, if you're just going to test the individual bits rather than use them as some sort of mask, you can directly test the bits that pmovmskb leaves in EAX; you don't have to coalesce them into a single byte.

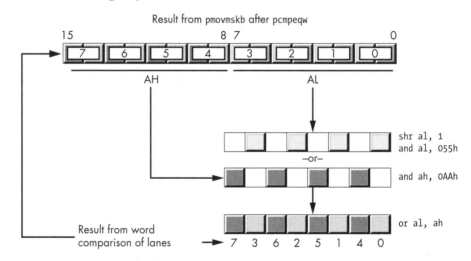

Figure 11-44: Merging bits from pcmpeqw

When using the double-word or quad-word packed comparisons, you could also use a scheme such as the one provided here for pcmpeqw. However, the floating-point mask move instructions (see "The (v)movmskps, (v)movmskpd Instructions" on page 676) do the job more efficiently by breaking the rule about using SIMD instructions that are appropriate for the data type.

11.10.11 *Integer Conversions*

The SSE and AVX instruction set extensions provide various instructions that convert integer values from one form to another. There are zero- and sign-extension instructions that convert from a smaller value to a larger one. Other instructions convert larger values to smaller ones. This section covers these instructions.

11.10.11.1 Packed Zero-Extension Instructions

The *move with zero-extension* instructions perform the conversions appearing in Table 11-21.

Table 11-21: SSE4.1 and AVX Packed Zero-Extension Instructions

Syntax	Description
pmovzxbw xmm_{dest}, xmm_{src}/mem_{64}	Zero-extends a set of eight byte values in the LO 8 bytes of XMM_{src}/mem_{64} to word values in XMM_{dest}.
pmovzxbd xmm_{dest}, xmm_{src}/mem_{32}	Zero-extends a set of four byte values in the LO 4 bytes of XMM_{src}/mem_{32} to dword values in XMM_{dest}.
pmovzxbq xmm_{dest}, xmm_{src}/mem_{16}	Zero-extends a set of two byte values in the LO 2 bytes of XMM_{src}/mem_{16} to qword values in XMM_{dest}.
pmovzxwd xmm_{dest}, xmm_{src}/mem_{64}	Zero-extends a set of four word values in the LO 8 bytes of XMM_{src}/mem_{64} to dword values in XMM_{dest}.
pmovzxwq xmm_{dest}, xmm_{src}/mem_{32}	Zero-extends a set of two word values in the LO 4 bytes of XMM_{src}/mem_{32} to qword values in XMM_{dest}.
pmovzxdq xmm_{dest}, xmm_{src}/mem_{64}	Zero-extends a set of two dword values in the LO 8 bytes of XMM_{src}/mem_{64} to qword values in XMM_{dest}.

A set of comparable AVX instructions also exists (same syntax, but with a v prefix on the instruction mnemonics). The difference, as usual, is that the SSE instructions leave the upper bits of the YMM register unchanged, whereas the AVX instructions store 0s into the upper bits of the YMM registers.

The AVX2 instruction set extensions double the number of lanes by allowing the use of the YMM registers. They take similar operands to the SSE/AVX instructions (substituting YMM for the destination register and doubling the size of the memory locations) and process twice the number of lanes to produce sixteen words, eight dwords, or four qwords in a YMM destination register. See Table 11-22 for details.

Table 11-22: AVX2 Packed Zero-Extension Instructions

Syntax	Description
vpmovzxbw ymm_{dest}, xmm_{src}/mem_{128}	Zero-extends a set of sixteen byte values in the LO 16 bytes of XMM_{src}/mem_{128} to word values in YMM_{dest}.
vpmovzxbd ymm_{dest}, xmm_{src}/mem_{64}	Zero-extends a set of eight byte values in the LO 8 bytes of XMM_{src}/mem_{64} to dword values in YMM_{dest}.
vpmovzxbq ymm_{dest}, xmm_{src}/mem_{32}	Zero-extends a set of four byte values in the LO 4 bytes of XMM_{src}/mem_{32} to qword values in YMM_{dest}.
vpmovzxwd ymm_{dest}, xmm_{src}/mem_{128}	Zero-extends a set of eight word values in the LO 16 bytes of XMM_{src}/mem_{128} to dword values in YMM_{dest}.
vpmovzxwq ymm_{dest}, xmm_{src}/mem_{64}	Zero-extends a set of four word values in the LO 8 bytes of XMM_{src}/mem_{64} to qword values in YMM_{dest}.
vpmovzxdq ymm_{dest}, xmm_{src}/mem_{128}	Zero-extends a set of four dword values in the LO 16 bytes of XMM_{src}/mem_{128} to qword values in YMM_{dest}.

11.10.11.2 Packed Sign-Extension Instructions

The SSE/AVX/AVX2 instruction set extensions provide a comparable set of instructions that sign-extend byte, word, and dword values. Table 11-23 lists the SSE packed sign-extension instructions.

Table 11-23: SSE Packed Sign-Extension Instructions

Syntax	Description
pmovsxbw xmm_{dest}, xmm_{src}/mem_{64}	Sign-extends a set of eight byte values in the LO 8 bytes of XMM_{src}/mem_{64} to word values in XMM_{dest}.
pmovsxbd xmm_{dest}, xmm_{src}/mem_{32}	Sign-extends a set of four byte values in the LO 4 bytes of XMM_{src}/mem_{32} to dword values in XMM_{dest}.
pmovsxbq xmm_{dest}, xmm_{src}/mem_{16}	Sign-extends a set of two byte values in the LO 2 bytes of XMM_{src}/mem_{16} to qword values in XMM_{dest}.
pmovsxwd xmm_{dest}, xmm_{src}/mem_{64}	Sign-extends a set of four word values in the LO 8 bytes of XMM_{src}/mem_{64} to dword values in XMM_{dest}.
pmovsxwq xmm_{dest}, xmm_{src}/mem_{32}	Sign-extends a set of two word values in the LO 4 bytes of XMM_{src}/mem_{32} to qword values in XMM_{dest}.
pmovsxdq xmm_{dest}, xmm_{src}/mem_{64}	Sign-extends a set of two dword values in the LO 8 bytes of XMM_{src}/mem_{64} to qword values in XMM_{dest}.

A set of corresponding AVX instructions also exists (whose mnemonics have the v prefix). As usual, the difference between the SSE and AVX instructions is that the SSE instructions leave the upper bits of the YMM register unchanged (if applicable), and the AVX instructions store 0s into those upper bits.

AVX2-capable processors also allow a YMM_{dest} destination register, which doubles the number of (output) values the instruction can handle; see Table 11-24.

Table 11-24: AVX Packed Sign-Extension Instructions

Syntax	Description
vpmovsxbw ymm_{dest}, xmm_{src}/mem_{128}	Sign-extends a set of sixteen byte values in the LO 16 bytes of XMM_{src}/mem_{128} to word values in YMM_{dest}.
vpmovsxbd ymm_{dest}, xmm_{src}/mem_{64}	Sign-extends a set of eight byte values in the LO 8 bytes of XMM_{src}/mem_{64} to dword values in YMM_{dest}.
vpmovsxbq ymm_{dest}, $xmms_{rc}/mem_{32}$	Sign-extends a set of four byte values in the LO 4 bytes of XMM_{src}/mem_{32} to qword values in YMM_{dest}.
vpmovsxwd ymm_{dest}, xmm_{src}/mem_{128}	Sign-extends a set of eight word values in the LO 16 bytes of XMM_{src}/mem_{128} to dword values in YMM_{dest}.
vpmovsxwq ymm_{dest}, xmm_{src}/mem_{64}	Sign-extends a set of four word values in the LO 8 bytes of XMM_{src}/mem_{64} to qword values in YMM_{dest}.
vpmovsxdq ymm_{dest}, xmm_{src}/mem_{128}	Sign-extends a set of four dword values in the LO 16 bytes of XMM_{src}/mem_{128} to qword values in YMM_{dest}.

11.10.11.3 Packed Sign Extension with Saturation

In addition to converting smaller signed or unsigned values to a larger format, the SSE/AVX/AVX2-capable CPUs have the ability to convert large values to smaller values via saturation; see Table 11-25.

Table 11-25: SSE Packed Sign-Extension with Saturation Instructions

Syntax	Description
packsswb xmm_{dest}, xmm_{src}/mem_{128}	Packs sixteen signed word values (from two 128-bit sources) into sixteen byte lanes in a 128-bit destination register using signed saturation.
packuswb xmm_{dest}, xmm_{src}/mem_{128}	Packs sixteen unsigned word values (from two 128-bit sources) into sixteen byte lanes in a 128-bit destination register using unsigned saturation.
packssdw xmm_{dest}, xmm_{src}/mem_{128}	Packs eight signed dword values (from two 128-bit sources) into eight word values in a 128-bit destination register using signed saturation.
packusdw xmm_{dest}, xmm_{src}/mem_{128}	Packs eight unsigned dword values (from two 128-bit sources) into eight word values in a 128-bit destination register using unsigned saturation.

The saturate operation checks its operand to see if the value exceeds the range of the result (–128 to +127 for signed bytes, 0 to 255 for unsigned bytes, –32,768 to +32,767 for signed words, and 0 to 65,535 for unsigned words). When saturating to a byte, if the signed source value is less than –128, byte saturation sets the value to –128. When saturating to a word, if the signed source value is less than –32,786, signed saturation sets the value to –32,768. Similarly, if a signed byte or word value exceeds +127 or +32,767, then saturation replaces the value with +127 or +32,767, respectively. For unsigned operations, saturation limits the value to +255 (for bytes) or +65,535 (for words). Unsigned values are never less than 0, so unsigned saturation clips values to only +255 or +65,535.

AVX-capable CPUs provide 128-bit variants of these instructions that support three operands: two source operands and an independent destination operand. These instructions (mnemonics the same as the SSE instructions, with a v prefix) have the following syntax:

```
vpacksswb   xmm_dest, xmm_src1, xmm_src2/mem_128
vpackuswb   xmm_dest, xmm_src1, xmm_src2/mem_128
vpackssdw   xmm_dest, xmm_src1, xmm_src2/mem_128
vpackusdw   xmm_dest, xmm_src1, xmm_src2/mem_128
```

These instructions are roughly equivalent to the SSE variants, except that these instructions use XMM_{src1} as the first source operand rather than XMM_{dest} (which the SSE instructions use). Also, the SSE instructions do not modify the upper bits of the YMM register (if present on the CPU), whereas the AVX instructions store 0s into the upper YMM register bits.

AVX2-capable CPUs also allow the use of the YMM registers (and 256-bit memory locations) to double the number of values the instruction can saturate (see Table 11-26). Of course, don't forget to check for AVX2 (and AVX) compatibility before using these instructions.

Table 11-26: AVX Packed Sign-Extension with Saturation Instructions

Syntax	Description
vpacksswb ymm_{dest}, ymm_{src1}, ymm_{src2}/mem_{256}	Packs 32 signed word values (from two 256-bit sources) into 32 byte lanes in a 256-bit destination register using signed saturation.
vpackuswb ymm_{dest}, ymm_{src1}, ymm_{src2}/mem_{256}	Packs 32 unsigned word values (from two 256-bit sources) into 32 byte lanes in a 256-bit destination register using unsigned saturation.
vpackssdw ymm_{dest}, ymm_{src1}, ymm_{src2}/mem_{256}	Packs 16 signed dword values (from two 256-bit sources) into 16 word values in a 256-bit destination register using signed saturation.
vpackusdw ymm_{dest}, ymm_{src1}, ymm_{src2}/mem_{256}	Packs 16 unsigned dword values (from two 256-bit sources) into 16 word values in a 256-bit destination register using unsigned saturation.

11.11   SIMD Floating-Point Arithmetic Operations

The SSE and AVX instruction set extensions provide packed arithmetic equivalents for all the scalar floating-point instructions in "SSE Floating-Point Arithmetic" in Chapter 6. This section does not repeat the discussion of the scalar floating-point operations; see Chapter 6 for more details.

The 128-bit SSE packed floating-point instructions have the following generic syntax (where *instr* is one of the floating-point instructions in Table 11-27):

```
instrps xmm_dest, xmm_src/mem_128
instrpd xmm_dest, xmm_src/mem_128
```

The *packed single* (*ps) instructions perform four single-precision floating-point operations simultaneously. The *packed double* (*pd) instructions perform two double-precision floating-point operations simultaneously. As is typical for SSE instructions, these packed arithmetic instructions compute

$$xmm_{dest}[lane] = xmm_{dest}[lane]\ op\ xmm_{src}/mem_{128}[lane]$$

where *lane* varies from 0 to 3 for packed single-precision instructions and from 0 to 1 for packed double-precision instructions. *op* represents the operation (such as addition or subtraction). When the SSE instructions are executed on a CPU that supports the AVX extensions, the SSE instructions leave the upper bits of the AVX register unmodified.

The 128-bit AVX packed floating-point instructions have this syntax:[15]

```
vinstrps xmm_dest, xmm_src1, xmm_src2/mem_128 ; For dyadic operations
vinstrpd xmm_dest, xmm_src1, xmm_src2/mem_128 ; For dyadic operations
vinstrps xmm_dest, xmm_src/mem_128           ; For monadic operations
vinstrpd xmm_dest, xmm_src/mem_128           ; For monadic operations
```

These instructions compute

$$xmm_{dest}[lane] = xmm_{src1}[lane] \; op \; xmm_{src2}/mem_{128}[lane]$$

where *op* corresponds to the operation associated with the specific instruction (for example, vaddps does a packed single-precision addition). These 128-bit AVX instructions clear the HO bits of the underlying YMM$_{dest}$ register.

The 256-bit AVX packed floating-point instructions have this syntax:

```
vinstrps ymm_dest, ymm_src1, ymm_src2/mem_256 ; For dyadic operations
vinstrpd ymm_dest, ymm_src1, ymm_src2/mem_256 ; For dyadic operations
vinstrps ymm_dest, ymm_src/mem_256           ; For monadic operations
vinstrpd ymm_dest, ymm_src/mem_256           ; For monadic operations
```

These instructions compute

$$ymm_{dest}[lane] = ymm_{src1}[lane] \; op \; ymm_{src}/mem_{256}[lane]$$

where *op* corresponds to the operation associated with the specific instruction (for example, vaddps is a packed single-precision addition). Because these instructions operate on 256-bit operands, they compute twice as many lanes of data as the 128-bit instructions. Specifically, they simultaneously compute eight single-precision (the v*ps instructions) or four double-precision results (the v*pd instructions).

Table 11-27 provides the list of SSE/AVX packed instructions.

Table 11-27: Floating-Point Arithmetic Instructions

Instruction	Lanes	Description
addps	4	Adds four single-precision floating-point values
addpd	2	Adds two double-precision floating-point values
vaddps	4/8	Adds four (128-bit/XMM operands) or eight (256-bit/YMM operands) single-precision values
vaddpd	2/4	Adds two (128-bit/XMM operands) or four (256-bit/YMM operands) double-precision values
subps	4	Subtracts four single-precision floating-point values
subpd	2	Subtracts two double-precision floating-point values

(continued)

---

15. Dyadic operations have two operands; for example, addition is dyadic: x + y. Monadic operations have a single operand; for example, sqrt(x).

Table 11-27: Floating-Point Arithmetic Instructions *(continued)*

Instruction	Lanes	Description
vsubps	4/8	Subtracts four (128-bit/XMM operands) or eight (256-bit/YMM operands) single-precision values
vsubpd	2/4	Subtracts two (128-bit/XMM operands) or four (256-bit/YMM operands) double-precision values
mulps	4	Multiplies four single-precision floating-point values
mulpd	2	Multiplies two double-precision floating-point values
vmulps	4/8	Multiplies four (128-bit/XMM operands) or eight (256-bit/YMM operands) single-precision values
vmulpd	2/4	Multiplies two (128-bit/XMM operands) or four (256-bit/YMM operands) double-precision values
divps	4	Divides four single-precision floating-point values
divpd	2	Divides two double-precision floating-point values
vdivps	4/8	Divides four (128-bit/XMM operands) or eight (256-bit/YMM operands) single-precision values
vdivpd	2/4	Divides two (128-bit/XMM operands) or four (256-bit/YMM operands) double-precision values
maxps	4	Computes the maximum of four pairs of single-precision floating-point values
maxpd	2	Computes the maximum of two pairs of double-precision floating-point values
vmaxps	4/8	Computes the maximum of four (128-bit/XMM operands) or eight (256-bit/YMM operands) pairs of single-precision values
vmaxpd	2/4	Computes the maximum of two (128-bit/XMM operands) or four (256-bit/YMM operands) pairs of double-precision values
minps	4	Computes the minimum of four pairs of single-precision floating-point values
minpd	2	Computes the minimum of two pairs of double-precision floating-point values
vminps	4/8	Computes the minimum of four (128-bit/XMM operands) or eight (256-bit/YMM operands) pairs of single-precision values
vminpd	2/4	Computes the minimum of two (128-bit/XMM operands) or four (256-bit/YMM operands) pairs of double-precision values
sqrtps	4	Computes the square root of four single-precision floating-point values
sqrtpd	2	Computes the square root of two double-precision floating-point values
vsqrtps	4/8	Computes the square root of four (128-bit/XMM operands) or eight (256-bit/YMM operands) single-precision values
vsqrtpd	2/4	Computes the square root of two (128-bit/XMM operands) or four (256-bit/YMM operands) double-precision values
rsqrtps	4	Computes the approximate reciprocal square root of four single-precision floating-point values[*]
vrsqrtps	4/8	Computes the approximate reciprocal square root of four (128-bit/XMM operands) or eight (256-bit/YMM operands) single-precision values

[*] The relative error is $\leq 1.5 \times 2^{-12}$.

The SSE/AVX instruction set extensions also include floating-point horizontal addition and subtraction instructions. The syntax for these instructions is as follows:

```
haddps    xmm_dest, xmm_src/mem_128
vhaddps   xmm_dest, xmm_src1, xmm_src2/mem_128
vhaddps   ymm_dest, ymm_src1, ymm_src2/mem_256
haddpd    xmm_dest, xmm_src/mem_128
vhaddpd   xmm_dest, xmm_src1, xmm_src2/mem_128
vhaddpd   ymm_dest, ymm_src1, ymm_src2/mem_256

hsubps    xmm_dest, xmm_src/mem_128
vhsubps   xmm_dest, xmm_src1, xmm_src2/mem_128
vhsubps   ymm_dest, ymm_src1, ymm_src2/mem_256
hsubpd    xmm_dest, xmm_src/mem_128
vhsubpd   xmm_dest, xmm_src1, xmm_src2/mem_128
vhsubpd   ymm_dest, ymm_src1, ymm_src2/mem_256
```

As for the integer horizontal addition and subtraction instructions, these instructions add or subtract the values in adjacent lanes in the same register and store the result in the destination register (lane 2), as shown in Figure 11-43.

11.12 SIMD Floating-Point Comparison Instructions

Like the integer packed comparisons, the SSE/AVX floating-point comparisons compare two sets of floating-point values (either single- or double-precision, depending on the instruction's syntax) and store a resulting Boolean value (all 1 bits for true, all 0 bits for false) into the destination lane. However, the floating-point comparisons are far more comprehensive than those of their integer counterparts. Part of the reason is that floating-point arithmetic is more complex; however, an ever-increasing silicon budget for the CPU designers is also responsible for this.

11.12.1 SSE and AVX Comparisons

There are two sets of basic floating-point comparisons: (v)cmpps, which compares a set of packed single-precision values, and (v)cmppd, which compares a set of packed double-precision values. Instead of encoding the comparison type into the mnemonic, these instructions use an imm_8 operand whose value specifies the type of comparison. The generic syntax for these instructions is as follows:

```
cmpps    xmm_dest, xmm_src/mem_128, imm_8
vcmpps   xmm_dest, xmm_src1, xmm_src2/mem_128, imm_8
vcmpps   ymm_dest, ymm_src1, ymm_src2/mem_256, imm_8

cmppd    xmm_dest, xmm_src/mem_128, imm_8
vcmppd   xmm_dest, xmm_src1, xmm_src2/mem_128, imm_8
vcmppd   ymm_dest, ymm_src1, ymm_src2/mem_256, imm_8
```

The imm_8 operand specifies the type of the comparison. There are 32 possible comparisons, as listed in Table 11-28.

Table 11-28: imm$_8$ Values for cmpps and cmppd Instructions[†]

imm$_8$	Description	Result				Signal
		A < B	A = B	A > B	Unord	
00h	EQ, ordered, quiet	0	1	0	0	No
01h	LT, ordered, signaling	1	0	0	0	Yes
02h	LE, ordered, signaling	1	1	0	0	Yes
03h	Unordered, quiet	0	0	0	1	No
04h	NE, unordered, quiet	1	0	1	1	No
05h	NLT, unordered, signaling	0	1	1	1	Yes
06h	NLE, unordered, signaling	0	0	1	1	Yes
07h	Ordered, quiet	1	1	1	0	No
08h	EQ, unordered, quiet	0	1	0	1	No
09h	NGE, unordered, signaling	1	0	0	1	Yes
0Ah	NGT, unordered, signaling	1	1	0	1	Yes
0Bh	False, ordered, quiet	0	0	0	0	No
0Ch	NE, ordered, quiet	1	0	1	0	No
0Dh	GE, ordered, signaling	0	1	1	0	Yes
0Eh	GT, ordered, signaling	0	0	1	0	Yes
0Fh	True, unordered, quiet	1	1	1	1	No
10h	EQ, ordered, signaling	0	1	0	0	Yes
11h	LT, ordered, quiet	1	0	0	0	No
12h	LE, ordered, quiet	1	1	0	0	No
13h	Unordered, signaling	0	0	0	1	Yes
14h	NE, unordered, signaling	1	0	1	1	Yes
15h	NLT, unordered, quiet	0	1	1	1	No
16h	NLE, unordered, quiet	0	0	1	1	No
17h	Ordered, signaling	1	1	1	0	Yes
18h	EQ, unordered, signaling	0	1	0	1	Yes
19h	NGE, unordered, quiet	1	0	0	1	No
1Ah	NGT, unordered, quiet	1	1	0	1	No
1Bh	False, ordered, signaling	0	0	0	0	Yes
1Ch	NE, ordered, signaling	1	0	1	0	Yes
1Dh	GE, ordered, quiet	0	1	1	0	No
1Eh	GT, ordered, quiet	0	0	1	0	No
1Fh	True, unordered, signaling	1	1	1	1	Yes

† The darker shaded entries are available only on CPUs that support AVX extensions.

The "true" and "false" comparisons always store true or false into the destination lanes. For the most part, these comparisons aren't particularly useful. The `pxor`, `xorps`, `xorpd`, `vxorps`, and `vxorpd` instructions are probably better for setting an XMM or a YMM register to 0. Prior to AVX2, using a true comparison was the shortest instruction that would set all bits in an XMM or a YMM register to 1, though `pcmpeqb` is commonly used as well (be aware of microarchitectural inefficiencies with this latter instruction).

Note that non-AVX CPUs do not implement the GT, GE, NGT, and NGE instructions. On these CPUs, use the inverse operation (for example, NLT for GE) or swap the operands and use the opposite condition (as was done for the packed integer comparisons).

11.12.2   Unordered vs. Ordered Comparisons

The unordered relationship is true when at least one of the two source operands being compared is a NaN; the ordered relationship is true when neither source operand is a NaN. Having ordered and unordered comparisons allows you to pass error conditions through comparisons as false or true, depending on how you interpret the final Boolean results appearing in the lanes. Unordered results, as their name implies, are incomparable. When you compare two values, one of which is not a number, you must always treat the result as a failed comparison.

To handle this situation, you use an ordered or unordered comparison to force the result to be false or true, the opposite of what you ultimately expect when using the comparison result. For example, suppose you are comparing a sequence of values and want the resulting masks to be true if all the comparisons are valid (for example, you're testing to see if all the src_1 values are greater than the corresponding src_2 values). You would use an ordered comparison in this situation that would force a particular lane to false if one of the values being compared is NaN. On the other hand, if you're checking to see if all the conditions are false after the comparison, you'd use an unordered comparison to force the result to true if any of the values are NaN.

11.12.3   Signaling and Quiet Comparisons

The signaling comparisons generate an invalid arithmetic operation exception (IA) when an operation produces a quiet NaN. The quiet comparisons do not throw an exception and reflect only the status in the MXCSR (see "SSE MXCSR Register" in Chapter 6). Note that you can also mask signaling exceptions in the MXCSR register; you must explicitly set the IM (*invalid operation mask*, bit 7) in the MXCSR to 0 if you want to allow exceptions.

11.12.4   Instruction Synonyms

MASM supports the use of certain synonyms so you don't have to memorize the 32 encodings. Table 11-29 lists these synonyms. In this table, *x1* denotes the destination operand (XMM_n or YMM_n), and *x2* denotes the source operand (XMM_n/mem_{128} or YMM_n/mem_{256}, as appropriate).

Table 11-29: Synonyms for Common Packed Floating-Point Comparisons

Synonym	Instruction	Synonym	Instruction
cmpeqps *x1, x2*	cmpps *x1, x2,* 0	cmpeqpd *x1, x2*	cmppd *x1, x2,* 0
cmpltps *x1, x2*	cmpps *x1, x2,* 1	cmpltpd *x1, x2*	cmppd *x1, x2,* 1
cmpleps *x1, x2*	cmpps *x1, x2,* 2	cmplepd *x1, x2*	cmppd *x1, x2,* 2
cmpunordps *x1, x2*	cmpps *x1, x2,* 3	cmpunordpd *x1, x2*	cmppd *x1, x2,* 3
cmpneqps *x1, x2*	cmpps *x1, x2,* 4	cmpneqpd *x1, x2*	cmppd *x1, x2,* 4
cmpnltps *x1, x2*	cmpps *x1, x2,* 5	cmpnltpd *x1, x2*	cmppd *x1, x2,* 5
cmpnleps *x1, x2*	cmpps *x1, x2,* 6	cmpnlepd *x1, x2*	cmppd *x1, x2,* 6
cmpordps *x1, x2*	cmpps *x1, x2,* 7	cmpordpd *x1, x2*	cmppd *x1, x2,* 7

The synonyms allow you to write instructions such as

```
cmpeqps  xmm0, xmm1
```

rather than

```
cmpps   xmm0, xmm1, 0      ; Compare xmm0 to xmm1 for equality
```

Obviously, using the synonym makes the code much easier to read and understand. There aren't synonyms for all the possible comparisons. To create readable synonyms for the instructions MASM doesn't support, you can use a macro (or a more readable symbolic constant). For more information on macros, see Chapter 13.

11.12.5   AVX Extended Comparisons

The AVX versions of these instructions allow three register operands: a destination XMM or YMM register, a source XMM or YMM register, and a source XMM or YMM register or 128-bit or 256-bit memory location (followed by the imm_8 operand specifying the type of the comparison). The basic syntax is the following:

```
vcmpps  xmm_dest, xmm_src1, xmm_src2/mem_128, imm_8
vcmpps  ymm_dest, ymm_src1, ymm_src2/mem_256, imm_8

vcmppd  xmm_dest, xmm_src1, xmm_src2/mem_128, imm_8
vcmppd  ymm_dest, ymm_src1, ymm_src2/mem_256, imm_8
```

The 128-bit vcmpps instruction compares the four single-precision floating-point values in each lane of the XMM_{src1} register against the values in the corresponding XMM_{src2}/mem_{128} lanes and stores the true (all 1 bits) or false (all 0 bits) result into the corresponding lane of the XMM_{dest} register. The 256-bit vcmpps instruction compares the eight single-precision floating-point values in each lane of the YMM_{src1} register against the values in the corresponding YMM_{src2}/mem_{256} lanes and stores the true or false result into the corresponding lane of the YMM_{dest} register.

The vcmppd instructions compare the double-precision values in the two lanes (128-bit version) or four lanes (256-bit version) and store the result into the corresponding lane of the destination register.

As for the SSE compare instructions, the AVX instructions provide synonyms that eliminate the need to memorize 32 imm_8 values. Table 11-30 lists the 32 instruction synonyms.

Table 11-30: AVX Packed Compare Instructions

imm_8	Instruction
00h	vcmpeqps or vcmpeqpd
01h	vcmpltps or vcmpltpd
02h	vcmpleps or vcmplepd
03h	vcmpunordps or vcmpunordpd
04h	vcmpneqps or vcmpneqpd
05h	vcmpltps or vcmpltpd
06h	vcmpleps or vcmplepd
07h	vcmpordps or vcmpordpd
08h	vcmpeq_uqps or vcmpeq_uqpd
09h	vcmpngeps or vcmpngepd
0Ah	vcmpngtps or vcmpngtpd
0Bh	vcmpfalseps or vcmpfalsepd
0Ch	vcmpneq_oqps or vcmpneq_oqpd
0Dh	vcmpgeps or vcmpgepd
0Eh	vcmpgtps or vcmpgtpd
0Fh	vcmptrueps or vcmptruepd
10h	vcmpeq_osps or vcmpeq_ospd
11h	vcmplt_oqps or vcmplt_oqpd
12h	vcmple_oqps or vcmple_oqpd
13h	vcmpunord_sps or vcmpunord_spd
14h	vcmpneq_usps or vcmpneq_uspd
15h	vcmpnlt_uqps or vcmpnlt_uqpd
16h	vcmpnle_uqps or vcmpnle_uqpd
17h	vcmpord_sps or vcmpord_spd
18h	vcmpeq_usps or vcmpeq_uspd
19h	vcmpnge_uqps or vcmpnge_uqpd
1Ah	vcmpngt_uqps or vcmpngt_uqpd
1Bh	vcmpfalse_osps or vcmpfalse_ospd
1Ch	vcmpneq_osps or vcmpneq_ospd

(continued)

Table 11-30: AVX Packed Compare Instructions *(continued)*

imm$_8$	Instruction
1Dh	vcmpge_oqps or vcmpge_oqpd
1Eh	vcmpgt_oqps or vcmpgt_oqpd
1Fh	vcmptrue_usps or vcmptrue_uspd

NOTE *The* vcmpfalse* *instructions always set the destination lanes to false (0 bits), and the* vcmptrue* *instructions always set the destination lanes to true (1 bits).*

11.12.6 Using SIMD Comparison Instructions

As for the integer comparisons (see "Using Packed Comparison Results" on page 662), the floating-point comparison instructions produce a vector of Boolean results that you use to mask further operations on data lanes. You can use the packed logical instructions (pand and vpand, pandn and vpandn, por and vpor, and pxor and vpxor) to manipulate these results. You could extract the individual lane values and test them with a conditional jump, though this is definitely not the SIMD way of doing things; the following section describes one way to extract these masks.

11.12.7 The (v)movmskps, (v)movmskpd Instructions

The movmskps and movmskpd instructions extract the sign bits from their packed single- and double-precision floating-point source operands and store these bits into the LO 4 (or 8) bits of a general-purpose register. The syntax is

```
movmskps   reg, xmm_src
movmskpd   reg, xmm_src
vmovmskps  reg, ymm_src
vmovmskpd  reg, ymm_src
```

where *reg* is any 32-bit or 64-bit general-purpose integer register.

The movmskps instruction extracts the sign bits from the four single-precision floating-point values in the XMM source register and copies these bits to the LO 4 bits of the destination register, as shown in Figure 11-45.

The movmskpd instruction copies the sign bits from the two double-precision floating-point values in the source XMM register to bits 0 and 1 of the destination register, as Figure 11-46 shows.

The vmovmskps instruction extracts the sign bits from the four and eight single-precision floating-point values in the XMM and YMM source register and copies these bits to the LO 4 and 8 bits of the destination register. Figure 11-47 shows this operation with a YMM source register.

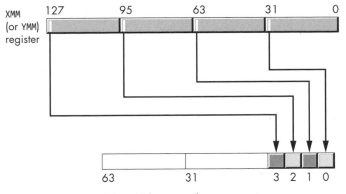

Figure 11-45: movmskps operation

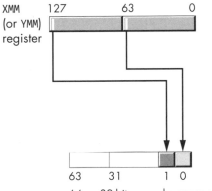

Figure 11-46: movmskpd operation

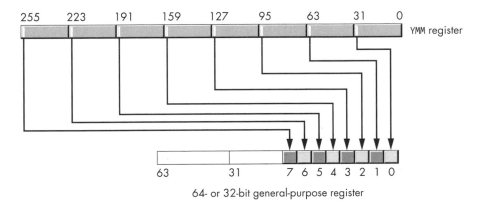

Figure 11-47: vmovmskps operation

The `vmovmskpd` instruction copies the sign bits from the four double-precision floating-point values in the source YMM register to bits 0 to 3 of the destination register, as shown in Figure 11-48.

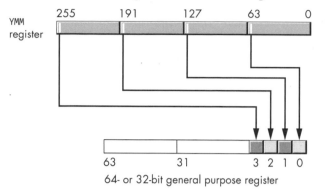

Figure 11-48: vmovmskpd operation

This instruction, with an XMM source register, will copy the sign bits from the two double-precision floating-point values into bits 0 and 1 of the destination register. In all cases, these instructions zero-extend the results into the upper bits of the general-purpose destination register. Note that these instructions do not allow memory operands.

Although the stated data type for these instructions is packed single-precision and packed double-precision, you will also use these instructions on 32-bit integers (movmskps and vmovmskps) and 64-bit integers (movmskpd and vmovmskpd). Specifically, these instructions are perfect for extracting 1-bit Boolean values from the various lanes after one of the (dword or qword) packed integer comparisons as well as after the single- or double-precision floating-point comparisons (remember that although the packed floating-point comparisons compare floating-point values, their results are actually integer values).

Consider the following instruction sequence:

```
            cmpeqpd  xmm0, xmm1
            movmskpd rax,  xmm0       ; Moves 2 bits into RAX
            lea      rcx,  jmpTable
            jmp      qword ptr [rcx][rax*8]

jmpTable    qword    nene
            qword    neeq
            qword    eqne
            qword    eqeq
```

Because `movmskpd` extracts 2 bits from XMM0 and stores them into RAX, this code can use RAX as an index into a jump table to select four different branch labels. The code at label `nene` executes if both comparisons produce not equal; label `neeq` is the target when the lane 0 values are equal but the lane 1 values are not equal. Label `eqne` is the target when the lane 0 values are not equal but the lane 1 values are equal. Finally, label `eqeq` is where this code branches when both sets of lanes contain equal values.

11.13 Floating-Point Conversion Instructions

Previously, I described several instructions to convert data between various scalar floating-point and integer formats (see "SSE Floating-Point Conversions" in Chapter 6). Variants of these instructions also exist for packed data conversions. Table 11-31 lists many of these instructions you will commonly use.

Table 11-31: SSE Conversion Instructions

Instruction syntax	Description
cvtdq2pd xmm_{dest}, xmm_{src}/mem_{64}	Converts two packed signed double-word integers from XMM_{src}/mem_{64} to two packed double-precision floating-point values in XMM_{dest}. If YMM register is present, this instruction leaves the HO bits unchanged.
vcvtdq2pd xmm_{dest}, xmm_{src}/mem_{64}	(AVX) Converts two packed signed double-word integers from XMM_{src}/mem_{64} to two packed double-precision floating-point values in XMM_{dest}. This instruction stores 0s into the HO bits of the underlying YMM register.
vcvtdq2pd ymm_{dest}, xmm_{src}/mem_{128}	(AVX) Converts four packed signed double-word integers from XMM_{src}/mem_{128} to four packed double-precision floating-point values in YMM_{dest}.
cvtdq2ps xmm_{dest}, xmm_{src}/mem_{128}	Converts four packed signed double-word integers from XMM_{src}/mem_{128} to four packed single-precision floating-point values in XMM_{dest}. If YMM register is present, this instruction leaves the HO bits unchanged.
vcvtdq2ps xmm_{dest}, xmm_{src}/mem_{128}	(AVX) Converts four packed signed double-word integers from XMM_{src}/mem_{128} to four packed single-precision floating-point values in XMM_{dest}. If YMM register is present, this instruction writes 0s to the HO bits.
vcvtdq2ps ymm_{dest}, ymm_{src}/mem_{256}	(AVX) Converts eight packed signed double-word integers from YMM_{src}/mem_{256} to eight packed single-precision floating-point values in YMM_{dest}. If YMM register is present, this instruction writes 0s to the HO bits.
cvtpd2dq xmm_{dest}, xmm_{src}/mem_{128}	Converts two packed double-precision floating-point values from XMM_{src}/mem_{128} to two packed signed double-word integers in XMM_{dest}. If YMM register is present, this instruction leaves the HO bits unchanged. The conversion from floating-point to integer uses the current SSE rounding mode.
vcvtpd2dq xmm_{dest}, xmm_{src}/mem_{128}	(AVX) Converts two packed double-precision floating-point values from XMM_{src}/mem_{128} to two packed signed double-word integers in XMM_{dest}. This instruction stores 0s into the HO bits of the underlying YMM register. The conversion from floating-point to integer uses the current AVX rounding mode.
vcvtpd2dq xmm_{dest}, ymm_{src}/mem_{256}	(AVX) Converts four packed double-precision floating-point values from YMM_{src}/mem_{256} to four packed signed double-word integers in XMM_{dest}. The conversion of floating-point to integer uses the current AVX rounding mode.

(continued)

Table 11-31: SSE Conversion Instructions *(continued)*

Instruction syntax	Description
cvtpd2ps xmm_{dest}, xmm_{src}/mem₁₂₈	Converts two packed double-precision floating-point values from XMM_{src}/mem₁₂₈ to two packed single-precision floating-point values in XMM_{dest}. If YMM register is present, this instruction leaves the HO bits unchanged.
vcvtpd2ps xmm_{dest}, xmm_{src}/mem₁₂₈	(AVX) Converts two packed double-precision floating-point values from XMM_{src}/mem₁₂₈ to two packed single-precision floating-point values in XMM_{dest}. This instruction stores 0s into the HO bits of the underlying YMM register.
vcvtpd2ps xmm_{dest}, ymm_{src}/mem₂₅₆	(AVX) Converts four packed double-precision floating-point values from YMM_{src}/mem₂₅₆ to four packed single-precision floating-point values in YMM_{dest}.
cvtps2dq xmm_{dest}, xmm_{src}/mem₁₂₈	Converts four packed single-precision floating-point values from XMM_{src}/mem₁₂₈ to four packed signed double-word integers in XMM_{dest}. If YMM register is present, this instruction leaves the HO bits unchanged. The conversion of floating-point to integer uses the current SSE rounding mode.
vcvtps2dq xmm_{dest}, xmm_{src}/mem₁₂₈	(AVX) Converts four packed single-precision floating-point values from XMM_{src}/mem₁₂₈ to four packed signed double-word integers in XMM_{dest}. This instruction stores 0s into the HO bits of the underlying YMM register. The conversion of floating-point to integer uses the current AVX rounding mode.
vcvtps2dq ymm_{dest}, ymm_{src}/mem₂₅₆	(AVX) Converts eight packed single-precision floating-point values from YMM_{src}/mem₂₅₆ to eight packed signed double-word integers in YMM_{dest}. The conversion of floating-point to integer uses the current AVX rounding mode.
cvtps2pd xmm_{dest}, xmm_{src}/mem₆₄	Converts two packed single-precision floating-point values from XMM_{src}/mem₆₄ to two packed double-precision values in XMM_{dest}. If YMM register is present, this instruction leaves the HO bits unchanged.
vcvtps2pd xmm_{dest}, xmm_{src}/mem₆₄	(AVX) Converts two packed single-precision floating-point values from XMM_{src}/mem₆₄ to two packed double-precision values in XMM_{dest}. This instruction stores 0s into the HO bits of the underlying YMM register.
vcvtps2pd ymm_{dest}, xmm_{src}/mem₁₂₈	(AVX) Converts four packed single-precision floating-point values from XMM_{src}/mem₁₂₈ to four packed double-precision values in YMM_{dest}.
cvttpd2dq xmm_{dest}, xmm_{src}/mem₁₂₈	Converts two packed double-precision floating-point values from XMM_{src}/mem₁₂₈ to two packed signed double-word integers in XMM_{dest} using truncation. If YMM register is present, this instruction leaves the HO bits unchanged.
vcvttpd2dq xmm_{dest}, xmm_{src}/mem₁₂₈	(AVX) Converts two packed double-precision floating-point values from XMM_{src}/mem₁₂₈ to two packed signed double-word integers in XMM_{dest} using truncation. This instruction stores 0s into the HO bits of the underlying YMM register.
vcvttpd2dq xmm_{dest}, ymm_{src}/mem₂₅₆	(AVX) Converts four packed double-precision floating-point values from YMM_{src}/mem₂₅₆ to four packed signed double-word integers in XMM_{dest} using truncation.
cvttps2dq xmm_{dest}, xmm_{src}/mem₁₂₈	Converts four packed single-precision floating-point values from XMM_{src}/mem₁₂₈ to four packed signed double-word integers in XMM_{dest} using truncation. If YMM register is present, this instruction leaves the HO bits unchanged.

Instruction syntax	Description
vcvttps2dq xmm_{dest}, xmm_{src}/mem_{128}	(AVX) Converts four packed single-precision floating-point values from XMM_{src}/mem_{128} to four packed signed double-word integers in XMM_{dest} using truncation. This instruction stores 0s into the HO bits of the underlying YMM register.
vcvttps2dq ymm_{dest}, ymm_{src}/mem_{256}	(AVX) Converts eight packed single-precision floating-point values from YMM_{src}/mem_{256} to eight packed signed double-word integers in YMM_{dest} using truncation.

11.14 Aligning SIMD Memory Accesses

Most SSE and AVX instructions require their memory operands to be on a 16-byte (SSE) or 32-byte (AVX) boundary, but this is not always possible. The easiest way to handle unaligned memory addresses is to use instructions that don't require aligned memory operands, like movdqu, movups, and movupd. However, the performance hit of using unaligned data movement instructions often defeats the purpose of using SSE/AVX instructions in the first place.

Instead, the trick to aligning data for use by SIMD instructions is to process the first few data items by using standard general-purpose registers until you reach an address that is aligned properly. For example, suppose you want to use the pcmpeqb instruction to compare blocks of 16 bytes in a large array of bytes. pcmpeqb requires its memory operands to be at 16-byte-aligned addresses, so if the memory operand is not already 16-byte-aligned, you can process the first 1 to 15 bytes in the array by using standard (non-SSE) instructions until you reach an appropriate address for pcmpeqb; for example:

```
cmpLp:  mov  al, [rsi]
        cmp  al, someByteValue
        je   foundByte
        inc  rsi
        test rsi, 0Fh
        jnz  cmpLp
Use SSE instructions here, as RSI is now 16-byte-aligned
```

ANDing RSI with 0Fh produces a 0 result (and sets the zero flag) if the LO 4 bits of RSI contain 0. If the LO 4 bits of RSI contain 0, the address it contains is aligned on a 16-byte boundary.[16]

The only drawback to this approach is that you must process as many as 15 bytes individually until you get an appropriate address. That's 6 × 15, or 90, machine instructions. However, for large blocks of data (say, more than about 48 or 64 bytes), you amortize the cost of the single-byte comparisons, and this approach isn't so bad.

To improve the performance of this code, you can modify the initial address so that it begins at a 16-byte boundary. ANDing the value in RSI

---

16. Logically AND with the value 1Fh for 32-byte alignment.

(in this particular example) with 0FFFFFFFFFFFFFFF0h (–16) modifies RSI so that it holds the address of the start of the 16-byte block containing the original address:[17]

```
        and   rsi, -16
```

To avoid matching unintended bytes before the start of the data structure, we can create a mask to cover the extra bytes. For example, suppose that we're using the following instruction sequence to rapidly compare 16 bytes at a time:

```
        sub     rsi, 16
cmpLp:  add     rsi, 16
        movdqa  xmm0, xmm2     ; XMM2 contains bytes to test
        pcmpeqb xmm0, [rsi]
        pmovmskb eax, xmm0
        ptest   eax, eax
        jz      cmpLp
```

If we use the AND instruction to align the RSI register prior to the execution of this code, we might get false results when we compare the first 16 bytes. To solve this, we can create a mask that will eliminate any bits from unintended comparisons. To create this mask, we start with all 1 bits and zero out any bits corresponding to addresses from the beginning of the 16-byte block to the first actual data item we're comparing. This mask can be calculated using the following expression:

```
-1 << (startAdrs & 0xF)  ; Note: -1 is all 1 bits
```

This creates 0 bits in the locations before the data to compare and 1 bit thereafter (for the first 16 bytes). We can use this mask to zero out the undesired bit results from the pmovmskb instruction. The following code snippet demonstrates this technique:

```
        mov   rcx, rsi
        and   rsi, -16   ; Align to 16 bits
        and   ecx, 0fH   ; Strip out offset of start of data
        mov   ebx, -1    ; 0FFFFFFFFh - all 1 bits
        shl   ebx, cl    ; Create mask

; Special case for the first 1 to 16 bytes:

        movdqa  xmm0, xmm2
        pcmpeqb xmm0, [rsi]
        pmovmskb eax, xmm0
        and     eax, ebx
        jnz     foundByte
```

17. One nice feature of the two's complement numbering system is that negating a power of 2 produces all 1 bits except for the LO $\log_2(pwr0f2)$ bits of the number. For example, –32 has 0s in the LO 5 bits, –16 has 0s in the LO 4 bits, –8 has 0s in the LO 3 bits, –4 has 0s in the LO 2 bits, and –2 has a 0 in the LO bit.

```
cmpLp:      add       rsi, 16
            movdqa    xmm0, xmm2    ; XMM2 contains bytes to test
            pcmpeqb   xmm0, [rsi]
            pmovmskb  eax, xmm0
            test      eax, eax
            jz        cmpLp
foundByte:
```
Do whatever needs to be done when the block of 16 bytes
   contains at least one match between the bytes in XMM2
   and the data at RSI

Suppose, for example, that the address is already aligned on a 16-byte boundary. ANDing that value with 0Fh produces 0. Shifting −1 to the left zero positions produces −1 (all 1 bits). Later, when the code logically ANDs this with the mask obtained after the pcmpeqb and pmovmskb instructions, the result does not change. Therefore, the code tests all 16 bytes (as we would want if the original address is 16-byte-aligned).

When the address in RSI has the value 0001b in the LO 4 bits, the actual data starts at offset 1 into the 16-byte block. So, we want to ignore the first byte when comparing the values in XMM2 against the 16 bytes at [RSI]. In this case, the mask is 0FFFFFFFEh, which is all 1s except for a 0 in bit 0. After the comparison, if bit 0 of EAX contains a 1 (meaning the bytes at offset 0 match), the AND operation eliminates this bit (replacing it with 0) so it doesn't affect the comparison. Likewise, if the starting offset into the block is 2, 3, . . . , 15, the shl instruction modifies the bit mask in EBX to eliminate bytes at those offsets from consideration in the first compare operation. The result is that it takes only 11 instructions to do the same work as (up to) 90+ instructions in the original (byte-by-byte comparison) example.

11.15   Aligning Word, Dword, and Qword Object Addresses

When aligning non-byte-sized objects, you increment the pointer by the size of the object (in bytes) until you obtain an address that is 16- (or 32-) byte-aligned. However, this works only if the object size is 2, 4, or 8 (because any other value will likely miss addresses that are multiples of 16).

For example, you can process the first several elements of an array of word objects (where the first element of the array appears at an even address in memory) on a word-by-word basis, incrementing the pointer by 2, until you obtain an address that is divisible by 16 (or 32). Note, though, that this scheme works only if the array of objects begins at an address that is a multiple of the element size. For example, if an array of word values begins at an odd address in memory, you will not be able to get an address that is divisible by 16 or 32 with a series of additions by 2, and you would not be able to use SSE/AVX instructions to process this data without first moving it to another location in memory that is properly aligned.

11.16 Filling an XMM Register with Several Copies of the Same Value

For many SIMD algorithms, you will want multiple copies of the same value in an XMM or a YMM register. You can use the (v)movddup, (v)movshdup, (v)pinsd, (v)pinsq, and (v)pshufd instructions for single-precision and double-precision floating-point values. For example, if you have a single-precision floating-point value, r4var, in memory and you want to replicate it throughout XMM0, you could use the following code:

```
movss  xmm0, r4var
pshufd xmm0, xmm0, 0    ; Lanes 3, 2, 1, and 0 from lane 0
```

To copy a pair of double-precision floating-point values from r8var into XMM0, you could use:

```
movsd  xmm0, r8var
pshufd xmm0, xmm0, 44h  ; Lane 0 to lanes 0 and 2, 1 to 1, and 3
```

Of course, pshufd is really intended for double-word integer operations, so additional latency (time) may be involved in using pshufd immediately after movsd or movss. Although pshufd allows a memory operand, that operand must be a 16-byte-aligned 128-bit-memory operand, so it's not useful for directly copying a floating-point value through an XMM register.

For double-precision floating-point values, you can use movddup to duplicate a single 64-bit float in the LO bits of an XMM register into the HO bits:

```
movddup xmm0, r8var
```

The movddup instruction allows unaligned 64-bit memory operands, so it's probably the best choice for duplicating double-precision values.

To copy byte, word, dword, or qword integer values throughout an XMM register, the pshufb, pshufw, pshufd, or pshufq instructions are a good choice. For example, to replicate a single byte throughout XMM0, you could use the following sequence:

```
movzx  eax, byteToCopy
movd   xmm0, eax
pxor   xmm1, xmm1   ; Mask to copy byte 0 throughout
pshufb xmm0, xmm1
```

The XMM1 operand is an array of bytes containing masks used to copy data from locations in XMM0 onto itself. The value 0 copies byte 0 in XMM0 throughout all the other bits in XMM0. This same code can be used to copy words, dwords, and qwords by simply changing the mask value in XMM1. Or you could use the `pshuflw` or `pshufd` instructions to do the job. Here's another variant that replicates a byte throughout XMM0:

```
movzx      eax, byteToCopy
mov        ah, al
movd       xmm0, eax
punpcklbw xmm0, xmm0    ; Copy bytes 0 and 1 to 2 and 3
pshufd     xmm0, xmm0, 0 ; Copy LO dword throughout
```

11.17 Loading Some Common Constants Into XMM and YMM Registers

No SSE/AVX instructions let you load an immediate constant into a register. However, you can use a couple of idioms (tricks) to load certain common constant values into an XMM or a YMM register. This section discusses some of these idioms.

Loading 0 into an SSE/AVX register uses the same idiom that general-purpose integer registers employ: exclusive-OR the register with itself. For example, to set all the bits in XMM0 to 0s, you would use the following instruction:

```
pxor xmm0, xmm0
```

To set all the bits in an XMM or a YMM register to 1, you can use the `pcmpeqb` instruction, as follows:

```
pcmpeqb xmm0, xmm0
```

Because any given XMM or YMM register is equal to itself, this instruction stores 0FFh in all the bytes of XMM0 (or whatever XMM or YMM register you specify).

If you want to load the 8-bit value 01h into all 16 bytes of an XMM register, you can use the following code (this comes from Intel):

```
pxor    xmm0, xmm0
pcmpeqb xmm1, xmm1
psubb   xmm0, xmm1    ; 0 - (-1) is (1)
```

You can substitute `psubw` or `psubd` for `psubb` in this example if you want to create 16- or 32-bit results (for example, four 32-bit dwords in XMM0, each containing the value 00000001h).

If you would like the 1 bit in a different bit position (rather than bit 0 of each byte), you can use the `pslld` instruction after the preceding sequence to reposition the bits. For example, if you want to load the XMM0 register with 8080808080808080h, you could use the following instruction sequence:

```
pxor    xmm0, xmm0
pcmpeqb xmm1, xmm1
```

```
psubb    xmm0, xmm1
pslld    xmm0, 7              ; 01h -> 80h in each byte
```

Of course, you can supply a different immediate constant to `pslld` to load each byte in the register with 02h, 04h, 08h, 10h, 20h, or 40h.

Here's a neat trick you can use to load $2^n - 1$ (all 1 bits up to the nth bit in a number) into all the lanes on an SSE/AVX register:[18]

```
; For 16-bit lanes:

pcmpeqd  xmm0, xmm0          ; Set all bits to 1
psrlw    xmm0, 16 - n        ; Clear top 16 - n bits of xmm0

; For 32-bit lanes:

pcmpeqd  xmm0, xmm0          ; Set all bits to 1
psrld    xmm0, 32 - n        ; Clear top 16 - n bits of xmm0

; For 64-bit lanes:

pcmpeqd  xmm0, xmm0          ; Set all bits to 1
psrlq    xmm0, 64 - n        ; Clear top 16 - n bits of xmm0
```

You can also load the inverse (NOT$(2^n - 1)$, all 1 bits in bit position n through the end of the register) by shifting to the left rather than the right:

```
; For 16-bit lanes:

pcmpeqd  xmm0, xmm0          ; Set all bits to 1
psllw    xmm0, n             ; Clear bottom n bits of xmm0

; For 32-bit lanes:

pcmpeqd  xmm0, xmm0          ; Set all bits to 1
pslld    xmm0, n             ; Clear bottom n bits of xmm0

; For 64-bit lanes:

pcmpeqd  xmm0, xmm0          ; Set all bits to 1
psllq    xmm0, n             ; Clear bottom n bits of xmm0
```

Of course, you can also load a "constant" into an XMM or a YMM register by putting that constant into a memory location (preferably 16- or 32-byte-aligned) and then using a `movdqu` or `movdqa` instruction to load that value into a register. Do keep in mind, however, that such an operation can be relatively slow if the data in memory does not appear in cache. Another possibility, if the constant is small enough, is to load the constant into a 32- or 64-bit integer register and use `movd` or `movq` to copy that value into an XMM register.

---

18. Suggested by Raymond Chen at *https://blogs.msdn.microsoft.com/oldnewthing/*.

11.18 Setting, Clearing, Inverting, and Testing a Single Bit in an SSE Register

Here's another set of tricks suggested by Raymond Chen (*https://blogs.msdn .microsoft.com/oldnewthing/20141222-00/?p=43333/*) to set, clear, or test an individual bit in an XMM register.

To set an individual bit (bit *n*, assuming that *n* is a constant) with all other bits cleared, you can use the following macro:

```
; setXBit - Sets bit n in SSE register xReg.

setXBit macro   xReg, n
        pcmpeqb xReg, xReg      ; Set all bits in xReg
        psrlq   xReg, 63        ; Set both 64-bit lanes to 01h
        if      n lt 64
        psrldq  xReg, 8         ; Clear the upper lane
        else
        pslldq  xReg, 8         ; Clear the lower lane
        endif
        if      (n and 3fh) ne 0
        psllq   xReg, (n and 3fh)
        endif
        endm
```

Once you can fill an XMM register with a single set bit, you can use that register's value to set, clear, invert, or test that bit in another XMM register. For example, to set bit *n* in XMM1, without affecting any of the other bits in XMM1, you could use the following code sequence:

```
setXBit xmm0, n     ; Set bit n in XMM1 to 1 without
por     xmm1, xmm0  ; affecting any other bits
```

To clear bit *n* in an XMM register, you use the same sequence but substitute the vpandn (AND NOT) instruction for the por instruction:

```
setXBit xmm0, n            ; Clear bit n in XMM1 without
vpandn  xmm1, xmm0, xmm1   ; affecting any other bits
```

To invert a bit, simply substitute pxor for por or vpandn:

```
setXBit xmm0, n     ; Invert bit n in XMM1 without
pxor    xmm1, xmm0  ; affecting any other bits
```

To test a bit to see if it is set, you have a couple of options. If your CPU supports the SSE4.1 instruction set extensions, you can use the ptest instruction:

```
setXBit xmm0, n     ; Test bit n in XMM1
ptest   xmm1, xmm0
jnz     bitNisSet   ; Fall through if bit n is clear
```

If you have an older CPU that doesn't support the ptest instruction, you can use pmovmskb as follows:

```
; Remember, psllq shifts bits, not bytes.
; If bit n is not in bit position 7 of a given
; byte, then move it there. For example, if n = 0, then
; (7 - (0 and 7)) is 7, so psllq moves bit 0 to bit 7.

movdqa    xmm0, xmm1
if        7 - (n and 7)
psllq     xmm0, 7 - (n and 7)
endif


; Now that the desired bit to test is sitting in bit position
; 7 of *some* byte, use pmovmskb to extract all bit 7s into AX:

pmovmskb eax, xmm0

; Now use the (integer) test instruction to test that bit:

test    ax, 1 shl (n / 8)
jnz     bitNisSet
```

11.19 Processing Two Vectors by Using a Single Incremented Index

Sometimes your code will need to process two blocks of data simultaneously, incrementing pointers into both blocks during the execution of the loop.

One easy way to do this is to use the scaled-indexed addressing mode. If R8 and R9 contain pointers to the data you want to process, you can walk along both blocks of data by using code such as the following:

```
          dec rcx
blkLoop:  inc rcx
          mov eax, [r8][rcx * 4]
          cmp eax, [r9][rcx * 4]
          je  theyreEqual
          cmp eax, sentinelValue
          jne blkLoop
```

This code marches along through the two dword arrays comparing values (to search for an equal value in the arrays at the same index). This loop uses four registers: EAX to compare the two values from the arrays, the two pointers to the arrays (R8 and R9), and then the RCX index register to step through the two arrays.

It is possible to eliminate RCX from this loop by incrementing the R8 and R9 registers in this loop (assuming it's okay to modify the values in R8 and R9):

```
          sub r8, 4
          sub r9, 4
blkLoop:  add r8, 4
```

```
        add r9, 4
        mov eax, [r8]
        cmp eax, [r9]
        je  theyreEqual
        cmp eax, sentinelValue
        jne blkLoop
```

This scheme requires an extra add instruction in the loop. If the execution speed of this loop is critical, inserting this extra addition could be a deal breaker.

There is, however, a sneaky trick you can use so that you have to increment only a single register on each iteration of the loop:

```
          sub r9, r8          ; R9 = R9 - R8
          sub r8, 4
blkLoop:  add r8, 4
          mov eax, [r8]
          cmp eax, [r9][r8 * 1] ; Address = R9 + R8
          je  theyreEqual
          cmp eax, sentinelValue
          jne blkLoop
```

The comments are there because they explain the trick being used. At the beginning of the code, you subtract the value of R8 from R9 and leave the result in R9. In the body of the loop, you compensate for this subtraction by using the [r9][r8 * 1] scaled-indexed addressing mode (whose effective address is the sum of R8 and R9, thus restoring R9 to its original value, at least on the first iteration of the loop). Now, because the cmp instruction's memory address is the sum of R8 and R9, adding 1 to R8 also adds 1 to the effective address used by the cmp instruction. Therefore, on each iteration of the loop, the mov and cmp instructions look at successive elements of their respective arrays, yet the code has to increment only a single pointer.

NOTE   *In this example, you always use the * 1 scale factor on the scaled-indexed addressing mode. Adjusting for the size of the operand (4 bytes) happens when adding 4 to the R8 register.*

This scheme works especially well when processing SIMD arrays with SSE and AVX instructions because the XMM and YMM registers are 16 and 32 bytes each, so you can't use normal scaling factors (1, 2, 4, or 8) to index into an array of packed data values. You wind up having to add 16 (or 32) to your pointers when stepping through the arrays, thus losing one of the benefits of the scaled-indexed addressing mode. For example:

```
; Assume R9 and R8 point at (32-byte-aligned) arrays of 20 double values.
; Assume R10 points at a (32-byte-aligned) destination array of 20 doubles.

        sub     r9, r8    ; R9 = R9 - R8
        sub     r10, r8   ; R10 = R10 - R8
        sub     r8, 32
```

```
            mov     ecx, 5       ; Vector with 20 (5 * 4) double values
addLoop:    add     r8, 32
            vmovapd ymm0, [r8]
            vaddpd  ymm0, ymm0, [r9][r8 * 1] ; Address = R9 + R8
            vmovapd [r10][r8 * 1], ymm0      ; Address = R10 + R8
            dec     ecx
            jnz     addLoop
```

11.20 Aligning Two Addresses to a Boundary

The vmovapd and vaddpd instructions from the preceding example require their memory operands to be 32-byte-aligned or you will get a general protection fault (memory access violation). If you have control over the placement of the arrays in memory, you can specify an alignment for the arrays. If you have no control over the data's placement in memory, you have two options: working with the unaligned data regardless of the performance loss, or moving the data to a location where it is properly aligned.

If you must work with unaligned data, you can substitute an unaligned move for an aligned move (for example, vmovupd for vmovdqa) or load the data into a YMM register by using an unaligned move and then operate on the data in that register by using your desired instruction. For example:

```
addLoop:    add     r8, 32
            vmovupd ymm0, [r8]
            vmovupd ymm1, [r9][r8 * 1]  ; Address = R9 + R8
            vaddpd  ymm0, ymm0, ymm1
            vmovupd [r10][r8 * 1], ymm0 ; Address = R10 + R8
            dec     ecx
            jnz     addLoop
```

Sadly, the vaddpd instruction does not support unaligned access to memory, so you must load the value from the second array (pointed at by R9) into another register (YMM1) before the packed addition operation. This is the drawback to unaligned access: not only are unaligned moves slower, but you also may need to use additional registers and instructions to deal with unaligned data.

Moving the data to a memory location whose alignment you can control is an option when you have a data operand you will be using over and over again in the future. Moving data is an expensive operation; however, if you have a standard block of data you're going to compare against many other blocks, you can amortize the cost of moving that block to a new location over all the operations you need to do.

Moving the data is especially useful when one (or both) of the data arrays appears at an address that is not an integral multiple of the sub-elements's size. For example, if you have an array of dwords that begin at an odd address, you will never be able to align a pointer to that array's data to a 16-byte boundary without moving the data.

11.21 Working with Blocks of Data Whose Length Is Not a Multiple of the SSE/AVX Register Size

Using SIMD instructions to march through a large data set processing 2, 4, 8, 16, or 32 values at a time often allows a SIMD algorithm (a *vectorized* algorithm) to run an order of magnitude faster than the SISD (scalar) algorithm. However, two boundary conditions create problems: the start of the data set (when the starting address might not be properly aligned) and the end of the data set (when there might not be a sufficient number of array elements to completely fill an XMM or a YMM register). I've addressed the issues with the start of the data set (misaligned data) already. This section takes a look at the latter problem.

For the most part, when you run out of data at the end of the array (and the XMM and YMM registers need more for a packed operation), you can use the same technique given earlier for aligning a pointer: load more data than is necessary into the register and mask out the unneeded results. For example, if only 8 bytes are left to process in a byte array, you can load 16 bytes, do the operation, and ignore the results from the last 8 bytes. In the comparison loop examples I've been using through these past sections, you could do the following:

```
movdqa    xmm0, [r8]
pcmpeqd   xmm0, [r9]
pmovmskb  eax, xmm0
and       eax, 0ffh      ; Mask out the last 8 compares
cmp       eax, 0ffh
je        matchedData
```

In most cases, accessing data beyond the end of the data structures (either the data pointed at by R8, R9, or both in this example) is harmless. However, as you saw in "Memory Access and 4K Memory Management Unit Pages" in Chapter 3, if that extra data happens to cross a memory management unit page, and that new page doesn't allow read access, the CPU will generate a general protection fault (memory access or segmentation fault). Therefore, unless you know that valid data follows the array in memory (at least to the extent the instruction references), you shouldn't access that memory area; doing so could crash your software.

This problem has two solutions. First, you can align memory accesses on an address boundary that is the same size as the register (for example, 16-byte alignment for XMM registers). Accessing data beyond the end of the data structure with an SSE/AVX instruction will not cross a page boundary (because 16-byte accesses aligned on 16-byte boundaries will always fall within the same MMU page, and ditto for 32-byte accesses on 32-byte boundaries).

The second solution is to examine the memory address prior to accessing memory. While you cannot access the new page without possibly triggering an access fault,[19] you can check the address itself and see if accessing 16 (or 32) bytes at that address will access data in a new page. If it would, you can take some precautions before accessing the data on the next page. For example, rather than continuing to process the data in SIMD mode, you could drop down to SISD mode and finish processing the data to the end of the array by using standard scalar instructions.

To test if a SIMD access will cross an MMU page boundary, supposing that R9 contains the address at which you're about to access 16 bytes in memory using an SSE instruction, use code like the following:

```
mov   eax, r9d
and   eax, 0fffh
cmp   eax, 0ff0h
ja    willCrossPage
```

Each MMU page is 4KB long and is situated on a 4KB address boundary in memory. Therefore, the LO 12 bits of an address provide an index into the MMU page associated with that address. The preceding code checks whether the address has a page offset greater than 0FF0h (4080). If so, then accessing 16 bytes starting at that address will cross a page boundary. Check for a value of 0FE0h if you need to check for a 32-byte access.

11.22 Dynamically Testing for a CPU Feature

At the beginning of this chapter, I mentioned that when testing the CPU feature set to determine which extensions it supports, the best solution is to dynamically select a set of functions based on the presence or absence of certain capabilities. To demonstrate dynamically testing for, and using (or avoiding), certain CPU features—specifically, testing for the presence of AVX extensions—I'll modify (and expand) the print procedure that I've been using in examples up to this point.

The print procedure I've been using is very convenient, but it doesn't preserve any SSE or AVX registers that a call to printf() could (legally) modify. A generic version of print should preserve the volatile XMM and YMM registers as well as general-purpose registers.

The problem is that you cannot write a generic version of print that will run on all CPUs. If you preserve the XMM registers only, the code will run on any x86-64 CPU. However, if the CPU supports the AVX extensions and the program uses YMM0 to YMM5, the print routine will preserve only the LO 128 bits of those registers, as they are aliased to the corresponding XMM registers. If you save the volatile YMM registers, that code will crash on a CPU that doesn't support the AVX extensions. So, the trick is to write code that will dynamically determine whether the CPU has the AVX registers and preserve them if they are present, and otherwise preserve only the SSE registers.

---

19. As far as I know, at least while this is being written, there is no convenient way to test a byte in memory to see if it is accessible without causing a fault; in theory, you could put in an exception handler, but triggering and handling the exception is far too expensive to consider.

The easy way to do this, and probably the most appropriate solution for the print function, is to simply stick the cpuid instruction inside print and test the results immediately before preserving (and restoring) the registers. Here's a code fragment that demonstrates how this could be done:

```
AVXSupport    =    10000000h              ; Bit 28

print       proc

; Preserve all the volatile registers
; (be nice to the assembly code that
; calls this procedure):

            push    rax
            push    rbx                    ; CPUID messes with EBX
            push    rcx
            push    rdx
            push    r8
            push    r9
            push    r10
            push    r11

; Reserve space on the stack for the AVX/SSE registers.
; Note: SSE registers need only 96 bytes, but the code
; is easier to deal with if we reserve the full 128 bytes
; that the AVX registers need and ignore the extra 64
; bytes when running SSE code.

            sub     rsp, 192

; Determine if we have to preserve the YMM registers:

            mov     eax, 1
            cpuid
            test    ecx, AVXSupport        ; Test bits 19 and 20
            jnz     preserveAVX

; No AVX support, so just preserve the XXM0 to XXM3 registers:

            movdqu  xmmword ptr [rsp + 00], xmm0
            movdqu  xmmword ptr [rsp + 16], xmm1
            movdqu  xmmword ptr [rsp + 32], xmm2
            movdqu  xmmword ptr [rsp + 48], xmm3
            movdqu  xmmword ptr [rsp + 64], xmm4
            movdqu  xmmword ptr [rsp + 80], xmm5
            jmp     restOfPrint

; YMM0 to YMM3 are considered volatile, so preserve them:

preserveAVX:
            vmovdqu ymmword ptr [rsp + 000], ymm0
            vmovdqu ymmword ptr [rsp + 032], ymm1
            vmovdqu ymmword ptr [rsp + 064], ymm2
            vmovdqu ymmword ptr [rsp + 096], ymm3
```

```
            vmovdqu ymmword ptr [rsp + 128], ymm4
            vmovdqu ymmword ptr [rsp + 160], ymm5

restOfPrint:
            The rest of the print function goes here
```

At the end of the print function, when it's time to restore everything, you could do another test to determine whether to restore XMM or YMM registers.[20]

For other functions, when you might not want the expense of cpuid (and preserving all the registers it stomps on) incurred on every function call, the trick is to write *three* functions: one for SSE CPUs, one for AVX CPUs, and a special function (that you call only once) that selects which of these two you will call in the future. The bit of magic that makes this efficient is *indirection*. You won't directly call any of these functions. Instead, you'll initialize a pointer with the address of the function to call and indirectly call one of these three functions by using the pointer. For the current example, we'll name this pointer print and initialize it with the address of the third function, choosePrint:

```
            .data
print       qword   choosePrint
```

Here's the code for choosePrint:

```
; On first call, determine if we support AVX instructions
; and set the "print" pointer to point at print_AVX or
; print_SSE:

choosePrint proc
            push    rax             ; Preserve registers that get
            push    rbx             ; tweaked by CPUID
            push    rcx
            push    rdx

            mov     eax, 1
            cpuid
            test    ecx, AVXSupport ; Test bit 28 for AVX
            jnz     doAVXPrint

            lea     rax, print_SSE  ; From now on, call
            mov     print, rax      ; print_SSE directly

; Return address must point at the format string
; following the call to this function! So we have
; to clean up the stack and JMP to print_SSE.

            pop     rdx
            pop     rcx
            pop     rbx
```

---

20. You could save the cpuid results and just test the flag, if that is more convenient for you.

```
                pop     rax
                jmp     print_SSE

doAVXPrint: lea     rax, print_AVX  ; From now on, call
                mov     print, rax      ; print_AVX directly

; Return address must point at the format string
; following the call to this function! So we have
; to clean up the stack and JMP to print_AUX.

                pop     rdx
                pop     rcx
                pop     rbx
                pop     rax
                jmp     print_AVX

choosePrint endp
```

The print_SSE procedure runs on CPUs without AVX support, and the print_AVX procedure runs on CPUs with AVX support. The choosePrint procedure executes the cpuid instruction to determine whether the CPU supports the AVX extensions; if so, it initializes the print pointer with the address of the print_AVX procedure, and if not, it stores the address of print_SSE into the print variable.

choosePrint is not an explicit initialization procedure you must call prior to calling print. The choosePrint procedure executes only *once* (assuming you call it via the print pointer rather than calling it directly). After the first execution, the print pointer contains the address of the CPU-appropriate print function, and choosePrint no longer executes.

You call the print pointer just as you would make any other call to print; for example:

```
call print
byte "Hello, world!", nl, 0
```

After setting up the print pointer, choosePrint must transfer control to the appropriate print procedure (print_SSE or print_AVX) to do the work the user is expecting. Because preserved register values are sitting on the stack, and the actual print routines expect only a return address, choosePrint will first restore all the (general-purpose) registers it saved and then jump to (not call) the appropriate print procedure. It does a jump, rather than a call, because the return address pointing to the format string is already sitting on the top of the stack. On return from the print_SSE or print_AVX procedure, control will return to whomever called choosePrint (via the print pointer).

Listing 11-5 shows the complete print function, with print_SSE and print_AVX, and a simple main program that calls print. I've extended print to accept arguments in R10 and R11 as well as in RDX, R8, and R9 (this function reserves RCX to hold the address of the format string following the call to print).

```
; Listing 11-5

; Generic print procedure and dynamically
; selecting CPU features.

        option  casemap:none

nl          =       10

; SSE4.2 feature flags (in ECX):

SSE42       =       00180000h       ; Bits 19 and 20
AVXSupport  =       10000000h       ; Bit 28

; CPUID bits (EAX = 7, EBX register)

AVX2Support =       20h             ; Bit 5 = AVX

            .const
ttlStr      byte    "Listing 11-5", 0

            .data
            align   qword
print       qword   choosePrint     ; Pointer to print function

; Floating-point values for testing purposes:

fp1         real8   1.0
fp2         real8   2.0
fp3         real8   3.0
fp4         real8   4.0
fp5         real8   5.0

            .code
            externdef printf:proc

; Return program title to C++ program:

            public  getTitle
getTitle    proc
            lea     rax, ttlStr
            ret
getTitle    endp

;***************************************************************

; print - "Quick" form of printf that allows the format string to
;         follow the call in the code stream. Supports up to five
;         additional parameters in RDX, R8, R9, R10, and R11.
```

; This function saves all the Microsoft ABI-volatile,
; parameter, and return result registers so that code
; can call it without worrying about any registers being
; modified (this code assumes that Windows ABI treats
; YMM4 to YMM15 as nonvolatile).

; Of course, this code assumes that AVX instructions are
; available on the CPU.

; Allows up to 5 arguments in:

;   RDX - Arg #1
;   R8 - Arg #2
;   R9 - Arg #3
;   R10 - Arg #4
;   R11 - Arg #5

; Note that you must pass floating-point values in
; these registers, as well. The printf function
; expects real values in the integer registers.

; There are two versions of this function, one that
; will run on CPUs without AVX capabilities (no YMM
; registers) and one that will run on CPUs that
; have AVX capabilities (YMM registers). The difference
; between the two is which registers they preserve
; (print_SSE preserves only XMM registers and will
; run properly on CPUs that don't have YMM register
; support; print_AVX will preserve the volatile YMM
; registers on CPUs with AVX support).

; On first call, determine if we support AVX instructions
; and set the "print" pointer to point at print_AVX or
; print_SSE:

```
choosePrint proc
            push    rax             ; Preserve registers that get
            push    rbx             ; tweaked by CPUID
            push    rcx
            push    rdx

            mov     eax, 1
            cpuid
            test    ecx, AVXSupport ; Test bit 28 for AVX
            jnz     doAVXPrint

            lea     rax, print_SSE  ; From now on, call
            mov     print, rax      ; print_SSE directly
```

; Return address must point at the format string
; following the call to this function! So we have
; to clean up the stack and JMP to print_SSE.

```
            pop     rdx
            pop     rcx
```

```
               pop     rbx
               pop     rax
               jmp     print_SSE

doAVXPrint: lea     rax, print_AVX  ; From now on, call
            mov     print, rax      ; print_AVX directly

; Return address must point at the format string
; following the call to this function! So we have
; to clean up the stack and JMP to print_AUX.

               pop     rdx
               pop     rcx
               pop     rbx
               pop     rax
               jmp     print_AVX

choosePrint endp

; Version of print that will preserve volatile
; AVX registers (YMM0 to YMM3):

print_AVX    proc

; Preserve all the volatile registers
; (be nice to the assembly code that
; calls this procedure):

               push    rax
               push    rbx
               push    rcx
               push    rdx
               push    r8
               push    r9
               push    r10
               push    r11

; YMM0 to YMM7 are considered volatile, so preserve them:

               sub     rsp, 256
               vmovdqu ymmword ptr [rsp + 000], ymm0
               vmovdqu ymmword ptr [rsp + 032], ymm1
               vmovdqu ymmword ptr [rsp + 064], ymm2
               vmovdqu ymmword ptr [rsp + 096], ymm3
               vmovdqu ymmword ptr [rsp + 128], ymm4
               vmovdqu ymmword ptr [rsp + 160], ymm5
               vmovdqu ymmword ptr [rsp + 192], ymm6
               vmovdqu ymmword ptr [rsp + 224], ymm7

               push    rbp

returnAdrs  textequ <[rbp + 328]>

               mov     rbp, rsp
               sub     rsp, 128
```

```
                    and     rsp, -16

; Format string (passed in RCX) is sitting at
; the location pointed at by the return address,
; load that into RCX:

                    mov     rcx, returnAdrs

; To handle more than 3 arguments (4 counting
; RCX), you must pass data on stack. However, to the
; print caller, the stack is unavailable, so use
; R10 and R11 as extra parameters (could be just
; junk in these registers, but pass them just
; in case):

                    mov     [rsp + 32], r10
                    mov     [rsp + 40], r11
                    call    printf

; Need to modify the return address so
; that it points beyond the zero-terminating byte.
; Could use a fast strlen function for this, but
; printf is so slow it won't really save us anything.

                    mov     rcx, returnAdrs
                    dec     rcx
skipTo0:            inc     rcx
                    cmp     byte ptr [rcx], 0
                    jne     skipTo0
                    inc     rcx
                    mov     returnAdrs, rcx

                    leave
                    vmovdqu ymm0, ymmword ptr [rsp + 000]
                    vmovdqu ymm1, ymmword ptr [rsp + 032]
                    vmovdqu ymm2, ymmword ptr [rsp + 064]
                    vmovdqu ymm3, ymmword ptr [rsp + 096]
                    vmovdqu ymm4, ymmword ptr [rsp + 128]
                    vmovdqu ymm5, ymmword ptr [rsp + 160]
                    vmovdqu ymm6, ymmword ptr [rsp + 192]
                    vmovdqu ymm7, ymmword ptr [rsp + 224]
                    add     rsp, 256
                    pop     r11
                    pop     r10
                    pop     r9
                    pop     r8
                    pop     rdx
                    pop     rcx
                    pop     rbx
                    pop     rax
                    ret
print_AVX           endp

; Version that will run on CPUs without
; AVX support and will preserve the
```

; volatile SSE registers (XMM0 to XMM3):

```
print_SSE    proc

; Preserve all the volatile registers
; (be nice to the assembly code that
; calls this procedure):

                push    rax
                push    rbx
                push    rcx
                push    rdx
                push    r8
                push    r9
                push    r10
                push    r11

; XMM0 to XMM3 are considered volatile, so preserve them:

                sub     rsp, 128
                movdqu  xmmword ptr [rsp + 00],  xmm0
                movdqu  xmmword ptr [rsp + 16],  xmm1
                movdqu  xmmword ptr [rsp + 32],  xmm2
                movdqu  xmmword ptr [rsp + 48],  xmm3
                movdqu  xmmword ptr [rsp + 64],  xmm4
                movdqu  xmmword ptr [rsp + 80],  xmm5
                movdqu  xmmword ptr [rsp + 96],  xmm6
                movdqu  xmmword ptr [rsp + 112], xmm7

                push    rbp

returnAdrs   textequ <[rbp + 200]>

                mov     rbp, rsp
                sub     rsp, 128
                and     rsp, -16

; Format string (passed in RCX) is sitting at
; the location pointed at by the return address,
; load that into RCX:

                mov     rcx, returnAdrs

; To handle more than 3 arguments (4 counting
; RCX), you must pass data on stack. However, to the
; print caller, the stack is unavailable, so use
; R10 and R11 as extra parameters (could be just
; junk in these registers, but pass them just
; in case):

                mov     [rsp + 32], r10
                mov     [rsp + 40], r11
                call    printf

; Need to modify the return address so
```

```
; that it points beyond the zero-terminating byte.
; Could use a fast strlen function for this, but
; printf is so slow it won't really save us anything.

            mov     rcx, returnAdrs
            dec     rcx
skipTo0:    inc     rcx
            cmp     byte ptr [rcx], 0
            jne     skipTo0
            inc     rcx
            mov     returnAdrs, rcx

            leave
            movdqu  xmm0, xmmword ptr [rsp + 00]
            movdqu  xmm1, xmmword ptr [rsp + 16]
            movdqu  xmm2, xmmword ptr [rsp + 32]
            movdqu  xmm3, xmmword ptr [rsp + 48]
            movdqu  xmm4, xmmword ptr [rsp + 64]
            movdqu  xmm5, xmmword ptr [rsp + 80]
            movdqu  xmm6, xmmword ptr [rsp + 96]
            movdqu  xmm7, xmmword ptr [rsp + 112]
            add     rsp, 128
            pop     r11
            pop     r10
            pop     r9
            pop     r8
            pop     rdx
            pop     rcx
            pop     rbx
            pop     rax
            ret
print_SSE   endp

;****************************************************************

; Here is the "asmMain" function.

            public  asmMain
asmMain     proc
            push    rbx
            push    rsi
            push    rdi
            push    rbp
            mov     rbp, rsp
            sub     rsp, 56         ; Shadow storage

; Trivial example, no arguments:

            call    print
            byte    "Hello, world!", nl, 0

; Simple example with integer arguments:

            mov     rdx, 1          ; Argument #1 for printf
            mov     r8, 2           ; Argument #2 for printf
```

```
            mov     r9, 3           ; Argument #3 for printf
            mov     r10, 4          ; Argument #4 for printf
            mov     r11, 5          ; Argument #5 for printf
            call    print
            byte    "Arg 1=%d, Arg2=%d, Arg3=%d "
            byte    "Arg 4=%d, Arg5=%d", nl, 0

; Demonstration of floating-point operands. Note that
; args 1, 2, and 3 must be passed in RDX, R8, and R9.
; You'll have to load parameters 4 and 5 into R10 and R11.

            mov     rdx, qword ptr fp1
            mov     r8,  qword ptr fp2
            mov     r9,  qword ptr fp3
            mov     r10, qword ptr fp4
            mov     r11, qword ptr fp5
            call    print
            byte    "Arg1=%6.1f, Arg2=%6.1f, Arg3=%6.1f "
            byte    "Arg4=%6.1f, Arg5=%6.1f ", nl, 0

allDone:    leave
            pop     rdi
            pop     rsi
            pop     rbx
            ret             ; Returns to caller
asmMain     endp
            end
```

Listing 11-5: Dynamically selected print procedure

Here's the build command and output for the program in Listing 11-5:

```
C:\>build listing11-5

C:\>echo off
 Assembling: listing11-5.asm
c.cpp

C:\>listing11-5
Calling Listing 11-5:
Hello, World!
Arg 1=1, Arg2=2, Arg3=3 Arg 4=4, Arg5=5
Arg1=   1.0, Arg2=   2.0, Arg3=   3.0 Arg4=   4.0, Arg5=   5.0
Listing 11-5 terminated
```

11.23   The MASM Include Directive

As you've seen already, including the source code for the print procedure
in every sample listing in this book wastes a lot of space. Including the new
version from the previous section in every listing would be impractical. In
Chapter 15, I discuss include files, libraries, and other functionality you can
use to break large projects into manageable pieces. In the meantime, however, it's worthwhile to discuss the MASM include directive so this book can
eliminate a lot of unnecessary code duplication in sample programs.

The MASM `include` directive uses the following syntax:

```
include  source_filename
```

where *source_filename* is the name of a text file (generally in the same directory of the source file containing this `include` directive). MASM will take the source file and insert it into the assembly at the point of the `include` directive, exactly as though the text in that file had appeared in the source file being assembled.

For example, I have extracted all the source code associated with the new print procedure (the `choosePrint`, `print_AVX`, and `print_SSE` procedures, and the `print` qword variable), and I've inserted them into the *print.inc* source file.[21] In listings that follow in this book, I'll simply place the following directive in the code in place of the print function:

```
include print.inc
```

I've also put the `getTitle` procedure into its own header file (*getTitle.inc*) to be able to remove that common code from sample listings.

11.24 And a Whole Lot More

This chapter doesn't even begin to describe all the various SSE, AVX, AVX2, and AVX512 instructions. As already mentioned, most of the SIMD instructions have a specific purpose (such as interleaving or deinterleaving bytes associated with video or audio information) that aren't very useful outside their particular problem domain. Other instructions (at least, as this book was being written) are sufficiently new that they won't execute on many CPUs in use today. If you're interested in learning about more of the SIMD instructions, check out the information in the next section.

11.25 For More Information

For more information about the `cpuid` instruction on AMD CPUs, see the 2010 AMD document "CPUID Specification" (*https://www.amd.com/system/files/TechDocs/25481.pdf*). For Intel CPUs, check out "Intel Architecture and Processor Identification with CPUID Model and Family Numbers" (*https://software.intel.com/en-us/articles/intel-architecture-and-processor-identification-with-cpuid-model-and-family-numbers/*).

Microsoft's website (particularly the Visual Studio documentation) has additional information on the MASM `segment` directive and x86-64 segments. A search for *MASM Segment Directive* on the internet, for example, brought up the page *https://docs.microsoft.com/en-us/cpp/assembler/masm/segment?view=msvc-160/*.

The complete discussion of all the SIMD instructions can be found in Intel's documentation: *Intel® 64 and IA-32 Architectures Software Developer's Manual*, Volume 2: *Instruction Set Reference*.

---

21. *.inc* is the typical suffix MASM programmers use for include files.

You can easily find this documentation online at Intel's website; for example:

- *https://software.intel.com/en-us/articles/intel-sdm/*
- *https://software.intel.com/content/www/us/en/develop/download/intel-64-and-ia -32-architectures-sdm-combined-volumes-1-2a-2b-2c-2d-3a-3b-3c-3d-and-4.html*

AMD's variant can be found at *https://www.amd.com/system/files/TechDocs/ 40332.pdf.*

Although this chapter has presented many of the SSE/AVX/AVX2 instructions and what they do, it has not spent much time describing how you would use these instructions in a typical program. You can easily find lots of useful high-performance algorithms that use SSE and AVX instructions on the internet. The following URLs provide some examples:

Tutorials on SIMD programming

- SSE Arithmetic, by Stefano Tommesani, *http://www.tommesani.com/index .php/simd/46-sse-arithmetic.html*
- x86/x64 SIMD Instruction List, *https://www.officedaytime.com/simd512e/*
- Basics of SIMD Programming, Sony Computer Entertainment, *http:// ftp.cvut.cz/kernel/people/geoff/cell/ps3-linux-docs/CellProgrammingTutorial/ BasicsOfSIMDProgramming.html*

Sorting algorithms

- "A Novel Hybrid Quicksort Algorithm Vectorized Using AVX-512 on Intel Skylake," by Berenger Bramas, *https://arxiv.org/pdf/1704.08579.pdf*
- "Register Level Sort Algorithm on Multi-Core SIMD Processors" by Tian Xiaochen et al., *http://olab.is.s.u-tokyo.ac.jp/~kamil.rocki/xiaochen _rocki_IA3_SC13.pdf*
- "Fast Quicksort Implementation Using AVX Instructions" by Shay Gueron and Vlad Krasnov, *http://citeseerx.ist.psu.edu/viewdoc/download?doi=10.1.1.100 9.7773&rep=rep1&type=pdf*

Search algorithms

- "SIMD-Friendly Algorithms for Substring Searching" by Wojciech Mula, *http://0x80.pl/articles/simd-strfind.html*
- "Fast Multiple String Matching Using Streaming SIMD Extensions Technology" by Simone Faro and M. Oğuzhan Külekci, *https://citeseerx .ist.psu.edu/viewdoc/download?doi=10.1.1.1041.3831&rep=rep1&type=pdf*
- "k-Ary Search on Modern Processors" by Benjamin Schlegel et al., *https://event.cwi.nl/damon2009/DaMoN09-KarySearch.pdf*

11.26 Test Yourself

1. How can you determine whether a particular SSE or AVX feature is available on the CPU?

2. Why is it important to check the manufacturer of the CPU?

3. What EAX setting do you use with cpuid to obtain the feature flags?

4. What feature flag bit tells you that the CPU supports SSE4.2 instructions?

5. What is the name of the default segment used by the following directives?

   a. .code

   b. .data

   c. .data?

   d. .const

6. What is the default segment alignment?

7. How would you create a data segment aligned on a 64-byte boundary?

8. Which instruction set extensions support the YMM*x* registers?

9. What is a lane?

10. What is the difference between a scalar instruction and a vector instruction?

11. SSE memory operands (XMM) must usually be aligned on what memory boundary?

12. AVX memory operands (YMM) must usually be aligned on what memory boundary?

13. AVX-512 memory operands (ZMM) must usually be aligned on what memory boundary?

14. What instruction would you use to move the data from a 32-bit general-purpose integer register into the LO 32 bits of an XMM and a YMM register?

15. What instruction would you use to move the data from a 64-bit general-purpose integer register into the LO 64 bits of an XMM and a YMM register?

16. What three instructions would you use to load 16 bytes from an aligned memory location into an XMM register?

17. What three instructions would you use to load 16 bytes from an arbitrary memory address into an XMM register?

18. If you want to move the HO 64 bits of an XMM register into the HO 64 bits of another XMM register without affecting the LO 64 bits of the destination, what instruction would you use?

19. If you want to duplicate a double-precision value in the LO 64 bits of an XMM register in the two qwords (LO and HO) of another XMM register, what instruction would you use?

20. Which instruction would you use to rearrange the bytes in an XMM register?

21. Which instruction would you use to rearrange the dword lanes in an XMM register?

22. Which instructions would you use to extract bytes, words, dwords, or qwords from an XMM register and move them into a general-purpose register?

23. Which instructions would you use to take a byte, word, dword, or qword in a general-purpose register and insert it somewhere in an XMM register?

24. What does the `andnpd` instruction do?

25. Which instruction would you use to shift the bytes in an XMM register one byte position to the left (8 bits)?

26. Which instruction would you use to shift the bytes in an XMM register one byte position to the right (8 bits)?

27. If you want to shift the two qwords in an XMM register n bit positions to the left, what instruction would you use?

28. If you want to shift the two qwords in an XMM register n bit positions to the right, what instruction would you use?

29. What happens in a `paddb` instruction when a sum will not fit into 8 bits?

30. What is the difference between a vertical addition and a horizontal addition?

31. Where does the `pcmpeqb` instruction put the result of the comparison? How does it indicate the result is true?

32. There is no `pcmpltq` instruction. Explain how to compare lanes in a pair of XMM registers for the less-than condition.

33. What does the `pmovmskb` instruction do?

34. How many simultaneous additions are performed by the following?

    a. `addps`

    b. `addpd`

35. If you have a pointer to data in RAX and want to force that address to be aligned on a 16-byte boundary, what instruction would you use?

36. How can you set all the bits in the XMM0 register to 0?

37. How can you set all the bits in the XMM1 register to 1?

38. What directive do you use to insert the content of a source file into the current source file during assembly?

12

BIT MANIPULATION

Manipulating bits in memory is, perhaps, the feature for which assembly language is most famous. Even the C programming language, known for bit manipulation, doesn't provide as complete a set of bit-manipulation operations.

This chapter discusses how to manipulate strings of bits in memory and registers by using x86-64 assembly language. It begins with a review of the bit-manipulation instructions covered thus far, introduces a few new instructions, then reviews information on packing and unpacking bit strings in memory, which is the basis for many bit-manipulation operations. Finally, this chapter discusses several bit-centric algorithms and their implementation in assembly language.

12.1 What Is Bit Data, Anyway?

Bit manipulation refers to working with *bit data*: data types that consist of strings of bits that are noncontiguous or not a multiple of 8 bits long.

Generally, such bit objects will not represent numeric integers, although we will not place this restriction on our bit strings.

A *bit string* is a contiguous sequence of 1 or more bits. It does not have to start or end at any special point. For example, a bit string could start in bit 7 of a byte in memory and continue through to bit 6 of the next byte in memory. Likewise, a bit string could begin in bit 30 of EAX, consume the upper 2 bits of EAX, and then continue from bit 0 through to bit 17 of EBX. In memory, the bits must be physically contiguous (that is, the bit numbers are always increasing except when crossing a byte boundary, and at byte boundaries the memory address increases by 1 byte). In registers, if a bit string crosses a register boundary, the application defines the continuation register, but the bit string always continues in bit 0 of that second register.

A *bit run* is a sequence of bits with all the same value. A *run of zeros* is a bit string that contains all 0s, and a *run of ones* is a bit string containing all 1s. The *first set bit* in a bit string is the bit position of the first bit containing a 1 in a bit string; that is, the first 1 bit following a possible run of zeros. A similar definition exists for the *first clear bit*. The *last set bit* is the last bit position in a bit string that contains 1s; the remainder of the string forms an uninterrupted run of zeros. A similar definition exists for the *last clear bit*.

A *bit set* is a collection of bits, not necessarily contiguous, within a larger data structure. For example, bits 0 to 3, 7, 12, 24, and 31 from a double word form a set of bits. Normally, we will deal with bit sets that are part of a *container object* (the data structure that encapsulates the bit set) no more than about 32 or 64 bits in size, though this limit is completely artificial. Bit strings are special cases of bit sets.

A *bit offset* is the number of bits from a boundary position (usually a byte boundary) to the specified bit. As noted in Chapter 2, we number the bits starting from 0 at the boundary location.

A *mask* is a sequence of bits that we'll use to manipulate certain bits in another value. For example, the bit string 0000_1111_0000b, when it's used with the and instruction, masks away (clears) all the bits except bits 4 through 7. Likewise, if you use the same value with the or instruction, it can set bits 4 through 7 in the destination operand. The term *mask* comes from the use of these bit strings with the and instruction. In those situations, the 1 and 0 bits behave like masking tape when you're painting something; they pass through certain bits unchanged while masking out (clearing) the other bits.

Armed with these definitions, we're ready to start manipulating some bits!

12.2　Instructions That Manipulate Bits

Bit manipulation generally consists of six activities: setting bits, clearing bits, inverting bits, testing and comparing bits, extracting bits from a bit string, and inserting bits into a bit string. The most basic bit-manipulation instructions are the and, or, xor, not, test, and shift and rotate instructions. The following paragraphs review these instructions, concentrating on how you could use them to manipulate bits in memory or registers.

12.2.1 The and Instruction

The and instruction provides the ability to replace unwanted bits in a bit sequence with 0s. This instruction is especially useful for isolating a bit string or a bit set that is merged with other, unrelated data (or, at least, data that is not part of the bit string or bit set). For example, suppose that a bit string consumes bit positions 12 through 24 of the EAX register; we can isolate this bit string by setting all other bits in EAX to 0 by using the following instruction (see Figure 12-1):

```
and eax, 1111111111111000000000000b
```

In theory, you could use the or instruction to mask all unwanted bits to 1s rather than 0s, but later comparisons and operations are often easier if the unneeded bit positions contain 0.

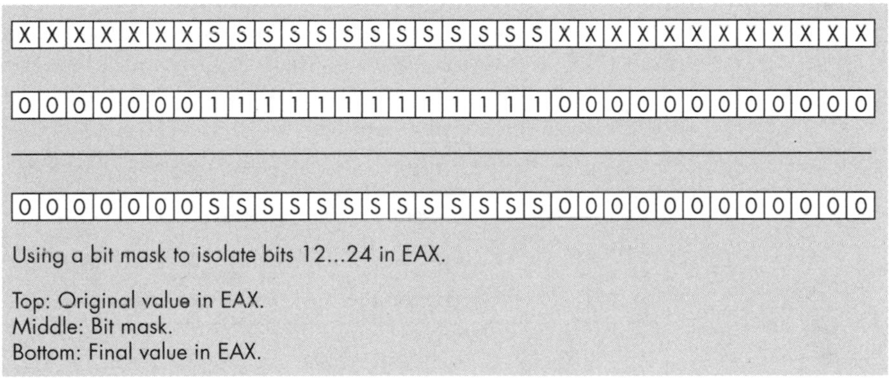

Using a bit mask to isolate bits 12...24 in EAX.

Top: Original value in EAX.
Middle: Bit mask.
Bottom: Final value in EAX.

Figure 12-1: Isolating a bit string by using the and instruction

Once you've cleared the unneeded bits in a set of bits, you can often operate on the bit set in place. For example, to see if the string of bits in positions 12 through 24 of EAX contains 12F3h, you could use the following code:

```
and eax, 1111111111111000000000000b
cmp eax, 1001011110011000000000000b
```

Here's another solution, using constant expressions, that's a little easier to digest:

```
and eax, 1111111111111000000000000b
cmp eax, 12F3h shl 12
```

To make the constants and other values you use in conjunction with this value easier to deal with, you can use the shr instruction to align the bit string with bit 0 after you've masked it, like this:

```
and eax, 1111111111111000000000000b
shr eax, 12
cmp eax, 12F3h
  Other operations that require the bit string at bit #0
```

12.2.2 The or Instruction

The or instruction is especially useful for inserting a bit set into another bit string, using the following steps:

1. Clear all the bits surrounding your bit set in the source operand.
2. Clear all the bits in the destination operand where you wish to insert the bit set.
3. OR the bit set and destination operand together.

For example, suppose you have a value in bits 0 to 12 of EAX that you wish to insert into bits 12 to 24 of EBX without affecting any of the other bits in EBX. You would begin by stripping out bits 13 and above from EAX; then you would strip out bits 12 to 24 in EBX. Next, you would shift the bits in EAX so the bit string occupies bits 12 to 24 of EAX. Finally, you would OR the value in EAX into EBX (see Figure 12-2), as shown here:

```
and eax, 1FFFh       ; Strip all but bits 0 to 12 from EAX
and ebx, 0FE000FFFh  ; Clear bits 12 to 24 in EBX
shl eax, 12          ; Move bits 0 to 12 to 12 to 24 in EAX
or ebx,eax           ; Merge the bits into EBX
```

In Figure 12-2, the desired bits (AAAAAAAAAAAAA) form a bit string. However, this algorithm still works fine even if you're manipulating a noncontiguous set of bits. All you have to do is to create a bit mask that has 1s in the appropriate places.

When you work with bit masks, it is incredibly poor programming style to use literal numeric constants as in the past few examples. You should always create symbolic constants in MASM. By combining these with some constant expressions, you can produce code that is much easier to read and maintain. The current example code is more properly written as the following:

```
StartPosn = 12
BitMask   = 1FFFh shl StartPosn ; Mask occupies bits 12 to 24

    .
    .
    .

    shl eax, StartPosn    ; Move into position
    and eax, BitMask      ; Strip all but bits 12 to 24 from EAX
    and ebx, not BitMask  ; Clear bits 12 to 24 in EBX
    or  ebx, eax          ; Merge the bits into EBX
```

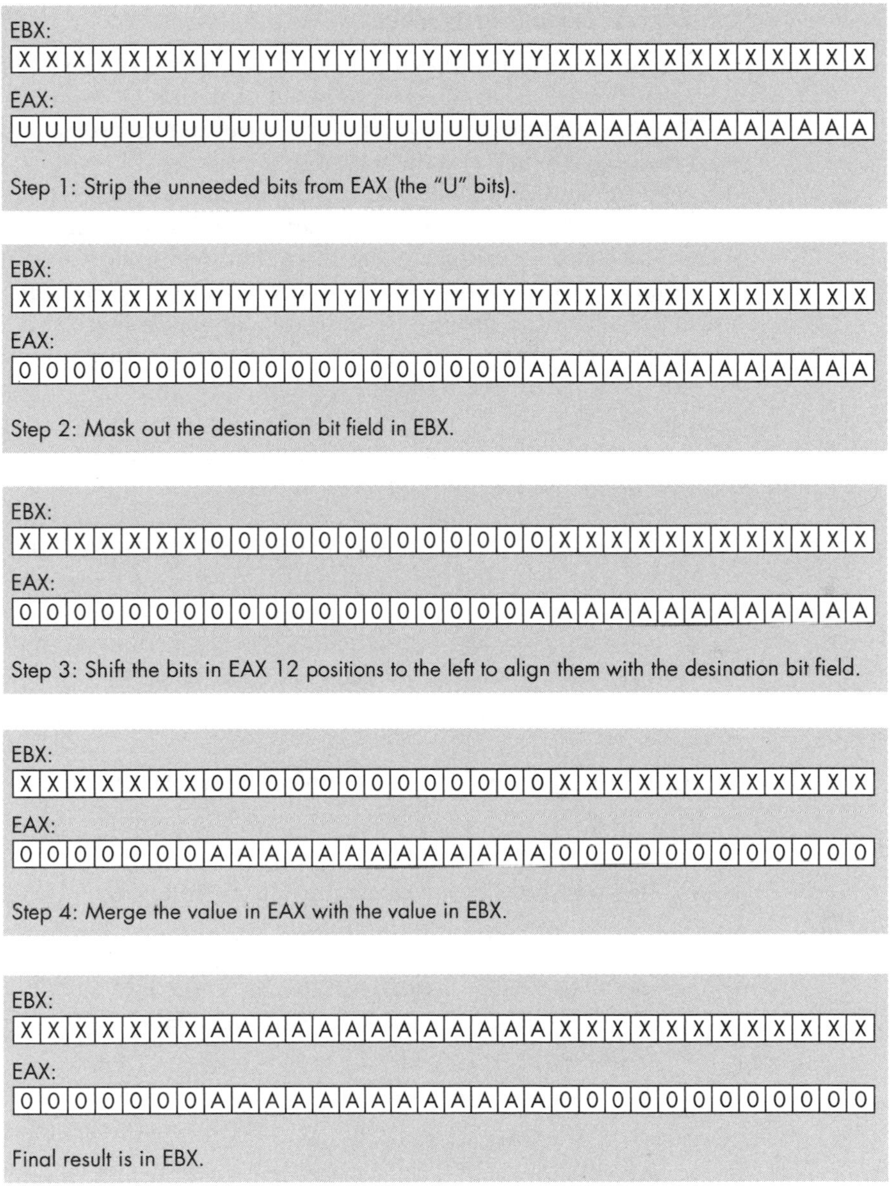

EBX:
`X X X X X X X Y Y Y Y Y Y Y Y Y Y Y Y Y X X X X X X X X X X X X`

EAX:
`U U U U U U U U U U U U U U U U U U U U A A A A A A A A A A A A`

Step 1: Strip the unneeded bits from EAX (the "U" bits).

EBX:
`X X X X X X X Y Y Y Y Y Y Y Y Y Y Y Y Y X X X X X X X X X X X X`

EAX:
`0 0 0 0 0 0 0 0 0 0 0 0 0 0 0 0 0 0 0 0 A A A A A A A A A A A A`

Step 2: Mask out the destination bit field in EBX.

EBX:
`X X X X X X X 0 0 0 0 0 0 0 0 0 0 0 0 0 X X X X X X X X X X X X`

EAX:
`0 0 0 0 0 0 0 0 0 0 0 0 0 0 0 0 0 0 0 0 A A A A A A A A A A A A`

Step 3: Shift the bits in EAX 12 positions to the left to align them with the desination bit field.

EBX:
`X X X X X X X 0 0 0 0 0 0 0 0 0 0 0 0 0 X X X X X X X X X X X X`

EAX:
`0 0 0 0 0 0 0 A A A A A A A A A A A A 0 0 0 0 0 0 0 0 0 0 0 0`

Step 4: Merge the value in EAX with the value in EBX.

EBX:
`X X X X X X X A A A A A A A A A A A A X X X X X X X X X X X X`

EAX:
`0 0 0 0 0 0 0 A A A A A A A A A A A A 0 0 0 0 0 0 0 0 0 0 0 0`

Final result is in EBX.

Figure 12-2: Inserting bits 0 to 12 of EAX into bits 12 to 24 of EBX

The use of the compile time not operator to invert the bit mask saves having to create another constant in the program that has to be changed anytime you modify the BitMask constant. Having to maintain two separate symbols whose values are dependent on one another is not a good thing in a program.

Of course, in addition to merging one bit set with another, the or instruction is also useful for forcing bits to 1 in a bit string. By setting various bits in a source operand to 1, you can force the corresponding bits in the destination operand to 1 by using the or instruction.

12.2.3 The xor Instruction

The xor instruction allows you to invert selected bits in a bit set. Of course, if you want to invert all the bits in a destination operand, the not instruction is more appropriate; however, if you want to invert selected bits while not affecting others, xor is the way to go.

One interesting fact about xor's operation is that it lets you manipulate known data in just about any way imaginable. For example, if you know that a field contains 1010b, you can force that field to 0 by XORing it with 1010b. Similarly, you can force it to 1111b by XORing it with 0101b. Although this might seem like a waste, because you can easily force this 4-bit string to 0 or all 1s by using and/or, the xor instruction has two advantages. First, you are not limited to forcing the field to all 0s or all 1s; you can actually set these bits to any of the 16 valid combinations via xor. Second, if you need to manipulate other bits in the destination operand at the same time, and/or may not be able to do the job.

For example, suppose you know that one field contains 1010b that you want to force to 0, and another field in the same operand contains 1000b and you wish to increment that field by 1 (that is, set the field to 1001b). You cannot accomplish both operations with a single and or or instruction, but you can with a single xor instruction; just XOR the first field with 1010b and the second field with 0001b. Remember, however, that this trick works only if you know the current value of a bit set within the destination operand.

12.2.4 Flag Modification by Logical Instructions

In addition to setting, clearing, and inverting bits in a destination operand, the and, or, and xor instructions also affect various condition codes in the FLAGS register. These instructions do the following:

- Always clear the carry and overflow flags.
- Set the sign flag if the result has a 1 in the HO bit. They clear it otherwise; that is, these instructions copy the HO bit of the result into the sign flag.
- Set or clear the zero flag if the result is zero or not zero, respectively.
- Set the parity flag if there is an even number of set bits in the LO byte of the destination operand, and clear the parity flag if there is an odd number of set bits.

Because these instructions always clear the carry and overflow flags, you cannot expect the system to preserve the state of these two flags across the execution of these instructions. A common mistake in many assembly language programs is the assumption that these instructions do not affect the carry flag. Many people will execute an instruction that sets or clears the carry flag; execute an and, or, or xor instruction; and then attempt to test the state of the carry from the previous instruction. This simply will not work.

One of the more interesting aspects to these instructions is that they copy the HO bit of their result into the sign flag. Therefore, you can easily test the HO bit by testing the sign flag (using cmovs and cmovns, sets and setns, or js and jns instructions). For this reason, many assembly language programmers will place an important Boolean variable in the HO bit of an operand so they can easily test the state of that variable by using the sign flag after a logical operation.

12.2.4.1 The Parity Flag

Parity is a simple error-detection scheme originally employed by telegraphs and other serial communication protocols. The idea was to count the number of set bits in a character and include an extra bit in the transmission to indicate whether that character contained an even or odd number of set bits. The receiving end of the transmission would also count the bits and verify that the extra *parity* bit indicated a successful transmission. The purpose of the parity flag is to help compute the value of this extra bit, though parity-checking has been taken over by hardware.[1]

The x86-64 and, or, and xor instructions set the parity bit if the LO byte of their operand contains an even number of set bits. An important fact bears repeating here: the parity flag reflects only the number of set bits in the *LO byte* of the destination operand; it does not include the HO bytes in a word, double-word, or other-sized operand. The instruction set uses the LO byte only to compute the parity because communication programs that use parity are typically character-oriented transmission systems (better error-checking schemes could be used if you transmit more than 8 bits at a time).

12.2.4.2 The Zero Flag

The zero flag setting is one of the more important results produced by the and, or, and xor instructions. Indeed, programs reference this flag so often after the and instruction that Intel added a separate instruction, test, whose main purpose is to logically AND two results and set the flags without otherwise affecting either instruction operand.

The zero flag has three main uses after the execution of an and or a test instruction: (1) checking to see if a particular bit in an operand is set, (2) checking to see if at least one of several bits in a bit set is 1, and (3) checking to see if an operand is 0. Using (1) is actually a special case of (2), in which the bit set contains only a single bit. We'll explore each of these uses in the following paragraphs.

To test whether a particular bit is set in a given operand, use the and and test instructions for an operand with a constant value containing a single set bit you wish to test. This clears all the other bits in the operand, leaving a 0 in the bit position under test if the operand contained a 0 in that bit position and a 1 if it contained a 1. Because all of the other bits in the result are 0, the entire result will be 0 if that particular bit is 0; the entire result will be nonzero if that bit position contains a 1. The x86-64

---

1. Serial communications chips and other communications hardware that use parity for error checking normally compute the parity in hardware; you don't have to use software for this purpose.

reflects this status in the zero flag (Z = 1 indicates a 0 bit; Z = 0 indicates a 1 bit). The following instruction sequence demonstrates how to test if bit 4 is set in EAX:

```
    test eax, 10000b  ; Check bit #4 to see if it is 0 or 1
    jnz  bitIsSet

    Do this if the bit is clear
       .
       .
       .
bitIsSet:    ; Branch here if the bit is set
```

You can also use the and and test instructions to see if any one of several bits is set. Simply supply a constant that has a 1 in all the positions you want to test (and 0s everywhere else). ANDing an operand with such a constant will produce a nonzero value if one or more of the bits in the operand under test contain a 1. The following example tests whether the value in EAX contains a 1 in bit positions 1, 2, 4, and 7:

```
    test eax, 10010110b
    jz   noBitsSet

    Do whatever needs to be done if one of the bits is set

noBitsSet:
```

You cannot use a single and or test instruction to see if all the corresponding bits in the bit set are equal to 1. To accomplish this, you must first mask out the bits that are not in the set and then compare the result against the mask itself. If the result is equal to the mask, all the bits in the bit set contain 1s. You must use the and instruction for this operation because the test instruction does not modify the result. The following example checks whether all the bits in a bit set (bitMask) are equal to 1:

```
    and eax, bitMask
    cmp eax, bitMask
    jne allBitsArentSet

; All the bit positions in EAX corresponding to the set
; bits in bitMask are equal to 1 if we get here.

    Do whatever needs to be done if the bits match

allBitsArentSet:
```

Of course, once we stick the cmp instruction in there, we don't really have to check whether all the bits in the bit set contain 1s. We can check for any combination of values by specifying the appropriate value as the operand to the cmp instruction.

Note that the test and and instructions will set the zero flag in the preceding code sequences only if all the bits in EAX (or other destination operand) have 0s in the positions where 1s appear in the constant operand. This suggests another way to check for all 1s in the bit set: invert the value in EAX prior to using the and or test instruction. Then if the zero flag is set, you know that there were all 1s in the (original) bit set. For example:

```
not  eax
test eax, bitMask
jnz  NotAllOnes

; At this point, EAX contained all 1s in the bit positions
; occupied by 1s in the bitMask constant.

    Do whatever needs to be done at this point

NotAllOnes:
```

The previous paragraphs all suggest that the bitMask (the source operand) is a constant, but you can use a variable or other register too. Simply load that variable or register with the appropriate bit mask before you execute the test, and, or cmp instructions in the preceding examples.

12.2.5 The Bit Test Instructions

Another set of instructions we've already seen that we can use to manipulate bits is the *bit test instructions*. These instructions include bt (*bit test*), bts (*bit test and set*), btc (*bit test and complement*), and btr (*bit test and reset*). The btx instructions use the following syntax:

```
btx  bits_to_test, bit_number
btx  reg₁₆, reg₁₆
btx  reg₃₂, reg₃₂
btx  reg₆₄, reg₆₄
btx  reg₁₆, constant
btx  reg₃₂, constant
btx  reg₆₄, constant
btx  mem₁₆, reg₁₆
btx  mem₃₂, reg₃₂
btx  mem₆₄, reg₆₄
btx  mem₁₆, constant
btx  mem₃₂, constant
btx  mem₆₄, constant
```

where *x* is nothing, c, s, or r.

The btx instructions' second operand is a bit number that specifies which bit to check in the first operand. If the first operand is a register, the second operand must contain a value between 0 and the size of the register (in bits) minus 1; because the x86-64's largest (general-purpose) registers are 64 bits, this value has the maximum value of 63 (for 64-bit registers). If the first operand is a memory location, the bit count is not limited to values in the range 0 to 63. If the second operand is a constant, it can be any 8-bit value in the range 0 to 255. If the second operand is a register, it has no (practical) limitation and, in fact, it allows negative bit offsets.

The bt instruction copies the specified bit from the second operand into the carry flag. For example, the bt eax, 8 instruction copies bit 8 of the EAX register into the carry flag. You can test the carry flag after this instruction to determine whether bit 8 was set or clear in EAX.

The bts, btc, and btr instructions manipulate the bit they test while they are testing it. These instructions may be slow (depending on the processor you're using), and you should avoid them if performance is your primary concern, particularly if you're using an older CPU. If performance (versus convenience) is an issue, you should always try two different algorithms—one that uses these instructions, and one that uses and and or instructions—and measure the performance difference; then choose the best of the two approaches.

12.2.6 Manipulating Bits with Shift and Rotate Instructions

The *shift and rotate instructions* are another group of instructions you can use to manipulate and test bits. These instructions move the HO (left shift and rotate) or LO (right shift and rotate) bits into the carry flag. Therefore, you can test the carry flag after you execute one of these instructions to determine the original setting of the operand's HO or LO bit; for example:

```
shr   al, 1
jc    LOBitWasSet
```

The nice thing about the shift and rotate instructions is that they automatically move bits up or down in their operand so the next bit to test is in place; this is especially useful when operating within a loop.

The shift and rotate instructions are invaluable for aligning bit strings and packing and unpacking data. Chapter 2 has several examples of this, and some earlier examples in this chapter also use the shift instructions for this purpose.

12.3   The Carry Flag as a Bit Accumulator

The btx, shift, and rotate instructions set or clear the carry flag depending on the operation and selected bit. Because these instructions place their "bit result" in the carry flag, it is often convenient to think of the carry flag as a 1-bit register or accumulator for bit operations. In this section, we will explore some of the operations possible with this bit result in the carry flag.

Instructions that use the carry flag as some sort of input value are useful for manipulating bit results in the carry flag. For example:

- adc, sbb
- rcl, rcr
- cmc, clc, and stc
- cmovc, cmovnc
- jc, jnc
- setc, setnc

The adc and sbb instructions add or subtract their operands along with the carry flag, so if you've computed a bit result into the carry flag, you can figure that result into an addition or a subtraction by using these instructions.

To save a carry flag result, you can use the rotate-through-carry instructions (rcl and rcr), which move the carry flag into the LO or HO bits of their destination operand. These instructions are useful for packing a set of bit results into a byte, word, or double-word value.

The cmc (*complement carry*) instruction lets you easily invert the result of a bit operation. You can also use the clc and stc instructions to initialize the carry flag prior to a string of bit operations involving the carry flag.

Instructions that test the carry flag, like jc, jnc, cmovc, cmovnc, setc, and setnc, are useful after a calculation that leaves a bit result in the carry flag.

If you have a sequence of bit calculations and would like to test whether those calculations produce a specific set of 1-bit results, you can clear a register or memory location and use the rcl or rcr instruction to shift each result into that location. Once the bit operations are complete, compare the register or memory location, holding the result against a constant value. If you want to test a sequence of results involving ANDs and ORs, you could use the setc and setnc instruction to set a register to 0 or 1 and then use the and and or instructions to merge the results.

12.4 Packing and Unpacking Bit Strings

A common bit operation is inserting a bit string into an operand or extracting a bit string from an operand. Chapter 2 provided simple examples of packing and unpacking such data; now it is time to formally describe how to do this.

For our purposes, I will assume that we're dealing with bit strings that fit within a byte, word, double-word, or quad-word operand. Large bit strings that cross object boundaries require additional processing; we'll discuss bit strings that cross quad-word boundaries later in this section.

When packing and unpacking a bit string, we must consider its starting bit position and length. The *starting bit position* is the bit number of the LO bit of the string in the larger operand. The *length* is the number of bits in the operand.

To insert (pack) data into a destination operand, you start with a bit string of the appropriate length that is right-justified (starts in bit position 0) and zero-extended to 8, 16, 32, or 64 bits; then insert this data at the appropriate starting position in another operand that is 8, 16, 32, or 64 bits wide. There is no guarantee that the destination bit positions contain any particular value.

The first two steps (which can occur in any order) are to clear out the corresponding bits in the destination operand and to shift (a copy of) the bit string so that the LO bit begins at the appropriate bit position. The third step is to OR the shifted result with the destination operand. This inserts the bit string into the destination operand (see Figure 12-3).

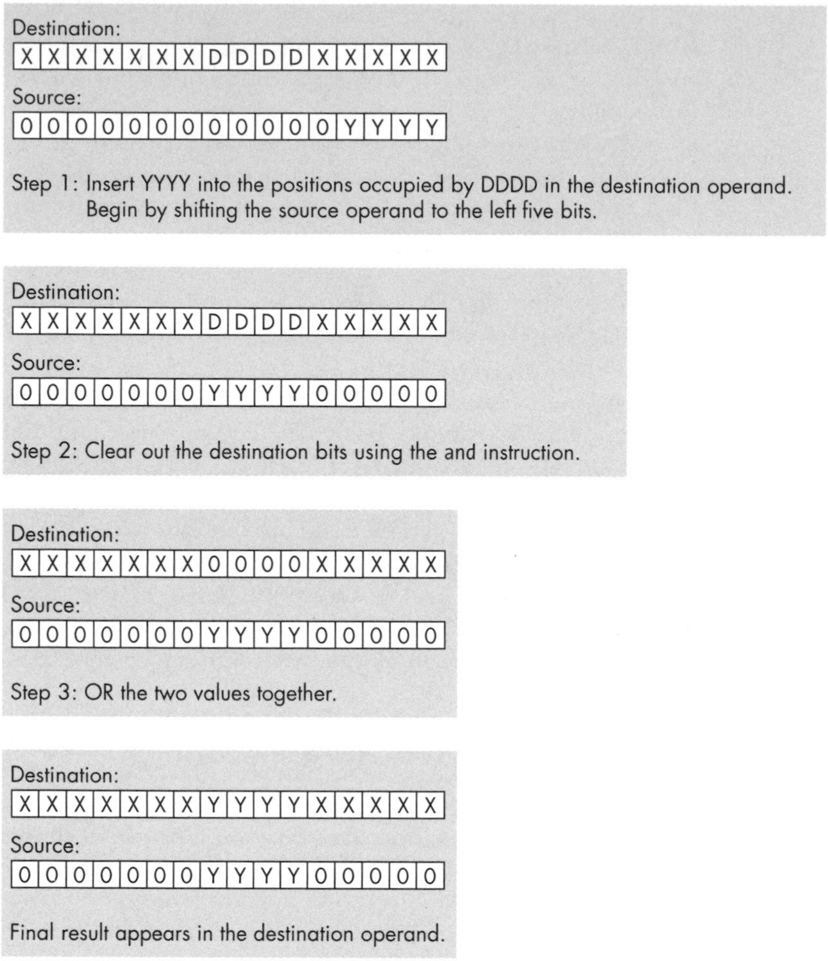

Destination:

X	X	X	X	X	X	X	D	D	D	D	X	X	X	X	X

Source:

0	0	0	0	0	0	0	0	0	0	0	0	Y	Y	Y	Y

Step 1: Insert YYYY into the positions occupied by DDDD in the destination operand. Begin by shifting the source operand to the left five bits.

Destination:

X	X	X	X	X	X	X	D	D	D	D	X	X	X	X	X

Source:

0	0	0	0	0	0	0	Y	Y	Y	Y	0	0	0	0	0

Step 2: Clear out the destination bits using the and instruction.

Destination:

X	X	X	X	X	X	X	0	0	0	0	X	X	X	X	X

Source:

0	0	0	0	0	0	0	Y	Y	Y	Y	0	0	0	0	0

Step 3: OR the two values together.

Destination:

X	X	X	X	X	X	X	Y	Y	Y	Y	X	X	X	X	X

Source:

0	0	0	0	0	0	0	Y	Y	Y	Y	0	0	0	0	0

Final result appears in the destination operand.

Figure 12-3: Inserting a bit string into a destination operand

The following three instructions insert a bit string of known length into a destination operand, as shown in Figure 12-3. These instructions assume that the source operand is in BX and the destination operand is in AX:

```
shl  bx, 5
and  ax, 1111111000011111b
or   ax, bx
```

If the length and the starting position aren't known when you're writing the program (that is, you have to calculate them at runtime), then you can use a lookup table to insert a bit string. Let's assume that we have two 8-bit values: a starting bit position for the field we're inserting and a nonzero 8-bit length value. Also assume that the source operand is in EBX and the destination operand is in EAX. The mergeBits procedure in Listing 12-1 demonstrates how to do this.

```
; Listing 12-1

; Demonstrate inserting bit strings into a register.

; Note that this program must be assembled and linked
; with the "LARGEADDRESSAWARE:NO" option.

        option  casemap:none

nl          =       10

            .const
ttlStr      byte    "Listing 12-1", 0

; The index into the following table specifies the length
; of the bit string at each position. There are 65 entries
; in this table (one for each bit length from 0 to 64).

            .const
MaskByLen   equ     this qword
    qword   0
    qword   1,          3,          7,          0fh
    qword   1fh,        3fh,        7fh,        0ffh
    qword   1ffh,       3ffh,       7ffh,       0fffh
    qword   1fffh,      3fffh,      7fffh,      0ffffh
    qword   1ffffh,     3ffffh,     7ffffh,     0fffffh
    qword   1fffffh,    3fffffh,    7fffffh,    0ffffffh
    qword   1ffffffh,   3ffffffh,   7ffffffh,   0fffffffh
    qword   1fffffffh,  3fffffffh,  7fffffffh,  0ffffffffh

    qword   1ffffffffh,         03ffffffffh
    qword   7ffffffffh,         0fffffffffh

    qword   1fffffffffh,        03fffffffffh
    qword   7fffffffffh,        0ffffffffffh

    qword   1ffffffffffh,       03ffffffffffh
    qword   7ffffffffffh,       0fffffffffffh

    qword   1fffffffffffh,      03fffffffffffh
    qword   7fffffffffffh,      0ffffffffffffh

    qword   1ffffffffffffh,     03ffffffffffffh
    qword   7ffffffffffffh,     0fffffffffffffh

    qword   1fffffffffffffh,    03fffffffffffffh
    qword   7fffffffffffffh,    0ffffffffffffffh

    qword   1ffffffffffffffh,   03ffffffffffffffh
    qword   7ffffffffffffffh,   0fffffffffffffffh

    qword   1fffffffffffffffh,  03fffffffffffffffh
    qword   7fffffffffffffffh,  0ffffffffffffffffh
```

```
Val2Merge    qword    12h, 1eh, 5555h, 1200h, 120h
LenInBits    byte     5,    9,    16,    16,    12
StartPosn    byte     7,    4,    4,     12,    18

MergeInto    qword    0ffffffffh, 0, 12345678h
             qword    11111111h, 0f0f0f0fh

             include getTitle.inc
             include print.inc

             .code

; mergeBits(Val2Merge, MergeWith, Start, Length):
; Length (LenInBits[i]) value is passed in DL.
; Start (StartPosn[i]) is passed in CL.
; Val2Merge (Val2Merge[i]) and MergeWith (MergeInto[i])
; are passed in RBX and RAX.

; mergeBits result is returned in RAX.

mergeBits    proc
             push    rbx
             push    rcx
             push    rdx
             push    r8
             movzx   edx, dl         ; Zero-extends to RDX
             mov     rdx, MaskByLen[rdx * 8]
             shl     rdx, cl
             not     rdx
             shl     rbx, cl
             and     rax, rdx
             or      rax, rbx
             pop     r8
             pop     rdx
             pop     rcx
             pop     rbx
             ret
mergeBits    endp

; Here is the "asmMain" function.

             public  asmMain
asmMain      proc
             push    rbx
             push    rsi
             push    rdi
             push    rbp
             mov     rbp, rsp
             sub     rsp, 56         ; Shadow storage

; The following loop calls mergeBits as
; follows:

;   mergeBits(Val2Merge[i], MergeInto[i],
;             StartPosn[i], LenInBits[i]);
```

```
            ; Where "i" runs from 4 down to 0.

            ; Index of the last element in the arrays:

                    mov     r10, (sizeof LenInBits) - 1
            testLoop:

            ; Fetch the Val2Merge element and write
            ; its value to the display while it is handy.

                    mov     rdx, Val2Merge[r10 * 8]
                    call    print
                    byte    "merge( %x, ", 0
                    mov     rbx, rdx

            ; Fetch the MergeInto element and write
            ; its value to the display.

                    mov     rdx, MergeInto[r10 * 8]
                    call    print
                    byte    "%x, ", 0
                    mov     rax, rdx

            ; Fetch the StartPosn element and write
            ; its value to the display.

                    movzx   edx, StartPosn[r10 * 1] ; Zero-extends to RDX
                    call    print
                    byte    "%d, ", 0
                    mov     rcx, rdx

            ; Fetch the LenInBits element and write
            ; its value to the display.

                    movzx   edx, LenInBits[r10 * 1] ; Zero-extends to RDX
                    call    print
                    byte    "%d ) = ", 0

            ; Call mergeBits(Val2Merge, MergeInto,
            ;                StartPosn, LenInBits)

                    call    mergeBits

            ; Display the function result (returned
            ; in RAX). For this program, the results
            ; are always 32 bits, so it prints only
            ; the LO 32 bits of RAX:

                    mov     edx, eax
                    call    print
                    byte    "%x", nl, 0

            ; Repeat for each element of the array.

                    dec     r10
```

```
            jns     testLoop

allDone:    leave
            pop     rdi
            pop     rsi
            pop     rbx
            ret     ; Returns to caller
asmMain     endp
            end
```

Listing 12-1: Inserting bits where the bit string length and starting position are variables

Here's the build command and output for the program in Listing 12-1. Because this program accesses arrays directly (rather than loading their addresses into registers, which obfuscates the code), this program must be built with the LARGEADDRESSAWARE:NO flag, hence the use of the *sbuild.bat* batch file (see the description of *sbuild.bat* in "Large Address Unaware Applications" in Chapter 3):

```
C:\>sbuild listing12-1

C:\>echo off
 Assembling: listing12-1.asm
c.cpp

C:\>listing12-1
Calling Listing 12-1:
merge(120, f0f0f0f, 18, 12) = 4830f0f
merge(1200, 11111111, 12, 16) = 11200111
merge(5555, 12345678, 4, 16) = 12355558
merge(1e, 0, 4, 9) = 1e0
merge(12, ffffffff, 7, 5) = fffff97f
Listing 12-1 terminated
```

Each entry in the MaskByLen table (in Listing 12-1) contains the number of 1 bits specified by the index into the table. Using the mergeBits Length parameter value as an index into this table fetches a value that has as many 1 bits as the Length value. The mergeBits function fetches an appropriate mask, shifts it to the left so that the LO bit of this run of 1s matches the starting position of the field into which we want to insert the data, and then inverts the mask and uses the inverted value to clear the appropriate bits in the destination operand.

To extract a bit string from a larger operand, all you have to do is mask out the unwanted bits and then shift the result until the LO bit of the bit string is in bit 0 of the destination operand. For example, to extract the 4-bit field starting at bit position 5 in EBX and leave the result in EAX, you could use the following code:

```
mov eax, ebx        ; Copy data to destination
and eax, 111100000b ; Strip unwanted bits
shr eax, 5          ; Right-justify to bit position 0
```

If you do not know the bit string's length and starting position when you're writing the program, you can still extract the desired bit string. The code is similar to insertion (though a little simpler). Assuming you have the Length and Start values we used when inserting a bit string, you can extract the corresponding bit string by using the following code (assuming source = EBX and dest = EAX):

```
movzx   edx, Length
lea     r8, MaskByLen       ; Table from Listing 12-1
mov     rdx, [r8][rdx * 8]
mov     cl, StartingPosition
mov     rax, rbx
shr     rax, cl
and     rax, rdx
```

The examples up to this point all assume that the bit string appears completely within a quad-word (or smaller) object. This will always be the case if the bit string is less than or equal to 64 bits in length. However, if the length of the bit string plus its starting position (modulo 8) within an object is greater than 64, the bit string will cross a quad-word boundary within the object.

Extracting such bit strings requires up to three operations: one operation to extract the start of the bit string (up to the first quad-word boundary), an operation that copies whole quad words (assuming the bit string is so long that it consumes several quad words), and a final operation that copies leftover bits in the last quad word at the end of the bit string. The actual implementation of this operation is left as an exercise for you.

12.5   BMI1 Instructions to Extract Bits and Create Bit Masks

If your CPU supports the BMI1 (*bit manipulation instructions, set 1*) instruction set extensions,[2] you can use the bextr (*bit extraction*) instruction to extract bits from a 32- or 64-bit general-purpose register. This instruction has the following syntax:

```
bextr  reg_dest,  reg_src,  reg_ctrl
bextr  reg_dest,  mem_src,  reg_ctrl
```

The operands must all be the same size and must be 32- or 64-bit registers (or memory locations).

The bextr instruction encodes two parameters into reg_{ctrl}:

- Bits 0 to 7 of reg_{ctrl} specify a starting bit position in the source operand (this must be a value in the range 0 to 31 for 32-bit operands and 0 to 63 for 64-bit operands).
- Bits 8 to 15 of reg_{ctrl} specify the number of bits to extract from the source operand.

---

2. See Listing 11-2 in Chapter 11 to see how to check for the presence of the BMI1 and BMI2 instruction set extensions.

The bextr instruction will extract the specified bits from reg_{src} or mem_{src} and store those bits (shifted down to bit 0) in reg_{dest}. As a general rule, you should attempt to use RAX and EAX, RBX and EBX, RCX and ECX, or RDX and EDX as the *ctrl* register because you can easily manipulate the starting and length values by using the AH and AL, BH and BL, CH and CL, and DH and DL 8-bit registers. Listing 12-2 provides a quick demonstration of the bextr instruction.[3]

```
; Listing 12-2

; Demonstrate extracting bit strings from a register.

        option  casemap:none

nl          =       10

            .const
ttlStr      byte    "Listing 12-2", 0

            include getTitle.inc
            include print.inc

; Here is the "asmMain" function.

            .code
            public  asmMain
asmMain     proc
            push    rbx
            push    rsi
            push    rdi
            push    rbp
            mov     rbp, rsp
            sub     rsp, 56         ; Shadow storage

; >>>> Unique code for various listings:

            mov     rax, 123456788abcdefh
            mov     bl, 4
            mov     bh, 16

            bextr   rdx, rax, rbx

            call    print
            byte    "Extracted bits: %x", nl, 0

; <<<< End of unique code.

allDone:    leave
            pop     rdi
            pop     rsi
```

---

3. This listing contains some common code that other listings in this chapter will share. The code unique to this listing appears between the ; >>>> and ; <<<< comments.

```
          pop    rbx
          ret    ; Returns to caller
asmMain   endp
          end
```

Listing 12-2: bextr instruction example

Listing 12-2 produces the following output:

```
C:\>build listing12-2

C:\>echo off
 Assembling: listing12-2.asm
c.cpp

C:\>listing12-2
Calling Listing 12-2:
Extracted bits: bcde
Listing 12-2 terminated
```

The BMI1 instruction set extension also includes an instruction that extracts the lowest-numbered set bit in a register: blsi (*extract lowest set isolated bit*). The syntax for this instruction is as follows:

```
blsi reg_dest, reg_src
blsi reg_dest, mem_src
```

The operands must be the same size and can be either 32 or 64 bits. This instruction locates the lowest set bit in the source operand (register or memory). It copies that bit to the destination register and zeroes out all other bits in the destination. If the source value is 0, blsi copies 0 to the destination register and sets the zero and carry flags. Listing 12-3 is a simple demonstration of this instruction (note that I've eliminated the common code from Listing 12-2).

```
; >>>> Unique code for various listings.

mov    r8, 12340000h
blsi   edx, r8

call   print
byte   "Extracted bit: %x", nl, 0

; <<<< End of unique code.
```

Listing 12-3: Simple demonstration of the blsi instruction

Inserting this into a shell sample program and running it produces the following output:

```
Extracted bit: 40000
```

The BMI1 `andn` instruction is useful in conjunction with `blsi`. The `andn` (*and not*) instruction has the following generic syntax:

```
andn reg_dest, reg_src1, reg_src2
andn reg_dest, reg_src1, mem_src2
```

The operands must all be the same size and must be 32 or 64 bits. This instruction logically ANDs an inverted copy of the value in reg_{src1} with the third operand (the *src2* operand) and stores the result into the reg_{dest} operand.

You can use the `andn` instruction immediately after a `blsi` instruction to remove the lowest-numbered bit from `blsi`'s source operand after extracting it. Listing 12-4 demonstrates this operation (as usual, omitting the common code).

```
; >>>> Unique code for various listings.

mov     r8, 12340000h
blsi    edx, r8
andn    r8, rdx, r8

; Output value 1 is in RDX (extracted bit),
; output value 2 in R8 (value with deleted bit).

call    print
byte    "Extracted bit: %x, result: %x", nl, 0

; <<<< End of unique code.
```

Listing 12-4: Extracting and removing the lowest set bit in an operand

Running this code produces the following output:

```
Extracted bit: 40000, result: 12300000
```

Extracting the LO bit and keeping the remaining bits (as was done with the `blsi` and `andn` instructions in Listing 12-4) are such a common operation that Intel created an instruction to specifically handle this task: `blsr` (*reset lowest set bit*). Here's its generic syntax:

```
blsr reg_dest, reg_src
blsr reg_dest, mem_src
```

Both operands must be the same size and must be either 32 or 64 bits. This instruction gets the data from the source operand, sets the lowest-numbered set bit to 0, and copies the result to the destination register. If the source operand contains 0, this instruction copies 0 to the destination and sets the carry flag.

Listing 12-5 demonstrates the usage of this instruction.

```
; >>>> Unique code for various listings.

mov     r8, 12340000h
blsr    edx, r8
```

```
; Output value 1 is in RDX (extracted bit), resulting value.

call    print
byte    "Value with extracted bit: %x", nl, 0

; <<<< End of unique code.
```

Listing 12-5: blsr instruction example

Here's the output from this code fragment (after inserting it into a test program shell):

```
Value with extracted bit: 12300000
```

Another useful BMI1 instruction is blsmsk. This instruction creates a bit mask by searching for the lowest-numbered set bit. Then it creates a bit mask consisting of all 1 bits up to and including the lowest set bit. The blsmsk instruction sets the remaining bits to 0. If the original value was 0, blsmsk sets all the bits in the destination register to 1 and sets the carry flag. Here's the generic syntax for blsmsk:

```
blsmsk reg_dest, reg_src
blsmsk reg_dest, mem_src
```

Listing 12-6 is a sample code fragment and the output it will produce.

```
; >>>> Unique code for various listings.

mov     r8, 12340000h
blsmsk  edx, r8

; Output value 1 is in RDX (mask).

call    print
byte    "Mask: %x", nl, 0

; <<<< End of unique code.
```

Listing 12-6: blsmsk example

Here is the sample output:

```
Mask: 7ffff
```

Especially note that the mask the blsmsk instruction produces includes a 1 bit in the bit position holding the lowest-numbered set bit in the source file. Often, you will actually want a bit mask containing 1 bits up to, but not including, the lowest-numbered set bit. This is easy to achieve using the blsi and dec instructions, as shown in Listing 12-7.

```
; >>>> Unique code for various listings.

mov     r8, 12340000h
blsi    rdx, r8
dec     rdx
```

```
; Output value 1 is in RDX (mask).

call    print
byte    "Mask: %x", nl, 0

; <<<< End of unique code.
```

Listing 12-7: Creating a bit mask that doesn't include the lowest-numbered set bit

Here's the output:

```
Mask: 3ffff
```

The last of the BMI1 instructions is tzcnt (*trailing zero count*). This instruction has the following generic syntax:

```
tzcnt reg_dest, reg_src
tzcnt reg_dest, mem_src
```

As usual, the operands must both be the same size. The tzcnt instruction is unique among the BMI1 instructions insofar as it allows 16-, 32-, and 64-bit operands.

The tzcnt instruction counts the number of LO 0 bits in the source (starting at the LO bit and working up toward the HO bit). It stores the 0 bit count into the destination register. Conveniently, the count of 0 bits is also the bit index of the first set bit in the source operand. This instruction sets the carry flag if the source operand is 0 (in which case it also sets the destination register to the size of the operands).

To search for and extract 0 bits with bextr, blsi, blsr, and blsmsk, invert the source operand before executing these instructions. Likewise, to count the number of trailing set bits with tzcnt, first invert the source operand.[4]

If you use bextr, blsi, blsr, blsmsk, tzcnt, or andn in your program, don't forget to test for the presence of the BMI1 instruction set extensions. Not all x86-64 CPUs support these instructions.

12.6   Coalescing Bit Sets and Distributing Bit Strings

Inserting and extracting bit sets are only a little different from inserting and extracting bit strings if the shape of the bit set you're inserting (or resulting bit set you're extracting) is the same as the shape of the bit set in the main object. The *shape* of a bit set is the distribution of the bits in the set, ignoring the starting bit position of the set. A bit set that includes bits 0, 4, 5, 6, and 7 has the same shape as that of a bit set that includes bits 12, 16, 17, 18, and 19 because the distribution of the bits is the same.

The code to insert or extract this bit set is nearly identical to that of the previous section; the only difference is the mask value you use. For

---

4. Certain AMD processors include instructions for these operations. See the AMD literature for more details.

example, to insert this bit set starting at bit 0 in EAX into the corresponding bit set starting at position 12 in EBX, you could use the following code:

```
and ebx, not 11110001000000000000b ; Mask out destination bits
shl eax, 12                         ; Move source bits into position
or  ebx, eax                        ; Merge the bit set into EBX
```

However, suppose you have 5 bits in bit positions 0 through 4 in EAX and want to merge them into bits 12, 16, 17, 18, and 19 in EBX. Somehow you have to distribute the bits in EAX prior to logically ORing the values into EBX. Given that this particular bit set is made of two runs of 1 bits, the process is somewhat simplified. The following code distributes the bits in a sneaky fashion:

```
and ebx, not 11110001000000000000b
and eax, 11110001000000000000b ; Mask out destination bits
shl eax, 2     ; Spread out bits: 1 to 4 goes to 3 to 6 and 0 goes to 2
btr eax, 2     ; Bit 2 -> carry and then clear bit 2
rcl eax, 13    ; Shift in carry and put bits into final position
or  ebx, eax   ; Merge the bit set into EBX
```

This trick with the btr (*bit test and reset*) instruction worked well because we had only 1 bit out of place in the original source operand. Alas, had the bits all been in the wrong location relative to one another, this scheme wouldn't be an efficient solution. We'll see a more general solution in just a moment.

Extracting this bit set and collecting (*coalescing*) the bits into a bit string is not quite as easy. However, we still have some sneaky tricks we can pull. Consider the following code that extracts the bit set from EBX and places the result into bits 0 to 4 of EAX:

```
mov eax, ebx
and eax, 11110001000000000000b  ; Strip unwanted bits
shr eax, 5                      ; Put bit 12 into bit 7, and so on
shr ah, 3                       ; Move bits 11 to 14 to 8 to 11
shr eax, 7                      ; Move down to bit 0
```

This code moves (original) bit 12 into bit position 7, the HO bit of AL. At the same time, it moves bits 16 to 19 down to bits 11 to 14 (bits 3 to 6 of AH). Then the code shifts bits 3 to 6 in AH down to bit 0. This positions the HO bits of the bit set so that they are adjacent to the bit remaining in AL. Finally, the code shifts all the bits down to bit 0. Again, this is not a general solution, but it shows a clever way to attack this problem if you think about it carefully.

The preceding coalescence and distribution algorithms apply only to their specific bit sets. A generalized solution (perhaps one that lets you specify a mask, then distributes or coalesces the bits accordingly) is going to be a bit more difficult. The following code demonstrates how to distribute the bits in a bit string according to the values in a bit mask:

```
; EAX - Originally contains a value into which we
;       insert bits from EBX.
; EBX - LO bits contain the values to insert into EAX.
```

```
; EDX - Bitmap with 1s indicating the bit positions in
;       EAX to insert.
; CL -  Scratchpad register.

            mov cl, 32      ; Count number of bits we rotate
            jmp DistLoop

CopyToEAX:
            rcr ebx, 1      ; Don't use SHR, must preserve Z-flag
            rcr eax, 1
            jz  Done
DistLoop:   dec cl
            shr edx, 1
            jc  CopyToEAX
            ror eax, 1      ; Keep current bit in EAX
            jnz DistLoop

Done:       ror eax, cl     ; Reposition remaining bits
```

If we load EDX with 11001001b, this code will copy bits 0 to 3 to bits 0, 3, 6, and 7 in EAX. Notice the short-circuit test that checks whether we've exhausted the values in EDX (by checking for a 0 in EDX). The rotate instructions do not affect the zero flag, but the shift instructions do. Hence, the preceding shr instruction will set the zero flag when there are no more bits to distribute (when EDX becomes 0).

The general algorithm for coalescing bits is a tad more efficient than general distribution. Here's the code that will extract bits from EBX via the bit mask in EDX and leave the result in EAX:

```
; EAX - Destination register.
; EBX - Source register.
; EDX - Bitmap with 1s representing bits to copy to EAX.
; EBX and EDX are not preserved.

        xor eax, eax    ; Clear destination register
        jmp ShiftLoop

ShiftInEAX:
        rcl ebx, 1      ; EBX to EAX
        rcl eax, 1
ShiftLoop:
        shl edx, 1      ; Check to see if we need to copy a bit
        jc  ShiftInEAX  ; If carry set, go copy the bit
        rcl ebx, 1      ; Current bit is uninteresting, skip it
        jnz ShiftLoop   ; Repeat as long as there are bits in EDX
```

This sequence also takes advantage of a sneaky trait of the shift and rotate instructions: the shift instructions affect the zero flag, whereas the rotate instructions do not. Therefore, the shl edx, 1 instruction sets the zero flag when EDX becomes 0 (after the shift). If the carry flag was also set, the code will make one additional pass through the loop in order to shift a bit into EAX, but the next time the code shifts EDX 1 bit to the left,

EDX is still 0 and so the carry will be clear. On this iteration, the code falls out of the loop.

Another way to coalesce bits is via table lookup. By grabbing a byte of data at a time (so your tables don't get too large), you can use that byte's value as an index into a lookup table that coalesces all the bits down to bit 0. Finally, you can merge the bits at the low end of each byte together. This might produce a more efficient coalescing algorithm in certain cases. The implementation is left to you.

12.7 Coalescing and Distributing Bit Strings Using BMI2 Instructions

Intel's BMI2 (*bit manipulation instructions, set 2*)[5] instruction set extensions include a handy set of instructions you can use to insert or extract arbitrary bit sets: pdep (*parallel bits deposit*) and pext (*parallel bits extract*). If these instructions are available on your CPU, they can handle many of the tasks presented with non-BMI instructions in this chapter. They are powerful instructions indeed.

These instructions have the following syntax:

---

pdep reg_{dest}, reg_{src}, reg_{mask}
pdep reg_{dest}, reg_{src}, mem_{mask}
pext reg_{dest}, reg_{src}, reg_{mask}
pext reg_{dest}, reg_{src}, mem_{mask}

All operands must be the same size and must be 32 or 64 bits.

The pext instruction extracts an arbitrary bit string from the source (second) register and coalesces those bits to contiguous bit locations starting at bit 0 in the destination register. The third operand, the mask, controls which bits pext extracts from the source.

The mask operand contains 1 bits in the bit positions that pext will extract from the source register. Figure 12-4 shows how this bit mask works. For each 1 bit in the mask operand, the pext instruction copies the corresponding bit in the source register to the next available bit position (starting from bit 0) in the destination register.

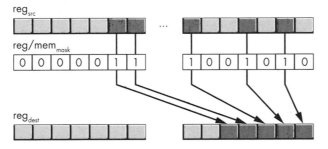

Figure 12-4: Bit mask for pext instruction

---

5. See Listing 11-2 in Chapter 11 to see how to check for the presence of the BMI1 and BMI2 instruction set extensions.

Listing 12-8 is a sample program fragment and the output it produces demonstrating the pext instruction (as usual, this listing eliminates the common code).

```
; >>>> Unique code for various listings.

mov     r8d, 12340000h
mov     r9d, 0F0f000Fh
pext    edx, r8d, r9d

; Output value 1 is in RDX (mask).

call    print
byte    "Extracted: %x", nl, 0

; <<<< End of unique code.
-------------------------------------------------------------------------------
Extracted: 240
```

Listing 12-8: pext instruction example

The pdep instruction does the converse of pext. It takes the contiguous set of bits starting with the LO bit of the source register operand and distributes those bits throughout the destination register by using the 1 bits in the mask operand to determine placement, as shown in Figure 12-5. The pdep instruction sets all other bits in the destination register to 0.

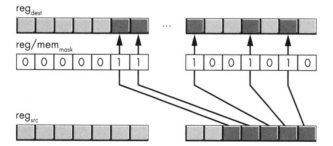

Figure 12-5: pdep instruction operation

Listing 12-9 is an example of the pdep instruction and the output it produces.

```
mov     r8d, 1234h
mov     r9d, 0F0FF00Fh
pdep    edx, r8d, r9d

; Output value 1 is in RDX (mask).

call    print
byte    "Distributed: %x", nl, 0
-------------------------------------------------------------------------------
Distributed: 1023004
```

Listing 12-9: pdep instruction example

If you use the pdep or pext instructions in your program, don't forget to test for the presence of the BMI2 instruction set extensions. Not all x86-64 CPUs support these instructions. See Listing 11-2 in Chapter 11 to see how to check for the presence of the BMI2 instruction set extensions.

12.8 Packed Arrays of Bit Strings

Though far less efficient, it is quite possible to create arrays of elements whose size is not a multiple of 8 bits. The drawback is that calculating the "address" of an array element and manipulating that array element involves a lot of extra work. In this section, we'll take a look at a few examples of packing and unpacking array elements in an array whose elements are an arbitrary number of bits long.

Why would you want arrays of bit objects? The answer is simple: space. If an object consumes only 3 bits, you can get 2.67 times as many elements into the same space if you pack the data rather than allocating a whole byte for each object. For very large arrays, this can be a substantial savings. Of course, the cost of this space savings is speed: you have to execute extra instructions to pack and unpack the data, thus slowing down access to the data.

The calculation for locating the bit offset of an array element in a large block of bits is almost identical to the standard array access:

```
element_address_in_bits =
    base_address_in_bits + index * element_size_in_bits
```

Once you calculate the element's address in bits, you need to convert it to a byte address (because we have to use byte addresses when accessing memory) and extract the specified element. Because the base address of an array element (almost) always starts on a byte boundary, we can use the following equations to simplify this task:

```
byte_of_1st_bit =
    base_address + (index * element_size_in_bits) / 8

offset_to_1st_bit =
    (index * element_size_in_bits) % 8
```

For example, suppose we have an array of 200 three-bit objects that we declare as follows:

```
        .data
AO3Bobjects  byte (200 * 3)/8 + 2 dup (?)  ; "+2" handles truncation
```

The constant expression in the preceding dimension reserves space for enough bytes to hold 600 bits (200 elements, each 3 bits long). As the comment notes, the expression adds 2 extra bytes at the end to ensure we don't lose any odd bits[6] as well as to allow us to access 1 byte beyond the end of the array (when storing data to the array).

---

6. That won't happen in this example because 600 is evenly divisible by 8, but in general you can't count on this; 2 extra bytes usually won't hurt things.

Now suppose you want to access the *i*th 3-bit element of this array. You can extract these bits by using the following code:

```
; Extract the ith group of 3 bits in AO3Bobjects
; and leave this value in EAX.

xor  ecx, ecx                ; Put i / 8 remainder here
mov  eax, i                  ; Get the index into the array
lea  rax, [rax + rax * 2]    ; RAX := RAX * 3 (3 bits/element)
shrd rcx, rax, 3             ; RAX / 8 -> RAX and RAX mod 8 -> RCX
                             ; (HO bits)
shr  rax, 3                  ; Remember, shrd doesn't modify EAX
rol  rcx, 3                  ; Put remainder into LO 3 bits of RCX

; Okay, fetch the word containing the 3 bits we want to
; extract. We have to fetch a word because the last bit or two
; could wind up crossing the byte boundary (that is, bit offset 6
; and 7 in the byte).

lea r8, AO3Bobjects
mov ax, [r8][rax * 1]
shr ax, cl                   ; Move bits down to bit 0
and eax, 111b                ; Remove the other bits (incl HO RAX)
```

Inserting an element into the array is a bit more difficult. In addition to computing the base address and bit offset of the array element, you also have to create a mask to clear out the bits in the destination where you're going to insert the new data. Listing 12-10 inserts the LO 3 bits of EAX into the *i*th element of the AO3Bobjects array.

```
; Listing 12-10

; Creating a bit mask with blsi and dec.

        option  casemap:none

nl          =       10

            .const
ttlStr      byte    "Listing 12-10", 0

Masks       equ     this word
            word    not 0111b,          not 00111000b
            word    not 000111000000b,  not 1110b
            word    not 01110000b,      not 001110000000b
            word    not 00011100b,      not 11100000b

            .data
i           dword   5
AO3Bobjects byte    (200*3)/8 + 2 dup (?)   ; "+2" handles truncation
```

```
                include getTitle.inc
                include print.inc

                .code

; Here is the "asmMain" function.

                public  asmMain
asmMain         proc
                push    rbx
                push    rsi
                push    rdi
                push    rbp
                mov     rbp, rsp
                sub     rsp, 56         ; Shadow storage

                mov     eax, 7          ; Value to store

                mov     ebx, i          ; Get the index into the array
                mov     ecx, ebx        ; Use LO 3 bits as index
                and     ecx, 111b       ; into Masks table
                lea     r8, Masks
                mov     dx, [r8][rcx * 2] ; Get bit mask

; Convert index into the array into a bit index.
; To do this, multiply the index by 3:

                lea     rbx, [rbx + rbx * 2]

; Divide by 8 to get the byte index into EBX
; and the bit index (the remainder) into ECX:

                shrd    ecx, ebx, 3
                shr     ebx, 3
                rol     ecx, 3

; Grab the bits and clear those we're inserting.

                lea     r8, AO3Bobjects
                and     dx, [r8][rbx * 1]

; Put our 3 bits in their proper location.

                shl     ax, cl

; Merge bits into destination.

                or      dx, ax

; Store back into memory.

                mov     [r8][rbx * 1], dx
```

```
            mov     edx, dword ptr A03Bobjects
            call    print
            byte    "value:%x", nl, 0

allDone:    leave
            pop     rdi
            pop     rsi
            pop     rbx
            ret     ; Returns to caller
asmMain     endp
            end
```

Listing 12-10: Storing the value 7 (111b) into an array of 3-bit elements

Inserting the code in Listing 12-10 into a shell assembly file produces the following output:

```
value:38000
```

The print statement prints the first 32 bits of A03Bobjects. Because each element is 3 bits, the array looks like

```
000 000 000 000 000 111 000 000 000 000 00 ...
```

where bit 0 is the leftmost bit. Flipping the 32 bits around to make them more readable, and grouping them in blocks of 4 bits (to make it easy to convert to hexadecimal), we get

```
0000 0000 0000 0011 1000 0000 0000 0000
```

which is 38000h.

Listing 12-10 uses a lookup table to generate the masks needed to clear out the appropriate position in the array. Each element of this array contains all 1s except for three 0s in the position we need to clear for a given bit offset (note the use of the not operator to invert the constants in the table).

12.9 Searching for a Bit

A common bit operation is to locate the end of a run of bits. A special case of this operation is to locate the first (or last) set or clear the bit in a 16-, 32-, or 64-bit value. In this section, we'll explore ways to handle this special case.

The term *first set bit* means the first bit in a value, scanning from bit 0 toward the high-order bit, which contains a 1. A similar definition exists for the *first clear bit*. The *last set bit* is the first bit in a value, scanning from the high-order bit toward bit 0, which contains a 1. A similar definition exists for the *last clear bit*.

One obvious way to scan for the first or last bit is to use a shift instruction in a loop and count the number of iterations before you shift out a 1 (or 0) into the carry flag. The number of iterations specifies the position.

Here's some sample code that checks for the first set bit in EAX and returns that bit position in ECX:

```
           mov ecx, -32    ; Count off the bit positions in ECX
TstLp:     shr eax, 1      ; Check to see if current bit
                           ; position contains a 1
           jc  Done        ; Exit loop if it does
           inc ecx         ; Bump up our bit counter by 1
           jnz TstLp       ; Exit if we execute this loop 32 times

Done:      add cl, 32      ; Adjust loop counter so it holds
                           ; the bit position

; At this point, CL contains the bit position of the
; first set bit. CL contains 32 if EAX originally
; contained 0 (no set bits).
```

The only thing tricky about this code is that it runs the loop counter from −32 up to 0 rather than 32 down to 0. This makes it slightly easier to calculate the bit position after the loop terminates.

The drawback to this particular loop is that it's expensive. This loop repeats as many as 32 times, depending on the original value in EAX. If the values you're checking often have lots of 0s in the LO bits of EAX, this code runs rather slowly.

Searching for the first (or last) set bit is such a common operation that Intel added a couple of instructions specifically to accelerate this process. These instructions are bsf (*bit scan forward*) and bsr (*bit scan reverse*). Their syntax is as follows:

```
bsr dest_reg, reg_src
bsr dest_reg, mem_src
bsf dest_reg, reg_src
bsf dest_reg, mem_src
```

The source and destination operands must be the same size (16, 32, or 64 bits). The destination operand has to be a register. The source operand can be a register or a memory location.

The bsf instruction scans for the first set bit (starting from bit position 0) in the source operand. The bsr instruction scans for the last set bit in the source operand by scanning from the HO bit toward the LO bit. If these instructions find a bit that is set in the source operand, they clear the zero flag and put the bit position into the destination register. If the source register contains 0 (that is, there are no set bits), then these instructions set the zero flag and leave an indeterminate value in the destination register. You should test the zero flag immediately after the execution of these instructions to validate the destination register's value. Here's an example:

```
mov ebx, SomeValue    ; Value whose bits we want to check
bsf eax, ebx          ; Put position of first set bit in EAX
jz  NoBitsSet         ; Branch if SomeValue contains 0
```

```
    mov FirstBit, eax    ; Save location of first set bit
        .
        .
        .
```

You use the bsr instruction in an identical fashion except that it computes the bit position of the last set bit in an operand (the first set bit it finds when scanning from the HO bit toward the LO bit).

The x86-64 CPUs do not provide instructions to locate the first bit containing a 0. However, you can easily scan for a 0 bit by first inverting the source operand (or a copy of the source operand if you must preserve the source operand's value) and then searching for the first 1 bit; this corresponds to the first 0 bit in the original operand value.

The bsf and bsr instructions are complex x86-64 instructions and may be slower than others. In some circumstances, it may be faster to locate the first set bit by using discrete instructions. However, because the execution time of these instructions varies widely from CPU to CPU, you should test the performance of these instructions prior to using them in time-critical code.

Note that the bsf and bsr instructions do not affect the source operand. A common operation is to extract (and clear) the first or last set bit you find in an operand. If the source operand is in a register, you can use the btr (or btc) instruction to clear the bit after you've found it. Here's some code that achieves this result:

```
    bsf ecx, eax        ; Locate first set bit in EAX
    jz  noBitFound      ; If we found a bit, clear it

    btr eax, ecx        ; Clear the bit we just found

noBitFound:
```

At the end of this sequence, the zero flag indicates whether we found a bit (note that btr doesn't affect the zero flag).

Because the bsf and bsr instructions support only 16-, 32-, and 64-bit operands, you will have to compute the first bit position of an 8-bit operand a little differently. There are a couple of reasonable approaches. First, you can zero-extend an 8-bit operand to 16 or 32 bits and then use the bsf or bsr instruction. Another alternative is to create a lookup table in which each entry contains the number of bits in the value you use as an index into the table; then you can use the xlat instruction to "compute" the first bit position in the value (you will have to handle the value 0 as a special case). Another solution is to use the shift algorithm appearing at the beginning of this section; for an 8-bit operand, this is not an entirely inefficient solution.

You can use bsf and bsr to determine the size of a run of bits, assuming that you have a single run of bits in your operand. Simply locate the first and last bits in the run (as in the previous example) and then compute the difference (plus 1) of the two values. Of course, this scheme is valid only if there are no intervening 0s between the first and last set bits in the value.

12.10 Counting Bits

The last example in the previous section demonstrates a specific case of a very general problem: counting bits. Unfortunately, that example has a severe limitation: it counts only a single run of 1 bits appearing in the source operand. This section discusses a more general solution to this problem.

Hardly a week goes by that someone doesn't ask on one of the internet newsgroups how to count the number of bits in a register operand. This is a common request, undoubtedly because many assembly language course instructors assign this task as a project to their students as a way to teach them about the shift and rotate instructions, as follows:

```
; BitCount1:

; Counts the bits in the EAX register,
; returning the count in EBX.

            mov cl, 32     ; Count the 32 bits in EAX
            xor ebx, ebx   ; Accumulate the count here
CntLoop:    shr eax, 1     ; Shift bit out of EAX and into carry
            adc bl, 0      ; Add the carry into the EBX register
            dec cl         ; Repeat 32 times
            jnz CntLoop
```

The "trick" is that this code uses the adc instruction to add the value of the carry flag into the BL register. Because the count is going to be less than 32, the result will fit comfortably into BL.

Tricky code or not, this instruction sequence is not particularly fast. The preceding loop always executes 32 times, so this code sequence executes 130 instructions (four instructions per iteration plus two extra instructions).

For a more efficient solution, use the popcnt instruction (*population count*, introduced in the SSE 4.1 instruction set), which counts the number of 1 bits in the source operand and stores the value into the destination operand:

```
popcnt reg_dest, reg_src
popcnt reg_dest, mem_src
```

The operands must be the same size and must be 16, 32, or 64 bits.

12.11 Reversing a Bit String

Another common programming project instructors assign, and a useful function in its own right, is a program that reverses the bits in an operand. This program swaps the LO bit with the HO bit, bit 1 with the next-to-HO bit, and so on. The typical solution an instructor expects is the following:

```
; Reverse the 32 bits in EAX, leaving the result in EBX:

            mov cl, 32     ; Move current bit in EAX to
RvsLoop:    shr eax, 1     ; the carry flag
```

```
        rcl ebx, 1      ; Shift the bit back into
                        ; EBX, backward
        dec cl
        jnz RvsLoop
```

As with the previous examples, this code suffers from repeating the loop 32 times, for a grand total of 129 instructions (for 32-bit operands, so double that for 64-bit operands). By unrolling the loop, you can get it down to 64 instructions, but this is still somewhat expensive.

The best solution to an optimization problem is often using a better algorithm rather than attempting to tweak your code by trying to choose faster instructions to speed it up. In the preceding section, for example, we were able to speed up counting the bits in a string by substituting a more complex algorithm for the simplistic "shift and count" algorithm. In the preceding example, the trick is to do as much work as possible in parallel.

Suppose that all we wanted to do was swap the even and odd bits in a 32-bit value. We can easily swap the even and odd bits in EAX by using the following code:

```
mov edx, eax        ; Make a copy of the odd bits
shr eax, 1          ; Move the even bits to the odd positions
and edx, 55555555h  ; Isolate the odd bits
and eax, 55555555h  ; Isolate the even bits
shl edx, 1          ; Move the odd bits to even positions
or  eax, edx        ; Merge the bits and complete the swap
```

Swapping the even and odd bits takes us part of the way to reversing all the bits in the number. After executing the preceding code sequence, you can swap adjacent pairs of bits to swap the bits in all the nibbles in the 32-bit value by using the following code:

```
mov edx, eax        ; Make a copy of the odd-numbered bit pairs
shr eax, 2          ; Move the even bit pairs to the odd position
and edx, 33333333h  ; Isolate the odd pairs
and eax, 33333333h  ; Isolate the even pairs
shl edx, 2          ; Move the odd pairs to the even positions
or  eax, edx        ; Merge the bits and complete the swap
```

After completing the preceding sequence, you swap the adjacent nibbles in the 32-bit register. Again, the only difference is the bit mask and the length of the shifts. Here's the code:

```
mov edx, eax        ; Make a copy of the odd-numbered nibbles
shr eax, 4          ; Move the even nibbles to the odd position
and edx, 0f0f0f0fh  ; Isolate the odd nibbles
and eax, 0f0f0f0fh  ; Isolate the even nibbles
shl edx, 4          ; Move the odd pairs to the even positions
or  eax, edx        ; Merge the bits and complete the swap
```

You can probably see the pattern developing and can figure out that in the next two steps you have to swap the bytes and then the words in this object. You can use code like the preceding example, but there is a better way: use bswap. The bswap (*byte swap*) instruction uses the following syntax:

bswap reg₃₂

The bswap instruction swaps bytes 0 and 3 and bytes 1 and 2 in the specified 32-bit register, exactly what you want when reversing bits (and when converting data between little-endian and big-endian data formats, the principal use of this instruction). Rather than sticking in another 12 instructions to swap the bytes and then the words, you can simply use a bswap eax instruction to complete the job after the preceding instructions. The final code sequence is shown here:

```
mov   edx, eax        ; Make a copy of the odd bits in the data
shr   eax, 1          ; Move the even bits to the odd positions
and   edx, 55555555h  ; Isolate the odd bits
and   eax, 55555555h  ; Isolate the even bits
shl   edx, 1          ; Move the odd bits to the even positions
or    eax, edx        ; Merge the bits and complete the swap

mov   edx, eax        ; Make a copy of the odd-numbered bit pairs
shr   eax, 2          ; Move the even bit pairs to the odd position
and   edx, 33333333h  ; Isolate the odd pairs
and   eax, 33333333h  ; Isolate the even pairs
shl   edx, 2          ; Move the odd pairs to the even positions
or    eax, edx        ; Merge the bits and complete the swap

mov   edx, eax        ; Make a copy of the odd-numbered nibbles
shr   eax, 4          ; Move the even nibbles to the odd position
and   edx, 0f0f0f0fh  ; Isolate the odd nibbles
and   eax, 0f0f0f0fh  ; Isolate the even nibbles
shl   edx, 4          ; Move the odd pairs to the even positions
or    eax,edx         ; Merge the bits and complete the swap

bswap eax             ; Swap the bytes and words
```

This algorithm requires only 19 instructions and executes much faster than does the bit-shifting loop appearing earlier. Of course, this sequence does consume a little more memory. If you're trying to save memory rather than clock cycles, the loop is probably a better solution.

12.12 *Merging Bit Strings*

Another common bit string operation is producing a single bit string by merging, or interleaving, bits from two different sources. The following example code sequence creates a 32-bit string by merging alternate bits from two 16-bit strings:

```
; Merge two 16-bit strings into a single 32-bit string.
; AX - Source for even-numbered bits.
; BX - Source for odd-numbered bits.
```

```
; CL  - Scratch register.
; EDX - Destination register.

           mov  cl, 16
MergeLp:   shrd edx, eax, 1     ; Shift a bit from EAX into EDX
           shrd edx, ebx, 1     ; Shift a bit from EBX into EDX
           dec  cl
           jne  MergeLp;
```

This particular example merges two 16-bit values together, alternating their bits in the result value. For a faster implementation of this code, unroll the loop to eliminate half the instructions.

With a few slight modifications, we can merge four 8-bit values together, or merge other bit sets from the source strings. For example, the following code copies bits 0 to 5 from EAX, then bits 0 to 4 from EBX, then bits 6 to 11 from EAX, then bits 5 to 15 from EBX, and finally bits 12 to 15 from EAX:

```
shrd edx, eax, 6
shrd edx, ebx, 5
shrd edx, eax, 6
shrd edx, ebx, 11
shrd edx, eax, 4
```

Of course, if you have BMI2 instructions available, you can also use the pextr instruction to extract various bits for insertion into another register.

12.13 Extracting Bit Strings

We can also extract and distribute bits in a bit string among multiple destinations. The following code takes the 32-bit value in EAX and distributes alternate bits among the BX and DX registers:

```
           mov cl, 16    ; Count the loop iterations
ExtractLp: shr eax, 1    ; Extract even bits to (E)BX
           rcr ebx, 1
           shr eax, 1    ; Extract odd bits to (E)DX
           rcr edx, 1
           dec cl        ; Repeat 16 times
           jnz ExtractLp
           shr ebx, 16   ; Need to move the results from the HO
           shr edx, 16   ; bytes of EBX and EDX to the LO bytes
```

This sequence executes 99 instructions (six inside the loop repeated 16 times plus three outside the loop). You can unroll the loop and pull other tricks, but it's probably not worth the added complexity when it's all said and done.

If you have the BMI2 instruction set extensions available, you can also use the pext instruction to do this job efficiently:

```
mov   ecx, 55555555h  ; Odd bit positions
pext edx, eax, ecx    ; Put odd bits into EDX
mov   ecx, 0aaaaaaaah ; Even bit positions
pext ebx, eax, ecx    ; Put even bits into EBX
```

12.14 Searching for a Bit Pattern

Another bit-related operation you may need is the ability to search for a particular bit pattern in a string of bits. For example, you might want to locate the bit index of the first occurrence of 1011b starting at some particular position in a bit string. In this section, we'll explore some simple algorithms to accomplish this task.

To search for a particular bit pattern, we need to know four things:

- The pattern to search for (the *pattern*)
- The length of the pattern we're searching for
- The bit string that we're going to search through (the *source*)
- The length of the bit string to search through

The basic idea behind the search is to create a mask based on the length of the pattern and mask a copy of the source with this value. Then we can directly compare the pattern with the masked source for equality. If they are equal, you're finished; if they're not equal, increment a bit position counter, shift the source one position to the right, and try again. You repeat this operation *length(source)* - *length(pattern)* times. The algorithm fails if it does not detect the bit pattern after this many attempts (because we will have exhausted all the bits in the source operand that could match the pattern's length). Here's a simple algorithm that searches for a 4-bit pattern throughout the EBX register:

```
        mov cl, 28      ; 28 attempts because 32 - 4 = 28
                        ; (len(src) - len(pat))
        mov ch, 1111b   ; Mask for the comparison
        mov al, pattern ; Pattern to search for
        and al, ch      ; Mask unnecessary bits in AL
        mov ebx, source ; Get the source value
ScanLp: mov dl, bl      ; Copy the LO 4 bits of EBX
        and dl, ch      ; Mask unwanted bits
        cmp al, dl      ; See if we match the pattern
        jz  Matched
        dec cl          ; Repeat specified number of times
        shr ebx, 1
        jnz ScanLp

; Do whatever needs to be done if we failed to
; match the bit string.
```

```
        jmp Done

Matched:

; If we get to this point, we matched the bit string.
; We can compute the position in the original source as 28 - CL.

Done:
```

Bit-string scanning is a special case of string matching. *String matching* is a well-studied problem in computer science, and many of the algorithms you can use for string matching are applicable to bit-string matching as well. Such algorithms are beyond the scope of this chapter, but to give you a preview of how this works, you compute a function (like xor or sub) between the pattern and the current source bits and use the result as an index into a lookup table to determine how many bits you can skip. Such algorithms let you skip several bits rather than shifting only once for each iteration of the scanning loop (as is done by the previous algorithm).

12.15 For More Information

The AMD Athlon optimization guide contains useful algorithms for bit-based computations. To learn more about bit-searching algorithms, pick up a textbook on data structures and algorithms and study the section on string-matching algorithms.

Probably the ultimate book on bit twiddling is *Hacker's Delight,* Second Edition, by Henry S. Warren (Addison-Wesley, 2012). While this book uses the C programming language for examples, almost all the concepts apply to assembly language programs as well.

12.16 Test Yourself

1. What general instruction(s) would you use to clear bits in a register?
2. What instruction could you use to clear a bit, specified by bit number, in a register?
3. What general instruction would you use to set bits in a register?
4. What instruction could you use to set a bit, specified by bit number, in a register?
5. What general instruction would you use to invert bits in a register?
6. What instruction could you use to invert a bit, specified by bit number, in a register?
7. What general instruction would you use to test a bit (or group of bits) for 0 and 1 in a register?
8. What instruction could you use to test a single bit, specified by bit number, in a register?

9. What single instruction could you use to extract and coalesce a set of bits?

10. What single instruction could you use to position and insert a set of bits in a register?

11. What single instruction could you use to extract a bit substring from a larger bit string?

12. What instruction allows you to search for the first set bit in a register?

13. What instruction allows you to search for the last set bit in a register?

14. How would you search for the first clear bit in a register?

15. How would you search for the last clear bit in a register?

16. What instruction can you use to count the number of bits in a register?

13

MACROS AND THE MASM COMPILE-TIME LANGUAGE

This chapter discusses the MASM compile-time language, including the very important *macro expansion facilities*. A *macro* is an identifier that the assembler will expand into additional text (often many lines of text), allowing you to abbreviate large amounts of code with a single identifier. MASM's macro facility is actually a *computer language inside a computer language*; that is, you can write short little programs inside a MASM source file whose purpose is to generate other MASM source code to be assembled by MASM.

This *language inside a language*, also known as a *compile-time language*, consists of macros (the compile-time language equivalent of a procedure), conditionals (if statements), loops, and other statements. This chapter covers many of the MASM compile-time language features and shows how you can use them to reduce the effort needed to write assembly language code.

13.1 Introduction to the Compile-Time Language

MASM is actually two languages rolled into a single program. The *runtime language* is the standard x86-64/MASM assembly language you've been reading about in all the previous chapters. This is called the runtime language because the programs you write execute when you run the executable file. MASM contains an interpreter for a second language, the MASM *compile-time language (CTL)*. MASM source files contain instructions for both the MASM CTL and the runtime program, and MASM executes the CTL program during assembly (compilation). Once MASM completes assembly, the CTL program terminates (see Figure 13-1).

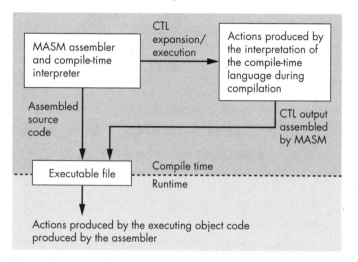

Figure 13-1: Compile-time versus runtime execution

The CTL application is not a part of the runtime executable that MASM emits, although the CTL application can *write* part of the runtime program for you, and, in fact, this is the major purpose of the CTL. Using automatic code generation, the CTL gives you the ability to easily and elegantly emit repetitive code. By learning how to use the MASM CTL and applying it properly, you can develop assembly language applications as rapidly as high-level language applications (even faster because MASM's CTL lets you create very high-level-language constructs).

13.2 The echo and .err Directives

You may recall that Chapter 1 began with the typical first program most people write when learning a new language, the "Hello, world!" program. Listing 13-1 provides the basic "Hello, world!" program written in the MASM compile-time language.

```
; Listing 13-1

; CTL "Hello, world!" program.
```

```
echo    Listing 13-1: Hello, world!
end
```

Listing 13-1: The CTL "Hello, world!" program

The only CTL statement in this program is the echo statement.[1] The end statement is needed just to keep MASM happy.

The echo statement displays the textual representation of its argument list during the assembly of a MASM program. Therefore, if you compile the preceding program with the command

```
ml64 /c listing13-1.asm
```

the MASM assembler will immediately print the following text:

```
Listing 13-1: Hello, world!
```

Other than displaying the text associated with the echo parameter list, the echo statement has no effect on the assembly of the program. It is invaluable for debugging CTL programs, displaying the progress of the assembly, and displaying assumptions and default actions that take place during assembly.

Though assembly language calls to print also emit text to the standard output, there is a big difference between the following two groups of statements in a MASM source file:

```
echo "Hello World"
```

```
call print
byte "Hello World", nl,0
```

The first statement prints "Hello World" (and a newline) during the assembly process and has no effect on the executable program. The last two lines don't affect the assembly process (other than the emission of code to the executable file). However, when you run the executable file, the second set of statements prints the string Hello World followed by a newline sequence.

The .err directive, like echo, will display a string to the console during assembly, though this must be a text string (delimited by < and >). The .err statement displays the text as part of a MASM error diagnostic. Furthermore, the .err statement increments the error count, and this will cause MASM to stop the assembly (without assembling or linking) after processing the current source file. You would normally use the .err statement to display an error message during assembly if your CTL code discovers something that prevents it from creating valid code. For example:

```
.err <Statement must have exactly one operand>
```

---

1. %out is a synonym for echo (just in case you see %out in any MASM source files).

13.3 Compile-Time Constants and Variables

Just as the runtime language does, the compile-time language supports constants and variables. You declare compile-time constants by using the textequ or equ directives. You declare compile-time variables by using the = directive (compile-time assignment statement). For example:

```
inc_by equ 1
ctlVar = 0
ctlVar = ctlVar + inc_by
```

13.4 Compile-Time Expressions and Operators

The MASM CTL supports constant expressions in the CTL assignment statement. See "MASM Constant Declarations" in Chapter 4 for a discussion of constant expressions (which are also the CTL expressions and operators).

In addition to the operators and functions appearing in that chapter, MASM includes several additional CTL operators, functions, and directives you will find useful. The following subsections describe these.

13.4.1 The MASM Escape (!) Operator

The first operator is the ! operator. When placed in front of another symbol, this operator tells MASM to treat that character as text rather than as a special symbol. For example, !; creates a text constant consisting of the semicolon character, rather than a comment that causes MASM to ignore all text after the ; symbol (for C/C++ programmers, this is similar to the backslash escape character, \, in a string constant).

13.4.2 The MASM Evaluation (%) Operator

The second useful CTL operator is %. The percent operator causes MASM to evaluate the expression following it and replace that expression with its value. For example, consider the following code sequence:

```
num10   =        10
text10  textequ  <10>
tn11    textequ  %num10 + 1
```

If you assemble this sequence in an assembly language source file and direct MASM to produce an assembly listing, it will report the following for these three symbols:

```
num10 . . . . . . . . . . . . .    Number   0000000Ah
text10 . . . . . . . . . . . .     Text     10
tn11 . . . . . . . . . . . . .     Text     11
```

The num10 is properly reported as a numeric value (decimal 10), text10 as a text symbol (containing the string 10), and tn11 as a text symbol (as you would expect, because this code sequence uses the textequ directive to define it). However, rather than containing the string %num10 + 1, MASM evaluates the expression num10 + 1 to produce the numeric value 11, which MASM then converts to text data. (By the way, to put a percent sign in a text string, use the text sequence <!%>.)

If you place the % operator in the first column of a source line, MASM will translate all numeric expressions on that line to textual form. This is handy with the echo directive. It causes echo to display the value of numeric equates rather than simply displaying the equate names.

13.4.3 The catstr Directive

The catstr function has the following syntax:

```
identifier   catstr  string1, string2, ...
```

The identifier is an (up to this point) undefined symbol. The *string1* and *string2* operands are textual data surrounded by < and > symbols. This statement stores the concatenation of the two strings into *identifier*. Note that *identifier* is a text object, not a string object. If you specify the identifier in your code, MASM will substitute the text string for the identifier and try to process that text data as though it were part of your source code input.

The catstr statement allows two or more operands separated by commas. The catstr directive will concatenate the text values in the order they appear in the operand field. The following statement generates the textual data Hello, World!:

```
helloWorld catstr <Hello>, <, >, <World!!>
```

Two exclamation marks are necessary in this example, because ! is an operator telling MASM to treat the next symbol as text rather than as an operator. With only one ! symbol, MASM thinks that you're attempting to include a > symbol as part of the string and reports an error (because there is no closing >). Putting !! in the text string tells MASM to treat the second ! symbol as a text character.

13.4.4 The instr Directive

The instr directive searches for the presence of one string within another. The syntax for the directive is

```
identifier   instr  start, source, search
```

where *identifier* is a symbol into which MASM will put the offset of the *search* string within the *source* string. The search begins at position *start* within *source*. Unconventionally, the first character in *source* has the position 1 (not 0). The following example searches for World within the string Hello World (starting at character position 1, which is the index of the H character):

```
WorldPosn  instr 1, <Hello World>, <World>
```

This statement defines WorldPosn as a number with the value 7 (as the string World is at position 7 in Hello World if you start counting from position 1).

13.4.5 The sizestr Directive

The sizestr directive computes the length of a string.[2] The syntax for the directive is

```
identifier sizestr string
```

where *identifier* is the symbol into which MASM will store the string's length, and *string* is the string literal whose length this directive computes. As an example,

```
hwLen sizestr <Hello World>
```

defines the symbol hwLen as a number and sets it to the value 11.

13.4.6 The substr Directive

The substr directive extracts a substring from a larger string. The syntax for this directive is

```
identifier substr source, start, len
```

where *identifier* is the symbol that MASM will create (type TEXT, initialized with the substring characters), *source* is the source string from which MASM will extract the substring, *start* is the starting position in the string to begin the extraction, and *len* is the length of the substring to extract. The *len* operand is optional; if it is absent, MASM will assume you want to use the remainder of the string (starting at position *start*) for the substring. Here's an example that extracts Hello from the string Hello World:

```
hString substr <Hello World>, 1, 5
```

13.5 Conditional Assembly (Compile-Time Decisions)

MASM's compile-time language provides an if statement, if, that lets you make decisions at assembly time. The if statement has two main purposes. The traditional use of if is to support *conditional assembly*, allowing you to include or exclude code during an assembly, depending on the status of

---

2. If you're wondering, MASM already uses the length reserved word for other purposes.

various symbols or constant values in your program. The second use is to support the standard if-statement decision-making process in the MASM compile-time language. This section discusses these two uses for the MASM if statement.

The simplest form of the MASM compile-time if statement uses the following syntax:

```
if constant_boolean_expression
    Text
endif
```

At compile time, MASM evaluates the expression after the if. This must be a constant expression that evaluates to an integer value. If the expression evaluates to true (nonzero), MASM continues to process the text in the source file as though the if statement were not present. However, if the expression evaluates to false (zero), MASM treats all the text between the if and the corresponding endif clause as though it were a comment (that is, it ignores this text), as shown in Figure 13-2.

```
if(constant_boolean_expression)
```

MASM compiles this code if the expression is true. Otherwise, MASM treats this code like a comment.

```
endif
```

Figure 13-2: Operation of a MASM compile-time if statement

The identifiers in a compile-time expression must all be constant identifiers or a MASM compile-time function call (with appropriate parameters). Because MASM evaluates these expressions at assembly time, they cannot contain runtime variables.

The MASM if statement supports optional elseif and else clauses that behave in an intuitive fashion. The complete syntax for the if statement looks like the following:

```
if constant_boolean_expression1
    Text
elseif constant_boolean_expression2
    Text
else
    Text
endif
```

If the first Boolean expression evaluates to true, MASM processes the text up to the elseif clause. It then skips all text (that is, treats it like a comment) until it encounters the endif clause. MASM continues processing the text after the endif clause in the normal fashion.

If the first Boolean expression evaluates to false, MASM skips all the text until it encounters an elseif, else, or endif clause. If it encounters an elseif clause (as in the preceding example), MASM evaluates the Boolean expression associated with that clause. If it evaluates to true, MASM processes the text between the elseif and the else clauses (or to the endif clause if the else clause is not present). If, during the processing of this text, MASM encounters another elseif or, as in the preceding example, an else clause, then MASM ignores all further text until it finds the corresponding endif. If both the first and second Boolean expressions in the previous example evaluate to false, MASM skips their associated text and begins processing the text in the else clause.

You can create a nearly infinite variety of if statement sequences by including zero or more elseif clauses and optionally supplying the else clause.

A traditional use of conditional assembly is to develop software that you can easily configure for several environments. For example, the fcomip instruction makes floating-point comparisons easy, but this instruction is available only on Pentium Pro and later processors. To use this instruction on the processors that support it and fall back to the standard floating-point comparison on the older processors, most engineers use conditional assembly to embed the separate sequences in the same source file (instead of writing and maintaining two versions of the program). The following example demonstrates how to do this:

```
; Set true (1) to use FCOMIxx instrs.

PentProOrLater = 0
        .
        .
        .
        if PentProOrLater

          fcomip st(0), st(1) ; Compare ST1 to ST0 and set flags

        else

          fcomp               ; Compare ST1 to ST0
          fstsw ax            ; Move the FPU condition code bits
          sahf                ; into the FLAGS register

        endif
```

As currently written, this code fragment will compile the three-instruction sequence in the else clause and ignore the code between the if and else clauses (because the constant PentProOrLater is false). By changing the value of PentProOrLater to true, you can tell MASM to compile the single fcomip instruction rather than the three-instruction sequence.

Though you need to maintain only a single source file, conditional assembly does not let you create a single *executable* that runs efficiently on all processors. When using this technique, you will still have to create two executable programs (one for Pentium Pro and later processors, one for the earlier processors) by compiling your source file twice: during the first assembly, you must set the PentProOrLater constant to false; during the second assembly, you must set it to true.

If you are familiar with conditional assembly in other languages, such as C/C++, you may be wondering if MASM supports a statement like C's #ifdef statement. The answer is yes, it does. Consider the following modification to the preceding code that uses this directive:

```
; Note: uncomment the following line if you are compiling this
; code for a Pentium Pro or later CPU.

; PentProOrLater = 0        ; Value and type are irrelevant
        .
        .
        .
ifdef PentProOrLater

    fcomip st(0), st(1)   ; Compare ST1 to ST0 and set flags

else

    fcomp                 ; Compare ST1 to ST0
    fstsw ax              ; Move the FPU condition code bits
    sahf                  ; into the FLAGS register

endif
```

Another common use of conditional assembly is to introduce debugging and testing code into your programs. A typical debugging technique that many MASM programmers use is to insert print statements at strategic points throughout their code; this enables them to trace through their code and display important values at various checkpoints.

A big problem with this technique, however, is that they must remove the debugging code prior to completing the project. Two further problems are as follows:

- Programmers often forget to remove some debugging statements, and this creates defects in the final program.

- After removing a debugging statement, these programmers often discover that they need that same statement to debug a different problem at a later time. Hence, they are constantly inserting and removing the same statements over and over again.

Conditional assembly can provide a solution to this problem. By defining a symbol (say, debug) to control debugging output in your program, you can activate or deactivate *all* debugging output by modifying a single line of source code. The following code fragment demonstrates this:

```
; Set to true to activate debug output.

debug   =    0
```

```
            .
            .
            .
        if debug

            echo *** DEBUG build

            mov  edx, i
            call print
            byte "At point A, i=%d", nl, 0

        else

        echo *** RELEASE build

        endif
```

As long as you surround all debugging output statements with an `if` statement like the preceding one, you don't have to worry about debugging output accidentally appearing in your final application. By setting the `debug` symbol to false, you can automatically disable all such output. Likewise, you don't have to remove all your debugging statements from your programs after they've served their immediate purpose. By using conditional assembly, you can leave these statements in your code because they are so easy to deactivate. Later, if you decide you need to view this same debugging information during assembly, you can reactivate it by setting the `debug` symbol to true.

Although program configuration and debugging control are two of the more common, traditional uses for conditional assembly, don't forget that the `if` statement provides the basic conditional statement in the MASM CTL. You will use the `if` statement in your compile-time programs the same way you would use an `if` statement in MASM or another language. Later sections in this chapter present lots of examples of using the `if` statement in this capacity.

13.6 Repetitive Assembly (Compile-Time Loops)

MASM's `while..endm`, `for..endm`, and `forc..endm` statements provide compile-time loop constructs.[3] The `while` statement tells MASM to process the same sequence of statements repetitively during assembly. This is handy for constructing data tables as well as providing a traditional looping structure for compile-time programs.

The `while` statement uses the following syntax:

```
while constant_boolean_expression
     Text
endm
```

---

3. `endm` stands for *end macro*, in case you're wondering. MASM considers all CTL looping instructions variants of the MASM macro facility. `irp` and `irpc` are synonyms for `for` and `forc`, respectively.

When MASM encounters the while statement during assembly, it evaluates the constant Boolean expression. If the expression evaluates to false, MASM will skip over the text between the while and the endm clauses (the behavior is similar to the if statement if the expression evaluates to false). If the expression evaluates to true, MASM will process the statements between the while and endm clauses and then "jump back" to the start of the while statement in the source file and repeat this process, as shown in Figure 13-3.

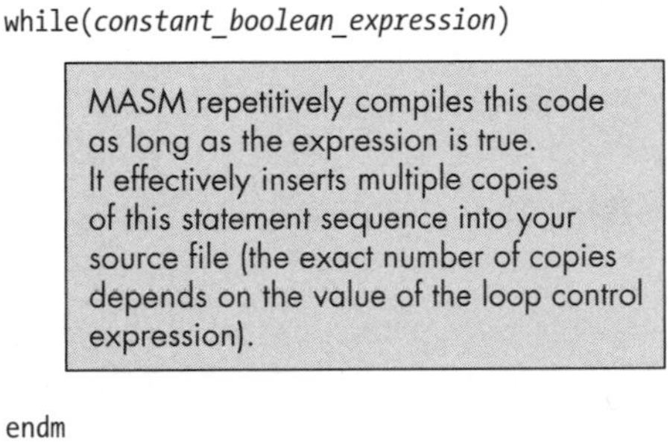

```
while(constant_boolean_expression)
```

> MASM repetitively compiles this code as long as the expression is true. It effectively inserts multiple copies of this statement sequence into your source file (the exact number of copies depends on the value of the loop control expression).

```
endm
```

Figure 13-3: MASM compile-time while statement operation

To understand how this process works, consider the program in Listing 13-2.

```
; Listing 13-2

; CTL while loop demonstration program.

        option  casemap:none

nl          =       10

        .const
ttlStr      byte    "Listing 13-2", 0

        .data
ary         dword   2, 3, 5, 8, 13

        include getTitle.inc
        include print.inc

        .code

; Here is the "asmMain" function.

        public  asmMain
asmMain     proc
        push    rbx
        push    rbp
        mov     rbp, rsp
        sub     rsp, 56         ; Shadow storage
```

```
i          =       0
           while   i LT lengthof ary ; 5

           mov     edx, i            ; This is a constant!
           mov     r8d, ary[i * 4]   ; Index is a constant
           call    print
           byte    "array[%d] = %d", nl, 0

i          =       i + 1
           endm

allDone:   leave
           pop     rbx
           ret     ; Returns to caller
asmMain    endp
           end
```

Listing 13-2: *while..endm demonstration*

Here's the build command and program output for Listing 13-2:

```
C:\>build listing13-2

C:\>echo off
 Assembling: listing13-2.asm
c.cpp

C:\>listing13-2
Calling Listing 13-2:
array[0] = 2
array[1] = 3
array[2] = 5
array[3] = 8
array[4] = 13
Listing 13-2 terminated
```

The while loop repeats five times during assembly. On each repetition of the loop, the MASM assembler processes the statements between the while and endm directives. Therefore, the preceding program is really equivalent to the code fragment shown in Listing 13-3.

```
       .
       .
       .
mov    edx, 0          ; This is a constant!
mov    r8d, ary[0]     ; Index is a constant
call   print
byte   "array[%d] = %d", nl, 0

mov    edx, 1          ; This is a constant!
mov    r8d, ary[4]     ; Index is a constant
call   print
byte   "array[%d] = %d", nl, 0
```

```
mov     edx, 2          ; This is a constant!
mov     r8d, ary[8]     ; Index is a constant
call    print
byte    "array[%d] = %d", nl, 0

mov     edx, 3          ; This is a constant!
mov     r8d, ary[12]    ; Index is a constant
call    print
byte    "array[%d] = %d", nl, 0

mov     edx, 4          ; This is a constant!
mov     r8d, ary[16]    ; Index is a constant
call    print
byte    "array[%d] = %d", nl, 0
```

Listing 13-3: Program equivalent to the code in Listing 13-2

As you can see in this example, the while statement is convenient for constructing repetitive-code sequences, especially for unrolling loops.

MASM provides two forms of the for..endm loop. These two loops take the following general form:

```
for identifier, <arg1, arg2, ..., argn>
    .
    .
    .
endm

forc identifier, <string>
    .
    .
    .
endm
```

The first form of the for loop (plain for) repeats the code once for each of the arguments specified between the < and > brackets. On each repetition of the loop, it sets *identifier* to the text of the current argument: on the first iteration of the loop, *identifier* is set to *arg1*, and on the second iteration it is set to *arg2*, and so on, until the last iteration, when it is set to *argn*. For example, the following for loop will generate code that pushes the RAX, RBX, RCX, and RDX registers onto the stack:

```
for  reg, <rax, rbx, rcx, rdx>
push reg
endm
```

This for loop is equivalent to the following code:

```
push rax
push rbx
push rcx
push rdx
```

The forc compile-time loop repeats the body of its loop for each character appearing in the string specified by the second argument. For example, the following forc loop generates a hexadecimal byte value for each character in the string:

```
        forc    hex, <0123456789ABCDEF>
hexNum  catstr  <0>,<hex>,<h>
        byte    hexNum
        endm
```

The for loop will turn out to be a lot more useful than forc. Nevertheless, forc is handy on occasion. Most of the time when you're using these loops, you'll be passing them a variable set of arguments rather than a fixed string. As you'll soon see, these loops are handy for processing macro parameters.

13.7 Macros (Compile-Time Procedures)

Macros are objects that a language processor replaces with other text during compilation. Macros are great devices for replacing long, repetitive sequences of text with much shorter sequences of text. In addition to the traditional role that macros play (for example, #define in C/C++), MASM's macros also serve as the equivalent of a compile-time language procedure or function.

Macros are one of MASM's main features. The following sections explore MASM's macro-processing facilities and the relationship between macros and other MASM CTL control constructs.

13.8 Standard Macros

MASM supports a straightforward macro facility that lets you define macros in a manner that is similar to declaring a procedure. A typical, simple macro declaration takes the following form:

```
macro_name macro arguments
        Macro body
            endm
```

The following code is a concrete example of a macro declaration:

```
neg128 macro

        neg rdx
        neg rax
        sbb rdx, 0

        endm
```

Execution of this macro's code will compute the two's complement of the 128-bit value in RDX:RAX (see the description of extended-precision neg in "Extended-Precision Negation Operations" in Chapter 8).

To execute the code associated with neg128, you specify the macro's name at the point you want to execute these instructions. For example:

```
mov     rax, qword ptr i128
mov     rdx, qword ptr i128[8]
neg128
```

This intentionally looks just like any other instruction; the original purpose of macros was to create synthetic instructions to simplify assembly language programming.

Though you don't need to use a call instruction to invoke a macro, from the point of view of your program, invoking a macro executes a sequence of instructions just like calling a procedure. You could implement this simple macro as a procedure by using the following procedure declaration:

```
neg128p  proc

         neg     rdx
         neg     rax
         sbb     rdx, 0
         ret

neg128p  endp
```

The following two statements will both negate the value in RDX:RAX:

```
neg128
call    neg128p
```

The difference between these two (the macro invocation versus the procedure call) is that macros expand their text inline, whereas a procedure call emits a call to the corresponding procedure elsewhere in the text. That is, MASM replaces the invocation neg128 directly with the following text:

```
neg rdx
neg rax
sbb rdx, 0
```

On the other hand, MASM replaces the procedure call neg128p with the machine code for the call instruction:

```
call neg128p
```

You should choose macro versus procedure call based on efficiency. Macros are slightly faster than procedure calls because you don't execute the call and corresponding ret instructions, but they can make your program larger because a macro invocation expands to the text of the macro's body on each invocation. If the macro body is large and you invoke the macro several times throughout your program, it will make your final executable much larger. Also, if the body of your macro executes more than a few simple instructions, the overhead of a call and ret sequence has little impact on the overall execution time of the code, so the execution time savings are nearly negligible. On the other hand, if the body of a procedure is very short (like the preceding neg128 example), the macro implementation can be faster and doesn't expand the size of your program by much. A good rule of thumb is as follows:

> Use *macros* for short, time-critical program units. Use *procedures* for longer blocks of code and when execution time is not as critical.

Macros have many other disadvantages over procedures. Macros cannot have local (automatic) variables, macro parameters work differently than procedure parameters, macros don't support (runtime) recursion, and macros are a little more difficult to debug than procedures (just to name a few disadvantages). Therefore, you shouldn't really use macros as a substitute for procedures except when performance is absolutely critical.

13.9 Macro Parameters

Like procedures, macros allow you to define *parameters* that let you supply different data on each macro invocation, which lets you write generic macros whose behavior can vary depending on the parameters you supply. By processing these macro parameters at compile time, you can write sophisticated macros.

Macro parameter declaration syntax is straightforward. You supply a list of parameter names as the operands in a macro declaration:

```
neg128  macro reg64HO, reg64LO

        neg     reg64HO
        neg     reg64LO
        sbb     reg64HO, 0

        endm
```

When you invoke a macro, you supply the actual parameters as arguments to the macro invocation:

```
neg128  rdx, rax
```

13.9.1 Standard Macro Parameter Expansion

MASM automatically associates the type text with macro parameters. This means that during a macro expansion, MASM substitutes the text you supply as the actual parameter everywhere the formal parameter name appears. The semantics of *pass by textual substitution* are a little different from *pass by value* or *pass by reference*, so exploring those differences here is worthwhile.

Consider the following macro invocations, using the `neg128` macro from the previous section:

```
neg128 rdx, rax
neg128 rbx, rcx
```

These two invocations expand into the following code:

```
; neg128 rdx, rax

    neg rdx
    neg rax
    sbb rdx, 0

; neg128 rbx, rcx

    neg rbx
    neg rcx
    sbb rbx, 0
```

Macro invocations do not make a local copy of the parameters (as *pass by value* does), nor do they pass the address of the actual parameter to the macro. Instead, a macro invocation of the form `neg128 rdx, rax` is equivalent to the following:

```
reg64H0  textequ <rdx>
reg64L0  textequ <rax>

        neg     reg64H0
        neg     reg64L0
        sbb     reg64H0, 0
```

The text objects immediately expand their string values inline, producing the former expansion for `neg128 rdx, rax`.

Macro parameters are not limited to memory, register, or constant operands as are instruction or procedure operands. Any text is fine as long as its expansion is legal wherever you use the formal parameter. Similarly, formal parameters may appear anywhere in the macro body, not just where memory, register, or constant operands are legal. Consider the following macro declaration and sample invocations that demonstrate how you can expand a formal parameter into a whole instruction:

```
chkError macro instr, jump, target

        instr
        jump  target

        endm

    chkError <cmp eax, 0>, jnl, RangeError  ; Example 1
        .
        .
        .
```

```
        chkError <test bl, 1>, jnz, ParityError ; Example 2

; Example 1 expands to:

        cmp   eax, 0
        jnl   RangeError

; Example 2 expands to:

        test bl, 1
        jnz  ParityError
```

We use the < and > brackets to treat the full `cmp` and `test` instructions as a single string (normally, the comma in these instructions would split them into two macro parameters).

In general, MASM assumes that all text between commas constitutes a single macro parameter. If MASM encounters any opening bracketing symbols (left parentheses, left braces, or left angle brackets), then it will include all text up to the appropriate closing symbol, ignoring any commas that may appear within the bracketing symbols. Of course, MASM does not consider commas (and bracketing symbols) within a string constant as the end of an actual parameter. So the following macro and invocation are perfectly legal:

```
_print macro strToPrint

        call print
        byte strToPrint, nl, 0

    endm
      .
      .
      .
    _print "Hello, world!"
```

MASM treats the string `Hello, world!` as a single parameter because the comma appears inside a literal string constant, just as your intuition suggests.

You can run into some issues when MASM expands your macro parameters, because parameters are expanded as text, not values. Consider the following macro declaration and invocation:

```
Echo2nTimes macro n, theStr
echoCnt     =     0
            while echoCnt LT n * 2

            call  print
            byte  theStr, nl, 0

echoCnt     =     echoCnt + 1
            endm
            endm
```

```
        .
        .
        .
        Echo2nTimes  3 + 1, "Hello"
```

This example displays Hello five times during assembly rather than the eight times you might intuitively expect. This is because the preceding while statement expands to

```
while  echoCnt LT 3 + 1 * 2
```

The actual parameter for n is 3 + 1; because MASM expands this text directly in place of n, you get an erroneous text expansion. At compile time MASM computes 3 + 1 * 2 as the value 5 rather than as the value 8 (which you would get if the MASM passed this parameter by value rather than by textual substitution).

The common solution to this problem when passing numeric parameters that may contain compile-time expressions is to surround the formal parameter in the macro with parentheses; for example, you would rewrite the preceding macro as follows:

```
Echo2nTimes macro n, theStr
echoCnt     =    0
            while echoCnt LT (n) * 2

            call  print
            byte  theStr, nl, 0

echoCnt     =    echoCnt + 1
            endm ; while
            endm ; macro
```

Now, the invocation expands to the following code that produces the intuitive result:

```
while  echoCnt LT (3 + 1) * 2
call   print
byte   theStr, nl, 0
endm
```

If you don't have control over the macro definition (perhaps it's part of a library module you use, and you can't change the macro definition because doing so could break existing code), there is another solution to this problem: use the MASM % operator before the argument in the macro invocation so that the CTL interpreter evaluates the expression before expanding the parameters. For example:

```
Echo2nTimes  %3 + 1, "Hello"
```

This will cause MASM to properly generate eight calls to the print procedure (and associated data).

13.9.2 Optional and Required Macro Parameters

As a general rule, MASM treats macro arguments as optional arguments. If you define a macro that specifies two arguments and invoke that argument with only one argument, MASM will not (normally) complain about the invocation. Instead, it will simply substitute the empty string for the expansion of the second argument. In some cases, this is acceptable and possibly even desirable.

However, suppose you left off the second parameter in the neg128 macro given earlier. That would compile to a neg instruction with a missing operand and MASM would report an error; for example:

```
neg128      macro   arg1, arg2      ; Line 6
            neg     arg1            ; Line 7
            neg     arg2            ; Line 8
            sbb     arg1, 0         ; Line 9
            endm                    ; Line 10
                                    ; Line 11
            neg128  rdx             ; Line 12
```

Here's the error that MASM reports:

```
listing14.asm(12) : error A2008:syntax error : in instruction
 neg128(2): Macro Called From
  listing14.asm(12): Main Line Code
```

The (12) is telling us that the error occurred on line 12 in the source file. The neg128(2) line is telling us that the error occurred on line 2 of the neg128 macro. It's a bit difficult to see what is actually causing the problem here.

One solution is to use conditional assembly inside the macro to test for the presence of both parameters. At first, you might think you could use code like this:

```
neg128  macro reg64HO, reg64LO

        if    reg64LO eq <>
        .err  <neg128 requires 2 operands>
        endif

        neg   reg64HO
        neg   reg64LO
        sbb   reg64O, 0
        endm
        .
        .
        .
        neg128 rdx
```

Unfortunately, this fails for a couple of reasons. First of all, the eq operator doesn't work with text operands. MASM will expand the text operands before attempting to apply this operator, so the if statement in the preceding example effectively becomes

```
    if  eq
```

because MASM substitutes the empty string for both the operands around the eq operator. This, of course, generates a syntax error. Even if there were non-blank textual operands around the eq operator, this would still fail because eq expects numeric operands. MASM solves this issue by introducing several additional conditional if statements intended for use with text operands and macro arguments. Table 13-1 lists these additional if statements.

Table 13-1: Text-Handling Conditional if Statements

Statement	Text operand(s)	Meaning
ifb*	arg	If blank: true if arg evaluates to an empty string.
ifnb	arg	If not blank: true if arg evaluates to a non-empty string.
ifdif	arg1, arg2	If different: true if arg1 and arg2 are different (case-sensitive).
ifdifi	arg1, arg2	If different: true if arg1 and arg2 are different (case-insensitive).
ifidn	arg1, arg2	If identical: true if arg1 and arg2 are exactly the same (case-sensitive).
ifidni	arg2, arg2	If identical: true if arg1 and arg2 are exactly the same (case-insensitive).

* ifb arg is shorthand for ifidn <arg>, <>.

You use these conditional if statements exactly like the standard if statement. You can also follow these if statements with an elseif or else clause, but there are no elseifb, elseifnb, . . . , variants of these if statements (only a standard elseif with a Boolean expression may follow these statements).

The following snippet demonstrates how to use the ifb statement to ensure that the neg128 macro has exactly two arguments. There is no need to check whether reg64HO is also blank; if reg64HO is blank, reg64LO will also be blank, and the ifb statement will report the appropriate error:

```
neg128  macro reg64HO, reg64LO

        ifb  <reg64LO>
        .err <neg128 requires 2 operands>
        endif
```

```
        neg   reg64HO
        neg   reg64LO
        sbb   reg64HO, 0
        endm
```

Be very careful about using `ifb` in your programs. It is easy to pass in a text symbol to a macro and wind up testing whether the name of that symbol is blank rather than the text itself. Consider the following:

```
symbol      textequ <>
            neg128  rax, symbol      ; Generates an error
```

The `neg128` invocation has two arguments, and the second one is not blank, so the `ifb` directive is happy with the argument list. However, inside the macro when `neg128` expands `reg64LO` after the `neg` instruction, the expansion is the empty string, producing an error (which is what the `ifb` was supposed to prevent).

A different way to handle missing macro arguments is to explicitly tell MASM that an argument is required with the `:req` suffix on the macro definition line. Consider the following definition for the `neg128` macro:

```
neg128  macro reg64HO:req, reg64LO:req
        neg   reg64HO
        neg   reg64LO
        sbb   reg64HO, 0
        endm
```

With the `:req` option present, MASM reports the following if you are missing one or more of the macro arguments:

```
listing14.asm(12) : error A2125:missing macro argument
```

13.9.3 Default Macro Parameter Values

One way to handle missing macro arguments is to define default values for those arguments. Consider the following definition for the `neg128` macro:

```
neg128  macro reg64HO:=<rdx>, reg64LO:=<rax>
        neg   reg64HO
        neg   reg64LO
        sbb   reg64HO, 0
        endm
```

The `:=` operator tells MASM to substitute the text constant to the right of the operator for the associated macro argument if an actual value is not present on the macro invocation line. Consider the following two invocations of `neg128`:

```
neg128          ; Defaults to "RDX, RAX" for the args
neg128 rbx      ; Uses RBX:RAX for the 128-bit register pair
```

13.9.4 Macros with a Variable Number of Parameters

It is possible to tell MASM to allow a variable number of arguments in a macro invocation:

```
varParms  macro varying:vararg

    Macro body

        endm
          .
          .
          .
        varParms 1
        varParms 1, 2
        varParms 1, 2, 3
        varParms
```

Within the macro, MASM will create a text object of the form *<arg1, arg2, ..., argn>* and assign this text object to the associated parameter name (varying, in the preceding example). You can use the MASM for loop to extract the individual values of the varying argument. For example:

```
varParms  macro varying:vararg
          for   curArg, <varying>
          byte  curArg
          endm  ; End of FOR loop
          endm  ; End of macro

          varParms 1
          varParms 1, 2
          varParms 1, 2, 3
          varParms <5 dup (?)>
```

Here's the listing output for an assembly containing this example source code:

```
00000000                      .data
                    varParms  macro varying:vararg
                              for   curArg, <varying>
                              byte  curArg
                              endm  ; End of FOR loop
                              endm  ; End of macro

                              varParms 1
00000000  01        2         byte  1
                              varParms 1, 2
00000001  01        2         byte  1
00000002  02        2         byte  2
                              varParms 1, 2, 3
00000003  01        2         byte  1
00000004  02        2         byte  2
```

```
00000005  03          2          byte  3
                                  varParms <5 dup (?)>
00000006  00000005 [ 2           byte  5 dup (?)
          00
        ]
```

A macro can have, at most, one vararg parameter. If a macro has more than one parameter and also has a vararg parameter, the vararg parameter must be the last argument.

13.9.5 The Macro Expansion (&) Operator

Inside a macro, you can use the & operator to replace a macro name (or other text symbol) with its actual value. This operator is active anywhere, even with string literals. Consider the following examples:

```
expand      macro   parm
            byte    '&parm', 0
            endm

            .data
            expand  a
```

The macro invocation in this example expands to the following code:

```
byte 'a', 0
```

If, for some reason, you need the string '&parm' to be emitted within a macro (that has parm as one of its parameters), you will have to work around the expansion operator. Note that '!&parm' will not escape the & operator. One solution that works in this specific case is to rewrite the byte directive:

```
expand      macro   parm
            byte    '&', 'parm', 0
            endm
```

Now the & operator is not causing the expansion of parm inside a string.

13.10 Local Symbols in a Macro

Consider the following macro declaration:

```
jzc     macro   target

        jnz     NotTarget
        jc      target
NotTarget:
        endm
```

This macro simulates an instruction that jumps to the specified target location if the zero flag is set *and* the carry flag is set. Conversely, if either the zero flag or the carry flag is clear, this macro transfers control to the instruction immediately following the macro invocation.

There is a serious problem with this macro. Consider what happens if you use this macro more than once in your program:

```
jzc Dest1
    .
    .
    .
jzc Dest2
    .
    .
    .
```

The preceding macro invocations expand to the following code:

```
        jnz NotTarget
        jc Dest1
NotTarget:
        .
        .
        .
        jnz NotTarget
        jc Dest2
NotTarget:
        .
        .
        .
```

These two macro invocations both emit the same label, `NotTarget`, during macro expansion. When MASM processes this code, it will complain about a duplicate symbol definition.

MASM's solution to this problem is to allow the use of *local symbols* within a macro. Local macro symbols are unique to a specific invocation of a macro. You must explicitly tell MASM which symbols must be local by using the local directive:

```
macro_name      macro   optional_parameters
                local   list_of_local_names
            Macro body
                endm
```

The *list_of_local_names* is a sequence of one or more MASM identifiers separated by commas. Whenever MASM encounters one of these names in a particular macro invocation, it automatically substitutes a unique name for that identifier. For each macro invocation, MASM substitutes a different name for the local symbol.

You can correct the problem with the `jzc` macro by using the following macro code:

```
jzc        macro   target
           local   NotTarget

           jnz     NotTarget
           jc      target
NotTarget:

           endm
```

Now whenever MASM processes this macro, it will automatically associate a unique symbol with each occurrence of `NotTarget`. This will prevent the duplicate symbol error that occurs if you do not declare `NotTarget` as a local symbol.

MASM generates symbols of the form ??*nnnn*, where *nnnn* is a (unique) four-digit hexadecimal number, for each local symbol. So, if you see symbols such as ??0000 in your assembly listings, you know where they came from.

A macro definition can have multiple `local` directives, each with its own list of local names. However, if you have multiple `local` statements in a macro, they should all immediately follow the `macro` directive.

NOTE *Unlike local symbols in a procedure, you do not attach a type to a local macro symbol. The* `local` *directive in a macro declaration accepts only a list of identifiers; the type of the symbols will always be* `text`.

13.11 The exitm Directive

The MASM `exitm` directive (which may appear only within a macro) tells MASM to immediately terminate the processing of the macro. MASM will ignore any additional lines of text within the macro. If you think of a macro as a procedure, `exitm` is the return statement.

The `exitm` directive is useful in a conditional assembly sequence. Perhaps after checking for the presence (or absence) of certain macro arguments, you might want to stop processing the macro to avoid additional errors from MASM. For example, consider the earlier `neg128` macro:

```
neg128  macro reg64HO, reg64LO

        ifb     <reg64LO>
        .err    <neg128 requires 2 operands>
        exitm
        endif

        neg     reg64HO
        neg     reg64LO
        sbb     reg64HO, 0
        endm
```

Without the `exitm` directive inside the conditional assembly, this macro would attempt to assemble the `neg reg64LO` instruction, generating another error because reg64LO expands to the empty string.

13.12 MASM Macro Function Syntax

Originally, MASM's macro design allowed programmers to create substitute mnemonics. A programmer could use a macro to replace a machine instruction or other statement (or sequence of statements) in an assembly language source file. Macros could create only *whole lines* of output text in the source file. This prevented programmers from using macro invocation such as the following:

```
mov rax, some_macro_invocation(arguments)
```

Today, MASM supports additional syntax that allows you to create *macro functions*. A MASM macro function definition looks exactly like a normal macro definition with one addition: you use an `exitm` directive with a textual argument to return a *function result* from the macro. Consider the upperCase macro function in Listing 13-4.

```
; Listing 13-4

; CTL while loop demonstration program.

        option  casemap:none

nl          =       10

            .const
ttlStr      byte    "Listing 13-4", 0

; upperCase macro function.

; Converts text argument to a string, converting
; all lowercase characters to uppercase.

upperCase   macro   theString
            local   resultString, thisChar, sep
resultStr   equ     <> ; Initialize function result with ""
sep         textequ <> ; Initialize separator char with ""

            forc    curChar, theString

; Check to see if the character is lowercase.
; Convert it to uppercase if it is, otherwise
; output it to resultStr as is. Concatenate the
; current character to the end of the result string
; (with a ", " separator, if this isn't the first
; character appended to resultStr).
```

```
              if      ('&curChar' GE 'a') and ('&curChar' LE 'z')
resultStr     catstr  resultStr, sep, %'&curChar'-32
              else
resultStr     catstr  resultStr, sep, %'&curChar'
              endif

; First time through, sep is the empty string. For all
; other iterations, sep is the comma separator between
; values.

sep           textequ <, >
              endm    ; End for

              exitm   <resultStr>
              endm    ; End macro

; Demonstration of the upperCase macro function:

              .data
chars         byte    "Demonstration of upperCase"
              byte    "macro function:"
              byte    upperCase(<abcdEFG123>), nl, 0

              .code
              externdef printf:proc

; Return program title to C++ program:

              public  getTitle
getTitle      proc
              lea     rax, ttlStr
              ret
getTitle      endp

; Here is the "asmMain" function.

              public  asmMain
asmMain       proc
              push    rbx
              push    rbp
              mov     rbp, rsp
              sub     rsp, 56          ; Shadow storage

              lea     rcx, chars       ; Prints characters converted to uppercase
              call    printf

allDone:      leave
              pop     rbx
              ret     ; Returns to caller
asmMain       endp
              end
```

Listing 13-4: Sample macro function

Whenever you invoke a MASM macro function, you must always follow the macro name with a pair of parentheses enclosing the macro's arguments. Even if the macro has no arguments, an empty pair of parentheses must be present. This is how MASM differentiates standard macros and macro functions.

Earlier versions of MASM included functions for directives such as sizestr (using the name @sizestr). Recent versions of MASM have removed these functions. However, you can easily write your own macro functions to replace these missing functions. Here's a quick replacement for the @sizestr function:

```
; @sizestr - Replacement for the MASM @sizestr function
;              that Microsoft removed from MASM.

@sizestr    macro   theStr
            local   theLen
theLen      sizestr <theStr>
            exitm   <&theLen>
            endm
```

The & operator in the exitm directive forces the @sizestr macro to expand the text associated with theLen local symbol inside the < and > string delimiters before returning the value to whomever invoked the macro function. Without the & operator, the @sizestr macro will return text of the form ??0002 (the unique symbol MASM creates for the local symbol theLen).

13.13 Macros as Compile-Time Procedures and Functions

Although programmers typically use macros to expand to a sequence of machine instructions, there is absolutely no requirement that a macro body contain any executable instructions. Indeed, many macros contain only compile-time language statements (for example, if, while, for, = assignments, and the like). By placing only compile-time language statements in the body of a macro, you can effectively write compile-time procedures and functions using macros.

The following unique macro is a good example of a compile-time function that returns a string result:

```
unique macro
       local   theSym
       exitm   <theSym>
       endm
```

Whenever your code references this macro, MASM replaces the macro invocation with the text theSym. MASM generates unique symbols such as ??0000 for local macro symbols. Therefore, each invocation of the unique macro will generate a sequence of symbols such as ??0000, ??0001, ??0002, and so forth.

13.14 Writing Compile-Time "Programs"

The MASM compile-time language allows you to write short programs *that write other programs*—in particular, to automate the creation of large or complex assembly language sequences. The following subsections provide simple examples of such compile-time programs.

13.14.1 Constructing Data Tables at Compile Time

Earlier, this book suggested that you could write programs to generate large, complex lookup tables for your assembly language programs (see the discussion of tables in "Generating Tables" in Chapter 10). Chapter 10 provides C++ programs that generate tables to paste into assembly programs. In this section, we will use the MASM compile-time language to construct data tables during assembly of the program that uses the tables.

One common use for the compile-time language is to build ASCII character lookup tables for alphabetic case manipulation with the xlat instruction at runtime. Listing 13-5 demonstrates how to construct an uppercase conversion table and a lowercase conversion table.[4] Note the use of a macro as a compile-time procedure to reduce the complexity of the table-generating code.

```
; Listing 13-5

; Creating lookup tables with macros.

        option  casemap:none

nl          =       10

            .const
ttlStr      byte    "Listing 13-5", 0
fmtStr1     byte    "testString converted to UC:", nl
            byte    "%s", nl, 0

fmtStr2     byte    "testString converted to LC:", nl
            byte    "%s", nl, 0

testString  byte    "This is a test string ", nl
            byte    "Containing UPPERCASE ", nl
            byte    "and lowercase chars", nl, 0

emitChRange macro   start, last
            local   index, resultStr
index       =       start
            while   index lt last
            byte    index
```

---

4. On modern processors, using a lookup table is probably not the most efficient way to convert between alphabetic cases. However, this is just an example of filling in the table using the compile-time language. The principles are correct, even if the code is not exactly the best it could be.

```
index          =          index + 1
               endm
               endm

; Lookup table that will convert lowercase
; characters to uppercase. The byte at each
; index contains the value of that index,
; except for the bytes at indexes "a" to "z".
; Those bytes contain the values "A" to "Z".
; Therefore, if a program uses an ASCII
; character's numeric value as an index
; into this table and retrieves that byte,
; it will convert the character to uppercase.

lcToUC         equ              this byte
               emitChRange      0, 'a'
               emitChRange      'A', %'Z'+1
               emitChRange      %'z'+1, 0ffh

; As above, but this table converts uppercase
; to lowercase characters.

UCTolc         equ              this byte
               emitChRange      0, 'A'
               emitChRange      'a', %'z'+1
               emitChRange      %'Z'+1, 0ffh

               .data

; Store the destination strings here:

toUC           byte     256 dup (0)
TOlc           byte     256 dup (0)

               .code
               externdef printf:proc

; Return program title to C++ program:

               public  getTitle
getTitle       proc
               lea     rax, ttlStr
               ret
getTitle       endp

; Here is the "asmMain" function.

               public  asmMain
asmMain        proc
               push    rbx
               push    rdi
               push    rsi
               push    rbp
               mov     rbp, rsp
```

```
              sub     rsp, 56              ; Shadow storage

; Convert the characters in testString to uppercase:

              lea     rbx, lcToUC
              lea     rsi, testString
              lea     rdi, toUC
              jmp     getUC

toUCLp:       xlat
              mov     [rdi], al
              inc     rsi
              inc     rdi
getUC:        mov     al, [rsi]
              cmp     al, 0
              jne     toUCLp

; Display the converted string:

              lea     rcx, fmtStr1
              lea     rdx, toUC
              call    printf

; Convert the characters in testString to lowercase:

              lea     rbx, UCTolc
              lea     rsi, testString
              lea     rdi, TOlc
              jmp     getLC

toLCLp:       xlat
              mov     [rdi], al
              inc     rsi
              inc     rdi
getLC:        mov     al, [rsi]
              cmp     al, 0
              jne     toLCLp

; Display the converted string:

              lea     rcx, fmtStr2
              lea     rdx, TOlc
              call    printf

allDone:      leave
              pop     rsi
              pop     rdi
              pop     rbx
              ret     ; Returns to caller
asmMain       endp
              end
```

Listing 13-5: Generating case-conversion tables with the compile-time language

Here's the build command and sample output for the program in Listing 13-5:

```
C:\>build listing13-5

C:\>echo off
 Assembling: listing13-5.asm
c.cpp

C:\>listing13-5
Calling Listing 13-5:
testString converted to UC:
THIS IS A TEST STRING
CONTAINING UPPERCASE
AND LOWERCASE CHARS

testString converted to LC:
this is a test string
containing uppercase
and lowercase chars

Listing 13-5 terminated
```

13.14.2   Unrolling Loops

Chapter 7 points out that you can unroll loops to improve the performance of certain assembly language programs. However, this requires a lot of extra typing, especially if you have many loop iterations. Fortunately, MASM's compile-time language facilities, especially the while loop, come to the rescue. With a small amount of extra typing plus one copy of the loop body, you can unroll a loop as many times as you please.

If you simply want to repeat the same code sequence a certain number of times, unrolling the code is especially trivial. All you have to do is wrap a MASM while..endm loop around the sequence and count off the specified number of iterations. For example, if you wanted to print Hello World 10 times, you could encode this as follows:

```
count = 0
while count LT 10
    call print
    byte "Hello World", nl, 0

count = count + 1
endm
```

Although this code looks similar to a high-level language while loop, remember the fundamental difference: the preceding code simply consists of 10 straight calls to print in the program. Were you to encode this using an actual loop, there would be only one call to print and lots of additional logic to loop back and execute that single call 10 times.

Unrolling loops becomes slightly more complicated if any instructions in that loop refer to the value of a loop control variable or another value, which changes with each iteration of the loop. A typical example is a loop that zeroes the elements of an integer array:

```
            xor eax, eax    ; Set EAX and RBX to 0
            xor rbx, rbx
            lea rcx, array
whlLp:      cmp rbx, 20
            jae loopDone
            mov [rcx][rbx * 4], eax
            inc rbx
            jmp whlLp


loopDone:
```

In this code fragment, the loop uses the value of the loop control variable (in RBX) to index into array. Simply copying mov [rcx][ebx * 4], eax 20 times is not the proper way to unroll this loop. You must substitute an appropriate constant index in the range 0 to 76 (the corresponding loop indices, times 4) in place of rbx * 4 in this example. Correctly unrolling this loop should produce the following code sequence:

```
mov   [rcx][0 * 4], eax
mov   [rcx][1 * 4], eax
mov   [rcx][2 * 4], eax
mov   [rcx][3 * 4], eax
mov   [rcx][4 * 4], eax
mov   [rcx][5 * 4], eax
mov   [rcx][6 * 4], eax
mov   [rcx][7 * 4], eax
mov   [rcx][8 * 4], eax
mov   [rcx][9 * 4], eax
mov [rcx][10 * 4], eax
mov [rcx][11 * 4], eax
mov [rcx][12 * 4], eax
mov [rcx][13 * 4], eax
mov [rcx][14 * 4], eax
mov [rcx][15 * 4], eax
mov [rcx][16 * 4], eax
mov [rcx][17 * 4], eax
mov [rcx][18 * 4], eax
mov [rcx][19 * 4], eax
```

You can easily do this using the following compile-time code sequence:

```
iteration = 0
while iteration LT 20
    mov [rcx][iteration * 4], eax
    iteration = iteration + 1
endm
```

If the statements in a loop use the loop control variable's value, it is possible to unroll such loops only if those values are known at compile time. You cannot unroll loops when user input (or other runtime information) controls the number of iterations.

Of course, if the code sequence loaded RCX with the address of array immediately prior to this loop, you could also use the following while loop to save the use of the RCX register:

```
iteration = 0
while iteration LT 20
    mov array[iteration * 4], eax
    iteration = iteration + 1
endm
```

NOTE *This macro expansion still uses the PC-relative addressing mode, so you don't have to use the LARGEADDRESSAWARE:NO option.*

13.15 Simulating HLL Procedure Calls

Calling procedures (functions) in assembly language is a real chore. Loading registers with parameters, pushing values onto the stack, and other activities are a complete distraction. High-level language procedure calls are far more readable and easier to write than the same calls to an assembly language function. Macros provide a good mechanism to call procedures and functions in a high-level-like manner.

13.15.1 HLL-Like Calls with No Parameters

Of course, the most trivial example is a call to an assembly language procedure that has no arguments at all:

```
someProc  macro
          call    _someProc
          endm

_someProc proc
             .
             .
             .
_someProc endp
             .
             .
             .
          someProc   ; Call the procedure
```

This simple example demonstrates a couple of conventions this book will use for calling procedures via macro invocation:

- If the procedure and all calls to the procedure occur within the same source file, place the macro definition immediately before the procedure to make it easy to find. (Chapter 15 discusses the placement of the macro if you call the procedure from several different source files.)
- If you would normally name the procedure someProc, change the procedure's name to _someProc and then use someProc as the macro name.

While the advantage to using a macro invocation of the form `someProc` versus a call to the procedure using `call someProc` might seem somewhat dubious, keeping all procedure calls consistent (by using macro invocations for all of them) helps make your programs more readable.

13.15.2 HLL-Like Calls with One Parameter

The next step up in complexity is to call a procedure with a single parameter. Assuming you're using the Microsoft ABI and passing the parameter in RCX, the simplest solution is something like the following:

```
someProc  macro   parm1
          mov     rcx, parm1
          call    _someProc
          endm
            .
            .
            .
          someProc Parm1Value
```

This macro works well if you're passing a 64-bit integer by value. If the parameter is an 8-, 16-, or 32-bit value, you would swap CL, CX, or ECX for RCX in the `mov` instruction.[5]

If you're passing the first argument by reference, you would swap an `lea` instruction for the `mov` instruction in this example. As reference parameters are always 64-bit values, the `lea` instruction would usually take this form:

```
lea     rcx, parm1
```

Finally, if you're passing a real4 or real8 value as the parameter, you'd swap one of the following instructions for the `mov` instruction in the previous macro:

```
movss  xmm0, parm1  ; Use this for real4 parameters
movsd  xmm0, parm1  ; Use this for real8 parameters
```

As long as the actual parameter is a memory variable or an appropriate integer constant, this simple macro definition works quite well, covering a very large percentage of the real-world cases.

For example, to call the C Standard Library `printf()` function with a single argument (the format string) using the current macro scheme, you'd write the macro as follows:[6]

```
cprintf macro parm1
        lea   rcx, parm1
        call  printf
        endm
```

---

5. Some people will even use `movzx ecx, parm1` for 8- or 16-bit values to ensure the HO bits of ECX and RCX are all 0 upon entry into the procedure.

6. We don't get to pick the name of the function here. We must call the `printf` function; we cannot arbitrarily name it `_printf` in our code. Therefore, this macro uses the identifier cprintf (for *call printf*).

So you can invoke this macro as

```
cprintf fmtStr
```

where `fmtStr` is (presumably) the name of a `byte` object in your `.data` section containing the `printf` format string.

For a more high-level-like syntax for our procedure calls, we should allow something like the following:

```
cprintf "This is a printf format string"
```

Unfortunately, the way the macro is currently written, this will generate the following (syntactically incorrect) statement:

```
lea   rcx, "This is a printf format string"
```

We could modify this macro to allow this invocation by rewriting it as follows:

```
cprintf macro  parm1
        local  fmtStr
        .data
fmtStr  byte   parm1, nl, 0
        .code
        lea    rcx, fmtStr
        call   printf
        endm
```

Invoking this macro by using a string constant as the argument expands to the following code:

```
        .data
fmtStr  byte   "This is a printf format string", nl, 0
        .code
        lea    rcx, fmtStr  ; Technically, fmtStr will really be something
        call   printf       ; like ??0001
```

NOTE *Inserting a `.data` segment into your code sequence is perfectly okay. When the `.code` directive comes along, MASM will continue emitting the new object code at the program counter offset in effect when it encounters the `.data` directive.*

The only problem with this new form of the macro is that it no longer accepts invocations such as

```
cprintf fmtStr
```

where `fmtStr` is a `byte` object in the `.data` section. We'd really like to have a macro that can accept *both* forms.

13.15.3 Using opattr to Determine Argument Types

The trick to this is the opattr operator (see Table 4-1 in Chapter 4). This operator returns an integer value with certain bits set based on the type of expression that follows. In particular, bit 2 will be set if the expression following is relocatable or otherwise references memory. Therefore, this bit will be set if a variable such as fmtStr appears as the argument, and it will be clear if you pass a string literal as the argument (opattr actually returns the value 0 for string literals that are longer than 8 characters, just so you know). Now consider the code in Listing 13-6.

```
; Listing 13-6

; opattr demonstration.

        option  casemap:none

nl          =       10

            .const
ttlStr      byte    "Listing 13-6", 0

fmtStr      byte    nl, "Hello, World! #2", nl, 0

            .code
            externdef printf:proc

; Return program title to C++ program:

            public  getTitle
getTitle    proc
            lea     rax, ttlStr
            ret
getTitle    endp

; cprintf macro:

;           cprintf fmtStr
;           cprintf "Format String"

cprintf     macro   fmtStrArg
            local   fmtStr, attr, isConst

attr        =       opattr fmtStrArg
isConst     =       (attr and 4) eq 4
            if      (attr eq 0) or isConst
            .data
fmtStr      byte    fmtStrArg, nl, 0
            .code
            lea     rcx, fmtStr

            else
```

```
                lea     rcx, fmtStrArg

                endif
                call    printf
                endm

atw     =       opattr "Hello World"
bin     =       opattr "abcdefghijklmnopqrstuvwxyz"

; Here is the "asmMain" function.

                public  asmMain
asmMain         proc
                push    rbx
                push    rdi
                push    rsi
                push    rbp
                mov     rbp, rsp
                sub     rsp, 56         ; Shadow storage

                cprintf "Hello World!"
                cprintf fmtStr

allDone:        leave
                pop     rsi
                pop     rdi
                pop     rbx
                ret     ; Returns to caller
asmMain         endp
                end
```

Listing 13-6: opattr operator in a macro

Here's the build command and sample output for Listing 13-6:

```
C:\>build listing13-6

C:\>echo off
 Assembling: listing13-6.asm
c.cpp

C:\>listing13-6
Calling Listing 13-6:
Hello World!
Hello, World! #2
Listing 13-6 terminated
```

This cprintf macro is far from perfect. For example, the C/C++ printf() function allows multiple arguments that this macro does not handle. But this macro does demonstrate how to handle two different calls to printf based on the type of the argument you pass cprintf.

13.15.4 HLL-Like Calls with a Fixed Number of Parameters

Expanding the macro-calling mechanism from one parameter to two or more (assuming a fixed number of parameters) is fairly easy. All you need to do is add more formal parameters and handle those arguments in your macro definition. Listing 13-7 is a modification of Listing 9-11 in Chapter 9 that uses macro invocations for calls to r10ToStr, e10ToStr, and some fixed calls to printf (for brevity, as this is a very long program, only the macros and a few invocations are included).

```
           .
           .       ; About 1200 lines from Listing 9-10.
           .


; r10ToStr - Macro to create an HLL-like call for the
;            _r10ToStr procedure.

; Parameters:

;   r10    - Must be the name of a real4, real8, or
;            real10 variable.
;   dest   - Must be the name of a byte buffer to hold
;            string result.

;   wdth   - Output width for the string. Either an
;            integer constant or a dword variable.

;   dPts   - Number of positions after the decimal
;            point. Either an integer constant or
;            a dword variable.

;   fill   - Fill char. Either a character constant
;            or a byte variable.

;   mxLen  - Maximum length of output string. Either
;            an integer constant or a dword variable.

r10ToStr    macro   r10, dest, wdth, dPts, fill, mxLen
            fld     r10

; dest is a label associated with a string variable:

            lea     rdi, dest

; wdth is either a constant or a dword var:

            mov     eax, wdth

; dPts is either a constant or a dword var
; holding the number of decimal point positions:

            mov     edx, dPts
```

```
; Process fill character. If it's a constant,
; directly load it into ECX (which zero-extends
; into RCX). If it's a variable, then move with
; zero extension into ECX (which also zero-
; extends into RCX).

; Note: bit 2 from opattr is 1 if fill is
; a constant.

            if      ((opattr fill) and 4) eq 4
            mov     ecx, fill
            else
            movzx   ecx, fill
            endif

; mxLen is either a constant or a dword var.

            mov     r8d, mxLen
            call    _r10ToStr
            endm

; e10ToStr - Macro to create an HLL-like call for the
;            _e10ToStr procedure.

; Parameters:

;   e10   - Must be the name of a real4, real8, or
;           real10 variable.
;   dest  - Must be the name of a byte buffer to hold
;           string result.

;   wdth  - Output width for the string. Either an
;           integer constant or a dword variable.

;   xDigs - Number of exponent digits.

;   fill  - Fill char. Either a character constant
;           or a byte variable.

;   mxLen - Maximum length of output string. Either
;           an integer constant or a dword variable.

e10ToStr    macro   e10, dest, wdth, xDigs, fill, mxLen
            fld     e10

; dest is a label associated with a string variable:

            lea     rdi, dest

; wdth is either a constant or a dword var:

            mov     eax, wdth
```

```
; xDigs is either a constant or a dword var
; holding the number of decimal point positions:

            mov     edx, xDigs

; Process fill character. If it's a constant,
; directly load it into ECX (which zero-extends
; into RCX). If it's a variable, then move with
; zero extension into ECX (which also zero-
; extends into RCX).

; Note: bit 2 from opattr is 1 if fill is
; a constant.

            if      ((opattr fill) and 4) eq 4
            mov     ecx, fill
            else
            movzx   ecx, fill
            endif

; mxLen is either a constant or a dword var.

            mov     r8d, mxLen
            call    _e10ToStr
            endm

; puts - A macro to print a string using printf.

; Parameters:

;    fmt    - Format string (must be a byte
;              variable or string constant).

;    theStr - String to print (must be a
;              byte variable, a register,
;              or a string constant).

puts        macro   fmt, theStr
            local   strConst, bool

            lea     rcx, fmt

            if      ((opattr theStr) and 2)

; If memory operand:

            lea     rdx, theStr

            elseif  ((opattr theStr) and 10h)

; If register operand:

            mov     rdx, theStr

            else
```

```
; Assume it must be a string constant.

            .data
strConst    byte      theStr, 0
            .code
            lea       rdx, strConst

            endif

            call      printf
            endm

            public    asmMain
asmMain     proc
            push      rbx
            push      rsi
            push      rdi
            push      rbp
            mov       rbp, rsp
            sub       rsp, 64          ; Shadow storage

; F output:

            r10ToStr r10_1, r10str_1, 30, 16, '*', 32
            jc        fpError
            puts      fmtStr1, r10str_1

            r10ToStr r10_1, r10str_1, 30, 15, '*', 32
            jc        fpError
            puts      fmtStr1, r10str_1

                .
                .     ; Similar code to Listing 9-10 with macro
                .     ; invocations rather than procedure calls.
; E output:

            e10ToStr e10_1, r10str_1, 26, 3, '*', 32
            jc        fpError
            puts      fmtStr3, r10str_1

            e10ToStr e10_2, r10str_1, 26, 3, '*', 32
            jc        fpError
            puts      fmtStr3, r10str_1

                .
                .     ; Similar code to Listing 9-10 with macro
                .     ; invocations rather than procedure calls.
```

Listing 13-7: Macro call implementation for converting floating-point values to strings

Compare the HLL-like calls to these three functions against the original procedure calls in Listing 9-11:

```
; F output:

fld     r10_1
lea     rdi, r10str_1
```

```
        mov     eax, 30         ; fWidth
        mov     edx, 16         ; decimalPts
        mov     ecx, '*'        ; Fill
        mov     r8d, 32         ; maxLength
        call    r10ToStr
        jc      fpError

        lea     rcx, fmtStr1
        lea     rdx, r10str_1
        call    printf

        fld     r10_1
        lea     rdi, r10str_1
        mov     eax, 30         ; fWidth
        mov     edx, 15         ; decimalPts
        mov     ecx, '*'        ; Fill
        mov     r8d, 32         ; maxLength
        call    r10ToStr
        jc      fpError

        lea     rcx, fmtStr1
        lea     rdx, r10str_1
        call    printf
        .
        .   ; Additional code from Listing 9-10.
        .
        ; E output:

        fld     e10_1
        lea     rdi, r10str_1
        mov     eax, 26         ; fWidth
        mov     edx, 3          ; expDigits
        mov     ecx, '*'        ; Fill
        mov     r8d, 32         ; maxLength
        call    e10ToStr
        jc      fpError

        lea     rcx, fmtStr3
        lea     rdx, r10str_1
        call    printf

        fld     e10_2
        lea     rdi, r10str_1
        mov     eax, 26         ; fWidth
        mov     edx, 3          ; expDigits
        mov     ecx, '*'        ; Fill
        mov     r8d, 32         ; maxLength
        call    e10ToStr
        jc      fpError

        lea     rcx, fmtStr3
        lea     rdx, r10str_1
        call    printf
```

```
    .
    .    ; Additional code from Listing 9-10.
    .
```

Clearly, the macro version is easier to read (and, as it turns out, easier to debug and maintain too).

13.15.5   HLL-Like Calls with a Varying Parameter List

Some procedures expect a varying number of parameters; the C/C++ printf() function is a good example. Some procedures, though they might support only a fixed number of arguments, could be better written using a varying argument list. For example, consider the print procedure that has appeared throughout the examples in this book; its string parameter (which follows the call to print in the code stream) is, technically, a single-string argument. Consider the following macro implementation for a call to print:

```
print       macro   arg
            call    _print
            byte    arg, 0
            endm
```

You could invoke this macro as follows:

```
print   "Hello, World!"
```

The only problem with this macro is that you will often want to supply multiple arguments in its invocation, such as this:

```
print   "Hello, World!", nl, "It's a great day!", nl
```

Unfortunately, this macro will not accept this list of parameters. However, this seems like a natural use of the print macro, so it makes a lot of sense to modify the print macro to handle multiple arguments and combine them as a single string after the call to the _print function. Listing 13-8 provides such an implementation.

```
; Listing 13-8

; HLL-like procedure calls with
; a varying parameter list.

        option  casemap:none

nl          =       10

            .const
ttlStr      byte    "Listing 13-8", 0

            .code
            externdef printf:proc
```

```
                include getTitle.inc

; Note: don't include print.inc here
; because this code uses a macro for
; print.

; print macro - HLL-like calling sequence for the _print
;                function (which is, itself, a shell for
;                the printf function).

; If print appears on a line by itself (no; arguments),
; then emit a string consisting of a single newline
; character (and zero-terminating byte). If there are
; one or more arguments, emit each argument and append
; a single 0 byte after all the arguments.

; Examples:

;               print
;               print   "Hello, World!"
;               print   "Hello, World!", nl

print           macro   arg1, optArgs:vararg
                call    _print

                ifb     <arg1>

; If print is used by itself, print a
; newline character:

                byte    nl, 0

                else

; If we have one or more arguments, then
; emit each of them:

                byte    arg1

                for     oa, <optArgs>

                byte    oa

                endm

; Zero-terminate the string.

                byte    0

                endif
                endm

_print          proc
                push    rax
                push    rbx
```

```
            push    rcx
            push    rdx
            push    r8
            push    r9
            push    r10
            push    r11

            push    rbp
            mov     rbp, rsp
            sub     rsp, 40
            and     rsp, -16

            mov     rcx, [rbp + 72]   ; Return address
            call    printf

            mov     rcx, [rbp + 72]
            dec     rcx
skipToO:    inc     rcx
            cmp     byte ptr [rcx], 0
            jne     skipToO
            inc     rcx
            mov     [rbp + 72], rcx

            leave
            pop     r11
            pop     r10
            pop     r9
            pop     r8
            pop     rdx
            pop     rcx
            pop     rbx
            pop     rax
            ret
_print      endp

p           macro   arg
            call    _print
            byte    arg, 0
            endm

; Here is the "asmMain" function.

            public  asmMain
asmMain     proc
            push    rbx
            push    rdi
            push    rsi
            push    rbp
            mov     rbp, rsp
            sub     rsp, 56         ; Shadow storage

            print   "Hello world"
            print
            print   "Hello, World!", nl
```

```
allDone:    leave
            pop     rsi
            pop     rdi
            pop     rbx
            ret     ; Returns to caller
asmMain     endp
            end
```

Listing 13-8: Varying arguments' implementation of print macro

Here's the build command and output for the program in Listing 13-8:

```
C:\>build listing13-8

C:\>echo off
 Assembling: listing13-8.asm
c.cpp

C:\>listing13-8
Calling Listing 13-8:
Hello world
Hello, World!
Listing 13-8 terminated
```

With this new print macro, you can now call the _print procedure in an HLL-like fashion by simply listing the arguments in the print invocation:

```
print "Hello World", nl, "How are you today?", nl
```

This will generate a byte directive that concatenates all the individual string components.

Note, by the way, that it is possible to pass a string containing multiple arguments to the original (single-argument) version of print. By rewriting the macro invocation

```
print "Hello World", nl
```

as

```
print <"Hello World", nl>
```

you get the desired output. MASM treats everything between the < and > brackets as a single argument. However, it's a bit of a pain to have to constantly put these brackets around multiple arguments (and your code is inconsistent, as single arguments don't require them). The print macro implementation with varying arguments is a much better solution.

13.16   The invoke Macro

At one time, MASM provided a special directive, invoke, that you could use to call a procedure and pass it parameters (it worked with the proc directive to determine the number and type of parameters a procedure expected). When Microsoft modified MASM to support 64-bit code, it removed the invoke statement from the MASM language.

However, some enterprising programmers have written MASM macros to simulate the invoke directive in 64-bit versions of MASM. The invoke macro not only is useful in its own right but also provides a great example of how to write advanced macros to call procedures. For more information on the invoke macro, visit *https://www.masm32.com/* and download the MASM32 SDK. This includes a set of macros (and other utilities) for 64-bit programs, including the invoke macro.

13.17 Advanced Macro Parameter Parsing

The previous sections provided examples of macro parameter processing used to determine the type of a macro argument in order to determine the type of code to emit. By carefully examining the attributes of an argument, a macro can make various choices concerning how to deal with that argument. This section presents some more advanced techniques you can use when processing macro arguments.

Clearly, the opattr compile-time operator is one of the most important tools you can use when looking at macro arguments. This operator uses the following syntax:

```
opattr expression
```

Note that a generic address expression follows opattr; you are not limited to a single symbol.

The opattr operator returns an integer value that is a bit mask specifying the opattr attributes of the associated expression. If the expression following opattr contains forward-referenced symbols or is an illegal expression, opattr returns 0. Microsoft's documentation indicates that opattr returns the values shown in Table 13-2.

Table 13-2: opattr Return Values

Bit	Meaning
0	There is a code label in the expression.
1	The expression is relocatable.
2	The expression is a constant expression.
3	The expression is uses direct (PC-relative) addressing.
4	The expression is a register.
5	The expression contains no undefined symbols (obsolete).
6	The expression is a stack-segment memory expression.
7	The expression references an external symbol.

(continued)

Table 13-2: opattr Return Values *(continued)*

Bit	Meaning	
8–11	Language type[*]	
	Value	Language
	0	No language type
	1	C
	2	SYSCALL
	3	STDCALL
	4	Pascal
	5	FORTRAN
	6	BASIC

* 64-bit code generally doesn't support a language type, so these bits are usually 0.

Quite honestly, Microsoft's documentation does not do the best job explaining how MASM sets the bits. For example, consider the following MASM statements:

```
codeLabel:
opcl        =   opattr codeLabel ; Sets opcl to 25h or 0010_0101b
opconst     =   opattr 0         ; Sets opconst to 36 or 0010_0100b
```

The opconst has bits 2 and 5 set, just as you would expect from Table 13-2. However, opcl has bits 0, 2, and 5 set; 0 and 5 make sense, but bit 2 (the expression is a constant expression) does not make sense. If, in a macro, you were to test only bit 2 to determine if the operand is a constant (as, I must admit, I have done in earlier examples in this chapter), you could get into trouble when bit 2 is set and you assume that it is a constant.

Probably the wisest thing to do is to mask off bits 0 to 7 (or maybe just bits 0 to 6) and compare the result against an 8-bit value rather than a simple mask. Table 13-3 lists some common values you can test against.

Table 13-3: 8-Bit Values for opattr Results

Value	Meaning
0	Undefined (forward-referenced) symbol or illegal expression
34 / 22h	Memory access of the form [*reg* + *const*]
36 / 24h	Constant
37 / 25h	Code label (proc name or symbol with a : suffix) or offset *code_label* form
38 / 26h	Expression of the form offset *label*, where *label* is a variable in the .data section
42 / 2Ah	Global symbol (for example, symbol in .data section)
43 / 2Bh	Memory access of the form [*reg* + *code_label*], where *code_label* is a proc name or symbol with : suffix

Value	Meaning
48 / 30h	Register (general-purpose, MM, XMM, YMM, ZMM, floating-point/ST, or other special-purpose register)
98 / 62h	Stack-relative memory access (memory addresses of the form [rsp + *xxx*] and [rbp + *xxx*])
165 / 0A5h	External code symbol (37 / 25h with bit 7 set)
171 / ABh	External data symbol (43 / 2Bh with bit 7 set)

Perhaps the biggest issue with opattr, as has already been pointed out, is that it believes that constant expressions are integers that can fit into 64 bits. This creates a problem for two important constant types: string literals (longer than 8 characters) and floating-point constants. opattr returns 0 for both.[8]

13.17.1 Checking for String Literal Constants

Although opattr won't help us determine whether an operand is a string, we can use MASM's string-processing operations to test the first character of an operand to see if it is a quote. The following code does just that:

```
; testStr is a macro function that tests its
; operand to see if it is a string literal.

testStr      macro    strParm
             local    firstChar

             ifnb     <strParm>
firstChar    substr   <strParm>, 1, 1

             ifidn    firstChar,<!">

; First character was ", so assume it's
; a string.

             exitm    <1>
             endif    ; ifidn
             endif    ; ifnb

; If we get to this point in the macro,
; we definitely do not have a string.

             exitm    <0>
             endm
```

NOTE *This macro looks only for a leading quote ("), but MASM strings can also be delimited by apostrophes. I'll leave it up to you to expand this macro to handle apostrophes as well as quotes.*

---

7. MASM will treat a sequence of one to eight characters as an integer value. So short strings (eight characters or less) work fine as expressions.

Consider the following two invocations of the testStr macro:

```
isAStr  = testStr("String Literal")
notAStr = testStr(someLabel)
```

MASM will set the symbol isAStr to the value 1, and notAStr to the value 0.

13.17.2 Checking for Real Constants

Real constants are another literal type that MASM's opattr operator doesn't support. Again, writing a macro to test for a real constant can resolve that issue. Sadly, parsing real numbers isn't as easy as checking for a string constant: there is no single leading character that we can use to say, "Hey, we've got a floating-point constant here." The macro will have to explicitly parse the operand character by character and validate it.

To begin with, here is a grammar that defines a MASM floating-point constant:

```
Sign     ::= (+|-)
Digit    ::= [0-9]
Mantissa ::= (Digit)+ | '.' Digit)+ | (Digit)+ '.' Digit*
Exp      ::= (e|E) Sign? Digit? Digit? Digit?
Real     ::= Sign? Mantissa Exp?
```

A real number consists of an optional sign followed by a mantissa and an optional exponent. A mantissa contains at least one digit; it can also contain a decimal point with a digit to its left or right (or both). However, a mantissa cannot consist of a decimal point by itself.

The macro function to test for a real constant should be callable as follows:

```
isReal = getReal(some_text)
```

where *some_text* is the textual data we want to test to see if it's a real constant. The macro for getReal could be the following:

```
; getReal - Parses a real constant.

; Returns:
;    true  - If the parameter contains a syntactically
;            correct real number (and no extra characters).
;    false - If there are any illegal characters or
;            other syntax errors in the numeric string.

getReal       macro  origParm
              local  parm, curChar, result

; Make a copy of the parameter so we don't
; delete the characters in the original string.

parm          textequ &origParm
```

```
; Must have at least one character:

            ifb     parm
            exitm   <0>
            endif

; Extract the optional sign:

            if      isSign(parm)
curChar     textequ extract1st(parm)        ; Skip sign char
            endif

; Get the required mantissa:

            if      getMant(parm) eq 0
            exitm   <0>                      ; Bad mantissa
            endif

; Extract the optional exponent:

result      textequ getExp(parm)
            exitm   <&result>

            endm    ; getReal
```

Testing for real constants is a complex process, so it's worthwhile to go through this macro (and all subservient macros) step by step:

1. Make a copy of the original parameter string. During processing, getReal will delete characters from the parameter string while parsing the string. This macro makes a copy to prevent disturbing the original text string passed in to it.

2. Check for a blank parameter. If the caller passes in an empty string, the result is not a valid real constant and getReal must return false. It's important to check for the empty string right away because the rest of the code makes the assumption that the string is at least one character long.

3. Call the getSign macro function. This function (its definition appears a little later) returns true if the first character of its argument is a + or - symbol; otherwise, it returns false.

4. If the first character is a sign character, invoke the extract1st macro:

```
curChar     textequ extract1st(parm)        ; Skip sign char
```

The extract1st macro returns the first character of its argument as the function result (which this statement assigns to the curChar symbol) and then deletes the first character of its argument. So if the original string passed to getReal was +1, this statement puts + into curChar and deletes the first character in parm (producing the string 1). The definition for extract1st appears a little later in this section.

getReal doesn't actually use the sign character assigned to curChar. The purpose of this extract1st invocation was strictly for the side effect of deleting the first character in parm.

5. Invoke getMant. This macro function will return true if the prefix of its string argument is a valid mantissa. It will return false if the mantissa does not contain at least one numeric digit. Note that getMant will stop processing the string on the first non-mantissa character it encounters (including a second decimal point, if there are two or more decimal points in the mantissa). The getMant function doesn't care about illegal characters; it leaves it up to getReal to look at the remaining characters after the return from getMant to determine if the whole string is valid. As a side effect, getMant deletes all leading characters from the parameter string that it processes.

6. Invoke the getExp macro function to process any (optional) trailing exponent. The getExp macro is also responsible for ensuring that no garbage characters follow (which results in a parse failure).

The isSign macro is fairly straightforward. Here's its implementation:

```
; isSign - Macro function that returns true if the
;          first character of its parameter is a
;          "+" or "-".

isSign      macro   parm
            local   FirstChar
            ifb     <parm>
            exitm   <0>
            endif

FirstChar   substr  parm, 1, 1
            ifidn   FirstChar, <+>
            exitm   <1>
            endif
            ifidn   FirstChar, <->
            exitm   <1>
            endif
            exitm   <0>
            endm
```

This macro uses the substr operation to extract the first character from the parameter and then compares this against the sign characters (+ or -). It returns true if it is a sign character, and false otherwise.

The extract1st macro function removes the first character from the argument passed to it and returns that character as the function result. As a side effect, this macro function also deletes the first character from the parameter passed to it. Here's extract1st's implementation:

```
extract1st  macro   parm
            local   FirstChar
            ifb     <%parm>
```

```
          exitm   <>
          endif
FirstChar substr  parm, 1, 1
          if      @sizestr(%parm) GE 2
parm      substr  parm, 2
          else
parm      textequ <>
          endif

          exitm   <FirstChar>
          endm
```

The ifb directive checks whether the parameter string is empty. If it is, extract1st immediately returns the empty string without further modification to its parameter.

Note the % operator before the parm argument. The parm argument actually expands to the name of the string variable holding the real constant. This turns out to be something like ??0005 because of the copy made of the original parameter in the getReal function. Were you to simply specify ifb <parm>, the ifb directive would see <??0005>, which is not blank. Placing the % operator before the parm symbol tells MASM to evaluate the expression (which is just the ??0005 symbol) and replace it by the text it evaluates to (which, in this case, is the actual string).

If the string is not blank, extract1st uses the substr directive to extract the first character from the string and assigns this character to the FirstChar symbol. The extract1st macro function will return this value as the function result.

Next, the extract1st function has to delete the first character from the parameter string. It uses the @sizestr function (whose definition appears a little earlier in this chapter) to determine whether the character string contains at least two characters. If so, extract1st uses the substr directive to extract all the characters from the parameter, starting at the second character position. It assigns this substring back to the parameter passed in. If extract1st is processing the last character in the string (that is, if @sizestr returns 1), then the code cannot use the substr directive because the index would be out of range. The else section of the if directive returns an empty string if @sizestr returns a value less than 2.

The next getReal subservient macro function is getMant. This macro is responsible for parsing the mantissa component of the floating-point constant. The implementation is the following:

```
getMant   macro   parm
          local   curChar, sawDecPt, rpt
sawDecPt  =       0
curChar   textequ extract1st(parm)        ; Get 1st char
          ifidn   curChar, <.>            ; Check for dec pt
sawDecPt  =       1
curChar   textequ extract1st(parm)        ; Get 2nd char
          endif
```

```
        ; Must have at least one digit:

                    if      isDigit(curChar) eq 0
                    exitm   <0>                     ; Bad mantissa
                    endif

        ; Process zero or more digits. If we haven't already
        ; seen a decimal point, allow exactly one of those.

        ; Do loop at least once if there is at least one
        ; character left in parm:

        rpt         =       @sizestr(%parm)
                    while   rpt

        ; Get the 1st char from parm and see if
        ; it is a decimal point or a digit:

        curChar     substr  parm, 1, 1
                    ifidn   curChar, <.>
        rpt         =       sawDecPt eq 0
        sawDecPt    =       1
                    else
        rpt         =       isDigit(curChar)
                    endif

        ; If char was legal, then extract it from parm:

                    if      rpt
        curChar     textequ extract1st(parm)        ; Get next char
                    endif

        ; Repeat as long as we have more chars and the
        ; current character is legal:

        rpt         =       rpt and (@sizestr(%parm) gt 0)
                    endm    ; while

        ; If we've seen at least one digit, we've got a valid
        ; mantissa. We've stopped processing on the first
        ; character that is not a digit or the 2nd "." char.

                    exitm   <1>
                    endm    ; getMant
```

A mantissa must have at least one decimal digit. It can have zero or one occurrence of a decimal point (which may appear before the first digit, at the end of the mantissa, or in the middle of a string of digits). The getMant macro function uses the local symbol sawDecPt to keep track of whether it has seen a decimal point already. The function begins by initializing sawDecPt to false (0).

A valid mantissa must have at least one character (because it must have at least one decimal digit). So the next thing getMant does is extract the first character from the parameter string (and place this character in curChar). If the first character is a period (decimal point), the macro sets sawDecPt to true.

The getMant function uses a while directive to process all the remaining characters in the mantissa. A local variable, rpt, controls the execution of the while loop. The code at the beginning of getMant sets rpt to true if the first character is a period or a decimal digit. The isDigit macro function tests the first character of its argument and returns true if it's one of the characters 0 to 9. The definition for isDigit will appear shortly.

If the first character in the parameter was a dot (.) or a decimal digit, the getMant function removes that character from the beginning of the string and executes the body of the while loop for the first time if the new parameter string length is greater than zero.

The while loop grabs the first character from the current parameter string (without deleting it just yet) and tests it against a decimal digit or a . character. If it's a decimal digit, the loop will remove that character from the parameter string and repeat. If the current character is a period, the code first checks whether it has already seen a decimal point (using sawDecPt). If this is a second decimal point, the function returns true (later code will deal with the second . character). If the code has not already seen a decimal point, the loop sets sawDecPt to true and continues with the loop execution.

The while loop repeats as long as it sees decimal digits, a single decimal point, or a string with length greater than zero. Once the loop completes, the getMant function returns true. The only way getMant returns false is if it does not see at least one decimal digit (either at the beginning of the string or immediately after the decimal point at the beginning of the string).

The isDigit macro function is a brute-force function that tests its first character against the 10 decimal digits. This function does not remove any characters from its parameter argument. The source code for isDigit is the following:

```
isDigit     macro   parm
            local   FirstChar
            if      @sizestr(%parm) eq 0
            exitm   <0>
            endif

FirstChar   substr  parm, 1, 1
            ifidn   FirstChar, <0>
            exitm   <1>
            endif
            ifidn   FirstChar, <1>
            exitm   <1>
            endif
            ifidn   FirstChar, <2>
            exitm   <1>
            endif
            ifidn   FirstChar, <3>
            exitm   <1>
            endif
            ifidn   FirstChar, <4>
            exitm   <1>
```

```
            endif
            ifidn   FirstChar, <5>
            exitm   <1>
            endif
            ifidn   FirstChar, <6>
            exitm   <1>
            endif
            ifidn   FirstChar, <7>
            exitm   <1>
            endif
            ifidn   FirstChar, <8>
            exitm   <1>
            endif
            ifidn   FirstChar, <9>
            exitm   <1>
            endif
            exitm   <0>
            endm
```

The only thing worth commenting on is the % operator in @sizestr (for reasons explained earlier).

Now we arrive at the last helper function appearing in getReal: the getExp (*get exponent*) macro function. Here's its implementation:

```
getExp      macro   parm
            local   curChar

; Return success if no exponent present.

            if      @sizestr(%parm) eq 0
            exitm   <1>
            endif

; Extract the next character, return failure
; if it is not an "e" or "E" character:

curChar     textequ extract1st(parm)
            if      isE(curChar) eq 0
            exitm   <0>
            endif

; Extract the next character:

curChar     textequ extract1st(parm)

; If an optional sign character appears,
; remove it from the string:

            if      isSign(curChar)
curChar     textequ extract1st(parm)        ; Skip sign char
            endif                           ; isSign

; Must have at least one digit:

            if      isDigit(curChar) eq 0
```

```
                exitm   <0>
                endif

; Optionally, we can have up to three additional digits:

                if      @sizestr(%parm) gt 0
curChar         textequ extract1st(parm)        ; Skip 1st digit
                if      isDigit(curChar) eq 0
                exitm   <0>
                endif
                endif


                if      @sizestr(%parm) gt 0
curChar         textequ extract1st(parm)        ; Skip 2nd digit
                if      isDigit(curChar) eq 0
                exitm   <0>
                endif
                endif


                if      @sizestr(%parm) gt 0
curChar         textequ extract1st(parm)        ; Skip 3rd digit
                if      isDigit(curChar) eq 0
                exitm   <0>
                endif
                endif

; If we get to this point, we have a valid exponent.

                exitm   <1>
                endm    ; getExp
```

Exponents are optional in a real constant. Therefore, the first thing this macro function does is check whether it has been passed an empty string. If so, it immediately returns success. Once again, the ifb <%parm> directive must have the % operator before the parm argument.

If the parameter string is not empty, the first character in the string must be an E or e character. This function returns false if this is not the case. Checking for an E or e is done with the isE helper function, whose implementation is the following (note the use of ifidni, which is case-insensitive):

```
isE         macro   parm
            local   FirstChar
            if      @sizestr(%parm) eq 0
            exitm   <0>
            endif


FirstChar   substr  parm, 1, 1
            ifidni  FirstChar, <e>
            exitm   <1>
            endif
            exitm   <0>
            endm
```

Next, the getExp function looks for an optional sign character. If it encounters one, it deletes the sign character from the beginning of the string.

At least one decimal digit, and at most four decimal digits, must follow the e or E and sign characters. The remaining code in getExp handles that.

Listing 13-9 is a demonstration of the macro snippets appearing throughout this section. Note that this is a pure compile-time program; all its activity takes place while MASM assembles this source code. It does not generate any executable machine code.

```
; Listing 13-9

; This is a compile-time program.
; It does not generate any executable code.

; Several useful macro functions:

; mout       - Like echo, but allows "%" operators.

; testStr    - Tests an operand to see if it
;                is a string literal constant.

; @sizestr   - Handles missing MASM function.

; isDigit    - Tests first character of its
;                argument to see if it's a decimal
;                digit.

; isSign     - Tests first character of its
;                argument to see if it's a "+"
;                or a "-" character.

; extract1st - Removes the first character
;                from its argument (side effect)
;                and returns that character as
;                the function result.

; getReal    - Parses the argument and returns
;                true if it is a reasonable-
;                looking real constant.

; Test strings and invocations for the
; getReal macro:

    Note: actual macro code appears in previous code snippets
      and has been removed from this listing for brevity

mant1         textequ <1>
mant2         textequ <.2>
mant3         textequ <3.4>
rv4           textequ <1e1>
rv5           textequ <1.e1>
rv6           textequ <1.0e1>
rv7           textequ <1.0e + 1>
```

```
rv8         textequ <1.0e - 1>
rv9         textequ <1.0e12>
rva         textequ <1.0e1234>
rvb         textequ <1.0E123>
rvc         textequ <1.0E + 1234>
rvd         textequ <1.0E - 1234>
rve         textequ <-1.0E - 1234>
rvf         textequ <+1.0E - 1234>
badr1       textequ <>
badr2       textequ <a>
badr3       textequ <1.1.0>
badr4       textequ <e1>
badr5       textequ <1ea1>
badr6       textequ <1e1a>

% echo get_Real(mant1) = getReal(mant1)
% echo get_Real(mant2) = getReal(mant2)
% echo get_Real(mant3) = getReal(mant3)
% echo get_Real(rv4)   = getReal(rv4)
% echo get_Real(rv5)   = getReal(rv5)
% echo get_Real(rv6)   = getReal(rv6)
% echo get_Real(rv7)   = getReal(rv7)
% echo get_Real(rv8)   = getReal(rv8)
% echo get_Real(rv9)   = getReal(rv9)
% echo get_Real(rva)   = getReal(rva)
% echo get_Real(rvb)   = getReal(rvb)
% echo get_Real(rvc)   = getReal(rvc)
% echo get_Real(rvd)   = getReal(rvd)
% echo get_Real(rve)   = getReal(rve)
% echo get_Real(rvf)   = getReal(rvf)
% echo get_Real(badr1) = getReal(badr1)
% echo get_Real(badr2) = getReal(badr2)
% echo get_Real(badr3) = getReal(badr3)
% echo get_Real(badr4) = getReal(badr4)
% echo get_Real(badr5) = getReal(badr5)
% echo get_Real(badr5) = getReal(badr5)
        end
```

Listing 13-9: Compile-time program with test code for getReal macro

Here's the build command and (compile-time) program output:

```
C:\>ml64 /c listing13-9.asm
Microsoft (R) Macro Assembler (x64) Version 14.15.26730.0
Copyright (C) Microsoft Corporation.  All rights reserved.

 Assembling: listing13-9.asm
get_Real(1) = 1
get_Real(.2) = 1
get_Real(3.4) = 1
get_Real(1e1)  = 1
get_Real(1.e1) = 1
get_Real(1.0e1) = 1
get_Real(1.0e + 1) = 1
```

```
get_Real(1.0e - 1) = 1
get_Real(1.0e12) = 1
get_Real(1.0e1234) = 1
get_Real(1.0E123) = 1
get_Real(1.0E + 1234) = 1
get_Real(1.0E - 1234) = 1
get_Real(-1.0E - 1234) = 1
get_Real(+1.0E - 1234) = 1
get_Real() = 0
get_Real(a) = 0
get_Real(1.1.0) = 0
get_Real(e1) = 0
get_Real(1ea1) = 0
get_Real(1ea1) = 0
```

13.17.3 Checking for Registers

Although the opattr operator provides a bit to tell you that its operand is an x86-64 register, that's the only information opattr provides. In particular, opattr's return value won't tell you which register it has seen; whether it's a general-purpose, XMM, YMM, ZMM, MM, ST, or other register; or the size of that register. Fortunately, with a little work on your part, you can determine all this information by using MASM's conditional assembly statements and other operators.

To begin with, here's a simple macro function, isReg, that returns 1 or 0 depending on whether its operand is a register. This is a simple shell around the opattr operator that returns the setting of bit 4:

```
isReg       macro   parm
            local   result
result      textequ %(((opattr &parm) and 10h) eq 10h)
            exitm   <&result>
            endm
```

While this function provides some convenience, it doesn't really provide any information that the opattr operator already provides. We want to know what register appears in the operand as well as the size of that register.

Listing 13-10 (available online at *http://artofasm.randallhyde.com/*) provides a wide range of useful macro functions and equates for processing register operands in your own macros. The following paragraphs describe some of the more useful equates and macros.

Listing 13-10 contains a set of equates that map register names to numeric values. These equates use symbols of the form reg*XXX*, where *XXX* is the register name (all uppercase). Examples include the following: regAL, regSIL, regR8B, regAX, regBP, regR8W, regEAX, regEBP, regR8D, regRAX, regRSI, regR15, regST, regST0, regMMO, regXMM0, and regYMM0.

There is also a special equate for the symbol regNone that represents a non-register entity. These equates give numeric values in the range 1 to 117 to each of these symbols (regNone is given the value 0).

The purpose behind all these equates (and, in general, assigning numeric values to registers) is to make it easier to test for specific registers (or ranges of registers) within your macros by using conditional assembly.

A useful set of macros appearing in Listing 13-10 converts textual forms of the register names (that is, AL, AX, EAX, RAX, and so forth) to their numeric form (regAL, regAX, regEAX, regRAX, and so on). The most generic macro function to do this is whichReg(*register*). This function accepts a text object and returns the appropriate reg*XXX* value for that text. If the text passed as an argument is not one of the valid general-purpose, FPU, MMX, XMM, or YMM registers, whichReg returns the value regNone. Here are some examples of calls to whichReg:

```
alVal   =        whichReg(al)
axTxt   textequ <ax>
axVal   =        whichReg(axTxt)

aMac    macro   parameter
        local   regVal
regVal  =        whichReg(parameter)
        if       regVal eq regNone
        .err     <Expected a register argument>
        exitm
        endif
          .
          .
          .
        endm
```

The whichReg macro function accepts any of the x86-64 general-purpose, FPU, MMX, XMM, or YMM registers. In many situations, you might want to limit the set of registers to a particular subset of these. Therefore, Listing 13-11 (also available online at *http://artofasm.randallhyde.com/*) provides the following macro functions:

isGPReg(*text*)   Returns a nonzero register value for any of the general-purpose (8-, 16-, 32-, or 64-bit) registers. Returns regNone (0) if the argument is not one of these registers.

is8BitReg(*text*)   Returns a nonzero register value for any of the general-purpose 8-bit registers. Otherwise, it returns regNone (0).

is16BitReg(*text*)   Returns a nonzero register value for any of the general-purpose 16-bit registers. Otherwise, it returns regNone (0).

is32BitReg(*text*)   Returns a nonzero register value for any of the general-purpose 32-bit registers. Otherwise, it returns regNone (0).

is64BitReg(*text*)   Returns a nonzero register value for any of the general-purpose 64-bit registers. Otherwise, it returns regNone (0).

isFPReg(*text*)   Returns a nonzero register value for any of the FPU registers (ST, and ST(0) to ST(7)). Otherwise, it returns regNone (0).

isMMReg(*text*)   Returns a nonzero register value for any of the MMX registers (MM0 to MM7). Otherwise, it returns regNone (0).

isXMMReg(*text*)   Returns a nonzero register value for any of the XMM registers (XMM0 to XMM15). Otherwise, it returns regNone (0).

isYMMReg(*text*)   Returns a nonzero register value for any of the YMM registers (YMM0 to YMM15). Otherwise, it returns regNone (0).

If you need other register classifications, it's easy to write your own macro functions to return an appropriate value. For example, if you want to test whether a particular register is one of the Windows ABI parameter registers (RCX, RDX, R8, or R9), you could create a macro function like the following:

```
isWinParm  macro  theReg
           local  regVal, isParm
regVal     =      whichReg(theReg)
isParm     =      (regVal eq regRCX) or (regVal eq regRDX)
isParm     =      isParm or (regVal eq regR8)
isParm     =      isParm or (regVal eq regR9)

           if     isParm
           exitm <%regVal>
           endif
           exitm <%regNone>
           endm
```

If you've converted a register in text form to its numeric value, at some point you might need to convert that numeric value back to text so you can use that register as part of an instruction. The toReg(*reg_num*) macro in Listing 13-10 accomplishes this. If you supply it a value in the range 1 to 117 (the numeric values for the registers), this macro will return the text that corresponds to that register value. For example:

```
mov toReg(1), 0    ; Equivalent to mov al, 0
```

(Note that regAL = 1.)

If you pass regNone to the toReg macro, toReg returns an empty string. Any value outside the range 0 to 117 will produce an undefined symbol error message.

When working in macros, where you've passed a register as an argument, you may find that you need to convert that register to a larger size (for example, convert AL to AX, EAX, or RAX; convert AX to EAX or RAX; or convert EAX to RAX). Listing 13-11 provides several macros to do the up conversion. These macro functions accept a register number as their parameter input and produce a textual result holding the actual register name:

reg8To16   Converts an 8-bit general-purpose register to its 16-bit equivalent[8]

reg8To32   Converts an 8-bit general-purpose register to its 32-bit equivalent

---

8. Registers AH, BH, CH, and DH get converted to the same registers as AL, BL, CL, and DL, respectively.

reg8To64   Converts an 8-bit general-purpose register to its 64-bit equivalent

reg16To32   Converts a 16-bit general-purpose register to its 32-bit equivalent

reg16To64   Converts a 16-bit general-purpose register to its 64-bit equivalent

reg32To64   Converts a 32-bit general-purpose register to its 64-bit equivalent

Another useful macro function in Listing 13-10 is the regSize(*reg_value*) macro. This function returns the size (in bytes) of the register value passed as an argument. Here are some example calls:

```
alSize    =  regSize(regAL)    ; Returns 1
axSize    =  regSize(regAX)    ; Returns 2
eaxSize   =  regSize(regEAX)   ; Returns 4
raxSize   =  regSize(regRAX)   ; Returns 8
stSize    =  regSize(regST0)   ; Returns 10
mmSize    =  regSize(regMM0)   ; Returns 8
xmmSize   =  regSize(regXMM0)  ; Returns 16
ymmSize   =  regSize(regYMM0)  ; Returns 32
```

The macros and equates in Listing 13-10 come in handy when you are writing macros to handle generic code. For example, suppose you want to create a putInt macro that accepts an arbitrary 8-, 16-, or 32-bit register operand and that will print that register's value as an integer. You would like to be able to pass any arbitrary (general-purpose) register and sign-extend it, if necessary, before printing. Listing 13-12 is one possible implementation of this macro.

```
; Listing 13-12

; Demonstration of putInt macro.

; putInt - This macro expects an 8-, 16-, or 32-bit
;          general-purpose register argument. It will
;          print the value of that register as an
;          integer.

putInt     macro    theReg
           local    regVal, sz
regVal     =        isGPReg(theReg)

; Before we do anything else, make sure
; we were actually passed a register:

           if       regVal eq regNone
           .err     <Expected a register>
           endif

; Get the size of the register so we can
; determine if we need to sign-extend its
```

```
        ; value:

sz            =         regSize(regVal)

; If it was a 64-bit register, report an
; error:

                if      sz gt 4
                .err    64-bit register not allowed
                endif

; If it's a 1- or 2-byte register, we will need
; to sign-extend the value into EDX:

                if      (sz eq 1) or (sz eq 2)
                movsx   edx, theReg

; If it's a 32-bit register, but is not EDX, we need
; to move it into EDX (don't bother emitting
; the instruction if the register is EDX;
; the data is already where we want it):

                elseif  regVal ne regEDX
                mov     edx, theReg
                endif

; Print the value in EDX as an integer:

                call    print
                byte    "%d", 0
                endm

        option  casemap:none

nl            =         10

                .const
ttlStr          byte    "Listing 13-12", 0
```

Note: several thousand lines of code omitted here for brevity. This includes most of the text from Listing 13-11 plus the putInt macro

```
                .code

                include getTitle.inc
                include print.inc
                public  asmMain
asmMain         proc
                push    rbx
                push    rbp
                mov     rbp, rsp
                sub     rsp, 56         ; Shadow storage
```

```
                    call    print
                    byte    "Value 1:", 0
                    mov     al, 55
                    putInt  al

                    call    print
                    byte    nl, "Value 2:", 0
                    mov     cx, 1234
                    putInt  cx

                    call    print
                    byte    nl, "Value 3:", 0
                    mov     ebx, 12345678
                    putInt  ebx

                    call    print
                    byte    nl, "Value 4:", 0
                    mov     edx, 1
                    putInt  edx
                    call    print
                    byte    nl, 0

allDone:            leave
                    pop     rbx
                    ret     ; Returns to caller
asmMain             endp
                    end
```

Listing 13-12: putInt macro function test program

Here's the build command and sample output for Listing 13-12:

```
C:\>build listing13-12

C:\>echo off
 Assembling: listing13-12.asm
c.cpp

C:\>listing13-11
Calling Listing 13-12:
Value 1:55
Value 2:1234
Value 3:12345678
Value 4:1
Listing 13-12 terminated
```

Though Listing 13-12 is a relatively simple example, it should give you a good idea of how you could make use of the macros in Listing 13-10.

13.17.4 Compile-Time Arrays

A compile-time *constant array* is an array that exists only at compile time—data for the array does not exist at runtime. Sadly, MASM doesn't provide direct support for this useful CTL data type. Fortunately, it's possible to use other MASM CTL features to simulate compile-time arrays.

This section considers two ways to simulate compile-time arrays: text strings and a list of equates (one equate per array element). The list of equates is probably the easiest implementation, so this section considers that first.

In Listing 13-11 (available online), a very useful function converts all the text in a string to uppercase (toUpper). The register macros use this macro to convert register names to uppercase characters (so that register name comparisons are case-insensitive). The toUpper macro is relatively straightforward. It extracts each character of a string and checks whether that character's value is in the range a to z, and if it is, it uses that character's value as an index into an array (indexed from a to z) to extract the corresponding array element value (which will have the values A to Z for each element of the array). Here's the toUpper macro:

```
; toUpper - Converts alphabetic characters to uppercase
;           in a text string.

toUpper     macro   lcStr
            local   result

; Build the result string in "result":

result      textequ <>

; For each character in the source string,
; convert it to uppercase.

            forc    eachChar, <lcStr>

; See if we have a lowercase character:

            if      ('&eachChar' ge 'a') and ('&eachChar' le 'z')

; If lowercase, convert it to the symbol "lc_*" where "*"
; is the lowercase character. The equates below will map
; this character to uppercase:

eachChar    catstr  <lc_>,<eachChar>
result      catstr  result, &eachChar

            else

; If it wasn't a lowercase character, just append it
; to the end of the string:

result      catstr  result, <eachChar>

            endif
            endm                    ; forc
```

```
            exitm    result  ; Return result string
            endm             ; toUpper
```

The "magic" statements, which handle the array access, are these two statements:

```
eachChar    catstr  <lc_>,<eachChar>
result      catstr  result, &eachChar
```

The eachChar catstr operation produces a string of the form lc_a, lc_b, ..., lc_z whenever this macro encounters a lowercase character. The result catstr operation expands a label of the form lc_a, ..., to its value and concatenates the result to the end of the result string (which is a register name). Immediately after the toUpper macro in Listing 13-11, you will find the following equates:

```
lc_a        textequ <A>
lc_b        textequ <B>
lc_c        textequ <C>
lc_d        textequ <D>
lc_e        textequ <E>
lc_f        textequ <F>
lc_g        textequ <G>
lc_h        textequ <H>
lc_i        textequ <I>
lc_j        textequ <J>
lc_k        textequ <K>
lc_l        textequ <L>
lc_m        textequ <M>
lc_n        textequ <N>
lc_o        textequ <O>
lc_p        textequ <P>
lc_q        textequ <Q>
lc_r        textequ <R>
lc_s        textequ <S>
lc_t        textequ <T>
lc_u        textequ <U>
lc_v        textequ <V>
lc_w        textequ <W>
lc_x        textequ <X>
lc_y        textequ <Y>
lc_z        textequ <Z>
```

Therefore, lc_a will expand to the character A, lc_b will expand to the character B, and so forth. This sequence of equates forms the lookup table (array) that toUpper uses. The array should be called lc_, and the index into the array is the suffix of the array's name (a to z). The toUpper macro accesses element lc_[*character*] by appending *character* to lc_ and then expanding the text equate lc_*character* (expansion happens by applying the & operator to the eachChar string the macro produces).

Note the following two things. First, the array index doesn't have to be an integer (or ordinal) value. Any arbitrary string of characters will suffice.[9] Second, if you supply an index that isn't within bounds (a to z), the toUpper macro will attempt to expand a symbol of the form lc_*xxxx* that results in an undefined identifier. Therefore, MASM will report an undefined symbol error should you attempt to supply an index that is not within range. This will not be an issue for the toUpper macro because toUpper validates the index (using a conditional if statement) prior to constructing the lc_*xxxx* symbol.

Listing 13-11 also provides an example of another way to implement a compile-time array: using a text string to hold array elements and using substr to extract elements of the array from that string. The is*XX*BitReg macros (is8BitReg, is16BitReg, and so forth) pass along a couple of arrays of data to the more generic lookupReg macro. Here's the is16BitReg macro:[10]

```
all16Regs   catstr <AX>,
                   <BX>,
                   <CX>,
                   <DX>,
                   <SI>,
                   <DI>,
                   <BP>,
                   <SP>,
                   <R8W>,
                   <R10W>,
                   <R11W>,
                   <R12W>,
                   <R13W>,
                   <R14W>,
                   <R15W>


all16Lens   catstr <2>, <0>,              ; AX
                   <2>, <0>,              ; BX
                   <2>, <0>,              ; CX
                   <2>, <0>,              ; DX
                   <2>, <0>,              ; SI
                   <2>, <0>,              ; DI
                   <2>, <0>,              ; BP
                   <2>, <0>,              ; SP
                   <3>, <0>, <0>,         ; R8W
                   <3>, <0>, <0>,         ; R9W
                   <4>, <0>, <0>, <0>,    ; R10W
                   <4>, <0>, <0>, <0>,    ; R11W
                   <4>, <0>, <0>, <0>,    ; R12W
                   <4>, <0>, <0>, <0>,    ; R13W
                   <4>, <0>, <0>, <0>,    ; R14W
                   <4>, <0>, <0>, <0>     ; R15W
```

---

9. Technically, this type of data structure is a *dictionary*, or *associative array*. However, it serves as a perfectly good array for our purposes.

10. This macro has a couple of slight modifications (using catstr rather than textequ) to make it more readable within this book. Functionally, it is the same as the macro appearing in the actual source code.

```
is16BitReg   macro   parm
             exitm   lookupReg(parm, all16Regs, all16Lens)
             endm    ; is16BitReg
```

The all16Regs string is a list of register names (all concatenated together into one string). The lookupReg macro will search for a user-supplied register (parm) in this string of register names by using the MASM instr directive. If instr does not find the register in the list of names, parm is not a valid 16-bit register and instr returns the value 0. If it does locate the string held by parm in all16Regs, then instr returns the (nonzero) index into all16Regs where the match occurs. By itself, a nonzero index does not indicate that lookupReg has found a valid 16-bit register. For example, if the user supplies PR as a register name, the instr directive will return a nonzero index into the all16Regs string (the index of the last character of the SP register, with the R coming from the first character of the R8W register name). Likewise, if the caller passes the string R8 to is16BitReg, the instr directive will return the index to the first character of the R8W entry, but R8 is not a valid 16-bit register.

Although instr can reject a register name (by returning 0), additional validation is necessary if instr returns a nonzero value; this is where the all16Lens array comes in. The lookupReg macro uses the index that instr returns as an index into the all16Lens array. If the entry is 0, the index into all16Regs is not a valid register index (it's an index to a string that is not at the start of a register name). If the index into all16Lens points at a nonzero value, lookupReg compares this value against the length of the parm string. If they are equal, parm holds an actual 16-bit register name; if they are not equal, parm is too long or too short and is not a valid 16-bit register name. Here's the full lookupReg macro:

```
; lookupReg - Given a (suspected) register and a lookup table, convert
;             that register to the corresponding numeric form.

lookupReg    macro   theReg, regList, regIndex
             local   regUpper, regConst, inst, regLen, indexLen

; Convert (possible) register to uppercase:

regUpper     textequ toUpper(theReg)
regLen       sizestr <&theReg>

; Does it exist in regList? If not, it's not a register.

inst         instr   1, regList, &regUpper
             if      inst ne 0

regConst     substr  &regIndex, inst, 1
             if      &regConst eq regLen

; It's a register (in text form). Create an identifier of
; the form "regXX" where "XX" represents the register name.
```

```
regConst    catStr   <reg>,regUpper

            ifdef    &regConst

; Return "regXX" as function result. This is the numeric value
; for the register.

              exitm   regConst
              endif
              endif
              endif

; If the parameter string wasn't in regList, then return
; "regNone" as the function result:

              exitm   <regNone>
              endm    ; lookupReg
```

Note that lookupReg also uses the register value constants (regNone, regAL, regBL, and so on) as an associative compile-time array (see the regConst definitions).

13.18   Using Macros to Write Macros

One advanced use of macros is to have a macro invocation create one or more new macros. If you nest a macro declaration inside another macro, invoking that (enclosing) macro will expand the enclosed macro definition and define that macro at that point. Of course, if you invoke the outside (enclosing) macro more than once, you could wind up with a duplicate macro definition unless you take care in the construction of the new macro (that is, by assigning it a new name with each new invocation of the outside macro). In a few cases, being able to generate macros on the fly can be useful.

Consider the compile-time array examples from the previous section. If you want to create a compile-time array by using the *multiple equates* method, you will have to manually define equates for all the array elements before you can use that array. This can be tedious, especially if the array has a large number of elements. Fortunately, it's easy to create a macro to automate this process for you.

The following macro declaration accepts two arguments: the name of an array to create and the number of elements to put into the array. This macro generates a list of definitions (using the = directive, rather than the textequ directive) with each element initialized to 0:

```
genArray    macro    arrayName, elements
            local    index, eleName, getName

; Loop over each element of the array:

index       =        0
            while    index lt &elements
```

```
; Generate a textequ statement to define a single
; element of the array, for example:

; aryXX = 0

; where "XX" is the index (0 to (elements - 1)).

eleName      catstr  <&arrayName>,%index,< = 0>

; Expand the text just created with the catstr directive.

        eleName

; Move on to next array index:

index       =       index + 1
            endm    ; while

            endm    ; genArray
```

For example, the following macro invocation creates 10 array elements, named ary0 to ary9:

```
genArray ary, 10
```

You can access the array elements directly by using the names ary0, ary1, ary2, . . . , ary9. If you want to access these array elements programmatically (perhaps in a compile-time while loop), you would have to use the catstr directive to create a text equate that has the array name (ary) concatenated with the index. Wouldn't it be more convenient to have a macro function that creates this text equate for you? It's easy enough to write a macro that does this:

```
ary_get     macro   index
            local   element
element     catstr  <ary>,%index
            exitm   <element>
            endm
```

With this macro, you can easily access elements of the ary array by using the macro invocation ary_get(*index*). You could also write a macro to store a value into a specified element of the ary array:

```
ary_set     macro   index, value
            local   assign
assign      catstr  <ary>, %index, < = >, %value
            assign
            endm
```

These two macros are so useful, you'd probably want to include them with each array you create with the genArray macro. So why not have the genArray macro write these macros for you? Listing 13-13 provides an implementation of genArray that does exactly this.

```
; Listing 13-13

; This is a compile-time program.
; It does not generate any executable code.

        option  casemap:none

genArray    macro   arrayName, elements
            local   index, eleName, getName

; Loop over each element of the array:

index       =       0
            while   index lt &elements

; Generate a textequ statement to define a single
; element of the array, for example:

; aryXX = 0

; where "XX" is the index (0 to (elements - 1)).

eleName     catstr  <&arrayName>,%index,< = 0>

; Expand the text just created with the catstr directive:

            eleName

; Move on to next array index:

index       =       index + 1
            endm    ; while

; Create a macro function to retrieve a value from
; the array:

getName     catstr  <&arrayName>,<_get>

getName     macro   theIndex
            local   element
element     catstr  <&arrayName>,%theIndex
            exitm   <element>
            endm

; Create a macro to assign a value to
; an array element.

setName     catstr  <&arrayName>,<_set>

setName     macro   theIndex, theValue
            local   assign
assign      catstr  <&arrayName>, %theIndex, < = >, %theValue
```

```
                assign
                endm


                endm      ; genArray

; mout - Replacement for echo. Allows "%" operator
;          in operand field to expand text symbols.

mout            macro    valToPrint
                local    cmd
cmd             catstr   <echo >, <valToPrint>
                cmd
                endm


; Create an array ("ary") with ten elements:

                genArray ary, 10

; Initialize each element of the array to
; its index value:

index           = 0
                while    index lt 10
                ary_set index, index
index           =        index + 1
                endm

; Print out the array values:

index           =        0
                while    indcx lt 10

value           =        ary_get(index)
                mout     ary[%index] = %value
index           =        index + 1
                endm


                end
```

Listing 13-13: A macro that writes another pair of macros

Here's the build command and sample output for the compile-time program in Listing 13-13:

```
C:\>ml64 /c /Fl listing13-13.asm
Microsoft (R) Macro Assembler (x64) Version 14.15.26730.0
Copyright (C) Microsoft Corporation.  All rights reserved.

 Assembling: listing13-13.asm
ary[0] = 0
ary[1] = 1
ary[2] = 2
ary[3] = 3
ary[4] = 4
ary[5] = 5
```

```
ary[6] = 6
ary[7] = 7
ary[8] = 8
ary[9] = 9
```

13.19 Compile-Time Program Performance

When writing compile-time programs, keep in mind that MASM is interpreting these programs during assembly. This can have a huge impact on the time it takes MASM to assemble your source files. Indeed, it is quite possible to create infinite loops that will cause MASM to (seemingly) hang up during assembly. Consider the following trivial example:

```
true        =    1
            while true
            endm
```

Any attempt to assemble a MASM source file containing this sequence will lock up the system until you press CTRL-C (or use another mechanism to abort the assembly process).

Even without infinite loops, it is easy to create macros that take a considerable amount of time to process. If you use such macros hundreds (or even thousands) of times in a source file (as is common for some complex print-type macros), it could take a while for MASM to process your source files. Be aware of this (and be patient if MASM seems to hang up—it could simply be your compile-time programs taking a while to do their job).

If you think a compile-time program has entered an infinite loop, the echo directive (or macros like mout, appearing throughout this chapter) can help you track down the infinite loop (or other bugs) in your compile-time programs.

13.20 For More Information

Although this chapter has spent a considerable amount of time describing various features of MASM's macro support and compile-time language features, the truth is this chapter has barely described what's possible with MASM. Sadly, Microsoft's documentation all but ignores the macro facilities of MASM. Probably the best place to learn about advanced macro programming with MASM is the MASM32 forum at *http://www.masm32.com/board/index.php*.

Although it is an older book, covering MASM version 6, *The Waite Group's Microsoft Macro Assembler Bible* by Nabajyoti Barkakati and this author (Sams, 1992) does go into detail about the use of MASM's macro facilities (as well as other directives that are poorly documented these days). Also, the MASM 6.*x* manual can still be found online at various sites. While this manual is woefully outdated with respect to the latest versions of MASM (it does not, for example, cover any of the 64-bit instructions or addressing modes), it does a decent job of describing MASM's macro facilities and many of MASM's directives. Just keep in mind when reading the older documentation that Microsoft has *disabled* many features that used to be present in MASM.

13.21 Test Yourself

1. What does *CTL* stand for?
2. When do CTL programs execute?
3. What directive would you use to print a message (not an error) during assembly?
4. What directive would you use to print an error message during assembly?
5. What directive would you use to create a CTL variable?
6. What is the MASM macro escape character operator?
7. What does the MASM % operator do?
8. What does the MASM macro & operator do?
9. What does the catstr directive do?
10. What does the MASM instr directive do?
11. What does the sizestr directive do?
12. What does the substr directive do?
13. What are the main (four) conditional assembly directives?
14. What directives could you use to create compile-time loops?
15. What directive would you use to extract the characters from a MASM text object in a loop?
16. What directives do you use to define a macro?
17. How do you invoke a macro in a MASM source file?
18. How do you specify macro parameters in a macro declaration?
19. How do you specify that a macro parameter is required?
20. How do you specify that a macro parameter is optional?
21. How do you specify a variable number of macro arguments?
22. Explain how you can manually test whether a macro parameter is present (without using the :req suffix).
23. How can you define local symbols in a macro?
24. What directive would you use (generally inside a conditional assembly sequence) to immediately terminate macro expansion without processing any additional statements in the macro?
25. How would you return a textual value from a macro function?
26. What operator could you use to test a macro parameter to see if it is a machine register versus a memory variable?

14

THE STRING INSTRUCTIONS

A *string* is a collection of values stored in contiguous memory locations. The x86-64 CPUs can process four types of strings: byte strings, word strings, double-word strings, and quad-word strings.

The x86-64 microprocessor family supports several instructions specifically designed to cope with strings. They can move strings, compare strings, search for a specific value within a string, initialize a string to a fixed value, and do other primitive operations on strings. The x86-64's string instructions are also useful for assigning and comparing arrays, tables, and records, and they may speed up your array-manipulation code considerably. This chapter explores various uses of the string instructions.

14.1 The x86-64 String Instructions

All members of the x86-64 family support five string instructions: movs*x*, cmps*x*, scas*x*, lods*x*, and stos*x*.[1] (*x* = b, w, d, or q for byte, word, double word, or quad word, respectively; this book generally drops the *x* suffix when talking about these string instructions in a general sense.) Moving, comparing, scanning, loading, and storing are the primitives on which you can build most other string operations.

The string instructions operate on *blocks* (contiguous linear arrays) of memory. For example, the movs instruction moves a sequence of bytes from one memory location to another, the cmps instruction compares two blocks of memory, and the scas instruction scans a block of memory for a particular value. The source and destination blocks (and any other values an instruction needs) are not provided as explicit operands, however. Instead, the string instructions use specific registers as operands:

- RSI (source index) register
- RDI (destination index) register
- RCX (count) register
- AL, AX, EAX, and RAX registers
- The direction flag in the FLAGS register

For example, the movs (*move string*) instruction copies RCX elements from the source address specified by RSI to the destination address specified by RDI. Likewise, the cmps instruction compares the string pointed at by RSI, of length RCX, to the string pointed at by RDI.

The sections that follow describe how to use these five instructions, starting with a prefix that makes the instructions do what you'd expect: repeat their operation for each value in the string pointed to by RSI.[2]

14.1.1 The rep, repe, repz, and the repnz and repne Prefixes

By themselves, the string instructions do not operate on strings of data. For example, the movs instruction will only copy a single byte, word, double word, or quad word. The repeat prefixes tell the x86-64 to do a multi-byte string operation—specifically, to repeat a string operation up to RCX times.[3]

The syntax for the string instructions with repeat prefixes is as follows:

```
rep prefix:
    rep movsx (x is b, w, d, or q)
```

---

1. The x86-64 processor supports two additional string instructions: ins, which inputs strings of data from an input port, and outs, which outputs strings of data to an output port. We do not consider these because they are privileged instructions, and you cannot execute them in a standard 64-bit OS application.

2. MASM overloads the meanings of the movsd and cmpsd instructions. With no operands, these are the *move string double* and *compare string double* instructions; with operands, they are the *move scalar double* and *compare scalar double* instructions.

3. The exceptions are the cmps and scas instructions, which repeat *at most* the number of times specified in the RCX register.

```
    rep  stosx
```

```
repe prefix: (Note: repz is a synonym for repe)
    repe  cmpsx
    repe  scasx
```

```
repne prefix: (Note: repnz is a synonym for repne)
    repne  cmpsx
    repne  scasx
```

You don't normally use the repeat prefixes with the lods instruction.

The rep prefix tells the CPU to "repeat this operation the number of times specified by the RCX register." The repe prefix says to "repeat this operation while the comparison is equal, or up to the number of times specified by RCX (whichever condition fails first)." The repne prefix's action is "repeat this operation while the comparison is not equal, or up to the number of times specified by RCX." As it turns out, you'll use repe for most character string comparisons; repne is used mainly with the scasx instructions to locate a specific character within a string (such as a zero-terminating byte).

You can use repeat prefixes to process entire strings with a single instruction. You can use the string instructions, without the repeat prefix, as string primitive operations to synthesize more powerful string operations.

14.1.2 The Direction Flag

The *direction flag* in the FLAGS register controls how the CPU processes strings. If the direction flag is clear, the CPU increments RSI and RDI after operating on each string element. For example, executing movs will move the byte, word, double word, or quad word at RSI to RDI and then increment RSI and RDI by 1, 2, 4, or 8 (respectively). When specifying the rep prefix before this instruction, the CPU increments RSI and RDI for each element in the string (the count in RCX specifies the number of elements). At completion, the RSI and RDI registers will be pointing at the first item beyond the strings.

If the direction flag is set, the x86-64 decrements RSI and RDI after it processes each string element (again, RCX specifies the number of string elements for a repeated string operation). Afterward, the RSI and RDI registers will be pointing at the first byte, word, or double word before the strings.

You can change the direction flag's value by using the cld (*clear direction flag*) and std (*set direction flag*) instructions.

The Microsoft ABI requires that the direction flag be clear upon entry into a (Microsoft ABI–compliant) procedure. Therefore, if you set the direction flag within a procedure, you should always clear that flag when you are finished using it (and especially before calling any other code or returning from the procedure).

14.1.3 The movs Instruction

The movs instruction uses the following syntax:

```
movsb
movsw
movsd
```

```
movsq
rep    movsb
rep    movsw
rep    movsd
rep    movsq
```

The movsb (*move string, bytes*) instruction fetches the byte at address RSI, stores it at address RDI, and then increments or decrements the RSI and RDI registers by 1. If the rep prefix is present, the CPU checks RCX to see whether it contains 0. If not, it moves the byte from RSI to RDI and decrements the RCX register. This process repeats until RCX becomes 0. If RCX contains 0 upon initial execution, the movsb instruction will not copy any data bytes.

The movsw (*move string, words*) instruction fetches the word at address RSI, stores it at address RDI, and then increments or decrements RSI and RDI by 2. If there is a rep prefix, the CPU repeats this procedure RCX times.

The movsd instruction operates in a similar fashion on double words. It increments or decrements RSI and RDI by 4 after each data movement.

Finally, the movsq instruction does the same thing on quad words. It increments or decrements RSI and RDI by 8 after each data movement.

For example, this code segment copies 384 bytes from CharArray1 to CharArray2:

```
CharArray1  byte 384 dup (?)
CharArray2  byte 384 dup (?)
              .
              .
              .
            cld
            lea  rsi, CharArray1
            lea  rdi, CharArray2
            mov  rcx, lengthof(CharArray1) ; = 384
        rep movsb
```

If you substitute movsw for movsb, the preceding code will move 384 words (768 bytes) rather than 384 bytes:

```
WordArray1  word 384 dup (?)
WordArray2  word 384 dup (?)
              .
              .
              .
            cld
            lea  rsi, WordArray1
            lea  rdi, WordArray2
            mov  rcx, lengthof(WordArray1) ; = 384
        rep movsw
```

Remember, the RCX register contains the element count, not the byte count; fortunately, the MASM lengthof operator returns the number of array elements (words), not the number of bytes.

If you've set the direction flag before executing a movsq, movsb, movsw, or movsd instruction, the CPU decrements the RSI and RDI registers after moving each string element. This means that the RSI and RDI registers must point at the last element of their respective strings before executing a movsb, movsw, movsd, or movsq instruction. For example:

```
CharArray1 byte  384 dup (?)
CharArray2 byte  384 dup (?)
            .
            .
            .
        std
        lea rsi, CharArray1[lengthof(CharArray1) - 1]
        lea rdi, CharArray2[lengthof(CharArray1) - 1]
        mov rcx, lengthof(CharArray1);
    rep movsb
        cld
```

Although sometimes processing a string from tail to head is useful (see "Comparing Extended-Precision Integers" on page 834), generally you'll process strings in the forward direction. For one class of string operations, being able to process strings in both directions is mandatory: moving strings when the source and destination blocks overlap. Consider what happens in the following code:

```
CharArray1  byte ?
CharArray2  byte 384 dup (?)
            .
            .
            .
        cld
        lea rsi, CharArray1
        lea rdi, CharArray2
        mov rcx, lengthof(CharArray2);
    rep movsb
```

This sequence of instructions treats CharArray1 and CharArray2 as a pair of 384-byte strings. However, the last 383 bytes in the CharArray1 array overlap the first 383 bytes in the CharArray2 array. Let's trace the operation of this code byte by byte.

When the CPU executes the movsb instruction, it does the following:

1. Copies the byte at RSI (CharArray1) to the byte pointed at by RDI (CharArray2).

2. Increments RSI and RDI, and decrements RCX by 1. Now the RSI register points at CharArray1 + 1 (which is the address of CharArray2), and the RDI register points at CharArray2 + 1.

3. Copies the byte pointed at by RSI to the byte pointed at by RDI. However, this is the byte originally copied from location CharArray1. So, the movsb instruction copies the value originally in location CharArray1 to both locations CharArray2 and CharArray2 + 1.

4. Again increments RSI and RDI, and decrements RCX.

5. Copies the byte from location CharArray1 + 2 (CharArray2 + 1) to location CharArray2 + 2. Once again, this is the value that originally appeared in location CharArray1.

Each repetition of the loop copies the next element in CharArray1 to the next available location in the CharArray2 array. Pictorially, it looks something like Figure 14-1. The result is that the movsb instruction replicates X throughout the string.

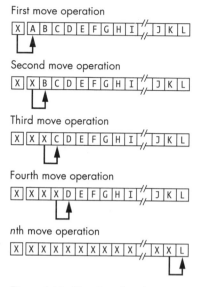

Figure 14-1: Copying data between two overlapping arrays (forward direction)

If you really want to move one array into another when they overlap like this, you should move each element of the source string to the destination string, starting at the end of the two strings, as shown in Figure 14-2.

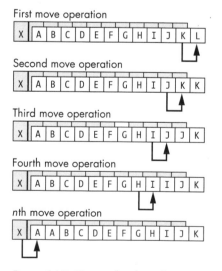

Figure 14-2: Using a backward copy to copy data in overlapping arrays

Setting the direction flag and pointing RSI and RDI at the end of the strings will allow you to (correctly) move one string to another when the two strings overlap and the source string begins at a lower address than the destination string. If the two strings overlap and the source string begins at a higher address than the destination string, clear the direction flag and point RSI and RDI at the beginning of the two strings.

If the two strings do not overlap, you can use either technique to move the strings around in memory. Generally, operating with the direction flag clear is the easiest.

You shouldn't use the movsx instruction to fill an array with a single byte, word, double-word, or quad-word value. Another string instruction, stos, is much better for this purpose.

If you are moving a large number of bytes from one array to another, the copy operation will be faster if you can use the movsq instruction rather than the movsb instruction. If the number of bytes you wish to move is an even multiple of 8, this is a trivial change; just divide the number of bytes to copy by 8, load this value into RCX, and then use the movsq instruction. If the number of bytes is not evenly divisible by 8, you can use the movsq instruction to copy all but the last 1, 2, . . . , 7 bytes of the array (that is, the remainder after you divide the byte count by 8). For example, if you want to efficiently move 4099 bytes, you can do so with the following instruction sequence:

```
    lea  rsi, Source
    lea  rdi, Destination
    mov  rcx, 512      ; Copy 512 qwords = 4096 bytes
rep movsq
    movsw              ; Copy bytes 4097 and 4098
    movsb              ; Copy the last byte
```

Using this technique to copy data never requires more than four movsx instructions because you can copy 1, . . . , 7 bytes with no more than one (each) of the movsb, movsw, and movsd instructions. The preceding scheme is most efficient if the two arrays are aligned on quad-word boundaries. If not, you might want to move the movsb, movsw, or movsd instruction (or all three) before or after the movsq instruction so that movsq works with quad-word–aligned data.

If you do not know the size of the block you are copying until the program executes, you can still use code like the following to improve the performance of a block move of bytes:

```
    lea  rsi, Source
    lea  rdi, Destination
    mov  rcx, Length
    shr  rcx, 3        ; Divide by 8
    jz   lessThan8     ; Execute movsq only if 8 or more bytes

rep movsq              ; Copy the qwords
```

```
lessThan8:
     mov  rcx, Length
     and  rcx, 111b      ; Compute (Length mod 8)
     jz   divisibleBy8   ; Execute movsb only if # of bytes/8 <> 0

  rep movsb             ; Copy the remaining 1 to 7 bytes

divisibleBy8:
```

On many computer systems, the movsq instruction provides about the fastest way to copy bulk data from one location to another. While there are, arguably, faster ways to copy data on certain CPUs, ultimately the memory bus performance is the limiting factor, and the CPUs are generally much faster than the memory bus. Therefore, unless you have a special system, writing fancy code to improve memory-to-memory transfers is probably a waste of time.

Also, Intel has improved the performance of the movsx instructions on later processors so that movsb operates as efficiently as movsw, movsd, and movsq when copying the same number of bytes. On these later processors, it may be more efficient to use movsb to copy the specified number of bytes rather than go through all the complexity outlined previously.

The bottom line is this: if the speed of a block move matters to you, try it several different ways and pick the fastest (or the simplest, if they all run the same speed, which is likely).

14.1.4 The cmps Instruction

The cmps instruction compares two strings. The CPU compares the value referenced by RDI to the value pointed at by RSI. RCX contains the number of elements in the source string when using the repe or repne prefix to compare entire strings. Like the movs instruction, MASM allows several forms of this instruction:

```
cmpsb
cmpsw
cmpsd
cmpsq

repe    cmpsb
repe    cmpsw
repe    cmpsd
repe    cmpsq

repne   cmpsb
repne   cmpsw
repne   cmpsd
repne   cmpsq
```

Without a repeat prefix, the cmps instruction subtracts the value at location RDI from the value at RSI and updates the flags according to the result (which it discards). After comparing the two locations, cmps increments or decrements the RSI and RDI registers by 1, 2, 4, or 8 (for cmpsb, cmpsw, cmpsd, and cmpsq, respectively). cmps increments the RSI and RDI registers if the direction flag is clear and decrements them otherwise.

Remember, the value in the RCX register determines the number of elements to process, not the number of bytes. Therefore, when using cmpsw, RCX specifies the number of words to compare. Likewise, for cmpsd and cmpsq, RCX contains the number of double and quad words to process.

The repe prefix compares successive elements in a string as long as they are equal and RCX is greater than 0. The repne prefix does the same as long the elements are not equal.

After the execution of repne cmps, either the RCX register is 0 (in which case the two strings are totally different), or the RCX contains the number of elements compared in the two strings until a match is found. While this form of the cmps instruction isn't particularly useful for comparing strings, it is useful for locating the first pair of matching items in a couple of byte, word, or double-word arrays.

14.1.4.1 Comparing Character Strings

Character strings are usually compared using *lexicographical ordering*, the standard alphabetical ordering you've grown up with. We compare corresponding elements until encountering a character that doesn't match or the end of the shorter string. If a pair of corresponding characters does not match, compare the two strings based on that single character. If the two strings match up to the length of the shorter string, compare their length. The two strings are equal if and only if their lengths are equal and each corresponding pair of characters in the two strings is identical. The length of a string affects the comparison only if the two strings are identical up to the length of the shorter string. For example, Zebra is less than Zebras because it is the shorter of the two strings; however, Zebra is greater than AAAAAAAAAAH! even though Zebra is shorter.

For (ASCII) character strings, use the cmpsb instruction in the following manner:

1. Clear the direction flag.
2. Load the RCX register with the length of the smaller string.
3. Point the RSI and RDI registers at the first characters in the two strings you want to compare.
4. Use the repe prefix with the cmpsb instruction to compare the strings on a byte-by-byte basis.

NOTE *Even if the strings contain an even number of characters, you cannot use the cmpsw or cmpsd instructions, because they do not compare strings in lexicographical order.*

5. If the two strings are equal, compare their lengths.

The following code compares a couple of character strings:

```
        cld
        mov   rsi, AdrsStr1
        mov   rdi, AdrsStr2
        mov   rcx, LengthSrc
        cmp   rcx, LengthDest
        jbe   srcIsShorter     ; Put the length of the
                               ; shorter string in RCX
        mov   rcx, LengthDest

srcIsShorter:
  repe cmpsb
        jnz   notEq            ; If equal to the length of the
                               ; shorter string, cmp lengths
        mov   rcx, LengthSrc
        cmp   rcx, LengthDest

notEq:
```

If you're using bytes to hold the string lengths, you should adjust this code appropriately (that is, use a `movzx` instruction to load the lengths into RCX).

14.1.4.2 Comparing Extended-Precision Integers

You can also use the `cmps` instruction to compare multi-word integer values (that is, extended-precision integer values). Because of the setup required for a string comparison, this isn't practical for integer values less than six or eight double words in length, but for large integer values, it's excellent.

Unlike with character strings, we cannot compare integer strings by using lexicographical ordering. When comparing strings, we compare the characters from the least significant byte to the most significant byte. When comparing integers, we must compare the values from the most significant byte, word, or double word down to the least significant. So, to compare two 32-byte (256-bit) integer values, use the following code:

```
        std
        lea   rsi, SourceInteger[3 * 8]
        lea   rdi, DestInteger[3 * 8]
        mov   rcx, 4
repe cmpsq
        cld
```

This code compares the integers from their most significant qword down to the least significant qword. The `cmpsq` instruction finishes when the two values are unequal or upon decrementing RCX to 0 (implying that the two values are equal). Once again, the flags provide the result of the comparison.

14.1.5 The scas Instruction

The scas (*scan string*) instruction is used to search for a particular element within a string—for example, to quickly scan for a 0 throughout another string.

Unlike the movs and cmps instructions, scas requires only a destination string (pointed at by RDI). The source operand is the value in the AL (scasb), AX (scasw), EAX (scasd), or RAX (scasq) register. The scas instruction compares the value in the accumulator (AL, AX, EAX, or RAX) against the value pointed at by RDI and then increments (or decrements) RDI by 1, 2, 4, or 8. The CPU sets the flags according to the result of the comparison.

The scas instructions take the following forms:

```
scasb
scasw
scasd
scasq

repe    scasb
repe    scasw
repe    scasd
repe    scasq

repne   scasb
repne   scasw
repne   scasd
repne   scasq
```

With the repe prefix, scas scans the string, searching for an element that does not match the value in the accumulator. When using the repne prefix, scas scans the string, searching for the first element that is equal to the value in the accumulator. This is counterintuitive, because repe scas actually scans through the string while the value in the accumulator is equal to the string operand, and repne scas scans through the string while the accumulator is not equal to the string operand.

Like the cmps and movs instructions, the value in the RCX register specifies the number of elements, not bytes, to process when using a repeat prefix.

14.1.6 The stos Instruction

The stos instruction stores the value in the accumulator at the location specified by RDI. After storing the value, the CPU increments or decrements RDI depending on the state of the direction flag. Although the stos instruction has many uses, its primary use is to initialize arrays and strings to a constant value. For example, if you have a 256-byte array that you want to clear out with 0s, use the following code:

```
    cld
    lea  rdi, DestArray
    mov  rcx, 32        ; 32 quad words = 256 bytes
    xor  rax, rax       ; Zero out RAX
rep stosq
```

This code writes 32 quad words rather than 256 bytes because a single stosq operation is faster (on some older CPUs) than four stosb operations.

The stos instructions take eight forms:

```
stosb
stosw
stosd
stosq

rep   stosb
rep   stosw
rep   stosd
rep   stosq
```

The stosb instruction stores the value in the AL register into the specified memory location(s), stosw stores the AX register into the specified memory location(s), stosd stores EAX into the specified location(s), and stosq stores RAX into the specified location(s). With the rep prefix, this process repeats the number of times specified by the RCX register.

If you need to initialize an array with elements that have different values, you cannot (easily) use stos.

14.1.7 The lods Instruction

The lods instruction copies the byte, word, double word, or quad word pointed at by RSI into the AL, AX, EAX, or RAX register, after which it increments or decrements the RSI register by 1, 2, 4, or 8. Use lods to fetch bytes (lodsb), words (lodsw), double words (lodsd), or quad words (lodsq) from memory for further processing.

Like stos, the lods instructions take eight forms:

```
lodsb
lodsw
lodsd
lodsq

rep   lodsb
rep   lodsw
rep   lodsd
rep   lodsq
```

You will probably never use a repeat prefix with this instruction, because the accumulator register will be overwritten each time lods repeats. At the end of the repeat operation, the accumulator will contain the last value read from memory.[4]

---

4. The repeat prefixes appear here simply because they are allowed. They're not very useful, but they are allowed. About the only use for this form of the instruction is to "touch" items in the cache so they are preloaded into the cache. However, there are better ways to accomplish this.

14.1.8 Building Complex String Functions from lods and stos

You can use the lods and stos instructions to generate any particular string operation. For example, suppose you want a string operation that converts all the uppercase characters in a string to lowercase. You could use the following code:

```
        mov rsi, StringAddress  ; Load string address into RSI
        mov rdi, rsi            ; Also point RDI here
        mov rcx, stringLength   ; Presumably, this was precomputed
        jrcxz skipUC            ; Don't do anything if length is 0
rpt:
        lodsb                   ; Get the next character in the string
        cmp    al, 'A'
        jb     notUpper
        cmp    al, 'Z'
        ja     notUpper
        or     al, 20h          ; Convert to lowercase
notUpper:
        stosb                   ; Store converted char into string
        dec    rcx
        jnz    rpt              ; Zero flag is set when RCX is 0
skipUC:
```

The rpt loop fetches the byte at the location specified by RSI, tests whether it is an uppercase character, converts it to lowercase if it is (leaving it unchanged if it is not), stores the resulting character at the location specified by RDI, and then repeats this process the number of times specified by the value in RCX.

Because the lods and stos instructions use the accumulator as an intermediary location, you can use any accumulator operation to quickly manipulate string elements. This could be something as simple as a toLower (or toUpper) function or as complex as data encryption. You might even use this instruction sequence to compute a hash, checksum, or CRC value while moving data from one string to another. Any operation you would do on a string on a character-by-character basis while moving the string data around is a candidate.

14.2 Performance of the x86-64 String Instructions

In the early x86-64 processors, the string instructions provided the most efficient way to manipulate strings and blocks of data. However, these instructions are not part of Intel's RISC Core instruction set and can be slower (though more compact) than if you did the same operations with discrete instructions. Intel has optimized movs and stos on later processors so that they operate as rapidly as possible, but the other string instructions can be fairly slow.

As always, it's a good idea to implement performance-critical algorithms by using different algorithms (with and without the string instructions) and comparing their performance to determine which solution to use. Because the string instructions run at different speeds relative to other instructions depending on which processor you're using, try your experiments on the processors where you expect your code to run.

NOTE *On most processors, the* movs *instruction is faster than the corresponding discrete instructions. Intel has worked hard to keep* movs *optimized because so much performance-critical code uses it.*

14.3 SIMD String Instructions

The SSE4.2 instruction set extensions include four powerful instructions for manipulating character strings. These instructions were first introduced in 2008, so some computers in use today still might not support them. Always use cpuid to determine if these instructions are available before attempting to use them in wide-distribution commercial applications (see "Using cpuid to Differentiate Instruction Sets" in Chapter 11).

The four SSE4.2 instructions that process text and string fragments are as follows:

PCMPESTRI   Packed compare explicit-length strings, return index

PCMPESTRM   Packed compare explicit-length strings, return mask

PCMPISTRI   Packed compare implicit-length strings, return index

PCMPISTRM   Packed compare implicit-length strings, return mask

Implicit-length strings use a sentinel (trailing) byte to mark the end of the string, specifically, a zero-terminating byte (or word, in the case of Unicode characters). *Explicit-length strings* are those for which you supply a string length.

Instructions that produce an index return the index of the first (or last) matching occurrence within the source string. Instructions that return a bit mask return an array of 0 or (all) 1 bits that mark each occurrence of the match within the two input strings.

The packed compare string instructions are among the most complex in the x86-64 instruction set. The syntax for these instructions is

pcmpXstrY xmm_{src1}, xmm_{src2}/mem_{src2}, imm_8
vpcmpXstrY xmm_{src1}, xmm_{src2}/mem_{src2}, imm_8

where X is E or I, and Y is I or M. Both forms use 128-bit operands (no 256-bit YMM registers for the v-prefixed form in this case), and, unlike most SSE instructions, the (v)pcmpXstrY instructions allow memory operands that are not aligned on a 16-byte boundary (they would be nearly useless for their intended operation if they required 16-byte-aligned memory operands).

The (v)pcmpXstrY instructions compare corresponding bytes or words in a pair of XMM registers, combine the results of the individual comparisons into a vector (bit mask), and return the results for all the comparisons. The imm_8 operand controls various comparison attributes as described in "Type of Comparison" on the following page.

14.3.1 Packed Compare Operand Sizes

Bits 0 and 1 of the immediate operand specify the size and type of the string elements. The elements can be bytes or words, or they can be treated as unsigned or signed values for the comparison (see Table 14-1).

Bit 0 specifies word (Unicode) or byte (ASCII) operands. Bit 1 specifies whether the operands are signed or unsigned. Generally, for character strings, you use unsigned comparisons. However, in certain situations (or when processing strings of integers rather than characters), you may want to specify signed comparisons.

Table 14-1: Packed Compare imm_8 Bits 0 and 1

Bit(s)	Bit value	Meaning
0–1	00	Both source operands contain 16 unsigned bytes.
	01	Both source operands contain 8 unsigned words.
	10	Both source operands contain 16 signed bytes.
	11	Both source operands contain 8 signed words.

14.3.2 Type of Comparison

Bits 2 and 3 of the immediate operand specify how the instruction will compare the two strings. There are four comparison types, which test characters from one string against the set of characters in the second, test characters from one string against a range of characters, do a straight string comparison, or search for a substring within another string (see Table 14-2).

Table 14-2: Packed Compare imm_8 Bits 2 and 3

Bit(s)	Bit value	Meaning
2–3	00	Equal any: compares each character in the second source string against a set of characters appearing in the first source operand.
	01	Ranges: compares each value in the second source operand against a set of ranges specified by the first source operand.
	10	Equal each: compares each corresponding element for equality (character-by-character comparison of the two operands).
	11	Equal ordered: searches for the substring specified by the first operand within the string specified by the second operand.

Bits 2 to 3 specify the type of comparison to perform (the *aggregate operation* in Intel terminology). *Equal each* (10b) is probably the easiest comparison to understand. The packed compare instruction will compare each corresponding character in the string (up to the length of the string—more on that later) and set a Boolean flag for the result of the comparison of each byte or word in the string, as shown in Figure 14-3. This is comparable to the operation of the C/C++ memcmp() or strcmp() functions.

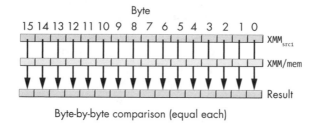

Byte

15 14 13 12 11 10 9 8 7 6 5 4 3 2 1 0

XMM$_{src1}$

XMM/mem

Result

Byte-by-byte comparison (equal each)

Figure 14-3: Equal each aggregate comparison operation

The *equal any* comparison compares each byte in the second source operand to see whether it is any of the characters found in the first source operand (XMM$_{src2}$/mem$_{src2}$). For example, if XMM$_{src1}$ contains the string abcdefABCDEF (and four 0 bytes), and XMM$_{src2}$/mem$_{src2}$ contains 12AF89C0, the resulting comparison would yield 00101100b (1s in the character positions corresponding to the A, F, and C characters). Also note that the first character (1) maps to bit 0, and the A and F characters map to bits 2 and 3. This is similar to the strspn() and strcspn() functions in the C Standard Library.

The *equal ordered* comparison searches for each occurrence of the string in XMM$_{src1}$ that can be found in the XMM$_{src2}$/mem$_{src2}$ operand. For example, if the XMM$_{src2}$/mem$_{src2}$ operand contains the string never need shine and the XMM$_{src1}$ operand has the string ne (padded with 0s), then the equal ordered comparison produces the vector 0100000001000001b. This is similar to the strstr() function in the C Standard Library.

The *ranges* comparison aggregate operation breaks the entries in the XMM$_{src1}$ operand into pairs (at even and odd indexes in the register). The first element (byte or word) specifies a lower bound, and the second entry specifies an upper bound. The XMM$_{src1}$ register supports up to eight byte ranges or four word ranges (if you need fewer ranges, pad the remaining pairs with 0s). This aggregate operation compares each character in the XMM$_{src2}$/mem$_{src2}$ operand against each of these ranges and stores true in the resultant vector if the character is within one of the specified ranges (inclusive) and false if it is outside all of these ranges.

14.3.3 Result Polarity

Bits 4 and 5 of the immediate operand specify the result polarity (see Table 14-3). This chapter will fully discuss the meaning of these bits in a moment (some additional commentary is necessary).

Table 14-3: Packed Compare *imm$_8$*
Bits 4 and 5

Bit(s)	Bit value	Meaning
4–5	00	Positive polarity
	01	Negative polarity
	10	Positive masked
	11	Negative masked

14.3.4 Output Processing

Bit 6 of the immediate operand specifies the instruction result (see Table 14-4). The packed compare instructions do not use bit 7; it should always be 0.

Table 14-4: Packed Compare imm_8 Bit 6 (and 7)

Bit(s)	Bit value	Meaning
6	0	(v)pcomXstri only, the index returned in ECX is the first result. (v)pcomXstrm only, the mask appears in the LO bits of XMM0 with zero extension to 128 bits.
	1	(v)pcomXstri only, the index returned in ECX is the last result. (v)pcomXstrm only, expand the bit mask into a byte or word mask.
7	0	This bit is reserved and should always be 0.

The (v)pcmpestrm and (v)pcmpistrm instructions produce a bit-mask result and store it into the XMM0 register (this is fixed—the CPU does not determine this by the operands to these instructions). If bit 6 of the imm_8 operand contains a 0, these two instructions pack this bit mask into 8 or 16 bits and store them into the LO 8 (or 16) bits of XMM0, zero-extending that value through the upper bits of XMM0. If imm_8 bit 6 contains a 1, these instructions will store the bit mask (all 1 bits per byte or word) throughout the XMM0 register.[5]

The (v)pcmpestri and (v)pcmpistri instructions produce an index result and return this value in the ECX register.[6] If bit 6 of the imm_8 operand contains a 0, these two instructions return the index of the LO set bit in the result bit mask (that is, the first matching comparison). If bit 6 of the imm_8 operand is 1, these instructions return the index of the highest-order set bit in the resultant bit mask (that is, the last matching comparison). If there are no set bits in the result bit mask, these instructions return 16 (for byte comparisons) or 8 (for word comparisons) in the ECX register. Although these instructions internally generate a bit mask result in order to calculate the index, they do not overwrite the XMM0 register (as do the (v)pcmpestrm and (v)pcmpistrm instructions).

14.3.5 Packed String Compare Lengths

The (v)pcmpXstrY instructions have a 16-byte (XMM register size) comparison limit. This is true even on AVX processors with 32-byte YMM registers. To compare larger strings requires executing multiple (v)pcmpXstrY instructions.

The (v)pcmpistri and (v)pcmpistrm instructions use an implicit string length. The strings appear in the XMM registers or memory with the first character (if any) appearing in the LO byte followed by the remaining

---

5. Byte comparisons will require 16 bits or 16 bytes, while word comparisons will require 8 bits or 8 bytes to hold the bit mask.

6. Zero-extended into RCX; that is, the upper 32 bits of RCX will contain 0 after the packed compare instructions that produce an index value.

characters in the string. The strings end with a zero-terminating byte or word. If there are more than 16 characters (if byte strings, or 8 characters if word strings), then the register (or 128-bit memory) size delimits the string.

The (v)pcmpestri and (v)pcmpestrm instructions use explicitly supplied string lengths. The RAX and EAX registers specify the string length for the string appearing in XMM$_{src1}$, and the RDX and EDX registers specify the string length for the string appearing in XMM$_{src2}$/mem$_{src2}$. If the string length is greater than 16 (for byte strings) or 8 (for word strings), the instruction saturates the length at 16 or 8. Also, the (v)pcmpestri and (v)pcmpestrm instructions take the absolute value of the length, so –1 to –16 is equivalent to 1 to 16.

The reason the explicit-length instructions saturate the length to 16 (or 8) is to allow a program to process larger strings in a loop. By processing 16 bytes (or 8 words) at a time in a loop and decrementing the overall string length (from some large value down to 0), the packed string operations will operate on 16 or 8 characters per loop iteration until the very last loop iteration. At that point, the instructions will process the remaining (total length mod 16 or 8) characters in the string.

The reason the explicit-length instructions take the absolute value of the length is to allow code that processes large strings to either decrement the loop counter (from a large positive value) to 0 or increment the loop counter (from a negative value) toward 0, whichever is more convenient for the program.

Whenever the length (implicit or explicit) is less than 16 (for bytes) or 8 (for words), certain characters in the XMM register (or 128-bit memory location) will be invalid. Specifically, every character after the zero-terminating character (for implicit-length strings) or beyond the count in RAX and EAX or RDX and EDX will be invalid. Regardless of the presence of invalid characters, the packed compare instructions still produce an intermediate bit vector result by comparing all characters in the string.

Because the string lengths of the two input strings (in XMM$_{src1}$ and XMM$_{src2}$/mem$_{src2}$) are not necessarily equal, there are four possible situations: src1 and src2 are both invalid, exactly one of the two source operands is invalid (and the other is valid, so there are two cases here), or both are valid. Depending on which operands are valid or invalid, the packed compare instructions may force the result to true or false. Table 14-5 lists how these instructions force results, based on the type of comparison (aggregate operation) specified by the imm$_8$ operand.

Table 14-5: Comparison Result When Source 1 and Source 2 Are Valid or Invalid

Src1	Src2	Equal any	Ranges	Equal each	Equal ordered
Invalid	Invalid	Force false	Force false	Force true	Force true
Invalid	Valid	Force false	Force false	Force false	Force true
Valid	Invalid	Force false	Force false	Force false	Force false
Valid	Valid	Result	Result	Result	Result

To understand the entries in this table, you must consider each comparison type individually.

The *equal any* comparison checks whether each character appearing in src2 appears anywhere in the set of characters specified by src1. If a character in src1 is invalid, that means the instructions are comparing against a character that is not in the set; in this situation, you want to return false (regardless of src2's validity). If src1 is valid but src2 is invalid, you're at (or beyond) the end of the string; that's not a valid comparison, so equal any also forces a false result in this situation.

The *ranges* comparison is also (in a sense) comparing a source string (src2) against a set of characters (specified by the ranges in src1). Therefore, the packed compare instructions force false if either (or both) operands are invalid for the same reasons as *equal any* comparisons.

The *equal each* comparison is the traditional string comparison operation, comparing the string in src2 to the string in src1. If the corresponding character in both strings is invalid, you've moved beyond the end of both strings. The packed compare instructions force the result to true in this situation because these instructions are, effectively, comparing empty strings at this point (and empty strings are equal). If a character in one string is valid but the corresponding character in the other string is invalid, you're comparing actual characters against an empty string, which is always *not equal*; hence, the packed string comparison instructions force a false result.

The *equal ordered* operation searches for the substring XMM_{src1} within the larger string XMM_{src2}/mem_{src2}. If you've gone beyond the end of both strings, you're comparing empty strings (and one empty string is always a substring of another empty string), so the packed comparison instructions return a true result. If you've reached the end of the string in src1 (the substring to search for), the result is true even if there are more characters in src2; hence, the packed comparisons return true in this situation. However, if you've reached the end of the src2 string but not the end of the src1 (substring) string, there is no way that *equal ordered* will return true, so the packed comparison instructions force a false in this situation.

If the polarity bits (bits 4 to 5 of *imm8*) contain 00b or 10b, the polarity bits do not affect the comparison operation. If the polarity bits are 01b, the packed string comparison instructions invert all the bits in the temporary bit map result before copying the data to XMM0 ((v)pcmpistrm and (v)pcmpestrm) or calculating the index ((v)pcmpestri and (v)pcmpistri). If the polarity setting is 11b, the packed string comparison instructions invert the resultant bit if and only if the corresponding src2 character is valid.

14.3.6 Packed String Comparison Results

The last thing to note about the packed string comparison instructions is how they affect the CPU flags. These instructions are unusual among the SSE/AVX instructions insofar as they affect the condition codes. However, they do not affect the condition codes in standard ways (for example, you cannot use the carry and zero flags to test for string less than or greater than, as you can with the cmps instructions). Instead, these instructions over-load the meanings of the carry, zero, sign, and overflow flags; furthermore, each instruction defines the meaning of these flags independently.

All eight instructions—(v)pcmpestri, (v)pcmpistri, (v)pcmpestrm, and (v)pcmpistrm—clear the carry flag if all of the bits in the (internal) result bit map are 0 (no comparison); these instructions set the carry flag if there is at least 1 bit set in the bit map. Note that the carry flag is set or cleared after the application of the polarity.

The zero flag indicates whether the src2 length is less than 16 (8 for word characters). For the (v)pcmpestri and (v)pcmpestrm instructions, the zero flag is set if EDX is less than 16 (8); for the (v)pcmpistri and (v)pcmpistrm instructions, the zero flag is set if XMM_{src2}/mem_{src2} contains a null character.

The sign flag indicates whether the src1 length is less than 16 (8 for word characters). For the (v)pcmpestri and (v)pcmpestrm instructions, the sign flag is set if EAX is less than 16 (8); for the (v)pcmpistri and (v)pcmpistrm instructions, the zero flag is set if XMM_{src1} contains a null character.

The overflow flag contains the setting for bit 0 of the result bit map (that is, whether the first character of the source string was a match). This can be useful after an equal ordered comparison to see if the substring is a prefix of the larger string (for example).

14.4   Alignment and Memory Management Unit Pages

The (v)pcmpXstrY instructions are nice insofar as they do not require their memory operand to be 16-byte aligned. However, this lack of alignment creates a special problem of its own: it is possible for a single (v)pcmpXstrY instruction memory access to cross an MMU page boundary. As noted in "Memory Access and 4K Memory Management Unit Pages" in Chapter 3, some MMU pages might not be accessible and will generate a general pro-tection fault if the CPU attempts to read data from them.

If the string is less than 16 bytes in length and ends before the page boundary, using (v)pcmpXstrY to access that data may cause an inadvertent page fault when it reads a full 16 bytes from memory, including data beyond the end of the string. Though accessing data beyond the string that crosses into a new, inaccessible MMU page is a rare situation, it can happen, so you want to ensure you don't access data across MMU page boundaries unless the next MMU page contains actual data.

If you have aligned an address on a 16-byte boundary and you access 16 bytes from memory starting at that address, you never have to worry about crossing into a new MMU page. MMU pages contain an integral multiple of 16 bytes (there are 256 16-byte blocks in an MMU page). If the CPU accesses 16 bytes starting at a 16-byte boundary, the last 15 bytes of that block will fall into the same MMU page as the first byte. This is why most SSE memory accesses are okay: they require 16-byte-aligned memory operands. The exceptions are the unaligned move instructions and the (v)pcmpXstrY instructions.

You typically use the unaligned move instructions (for example, `movdqu` and `movupd`) to move 16 actual bytes of data into an SSE/AVX register; therefore, these instructions don't usually access extra bytes in memory. The `(v)pcmpXstrY` instructions, however, often access data bytes beyond the end of the actual string. These instructions read a full 16 bytes from memory even if the string consumes fewer than 16 of those bytes. Therefore, when using the `(v)pcmpXstrY` instructions (and the other unaligned moves, if you're using them to read beyond the end of a data structure), you should ensure that the memory address you are supplying is at least 16 bytes before the end of an MMU page, or that the next page in memory contains valid data.

As Chapter 3 notes, there is no machine instruction that lets you test a page in memory to see if the application can legally access that page. So you have to ensure that no memory accesses by the `(v)pcmpXstrY` instructions will cross a page boundary. The next chapter provides several examples.

14.5 For More Information

Agner Fog is one of the world's foremost experts on optimization of x86(-64) assembly language. His website (*https://www.agner.org/optimize/#manuals/*) has a lot to say about optimizing memory moves and other string instructions. This website is highly recommended if you want to write fast string code in x86 assembly language.

T. Herselman has spent a huge amount of time writing fast `memcpy` functions. You can find his results at *https://www.codeproject.com/Articles/1110153/ Apex-memmove-the-fastest-memcpy-memmove-on-x-x-EVE/* (or just search the web for *Apex memmove*). The length of this code will, undoubtedly, convince you to stick with the `movs` instruction (which runs fairly fast on modern x86-64 CPUs).

14.6 Test Yourself

1. What size operands do the generic string instructions support?
2. What are the five general-purpose string instructions?
3. What size operands do the `pcmpXstrY` instructions support?
4. What registers does the `rep movsb` instruction use?
5. What registers does the `cmpsw` instruction use?
6. What registers does the `repne scasb` instruction use?
7. What registers does the `stosd` instruction use?
8. If you want to increment the RSI and RDI registers after each string operation, what direction flag setting do you use?
9. If you want to decrement the RSI and RDI registers after each string operation, what direction flag setting do you use?
10. If a function or procedure modifies the direction flag, what should that function do before returning?

11. The Microsoft ABI requires a function to _____ the direction flag before returning if it modifies the flag's value.

12. Which string instructions have Intel optimized for performance on later x86-64 CPUs?

13. When would you want to set the direction flag prior to using a movs instruction?

14. When would you want to clear the direction flag prior to using a movs instruction?

15. What can happen if the direction flag is not set properly when you are executing a movs instruction?

16. Which string prefix would you normally use with cmpsb to test two strings to see if they are equal?

17. When comparing two character strings, how should the direction flag normally be set?

18. Do you need to test whether RCX is 0 before executing a string instruction with a repeat prefix?

19. If you wanted to search for a zero-terminating byte in a C/C++ string, what (general-purpose) string instruction would be most appropriate?

20. If you wanted to fill a block of memory with 0s, what string instruction would be most appropriate?

21. If you wanted to concoct your own string operations, what string instruction(s) would you use?

22. Which string instruction would you typically never use with a repeat prefix?

23. Before using one of the pcmpXstrY instructions, what should you do?

24. Which SSE string instructions automatically handle zero-terminated strings?

25. Which SSE string instructions require an explicit length value?

26. Where do you pass explicit lengths to the pcmpXstrY instructions?

27. Which pcmpXstrY aggregate operation searches for characters belonging to a set of characters?

28. Which pcmpXstrY aggregate operation compares two strings?

29. Which pcmpXstrY aggregate operation checks whether one string is a substring of another?

30. What is the problem with the pcmpXstrY instruction and MMU pages?

15

MANAGING COMPLEX PROJECTS

Most assembly language source files aren't stand-alone programs. They're components of a large set of source files, in different languages, compiled and linked together to form complex applications. *Programming in the large* is the term software engineers have coined to describe the processes, methodologies, and tools for handling the development of large software projects.

While everyone has their own idea of what *large* is, *separate compilation* is one of the more popular techniques that support programming in the large. Using separate compilation, you first break your large source files into manageable chunks. Then you compile the separate files into object code modules. Finally, you link the object modules together to form a complete program. If you need to make a small change to one of the modules, you need to reassemble only that one module; you do not need to reassemble the entire program. Once you've debugged and tested a large section of your code, continuing to assemble that same code when you make a small change to another part of your program is a waste of time. Imagine having to wait 20 or 30 minutes on a fast PC to assemble a program to which you've made a one-line change!

The following sections describe the tools MASM provides for separate compilation and how to effectively employ these tools in your programs for modularity and reduced development time.

15.1 The include Directive

The include directive, when encountered in a source file, merges a specified file into the compilation at the point of the include directive. The syntax for the include directive is

---

include *filename*

---

where *filename* is a valid filename. By convention, MASM include files have an *.inc* (include) suffix, but the name of any file containing MASM assembly language source will work fine. A file being included into another file during assembly may itself include files.

Using the include directive by itself does not provide separate compilation. You *could* use the include directive to break a large source file into separate modules and join these modules together when you compile your file. The following example would include the *print.inc* and *getTitle.inc* files during the compilation of your program:

```
include  print.inc
include  getTitle.inc
```

Now your program will benefit from modularity. Alas, you will not save any development time. The include directive inserts the source file at the point of the include during compilation, exactly as though you had typed that code yourself. MASM still has to compile the code, and that takes time. If you are including a large number of source files (such as a huge library) into your assembly, the compilation process could take *forever*.

In general, you should *not* use the include directive to include source code as shown in the preceding example.[1] Instead, you should use the include directive to insert a common set of constants, types, external procedure declarations, and other such items into a program. Typically, an assembly language include file does *not* contain any machine code (outside of a macro; see Chapter 13 for details). The purpose of using include files in this manner will become clearer after you see how the external declarations work.

---

1. There is nothing wrong with this, except that it does not take advantage of separate compilation.

15.2   Ignoring Duplicate Include Operations

As you begin to develop sophisticated modules and libraries, you will eventually discover a big problem: some header files need to include other header files. Well, this isn't actually a big problem, but a problem will occur when one header file includes another, and that second header file includes another, and that third header file includes another, and . . . that last header file includes the first header file. Now *this* is a big problem, because it creates an infinite loop in the compiler and makes MASM complain about duplicate symbol definitions. After all, the first time it reads the header file, it processes all the declarations in that file; the second time around, it views all those symbols as duplicate symbols.

The standard technique for ignoring duplicate includes, well-known to C/C++ programmers, is to use conditional assembly to have MASM ignore the content of an include file. (See "Conditional Assembly (Compile-Time Decisions)" in Chapter 13.) The trick is to place an ifndef (*if not defined*) statement around all statements in the include file. You specify the include file's filename as the ifndef operand, substituting underlines for periods (or any other undefined symbol). Then, immediately after the ifndef statement, you define that symbol (using a numeric equate and assigning the symbol the constant 0 is typical). Here's an example of this ifndef usage in action:

```
           ifndef  myinclude_inc   ; Filename: myinclude.inc
myinclude_inc =      0

Put all the source code lines for the include file here

; The following statement should be the last non-blank line
; in the source file:

           endif  ; myinclude_inc
```

On the second inclusion, MASM simply skips over the contents of the include file (including any include directives), which prevents the infinite loop and all the duplicate symbol definitions.

15.3   Assembly Units and External Directives

An *assembly unit* is the assembly of a source file plus any files it includes or indirectly includes. An assembly unit produces a single *.obj* file after assembly. The Microsoft linker takes multiple object files (produced by MASM or other compilers, such as MSVC) and combines them into a single executable unit (an *.exe* file). The main purpose of this section (and, indeed, this whole chapter) is to describe how these assembly units (*.obj* files) communicate linkage information to one another during the linking process. Assembly units are the basis for creating modular programs in assembly language.

To use MASM's assembly unit facilities, you must create at least two source files. One file contains a set of variables and procedures used by the second. The second file uses those variables and procedures without knowing how they're implemented.

Instead of using the include directive to create modular programs, which wastes time because MASM must recompile bug-free code every time you assemble the main program, a much better solution would be to preassemble the debugged modules and link the object code modules together. This is what the public, extern, and externdef directives allow you to do.

Technically, all of the programs appearing in this book up to this point have been separately assembled modules (which happen to link with a C/C++ main program rather than another assembly language module). The assembly language main program named asmMain is nothing but a function compatible with C++ that the generic *c.cpp* program has called from its main program. Consider the body of asmMain from Listing 2-1 in Chapter 2:

```
; Here is the "asmMain" function.

        public   asmMain
asmMain proc
           .
           .
           .
asmMain endp
```

The public asmMain statement has been included in every program that has had an asmMain function without any definition or explanation. Well, now it's time to deal with that oversight.

Normal symbols in a MASM source file are *private* to that particular source file and are inaccessible from other source files (which don't directly include the file containing those private symbols, of course). That is, the *scope* of most symbols in a source file is limited to those lines of code within that particular source file (and any files it includes). The public directive tells MASM to make the specified symbol global to the assembly unit—accessible by other assembly units during the link phase. Through the public asmMain statement in the example programs appearing throughout this book, these sample programs have made the asmMain symbol global to the source file containing them so that the *c.cpp* program can call the asmMain function.

Simply making a symbol public is insufficient to use that symbol in another source file. The source file that wants to use the symbol must also declare that symbol as an *external* symbol. This notifies the linker that it will have to patch in the address of a public symbol whenever the file with the external declaration uses that symbol. For example, the *c.cpp* source file defines the asmMain symbol as external in the following lines of code (for what it's worth, this declaration also defines the external symbols getTitle and readLine):

```
// extern "C" namespace prevents
// "name mangling" by the C++
// compiler.

extern "C"
{
```

```
// asmMain is the assembly language
// code's "main program":

void asmMain(void);

// getTitle returns a pointer to a
// string of characters from the
// assembly code that specifies the
// title of that program (which makes
// this program generic and usable
// with a large number of sample
// programs in "The Art of 64-Bit
// Assembly").

char *getTitle(void);

// C++ function that the assembly
// language program can call:

int readLine(char *dest, int maxLen);

};
```

Note, in this example, that readLine is a C++ function defined in the *c.cpp* source file. C/C++ does not have an explicit public declaration. Instead, if you supply the source code for a function in a source file that declares that function to be external, C/C++ will automatically make that symbol public by virtue of the external declaration.

MASM actually has two external symbol declaration directives: extern and externdef.[2] These two directives use the syntax

```
extern    symbol:type  {optional_list_of_symbol:type_pairs}
externdef symbol:type  {optional_list_of_symbol:type_pairs}
```

where *symbol* is the identifier you want to use from another assembly unit, and *type* is the data type of that symbol. The data type can be any of the following:

- proc, which indicates that the symbol is a procedure (function) name or a statement label
- Any MASM built-in data type (such as byte, word, dword, qword, oword, and so on)
- Any user-defined data type (such as a struct name)
- abs, which indicates a constant value

The abs type isn't for declaring generic external constants such as someConst = 0. Pure constant declarations, such as this one, would normally appear in a header file (an include file), which this section will describe

---

2. Technically, MASM has three external directives; extrn is an older name for extern. They are just synonyms. This book uses the extern variant.

shortly. Instead, the abs type is generally reserved for constants that are based on code offsets within an object module. For example, if you have the following code in an assembly unit,

```
         public someLen
someStr  byte    "abcdefg"
someLen  =       $-someStr
```

someLen's type, in an extern declaration, would be abs.

Both directives use a comma-delimited list to allow multiple symbol declarations; for example:

```
extern p:proc, b:byte, d:dword, a:abs
```

I'd argue, however, that your programs will be more readable if you limit your external declarations to one symbol per statement.

When you place an extern directive in your program, MASM treats that declaration the same as any other symbol declaration. If the symbol already exists, MASM will generate a symbol-redefinition error. Generally, you should place all external declarations near the beginning of the source file to avoid any scoping or forward reference issues. Because the public directive does not actually define the symbol, the placement of the public directive is not as critical. Some programmers put all the public declarations at the beginning of a source file; others put the public declaration right before the definition of the symbol (as I've done with the asmMain symbol in most of the same programs). Either position is fine.

15.4 Header Files in MASM

Because a public symbol from one source file can be used by many assembly units, a small problem develops: you have to replicate the extern directive in all the files that use that symbol. For a small number of symbols, this is not much of a problem. However, as the number of external symbols increases, maintaining all these external symbols across multiple source files becomes burdensome. The MASM solution is the same as the C/C++ solution: header files.

Header files are include files that contain external (and other) declarations that are common among multiple assembly units. They are called *header files* because the include statement that injects their code into a source file normally appears at the beginning (at the *head*) of the source file that uses them. This turns out to be the primary use of include files in MASM: to include external (and other) common declarations.

15.5 The externdef Directive

When you start using header files with large sets of library modules (assembly units), you'll quickly discover a huge problem with the extern directive. Typically, you will create a single header file for a large set of library functions, with each function possibly appearing in its own assembly unit. Some library functions might use other functions in the same *library module* (a collection of object files); therefore, that particular library function's source file might want to include the header file for the library in order to reference the external name of the other library function.

Unfortunately, if the header file contains the external definition for the function in the current source file, a symbol redefinition error occurs:

```
; header.inc
            ifndef    header_inc
header_inc =        0

            extern    func1:proc
            extern    func2:proc

            endif   ; header_inc
```

Assembly of the following source file produces an error because func1 is already defined in the *header.inc* include file:

```
; func1.asm

            include header.inc

            .code

func1       proc
               .
               .
               .
            call  func2
               .
               .
               .
func1       endp
            end
```

C/C++ doesn't suffer from this problem because the external keyword doubles as both a public and an external declaration.

To overcome this problem, MASM introduced the externdef directive. This directive is similar to C/C++'s external directive: it behaves like an extern directive when the symbol is not present in a source file, and it behaves like a public directive when the symbol is defined in a source file. In addition, multiple externdef declarations for the same symbol may appear in a source file (though they should specify the same type for the symbol if multiple declarations do appear). Consider the previous *header.inc* header file modified to use externdef definitions:

```
; header.inc
            ifndef    header_inc
header_inc =        0
```

```
            externdef   func1:proc
            externdef   func2:proc

       endif        ; header_inc
```

Using this header file, the *func1.asm* assembly unit will compile correctly.

15.6 Separate Compilation

Way back in "The MASM Include Directive" in Chapter 11, I started putting the print and getTitle functions in include files so that I could simply include them in every source file that needed to use these functions rather than manually cutting and pasting these functions into every program. Clearly, these are good examples of programs that should be made into assembly units and linked with other programs rather than being included during assembly.

Listing 15-1 is a header file that incorporates the necessary print and getTitle declarations:[3]

```
; aoalib.inc - Header file containing external function
;               definitions, constants, and other items used
;               by code in "The Art of 64-Bit Assembly."

            ifndef      aoalib_inc
aoalib_inc  equ         0

; Constant definitions:

; nl (newline constant):

nl          =           10

; SSE4.2 feature flags (in ECX):

SSE42       =           00180000h       ; Bits 19 and 20
AVXSupport  =           10000000h       ; Bit 28

; CPUID bits (EAX = 7, EBX register):

AVX2Support =           20h             ; Bit 5 = AVX

************************************************************

; External data declarations:

            externdef   ttlStr:byte
```

---

3. This source file is also part of the generic *aoalib.inc* header file used to encompass various
library functions appearing throughout this book.

```
*********************************************************

; External function declarations:

            externdef    print:qword
            externdef    getTitle:proc

; Definition of C/C++ printf function that
; the print function will call (and some
; AoA sample programs call this directly,
; as well).

            externdef    printf:proc

            endif        ; aoalib_inc
```

Listing 15-1: aoalib.inc header file

Listing 15-2 contains the print function used in "The MASM Include Directive" in Chapter 11 converted to an assembly unit.

```
; print.asm - Assembly unit containing the SSE/AVX dynamically
;              selectable print procedures.

            include aoalib.inc

            .data
            align    qword
print       qword    choosePrint    ; Pointer to print function

            .code

; print - "Quick" form of printf that allows the format string to
;          follow the call in the code stream. Supports up to five
;          additional parameters in RDX, R8, R9, R10, and R11.

; This function saves all the Microsoft ABI-volatile,
; parameter, and return result registers so that code
; can call it without worrying about any registers being
; modified (this code assumes that Windows ABI treats
; YMM6 to YMM15 as nonvolatile).

; Of course, this code assumes that AVX instructions are
; available on the CPU.

; Allows up to 5 arguments in:

;   RDX - Arg #1
;   R8  - Arg #2
;   R9  - Arg #3
;   R10 - Arg #4
;   R11 - Arg #5
```

```
                ; Note that you must pass floating-point values in
                ; these registers as well. The printf function
                ; expects real values in the integer registers.

                ; There are two versions of this program, one that
                ; will run on CPUs without AVX capabilities (no YMM
                ; registers) and one that will run on CPUs that
                ; have AVX capabilities (YMM registers). The difference
                ; between the two is which registers they preserve
                ; (print_SSE preserves only XMM registers and will
                ; run properly on CPUs that don't have YMM register
                ; support; print_AVX will preserve the volatile YMM
                ; registers on CPUs with AVX support).

                ; On first call, determine if we support AVX instructions
                ; and set the "print" pointer to point at print_AVX or
                ; print_SSE:

choosePrint proc
                push    rax             ; Preserve registers that get
                push    rbx             ; tweaked by CPUID
                push    rcx
                push    rdx

                mov     eax, 1
                cpuid
                test    ecx, AVXSupport ; Test bit 28 for AVX
                jnz     doAVXPrint

                lea     rax, print_SSE  ; From now on, call
                mov     print, rax      ; print_SSE directly

; Return address must point at the format string
; following the call to this function! So we have
; to clean up the stack and JMP to print_SSE.

                pop     rdx
                pop     rcx
                pop     rbx
                pop     rax
                jmp     print_SSE

doAVXPrint: lea     rax, print_AVX  ; From now on, call
                mov     print, rax      ; print_AVX directly

; Return address must point at the format string
; following the call to this function! So we have
; to clean up the stack and JMP to print_AUX.

                pop     rdx
                pop     rcx
                pop     rbx
                pop     rax
                jmp     print_AVX
```

```
choosePrint endp

; Version of print that will preserve volatile
; AVX registers (YMM0 to YMM3):

thestr      byte "YMM4:%I64x", nl, 0
print_AVX   proc

; Preserve all the volatile registers
; (be nice to the assembly code that
; calls this procedure):

            push    rax
            push    rbx
            push    rcx
            push    rdx
            push    r8
            push    r9
            push    r10
            push    r11

; YMM0 to YMM7 are considered volatile, so preserve them:

            sub     rsp, 256
            vmovdqu ymmword ptr [rsp + 000], ymm0
            vmovdqu ymmword ptr [rsp + 032], ymm1
            vmovdqu ymmword ptr [rsp + 064], ymm2
            vmovdqu ymmword ptr [rsp + 096], ymm3
            vmovdqu ymmword ptr [rsp + 128], ymm4
            vmovdqu ymmword ptr [rsp + 160], ymm5
            vmovdqu ymmword ptr [rsp + 192], ymm6
            vmovdqu ymmword ptr [rsp + 224], ymm7


            push    rbp

returnAdrs  textequ <[rbp + 328]>

            mov     rbp, rsp
            sub     rsp, 256
            and     rsp, -16

; Format string (passed in RCX) is sitting at
; the location pointed at by the return address;
; load that into RCX:

            mov     rcx, returnAdrs

; To handle more than three arguments (four counting
; RCX), you must pass data on stack. However, to the
; print caller, the stack is unavailable, so use
; R10 and R11 as extra parameters (could be just
; junk in these registers, but pass them just
; in case).
```

```
                mov     [rsp + 32], r10
                mov     [rsp + 40], r11
                call    printf

; Need to modify the return address so
; that it points beyond the zero-terminating byte.
; Could use a fast strlen function for this, but
; printf is so slow it won't really save us anything.

                mov     rcx, returnAdrs
                dec     rcx
skipTo0:        inc     rcx
                cmp     byte ptr [rcx], 0
                jne     skipTo0
                inc     rcx
                mov     returnAdrs, rcx

                leave
                vmovdqu ymm0, ymmword ptr [rsp + 000]
                vmovdqu ymm1, ymmword ptr [rsp + 032]
                vmovdqu ymm2, ymmword ptr [rsp + 064]
                vmovdqu ymm3, ymmword ptr [rsp + 096]
                vmovdqu ymm4, ymmword ptr [rsp + 128]
                vmovdqu ymm5, ymmword ptr [rsp + 160]
                vmovdqu ymm6, ymmword ptr [rsp + 192]
                vmovdqu ymm7, ymmword ptr [rsp + 224]
                add     rsp, 256
                pop     r11
                pop     r10
                pop     r9
                pop     r8
                pop     rdx
                pop     rcx
                pop     rbx
                pop     rax
                ret
print_AVX       endp

; Version that will run on CPUs without
; AVX support and will preserve the
; volatile SSE registers (XMM0 to XMM3):

print_SSE       proc

; Preserve all the volatile registers
; (be nice to the assembly code that
; calls this procedure):

                push    rax
                push    rbx
                push    rcx
                push    rdx
                push    r8
                push    r9
```

```
              push    r10
              push    r11

; XMM0 to XMM3 are considered volatile, so preserve them:

              sub     rsp, 128
              movdqu  xmmword ptr [rsp + 00],   xmm0
              movdqu  xmmword ptr [rsp + 16],   xmm1
              movdqu  xmmword ptr [rsp + 32],   xmm2
              movdqu  xmmword ptr [rsp + 48],   xmm3
              movdqu  xmmword ptr [rsp + 64],   xmm4
              movdqu  xmmword ptr [rsp + 80],   xmm5
              movdqu  xmmword ptr [rsp + 96],   xmm6
              movdqu  xmmword ptr [rsp + 112],  xmm7

              push    rbp

returnAdrs    textequ <[rbp + 200]>

              mov     rbp, rsp
              sub     rsp, 128
              and     rsp, -16

; Format string (passed in RCX) is sitting at
; the location pointed at by the return address;
; load that into RCX:

              mov     rcx, returnAdrs

; To handle more than three arguments (four counting
; RCX), you must pass data on stack. However, to the
; print caller, the stack is unavailable, so use
; R10 and R11 as extra parameters (could be just
; junk in these registers, but pass them just
; in case):

              mov     [rsp + 32], r10
              mov     [rsp + 40], r11
              call    printf

; Need to modify the return address so
; that it points beyond the zero-terminating byte.
; Could use a fast strlen function for this, but
; printf is so slow it won't really save us anything.

              mov     rcx, returnAdrs
              dec     rcx
skipTo0:      inc     rcx
              cmp     byte ptr [rcx], 0
              jne     skipTo0
              inc     rcx
              mov     returnAdrs, rcx

              leave
```

```
            movdqu   xmm0, xmmword ptr [rsp + 00]
            movdqu   xmm1, xmmword ptr [rsp + 16]
            movdqu   xmm2, xmmword ptr [rsp + 32]
            movdqu   xmm3, xmmword ptr [rsp + 48]
            movdqu   xmm4, xmmword ptr [rsp + 64]
            movdqu   xmm5, xmmword ptr [rsp + 80]
            movdqu   xmm6, xmmword ptr [rsp + 96]
            movdqu   xmm7, xmmword ptr [rsp + 112]
            add      rsp, 128
            pop      r11
            pop      r10
            pop      r9
            pop      r8
            pop      rdx
            pop      rcx
            pop      rbx
            pop      rax
            ret
print_SSE   endp
            end
```

Listing 15-2: The print function appearing in an assembly unit

To complete all the common *aoalib* functions used thus far, here is Listing 15-3.

```
; getTitle.asm - The getTitle function converted to
;                an assembly unit.

; Return program title to C++ program:

            include aoalib.inc

            .code
getTitle    proc
            lea      rax, ttlStr
            ret
getTitle    endp
            end
```

Listing 15-3: The getTitle function as an assembly unit

Listing 15-4 is a program that uses the assembly units in Listings 15-2 and 15-3.

```
; Listing 15-4

; Demonstration of linking.

            include aoalib.inc

            .data
ttlStr      byte     "Listing 15-4", 0
```

```
**********************************************************

; Here is the "asmMain" function.

            .code
            public  asmMain
asmMain     proc
            push    rbx
            push    rsi
            push    rdi
            push    rbp
            mov     rbp, rsp
            sub     rsp, 56         ; Shadow storage

            call    print
            byte    "Assembly units linked", nl, 0

            leave
            pop     rdi
            pop     rsi
            pop     rbx
            ret     ; Returns to caller
asmMain     endp
            end
```

Listing 15-4: A main program that uses the print *and* getTitle *assembly modules*

So how do you build and run this program? Unfortunately, the *build.bat* batch file this book has been using up to this point will not do the job. Here's a command that will assemble all the units and link them together:

```
ml64 /c print.asm getTitle.asm listing15-4.asm
cl /EHa c.cpp print.obj getTitle.obj listing15-4.obj
```

These commands will properly compile all source files and link together their object code to produce the executable file *c.exe*.

Unfortunately, the preceding commands defeat one of the major benefits of separate compilation. When you issue the ml64 /c print.asm getTitle .asm listing15-4.asm command, it will compile all the assembly source files. Remember, a major reason for separate compilation is to reduce compilation time on large projects. While the preceding commands work, they don't achieve this goal.

To separately compile the two modules, you must run MASM separately on them. To compile the three source files separately, break the ml64 invocation into three separate commands:

```
ml64 /c print.asm
ml64 /c getTitle.asm
ml64 /c listing15-4.asm
cl /EHa c.cpp print.obj getTitle.obj listing15-4.obj
```

Of course, this sequence still compiles all three assembly source files. However, after the first time you execute these commands, you've built the *print.obj* and *getTitle.obj* files. From this point forward, as long as you don't change the *print.asm* or *getTitle.asm* source files (and don't delete the *print.obj* or *getTitle.obj* files), you can build and run the program in Listing 15-4 by using these commands:

```
ml64 /c listing15-4.asm
cl /EHa c.cpp print.obj getTitle.obj listing15-4.obj
```

Now, you've saved the time needed to compile the *print.asm* and *getTitle.asm* files.

15.7 An Introduction to Makefiles

The *build.bat* file used throughout this book has been far more convenient than typing the individual build commands. Unfortunately, the build mechanism that *build.bat* supports is really good for only a few fixed source files. While you could easily construct a batch file to compile all the files in a large assembly project, running the batch file would reassemble every source file in the project. Although you can use complex command line functions to avoid some of this, there is an easier way: makefiles.

A *makefile* is a script in a special language (designed in early releases of Unix) that specifies how to execute a series of commands based on certain conditions, executed by the program make. If you've installed MSVC and MASM as part of Visual Studio, you've probably also installed (as part of that same process) Microsoft's variant of make: nmake.exe.[4] To use nmake.exe, you execute it from a Windows command line as follows:

```
nmake optional_arguments
```

If you execute nmake on a command line by itself (without any arguments), nmake.exe will search for a file named *makefile* and attempt to process the commands in that file. For many projects, this is very convenient. You will have all your project's source files in a single directory (or in subdirectories hanging off that directory), and you will place a single makefile (named *makefile*) in that directory. By changing into that directory and executing nmake (or make), you can build the project with minimal fuss.

If you want to use a different filename than *makefile*, you must preface the filename with the /f option, as follows:

```
nmake /f mymake.mak
```

The filename doesn't have to have the extension *.mak*. However, this is a popular convention when using makefiles that are not named *makefile*.

---

4. nmake stands for *new make*, which is Microsoft's way of saying that it didn't adhere to the standard make language. That's fine; nmake will behave just like the Unix variants for the simple operations we need.

The nmake program does provide many command line options, and /help will list them. Look up nmake documentation online for a description of the other command line options (most of them are advanced and are unnecessary for most tasks).

15.7.1 Basic Makefile Syntax

A makefile is a standard ASCII text file containing a sequence of lines (or a set of multiple occurrences of this sequence) as follows:

```
target: dependencies
    commands
```

The `target: dependencies` line is optional. The `commands` item is a list of one or more command line commands, also optional. The `target` item, if present, must begin in column 1 of the source line it is on. The `commands` items must have at least one whitespace character (space or tab) in front of them (that is, they must not begin in column 1 of the source line). Consider the following valid makefile:

```
c.exe:
    ml64 /c print.asm
    ml64 /c getTitle.asm
    ml64 /c listing15-4.asm
    cl /EHa c.cpp print.obj getTitle.obj listing15-4.obj
```

If these commands appear in a file named *makefile* and you execute nmake, then nmake will execute these commands exactly like the command line interpreter would have executed them had they appeared in a batch file.

A *target* item is an identifier or a filename of some sort. Consider the following makefile:

```
executable:
    ml64 /c listing15-4.asm
    cl /EHa c.cpp print.obj getTitle.obj listing15-4.obj

library:
    ml64 /c print.asm
    ml64 /c getTitle.asm
```

This separates the build commands into two groups: one group specified by the executable label and one group specified by the library label.

If you run nmake without any command line options, nmake will execute only those commands associated with the very first target in the makefile. In this example, if you run nmake by itself, it will assemble *listing15-4.asm*, *print.asm*, and *getTitle.asm*; compile *c.cpp*; and attempt to link the resulting *c.obj* with *print.obj*, *getTitle.obj*, and *listing15-4.obj*. This should successfully produce the *c.exe* executable.

To process the commands after the library target, specify the target name as an nmake command line argument:

```
nmake library
```

This nmake command compiles *print.asm* and *getTitle.asm*. So if you execute this command once (and never change *print.asm* or *getTitle.asm* thereafter), you need only execute the nmake command by itself to generate the executable file (or use nmake executable if you want to explicitly state that you are building the executable).

15.7.2 Make Dependencies

Although the ability to specify which targets you want to build on the command line is very useful, as your projects get larger (with many source files and library modules), keeping track of which source files you need to recompile all the time can be burdensome and error prone; if you're not careful, you'll forget to compile an obscure library module after you've made changes to it and wonder why the application is still failing. The make dependencies option allows you to automate the build process to help avoid these problems.

A list of one or more (whitespace-separated) dependencies can follow a target in a makefile:

```
target: dependency1 dependency2 dependency3 ...
```

Dependencies are either target names (of targets appearing in that makefile) or filenames. If a dependency is a target name (that is not also a filename), nmake will go execute the commands associated with that target. Consider the following makefile:

```
executable:
  ml64 /c listing15-4.asm
  cl /EHa c.cpp print.obj getTitle.obj listing15-4.obj

library:
  ml64 /c print.asm
  ml64 /c getTitle.asm

all: library executable
```

The all target depends on the library and executable targets, so it will go execute the commands associated with those targets (and in the order library, executable, which is important because the library object files must be built before the associated object modules can be linked into the executable program). The all identifier is a common target in makefiles. Indeed, it is often the first or second target to appear in a makefile.

If a *target: dependencies* line becomes too long to be readable (nmake doesn't really care too much about line length), you can break the line into multiple lines by putting a backslash character (\) as the last character on a line. The nmake program will combine source lines that end with a backslash with the next line in the makefile.

NOTE *The backslash must be the very last character on the line. Whitespace characters (tabs and spaces) are not allowed.*

Target names and dependencies can also be filenames. Specifying a filename as a target name is generally done to tell the make system how to build that particular file. For example, we could rewrite the current example as follows:

```
executable:
  ml64 /c listing15-4.asm
  cl /EHa c.cpp print.obj getTitle.obj listing15-4.obj

library: print.obj getTitle.obj

print.obj:
  ml64 /c print.asm

getTitle.obj:
  ml64 /c getTitle.asm

all: library executable
```

When dependencies are associated with a target that is a filename, you can read the *target*: *dependencies* statement as "*target* depends on *dependencies*." When processing a make command, nmake compares the modification date and time stamp of the files specified as target filenames and dependency filenames.

If the date and time of the target are older than *any* of the dependencies (or the target file doesn't exist), nmake will execute the commands after the target. If the target file's modification date and time are later (newer) than *all* of the dependent files, nmake will not execute the commands. If one of the dependencies after a target is itself a target elsewhere, nmake will first execute that command (to see if it modifies the target object, changing its modification date and time, and possibly causing nmake to execute the current target's commands). If a target or dependency is just a label (it is not a filename), nmake will treat its modification date and time as older than any file.

Consider the following modification to the running makefile example:

```
c.exe: print.obj getTitle.obj listing15-4.obj
  cl /EHa c.cpp print.obj getTitle.obj listing15-4.obj

listing15-4.obj: listing15-4.asm
  ml64 /c listing15-4.asm

print.obj: print.asm
  ml64 /c print.asm

getTitle.obj: getTitle.asm
  ml64 /c getTitle.asm
```

Note that the all and library targets were removed (they turn out to be unnecessary) and that executable was changed to *c.exe* (the final target executable file).

Consider the *c.exe* target. Because *print.obj*, *getTitle.obj*, and *listing15-4.obj* are all targets (as well as filenames), nmake will first go execute those targets. After executing those targets, nmake will compare the modification date and time of *c.exe* against that of the three object files. If *c.exe* is older than any of those object files, nmake will execute the command following the *c.exe* target line (to compile *c.cpp* and link it with the object files). If *c.exe* is newer than its dependent object files, nmake will not execute the command.

The same process happens, recursively, for each of the dependent object files following the *c.exe* target. While processing the *c.exe* target, nmake will go off and process the *print.obj*, *getTitle.obj*, and *listing15-4.obj* targets (in that order). In each case, nmake will compare the modification date and time of the *.obj* file with the corresponding *.asm* file. If the *.obj* file is newer than the *.asm* file, nmake returns to processing the *c.exe* target without doing anything; if the *.obj* file is older than the *.asm* file (or doesn't exist), nmake executes the corresponding ml64 command to generate a new *.obj* file.

If *c.exe* is newer than all the *.obj* files (and they are all newer than the *.asm* files), executing nmake does nothing (well, it will report that *c.exe* is up to date, but it will not process any of the commands in the makefile). If any of the files are out of date (because they've been modified), this makefile will compile and link only the files necessary to bring *c.exe* up to date.

The makefiles thus far are missing an important dependency: all of the *.asm* files include the *aoalib.inc* file. A change to *aoalib.inc* could possibly require a recompilation of these *.asm* files. This dependency has been added to Listing 15-5. This listing also demonstrates how to include comments in a makefile by using the # character at the beginning of a line.

```
# listing15-5.mak

# makefile for Listing 15-4.

listing15-4.exe:print.obj getTitle.obj listing15-4.obj
    cl /nologo /O2 /Zi /utf-8 /EHa /Felisting15-4.exe c.cpp \
        print.obj getTitle.obj listing15-4.obj

listing15-4.obj: listing15-4.asm aoalib.inc
  ml64 /nologo /c listing15-4.asm

print.obj: print.asm aoalib.inc
  ml64 /nologo /c print.asm

getTitle.obj: getTitle.asm aoalib.inc
  ml64 /nologo /c getTitle.asm
```

Listing 15-5: Makefile to build Listing 15-4

Here's the nmake command to build the program in Listing 15-4 by using the makefile (*listing15-5.mak*) in Listing 15-5:

```
C:\>nmake /f listing15-5.mak

Microsoft (R) Program Maintenance Utility Version 14.15.26730.0
Copyright (C) Microsoft Corporation.  All rights reserved.
```

```
        ml64 /nologo /c print.asm
Assembling: print.asm
        ml64 /nologo /c getTitle.asm
Assembling: getTitle.asm
        ml64 /nologo /c listing15-4.asm
Assembling: listing15-4.asm
        cl /nologo /O2 /Zi /utf-8 /EHa /Felisting15-4.exe c.cpp  print.obj
getTitle.obj listing15-4.obj
c.cpp

C:\>listing15-4
Calling Listing 15-4:
Assembly units linked
Listing 15-4 terminated
```

15.7.3 Make Clean and Touch

One common target you will find in most professionally made makefiles
is clean. The clean target will delete an appropriate set of files to force the
entire system to be remade the next time you execute the makefile. This
command typically deletes all the *.obj* and *.exe* files associated with the project. Listing 15-6 provides a clean target for the makefile in Listing 15-5.

```
# listing15-6.mak

# makefile for Listing 15-4.

listing15-4.exe:print.obj getTitle.obj listing15-4.obj
    cl /nologo /O2 /Zi /utf-8 /EHa /Felisting15-4.exe c.cpp \
        print.obj getTitle.obj listing15-4.obj

listing15-4.obj: listing15-4.asm aoalib.inc
    ml64 /nologo /c listing15-4.asm

print.obj: print.asm aoalib.inc
    ml64 /nologo /c print.asm

getTitle.obj: getTitle.asm aoalib.inc
    ml64 /nologo /c getTitle.asm

clean:
    del getTitle.obj
    del print.obj
    del listing15-4.obj
    del c.obj
    del listing15-4.ilk
    del listing15-4.pdb
    del vc140.pdb
    del listing15-4.exe

# Alternative clean (if you like living dangerously):

# clean:
#   del *.obj
#   del *.ilk
```

```
#    del *.pdb
#    del *.exe
```

Listing 15-6: A clean target example

Here is a sample clean and remake operation:

```
C:\>nmake /f listing15-6.mak clean

Microsoft (R) Program Maintenance Utility Version 14.15.26730.0
Copyright (C) Microsoft Corporation.  All rights reserved.

        del getTitle.obj
        del print.obj
        del listing15-4.obj
        del c.obj
        del listing15-4.ilk
        del listing15-4.pdb
        del listing15-4.exe

C:\>nmake /f listing15-6.mak

Microsoft (R) Program Maintenance Utility Version 14.15.26730.0
Copyright (C) Microsoft Corporation.  All rights reserved.

        ml64 /nologo /c print.asm
 Assembling: print.asm
        ml64 /nologo /c getTitle.asm
 Assembling: getTitle.asm
        ml64 /nologo /c listing15-4.asm
 Assembling: listing15-4.asm
        cl /nologo /O2 /Zi /utf-8 /EHa /Felisting15-4.exe c.cpp
            print.obj getTitle.obj listing15-4.obj
c.cpp
```

If you want to force the recompilation of a single file (without manually editing and modifying it), a Unix utility comes in handy: touch. The touch program accepts a filename as its argument and goes in and updates the modification date and time of the file (without otherwise modifying the file). For example, after building Listing 15-4 by using the makefile in Listing 15-6, were you to execute the command

```
touch listing15-4.asm
```

and then execute the makefile in Listing 15-6 again, it would reassemble the code in Listing 15-4, recompile *c.cpp*, and produce a new executable.

Unfortunately, while touch is a standard Unix application and comes with every Unix and Linux distribution, it is not a standard Windows application.[5] Fortunately, you can easily find a version of touch for Windows on the internet. It's also a relatively simple program to write.

---

5. Also see *https://docs.microsoft.com/en-us/windows/wsl/install-win10/* to see how to gain access to Linux utilities under Windows.

15.8 The Microsoft Linker and Library Code

Many common projects reuse code that developers created long ago (or they use code that came from a source outside the developer's organization). These libraries of code are relatively *static*: they rarely change during the development of a project that uses the library code. In particular, you would not normally incorporate the building of the libraries into a given project's makefile. A specific project might list the library files as dependencies in the makefile, but the assumption is that the library files are built elsewhere and supplied as a whole to the project. Beyond that, one major difference exists between a library and a set of object code files: packaging.

Dealing with a myriad of separate object files can become troublesome when you're working with true sets of library object files. A library may contain tens, hundreds, or even thousands of object files. Listing all of these object files (or even just the ones a project uses) is a lot of work and can lead to consistency errors. A common way to deal with this problem is to combine various object files into a separate package (file) known as a *library file*. Under Windows, library files typically have a *.lib* suffix.

For many projects, you will be given a library (*.lib*) file that packages together a specific library module. You supply this file to the linker when building your program, and the linker automatically picks out the object modules it needs from the library. This is an important point: including a library while building an executable does not automatically insert all of the code from that library into the executable. The linker is smart enough to extract only the object files it needs and to ignore the object files it doesn't use (remember, a library is just a package containing a bunch of object files).

So the question is, "How do you create a library file?" The short answer is, "By using the Microsoft Library Manager program (*lib.exe*)." The basic syntax for the lib program is

```
lib /out:libname.lib list_of_.obj_files
```

where `libname.lib` is the name of the library file you want to produce, and `list_of_.obj_files` is a (space-separated) list of object filenames you want to collect into the library. For example, if you want to combine the *print.obj* and *getTitle.obj* files into a library module (*aoalib.lib*), here's the command to do it:

```
lib /out:aoalib.lib getTitle.obj print.obj
```

Once you have a library module, you can specify it on a linker (or ml64 or cl) command line just as you would an object file. For example, to link in the *aoalib.lib* module with the program in Listing 15-4, you could use the following command:

```
cl /EHa /Felisting15-4.exe c.cpp listing15-4.obj aoalib.lib
```

The lib program supports several command line options. You can get a list of those options by using this command:

```
lib /?
```

See the online Microsoft documentation for a description of the various commands. Perhaps the most useful of the options is

```
lib /list lib_filename.lib
```

where `lib_filename.lib` represents a library filename. This will print a list of the object files contained within that library module. For example, `lib /list aoalib.lib` produces the following output:

```
C:\>lib /list aoalib.lib
Microsoft (R) Library Manager Version 14.15.26730.0
Copyright (C) Microsoft Corporation.  All rights reserved.

getTitle.obj
print.obj
```

MASM provides a special directive, `includelib`, that lets you specify libraries to include. This directive has the syntax

```
includelib lib_filename.lib
```

where `lib_filename.lib` is the name of the library file you want to include. This directive embeds a command in the object file that MASM produces that passes this library filename along to the linker. The linker will then automatically load the library file when processing the object module containing the `includelib` directive.

This activity is identical to manually specifying the library filename to the linker (from the command line). Whether you prefer to put the `includelib` directive in a MASM source file, or include the library name on the linker (or `ml64/cl`) command line, is up to you. In my experience, most assembly language programmers (especially when writing stand-alone assembly language programs) prefer the `includelib` directive.

15.9 Object File and Library Impact on Program Size

The basic unit of linkage in a program is the object file. When combining object files to form an executable, the Microsoft linker will take all of the data from a single object file and merge it into the final executable. This is true even if the main program doesn't call all the functions (directly or indirectly) in the object module or use all the data in that object file. So, if you put 100 routines in a single assembly language source file and compile them into an object module, the linker will include the code for all 100 routines in your final executable even if you use only one of them.

If you want to avoid this situation, you should break those 100 routines into 100 separate object modules and combine the resulting 100 object files into a single library. When the Microsoft linker processes that library file, it will pick out the single object file containing the function the program uses and incorporate only that object file into the final executable. Generally, this is far more efficient than linking in a single object file with 100 functions buried in it.

The key word in that last sentence is *generally*. In fact, there are some good reasons for combining multiple functions into a single object file. First of all, consider what happens when the linker merges an object file into an executable. To ensure proper alignment, whenever the linker takes a section or segment (for example, the `.code` section) from an object file, it adds sufficient padding so that the data in that section is aligned on that section's specified alignment boundary. Most sections have a default 16-byte section alignment, so the linker will align each section from the object file it links in on a 16-byte boundary. Normally, this isn't too bad, especially if your procedures are large. However, suppose those 100 procedures you've created are all really short (a few bytes each). Then you wind up wasting a lot of space.

Granted, on modern machines, a few hundred bytes of wasted space won't amount to much. However, it might be more practical to combine several of these procedures into a single object module (even if you don't call them all) to fill in some of the wasted space. Don't go overboard, though; once you've gone beyond the alignment, whether you're wasting space because of padding or wasting space because you're including code that never gets called, you're still wasting space.

15.10 For More Information

Although it is an older book, covering MASM version 6, *The Waite Group's Microsoft Macro Assembler Bible* by Nabajyoti Barkakati and this author (Sams, 1992) goes into much greater detail about MASM's external directives (extern, externdef, and `public`) and include files.

You can also find the MASM 6 manual (the last published edition) online.

For more information about makefiles, check out these resources:

- Wikipedia: *https://en.wikipedia.org/wiki/Make_(software)*
- *Managing Projects with GNU Make*, Third Edition, by Robert Mecklenburg (O'Reilly Media, 2004)
- *The GNU Make Book* by John Graham-Cumming (No Starch Press, 2015)

15.11 Test Yourself

1. What statement(s) would you use to prevent recursive include files?
2. What is an assembly unit?
3. What directive would you use to tell MASM that a symbol is global and visible outside the current source file?
4. What directive(s) would you use to tell MASM to use a global symbol from another object module?

5. Which directive prevents duplicate symbol errors when an external symbol is defined within an assembly source file?

6. What external data type declaration would you use to access an external constant symbol?

7. What external data type declaration would you use to access an external procedure?

8. What is the name of Microsoft's make program?

9. What is the basic makefile syntax?

10. What is a makefile-dependent file?

11. What does a makefile clean command typically do?

12. What is a library file?

16

STAND-ALONE ASSEMBLY LANGUAGE PROGRAMS

Until now, this book has relied upon a C/C++ main program to call the example code written in assembly language. Although this is probably the biggest use of assembly language in the real world, it is also possible to write stand-alone code (no C/C++ main program) in assembly language.

In the context of this chapter, *stand-alone assembly language programs* means that you're writing an executable program in assembly that does not directly link into a C/C++ program for execution. Without a C/C++ main program calling your assembly code, you're not dragging along the C/C++ library code and runtime system, so your programs can be smaller and you won't have external naming conflicts with C/C++ public names. However, you'll have to do much of the work yourself that C/C++ libraries do by writing comparable assembly code or calling the Win32 API.

The *Win32 API* is a bare-metal interface to the Windows operating system that provides thousands of functions you can call from a stand-alone assembly language program—far too many to consider in this chapter. This chapter provides a basic introduction to Win32 applications (especially console-based applications). This information will get you started writing stand-alone assembly language programs under Windows.

To use the Win32 API from your assembly programs, you'll need to download the MASM32 library package from *https://www.masm32.com/*.[1] Most of the examples in this chapter assume the MASM32 64-bit include files are available on your system in the *C:\masm32* subdirectory.

16.1 Hello World, by Itself

Before showing you some of the wonders of Windows stand-alone assembly language programming, perhaps the best place to start is at the beginning: with a stand-alone "Hello, world!" program (Listing 16-1).

```
; Listing 16-1.asm

; A stand-alone assembly language version of
; the ubiquitous "Hello, world!" program.

; Link in the Windows Win32 API:

            includelib kernel32.lib

; Here are the two Windows functions we will need
; to send "Hello, world!" to the standard console device:

            extrn   __imp_GetStdHandle:proc
            extrn   __imp_WriteFile:proc


            .code
hwStr       byte      "Hello World!"
hwLen       =         $-hwStr

; This is the honest-to-goodness assembly language
; main program:

main        proc

; On entry, stack is aligned at 8 mod 16. Setting aside
; 8 bytes for "bytesWritten" ensures that calls in main have
; their stack aligned to 16 bytes (8 mod 16 inside function),
; as required by the Windows API (which __imp_GetStdHandle and
; __imp_WriteFile use. They are written in C/C++).

            lea     rbx, hwStr
            sub     rsp, 8
            mov     rdi, rsp       ; Hold # of bytes written here

; Note: must set aside 32 bytes (20h) for shadow registers for
; parameters (just do this once for all functions).
; Also, WriteFile has a 5th argument (which is NULL),
```

---

1. Despite its name, the MASM32 library includes header files for both 32-bit and 64-bit assembly language programmers. Obviously, we're interested in the 64-bit libraries.

```
; so we must set aside 8 bytes to hold that pointer (and
; initialize it to zero). Finally, stack must always be
; 16-byte-aligned, so reserve another 8 bytes of storage
; to ensure this.

            sub     rsp, 030h  ; Shadow storage for args

; Handle = GetStdHandle(-11);
; Single argument passed in ECX.
; Handle returned in RAX.

            mov     rcx, -11                      ; STD_OUTPUT
            call    qword ptr __imp_GetStdHandle  ; Returns handle
                                                  ; in RAX

; WriteFile(handle, "Hello World!", 12, &bytesWritten, NULL);
; Zero out (set to NULL) "lpOverlapped" argument:

            xor     rcx, rcx
            mov     [rsp + 4 * 8], rcx

            mov     r9, rdi    ; Address of "bytesWritten" in R9
            mov     r8d, hwLen ; Length of string to write in R8D
            lea     rdx, hwStr ; Ptr to string data in RDX
            mov     rcx, rax   ; File handle passed in RCX
            call    qword ptr __imp_WriteFile

; Clean up stack and return:

            add     rsp, 38h
            ret
main        endp
            end
```

Listing 16-1: Stand-alone "Hello, world!" program

The __imp_GetStdHandle and __imp_WriteFile procedures are functions inside Windows (they are part of the so-called Win32 API, even though this is 64-bit code that is executing). The __imp_GetStdHandle procedure, when passed the (admittedly magic) number –11 as an argument, returns a handle to the standard output device. With this handle, calls to __imp_WriteFile will send the output to the standard output device (the console). To build and run this program, use the following command:

```
ml64 listing16-1.asm /link /subsystem:console /entry:main
```

The MASM /link command line option tells it that the following commands (to the end of the line) are to be passed on to the linker. The /subsystem:console (linker) command line option tells the linker that this program is a console application (that is, it will run in a command line window). The /entry:main linker option passes along the name of the main program to the linker. The linker stores this address in a special location in the executable file so Windows can determine the starting address of the main program after it loads the executable file into memory.

16.2 Header Files and the Windows Interface

Near the beginning of the "Hello, world!" example in Listing 16-1, you'll notice the following lines:

```
includelib kernel32.lib

; Here are the two Windows functions we will need
; to send "Hello, world!" to the standard console device:

extrn __imp_GetStdHandle:proc
extrn __imp_WriteFile:proc
```

The *kernel32.lib* library file contains the object module definitions for many of the Win32 API functions, including the __imp_GetStdHandle and __imp_WriteFile procedures. Inserting extrn directives for all the Win32 API functions into your assembly language programs is an incredible amount of work. The proper way to deal with these function definitions is to include them in a header (include) file and then include that file in every application you write that uses the Win32 API functions.

The bad news is that creating an appropriate set of header files is a gargantuan task. The good news is that somebody else has already done all that work for you: the MASM32 headers. Listing 16-2 is a rework of Listing 16-1 that uses the MASM32 64-bit include files to obtain the Win32 external declarations. Note that we incorporate MASM32 via an include file, *listing16-2.inc*, rather than use it directly. This will be explained in a moment.

```
; Listing 16-2

            include    listing16-2.inc
            includelib kernel32.lib                ; File I/O library

; Include just the files we need from masm64rt.inc:

;           include \masm32\include64\masm64rt.inc
;           OPTION DOTNAME                         ; Required for macro files
;           option casemap:none                    ; Case sensitive
;           include \masm32\include64\win64.inc
;           include \masm32\macros64\macros64.inc
;           include \masm32\include64\kernel32.inc

            .data
bytesWrtn   qword   ?
hwStr       byte    "Listing 16-2", 0ah, "Hello, World!", 0
hwLen       =       sizeof hwStr

            .code

*********************************************************
```

; Here is the "asmMain" function.

```
            public  asmMain
asmMain     proc
            push    rbx
            push    rsi
            push    rdi
            push    r15
            push    rbp
            mov     rbp, rsp
            sub     rsp, 56         ; Shadow storage
            and     rsp, -16

            mov     rcx, -11        ; STD_OUTPUT
            call    __imp_GetStdHandle ; Returns handle

            xor     rcx, rcx
            mov     bytesWrtn, rcx

            lea     r9, bytesWrtn   ; Address of "bytesWritten" in R9
            mov     r8d, hwLen      ; Length of string to write in R8D
            lea     rdx, hwStr      ; Ptr to string data in RDX
            mov     rcx, rax        ; File handle passed in RCX
            call    __imp_WriteFile

allDone:    leave
            pop     r15
            pop     rdi
            pop     rsi
            pop     rbx
            ret     ; Returns to caller
asmMain     endp
            end
```

Here's the *listing16-2.inc* include file:

```
; listing16-2.inc

; Header file entries extracted from MASM32 header
; files (placed here rather than including the
; full MASM32 headers to avoid namespace pollution
; and speed up assemblies).

PPROC           TYPEDEF PTR PROC        ; For include file prototypes

externdef __imp_GetStdHandle:PPROC
externdef __imp_WriteFile:PPROC
```

Listing 16-2: Using the MASM32 64-bit include files

Here's the build command and sample output:

```
C:\>ml64 /nologo listing16-2.asm kernel32.lib /link /nologo /subsystem:console
/entry:asmMain
 Assembling: listing16-2.asm
```

```
C:\>listing16-2
Listing 16-2
Hello, World!
```

The MASM32 include file

```
include \masm32\include64\masm64rt.inc
```

includes all the other hundreds of include files that are part of the MASM32 64-bit system. Sticking this include directive into your programs provides your application with access to a huge number of Win32 API functions, data declarations, and other goodies (such as MASM32 macros).

However, your computer will pause for a bit when you assemble your source file. That's because that single include directive winds up including many tens of thousands of lines of code into your program during assembly. If you know which header file(s) contain the actual declarations you want to use, you can speed up your compilations by including just the files you need (as was done in *listing16-2.asm* using the MASM32 64-bit include files).

Including *masm64rt.inc* into your programs has one other problem: *namespace pollution*. The MASM32 include file introduces thousands and thousands of symbols into your program, and there is a chance a symbol you want to use has already been defined in the MASM32 include files (for a different purpose than the one you have in mind). If you have a *file grep* utility, a program that searches through files in a directory and recursively in subdirectories for a particular string, you can easily locate all occurrences of a particular symbol you want to use in your file and copy that symbol's definition into your own source file (or, better yet, into a header file you create specifically for this purpose). This is the approach this chapter uses for many of the example programs.

16.3   The Win32 API and the Windows ABI

The Win32 API functions all adhere to the Windows ABI calling convention. This means that calls to these functions can modify all the volatile registers (RAX, RCX, RDX, R8, R9, R10, R11, and XMM0 to XMM5) but must preserve the nonvolatile registers (the others not listed here). Also, API calls pass parameters in RDX, RCX, R8, R9 (and XMM0 to XMM3), and then on the stack; the stack must be 16-byte-aligned prior to the API call. See the discussion of the Windows ABI throughout this book for more details.

16.4   Building a Stand-Alone Console Application

Take a look at the (simplified) build command from the preceding section:[2]

```
ml64 listing16-2.asm /link /subsystem:console /entry:asmMain
```

---

2. I've removed the /nologo options to save space on the line. They don't affect the operation of the compilation other than to reduce some Microsoft output.

The /subsystem:console option tells the linker that in addition to possible GUI windows the application might create, the system must also create a special window for the application to display console information. If you run the program from a Windows command line, it uses the already-open console window of the *cmd.exe* program.

16.5 Building a Stand-Alone GUI Application

To create a pure Windows GUI application that does not also open up a console window, you can specify /subsystem:windows rather than /subsystem:console. The simple dialog box application in Listing 16-3 is an example of an especially simple Windows application. It displays a simple dialog box and then quits when the user clicks the OK button in the dialog box.

```
; Listing 16-3

; Dialog box demonstration.

            include     listing16-3.inc
            includelib user32.lib

          ; include \masm32\include64\masm64rt.inc

            .data

msg         byte      "Dialog Box Demonstration",0
DBTitle     byte      "Dialog Box Title", 0

            .code


;***********************************************************

; Here is the "asmMain" function.

            public  asmMain
asmMain     proc
            push    rbp
            mov     rbp, rsp
            sub     rsp, 56         ; Shadow storage
            and     rsp, -16

            xor     rcx, rcx        ; HWin = NULL
            lea     rdx, msg        ; Message to display
            lea     r8, DBTitle     ; Dialog box title
            mov     r9d, MB_OK      ; Has an "OK" button
            call    MessageBox

allDone:    leave
            ret     ; Returns to caller
asmMain     endp
            end
```

Listing 16-3: A simple dialog box application

Here's the *listing16-3.inc* include file:

```
; listing16-3.inc

; Header file entries extracted from MASM32 header
; files (placed here rather than including the
; full MASM32 headers to avoid namespace pollution
; and speed up assemblies).

PPROC              TYPEDEF PTR PROC        ; For include file prototypes

MB_OK                                   equ 0h

externdef __imp_MessageBoxA:PPROC
MessageBox equ <__imp_MessageBoxA>
```

Here is the build command for the program in Listing 16-3:

```
C:\>ml64 listing16-3.asm /link /subsystem:windows /entry:asmMain
```

Figure 16-1 shows the runtime output from Listing 16-3.

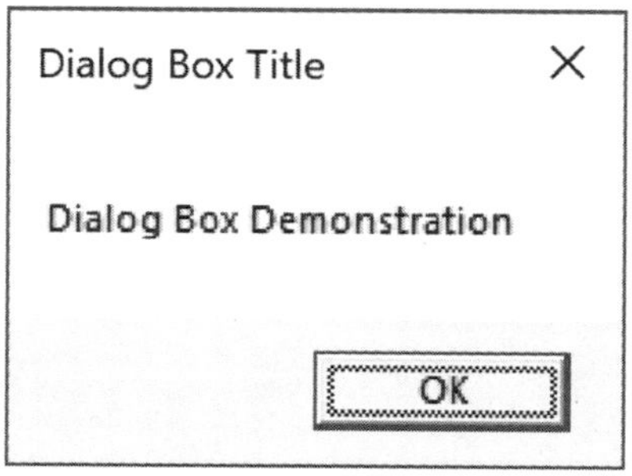

Figure 16-1: Sample dialog box output

16.6 A Brief Look at the MessageBox Windows API Function

Although creating GUI applications in assembly language is well beyond the scope of this book, the MessageBox function is sufficiently useful (even in console applications) to be worth a special mention.

The MessageBox function has four parameters:

RCX Window handle. This is usually NULL (0), implying that the message box is a stand-alone dialog box that is not associated with any particular window.

RDX Message pointer. RDX contains a pointer to a zero-terminated string that will be displayed in the body of the message box.

R8 Window title. R8 contains a pointer to a zero-terminated string that is displayed in the title bar of the message box window.

R9D Message box type. This is an integer value that specifies the type of buttons and other icons appearing in the message box. Typical values are the following: `MB_OK`, `MB_OKCANCEL`, `MB_ABORTRETRYIGNORE`, `MB_YESNOCANCEL`, `MB_YESNO`, and `MB_RETRYCANCEL`.

The `MessageBox` function returns an integer value in RAX corresponding to the button that was pressed (if `MB_OK` was specified, that's the value that the message box returns when the user clicks the OK button).

16.7 Windows File I/O

One thing missing from most of the example code in this book has been a discussion of file I/O. Although you can easily make C Standard Library calls to open, read, write, and close files, it seemed appropriate to use file I/O as an example in this chapter to cover this missing detail.

The Win32 API provides many useful functions for *file I/O*: reading and writing file data. This section describes a small number of these functions:

CreateFileA A function (despite its name) that you use to open existing files or create new files

WriteFile A function that writes data to a file

ReadFile A function that reads data from a file

CloseHandle A function that closes a file and flushes any cached data to the storage device

GetStdHandle A function, which you've already seen, that returns the handle of one of the standard input or output devices (standard input, standard output, or standard error)

GetLastError A function you can use to retrieve a Windows error code if an error occurs in the execution of any of these functions

Listing 16-4 demonstrates the use of these functions as well as the creation of some useful procedures that call these functions. Note that this code is rather long, so I've taken the liberty of breaking it into smaller chunks, with individual explanations in front of each section.

The Win32 file I/O functions are all part of the *kernel32.lib* library module. Therefore, Listing 16-4 uses the `includelib kernel32.lib` statement to automatically link in this library during the build phase. To speed up assembly and reduce namespace pollution, this program does not automatically include all of the MASM32 equate files (via an `include \masm32 \include64\masm64rt.inc` statement). Instead, I've collected all the necessary equates and other definitions from the MASM32 header files and placed them in the *listing16-4.inc* header file (which appears a little later in this chapter). Finally, the program also includes the *aoalib.inc* header file, just to use a few of the constants defined in that file (such as cr and nl):

```
; Listing 16-4

; File I/O demonstration.

            include    listing16-4.inc
            include    aoalib.inc   ; To get some constants
            includelib kernel32.lib ; File I/O library

            .const
prompt      byte    "Enter (text) filename:", 0
badOpenMsg  byte    "Could not open file", cr, nl, 0

            .data

inHandle    dword   ?
inputLn     byte    256 dup (0)

fileBuffer  byte    4096 dup (0)
```

The following code constructs *wrapper code* around each of the file I/O functions to preserve the volatile register values. These functions use the following macro definitions to save and restore the register values:

```
            .code

rcxSave     textequ <[rbp - 8]>
rdxSave     textequ <[rbp - 16]>
r8Save      textequ <[rbp - 24]>
r9Save      textequ <[rbp - 32]>
r10Save     textequ <[rbp - 40]>
r11Save     textequ <[rbp - 48]>
xmm0Save    textequ <[rbp - 64]>
xmm1Save    textequ <[rbp - 80]>
xmm2Save    textequ <[rbp - 96]>
xmm3Save    textequ <[rbp - 112]>
xmm4Save    textequ <[rbp - 128]>
xmm5Save    textequ <[rbp - 144]>
var1        textequ <[rbp - 160]>

mkActRec    macro
            push    rbp
            mov     rbp, rsp
            sub     rsp, 256        ; Includes shadow storage
            and     rsp, -16        ; Align to 16 bytes
            mov     rcxSave, rcx
            mov     rdxSave, rdx
            mov     r8Save, r8
            mov     r9Save, r9
            mov     r10Save, r10
            mov     r11Save, r11
            movdqu  xmm0Save, xmm0
            movdqu  xmm1Save, xmm1
```

```
            movdqu  xmm2Save, xmm2
            movdqu  xmm3Save, xmm3
            movdqu  xmm4Save, xmm4
            movdqu  xmm5Save, xmm5
            endm

rstrActRec  macro
            mov     rcx, rcxSave
            mov     rdx, rdxSave
            mov     r8, r8Save
            mov     r9, r9Save
            mov     r10, r10Save
            mov     r11, r11Save
            movdqu  xmm0, xmm0Save
            movdqu  xmm1, xmm1Save
            movdqu  xmm2, xmm2Save
            movdqu  xmm3, xmm3Save
            movdqu  xmm4, xmm4Save
            movdqu  xmm5, xmm5Save
            leave
            endm
```

NOTE *These macros assume that the code does not need to preserve the AVX registers (YMM, or even ZMM, registers). If you're running on a CPU that supports the AVX extensions (and you need to preserve YMM0 to YMM5 or even ZMM0 to ZMM5), you will need to modify these macros to handle the preservation of those registers. These macros also do not preserve the value in the RAX register, because almost all Win32 API functions return a function result in RAX (an error code, if nothing else).*

The first function appearing in Listing 16-4 is getStdOutHandle. This is a wrapper function around __imp_GetStdHandle that preserves the volatile registers and explicitly requests the standard output device handle. This function returns the standard output device handle in the RAX register. Immediately following getStdOutHandle are comparable functions that retrieve the standard error handle and the standard input handle:

```
; getStdOutHandle - Returns stdout handle in RAX:

getStdOutHandle proc
            mkActRec
            mov     rcx, STD_OUTPUT_HANDLE
            call    __imp_GetStdHandle  ; Returns handle
            rstrActRec
            ret
getStdOutHandle endp

; getStdErrHandle - Returns stderr handle in RAX:

getStdErrHandle proc
            mkActRec
            mov     rcx, STD_ERROR_HANDLE
            call    __imp_GetStdHandle  ; Returns handle
            rstrActRec
            ret
```

```
getStdErrHandle endp

; getStdInHandle - Returns stdin handle in RAX:

getStdInHandle proc
            mkActRec
            mov     rcx, STD_INPUT_HANDLE
            call    __imp_GetStdHandle   ; Returns handle
            rstrActRec
            ret
getStdInHandle endp
```

Now consider the wrapper code for the write function:

```
; write - Write data to a file handle.

; RAX - File handle.
; RSI - Pointer to buffer to write.
; RCX - Length of buffer to write.

; Returns:

; RAX - Number of bytes actually written
;       or -1 if there was an error.

write       proc
            mkActRec

            mov     rdx, rsi        ; Buffer address
            mov     r8, rcx         ; Buffer length
            lea     r9, var1        ; bytesWritten
            mov     rcx, rax        ; Handle
            xor     r10, r10        ; lpOverlapped is passed
            mov     [rsp+4*8], r10  ; on the stack
            call    __imp_WriteFile
            test    rax, rax        ; See if error
            mov     rax, var1       ; bytesWritten
            jnz     rtnBytsWrtn     ; If RAX was not zero
            mov     rax, -1         ; Return error status

rtnBytsWrtn:
            rstrActRec
            ret
write       endp
```

The write function writes data from a memory buffer to the output file specified by a file handle (which could also be the standard output or standard error handle, if you want to write data to the console). The write function expects the following parameter data:

RAX   File handle specifying the write destination. This is typically a handle obtained by the open or openNew functions (a little later in the program) or the getStdOutHandle and getStdErrHandle functions.

RSI Address of the buffer containing the data to write to the file.

RCX Number of bytes of data to write to the file (from the buffer).

This function does not follow the Windows ABI calling convention. Although there isn't an official *assembly language calling convention*, many assembly language programmers tend to use the same registers that the x86-64 string instructions use. For example, the source data (buffer) is passed in RSI (the source index register), and the count (buffer size) parameter appears in the RCX register. The write procedure moves the data to appropriate locations for the call to __imp_WriteFile (as well as sets up additional parameters).

The __imp_WriteFile function is the actual Win32 API write function (technically, __imp_WriteFile is a pointer to the function; the call instruction is an indirect call through this pointer). The __imp_WriteFile has the following arguments:

RCX File handle.

RDX Buffer address.

R8 Buffer size (really, 32 bits in R8D).

R9 Address of a dword variable to receive the number of bytes written to the file; this will equal the buffer size if the write operation is successful.

[rsp + 32] lpOverlapped value; just set this to NULL (0). As per the Windows ABI, callers pass all parameters beyond the fourth parameter on the stack, leaving room (shadow parameters) for the first four.

On return from __imp_WriteFile, RAX contains a nonzero value (true) if the write was successful, and zero (false) if there was an error. If there was an error, you can call the Win32 GetLastError function to retrieve the error code.

Note that the write function returns the number of bytes written to the file in the RAX register. If there was an error, write returns -1 in the RAX register.

Next up are the puts and newLn functions:

```
; puts - Outputs a zero-terminated string to standard output device.

; RSI - Address of string to print to standard output.

            .data
stdOutHnd   qword   0
hasSOHndl   byte    0

            .code
puts        proc
            push    rax
            push    rcx
            cmp     hasSOHndl, 0
            jne     hasHandle
```

```
            call    getStdOutHandle
            mov     stdOutHnd, rax
            mov     hasSOHndl, 1

; Compute the length of the string:

hasHandle:  mov     rcx, -1
lenLp:      inc     rcx
            cmp     byte ptr [rsi][rcx * 1], 0
            jne     lenLp

            mov     rax, stdOutHnd
            call    write

            pop     rcx
            pop     rax
            ret
puts        endp

; newLn - Outputs a newline sequence to the standard output device:

newlnSeq    byte    cr, nl

newLn       proc
            push    rax
            push    rcx
            push    rsi
            cmp     hasSOHndl, 0
            jne     hasHandle

            call    getStdOutHandle
            mov     stdOutHnd, rax
            mov     hasSOHndl, 1

hasHandle:  lea     rsi, newlnSeq
            mov     rcx, 2
            mov     rax, stdOutHnd
            call    write

            pop     rsi
            pop     rcx
            pop     rax
            ret
newLn       endp
```

The puts and newLn procedures write strings to the standard output device. The puts function writes a zero-terminated string whose address you pass in the RSI register. The newLn function writes a newline sequence (carriage return and line feed) to the standard output device.

These two functions have a tiny optimization: they call getStdOutHandle only once to obtain the standard output device handle. On the first call to either of these functions, they call getStdOutHandle and cache the result (in the stdOutHnd variable) and set flag (hasSOHndl) that indicates that the cached value is valid. Thereafter, these functions use the cached value rather than continually calling getStdOutHandle to retrieve the standard output device handle.

The write function requires a buffer length; it does not work on zero-terminated strings. Therefore, the puts function must explicitly determine the length of the zero-terminated string before calling write. The newLn function doesn't have to do this because it knows the length of the carriage return and line feed sequence (two characters).

The next function in Listing 16-4 is the wrapper for the read function:

```
; read - Read data from a file handle.

; EAX - File handle.
; RDI - Pointer to buffer receive data.
; ECX - Length of data to read.

; Returns:

; RAX - Number of bytes actually read
;       or -1 if there was an error.

read        proc
            mkActRec

            mov     rdx, rdi          ; Buffer address
            mov     r8, rcx           ; Buffer length
            lea     r9, var1          ; bytesRead
            mov     rcx, rax          ; Handle
            xor     r10, r10          ; lpOverlapped is passed
            mov     [rsp+4*8], r10    ; on the stack
            call    __imp_ReadFile
            test    rax, rax          ; See if error
            mov     rax, var1         ; bytesRead
            jnz     rtnBytsRead       ; If RAX was not zero
            mov     rax, -1           ; Return error status

rtnBytsRead:
            rstrActRec
            ret
read        endp
```

The read function is the input analog to the write function. The parameters are similar (note, however, that read uses RDI as the *destination address* for the buffer parameter):

RAX File handle.

RDI Destination buffer to store data read from file.

RCX Number of bytes to read from the file.

The read function, a wrapper around the Win32 API __imp_ReadFile function, has the following arguments:

RCX File handle.

RDX File buffer address.

R8   Number of bytes to read.

R9   Address of dword variable to receive the number of bytes actually read.

[rsp + 32]   Overlapped operation; should be NULL (0). As per the Windows ABI, callers pass all parameters beyond the fourth parameter on the stack, leaving room (shadow parameters) for the first four.

The read function returns -1 in RAX if there was an error during the read operation. Otherwise, it returns the actual number of bytes read from the file. This value can be less than the requested read amount if the read operation reaches the end of the file (EOF). A 0 return value generally indicates EOF has been reached.

The open function opens an existing file for reading, writing, or both. It is a wrapper function for the Windows CreateFileA API call:

```
; open - Open existing file for reading or writing.

; RSI - Pointer to filename string (zero-terminated).
; RAX - File access flags.
;       (GENERIC_READ, GENERIC_WRITE, or
;       "GENERIC_READ + GENERIC_WRITE")

; Returns:

; RAX - Handle of open file (or INVALID_HANDLE_VALUE if there
;       was an error opening the file).

open        proc
            mkActRec

            mov     rcx, rsi                ; Filename
            mov     rdx, rax                ; Read and write access
            xor     r8, r8                  ; Exclusive access
            xor     r9, r9                  ; No special security
            mov     r10, OPEN_EXISTING      ; Open an existing file
            mov     [rsp + 4 * 8], r10
            mov     r10, FILE_ATTRIBUTE_NORMAL
            mov     [rsp + 5 * 8], r10
            mov     [rsp + 6 * 8], r9       ; NULL template file
            call    __imp_CreateFileA
            rstrActRec
            ret
open        endp
```

The open procedure has two parameters:

RSI   A pointer to a zero-terminated string containing the filename of the file to open.

RAX   A set of file access flags. These are typically the constants GENERIC _READ (to open a file for reading), GENERIC_WRITE (to open a file for writing), or GENERIC_READ + GENERIC_WRITE (to open a file for reading and writing).

The open function calls the Windows CreateFileA function after setting up the appropriate parameters for the latter. The A suffix on CreateFileA stands for *ASCII*. This particular function expects the caller to pass an ASCII filename. Another function, CreateFileW, expects Unicode filenames, encoded as UTF-16. Internally, Windows uses Unicode filenames; when you call CreateFileA, it converts the ASCII filename to Unicode and then calls CreateFileW. The open function sticks with ASCII characters.

The CreateFileA function has the following parameters:

RCX   Pointer to zero-terminated (ASCII) string holding the name of the file to open.

RDX   Read and write access flags (GENERIC_READ and GENERIC_WRITE).

R8   Sharing mode flag (0 means exclusive access). Controls whether another process can access the file while the current process has it open. Possible flag values are FILE_SHARE_READ, FILE_SHARE_WRITE, and FILE_SHARE_DELETE (or a combination of these).

R9   Pointer to a security descriptor. The open function doesn't specify any special security; it simply passes NULL (0) as this argument.

[rsp + 32]   This parameter holds the creation disposition flag. The open function opens an existing file, so it passes OPEN_EXISTING here. Other possible values are CREATE_ALWAYS, CREATE_NEW, OPEN_ALWAYS, OPEN_EXISTING, or TRUNCATE_EXISTING. The OPEN_EXISTING value requires that the file exists, or it will return an open error. Being the fifth parameter, this is passed on the stack (in the fifth 64-bit slot).

[rsp + 40]   This parameter contains the file attributes. This function simply uses the FILE_ATTRIBUTE_NORMAL attribute (for example, not read-only).

[rsp + 48]   This parameter is a pointer to a file template handle. The open function doesn't use a file template, so it passes NULL (0) in this argument.

The open function returns a file handle in the RAX register. If there was an error, this function returns INVALID_HANDLE_VALUE in RAX.

The openNew function is also a wrapper around the CreateFileA function:

```
; openNew - Creates a new file and opens it for writing.

; RSI - Pointer to filename string (zero-terminated).

; Returns:

; RAX - Handle of open file (or INVALID_HANDLE_VALUE if there
;       was an error opening the file).

openNew     proc
            mkActRec

            mov     rcx, rsi                        ; Filename
            mov     rdx, GENERIC_WRITE+GENERIC_WRITE ; Access
```

```
              xor     r8, r8                      ; Exclusive access
              xor     r9, r9                      ; No security
              mov     r10, CREATE_ALWAYS          ; Open a new file
              mov     [rsp + 4 * 8], r10
              mov     r10, FILE_ATTRIBUTE_NORMAL
              mov     [rsp + 5 * 8], r10
              mov     [rsp + 6 * 8], r9           ; NULL template
              call    __imp_CreateFileA
              rstrActRec
              ret
openNew       endp
```

openNew creates a new (empty) file on the disk. If the file previously existed, openNew will delete it before opening the new file. This function is almost identical to the preceding open function, with the following two differences:

- The caller does not pass the file access flags in the RAX register. The file access is always assumed to be GENERIC_WRITE.

- This function passes the CREATE_ALWAYS creation disposition flag to CreateFileA rather than OPEN_EXISTING.

The closeHandle function is a simple wrapper around the Windows CloseHandle function. You pass the file handle of the file to close in the RAX register. This function returns 0 in RAX if there was an error, or a nonzero file if the file close operation was successful. The only purpose of this wrapper is to preserve all the volatile registers across the call to the Windows CloseHandle function:

```
; closeHandle - Closes a file specified by a file handle.

; RAX - Handle of file to close.

closeHandle proc
            mkActRec

            call    __imp_CloseHandle

            rstrActRec
            ret
closeHandle endp
```

Although this program doesn't explicitly use getLastError, it does provide a wrapper around the getLastError function (just to show how it would be written). Whenever one of the Windows functions in this program returns an error indication, you have to call getLastError to retrieve the actual error code. This function has no input parameters. It returns the last Windows error code generated in RAX.

It is very important to call getLastError immediately after a function returns an error indication. If you call any other Windows functions between the error and retrieval of the error code, those intervening calls will reset the last error code value.

As was the case for the closeHandle function, the getLastError procedure is a very simple wrapper around the Windows GetLastError function that preserves volatile register values across the call:

```
; getLastError - Returns the error code of the last Windows error.

; Returns:

; RAX - Error code.

getLastError proc
            mkActRec
            call    __imp_GetLastError
            rstrActRec
            ret
getLastError endp
```

The stdin_read is a simple wrapper function around the read function that reads its data from the standard input device (rather than from a file on another device):

```
; stdin_read - Reads data from the standard input.

; RDI - Buffer to receive data.
; RCX - Buffer count (note that data input will
;       stop on a newline character if that
;       comes along before RCX characters have
;       been read).

; Returns:

; RAX - -1 if error, bytes read if successful.

stdin_read  proc
            .data
hasStdInHnd byte    0
stdInHnd    qword   0
            .code
            mkActRec
            cmp     hasStdInHnd, 0
            jne     hasHandle

            call    getStdInHandle
            mov     stdInHnd, rax
            mov     hasStdInHnd, 1

hasHandle:  mov     rax, stdInHnd   ; Handle
            call    read

            rstrActRec
            ret
stdin_read  endp
```

stdin_read is similar to the puts (and newLn) procedure insofar as it caches the standard input handle on its first call and uses that cached value on subsequent calls. Note that stdin_read does not (directly) preserve the volatile registers. This function does not directly call any Windows functions, so it doesn't have to preserve the volatile registers (stdin_read calls the read function, which preserves the volatile registers). The stdin_read function has the following parameters:

RDI Pointer to destination buffer that will receive the characters read from the standard input device.

RCX Buffer size (maximum number of bytes to read).

This function returns the actual number of bytes read in the RAX register. This value may be less than the value passed in RCX. If the user presses ENTER, this function immediately returns. This function does not zero-terminate the string read from the standard input device. Use the value in the RAX register to determine the string's length. If this function returns because the user pressed ENTER on the standard input device, that carriage return will appear in the buffer.

The stdin_getc function reads a single character from the standard input device and returns that character in the AL register:

```
; stdin_getc - Reads a single character from the standard input.
;               Returns character in AL register.

stdin_getc  proc
            push    rdi
            push    rcx
            sub     rsp, 8

            mov     rdi, rsp
            mov     rcx, 1
            call    stdin_read
            test    eax, eax        ; Error on read?
            jz      getcErr
            movzx   rax, byte ptr [rsp]

getcErr:    add     rsp, 8
            pop     rcx
            pop     rdi
            ret
stdin_getc  endp
```

The readLn function reads a string of characters from the standard input device and places them in a caller-specified buffer. The arguments are as follows:

RDI Address of the buffer.

RCX Maximum buffer size. (readLn allows the user to enter a maximum of RCX − 1 characters.)

This function will put a zero-terminating byte at the end of the string input by the user. Furthermore, it will strip out the carriage return (or newline or line feed) character at the end of the line. It returns the character count in RAX (not counting the ENTER key):

```
; readLn - Reads a line of text from the user.
;          Automatically processes backspace characters
;          (deleting previous characters, as appropriate).
;          Line returned from function is zero-terminated
;          and does not include the ENTER key code (carriage
;          return) or line feed.

; RDI - Buffer to place line of text read from user.
; RCX - Maximum buffer length.

; Returns:

; RAX - Number of characters read from the user
;        (does not include ENTER key).

readLn      proc
            push    rbx

            xor     rbx, rbx        ; Character count
            test    rcx, rcx        ; Allowable buffer is 0?
            je      exitRdLn
            dec     rcx             ; Leave room for 0 byte
readLp:
            call    stdin_getc      ; Read 1 char from stdin
            test    eax, eax        ; Treat error like ENTER
            jz      lineDone
            cmp     al, cr          ; Check for ENTER key
            je      lineDone
            cmp     al, nl          ; Check for newline code
            je      lineDone
            cmp     al, bs          ; Handle backspace character
            jne     addChar

; If a backspace character came along, remove the previous
; character from the input buffer (assuming there is a
; previous character).

            test    rbx, rbx        ; Ignore BS character if no
            jz      readLp          ; chars in the buffer
            dec     rbx
            jmp     readLp

; If a normal character (that we return to the caller),
; then add the character to the buffer if there is
; room for it (ignore the character if the buffer is full).

addChar:    cmp     ebx, ecx        ; See if we're at the
            jae     readLp          ; end of the buffer
            mov     [rdi][rbx * 1], al ; Save char to buffer
```

```
            inc      rbx
            jmp      readLp

; When the user presses ENTER (or the line feed) key
; during input, come down here and zero-terminate the string.

lineDone:   mov      byte ptr [rdi][rbx * 1], 0

exitRdLn:   mov      rax, rbx         ; Return char cnt in RAX
            pop      rbx
            ret
readLn      endp
```

Here's the main program for Listing 16-4, which reads a filename from the user, opens that file, reads the file data, and displays the data on the standard output device:

```
*********************************************************

; Here is the "asmMain" function.

            public   asmMain
asmMain     proc
            push     rbx
            push     rsi
            push     rdi
            push     rbp
            mov      rbp, rsp
            sub      rsp, 64          ; Shadow storage
            and      rsp, -16

; Get a filename from the user:

            lea      rsi, prompt
            call     puts

            lea      rdi, inputLn
            mov      rcx, lengthof inputLn
            call     readLn

; Open the file, read its contents, and display
; the contents to the standard output device:

            lea      rsi, inputLn
            mov      rax, GENERIC_READ
            call     open

            cmp      eax, INVALID_HANDLE_VALUE
            je       badOpen

            mov      inHandle, eax
```

```
; Read the file 4096 bytes at a time:

readLoop:   mov     eax, inHandle
            lea     rdi, fileBuffer
            mov     ecx, lengthof fileBuffer
            call    read
            test    eax, eax        ; EOF?
            jz      allDone
            mov     rcx, rax        ; Bytes to write

            call    getStdOutHandle
            lea     rsi, fileBuffer
            call    write
            jmp     readLoop

badOpen:    lea     rsi, badOpenMsg
            call    puts

allDone:    mov     eax, inHandle
            call    closeHandle

            leave
            pop     rdi
            pop     rsi
            pop     rbx
            ret     ; Returns to caller
asmMain     endp
            end
```

Listing 16-4: File I/O demonstration program

Here's the build command and sample output for Listing 16-4:

```
C:\>nmake /nologo /f listing16-4.mak
        ml64 /nologo listing16-4.asm  /link /subsystem:console /entry:asmMain
 Assembling: listing16-4.asm
Microsoft (R) Incremental Linker Version 14.15.26730.0
Copyright (C) Microsoft Corporation.  All rights reserved.

/OUT:listing16-4.exe
listing16-4.obj
/subsystem:console
/entry:asmMain

C:\>listing16-4
Enter (text) filename:listing16-4.mak
listing16-4.exe: listing16-4.obj listing16-4.asm
        ml64 /nologo listing16-4.asm \
              /link /subsystem:console /entry:asmMain
```

Here's the *listing16-4.inc* include file:

```
; listing16-4.inc

; Header file entries extracted from MASM32 header
; files (placed here rather than including the
; entire set of MASM32 headers to avoid namespace
; pollution and speed up assemblies).

STD_INPUT_HANDLE                    equ -10
STD_OUTPUT_HANDLE                   equ -11
STD_ERROR_HANDLE                    equ -12
CREATE_NEW                          equ 1
CREATE_ALWAYS                       equ 2
OPEN_EXISTING                       equ 3
OPEN_ALWAYS                         equ 4
FILE_ATTRIBUTE_READONLY             equ 1h
FILE_ATTRIBUTE_HIDDEN               equ 2h
FILE_ATTRIBUTE_SYSTEM               equ 4h
FILE_ATTRIBUTE_DIRECTORY            equ 10h
FILE_ATTRIBUTE_ARCHIVE              equ 20h
FILE_ATTRIBUTE_NORMAL               equ 80h
FILE_ATTRIBUTE_TEMPORARY            equ 100h
FILE_ATTRIBUTE_COMPRESSED           equ 800h
FILE_SHARE_READ                     equ 1h
FILE_SHARE_WRITE                    equ 2h
GENERIC_READ                        equ 80000000h
GENERIC_WRITE                       equ 40000000h
GENERIC_EXECUTE                     equ 20000000h
GENERIC_ALL                         equ 10000000h
INVALID_HANDLE_VALUE                equ -1

PPROC           TYPEDEF PTR PROC        ; For include file prototypes

externdef __imp_GetStdHandle:PPROC
externdef __imp_WriteFile:PPROC
externdef __imp_ReadFile:PPROC
externdef __imp_CreateFileA:PPROC
externdef __imp_CloseHandle:PPROC
externdef __imp_GetLastError:PPROC
```

Here's the *listing16-4.mak* makefile:

```
listing16-4.exe: listing16-4.obj listing16-4.asm
    ml64 /nologo listing16-4.asm \
        /link /subsystem:console /entry:asmMain
```

16.8 Windows Applications

This chapter has provided just a glimpse of what is possible when writing pure assembly language applications that run under Windows. The *kernel32.lib* library provides hundreds of functions you can call, covering such diverse topic areas as manipulating filesystems (for example, deleting files, looking up filenames in a directory, and changing directories), creating threads and synchronizing them, processing environment strings, allocating and deallocating memory, manipulating the Windows registry, sleeping for a certain time period, waiting for events to occur, and much, much more.

The *kernel32.lib* library is but one of the libraries in the Win32 API. The *gdi32.lib* library contains most of the functions needed to create GUI applications running under Windows. Creating such applications is well beyond the scope of this book, but if you want to create stand-alone Windows GUI applications, you need to become intimately familiar with this library. The following "For More Information" section provides links to internet resources if you're interested in creating stand-alone Windows GUI applications in assembly language.

16.9 For More Information

If you want to write stand-alone 64-bit assembly language programs that run under Windows, your first stop should be *https://www.masm32.com/*. Although this website is primarily dedicated to creating 32-bit assembly language programs that run under Windows, it has a large amount of information for 64-bit programmers as well. More importantly, this site contains the header files you will need to access the Win32 API from your 64-bit assembly language programs.

If you're serious about writing Win32 API–based Windows applications in assembly language, Charles Petzold's *Programming Windows*, Fifth Edition (Microsoft, 1998) is an absolutely essential purchase. This book is old (do not get the newer edition for C# and XAML), and you likely will have to purchase a used copy. It was written for C programmers (not assembly), but if you know the Windows ABI (which you should by now), translating all the C calls into assembly language isn't that difficult. Though much of this information about the Win32 API is available online (such as at the MASM32 site), having all the information available in a single (very large!) book is essential.

Another good source on the web for Win32 API calls is software analyst Geoff Chappell's Win32 Programming page (*https://www.geoffchappell.com/studies/windows/win32/*).

The Iczelion tutorials were the original standard for writing Windows programs in x86 assembly language. Although they were originally written for 32-bit x86 assembly language, there have been several translations of this code to 64-bit assembly language, for example: *http://masm32.com/board/index.php?topic=4190.0/*.

The HLA Standard Library and examples (which can be found at *https://www.randallhyde.com/*) contain a ton of Windows code and API function calls. Though this code is all 32-bit, translating it to 64-bit MASM code is easy.

16.10 Test Yourself

1. What is the linker command line option needed to tell MASM that you're building a console application?
2. What website should you visit to get Win32 programming information?
3. What is the major drawback to including *\masm32\include64\masm64rt.inc* in all your assembly language source files?
4. What linker command line option lets you specify the name of your assembly language main program?
5. What is the name of the Win32 API function that lets you bring up a dialog box?
6. What is wrapper code?
7. What is the Win32 API function you would use to open an existing file?
8. What Win32 API function do you use to retrieve the last Windows error code?

PART III

REFERENCE MATERIAL

A

ASCII CHARACTER SET

Binary	Hex	Decimal	Character
0000_0000	00	0	NUL
0000_0001	01	1	CTRL-A
0000_0010	02	2	CTRL-B
0000_0011	03	3	CTRL-C
0000_0100	04	4	CTRL-D
0000_0101	05	5	CTRL-E
0000_0110	06	6	CTRL-F
0000_0111	07	7	Bell
0000_1000	08	8	BACKSPACE
0000_1001	09	9	TAB
0000_1010	0A	10	Line feed
0000_1011	0B	11	CTRL-K
0000_1100	0C	12	Form feed
0000_1101	0D	13	Carriage return
0000_1110	0E	14	CTRL-N
0000_1111	0F	15	CTRL-O
0001_0000	10	16	CTRL-P
0001_0001	11	17	CTRL-Q

(continued)

Binary	Hex	Decimal	Character
0001_0010	12	18	CTRL-R
0001_0011	13	19	CTRL-S
0001_0100	14	20	CTRL-T
0001_0101	15	21	CTRL-U
0001_0110	16	22	CTRL-V
0001_0111	17	23	CTRL-W
0001_1000	18	24	CTRL-X
0001_1001	19	25	CTRL-Y
0001_1010	1A	26	CTRL-Z
0001_1011	1B	27	ESC (CTRL-[)
0001_1100	1C	28	CTRL-\
0001_1101	1D	29	CTRL-]
0001_1110	1E	30	CTRL-^
0001_1111	1F	31	CTRL-_
0010_0000	20	32	Space
0010_0001	21	33	!
0010_0010	22	34	"
0010_0011	23	35	#
0010_0100	24	36	$
0010_0101	25	37	%
0010_0110	26	38	&
0010_0111	27	39	'
0010_1000	28	40	(
0010_1001	29	41	)
0010_1010	2A	42	*
0010_1011	2B	43	+
0010_1100	2C	44	,
0010_1101	2D	45	-
0010_1110	2E	46	.
0010_1111	2F	47	/
0011_0000	30	48	0
0011_0001	31	49	1
0011_0010	32	50	2
0011_0011	33	51	3
0011_0100	34	52	4
0011_0101	35	53	5
0011_0110	36	54	6

Binary	Hex	Decimal	Character
0011_0111	37	55	7
0011_1000	38	56	8
0011_1001	39	57	9
0011_1010	3A	58	:
0011_1011	3B	59	;
0011_1100	3C	60	<
0011_1101	3D	61	=
0011_1110	3E	62	>
0011_1111	3F	63	?
0100_0000	40	64	@
0100_0001	41	65	A
0100_0010	42	66	B
0100_0011	43	67	C
0100_0100	44	68	D
0100_0101	45	69	E
0100_0110	46	70	F
0100_0111	47	71	G
0100_1000	48	72	H
0100_1001	49	73	I
0100_1010	4A	74	J
0100_1011	4B	75	K
0100_1100	4C	76	L
0100_1101	4D	77	M
0100_1110	4E	78	N
0100_1111	4F	79	O
0101_0000	50	80	P
0101_0001	51	81	Q
0101_0010	52	82	R
0101_0011	53	83	S
0101_0100	54	84	T
0101_0101	55	85	U
0101_0110	56	86	V
0101_0111	57	87	W
0101_1000	58	88	X
0101_1001	59	89	Y
0101_1010	5A	90	Z

(continued)

Binary	Hex	Decimal	Character
0101_1011	5B	91	[
0101_1100	5C	92	\
0101_1101	5D	93	]
0101_1110	5E	94	^
0101_1111	5F	95	_
0110_0000	60	96	`
0110_0001	61	97	a
0110_0010	62	98	b
0110_0011	63	99	c
0110_0100	64	100	d
0110_0101	65	101	e
0110_0110	66	102	f
0110_0111	67	103	g
0110_1000	68	104	h
0110_1001	69	105	i
0110_1010	6A	106	j
0110_1011	6B	107	k
0110_1100	6C	108	l
0110_1101	6D	109	m
0110_1110	6E	110	n
0110_1111	6F	111	o
0111_0000	70	112	p
0111_0001	71	113	q
0111_0010	72	114	r
0111_0011	73	115	s
0111_0100	74	116	t
0111_0101	75	117	u
0111_0110	76	118	v
0111_0111	77	119	w
0111_1000	78	120	x
0111_1001	79	121	y
0111_1010	7A	122	z
0111_1011	7B	123	{
0111_1100	7C	124		
0111_1101	7D	125	}
0111_1110	7E	126	~
0111_1111	7F	127	DELETE

B

GLOSSARY

Symbols

.code
A section for program code.

.const
A declaration section for initialized read-only values.

.data
A declaration section for initialized variables.

.data?
A declaration section for uninitialized variables.

A

ABI
See *application binary interface*.

address bus
A set of electronic signals that hold a binary address of a memory element.

aggregate data types

Data types composed of one or more smaller data types.

API

Application programming interface.

application binary interface

A set of conventions that code uses to ensure interoperability between code that calls other functions or procedures and the functions or procedures being called.

ASCII

American Standard Code for Information Interchange.

assembly unit

The assembly of a source file plus any files it includes or indirectly includes.

associativity

Associativity dictates the grouping of operations within a complex expression in which the operators all have the same precedence. For example, if you have two operators, *op1* and *op2*, associativity determines the order of evaluation of the expression *x op1 y op2 z*. Left-associative operators would produce the result of the evaluation (*x op1 y*) *op2 z*, whereas right-associative operators would produce the result of the evaluation *x op1* (*y op2 z*).

automatic variables

See *local variables*.

AVX

Advanced Vector Extensions.

B

BCD

Binary-coded decimal.

big endian

Multi-byte data objects in memory are big endian if their HO byte appears at the lowest address in memory and their LO byte appears at the highest address in memory.

C

calling convention

The protocol for passing data to and from a procedure, including where the data is to be passed, the alignment of the data, and the size of the data.

CLI

Command line interface, or command line interpreter (Windows *cmd.exe* application).

code snippets

See *snippets*.

coercion

Forcing a data type to behave as another data type; for example, treating a character value as an integer.

column-major ordering

A function for storing elements of multidimensional array elements in linear memory by storing the elements of a column in contiguous locations and then placing each column after the previous column in memory.

commutative

An operation is commutative if (*A op B*) is always equal to (*B op A*).

composite data types

See *aggregate data types*.

control bus

A set of electronic signals from the CPU that control activities such as reading, writing, and generating wait states.

control characters

Special nonprinting characters that control aspects of the machine printing the characters. This includes operations such as carriage return (moving the printer carriage to the beginning of the line), line feed (moving the printer device down one line), and backspace (moving the print position back one character on the current line).

CTL

Compile-time language.

D

dangling pointer

Use of a pointer to allocated memory after that memory has been freed and returned to the system (and is possibly being used for another purpose).

data bus

A set of electronic signals from the CPU that transfer data between the CPU and external devices (such as memory or I/O).

delimiter characters

Characters that separate a sequence of other characters belonging to a set (such as a string of numeric characters delimited by spaces or commas).

dependencies

In a makefile, one file is dependent on another if changing that other file requires a recompilation (or other operation) on the original file.

dereference

Access data at an address specified by a pointer variable.

descriptor

A data structure that describes another data structure. Typically, a descriptor contains information such as a pointer to the actual data, type information, or length information.

directive

An assembly language statement that provides information to the assembler but is not a machine instruction and does not generate any code.

domain (of a function)

The set of all possible input values that a function accepts.

dword

Double word (two 16-bit words, forming a 32-bit value).

dynamic type system

A program organization that allows types of objects to change during runtime.

E

effective address

The ultimate address in memory that an instruction will access, after all the address calculations are complete.

epilogue

The standard exit sequence that cleans up local variable storage for a procedure. Typically, this consists of the following statements:

```
leave
ret
```

F

facade code
Code that changes the parameter or return result interface between calling code and a function or procedure being called to make the calling sequences compatible.

false precision
Extra bits in a computed result that contain garbage values; their presence indicates more precision than is actually present in the result.

field
A member of a record and struct or object.

floating-point unit
A section of a CPU that implements floating-point arithmetic.

FPU
See *floating-point unit*.

full pathname
A pathname beginning with a backslash (\) character, specifying a path that starts at the root directory. Also see *pathnames*.

G

granularity
The smallest unit of access; for example, an MMU may access memory by using page granularity, where the granularity is 4096 bytes.

guard digits (or bits)
Extra digits (or bits) maintained during a calculation to enhance the accuracy of a long chain of calculations.

H

heap
An area in memory where a program keeps dynamically allocated memory objects.

HLL
High-level language.

HO
High order.

horizontal addition or subtraction

Adding or subtracting adjacent lanes in an XMM or a YMM register rather than the usual corresponding lanes in separate XMM or YMM registers. Also see *vertical addition or subtraction*.

I

I/O

Input/output.

IDE

See *integrated development environment*.

idiom

An idiosyncrasy of the machine.

indirection

A technique in which an instruction's operand provides the location where the instruction can find the address of the object, rather than the object itself.

induction variable

A variable whose value depends entirely on the value of another variable (typically during the execution of a loop).

integrated development environment

A set of programmer tools including compilers and assemblers, linkers, debuggers, and editors that allow you to develop software all within the same system.

L

lane

An element of a vector (SSE/AVX packed data types).

leaf function

A function that does not call any other functions. The name comes from a call tree graph, in which its leaf nodes are those procedures that do not call any other procedures (and have no edges coming out of their nodes).

lexicographical ordering

Alphabetical ordering (or, more correctly, ordering based on the character code). Strings are compared on a character-by-character basis from the first character to the length of the shorter string. If two strings are equal to the length of the shorter string, the longer string is the greater of the two. Two strings are equal only if they have the same length and all characters in the string are equal.

library module

A collection of object files. Typically organized into a *.lib* file (though this is not a requirement for a library module).

lifetime

A period of time, ranging from when storage is first bound to a variable to the point when the storage is no longer available for that variable.

LIFO

Last in, first out.

little endian

Multi-byte data objects in memory are little endian if their LO byte appears at the lowest address in memory and their HO byte appears at the highest address in memory.

LO

Low order.

local variables

Variables (more properly called *automatic variables*) that have their storage allocated upon entry into a procedure and that storage is returned for other use when the procedure returns to its caller.

loop-invariant computation

A calculation that appears within a loop and always yields the same result on each iteration.

M

machine code

Binary (or numeric) encoding of assembly language instructions.

macro

A textual sequence that a macro processor will substitute for a macro identifier everywhere that identifier appears in the source file.

macroarchitecture

That view of the CPU's architecture that is visible to software.

macro function

A macro that you can invoke anywhere in the body of the source file (including in the operand field of an instruction or directive); the macro returns a textual string that the macro invocation substitutes for the invocation.

manifest constant

An identifier representing a constant value. MASM directly substitutes the value of the manifest constant everywhere the identifier appears in the program.

MASM

Microsoft Macro Assembler.

memory management unit

A component of the CPU that translates program addresses into physical memory addresses and handles illegal memory accesses.

microarchitecture

The design of the CPU below the level that is visible to software.

MMU

See *memory management unit.*

MMX

Multimedia Extensions (extended instruction set for the x86 CPU to support multimedia operations).

mnemonic

Literally, this means *memory aid.* Applied to instruction names, mnemonic effectively means *abbreviation.* For example, the mnemonic *lea* stands for *load effective address.*

MSVC

Microsoft Visual C++.

N

namespace pollution

Having many names in a source file, thus limiting the number of available new names a programmer can use. (When a source file contains a large number of symbols, programmers commonly create conflicts by reusing the same name, leading to duplicate symbol errors in the compilation process.)

NaN

Not a number. A floating-point exceptional value indicating that a valid numeric result is unobtainable.

O

opcode

Operation code. The numeric encoding of a machine instruction.

ordered comparisons
Comparisons between two values, neither of which are NaNs.

oword
Octal word (eight 16-bit words, or a 16-byte value).

P

partial pathname
A pathname that begins with a directory name (not a backslash character), denoting a path off the current (default) directory.

pass by reference
A parameter-passing mechanism whereby the caller passes the address of the actual parameter data to a procedure or function.

pass by value
A parameter-passing mechanism whereby the caller passes the actual value of a parameter to a procedure or function.

pathnames
A sequence of (sub)directory names separated by backslash (\\) characters, possibly ending with a filename.

PC
Program counter. The current instruction or directive address in an assembly language program. PC-relative addressing is an offset from the current machine instruction.

powerset
A set data type implemented by using a single bit to represent each object in the set. If the cardinality of the set (number of members in the set) is n, the set data type will require n bits. In mathematics, the power set of any set S is the set of all subsets of S, including the empty set and S itself; this requires 2^n different sets, which is representable by an n-bit bit string.

precedence
When two different operators appear in an expression (without parentheses to denote the order of evaluation), precedence controls which operations occur first. For example, with the operators *op1* and *op2*, and the expression x *op1* y *op2* z, the order of evaluation is determined by the precedence of the operators. If *op1* has higher precedence than *op2*, the expression is evaluated as $(x$ *op1* $y)$ *op2* z. If *op2* has a higher precedence than *op1*, the expression is evaluated as x *op1* $(y$ *op2* $z)$. If both operators have the same precedence, associativity rules control the order of evaluation (see also *associativity*).

precision

The number of digits or bits maintained in a computation.

programming in the large

Using processes, methodologies, and tools to handle the development of large software systems.

prologue

The standard entry sequence to a procedure, typically consisting of these statements:

```
push   rbp
mov    rbp, rsp
sub    rsp, size_of_local_variables
```

proper subset

A set whose elements are all contained within another set, and the two sets are not equal.

proper superset

A set that contains all the elements of another set, and the two sets are not equal.

Q

qword

Quad word (four 16-bit values, forming a 64-bit value).

R

range (of a function)

The set of all possible output values a function produces.

record

See *struct*.

row-major ordering

A function for arranging multidimensional arrays in linear memory by storing elements of each row in contiguous memory locations and then placing each row, one after the other, in memory.

S

saturation

The process of converting a larger (bit-sized) value to a smaller one by clipping (that is, forcing the maximum- or minimum-sized value if the original value is too large to fit in the smaller result).

scalar data type

A primitive, indivisible data type (for example, an integer or a floating-point value) that cannot be broken into any smaller parts (other than individual bits).

scope

The scope of an identifier determines where that identifier is visible (accessible) in the source file during compilation. In most HLLs, the scope of a procedure local variable is the body of that procedure; the identifier is inaccessible outside that procedure.

sign contraction

The process of converting a larger signed value to a smaller signed value.

significant digits

The (number of) digits whose values are maintained during a calculation.

SIMD

See *single-instruction, multiple-data instructions*.

single-instruction, multiple-data instructions

Specialized machine instructions that operate on two or more pieces of data simultaneously. Provides higher-performance operations for certain multimedia and other applications.

SISD

Single instruction, single data.

snippets

Small pieces of code that demonstrate a concept.

SSE

Streaming SIMD Extensions.

state machine

Programming logic that maintains a history of prior execution via a *state* maintained by the program. The state could be maintained in variables or in the current execution location of the state machine.

static variables

Variables whose lifetime is the execution time of the whole program; typically, you declare static variables in the .data, .data?, or .const section of an assembly language program.

strength-reduction optimizations

Using a less expensive operation to compute the same result as a more expensive operation.

string descriptor

A data structure that provides information about string data. Typically, a string descriptor contains a pointer to the actual string data, the number of characters in the string (its length), and possibly the string type or encoding (such as ASCII, UTF-8, or information describing other encoding).

struct

A composite data structure composed of a collection of heterogeneous (different typed) objects.

system bus

A collection of electronic signals comprising the address, data, and control buses.

T

timestamp

A numeric (usually time-based) value associated with an event in the system. Timestamps are monotonically increasing; that is, if two events have timestamps associated with them, the later event will have a larger timestamp value.

TOS

Top of stack.

trampoline

A fixed point in the code where a program can jump (or call) to transfer to another point in the code that is outside the normal range of a `jmp` or `call` instruction.

tricky programming

Programming constructs that use non-obvious results of a computation.

U

unordered comparisons

Comparisons between two values, where at least one of the values is a NaN.

unraveling loops

Pulling the body out of a loop and expanding it in place several times (once for each loop iteration) to avoid the overhead of loop control at runtime.

URL

Uniform resource locator (web address).

V

variant type
A data type that can change dynamically during program execution (that is, it is a *varying* type).

vector instructions
Instructions that operate on multiple pieces of data simultaneously (SIMD instructions). Specifically, an array of two or more data values.

vertical addition or subtraction
Adding or subtracting corresponding lanes in two XMM or YMM registers. Also see *horizontal addition or subtraction*.

W

whitespace characters
Characters that reserve space on a display but don't otherwise have a printable glyph (such as the space and tab characters).

word
A 16-bit value.

wrapper code
Code that is written to change the behavior of a function call without directly modifying that function (such as changing where the caller passes parameters to the underlying function). Wrapper code is also known as a *facade*.

INSTALLING AND USING
VISUAL STUDIO

The Microsoft Macro Assembler (MASM), Microsoft C++ compiler, Microsoft linker, and other tools this book uses are all available in the Microsoft Visual Studio package. At the time of this writing, you can download the Visual Studio Community edition for Windows at *https://visualstudio .microsoft.com/vs/community/*. Of course, URLs change over time. A web-based search for *Microsoft Visual Studio download* should lead you to the appropriate spot.

C.1   Installing Visual Studio Community

Once you download the Visual Studio Community edition, run the installer program. This appendix does not provide step-by-step directions as Microsoft is famous for completely changing the user interface of programs even when minor updates occur. Any directions appearing here would probably be obsolete when you try to run them. However, the main thing you want to do is ensure that you download and install the Microsoft Visual C++ desktop tools.

C.2   Creating a Command Line Prompt for MASM

To use the Microsoft Visual C++ (MSVC) compiler and MASM, we need to initialize the environment by using a batch file provided by Visual Studio and then leave the command line interpreter (CLI) open so we can build and run programs. We have two options: use an environment created by the Visual Studio installer, or create a custom environment.

At the time of this writing, the Visual Studio 2019 installer creates various CLI environments:

- Developer Command Prompt for VS 2019
- Developer PowerShell for VS 2019
- x64 Native Tools Command Prompt for VS 2019
- x64_x86 Cross Tools Command Prompt for VS 2019
- x86 Native Tools Command Prompt for VS 2019
- x86_x64 Cross Tools Command Prompt for VS 2019

You can find these by clicking **Start** (the Windows icon) on the Windows taskbar and then navigating to and clicking the **Visual Studio 2019** folder. *x86* refers to 32-bit, and *x64* refers to 64-bit versions of Windows.

The Developer Command Prompt, Developer PowerShell, x86 Native Tools, and x64_x86 Cross Tools target the 32-bit versions of Windows, so they are outside the scope of this book. x86_x64 Cross Tools targets 64-bit Windows, but the tools available in the environment are themselves 32-bit. Basically, these are the tools for people running a 32-bit version of Windows. x64 Native Tools are for people targeting and running a 64-bit version of Windows. The 32-bit versions of Windows are rare today, so we have not used nor tested this book's code under x86_x64 Cross Tools. In theory, it should work to assemble and compile 64-bit code, but we would not be able to run it in this 32-bit environment.

x64 Native Tools running under 64-bit Windows is what we have used and tested. If you right-click **x64 Native Tools**, you can pin it to Start, or if you select **More**, you can pin it to the taskbar.

Alternatively, you can create your own custom environment, and we will now go through that process. We'll create a shortcut to a MASM-ready command line prompt by using the following steps:

1. Find the batch file named *vcvars64.bat* (or something similar). If you cannot find *vcvars64.bat*, try *vcvarsall.bat* instead. At the time of writing this chapter (using Visual Studio 2019), I found the *vcvars64.bat* file in the following directory: *C:\Program Files (x86)\Microsoft Visual Studio\2019\ Community\VC\Auxiliary\Build*.

vcvars.bat *or* vcvars32.bat *will not work (these set up the environment variables for the 32-bit version of the assembler and C++ compiler, which we don't want to use).*

2. Create a shortcut to the file (by right-clicking it in the Windows Explorer and selecting **Create Shortcut** from the pop-up). Move this shortcut to your Windows desktop and rename it *VSCmdLine.*

3. Right-click the shortcut icon on the desktop and click **Properties ▸ Shortcut**. Find the Target text box that contains the path to the *vcvars64.bat* file; for example:

```
"C:\Program Files (x86)\Microsoft Visual Studio\2019\Community\VC\Auxiliary\Build\vcvars64.bat"
```

Add the prefix `cmd /k` in front of this path:

```
cmd /k "C:\Program Files (x86)\Microsoft Visual Studio\2019\Community\VC\Auxiliary\Build\
vcvars64.bat"
```

The `cmd` command is the Microsoft *cmd.exe* command line interpreter. The /k option tells *cmd.exe* to execute the command that follows (that is, the *vcvars64.bat* file) and then leave the window open when the command finishes execution. Now, when you double-click the shortcut icon on the desktop, it will initialize all the environment variables and leave the command window open so you can execute the Visual Studio tools (for example, MASM and MSVC) from the command line.

If you can't find *vcvars64.bat* but there is a *vcvarsall.bat*, also add **x64** to the end of the command line:

```
cmd /k "C:\Program Files (x86)\Microsoft Visual Studio\2019\Community\VC\Auxiliary\Build\
vcvarsall.bat" x64
```

4. Before closing the shortcut's Properties dialog, modify the **Start In** text box to contain **C:** or another directory where you will normally be working when first starting the Visual Studio command line tools.

Double-click the shortcut icon on the desktop; you should be presented with a command window that has text like the following:

```
**********************************************************************
** Visual Studio 2019 Developer Command Prompt v16.9.0
** Copyright (c) 2019 Microsoft Corporation
**********************************************************************
[vcvarsall.bat] Environment initialized for: 'x64'
```

From the command line, type `ml64`. This should produce output similar to the following:

```
C:\>ml64
Microsoft (R) Macro Assembler (x64) Version 14.28.29910.0
Copyright (C) Microsoft Corporation.  All rights reserved.
```

```
usage: ML64 [options] filelist [/link linkoptions]
Run "ML64 /help" or "ML64 /?" for more info
```

Although MASM is complaining that you haven't supplied a filename to compile, the fact that you've gotten this message means that *ml64.exe* is in the execution path, so the system has properly set up the environment variables so you can run the Microsoft Macro Assembler.

5. As a final test, execute the **cl** command to verify that you can run MSVC. You should get output similar to the following:

```
C:\>cl
Microsoft (R) C/C++ Optimizing Compiler Version 19.28.29910 for x64
Copyright (C) Microsoft Corporation.  All rights reserved.

usage: cl [option...] filename... [/link linkoption...]
```

6. Finally, as one last check, locate the Visual Studio application in the Windows Start menu. Click it and verify that this brings up the Visual Studio IDE. If you like, you can make a copy of this shortcut and place it on the desktop so you can bring up Visual Studio by double-clicking the shortcut icon.

C.3 Editing, Assembling, and Running a MASM Source File

You will use a text editor of some sort to create and maintain MASM assembly language source files. If you're not already familiar with Visual Studio and want an environment that's easier to learn and use, consider downloading the (free) Notepad++ text editor application. Notepad++ provides excellent support for MASM, is fast, and is easy to learn and use. Regardless of which text editor you choose (I use a commercial product called CodeWright), the first step is to create a simple assembly language source file.

MASM requires that all source files have a *.asm* suffix, so create the file *hw64.asm* with your editor and enter the following text into that file:

```
includelib kernel32.lib

        extrn __imp_GetStdHandle:proc
        extrn __imp_WriteFile:proc

        .CODE
hwStr   byte    "Hello World!"
hwLen   =       $-hwStr

main    PROC

; On entry, stack is aligned at 8 mod 16. Setting aside 8
; bytes for "bytesWritten" ensures that calls in main have
; their stack aligned to 16 bytes (8 mod 16 inside function).
```

```
        lea     rbx, hwStr
        sub     rsp, 8
        mov     rdi, rsp            ; Hold # of bytes written here

; Note: must set aside 32 bytes (20h) for shadow registers for
; parameters (just do this once for all functions).
; Also, WriteFile has a 5th argument (which is NULL),
; so we must set aside 8 bytes to hold that pointer (and
; initialize it to zero). Finally, the stack must always be
; 16-byte-aligned, so reserve another 8 bytes of storage
; to ensure this.

; Shadow storage for args (always 30h bytes).

        sub     rsp, 030h

; Handle = GetStdHandle(-11);
; Single argument passed in ECX.
; Handle returned in RAX.

        mov     rcx, -11        ; STD_OUTPUT
        call    qword ptr __imp_GetStdHandle

; WriteFile(handle, "Hello World!", 12, &bytesWritten, NULL);
; Zero out (set to NULL) "LPOverlapped" argument:

        mov     qword ptr [rsp + 4 * 8], 0  ; 5th argument on stack

        mov     r9, rdi         ; Address of "bytesWritten" in R9
        mov     r8d, hwLen      ; Length of string to write in R8D
        lea     rdx, hwStr      ; Ptr to string data in RDX
        mov     rcx, rax        ; File handle passed in RCX
        call    qword ptr __imp_WriteFile
        add     rsp, 38h
        ret
main    ENDP
        END
```

This (pure) assembly language program is offered without explanation. Various chapters in this book explain the machine instructions.

Look back at the source code, and you'll see the first line is as follows:

```
includelib kernel32.lib
```

The *kernel32.lib* is a Windows library that includes, among other things, the GetStdHandle and WriteFile functions this assembly language program uses. The Visual Studio installation includes this file and, presumably, the *vcvars64.bat* file will put it in an include path so the linker can find it. If you have problems assembling and linking the program (in the next step), simply make a copy of this file (wherever you can find it in the Visual Studio installation) and include that copy in the directory where you are building the *hw64.asm* file.

To compile (assemble) this file, open the command window (whose shortcut you created earlier) to get a command prompt. Then enter the following command:

```
ml64 hw64.asm /link /subsystem:console /entry:main
```

Assuming you entered the code without error, the command window should have output similar to the following:

```
C:\MASM64>ml64 hw64.asm /link /subsystem:console /entry:main
Microsoft (R) Macro Assembler (x64) Version 14.28.29910.0
Copyright (C) Microsoft Corporation.  All rights reserved.

 Assembling: hw64.asm
Microsoft (R) Incremental Linker Version 14.28.29910.0
Copyright (C) Microsoft Corporation.  All rights reserved.

/OUT:hw64.exe
hw64.obj
/subsystem:console
/entry:main
```

You can run the *hw64.exe* output file that this assembly produces by typing the command **hw64** at the command line prompt. The output should be the following:

```
C:\MASM64>hw64
Hello World!
```

D

THE WINDOWS COMMAND LINE INTERPRETER

Microsoft's MASM is (mostly) a tool that you use from the Windows command line. Therefore, to use MASM properly (at least with respect to all the examples in this book), you will need to be comfortable using the Windows command line interpreter (CLI).

Appendix C shows how to set up the Windows CLI so you can use it. This appendix briefly describes some common commands you will use in the CLI.

D.1 Command Line Syntax

A basic Windows CLI command takes the form

command options

where *command* is either a built-in CLI command, an executable program on disk (typically having an *.exe* filename suffix), or a batch filename (with a *.bat* suffix), and *options* is a list of zero or more options for the command. The options are command-specific.

Probably the most common example in this book of an executable program you would run from the command line is the *ml64.exe* program (the MASM assembler). The Microsoft linker (*link.exe*), librarian (*lib.exe*), nmake (*nmake.exe*), and the MSVC compiler (*cl.exe*) are also examples of executable programs you might run from the command line.

All of the sample programs appearing in this book are also examples of commands you could run from the command line. For example, the following command executes the *build.bat* batch file to build the *listing2-1.exe* executable file (from Chapter 2):

```
build listing2-1
```

Immediately after building the *listing2-1.exe* executable file, you can run it from the command line. Here's the command and the output it produces:

```
C:\>listing2-1
Calling Listing 2-1:
i=1, converted to hex=1
j=123, converted to hex=7b
k=456789, converted to hex=6f855
Listing 2-1 terminated
```

The *listing2-1.exe* executable file doesn't support any command line options. If you type anything after the listing2-1 command on the command line, the *listing2-1.exe* program will ignore that text.

Although most options are command-specific, you can apply certain command line options to most programs you run from the command line: specifically, *I/O redirection*. Many console applications write data to the *standard output device* (the console window). All of the print and printf function calls appearing throughout this book, for example, write their data to the standard output device. Normally, all output sent to the standard output device appears as text written to the command line (console) window.

However, you can tell Windows to send this data to a file (or even another device) by using an *output redirection option*. The output redirection option takes the form

```
command options >filename more_options
```

where *command* is the command name, *options* and *more_options* are zero or more command line options (not containing an output redirection option), and *filename* is the name of the file where you would like to have the output from *command* sent. Consider the following command line:

```
listing2-1 >listing2-1.txt
```

Executing this command produces no output to the display. However, you will discover that this command creates a new text file on the disk. That text file will contain the output from the *listing2-1.exe* program (given earlier).

The Windows CLI also supports *standard input redirection* using the syntax

---

```
command options <filename more_options
```

---

where `command` is the command name, `options` and `more_options` are zero or more command line options (not containing an input redirection option), and `filename` is the name of the file from which `command` will read its input.

Input redirection causes a program that would normally read data from the user (at the keyboard, which is the standard input device) to instead read the data from a text file. For example, suppose you executed the `listing2-1` command given earlier and redirected the output to the *listing2-1.txt* output file. Consider the following command (from Chapter 1) that reads a line of text from the user (in this particular example, I typed **hello** in response to the program's request for input):

```
C:\>build listing1-8
C:\>echo off
 Assembling: listing1-8.asm
c.cpp
C:\>listing1-8
Calling Listing 1-8:
Enter a string: hello
User entered: 'hello'
Listing 1-8 terminated
```

Now consider the following command:

```
C:\>listing1-8 <listing2-1.txt
Calling Listing 1-8:
Enter a string: User entered: 'Calling Listing 2-1:'
Listing 1-8 terminated
```

In this example, the input is redirected from the *listing2-1.txt* file produced by the earlier execution of *listing2-1.exe*. The *listing1-8.exe* program reads the first line of that file as input (rather than reading a line of text from the keyboard). The program doesn't echo the text read from the file (including the newline character); this is why the `User entered: 'Calling Listing 2-1:'` text appears on the same line as the `Enter a string:` prompt. When actually reading data from the keyboard, the system echoes the data to the display (including the newline character). This doesn't happen when redirecting the input from a file.

The file contains several lines of text. However, *listing1-8.exe* reads only one line of text, so it ignores the remaining lines in the *listing2-1.txt* file.

You can redirect both the standard input and the standard output on the same command. Consider the following:

```
C:\>listing1-8 <listing2-1.txt >listing1-8.txt
```

This reads the data from the *listing2-1.txt* file and sends all the output to the *listing1-8.txt* file.

When redirecting the output from a program to a text file, if the output file already exists, Windows will delete that file prior to writing the standard output text to that file. You can also instruct Windows to append the output from the command to the existing file by using the following output redirection syntax (using two greater-than symbols):

```
command options >>filename more_options
```

Command line options other than the redirection options are usually filenames (for example, ml64 mySource.asm) or options that control the command's behavior (such as ml64's /c or /Fl command line options you'll find used throughout this book). By convention, most Windows CLI commands use a slash character (/) as a prefix before actual options (as opposed to filenames). This is a convention, not a hard requirement.

Some commands, for example, use the Unix convention of a dash or hyphen character (-) instead of (or in addition to) the slash character. It's really an application-specific choice. See the documentation for the particular program you are using for the details. All the built-in CLI commands, and most Microsoft CLI programs, use the slash character to designate options.

D.2　Directory Names and Drive Letters

Many commands accept or require a file or directory pathname as a command line option. Pathnames consist of two major components: a drive letter and the directory or file pathname. A drive letter is a single alphabetic character (A to Z) followed by a colon; for example:

```
A: B: C: etc.
```

Drive letters are not case-sensitive. A: is equivalent to a: on the command line. Windows reserves drive letters A: and B: for floppy drives. As you don't often see floppy disk drives on modern machines, you won't likely use these drive letters. However, if you have a really old machine . . .

C: is the default drive letter for the boot drive. If you have only one hard drive (or SSD) in your machine, Windows will probably associate C: with that drive. The examples appearing throughout this book assume you're operating on drive C: (though this is by no means a requirement).

If you have multiple drives (either multiple physical drive units, or you've partitioned your hard drive into multiple logical drives), Windows usually associates consecutive drive letters (D:, E:, and so forth) with these additional drives. You can reassign drive letters, if you like, so there is no guarantee that all drive letters will be contiguous in the alphabet.

You can switch the default drive letter by typing the letter and a colon, by themselves, on the command line. For example,

```
D:
```

switches the default drive to D:, assuming such a drive exists. If the drive does not exist, Windows will complain that the system cannot find the specified drive and will not change the default drive.

Normally (you can change this), Windows displays the current drive letter as part of the command line prompt (by default, it displays the default pathname as well). For example, a typical Windows command line prompt looks like this:

```
C:\>
```

The \ character appearing in the command prompt is the current (default) directory. In this case, \ by itself indicates the root (or main) directory on the C: drive. Had the current directory been something else, Windows would have listed that after the drive letter. For example, had the current directory been \WINDOWS, the CLI would have displayed the following as the command line prompt:

```
C:\WINDOWS>
```

Windows, as you're probably aware, has a hierarchical filesystem, allowing subdirectories inside (sub)directories. The backslash character separates directory names in a full pathname. You'll commonly see two pathname forms in Windows: full pathnames and partial pathnames.

Full pathnames begin with a backslash (\) character and start from the root directory. *Partial pathnames* do not begin with a backslash, and the path begins with the current (default) directory (the first subdirectory in the partial pathname must appear in the current default subdirectory).

Spaces normally separate options on a command line. If a space appears in a pathname, you must surround the entire pathname with quotes; for example:

```
"\This\Path name\has\a\space"
```

The CLI supports a pair of *wildcard* characters in pathnames. The asterisk character (*) will match zero or more characters. The question mark character (?) will match zero or one character.

A command must explicitly support wildcard characters; the Windows CLI commands support wildcard options, as do most Microsoft tools (for example, *ml64.exe*). Not all executable files support wildcards in filenames, however. Wildcard characters are usable in directory names as well as filenames. They will not, however, replace the backslash character (\) in a pathname.

D.3 Some Useful Built-in Commands

The Windows CLI contains many built-in commands (commands that are part of the *cmd.exe* program and don't require a separate *.exe* or *.bat* file). There are far too many built-in commands to consider here (and you wouldn't use most of them); therefore, this section presents just a handful of the most commonly used commands.

D.3.1 The cd and chdir Commands

The cd (*change directory*) command switches the default directory to the directory you specify as the command line option. Note that chdir is a synonym for cd. Its syntax is

```
cd directory_name
```

where *directory_name* is a full or partial pathname to the new directory. For example:

```
cd \masm32\examples
```

The cd command does not normally change the default drive letter, even if you specify it as part of the pathname. For example, if the current drive letter is D:, the following command will not directly change the default drive letter and pathname:

```
D:\>cd C:\masm32\examples
D:\>
```

Notice that the command prompt remains D:\> after the cd command. However, if you switch to the C: drive (using the C: command), Windows will set the default directory as per the previous command:

```
D:>C:
C:\masm32\examples>
```

As you can see, the default directory is associated with a drive letter (and each drive letter maintains its own default directory).

If you want to switch both the drive letter and the pathname with the cd command, just supply the /d option before the pathname:

```
D:\>cd /d C:\masm32\examples
C:\masm32\examples
```

Don't forget that if a pathname contains spaces, you must enclose the pathname in quotes when using the cd command:

```
cd /d "C:\program files"
```

The following displays help information about the cd command:

```
cd /?
```

If you issue the cd command by itself (no command line arguments), this command displays the current (default) pathname.

D.3.2   The cls Command

The cls command clears the screen (at least, the command window). This is useful when you want to clear the screen prior to a compilation and want to see only the messages associated with that particular compilation when scrolling back through the command window.

D.3.3   The copy Command

The copy command copies one or more files to a different location. Typically, you use this command to make backup copies of a file in the current directory or to make a copy of a file into a different subdirectory. The syntax for this command is as follows:

```
copy source_filename destination_filename
```

This command duplicates the file specified by *source_filename* and names that duplicate *destination_filename*. Both names can be full or partial pathnames.

The copy command supports several command line options (in addition to the source and destination filenames). You probably won't use those options very often. For more details, issue the following help command:

```
copy /?
```

D.3.4   The date Command

The date command, by itself, displays the current system date and prompts you to enter a new date (which will permanently set the system date—so be careful using this!). With a /t command line option, this command will only display the date and not ask you to change it. Here's an example:

```
C:\>date /t
Sat 02/23/2019
```

As usual, date /? displays the help information for this command.

D.3.5 The del (erase) Command

The del command (erase is a synonym for del) will delete the file(s) you specify as the command line options. The syntax is

```
del options files_to_delete
```

where *options* is command line options beginning with a slash, and *files _to_delete* is a list of filenames (pathnames), separated by spaces or commas, to be deleted. This command accepts wildcard characters; for example, the following command deletes all the *.obj* files appearing in the current directory:

```
del *.obj
```

It goes without saying that you should be very careful when using this command, especially when using wildcard characters. For example, consider the following command (which is probably a typo):

```
del * .obj
```

This deletes all the files in the current directory and then attempts to delete a file named *.obj* (which won't exist after this command has deleted all the files in the subdirectory).

Some useful command line options are associated with this command. Use the /? option to learn about them:

```
C:\>del /?
```

D.3.6 The dir Command

The dir (*directory*) command is one of the more useful CLI commands. It displays a directory listing (a list of files in a directory).

Without any command line options, this command displays all the files in the current directory. With a single drive letter (and colon) as the argument, this command displays all the files in the default directory on the specified drive. With a pathname that leads to a subdirectory, this command displays all the files in the specified directory. With a pathname that leads to a single filename, this command displays the directory information about that particular file.

As usual, this command supports several command line options beginning with the slash character. Use dir /? to get the help information for this command.

D.3.7 The more Command

The more command displays the text in a text file one screenful at a time. After displaying a screenful of text, it waits for the user to press ENTER or spacebar on the keyboard. Pressing spacebar advances the output another screenful of text; pressing ENTER advances the output by one line. Pressing Q terminates the program.

The more command expects one or more filenames on the command line as arguments. If you specify two or more files, more will display the output in order. The more command also allows several command line options. You can use the following command to learn about them:

```
more /?
```

D.3.8 The move Command

The move command moves a file from one location to another (possibly renaming the file while moving it). It is similar to copy, though move deletes the file from its original location after moving it. The basic syntax for this command is the following:

```
move original_file new_file
```

As usual, the /? command line option provides help for this command.

D.3.9 The ren and rename Commands

The ren command (rename is a synonym) changes the name of a file. The syntax is

```
ren original_filename new_filename
```

where (obviously) *original_filename* is the old filename you want to change and *new_filename* is the new name of the file you want to use. The new and old files must be in the same directory. Use the move command if you want to move the file to a new directory while renaming it.

D.3.10 The rd and rmdir Commands

The rd command (rmdir is a synonym) removes (deletes) a directory. The directory must be empty before using this command (though the /s option can override this). The basic syntax for this command is

```
rd directory_path
```

where *directory_path* is the path to the directory you wish to remove. Use the rd /? command to get help.

D.3.11 The time Command

With no arguments, the time command displays the current system time and prompts you to change it. With a /t command line argument, time simply displays the current time. Use /? to display help information for this command.

D.4 For More Information

This appendix has provided only the tiniest introduction to the Windows command line interpreter—just enough information to be able to effectively compile and run assembly language programs using MASM. The CLI supports many dozens of built-in commands (if not over a hundred). One place to learn about these commands is *https://docs.microsoft.com/en-us/windows-server/administration/windows-commands/cmd/*.

ANSWERS TO QUESTIONS

E.1 Answers to Questions in Chapter 1

1. *cmd.exe*
2. *ml64.exe*
3. Address, data, and control
4. AL, AH, AX, and EAX
5. BL, BH, BX, and EBX
6. SIL, SI, and ESI
7. R8B, R8W, and R8D
8. FLAGS, EFLAGS, or RFLAGS
9. (a) 2, (b) 4, (c) 16, (d) 32, (e) 8
10. Any 8-bit register and any constant that can be represented with 8 bits
11. 32

12.

Destination	Constant size
RAX	32
EAX	32
AX	16
AL	8
AH	8
mem$_{32}$	32
mem$_{64}$	32

NOTE *64-bit add operands support only 32-bit constants.*

13. 64

NOTE *Technically the x86-64 allows 16- and 32-bit registers as* lea *destination operands for legacy reasons; however, such instructions are not generally useful for calculating actual memory addresses (though they might be useful for sneaky addition operations).*

14. Any memory operand will work, regardless of its size.

15. call

16. ret

17. Application binary interface

18. (a) AL, (b) AX, (c) EAX, (d) RAX, (e) XMM0, (f) RAX

19. RCX for integer operands, XMM0 for floating-point/vector operands

20. RDX for integer operands, XMM1 for floating-point/vector operands

21. R8 for integer operands, XMM2 for floating-point/vector operands

22. R9 for integer operands, XMM3 for floating-point/vector operands

23. dword or sdword

24. qword

E.2 Answers to Questions in Chapter 2

1. $9 \times 10^3 + 3 \times 10^2 + 8 \times 10^1 + 4 \times 10^0 + 5 \times 10^{-1} + 7 \times 10^{-2} + 6 \times 10^{-3}$

2. (a) 10, (b) 12, (c) 7, (d) 9, (e) 3, (f) 15

3. (a) A, (b) E, (c) B, (d) D, (e) 2, (f) C, (g) CF, (h) 98D1

4. (a) 0001_0010_1010_1111, (b) 1001_1011_1110_0111, (c) 0100_1010, (d) 0001_0011_0111_1111, (e) 1111_0000_0000_1101, (f) 1011_1110 _1010_1101, (g) 0100_1001_0011_1000

5. (a) 10, (b) 11, (c) 15, (d) 13, (e) 14, (f) 12

6. (a) 16, (b) 64, (c) 128, (d) 32, (e) 4, (f) 8, (g) 4

7. (a) 2, (b) 4, (c) 8, (d) 16

8. (a) 16, (b) 256, (c) 65,636, (d) 2

9. 4

10. 0 through 7

11. Bit 0

12. Bit 31

13. (a) 0, (b) 0, (c) 0, (d) 1

14. (a) 0, (b) 1, (c) 1, (d) 1

15. (a) 0, (b) 1, (c) 1, (d) 0

16. 1

17. AND

18. OR

19. NOT

20. XOR

21. not

22. 1111_1011

23. 0000_0010

24. (a) and (c) and (e)

25. neg

26. (a) and (c) and (d)

27. jmp

28. *label:*

29. Carry, overflow, zero, and sign

30. JZ

31. JC

32. JA, JAE, JBE, JB, JE, JNE (and the synonyms JNA, JNAE, JNB, JNBE, plus other synonyms)

33. JG, JGE, JL, JLE, JE, JNE (and the synonyms JNG, JNGE, JNL, and JNLE)

34. ZF = 1 if the result of the shift is 0.

35. The HO bit shifted out of the operand goes into the carry flag.

36. If the next-to-HO bit is different from the HO bit *before* the shift, the OF will be set; otherwise, it is cleared, though only for 1-bit shifts.

37. The SF is set equal to the HO bit of the result.

38. ZF = 1 if the result of the shift is 0.

39. The LO bit shifted out of the operand goes into the carry flag.

40. If the next-to-HO bit is different from the HO bit *before* the shift, the OF will be set; otherwise, it is cleared, but only for 1-bit shifts.

41. The SF is always clear after the SHR instruction because a 0 is always shifted into the HO bit of the result.

42. ZF = 1 if the result of the shift is 0.

43. The LO bit shifted out of the operand goes into the carry flag.

44. The OF is always clear after SAR as it is impossible for the sign to change.

45. The SF is set equal to the HO bit of the result, though technically it will never change.

46. The HO bit shifted out of the operand goes into the carry flag.

47. It doesn't affect the ZF.

48. The LO bit shifted out of the operand goes into the carry flag.

49. It doesn't affect the sign flag.

50. Multiplication by 2

51. Division by 2

52. Multiplication and division

53. Subtract them and see if their difference is less than a small error value.

54. A value that has a 1 bit in the HO mantissa position

55. 7

56. 30h through 39h

57. Apostrophes and quotes

58. UTF-8, UTF-16, and UTF-32

59. A scalar integer value that represents a single Unicode character

60. A block of 65,536 different Unicode characters

E.3   Answers to Questions in Chapter 3

1. RIP

2. Operation code, the numeric encoding for a machine instruction

3. Static and scalar variables

4. ±2GB

5. The address of the memory location to access

6. RAX

7. lea

8. The final address obtained after all addressing mode calculations are completed

9. 1, 2, 4, or 8

10. 2GB total memory

11. You can use the VAR[REG] addressing mode(s) to directly access elements of an array using a 64-bit register as an index into the array without first loading the address of the array into a separate base register.

12. The `.data` section can hold initialized data values; the `.data?` section can contain only uninitialized variables.

13. `.code` and `.const`

14. `.data` and `.data?`

15. An offset into a particular section (for example, `.data`)

16. Use *some_ID* `label` *some_type* to inform MASM that the following data is of type *some_type* when, in fact, it could be another type.

17. MASM will combine them into a single section.

18. Use the `align 8` statement.

19. Memory management unit

20. If `b` is at an address that is at the last byte in an MMU page and the next page is not readable, loading a word from the memory location starting with `b` will produce a general protection fault.

21. A constant expression plus the base address of a variable in memory

22. To coerce the following operand type to a different type

23. Little-endian values appear in memory with their LO byte at the lowest address and the HO byte at the highest address. Big-endian values are the opposite: their HO byte appears at the lowest address, and their LO byte appears at the highest address in memory.

24. `xchg al, ah` or `xchg ah, al`

25. `bswap eax`

26. `bswap rax`

27. (a) Subtract 8 from RSP, (b) Store the value in RAX at the location pointed at by RSP.

28. (a) Load RAX from the 8 bytes pointed at by RSP, (b) Add 8 to RSP.

29. Reverse

30. Last in, first out

31. Move the data to and from the stack using the [`RSP` ± *const*] addressing mode.

32. The Windows ABI requires the stack to be aligned on a 16-byte boundary; pushing RAX might make the stack aligned on an 8-byte (but not 16-byte) boundary.

E.4 Answers to Questions in Chapter 4

1. `imul` *reg, constant*

2. `imul` *destreg, srcreg, constant*

3. `imul` *destreg, srcreg*

4. A symbolic (named) constant for which MASM will substitute the literal constant for the name everywhere it appears in the source file

5. `=, equ, textequ`

6. Text equates substitute a textual string that can be any text; numeric equates must be assigned a numeric constant value that can be represented with a 64-bit integer.

7. Use the text delimiters < and > around the string literal; for example, <"a long string">.

8. An arithmetic expression whose value MASM can calculate during assembly

9. `lengthof`

10. The offset into the current section

11. `this` and `$`

12. Use the constant expression `$-startingLocation`.

13. Use a series of (numeric) equates, with each successive equate set to the value of the previous equate plus one; for example:

```
val1 = 0
val2 = val1 + 1
val3 = val2 + 1
etc.
```

14. Using the `typedef` directive

15. A pointer is a variable in memory that holds the address of another object in memory.

16. Load the pointer variable into a 64-bit register and use the register-indirect addressing mode to reference that address.

17. Using a `qword` data declaration, or another data type that is 64 bits in size

18. The `offset` operator

19. (a) Uninitialized pointers, (b) Using pointers to hold an illegal value, (c) Using a pointer after its storage has been freed (dangling pointers), (d) Failing to free storage after it is no longer being used (memory leak), (e) Accessing indirect data by using the wrong data type

20. Using a pointer after its storage has been freed

21. Failing to free storage after you are done using it

22. An aggregate type composed of smaller data objects

23. A sequence of characters ending with a 0 byte (or other 0 value)

24. A string containing a length value as its first element

25. A descriptor is a data type containing a pointer (to the character data), string length, and possibly other information that describes the string data.

26. A homogenous collection of data elements (all with the same type)

27. The memory address of the first element of the array

28. `array byte 10 dup (?)` (as an example)

29. Simply fill in the initial values as the operand field of a byte, word, dword, or other data declaration directive. Also, you could use a sequence of one or more constant values as the dup operator operand; for example, 5 dup (2, 3).

30. (a) *base_address* + *index* * 4 (4 is the element size), (b) W[i,j] = *base_address* + (i * 8 + j) * 2 (2 is the element size), (c) R[i,j,k] = *base_address* +(((i * 4) + j) * 6 + k) * 8 (8 is the element size)

31. An organization for multidimensional arrays where you store the elements of each row in the array in contiguous memory locations and then store each row, one after the other, in memory

32. An organization for multidimensional arrays where you store the elements of each column in the array in contiguous memory locations and then store each column, one after the other, in memory

33. W word 4 dup (8 dup (?))

34. A heterogeneous collection of data elements (each field could have different types)

35. struct and ends

36. The dot operator

37. A heterogeneous collection of data elements (each field could have different types); the offset of each field in the union begins at 0.

38. union and ends

39. The fields of a record and struct appear at successive memory locations within the struct (each field has its own block of bytes); the fields of a union overlap one another, with each field beginning at offset zero in the union.

40. An unnamed union whose fields are treated as fields of the enclosing struct

E.5 Answers to Questions in Chapter 5

1. It pushes the return address onto the stack (the address of the next instruction after the call) and then jumps to the address specified by the operand.

2. It pops a return address off the stack and moves the address into the RIP register, transferring control to the instruction just beyond the call to the current procedure.

3. After popping the return address, the CPU adds this value to RSP, removing that number of bytes of parameters from the stack.

4. The address of the instruction just beyond the call to the procedure

5. Namespace pollution occurs when so many symbols, identifiers, or names are defined in a source file that it becomes difficult to select new, unique names to use in that source file.

6. Put two colons after the name; for example, id::.

7. Use the `option noscoped` directive just before the procedure.

8. Use the `push` instruction to save the register values on the stack upon entry into the procedure; then use the `pop` instruction to restore the register values immediately before returning from the procedure.

9. Code is difficult to maintain. (A secondary issue, though minor, is that it takes more space.)

10. Performance—because you're often preserving registers that don't need to be preserved for the calling code

11. When the subroutine attempts to return, it uses the garbage you left on the stack as the return address, which usually produces undefined results (a program crash).

12. The subroutine uses whatever was on the stack prior to the call as the return address, with undefined results.

13. A collection of data, including parameters, local variables, the return address, and other items, associated with the call (activation) of a procedure

14. RBP

15. 8 bytes (64 bits)

16. _____

```
push rbp
mov  rbp, rsp
sub  rsp, sizeOfLocals ; Assuming there are local variables
```

17. _____

```
leave
ret
```

18. `and rsp, -16`

19. The section of the source file (usually the body of a procedure) where the symbol is visible and usable in the program

20. From the moment storage is allocated for the variable to the point the system deallocates that storage

21. Variables whose storage is automatically allocated upon entry into a block of code (usually a procedure) and automatically deallocated upon exiting that block of code

22. Upon entry into a procedure (or the block of code associated with that automatic variable)

23. Using `textequ` directives or the MASM `local` directive

24. `var1`: −2; `local2`: −8 (MASM aligns variable on dword boundary); `dVar`: −9; `qArray`: −32 (base address of array is the lowest memory address); `rlocal`: −40 (base address of array is the lowest memory address); `ptrVar`: −48

25. `option prologue:PrologueDef` and `option epilogue:EpilogueDef`. Should also supply `option prologue:none` and `option epilogue:none` to turn this off.

26. Before MASM emits any code for the procedure, after all the local directives

27. Wherever a ret instruction appears

28. The actual parameter's value

29. The memory address of the actual parameter's value

30. RCX, RDX, R8, and R9 (or smaller subcomponents of these registers)

31. XMM0, XMM1, XMM2, or XMM3

32. On the stack, above the shadow locations (32 bytes) reserved for the arguments passed in the registers

33. Procedures are free to modify volatile registers without preserving their values; procedures must preserve the values of nonvolatile registers across a procedure invocation.

34. RAX, RCX, RDX, R8, R9, R10, R11, XMM0, XMM1, XMM2, XMM3, XMM4, XMM5, and the HO 128 bits of all the YMM and ZMM registers

35. RBX, RSI, RDI, RBP, RSP, R12, R13, R14, R15, and XMM6–XMM15. Also, the direction flag must be clear upon return from a procedure.

36. Using positive offsets from the RBP register

37. Storage reserved on the stack for parameters the caller passes in the RCX, RDX, R8 and R9 registers

38. 32 bytes

39. 32 bytes

40. 32 bytes

NOTE *Shadow storage is the same regardless of how many parameters you pass (including none).*

41. parm1: RBP + 16; parm2: RBP + 24; parm3: RBP + 32; parm4: RBP + 40

42. _____

```
mov rax, parm4
mov al, [rax]
```

43. lclVar1: RBP − 1; lclVar2: RBP − 4 (aligned to 2-byte boundary); lclVar3: RBP − 8; lclVar4: RBP − 16

44. By reference

45. Application binary interface

46. In the RAX register

47. The address of a procedure passed as a parameter

48. Indirectly. Typically by using a call *parm* instruction, where *parm* is the procedural parameter, a qword variable containing the address of the procedure. You could also load the parameter value into a 64-bit register and indirectly call the procedure through that register.

49. Allocate local storage to hold the register values to preserve and move the register data into that storage upon procedure entry, and then move the data back into the registers just before returning from the procedure.

E.6   Answers to Questions in Chapter 6

1. AL for 8-bit operands, AX for 16-bit operands, EAX for 32-bit operands, and RAX for 64-bit operands

2. 8-bit mul operation: 16 bits; 16-bit mul operation: 32 bits; 32-bit mul operation: 64 bits; 64-bit mul operator: 128 bits. The CPU put the products at AX for 8×8 products, DX:AX for 16×16 products, EDX:EAX for 32×32 products, and RDX:RAX for 64×64 products.

3. The quotient in AL, AX, EAX, or RAX and the remainder in AH, DX, EDX, or RDX

4. Sign-extend AX into DX.

5. Zero-extend EAX into EDX.

6. A division by 0 and producing a quotient that will not fit into the accumulator register (AL, AX, EAX, or RAX)

7. By setting the carry and overflow flags

8. They scramble the flag; that is, they leave it in an undefined state.

9. The extended-precision imul instruction produces a $2 \times n$-bit result, uses implied operands (AL, AX, EAX, and RAX), and modifies the AH, DX, EDX, and RDX registers. Also, the extended-precision imul instruction does not allow constant operands, whereas the generic imul instruction does.

10. cbw, cwd, cdq, and cqo

11. They scramble all the flags, leaving them in an undefined state.

12. It sets the zero flag if the two operands are equal.

13. It sets the carry flag if the first operand is less than the second operand.

14. The sign and overflow flags are different if the first operand is less than the second operand; they are the same if the first operand is greater than or equal to the second operand.

15. An 8-bit register or memory location

16. They set the operand to 1 if the condition is true, or to false if the condition is not true.

17. The test instruction is the same as the and instruction except it does not store the result to the destination (first) operand; it only sets the flags.

18. They both set the condition code flags the same way.

19. Supply the operand to be tested as the first (destination) operand and an immediate constant containing a single 1 bit in the bit position to test. After the test instruction, the zero flag will contain the state of the desired bit.

20. The following are some possible, not the only, solutions:

```
x = x + y
```

```
mov eax, x
add eax, y
mov x, eax
```

```
x = y - z
```

```
mov eax, y
sub eax, z
mov x, eax
```

```
x = y * z
```

```
mov  eax, y
imul eax, z
mov  x, eax
```

```
x = y + z * t
```

```
mov  eax, z
imul eax, t
add  eax, y
mov  x, eax
```

```
x = (y + z) * t
```

```
mov  eax, y
add  eax, z
imul eax, t
mov  x, eax
```

```
x = -((x*y)/z)
```

```
mov  eax, x
imul y           ; Note: Sign-extends into EDX
idiv z
mov  x, eax
```

```
x = (y == z) && (t != 0)
```

```
mov   eax, y
cmp   eax, z
sete  bl
cmp   t, 0
setne bh
and   bl, bh
movzx eax, bl    ; Because x is a 32-bit integer
mov   x, eax
```

21. The following are some possible, not the only, solutions:

```
x = x * 2
```

```
shl    x, 1
```

```
x = y * 5
```

```
mov    eax, y
lea    eax, [eax][eax*4]
mov    x, eax
```

Here is another solution:

```
mov    eax, y
mov    ebx, eax
shl    eax, 2
add    eax, ebx
mov    x, eax
```

```
x = y * 8
```

```
mov    eax, y
shl    eax, 3
mov    x, eax
```

22. x = x /2

```
shr    x, 1
```

```
x = y / 8
```

```
mov    ax, y
shr    ax, 3
mov    x, ax
```

```
x = z / 10
```

```
movzx eax, z
imul  eax, 6554   ; Or 6553
shr   eax, 16
mov   x, ax
```

23. x = x + y

```
fld    x
fld    y
faddp
fstp   x
```

```
x = y - z
```

```
fld    y
fld    z
```

```
fsubp
fstp   x
```

x = y * z

```
fld    y
fld    z
fmulp
fstp   x
```

x = y + z * t

```
fld    y
fld    z
fld    t
fmulp
faddp
fstp   x
```

x = (y + z) * t

```
fld    y
fld    z
faddp
fld    t
fmulp
fstp   x
```

x = -((x * y)/z)

```
fld    x
fld    y
fmulp
fld    z
fdivp
fchs
fstp   x
```

24. x = x + y

```
movss xmm0, x
addss xmm0, y
movss x, xmm0
```

x = y - z

```
movss xmm0, y
subss xmm0, z
movss x, xmm0
```

x = y * z

```
movss xmm0, y
```

```
mulss   xmm0, z
movss   x, xmm0
```

```
x = y + z * t
```

```
movss   xmm0, z
mulss   xmm0, t
addss   xmm0, y
movss   x, xmm0
```

25. b = x < y

```
fld     y
fld     x
fcomip  st(0), st(1)
setb    b
fstp    st(0)
```

```
b = x >= y && x < z
```

```
fld     y
fld     x
fcomip  st(0), st(1)
setae   bl
fstp    st(0)
fld     z
fld     x
fcomip  st(0), st(1)
setb    bh
fstp    st(0)
and     bl, bh
mov     b, bl
```

E.7   Answers to Questions in Chapter 7

1. Use the `lea` instruction or the `offset` operator.
2. `option noscoped`
3. `option scoped`
4. `jmp` reg_{64} and `jmp` mem_{64}
5. A piece of code that maintains history information in variables or via the program counter
6. If the second letter of the jump mnemonic is n, remove the n; otherwise, insert an n as the second character.
7. `jpo` and `jpe`

> **NOTE**   *Technically, the* `jcxz`*,* `jecxz`*, and* `jrcxz` *instructions are also exceptions.*

8. A short code sequence used to extend the range of a jump or call instruction beyond the ±2GB range

9. `cmovcc reg, src`, where *cc* is one of the conditional suffixes (which follow a conditional jump), *reg* is a 16-, 32-, or 64-bit register, and *src* is a source register or memory location that is the same size as *reg*.

10. You can conditionally execute a large set of different types of instructions by using a conditional jump without the time penalty of a control transfer.

11. The destination has to be a register, and 8-bit registers are not allowed.

12. Complete Boolean evaluation of an expression evaluates all components of the expression, even if it is not logically necessary to do so; short-circuit evaluation stops as soon as it determines that the expression must be true or false.

13.

```
if(x == y || z > t)
{
    Do something
}
    mov   eax, x
    cmp   eax, y
    sete  bl
    mov   eax, z
    cmp   eax, t
    seta  bh
    or    bl, bh
    jz    skipIF
        Code for statements that "do something"
skipIF:

if(x != y && z < t)
{
    THEN statements
}
Else
{
    ELSE statements
}
    mov   eax, x
    cmp   eax, y
    setne bl
    mov   eax, z
    cmp   eax, t
    setb  bh
    and   bl, bh
    jz    doElse
        Code for THEN statements
    jmp   endOfIF

doElse:
        Code for ELSE statements
endOfIF:
```

14.

```
1st IF:
        mov   ax, x
        cmp   ax, y
        jeq   doBlock
        mov   eax, z
        cmp   eax, t
        jnl   skipIF
doBlock:      Code for statements that "do something"
skipIF:


2nd IF:
        mov   eax, x
        cmp   eax, y
        je    doElse
        mov   eax, z
        cmp   eax, t
        jnl   doElse
         Code for THEN statements
        jmp   endOfIF


doElse:
        Code for ELSE statements
endOfIF:
```

15.

```
switch(s)
{
    case 0:   case 0 code   break;
    case 1:   case 1 code   break;
    case 2:   case 2 code   break;
    case 3:   case 3 code   break;
}


    mov eax, s ; Zero-extends!
    cmp eax, 3
    ja  skipSwitch
    lea rbx, jmpTbl
    jmp [rbx][rax * 8]
jmpTbl qword case0, case1, case2, case3

case0: case 0 code
       jmp skipSwitch

case1: case 1 code
       jmp skipSwitch

case2: case 2 code
       jmp skipSwitch

case3: case 3 code
```

```
skipSwitch:

switch(t)
{
   case 2:  case 0 code break;
   case 4:  case 4 code break;
   case 5:  case 5 code break;
   case 6:  case 6 code break;
   default: default code
}
    mov eax, t ; Zero-extends!
    cmp eax, 2
    jb  swDefault
    cmp eax, 6
    ja  swDefault
    lea rbx, jmpTbl
    jmp [rbx][rax * 8 - 2 * 8]
jmpTbl qword case2, swDefault, case4, case5, case6

swDefault: default code
       jmp endSwitch

case2: case 2 code
       jmp endSwitch

case4: case 4 code
       jmp endSwitch

case5: case 5 code
       jmp endSwitch

case6: case 6 code

endSwitch:

switch(u)
{
   case 10:   case 10 code  break;
   case 11:   case 11 code  break;
   case 12:   case 12 code  break;
   case 25:   case 25 code  break;
   case 26:   case 26 code  break;
   case 27:   case 27 code  break;
   default:   default code
}
    lea rbx, jmpTbl1  ; Assume cases 10-12
    mov eax, u        ; Zero-extends!
    cmp eax, 10
    jb  swDefault
    cmp eax, 12
    jbe sw1
    cmp eax, 25
    jb  swDefault
    cmp eax, 27
```

```
        ja  swDefault
        lea rbx, jmpTbl2
        jmp [rbx][rax * 8 - 25 * 8]
sw1: jmp [rbx][rax*8-2*8]
jmpTbl1 qword case10, case11, case12
jmpTbl2 qword case25, case26, case27

swDefault: default code
        jmp endSwitch

case10: case 10 code
        jmp endSwitch

case11: case 11 code
        jmp endSwitch

case12: case 12 code
        jmp endSwitch

case25: case 25 code
        jmp endSwitch

case26: case 26 code
        jmp endSwitch

case27: case 27 code

endSwitch:
```

16. _____

```
while(i < j)
{
    Code for loop body
}

whlLp:
    mov eax, i
    cmp eax, j
    jnl endWhl
     Code for loop body
    jmp whlLp
endWhl:

while(i < j && k != 0)
{
    Code for loop body, part a
    if(m == 5) continue;
    Code for loop body, part b
    if(n < 6) break;
    Code for loop body, part c
}

; Assume short-circuit evaluation:
```

```
whlLp:
    mov eax, i
    cmp eax, j
    jnl endWhl
    mov eax, k
    cmp eax, 0
    je  endWhl
     Code for loop body, part a
    cmp m, 5
    je  whlLp
     Code for loop body, part b
    cmp n, 6
    jl  endWhl
     Code for loop body, part c
    jmp whlLp
endWhl:

do
{
   Code for loop body
} while(i != j);

doLp:
   Code for loop body
    mov eax, i
    cmp eax, j
    jne doLp

do
{
   Code for loop body, part a
   if(m != 5) continue;
   Code for loop body, part b
   if(n == 6) break;
   Code for loop body, part c
} while(i < j && k > j);

doLp:
   Code for loop body, part a
    cmp m, 5
    jne doCont
   Code for loop body, part b
    cmp n, 6
    je  doExit
   Code for loop body, part c
doCont:    mov eax, i
    cmp eax, j
    jnl doExit
    mov eax, k
    cmp eax, j
    jg  doLp
doExit:

for(int i = 0; i < 10; ++i)
```

```
{
   Code for loop body
}

        mov i, 0
forLp: cmp i, 10
        jnl forDone
         Code for loop body
        inc i
        jmp forLp
forDone:
```

E.8 Answers to Questions in Chapter 8

1. You compute $x = y + z$ as follows:

   a.
   ```
   mov rax, qword ptr y
   add rax, qword ptr z
   mov qword ptr x, rax
   mov rax, qword ptr y[8]
   adc rax, qword ptr z[8]
   mov qword ptr x[8], rax
   ```

   b.
   ```
   mov rax, qword ptr y
   add rax, qword ptr z
   mov qword ptr x, rax
   mov eax, dword ptr z[8]
   adc eax, qword ptr y[8]
   mov dword ptr x[8], eax
   ```

   c.
   ```
   mov eax, dword ptr y
   add eax, dword ptr z
   mov dword ptr x, eax
   mov ax, word ptr z[4]
   adc ax, word ptr y[4]
   mov word ptr x[4], ax
   ```

2. You compute $x = y - z$ as follows:

   a.
   ```
   mov rax, qword ptr y
   sub rax, qword ptr z
   mov qword ptr x, rax
   mov rax, qword ptr y[8]
   sbb rax, qword ptr z[8]
   mov qword ptr x[8], rax
   ```

```
      mov rax, qword ptr y[16]
      sbb rax, qword ptr z[16]
      mov qword ptr x[16], rax
```

b. _____

```
      mov rax, qword ptr y
      sub rax, qword ptr z
      mov qword ptr x, rax
      mov eax, dword ptr y[8]
      sbb eax, dword ptr z[8]
      mov dword ptr x[8], eax
```

3. _____

```
mov rax, qword ptr y
mul qword ptr z
mov qword ptr x, rax
mov rbx, rdx

mov rax, qword ptr y
mul qword ptr z[8]
add rax, rbx
adc rdx, 0
mov qword ptr x[8], rax
mov rbx, rdx

mov rax, qword ptr y[8]
mul qword ptr z
add x[8], rax
adc rbx, rdx

mov rax, qword ptr y[8]
mul qword ptr z[8]
add rax, rbx
mov qword ptr x[16], rax
adc rdx, 0
mov qword ptr x[24], rdx
```

4. _____

```
mov  rax, qword ptr y[8]
cqo
idiv qword ptr z
mov  qword ptr x[8], rax
mov  rax, qword ptr y
idiv qword ptr z
mov  qword ptr x, rax
```

5. The conversions are as follows:

a. _____

```
; Note: order of comparison (HO vs. LO) is irrelevant
; for "==" comparison.
```

```
        mov rax, qword ptr x[8]
        cmp rax, qword ptr y[8]
        jne skipElse
        mov rax, qword ptr x
        cmp rax, qword ptr y
        jne skipElse
        then code
    skipElse:
```

b. _____

```
        mov rax, qword ptr x[8]
        cmp rax, qword ptr y[8]
        jnb skipElse
        mov rax, qword ptr x
        cmp rax, qword ptr y
        jnb skipElse
        then code
    skipElse:
```

c. _____

```
        mov rax, qword ptr x[8]
        cmp rax, qword ptr y[8]
        jna skipElse
        mov rax, qword ptr x
        cmp rax, qword ptr y
        jna skipElse
        then code
    skipElse:
```

d. _____

```
    ; Note: order of comparison (HO vs. LO) is irrelevant
    ; for "!=" comparison.

        mov rax, qword ptr x[8]
        cmp rax, qword ptr y[8]
        jne doElse
        mov rax, qword ptr x
        cmp rax, qword ptr y
        je skipElse
    doElse:
        then code
    skipElse:
```

6. The conversions are as follows:

a. _____

```
    ; Note: order of comparison (HO vs. LO) is irrelevant
    ; for "==" comparison.

        mov eax, dword ptr x[8]
        cmp eax, dword ptr y[8]
```

```
        jne skipElse
        mov rax, qword ptr x
        cmp rax, qword ptr y
        jne skipElse
        then code
skipElse:
```

b.
```
        mov eax, dword ptr x[8]
        cmp eax, dword ptr y[8]
        jnb skipElse
        mov rax, qword ptr x
        cmp rax, qword ptr y
        jnb skipElse
        then code
skipElse:
```

c.
```
        mov eax, dword ptr x[8]
        cmp eax, dword ptr y[8]
        jna skipElse
        mov rax, qword ptr x
        cmp rax, qword ptr y
        jna skipElse
        then code
skipElse:
```

7. The conversions are as follows:

a.
```
neg qword ptr x[8]
neg qword ptr x
sbb qword ptr x[8], 0

xor rax, rax
xor rdx, rdx
sub rax, qword ptr x
sbb rdx, qword ptr x[8]
mov qword ptr x, rax
mov qword ptr x[8], rdx
```

b.
```
mov rax, qword ptr y
mov rdx, qword ptr y[8]
neg rdx
neg rax
sbb rdx, 0
mov qword ptr x, rax
mov qword ptr x[8], rdx
```

```
xor rdx, rdx
xor rax, rax
sub rax, qword ptr y
sbb rdx, qword ptr y[8]
mov qword ptr x, rax
mov qword ptr x[8], rdx
```

8. The conversions are as follows:

a.

```
mov rax, qword ptr y
and rax, qword ptr z
mov qword ptr x, rax
mov rax, qword ptr y[8]
and rax, qword ptr z[8]
mov qword ptr x[8], rax
```

b.

```
mov rax, qword ptr y
or  rax, qword ptr z
mov qword ptr x, rax
mov rax, qword ptr y[8]
or  rax, qword ptr z[8]
mov qword ptr x[8], rax
```

c.

```
mov rax, qword ptr y
xor rax, qword ptr z
mov qword ptr x, rax
mov rax, qword ptr y[8]
xor rax, qword ptr z[8]
mov qword ptr x[8], rax
```

d.

```
mov rax, qword ptr y
not rax
mov qword ptr x, rax
mov rax, qword ptr y[8]
not rax
mov qword ptr x[8], rax
```

e.

```
mov rax, qword ptr y
shl rax, 1
mov qword ptr x, rax
mov rax, qword ptr y[8]
rcl rax, 1
mov qword ptr x[8], rax
```

f.
```
    mov rax, qword ptr y[8]
    shr rax, 1
    mov qword ptr x[8], rax
    mov rax, qword ptr y
    rcr rax, 1
    mov qword ptr x rax
```

9.
```
mov rax, qword ptr y[8]
sar rax, 1
mov qword ptr x[8], rax
mov rax, qword ptr y
rcr rax, 1
mov qword ptr x, rax
```

10.
```
rcl qword ptr x, 1
rcl qword ptr x[8], 1
```

11.
```
rcr qword ptr x[8], 1
rcr qword ptr x, 1
```

E.9 Answers to Questions in Chapter 9

1.
```
btoh        proc

            mov     ah, al       ; Do HO nibble first
            shr     ah, 4        ; Move HO nibble to LO
            or      ah, '0'      ; Convert to char
            cmp     ah, '9' + 1  ; Is it "A" to "F"?
            jb      AHisGood

; Convert 3Ah to 3Fh to "A" to "F".

            add     ah, 7

; Process the LO nibble here.

AHisGood:   and     al, 0Fh      ; Strip away HO nibble
            or      al, '0'      ; Convert to char
            cmp     al, '9' + 1  ; Is it "A" to "F"?
            jb      ALisGood

; Convert 3Ah to 3Fh to "A" to "F".
```

```
                  add       al, 7
ALisGood:         ret
btoh              endp
```

2. 8

3. Call qToStr twice: once with the HO 64 bits and once with the LO
   64 bits. Then concatenate the two strings.

4. fbstp

5. If the input value is negative, emit a hyphen (-) character and negate
   the value; then call the unsigned decimal conversion function. If the
   number is 0 or positive, just call the unsigned decimal conversion
   function.

6. _____

```
; Inputs:
;    RAX -   Number to convert to string.
;    CL  -   minDigits (minimum print positions).
;    CH  -   Padding character.
;    RDI -   Buffer pointer for output string.
```

7. It will produce the full string required; the minDigits parameter specifies
   the minimum string size.

8. _____

```
; On Entry:

    ; r10         - Real10 value to convert.
    ;                 Passed in ST(0).

    ; fWidth      - Field width for the number (note that this
    ;                 is an *exact* field width, not a minimum
    ;                 field width).
    ;                 Passed in EAX (RAX).

    ; decimalpts  - # of digits to display after the decimal pt.
    ;                 Passed in EDX (RDX).

    ; fill        - Padding character if the number is smaller
    ;                 than the specified field width.
    ;                 Passed in CL (RCX).

    ; buffer      - r10ToStr stores the resulting characters
    ;                 in this string.
    ;                 Address passed in RDI.

    ; maxLength   - Maximum string length.
    ;                 Passed in R8D (R8).
```

9. A string containing fWidth # characters.

10. _____ , _____

```
; On Entry:

;     e10      - Real10 value to convert.
;                Passed in ST(0).

;     width    - Field width for the number (note that this
;                is an *exact* field width, not a minimum
;                field width).
;                Passed in RAX (LO 32 bits).

;     fill     - Padding character if the number is smaller
;                than the specified field width.
;                Passed in RCX.

;     buffer   - e10ToStr stores the resulting characters in
;                this buffer (passed in EDI).
;                Passed in RDI (LO 32 bits).

;     expDigs  - Number of exponent digits (2 for real4,
;                3 for real8, and 4 for real10).
;                Passed in RDX (LO 8 bits).
```

11. A character that separates a sequence of characters from other such sequences, such as beginning or ending a numeric string

12. Illegal character on input and numeric overflow during conversion

E.10 Answers to Questions in Chapter 10

1. The set of all possible input (parameter) values
2. The set of all possible function output (return) values
3. Computes AL = [RBX + AL × 1]
4. Byte values: domain is the set of all integers in the range 0 to 255, and the range is also the set of all integers in the range 0 to 255.
5. The code implementing the functions is as follows:

   a. _____

   ```
   lea rbx, f
   mov al, input
   xlat
   ```
   _____

   b. _____

   ```
   lea rbx, f
   movzx rax, input
   mov ax, [rbx][rax * 2]
   ```
   _____

c.

```
lea rbx, f
movzx rax, input
mov al, [rbx][rax * 1]
```

d.

```
lea rbx, f
movzx rax, input
mov ax, [rbx][rax * 2]
```

6. Modifying input values that are out of a specific range so that they lie within the input domain of the function

7. Main memory is so slow that it might be faster to compute the value than to look it up via a table.

E.11   Answers to Questions in Chapter 11

1. Use the cpuid instruction.
2. Because Intel and AMD have different feature sets
3. EAX = 1
4. ECX bit 20
5. (a) _TEXT, (b) _DATA, (c) _BSS, (d) CONST
6. PARA or 16 bytes
7.

```
data   segment align(64) 'DATA'
         .
         .
         .
data   ends
```

8. AVX/AVX2/AVX-256/AVX-512
9. A data type within a SIMD register; typically, 1, 2, 4, or 8 bytes wide
10. Scalar instructions operate on a single piece of data; vector instructions operate, simultaneously, on two or more pieces of data.
11. 16 bytes
12. 32 bytes
13. 64 bytes
14. movd
15. movq
16. movaps, movapd, and movdqa
17. movups, movupd, and movdqu

NOTE   *lddqu also works.*

18. movhps or movhpd

19. movddup

20. pshufb

21. pshufd, though pshufb could also work

22. (v)pextrb, (v)pextrw, (v)pextrd, or (v)pextrq

23. (v)pinsrb, (v)pinsrw, (v)pinsrd, or (v)pinsrq

24. It takes the bits in the second operand, inverts them, and then logically ANDs these inverted bits with the first (destination) operand.

25. pslldq

26. pslrdq

27. psllq

28. pslrq

29. The carry out of the HO bit is lost.

30. In a vertical addition, the CPU sums values found in the same lane of two separate XMM registers; in a horizontal addition, the CPU sums values found in adjacent lanes of the same XMM register.

31. In the destination XMM register, by storing 0FFh in the corresponding lane of the destination XMM register (0 for false)

32. Swap the operands of the pcmpgtq instruction.

33. It copies the HO bit of each byte in an XMM register into the corresponding bit position of a general-purpose 16-bit register; for example, bit 7 of lane 0 goes into bit 0.

34. (a) 4 on SSE, 8 on AVX2, (b) 2 on SSE, 4 on AVX2

35. and rax, -16

36. pxor xmm0, xmm0

37. pcmpeqb xmm1, xmm1

38. include

E.12   Answers to Questions in Chapter 12

1.   and/andn

2.   btr

3.   or

4.   bts

5.   xor

6.   btc

7.   test/and

8.   bt

9.   pext

10. pdep

11. bextr

12. `bsf`

13. `bsr`

14. Invert the register and use `bsf`.

15. Invert the register and use `bsr`.

16. `popcnt`

E.13   Answers to Questions in Chapter 13

1. Compile-time language

2. During the assembly and compilation process

3. `echo` (or `%out`)

4. `.err`

5. The `=` directive

6. `!`

7. It replaces an expression with text representing the value of that compile-time expression.

8. It replaces a text symbol with the expansion of its text.

9. It concatenates two or more textual strings at assembly time and stores the result into a text symbol.

10. It searches for a substring within a larger string in a MASM text object and returns the index of the substring into that object; 0 if the substring does not appear in the larger string.

11. It returns the length of a MASM text string.

12. It returns a substring from a larger MASM text string.

13. `if`, `elseif`, `else`, and `endif`

14. `while`, `for`, `forc`, and `endm`

15. `forc`

16. `macro`, `endm`

17. Specify the macro's name where you want the text expansion to occur.

18. As operands to the macro directive

19. Specify `:req` after the parameter name in the macro operand field.

20. Macro parameters are optional, by default, if they don't have the `:req` suffix.

21. Use the `:vararg` suffix after the last macro parameter declaration.

22. Use conditional assembly directives such as `ifb` or `ifnb` to see if the actual macro argument is blank.

23. Use the `local` directive.

24. `exitm`

25. Use `exitm <text>`.

26. `opattr`

E.14   Answers to Questions in Chapter 14

1. Bytes, words, dwords, and qwords
2. movs, cmps, scas, stos, and lods
3. Bytes and words
4. RSI, RDI, and RCX
5. RSI and RDI
6. RCX, RSI, and AL
7. RDI and EAX
8. Dir = 0
9. Dir = 1
10. Clear the direction flag; alternatively, preserve its value.
11. Clear
12. movs and stos
13. When the source and destination blocks overlap and the source address starts at a lower memory address than the destination block
14. This is the default condition; you would also clear the direction flag when the source and destination blocks overlap and the source address starts at a higher memory address than the destination block.
15. Portions of the source block can be replicated in the destination block.
16. repe
17. Direction flag should be clear.
18. No, string instructions test RCX prior to the string operation when using a repeat prefix.
19. scasb
20. stos
21. lods and stos
22. lods
23. Verify that the CPU supports SSE 4.2 instructions.
24. pcmpistri and pcmpistrm
25. pcmpestri and pcmpestrm
26. RAX holds the src1 length, and RDX holds the src2 length.
27. Equal any, or possibly, equal range
28. Equal each
29. Equal ordered
30. The pcmpXstrY instructions always read 16 bytes of memory, even if the string is shorter than this, and there is the possibility of an MMU page fault when it reads data beyond the end of the string.

E.15 Answers to Questions in Chapter 15

1. `.ifndef` and `endif`
2. The assembly of a source file plus any files it includes or indirectly includes
3. `public`
4. `extern` and `externdef`
5. `externdef`
6. `abs`
7. `proc`
8. *nmake.exe*
9. Multiple blocks of the following form:

   ```
   target: dependencies
       commands
   ```

10. A dependent file is one that the current file depends on for its proper operation; the dependent file must be updated and built prior to the compilation and linking of the current file.
11. Delete old object and executable files, and delete other cruft.
12. A collection of object files

E.16 Answers to Questions in Chapter 16

1. `/subsystem:console`
2. *https://www.masm32.com/*
3. It slows the assembly process.
4. `/entry:procedure_name`
5. `MessageBox`
6. Code that surrounds a call to a function and that changes the way you call the function (for example, parameter order and location)
7. `__imp_CreateFileA`
8. `__imp_GetLastError`

INDEX

Numbers

8-bit excess-127 exponent, 88
8-bit registers, 10
16-bit integer variables, 54
16-bit registers, 10
16-byte-aligned addresses, 606
32-bit integer variables, 54
32-bit registers, 10
32-byte alignment within a segment, 605
64-byte alignment within a segment, 605
64-byte memory alignment, 607
80x86 memory addressing modes, 105
96-bit rcl and rcr operations, 484
128-bit comparisons, 461
128-bit decimal output (conversion to string), 508
256-bit by 64-bit division, 468
8087 FPU, 317

Symbols

%1 (batch file parameter), 34
/c MASM command line option, 9
.code section, 108
.const declaration section, 109
.data declaration section, 108
.data? declaration section, 110
.data directive, 14
.err CTL statement, 748
! escape operator (MASM macros), 750
#IA exception (invalid arithmetic operation), 673
.inc files (include files), 848
+infinity, 90
−infinity, 90
.lib files, 869
$ operator, 154
% operator in the first column of a source line, 751
% operator (MASM macros), 750
− (unary negation, within a constant expression), 153
+ (within a constant expression), 153
[ ] (within a constant expression), 153
* (within a constant expression), 153
/ (within a constant expression), 153

A

ABI (application binary interface), 27, 261
ABI (Microsoft) register usage, 38
abs external symbol type, 851
absolute value (floating-point), 349
absolute value (SIMD), 659
access fields of a struct/record, 199
accessing
    an element of a single dimensional array, 182
    data on the stack, 142
    data via a pointer, 162
    elements of an array, 183
    elements of multidimensional arrays, 196
    elements of three- and four-dimensional arrays, 191
    fields of a struct/record via a pointer, 199
    fields of a union, 206
    local variables, 235
    record/struct fields, 199
    reference parameters, 256
    subfields of a nested structure, 200
    value parameters, 253
accumulated errors in a floating-point calculation, 315
activation record
    construction at runtime, 228
    definition, 228
adc instruction, 455, 716

adding 1 to a register or memory location, 149

add instruction, 21

addition (extended-precision), 454

addition (horizontal, packed), 650

addition (SIMD), 648

addition (vertical, packed), 649

addpd instruction, 669

addps instruction, 669

addresses, 9

address expressions, 130

addressing modes, 122
    indirect, 124
    indirect-plus-offset, 125
    register indirect, 124
    scaled-indexed, 126
    scaling factor, 126

address of an object, 22

addsd instruction, 371

addss instruction, 371

Advanced Vector Extensions (AVX), 596

aggregate data types, 174

AH register, 10
    copying AH to FLAGS register, 86, 350

AL/AX/EAX register usage in string instructions, 826

algorithm to convert a string to an integer, 546

aliases, 207

aliasing registers, 10, 623

align directive, 121

aligned data movement instructions (SSE/AVX), 610

aligning
    bit strings, 710
    data in a segment, 605
    data objects on the stack or heap, 607
    within a record, 204

alignment
    data alignment, 119
    variable alignment, 121
    within a record, 204

allocating storage for arrays, 194. *See also* arrays

allocating storage for uninitialized arrays, 183

AL register, 10

anatomy of a MASM program, 5

and instruction, 58, 309, 709

ANDN (and not) operation, 645

andnpd instruction, 645

AND operation, 55

AND operator, 153

andpd instruction, 645

anonymous
    unions, 208
    variables, 125

application binary interface (ABI), 27, 261

application programming interface (API), 35

arbitrary alignment within a segment, 605

arctangent, 361

arithmetic
    expressions, 299, 302
    idioms, 310
    logical systems, 310
    operators within a constant expression, 153
    shift right, 77

arithmetic shifts (SSE/AVX), 647

arrays, 191
    accessing elements of an array, 183
    accessing elements of multidimensional arrays, 196
    allocating storage for a multidimensional array, 194
    arrays of arrays, 192
    arrays of structs, 203
    base address, 182
    bubble sort, 188
    column-major ordering, 193
    declarations, 182
    definition, 181
    dup operator, 182
    four-dimensional array access (row major), 191
    indexing operator, 181
    initialized arrays, 183
    LARGEADDRESSAWARE, 183
    multidimensional, 189, 192
    row-major ordering, 190
    sorting, 185

three-dimensional array access (row major), 191
two or more dimensions, 189
uninitialized storage, 183
array variables, 182
ASCII
    character set, 53, 93
    codes for numeric digits, 95
    groups, 94
assembly language procedures, xxviii, 22
assembly-time initialization of structures, 200
assigning, 299
    constant to a variable, 299
    one variable to another, 299
associativity, 302, 304
automatic allocation, 240
automatic code generation, 748
automatic (local) variables, 235
automatic variables, 234
    in a procedure, 234
average computation (SIMD), 657
avoiding branches by using calculations, 409
AVX
    aligned data movement instructions, 610
    AVX-512 memory alignment, 607
    AVX, AVX2, AVX-256, AVX-512, 596
    AVX/SSE comparison synonyms, 673
    extensions, 596
    floating-point arithmetic (SIMD), 668
    floating-point conversions, 679
    instruction operands, 606
    memory alignment requirements, 606
    packed byte data types, 597
    packed dword data types, 598
    packed qword data types, 598
    packed word data types, 597
    programming model, 596
    sign extension, 666
    unaligned memory access, 606, 612
    zero extension, 665
AX register, 10

B

backspace, 93
base address (of an array), 182
Base Pointer register (RBP), 230
Basic Multilingual Plane (Unicode BMP), 97
batch files, 33
BCD (binary coded decimal), 91
    arithmetic, 486
    numbers, 51
    representation, 91, 487
BH register, 10
biased (excess) exponents, 88
big-endian data organization, 115
big-endian to little-endian conversion, 116
binary
    data types, 51
    digits, 44
    formats, 45
    numbering system, 43
    point (binary fractions), 87
binary-coded decimal (BCD), 91
    arithmetic, 487
    numbers, 51
    representation, 91
binary search, 422
bit, 45, 51
    complement, 708
    counting, 739
    data, 707
    fields, 79
    inversion, 708
    manipulation, 707, 708
    mask, 708
    offset, 708
    packed data, 79
    pattern search, 743
    runs, 708
    sets, 708
    strings, 57, 708
        arrays, 733
        extraction, 742
        merging, 741
        reversal, 739
        test for 1 bits, 714
bit-by-bit operations, 58
bit string alignment, 710

bit string masking, 58
bitwise operations, 58
blank macro arguments, 767
BL register, 10
BMP (Unicode Basic Multilingual
        Plane), 97
Boolean
        evaluation
                complete, 400
                short-circuit, 401
        expressions, 308
        logical systems, 310
        values, 51
BP register, 10
bracketing characters in macro
        parameters, 764
branch out of range, 393
branch-prediction hardware, 448
break statement, 438
bsf instruction, 737
bsr instruction, 737
bswap instruction, 116
btc instruction, 715
bt instruction, 715
btoStr (byte to string) function, 493
btr instruction, 715
bts, btc, and btr instructions and CPU
        performance, 716
bts instruction, 715
bubble sort, 185
busy bit (FPU), 324
BX register, 10
byte, 52
        alignment in a segment, 605
        data directive, 53
        directive, 15
byte-sized lanes, 598
byte strings, 825
byte vectors (packed bytes), 597

C

C++ compiler, 4
callee register preservation, 222
caller register preservation, 222
call indirect, 278
calling assembly code from C/C++, 4
calling C/C++ code from assembly, 4
call instruction, 22, 216, 218

carriage return, 93
carry flag, 12, 294
        and, or, and xor instruction
                effect, 712
        as a bit accumulator, 716
        setting after an arithmetic
                operation, 71
case
        labels (noncontiguous), 418
        statement, 396, 410
case-sensitive identifiers, 8
catstr directive, 751
cbw instruction, 288
C/C++ Standard Library, 4
cd command, 930
cdecl calling convention, 262
cdqe instruction, 288
cdq instruction, 288
central processing unit, 9
change sign (floating-point), 349
char
        data type, 96
        declaring characters in a MASM
                program, 96
character
        data type, 92
        literal constants, 95
        strings, 174
chdir command, 930
checking a bit to see if it is zero or
        one, 298
checking to see if a macro argument is
        blank, 767
checking whether a bit string contains
        all 1 bits, 714
choosing an alignment value for
        variables, 121
CH register, 10
C integer types, 454
class argument for segment
        directive, 605
clc instruction, 86, 716
cld instruction, 86
clearing
        bits, 708
        clearing bits prior to comparing
                them, 709
        FPU exception bits, 363

CLI (command line interpreter), xxx
cd command, 930
del command, 932
cli instruction, 86
clipping (saturation), 68
closeHandle function, 890
CL register, 10
in rotate operations, 79
in shl instruction, 75
cls command, 931
cmc instruction, 86, 716
cmd.exe (command line interpreter), xxx
cmovae instruction, 395
cmova instruction, 395
cmovbe instruction, 395
cmovb instruction, 395
cmovc instruction, 394, 716
cmove instruction, 395
cmovge instruction, 395
cmovg instruction, 395
cmovnp instruction, 395
cmovpe instruction, 395
cmovp instruction, 395
cmovle instruction, 395
cmovl instruction, 395
cmovnae instruction, 395
cmovna instruction, 395
cmovnbe instruction, 395
cmovnb instruction, 395
cmovnc instruction, 394, 716
cmovne instruction, 395
cmovnge instruction, 395
cmovng instruction, 395
cmovnle instruction, 395
cmovnl instruction, 395
cmovno instruction, 395
cmovns instruction, 394
cmovnz instruction, 394
cmovo instruction, 394
cmovpo instruction, 395
cmovs instruction, 394
cmovz instruction, 394
cmpeqps instruction, 674
cmpeqsd instruction, 373
cmpeqss instruction, 372
cmp instruction, 72, 293
cmpleps instruction, 674
cmplesd instruction, 373

cmpless instruction, 372
cmpltps instruction, 674
cmpltsd instruction, 373
cmpltss instruction, 372
cmpneps instruction, 674
cmpnesd instruction, 373
cmpness instruction, 372
cmpnleps instruction, 674
cmpnless instruction, 372
cmpnltps instruction, 674
cmpnltsd instruction, 373
cmpnltss instruction, 372
cmpordps instruction, 674
cmpordsd instruction, 373
cmpordss instruction, 372
cmppd instruction, 671
cmpps instruction, 671, 674
cmpsd instruction, 372
cmpss instruction, 372
cmps string instruction, 832
cmpunordps instruction, 674
cmpunordsd instruction, 373
cmpunordss instruction, 372
coalescing bit strings, 728
code planes (Unicode), 97
code points (Unicode), 96
code sections, 108
code snippets, xxviii
coercion, 157
collecting disparate bits into a bit
string, 728
collecting macro parameters, 764
column major ordering, 193
formula, 193
command line, xxx
command line assembler, 6
command line interpreter. See CLI
common C++ data type sizes, 35
commutative operators, 307
comparing
a register to zero, 298
bits, 708
dates, 85
strings, 825
comparison for less than (packed/
vector/SIMD), 662
comparison operators in a constant
expression, 153

comparison results (SIMD), 663, 678
comparisons
    dates, 85
    floating point, 323
    SIMD, 660
comparison synonyms (AVX/SSE), 673
compile-time
    decisions, 752
    expressions and operators, 750
    language, 748
    loops, 756
    procedures, 760
compile-time function
    sizeof, 207
compile-time language. *See* CTL
compile-time statement
    echo, 748
    else, 753
    elseif, 753
    endm, 756, 759
    .err, 748
    for, 756, 759
    forc, 756
    if, 752
    while, 756
compile-time versus runtime
    expressions, 155–156
complete Boolean evaluation, 400
complex arithmetic expressions, 302
complex string functions, 837
composite data types, 174
computation via table lookup, 584
computing
    arctangent, 362
    cos, 361
    cosine, 361
    $\log_2(x)$, 362
    $\log_2(x)$ plus one, 362
    sine, 361
    square root, 327, 347
    tangent, 361
    2^x minus one, 361
computing the address of a memory
    variable, 22
computing the length of a string at
    assembly time, 176
concatenation of text values in
    MASM, 751

conditional
    compilation, 752
    jmp aliases, 392
    jmp instructions (opposite
        conditions), 391–392
    statements, 396
conditional jump instructions, 70
conditional jumps
    ja, 391
    jae, 391
    jb, 391
    jbe, 391
    jc, 391, 716
    je, 391
    jg, 391
    jge, 391
    jl, 391
    jle, 391
    jna, 391
    jnae, 391
    jnb, 391
    jnbe, 391
    jnc, 391, 716
    jne, 391
    jng, 391
    jnge, 391
    jnl, 391
    jnle, 391
    jno, 391
    jnp, 391
    jns, 391
    jnz, 391
    jo, 391
    jp, 391
    jpe, 391
    jpo, 391
    js, 391
    jz, 391
conditional move (if carry), 716
conditional move instructions, 394
condition code
    flags, 12
    FPU condition codes, 322
    settings after cmp instruction, 294
conditioning inputs, 589
configuring software for several
    environments, 754

constant
    0.0 (FPU load instruction), 360
    expressions, 131, 152
    expressions in CTL
        statements, 750
    $\log_2(10)$, 361
    $\log_2(e)$, 361
    $\log_{10}(2)$, 361
    $\log_e(2)$, 361
    pi, 360
constant declarations, 18, 149
constant expression evaluation, 156
constant expressions, 164
constant values, 18
construction of an activation record, 228
continue statement, 438
control characters, 93
control word, 321, 363
conversions (floating-point
      instructions), 328
converting
    32-bit integers to floating-point, 679
    arithmetic expressions to postfix
        notation, 366
    ASCII digit code (0 to 9) to its
        corresponding integer value, 95
    BCD to floating-point, 329
    between big-endian and little-
        endian forms, 116
    binary to hexadecimal, 48
    binary value (0 to 9) to its ASCII
        character representation, 95
    break statements to pure
        assembly, 438
    complex expressions to
        assembly, 302
    continue statements to pure
        assembly, 439
    double-precision floating-point
        values to single-precision, 680
    floating-point expressions to
        assembly, 364
    floating-point values to a decimal
        string, 527
    floating-point values to an integer,
        319, 679
        with truncation, 680
    floating-point values to
        exponential form, 537
    forever statements to pure
        assembly, 436
    for statements to pure assembly, 437
    hexadecimal digit to a
        character, 493
    hexadecimal to binary, 47
    if statements to pure assembly, 396
    integer to floating-point, 328
    larger integer object to a smaller
        one (via saturation), 667
    noncommutative arithmetic
        operators to assembly, 305
    numbers to strings using fbstp, 503
    postfix notation to assembly, 367
    repeat..until loop to pure
        assembly, 434
    simple expressions to assembly, 300
    single-precision floating-point
        values to double-precision, 680
    strings to integers, 546
    while loops to pure assembly, 433
copy command (CLI), 931
copying
    arbitrary number of bytes using
        the movsd instruction, 831
    overlapping arrays using the movs
        string instructions, 830
cosine, 361
counting bits, 739
cpuid instruction, 599
CPU registers, 10
cqo instruction, 288
creating lookup tables, 590
CTL (compile-time language), 748
    conditional assembly, 752
    decisions, 752
    else, 753
    elseif, 753
    endif, 753
    endm, 756
    forc, 756
    for loop, 756
    if statement, 752
    instr operator, 751
    loops, 756

CTL (*continued*)

 macros, 760

 ! operator, 750

 % operator, 750

 procedures (compile-time), 760

 sizestr operator, 752

 substring operator, 752

 while statement, 756

cvtdq2pd instruction, 679

cvtdq2ps instruction, 679

cvtpd2dq instruction, 679

cvtpd2ps instruction, 680

cvtps2dq instruction, 680

cvtps2pd instruction, 680

cvttpd2dq instruction, 680

cvttps2dq instruction, 680

cwde instruction, 288

cwd instruction, 288

CX register, 10

D

dangling pointers, 169

data alignment, 119

 in a segment, 605

 Microsoft ABI, 144

data declaration directives, 15

data representation, 147

data type coercion, 157

data types associated with SSE/AVX

 move instructions, 622

data type sizes (C++), 35

date command (CLI), 931

date comparison, 85

date/time stamp of a file in a make

 operation, 865

db directive, 15

dd directive, 15

debugging CTL programs, 749

debugging with conditional

 compilation, 755

decimal arithmetic, 453, 486, 581

decimal numbering system, 44

decimal (signed) to string conversion

 (extended-precision), 513

decimal string-to-integer conversion, 546

decimal string-to-numeric conversion

 (extended-precision), 569

decimal-to-string conversion, 500

dec instruction, 149

decisions in MASM, 397

declarations

 .code section, 108

 .const, 109

 .data, 108

 .data?, 110

 typedef, 156

declaring character variables in a

 MASM program, 96

declaring constants, 18

declaring parameters with the proc

 directive, 255

default macro parameter values, 768

default segment alignment, 605

defining read-only data in a user-

 defined segment, 605

definite loop, 437

del command (CLI), 932

delimiter characters, 546

delimiting macro parameters, 764

denormal exception flag (DE, SSE), 369

denormalized

 exception (FPU), 320

 floating-point values, 325

 values, 90

denormal mask (DM, SSE), 370

denormals are zero (DAZ, SSE), 370

dependencies (in a makefile), 864

destructuring, 407

determining which CPU a piece of

 software is running on, 599

DH register, 10

dialog box (example code), 879

differences in the imul instructions, 291

different-size operands, 485

dir command, 932

direction flag and the string

 instructions, 826

directives, 6

 ?, 15

 align, 121

 byte, 15, 53

 catstr, 751

 db, 15

 dd, 15

 dq, 15

 dt, 15

dw, 15
dword, 15, 55
else, 753
elseif, 753
endif, 753
endm, 756, 759, 760
endp, 216
ends (for structs), 198
equ, 18, 150
extern, 850
externdef, 24, 850
for, 756, 759
forc, 756, 760
if, 753
ifb, 767
ifdef, 849
ifdif, 767
ifdifi, 767
ifidn, 767
ifidni, 767
ifnb, 767
include, 848
instr, 751
label, 156
local (in procedures), 237
macro, 760
option, 8, 238
option epilogue, 238
option prologue, 238
oword, 15, 55
proc, 216, 255
public, 8, 850
qword, 15, 55
real4, 15
real8, 15
real10, 15
sdword, 15
sizestr, 752
sqword, 15
struct, 198
substr, 752
sword, 15
tbyte, 15
textequ, 151
typedef, 156
while, 756
word, 15, 54

direct jump instructions, 382
DI register, 10
disadvantages of macros (versus
    procedures), 762
displacements, 113
displaying equate values during
    assembly, 751
distributing bit strings, 728
div and idiv instructions, 291, 466
divide-by-zero exception (FPU), 320
divide-by-zero mask (ZM, SSE), 370
division without div or idiv, 312
divpd instruction, 670
divps instruction, 670
divsd instruction, 371
divss instruction, 371
DL register, 10
domain conditioning, 589
dot notation for accessing struct/
    record fields, 199
dot operator, 199
double-precision floating-point
    format, 88
double-precision (floating-point)
    lanes, 599
double-precision vector types, 597
double word, 51, 54. See also dword
double-word strings, 825
dq directive, 15
dt directive, 15
dtoStr (double word to string)
    function, 493
duplicate include files/operations
    (preventing), 849
duplicating data in an XMM/YMM
    register, 620
dup operator, 182, 195
dw directive, 15, 55
dword, 51, 54
    alignment within a segment, 605
    directive, 15, 55
    dword-sized lanes, 598
    vectors (packed dwords), 598
DX register, 10
dyadic operations, 55
dynamic
    memory allocation, 106, 166
    type systems, 209

E

e10toStr function, 537

EAX, EBX, ECX, EDX, ESI, EDI, EBP, and ESP registers, 10

echo CTL statement, 748

effective address, 125

EFLAGS register, 12

else compile-time statement, 753

else directive, 753

elseif compile-time statement, 753

elseif directive, 753

else statement, 397

empty macro arguments, 767

endian byte organization, 114

endian conversions, 116

endif directive, 753

endm compile-time statement, 756, 759

endm directive, 756, 759, 760

endp directive, 216

ends directive (for structs), 198

ends (end segment) directive, 604

enumerated data constants in MASM, 156

epiloguedef option, 239

epilogue (operand for option directive), 238

eq operator, 153

equality (macro arguments), 767

equates, 149

equ directive, 18, 150

erase command (CLI), 932

escape character in MASM expressions, 750

exception-handling in C++, 30

exceptions

    divide by zero (FPU), 320

    flags (FPU), 322

    FPU exception bits, 363

    masks (FPU), 320

    overflow (FPU), 320

excess-127 exponent, 87, 88

excess-1023 exponent, 88

excess (biased) exponents, 88

exclusive-or operation, 55, 57

executing a loop backward, 445

exponent of a floating-point number, 88

expressions, 302

    and temporary values, 307

extended-precision

    addition, 454

    AND, 479

    arithmetic, 453

    comparisons, 458

    conversions

        decimal-to-string (signed), 513

        decimal-to-string (unsigned), 566

        string-to-numeric, 555

        unsigned integer-to-string, 508

    division, 466

    floating-point format, 89

    formatted I/O, 514

    I/O, 491

    multiplication, 461

    neg, 477

    NOT, 480

    numeric conversion routines, 546

    OR, 479

    rotates, 484

    shifts, 480

    shifts and the flags, 482

    XOR, 480

external directives, 849

external symbols, 850

external symbol types, 851

externdef directive, 24, 849, 851

extern directive, 849, 851

extracting

    bits, 708

    bit strings, 742

    sign bits from SSE/AVX floating-point values, 676

extractps instruction, 643

F

f2xm1 instruction, 361

fabs instruction, 349

facade code, 27

fadd instruction, 330

faddp instruction, 330

false precision, 315

false (representation), 308

FASTCALL calling convention, 263

fbld instruction, 329, 488, 566

fbstp instruction, 329, 488, 503, 566

fchs instruction, 349

fclex instruction, 363

fcomi instruction, 357

fcom instruction, 322, 350

fcomip instruction, 357

fcomp instruction, 322, 350

fcompp instruction, 322, 350

fcos instruction, 361

fdiv instruction, 343

fdivp instruction, 343

fdivr instruction, 343

fdivrp instruction, 343

ficom instruction, 322

ficomp instruction, 322

field, 197

field access (of a record/struct) via a
    pointer, 199

field alignment within a record, 204

fild instruction, 328

finit instruction, 363

first clear bit, 708, 736

first set bit, 708, 736

fist instruction, 328

fistp instruction, 328

fisttp instruction, 328

flags, 12

    and instruction, 712

    carry, 12, 294

    cmp instruction effect on flags, 293

    copying AH register to flags, 86, 350

    direction, 826

    lahf instruction, 86

    or instruction, 712

    overflow, 293

    sign, 293

    xor instruction, 712

    zero, 293

flag settings for the logical instructions
    (and, or, xor, and not), 71

FLAGS register, 12

fld1 instruction, 360

fldcw instruction, 321, 363

fld instruction, 326

fldl2e instruction, 361

fldl2t instruction, 361

fldlg2 instruction, 361

fldln2 instruction, 361

fldpi instruction, 360

fldz instruction, 360

floating-point

    arithmetic, 317

    calculations, 317

    comparisons, 323, 350

        SIMD, 671

    control register, 317

    control word, 321, 363

    conversion to integer, 319, 328

    conversion to string, 519, 527

        exponential form, 537

    data registers, 317

    data types, 324

    division, 343

    exchange registers, 327

    FPU (floating-point unit), 11, 317

    multiplication, 339

    negation, 349

    normalized format, 325

    overflow, 316

    overflow exception, 320

    partial remainder, 348

    precision control, 320

    pushing a value onto the FPU
        stack, 326

    pushing the constant 1.0 onto the
        FPU stack, 360

    registers, 11, 317

    remainder, 348

    rounding control, 319

    status register, 317

    string conversion (to real), 570

    string output, 519

    subtraction, 334

    test for zero, 322, 360

    underflow, 316

    unordered comparisons, 357, 360

    unit. *See* FPU

    values, 54

        as parameters, 244

flush to zero (FZ, SSE), 370

fmul instruction, 339

fmulp instruction, 339

fnclex instruction, 363

fninit instruction, 363

fnstsw instruction, 364

forc directive, 756, 759

forcing
a zero result, 56
bits to one, 58
bits to zero, 58
for directive, 756, 759
for and endm compile-time statement,
756, 759
for loops, 437
format specifiers (printf), 24
formatted numeric-to-string
conversions, 514
formula for two-dimensional row-major
access, 191
FORTRAN programming language, 424
four-dimensional array element
access, 191
fpatan instruction, 362
fprem1 instruction, 348
fprem instruction, 348
fptan instruction, 361
FPU (floating-point unit), 11, 317
busy bit, 324
condition code bits, 322
control register, 318
control word, 321, 363
data movement instructions, 326
data registers, 317
data types, 324
denormalized result exception, 320
divide-by-zero exception, 320
exception bits, 363
exception flags, 322
exception masks, 320
floating-point unit, 317
invalid operation exception, 320
overflow exception, 320
popping the FPU stack, 326
precision exception, 321
registers, 317
rounding control, 319
round-up and round-down, 319
stack fault flag, 322
status register, 321, 364
status word, 321
top of stack pointer, 324
truncate during computations, 319
underflow exception, 321

free (memory deallocation) function, 170
frndint instruction, 349
fsincos instruction, 361
fsin instruction, 361
fsqrt instruction, 327, 347
fstcw instruction, 321, 363
fst instruction, 326
fstp instruction, 326
fstsw instruction, 321, 350, 364
fsub instruction, 334
fsubp instruction, 334
fsubr instruction, 334
fsubrp instruction, 334
ftst instruction, 322, 360
fucom instruction, 323
fucomp instruction, 323
fucompp instruction, 323
function
computation via table lookup, 584
results, 270
fxam instruction, 323
fxch instruction, 327
fyl2x instruction, 362
fyl2xp1 instruction, 362

G

general protection fault, 107
general purpose registers, 10, 12
ge operator, 153
getLastError function, 891
getStdErrHandle function, 883
GetStdHandle (Win32 API
function), 875
getStdInHandle function, 884
getStdOutHandle function, 883
getting the address of a variable, 22
granularity (MMU pages), 111
greater-than comparisons on SSE
CPUs, 673
GT operator, 153
guard digits/bits, 314

H

haddpd instruction, 671
haddps instruction, 671
handling SIMD comparisons, 663
header files, 849, 852

heap variable address alignment, 607
Hello, world!
    compile-time program, 748
    MASM program, 6
    stand-alone version, 874
hexadecimal
    digit-to-character conversion, 493
    hexadecimal-to-string
      conversion, 492
        using table lookup, 497
    numbering system, 43, 46
    numbers, 51
    output (extended-precision), 499
    string-to-numeric conversion, 556
high32 operator, 153
high operator, 153
high-order (HO), 46
    bit, 46, 52
    byte, 53
    nibble, 52
    word, 54
highword operator, 153
HO (high-order), 46
horizontal addition, 650
    and subtraction (floating-point), 671
hsubpd instruction, 671
hsubps instruction, 671
hybrid programs (assembly and
    C/C++), 7

I

i128toStr function, 513
identifiers, 8
idiom, 685
    machine idiosyncrasies, 310
idiv instruction, 291, 407, 466
IEEE
    floating-point standard, 86, 318, 320
ifb directive, 767
if compile-time statement, 752
if conditional statement, 396
ifdef directive, 849
ifdif directive, 767
ifdifi directive, 767
if directive, 753
ifidn directive, 767
ifidni directive, 767
ifnb directive, 767

imul instruction, 148, 289, 461
inc instruction, 149
include directive, 848
inclusive or operation, 90
indirect
    addressing modes, 124
      indirect and scaled-indexed
        addressing modes, 106
      indirect-plus-offset addressing
        mode, 125
    calls, 278
    jump instructions, 383
    jumps, 396, 424
      through a memory pointer, 389
induction variables, 449
infinite loops, 433
infinite-precision arithmetic, 313
infinity (IEEE representation), 90
infix notation, 364
initialized arrays, 183
initializing struct fields, 200
initializing the FPU, 363
input conditioning, 589
input/output (I/O), 9
input redirection, 927
inserting
    a bit into a bit array, 734
    a bit set into another bit string, 710
    a bit string into a larger bit
      string, 718
insertps instruction, 643
instr directive, 751
instructions
    adc, 455, 716
    add, 21
    addpd, 669
    addps, 669
    addsd, 371
    adss, 371
    and, 58, 309, 709
    andnpd, 645
    andpd, 645
    bsf, 737
    bsr, 737
    bswap, 116
    bt, 715
    btc, 715
    btr, 715

instructions *(continued)*

bts, 715

call, 22, 216, 218

cbw, 288

cdq, 288

cdqe, 288

clc, 86, 716

cld, 86

cli, 86

cmc, 86, 716

cmova, 395

cmovae, 395

cmovb, 395

cmovbe, 395

cmovc, 394, 716

cmove, 395

cmovg, 395

cmovge, 395

cmovl, 395

cmovle, 395

cmovna, 395

cmovnae, 395

cmovnb, 395

cmovnbe, 395

cmovnc, 394, 716

cmovne, 395

cmovng, 395

cmovnge, 395

cmovnl, 395

cmovnle, 395

cmovno, 395

cmovnp, 395

cmovns, 394

cmovnz, 394

cmovo, 394

cmovp, 395

cmovpe, 395

cmovpo, 395

cmovs, 394

cmovz, 394

cmp, 72, 293

cmpeqps, 674

cmpeqsd, 373

cmpeqss, 372

cmpleps, 674

cmplesd, 373

cmpless, 372

cmpltps, 674

cmpltsd, 373

cmpltss, 372

cmpneps, 674

cmpnesd, 373

cmpness, 372

cmpnleps, 674

cmpnless, 373

cmpnltps, 674

cmpnltsd, 373

cmpnltss, 372

cmpordps, 674

cmpordsd, 373

cmpordss, 373

cmppd, 671

cmpps, 671, 674

cmps, 832

cmpsd, 372

cmpss, 372

cmpunordps, 674

cmpunordsd, 373

cmpunordss, 372

cqo, 288

cvtdq2pd, 679

cvtdq2ps, 679

cvtpd2dq, 679

cvtpd2ps, 680

cvtps2dq, 680

cvtps2pd, 680

cvttpd2dq, 680

cvttps2dq, 680

cwd, 288

cwde, 288

dec, 149

div, 291, 466

divpd, 670

divps, 670

divsd, 371

divss, 371

extractps, 643

f2xm1, 361

fabs, 349

fadd, 330

faddp, 330

fbld, 329, 488, 503

fbstp, 329, 488, 503, 566

fchs, 349

fclex, 363

fcom, 322, 350

fcomi, 357

fcomip, 357

fcomp, 322, 350

fcompp, 322, 350

fcos, 361

fdiv, 343

fdivp, 343

fdivr, 343

fdivrp, 343

ficom, 322

ficomp, 322

fild, 328

finit, 363

fist, 328

fistp, 328

fisttp, 328

fld, 326

fld1, 360

fld2e, 361

fldcw, 321, 363

fldl2t, 361

fldlg2, 361

fldln2, 361

fldpi, 360

fldz, 360

floating-point comparisons, 350

floating-point conversions, 328

fmul, 339

fmulp, 339

fnclex, 363

fninit, 363

fnstsw, 364

fpatan, 362

fprem, 348

fprem1, 348

fptan, 361

FPU data movement, 326

frndint, 349

fsin, 361

fsincos, 361

fsqrt, 327, 347

fst, 326

fstcw, 321, 363

fstp, 326

fstsw, 321, 350, 364

fsub, 334

fsubp, 334

fsubr, 334

fsubrp, 334

ftst, 322, 360

fucom, 323

fucomp, 323

fxam, 323

fxch, 327

fyl2x, 362

fyl2xp1, 362

haddpd, 671

haddps, 671

hsubpd, 671

hsubps, 671

idiv, 291, 407, 466

imul, 148, 289, 461

inc, 149

indirect jumps, 383

insertps, 643

intmul, 291

ja, 73, 391

jae, 73, 391

jb, 73, 391

jbe, 73, 391

jc, 70, 74, 391, 716

je, 72, 74, 391–392

jg, 73, 391

jge, 73, 391–392

jl, 73, 391–392

jle, 73, 391–392

jmp, 69, 382

jna, 74, 391–392

jnae, 74, 391

jnb, 74, 391

jnbe, 74, 391

jnc, 70, 74, 391, 716

jne, 72, 74, 391–392

jng, 74, 391–392

jnge, 74, 391–392

jnl, 74, 391–392

jnle, 74, 391

jno, 70, 391

jnp, 70, 391

jns, 70, 391

jnz, 70, 74, 298, 391

jo, 70, 391

jp, 391

jpe, 391

jpo, 391

js, 70, 391

instructions *(continued)*

jz, 70, 74, 298, 391
lahf, 86
lddqu, 622
ldmxcsr, 370
lea, 22, 125, 378
leave, 234
lods, 836
maxpd, 670
maxps, 670
maxsd, 371
maxss, 371
minpd, 670
minps, 670
minsd, 371
minss, 371
mov, 18, 122
movapd, 610
movaps, 610
movd, 371, 609
movddup, 621
movdqa, 610
movdqu, 612
movhlps, 619
movhpd, 617
movhps, 617
movlhps, 619
movlpd, 615
movlps, 615
movmskpd, 676
movmskps, 676
movq, 371, 609
movs, 826
movsb, 826
movsd, 370, 826
movshdup, 620
movsldup, 620
movss, 370
movsw, 826
movupd, 612
movups, 612
mul, 289, 461
mulpd, 670
mulps, 670
mulsd, 371
mulss, 371
neg, 478
not, 58, 309, 709

or, 58, 309, 709
orpd, 645
pabsb, 659
pabsd, 659
pabsw, 659
packssdw, 667
packsswb, 667
packusdw, 667
packuswb, 667
paddb, 648
paddd, 649
paddq, 649
paddw, 648–649
pavgb, 657
pavgw, 657
pclmulqdq, 656
pcmpeqb, 660
pcmpeqd, 660
pcmpeqq, 660
pcmpeqw, 660
pcmpgtb, 660
pcmpgtd, 660
pcmpgtq, 660
pcmpgtw, 660
pextrb, 641
pextrd, 642
pextrq, 642
pextrw, 642
phaddd, 650
phaddw, 650
pinsrd, 642
pinsrq, 642
pinsrw, 642
pmaxsb, 657
pmaxsd, 658
pmaxsq, 658
pmaxsw, 657
pmaxub, 658
pmaxud, 658
pmaxuq, 658
pmaxuw, 658
pminsb, 658
pminsd, 658
pminsw, 658
pminub, 658
pminud, 658
pminuq, 658
pminuw, 658

pmovmskb, 662

pmovsxbd, 666

pmovsxbq, 666

pmovsxbw, 666

pmovsxdq, 666

pmovsxwd, 666

pmovsxwq, 666

pmovzxbd, 665

pmovzxbq, 665

pmovzxbw, 665

pmovzxdq, 665

pmovzxwd, 665

pmovzxwq, 665

pmuldq, 656

pmulld, 655

pmuludq, 656

pop, 135, 222

popf, 140

popfd, 140

pshufb, 625

pshufd, 626

pshufhw, 628

pshuflw, 628

psignb, 659

psignd, 660

psignw, 659

pslldq, 647

psllw, 647

psrldq, 647

psubb, 654

psubd, 653

psubq, 653

psubw, 654

ptest, 646

punpckhbw, 637

punpckhdq, 637

punpckhqdq, 637

punpcklbw, 637

punpckldq, 637

punpcklqdq, 637

punpcklwd, 637

push, 134, 222

pushf, 140

pushfq, 140

pushw, 134

rcl, 79, 716

rcpss, 372

rcr, 79, 716

repe prefix on cmpsb, cmpsw, cmpsd, and cmpsq, 827

repne prefix on cmpsb, cmpsw, cmpsd, and cmpsq, 827

rep prefix on movsb, movsw, movsd, and movsq, 826

ret, 22, 218

rol, 78

ror, 78

rsqrtps, 670

rsqrtss, 372

sahf, 86, 350

sar, 77, 312

sbb, 457, 716

scas, 835

seta, 296

setae, 296

setb, 296

setbe, 296

setc, 295, 716

sete, 296

setg, 296

setge, 297

setl, 297

setna, 296

setnae, 296

setnb, 296

setnbe, 296

setnc, 295, 716

setne, 296

setng, 297

setnge, 297

setnl, 297

setnle, 296

setno, 295

setnp, 295

setns, 295

setnz, 295, 298

seto, 295

setp, 295

setpe, 295

setpo, 295

sets, 295

setz, 295, 298

shl, 75, 310

shld, 482

shr, 76, 312

shrd, 482

instructions *(continued)*

shufpd, 630
shufps, 630
sqrtpd, 670
sqrtps, 670
sqrtsd, 372
sqrtss, 372
stc, 716
std, 86
sti, 86
stmxcsr, 370
stos, 835
sub, 21
subpd, 669
subps, 669
subsd, 371
subss, 371
test, 297, 709
unpckhpd, 633
unpckhps, 633
unpcklpd, 633
unpcklps, 633
vaddpd, 669
vaddps, 669
vandnpd, 645
vandpd, 645
vcmppd, 671, 674
vcmpps, 671, 674
vcvtdq2pd, 679
vcvtdq2ps, 679
vcvtpd2dq, 679
vcvtpd2ps, 680
vcvtps2dq, 680
vcvtps2pd, 680
vcvttpd2dq, 680
vcvttps2dq, 680
vdivpd, 670
vdivps, 670
vextractps, 643
vhaddpd, 671
vhaddps, 671
vhsubpd, 671
vhsubps, 671
vinsertps, 643
vlddqu, 622
vmaxpd, 670
vmaxps, 670
vminpd, 670

vminps, 670
vmovapd, 610
vmovaps, 610
vmovd, 609
vmovddup, 621
vmovdqa, 610
vmovdqu, 612
vmovhlps, 619
vmovhpd, 618
vmovhps, 618
vmovlhps, 619
vmovlpd, 615
vmovlps, 615
vmovmskpd, 676
vmovmskps, 676
vmovq, 609
vmovshdup, 620
vmovsldup, 620
vmovupd, 612
vmovups, 612
vmulpd, 670
vmulps, 670
vorpd, 645
vpabsb, 659
vpabsd, 659
vpabsw, 659
vpackssdw, 667
vpacksswb, 667
vpackusdw, 667
vpackuswb, 667
vpaddb, 649
vpaddd, 649
vpaddq, 649
vpaddw, 648–649
vpavgb, 657
vpavgw, 657
vpclmulqdq, 656
vpcmpeqb, 661
vpcmpeqd, 661
vpcmpeqq, 661
vpcmpeqw, 661
vpcmpgtb, 661
vpcmpgtd, 661
vpcmpgtq, 661
vpcmpgtw, 661
vpextrb, 642
vpextrd, 642
vpextrq, 642

vpextrw, 642
vphaddd, 650
vphaddw, 650
vpinsrd, 643
vpinsrq, 643
vpinsrw, 643
vpmaxsb, 657
vpmaxsd, 658
vpmaxsq, 658
vpmaxsw, 657
vpmaxub, 658
vpmaxud, 658
vpmaxuq, 658
vpmaxuw, 658
vpminsb, 658
vpminsd, 658
vpminsw, 658
vpminub, 658
vpminud, 658
vpminuq, 658
vpminuw, 658
vpmovmskb, 662
vpmovsxbd, 666
vpmovsxbq, 666
vpmovsxbw, 666
vpmovsxdq, 666
vpmovsxwd, 666
vpmovsxwq, 666
vpmovzxbd, 665
vpmovzxbq, 665
vpmovzxbw, 665
vpmovzxdq, 665
vpmovzxwd, 665
vpmovzxwq, 665
vpmuldq, 656
vpmulld, 655
vpmuludq, 656
vpshufb, 625
vpshufd, 626
vpshufhw, 628
vpshuflw, 628
vpshufps, 632
vpsignb, 659
vpsignd, 660
vpsignw, 659
vpslldq, 647
vpsllw, 647

vpsrldq, 647
vpsubb, 654
vpsubd, 653
vpsubq, 653
vpsubw, 654
vptest, 646
vpunpckhbw, 640
vpunpckhdq, 641
vpunpckhqdq, 641
vpunpckhwd, 640
vpunpcklbw, 640
vpunpckldq, 640
vpunpcklqdq, 641
vrsqrtps, 670
vshufpd, 632
vsqrtpd, 670
vsqrtps, 670
vsubpd, 669
vsubps, 669
vunpckhpd, 633
vunpckhps, 633
vunpcklpd, 633
vunpcklps, 633
vxorpd, 645
xchg, 116
xlat, 584
xor, 58, 309, 709, 712
xorpd, 645
integer
    addition (SIMD), 648
    arithmetic (SIMD), 648
    average computation (SIMD), 657
    comparisons (SIMD), 660
    conversions (SIMD), 664
    integer portion of a floating-point
        number, 349
    integer-to-floating-point
        conversion, 328
    integer-to-string conversion
        (extended precision,
        unsigned), 508
    integer-to-string conversion
        (signed), 507
    less-than comparison (SIMD), 662
    multiplication (SIMD), 654
    signed remainder/modulo, 407
    subtraction (SIMD), 653
integer types in C, 454

integer unpack instructions (SSE/AVX), 637

interleaving comparison results (SIMD), 664

imul instruction, 291

invalid arithmetic operation (IA), 673

invalid operation exception flag (IE, SSE), 369

invalid operation exception (FPU), 320

invalid operation mask (IM, SSE), 370

invariant computations, 446

inverting

> bits, 58, 708
>
> bits in a bit string, 57
>
> selected bits in a bit set, 712

I/O (input/output), 9

iSize function, 516

itoStrSize function, 517–518

J

jae instruction, 73, 391

ja instruction, 73, 390

jbe instruction, 73, 390

jb instruction, 73, 390

jc instruction, 70, 74, 390, 716

je instruction, 72, 74, 390, 390–391

jge instruction, 73, 390, 392

jg instruction, 73, 391

jle instruction, 73, 390, 392

jl instruction, 73, 390, 392

jmp instruction, 69, 382

jnae instruction, 74, 390

jna instruction, 74, 390

jnbe instruction, 74, 390

jnb instruction, 74, 390

jnc instruction, 70, 74, 390, 716

jne instruction, 72, 74, 390, 390–391

jnge instruction, 74, 390, 392

jng instruction, 74, 390, 392

jnle instruction, 74, 390

jnl instruction, 74, 390, 392

jno instruction, 70, 390

jnp instruction, 390

jns instruction, 70, 390

jnz instruction, 70, 74, 298, 390

jo instruction, 70, 390

jpe instruction, 390

jp instruction, 390

jpo instruction, 390

js instruction, 70, 390

jump instructions, 382

jz instruction, 70, 74, 298, 390

K

KCS Floating-Point Standard, 87

L

label declaration, 114

label directive, 156

labels, 378

> in a procedure, 219

lahf instruction, 86

lanes (elements of an SSE/AVX packed array), 598

LARGEADDRESSAWARE, 127

> and arrays, 183

large address unaware applications, 127

large parameters, 258

last clear bit, 708, 736

last-in, first-out (LIFO) data structures, 137

last set bit, 736

lddqu instruction, 622

ldmxcsr instruction, 370

leaf function, 278

lea instruction, 22, 125, 378

least significant bit, 46, 52

leave instruction, 234

left

> rotates, 78
>
> shifts, 75

left-associative operators, 304

lengthof operator, 153

length of text string in MASM textual constants, 752

length-prefixed strings, 175

le operator, 153

less-than comparison (SIMD), 662

lexical scope, 378

lexicographical ordering, 833

library file, 869

library module, 853

lifetime of a local variable, 234

LIFO (last in, first out), 137

linear search, 422

line feed, 93

listings, xxviii
literal constant, 18
little-endian data organization, 114
little-endian to big-endian
    conversion, 116
LO (low-order), 46
load effective address, 378
    instruction, 22
loading data into an SSE/AVX
    register, 610
loading single-precision vectors into
    SSE/AVX registers, 612
loading the flags register from AH, 86
loading the FPU control word, 363
local directive (in procedures), 237
local symbols in procedures, 378
local symbols (statement labels) in a
    procedure, 219
local variable access, 235
local variable address alignment, 607
local variables, 234
location counter, 113, 154
lods instruction, 836
$\log_2(e)$, 361
$\log_2(x)$, 362
logical
    AND operation, 55, 309
    exclusive-or operation, 55, 57
    NOT operation, 55, 57
    operations on binary numbers, 57
    operations on bits, 55
    operators within a constant
      expression, 153
    OR operation, 55, 309
    shift right, 77
    XOR operation, 55, 309
logical systems
    arithmetic, 310
    Boolean, 310
loops, 433, 437
    invariant computations, 446
    loop-control variables, 433
    register usage, 442
    termination, 443
    unraveling/unrolling, 447
loops in the MASM compile-time
    language, 756
low32 operator, 154

low-level control structures, 378
low operator, 153
low-order (LO), 46
    bit, 46, 52
    byte, 53
    nibble, 52
    word, 54
lowword operator, 153
lt operator, 153

M

machine code encoding, 73
machine idioms, 310
machine state (preservation), 220
machine state, saving the, 220
macro
    default parameter values, 768
    optional parameters, 766
    parameter delimiters, 764
    parameter expansion, 762
    parameter expansion issues, 765
    parameters, 762
    required parameters, 766
macroarchitecture, 622
macro directive, 760
macros, 760
make dependencies, 864
makefiles, 34
makefile syntax, 863
making symbols case-sensitive in
    MASM, 8
malloc (C Standard Library
    function), 166
manifest constants, 18, 149
manipulating bits in memory, 707
mantissa, 87
mask (bits), 708
masking
    bit strings, 58
    masking in bits, 58
    masking out bits, 58
MASM (Microsoft Macro Assembler)
    dup operator in a data
      declaration, 31
    enumerated constants, 156
    pointers, 162
    procedures, 22
    structures (struct), 198

MASM (*continued*)

    support for ASCII characters, 95

    variables, 14

masm32.com website, 874

MASM /c command line option, 9

MASM/C++ hybrid programs, 7

maximum instructions (SIMD), 657

maxpd instruction, 670

maxps instruction, 670

maxsd instruction, 372

maxss instruction, 371

memory, 9

    addressing modes, 105, 122

    allocation, 105

    indirect jump through memory, 389

    organization, 106

    read operation, 14

    subsystem, 13

    write operation, 13

memory access violation exception, 169

memory addresses, 9

memory alignment requirements

    (SSE/AVX/SIMD), 606

memory leaks, 171

memory management unit (MMU), 111

merging bit strings, 741

merging source files during

    assembly, 848

microarchitecture, 622

Microsoft ABI, 35

    data alignment boundary, 144

    register usage, 38

    volatile registers, 38

Microsoft Macro Assembler. *See* MASM

Microsoft Visual C++ (MSVC), 9, 920

minimal procedures, 218

minimum instructions (SIMD), 657

minpd instruction, 670

minps instruction, 670

minsd instruction, 371

minss instruction, 371

misaligned data and the system

    cache, 121

mkActRec (macro), 882

MMU (memory management unit), 111

MMX (Multimedia Extensions), 624

MMX register set, 11

mnemonic, 289

modulo

    floating-point remainder, 348

    integer remainder, 407

modulo-*n* counters, 312

mod (within a constant expression), 153

monadic operations, 57

more command (CLI), 932

most significant bit, 46, 52

movapd instruction, 610

movapd operands (MASM), 611

movaps instruction, 610

movaps operands (MASM), 611

movddup instruction, 621

movd instruction, 371, 609

movdqa instruction, 610

movdqa operands (MASM), 611

movdqu instruction, 612

move command (CLI), 933

movhlps instruction, 619

movhpd instruction, 617

movhps instruction, 617

moving string data, 825

mov instruction, 18, 122

mov instruction operands, 20

movlhps instruction, 619

movlpd instruction, 615

movlps instruction, 615

movmskpd instruction, 676

movmskps instruction, 676

movq instruction, 371, 609

movsb instruction, 827

movsd instruction, 370, 827

movshdup instruction, 620

movs instruction, 827

movs instruction performance, 831

movsldup instruction, 620

movss instruction, 370

movsw instruction, 827

movsx instruction, 288

movupd instruction, 612

movups instruction, 612

MSVC (Microsoft Visual C++), 9, 920

mul instruction, 289, 461

mulpd instruction, 670

mulps instruction, 670

mulsd instruction, 371

mulss instruction, 371

multi-byte data structure organization (in memory), 114
multilingual planes (Unicode), 97
Multimedia Extensions (MMX), 624
multiple data values in a single data declaration, 16
multiplication, 148, 289, 291, 461
    floating-point, 339
multiplying
    by a reciprocal to simulate division, 312
    register value by ten, 311
    without `mul` or `imul`, 310
multiprecision
    addition, 454
    comparisons, 458
    operations, 454, 703
    subtraction, 457

N

namespace pollution, 220, 878
naming a segment, 604
NaN (not a number), 90, 296, 320
natural data alignment boundary, 144
`neg128` (macro), 760
negating large values, 478
negation (floating-point), 349
`neg` instruction, 478
`ne` operator, 153
nested array constants, 195
nested `dup` operator, 195
nested structs, 200
nested subfield access (of a structure), 200
`newLn` function, 886
nibble, 51
N/No N rule, 392
noncommutative binary operators, 308
nonvolatile registers, 265
nonvolatile registers (Microsoft ABI), 39
normalized floating-point numbers, 89, 325
not a number (NaN), 90, 296
`not` instruction, 58, 309, 709
NOT operation, 55, 57
NOT operator, 153
NUL character, 176, 248
`NULL` pointer references, 107

numbering system, 44
    binary, 44
    decimal, 44
    hexadecimal, 46
    positional, 44
numeric
    conversion from string, 546
    memory addresses, 9
    numeric-to-string conversion performance, 507
    numeric-to-string conversions, 491
    representation, 48

O

octal words, 55
`offset` operator, 154, 378
offsets, 113
one's complement format, 87
`opattr` operator, 154
opcode, 123
`open` function, 888
`openNew` function, 889
operation code (opcode), 123
operations
    AND, 309
    NOT, 309
    on binary numbers, 57
    OR, 56, 309
    rotation, 74
    shift arithmetic right, 77
    shifts, 74
    XOR, 57, 309
operator precedence, 303
operators, 195
    $, 154
    AND, 153
    dot (structure/record field access), 199
    dup, 182, 195
    eq, 153
    ge, 153
    gt, 153
    high, 153
    high32, 153
    highword, 153
    le, 153
    lengthof, 153
    logical operators, 153

operators *(continued)*
    low, 153
    low32, 154
    lowword, 153
    lt, 153
    ne, 153
    NOT, 153
    offset, 154, 378
    opattr, 154
    OR, 153
    size, 154
    sizeof, 154
    this, 154
    type, 159
opposite jumps, 392
optional macro parameters, 766
option directive, 8, 238
    epilogue operand, 238
    prologue operand, 238
ordered comparison, 90, 373
or instruction, 58, 309, 709
OR operation, 55
OR operator, 153
orpd instruction, 645
output redirection (standard output), 926
overflow exception flag (OE, SSE), 369
overflow exception (FPU), 320
overflow flag, 12, 293
    setting after an arithmetic
        operation, 71
overflow mask (OM, SSE), 370
overlaid registers (XMM/YMM), 623
oword, 51
oword directive, 15, 55

P

pabsb instruction, 659
pabsd instruction, 659
pabsw instruction, 659
packed
    absolute value (integer), 659
    addition, 648
    arrays of bit strings, 733
    byte data types, 597
    data, 79
    decimal arithmetic, 488
    double (precision) arithmetic
        instructions, 668

dword data types, 598
floating-point arithmetic, 668
integer comparisons, 660
integer multiplication, 654
memory operands (SSE/AVX), 606
operands for SSE/AVX
    instructions, 606
qword data types, 598
shifts, 647
sign extension, 666
sign transfer, 659
(SIMD) integer comparison for
    less than, 662
single (precision) arithmetic
    instructions, 668
word data types, 597
zero extension, 665
packing and unpacking bit strings, 717
packssdw instruction, 667
packsswb instruction, 667
packusdw instruction, 667
packuswb instruction, 667
paddb instruction, 649
paddd instruction, 649
paddq instruction, 649
paddw instruction, 648–649
page (256-byte) alignment within a
    segment, 605
pages (memory management), 111
paragraph memory alignment, 606
paragraph (para/16-byte) alignment
    within a segment, 605
parameter declarations with the proc
    directive, 255
parameter expansion in macros, 762
parameters, 240
    variable length, 248
partial remainder, 348
pass by reference
    efficiency, 243
passing
    large objects as parameters, 258
    parameters by reference, 241
    parameters by value, 241
    parameters in registers, 243
    parameters in the code stream, 246
    parameters on the stack, 249
pavgb instruction, 657

pavgw instruction, 657

pclmulqdq instruction, 656

pcmpeqb instruction, 660

pcmpeqd instruction, 660

pcmpeqq instruction, 660

pcmpeqw instruction, 660

pcmpgtb instruction, 660

pcmpgtd instruction, 660

pcmpgtq instruction, 660

pcmpgtw instruction, 660

PC-relative addressing mode, 122

performance improvements for
loops, 443

performance of numeric-to-string
conversion, 507

performance of the string
instructions, 837

pextrb instruction, 641

pextrd instruction, 641

pextrq instruction, 641

pextrw instruction, 641

phaddd instruction, 650

phaddsw instruction, 650

phaddw instruction, 650

pi (FPU load instruction), 360

pinsrb instruction, 642

pinsrd instruction, 642

pinsrq instruction, 642

pinsrw instruction, 642

pmaxsb instruction, 657

pmaxsd instruction, 658

pmaxsq instruction, 658

pmaxsw instruction, 657

pmaxub instruction, 658

pmaxud instruction, 658

pmaxuq instruction, 658

pmaxuw instruction, 658

pminsb instruction, 658

pminsd instruction, 658

pminsq instruction, 658

pminsw instruction, 658

pminub instruction, 658

pminud instruction, 658

pminuq instruction, 658

pminuw instruction, 658

pmovmskb instruction, 662

pmovmskd simulation, 663

pmovmskw simulation, 663

pmovmsq simulation, 663

pmovsxbd instruction, 666

pmovsxbq instruction, 666

pmovsxbw instruction, 666

pmovsxdq instruction, 666

pmovsxwq instruction, 666

pmovzxbd instruction, 665

pmovzxbq instruciton, 665

pmovzxbw instruction, 665

pmovzxdq instruction, 665

pmovzxwd instruction, 666

pmovzxwq instruction, 665

pmuldq instruction, 656

pmulld instruction, 655

pmuludq instruction, 656

pointer constants and pointer constant
expressions, 164

pointer data access, 162

pointer problems, 167

pointers, 161

popfd instruction, 140

popf instruction, 140

pop instruction, 135, 222

popping the FPU stack, 326

postfix notation, 364
conversion to assembly
language, 367

precedence
of arithmetic operators, 303
rules, 303

precision, 314
control bits (FPU), 320
control during floating-point
computations, 320
exception (FPU), 321
precision exception flag
(PE, SSE), 369
precision mask (PM, SSE), 370

preserving
machine state, 220
registers, 38, 137, 220
in loops, 442

printf format specifiers, 24

problems with macro parameter
expansion, 765

proc directive, 216, 255
parameter declarations, 255

procedural parameters, 280
 passing procedures as
  parameters, 280
procedure invocation, 216
procedure pointers, 278
procedures, 22, 216
 effect on the stack, 278
 in MASM, 22
processing SIMD comparison results, 678
proc external symbol type, 851
program counter in a section, 154
programming in the large, 847
programming language
 FORTRAN, 424
program size and object/library files, 870
prolog (standard entry sequence
  code), 239
 option, 239
prologue (operand for option
  directive), 238
pshufb instruction, 625
pshufd instruction, 626
pshufhw instruction, 628
pshuflw instruction, 628
psignb instruction, 659
psignd instruction, 660
psignw instruction, 659
pslldq instruction, 647
psllw instruction, 647
psrldq instruction, 647
psubb instruction, 654
psubd instruction, 653
psubq instruction, 653
psubw instruction, 654
ptest instruction, 646
public directive, 8, 849
punpckhbw instruction, 637
punpckhdq instruction, 637
punpckhqdq instruction, 637
punpckhwd instruction, 637
punpcklbw instruction, 637
punpckldq instruction, 637
punpcklqdq instruction, 637
punpcklwd instruction, 637
pushf instruction, 140
pushfq instruction, 140
pushing a value onto the floating-point
  stack, 326

pushing the constant 1.0 onto the FPU
  stack, 360
push instruction, 134, 222
pushw instruction, 134
puts function, 885

Q

qtoStr (quad word to string)
  function, 493
quad words, 55
quad-word strings, 825
question mark in a data declaration
  directive, 15
quicksort, 272
qword, 51
qword data declarations, 55
qword directive, 15
qword-sized lanes, 599
qword vectors (packed qwords), 598

R

R8B, R9B, R10B, R11B, R12B, R13B,
  R14B, and R15B registers, 10
R8D, R9D, R10D, R11D, R12D, R13D,
  R14D, and R15D registers, 10
R8W, R9W, R10W, R11W, R12W, R13W,
  R14W, and R15W registers, 10
r10toStr function, 527, 530
radix, 46
range of a function, 586
RAX, RBX, RCX, RDX, RSI, RDI,
  RBP, RSP, R8, R9, R10, R11,
  R12, R13, R14, and R15
  registers, 10
RBP register, 13, 230
rcl instruction, 79, 716
rcpss instruction, 372
rcr instruction, 79, 716
RCX register usage in string
  instructions, 826
RDI register usage in string
  instructions, 826
rd/rmdir commands (CLI), 933
read function, 887
reading from memory, 13
readLine() function, 30
readLn function, 893

readonly
    segment argument, 605
    variables as constants, 150
real4 directive, 15
real8 directive, 15
real10 directive, 15
real values as parameters, 244
rearranging bytes in an XMM/YMM
    register, 625
rearranging expressions
    in if statements to improve
        performance, 406
    to make them more efficient, 406
record, 197
    declarations, 198
    field access, 199
    field alignment, 204
record/struct field access via pointer, 200
recursion, 271
recursively converting numbers to
    strings, 500
reference parameters, 241, 256
register
    8-bit, 10
    16-bit, 10
    32-bit, 10
    64-bit, 10
    addressing modes, 122
    aliasing, 10, 623
    as a procedure parameters, 243
    comparison to zero, 298
    FPU, 317
    indirect addressing mode, 124
    indirect jump instruction, 383
    overlaying, 10
    preservation, 137, 220, 442
        callee, 222
        caller, 222
    usage in loops, 442
    usage in string instructions, 826
    usage in the Microsoft ABI, 38
remainder
    floating point, 348
    signed integer, 407
removing unwanted data from the
    stack, 140
ren/rename commands, 933

repeat..until loop, 433, 434
repe prefix on cmpsb, cmpsw, cmpsd, and
    cmpsq instructions, 827
repetitive compilation, 756
repne prefix on cmpsb, cmpsw, cmpsd, and
    cmpsq instructions, 827
rep prefix on movsb, movsw, movsd, and
    movsq instructions, 826
rep/repe/repz and repnz/repne string
    instruction prefixes, 826
required macro parameters, 766
restrictions in simple switch statement
    implementations, 414
ret instruction, 22, 218
return address, 218
returning a result to a C++ program
    from an assembly language
    function, 30
reverse
    division (floating-point), 343
    Polish notation (RPN), 364
    subtraction (floating-point), 334
reversing bits in a bit string, 739
RFLAGS register, 12, 140
right
    rotates, 78
    shift operation, 76, 77
    shifts, 75
right associative operators, 304
RIP-relative addressing mode, 123
rol instruction, 78
ror instruction, 78
rotate
    left, 77
    operations, 74
    right, 77
rounding
    control (FPU), 319
    control (SSE), 370
    floating-point numbers, 349
    floating-point value to an
        integer, 349
round-up and round-down options
    during floating-point
    computations, 319
row-major array access for three-
    dimensional arrays, 191
row-major ordering, 190

RPN (reverse Polish notation), 364. *See also* postfix notation

RSI register usage in string instructions, 826

rsqrtps instruction, 670

rsqrtss instruction, 372

rstrActRec (macro), 883

run of zeros bit string, 708

runtime

language, 748

memory organization, 106

runtime versus compile-time expressions, 155

S

sahf instruction, 86, 350

sar instruction, 77, 312

saturation addition (horizontal), 650, 652

saturation (SSE/AVX/SIMD), 667

saving the machine state, 220

sbb instruction, 457, 716

sbyte directive, 15

scalar data types, 597

scaled-indexed addressing mode, 126

scaling factor, 126

scas instruction, 835

scope, 378, 850

of a local variable, 234

sdword directive, 15

searching

for a bit, 736

for a bit pattern, 743

for a substring within another string in MASM textual constants, 751

for the first (or last) set bit, 737

section location counter, 154

segment

alignment option, 605

alignment (powers of 2), 605

class argument, 605

declarations, 604

directive, 604

directive align option (for 32-byte alignment), 606

faults, 107

faults on unaligned memory accesses (SSE/AVX), 606

names, 604

registers, 10

separate assembly, 854

separate compilation, 847, 854

setae instruction, 296

seta instruction, 296

setbe instruction, 296

setb instruction, 296

setcc instructions, 295

setc instruction, 295, 716

sete instruction, 296

setge instruction, 297

setg instruction, 296

setl instruction, 297

setnae instruction, 296

setna instruction, 296

setnbe instruction, 296

setnb instruction, 296

setnc instruction, 295, 716

setne instruction, 296

setnge instruction, 297

setng instruction, 297

setnle instruction, 296

setnl instruction, 297

setno instruction, 295

setnp instruction, 295

setns instruction, 295

setnz instruction, 295, 298

seto instruction, 295

set on condition instructions, 295

setpe instruction, 295

setp instruction, 295

setpo instruction, 295

sets instruction, 295

setting bits, 708

setz instruction, 295, 298

shadow storage (for parameters), 255, 264

shift

arithmetic right operation, 77

left operation, 75

operations, 74

operations (SSE/AVX), 647

right operation, 76

shift and rotate instructions, 709, 716

shld instruction, 482

shl instruction, 75, 310

short-circuit

Boolean evaluation, 401

short-circuit versus complete
 Boolean evaluation, 403
shrd instruction, 482
shr instruction, 76, 312
shuffle instructions, 625
shufpd instruction, 630
shufps instruction, 630
side effects, 403
sign
 bit, 62
 contraction, 67
 extension, 67, 292
 extension prior to division, 305
sign and zero flag settings after mul and
 imul instructions, 291
signed
 comparison flag settings, 294
 comparisons, 296
 decimal input (extended-
  precision), 569
 decimal output (extended-
  precision), 513
 division, 292
 integer remainder/modulo, 407
 integer-to-string conversion, 507
 multiplication, 148, 289, 291, 461
 numbers, 62
signed and unsigned numbers, 62
sign extension (SIMD/SSE/AVX), 666
sign flag, 12, 293
 setting after an arithmetic
  operation, 71
sign flag and the and, or, and xor
 instructions, 712
significant digits, 314
sign transfer, 659
SIMD (single instruction, multiple
 data), 11, 55, 595
 arithmetic/logical operations, 644
 bitwise instructions, 645
 comparison instructions (floating-
  point), 671
 comparison results (processing
  multiple comparisons), 663
 floating-point arithmetic
  operations, 668
 floating-point conversions, 679
 integer absolute value, 659

integer addition, 648
integer arithmetic instructions, 648
integer average instructions, 657
integer comparison
 instructions, 660
integer conversions, 664
integer minimum and
 maximum, 657
integer multiplication, 654
integer sign-transfer
 instructions, 659
integer subtraction, 653
memory alignment
 requirements, 606
programming model, 596
saturation, 667
SIMD string instructions, 838
SIMD zero-extension
 instructions, 665
simple assignments (conversion to
 assembly language), 299
simulating div, 312
sine, 361
single-instruction, multiple-data
 (SIMD) instructions. *See* SIMD
single-instruction, single-data (SISD)
 instructions. *See* SISD
single-precision floating-point format, 87
single-precision (floating-point)
 lanes, 598
single-precision vector types, 597
SI register, 10
SISD (single instruction, single data),
 595
sizeof function (applied to
 UNIONs), 207
sizeof operator, 154
size operator, 154
sizestr directive, 752
software configuration via conditional
 compilation, 754
sorting, 185
 bubble sort, 185
 quicksort, 272
special-purpose application-accessible
 registers, 10
special-purpose kernel-mode
 registers, 10

specifying a variable name and type
without allocating storage, 114
SP register, 10
sqrtpd instruction, 670
sqrtps instruction, 670
sqrtsd instruction, 372
sqrtss instruction, 372
square root, 327, 347
sqword directive, 15
SSE (Streaming SIMD Extensions),
596, 624
  aligned data movement
instructions, 610
  denormal exception flag (DE), 369
  denormal mask (DM), 370
  denormals are zero (DAZ), 370
  divide-by-zero mask (ZM), 370
  floating-point arithmetic
(SIMD), 668
  floating-point conversions, 679
  flush to zero (FZ), 370
  instruction operands, 606
  invalid operation mask (IM), 370
  memory alignment
requirements, 606
  overflow exception flag (OE), 369
  overflow exception flag (UE), 369
  overflow mask (OM), 370
  packed byte data types, 597
  packed dword data types, 598
  packed qword data types, 598
  packed word data types, 597
  precision exception flag (PE), 369
  precision mask (PM), 370
  programming model, 596
  rounding control, 370
  sign extension, 666
  string instructions, 838
  unaligned memory access, 606, 612
  underflow mask (UM), 370
  zero exception flag (ZE), 369
  zero extension, 665
SSE2, SSE3, SSSE3, SSE4, SSE4.1,
SSE4.2, 596
SSE/AVX comparison synonyms, 673
SSE/SSE2 instruction set, 11
ST0, 318
ST1, 318

stack, 134
stack fault flag (FPU), 322
stack manipulation by procedure
calls, 224
stack operations
  pop, 135, 222
  popf, 140
  popfd, 140
  push, 134, 222
  pushf, 140
  pushfd, 140
  pushw, 134
stack pointer register, 13
stack segment, 134
stack variable address alignment, 607
standard entry sequence (to a
procedure), 231
standard exit sequence (from a
procedure), 233
standard input redirection, 927
standard macro parameter
expansion, 762
standard macros, 760
standard output redirection, 926
state machine, 424
statement labels, 378
statements
  break, 438
  case, 396, 410
  conditional, 396
  continue, 438
  else, 397
  for, 437
  if, 396
  repeat..until, 433
  while, 433
state variable, 424
static variable declaration section, 108
status register (FPU), 321, 364
status word, 350, 364
stc instruction, 716
STDCALL calling convention, 263
stdin_getc function, 892
stdin_read function, 891
std instruction, 86
sti instruction, 86
stmxcsr instruction, 370

store data from an SSE/AVX register into memory, 610
storing AH register into flags, 86, 350
storing single-precision vectors from SSE/AVX registers to memory, 612
storing the FPU control word, 321
storing the FPU status word, 321, 350, 364
stos instruction, 835
streaming data types, 596
streaming SIMD extensions. *See* SSE
strength-reduction optimizations, 311
strfill procedure, 244
strings, 174
    comparisons, 825
    descriptors, 176
    equality test for macro/text arguments, 767
    instruction performance, 837
    instructions, 825, 836
    length, 174
    length calculated at assembly time, 176
    length operator in MASM textual constants, 752
    length-prefixed, 175
    SSE instructions, 838
    zero-terminated, 174
string-to-decimal conversion (unsigned), 563
string-to-floating-point conversion, 570
string-to-integer conversion, 546
string-to-numeric conversion (hexadecimal), 556
string-to-numeric conversions, 546
string-to-numeric conversion (signed, extended-precision), 569
strtoh128 function, 561
strtoh function, 557
strtoi function, 550
strToR10 function, 573
strtou128 function, 567
strtou function, 548, 564
struct arrays, 203
struct assembler directive, 198
struct declarations, 198
struct directive, 198
struct/record field access via pointer, 199

structs, 197
    nested, 200
structure field access, 199
structure field initialization, 200
sub instruction, 21
subpd instruction, 669
subps instruction, 669
subregisters, 623
subsd instruction, 371
subss instruction, 371
substr directive, 752
substring operator (MASM text strings), 752
substring search in MASM textual constants, 751
subtraction, 457, 716
    floating-point, 334
subtract with borrow, 457, 716
swapping bytes in a multi-byte object, 116
swapping registers on the FPU stack, 327
switch statement, 410
sword directive, 15
synthesizing
    break statements in assembly language, 438
    continue statements in assembly language, 439
    forever..endfor loops in assembly language, 436
    for statements in assembly language, 437
    repeat..until loops in assembly language, 434
    while loops in assembly language, 433
system bus, 9

T

tables and table lookups, 583
    table lookup computations, 584
    table lookup (hexadecimal-to-string conversion), 497
tag field, 209
taking the address of a statement label, 378
tangent, 361

tbyte directive, 15
tbyte values (BCD), 488
temporary values in an expression, 307
temporary variables, 306
test for zero (floating-point), 360
testing a floating-point operand for
    zero, 322, 360
testing bits, 708
testing to see if a macro argument is
    the empty string, 767
testing two text objects for equality, 767
test instruction, 297, 709
text delimiters, 151
textequ directive, 151
this operator, 154
three-dimensional array element access
    (row-major), 191
time command (CLI), 933
top of stack pointer (FPU), 324
trampoline, 393
transcendental function instructions, 361
translate arithmetic expressions into
    assembly language, 287
translate instruction, 585
tricky programming, 310
true (representation), 308
truncation during FPU calculations, 319
truth table, 55
try..catch statement (C++), 30
two-dimensional row-major ordered
    array formula (for accessing
    array elements), 191
two's complement
    numbering system, 54
    numeric representation, 62
    operation, 63
type checking, 20
    coercion, 157
type coercion, 157, 159
type declaration section, 156
typedef directive, 156
type operator, 159

U

unaligned loads (to XMM/YMM
    registers), 622
unaligned SSE/AVX data
    movements, 612

unaligned SSE/AVX memory
    accesses, 606
unary operator (conversion to assembly
    language), 301
unconditional jump instruction, 69
underflow, 316
underflow exception flag (UE,
    SSE), 369
underflow exception (FPU), 321
underflow mask (UM, SSE), 370
Unicode, 54, 96
    BMP (Basic Multilingual Plane), 97
    UTF-8 encoding, 98
    UTF-16 encoding, 98
    UTF-32 encoding, 98
    code planes, 97
    code points, 96
    encodings, 97
    multilingual planes, 97
uninitialized pointers, 168
unions, 206
    accessing fields of a union, 206
    anonymous, 208
    definition, 206
    syntax (declaration), 206
unordered comparisons, 90, 360, 373, 673
    floating-point, 357
unpacking bit strings, 717
unpack instructions, 625
unpckhpd instruction, 633
unpckhps instruction, 633
unpcklpd instruction, 633
unpcklps instruction, 633
unraveling loops, 447
unrolling loops, 448
unsigned
    comparisons, 296
    decimal input (extended-
        precision), 566
    decimal output, 500
    division, 291
    integer-to-string conversion
        (extended-precision), 508
    multiplication, 289, 461
    numbers, 62
    string-to-decimal conversion, 563
untyped reference parameters, 284
using echo to display equate values, 751

uSize function, 514
UTF-8 encoding, 98
UTF-16 encoding (Unicode), 98
UTF-32 encoding (Unicode), 98
utoStrSize function, 517

V

vaddpd instruction, 669
vaddps instruction, 669
value parameters, 241, 253
vandnpd instruction, 645
vandpd instruction, 645
variable-length parameters, 248
variable names, 14
variables in MASM, 14
variant objects, 209
variant types, 209
vcmppd instruction, 671, 674
vcmpps instruction, 671, 674
vcvtdq2pd instruction, 679
vcvtdq2ps instruction, 679
vcvtpd2dq instruction, 679
vcvtpd2ps instruction, 680
vcvtps2dq instruction, 680
vcvtps2pd instruction, 680
vcvttpd2dq instruction, 680
vcvttps2dq instruction, 680
vdivpd instruction, 670
vdivps instruction, 670
vector
    absolute value (integer), 659
    addition, 648
    data types, 597
    floating-point arithmetic, 668
    instructions, 595
    integer comparisons, 660
    integer multiplication, 654
    memory operands, 606
    operands for SSE/AVX
        instructions, 606
    shifts, 647
    sign extension, 666
    sign transfer, 659
    (SIMD) integer comparison for
        less than, 662
    zero extension, 665
vertical addition, 649
vextractps instruction, 643

vhaddpd instruction, 671
vhaddps instruction, 671
vhsubpd instruction, 671
vhsubps instruction, 671
vinsertps instruction, 643
vlddqu instruction, 622
vmaxpd instruction, 670
vmaxps instruction, 670
vminpd instruction, 670
vminps instruction, 670
vmovapd instruction, 610
vmovapd operands (MASM), 611
vmovaps instruction, 610
vmovaps operands (MASM), 611
vmovddup instruction, 621
vmovd instruction, 609
vmovdqa instruction, 610
vmovdqa operands (MASM), 611
vmovdqu instruction, 612
vmovhlps instruction, 619
vmovhpd instruction, 618
vmovhps instruction, 618
vmovlhps instruction, 619
vmovlpd instruction, 615
vmovlps instruction, 615
vmovmskpd instruction, 676
vmovmskps instruction, 676
vmovq instruction, 609
vmovshdup instruction, 620
vmovsldup instruction, 620
vmovupd instruction, 612
vmovups instruction, 612
vmulpd instruction, 670
vmulps instruction, 670
volatile registers, 265
    Microsoft ABI, 38
von Neumann architecture, 9
vorpd instruction, 645
vpabsb instruction, 659
vpabsd instruction, 659
vpabsw instruction, 659
vpackssdw instruction, 667
vpacksswb instruction, 667
vpackusdw instruction, 667
vpackuswb instruction, 667
vpaddb instruction, 649
vpaddd instruction, 649
vpaddq instruction, 649

vpaddw instruction, 648–649
vpavgb instruction, 657
vpavgw instruction, 657
vpclmulqdq instruction, 656
vpcmpeqb instruction, 661
vpcmpeqd instruction, 661
vpcmpeqq instruction, 661
vpcmpeqw instruction, 661
vpcmpgtb instruction, 661
vpcmpgtd instruction, 661
vpcmpgtq instruction, 661
vpcmpgtw instruction, 661
vpextrb instruction, 642
vpextrd instruction, 642
vpextrq instruction, 642
vpextrw instruction, 642
vphaddd instruction, 650
vphaddw instruction, 650
vpinsrb instruction, 642
vpinsrd instruction, 643
vpinsrq instruction, 643
vpinsrw instruction, 643
vpmaxsb instruction, 657
vpmaxsd instruction, 658
vpmaxsq instruction, 658
vpmaxsw instruction, 657
vpmaxub instruction, 658
vpmaxud instruction, 658
vpmaxuq instruction, 658
vpmaxuw instruction, 658
vpminsb instruction, 658
vpminsd instruction, 658
vpminsw instruction, 658
vpminub instruction, 658
vpminud instruction, 658
vpminuq instruction, 658
vpminuw instruction, 658
vpmovmskb instruction, 662
vpmovsxbd instruction, 666
vpmovsxbq instruction, 666
vpmovsxbw instruction, 666
vpmovsxdq instruction, 666
vpmovsxwd instruction, 666
vpmovsxwq instruction, 666
vpmovzxbd instruction, 665
vpmovzxbq instruction, 665
vpmovzxbw instruction, 665
vpmovzxdq instruction, 665

vpmovzxwd instruction, 665
vpmovzxwq instruction, 665
vpmuldq instruction, 656
vpmulld instruction, 655
vpmuludq instruction, 656
vpshufb instruction, 625
vpshufd instruction, 626
vpshufhw instruction, 628
vpshuflw instruction, 628
vpsignb instruction, 659
vpsignd instruction, 660
vpsignw instruction, 659
vpslldq instruction, 647
vpsllw instruction, 647
vpsrldq instruction, 647
vpsubd instruction, 653
vpsubq instruction, 653
vpsubsb instruction, 654
vpsubw instruction, 654
vptest instruction, 646
vpunpckhbw instruction, 640
vpunpckhdq instruction, 641
vpunpckhqdq instruction, 641
vpunpckhwd instruction, 640
vpunpcklbw instruction, 640
vpunpckldq instruction, 640
vpunpcklqdq instruction, 641
vpunpcklwd instruction, 640
vrsqrtps instruction, 670
vshufpd instruction, 632
vshufps instruction, 632
vsqrtpd instruction, 670
vsqrtps instruction, 670
vsubpd instruction, 670
vsubps instruction, 670
vunpckhpd instruction, 633
vunpckhps instruction, 633
vunpcklpd instruction, 633
vunpcklps instruction, 633
vxorpd instruction, 645

W

while directive, 756
while..endm compile-time
        statement, 756
while statement, 433
Win32 API, 876
Windows command line, xxx

word, 51, 53
    16-bit variables, 54
    alignment in a segment, 605
    directive, 15, 54
    strings, 825
    vectors (packed words), 597
    word-sized lanes, 598
wrapper code, 882
WriteFile (Win32 API function), 875
write function, 884
wtoStr (word to string) function, 493

X

xchg instruction, 116
xlat instruction, 584
XMM registers, 11
xor instruction, 58, 309, 709, 712
XOR operation, 55, 57
xorpd instruction, 645

Y

Y2K, 85
YMM registers, 11

Z

zero and sign flag settings after mul and
    imul, 291
zero-divide exception (FPU), 320
zero exception flag (ZE, SSE), 369
zero-extension, 292
zero-extension (SIMD), 665
zero flag, 12, 293, 713
    setting after a multiprecision
      OR, 479
    setting after an arithmetic
      operation, 71
    settings after mul and imul
      instructions, 291
zero-terminated strings, 174

RESOURCES

Visit *https://nostarch.com/art-64-bit-assembly/* for errata and more information.

More no-nonsense books from  **NO STARCH PRESS**

WRITE GREAT CODE, VOLUME 2, 2ND EDITION

THINKING LOW-LEVEL, WRITING HIGH-LEVEL

BY RANDALL HYDE
656 PP., $49.95
ISBN 978-1-71850-038-9

HOW COMPUTERS REALLY WORK

A HANDS-ON GUIDE TO THE INNER WORKINGS OF THE MACHINE

BY MATTHEW JUSTICE
392 PP., $39.95
ISBN 978-1-71850-066-2

THE LINUX COMMAND LINE, 2ND EDITION

A COMPLETE INTRODUCTION

BY WILLIAM SHOTTS
504 PP., $39.95
ISBN 978-1-59327-952-3

EFFECTIVE C

AN INTRODUCTION TO PROFESSIONAL C PROGRAMMING

BY ROBERT C. SEACORD
272 PP., $49.95
ISBN 978-1-71850-104-1

C++ CRASH COURSE

A FAST-PACED INTRODUCTION

BY JOSH LOSPINOSO
792 PP., $59.95
ISBN 978-1-59327-888-5

THE ART OF ASSEMBLY LANGUAGE, 2ND EDITION

BY RANDALL HYDE
768 PP., $59.95
ISBN 978-1-59327-207-4

PHONE:
800.420.7240 OR
415.863.9900

EMAIL:
SALES@NOSTARCH.COM
WEB:
WWW.NOSTARCH.COM